The Handbook of
Multilevel Theory,
Measurement,
and Analysis

The Handbook of Multilevel Theory, Measurement, and Analysis

Edited by
Stephen E. Humphrey
James M. LeBreton

AMERICAN PSYCHOLOGICAL ASSOCIATION
Washington, DC

Published by
American Psychological Association
750 First Street, NE
Washington, DC 20002
www.apa.org

APA Order Department
P.O. Box 92984
Washington, DC 20090-2984
Phone: (800) 374-2721; Direct: (202) 336-5510
Fax: (202) 336-5502; TDD/TTY: (202) 336-6123
Online: http://www.apa.org/pubs/books
E-mail: order@apa.org

In the U.K., Europe, Africa, and the Middle East, copies may be ordered from
Eurospan Group
c/o Turpin Distribution
Pegasus Drive
Stratton Business Park
Biggleswade, Bedfordshire
SG18 8TQ United Kingdom
Phone: +44 (0) 1767 604972
Fax: +44 (0) 1767 601640
Online: https://www.eurospanbookstore.com/apa
E-mail: eurospan@turpin-distribution.com

Typeset in Berkeley by Circle Graphics, Inc., Reisterstown, MD

Printer: Sheridan Books, Chelsea, MI
Cover Designer: Nicci Falcone, Gaithersburg, MD

Library of Congress Cataloging-in-Publication Data

Names: Humphrey, Stephen E. (Stephen Earle), editor. | LeBreton, James M., editor.
Title: The handbook of multilevel theory, measurement, and analysis / edited by Stephen E. Humphrey and James M. LeBreton.
Description: First Edition. | Washington, DC : American Psychological Association, [2019] | Includes bibliographical references and index. | Description based on print version record and CIP data provided by publisher; resource not viewed.
Identifiers: LCCN 2018027316 (print) | LCCN 2018043700 (ebook) | ISBN 9781433830099 (eBook) | ISBN 1433830094 (eBook) | ISBN 9781433830013 (hardcover : alk. paper) | ISBN 1433830019 (hardcover : alk. paper)
Subjects: LCSH: Interpersonal relations—Research. | Industrial sociology—Research. | Psychology—Research. | Social sciences—Research.
Classification: LCC HM1106 (ebook) | LCC HM1106 .H364 2019 (print) | DDC 302.01—dc23
LC record available at https://lccn.loc.gov/2018027316

British Library Cataloguing-in-Publication Data
A CIP record is available from the British Library.

Printed in the United States of America

http://dx.doi.org/10.1037/0000115-000

10 9 8 7 6 5 4 3 2 1

Contents

Contributors

Juliet R. Aiken, PhD, Department of Psychology, University of Maryland, College Park

Valeria Alterman, BS, Doctoral Candidate, Department of Management, University of Florida, Gainesville

Gary A. Ballinger, PhD, Department of Management, University of Virginia, Charlottesville

Daniel J. Beal, PhD, Department of Management, Virginia Tech, Blacksburg

Laura J. Bird, MPsych, Doctoral Candidate, Melbourne School of Psychological Sciences, University of Melbourne, Melbourne, Australia

Caitlin E. Blackmore, MS, Doctoral Candidate, Department of Psychology, Wright State University, Dayton, OH

Paul D. Bliese, PhD, Department of Management, Darla Moore School of Business, University of South Carolina, Columbia

Stephen P. Borgatti, PhD, LINKS Center for Social Network Analysis, Department of Management, University of Kentucky, Lexington

Daniel J. Brass, PhD, LINKS Center for Social Network Analysis, Department of Management, University of Kentucky, Lexington

Kinsey B. Bryant-Lees, MA, Doctoral Candidate, Department of Psychology, Wright State University, Dayton, OH

David Chan, PhD, School of Social Sciences, Singapore Management University, Singapore

Gilad Chen, PhD, Department of Management & Organization, University of Maryland, College Park

Tiancheng Chen, MPS, Doctoral Candidate, Department of Psychology, George Mason University, Fairfax, VA

Matthew A. Cronin, PhD, School of Business, George Mason University, Fairfax, VA

Fred Dansereau, PhD, School of Management, State University of New York at Buffalo

Katie England, MS, Department of Psychology, Pennsylvania State University, University Park

Allison S. Gabriel, PhD, Department of Management and Organizations, University of Arizona, Tucson

Martin C. Goossen, PhD, Department of Management, Tilburg University, Tilburg, The Netherlands

Janaki Gooty, PhD, Department of Management, Belk College of Business, University of North Carolina at Charlotte

Simon Grund, PhD, Leibniz Institute for Science and Mathematics Education, and Centre for International Student Assessment, Kiel, Germany

Stanley M. Gully, PhD, School of Labor and Employment Relations, Pennsylvania State University, University Park

Paul J. Hanges, PhD, Department of Psychology, University of Maryland, College Park

Andrew Helbling, BS, School of Psychology, Georgia Institute of Technology, Atlanta

Jonathan L. Hendricks, BA, Doctoral Candidate, Department of Management, University of South Carolina, Columbia

Michael E. Hoffman, MS, Doctoral Candidate, Department of Psychology, Pennsylvania State University, University Park

Stephen E. Humphrey, PhD, Department of Management and Organization, Pennsylvania State University, University Park

Andrew T. Jebb, MA, Doctoral Candidate, Department of Psychological Sciences, Purdue University, West Lafayette, IN

Elnora D. Kelly, MS, School of Psychology, Georgia Institute of Technology, Atlanta

Andrew P. Knight, PhD, Department of Organizational Behavior, Washington University in St. Louis, St. Louis, MO

Dina V. Krasikova, PhD, Department of Management, University of Texas at San Antonio

David M. LaHuis, PhD, Department of Psychology, Wright State University, Dayton, OH

Jonas W. B. Lang, PhD, Department of Personnel Management and Work and Organizational Psychology, Ghent University, Ghent, Belgium

James M. LeBreton, PhD, Department of Psychology, Pennsylvania State University, University Park

MinShuou Li, BS, School of Psychology, Georgia Institute of Technology, Atlanta

Yihao Liu, PhD, School of Labor and Employment Relations, University of Illinois, Urbana-Champaign

Margaret M. Luciano, PhD, Department of Management and Entrepreneurship, Arizona State University, Tempe

Oliver Lüdtke, PhD, Leibniz Institute for Science and Mathematics Education, and Centre for International Student Assessment, Kiel, Germany

John E. Mathieu, PhD, Management Department, University of Connecticut, Storrs

Rustin D. Meyer, PhD, Department of Psychology, Pennsylvania State University, University Park

Curt B. Moore, PhD, School of Entrepreneurship, Oklahoma State University, Stillwater

Daniel A. Newman, PhD, Department of Psychology and School of Labor & Employment Relations, University of Illinois, Urbana-Champaign

Vincent Ng, MS, Doctoral Candidate, Department of Psychological Sciences, Purdue University, West Lafayette, IN

Cheri Ostroff, PhD, School of Management, University of South Australia, Adelaide, Australia

Donna Outten, BA, Department of Psychology, Georgia State University, Atlanta

Srikanth Paruchuri, PhD, Department of Management and Organization, Smeal College of Business, Pennsylvania State University, University Park

Erik Pesner, MS, Department of Psychology, The Graduate Center and Baruch College, City University of New York, New York

Corey Phelps, PhD, Faculty of Management, McGill University, Montreal, Quebec, Canada

Jean M. Phillips, PhD, School of Labor and Employment Relations, Pennsylvania State University, University Park

Robert E. Ployhart, PhD, Department of Management, University of South Carolina, Columbia

Kristopher J. Preacher, PhD, Department of Psychology and Human Development, Vanderbilt University, Nashville, TN

Hettie A. Richardson, PhD, Department of Management, Entrepreneurship, and Leadership, Texas Christian University, Fort Worth

Alexander Robitzsch, PhD, Leibniz Institute for Science and Mathematics Education, and Centre for International Student Assessment, Kiel, Germany

Denise Rousseau, PhD, Tepper School of Business, Carnegie Mellon University, Pittsburgh, PA

Charles A. Scherbaum, PhD, Department of Psychology, Baruch College, City University of New York, New York

Benjamin Schneider, PhD, MBA, Department of Psychology, University of Maryland, College Park

Levi K. Shiverdecker, MS, Doctoral Candidate, Department of Psychology, Pennsylvania State University, University Park

Yifan Song, BS, Doctoral Candidate, Department of Management, University of Florida, Gainesville

Louis Tay, PhD, Department of Psychological Sciences, Purdue University, West Lafayette, IN

Jeffrey B. Vancouver, PhD, Department of Psychology, Ohio University, Athens

Robert J. Vandenberg, PhD, Department of Management, Terry College of Business, University of Georgia, Athens

Mo Wang, PhD, Department of Management, University of Florida, Gainesville

Wei Wang, PhD, School of Communication, Northwestern University, Evanston, IL

Sang Woo, PhD, Department of Psychological Sciences, Purdue University, West Lafayette, IN

Francis J. Yammarino, PhD, School of Management and Center for Leadership Studies, State University of New York at Binghamton

Miles A. Zachary, PhD, Department of Management, Auburn University, Auburn, AL

Zhen Zhang, PhD, Department of Management and Entrepreneurship, Arizona State University, Tempe

Le Zhou, PhD, Department of Work and Organization, University of Minnesota, Minneapolis

Michael J. Zyphur, PhD, Department of Management and Marketing, University of Melbourne, Melbourne, Australia

The Handbook of
Multilevel Theory,
Measurement,
and Analysis

INTRODUCTION

Stephen E. Humphrey and James M. LeBreton

The domain of social science is that of inter- actions between people—how people think, feel, and behave, and how the collectives to which they belong do the same. In different disciplines, there is often a particular focus on one aspect of this (e.g., psychology generally begins with a focus on the individual, sociology on the system), but resident in all of these disciplines is the idea that there are multiple levels within which the focal units reside.

For example, within the organizational sciences (broadly and liberally defined), there has been a growing awareness of the importance of unpacking multilevel relationships to explain social phenomena in work contexts. Employees are frequently members of a team (or multiple teams); they exist within a social network of relationships, working under a supervisor (or multiple supervisors), within or spanning organizations (Klein & Kozlowski, 2000). Teams are composed of individuals who are embedded in multiple dyadic relationships; the teams reside within or span departments and are nested within or across organizations (Humphrey & Aime, 2014). Organizations are composed of many individuals, residing in multiple departments or functions, and the organizations themselves may be embedded within multiple joint ventures or alliances (Lepak, Smith, & Taylor, 2007). Moreover, all of these subjects exist across time. These levels define organizational research, bounding theories and shaping discourse.

Scholars often like to focus solely on one level to simplify theoretical and empirical challenges. In contrast, this handbook begins with the premise that social science is fundamentally multilevel in nature—the specific level or levels that are the focus on a particular scholar (or normatively studied within disciplines) may vary. However, the thesis of this handbook is that ignoring that multiple levels exist (and concentrating on only one level) is no longer a productive option for social scientists. For example, studying organizations without considering their industry is a fatal flaw within strategic management research; studying students without considering their classroom, their school, or their area is a nonstarter in educational psychology.

Even when scholars explicitly acknowledge the multilevel nature of the field (e.g., Chan, 1998; Klein & Kozlowski, 2000; Morgeson & Hofmann, 1999), the guidance they have produced has been isolated to a small subsection of the broader organizational domain. Surprisingly, micro research (i.e., research focused on intra- and interindividual phenomena) has had little cross-pollination with macro research (i.e., research focused on intra- and interorganizational phenomena). This lack of cross-disciplinary connections has occurred despite the fact that both micro and macro researchers are inherently interested in the multilevel nature of (organizationally relevant) phenomena. Essentially,

http://dx.doi.org/10.1037/0000115-001
The Handbook of Multilevel Theory, Measurement, and Analysis, S. E. Humphrey and J. M. LeBreton (Editors-in-Chief)

what the literature has been sorely lacking is an inclusive guide to multilevel research that recapitulates and extends the current state of the science.

We thus felt that it was time for a systematic and inclusive treatment of multilevel research, one that reviews and melds the three core "silos" of multilevel research (multilevel theory, multilevel measurement, and multilevel analysis) and does so from a perspective that considers micro, meso, and macro frameworks. The purpose of this handbook is therefore to provide guidance for scholars working in the social and behavioral sciences who wish to consider the implications that multilevel research (i.e., theory, measurement, and analysis) may have for their research programs. Although the majority of contributors to this handbook have backgrounds in the organizational sciences, the chapters have been largely written in a manner that should be accessible to researchers from a wide array of research disciplines including (but not limited to) communication, education, sociology, psychology (clinical, developmental, industrial, social), management (strategy, human resources, organizational behavior), and nursing.

PART I: MULTILEVEL THEORY

In the first part of the handbook, scholars focus on providing guidance on how to improve theory by integrating a multilevel perspective. Gully and Phillips (Chapter 1) begin this part by positing the most fundamental question for multilevel research: What is the appropriate level for your research? These authors define *identifying the appropriate level* as determining which level has the most explanatory power for the particular outcome of interest; they discuss the challenges scholars face in determining the appropriate level before shifting to a more grounded process of figuring out what is appropriate to one's own research. Their chapter serves to orient readers as to how to begin thinking as a multilevel scholar.

In the next chapter, Ostroff (Chapter 2) engages readers with a discussion of how to "contextualize context." As she documents, context is omnipresent

within the social and organizational sciences, and failure to consider context severely limits the application and interpretation of theoretical models. After reviewing where the study of context has been, she introduces a structure for interpreting, assessing, and analyzing context. This chapter is an important addition to the growing discussion of the importance of context in organizational research, providing a practical and user-friendly guide to integrating context into theory and empirical research.

Next, Meyer, England, Kelly, Helbling, Li, and Outten (Chapter 3) extend the previous chapter by presenting three metatheoretical frameworks for understanding context. After reviewing the three frameworks, the authors review several empirical conceptualizations of context, interpreting these papers through the lenses of the metatheoretical frameworks. They conclude by providing guidance, derived from this exercise, for conceptualizing context in one's own work.

Shifting the focus from context to dynamics, Cronin and Vancouver (Chapter 4) provide an in-depth examination of "dynamics" in the context of multilevel theory. Recognizing that behavior is a series of ongoing events and happenings (rather than a singular, static perspective of a stimulus and response), Cronin and Vancouver discuss how to theorize in a way that incorporates time and change. After developing five principles of multilevel dynamics, they apply their model to a concrete example. This chapter is extremely helpful for making sense of dynamics in social and organizational research. Despite the fact that scholars intuitively recognize that behavior is continuous, research has consistently neglected to theorize or test dynamic models. With this chapter, scholars are provided with a clear and concise set of instructions for creating dynamic models.

In Chapter 5, Aiken, Hanges, and Chen shift to a discussion of complexity science. Similar to the surrounding chapters, Aiken et al. are interested in emergence—the idea that constructs evolve and "emerge" over time. In contrast to the other chapters, however, they focus on emergence within the context of complex adaptive systems. In such systems, emergence is expressed in patterns of relationships that are nonlinear and nondeterministic. This chapter provides a thoughtful summary of complexity theory, particularly as it intersects with multilevel theory, giving readers a fantastic introduction to how one might better integrate concepts from complexity theory into their multilevel research.

In the next chapter, Ployhart and Hendricks (Chapter 6) begin a conversation about bottom-up theory and methods. Combining the micro and macro organizational literatures, they propose a framework for conducting microfoundations research—that is, research that connects the individual to organizational- or group-level outcomes. Their four-step process connects theorizing, measurement, and analysis in this domain. This chapter is invaluable for those scholars interested in looking "inside the box" to understand how lower level antecedents may emerge to influence higher level (e.g., organizational) outcomes.

Mathieu and Luciano (Chapter 7) integrate several themes in their chapter: construct clarification, emergence, and temporal dynamics. The goal of this integration was to propose an authentic and dynamic way of considering emergence, one that focused less on statistical processes and more on theoretical mechanisms. Within multilevel research, understanding emergence is fundamental because constructs at a higher level are dependent on, connected to, or otherwise affected by lower level phenomena, yet without a clear understanding of how focal constructs are connected to others, models are likely misspecified.

The next two chapters focus on social networks within organizational sciences. First, as Brass and Borgatti (Chapter 8) note, social networks are inherently multilevel in nature. They suggest that taking a social network approach to research will open both theoretical and empirical avenues, allowing researchers the opportunity to better specify and analyze relationships. With this as their focus, they spend the majority of the chapter orienting the reader to the complexities of social network research, particularly as they pertain to multilevel research questions.

Paruchuri, Goossen, and Phelps (Chapter 9) expand on this introduction to social network research in by presenting a guide for theorizing and specifying multilevel social networks. Whereas most social network research collapses multilevel data (e.g., individuals nested in dyads nested in departments) to a single level (e.g., individuals), Paruchuri and colleagues argue that much may be gained by scholars simultaneously examining multiple levels. In their chapter, they present a primer on social network research, moving from single-level to multilevel networks. Throughout the chapter, they couple an organizing framework with illustrative examples, grounding the reader in current science. Finally, they conclude by providing multiple avenues for future research, laying out a broad research agenda for aspiring scholars.

PART II: MULTILEVEL MEASUREMENT AND DESIGN

In this part of the handbook, we transition from focusing largely on issues related to multilevel theory, to a discussion of issues related to multilevel measurement and research design. These chapters are particularly important for those readers who have specified their theory and are now ready to set about collecting data to test it.

Zhou, Song, Alterman, Liu, and Wang (Chapter 10) present a valuable and detailed guide for collecting multilevel data. As they note, there are unique challenges associated with multi-level data collection—beyond what is required for single-level data collection—and understanding how to avoid fatal flaws is critical for anyone pursuing a multilevel research agenda. In addition to the in-depth guidance, they provide a pocket guide to their recommendations, which is likely to be a go-to handout for aspiring multilevel scholars.

Jebb, Tay, Ng, and Woo (Chapter 11) offer a primer on multilevel construct validation. Construct validation is an important component of research, serving as the bedrock on which theory testing rests. In this chapter, Jebb and colleagues walk the reader through the process of construct validation for multilevel studies, giving readers guidance for several construct forms. Finally, they include syntax for replicating their analyses, giving readers the opportunity to easily apply Jebb et al.'s guidance to their own work.

Chapter 12, by Krasikova and LeBreton, has three goals: to provide readers with a summary of the reliability and agreement indices that are most commonly used in multilevel research, to present a user-friendly guide to these indices, and to extend the application of these indices to the study of dyadic phenomena. In an effort to summarize this topic as succinctly as possible, the authors present a clear and interpretable set of guidelines for assessing agreement and reliability. Finally, within their illustrative example, they present syntax for replicating and extending their analyses.

Beal and Gabriel (Chapter 13) shift the focus to the unique challenges associated with measurement within the contexts of within-person research designs. Given the benefit to theory stemming from examining intraindividual development and change, understanding how to conduct these types of studies is imperative. They discuss several types of within-person research designs and highlight the strengths and weaknesses of each design. Finally, they connect the within-person methods to the between-person level, expanding the number of levels that may be studied.

Next, Scherbaum and Pesner (Chapter 14) deal with a crucial issue for multilevel research: determining whether one has sufficient power to adequately test his or her hypotheses. As the authors note, although power analysis is rather straight-forward and well documented within single-level research, the issue is appreciably more complex (and less well documented) in multilevel research. After reviewing the state of the literature and discussing the central equations, they present several tools for estimating multilevel power analysis. Finally, they walk readers through the use of these tools, providing a hands-on tutorial or guide to estimating power in multilevel research.

LaHuis, Blackmore, and Bryant-Lees (Chapter 15) examine how to calculate, interpret, and present estimates of explained variance in multilevel research. Given the movement to better integrate information about effect sizes into research

summaries, it is both logical and necessary for scholars to understand how variance is partitioned in multilevel research, as well as have the tools to estimate explained variance in their own research. After discussing several ways to estimate explained variance, the authors walk readers through the estimations, providing syntax for running the estimations in their own models.

In Chapter 16, Grund, Lüdtke, and Robitzsch address a common problem in multilevel research: missing data. Although scholars may be tempted to simply drop missing data from their analyses (listwise deletion), there are two clear problems: potential reductions in statistical power and the potential for biased estimates of population parameters. The authors discuss two solutions to this problem (multiple imputation and maximum likelihood estimation), followed by an illustration that walks the reader through the application of these methods. Similar to several other chapters, the authors provide their syntax for implementing these solutions.

PART III: MULTILEVEL ANALYSIS

The third part of the book deals with questions of analysis—now that you have a theory and have collected the data, how do you go about testing your hypotheses? The first chapter in this part, written by Shiverdecker and LeBreton (Chapter 17), presents a simple primer for conducting multilevel (random coefficients) regression analyses. In an effort to be comprehensive, the authors walk through both the mathematical models that underlie multilevel regression and the actual steps for running these models. Using an illustrative example and providing syntax, the authors offer even the most novice multilevel researcher the tools for modeling multilevel relationships.

Next, Knight and Humphrey (Chapter 18) discuss how to analyze dyadic data. They begin by providing a detailed introduction to dyadic data analysis, describing the different levels that exist in dyadic data structures (using both theoretical and empirical terminology). They then provide an empirical illustration of social relations modeling (one specific dyadic data analysis technique), walking the reader through each step (from structuring the data set to interpreting the results). After providing the syntax used in their chapter, they conclude by discussing alternative software packages for analyzing dyadic data.

In Chapter 19, Vandenberg and Richardson provide an introductory, "nuts and bolts" guide to multilevel structural equation modeling (MLSEM). After discussing the benefits of MLSEM, the authors build a testable model, walking the reader through each step necessary for eventually running an MLSEM. They not only present syntax for running an MLSEM but also discuss each component of the syntax and the output, giving readers in-depth knowledge of an MLSEM.

Going beyond the in-depth primer from the prior chapter, Zyphur, Zhang, Preacher, and Bird dedicate Chapter 20 to discussing moderated mediation in MLSEM. After discussing moderation, mediation, and moderated mediation, they provide an illustrative example of testing multilevel moderated mediation. In this example, they introduce a "Bayesian 'plausible values' approach to latent variable interactions" to avoid numerical integration (which ultimately ensures convergence in their analyses). These authors also provide the syntax they used to run the models in their chapter.

In Chapter 21, Zachary, Moore, and Ballinger focus on how to analyze nonnormal data in multilevel models. They begin by discussing the challenges associated with analyzing nonnormal data in multilevel analyses. They follow this by describing the benefits of generalized linear mixed modeling before providing an illustrative example. In walking the reader through the example, they provide relevant syntax for replicating their analyses.

Lang and Bliese (Chapter 22) offer a new statistical framework for detecting a specific form of emergence—consensus among lower level units nested in higher level collectives—over time. They develop a three-level emergence model that both provides a formal test of consensus emergence and allows researchers to include variables that might help to predict consensus. The authors conclude by demonstrating their model with two examples and again offer syntax so that others may verify and extend the results from this chapter to their own work.

In the final chapter of this part of the handbook, Newman and Wang (Chapter 23) provide an alternative method for assessing emergence through the use of network analysis. They begin by deriving the equations for their model, which they use to develop a computational model of climate emergence. They demonstrate the applicability of their model, providing useful syntax for applying their model to other contexts.

Some appendices for Chapters 11, 12, 16, 17, 18, 21, 22, and 23 include R codes. These appendices can also be found on the American Psychological Association website at http://pubs.apa.org/books/supp/humphrey/.

PART IV: REFLECTIONS ON MULTILEVEL RESEARCH

The two concluding chapters provide perspective on the development of multilevel research. In Chapter 24, Yammarino and Gooty discuss the use of cross-level models within the organizational sciences. They begin by providing a historical perspective on cross-level models, examining the similarities and differences in how the concept of "cross-level models" has been applied by various groups of researchers. They then transition to the presentation of an integrative cross-level model, discussing its applicability to theory building and testing within the organizational sciences.

The final chapter of the handbook (Chapter 25) consists of a series of interviews (conducted by Michael Hoffman) with five distinguished multilevel scholars: David Chan, Gilad Chen, Fred Dansereau, Denise Rousseau, and Benjamin Schneider. In these interviews, the scholars reflected on their experiences working on multilevel research, discussing the challenges they faced and the seminal work that influenced their thinking and their work. They then discuss where multilevel research is going, sharing their individual visions for the future.

References

Chan, D. (1998). Functional relations among constructs in the same content domain at different levels of analysis: A typology of composition models. *Journal of Applied Psychology, 83,* 234–246. http://dx.doi.org/10.1037/0021-9010.83.2.234

Humphrey, S. E., & Aime, F. (2014). Team microdynamics: Toward an organizing approach to teamwork. *The Academy of Management Annals, 8*, 443–503. http://dx.doi.org/10.5465/19416520.2014.904140

Klein, K. J., & Kozlowski, S. W. J. (2000). *Multilevel theory, research, and methods in organizations: Foundations, extensions, and new directions.* San Francisco, CA: Jossey-Bass.

Lepak, D. P., Smith, K. G., & Taylor, M. S. (2007). Value creation and value capture: A multilevel perspective. *Academy of Management Review, 32*, 180–194.

Morgeson, F. P., & Hofmann, D. A. (1999). The structure and function of collective constructs: Implications for multilevel research and theory development. *Academy of Management Review, 24*, 249–265.

## PART I

MULTILEVEL THEORY

## CHAPTER 1

ON FINDING YOUR LEVEL

Stanley M. Gully and Jean M. Phillips

We encourage scholars to think more deeply about the concept of the appropriate level of analysis in research. By *appropriate level*, we are not referring to the stated level of interest, the level of data collection, or the appropriate level of statistical analysis. For the purpose of this chapter, *identifying the appropriate level* means finding the level that has the most explanatory power for the outcome of interest. When we wish to identify the level that explains what is happening in a dynamic and complex system, how do we know where the "action" is in a multilevel framework? To answer this question, we focus on three key issues. First, we discuss why identifying the appropriate level is more challenging than it might initially appear. Some scholars have suggested that contiguity in levels creates the strong interactions necessary to create bonds, close coupling, and embeddedness. We agree in general but propose that focusing on tightly coupled levels can overlook key determinants of process dynamics that may skip levels. Second, we examine the notions of causality and variance and discuss the implications of these concepts in a multilevel framework. Third, we offer ideas and examples of how we can expand our thinking to consider what is meant when we refer to the appropriate level of analysis. By examining variance creation and variance restriction, we highlight a number of key processes that lead to the generation and dissolution of higher and lower level effects. We provide several examples and propose

some potential solutions to the thorny challenge of thinking about levels in the social sciences.

The concept *level of analysis* is pertinent to all social sciences, including research on family dynamics (Snijders & Kenny, 1999), education (Raudenbush & Bryk, 1988), health (Blakely & Woodward, 2000), crime (Groff, Weisburd, & Yang, 2010), emotions (Keltner & Haidt, 1999), international relations (Singer, 1961), community psychology (Shinn & Rapkin, 2000), applied psychology (Chan, 1998), and social and personality psychology (Nezlek, 2001). Similarly, we see levels issues in the micro–macro divide in the disciplines of sociology and economics (Gerstein, 1987; Hodgson, 1998; Jepperson & Meyer, 2011). The following discussion pertains to levels issues in all of these fields and more. We use a variety of examples drawn from different fields but applicable to all of the above social science disciplines, as well as others.

We begin with the following simple question: What is the appropriate level of analysis? To answer this question, we must first define what is meant by *level*. We define a *level* as a focal plane in social, psychological, or physical space that exists within a hierarchical structure among things or constructs (Gully & Phillips, 2005; K. J. Klein, Dansereau, & Hall, 1994; Rousseau, 1985). *Levels* refer to distinct hierarchical structures within a system, with some entities existing within or as a part of others. We can conceive of the hierarchical structure as a series

http://dx.doi.org/10.1037/0000115-002
The Handbook of Multilevel Theory, Measurement, and Analysis, S. E. Humphrey and J. M. LeBreton (Editors-in-Chief)

of nested relationships with, for example, repeated observations nested within individuals, individuals nested within families, and families within communities. Communities, in turn, can be nested within regions, and regions can be nested within countries.

Typically, what is defined as a higher or lower level depends on the phenomenon of interest. In a business context, teams are a higher level of analysis when compared to individuals, but they are a lower level of analysis when compared to organizations, unless the "teams" are policy makers in governments that affect organizational regulation, in which case the teams may be at a higher level than organizations. To be clear, *higher* and *lower levels* do not refer to power relationships or echelons (Rousseau, 1985), although they may be related. Also, we do not mean to imply that all levels are equally present in all organizations or all contexts. Some organizations may not have teams within their hierarchical structure (i.e., flatter organizations), whereas other organizations may or may not have distinct business units within their overall organizational structure. We are merely trying to highlight the possibilities in levels as we pursue our discussion.

Figure 1.1 shows the levels most often considered by organizational scientists. Given our backgrounds in industrial and organizational psychology and management, we draw from examples that tend to focus largely on the individual (e.g., individual attitudes, individual behavior, and individual performance) or team levels (e.g., team cohesion, team potency, team performance, team conflict), but the same principles we describe also apply to other levels and other contexts of social science. For example, we can envision students within classrooms within schools within school districts within states or regions within nations. Also, as we seek to answer the question "what is the appropriate level," we find that our focal level may not be the individual level, even if we wish to understand individual outcomes. In any case, much of our attention as social scientists has been targeted toward the lower regions (as indicated by the shading), ranging from social collectives (e.g., organizations) to individuals. Some scholars might suggest that we look at levels below that of individuals by trying to understand what happens to individuals over time (e.g., mood). This is a lower level because it is within the person

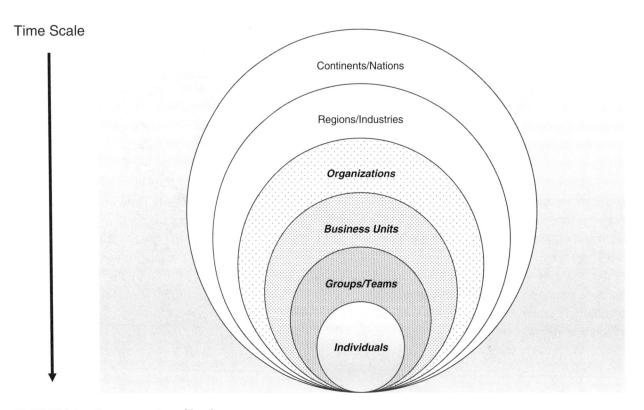

FIGURE 1.1.   Representation of levels.

over time. This argument is correct, but we address time as a distinct topic in subsequent discourse for reasons that will soon become clear. For now, we focus on physical, psychological, or social structures that exist above and below the level of groups–teams.

One issue that should be apparent is that levels have semipermeable boundaries. For example, some individuals are members of multiple teams within organizations and some countries are somewhat homogenous internally, whereas others may have varying characteristics across regions (as in the United States). We see the same thing in high schools with students attending several classes within the same school or teachers working in more than one school within the same district.

Additionally, it is not always clear where some levels reside. Some levels cut across other levels. Consider for example, the notions of "job" or "vocation." Does a job or vocation exist within (i.e., hierarchically nested under) an organization? Often, we place jobs at a lower level than the work unit (different jobs within the unit) and the individual who fills a given job at the level below the job level (one type of job can be filled by different people, so job is the higher level). The organization would be at a higher level than the individual, job, or work unit, because the work unit is nested within the organization. Yet individuals have allegiances to their jobs that transcend work units and even organizations. Moreover, many jobs share common characteristics that transcend organizations or even geographic regions (O*Net, 2017). Similarly, many of us see our membership within professional societies as part of our job, but our membership both defines and is defined by our roles outside the university or college to which we belong.

Consider the job of professor. A person in such a position is nested in multiple sets of structures, including formal hierarchical job structures (e.g., rank, department, college, university) and professional semi- or nonhierarchical structures (leadership in professional societies, editorial boards, multiple research teams). Thus, the person is nested within the job (e.g., associate professor) nested within the department (e.g., Sociology) within the university (e.g., Penn State), but that same person may also be nested within several research teams that may be further nested within distinct geographic or cultural regions. Professional structures and research teams often exist independently of the department or university within which the person is employed, yet the particular individual and associated job of professor is relevant to all these contexts. This is what we mean when we say that some levels cut across levels and that levels are semi-permeable. One challenge is trying to pick the correct level of analysis for understanding an outcome when the level itself may be semi-permeable (and as we shall see in the section Dual Processes in Multilevel Systems, impermanent). As scientists, we need to be clear about our basis for grouping entities and articulate reasons for ignoring other potentially relevant grouping systems (Mathieu & Chen, 2011).

PROBLEMS WITH IDENTIFYING THE LEVEL

It may seem that a chapter exploring the identification of the appropriate level isn't needed because if we want to know the level, we need only think about the outcome we are trying to understand. If we want to understand individual behavior (e.g., student achievement), then the level is the individual (i.e., the student). There may be factors residing both above the individual level (e.g., teacher experience, availability of classroom technology) and below the individual level (e.g., day-to-day patterns of sleep, nutrition, or affect) that may impact or influence individual behavior, but the level is clearly the individual. Likewise, if we want to understand outcomes residing at the level of a social collective (e.g., team performance), then the level is the team. Similarly, a focus on trust in married couples implies that the level is the couple; a focus on organizational profitability implies that the "appropriate" level is the organization.

However, what if it isn't so simple? When we ask, "What is the appropriate level?" we don't mean "What is the level of your dependent variable?" or "What is the level at which I should analyze my data?" Rather, we are asking, "What is the level that will enable deep understanding of a particular phenomenon?" Or, in plain language, "Where's the action?" This question is more difficult to answer for a variety of reasons. First, our theory and disciplinary backgrounds affect what we attend to. Perhaps if we want to understand individual student health, then we might surmise that the level is the individual student. We could incorporate a level up, so we could examine social structures (e.g., peer social support, school lunch programs) to understand individual student stress and wellness. This is an obvious approach to the levels question. Think about the outcome of interest, and that tells you the level of action.

Unless, of course, you work at the Centers for Disease Control and Prevention (CDC) and are trying to understand student health; then the level might be within-person, at the biological or cellular level. Or suppose you work at the CDC and you are trying to understand a pandemic in schools, in which case the level might be international or global travel patterns. We may not be able to understand individual health without understanding global infection patterns (global level), and we can't understand global patterns if we don't understand the biological pathways through which an infection occurs (viral or bacterial level). Additionally, we may need to understand individual travel patterns (within or across national levels) as well as within-person level behaviors and genetics (Are particular people predisposed? Does the individual wash his or her hands and when? What did he or she eat? With whom did she or he interact?). Understanding student health at the CDC to stop a global pandemic requires an understanding of all these levels.

Our choice of theory affects everything. It determines what level of analysis we use for sampling, who or what we sample, how we measure, what we measure, when we measure, and how we analyze the data. If we believe that student health is an individual-level phenomenon, then we might go to a single school; gather data on 1,000 students, including classrooms, teachers, classmates, and so forth; and then analyze the data. Given that we believe it is an individual-level phenomenon, we will ask how the *individual* feels, thinks, and acts. But what if it is a group phenomenon? Perhaps instead of asking whether the individual worries about wellness, we need to ask whether other

students in the classroom worry about wellness because that sets the social context for taking care of oneself. We know the wording matters. Asking whether I feel self-efficacious is not the same as asking whether classmates feel efficacious (Chan, 1998), even if we aggregate individual perceptions to the level of the classroom. How we word the questions affects the variability we observe and the intrinsic meaning of the construct (Baltes, Zhdanova, & Parker, 2009; Chen, Mathieu, & Bliese, 2004; K. J. Klein, Conn, Smith, & Sorra, 2001). What if student health is influenced by school-level or districtwide phenomena, as it almost certainly is (e.g., McNeely, Nonnemaker, & Blum, 2002), but we focus on the individual?

For another context, consider employees working in the technology industry. Gathering data (even a large sample; $N = 5,000$) from individuals nested within a single company or individuals nested within two companies (e.g., IBM and Google; $N = 5,000$ per organization) necessarily excludes key factors that determine employee health such as industrial safety records. Our initial focus on the individual may overlook the large-scale patterns of health and wellness across industries, organizations, and occupations (Bureau of Labor Statistics, 2015a, 2015b, 2016; Johnson et al., 2005), and we miss the big picture. Our theory determines what we sample and what we measure. If we believe that occupations (or grades), organizations (or schools), or industries (or school districts) matter, then we gather data on units at that level. If we believe individuals matter, then that's where we seek our samples.

If our theory determines how we sample, measure, and analyze, and if the way in which we approach these decisions then constricts (or enhances) our ability to see effects at a particular level, then how do we know when we've got the right level or levels? There have been multilevel analytic systems that purport to tell us the level at which effects exist (Dansereau, Alutto, & Yammarino, 1984). Although such approaches can be useful because they can tell us the level at which we observe variance, the findings are unlikely to generalize to other, more diverse samples or data sets. These approaches cannot tell you where the variance lives in the system, out there in the wild, because the variance of the data is itself determined by what and how we measure and sample. We won't see variance, even if it's important, if we don't sample and measure in ways that enable us to see it.

In a way, James, Demaree, and Wolf (1984) recognized this conundrum when they introduced their measure of agreement: r_{WG}. Simply because there is insufficient variance across units to see differences doesn't mean that agreement isn't present or that a higher level construct doesn't exist. Most existing measures for agreement at the time examined it from a reliability perspective or from a group effects perspective [e.g., F tests, intraclass correlation coefficient (ICC)(1), ICC(2)] and thus relied on the proportion of variance across units as compared to the proportion of variance within units to tell us whether members within units responded reliably or consistently (James, 1982). Simply because all units are relatively similar in terms of their mean levels on a construct (and thus, there is very little between-unit variance) doesn't mean that there isn't a higher level construct worth assessing and understanding.

Our choice of theory can and will lead us to focus on a given level, but we bring with us a certain myopia for looking at a given research problem. A public health researcher might look at employee health at the governmental and community levels (e.g., health policy), and a sociologist might look at employee health as a social problem, at the level of structures within our society (e.g., poverty, access to health care). A management researcher studying teams might look at employee wellness as a function of social and team dynamics or leadership (e.g., social support, abusive supervision, access to wellness programs). A personality theorist might look at employees' mental health as a function of individual characteristics (e.g., self-identity, self-esteem, sensation seeking, depression). Which level is "correct"? The point is that selecting the focal level of interest can excise meaningful other variables from the equation.

How then do we find the correct level? For now, it's enough to assert that no statistical system can identify whether we have the correct level because our statistical results are determined by what we do. Furthermore, theory drives what we do, which then tells us what we see and have done. It is difficult to determine the correct level theoretically because the theory gives us tunnel vision. Unfortunately, there's no recipe to follow to know that we've found the right level. Instead, we have to operate as detectives, picking up a clue here or there, fencing off areas for careful examination to reduce contamination of evidence, making observations over time. It is only then that we will uncover where (i.e., at what level or levels) the (majority of) variance truly resides. In most circumstances, we are not looking for a single level. Instead, we have to think about identifying a multilevel nomological network (Cronbach & Meehl, 1955). The following sections provide thoughts on how we can proceed more effectively as detectives and provide some fodder for thinking beyond our respective disciplinary foci.

ASSUMPTIONS OF TIGHT COUPLING

Previous scholars (Hackman, 2003; Kozlowski & Klein, 2000; Simon, 1973) have suggested that contiguity in levels creates the strong interactions necessary to create bonds, close coupling, and embeddedness. In general, we agree with this sentiment, but we caution that by focusing on tightly coupled levels we may overlook key determinants of process dynamics that may skip levels. Scholars (ourselves included) frequently assume that stronger relationships may be detected among variables that exist at the same level of analysis. So, for example, it is thought that the best predictors of individual performance will be individual factors (e.g., intelligence, conscientiousness, work ethic; Schmidt & Hunter, 1998). Likewise, many scholars would argue that we need to examine team-level input and process factors to understand team-level outcomes, even when those input or process factors represent aggregations of individual-level variables (e.g., team ability or team personality; Barrick, Stewart, Neubert, & Mount, 1998; Baysinger, Scherer, & LeBreton, 2014). It's such a compelling argument that it nearly seems tautological, and there is a long history of this type of thinking.

Indik (1968) was an early systems scholar who presented a figure with panels representing variables for structure, process, and function at the organizational, group, and individual levels. He stated,

> Specifically, we expect larger relationships to occur between variables in panels closer together in the schema. For example, organization size, a Panel One variable, should be more clearly related to variables of organization function or process such as communication, control, or coordination than to Panel Five [individual] variables such as attitude toward the organization, attitude toward the work group, and achievement motivation. (p. 22)

Here he is making the clear argument that we will find stronger connections for variables connected at a given level, or across contiguous levels, than jumping across levels.

Simon (1973) made a similar argument when describing the nature of hierarchical systems. He described a hierarchy that "leads from human societies to organizations, to small groups, to individual human beings, to cognitive programs in the central nervous system, to elementary information processes" (p. 9). He went on to state the following:

> Most interactions that occur in nature, between systems of all kinds, decrease in strength with distance. Hence, any given "particle" has most of its strong interactions with nearby particles. As a result, a system is likely to behave either as made up of a collection of localized subsystems or to form a more or less uniform "tissue" of equally strong interactions. (p. 9)

This perspective suggests that everything is connected but that some things are more connected than others, and those factors closest to others at the same level are most important for understanding a particular phenomenon. We once believed this as well, and perhaps it is often true. But there is evidence to suggest otherwise, and we think the "skip level effect" may be more common than we typically consider.

Hackman (2003) questioned the utility of seeking explanations solely at the same or lower levels of analysis. Data were collected on 300 flight crews in nine different types of aircraft at seven different airlines. The conceptual model tested was Hackman's own (1987), which posited that the design of the flying task and the design of the aircrew would determine whether aircrews developed into self-correcting high-performing units. As he put it,

> We knew we were in trouble when we performed a simple one-way analysis of variance on our measures of crew structure and behavior across the seven diverse airlines. There was almost no variation across airlines on precisely those crew-level variables that we had expected to be most consequential for performance. (p. 910)

Where was the team level (i.e., crew-level) variance? When they turned to the organizational and institutional contexts within which aircrews operated, they found variation in perceived contextual factors, including adequacy of material resources, clarity of performance objectives, recognition and reinforcement for excellent crew performance, availability of educational and technical assistance, and availability of informational resources. Between-airline differences accounted for 23% of the variation in the composite measure of context supportiveness and context related to pilot satisfaction. However, none of these factors predicted pilot behavior and aircrew effectiveness. Why?

According to Hackman (2003), there were three dominant influences on aircrew performance, none of which were under the control of the flight crews or even the airlines for which they worked. First, there was aircraft and cockpit technology. Standard cockpit technology was generated by designers and engineers at Airbus and Boeing, and there are finite sets of configurations and technologies, all of which were designed for efficiency and safety. They found no aircrew differences associated with aircraft differences, because the consistency of technology determined how aircrew members interacted with one another and with others external to the flight crew. Even though there was limited observable variance, there was a higher level aircraft manufacturer effect that determined how aircrews behaved.

Second, there is a clearly defined set of regulatory procedures and standards developed over the years by the U.S. Federal Aviation Administration (FAA), in cooperation with airline manufacturers and flight operations departments of U.S. airlines. These FAA procedures and standards have been adopted globally, often with little modification, by airlines and regulatory agencies around the world. This creates consistency in how aircrews operate in widely varying contexts. Again, although we see limited variance, there is a higher level effect of institutionalized regulatory procedures and standards on aircrew behavior.

Hackman (2003) described the pervasive "culture of flying" that is rooted in a shared individualized experience that affects how pilots perceive and behave. Every pilot has a shared, nearly institutionalized experience as a pilot. All pilots worry about medical checks, and each pilot recognizes the importance of proficiency checks. This creates a consistency in the values and mindset of pilots regardless of background or location. There is limited variance across individuals for this "pilot" cultural effect, but the consistency across individual experiences affects what happens in flight crews. There is empirical evidence in other domains that when decision makers engage in consistent behaviors and interventions across time and situations, restriction of variance in performance can result. In other words, effective organizational or policy interventions attenuate or restrict variance in behavior or performance (Lebreton, Burgess, Kaiser, Atchley, & James, 2003).

Hackman (2003) detailed other examples of how factors at higher or lower levels of analysis than the team impinge on team processes and outcomes across a diverse array of examples including orchestral performance (influenced by national level cultures regarding gender and strength of ties with the orchestral community) and hospital patient care teams (influenced by nurse managers' reporting of errors).

Upon reflection, these findings make intuitive sense. Higher and lower level factors can shape the variance and outcomes observed at a particular level, sometimes many levels apart. Organizational differences can enhance or impede variation in team processes, so it may be the case that team effectiveness is not an outgrowth of team-level process or input factors but a result of contextual factors that determine how the team is structured and behaves. Likewise, family dynamics within a given society may be equally or more influenced by cultural factors than by individual factors. This is actually an old idea, but one that we believe theorists should re-embrace.

We concur with Hackman (2003) that we should consider "bracketing" higher and lower levels when investigating processes at a given level. Bracketing can enhance one's understanding of targeted phenomena; help discover factors that drive those phenomena, even when variance doesn't initially appear to exist; uncover boundary conditions and interactions that shape an outcome of interest; and inform choice of constructs within a nomological network (Cronbach & Meehl, 1955) representing a multilevel theoretic framework.

We hope that we've convinced you that (a) phenomena often cannot be easily understood with a focus on a single level of analysis; (b) we can't simply use theory to know the correct levels to consider because theory can be blinding; (c) we can't simply use statistics to know the correct levels to consider because our observations are driven by what we do (i.e., what data we consider and how we analyze it); and (d) simply assuming that factors at the same or contiguous levels are the most important for understanding outcomes at a given level may be misleading. Next, we turn to some thorny issues associated with finding the correct levels to consider and offer some possible solutions to these challenges.

EXPLANATIONS OF CAUSE AND EFFECT

From an epistemological perspective, why do scholars and researchers examine multilevel issues, or for that matter, any research domain? Presumably we do so because we wish to understand particular phenomena of interest. Inherent in this statement, despite limitations of our research methodologies and data analytic techniques, is the notion that we wish to understand *causality or causal systems*, or to answer the "why" question. If we aren't trying to understand what causes what, and why, then what is the point of theory and research? We could merely describe what we see.

Implicit in the work we do is the idea that we want to understand cause and effect relationships. If we adopt John Stuart Mill's approach to determining causality (Cook & Campbell, 1979), then three conditions must hold: (a) the cause must precede the effect in time, (b) the cause and effect have to be related (covary), and (c) other explanations of cause and effect have to be eliminated. These three conditions pose unique challenges and opportunities in a multilevel context. We begin with condition (c), that other explanations of cause and effect have to be eliminated.

Almost by definition, our world is made up of complex multilevel systems, including geographical tracts, nations, religions, schools, families, and neighborhoods. Organizations and the people who work in them are a sliver of that complex multilevel context. This is important because by acknowledging complexity across levels, we are acknowledging that most levels (actually, we would argue all levels) operate as part of an open rather than a closed system. As Katz and Kahn (1978) noted, a closed system walls off external influences on the relationships between inputs, processes, and outcomes, so that it becomes easier to see when movement in one part of the system leads to predictable patterns of movement or outcomes in other parts of the system. In contrast, in an open system the inputs, processes, and outcomes of a given part of the system may be influenced by inputs and disruptions from factors external to the system.

For example, in a closed system we could raise an individual in a box and control all aspects of the environment so that we could see how inputs (e.g., rewards) translate into outcomes (e.g., productivity) in a relatively deterministic pattern. This would be Skinner's box applied to an individual's life. Reality, however, is quite different. Individuals are buffeted by a variety of factors ranging from genetic and family effects to work, school, and national effects. We see external influences on individuals resulting

from major wars (e.g., World War II, Vietnam, Iraq), unusual opportunities (e.g., the Internet), and disasters (e.g., tsunamis), as well as other geophysical events that shape food and resource accessibility (e.g., volcanic eruptions, water scarcity). Our planet is the ultimate open system, with the constant energization on earth provided by the sun allowing life to fight the constant downhill ride toward entropy and enabling it to build structure where otherwise there would be disorder. In open systems, higher levels can be affected by lower level inputs as well. For example, individuals can become infected by parasites or bombarded by high-energy particles that can alter DNA, eventually leading to adaptations or cancer.

Within such dynamic, open systems, how are we to resolve condition (c), eliminating other explanations of cause and effect? It seems impossible because of the nearly infinite array of multilevel influences that can serve as an alternative explanation of cause and effect. To address this issue, we adopt a different but related point of view. Rather than completely eliminating other explanations of cause and effect, we suggest that we should incorporate them, theorize about them, and analyze and test them. We must consider bracketing levels (Hackman, 2003) by imagining a larger box (a theoretically closed system that doesn't exist in reality) that incorporates input and disruptive factors at levels below and above the focal level of interest. In this system, we may need to bracket levels much higher or lower than the outcome of interest. This is the foundation for the multilevel nomological network we mentioned in the section Assumptions of Tight Coupling.

For example, we have studies examining how organizational factors influence happiness and job satisfaction (Grant, Christianson, & Price, 2007; Takeuchi, Chen, & Lepak, 2009), how cross-national differences are related to happiness (Schyns, 1998), how teams affect happiness (Cheshin, Rafaeli, & Bos, 2011), how marital and family factors relate to happiness over time (Tsang, Harvey, Duncan, & Sommer, 2003), and how individual attributes are related to happiness 10 years later (Costa & McCrae, 1980). Our point is that such examinations have been piecemeal, taking one or two points of a larger system. This is not enough because happiness is likely to be influenced by all of these factors plus other factors such as macroeconomic patterns (Di Tella, MacCulloch, & Oswald, 2003).

It's fine enough if we, as scholars, tackle different components of a problem, but we tend to stay on our disciplinary tracks, rarely peering up, down, or across to take in the perspectives of scientists in other disciplines working on the same or related problems. At a recent conference on multilevel issues, we saw some of this in action. Some scholars focused on factors proximal to the individual, whereas others focused on organizational contextual factors. This led to an interesting dialogue about what matters more: organizational context or proximal team characteristics. The reality is that both perspectives are valid and we need to bridge them (Hitt, Beamish, Jackson, & Mathieu, 2007; House, Rousseau, & Thomas-Hunt, 1995). The effort to create precision in our theorizing may have the unintended side effect of creating ambiguity in what is the appropriate level of focus, because it is rarely a single level.

It is often said that the *level of theory* refers to the focal level to which generalizations are meant to apply (Mathieu & Chen, 2011; Rousseau, 1985). We can and should attempt to specify levels of theoretical interest, but we fear the process creates blinders that inhibit our ability to see the system as a system, particularly one with open inputs and disruptions. As Kozlowski and Klein (2000) stated: "The system is sliced into organization, group, and individual levels, each level the province of different disciplines, theories, and approaches. The organization may be an integrated system, but organizational science is not" (p. 3). We wholeheartedly concur and would argue that this criticism is not unique to organizational science, but more generally to social science (inclusively defined). Furthermore, at the higher level the system is also sliced into clusters (e.g., industries, economies, social and political structures), and at the lower level individuals are sliced into within-person constructs (e.g., moods, intraindividual variation in performance, neural patterns, even genetics). Scientists (including ourselves) are typically trained to slice and dice; we are trained to isolate and test. However, even theories that purport to be "integrative" rarely offer

a unified treatment of phenomena considering possible antecedents, correlates, and consequences of the phenomena across four, five, or even more interacting "levels."

Rousseau (1985) pointed out an idea on which House et al. (1995) later elaborated: Processes across several different levels are often connected, and the appropriate units of analysis may span from individuals to teams to organizations to clusters of organizations. Phenomena such as marital satisfaction, learning, group decision making, altruism, and technological systems are not single-level systems. To understand them and their associated causal determinants and effects, we must adopt a more holistic and integrative mode of thinking. The "appropriate" level is the system. It is all of the levels. Truly understanding phenomena requires a comprehensive understanding of many parts of a system or a clearer definition of what you are interested in studying (recognizing that you may be excising important determining factors). There is no single focal level because the phenomenon transcends the distinct slices. The mind is more than a cluster of neurons, the individual is more than a pile of organs, the family is more than an aggregation of individuals, the organization is more than a group of people with similar attitudes or goals, and an organizational strategy is more than the CEO's vision.

Consider another example to further elucidate the importance of this type of thinking. It is well accepted that the laboratory experiment is the epitome of research designs to assess causality because of its high internal validity and ability to eliminate or control extraneous influences (Shadish, Cook, & Campbell, 2002). However, experiments are part of an open system and exist within higher levels (Hanges & Wang, 2012). Consider the psychology undergraduate who expected to participate in laboratory studies as part of the requirements for course credit. The broader context is the cause for participation in the study, and the student carries these external influences into the closed box of the laboratory environment. The student will almost certainly behave differently if he or she feels like a lab rat forced to participate as compared to a student who feels that his or her participation is making a fundamental contribution to science. Additionally, it's possible that there is a social influence process operating, perhaps at the department or university level, so that in some universities students are happy to participate whereas at others they begrudgingly give their time. Laboratories are not as pure as we might like to believe. How might the outcome of an experiment vary as a function of the open system input factors?

How do we build a science of understanding causal connections to individual behavior when such effects can cascade across systems and levels? Our answer is to build theory that examines, tests, and incorporates the possible effects of such multi-level input factors into our models of causality. Failure to do so may lead us terribly astray because we cannot know what to conclude from even an excellently designed experiment without understanding the context.

How does this line of thinking help us with the causal problem at hand? By integrating causal factors across levels, we eliminate or reduce the likelihood that other unspecified causal factors are at play. "Other unspecified causal factors" is analogous to the omitted variables problem (see James, 1980; James, Mulaik, & Brett, 1982). Failure to include key causal variables in our models creates bias and misspecification of effects. By integrating other causal mechanisms across levels, we reduce the likelihood of omitted variables and overlooking other causal factors. As Katz and Kahn (1978) suggested,

> The closed system view implies that irregularities in the functioning of a system due to environmental influences are error variances and should be treated accordingly. According to this conception, they should be controlled out of studies of organizations. From the organization's own operations they should be excluded as irrelevant and should be guarded against. . . . Open system theory, on the other hand, would maintain that environmental influences are not sources of error variance but are integral to the functioning of a social

system, and that we cannot understand a system without a constant study of the forces that impinge upon it. (p. 32)

Additionally, if we are able to understand the operation of complex causal open systems across levels, then it becomes inordinately difficult for an unspecified and unmeasured causal factor to explain the interwoven chains of events unfolding across levels. Similarly, if there is an important yet overlooked causal variable in the system, then we should be able to note its presence by perturbations within some particular level or across levels.

Pragmatically, no scholar can know or study everything. For this integration we need partnerships across disciplines, and we must learn to speak the language of other scholars investigating the same or similar phenomena. We may learn that when economists speak of shirking (Kim, Han, Blasi, & Kruse, 2015), it appears similar to social loafing (Lount & Wilk, 2014). And when economists speak of moral hazard and the $1/n$ problem (Thompson, McWilliams, & Shanley, 2014), it reminds us of social dilemmas in social psychology (Bridoux & Stoelhorst, 2016; Van Lange, Joireman, Parks, & Van Dijk, 2013). In the process, we may begin to recognize how economic forces at the national and global level such as the labor market affect the feelings, decision making, and actions of individuals within families or employees in particular organizations. Working with engineers, we may discover that they think about the effect of individual "forgetting" over time on team productivity (Nembhard, 2014; Shafer, Nembhard, & Uzumeri, 2001) and that failure to consider forgetting as a process leads to an incomplete picture about what makes some teams more effective than others. We propose that social scientists should make a concerted effort to work with scholars across diverse disciplines to explore other levels of analysis and to think more broadly about the causal systems at play. This may improve our collective understanding of why things happen the way they do.

> **Principle 1:** Adopting a holistic, open systems view of social systems and building multilevel theory to account

for phenomena will reduce the likelihood that important causal variables will be omitted.

CAUSE AND EFFECT COVARIANCE

The next issue we contemplate as a vexing challenge is condition (b): that the cause and effect have to be related (covary). It is nice to believe that when *X* happens, *Y* follows consistently and deterministically. This certainly would allow us to build a strong causal theory for *X* to *Y* effects. However, two key issues limit our ability to see such relationships: probabilistic outcomes and equifinality. First, when dealing with social phenomena, most outcomes we observe are probabilistic. It's probably nearly axiomatic that if you are hungry, you eat. There's a clear causal connection: hunger → eating. If you are hungry and it's lunchtime, do you always eat? Do you always stop your work to go get lunch? Do all people eat at lunchtime when they are hungry? Do people only eat when they are hungry? If we required hunger to precede eating and hunger to be associated with eating each and every time that hunger is present, and if we further required that in the absence of hunger, eating would not occur, how well could we establish the causal link between hunger and eating? The simple answer is that we cannot do it if we require such deterministic and absolute relationships.

In a multilevel system, we must take into account multiple factors across levels and assume that they relate to the outcome in a probabilistic, not deterministic, fashion. In addition to hunger, eating behavior at lunchtime may be influenced by contextual factors such as workload (is there a chapter to be finished?), social influence (are others going to lunch and inviting you?), and cost (is lunch expensive at the diner?). It is influenced by individual factors such as memory (did I bring my lunch today?), self-image (is it okay to eat?), and so forth. When we combine the various factors, we can begin to see the causal patterns at play, but it's important to recognize that outcomes are caused by combinations of input factors, often across levels.

One approach to determining causal patterns is to conduct the necessary condition analysis (Dul, 2016).

In multicausal situations in which many factors contribute to outcomes, identifying those factors that are necessary but not sufficient to generate the outcome is helpful. Within a multilevel system, this can allow us to begin to parse the causal system into its dynamic components. Necessary conditions include those that are essential, critical, and not easily replaced by other factors but that are not sufficient by themselves to generate the outcome.

The second issue is equifinality. Multilevel and open systems are often characterized by the principle of equifinality, which means that a system can reach the same final state from differing initial conditions and by a variety of paths (Katz & Kahn, 1978). Katz and Kahn (1978) stated, "The equifinality principle simply asserts that there are more ways than one of producing a given outcome" (p. 30). If there are different paths to the outcome, then it also means that a given cause will inconsistently covary with the phenomenon of interest. In closed systems, the same initial operating parameters and inputs yield consistent outcomes. In open systems, there are many paths to any given outcome, and thus, many ways to achieve any given outcome. For example, employees might become more committed by treating them fairly and justly (Colquitt & Zipay, 2015), involving them in important decisions (Cox, Zagelmeyer, & Marchington, 2006), or empowering them to work in a more autonomous manner (Avolio, Zhu, Koh, & Bhatia, 2004). In short, there may be no single *X* that results in *Y*. There are many Xs and permutations of *X*, as well as other factors such as *Z*, *W*, and *Q*. To make the point, K. H. Roberts, Hulin, and Rousseau (1978) quoted Piaget (1971, p. 37): "Behavior is at the mercy of every possible disequilibrating factor, since it is always dependent on an environment which has no fixed limits and is constantly fluctuating" (p. 57).

How, then, do we establish causality when we don't know when or whether *X* will covary with *Y* (or whether *Z*, *W*, or *Q* will also covary with *Y*)? Again, the solution is to adopt a more holistic and integrated view of the phenomenon of interest. If we incorporate factors across levels and see that *X* probabilistically covaries with *Y* and also that *A*, *B*, and *C* covary with *X* and *Y*, then we can begin to build models of the conditions under which *X* will or will not covary with the Y outcome. We suggest that even though inputs from multiple levels are complex and dynamic, there are predictable dynamics that can be quantified and understood if we examine the system as a system. We can also begin to identify the necessary conditions for phenomena (Dul, 2016).

It's not easy, but we must find and explore the multiple paths to the outcomes so that we can better understand the conditions (and boundary conditions) in which the cause and effect are related. This is more important than scholars might readily acknowledge. For example, within applied psychology, there is a belief that hiring top performers (X) will yield high performance (Y). This tends to be true . . . except when it isn't (Groysberg, Nanda, & Nohria, 2004). What might affect the ability of stars to perform in a new job? Factors include the technology of the system, the social support of the new work group, firm resources, and developmental culture (Groysberg, 2010). We cannot assume simple $X \rightarrow Y$ causal patterns when equifinality and probabilistic outcomes exist. Yet, just because it's difficult doesn't mean we shouldn't try. As K. H. Roberts et al. (1978) stated,

> We can and should try to observe, quantify, and explain regularities in responses of individuals and groups in organizational contexts. By regularities we do not mean there must be a one-to-one correspondence between a stimulus and a response or between two responses. (p. 6)

These efforts will result in the development of multilevel nomological networks. Nomological networks are interlocking systems of constructs and relationships that constitute the fundamental components of our theories (cf. Binning & Barrett, 1989; Cronbach & Meehl, 1955; Messick, 1995).

> **Principle 2:** Adopting a holistic, open systems view of social systems and building multilevel theory to account for phenomena will improve our understanding and increase the likelihood that causal relationships will be properly specified.

CAUSE AND TEMPORAL PRECEDENCE

We now turn our attention to the final remaining condition for establishing causality—condition (a), that the cause must temporally precede the effect. This requirement seems both obvious and reasonable. If X is to cause Y, then surely X must precede Y in time. In some ways, however, this condition of determining causality may well be the most difficult of all to establish in multilevel open systems for three reasons: scaling of time, lagged outcomes, and fragile homeostasis.

Scaling of Time
Scaling of time refers to the notion that the rate at which processes unfold often varies across the level of hierarchy within a system. To discuss time, we must first recognize that time can cut across all focal levels yet can also exist at a lower level than the focal level. All units, whatever the level, change or evolve in some way. This means that repeated observations of a given entity (e.g., person, group, organization) reside at a lower level of analysis than the level of the entity itself (e.g., within-person, within-group, within-organization). For example, if data on student reading proficiency were collected four times throughout the academic year, then the repeated observations over time would be considered a within-person (student) factor.

However, this is not to imply that all observations over time reside at the lowest level. To make this statement clear, we provide an example. Assume we are interested in employee performance and believe it is affected by the employees' levels of task-specific self-efficacy and their individual levels of conscientiousness. In addition, we hypothesize that individual-level performance is also influenced by organizational culture. To test these hypotheses, we measure employee performance over four quarters with self-efficacy assessed each time (within-persons). We measure employee conscientiousness once, at the beginning of the study (person-level). We obtain a measure of organizational culture based on a survey completed the previous year by employees and subsequently aggregated up to the organizational level (organizational level; i.e., all individuals residing in a given organization are assigned the score for culture). In this model, time exists at the bottommost level, because observations take place within individuals (time or quarters), individual conscientiousness is at Level 2 (individual), and organizational success (i.e., previous performance) at Level 3 (organizational):

Level 1 $\quad Y_{tij} = \pi_{0ij} + \pi_{1ij}(\text{Self-Efficacy}_{tij}) + e_{tij}$

Level 2 $\quad \pi_{0ij} = \beta_{00j} + \beta_{01k}(\text{Conscientiousness}_{ij}) + r_{0ij}$

$\qquad\quad \pi_{1ij} = \beta_{10j} + r_{1ij}$

Level 3 $\quad \beta_{00j} = \gamma_{000} + \gamma_{001}(\text{Organizational Culture}_k)$

$\qquad\qquad\qquad + u_{00j}$

$\qquad\quad \beta_{01j} = \gamma_{010} + u_{01j}$

$\qquad\quad \beta_{10j} = \gamma_{100} + u_{10j}.$

In most hierarchical linear or random coefficient models, time is treated at the lowest level. Now imagine the same study but instead of a single measure of organizational culture based on the previous year's annual culture survey, we instead obtained ratings of culture each quarter. This situation creates substantial complexity not present in the previous example because we cannot simply stick several observations of organizational culture under the level of individuals. Time is a lower level than each entity, but multiple observations over time do not necessarily exist at the bottom rung of levels effects. In this latter example, we might be interested in the magnitude and trajectory of organizational culture. For example, if the organization is increasing in its culture for innovation, then perhaps that stimulates individuals to try harder and perform better, whereas decreasing culture for innovation might have the opposite effect. Conversely, from a social loafing perspective, perhaps individuals try less hard when the organization is doing increasingly well, but they work harder if the trend is diminishing because they perceive a threat to the organization (and therefore, their jobs).

Our typical multilevel model is not generally well suited to handling analyses of this type because we are now looking at intercepts and slope coefficients of the higher level construct (i.e., culture) over time

as inputs to the lower level effects. Normally the intercepts and slope coefficients of the lower level are used as outcomes to be predicted by higher level effects. Here we have intercepts and slope coefficients of both lower level and higher level entities. It can be done, but it's not business as usual, and we can't simply tuck repeated observations under individuals as a lower level factor.

We introduced this example because entities evolve over time, and temporal effects may reside at higher or lower levels depending on what's being measured (and when it is being measured). However, temporal assessments always reside at a lower level than the entity being measured because they are nested within the entity or unit. We also used this example because it brings up a second factor: the scaling of time. It is generally understood that processes at lower levels take place more rapidly than higher levels. Chemical transition states have incredibly short lifetimes of a few femtoseconds (10^{-15} seconds), the time required for electron redistribution (Schramm, 2011), and neurons fire in milliseconds (Diba, Amarasingham, Mizuseki, & Buzsáki, 2014); people may make decisions in split-seconds (G. A. Klein, 1998), whereas other behaviors or decisions might take minutes, hours, days, or even longer to unfold (e.g., Bragger, Hantula, Bragger, Kirnan, & Kutcher, 2003). If we wish to say X must precede Y to establish causality, what does this mean when all parts of a multilevel system are in motion and some parts move or evolve more rapidly than others? Furthermore, various relationships may have rhythms or patterns over time in addition to having different scaling (Mitchell & James, 2001; Zaheer, Albert, & Zaheer, 1999).

We might ask, "Does the cue ball cause the eight ball to go in the pocket?" If the cue ball moves first and strikes the eight ball, and then the eight ball goes in the pocket, we may be able to argue that the cue ball caused the eight ball to go in the pocket. What if we ask, "Does training in billiards cause the eight ball to go in the pocket?" Training is a process that takes place over weeks, months, and years, whereas the strike of a cue ball takes a fraction of a second. How do we relate training, with its long time frame, with the eight ball going in a pocket in less than a second? Additionally, training effects often dissipate with time. We face similar challenges when trying to relate something like FAA regulations to aircrew behavior on a flight.

It doesn't seem controversial to suggest that FAA regulations alter flight crew behavior. That's their raison d'etre. But how would we measure and model this relationship? It would be difficult. If we gather measures of the FAA regulations today and relate them to pilot behavior tomorrow, we wouldn't see much, if any, relationship. X (FAA regulations) most likely causes Y (pilot behavior), and we see and measure X preceding Y. However, we are unlikely to detect the relationship because X is nearly invariant over this time window. This is true even if we measured FAA regulations first and then assessed pilot behavior 6 months later. FAA regulations evolve over months and years, whereas aircrew behavior can take place in minutes, hours, and days. We have a mismatch in timescale associated with levels.

To see the causal connection between FAA regulations and flight crew behavior, we require either molar observations that transcend time (e.g., number of regulations or content of regulations; aircrew safe landings, aircrew errors, flight disruptions over time) or multiple observations over time at the timescale of each of the entities involved (regulation time 0; aircrew safety time 1; regulation time 1; aircrew safety time 2; and so forth). Thus, we need to know the durations, scaling, and time lag (Mitchell & James, 2001; Zaheer et al., 1999). As an illustration, if the idea is that FAA regulations involving pilot training influence aircrew behavior, then we might explore the impact of this intervention using an interrupted time-series design over years or decades wherein we collect data on pilot behavior both before and after changes were made regarding FAA regulations (Shadish et al., 2002). The types of measures of FAA regulations would depend on what is being measured and the rate at which FAA regulations can evolve. The time frame for the subsequent assessments of aircrew behavior would be dependent on whether FAA changes are likely to have immediate impact or whether it takes 6 months or a year to see the changes. Pick the wrong time frame and nothing will be seen (George & Jones, 2000). Another option might be to approach the question qualitatively, talking with pilots and regulators

before and after the changes to see what evidence might exist for various causal relationships.

The point being made is that powerful causal influences of higher level variables can be hidden because of differing time frames across levels and the inability to connect the time frames across levels in a meaningful fashion. Governmental laws (e.g., Civil Rights Act of 1964) almost certainly affect human behavior, but getting a quantitative measure of governmental regulation to correlate with specific individual behaviors may prove difficult unless we pay attention to the role of time.

We can't ignore important causal influences of higher level variables simply because they evolve more slowly or because it's difficult to assess causality. Some of the most important variables may be of this sort—slowly changing, difficult to measure, yet powerful as a causal antecedent.

Lagged Outcomes

The second issue relevant to time and temporal precedence in multilevel systems is the potential delay between a cause and the effect. Consider a study that purports to examine whether new CEOs tend to implement a new strategy that affects organizational performance. If we stay at the CEO and organizational level and do not approach this question from a multilevel systems perspective, then it might seem reasonable to assess the outcome a year later. But if we adopt a more sophisticated multilevel perspective, we may realize that CEO changes in strategy unfold at different rates across different levels across the organization. Consider an organization that hires a new CEO. She comes on board and after a few months of talking with executives, employees, and customers, she decides on a new strategic approach for the company. The top-level executives then work on plans, the organization's information technology professionals identify technologies to enable strategic pursuit, human resources decision makers implement changes to organizational structure and culture, training and development specialists train employees, and everyone adjusts to the inevitable bumps along the way. Sometime later the strategy begins to effect changes in relationships with customers, and as word spreads among customers through marketing and spillover effects, changes in sales and earnings become apparent. How long might it take for the CEO's changes to show their impact on return on equity measures? Is a year enough? Two years? The delayed effect on outcomes can easily mask our ability to detect relationships (covariance) if we don't think about the multilevel system generating those outcomes.

Fragile Homeostasis

The final issue to consider with the idea of seeing the cause preceding the effect in a multilevel system is the notion of fragile homeostasis. This is related to the idea of lagged effects, but it's the result of a distinct process. Lagged effects take time to manifest, but there's a smooth and even connection to the outcome. The challenge is getting the timing right in order to unveil the causal connection. Fragile homeostasis and homeostatic breakdown (or breakout) is different because it is more abrupt.

Complex social structures ranging from teams to governments and societies exist in a state of quasi-homeostasis. Many social collectives (e.g., teams, schools, organizations, professional societies) have a clearly defined structure and set of processes that allow them to exist independent of individual membership. Members may come and go, but the overall structure of the social collective remains largely static. The higher level entities are in homeostasis, but it is a partial homeostasis because they are changing, growing, shrinking, and evolving. When a cause enters the system, it may exhibit no easily discernable effect on the outcome, yet a change may occur. Over time the social system can reach a critical state preceding homeostatic breakdown, when abrupt change can take place. It's similar to conditions in chemistry when water can be superheated yet not boil. Then, when jostled even slightly the water roils and boils over the edge of the cup. Or conversely, liquids can be supercooled but still in a liquid state, but then the smallest perturbation can result in a nearly instant shift to a solid state. George and Jones (2000) referred to this process as *discontinuous change*.

What does it look like when applied to social structures? Consider Rosa Parks. She didn't cause the civil rights movement. Society was pressurized, with inequality, prejudice, and even violence creating differences in quality of life and opportunity for a large segment of the population. As slight was heaped upon slight, the social context became ripened for a phase shift—a change to something new. Then something happens to disturb the system and the structure abruptly changes. For another example, the assassination of the Archduke Ferdinand didn't cause World War I. The world was poised for war and the assassination precipitated the outcome. Teams abruptly coalesce and rally to become something special, and they sometimes explode unexpectedly. Organizations appear fine until a tightly wound spring such as excess leverage precipitates a dramatic fall. Marriages seem fine until financial difficulties rattle the relationship.

Fragile homeostasis and homeostatic breakdowns (or breakouts) make it difficult to determine whether the temporal sequencing of X before Y is in fact causing Y. Perhaps X does cause Y, over time, creating a state of fragile homeostasis, but then Z occurs and creates the homeostatic breakdown and abrupt phase shift in Y. As a result, we may ascribe the cause to Z, not X, but both Z and X could be the primary causative factor creating the breakdown in fragile homeostasis. Consider a student who has been generally unhappy and disconnected for a large number of years. What causes the student to drop out of school isn't necessarily some specific triggering event, Z (e.g., moving to a new school because a parent takes a new job, a failing grade), but rather Z creates a context in which the impact of X on Y became more salient or pronounced. If X is educational engagement and Y is school satisfaction (or staying in school), then levels of engagement may be correlated with satisfaction. However, even the least engaged student may not plan to quit school unless some triggering event strengthens the relationship between lack of engagement and dissatisfaction (e.g., moving to a new school, failing a class).

Addressing the condition of temporal precedence is not an easy task to accomplish. Levels often operate on a different scaling of time, but fragile homeostasis and homeostatic breakdown can make the situation more complex to understand. Stars evolve over billions of years, but when the conditions are right, massive stars can become supernovas within minutes. National governments and societies may lumber along, and it's business as usual for decades or centuries, but then when conditions are right, homeostatic breakdown takes place and revolutions occur.

We can and must do a better job of attending to the role of time in the complex open environments we call *multilevel systems* (George & Jones, 2000; Mitchell & James, 2001). We have to think more carefully about time-boundedness, the role of time scaling, lagged effects, and homeostatic breakdowns. As K. H. Roberts et al. (1978) stated:

> Many relations we study are time- and place-bound. That is, a relation observed in an organization today may not be observed in another organization and may not be observed in the same organization next year. Although we are reasonably sensitive to environmental influences on relations, we are generally insensitive to the time boundaries of our data. (p. 22)

We tend to be insensitive to the time boundaries and evolutionary processes of our theories. We haven't even mentioned reciprocal dynamics and the mediation that occurs between any putative cause and effect (cf. James et al., 1982; Mathieu & Taylor, 2007; Zhang, Zyphur, & Preacher, 2009). For every action and reaction, there's a potential intermediating effect that might also deserve examination, and sometimes it is the reciprocal effects of X and Y over time. Additionally, there can be other variables mediating effects. Indeed, between any two mediators there exists the possibility of a third mediator. If we want to truly understand a system, we may need to capture the micromediation processes taking place over time. Another issue is that in an open system for every 0 point in time, there's a $t-1$ point in time. That is, in open systems there's always the possibility of a time frame that precedes the time frame being investigated, and the preceding time frame could contain a key causative factor. With all this challenge and complexity, what should we do?

Social scientists can begin to address these issues by being more aware of the multifaceted ways that time exerts effects in multilevel contexts. With the long time frame for some effects, we may need to borrow from other disciplines such as historiography, ethnography, and econometrics to consider how best to predict and test potential cause and effect relationships. We may also need to use both qualitative designs and computational modeling or simulations to understand the dynamics involved (Kozlowski, Chao, Grand, Braun, & Kuljanin, 2013). We can borrow ideas from other sciences, even chemistry, astronomy, or physics, to metaphorically (and perhaps analytically) grasp how partially homeostatic systems in a quasi-equilibrium function as causal influences. We have to try new and different approaches to our theoretical and mathematical modeling of causes and effects.

> **Principle 3:** Adopting a holistic, open systems view of social systems and building multilevel theory to account for phenomena will enable scholars to more effectively detect cause and effect patterns over time, with lagged effects, and in the presence of fragile homeostasis.

SUBJECTIVE VERSUS OBJECTIVE EFFECTS

When trying to identify the multilevel effects at play within a system, we should consider the distinction between subjective, or perceived, effects and objective or physically manifested effects. Can effects at the level of cosmological events affect human behavior at work? Perhaps this is a laughable question, because who would care? The skip between levels seems simply too vast. But consider that objective cosmological effects have physically shaped our reality, and they include asteroid strikes that have led to the large-scale extinction of dinosaurs and supernovas that may have disrupted our atmosphere and caused small-scale extinctions. Mass coronal ejections have disrupted our electrical grids and are highly likely to do so again in the future. We can consider the impact of solar flares on communication patterns of individuals and societies. We don't need to turn to astrology to find strong evidence that physical cosmological events can and most likely will shape human behavior in the future. However, the vast scaling of time influences whether we attend to these issues.

The long time frame for such events makes studying such phenomena uninteresting to most organizational scientists. It's unlikely to happen in their lifetimes, and it's a rare event, so why bother? Yet these questions and issues are germane to human productivity and survival. Planetary-level effects such as climate change alter availability of food and water, and these will later affect geopolitical power and stability among nations. It's difficult to consider these relationships and their impact on individuals, families, and organizations, but it's important to try.

Cosmology or planetary change doesn't have to manifest as a physical event to influence human behavior. As long as people think about and perceive cosmological events as important, then they will exert effects on people. For example, we would never advocate taking astrology seriously as a science. However, in 2012 as much as 42% of the U.S. population thought astrology was either "sort of scientific" or "very scientific" (National Science Foundation, 2014). For believers, it doesn't matter if it's real; it's enough to believe. Thus, we can ask, "do astrological perceptions affect individual behavior?" Most likely they do for a subset of people. Ronald Reagan and his wife Nancy were said to have taken astrology seriously during his presidency; it affected the scheduling of important events (S. V. Roberts, 1988). Do others in work environments take astrology seriously? Might such beliefs affect perceived risk (Sjöberg & af Wåhlberg, 2002)?

We can also ask whether actual organizational policies affect employee behavior or whether perceptions and attributions about organizational policies matter more. We are reminded of a friend who lamented working long work weeks at a law firm when he had a newborn at home. We asked, "Doesn't your firm have paternity leave policies?" He said, "Yes, but everyone knows you'll never make partner if you take it." In many respects, it doesn't matter if the statement is true, because the statement is true for him. If he believes in his perceptions, then he will act accordingly regardless of whether the perceptions are objectively true. If such perceptions are shared, they manifest as collective constructs,

shaping individual behavior whether or not they are accurate. There are many instances in human history of behavior being shaped not by reality but by the perception of reality.

Objective impact of lower level factors can exist. People can be exposed to chemical compounds, viruses, or bacteria that alters human chemistry and changes our cognitions and behaviors over time. Genetics (which focuses on the molecular level) can affect people. Using twin studies, researchers have found that as much as 30% of the variance in job satisfaction may be associated with genetic factors (Arvey, Bouchard, Segal, & Abraham, 1989). Changes in brain structure or chemistry over time clearly can shape behavior. Researchers have associated ethical decision processes with neural activation patterns in the brain using fMRI techniques (Greene, Sommerville, Nystrom, Darley, & Cohen, 2001; Robertson et al., 2007).

Perceptions of lower level phenomena may be important too. If people think there are deadly germs all around them, then this will shape their behavior regardless of whether the germs actually exist. If people believe in a heritable trait theory of intelligence, then they will act and react differently to mistakes and errors than people who believe in malleable, contextually driven intelligence (Dweck & Leggett, 1988; James & LeBreton, 2012). Again, the more shared the perceptions, the more mutually reinforcing they become, eventually manifesting as higher level effects, even if they are higher level effects about perceptions of lower level phenomena.

> **Principle 4:** Scholars must attend to potential objective and subjective effects across levels of analysis to build a more integrated understanding of how a multilevel system influences outcomes.

ON VARIANCE AND VARIATION

Our typical modeling approach for multilevel data is to gather data, set up identifiers for units at two or more levels, partition the variance into higher- and lower level portions, and then determine the significance of predictor variables at a particular level for predicting the outcome variance at that level (cf. Dansereau et al., 1984; Raudenbush & Bryk, 2002). When modeling group effects, we are testing group predictors against the component of variance in individual-level scores that exists across groups. And when modeling individual level effects, we are testing individual predictors against the component of variance that represents variation of individuals within groups. This approach does well for what it is supposed to do: provide significance tests of specific effects within a given set of data. However, this approach will not tell us where the variance lives, unless we happen to get lucky and sample, measure, and analyze the correct variables at the correct level at the correct point in time.

By thinking of variance as a fixed pie to be sliced up into appropriate tests at various levels, we ignore some very important issues. First, the variance we see in our data may or may not be the important variance that exists. Second, we tend to collect data as a snapshot, yet phenomena unfold over time. Finally, we argue that variance is not a fixed pie. As shown in Figure 1.2, variance can increase and decrease over time, both within and across levels, as part of an adaptive or evolutionary process. Sometimes both individual and team variance can increase over time as in the propagation and adoption of innovations. At other times or in other contexts, individual variance can shrink while variance across teams can increase, such as when there are strong team effects influencing individual behavior. There are probably occasions when both individual variance within teams and variance between teams shrink. Perhaps this could be the result of strong socialization processes within an organization organized by units such as the military (James, Demaree, Mulaik, & Ladd, 1992). All of these patterns have profound effects on how much variance is seen at what level over time and our ability to see what is going on. This attaches to our previous conversation about time: what is increasing or decreasing over time and why?

Variance is not fixed to a particular level over time; it shifts and morphs as social systems unfurl their effects. Consider a brief thought experiment: Imagine for a moment that we have 500 individuals within 100 teams. On a measure of work satisfaction

(assessed using a 10-point Likert-type scale), nearly all of the teams have a mean work satisfaction score of 8 (within sampling error). All of the individual-level ratings of work satisfaction (i.e., each employee within each team) also hover around an 8. Thus, there are no significant differences between teams and no significant differences within teams (i.e., between individuals nested in a particular team). At what level in the system does the action exist for the work satisfaction construct? Answer: No one can tell you on the basis of variance. Individual and team effects are indistinguishable, and there's no evidence to suggest there is a particular level effect (or there are both individual and team effects and they can't be separated).

Now, what if we told you that previously, the individual-level scores vary widely from 1 to 10, but there were no specific team-level differences? Assume we've collected data moment by moment for many weeks. Scores are all over the place in the beginning, but there's a small team of three people, with one new charismatic member, all with scores of 7 or 8. Then we see the small group with scores around 8 expand to five. Eventually, the entire work unit averages close to 8. Over time, the initial team solidifies, individual scores drawing tighter around 8. Abruptly a second team rapidly transitions from scores ranging from 1 to 10 to a mean around 8. Then a third team follows the same pattern. This continues until all 100 teams average near 8. What is the level at which the system is operating? Clearly, the initial level was individual within team, with emergence or social contagion processes drawing people together. The next phase, however, operated at the team level, with the contagion "jumping" from one team to another. Perhaps because of the initial team, the organizational leaders realized there was a better way to do things and began to implement new best practices, one team at a time. Or perhaps other teams saw something working for one team and incorporated the practices into their own unit.

We can imagine other possibilities. What if the means of each team vary widely but individuals within each team begin to converge on similar values so that one team averages near 3 while another averages near 7 or 8, with all members within a

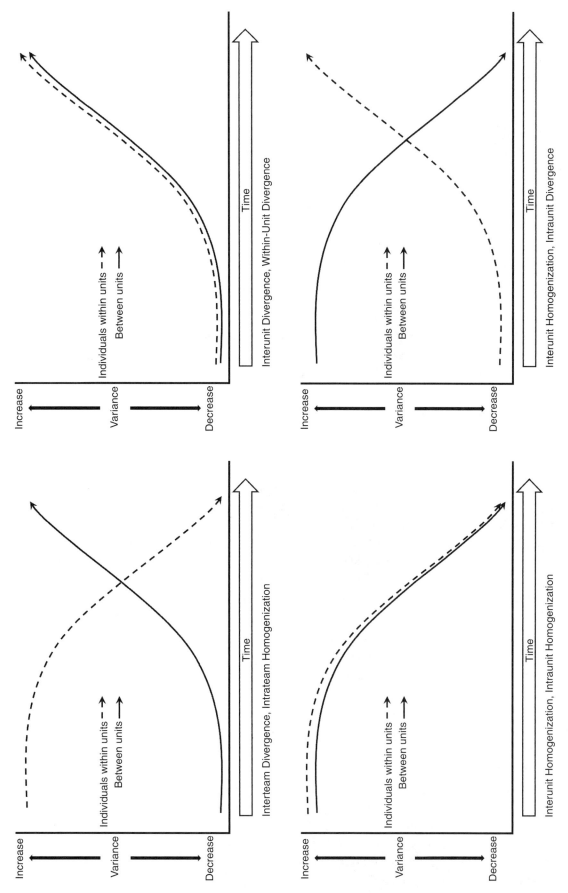

FIGURE 1.2.   Variance shifts over time.

team clustering. For a long time the teams vary from one another, but individuals within teams converge around their respective team means. After some time, all teams begin to slowly converge toward 8, so that the final result is that both individuals and teams hover around 8. This is a very different pattern than the preceding one. This situation clearly indicates that team context effects exist, so at least part of the action is at the team level. Over time, however, the teams converge, perhaps through the sharing of team best practices that make all of the teams more effective and therefore more satisfying. This might occur, for example, if innovation diffuses across teams.

There are three key points to consider in this thought experiment. First, by examining how variance changes across levels over time, we went from having no clear idea as to how the multiple-level system was operating to having a pretty good idea of what might have happened in each situation. Second, we see that effects can shift up and down levels over time as the variance components shift. Third, we have to measure processes over time to see the change in variance components.

The important issue to keep in mind is that structures or entities across levels come and go. There was once no Google, but a couple of people got together and began to change the world. Perhaps Google will continue to change the world for centuries, but it's worth remembering that a large-scale survival analysis suggested the average lifespan of a business is about a decade (Daepp, Hamilton, West, & Bettencourt, 2015). Teams form, storm, norm, perform (Chang, Bordia, & Duck, 2003; Mannix & Jehn, 2004) and then many disband, get reassigned or restructured, or become incorporated into some other entity. Members come and go and sometimes they change the character of the teams they join or leave (Mathieu & Chen, 2011). Most social structures have some degree of impermanence.

There was a time when there was little or no variance across large manufacturing companies in the use of assembly line production technologies. Companies didn't use this approach, so the variance was near zero—no organizational effect on assembly line technology. Then certain companies implemented the assembly line system, and variance on this technology increased. Other large manufacturing

companies began to adopt the approach, and variance across companies increased in the use of this technology. Now an organizational effect on the use of assembly lines could be detected; there was unit-level variance. However, variance in the types of jobs performed by each individual decreased as the assembly line technology was implemented. Eventually, nearly all large manufacturing companies adopted assembly line production methods, and the variance returned to near zero.

Where does the level exist for the diffusion of innovation of assembly line production techniques? It may exist at the organizational level, but many factors are in operation and we could only detect the organizational effect using organizational level prediction of variance during a small window of time (George & Jones, 2000; Mitchell & James, 2001). Today we won't see much variance in whether or not assembly line technologies are used. But these manufacturing systems have a profound effect on how employees work and feel on the job. Are we to say that there's no organizational effect of assembly line production technologies on employee behavior because we can't see variance? This would be a highly misleading conclusion because everything about the system, which exists at the organizational level, affects what employees do (and cannot do).

As scholars, we must be more sensitive to how variance changes over time and across levels. This means we have to think more carefully about the meaning of time, its scaling, and the types of effects we may see (lagged, homeostatic breakdown). By observing how units at multiple levels shift in variance, we can begin to detect the fundamental processes at play (e.g., social contagion, innovation diffusion). Failure to see variance does not mean that a higher level effect does not exist. The effects may be at play and they may be profound and powerful, but precisely because they are profound and powerful, there's little variance across higher units.

Returning to the example of FAA regulations: They work so everyone uses them, and the variance is not discernible. However, it drives the system, process, and outcomes regardless of the variance components. One merely needs to look at the history of aviation (e.g., Bryson, 2013) to see the reckless and wild early days of flight. Indeed, variance in flight safety was high in the 1930s. The FAA came to exist to reduce this variance and create standard operating procedures that would lead to flight safety, and it worked. The variance is gone but the system is there, nevertheless.

> Principle 5: Developing a deep understanding of complex multilevel systems requires scholars to move beyond snapshots of variance to reframing the relative partitioning of variance within and between units over time.

DUAL PROCESSES IN MULTILEVEL SYSTEMS

A final issue to consider when thinking about identifying the correct level are the dual processes of variance creation and restriction in multilevel systems. As shown in our earlier examples, units within a multilevel system change, adapt, and evolve over time. Families, teams, organizations, societies, and nations are not static entities. For example, a given team has not existed for an eternity. It comes into being for an externally driven purpose or because a collection of individuals shares a common vision and set of goals. Eventually, a group of individuals begin to restrict variance on key attitudes and share core values. This is one example of the process of emergence (Kozlowski et al., 2013). We see variance between groups/teams increasing and variance within teams decreasing on core values. Teams can also experience divergence, cases in which team members increasingly drift apart, eventually leading to the dissolution of the team.

The dual processes of variance creation and variance restriction forge and dissolve higher and lower level entities and their associated effects. The processes of variance creation and restriction occur both within units as well as across units. Exhibit 1.1 introduces some potential factors that can create or restrict variance within or across units.

This list is not meant to be exhaustive. Instead, it is meant to be a point of departure for thinking about the systems and process that drive variance creation and reduction and eventually lead to the existence and dissolution of higher and lower

---

EXHIBIT 1.1

Variance Creation and Restriction Processes

Variance creation	Variance restriction
Exploration	Exploitation
Innovation	Assimilation
Serendipity	Structuration
Adaptation	Elimination
Differentiation	Conformation
Contagion	Truncation
Deregulation	Regulation

---

entities and their associated effects. We attempt to highlight how countervailing forces act to create levels effects.

March (1991) described *exploration* as the process of experimenting, investigating, and innovating to find new products, markets, technologies, and services. The process of looking for and finding these new innovations necessarily creates variance across work units and organizations as each pursues a distinct path. Eventually, however, once the innovation is created or identified, organizations must become organized to take advantage of, or *exploit*, this new opportunity. Apple created the iPod and organized its marketing and manufacturing units to pursue the common goal of taking advantage of this new product. Initially the systems and processes innovating the iPod created variance, and then the systems and processes geared to take advantage of the iPod reduced certain types of variance (e.g., product goals). It happened at the industry level as well. The entry of the iPod created variance as other organizations rushed to take advantage of the opportunity, and eventually many technology players had some type of mp3 player on the market, reducing variance. We've seen this cycle many times, ranging from electricity, to the Internet, to smartphones and tablets.

There are similar forces with innovation and assimilation. New ideas, technologies, services, and markets can create competitive advantage for certain firms or teams. This creates variance among units as some are "haves" and some are "have nots." As other units see the success of the early adopters, they are more likely to assimilate the innovations into their own systems and structures. Over time, best practices become institutionalized, and nearly all units become "haves," thus restricting variance. Thus, we see that variance becomes an indicator for the ebb and flow of new approaches toward success. This sometimes results in a physical assimilation such as in an acquisition when a firm acquires another for people, products, or technologies. Assimilation of values or process approaches happens at not only the organizational level but the teams level as well, as some teams observe others engaging in practices that enable success. Over time, variance increases as some teams branch out, then variance decreases as teams become increasingly similar due to consistency in values, practices, and technologies. Most firefighting, hospital, and police units are similar, yet some show variance on key factors. Some hospitals are embracing a professional and open approach to communication, some police units are reaching out to the community, and some firefighting crews are embracing diversity. This creates variance and as we see which approaches work, other units adopt effective approaches, eventually reducing variance.

Serendipity should not be discounted as a force for variance. Random mutations create speciation over time, and random errors can result in fortunate discoveries (R. M. Roberts, 1989). Post-it® notes were the unexpected result of an adhesive experiment. For some time, 3M was the only firm to have this technology but over time other firms obtained it, creating variance. Now it seems that low adhesion adhesives are used in products everywhere, and many firms have it, reducing variance. Through *structuration* organizations become highly structured to take advantage of the new discoveries. Random changes that result in powerful positive outcomes eventually lead to new structures that are designed to take advantage of the serendipity. Teams and other social units can experience this. There has been a long tradition of people who get together to play games socially. Some of these groups began doing it online and today, many social gamers interact virtually. Groups adopt what works for other groups, eventually restricting variance of certain types.

The forces described above create adaptation at the individual, group, and organizational levels. Entities that adapt and evolve continue to exist as

the context changes. However, failure to adapt to contextual forces results in *elimination* or *dissolution* of the entity. Adaptation creates variance until the adaptation is generally embraced or assimilated across units. Elimination reduces variance as units that fail to adapt fall out of existence. These forces can have strong influences on our ability to detect higher level effects. Consider, for example, the idea that strategic human resource management practices need to be aligned with organizational strategies. This seems obvious, even intuitive, yet the empirical research supporting this perspective is notably weak (e.g., Huselid, 1995). One possibility is that organizations that have not aligned their talent strategies with their business strategies are eliminated from the competitive landscape. If true, it would mean a key quadrant enabling detection of the alignment hypothesis would be missing. In other words, if the theory that businesses need to align their talent strategies with their business strategies to succeed is correct, then the ability to test that theory would be compromised because the firms that fail to do so would drop out of the variance space. This can play out at the individual or team level as well. We might have a theory that people who are poor fits with an organization and who perform poorly have a different value system from those who are poor fits and perform well or those who are good fits and perform poorly. If we tried to run such a study, how many people do we expect to see remain in an organization who are poor fits, performing poorly? The elimination process would drive most of these people out. Adaptation and elimination processes can have profound effects on the variances we are able to see, both within and between units of interest.

We also see forces for *differentiation* and *conformation*. Some people, groups, and organizations embrace difference and actively try to be different from others. If everyone was the same, the world would be uninteresting. If all organizations are the same, there is no competitive advantage and they would all be subject to the tyranny of mediocrity. But there's a certain inelasticity to difference. If an entity is too different, too out there, then it can struggle, whether the entity is an individual, team, or organization. There are pressures for conformity that restrict variance. You wouldn't go to a restaurant and expect wait staff to be rude or dressed in pajamas or both. Individuals can't go to stores with pants on their heads and shirts on their legs. Part of the conformance effect is practical. Some things don't work and they are eliminated from the repertoire. However, social constraints driving conformance are powerful but don't necessarily have a pragmatic purpose. There's no reason that certain hand gestures (e.g., the "okay sign") have to mean something positive in some cultures and something negative in others. These are socially constructed interpretations. But conformance in each culture means that it is or is not appropriate to engage in the behavior. It's true for organizational strategy, too. Businesses operate differently in China, Germany, and France than they do in the United States.

Social and physical *contagion* processes have the ability to generate variance through bottom-up emergence effects. An individual or small group of people can start a social movement, create a new product, or develop a better service, and this can cascade out through a team, an organization, an industry, or a nation. Physical contagion can cascade out as well, changing how people interact with each other. As the contagion takes hold, variance is created but over time, either it is assimilated or truncated. Social *truncation* occurs when opposing forces work to squelch, control, or sometimes adopt and assimilate the social contagion. Eventually, either contagion wins and variance is restricted because most units adopt the new "thing," or truncation wins by squeezing the contagion out.

Regulation, including legislation, is designed to reduce variance by fiat, usually to enhance efficiency or increase safety. Regulations can also be derived from social construction. We have regulations intended to reduce risk in the finance industry, but they also restrict variance in the business practices and investment strategies that can be pursued. Some hospitals have regulations for surgical teams to use checklists because they've been shown to reduce surgical errors by ensuring that all teams engage in consistent effective practices. Likewise, the FAA has checklists for aircrews. We also have regulations for what people can do, what they eat, or how they act. The counter force for regulation is *deregulation*.

By removing constraints on individual, team, and organizational behavior, we allow variation in behaviors and practices. At times such variation can result in innovation and adaptation, at other times it can result in negative outcomes.

We suggest that the dual forces of variance creation and variance restriction shape the formation, evolution, and dissolution of units across levels over time. Attending to how various types of forces affect variance will help us better understand the system, as a system, rather than thinking about piecemeal slices of the system. As Kozlowski et al. (2013) pointed out, the emergence of levels is complex because it incorporates both process and structure. Process involves dynamic interactions among entities, and structure is the manifestation over time of a collective property. Both process and structure show their effects by transitions over time, and we further suggest that process and structure evolve in response to the dual forces of variance creation and variance restriction over time. As Kerlinger (1973) discussed, the concept of variation, or variance, is essential to all scientific efforts as the research process seems to understand or explain variation.

We agree and take this statement further in two ways. First, we suggest that understanding phenomena in open systems requires an understanding and explanation of variation at multiple levels of analysis. Second, we argue that variance is not static; it shifts and changes over time in response to dual forces of creation and restriction, and this occurs at multiple levels. Third, we need to think about the variance of the system as a whole in order to understand the phenomena of interest. We can begin by examining variance of the component parts, but eventually we need to build a more integrative understanding of the sources and outcomes of variance across levels.

SUMMARY

We suggest that researchers must think in more complex ways about the phenomena being studied. As Hanges and Wang (2012) noted, complex multi-level and adaptive systems have tangled feedback loops among the system's elements. As a result, causal influences flow in multiple directions within the system and across levels. We have to think more carefully about the system as a system and work toward interdisciplinary understanding of the phenomena we care about.

As we progress, we have to take seriously the notion that even if there are multiple Xs across levels predicting *Y*, understanding which *X* is causing *Y* is challenging because *X* doesn't always cause *Y*, seeing *X* precede *Y* doesn't mean it is the only influence on *Y*, and not seeing *Y* when *X* is present doesn't mean that *X* isn't important. Additionally, we have to be much more serious about the role of time in multilevel phenomena. In particular, we have to be sensitive to scaling of time, lagged effects, and fragile homeostasis. Timescales can mask or enhance our observed of relationships among variables of interest.

Finally, we have to think about variance creation and restriction processes that can influence our ability to see and detect phenomena. Most things are in a process of dynamic change at different timescales. As a result, we should think about how different forces for variance creation and restriction operate over time to influence outcomes. Do laws affect marital behavior? Certainly. But if laws change slowly and we gather observations over a year when they are unchanging, we may not detect the effects unless we adopt qualitative approaches of inquiry.

We began with the question "What is the appropriate level?" The answer is, there is no appropriate level. The level is the system, which is what we should examine if we want to understand multilevel causality. The ability to examine the system depends on timing of observation, and bracketing is not enough. Our efforts to understand such multilevel systems may require new interdisciplinary approaches and a willingness to broaden our own perspectives and conceptualizations of phenomena at hand.

References

Arvey, R. D., Bouchard, T. J., Segal, N. L., & Abraham, L. M. (1989). Job satisfaction: Environmental and genetic components. *Journal of Applied Psychology*, *74*, 187–192. http://dx.doi.org/10.1037/0021-9010.74.2.187

Avolio, B. J., Zhu, W., Koh, W., & Bhatia, P. (2004). Transformational leadership and organizational commitment: Mediating role of psychological empowerment and moderating role of structural distance. *Journal of Organizational Behavior*, *25*, 951–968. http://dx.doi.org/10.1002/job.283

Baltes, B. B., Zhdanova, L. S., & Parker, C. P. (2009). Psychological climate: A comparison of organizational and individual level referents. *Human Relations*, *62*, 669–700. http://dx.doi.org/10.1177/0018726709103454

Barrick, M. R., Stewart, G. L., Neubert, M. J., & Mount, M. K. (1998). Relating member ability and personality to work-team processes and team effectiveness. *Journal of Applied Psychology*, *83*, 377–391. http://dx.doi.org/10.1037/0021-9010.83.3.377

Baysinger, M. A., Scherer, K. T., & LeBreton, J. M. (2014). Exploring the disruptive effects of psychopathy and aggression on group processes and group effectiveness. *Journal of Applied Psychology*, *99*, 48–65. http://dx.doi.org/10.1037/a0034317

Binning, J. F., & Barrett, G. V. (1989). Validity of personnel decisions: A conceptual analysis of the inferential and evidential bases. *Journal of Applied Psychology*, *74*, 478–494. http://dx.doi.org/10.1037/0021-9010.74.3.478

Blakely, T. A., & Woodward, A. J. (2000). Ecological effects in multi-level studies. *Journal of Epidemiology and Community Health*, *54*, 367–374. http://dx.doi.org/10.1136/jech.54.5.367

Bragger, J. D., Hantula, D. A., Bragger, D., Kirnan, J., & Kutcher, E. (2003). When success breeds failure: History, hysteresis, and delayed exit decisions. *Journal of Applied Psychology*, *88*, 6–14. http://dx.doi.org/10.1037/0021-9010.88.1.6

Bridoux, F., & Stoelhorst, J. W. (2016). Stakeholder relationships and social welfare: A behavioral theory of contributions to joint value creation. *Academy of Management Review*, *41*, 229–251. http://dx.doi.org/10.5465/amr.2013.0475

Bryson, B. (2013). *One summer: America, 1927*. Toronto, Ontario, Canada: Doubleday Canada.

Bureau of Labor Statistics. (2015a). *Census of fatal occupational injuries charts, 1992–2015 (final data)*. Retrieved from https://www.bls.gov/iif/oshwc/cfoi/cfch0014.pdf

Bureau of Labor Statistics. (2015b). *Employer-reported workplace injuries and illnesses—2015*. Retrieved from https://www.bls.gov/news.release/archives/osh_10272016.pdf

Bureau of Labor Statistics. (2016). *Career outlook: Adrenaline jobs: High-intensity careers*. Retrieved from https://www.bls.gov/careeroutlook/2016/article/adrenaline-jobs.htm

Chan, D. (1998). Functional relations among constructs in the same content domain at different levels of analysis: A typology of composition models. *Journal of Applied Psychology, 83*, 234–246. http://dx.doi.org/10.1037/0021-9010.83.2.234

Chang, A., Bordia, P., & Duck, J. (2003). Punctuated equilibrium and linear progression: Toward a new understanding of group development. *Academy of Management Journal, 46*, 106–117. http://dx.doi.org/10.5465/30040680

Chen, G., Mathieu, J. E., & Bliese, P. D. (2004). A framework for conducting multilevel construct validation. In F. J. Yammarino & F. Dansereau (Eds.), *Research in multilevel issues: Multilevel issues in organizational behavior and processes* (Vol. 3, pp. 273–303). Oxford, UK: Elsevier. http://dx.doi.org/10.1016/S1475-9144(04)03013-9

Cheshin, A., Rafaeli, A., & Bos, N. (2011). Anger and happiness in virtual teams: Emotional influences of text and behavior on others' affect in the absence of non-verbal cues. *Organizational Behavior and Human Decision Processes, 116*, 2–16. http://dx.doi.org/10.1016/j.obhdp.2011.06.002

Civil Rights Act of 1964, Pub. L. No. 88-352, 78 Stat. 241, July 2, 1964.

Colquitt, J. A., & Zipay, K. P. (2015). Justice, fairness, and employee reactions. *Annual Review of Organizational Psychology and Organizational Behavior, 2*, 75–99. http://dx.doi.org/10.1146/annurev-orgpsych-032414-111457

Cook, T. D., & Campbell, D. T. (1979). *Quasi-experimentation: Design and analysis issues for field settings.* Boston, MA: Houghton Mifflin.

Costa, P. T., Jr., & McCrae, R. R. (1980). Influence of extraversion and neuroticism on subjective well-being: Happy and unhappy people. *Journal of Personality and Social Psychology, 38*, 668–678. http://dx.doi.org/10.1037/0022-3514.38.4.668

Cox, A., Zagelmeyer, S., & Marchington, M. (2006). Embedding employee involvement and participation at work. *Human Resource Management Journal, 16*, 250–267. http://dx.doi.org/10.1111/j.1748-8583.2006.00017.x

Cronbach, L. J., & Meehl, P. E. (1955). Construct validity in psychological tests. *Psychological Bulletin, 52*, 281–302. http://dx.doi.org/10.1037/h0040957

Daepp, M. I. G., Hamilton, M. J., West, G. B., & Bettencourt, L. M. A. (2015). The mortality of companies. *Journal of the Royal Society Interface, 12*, 20150120. http://dx.doi.org/10.1098/rsif.2015.0120. Published 1 April 2015.

Dansereau, F., Alutto, J. A., & Yammarino, F. J. (1984). *Theory testing in organizational behavior: The variant approach.* Englewood Cliffs, NJ: Prentice-Hall.

Diba, K., Amarasingham, A., Mizuseki, K., & Buzsáki, G. (2014). Millisecond timescale synchrony among hippocampal neurons. *The Journal of Neuroscience,*

34, 14984–14994. http://dx.doi.org/10.1523/JNEUROSCI.1091-14.2014

Di Tella, R., MacCulloch, R. J., & Oswald, A. J. (2003). The macroeconomics of happiness. *The Review of Economics and Statistics, 85*, 809–827. http://dx.doi.org/10.1162/003465303772815745

Dul, J. (2016). Necessary condition analysis (NCA): Logic and methodology of "Necessary but Not Sufficient" causality. *Organizational Research Methods, 19*, 10–52. http://dx.doi.org/10.1177/1094428115584005

Dweck, C. S., & Leggett, E. L. (1988). A social-cognitive approach to motivation and personality. *Psychological Review, 95*, 256–273. http://dx.doi.org/10.1037/0033-295X.95.2.256

George, J. M., & Jones, G. R. (2000). The role of time in theory and theory building. *Journal of Management, 26*, 657–684. http://dx.doi.org/10.1177/014920630002600404

Gerstein, D. R. (1987). To unpack micro and macro: Link small with large and part with whole. In J. C. Alexander, B. Giesen, R. Münch, & N. J. Smelser (Eds.), *The micro–macro link* (pp. 86–111). Los Angeles: University of California Press.

Grant, A. M., Christianson, M. K., & Price, R. H. (2007). Happiness, health, or relationships? Managerial practices and employee well-being tradeoffs. *The Academy of Management Perspectives, 21*, 51–63. http://dx.doi.org/10.5465/AMP.2007.26421238

Greene, J. D., Sommerville, R. B., Nystrom, L. E., Darley, J. M., & Cohen, J. D. (2001). An fMRI investigation of emotional engagement in moral judgment. *Science, 293*, 2105–2108. http://dx.doi.org/10.1126/science.1062872

Groff, E. R., Weisburd, D., & Yang, S. M. (2010). Is it important to examine crime trends at a local "micro" level? A longitudinal analysis of street to street variability in crime trajectories. *Journal of Quantitative Criminology, 26*, 7–32. http://dx.doi.org/10.1007/s10940-009-9081-y

Groysberg, B. (2010). *Chasing stars: The myth of talent and the portability of performance.* Princeton, NJ: Princeton University Press. http://dx.doi.org/10.1515/9781400834389

Groysberg, B., Nanda, A., & Nohria, N. (2004). The risky business of hiring stars. *Harvard Business Review, 82*, 92–100, 151.

Gully, S. M., & Phillips, J. M. (2005). A multilevel application of learning and performance orientations to individual, group, and organizational outcomes. In J. Martocchio (Ed.), *Research in personnel and human resources management* (Vol. 24, pp. 1–51). Greenwich, CT: JAI Press/Elsevier Science. http://dx.doi.org/10.1016/S0742-7301(05)24001-X

Hackman, J. R. (1987). The design of work teams. In *Handbook of organizational behavior* (pp. 315–342). Englewood Cliffs, NJ: Prentice-Hall.

Hackman, J. R. (2003). Learning more by crossing levels: Evidence from airplanes, hospitals, and orchestras. *Journal of Organizational Behavior, 24,* 905–922. http://dx.doi.org/10.1002/job.226

Hanges, P. J., & Wang, M. (2012). Seeking the Holy Grail in organizational science: Uncovering causality through research design. In S. W. J. Kozlowski (Ed.), *The Oxford handbook of organizational psychology* (pp. 79–116). New York, NY: Oxford University Press. http://dx.doi.org/10.1093/oxfordhb/9780199928309.013.0003

Hitt, M. A., Beamish, P. W., Jackson, S. E., & Mathieu, J. E. (2007). Building theoretical and empirical bridges across levels: Multilevel research in management. *Academy of Management Journal, 50,* 1385–1399. http://dx.doi.org/10.5465/AMJ.2007.28166219

Hodgson, G. M. (1998). The approach of institutional economics. *Journal of Economic Literature, 36,* 166–192.

House, R. J., Rousseau, D. M., & Thomas-Hunt, M. (1995). The third paradigm: Meso organizational research comes to age. *Research in Organizational Behavior, 17,* 71–114.

Huselid, M. A. (1995). The impact of human resource management practices on turnover, productivity, and corporate financial performance. *Academy of Management Journal, 38,* 635–672. http://dx.doi.org/10.5465/256741

Indik, B. (1968). The scope of the problem and some suggestions toward a solution. In B. P. Indik & F. K. Berrien (Eds.), *People, groups and organizations* (pp. 3–26). New York, NY: Teachers College Press.

James, L. R. (1980). The unmeasured variables problem in path analysis. *Journal of Applied Psychology, 65,* 415–421. http://dx.doi.org/10.1037/0021-9010.65.4.415

James, L. R. (1982). Aggregation bias in estimates of perceptual agreement. *Journal of Applied Psychology, 67,* 219–229. http://dx.doi.org/10.1037/0021-9010.67.2.219

James, L. R., Demaree, R. G., Mulaik, S. A., & Ladd, R. T. (1992). Validity generalization in the context of situational models. *Journal of Applied Psychology, 77,* 3–14. http://dx.doi.org/10.1037/0021-9010.77.1.3

James, L. R., Demaree, R. G., & Wolf, G. (1984). Estimating within-group interrater reliability with and without response bias. *Journal of Applied Psychology, 69,* 85–98. http://dx.doi.org/10.1037/0021-9010.69.1.85

James, L. R., & LeBreton, J. M. (2012). *Assessing implicit personality through conditional reasoning.*

Washington, DC: American Psychological Association. http://dx.doi.org/10.1037/13095-000

James, L. R., Mulaik, S. A., & Brett, J. M. (1982). *Causal analysis: Assumptions, models, and data.* Beverly Hills, CA: Sage.

Jepperson, R., & Meyer, J. W. (2011). Multiple levels of analysis and the limitations of methodological individualisms. *Sociological Theory, 29,* 54–73. http://dx.doi.org/10.1111/j.1467-9558.2010.01387.x

Johnson, S., Cooper, C., Cartwright, S., Donald, I., Taylor, P., & Millet, C. (2005). The experience of work-related stress across occupations. *Journal of Managerial Psychology, 20,* 178–187. http://dx.doi.org/10.1108/02683940510579803

Katz, D., & Kahn, R. L. (1978). *The social psychology of organizations* (2nd ed.). New York, NY: Wiley.

Keltner, D., & Haidt, J. (1999). Social functions of emotions at four levels of analysis. *Cognition and Emotion, 13,* 505–521. http://dx.doi.org/10.1080/026999399379168

Kerlinger, F. N. (1973). *Foundations of behavioral research* (2nd ed.). New York, NY: Holt, Rinehart and Winston.

Kim, A., Han, K., Blasi, J. R., & Kruse, D. L. (2015). Anti-shirking effects of group incentives and human-capital-enhancing HR practices. In A. Kauhanen (Ed.), *Advances in the economic analysis of participatory & labor-managed firms* (pp. 199–221). Bingley, England: Emerald Group. http://dx.doi.org/10.1108/S0885-333920150000016014

Klein, G. A. (1998). *Sources of power: How people make decision.* Cambridge, MA: MIT Press.

Klein, K. J., Conn, A. B., Smith, D. B., & Sorra, J. S. (2001). Is everyone in agreement? An exploration of within-group agreement in employee perceptions of the work environment. *Journal of Applied Psychology, 86,* 3–16. http://dx.doi.org/10.1037/0021-9010.86.1.3

Klein, K. J., Dansereau, F., & Hall, R. J. (1994). Levels issues in theory development, data collection, and analysis. *Academy of Management Review, 19,* 195–229.

Kozlowski, S. W. J., Chao, G. T., Grand, J. A., Braun, M. T., & Kuljanin, G. (2013). Advancing multilevel research design: Capturing the dynamics of emergence. *Organizational Research Methods, 16,* 581–615. http://dx.doi.org/10.1177/1094428113493119

Kozlowski, S. W. J., & Klein, K. J. (2000). A multilevel approach to theory and research in organizations: Contextual, temporal, and emergent processes. In K. J. Klein & S. W. J. Kozlowski (Eds.), *Multilevel theory, research, and methods in organizations: Foundations, extensions, and new directions* (pp. 3–90). San Francisco, CA: Jossey-Bass.

Lebreton, J. M., Burgess, J. R. D., Kaiser, R. B., Atchley, E. K. P., & James, L. R. (2003). The restriction of variance hypothesis and interrater reliability and agreement: Are ratings from multiple sources really dissimilar? *Organizational Research Methods, 6*, 80–128. http://dx.doi.org/10.1177/1094428102239427

Lount, R. B., Jr., & Wilk, S. L. (2014). Working harder or hardly working? Posting performance eliminates social loafing and promotes social laboring in workgroups. *Management Science, 60*, 1098–1106. http://dx.doi.org/10.1287/mnsc.2013.1820

Mannix, E., & Jehn, K. A. (2004). Let's norm and storm, but not right now: Integrating models of group development and performance. In E. Salas (Ed.), *Research on managing groups and teams: Vol. 6. Time in groups* (pp. 11–37). Bingley, England: Emerald Group. http://dx.doi.org/10.1016/S1534-0856(03)06002-X

March, J. G. (1991). Exploration and exploitation in organizational learning. *Organization Science, 2*, 71–87. http://dx.doi.org/10.1287/orsc.2.1.71

Mathieu, J. E., & Chen, G. (2011). The etiology of the multilevel paradigm in management research. *Journal of Management, 37*, 610–641. http://dx.doi.org/10.1177/0149206310364663

Mathieu, J. E., & Taylor, S. R. (2007). A framework for testing meso-mediational relationships in organizational behavior. *Journal of Organizational Behavior, 28*, 141–172. http://dx.doi.org/10.1002/job.436

McNeely, C. A., Nonnemaker, J. M., & Blum, R. W. (2002). Promoting school connectedness: Evidence from the national longitudinal study of adolescent health. *The Journal of School Health, 72*, 138–146. http://dx.doi.org/10.1111/j.1746-1561.2002.tb06533.x

Messick, S. (1995). Validity of psychological assessment: Validation of inferences from persons' responses and performances as scientific inquiry into score meaning. *American Psychologist, 50*, 741–749. http://dx.doi.org/10.1037/0003-066X.50.9.741

Mitchell, T. R., & James, L. R. (2001). Building better theory: Time and the specification of when things happen. *Academy of Management Review, 26*, 530–547.

National Science Foundation. (2014). Science and technology: Public attitudes and understanding. In *Science and engineering indicators 2014* (NSB 14-01). Arlington, VA: National Center for Science and Engineering Statistics. https://www.nsf.gov/statistics/seind14/content/chapter-7/chapter-7.pdf

Nembhard, D. (2014). Cross training efficiency and flexibility with process change. *International Journal of Operations & Production Management, 34*, 1417–1439. http://dx.doi.org/10.1108/IJOPM-06-2012-0197

Nezlek, J. B. (2001). Multilevel random coefficient analyses of event- and interval-contingent data in social and personality psychology research. *Personality and Social Psychology Bulletin, 27*, 771–785. http://dx.doi.org/10.1177/0146167201277001

O*Net. (2017). *Occupational Information Network (O*NET)*. Retrieved from https://www.onetcenter.org/overview.html

Piaget, J. (1971). *Biology and knowledge: An essay on the relations between organic regulations and cognitive processes*. Chicago, IL: University of Chicago Press.

Raudenbush, S. W., & Bryk, A. S. (1988). Methodological advances in analyzing the effects of schools and classrooms on student learning. *Review of Research in Education, 15*, 423–475. http://dx.doi.org/10.3102/0091732X015001423

Raudenbush, S. W., & Bryk, A. S. (2002). *Hierarchical linear models: Applications and data analysis methods*. Newbury Park, CA: Sage.

Roberts, K. H., Hulin, C. L., & Rousseau, D. M. (1978). *Developing an interdisciplinary science of organizations*. San Francisco, CA: Jossey-Bass.

Roberts, R. M. (1989). *Serendipity: Accidental discoveries in science*. Hoboken, NJ: Wiley & Sons.

Roberts, S. V. (1988, May 4). White House confirms Reagans follow astrology, up to a point. *New York Times*. http://www.nytimes.com/1988/05/04/us/white-house-confirms-reagans-follow-astrology-up-to-a-point.html.

Robertson, D., Snarey, J., Ousley, O., Harenski, K., DuBois Bowman, F., Gilkey, R., & Kilts, C. (2007). The neural processing of moral sensitivity to issues of justice and care. *Neuropsychologia, 45*, 755–766. http://dx.doi.org/10.1016/j.neuropsychologia.2006.08.014

Rousseau, D. M. (1985). Issues of level in organizational research: Multilevel and crosslevel perspectives. In L. L. Cummings & B. Staw (Eds.), *Research in organizational behavior* (Vol. 7, pp. 1–37). Greenwich, CT: JAI Press.

Schmidt, F. L., & Hunter, J. E. (1998). The validity and utility of selection methods in personnel psychology: Practical and theoretical implications of 85 years of research findings. *Psychological Bulletin, 124*, 262–274. http://dx.doi.org/10.1037/0033-2909.124.2.262

Schramm, V. L. (2011). Enzymatic transition states, transition-state analogs, dynamics, thermo-dynamics, and lifetimes. *Annual Review of Biochemistry, 80*, 703–732. http://dx.doi.org/10.1146/annurev-biochem-061809-100742

Schyns, P. (1998). Crossnational differences in happiness: Economic and cultural factors explored. *Social Indicators Research, 43*, 3–26. http://dx.doi.org/10.1023/A:1006814424293

Shadish, W. R., Cook, T. D., & Campbell, D. T. (2002). *Experimental and quasi-experimental designs for generalized causal inference*. Boston, MA: Houghton Mifflin.

Shafer, S. M., Nembhard, D. A., & Uzumeri, M. V. (2001). The effects of worker learning, forgetting, and heterogeneity on assembly line productivity. *Management Science, 47,* 1639–1653. http://dx.doi.org/10.1287/mnsc.47.12.1639.10236

Shinn, M., & Rapkin, B. D. (2000). Cross-level research without cross-ups in community psychology. In J. Rappaport & E. Seidman (Eds.), *Handbook of community psychology* (pp. 669–695). New York, NY: Kluwer/Springer. http://dx.doi.org/10.1007/978-1-4615-4193-6_28

Simon, H. A. (1973). The organization of complex systems. In H. H. Pattee (Ed.), *Hierarchy theory: The challenge of complex systems* (pp. 1–27). New York, NY: George Braziller.

Singer, J. D. (1961). The level-of-analysis problem in international relations. *World Politics, 14,* 77–92. http://dx.doi.org/10.2307/2009557

Sjöberg, L., & af Wåhlberg, A. (2002). Risk perception and new age beliefs. *Risk Analysis, 22,* 751–764. http://dx.doi.org/10.1111/0272-4332.00066

Snijders, T. A., & Kenny, D. A. (1999). The social relations model for family data: A multilevel approach. *Personal Relationships, 6,* 471–486. http://dx.doi.org/10.1111/j.1475-6811.1999.tb00204.x

Takeuchi, R., Chen, G., & Lepak, D. P. (2009). Through the looking glass of a social system: Cross-level effects of high-performance work systems on employees' attitudes. *Personnel Psychology, 62,* 1–29. http://dx.doi.org/10.1111/j.1744-6570.2008.01127.x

Thompson, P. B., McWilliams, A., & Shanley, M. (2014). Creating competitive advantage: A stakeholder view of employee ownership. *International Journal of Strategic Change Management, 5,* 262–279. http://dx.doi.org/10.1504/IJSCM.2014.064468

Tsang, L. L. W., Harvey, C. D., Duncan, K. A., & Sommer, R. (2003). The effects of children, dual earner status, sex role traditionalism, and marital structure on marital happiness over time. *Journal of Family and Economic Issues, 24,* 5–26. http://dx.doi.org/10.1023/A:1022478919443

Van Lange, P. M., Joireman, J., Parks, C. D., & Van Dijk, E. (2013). The psychology of social dilemmas: A review. *Organizational Behavior and Human Decision Processes, 120,* 125–141. http://dx.doi.org/10.1016/j.obhdp.2012.11.003

Zaheer, S., Albert, S., & Zaheer, A. (1999). Time scales and organizational theory. *Academy of Management Review, 24,* 725–741.

Zhang, Z., Zyphur, M. J., & Preacher, K. J. (2009). Testing multilevel mediation using hierarchical linear models: Problems and solutions. *Organizational Research Methods, 12,* 695–719. http://dx.doi.org/10.1177/1094428108327450

## CHAPTER 2

CONTEXTUALIZING CONTEXT IN ORGANIZATIONAL RESEARCH

Cheri Ostroff

Context is crucial for understanding collective entities and inherently entails a multilevel perspective. Top-down models focus on contextual factors that influence lower level phenomena, while bottom-up models address the emergence of phenomena from lower levels to create the context (Kozlowski & Klein, 2000). In organizational science, organizations are viewed as integrated, multilevel systems that provide the context for understanding responses and behaviors (Roberts, Hulin, & Rousseau, 1978). Direct consideration of the context makes theory and research more precise and robust (Schneider, 1985) and bridges the micro–macro divide (Bamberger, 2008). "Context effects are so central to an understanding of organizational phenomena that contextual analysis should become a distinctive feature of organizational scholarship" (Whetten, 2009, p. 30).

In the 1970s, 70% of the studies in organizational behavior were conducted solely at the individual level of analysis; by the 1990s, that figure had fallen to 38% (O'Reilly, 1991). Since then, articles specifically about context began appearing with more regularity (e.g., Cappelli & Sherer, 1991; Johns, 2001, 2006; Mowday & Sutton, 1993; Rousseau & Fried, 2001). Today, the term *context* has become almost ubiquitous in organizational research. An Internet search yields thousands of articles with "organizational context" in the article title across many topics such as social networking, knowledge brokering, obesity, personnel selection, managerial

actions, human capital, entrepreneurship, and leadership. Similarly, nearly every article includes phrases such as future research is needed to determine if the findings generalize to other contexts, the context is appropriate for this study, and within the organizational context. One might be tempted to think that the field of organizational science has finally conquered the issue of context. Yet scholars have continually pointed out that the impact of context has been and continues to be insufficiently recognized (e.g., Cappelli & Sherer, 1991; Härtel & O'Connor, 2014; Ilgen & Klein, 1988; Johns, 2001, 2006; O'Reilly, 1991; Pettigrew, 1987; Rousseau & Fried, 2001; Whetten, 2009).

The importance of context, and laments about failures to adequately consider it, have been noted in related fields. For example, strategic management scholars have argued that research about the organizational context in which strategy is situated has been piecemeal and unsystematic (e.g., MacKay & McKiernan, 2010). In anthropology, researchers have decried the importance of placing cultural and social phenomena in context (e.g., Dilley, 1999). Linguistics and communication scholars have long purported that discourse has little meaning unless the context is taken into consideration (e.g., Adair, Buchan, Chen, & Liu, 2016). The social context perspective in sociology focuses on how different types of collective social arrangements, such as community, social class, and country, shape

http://dx.doi.org/10.1037/0000115-003
The Handbook of Multilevel Theory, Measurement, and Analysis, S. E. Humphrey and J. M. LeBreton (Editors-in-Chief)

daily lives (e.g., Zusman, Knox, & Gardner, 2009). Behavioral economists (e.g., Camerer & Loewenstein, 2004) have debated whether context should be viewed as a nuisance variable or a treatment variable while at the same time acknowledging that context matters.

WHY CONTEXT IS IMPORTANT

Understanding the role of context can progress contemporary research and theory across different levels of analysis. Incorporating dimensions of context directly into research design allows for effects and relationships to emerge that may otherwise have remained undetected or misinterpreted. Furthermore, given that research has increasingly become more international and work and organizational settings have become increasingly diversified, attending to context can provide greater insight into the nature of factors and processes that influence behavior and outcomes in organizations and can better elucidate when, how, and why a phenomenon happens (Rousseau & Fried, 2001; Welter, 2011).

If context matters, why are we still struggling with our approach to context? One reason may be that definitions of context are often vague. "Context is one of those words you will encounter again and again, without anyone offering anything like a useful definition" (N. R. Williams, 2004, p. 105). Typical definitions take a top-down approach, deeming context as something outside of the focal entity, which affects the focal entity, and resides at a higher level of analysis. This type of broad generic definition has its usefulness. However, there is an absence of holistic theorizing about context (Bamberger, 2008). Building upon this prior work about the dimensions of context (cf. Johns, 2006; Rousseau & Fried, 2001), a more nuanced and comprehensive framework for considering the dimensions of context—the *what* of context—could help point scholars to more specific aspects of context to consider in any given study.

In addition, less explicit attention has been devoted to approaches for *how* to study context. A broad distinction has been drawn between direct or context approaches that incorporate measures of the context in the study, and indirect or contextualization approaches where context is used as a frame for the

study and to interpret results (Bamberger, 2008; Härtel & O'Connor, 2014). Configural approaches have been highlighted by some authors (e.g., Johns, 2006; Rousseau & Fried, 2001), and strength of the situational context has become an emerging trend (e.g., Schneider, González-Romá, Ostroff, & West, 2017). Yet the primary approach in articles that include context has been top-down and cross-level, tending to ignore the dynamic interplay between the micro and macro levels and the notion that the social context emerges from individuals. A more comprehensive treatment of how we can approach the study of context may promote thinking about context in new and different ways.

The overarching purpose of this chapter is to begin the process of developing a more refined framework for considering both the "what" of context in terms of broad dimensions and the "how" of context in terms of methodological approaches. In what follows, the rise of attention to context and definitions of context are first briefly reviewed with particular emphasis on why context is important and has its effect. The distinction between context that is external to the focal entity and context that is an internal part of the focal is acknowledged, although the focus in this chapter is primarily on internal context. Meta-dimensions of internal context are categorized (physical–technological, structure–practices, higher order social-psychological constructs, person-based), followed by consideration of approaches to study context (indirectly, directly, dimensions vs. configurations, idiosyncratic perceptions, collectives, relative standing, variability, and emergence). Together, the "what" dimensions and "how" approaches offer a framework that shows the array of ways to consider context. Although most of the illustrative examples in this chapter are based on organizational phenomena, context is important to the study of any social collective across disciplines in the social and behavioral sciences.

BRIEF HISTORY: FROM INTERACTIONISM TO OPEN SYSTEMS TO CONTEXT

Contextualization and context are related but distinct notions. *Contextualization* is the "linking of observations to a set of relevant facts, events or point of view that make possible research and theory that form part of a larger whole" (Rousseau & Fried, 2001, p. 1). Contextualized research takes into account features of the setting, location, time, organization, or collective to provide a richer understanding of the phenomenon, and promotes theory building (e.g., Bacharach, 1989). In general terms, *context* refers to the specific set of factors and features in the situation that have some influence on the phenomenon of interest, provides insights into the interpretation of results, and/or serves as boundary conditions for the phenomenon (e.g., Cappelli & Sherer, 1991; Heath & Sitkin, 2001; Johns, 2006; Whetten, 2009).

In the micro tradition, the focus on context has its roots in the interactionist perspective from psychology, which emphasized that neither traits nor situations are the primary drivers of individuals' responses, but it is their interaction that is important (Ekehammar, 1974; Mischel, 1973; Schneider, 1983). The emergence of the human relations movement in the 1920s spurred psychologists to examine how situational factors such as the structural features or culture of the organization influenced individual responses (Üsdiken & Leblebici, 2001). Kantor (1926) proposed that the unit of study should be the individual interacting with different types of situations. Murray's (1938) need-press theory emphasized that individual's needs could be fulfilled or hindered by the environment, and Goldstein (1939) focused on the relationship between a person's qualities and the nature of the tasks he or she confronts in the environment. However, Kurt Lewin was arguably the most influential scholar in bringing context to the forefront in psychological research by explicating "psychological forces" (Lewin, 1938), "social climate" (Lewin, Lippitt, & White, 1939), and the "total social field" (Lewin, 1947) as important contextual factors for understanding how individuals behave in their environment (Lewin, 1951).

A transition to the macro perspective began in the 1960s and 1970s. The open systems paradigm was applied to conceptualizing organizations as social systems (Katz & Kahn, 1978). The importance of understanding interrelationships among structural features of organizations began to be emphasized, with organizational effectiveness purported to depend on the alignment of input, transformation, and output processes and acknowledging dependence on external environmental resources (e.g., Yuchtman & Seashore, 1967). Structural-contingency models emphasized alignment between the internal structural arrangement of the organization and environmental constraints such as uncertainty (e.g., Pennings, 1975). Later developments showed increased complexity, focusing on environmental resource dependencies (e.g., Pfeffer & Salancik, 1978); institutional environments (e.g., Scott, 1995); environmental niches (e.g., Hannan & Freeman, 1989); configurations of environmental, contextual, structural, and strategic factors (e.g., Doty, Glick, & Huber, 1993); and transactions between managers, stockholders, board members, and organizations (e.g., Eisenhardt, 1989).

At the same time, the psychological tradition from the human relations movement was integrated with systems views of organizations (Üsdiken & Leblebici, 2001). For example, Likert (1961, 1967) emphasized that internally consistent structural arrangements (e.g., communication, decision-making, reward processes) facilitate the development and self-actualization of employees and facilitate stability. Sociotechnical theories of organizations (e.g., Emery & Trist, 1969) emphasized the fit between social (interrelationships among people) and technical (technologically based) subsystems and by extension between those aspects of organization and the needs and abilities of individuals (Katz & Kahn, 1978).

CONTEXT AS CONSTRAINTS AND OPPORTUNITIES IS MORE THAN TOP-DOWN

Context has been deemed important for nearly 100 years in the social and behavioral sciences. But what is context? "Almost universally, we find context to be an overworked word in everyday dialogue but a massively understudied and misunderstood concept" (Bate, 2014, p. 4). Definitions abound (see Exhibit 2.1 for representative examples) but are fairly generic. Common themes include context as something outside of the focal entity, typically at a higher level of analysis, which affects

---

EXHIBIT 2.1

Representative Definitions of Context

Authors	Definition
Cappelli and Sherer (1991)	The surroundings associated with the phenomena, which help to illuminate that phenomena, typically factors associated with units of analysis above those expressly under investigation
Mowday and Sutton (1993)	Stimuli and phenomena that surround and thus exist in the environment external to the individual, most often at a different level of analysis
Ghoshal and Bartlett (1994)	Systems, processes, and beliefs that shape individual-level behavior
Johns (2006)	Situational opportunities and constrains that affect the occurrence and meaning of organizational behavior as well as the functional relationships between variables
Griffin (2007)	The set of circumstances in which phenomena (events, processes, or entities) are situated; it typically exists at a unit of analysis above the phenomena being investigated and can explain some salient aspect of the phenomena
Whetten (2009)	The set of factors surrounding a phenomenon that exert some direct or indirect influence on it–also characterized as explanatory factors associated with higher levels of analysis than those expressly under investigation
Michailova (2011)	A dynamic array of factors, features, processes, or events which have an influence on a phenomenon that is examined . . . something that is multifaceted and that both influences and is influenced by the phenomenon under investigation
Bate (2014)	All of those variables (z) that influence or could influence the "independent" (x) and dependent (y) variables directly under study

or shapes experiences and explains phenomena. Context has been viewed as a sensitizing device that serves as a boundary condition to put the research study into perspective and a critical driver or moderator of lower level phenomenon (Bamberger, 2008). With respect to theory, *context theorizing* has been defined as "theories that specify how surrounding phenomena or temporal conditions directly influence lower-level phenomena, condition relations between one or more variables at different levels of analysis, or are influenced by the phenomena nested within them" (Bamberger, 2008, p. 841).

Yet context has roots in interactionism and systems theory. Relatively few recent articles devoted to context address the potential for dynamic interplay with the entity being influenced by and influencing the context. Likewise, context is more often viewed as something that resides at a higher level of analysis rather than a factor that can exist at the same level or emerge through a bottom-up process (Bamberger, 2008; Griffin, 2007). Context, however, may not always be a direct or moderating influence but may be an interaction of elements within the system, or it may operate through alignment with other factors at the same

or higher levels of analysis (Maloney, Bresman, Zellmer-Bruhn, & Beaver, 2016; Pettigrew, 1987). For example, characteristics of team members can become shared to serve as the context that influences a focal member (downward); other teams in the organization may act as the context and affect the dynamics of the focal team (horizontal), and the strategy adopted as being relevant for a particular industry may drive the system of human resources (HR) practices and ensuing climate (alignment).

A consideration of context through constraints and opportunities can help illuminate why the view of context as predominately a top-down influence or moderator is limiting. Organizations (or a social collective) are fundamentally social systems comprised of patterned activities across a number of individuals (Katz & Kahn, 1978). Patterns of social interaction are based on both contextual *constraints* and *opportunities* for social relations created by the composition of the population and structure of positions (Blau, 1974; Johns, 1991, 2001, 2006).

Context can constrain behavior and responses by decreasing variability in the phenomenon of interest (Kozlowski & Klein, 2000), thereby creating what Mischel (1973) referred to as a *strong situation*.

Human variability in organizations is reduced through task requirements that induce coordination of efforts for effective organizational functioning, shared values and expectations about how to behave, rule enforcement with sanctions for rule violations, and extrinsic rewards to condition people about how to behave (Katz & Kahn, 1978).

In contrast, some organizations are designed to allow a range of different employee responses to work requirements through providing greater autonomy, discretion, and flexibility (Bowen, Ledford, & Nathan, 1991). Stemming from the human relations approach (Likert, 1961) and now often referred to as *high-commitment, high-involvement* or *high performance work systems* (e.g., Boxall & Macky, 2009; Toh, Morgeson, & Campion, 2008), decision-making is pushed down the line, voice is provided at all levels, and discretion over how to accomplish work is provided. This type of organizational context provides opportunities such as engaging in job crafting (e.g., Wrzesniewski & Dutton, 2001) and role innovation (Ashforth, 2001).

Because context is so broad and multifaceted and often invisible (Rousseau & Fried, 2001), perhaps the definition needs to remain very broad. One avenue for deriving a more nuanced understanding of context has been outlining the characteristics of what contextualized research would entail such as multilevel, vertical and horizontal analysis of context features and incorporation of process, time, and setting (cf. Johns, 2006; Pettigrew, 1987; Rousseau & Fried, 2001). At this juncture, it may be fruitful to expand existing frameworks about the dimensions of context that are most relevant for organizational research and how we can best study those aspects.

External Environmental and Internal Context

Defining the boundaries of social collectives (e.g., groups, families, work teams, cultures) is often challenging, as individuals often have multiple roles; different social collectives may overlap in their membership, resources, and functions (Ashforth, 2001; Cummings & Haas, 2012); and boundaries can be defined in multiple ways (Santos & Eisenhardt, 2005). Nevertheless, it is useful to

attempt to draw some distinction between external environmental and internal organizational context (Katz & Kahn, 1978). External context consists of factors, stimuli, or processes that are often, but not always, outside of the control of the social collective of focal interest (e.g., family, team, organization) and that have some type of effect on the social collective. Internal context is created within the social collective through its people, structural choices, norms or practices leadership, and/or use of technology.

Katz and Kahn (1978) provided an overarching framework of external context characteristics by crossing five environmental sectors—societal values (cultural legitimation), political (legal norms and statutes), economic (markets and inputs of labor and materials), informational and technological, and physical (geography and natural resources)—with the general dimensions of stability–turbulence, uniformity–diversity, clustered–random, and scarcity–munificence. While developed for understanding organizations, these same external dimensions also influence other social collectives such as family dynamics and friendship networks (e.g., Kraut et al., 1998; Van den Broek, Dykstra, & Schenk, 2014).

It is beyond the scope of this chapter to examine external contextual factors in depth, but it is important to note that the external environment is a salient context for the internal context. Focusing on the external context is important because the exchanges between the social collective or organization and the environment shape and affect conditions within the organization (e.g., Sutton & Rousseau, 1979). As examples, the industry characteristics of capital intensity, differentiation, and growth influenced relationships between high performance work systems and firm productivity (Datta, Guthrie, & Wright, 2005). The racial composition of the local community moderated relationships between the racial composition in bank branches and their diversity climate (Pugh, Dietz, Brief, & Wiley, 2008). Industry and occupation moderated relationships between team task-oriented and relations-oriented diversity and performance (Joshi & Roh, 2009). By far, the preponderance of studies on external contextual influences on organizations focus on the organizational level of analysis from organizational theory and strategic management perspectives (e.g., Bluedorn, Johnson, Cartwright, & Barringer, 1994; Van de Ven, Ganco, & Hinings, 2013). Yet the external context is also critical at other levels of analysis.

The external environment provides a context for understanding the antecedents and consequences of the linkages and depths of bonds between people or between employees and organizations. "Changes going on in the external (to the organizations) environment provide a sort of 'ground' for the 'figure' of employee–organization linkages" (Mowday, Porter, & Steers, 2013, p. 8). As illustrations, external linkages help ensure that units and teams are aligned appropriately with their external environment (e.g., Bresman & Zellmer-Bruhn, 2013; Vera, Nemanich, Vélez-Castrillón, & Werner, 2016), and the degree to which individuals conform to the group has been shown to depend on societal culture (R. Bond & Smith, 1996). Many theories explicitly acknowledge the impact of the external environment on employees. For example, the extent of ties to the local community is an integral part of job embeddedness (e.g., William Lee, Burch, & Mitchell, 2014), unemployment rates have long been a key factor in models of employee turnover (e.g., Hom, Caranikas-Walker, Prussia, & Griffeth, 1992), and economic downturns have been shown to decrease helping behavior (Sirola & Pitesa, 2017). Thus, more holistic, theoretical development and additional research is encouraged that takes into account the direct and indirect effects of the external environment on lower level phenomena in organizations.

Omnibus and Discrete Context

Much like Katz and Kahn's (1978) observation that "everything in the universe, except for the organization under study, is treated as a single category of environment" (p. 122) and that more specification is needed, the same applies to the internal context. To date, Johns (2006) has provided the most comprehensive treatment of organizational context. He drew a distinction between omnibus and discrete contexts. The omnibus context addresses who (e.g., occupation or gender composition in the organization), where (e.g., location, country, community),

when (e.g., year, time of data collection), and why (e.g., why information is being collected). Discrete context reflects the internal context with three dimensions of task (e.g., autonomy, resources), social (e.g., social density, social influence), and physical (e.g., lighting, décor). Discrete context, in Johns's view, comprises situational variables that directly influence or moderate relationships between variables, while omnibus context dimensions are generally treated as "frames" for the study that can impact interpretation of results. Arguably, omnibus dimensions reflect both external and internal context features and can operate in the same direct or moderating way as dimensions of the discrete context. For example, demographic composition of units was related to unit climate for diversity, with racial composition of the local community found to moderate this relationship (e.g., Pugh et al., 2008). Given the increasing attention to contextual influences and continued questions about what context is, the time seems ripe to refocus attention on a richer view of the internal context by providing greater specification of the dimensions of internal context, incorporating a range of fundamental theoretical rationales for why those dimensions are important, and updating the array of ways in which context can be studied.

META-DIMENSIONS OF INTERNAL CONTEXT

The foundation for the dimensions of internal context resides in the premise that organizations and social collectives are socio-technical systems that require integration of the technological system (equipment, technology, and physical layout) with the social-psychological system comprising culture, values, norms, structure, practices, climate, and collective employee attributes. Although the technological system is somewhat constraining, for any given technological system a number of possible work arrangements and social-psychological systems can exist (Katz & Kahn, 1978). With this as a basis, four meta-dimensions of internal context are proposed: physical and technological, structure and practices, culture and climate, and person based (influential agents, the personal characteristics of others, and collective attitudes and behaviors). The physical and technological dimension is based on the physical layout and technology employed and reflects tangible or visible dimensions of context. Structure and practices are contrived aspects of context, often determined through leader or managerial decisions, and focus on how tasks are to be accomplished. Culture and climate represent higher order socially constructed variables that reflect values, norms, and perceptions of what is expected and valued (Ferris et al., 1998). Attributes and responses of people as the context points attention to the fact that the people around us exert direct and indirect influences on attitudes, affect, and behavior (M. Bond, 2014). Parsing the socio-technical system into meta-dimensions provides an organizing heuristic for focusing attention to broad aspects of the context with common underlying themes (e.g., tangible, contrived, socially constructed, person based). It is also important to note that contextual dimensions operate together and are mutually influential in creating the organizational system (Pettigrew, 1987).

Tangible Context—Physical and Technological

Research attention devoted to the impact of the physical and technological context can be traced back to the Hawthorne studies (Roethlisberger & Dickson, 1939). Although the original purpose was to examine the effects of physical conditions such as lighting and clean work stations on productivity, the conclusion was that it was not physical conditions, but rather that someone was concerned about the employees' workplace that resulted in the increased productivity. Since that time, research from environmental psychology, human factors, ergonomics, and management has consistently documented constraints and opportunities arising from the physical context.

A prominent theoretical basis underpinning studies of the physical layout as context is that noise, density, and crowding represent environmental stressors, which can have an adverse effect on mood (Proshansky, 1987). Housing and building features such as windows, high ceilings, and providing control over physical context such as

ventilation can reduce stress and negative feelings. The emerging research on open office plans speaks to the issue. In open office plans, close proximity, noise, and uncontrolled social contact purportedly creates overstimulation leading to a perceived loss of task and communication privacy, feelings of crowding, and lower satisfaction (Kim & De Dear, 2013; Oldham, 1988)—that is, constraining effects. At the same time, from a social relations view, open office layouts can provide opportunities for greater communication, development of interpersonal relationships, knowledge sharing, and creativity (Zalesny & Farace, 1987). Likewise, stripping organizational space of extraneous decoration provides the organization opportunities to accommodate changes in the number of people and functions in the same area, but it has a constraining effect on employees' ability to personalize their workspace. Providing employees the opportunity to personalize workspaces (Brunia & Hartjes-Gosselink, 2009) has been related to more positive perceptions of concentration, satisfaction, and productivity. Taken together, although underexplored in organizational research, social science research suggests that the organizational physical context may fulfill social, psychological, or cultural needs that are incorporated into self-identity creating place identity (Proshansky, 1987) or place attachment stemming from emotional or affective ties (Low & Altman, 1992; Stedman, 2002), which could have implications for employee responses such as engagement, involvement, and turnover.

Similarly, the technology and equipment can constrain what is accomplished but may also afford opportunities for coordination, different types of work arrangements, and means for increasing productivity (Katz & Kahn, 1978; Orlikowski, 2000) in dyads, families, classrooms, or organizations. Based on adaptive structuration theory (DeSanctis & Poole, 1994), routines, social structures of interpersonal interaction, work arrangements, rules, and norms develop around existing technology and reinforce a sense of stability (Orlikowski, 2000). In this view, technology creates new structures and practices as well as the social-psychological dimensions such as culture and climate, and once created provide stability and constraints on behavior. For example, meta-analytic results indicate that computer-mediated groups are characterized by less interaction and information exchange and take longer to complete tasks, suggesting that technological integrations may constrain some important social dynamics that are necessary for effective decision-making and performance (Baltes, Dickson, Sherman, Bauer, & LaGanke, 2002). At the same time, the existing social-psychological context can provide opportunities for more successful adoption of new technology and the changes in routines needed to maximize the benefits of a new technology (Mirvis, Sales, & Hackett, 1991). As an example, in cardiac surgical departments, the successful implementation of new technology depended on having a culture and climate that allowed for motivating the team, providing psychological safety, and promoting shared meanings (Edmondson, Bohmer, & Pisano, 2001).

Beyond these views of technology as context, the International Federation of Robotics (2017) estimated that the world's industrial robot population is close to 2 million, with robots being increasingly used in industries such as manufacturing, banking, health care, police, and the military. A growing body of research indicates that people anthropomorphize robots and technology; make assumptions about its personality, sensitivity, and gender; and become attached (Fussell, Kiesler, Setlock, & Yew, 2008; Turkle, 2012). While creating opportunities for new ways of interacting with people in the collective, working, and providing customer service, the attachment to technology or robots may constrain or substitute for social relationships and interactions with coworkers.

Contrived Context—Structure and Practices Context

Collectives, whether they be friendship networks, families, sporting groups, organizations, or societies, also develop similar features in terms of structure, authority, formalization, routines, and practices that shape social relations and social capital (Lin, 2002). In organizations, structure and practices are contrived dimensions of context that are created and renewed through concrete management actions (Ghoshal & Bartlett, 1994). All organizations have

a structure of authority and regulatory mechanisms that coordinate work effort and provide channels for carrying out organizational decisions. These structures encompass hierarchy, formal rules, policies, and procedures. They differ across organizations in terms of the degree of formalization, standardization of work tasks and workflow, and centralization of decision-making (Katz & Kahn, 1978). Highly mechanized structures can constrain responses through monitoring, regulation, and coercing employees into compliance, whereas less mechanistic structures afford greater opportunities for individual discretion in carrying out roles and work activities (Burns & Stalker, 1966).

Like technology, structural elements provide a context for the creation of habitual routines, or repeated patterns of interdependent behavior bound by rules and customs that reflect much of the organization's (or collective's) ongoing activity (Cyert & March, 1963). Routines reside in employees' procedural memory for how things are done and are a source of the reliability and speed of organizational performance, without which the organization would lose its capacity for collective action (Cohen & Bacdayan, 1994). The emphasis on routines as interactions makes them collective phenomena and hence an aspect of the context (Felin, Foss, Heimeriks, & Madsen, 2012). Routines can be constraining or a source of opportunity. Known, rigid routines that prescribe standard ways of behaving provide stability and prompt almost automatic action; as such, they can inhibit actively seeking out alternative ways of doing things (Levitt & March, 1988). Flexible routines can be more dynamic and allow for more discretion in how they are executed, leading to greater variability in behavior (Feldman & Pentland, 2003; Felin et al., 2012). For example, structural coordination mechanisms (e.g., job rotation, cross-functional interfaces) enhance a unit's potential absorptive capacity of being able to recognize the value of new information and assimilate it (Jansen, Van Den Bosch, & Volberda, 2005).

Similarly, role theory views a collective as a system of formal roles that exist apart from any current occupant and that serve to convey standardized information to employees about expected patterns of activity (Ashforth, 2001). The degree of uncertainty and interdependence in the structure provides a context for whether members can be effective by complying with requirements or by adapting and initiating change (Griffin, Neal, & Parker, 2007).

HR practices are also contrived through managerial decisions, are strategic in nature, and provide the foundation for human capital (Wright, McMahan, & McWilliams, 1994). The primary purpose of HR practices is to acquire and develop human capital (knowledge, skills, and abilities) and to motivate employees to work toward the achievement of organizational goals (e.g., Allen & Wright, 2007). HR practices provide a signaling function to employees about what behaviors and responses are valued, expected, and rewarded (Guzzo & Noonan, 1994; Rousseau & Wade-Benzoni, 1994) and why the practices are in place (Nishii, Lepak, & Schneider, 2008). The practices provide a context from which employees derive meaning about how to respond and behave in the organization (Nishii et al., 2008; Wright & Nishii, 2008). The set or types of HR practices adopted can be more or less constraining. For example, structural features such as the degree of centralization (Jansen, Simsek, & Cao, 2012) and the formality of the performance management practices (Gibson & Birkinshaw, 2004) influence unit ambidexterity (the capacity to simultaneously achieve alignment with current demands and adaptability to changing environments); decentralization and broad roles provide opportunities while practices such as rewards or punishment based on rigorous measurement are more constraining.

The degree of constraint or opportunities afforded by the set of HR practices depends on the combination of the set of HR practices and the strength of the HR system. As explained by Ostroff and Bowen (2000, 2016; Bowen & Ostroff, 2004), idiosyncratic interpretations of expected responses derived from the HR practices will result, unless there are strong HR process mechanisms so that HR practices are distinctive and understandable, delivered in consistent ways, and have consensus among message senders. The outcome of a strong HR system is more uniform expectations across employees. Although a strong HR system creates a strong situation, it is not necessarily constraining. A strong HR system that sends a clear message that the set of practices represents a traditional, bureaucratic philosophy with strong monitoring and control will constrain behavior, whereas a strong HR system that sends clear messages that the set of practices support autonomy, participation, and job crafting provides opportunities for employees.

Socially Constructed Context— Culture and Climate

Individuals, through their perceptions and cognitions, actively socially construct the external situation (Weick, 1995). As such, this aspect of context is not about the physical or actual situation per se, but rather the situation as people see and experience it. Collective entities and organizations develop a culture and climate that represents the social fabric of organizational life (Schneider et al., 2017); focuses on how participants observe, experience, and make sense of their environment (Schneider, Ehrhart, & Macey, 2011); and are fundamental for describing the social side of organizational phenomena (Schein, 2010). Culture and climate are higher order socially interactive constructs in that they cannot be reduced to an aggregation of the perceptions of the individuals currently comprising the collective or organization (Ferris et al., 1998).

Culture is conceptualized as organizationally embedded assumptions, ideologies, and values that exist at a fundamental and often subliminal level of awareness (Schein, 2010) and is grounded in history and tradition (Ehrhart, Schneider, & Macey, 2014). Culture is typically considered a property of the organization (Martin, 1992) stemming from the founders of the organization and top leadership and is continually reinforced and transmitted to members through symbolic interpretation of organizational events and artifacts (Hatch, 2011).

Climate, a related construct, is defined as shared perceptions of what the organization is like and is derived from employee perceptions of practices, policies, procedures, and routines (Jones & James, 1979). Climate is viewed as an emergent property because perceptions of climate reside within individuals, but when shared, become an emergent property of the organization that exists outside of any individual member (James et al., 2008). The focus in climate is on experientially based perceptions of the situation and can be viewed as temporal, subjective, and possibly subject to manipulation by authority figures (Denison, 1996).

The social and symbolic processes associated with organizational culture and climate shape individual responses, behaviors, and organizational performance (Schneider et al., 2017). For example, organizational culture has been related to individuals' attitudes and performance (Liden, Wayne, Liao, & Meuser, 2014). Cultural practices may be transmitted through explicit instructions to newcomers and imitation based on newcomers' observations of old-timers' performance (Kashima et al., 2015). Climate has been consistently related to individual attitudes and performance (Carr, Schmidt, Ford, & DeShon, 2003) and to unit and organizational effectiveness (Ostroff, Kinicki, & Muhammad, 2012).

One way in which culture and climate operate as contextual variables is by setting the stage for the development of normative behavior in organizations. System norms are shared by members, make explicit the appropriate forms of behavior, and are a justification for the activities and functions of the system (Katz & Kahn, 1978). They emanate from the socially constructed context of organizational cultural values and climate, vary markedly across organizations (Peysakhovich & Rand, 2015), and are conceptualized as context-specific regulators of behavior (Morris, Hong, Chiu, & Liu, 2015). While norms generally constrain behavior, adherence to norms is not always automatic and may provide opportunities. Norms can guide thoughts and behavior through what Morris and his colleagues (2015) termed *social autopilot* and *social radar*. When functioning like an autopilot, norms guide immediate responses and behaviors without conscious deliberation in a socially safe direction. Alternately, adherence to norms can be based on an iterative process much like radar, in which individuals deliberate on the system norms, send signals about adherence to them through behavior, and have that reflected back to decide whether they want to continue to adhere to the norm.

Taken together, culture and climate can represent strong or weak situation in at least two ways (Ostroff et al., 2012). First, it depends on the degree to which they lead employees to construe and encode the organizational situation similarly and induce uniform expectations about the most appropriate responses (e.g., González-Romá & Hernández, 2014; Lindell & Brandt, 2000; Schneider, Salvaggio, & Subirats, 2002). Second, pertains to the degree to which the culture and climate is pervasive and all-encompassing throughout all aspects of organizational life, with strong socialization and sanctions for behaving outside norms (e.g., R. L. Payne, 2000).

People as Context—Influential Agent, Collective Responses, and Personal Characteristics

Considerable research across social science disciplines shows that others around us can have powerful influences on our thoughts, perceptions, feelings, and behaviors (M. Bond, 2014). Meta-analytic results of 100 years of social psychology research indicate that group processes and leadership generally have stronger effects on attitudes and behaviors than individual-level relationships (Richard, Bond, & Stokes-Zoota, 2003). Schneider (1987) prompted organizational scientists to shift their focus from technological and structural context to people-based dimensions:

> We attribute cause not to the people attracted to, selected by, and remaining within the organization, but to the signs of their existence in the organization: to structure, process, and technology . . . let us seek explanation in people . . . the people make the place. (p. 451)

The people-based context is organized around three categories—an influential agent, the collective attitudes and responses of others in the unit or organization, and the background and demographic characteristics or members.

Influential agents. Influential agents, such as a leader, parent, teacher, mentor, or influential group member, are one source of people as context. Beginning with early studies on obedience and conformity (e.g., Milgram, 1963; Zimbardo, 1972), considerable research has documented that individuals tend to cede responsibility to authority figures and obey them, with little evidence that this has declined much over the years (e.g., Burger, 2009). Theoretical rationales for this phenomenon have a long history but generally focus on three core social influence mechanisms developed by Kelman (1958). First, compliance to the authority figure occurs when he or she is seen to have control or legitimate authority and engages in surveillance. Here, the individual's concern is with the social effect of his or her behavior and with conforming to the rules of the social system. A second mechanism operates through identification with the authority figure, typically based on liking or personal attributes. The individual's concern is with embedding their role in the social system by anchoring his or her behavior to meet the role and performance expectations of the figure. Third, internalization is based on the credibility, expertise, or trustworthiness of the authority figure. Willingness to be influenced from the agent depends on how the expected responses fit with the individual's own value system and the degree to which the values in the system are ones the individual shares. The internalization mechanism is more idiosyncratic, flexible, and complex (Kelman, 2006) and hence may be viewed as a less constraining type of influence.

Parents, teachers, leaders, and supervisors operate as powerful social influence agents through all three mechanisms. For example, leaders can induce compliance based on their legitimacy authority, position power, control of resources, and the ability to reward and punish (Magee & Galinsky, 2008), which can have positive effects such as inducing subordinates to work toward unit or organizational goals (e.g., Ouchi, 1980) or negative effects such as engaging in corruption (e.g., Pinto, Leana, & Pil, 2008). Charismatic leaders tend to be liked, often evoke identification and internationalization on the part of subordinates, and prompt employees to work toward a common goal (van Knippenberg & Sitkin, 2013). In addition, leaders are viewed as climate and culture engineers, meaning makers, and role models of appropriate behavior, thereby helping to

create and shape the socially constructed climate and culture context (e.g., Mowday & Sutton, 1993; Rentsch, 1990; Schein, 2010).

Other influential agents or groups can also shape the context and employees' thoughts, feelings, and actions (e.g., Mowday & Sutton, 1993). Although mentors rarely operate through compliance, they can be a source of legitimate authority based on their expertise, credibility, and trustworthiness, thereby inducing identification and internalization. Mentors also provide psychosocial support and opportunities for career development activities (e.g., Eby, Allen, Evans, Ng, & Dubois, 2008), and they are a critical source for imputing meaning about a multitude of facets of the organization context (Chao, 2012). Likewise, a single individual in the group can influence the context. For example, the mood of one person has been shown to have a ripple effect resulting in collective emotions of the group that in turn effect interactions and group performance (Barsade, 2002). Individuals more central and with greater information brokerage in social networks have the ability to influence others through exchanges (Fang et al., 2015).

Collective attitudes and responses. A second source of people-based context resides in the aggregate attitudes and behaviors of unit or organizational members (e.g., Mowday & Sutton, 1993). Since Sherif's (1936) and Asch's (1955) studies documenting that people's judgments about a stimulus were affected by the judgments made by others in their group, a multitude of collective group influences have been examined. While culture and climate are based on shared meanings, interpretations, and perceptions, in this section the focus is on unit members' feelings, attitudes, and behaviors. Theoretically, the group provides context through social, identity, cognitive, and emotional processes.

From a social and identity lens, the principle of homophily (Lazarsfeld & Merton, 1954) and similarity attraction (Byrne, 1971) posit that individuals are attracted to and make connections with similar others. Social identity theory (Tajfel & Turner, 1979) and self-categorization theory (J. C. Turner, Hogg, Oakes, Reicher, & Wetherell, 1987) indicate that people come to understand who they are through the internalization of the group into their own identity. As a result, individuals come to identify with the group, begin to shift thinking from "me" to "we," and create a shared social and group identity. In accordance with group effects theory (Blau, 1960), the desire to seek social approval in groups means that employees are guided by their own values and perceptions but also act in congruence with group values. Social comparison theory (Festinger, 1954) indicates that people evaluate their opinions and abilities in comparison to others around them. Identification with or the importance of the comparison group increases pressure toward uniformity in the group, prompting individuals to either persuade others to their view or to change their own views to be in accordance with the group. Similarly, individuals' desire for belongingness leads them to tune their attitudes and beliefs to be consistent with others in the group when they desire to get along or acquire knowledge (e.g., Hardin & Higgins, 1996; Lun, Sinclair, Whitchurch, & Glenn, 2007). Similar processes occur as individuals interpret and derive meaning from the context.

From a social cognitive perspective, according to social information processing theory, the complexity of the work environment requires individuals to rely on social cues from others as well as their own cognitions and perceptions to understand the context (Salancik & Pfeffer, 1978). Furthermore, individuals' cognitive representation of the organizational context is determined by individual patterns of understanding as well as by influential relationships with individuals and group members and organizational norms (Gioia & Poole, 1984). As such, through interactions with others in the unit or organization, individuals' own views of the context (e.g., climate perceptions) are influenced by others (e.g., Schulte, Ostroff, & Kinicki, 2006).

Finally, through emotional contagion processes, collective emotional states (both positive and negative) can arise and impact group functioning and behavior (George, 1990). Mood linking and contagion across individuals was found to be greater when individuals were engaged in a collective activity, with collective positive moods affording opportunities for better performance (e.g., Totterdell, 2000).

Positive emergent collective attitudes such as satisfaction and engagement can lead to opportunities for developing strong group norms and process that in turn relate to unit productivity, turnover, accidents, and customer satisfaction (Harter, Schmidt, & Hayes, 2002). At the same time, these processes can create constraining effects. Being in a group of similar or like-minded individuals, and wanting to maintain group identity and group harmony can lead to the classic problems of groupthink (Janis, 1982) and polarization (Myers & Lamm, 1976).

Skill, background, and demographic composition. Aggregate knowledge, skills, and abilities (KSAs) and demographic characteristics are another form of people-based context. At the unit or organizational level, aggregated KSAs create the human capital whereby individual-level KSAs are amplified through the interaction patterns and coordinated work to become a valuable resource for the unit or organization (Ployhart & Moliterno, 2011). For individuals, based on Festinger's (1954) social comparison theory, people tend to make upward comparisons to others in terms of similar ability, which can prompt efforts to improve; but when the abilities are perceived as different from the self, those comparisons weaken.

Demographic composition also provides context. For example, organizational demography assumes that heterogeneity in demographic characteristics can provide opportunities for growth and creativity, whereas homogeneity can constrain ideas and lead to stagnation in the unit (Jackson, Joshi, & Erhardt, 2003). The composition of the top management team is viewed as a reflection of the organization (Hambrick & Mason, 1984), with diversity in background shown to be related to firm performance (e.g., Cannella, Park, & Lee, 2008). Yet the belief that greater demographic diversity is needed to provide different perspectives and opportunities for improved performance and innovation did not hold at the unit level; instead, meta-analytic results found a positive relationship for job-relevant (e.g., different functions, education) diversity (Horwitz & Horwitz, 2007; Hülsheger, Anderson, & Salgado, 2009). Within units, fault lines can be created based on categorizations of race, sex, and language that impede unit and organizational functioning (e.g., Kulkarni, 2015; Lau & Murnighan, 1998).

The demographic makeup of the people in the context also influences individual reactions. For example, bystander effects (lack of helping when someone is in trouble) are reduced if the bystanders are predominately males (Fischer et al., 2011). Considerable research indicates that demographic similarity in groups and units is related to more positive individual attitudes and responses (e.g., Mannix & Neale, 2005). Other research highlights how the characteristics of others, beyond individuals' own demographic characteristics, impacts responses. For example, the sex and age composition of managers' subordinate and peer groups and supervisors was found to impact manager's pay (Ostroff & Atwater, 2003).

Social identity theory is a useful theoretical basis for understanding the role of demographic context. People tend to perceive the group they identify with (the ingroup) as more positive compared with others (the outgroup). Similarly, social dominance theory (Sidanius & Pratto, 1999) focuses on the desire to maintain social hierarchies in ingroup–outgroup relations. These theories help explain how unit or organizational members compare themselves and their group to other individuals and groups and have been used to explain a number of people-based contextual phenomena.

APPROACHES FOR EXAMINING CONTEXT

Given the complexity and multifaceted nature of context highlighted above, it is no surprise that studies incorporating context have taken an array of approaches. To provide a framework for "how" to study context, approaches were grouped into indirect, direct, variability, and emergence. Indirect approaches entail using context to frame the findings. Direct approaches include direct assessment of contextual variables. Variability approaches focus on the degree of dispersion or homogeneity in the environment, and emergence approaches examine how collectively based contextual constructs emerge from lower levels of analysis.

Indirect

Indirect approaches rely on contextualization. Dimensions of context are not directly assessed and incorporated into the study design. Rather, rich descriptions of the context within which the study was conducted are provided to better evaluate the applicability of the theory or findings (e.g., Härtel & O'Connor, 2014; Johns, 2006). The set of descriptors include temporal, internal and external environment, setting, location, country, and frame of reference (see Johns, 2006, and Rousseau & Fried, 2001, for more details). Not only do rich descriptions provide a means for better understanding the results, but cumulatively they also can be useful for examining contextual factors as moderators in meta-analyses (Bamberger, 2008) or comparative case studies (Rousseau & Fried, 2001).

Direct Assessment of Dimensions

In this approach, contextual dimensions and factors (e.g., structure, practices) are assessed across different collectives, units, or organizations and become a between-unit variable. This approach has been most often conceptualized and analyzed across levels, with the assumption that a contextual variable has a top-down effect on a lower level phenomenon (Kozlowski & Chao, 2012). However, given that the context variables are interdependent in the larger system (Katz & Kahn, 1978), examinations of context can be based on their nomological network and relationships—for example, relationships between organizational structure and HR practices (Toh et al., 2008) and between HR practices, human capital, collective motivation, and effectiveness (Jiang, Lepak, Hu, & Baer, 2012).

DIRECT ASSESSMENT OF COLLECTIVE PERCEPTIONS AND ATTRIBUTES: MEANS AND AMOUNTS

One subset of direct assessments of dimensions is based on the notion that many contextual constructs reside in the cognitions, perceptions, attitudes, and attributes of employees, and that when they coalesce, they create social-psychological and person-based attributes of the context (Kozlowski & Klein, 2000). Here, aggregated or mean scores are used to represent the context (e.g., climate, collective satisfaction). To the extent that the definition of the construct rests upon an assumption of some degree of similarity or sharedness, the aggregated variables can be taken to represent the contextual variable once sufficient agreement within units has been demonstrated (Chan, 1998). Additive models (Chan, 1998) are based on the notion that, on average, differences between units or organizations on the attribute of interest exist but do not need to be shared across employees. A common example is turnover rates. Finally, some background and attributes of group members have been used to represent the context—the amount of diversity among members of the unit or organization is an example.

Direct Assessment: Configurations

Configural approaches move beyond independent dimensions to examine contextual features through patterns or as a gestalt system. (See Ostroff & Schulte, 2014, for a theoretical review of configural approaches and Short, Payne, & Ketchen, 2008, for a review of research on configurations in organizations.) The premise behind the configural approach is that a set of factors, considered together as a bundle or configuration, exhibit more theoretically meaningful results than the study of independent factors (Cappelli & Sherer, 1991; Johns, 2006; Rousseau & Fried, 2001). Because the contextual elements or dimensions are interrelated and interact together as a system in achieving their effects, configural approaches allow for explaining more than the sum of the parts of the independent dimensions. Configural approaches have been used in a number of contextual areas such as bundles or configurations of HR practices (e.g., Toh et al., 2008); patterns of climate dimensions (e.g., Schulte, Ostroff, Shmulyian, & Kinicki, 2009); patterns of goals, climate, and resources (Ostroff & Schmitt, 1993); and alignment between ideal and actual organizational designs (G. T. Payne, 2006).

Direct Assessments: Idiosyncratic Perceptions

This approach is based on the assumption that individuals' *own* perceptions of the situational context, not the actual context, is the primary driving force for influencing individual responses (e.g., Magnusson & Endler, 1977; Mischel, 1973). For example, psychological climate perceptions have been related to individual attitudes, behaviors, and performance (Carr et al., 2003), perceptions of HR practices to attitudes and performance (e.g., Den Hartog, Boon, Verburg, & Croon, 2013), and individuals' perceptions of their own interdependence with other groups to trustworthiness and affect for their group members (M. Williams, 2001).

Direct Assessments: Relative Standing

In this approach, the individual's standing relative to other members in the unit, or the unit's or organization's standing relative to other units or organizations, is of interest. Because local comparisons with a smaller group supersede the effect of comparisons with a much larger pool (e.g., Zell & Alicke, 2010), the more immediate group (units) is often the context with which the focal individual (or unit) is compared—for example, an individual's performance ranking relative to peers in their unit, or an organization's performance compared with other organizations in the same industry. These contextual effects, often referred to as *frog-pond effects* (Kozlowski & Klein, 2000), focus on the relative ranking of the focal entity within the context, without considering how "high" or "low" the context is on the attribute. In other words, the degree to which the unit is high or low on performance (for example) is irrelevant; it is only the focal entity's standing within that unit or organization. Big-fish little-pond effects take into account both relative standing and the quality of the pond. An example would be an individual's level of trust in his or her leader relative to other members' trust in their leader, and that some groups have more trust in leaders overall than others. This effect is particularly relevant when changing contexts; for example, a little fish in a big pond has a different experience when becoming a big fish in a little pond (e.g., Marsh, 1987).

Variability

The amount of variability around the mean is a meaningful construct that reflects the amount and type of homogeneity in the context (e.g., Lindell

& Brandt, 2000; Schneider, Salvaggio, & Subirats, 2002). As Ostroff and Fulmer (2014) demonstrated, variability is a construct that can be studied at multiple levels. For example, individuals, units, and organizations simultaneously face pressures that drive conformity or similarity and pressures that drive divergence and variance. Individuals' responses can vary across different contexts and over time. The degree of similarity in attributes, perceptions, and attitudes among groups is a feature of the context that can constrain responses because low variability creates a strong situation. The degree of between-unit similarity and variability indicates the extent to which different units or organizations converge or diverge from one another in terms of contextual features such as structure, culture, human capital, collective attitudes, or performance. Thus, the amount and type of variance can represent a constraining effect or an opportunity effect of the context. Four approaches to examining variance were delineated: amount (more or less variance), optimal (nonlinearity, with the assumption that too little or too much variance is less desirable), patterned or configural variance (based on the notion that people or elements vary but do so in a way that the pattern is a substantive representation of the context), and clustered (based on a networking perspective such that in a system with variance, those similar to one another may be clustered or have stronger ties to one another).

Emergence

Social-psychological and people-based contextual variables exist at a higher level of analysis but are anchored in the cognitions, perceptions, emotions, and normative behaviors of individual employees. An emergent contextual property of the organization arises when experiences, interactions, or features in the organization drive similar reactions or when a coherent structure can be recognized among people or elements in the context (Kozlowski & Klein, 2000). One interest is in studying what leads to convergence in organizations, that is, the factors such as interaction patterns, leadership, and structures that lead to the emergence of a contextual property. In this case, the focus is on what creates convergence or variability, with vari-

ance as the dependent variable at a given point in time (see Fulmer & Ostroff, 2016, for a review). A second focus is on the emergent process or how convergence occurs over time, and it can be studied through ethnographic processes, longitudinal designs, and computer simulations, although few studies to date have emergent processes (Kozlowski & Chao, 2012).

MOVING FORWARD: IMPLICATIONS AND CONCLUSIONS

Up to this point, meta-dimensions of the context have been delineated for considering features of the context, associated with primary underlying theoretical rationales. Furthermore, a range of approaches for how to study and examine were reviewed. The dimensions and approaches can be crossed to provide a framework that illuminates what dimensions and what approaches might be considered in any given study of context. Table 2.1 provides an illustrative example of a research topic for each meta-dimension by approach box. As can be seen in the range of examples in Table 2.1, a vast array of topics and approaches are available that reflect the complexity of organizations as a system that operates across multiple levels of analysis. Researchers are encouraged to use this framework to expand the "what" dimensions of context they study and the "how" to study them, with an emphasis on comparisons of multiple dimensions and approaches simultaneously.

Examining Multiple Dimensions Simultaneously

The framework highlights the primary contextual dimensions that can be examined in research so that researchers can consider a greater range of contextual factors. A more comprehensive understanding of the role of context requires simultaneously examining the relative importance of different contextual features for a particular phenomenon of interest. For example, examining the relative importance of structural variables, HR practices, leaders, interaction patterns, and demographic composition in creating consensus (low variability) in climate perceptions is important for determining the levers

TABLE 2.1

Meta-Dimensions and Approaches to Context: Illustrative Examples

Approaches	Meta-dimensions of context				
	External	Tangible (physical, technology)	Contrived (structure, practices)	Social-psychological (culture, climate)	People-based (influential agent, collective attributes, collective attitudes and behavior)
Indirect	Industry and country used to frame the study and findings	Communication technology in virtual teams as the setting for communication quality	Outcome-based reward system as the context for organizational citizenship behavior	Culture of corruption in the organization as the setting for individual deviance	Percentage of women in the organization used to frame findings about workplace support
Dimensions	Environmental stability	Types of open office plans	Degree of standardization and formalization	Organizational cultural values	Leader visibility
Collective attributes	Aggregated cultural/societal values	Overall degree to which employees use a new technology	Collective perceptions of degree of mechanization	Shared perception of service climate	Racial composition in groups, clubs, or classes
Configurations	Pattern across industry capital intensity, turbulence, differentiation and regulation	Configuration across technology types used in organizations	Pattern of structural features compared to ideal types	Configuration of climate dimensions	Pattern of goal orientation across people in a unit
Idiosyncratic perceptions	Perceptions of the economic stability	Perceptions of physical space	Perceptions of strength of the human resource system	Psychological climate	Evaluation of leader behaviors
Relative standing	Resource-based view of relative standing within the industry	Relative use of computerized technology compared to other units in the organization	Relative use of pay incentives compared to organizations in the industry	Team innovative culture relative to other teams in the division	Quality of relationship with leader relative to other members in the unit
Variability	Spread of wealth across people in society	Amount of variance in office size in organizations	Optimal levels of formalization	Strength of the climate—low variability in perceptions	Optimal level of functional diversity
Emergence	Emergence of new industry grouping over time	Interaction patterns with new technology that create routines	Trend over time in hybrid forms of structure in a growing economy	Interactions patterns that facilitate formation of unit climate	Contagion process that creates collective mood in a dyad or group

for consensus that can effectively be put in place in organizations (Ostroff et al., 2012). Or, examining the relative importance of contextual factors beyond team climate, aggregated team personality, and team personality for understanding creativity and innovation (Somech & Drach-Zahavy, 2013).

Uncovering Complementarities and Substitutes

A deeper and more nuanced understanding of context can be gained through studies that examine the notions of complementarities versus substitutes. Largely introduced by Milgrom and Roberts (e.g., 1990a, 1990b) in the 1990s in the field of microeconomics, a complementarity is said to exist when the relationship between two or more elements enhance the value of one another. In organizational research, Ichniowski, Shaw, and Prennushi (1997) were among the first to study complementarities among HR practices, showing that they can enhance the effect of one another on productivity in manufacturing plants, and when considered together, explain variance beyond the independent practices. Ennen and Richter (2010) conducted a comprehensive review of studies examining complementarities in organizational contextual features and found mixed support for the notion. They concluded that technological and human capital dimensions combined with structural and policy dimensions yield some promise as complementary features of the context. Complementarities among HR practices were sometimes evident but sometimes not. Not only does this suggest the importance of future research aimed at addressing whether contextual dimensions together produce complementarities, the mixed and weaker findings also suggest the need to examine whether substitution effects exist among contextual dimensions. For example, Costa and Bijlsma-Frankema (2007) suggested that trust and control as governance mechanisms in organizations may operate as substitutes for one another, whereas Machin and Wood (2005) found that new types of HR systems were neither a substitute nor a complementarity for unions. Keller (2006) showed that collective subordinate ability and task attributes can act as substitutes for leadership in research and development teams. The framework can be used by

researchers to think through theoretically which of the range dimensions might create substitutability or complementarities, such as open office plans fostering communication as a substitute for leader visibility in creating a positive team climate.

Analyzing Multiple Approaches Simultaneously

The framework in Table 2.1 highlights the many ways to approach the study of context. Our understanding of the context and contextual effects will be heightened when multiple approaches are used simultaneously when studying a phenomenon of interest. Not only will this allow for determining which approach has more or less utility for examining a meta-dimension of context, but it can help unpack the way context operates.

For example, as noted above, simultaneously using a configural or system approach and a dimension approach to the study of HR practices revealed that complementarities among practices exist beyond the effect of the individual dimensions of practices in the relationship to productivity (Ichniowski et al., 1997). Configurations of climate explained variance beyond independent climate dimensions in individuals' attitudes (Schulte et al., 2006) and also highlighted the role of unit shared climate beyond individual perceptions of climate. Individuals who had better exchange relationships with their leader relative to group members (relative standing approach), the overall quality of exchanges relationships with the leader in the group (collective approach), and group-level variability in exchanges with the leader (variability approach) had differential relationships to perceptions of psychological contract fulfillment, sportsmanship behavior, and performance (Henderson, Wayne, Shore, Bommer, & Tetrick, 2008).

Focusing on Time and Changing Contexts

Temporal conditions have been noted by many (e.g., Bamberger, 2008; Johns, 2006; Rousseau & Fried, 2001) as an important aspect of the context because the time or year in which the phenomenon is examined carries with it information about what is happening in the organization, industry, or society. Two additional temporal elements that are particularly worth noting are turnover and temporal perceptions of a phenomenon. First, the movement of people in and out of contexts produces dynamic changes in the context through recomposition and cultural change (Hopkins & Hopkins, 2002), not just in organizations but families, sports teams, and other social collectives. Second, individuals engage in retrospective, current, and future-oriented thinking about events and behaviors that influences their sensemaking of the context, fit to the context, and subsequent responses (Shipp & Jansen, 2011) and has implications for change processes in organizations (Gioia, Corley, & Fabbri, 2002).

Finally, context can operate through both a top-down and bottom-up processes. In bottom-up processes, the social-psychological and collective context emerge from a process of coalescence based on interaction patterns among individuals that, over time, allow the higher level construct to manifest. The resultant higher level construct is an emergent property of the context that can then have a top-down effect (Fulmer & Ostroff, 2016; Kozlowski & Chao, 2012). Shocks to the system can destroy the social context, resulting in wide variability across individuals, and the process of emergence needs to begin anew (Dansereau, Yammarino, & Kohles, 1999). For example, a new leader or a public scandal can cause tension within the system leading to boundary shifts, rule changes, new interaction patterns, and new ways of interpreting the organization (Hazy, 2006; Lissack & Letiche, 2002).

Emergent norm theory (R. H. Turner, 1964) proposes that new collective behavior emerges from a precipitating event, and when collectively interpreted by participants, creates a normative crisis that sparks new normative guidelines for behavior. After a crisis, people are forced to abandon prior perceptions about how to behave, and new behavior patterns arise from a social rather than cognitive or rationale process. Emergent norm theory has been primarily based in sociology to explain collective behavior after crises, such as the evacuation behavior of occupants of the World Trade Center bombing in 1993 (Aguirre, Wenger, & Vigo, 1998) but has obvious implications for emergence of social context in organizational settings. In organizational

research, Allport's (1954) notion of event structures and cycles are typically used to explain emergence of social context constructs. After an event that breaks apart the emergent property, a series of ongoing interaction patterns and event cycles then needs to occur to recreate a new social contextual factor (Morgeson & Hofmann, 1999). Research on these effects is in its infancy, and an emphasis on temporal and emergent effects in contexts can elucidate how context is formed and how its effect dissipates or changes over time.

CONCLUSION

Consideration of the array of dimensions (the what of context) coupled with an array of approaches (the how to study context) reveals just how complex understanding context is. This is not surprising from a system perspective (Katz & Kahn, 1978) because the interplay of elements from multiple levels of analysis is what an organization represents. While considerable strides have been made in understanding contexts in organizations, there is still much work to be done. As others have before me, I urge continued work that contextualizes research by putting the study in context and that studies the context, relationships among contextual elements, their effects, and changes in context with a strong theoretical lens to explain the contextual effects. Particularly fruitful avenues may stem from the consideration of both multiple dimensions and multiple approaches simultaneously based on Table 2.1, or what Pettigrew (1987) referred to as *vertical analysis*, linking contextual elements across different levels of analysis and linking elements horizontally within a level of analysis to show the process of context as a constraint but also one that can be shaped.

References

Adair, W., Buchan, N., Chen, X., & Liu, D. (2016). A model of communication context and measure of context dependence. *Academy of Management Discoveries, 2*, 198–217. http://dx.doi.org/10.5465/amd.2014.0018

Aguirre, B. E., Wenger, D., & Vigo, G. (1998). A test of the emergent norm theory of collective behavior. *Sociological Forum, 13*, 301–320.

Allen, M. R., & Wright, P. M. (2007). Strategic management and HRM. In P. F. Boxall, J. Purcell, & P. M. Wright (Eds.), *The Oxford handbook of human resource management* (pp. 88–107). Oxford, England: Oxford University Press.

Allport, F. H. (1954). The structuring of events: Outline of a general theory with applications to psychology. *Psychological Review, 61,* 281–303. http://dx.doi.org/10.1037/h0062678

Asch, S. E. (1955). Opinions and social pressure. *Scientific American, 193,* 31–35. http://dx.doi.org/10.1038/scientificamerican1155-31

Ashforth, B. E. (2001). *Role transitions in organizational life: An identity-based perspective.* Mahwah, NJ: Lawrence Erlbaum.

Bacharach, S. B. (1989). Organizational theories: Some criteria for evaluation. *Academy of Management Review, 14,* 496–515.

Baltes, B. B., Dickson, M. W., Sherman, M. P., Bauer, C. C., & LaGanke, J. S. (2002). Computer-mediated communication and group decision making: A meta-analysis. *Organizational Behavior and Human Decision Processes, 87,* 156–179. http://dx.doi.org/10.1006/obhd.2001.2961

Bamberger, P. (2008). Beyond contextualization: Using context theories to narrow the micro–macro gap in management research. *Academy of Management Journal, 51,* 839–846. http://dx.doi.org/10.5465/AMJ.2008.34789630

Barsade, S. (2002). The ripple effect: Emotional contagion and its influence on group behavior. *Administrative Science Quarterly, 47,* 644–675. http://dx.doi.org/10.2307/3094912

Bate, P. (2014). *Context is everything.* Perspectives on Context Series. London, England: The Health Foundation.

Blau, P. M. (1960). Structural effects. *American Sociological Review, 25,* 178–193. http://dx.doi.org/10.2307/2092624

Blau, P. M. (1974). Presidential address: Parameters of social structure. *American Sociological Review, 39,* 615–635. http://dx.doi.org/10.2307/2094309

Bluedorn, A. C., Johnson, R. A., Cartwright, D. K., & Barringer, B. R. (1994). The interface and convergence of the strategic management and organizational environment domains. *Journal of Management, 20,* 201–262. http://dx.doi.org/10.1177/014920639402000201

Bond, M. (2014). *The power of others: Peer pressure, groupthink, and how the people around us shape everything we do.* London, England: Oneworld.

Bond, R., & Smith, P. B. (1996). Culture and conformity: A meta-analysis of studies using Asch's (1952b, 1956) line judgment task. *Psychological Bulletin, 119,* 111–137. http://dx.doi.org/10.1037/0033-2909.119.1.111

Bowen, D. E., Ledford, G. E., Jr., & Nathan, B. R. (1991). Hiring for the organization, not the job. *The Academy of Management Executive, 5,* 35–51. http://dx.doi.org/10.5465/AME.1991.4274747

Bowen, D. E., & Ostroff, C. (2004). Understanding HRM–firm performance linkages: The role of the "strength" of the HRM system. *Academy of Management Review, 29,* 203–221.

Boxall, P., & Macky, K. (2009). Research and theory on high-performance work systems: Progressing the high-involvement stream. *Human Resource Management Journal, 19,* 3–23. http://dx.doi.org/10.1111/j.1748-8583.2008.00082.x

Bresman, H., & Zellmer-Bruhn, M. (2013). The structural context of team learning: Effects of organizational and team structure on internal and external learning. *Organization Science, 24,* 1120–1139. http://dx.doi.org/10.1287/orsc.1120.0783

Brunia, S., & Hartjes-Gosselink, A. (2009). Personalization in non-territorial offices: A study of a human need. *Journal of Corporate Real Estate, 11,* 169–182. http://dx.doi.org/10.1108/14630010910985922

Burger, J. M. (2009). Replicating Milgram: Would people still obey today? *American Psychologist, 64,* 1–11. http://dx.doi.org/10.1037/a0010932

Burns, T., & Stalker, G. M. (1966). *The management of innovation* (2nd ed.). London, England: Tavistock.

Byrne, D. E. (1971). *The attraction paradigm* (Vol. 11). New York, NY: Academic Press.

Camerer, C. F., & Loewenstein, G. (2004). Behavioral economics: Past, present, future. In C. F. Camerer, G. Loewenstein, & M. Rabin (Eds.), *Advances in behavioral economics* (pp. 3–51). Princeton, NJ: Princeton University Press.

Cannella, A. A., Park, J. H., & Lee, H. U. (2008). Top management team functional background diversity and firm performance: Examining the roles of team member colocation and environmental uncertainty. *Academy of Management Journal, 51,* 768–784. http://dx.doi.org/10.5465/amr.2008.33665310

Cappelli, P., & Sherer, P. D. (1991). The missing role of context in OB—The need for a meso-level approach. *Research in Organizational Behavior, 13,* 55–110.

Carr, J. Z., Schmidt, A. M., Ford, J. K., & DeShon, R. P. (2003). Climate perceptions matter: A meta-analytic path analysis relating molar climate, cognitive and affective states, and individual level work outcomes. *Journal of Applied Psychology, 88,* 605–619. http://dx.doi.org/10.1037/0021-9010.88.4.605

Chan, D. (1998). Functional relations among constructs in the same content domain at different levels of analysis: A typology of composition models. *Journal of Applied Psychology, 83,* 234–246. http://dx.doi.org/10.1037/0021-9010.83.2.234

Chao, G. T. (2012). Organizational socialization: Background, basics and a blueprint for adjustment at work. In S. W. J. Kozlowski (Ed.), *The Oxford handbook of organizational psychology* (pp. 579–614). Oxford, England: Oxford University Press. http://dx.doi.org/10.1093/oxfordhb/9780199928309.013.0018

Cohen, M. D., & Bacdayan, P. (1994). Organizational routines are stored as procedural memory: Evidence from a laboratory study. *Organization Science, 5,* 554–568. http://dx.doi.org/10.1287/orsc.5.4.554

Costa, A. C., & Bijlsma-Frankema, K. (2007). Trust and control interrelations: New perspectives on the trust–control nexus. *Group & Organization Management, 32,* 392–406. http://dx.doi.org/10.1177/1059601106293871

Cummings, J. N., & Haas, M. R. (2012). So many teams, so little time: Time allocation matters in geographically dispersed teams. *Journal of Organizational Behavior, 33,* 316–341. http://dx.doi.org/10.1002/job.777

Cyert, R. M., & March, J. G. (1963). *A behavioral theory of the firm.* Englewood Cliffs, NJ: Prentice Hall.

Dansereau, F., Yammarino, F. J., & Kohles, J. C. (1999). Multiple levels of analysis from a longitudinal perspective: Some implications for theory building. *Academy of Management Review, 24,* 346–357.

Datta, D. K., Guthrie, J. P., & Wright, P. M. (2005). Human resource management and labor productivity: Does industry matter? *Academy of Management Journal, 48,* 135–145. http://dx.doi.org/10.5465/AMJ.2005.15993158

Den Hartog, D. N., Boon, C., Verburg, R. M., & Croon, M. A. (2013). HRM, communication, satisfaction, and perceived performance: A cross-level test. *Journal of Management, 39,* 1637–1665. http://dx.doi.org/10.1177/0149206312440118

Denison, D. (1996). What IS the difference between organizational culture and organizational climate? A native's point of view on a decade of paradigm wars. *Academy of Management Review, 21,* 619–654.

DeSanctis, G., & Poole, M. S. (1994). Capturing the complexity in advanced technology use: Adaptive structuration theory. *Organization Science, 5,* 121–147. http://dx.doi.org/10.1287/orsc.5.2.121

Dilley, R. (1999). *The problem of context* (Vol. 4). New York, NY: Berghahn Books.

Doty, D. H., Glick, W. H., & Huber, G. P. (1993). Fit, equifinality, and organizational effectiveness: A test of two configurational theories. *Academy of Management Journal, 36,* 1196–1250. http://dx.doi.org/10.2307/256810

Eby, L. T., Allen, T. D., Evans, S. C., Ng, T., & Dubois, D. (2008). Does mentoring matter? A multidisciplinary meta-analysis comparing mentored and non-mentored individuals. *Journal of Vocational Behavior, 72,* 254–267. http://dx.doi.org/10.1016/j.jvb.2007.04.005

Edmondson, A. C., Bohmer, R. M., & Pisano, G. P. (2001). Disrupted routines: Team learning and new technology implementation in hospitals. *Administrative Science Quarterly, 46,* 685–716. http://dx.doi.org/10.2307/3094828

Ehrhart, M. G., Schneider, B., & Macey, W. H. (2014). *Organizational climate and culture: An introduction to theory, research, and practice.* New York, NY: Routledge.

Eisenhardt, K. M. (1989). Agency theory: An assessment and review. *Academy of Management Review, 14,* 57–74.

Ekehammar, B. (1974). Interactionism in personality from a historical perspective. *Psychological Bulletin, 81,* 1026–1048. http://dx.doi.org/10.1037/h0037457

Emery, F. E., & Trist, E. L. (1969). Socio-technical systems. In F. E. Emery (Ed.), *Systems thinking.* Harmondsworth, England: Penguin.

Ennen, E., & Richter, A. (2010). The whole is more than the sum of its parts—Or is it? A review of the empirical literature on complementarities in organizations. *Journal of Management, 36,* 207–233. http://dx.doi.org/10.1177/0149206309350083

Fang, R., Landis, B., Zhang, Z., Anderson, M., Shaw, J., & Kilduff, M. (2015). Integrating personality and social networks: A meta-analysis of personality, network position, and work outcomes in organizations. *Organization Science, 26,* 1243–1260. http://dx.doi.org/10.1287/orsc.2015.0972

Feldman, M. S., & Pentland, B. T. (2003). Reconceptualizing organizational routines as a source of flexibility and change. *Administrative Science Quarterly, 48,* 94–118. http://dx.doi.org/10.2307/3556620

Felin, T., Foss, N. J., Heimeriks, K. H., & Madsen, T. L. (2012). Microfoundations of routines and capabilities: Individuals, processes, and structure. *Journal of Management Studies, 49,* 1351–1374. http://dx.doi.org/10.1111/j.1467-6486.2012.01052.x

Ferris, G. R., Arthur, M. M., Berkson, H. M., Kaplan, D. M., Harrell-Cook, G., & Frink, D. D. (1998). Toward a social context theory of the human resource management–organization effectiveness relationship. *Human Resource Management Review, 8,* 235–264. http://dx.doi.org/10.1016/S1053-4822(98)90004-3

Festinger, L. (1954). A theory of social comparison processes. *Human Relations, 7,* 117–140. http://dx.doi.org/10.1177/001872675400700202

Fischer, P., Krueger, J. I., Greitemeyer, T., Vogrincic, C., Kastenmüller, A., Frey, D., . . . Kainbacher, M. (2011). The bystander-effect: A meta-analytic review on bystander intervention in dangerous and non-dangerous emergencies. *Psychological Bulletin, 137*, 517–537. http://dx.doi.org/10.1037/a0023304

Fulmer, C. A., & Ostroff, C. (2016). Convergence and emergence in organizations: An integrative framework and review. *Journal of Organizational Behavior, 37*(S1), S122–S145. http://dx.doi.org/10.1002/job.1987

Fussell, S. R., Kiesler, S., Setlock, L. D., & Yew, V. (2008, March). How people anthropomorphize robots. In *Proceedings of the 3rd ACM/IEEE International Conference on Human–Robot Interaction* (pp. 145–152). New York, NY: Association for Computing Machinery.

George, J. M. (1990). Personality, affect, and behavior in groups. *Journal of Applied Psychology, 75*, 107–116. http://dx.doi.org/10.1037/0021-9010.75.2.107

Ghoshal, S., & Bartlett, C. A. (1994). Linking organizational context and managerial action: The dimensions of quality of management. *Strategic Management Journal, 15*(S2), 91–112. http://dx.doi.org/10.1002/smj.4250151007

Gibson, C. B., & Birkinshaw, J. (2004). The antecedents, consequences, and mediating role of organizational ambidexterity. *Academy of Management Journal, 47*, 209–226. http://dx.doi.org/10.2307/20159573

Gioia, D. A., Corley, K. G., & Fabbri, T. (2002). Revising the past (while thinking in the future perfect tense). *Journal of Organizational Change Management, 15*, 622–634. http://dx.doi.org/10.1108/09534810210449532

Gioia, D. A., & Poole, P. P. (1984). Scripts in organizational behavior. *Academy of Management Review, 9*, 449–459.

Goldstein, K. (1939). *The organism: A holistic approach to biology derived from pathological data in man.* Salt Lake City, UT: American Book Publishing. http://dx.doi.org/10.1037/10021-000

González-Romá, V., & Hernández, A. (2014). Climate uniformity: Its influence on team communication quality, task conflict, and team performance. *Journal of Applied Psychology, 99*, 1042–1058. http://dx.doi.org/10.1037/a0037868

Griffin, M. A. (2007). Editorial: Specifying organizational contexts: Systematic links between contexts and processes in organizational behavior. *Journal of Organizational Behavior, 28*, 859–863. http://dx.doi.org/10.1002/job.489

Griffin, M. A., Neal, A., & Parker, S. K. (2007). A new model of work role performance: Positive behavior in uncertain and interdependent contexts. *Academy of Management Journal, 50*, 327–347. http://dx.doi.org/10.5465/AMJ.2007.24634438

Guzzo, R. A., & Noonan, K. A. (1994). Human resource practices as communications and the psychological contract. *Human Resource Management, 33*, 447–462. http://dx.doi.org/10.1002/hrm.3930330311

Hambrick, D. C., & Mason, P. A. (1984). Upper echelons: The organization as a reflection of its top managers. *Academy of Management Review, 9*, 193–206.

Hannan, M. T., & Freeman, J. (1989). *Organizational ecology.* Cambridge, MA: Harvard University Press.

Hardin, C. D., & Higgins, E. T. (1996). Shared reality: How social verification makes the subjective objective. In R. M. Sorrentino & E. T. Higgins (Eds.), *Handbook of motivation and cognition: The interpersonal context* (Vol. 3, pp. 28–84). New York, NY: Guilford Press.

Härtel, C. E., & O'Connor, J. M. (2014). Contextualizing research: Putting context back into organizational behavior research. *Journal of Management & Organization, 20*, 417–422. http://dx.doi.org/10.1017/jmo.2014.61

Harter, J. K., Schmidt, F. L., & Hayes, T. L. (2002). Business-unit-level relationship between employee satisfaction, employee engagement, and business outcomes: A meta-analysis. *Journal of Applied Psychology, 87*, 268–279. http://dx.doi.org/10.1037/0021-9010.87.2.268

Hatch, M. J. (2011). Material and meaning in the dynamics of organizational culture and identity with implications for the leadership of organizational change. In N. M. Ashkanasy, C. P. M. Wilderom, & M. F. Peterson (Eds.), *Handbook of organizational culture & climate* (2nd ed., pp. 341–358). Thousand Oaks, CA: Sage. http://dx.doi.org/10.4135/9781483307961.n19

Hazy, J. K. (2006). Measuring leadership effectiveness in complex socio-technical systems. *Emergence, 8*, 58–64.

Heath, C., & Sitkin, S. B. (2001). Big-B versus Big-O: What is organizational about organizational behavior? *Journal of Organizational Behavior, 22*, 43–58. http://dx.doi.org/10.1002/job.77

Henderson, D. J., Wayne, S. J., Shore, L. M., Bommer, W. H., & Tetrick, L. E. (2008). Leader–member exchange, differentiation, and psychological contract fulfillment: A multilevel examination. *Journal of Applied Psychology, 93*, 1208–1219. http://dx.doi.org/10.1037/a0012678

Hom, P. W., Caranikas-Walker, F., Prussia, G. E., & Griffeth, R. W. (1992). A meta-analytical structural equations analysis of a model of employee turnover. *Journal of Applied Psychology, 77*, 890–909. http://dx.doi.org/10.1037/0021-9010.77.6.890

Hopkins, W. E., & Hopkins, S. A. (2002). Effects of cultural recomposition on group interaction processes. *Academy of Management Review, 27*, 541–553.

Horwitz, S. K., & Horwitz, I. B. (2007). The effects of team diversity on team outcomes: A meta-analytic review of team demography. *Journal of Management, 33*, 987–1015. http://dx.doi.org/10.1177/0149206307308587

Hülsheger, U. R., Anderson, N., & Salgado, J. F. (2009). Team-level predictors of innovation at work: A comprehensive meta-analysis spanning three decades of research. *Journal of Applied Psychology, 94*, 1128–1145. http://dx.doi.org/10.1037/a0015978

Ichniowski, C., Shaw, K., & Prennushi, G. (1997). The effects of human resource management practices on productivity: A study of steel finishing lines. *The American Economic Review, 87*, 291–313.

Ilgen, D. R., & Klein, H. J. (1988). Individual motivation and performance: Cognitive influences on effort and choice. In J. P. Campbell & R. J. Campbell (Eds.), *Productivity in organizations: New perspectives from industrial and organizational psychology* (pp. 143–176). San Francisco, CA: Jossey-Bass.

International Federation of Robotics. (2017). *Executive summary world robotics 2017 industrial robots.* Retrieved from https://ifr.org/downloads/press/Executive_Summary_WR_2017_Industrial_Robots.pdf

Jackson, S. E., Joshi, A., & Erhardt, N. L. (2003). Recent research on team and organizational diversity: SWOT analysis and implications. *Journal of Management, 29*, 801–830. http://dx.doi.org/10.1016/S0149-2063(03)00080-1

James, L., Choi, C., Ko, C. H. E., Mcneil, P., Minton, M., Wright, M. A., & Kim, K. I. (2008). Organizational and psychological climate: A review of theory and research. *European Journal of Work and Organizational Psychology, 17*, 5–32. http://dx.doi.org/10.1080/13594320701662550

Janis, I. L. (1982). *Groupthink: Psychological studies of policy decisions and fiascoes.* Boston, MA: Houghton Mifflin.

Jansen, J. J., Simsek, Z., & Cao, Q. (2012). Ambidexterity and performance in multiunit contexts: Cross-level moderating effects of structural and resource attributes. *Strategic Management Journal, 33*, 1286–1303. http://dx.doi.org/10.1002/smj.1977

Jansen, J. J., Van Den Bosch, F. A., & Volberda, H. W. (2005). Managing potential and realized absorptive capacity: How do organizational antecedents matter? *Academy of Management Journal, 48*, 999–1015. http://dx.doi.org/10.5465/AMJ.2005.19573106

Jiang, K., Lepak, D. P., Hu, J., & Baer, J. C. (2012). How does human resource management influence organizational outcomes? A meta-analytic investigation of mediating mechanisms. *Academy of Management Journal, 55*, 1264–1294. http://dx.doi.org/10.5465/amj.2011.0088

Johns, G. (1991). Substantive and methodological constraints on behavior and attitudes in organizational research. *Organizational Behavior and Human Decision Processes, 49*, 80–104. http://dx.doi.org/10.1016/0749-5978(91)90043-S

Johns, G. (2001). In praise of context. *Journal of Organizational Behavior, 22*, 31–42. http://dx.doi.org/10.1002/job.80

Johns, G. (2006). The essential impact of context on organizational behavior. *Academy of Management Review, 31*, 386–408. http://dx.doi.org/10.5465/AMR.2006.20208687

Jones, A. P., & James, L. R. (1979). Psychological climate: Dimensions and relationships of individual and aggregated work environment perceptions. *Organizational Behavior and Human Performance, 23*, 201–250. http://dx.doi.org/10.1016/0030-5073(79)90056-4

Joshi, A., & Roh, H. (2009). The role of context in work team diversity research: A meta-analytic review. *Academy of Management Journal, 52*, 599–627. http://dx.doi.org/10.5465/AMJ.2009.41331491

Kantor, J. R. (1926). *Principles of psychology* (Vol. 2). Bloomington, IN: Principia Press.

Kashima, Y., Laham, S. M., Dix, J., Levis, B., Wong, D., & Wheeler, M. (2015). Social transmission of cultural practices and implicit attitudes. *Organizational Behavior and Human Decision Processes, 129*, 113–125. http://dx.doi.org/10.1016/j.obhdp.2014.05.005

Katz, D., & Kahn, R. L. (1978). *The social psychology of organizations* (2nd ed.). New York, NY: Wiley.

Keller, R. T. (2006). Transformational leadership, initiating structure, and substitutes for leadership: A longitudinal study of research and development project team performance. *Journal of Applied Psychology, 91*, 202–210. http://dx.doi.org/10.1037/0021-9010.91.1.202

Kelman, H. C. (1958). Compliance, identification, and internalization: Three processes of attitude change. *The Journal of Conflict Resolution, 2*, 51–60. http://dx.doi.org/10.1177/002200275800200106

Kelman, H. C. (2006). Interests, relationships, identities: Three central issues for individuals and groups in negotiating their social environment. *Annual Review of Psychology, 57*, 1–26. http://dx.doi.org/10.1146/annurev.psych.57.102904.190156

Kim, J., & De Dear, R. (2013). Workspace satisfaction: The privacy–communication trade-off in open-plan offices. *Journal of Environmental Psychology, 36*, 18–26. http://dx.doi.org/10.1016/j.jenvp.2013.06.007

Kozlowski, S. W. J., & Chao, G. T. (2012). The dynamics of emergence: Cognition and cohesion in work teams. *Managerial and Decision Economics, 33*, 335–354. http://dx.doi.org/10.1002/mde.2552

Kozlowski, S. W. J., & Klein, K. J. (2000). A multilevel approach to theory and research in organizations: Contextual, temporal, and emergent processes. In K. J. Klein & S. W. J. Kozlowski (Eds.), *Multilevel theory, research and methods in organizations: Foundations, extensions, and new directions* (pp. 3–90). San Francisco, CA: Jossey-Bass.

Kraut, R., Patterson, M., Lundmark, V., Kiesler, S., Mukophadhyay, T., & Scherlis, W. (1998). Internet paradox. A social technology that reduces social involvement and psychological well-being? *American Psychologist, 53*, 1017–1031. http://dx.doi.org/10.1037/0003-066X.53.9.1017

Kulkarni, M. (2015). Language-based diversity and faultlines in organizations. *Journal of Organizational Behavior, 36*, 128–146. http://dx.doi.org/10.1002/job.1954

Lau, D. C., & Murnighan, J. K. (1998). Demographic diversity and faultlines: The compositional dynamics of organizational groups. *Academy of Management Review, 23*, 325–340.

Lazarsfeld, P. F., & Merton, R. K. (1954). Friendship as a social process: A substantive and methodological analysis. In M. Berger, T. Abel, & C. H. Page (Eds.), *Freedom and control in modern society* (pp. 18–66). New York, NY: Van Nostrand.

Levitt, B., & March, J. (1988). Organizational learning. *Annual Review of Sociology, 14*, 319–338. http://dx.doi.org/10.1146/annurev.so.14.080188.001535

Lewin, K. (1938). *The conceptual representation and the measurement of psychological forces*. Durham, NC: Duke University Press. http://dx.doi.org/10.1037/13613-000

Lewin, K. (1947). Frontiers in group dynamics: Concept, method and reality in social science; Social equilibria and social change. *Human Relations, 1*, 5–41. http://dx.doi.org/10.1177/001872674700100103

Lewin, K. A. (1951). *Field theory in social science: Selected theoretical papers*. New York, NY: Harper.

Lewin, K., Lippitt, R., & White, R. K. (1939). Patterns of aggressive behavior in experimentally created "social climates." *The Journal of Social Psychology, 10*, 269–299. http://dx.doi.org/10.1080/00224545.1939.9713366

Liden, R. C., Wayne, S. J., Liao, C., & Meuser, J. D. (2014). Servant leadership and serving culture: Influence on individual and unit performance. *Academy of Management Journal, 57*, 1434–1452. http://dx.doi.org/10.5465/amj.2013.0034

Likert, R. (1961). *New patterns of management*. New York, NY: McGraw-Hill.

Likert, R. (1967). *The human organization: Its management and value*. New York, NY: McGraw-Hill.

Lin, N. (2002). *Social capital: A theory of social structure and action* (Vol. 19). Cambridge, England: Cambridge University Press.

Lindell, M. K., & Brandt, C. J. (2000). Climate quality and climate consensus as mediators of the relationship between organizational antecedents and outcomes. *Journal of Applied Psychology, 85*, 331–348. http://dx.doi.org/10.1037/0021-9010.85.3.331

Lissack, M. R., & Letiche, H. (2002). Complexity, emergence, resilience, and coherence: Gaining perspective on organizations and their study. *Emergence, a Journal of Complexity Issues in Organizations and Management, 4*, 72–94.

Low, S. M., & Altman, I. (1992). Place attachment: A conceptual inquiry. In I. Altman & S. M. Low (Eds.), *Place attachment* (pp. 1–12). New York, NY: Plenum Press. http://dx.doi.org/10.1007/978-1-4684-8753-4_1

Lun, J., Sinclair, S., Whitchurch, E. R., & Glenn, C. (2007). (Why) do I think what you think? Epistemic social tuning and implicit prejudice. *Journal of Personality and Social Psychology, 93*, 957–972. http://dx.doi.org/10.1037/0022-3514.93.6.957

Machin, S., & Wood, S. (2005). Human resource management as a substitute for trade unions in British workplaces. *Industrial & Labor Relations Review, 58*, 201–218. http://dx.doi.org/10.1177/001979390505800202

MacKay, B., & McKiernan, P. (2010). Creativity and dysfunction in strategic processes: The case of scenario planning. *Futures, 42*, 271–281. http://dx.doi.org/10.1016/j.futures.2009.11.013

Magee, J. C., & Galinsky, A. D. (2008). Social hierarchy: The self-reinforcing nature of power and status. *The Academy of Management Annals, 2*, 351–398. http://dx.doi.org/10.5465/19416520802211628

Magnusson, D., & Endler, N. S. (1977). *Personality at the crossroads: Current issues in interactional psychology*. New York, NY: Wiley.

Maloney, M. M., Bresman, H., Zellmer-Bruhn, M. E., & Beaver, G. R. (2016). Contextualization and context theorizing in teams research: A look back and a path forward. *The Academy of Management Annals, 10*, 891–942. http://dx.doi.org/10.5465/19416520.2016.1161964

Mannix, E., & Neale, M. A. (2005). What differences make a difference? The promise and reality of diverse teams in organizations. *Psychological Science in the Public Interest, 6*, 31–55. http://dx.doi.org/10.1111/j.1529-1006.2005.00022.x

Marsh, H. W. (1987). The big-fish-little-pond effect on academic self-concept. *Journal of Educational Psychology, 79*, 280–295. http://dx.doi.org/10.1037/0022-0663.79.3.280

Martin, J. (1992). *The culture of organizations: Three perspectives*. New York, NY: Oxford University Press.

Michailova, S. (2011). Contextualizing in international business research: Why do we need more of it and how can we be better at it? *Scandinavian Journal of Management, 27*, 129–139. http://dx.doi.org/10.1016/j.scaman.2010.11.003

Milgram, S. (1963). Behavioral study of obedience. *Journal of Abnormal and Social Psychology, 67*, 371–378. http://dx.doi.org/10.1037/h0040525

Milgrom, P., & Roberts, J. (1990a). The economics of modern manufacturing: Technology, strategy, and organization. *The American Economic Review, 80*, 511–528.

Milgrom, P., & Roberts, J. (1990b). Rationalizability, learning, and equilibrium in games with strategic complementarities. *Econometrica, 58*, 1255–1277. http://dx.doi.org/10.2307/2938316

Mirvis, P. H., Sales, A. L., & Hackett, E. J. (1991). The implementation and adoption of new technology in organizations: The impact on work, people, and culture. *Human Resource Management, 30*, 113–139. http://dx.doi.org/10.1002/hrm.3930300107

Mischel, W. (1973). Toward a cognitive social learning reconceptualization of personality. *Psychological Review, 80*, 252–283. http://dx.doi.org/10.1037/h0035002

Morgeson, F. P., & Hofmann, D. A. (1999). The structure and function of collective constructs: Implications for multilevel research and theory development. *Academy of Management Review, 24*, 249–265.

Morris, M. W., Hong, Y. Y., Chiu, C. Y., & Liu, Z. (2015). Normology: Integrating insights about social norms to understand cultural dynamics. *Organizational Behavior and Human Decision Processes, 129*, 1–13. http://dx.doi.org/10.1016/j.obhdp.2015.03.001

Mowday, R. T., Porter, L. W., & Steers, R. M. (2013). *Employee–organization linkages: The psychology of commitment, absenteeism, and turnover.* Cambridge, MA: Academic Press.

Mowday, R. T., & Sutton, R. I. (1993). Organizational behavior: Linking individuals and groups to organizational contexts. *Annual Review of Psychology, 44*, 195–229. http://dx.doi.org/10.1146/annurev.ps.44.020193.001211

Murray, H. A. (1938). *Explorations in personality.* New York, NY: Oxford University Press.

Myers, D. G., & Lamm, H. (1976). The group polarization phenomenon. *Psychological Bulletin, 83*, 602–627. http://dx.doi.org/10.1037/0033-2909.83.4.602

Nishii, L. H., Lepak, D. P., & Schneider, B. (2008). Employee attributions of the "why" of HR practices: Their effects on employee attitudes and behaviors, and customer satisfaction. *Personnel Psychology, 61*, 503–545. http://dx.doi.org/10.1111/j.1744-6570.2008.00121.x

Oldham, G. R. (1988). Effects of changes in workspace partitions and spatial density on employee reactions: A quasi-experiment. *Journal of Applied Psychology, 73*, 253–258. http://dx.doi.org/10.1037/0021-9010.73.2.253

O'Reilly, C. A., III. (1991). Organizational behavior: Where we've been, where we're going. *Annual Review of Psychology, 42*, 427–458. http://dx.doi.org/10.1146/annurev.ps.42.020191.002235

Orlikowski, W. J. (2000). Using technology and constituting structures: A practice lens for studying technology in organizations. *Organization Science, 11*, 404–428. http://dx.doi.org/10.1287/orsc.11.4.404.14600

Ostroff, C., & Atwater, L. E. (2003). Does whom you work with matter? Effects of referent group gender and age composition on managers' compensation. *Journal of Applied Psychology, 88*, 725–740. http://dx.doi.org/10.1037/0021-9010.88.4.725

Ostroff, C., & Bowen, D. E. (2000). Moving HR to a higher level: Human resource practices and organizational effectiveness. In K. J. Klein & S. W. J. Kozlowski (Eds.), *Multi-level theories, research and methods in organizations* (pp. 211–266). San Francisco, CA: Jossey-Bass.

Ostroff, C., & Bowen, D. E. (2016). Reflections on the 2014 decade award: Is there strength in the construct of HR system strength? *Academy of Management Review, 41*, 196–214. http://dx.doi.org/10.5465/amr.2015.0323

Ostroff, C., & Fulmer, A. (2014). Variance as a construct: Understanding variability beyond the mean. In J. K. Ford, J. R. Hollenbeck, & A. M. Ryan (Eds.), *The nature of work: Advances in psychological theory, methods, and practice* (pp. 185–210). Washington, DC: American Psychological Association.

Ostroff, C., Kinicki, A. J., & Muhammad, R. S. (2012). Organizational culture and climate. In I. B. Weiner, N. W. Schmitt, & S. Highhouse (Eds.), *Handbook of psychology: Vol. 12. Industrial and organizational psychology* (pp. 643–676). Hoboken, NJ: Wiley.

Ostroff, C., & Schmitt, N. (1993). Configurations of organizational effectiveness and efficiency. *Academy of Management Journal, 36*, 1345–1361. http://dx.doi.org/10.5465/256814

Ostroff, C., & Schulte, M. (2014). A configural approach to the study of organizational culture and climate. In B. Schneider & K. M. Barbera (Eds.), *The Oxford handbook of organizational climate and culture* (pp. 532–552). Oxford, England: Oxford University Press.

Ouchi, W. G. (1980). Markets, bureaucracies, and clans. *Administrative Science Quarterly, 25*, 129–141. http://dx.doi.org/10.2307/2392231

Payne, G. T. (2006). Examining configurations and firm performance in a suboptimal equifinality context. *Organization Science, 17,* 756–770. http://dx.doi.org/10.1287/orsc.1060.0203

Payne, R. L. (2000). Climate and culture: How close can they get? In N. M. Ashkanasy, C. P. M. Wilderom, & M. F. Peterson (Eds.), *Handbook of organizational culture and climate* (pp. 163–176). Thousand Oaks, CA: Sage.

Pennings, J. M. (1975). The relevance of the structural-contingency model of organizational effectiveness. *Administrative Science Quarterly, 20,* 393–410. http://dx.doi.org/10.2307/2391999

Pettigrew, A. M. (1987). Context and action in the transformation of the firm. *Journal of Management Studies, 24,* 649–670. http://dx.doi.org/10.1111/j.1467-6486.1987.tb00467.x

Peysakhovich, A., & Rand, D. G. (2015). Habits of virtue: Creating norms of cooperation and defection in the laboratory. *Management Science, 62,* 631–647. http://dx.doi.org/10.1287/mnsc.2015.2168

Pfeffer, J., & Salancik, G. R. (1978). *The external control of organizations.* New York, NY: Harper & Row.

Pinto, J., Leana, C. R., & Pil, F. K. (2008). Corrupt organizations or organizations of corrupt individuals? Two types of organizational-level corruption. *Academy of Management Review, 33,* 685–709. http://dx.doi.org/10.5465/AMR.2008.32465726

Ployhart, R. E., & Moliterno, T. P. (2011). Emergence of the human capital resource: A multilevel model. *Academy of Management Review, 36,* 127–150. http://dx.doi.org/10.5465/amr.2009.0318

Proshansky, H. M. (1987). The field of environmental psychology: Securing its future. In D. Stokols & I. Altman (Eds.), *Handbook of environmental psychology* (Vol. 2, pp. 1467–1488). New York, NY: Wiley.

Pugh, S. D., Dietz, J., Brief, A. P., & Wiley, J. W. (2008). Looking inside and out: The impact of employee and community demographic composition on organizational diversity climate. *Journal of Applied Psychology, 93,* 1422–1428. http://dx.doi.org/10.1037/a0012696

Rentsch, J. R. (1990). Climate and culture: Interaction and qualitative differences in organizational meanings. *Journal of Applied Psychology, 75,* 668–681. http://dx.doi.org/10.1037/0021-9010.75.6.668

Richard, F. D., Bond, C. F., & Stokes-Zoota, J. J. (2003). One hundred years of social psychology quantitatively described. *Review of General Psychology, 7,* 331–363. http://dx.doi.org/10.1037/1089-2680.7.4.331

Roberts, K. H., Hulin, C. L., & Rousseau, D. M. (1978). *Developing an interdisciplinary science of organizations.* San Francisco, CA: Jossey-Bass.

Roethlisberger, F. J., & Dickson, W. J. (1939). *Management and the worker: An account of a research program conducted by the Western Electric Company, Hawthorne Works, Chicago.* London, England: Harvard University Press.

Rousseau, D. M., & Fried, Y. (2001). Location, location, location: Contextualizing organizational research [Editorial]. *Journal of Organizational Behavior, 22,* 1–13. http://dx.doi.org/10.1002/job.78

Rousseau, D. M., & Wade-Benzoni, K. A. (1994). Linking strategy and human resource practices: How employee and customer contracts are created. *Human Resource Management, 33,* 463–489. http://dx.doi.org/10.1002/hrm.3930330312

Salancik, G. R., & Pfeffer, J. (1978). A social information processing approach to job attitudes and task design. *Administrative Science Quarterly, 23,* 224–253. http://dx.doi.org/10.2307/2392563

Santos, F. M., & Eisenhardt, K. M. (2005). Organizational boundaries and theories of organization. *Organization Science, 16,* 491–508. http://dx.doi.org/10.1287/orsc.1050.0152

Schein, E. H. (2010). *Organizational culture and leadership* (4th ed.). San Francisco, CA: Jossey-Bass.

Schneider, B. (1983). Interactional psychology and organizational behavior. *Research in Organizational Behavior, 5,* 1–31.

Schneider, B. (1985). Organizational behavior. *Annual Review of Psychology, 36,* 573–611. http://dx.doi.org/10.1146/annurev.ps.36.020185.003041

Schneider, B. (1987). The people make the place. *Personnel Psychology, 40,* 437–453. http://dx.doi.org/10.1111/j.1744-6570.1987.tb00609.x

Schneider, B., Ehrhart, M. G., & Macey, W. H. (2011). Perspectives on organizational climate and culture. In S. Zedeck (Ed.), *APA handbook of industrial and organizational psychology* (pp. 373–414). Washington, DC: American Psychological Association.

Schneider, B., González-Romá, V., Ostroff, C., & West, M. A. (2017). A history of culture of climate. *Journal of Applied Psychology, 102,* 468–482.

Schneider, B., Salvaggio, A. N., & Subirats, M. (2002). Climate strength: A new direction for climate research. *Journal of Applied Psychology, 87,* 220–229. http://dx.doi.org/10.1037/0021-9010.87.2.220

Schulte, M., Ostroff, C., & Kinicki, A. J. (2006). Organizational climate systems and psychological climate perceptions: A cross-level study of climate-satisfaction relationships. *Journal of Occupational and Organizational Psychology, 79,* 645–671. http://dx.doi.org/10.1348/096317905X72119

Schulte, M., Ostroff, C., Shmulyian, S., & Kinicki, A. (2009). Organizational climate configurations:

Relationships to collective attitudes, customer satisfaction, and financial performance. *Journal of Applied Psychology, 94,* 618–634. http://dx.doi.org/10.1037/a0014365

Scott, W. R. (1995). *Institutions and organizations. Foundations for organizational science.* London, England: Sage.

Sherif, M. (1936). *The psychology of social norms.* New York, NY: Harper.

Shipp, A. J., & Jansen, K. J. (2011). Reinterpreting time in fit theory: Crafting and recrafting narratives of fit in medias res. *Academy of Management Review, 36,* 76–101. http://dx.doi.org/10.5465/amr.2009.0077

Short, J. C., Payne, G. T., & Ketchen, D. J., Jr. (2008). Research on organizational configurations: Past accomplishments and future challenges. *Journal of Management, 34,* 1053–1079. http://dx.doi.org/10.1177/0149206308324324

Sidanius, J., & Pratto, F. (1999). *Social dominance: An intergroup theory of social hierarchy and oppression.* Cambridge, England: Cambridge University Press. http://dx.doi.org/10.1017/CBO9781139175043

Sirola, N., & Pitesa, M. (2017). Economic downturns undermine workplace helping by promoting a zero-sum construal of success. *Academy of Management Journal, 60,* 1339–1359.

Somech, A., & Drach-Zahavy, A. (2013). Translating team creativity to innovation implementation the role of team composition and climate for innovation. *Journal of Management, 39,* 684–708. http://dx.doi.org/10.1177/0149206310394187

Stedman, R. C. (2002). Toward a social psychology of place predicting behavior from place-based cognitions, attitude, and identity. *Environment and Behavior, 34,* 561–581. http://dx.doi.org/10.1177/0013916502034005001

Sutton, R. I., & Rousseau, D. M. (1979). Structure, technology, and dependence on a parent organization: Organizational and environmental correlates of individual responses. *Journal of Applied Psychology, 64,* 675–687. http://dx.doi.org/10.1037/0021-9010.64.6.675

Tajfel, H., & Turner, J. C. (1979). The social identity theory of intergroup behavior. In S. Worchel & W. G. Austin (Eds.), *Psychology of intergroup relations* (2nd ed., pp. 7–24). Chicago, IL: Nelson-Hall.

Toh, S. M., Morgeson, F. P., & Campion, M. A. (2008). Human resource configurations: Investigating fit with the organizational context. *Journal of Applied Psychology, 93,* 864–882. http://dx.doi.org/10.1037/0021-9010.93.4.864

Totterdell, P. (2000). Catching moods and hitting runs: Mood linkage and subjective performance in professional sport teams. *Journal of Applied Psychology, 85,* 848–859. http://dx.doi.org/10.1037/0021-9010.85.6.848

Turkle, S. (2012). *Alone together: Why we expect more from technology and less from each other.* New York, NY: Basic Books.

Turner, J. C., Hogg, M., Oakes, P., Reicher, S., & Wetherell, M. (1987). *Rediscovering the social group: A self-categorization theory.* Oxford, England: Basil Blackwell.

Turner, R. H. (1964). New theoretical frameworks. *The Sociological Quarterly, 5,* 122–132. http://dx.doi.org/10.1111/j.1533-8525.1964.tb01611.x

Üsdiken, B., & Leblebici, H. (2001). Organization theory. In N. Anderson, D. S. Ones, H. K. Sinangil, & C. Viswesvaran (Eds.), *Handbook of industrial, work & organizational psychology* (Vol. 2, pp. 377–397). London, England: Sage.

Van den Broek, T., Dykstra, P. A., & Schenk, N. (2014). Regional economic performance and distance between parents and their employed children: A multilevel analysis. *Population Space and Place, 20,* 222–234. http://dx.doi.org/10.1002/psp.1757

Van de Ven, A. H., Ganco, M., & Hinings, C. R. (2013). Returning to the frontier of contingency theory of organizational and institutional designs. *The Academy of Management Annals, 7,* 393–440. http://dx.doi.org/10.5465/19416520.2013.774981

van Knippenberg, D., & Sitkin, S. B. (2013). A critical assessment of charismatic–transformational leadership research: Back to the drawing board? *The Academy of Management Annals, 7,* 1–60. http://dx.doi.org/10.1080/19416520.2013.759433

Vera, D., Nemanich, L., Vélez-Castrillón, S., & Werner, S. (2016). Knowledge-based and contextual factors associated with R&D teams' improvisation capability. *Journal of Management, 42,* 1874–1903.

Weick, K. E. (1995). *Sensemaking in organizations.* Thousand Oaks, CA: Sage.

Welter, F. (2011). Contextualizing entrepreneurship-conceptual challenges and ways forward. *Entrepreneurship Theory and Practice, 35,* 165–184. http://dx.doi.org/10.1111/j.1540-6520.2010.00427.x

Whetten, D. A. (2009). An examination of the interface between context and theory applied to the study of Chinese organizations. *Management and Organization Review, 5,* 29–55.

William Lee, T. W., Burch, T. C., & Mitchell, T. R. (2014). The story of why we stay: A review of job embeddedness. *Annual Review of Organizational Psychology and Organizational Behavior, 1,* 199–216. http://dx.doi.org/10.1146/annurev-orgpsych-031413-091244

Williams, M. (2001). In whom we trust: Group membership as an affective context for trust development. *Academy of Management Review, 26,* 377–396.

Williams, N. R. (2004). *How to get a 2:1 in media, communication and cultural studies.* London, England: Sage.

Wright, P. M., McMahan, G. C., & McWilliams, A. (1994). Human resources and sustained competitive advantage: A resource-based perspective. *International Journal of Human Resource Management, 5,* 301–326. http://dx.doi.org/10.1080/09585199400000020

Wright, P. M., & Nishii, L. H. (2008). Strategic HRM and organizational behaviour: Integrating multiple levels of analysis. In D. Guest (Ed.), *HRM and performance: Achievements and challenges* (pp. 97–110). Oxford, England: Blackwell.

Wrzesniewski, A., & Dutton, J. E. (2001). Crafting a job: Revisioning employees as active crafters of their work. *Academy of Management Review, 26,* 179–201.

Yuchtman, E., & Seashore, S. (1967). A system resource approach to organizational effectiveness. *American Sociological Review, 32,* 891–902. http://dx.doi.org/10.2307/2092843

Zalesny, M. D., & Farace, R. V. (1987). Traditional versus open offices: A comparison of sociotechnical, social relations, and symbolic meaning perspectives. *Academy of Management Journal, 30,* 240–259. http://dx.doi.org/10.5465/256272

Zell, E., & Alicke, M. D. (2010). The local dominance effect in self-evaluation: Evidence and explanations. *Personality and Social Psychology Review, 14,* 368–384. http://dx.doi.org/10.1177/1088868310366144

Zimbardo, P. G. (1972). Comment: Pathology of imprisonment. *Society, 9,* 4–8. http://dx.doi.org/10.1007/BF02701755

Zusman, M. E., Knox, D., & Gardner, T. (2009). *The social context view of sociology.* Chapel Hill, NC: Carolina Academic Press.

## CHAPTER 3

ASK NOT WHAT THE STUDY OF CONTEXT CAN DO FOR YOU: ASK WHAT YOU CAN DO FOR THE STUDY OF CONTEXT

Rustin D. Meyer, Katie England, Elnora D. Kelly, Andrew Helbling, MinShuou Li, and Donna Outten

The present handbook, in combination with decades of published empirical studies, demonstrates that multilevel research is alive and well in the social sciences. Although not always explicitly stated, a core component of multilevel research is context. Specifically, when scholars attempt to model the direct and/or indirect effects of social environments on relationships across levels (ranging from within-persons to larger social collectives, including groups, families, classrooms, organizations), they often must attempt to account for context (or some aspect thereof). In theory, then, a mature science dedicated to understanding the nature and structure of context would be a boon for multilevel scholars across disciplines as they continue to study the influence of social environments across levels of analysis.

Unfortunately, however, the study of context is not yet mature enough to offer definitive guidance about how context operates and how to best conceptualize it. Although many important advances have been made in this regard (some of which are outlined subsequently), substantive multilevel scholars are often left to their own devices to determine how to best conceptualize context for their unique needs. For example, a clinical psychologist who is interested in studying the moderating effects of supportive family environments on the relationship between early childhood trauma and adolescent suicidal ideation would ideally be able to look to the study of context to determine how supportive family environments are similar to and different from related social contexts. Such an end state would provide those who seek to understand the role of context with tools comparable to those who seek to understand the role of various individual differences. The latter group of scholars is able to turn to available conceptualizations of personality, abilities, and interests, whereas the former group of scholars is typically forced to rely on conceptualizations that lack a similar level of connective tissue.

This lack of definitive guidance essentially means that the study of context has not yet lived up to its full potential. In a perfect world, contextual scholars would be able to provide substantive researchers with all of the information they need to operationalize their key contextual variables of interest, predict relevant effects, and dynamically model these relationships. We argue instead that those of us who study context have much more to gain from substantive multilevel scholars than we are presently able to offer in return. Namely, our continued efforts to create and refine useful taxonomies of context would be improved greatly by diverse primary studies that, if structured and reported in ways that provide maximally useful data, would have the potential to create a positive feedback loop whereby the study of context informs substantive multilevel research, which in turn informs the study of context,

The last three authors contributed equally to the development and writing of this chapter.

http://dx.doi.org/10.1037/0000115-004
The Handbook of Multilevel Theory, Measurement, and Analysis, S. E. Humphrey and J. M. LeBreton (Editors-in-Chief)

which in turn informs substantive multilevel research.

The two key questions from this perspective thus become: (a) Where are we in our progress toward a future wherein the study of context can maximally benefit diverse substantive areas of multilevel research (i.e., "what the study of context can do for you") and (b) how do we get to a more mutually advantageous future from where we are now (i.e., "what you can do for the study of context")? These two questions form the basis for the present chapter, with relevant details taking three forms. First, we provide descriptions of three metatheoretical perspectives that have been put forward to help social scientists better understand (a) what context is and how it operates (Johns, 2006), (b) the nomenclature we might use to consistently discuss context (Rauthmann, Sherman, & Funder, 2015), and (c) the various ways in which context is shaped and studied (Ostroff, see Chapter 2, this volume). Second, we provide summaries (rooted in the aforementioned metatheories) of numerous constructs and taxonomies that have been published to help scholars better operationalize context. Finally, we provide specific guidance to substantive multilevel scholars who are interested in conducting their research in ways that maximally contribute to the aforementioned positive feedback loop.

EXTANT METATHEORIES OF CONTEXT

Before describing the three metatheories of context from which we draw throughout much of the remainder of this chapter, it is first important to describe what we mean (and do not mean) by the phrase *metatheory of context* (*metatheories* from this point forward). The metatheories discussed here can be thought of as conceptual road maps various contextual scholars have provided to help define what is meant by the term *context* and to establish some of the basic parameters for understanding how it can best be studied, how it operates, and so forth. These metatheories were not intended to be end states (or even tentative dimensional solutions) in and of themselves but were instead intended to serve as relatively high-level efforts to start a dialogue about the nature of context. Just as early differential psychologists may have discussed the broad ways in

which individuals are similar to and different from each other (e.g., by drawing distinctions between cognitive and dispositional traits) without necessarily offering dimensional solutions for the specific structures of any of these distinctions, the authors of the metatheories discussed here were primarily focused on establishing important conceptual foundations upon which later empirical work could be built.

Objective Versus Subjective Context

Although not technically a metatheory in and of itself, the first basic distinction that those interested in the nature of context typically draw is the importance of understanding that context can simultaneously refer to objective characteristics, subjective characteristics, or some hybrid thereof (Frederiksen, 1972). Perhaps the earliest distinction here was what Murray (1938) called *alpha-press* and *beta-press*, where the term *press* refers to characteristics of the environment that benefit or hinder a person (Murray considered everything else in the situation to be inert). Specifically, alpha-press refers to characteristics that objectively exist, whereas beta-press refers to individuals' interpretations of relevant characteristics. Although Murray's theory contains several additional elements pertaining to context (e.g., a discussion of the various environments that afford the expression of psychological needs), only the distinction between alpha- and beta-press is covered here because it is the only component of his model that can be considered a meta-aspect of context, given that it is the only component of his model that helps to inform the study of context.

Block and Block (1981) extended this distinction by arguing that environmental characteristics can be divided into three broad categories of perceptual concreteness. First, they argued that "physico-biological" aspects of the environment are "perceptually unfiltered and uninterpreted" (p. 86) characteristics that are absorbed naturally through the senses but rarely seen. Second, they argued that the "canonical situation" represents those aspects of context that are generally agreed upon by most individual who experience them. Last, they argued that the "functional situation," much like Murray's

(1938) beta-press, represents those aspects of context that are uniquely perceived by each individual. Block and Block's tripartite distinction is typically favored over Murray's "presses" because of the former's more contemporary and fine-grained nature, but the latter is also often referenced, though primarily for its historical relevance.

Johns (2006)

The first metatheory described here was presented by Johns (2006), who argued that context is frequently understudied and underappreciated in the organizational sciences (although the commensurate influence of context and its relative neglect is likely also common in many other social science domains). To improve this state of affairs, he outlined several key aspects of context and described how its nature could influence organizational research. First, Johns defined context as "situational opportunities and constraints that affect the occurrence and meaning of organizational behavior as well as functional relationships between variables" (p. 386). This definition is important because it specifies that context *does* something (i.e., it is more than the mundane and inert) and that it affects both people and variables. Second, he explicitly recognized that context typically exists at a level of analysis higher than the focal relationship(s). Although this statement may seem self-evident, it is important to note that it is not always necessarily true. Namely, scholars who are interested in a truly functional situation perspective (i.e., one wherein the force in consideration exists purely in the minds of participants) would not have any true Level 2 variables. For example, when studying a sample of people with paranoid schizophrenia, the delusions that influence their behavior are, by definition, intrapsychic phenomena as opposed to legitimate interpretations of some identifiable aspect of reality.

Most germane to the present chapter, Johns (2006) also (a) made a key distinction between "omnibus context" and "discrete context" and (b) delineated the possible effects of context on organizational behavior. Regarding the former, *omnibus context* is the broad social milieu that comprises a combination of elements that can be categorized into several broad categories. Johns derived the concept of omnibus context from journalism and argued that it is composed of the "5Ws and an H" of the social environment (i.e., who, what, when, where, why, and how), which combine to serve as an overarching force that operates through specific "levers" of more narrow context (i.e., characteristics of context that directly and specifically influence human cognition, emotion, motivation, behavior, etc.). Johns referred to these levers as discrete context, which fall into the domains of task-based considerations (e.g., autonomy), social considerations (e.g., social structure), and physical considerations (e.g., temperature). Although the examples Johns provided specifically reference organizational behavior, all three of these considerations are likely relevant to context in any domain of life (even domains that lack truly task-based considerations, such as leisure and family environments, still likely have desired end states such as experiencing pleasure and/or contentedness).

Regarding the latter contribution, Johns (2006) outlined seven possible effects that context might exert on relationships of interest. First, context restricts range such that the observed variation in either independent or dependent variables may become truncated in certain contexts, thereby limiting the generalizability of relevant effects (e.g., performance distributions are tighter in jobs wherein behaviors and procedures are highly prescribed by tasks, supervisors, or regulations compared with the performance distributions in jobs with high levels of autonomy). Second, context affects base rates such that certain effects can appear more or less common under some conditions than they appear under other conditions (e.g., living in a neighborhood that lacks access to fresh fruits and vegetables may make various metabolic diseases appear more common in certain demographic subgroups than in others). Third, context can change causal directions such that effects are best viewed as causes and/or causes are best viewed as effects in particular environments (e.g., in authoritarian cultures, psychologists might conceptualize acting out in school as a cause of corporeal punishment at home, whereas in egalitarian cultures, acting out might be viewed as an effect of corporeal punishment at home). Fourth, context reverses signs such that certain positive relationships become negative as a function of context, whereas certain negative relationships become positive (e.g., trait agreeableness may have a positive effect on performance in customer service positions but a negative effect in sales roles). Fifth, context may engender curvilinear effects such that various relationships might be positive at certain levels of a given contextual dimension but nonsignificant or even negative at other levels of context (e.g., there may be a positive relationship between family social support in the management of complex chronic diseases such as diabetes, but no relationship among simpler-to-manage diseases such as hypothyroidism). Sixth, context tips precarious relationships such that small changes on a given dimension can sometimes make an otherwise trivial relationship become practically meaningful (e.g., the nature of military environments may make certain social dynamics that are inert in other team-based environments important determinants of survival in combat). Seventh, context threatens validity such that certain contextual variables can mask effects by creating "experimental confounds or unrecognized interaction effects" (p. 400; e.g., a classic task of economic decision making in an experiment may fail to replicate during a recession).

Rauthmann et al. (2015)

In 2015, Rauthmann and his colleagues published a metatheoretical effort to identify and consistently label relevant principles and terms in the study of context (what the authors refer to exclusively as "situations"). Specifically, these authors reviewed several traditions across a variety of disciplines to posit that three core principles have historically underlain the study of context. First, the *processing principle* focuses on the idea that context is important only to the extent that someone is present to experience it (in either a consciously or not-consciously detectable manner), regardless of whether that experience is based on objective or subjective aspects of context. Indeed, the entire universe (writ large) is technically context, but the vast majority of it is irrelevant to human perception and behavior. Second, the *reality principle* reflects the idea that behaviorally relevant contextual cues

can come in a variety of forms (e.g., objective, subjective), so long as they are perceived as real by the affected individual(s). Third, the *circularity principle* recognizes that researchers often make inferences about context exclusively on the basis of individual-level variables (e.g., perceptions, behaviors), thereby potentially putting themselves at risk of relying on tautological arguments when assessing context and its effects.

More germane to the present chapter, Rauthmann et al. (2015) also pointed out that contextual scholars typically focus their efforts on one of three concepts. First, *cues* are the component parts of situations, which in and of themselves do not convey any particular psychological meaning but which are instead given meaning by the perceiver(s). For example, knowing that other people are present in a given situation or knowing that the situation takes place outdoors is simply descriptive information that could be interpreted in a variety of ways, depending on both other cues present as well as the individual differences profile of the person or people in question. The meaning given to a particular situation represents what these authors called *characteristics*, which are the psychologically meaningful dimensions that can be used to define and quantify situations. Just like the Big Five is a prominent dimensional solution for conceptualizing human personality, various efforts (some of which are outlined subsequently) have been put forward to create parsimonious solutions that can be used to conceptualize context across a variety of broad life domains. Third, the aforementioned broad life domains represent what Rauthmann et al. called *classes*, which are nominal labels for categories of similar situations (e.g., work situations, social situations) that likely differ from each other on important characteristics (as defined previously). That being said, determining precisely how and to what degree various classes are similar to and different from other classes is contingent upon having a viable set of underlying characteristics upon which to compare these classes (though holistic similarity judgments can also be used to glean the characteristics that implicitly guided participants' perceptions of various classes).

Rauthmann et al. (2015) also denoted five approaches through which situational stimuli can be detected and studied. These approaches range from those that focus on relatively objective stimuli to those that focus on relatively subjective stimuli, but they also differ according to the nature of the specific methods used. First, those who use "objective assumption" approaches make a (typically post hoc) claim that a given environmental characteristic was likely present in a given situation on the basis of the behavior of the people involved (e.g., the concertgoers were smiling as they left, so the show must have been enjoyable). Second, those who use "objective physical" approaches focus on the extent to which relevant physical characteristics define a particular situation (e.g., a blue-collar work environment likely involves similarly dressed employees using tools to perform utilitarian tasks, whereas a religious worship environment likely involves similarly dressed individuals engaging in scripted rituals). Third, those who use "objective consensus" approaches conclude that a given situation is best defined in a particular way because "ordinarily socially competent judges" (p. 365) show a statistically acceptable level of perceptual agreement about either (a) the situation's standing on relevant underlying characteristics or (b) its similarity to or difference from one or more comparison situations (e.g., participants might generally agree that weddings are more similar to graduation ceremonies than they are to doctor appointments). Fourth, those who use "subjective phenomenological" approaches define situations on the basis of how they are described by those who experience them, presumably using open-ended responses or ratings on a standardized instrument (e.g., the average score of a yoga session may be a 6 out of 7 on a scale developed to assess the perceived tranquility of a situation). Last, those who use "subjective idiosyncrasy" approaches define situations uniquely for each individual participant in a study, such that the perceptions of every person who experiences a given situation are viewed as equally valid, even if there is no agreement across observers (e.g., Pat thought the movie was funny, whereas Terry found it offensive).

Ostroff (Chapter 2, This Volume)

Finally, Ostroff sheds light on the study of organizational context in several important ways (though,

again, many of these distinctions can be applied to a variety of domains of study). Although not an integral part of her model, one of Ostroff's first points is that context not only operates in a top-down fashion by influencing lower-level relationships (the most common approach when considering the effects of context) but also emerges in a bottom-up fashion over time (a less common, but equally important approach). This is an especially important insight because studying context from the bottom up (i.e., by understanding the people involved, their perspectives, their roles, and their relationships) provides a solid foundation for subsequent contextual analysis by enabling deep anthropological insights that are not necessarily evident when context is viewed as a purely stable entity that exerts a unidirectional force from above.

More germane to the specific components of her model, Ostroff next distinguishes between "internal" and "external" context, with the former referring to characteristics within a given organization (e.g., policies, supervisors) that shape employees' experiences and the latter referring to characteristics outside of the organization (e.g., national culture, industry norms) that affect employees' experiences. Although this distinction pertains to what is inside versus outside organizations, it could also apply to essentially any entity of interest (e.g., communities, cultures, family units).

Ostroff next outlines five metadimensions of context that represent broad categories of considerations that are likely to affect the nature of a given context. It should be noted here, however, that these metadimensions differ from the dimensional (i.e., characteristic-based) solutions outlined subsequently because the latter represent parsimonious sets of factors that can be used to define and (ideally) quantify contextual characteristics, whereas the former represent heuristic categories that are likely *sources* of these characteristics. Specifically, she posits that context can be influenced by (a) external considerations such as industry or national culture, (b) tangible considerations such as artifacts or technology, (c) contrived considerations such as power structures or policies, (d) social-psychological considerations such as organizational culture or climate, and (e) people-based considerations such as influential agents or collective attributes of employees. Whereas these categories of contextual influencers can help researchers think through how context is affected, they do not represent measurable characteristics of context in and of themselves. In individual differences parlance, Ostroff's meta-dimensions are akin to saying that one's personality can be influenced by genetics, early life experiences, parenting style, and so forth, whereas the subsequently described dimensional solutions are akin to the Big Five as a model for understanding and measuring the nature of a given individual's personality.

Similar to Johns (2006) and Rauthmann et al. (2015), Ostroff also stresses the importance of distinguishing between empirical treatments wherein context is directly detected (i.e., formally operationalized/measured) versus those wherein it is conceived of indirectly (e.g., assumed to exist, used to frame findings in the absence of measurement). It is important to note, however, that this distinction applies to how specific *primary studies* assess context, as opposed to how various *dimensional solutions* treat context. For example, the authors of a given study might observe different base rates for a given phenomenon across broad contexts (e.g., aggressive behaviors at school vs. at home) and infer that this difference results at least in part from differences in negative versus positive role modeling (for example). Given that the authors of the dimensional solutions outlined subsequently presumably always advocate that context be assessed directly as opposed to inferred indirectly, this distinction does not factor into the subsequent summaries of empirical contextual solutions.

Ostroff also recognizes that context is not necessarily a constant and, instead, has the potential to be treated as something that changes over time. Thus, the subsequent summaries indicate the extent to which a given dimensional solution accounts for this possibility. Finally, Ostroff also points out the importance of studying the relative impact of various dimensions of context so as to more fully appreciate its influence on a necessarily complex phenomenon. Thus, the subsequent summaries also indicate the extent to which a given dimensional solution permits relevant characteristics to be empirically separated in analyses.

Metatheories Summary

The preceding metatheories (as well as the specific conceptualizations of context discussed subsequently) suggest that context is a reasonably "hot topic" in the social sciences (e.g., Johns, 2006, has been cited more than 2,100 times as of May 2018), but it is also an area of research that has not yet fully "found a home" in any specific discipline. For example, "contextual psychology" does not exist as a subdiscipline, no journals are especially well known for publishing research on the nature and effects of context, extant metatheories and dimensional structures come from scholars across a diverse array of subdisciplines. This is not to say that social scientists would generally deny the importance of context but instead suggests that there is no ideal place to start when attempting to give context serious empirical attention. For example, when asked, "What is context?" "How does context operate?" "What are the best ways to go about defining and measuring context?" we fear that many in our ranks would not be able to offer much beyond platitudes (e.g., "It depends on the nature of the question," "There are so many ways to think about this issue that it is impossible to provide specific guidance"). Unfortunately, this state of affairs is justifiable in the sense that those who are interested in the effects of context must go out of their way to find relevant and useful information. Further, once this information is located, the presence of multiple perspectives and competing frameworks makes deciding on a specific course of action difficult.

The remaining sections are intended to help rectify this state of affairs. Specifically, the next section provides summaries of several empirical solutions that have been published in an attempt to identify and define a finite set of dimensions that can be used to parsimoniously represent various aspects of context. In addition to reporting on the distinctions discussed in each of the previously described metatheories, we also report whether a given empirical conceptualization utilizes any particular theoretical rationale for its choice of stimuli and/or dimensions and report whether the solution was intended to represent a holistic framework of context (i.e., incorporate all aspects of context at a broad level of abstraction) or to simply elucidate the facet structure of some specific aspect of context. After providing these details for several conceptualizations, in the last section we outline a series of steps that substantive researchers can take to help increase the probability that their efforts are structured in a way that contributes to the ongoing study of context.

EXTANT CONCEPTUALIZATIONS OF CONTEXT

In terms of the content of the subsequent summaries, we erred on the side of conveying those qualities of each solution that best highlight the unique purpose or character of the model as opposed to attempting to provide an exhaustive description. Further, we also erred on the side of including the most contemporary conceptualizations of context because although many models exist that are decades old, none have been widely adopted. We posit, instead, that the taxonomies likely to be most useful for substantive multilevel scholars are those that incorporate contemporary theorizing, employ modern analytic strategies, and utilize large and diverse samples of both stimuli and respondents. Said differently, we make no attempt to cover every possible conceptualization of context, nor every key point within each conceptualization. Instead, our primary goal is to provide an overview of several extant taxonomies so that readers can select among those that might be appropriate for a specific research question. Entries are arranged alphabetically by framework name or relevant keywords.

THE CAPTION MODEL

Background and Definitions

The CAPTION model (Parrigon, Woo, Tay, & Wang, 2016) represents one of several recent attempts to empirically isolate and define a parsimonious set of the basic active ingredients of context. This approach is based on the lexical hypothesis (Galton, 1884), which posits that those concepts that a given culture identifies as psychologically important will be represented in that culture's language. As such, the CAPTION model is based on the notion that the basic structure of situations should be able to

be gleaned from a systematic analysis of any comprehensive population of situational stimuli. Although the CAPTION model is not the first to draw from the lexical approach when creating a taxonomy of situations, it is the most comprehensive from the standpoint of the raw number of situational stimuli used (discussed subsequently).

According to the authors, the lexical approach is an effective way to create a database of situational stimuli because it meets three important criteria: it must "a) capture the full domain of the general, evaluative *psychological* situation characteristics, b) be able to integrate the findings from diverse lines of research using different theoretical perspectives, and c) be generalizable and replicable" (Parrigon, Woo, Tay, & Wang, 2016, pp. 7–8). The authors' search for an initial set of relevant lexical stimuli yielded between 535 and 851 adjectives (depending on the approach used), which were subsequently used across four studies using diverse methods (i.e., qualitative integration, factor analysis, hierarchical cluster analysis, and neural-network-based models).

As the acronym suggests, the final CAPTION framework consists of seven dimensions: Complexity, Adversity, Positive Valence, Typicality, Importance, Humor, and Negative Valence. *Complexity* refers to the extent to which the situation demands complex thinking or problem solving (the cognitive component of this dimension) or nuanced emotional or ethical experiences (the general component of this dimension). *Adversity* represents the overall difficulty of a situation, which can refer to both the amount of energy required in the situation or the amount of stress or depletion that results from a situation (e.g., studying for final exams would score high on this dimension, whereas relaxing on the beach would score low on this dimension). *Positive Valence* refers to the overall valence of a situation and those aspects of the situation that are focused on interpersonal relationship development (e.g., chatting with a friend over lunch would score high on this dimension, whereas having your taxes professionally calculated would score low). *Typicality* refers to the extent to which the situation meets one's expectations in a straightforward manner (e.g., grocery shopping in a familiar location would score high on this dimension, whereas attending a surprise birthday party thrown in your honor would score low). *Importance* represents the extent to which a situation is conducive to the achievement of one's goals (e.g., receiving treatment for a medical condition would score high on this dimension, whereas tossing and turning with insomnia would score low). *Humor* represents the extent to which the situation is fun and lighthearted or, put slightly differently, even sophomoric or silly (e.g., attending a costume party would score high on this dimension, whereas attending a funeral would score low). And *Negative Valence* represents various unpleasant aspects of situations (e.g., having a root canal would score high on this dimension, whereas meditating would score low).

Categorization Within Extant Metatheories

Owing to its broad purpose and multidimensional structure, CAPTION is best characterized as a holistic framework as opposed to a multifaceted construct. This is the case because the dimensions are not necessarily intended to relate to each other, except insofar as they represent core aspects of situations in general. In terms of how they can be detected in scientific and applied settings, the CAPTION dimensions are best considered an instantiation of Murray's (1938) beta-press, Block and Block's (1981) canonical situation, and Rauthmann et al.'s (2015) subjective phenomenological classification given that the methods used to detect them (e.g., factor analysis) are based on shared perceptions as opposed to objective characteristics of situations.

From Johns's (2006) perspective, the CAPTION framework is best treated as a form of discrete context because its dimensions function as individual situational levers that operate through both task-based and social mechanisms (e.g., a situation might score high on the Importance dimension because of structural characteristics that convey a sense of seriousness as well as the presence of authority figures).

Using Rauthmann et al.'s (2015) terminology, each of the CAPTION dimensions is best conceptualized as a characteristic of situations because the framework as a whole represents an effort to "capture the *psychologically important meanings*

of perceived cues, thus summarizing a situation's psychological 'power'" (p. 364, emphasis in original). The CAPTION framework is also best viewed as a "cognitive attributional approach" to categorization because it emphasizes "mental constructs and declarative representations of situations" (p. 366) owing to the fact that each of the seven dimensions is ultimately based on individuals' perceptions and is best detected via subjective phenomenological means because it is dependent upon how people similarly perceive and experience it.

From the perspective of Ostroff (see Chapter 2, this volume), the CAPTION framework could represent either internal or external aspects of context, depending on how it is used within a given study. Further, it is likely that each of the CAPTION dimensions would be directly detected (as opposed to indirectly assumed to exist) and would be treated as stable, but these determinations are ultimately contingent upon the specific study in question. Given the separable nature of the CAPTION characteristics, however, it is possible to understand the relative standing and impact of each dimension individually, assuming appropriate analytic techniques are used to do so.

Key Additional Points and Issues

It is also important to point out that a key purpose of the CAPTION model was to develop and validate a measure that could be used to assess the CAPTION framework itself. Specifically, the authors developed the CAPTION scale (or CAPTIONs), which is a 70-item, adjective-based instrument, as well as a CAPTIONs short form, which consists of 28 items. Both of these instruments not only confirm the original seven-dimensional structure but also predict meaningful behavioral and affective outcomes and show significant incremental validity above and beyond extant situational measures.

A CHINESE IDIOMS-BASED APPROACH

Background and Definitions

One of the most difficult issues associated with developing any taxonomy of situations is deriving an initial stimulus set. This process is challenging because context is inherently rich, yet relevant descriptors (e.g., single parts of speech, brief statements) are inherently somewhat impoverished. Yang, Read, and Miller (2006) developed an ingenious and parsimonious solution to this conundrum by utilizing Chinese idioms as their stimuli, which also makes theirs an instantiation of the lexical approach to stimuli creation (albeit one that is substantially different from others that have used single-term lexical approaches). According to the authors, an idioms-based approach is advantageous for several reasons. First, there is a strong emphasis on context in the Chinese language and in East Asian culture more generally. Second, many Chinese idioms come in a standardized four-character form and are widely used and understood among Chinese laypeople. Third, these idioms capture a wide range of psychologically meaningful situations that individuals are likely to experience (examples provided by the authors include "too late for regrets" and "catching up from behind"). Fourth, Chinese idioms are both dynamic and timeless, meaning that they capture general activities that were developed in ancient times but are abstract enough to apply to modern life. Finally, Chinese idioms are easily translated into other languages without losing their meaning (as evidenced by the consistency in identified clusters across cultural groups).

Two native speakers used Chinese idiom dictionaries to select stimuli "that they thought described situations" (Yang et al., 2006, p. 757), broadly defined. Two lists of 140 idioms were randomly selected from the 928 idioms the two judges identified in common, which were then translated, back translated, and refined by bilingual individuals who speak Chinese and English. After screening the resultant 140 stimuli for usability, lists of 115 and 125 stimuli remained. Four separate online samples of either native Chinese or native English speakers sorted stimuli as a function of similarity. Resultant data based on each list were analyzed separately via hierarchical cluster analyses, with the first sample resulting in 17 clusters of stimuli, the second resulting in 18 clusters, the third resulting in 27 clusters, and the fourth resulting in 27 clusters (clusters contained anywhere between one and 94 idioms). Ultimately, however, the authors chose

a 17-cluster solution for reasons of both parsimony and conceptual clarity, then identified themes that emerged among these clusters.

The first theme that emerged across all four of the aforementioned online samples focused on the extent to which one's goals succeed or fail. The second theme focused on the extent to which one's goals are or are not supported by others. The third theme focused on the social appropriateness of one's goal-related pursuits. Indeed, Yang et al. (2006) ultimately posited that "for the diverse everyday situations captured by the abstract idioms, goal processes are a central organizing principle in differentiating them" (p. 773). Unfortunately, however, it is difficult to derive much in the way of additional specificity from their ultimate solution(s), given the large number of clusters and diversity across samples as well as the somewhat disconnected nature of the remaining cluster solutions.

As such, the ultimate usability of this solution for scientific purposes beyond an intuitive assessment of the aforementioned three relatively robust (yet ultimately interrelated) themes is limited because no standardized instrument is offered to help assess the extent to which a given situation scores high versus low on any resultant dimension. Further, it is also an open question whether Chinese idioms are appropriate stimuli. For example, Chinese idioms are rich in context, but little is known about the extent to which they represent the full domain of situations people might encounter—indeed, the results of the Yang et al. (2006) taxonomy suggest a potential overreliance on goal-relevant situations, perhaps at the potential exclusion of more mundane situations.

Categorization Within Extant Metatheories

Owing to its holistic purpose and multidimensional structure, Yang et al.'s (2006) Chinese idiom model is best characterized as an overall framework as opposed to a delineation of a single, multifaceted construct. That being said, it is also important to highlight that the authors specifically stated that, despite its breadth, this taxonomy should not be viewed as "an exhaustive list of all the distinctions that one can find across all situations," nor did they "consider that goal processes are the only way to conceptualize psychologically meaningful situations" (p. 773). Given that "goal striving" (broadly conceptualized) was ultimately a common theme that emerged across multiple clusters and multiple levels of abstraction, one could argue that their solution could be viewed as applied primarily to goal-relevant situations, but this focus was one that emerged from the data, so any such truncation of scope or purpose would necessarily be post hoc and at least somewhat inconsistent with the authors' original intent. That being said, it could also be the case that Chinese idioms inherently tend to focus more so on goal-relevant situations and/or that the individuals responsible for randomly selecting the idioms were biased by instructions given to them or by their own personalities.

In terms of how the primary dimensions can be detected in scientific and applied settings, Yang et al.'s (2006) solution is best considered an instantiation of Murray's (1938) beta-press, Block and Block's (1981) canonical situation, and Rauthmann et al.'s (2015) subjective phenomenological classification given that the methods used to detect them (e.g., cluster analysis) are based on perceived similarity.

From Johns's (2006) perspective, Yang et al.'s (2006) framework is best treated as a form of discrete, task-based, and social context because its dimensions function as individual situational levers that operate through a variety of potential mechanisms (e.g., a situation might be viewed as highly relevant to "achieving one's goals" either because of the nature of the task at hand or because of the quality of one's supporting cast).

Using Rauthmann et al.'s (2015) terminology, each of Yang et al.'s (2006) clusters is best conceptualized as a "class of cues" because cluster solutions yield similarity-based groups that do not inherently contain any dimensional information, but the stimuli used to form relevant classes were ultimately cues because the idioms used focused on the people involved, events that occurred to them, and descriptions of the (re)actions of others involved. That being said, the authors also identified several broad themes that these classes shared in common (which could be viewed as characteristics), but

this differentiation was not their primary focus. Further, it is also important to note that the Yang et al. taxonomy is also best viewed as a cognitive attributional approach to categorization because its ultimate focus on relevance to goal attainment is an important form of declarative representation based on perceived situational meaning (though the authors specifically mentioned that their taxonomy could have implications for better understanding the expression of personality traits). Last, this framework is best detected via subjective phenomenological means because it is dependent upon how people similarly perceive and experience relevant situational cues.

From the perspective of Ostroff, the Yang et al. (2006) framework represents relatively stable aspects of situations, though it is worth pointing out that one's perceptions of the key components of this framework might change as one's goals (or striving toward these goals) change. For example, at the beginning of a task, one might conclude that he is failing, but as proficiency and comfort levels increase, he may begin to believe that he will eventually succeed. Further, given that most of this solution's idiom clusters were focused on goal achievement (coupled with the lack of a standardized instrument), it is difficult to say whether one could readily determine the relative standing and impact of each cue or broad theme individually. Last, the question of internal versus external is not relevant given that goal processes could pertain to behavior within or outside of a focal unit of analysis.

THE DIAMONDS MODEL

Background and Definitions

The Situational Eight DIAMONDS (Rauthmann et al., 2014) represents another recent attempt to empirically define the active ingredients of situations. This approach uses the Riverside Situational Q-Sort (RSQ), which is an 89-item measure of situational affordances (i.e., those characteristics of situations that permit the expression of particular behaviors). Although the RSQ was originally designed to represent "as wide a range of situations as possible" (Sherman, Nave, & Funder, 2010), it is important to point out that it is not based on any underlying theory per se but was instead developed with the following principles in mind:

> (a) the instrument should be applicable to as wide a range of situations as possible, (b) the instrument should be able to quantify the degree of similarity or dissimilarity between any two situations across a wide range of psychological properties, and (c) the instrument should be related to important outcomes relevant to personality (e.g., behaviors, emotions). (Sherman et al., 2010, p. 332)

As the acronym suggests, the final DIAMONDS framework consists of eight dimensions: Duty, Intellect, Adversity, Mating, Positivity, Negativity, Deception, and Sociality (Rauthmann et al., 2014). *Duty* refers to the extent to which people perceive that the situation requires work, performing duties, completing tasks, problem solving, and other forms of diligence. *Intellect* refers to the extent to which people perceive that the situation requires thinking but can also refer to other forms of cognition such as daydreaming and rumination. *Adversity* refers to the extent to which people perceive that the situation contains any form of hostility from tasks or others, including threats, problems, challenges, and difficulties. *Mating* refers to the extent to which the situation is perceived as conducive to developing or maintaining amorous relationships. *Positivity* refers to the perceived presence of pleasant stimuli, fun, or easy-to-navigate experiences. *Negativity* refers to the perceived presence of stimuli that are likely to lead to negative emotional experiences such as anxiety, frustration, or anger. *Deception* refers to the extent to which it is possible to trick or betray someone or experience mistrust or hostility from others. *Sociality* refers to the extent to which participants can engage in positive interactions with others.

Categorization Within Extant Metatheories

Owing to its holistic purpose and multidimensional structure, the Situational Eight DIAMONDS is best characterized as an overall framework as opposed to a multifaceted construct.

This is the case because the dimensions are not necessarily intended to relate to each other, except insofar as they represent core aspects of situations in general. In terms of how they can be detected in scientific and applied settings, the DIAMONDS dimensions are best considered an instantiation of Murray's (1938) beta-press, Block and Block's (1981) canonical situation, and Rauthmann et al.'s (2015) subjective phenomenological classification given that the methods used to detect them (e.g., factor analysis) are based on shared perceptions as opposed to objective characteristics of situations.

From Johns's (2006) perspective, the DIAMONDS framework is best treated as a form of discrete, task-based, and social context because its dimensions function as individual situational levers that operate through a variety of potential mechanisms (e.g., a situation might score high on the Positivity dimension because of structural characteristics as well as the people who are present).

Using Rauthmann et al.'s (2015) terminology, each of the DIAMONDS dimensions is best conceptualized as a characteristic of situations because the framework as a whole represents an effort to "capture the *psychologically important meanings* of perceived cues, thus summarizing a situation's psychological 'power'" (p. 364, emphasis in original). Further, it is also important to note that the DIAMONDS framework is intended to fully capture the totality of situational characteristics at a broad level of abstraction. The DIAMONDS framework is also best viewed as a "trait-psychological approach" to categorization because it "emphasizes situations' affordances of trait expression" (p. 366). Last, the DIAMONDS framework is best detected via subjective phenomenological means because any assessment of its dimensions is dependent upon how raters similarly perceive and experience relevant contextual stimuli.

From the perspective of Ostroff (see Chapter 2, this volume), the DIAMONDS framework could represent either internal or external aspects of context, depending on the specific purpose of a given study. Further, it is likely that each of the DIAMONDS dimensions would be directly detected (as opposed to indirectly assumed to exist) and would be treated as a stable characteristic, but these determinations are ultimately contingent upon the specific study in question. Given the separable nature of the DIAMONDS dimensions, it is possible to understand the relative standing and impact of each characteristic individually, assuming appropriate analytic techniques are used to do so.

Key Additional Points and Issues

It is also important to point out that an additional key purpose of the DIAMONDS model was to develop and validate a measure that could be used to assess the DIAMONDS framework itself. Specifically, the authors developed the RSQ-8, which is based on the original RSQ refined using factor analysis to include only the 32 best-functioning items (i.e., four items per dimension). This instrument not only reflects the originally posited eight-dimensional structure but also predicts meaningful behavioral and affective outcomes and shows significant incremental validity above and beyond extant situational measures and measures of Big Five personality.

PERCEIVED QUALITIES OF SITUATIONS

Background and Definitions

Although scholars as far back as the 1970s recognized that situations, much like people, possess attributes that can be used to differentiate them, John Edwards and Angela Templeton (2005) were among the first to recognize that this perspective can be used to better understand the taxonomic structure of situations (assuming adequate sampling procedures, both from the perspective of adjectives used and situations rated).

Using samples of undergraduate participants, these authors concluded that four underlying characteristics could be used to describe situations broadly (Edwards & Templeton, 2005). First, *Positivity* represents the extent to which situations facilitate the achievement of favorable outcomes. Second, *Negativity* represents the extent to which situations facilitate the achievement of unfavorable outcomes. Third, *Productivity* represents the extent to which situations influence goal attainment or task completion. Fourth, *Ease of Negotiation* represents the extent to which situations are familiar and easy for participants to navigate. It is important

to note, however, that these authors ultimately treat Positivity–Negativity as a single underlying characteristic, thereby resulting in a three-dimensional solution.

Categorization Within Extant Metatheories

Owing to its breadth and comprehensive nature, this effort is best viewed as a taxonomic framework as opposed to a single construct or group of constructs. Namely, the authors used diverse empirical methods to derive an intentionally broad structural solution. In terms of how these characteristics can be detected in scientific and applied settings, they are an instantiation of Murray's (1938) beta-press, Block and Block's (1981) canonical situation, and Rauthmann et al.'s (2015) subjective phenomenological classification because the meaning assigned to a given situation vis-à-vis the dimensional structure provided here is at least partially a function of the perceivers' goals because "people may have a basic orientation towards viewing the world in terms of personal outcomes" (Edwards & Templeton, 2005, p. 717).

From Johns's (2006) perspective, this solution is best treated as dimensions of discrete, task- and social-based context because the resultant situational characteristics are posited, in conjunction with one's goals and perceptions, to influence behavior. Further, these four dimensions can and do apply to both task-based information and socially derived information. For example, it is possible that a situation could be perceived as highly positive because an employee is able to perform well on a task and earn substantial compensation (task-based goals) or because an extravert is able to socialize with others at a stimulating party (socially based goals).

Using Rauthmann et al.'s (2015) terminology, the four dimensions highlighted here are best conceptualized as characteristics of situations because they derive their power from the significance people give to them as a function of their goals, perspectives, and other personal characteristics. Further, Edwards and Templeton's (2005) solution was posited to be comprehensive, in that the authors argued that the proposed four-dimensional solution could be used to create profiles of the entire milieu of situations that individuals might experience—that is, these dimensions could be used as a universal language for describing the behavioral "power" of situations in general. For this reason, then, this solution is also best viewed as a "behavioral approach" to categorization because it utilized the perspective that "people see situations as having underlying qualities akin to human personality traits, which are often seen as specifying the causal power of the situation" (p. 706), which also makes this approach inherently subjective phenomenological because the causal power of the situation is inherently a function of the attributions made by those who experience it.

From the perspective of Ostroff (see Chapter 2, this volume), this solution seems to represent a relatively stable characteristic of situations, though it is also implied that one's perception of a given situation would change as one's goals, values, and perceptions change. For example, a party that enabled an extraverted individual to achieve her goal of obtaining social stimulation might become dull and monotonous after she has run out of conversation partners. That being said, changes such as this are somewhat fleeting in the sense that an extravert would likely generally view stimulating parties in positive terms, though any given party inevitably loses some of its luster. However, it is also important to point out that the authors seem to suggest that situations should be holistically judged as a function of all four dimensions (i.e., in terms of their overall profile) as opposed to determining which dimensions are most versus least relevant for a given individual.

Key Additional Points and Issues

Although the purpose of the Edwards and Templeton (2005) taxonomy was not to create or validate a specific instrument, per se, it is worth noting that they do provide access to all of the adjectives they used in their studies as well as to their factor loadings for each of the resultant four factors. Further, they also provide the specific stimuli they used to obtain these structures and loadings, thereby making it possible for interested scholars not only to replicate their findings but also to use their materials in continued examinations for relevant questions. For example, they stress the importance of having

a thorough conceptualization of the structure of situations when attempting to better understand concepts that are fundamental to social psychology, such as the fundamental attribution error.

SITUATIONAL AFFORDANCES FOR ADAPTIVE PROBLEMS

Background and Definitions

Most conceptualizations of context to date are primarily empirically driven as opposed to being based on a priori theory. One recent exception to this trend is the situational affordances for adaptive problems (SAAP) framework put forth by Brown, Neel, and Sherman (2015). Specifically, this model is based on the fundamental-motives framework (Kenrick, Neuberg, Griskevicius, Becker, & Schaller, 2010), which posits that our species has evolved seven deep-seated goals that served to help humans solve problems that were common in our evolutionary history. Specifically, these motives pertain to avoiding disease, protecting oneself, forming groups and allies, gaining status, attracting mates, retaining mates, and caring for one's kin.

Brown et al. (2015) used this model to develop and validate the SAAP scale, which was intended to assess the extent to which a given situation evokes or affords behaviors that are relevant to these seven motives. Although some of the details associated with item development and testing are not thoroughly described by the SAAP's authors (e.g., the process through which their initial set of 85 items was developed and refined, sample size decisions, their decision to not compare plausible alternative factor solutions), the SAAP is still admirable in the sense that it attempted to base contextual perceptions and assessment on a preexisting model of evolutionarily driven human psychology. Further, it also benefits from the presence of a parsimonious (28-item) scale that can help scholars across disciplines assess the extent to which the context of interest is defined by the aforementioned underlying motives.

Despite these generally positive characteristics, however, it should be noted that being so tightly hewn to an underlying theory also creates a host of potential problems and issues. For example, the fundamental-motives framework is but one possible solution to the question of determining the number and nature of goals that we faced in our evolutionary past. Other evolutionary psychologists might convincingly argue that our primary goals were to (a) survive (b) long enough to pass on our genes, and all other goals could be subsumed under these two. Further, inherent in evolutionary psychology is the idea that the modern Holocene epoch may differ in various critical respects from the Pleistocene epoch in which our species evolved such that we may have goals that did not exist in the past and/or that goals that existed in the past are no longer relevant. Thus, when attempting to determine the structure of modern context, one could argue that an evolutionary perspective is inherently anachronistic.

Categorization Within Extant Metatheories

Owing to its broad purpose and comprehensive structure, the SAAP typology is best characterized as a full framework. This is the case because an attempt was made to use evolutionary theory to distill a parsimonious set of dimensions that could be used to conceptualize context from a high level of abstraction (arguably the highest possible level of abstraction because it was based on survival issues in humans' evolutionary history). In terms of how these dimensions can be detected in scientific and applied settings, these motives are best considered instantiations of Murray's (1938) beta-press because they are ultimately rooted in one's unique perceptions of the extent to which a given motive is afforded in a given context (e.g., as the authors pointed out, research on human aggression shows that there are important individual differences in the extent to which people perceive situations reasonably require them to protect themselves). Further, this model also reflects Block and Block's (1981) canonical situation and Rauthmann et al.'s (2015) objective consensus because, despite individual differences, the authors demonstrated that ratings of vignettes intentionally written to represent a specific motive were generally rated as higher on this dimension than on other dimensions (though some important exceptions to this trend existed in their data).

From Johns's (2006) perspective, the SAAP model is best treated as a form of discrete, task-based context because its dimensions function as individual situational levers that operate primarily through goal-driven mechanisms (although Johns's metatheory focused on tasks in organizations, we posit here that surviving and thriving in life more generally is akin to a task-based consideration).

Using Rauthmann et al.'s (2015) terminology, the SAAP dimensions are best conceptualized as characteristics because they each represent an effort to quantify the extent to which individual cues (e.g., the presence or absence of other people) affect the seven underlying dimensions (e.g., are the other people involved potential friends, foes, mates, etc.?). Further, it is also important to note that the authors implicitly (if not explicitly) claimed that the seven dimensions assessed in the SAAP model represent all of the broadest characteristics of human contexts (though their data suggest that participants sometimes have a difficult time distinguishing between "mate attracting" and "mate retaining" and one could argue that "avoiding disease" is a logical subset of "protecting oneself"). Also, this solution is best viewed as a "cognitive attributional approach" to categorization because it "emphasized mental constructs and declarative representations of the situation" (p. 366) because of the fact that a given situation is ultimately rated on the seven dimensions on the basis of individuals' perceptions (though one could argue that a truly objective standard exists to the extent that a given situation actually does or does not afford the fulfillment of the various motives in question—e.g., to the extent that the person experiencing the situation does not die, the situation by definition afforded "self-protection").

From Ostroff's (see Chapter 2) perspective, the SAAP framework is an internal aspect of context because it, by definition, pertains to the extent to which a given situation enables individuals to fulfill their motives in an environment that they are an intimate part of. Further, it is likely that each of the SAAP dimensions would be directly detected (as opposed to indirectly assumed to exist) given the presence of a standardized instrument. Last, given that individuals' motives are relatively stable aspects of themselves, it would make logical sense that the extent to which a given environment fulfills or thwarts a given motive would also be relatively stable unless and until the situation fundamentally changes.

SITUATIONAL STRENGTH

Background and Definitions

Situational strength has a long history in the social sciences (see Meyer, Dalal, & Hermida, 2010, for a review). Not until recently, however, has research begun treating it as a construct in its own right—including providing a formal definition, a facet structure (Meyer et al., 2010), the beginnings of a nomological network, and a standardized measurement system (i.e., the Situational Strength at Work [SSW] scale—Meyer et al., 2014).

Broadly conceptualized, situational strength can be thought of as any aspect of context (work or otherwise) that encourages or discourages specific behaviors. Those situations that send unmistakable signals about prescribed behaviors are said to be "strong," whereas those that permit individual discretion are said to be "weak." The classic example of situational strength is a traffic signal, with red and green lights representing prototypically strong situations because the externally sanctioned behavior is known by all who experience it, whereas yellow lights are prototypically weak situations because "acceptable" behaviors are more varied because they are likely to be chosen as a function of one's individual differences profile.

Given such a broad conceptualization, it is not particularly surprising that situational strength not only has been used frequently as a framework for studying a variety of contextual influences (Barrick & Mount, 1993; Tett & Burnett, 2003) but also has "been institutionalized as an axiom in textbooks—particularly those in organizational behavior" (Cooper & Withey, 2009, p. 64). More specifically, recent theoretical and empirical research suggests that situational strength can be defined as "implicit or explicit cues provided by one's environment regarding the desirability of potential behaviors" (Meyer et al., 2010, p. 122) and consists of the four interrelated facets of Clarity, Consistency, Constraints, and Consequences.

Categorization Within Extant Metatheories

Although rather broad in scope, situational strength is best viewed as a multifaceted single construct as opposed to a comprehensive taxonomic framework. This is the case because its facets operate through the same basic behavioral mechanism and it is intended to represent only one characteristic of situations (i.e., their effects on behavior). In terms of how it can be detected in scientific and applied settings, it is an instantiation of Murray's (1938) beta-press, Block and Block's (1981) canonical situation, and Rauthmann et al.'s (2015) subjective phenomenological classification, because its meaning and effects occur primarily through the subjective interpretations of those who experience situations.

From Johns's (2006) perspective, situational strength is best treated as a dimension of discrete, task-based context because its four facets can be thought of as "specific situational variables that influence behavior directly or moderate relationships between variables" (p. 393) and pertain to task-relevant characteristics of the job. This is not to say that situational strength is unrelated to omnibus context but rather that it reflects the notion that discrete context variables serve as the levers through which omnibus context operates on specific relationships.

Using Rauthmann et al.'s (2015) terminology, situational strength is best conceptualized as a characteristic of situations because it represents an effort to "capture the *psychologically important meanings* of perceived cues, thus summarizing a situation's psychological 'power'" (p. 364, emphasis in original). It is important to note, however, that situational strength is by no means the only important characteristic of situations (as outlined throughout the rest of this chapter, several other efforts to define critical characteristics of situations exist), but it is unique in the sense that it is the only conceptualization to focus exclusively on characteristics that explicitly operate by influencing (i.e., homogenizing) human behavior. This is not to say that some of the characteristics outlined in other frameworks cannot influence or even homogenize behavior but simply to recognize that situational strength exclusively focuses on this particular effect of situational characteristics. For this reason, then, situational strength is also best viewed as a "behavioral approach" to categorization because it emphasizes stimulus–response configurations, with strength serving as the stimulus and specific behaviors serving as the response, and is best detected via subjective phenomenological means because it is dependent upon how people similarly perceive and experience it.

From the perspective of Ostroff (see Chapter 2), situational strength could represent either internal or external aspects of context, depending on the nature of one's question. For example, an organizational psychologist might be interested in the effects of the strength of a given occupation on a particular trait–outcome relationship, whereas a cross-cultural psychologist might be interested in the relationship between the strength of a given national culture on the same relationship. Further, strength is a relatively stable characteristic of situations, and it is possible to understand the relative standing and impact of each of its facets individually. In terms of stability, we say *relatively stable* because past research has shown that it can be viewed as a meaningful characteristic of situations at the job level (e.g., Barrick & Mount, 1993; Meyer, Dalal, & Bonaccio, 2009), but recently collected data also indicate that it varies from moment to moment across work contexts, with about 25% of variance occurring at the person level (Kelly, 2015). Last, given the separable nature of the four facets of situational strength, it is possible to assess the relative standing or impact of each dimensionally, but it can also be useful to assess the net or "global" strength of a given situation, especially when making practical recommendations.

Key Additional Points and Issues

It is also important to point out that situational strength has traditionally been viewed primarily as a moderator of personality–outcome relationships, such that relevant correlations are expected to be stronger in weak situations and weaker in strong situations. That being said, it is also important to point out that these effects are argued to exist in large part because situational strength encourages

behaviors among those who would be unlikely to engage in them when left to their own devices, thereby potentially leading to both main effects and restrictions of range on both predictor and outcome variables. For example, trait conscientiousness has been shown to lead to increased job performance because highly conscientious individuals are more likely to remain focused, spend additional time on their tasks, plan their work, and so forth. But when situations are strategically strengthened by entities outside the individual (e.g., formal policies, influential supervisors) in ways that encourage these behaviors among less conscientious individuals, at least some of conscientiousness's strategic advantage is eliminated, thereby attenuating its observed correlation with job performance (Barrick & Mount, 1993; Meyer et al., 2009).

TEN BERGE AND DE RAAD'S PERSONALITY PERSPECTIVE

Background and Definitions

The main objective of the taxonomy created by ten Berge and De Raad (2002) was to "describe situations from a personality psychology perspective" based on the idea that "trait information is systematically complemented by situational information" (p. 82). In this taxonomy, personality traits and situations are not considered separate entities, but rather situations are the "situational specification of traits" (p. 83).

Through the use of a principal components analysis of self-ratings and other ratings, four categories of situations were derived: (a) situations of pleasure (e.g., getting a paycheck, hearing good news), (b) situations of individual adversity (e.g., being ill, having a slight accident), (c) situations of interpersonal conflict (e.g., being teased, someone trying to pull your leg), and (d) situations of social demand (e.g., being in an unfamiliar environment, being in charge). Given this taxonomy's overlap with traits, individuals who score high on a particular Big Five personality dimension are predicted to be better equipped to deal with situations that are conceptually related to that factor (e.g., emotional stability and situations of individual adversity).

Categorization Within Extant Metatheories

This taxonomy is best viewed as a framework because it ties together multiple situational components as well as personality factors, although this taxonomy is more limited in scope than most of the other frameworks included in this chapter. Namely, rather than distilling the active ingredients (i.e., characteristics) of situations in general, this taxonomy simply provides four broad categories (i.e., classes) into which situations can be classified. In terms of how they can be detected in scientific and applied settings, this framework is an instantiation of Murray's (1938) beta-press and Block and Block's (1981) canonical situation, though this taxonomy's connection with personality traits (and the role these traits are likely to play in reactions to situations within each category) also make it relevant to Block and Block's functional situation.

From Johns's (2006) perspective, this taxonomy is best treated as a dimension of omnibus context because it pertains more to the 5Ws and an H of a situation as opposed to the situation's defining dimensions. Using Rauthmann et al.'s (2015) terminology, this system is best viewed as a "trait-psychological" approach to categorization because it necessarily emphasizes the relationship between types of situations and individuals' personality—namely, the relationship between the four components of situations and the Big Five structure of personality.

From the perspective of Ostroff (see Chapter 2), this taxonomy represents direct, stable characteristics of context. Although it is not possible to understand the relative standing and impact of each of this taxonomy's components individually because the focus of the present effort is not on situational characteristics, it is possible to determine the trait relevance of each class of situation—that is, to determine whether the expression of certain personality traits is more versus less common in certain situations.

SUMMARY OF EXTANT FRAMEWORKS

In the previous section we outlined a number of extant efforts to create taxonomies of context. Again, we do not claim that this summary is comprehensive but instead hope that it provides a reasonable sampling of the current state of the science. Indeed, numerous other frameworks and perspectives could have been selected for review, but we made a concerted effort to err on the side of including more-contemporary models. It is also important to highlight that, despite this diversity, the solutions outlined here share several areas of both methodological and substantive overlap.

First, it is clear that recent contextual research has favored characteristic-based solutions (as opposed to cue-based or class-based solutions) at a relatively broad level of abstraction. Perhaps the clearest and most recent examples of these trends are the CAPTION, DIAMONDS, and SAAP frameworks, which all show substantial promise as useful dimensional solutions. That being said, they also share a number of potential issues and limitations. For example, one question that remains regarding the nature of these (and similar) solutions is: Have they adequately captured the structure of context at the broadest possible level of abstraction? Said differently, have they isolated the structure of context in a truly parsimonious way (i.e., using the smallest number of meaningful dimensions), or is there a more basic set of dimensions that might be found if other stimulus-development or analytical approaches were used? Looking across solutions, valence tends to emerge consistently, yet various solutions also include dimensions that seem inherently positive or negative. For example, the CAPTION model includes both Negative Valence and Adversity (which seems inherently negatively valenced) as well as Positive Valence and Humor (which seems inherently positively valenced). Similarly, the DIAMONDS model shows a similar trend with Negativity and Adversity, on the one hand, and Positivity and Mating, on the other hand, which may suggest a hierarchical structure worthy of future conceptual and empirical attention.

Second, it is also clear that recent contextual research has favored lexically driven stimulus-development techniques. Although the lexical approach is a useful and thorough way of capturing important ideas, we are concerned that single-word stimuli lack the richness necessary to meaningfully capture the essence of context. We recommend instead that contextual scholars explore the feasibility of using alternative stimuli such as brief descriptions of situations that include information about the 5Ws and an H (e.g., "attending a symphony with my spouse on our anniversary" instead of single adjectives such as "romantic" or individual nouns such as "symphony") or perhaps even multimedia depictions of stimuli that clearly convey what is happening and, potentially, why.

Third, despite important progress, our collective understanding of context has not yet advanced to the point where contextual scholars are able to provide definitive guidance to substantive scholars who are interested in incorporating critical elements of context into their studies. In a perfect world, contextual scholars would develop algorithms or decision trees that could be used by substantive multilevel scholars to help determine how to best conceptualize context in a specific domain of study. Recognizing that the study of context has not yet developed to this point, the following section outlines a series of steps that substantive scholars can take to help those who study context do so more effectively (i.e., showing "what you can do for the study of context") and highlights how doing so is likely to help substantive multilevel scholars increase the availability of useful conceptualizations of context in the future.

STEPS TO TAKE WHEN CONCEPTUALIZING CONTEXT

As evidenced in the previous section, extant taxonomies of context tend to provide relatively broad dimensional solutions, whereas substantive multilevel research has traditionally conceptualized context in more focused ways that best fit the specific needs of the question at hand (i.e., a classic "bandwidth versus fidelity" conundrum—Cronbach & Glesser, 1965). This state of affairs is understandable but also underscores potential synergies that can theoretically benefit both substantive areas of research as well as contextual, given that broad conceptualizations of context can provide meaningful shared anchor points and that the specific operationalizations of context used in published studies can serve as a rich and diverse source of data for

continued contextual research. The purpose of this section is to detail some relatively simple steps that substantive researchers can take to help these synergies develop efficiently.

First, in those cases in which substantive scholars examine the effects of context, it would be useful if they included a subsection entitled "the role of context" (or similar) in their introduction near where context-relevant hypotheses are presented. In this section they should explicitly state that they are attempting to examine the role of context in a given relationship. We advocate following the guidance of Johns (2006), who said that a given research question involves context if it helps to explicate the extent to which who, what, when, where, why and/or how variables influence a given relationship (e.g., mediate it, moderate it, reverse its sign). Further, it would be beneficial to contextual scholars if this subsection also contained a discussion of how or why the substantive scholars chose to operationalize context in the way they ultimately did, including a discussion of the ways in which their contextual variables related to relevant characteristics from any of the previously discussed dimensional solutions. This could also include a discussion of the extent to which scholars are interested in assessing the effects of objective context, subjective context, or idiosyncratically interpreted context. We advocate using Block and Block's (1981) nomenclature, given that it subsumes Murray's (1938) system and adds another important distinction.

It is when agreed-upon subjective characteristics are the focus (i.e., the canonical situation) that substantive multilevel scholars have the most choices—namely, which model(s) of context to use and/or whether to "reinvent the wheel" by formulating a novel conceptualization of context. We make no specific recommendations about which existing taxonomy is best but hope this chapter helps to shed useful light on potential options. We do, however, advocate that scholars who choose to operationalize context in a way that is not derived from an existing taxonomy collect supplementary contextual data from an existing taxonomy (more on this point subsequently). If idiosyncratic conceptualizations of context (i.e., the functional situation) are the focus, then anthropological approaches are needed to more deeply understand the meaning each unique individual gives to context, though extant taxonomies can be used as a guide here as well.

Second, it is also important that substantive scholars explicate precisely what they expect context will *do* and how it will do it. Again, Johns's (2006) guidance is especially useful here because his work provides a reasonably comprehensive description of the ways in which context might operate. For example, is a particular dimension of context treated as a statistical moderator that constrains behavioral variability, a statistical moderator that encourages behavioral variability, or is context being treated as a threat to validity? Although there may not be any substantive differences in the actual role of context based on these purposes (e.g., a contextual threat to validity could be modeled as a statistical interaction given the appropriate data and analysis), it is important that scholars explicate the specific lens through which they are interpreting their particular research question so that subsequent reviews and meta-analyses can take these perspectives into account.

Third, we encourage substantive multilevel scholars to use a common nomenclature when discussing the aspect(s) of context in which they are interested. We believe that Rauthmann et al.'s (2015) distinction between cues, classes, and characteristics is especially useful in this regard. For example, an experimental psychologist who studies the influence of subtle environmental manipulations would use the term *cues*, a community psychologist who is interested in how a given relationship changes when studied in social clubs versus in religious institutions would use the term *classes*, whereas the hypothetical scholars referenced throughout who are interested in the moderating effects of family supportiveness would use the term *characteristics*.

Fourth, when using ad hoc operationalizations, substantive scholars would help to further the study of context by measuring and reporting relationships between their operationalizations of context and those derived from one or more of the broad taxonomies described previously. Using the ongoing example, scholars who recognize that their operationalization of "supportive family environments" is related to the broader contextual dimensions of positivity (Parrigon et al., 2016; Rauthmann et al., 2014),

facilitation/inhibition of important goals (Yang et al., 2006), and caring for one's kin (Brown et al., 2015) would benefit the ongoing study of context by measuring one or more of these broader dimensions alongside their specific operationalization. Contextual scholars could then use the resulting correlation matrix as a valuable source of secondary data in future reviews, meta-analyses, and/or data reduction efforts.

Last, substantive researchers who are interested in helping contextual researchers develop better systems and taxonomies can facilitate this process by mapping their specific conceptualizations of context onto one or more metatheories of context. Drawing again from the ongoing example, scholars should specifically state that "family supportiveness" is a form of discrete context, in that it serves as a specific lever through which an important aspect of omnibus context (i.e., family members) help to encourage coping patterns that are less likely to lead to suicidal thoughts than those experienced by abuse victims in less supportive family units. Similarly, these authors might also point out that their operationalization of a supportive family environment may be based on Rauthmann et al.'s (2015) objective physical category if supportiveness is quantified as the number of family members a participant reports interacting with in a typical week (for example) or may be based on Rauthmann et al.'s subjective phenomenological category if supportiveness is quantified as participants' self-reports on a scale designed to assess supportive familial behaviors.

We recognize that the aforementioned guidance creates a somewhat onerous burden for multilevel scholars. It is important to highlight, however, that the prescribed courses of action can be viewed as a long-term investment because the data contained in resultant studies will provide a rich source of information for contextual scholars as they develop future taxonomic solutions. Recognizing our interdependence, therefore, has the potential to help both substantive and contextual scholars because taxonomies of context are only useful to the extent that they realistically reflect the scope and depth of the reality in which multilevel scholars conduct their science and "help point scholars to more specific aspects of context to consider in any given study" (Ostroff, see Chapter 2, this volume).

DISCUSSION

We intended the present chapter to serve as a starting point for substantive multilevel scholars who are interested in (a) more actively incorporating the effects of context in their study of diverse phenomena and (b) helping to further the continued study of context. The present state of affairs suggests that, at a minimum, the following conclusions are warranted regarding progress toward a sufficient taxonomic understanding of context. First, how to best conceptualize context is an active area of research in several psychological subdisciplines. Indeed, one could reasonably argue that the study of context is presently experiencing the beginning of a significant renaissance. Indeed, in just the last few years, several new lines of thinking and many related empirical solutions have emerged that will surely help shape the future of contextual research. The most promising efforts have used impressive stimulus-development and analytic methods to specifically identify a comprehensive set of characteristics that underlie context either generally or in a specific area of study. This is not to say that these solutions are without limitations, but they do likely represent important steps in an evolving process. Indeed, these efforts are similar in scope and purpose to those that ultimately resulted in the Big Five model of personality. It is our hope (as well as the expressly stated hope of others in this area) that a similar consensus will be reached vis-à-vis a comprehensive, yet parsimonious structure of context.[1]

Second, despite important progress, continued inquiry into the taxonomic structure of context is needed before a true consensus can be reached. That being said, recent efforts in this regard show not only general promise but also substantial overlap in their conclusions. Specifically, between four and eight broad dimensions consistently emerge in analyses of the construct space of situations

and context in general, with more comprehensive frameworks published in the last few years leaning toward the high end of this estimate. Looking across solutions, the following characteristics often appear in common. One dimension in common is valence, which all present solutions that contain it treat as two separate dimensions (though one could conceivably treat it as a single bipolar dimension). A second dimension often found in common is importance/duty/productivity (on the one hand) versus triviality/mundaneness/leisure (on the other hand)—again, however, it is not clear whether these are separate dimensions or a single bipolar dimension. A third dimension often found in common is the extent to which some sort of difficulty or adversity is present, but substantial conceptual overlap exists between the components of this dimension and general negative valence. A fourth dimension often found in common is some fun/social aspects of context. A fifth dimension often found in common pertains to the cognitive demands of situations, though it is not clear whether the lack of characteristics pertaining to physical demands and/or emotional demands is a legitimate reflection of reality or is the result of sampling error among the stimuli used (for example).

It is important to expressly state here, however, that we believe that scholars should not conflate evidence of overlap with evidence of the higher-order structure of context. For example, one might be tempted to argue that, because extant conceptualizations of context share X dimensions in common (with X in this case somewhere between three and six), these X dimensions ipso facto represent the structure of context at the highest level of abstraction. Such an argument is potentially fallacious if (a) the taxonomies in question did not each have as their express purpose determining the factor structure of context at the broadest possible level of abstraction or (b) larger scale, more inclusive primary studies using more comprehensive stimulus-development approaches or more appropriate data reduction techniques are feasible. For example, no qualitative

---

[1]Although we explicitly recognize that the five-factor model is not without its limitations and detractors (e.g., Block, 2001), we also recognize that it helped to provide some order to an area of important inquiry. We expect that similar critiques and debates will happen with resultant taxonomies of context but view these discussions as an inevitable part of healthy scientific dialogue.

summary of extant dimensional structures would be able to determine whether *valence* should be treated as a single bipolar dimension or whether *positivity* and *negativity* should be treated as separate dimensions. Similarly, although *disease avoidance* could conceptually be viewed as a subset of *self-protection*, it is ultimately an empirical question whether these dimensions should be combined or kept separate. As such, we posit that if one's goal is to determine the basic dimensions of context, quantitative data and methods should be used to assess this question as directly as possible.

Third, even if a consensus is ultimately reached regarding the structure of context in general, it may be the case that conceptualizing context within some specific domains (e.g., organizational, educational, familial) will inherently emphasize some characteristics over others. For example, it may be the case that dimensions such as *duty*, *intellect*, *complexity*, and *typicality* (to name a few) may be especially relevant to organizations, whereas characteristics such as *humor*, *mating*, and *sociality* may be more relevant to familial contexts (although perhaps not completely irrelevant to the workplace). Similarly, it may be the case that focusing on specific domains may reveal new and important dimensions of context that have not yet been uncovered in any of the extant taxonomies. This is not to say that broad taxonomies should necessarily be eschewed but is instead meant to imply that scholars in specific subdisciplines (a) can contribute to broad efforts by identifying which characteristics are most versus least relevant to their specific area of study, (b) might find that subdimensions of the aforementioned broader characteristics may be needed when conceptualizing context in their specific domain, and/or (c) may conclude that other ways of conceptualizing context altogether are more useful for their purposes (e.g., focusing on cues vs. characteristics of the situations in question, anthropometric approaches paired with qualitative methods).

CONCLUSION

The study of context is alive and well in the social sciences and, indeed, appears to be coming of age. In addition to the specific conceptualizations of

context that formed the basis of the present chapter, it is also important to recognize the critical meta-theoretical work that has helped get scholars on the same page regarding critical issues of nomenclature (e.g., cues vs. characteristics vs. classes), levels of abstraction, areas of focus (e.g., characteristics of situations as captured by adjectives, affordances of situations as captured by verbs), stimulus generation (e.g., lexical approaches vs. self-reports of experiences), and methodological issues. Although there are difficult challenges in front of us, the net impact of the recent flurry of work in this area is that now a host of options is available for those who are interested in accounting for the important role of context in multilevel research. Although none of these approaches is perfect, they are a substantial improvement over the "jingle-jangle jungle" (Rauthmann et al., 2015, p. 372) that defined the study of context in the 20th century.

References

Barrick, M. R., & Mount, M. K. (1993). Autonomy as a moderator of the relationships between the Big Five personality dimensions and job performance. *Journal of Applied Psychology*, 78, 111–118. http://dx.doi.org/10.1037/0021-9010.78.1.111

Block, J. (2001). Millennial contrarianism: The five-factor approach to personality description 5 years later. *Journal of Research in Personality*, 35, 98–107. http://dx.doi.org/10.1006/jrpe.2000.2293

Block, J., & Block, J. H. (1981). Studying situational dimensions: A grand perspective and some limited empiricism. In D. M. Magnusson (Ed.), *Toward a psychology of situations: An interactional perspective* (pp. 85–103). Hillsdale, NJ: Lawrence Erlbaum.

Brown, N. A., Neel, R., & Sherman, R. A. (2015). Measuring the evolutionarily important goals of situations: Situational Affordances for Adaptive Problems. *Evolutionary Psychology*, 3, 1–15.

Cooper, W. H., & Withey, M. J. (2009). The strong situation hypothesis. *Personality and Social Psychology Review*, 13, 62–72. http://dx.doi.org/10.1177/1088868308329378

Cronbach, L., & Glesser, G. (1965). *Psychological tests and personnel decisions* (2nd ed.). Urbana: University of Illinois Press.

Edwards, J. A., & Templeton, A. (2005). The structure of perceived qualities of situations. *European Journal of Social Psychology*, 35, 705–723. http://dx.doi.org/10.1002/ejsp.271

Frederiksen, N. (1972). Toward a taxonomy of situations. *American Psychologist, 27,* 114–123. http://dx.doi.org/10.1037/h0032705

Galton, F. (1884). The measurement of character. *Fortnightly Review,* 179–185.

Johns, G. (2006). The essential impact of context on organizational behavior. *Academy of Management Review, 31,* 386–408. http://dx.doi.org/10.5465/AMR.2006.20208687

Kelly, E. D. (2015). *Examining the counterproductive work behavior process: Momentary relationships among personality, affect, and situational strength* (Master's thesis, Georgia Institute of Technology). Retrieved from https://smartech.gatech.edu/bitstream/handle/1853/58136/KELLY-THESIS-2015.pdf

Kenrick, D. T., Neuberg, S. L., Griskevicius, V., Becker, D. V., & Schaller, M. (2010). Goal-driven cognition and functional behavior: The fundamental-motives framework. *Current Directions in Psychological Science, 19,* 63–67. http://dx.doi.org/10.1177/0963721409359281

Meyer, R. D., Dalal, R. S., & Bonaccio, S. (2009). A meta-analytic investigation into the moderating effects of situational strength on the conscientiousness-performance relationship. *Journal of Organizational Behavior, 30,* 1077–1102. http://dx.doi.org/10.1002/job.602

Meyer, R. D., Dalal, R. S., & Hermida, R. (2010). A review and synthesis of situational strength in the organizational sciences. *Journal of Management, 36,* 121–140. http://dx.doi.org/10.1177/0149206309349309

Meyer, R. D., Dalal, R. S., José, I. J., Hermida, R., Chen, T. R., Vega, R. P., . . . Khare, V. P. (2014). Measuring job-related situational strength and assessing its interactive effects with personality on voluntary work behavior. *Journal of Management, 40,* 1010–1041. http://dx.doi.org/10.1177/0149206311425613

Murray, H. A. (1938). *Explorations in personality.* New York, NY: Oxford University Press.

Parrigon, S., Woo, S. E., Tay, L., & Wang, T. (2016). CAPTION-ing the situation: A lexically-derived taxonomy of psychological situation characteristics. *Journal of Personality and Social Psychology, 112,* 642–681.

Rauthmann, J. F., Gallardo-Pujol, D., Guillaume, E. M., Todd, E., Nave, C. S., Sherman, R. A., . . . Funder, D. C. (2014). The Situational Eight DIAMONDS: A taxonomy of major dimensions of situation characteristics. *Journal of Personality and Social Psychology, 107,* 677–718. http://dx.doi.org/10.1037/a0037250

Rauthmann, J. F., Sherman, R. A., & Funder, D. C. (2015). Principles of situation research: Towards a better understanding of psychological situations. *European Journal of Personality, 29,* 363–381. http://dx.doi.org/10.1002/per.1994

Sherman, R. A., Nave, C. S., & Funder, D. C. (2010). Situational similarity and personality predict behavioral consistency. *Journal of Personality and Social Psychology, 99,* 330–343. http://dx.doi.org/10.1037/a0019796

ten Berge, M. A., & De Raad, B. (2002). The structure of situations from a personality perspective. *European Journal of Personality, 16,* 81–102. http://dx.doi.org/10.1002/per.435

Tett, R. P., & Burnett, D. D. (2003). A personality trait-based interactionist model of job performance. *Journal of Applied Psychology, 88,* 500–517. http://dx.doi.org/10.1037/0021-9010.88.3.500

Yang, Y., Read, S. J., & Miller, L. C. (2006). A taxonomy of situations from Chinese idioms. *Journal of Research in Personality, 40,* 750–778. http://dx.doi.org/10.1016/j.jrp.2005.09.007

## CHAPTER 4

THE ONLY CONSTANT
IS CHANGE: EXPANDING
THEORY BY INCORPORATING
DYNAMIC PROPERTIES
INTO ONE'S MODELS

Matthew A. Cronin and Jeffrey B. Vancouver

Many scholars are dissatisfied with our "science of statics," which is dominated by conceptual models that offer no explanation, prediction, or control regarding a phenomenon's evolution over time. Many scholars are also endeavoring to move us beyond such static models, especially in the realm of multilevel research, where static models are particularly limiting. Much of this work on dynamics is done via creating new, or extending old, empirical methods. Yet, the impact of such endeavors is likely limited because theoretical understanding of dynamics within the field is nascent. In particular, researchers have limited conceptual tools with which to model the dynamics inherent in the phenomena we study. Without such tools, the same old kinds of static theoretical models are tested, just with more sophisticated methods. To address this conceptual gap, we discuss four properties of dynamic processes that, when considered as part of theorizing about a phenomenon, can help us move the field from static to dynamic models. The four properties are inertia, feedback, asymmetric influence, and endogenous change. Specifically, we define these properties, explain their importance, describe methods for representing them graphically and mathematically, and illustrate their usefulness. Our hope is that the more facility we have in creating theory about how and why dynamics occur in a phenomenon,

the more refined our research will be and the more sophisticated our science will become.

INTRODUCTION

"Organizations are multilevel systems" (p. 3); so began Kozlowski and Klein's (2000) opening chapter on multilevel theory and analysis. This groundbreaking text consolidated thinking and methods for conducting multilevel research in organizational contexts. It emphasized the nested nature of systems (i.e., systems are composed of nested subsystems), the ways this nesting needs to be recognized (e.g., observations are not independent within units), and how it should be studied (e.g., referencing the desired target level of a construct during assessment; analyzed with random coefficient models). In this chapter, we similarly acknowledge the nested nature of systems, but we wish to emphasize a property of systems largely absent from that groundbreaking work—namely, their dynamics. Dynamics are about change over time. For example, teams can experience stress (a group-level construct), perhaps due to actions of teammates (individual-level behavior), that initiates reactions from the team and the team leader that may, over time, reduce the stress experienced. This kind of dynamism is not, we argue, well represented within multilevel research, and such an omission

http://dx.doi.org/10.1037/0000115-005
The Handbook of Multilevel Theory, Measurement, and Analysis, S. E. Humphrey and J. M. LeBreton (Editors-in-Chief)

can seriously undermine the validity of findings from research that ignores such dynamics (DeShon, 2013; Hanges & Wang, 2012).

The usual explanations for why such dynamism is absent from organizational theory and research tend to be operational. For example, testing dynamic models generally requires longitudinal designs with multiple, repeated measures (Ployhart & Vandenberg, 2010). Such empirical designs are costly, time-consuming, and difficult to procure. Even if one can gather such data, the statistical methods that incorporate change over time are complicated, especially when causes and effects are occurring across multiple levels or those cause-and-effect relationships are reciprocally related. Fortunately, new techniques are being developed to accommodate this complexity (e.g., Hamaker & Wichers, 2017; Humphrey & Aime, 2014), and some of these techniques are highlighted in Chapters 22 and 23 of this volume.

Another reason why the consideration of dynamics may be proceeding at a languid pace, as Waller, Okhuysen, and Saghafian (2016) recently noted, is that our training on how to theorize about change is very limited. Specifically, most are trained to distill phenomena into constructs and the flow of cause between them. These notions are put together into linear causal chains called *path diagrams* that imply covariation or conditional covariation of the constructs (e.g., the level of X impacts the level of Y mediated or moderated by Z). Yet, such models leave little room for the articulation of dynamics because time is not really represented. That is, these models lead us to think superficially how an antecedent construct precedes a consequence construct but not how those properties change over time or how such change manifests in the system that is being conceptualized.

To be sure, scientific understanding begins with descriptions of key constructs and important classifications (i.e., taxonomies), followed by specifications of relationships among the constructs. Moreover, this kind of description is very much amenable to path diagrams and structural equation modeling—perhaps too amenable. However, the next step in the development of a scientific field is to specify how the constructs change (or do

not change) over time within the units of inquiry, preferably where the timescale is explicit. Thus, to move to this next level of explanation, prediction, and control, a field must incorporate temporal features into the structure of such models. Such features require theorists and researchers to think explicitly about how a phenomenon evolves over time and to represent such systematic change in their theory. This allows for not only new and more precise theory but also new avenues of research on existing theory.

To theorize about truly dynamic processes, we argue that four critical properties should ultimately be integrated into our conceptual modeling capabilities. These properties are (a) inertia, (b) feedback loops, (c) potential asymmetric influences, and (d) endogenous change. These four elements can be intrinsic to the real-world phenomena being modeled, and they can have dramatic effects on how theories are represented or data are interpreted. Thus, in the current chapter, we seek to inspire theorizing that will lead to a more sophisticated understanding of dynamics. In particular, we explain how to incorporate the four dynamic elements named above into the traditional ways theories are formalized. In each section, we explain what the dynamic element means, why it is problematic to ignore it, and how it should be incorporated into the models we build. In this way, we provide the tools for thinking about and representing the dynamic processes that are intrinsic to the phenomena that social science scholars are tasked with explaining. To put into perspective the importance of a sophisticated dynamic approach to theorizing, we begin by describing the current situation with regard to theorizing and dynamics.

CURRENT CONCEPTUALIZATIONS OF THEORY AND DYNAMICS

Given the ambiguity of language, we need to begin by defining some terms. First, as Whetten (1989) noted, *theory* is used to describe a set of constructs and their causal relationships (i.e., what factors influence each other) as well as provide the explanation for those relationships (i.e., how or why factors influence each other). Theory is typically formalized using a model that articulates the concepts (conventionally represented as ovals or boxes) that are linked together in a structure of causal relationships (conventionally represented as arrows). The model corresponds to the causal theory one seeks to test in relation to some phenomenon of interest. Figure 4.1 represents via a path diagram the most common structural features found in causal models concerned with the relationship between X and Y, including black ovals that represent where antecedents, mediators, and moderators might go. Note we could add or remove constructs, and we could position some of the constructs at different levels of analysis to make it multilevel. We could also represent the theory formally. Keeping it simple, for instance, we could say that Y is a function of X [e.g., $y = f(x)$]. We could also represent the theory analytically (e.g., $y = b_1 + b_2x$), where b_1 is an intercept and b_2 represents the effect size of x's influence on y.

In light of the fact that the colloquial definition of *dynamic* means change, the immediate question is: How are dynamics represented in the conventional path diagram or functional depictions of a model? The dynamics that we want to be able to model are about how the properties or conditions in a system change over time (Boulding, 1956; Sterman, 2000). For example, if one suggested coping behavior (X) affects stress (Y), the traditional model is $X \rightarrow Y$ with a hypothesized negative value for the b_2 coefficient. Yet, this leaves much unspecified and much to be desired. Specifically, it presumably means that any particular amount of coping behavior, represented by the x value, exhibited over some (unspecified) amount of time by a unit (e.g., a person), will result, after some (unspecified) amount of time, in some level of stress, represented by a y value, of a unit (e.g., a person or team). This assumption is necessary for testing the theory using a structural equation model, in which the variances arise from differences between units (James, Mulaik, & Brett, 1982). That is, James et al. (1982) noted that whatever changes in the x and y values might have occurred in the past, they would have had to have settled if one were using cross-sectional data to estimate the effect sizes of causal influences.

Yet, the inadequacy of the "theory" becomes immediately clear if one realizes that the probable reason for the coping behavior, X, was the unit's level of stress (i.e., the behavior was part of a feedback process caused by the level of stress, Y). Moreover, one might also realize that the level of stress, if experienced and not addressed with coping behavior, will remain at its level (i.e., exhibit inertia) whereas coping behavior may change instantaneously (i.e., not exhibit inertia). Meanwhile, one should also realize that decreasing coping will not increase stress but rather only determine the rate at which it might be mitigated (i.e., an asymmetric effect). Indeed, one might realize that various processes might decrease or increase stress, which, if not represented, limit one's understanding of the processes and/or undermine the interpretations of data about the (reciprocal) processes. This last point is a key one for those who take dynamics seriously; that is, one must represent the nature of endogenous change in a system to properly capture the system's dynamics (Forrester, 1968; Richardson, 2011). It is also similar

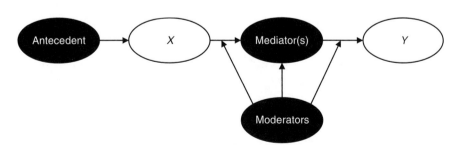

FIGURE 4.1. A depiction of how a simple cause-and-effect model is conceptualized and enriched. Note that the antecedents, mediators, and moderators could all represent multiple constructs or other systems and that any of the boxes could be positioned at different levels of analysis.

to the self-containment criteria James et al. (1982) discussed in terms of causal modeling.

Part of the challenge in representing change over time is that time can be conceptualized in several ways. For example, the *Academy of Management Review* devoted a special issue to the multitude of ways in which time could be used as a lens for understanding how phenomena unfold in organizational contexts (Ancona, Goodman, Lawrence, & Tushman, 2001). One such lens incorporated time by making temporally based constructs into perceptions, individual differences, and behaviors. Such constructs could be predictor constructs (e.g., temporal norms, rhythms, schedules; see Blount & Janicik, 2001), outcome constructs (e.g., speed; see Lawrence, Winn, & Jennings, 2001), or moderator/mediator constructs (future/present orientation; see Waller, Conte, Gibson, & Carpenter, 2001). Yet, these types of conceptualizations do not help facilitate an understanding of how to incorporate dynamics into theories because they fix the effects of the temporal construct. For example, future orientation may be constructed with reference to the experience of time, but its effect on other constructs is still conceptualized as some average effect size.

Another part of the challenge is that time can be analyzed in many ways (e.g., growth curve modeling, lagged regression), yet the dynamics within a phenomenon can lead to errors in the application of such analytical techniques. Consider the stress example. At a very abstract level, it is a kind of problem–remedy question. For example, one might ask if leader support is a remedy for unit stress. To assess this dynamically, one might have measured the level of stress units' experience and the amount of support provided across many waves of data collection. These would presumably be "at this moment" or "since the last survey" measures, for which the time periods of data collection are specified (e.g., daily or weekly). Because of a concern that support might be a function of stress, a lagged analytic approach was used to analyze the data. For example, Time 1's support report was paired with Time 2, 3, or 4's stress report (i.e., to assess the effects of support across 1, 2, or 3 degrees of lag, respectively), and this pairing was

continued across many waves of data. Moreover, many units were included in the study, and thus multilevel analysis methods were used to recognize the fact that observations were nested within units. Yet surprisingly, the result of such a design and analysis would likely be that support appears to be an enabling mechanism because the effect, b_2, of support on subsequent stress is positive, though it drops the longer the lag. This result would occur if stress occurs only periodically, if stress evokes a support response, and if it takes time for that support to reduce the stress. In fact, any response that is evoked because of and perhaps proportional to a problem but that takes time to remedy can seem to increase the problem. This pattern could easily be interpreted as a backfiring or "making the matter worse" type of effect. Indeed, this may explain why some studies appear to show that social support is harmful (e.g., Nahum-Shani, Henderson, Lim, & Vinokur, 2014). But this interpretation can be mistaken because of the way longitudinal analysis misinterprets the underlying dynamics when feedback and time lags are present.

Change must occur over time, and in a dynamic model, the nature of this change must be a fundamental aspect of the phenomenon being represented. Hence, it must pervade the theory that is being modeled. Getting it right requires asking several questions about how to conceptualize time in the theoretical model one is building. Indeed, one of the first issues is to think about the way to conceptualize the passage of time. For example, Ancona, Okhuysen, and Perlow (2001) reviewed several ways that time could be conceptualized as progressing (e.g., clock time, growth, transformation) and thus parameterized (regular vs. irregular intervals). Such questions are fundamental to characterizing change in a model on a scale that makes it detectable. Mitchell and James (2001) demonstrated the danger of misestimating the effect of an event if one failed to understand how its influence may rise and fall over time or if one misspecified how long it took for some effect to influence subsequent outcomes or events. Similarly, Huy (2001) explained how planned change, which was the phenomenon under study, had different subprocesses, which each had different kinds of emergence. These examples illustrate why timescale needs to be thought of somewhat like a level of analysis—something that ensures that change in the phenomenon is detectable and that causes can reasonably have enough time to affect consequences.

Yet, to fully incorporate dynamics into one's theories, one must think about how temporal change can manifest in the components of the model itself. To do that, one must dispense with certain habits inherent in the traditional modeling approaches. To capture the dynamics of a phenomenon, the field must enrich the capabilities for conceptualizing causal structures. There are four properties we will use to do this: (a) inertia, (b) feedback, (c) asymmetric influence, and (d) endogenous change (see Table 4.1 for a summary). In the next section, we more fully articulate what these properties mean, why they matter, and how one could model them both visually and mathematically. These properties are conceptual tools that can make concrete and explicit the dynamics that are either ignored or inconsistently assumed in the models typically constructed. We hope these new conceptual tools will expand thinking beyond the current static or superficial dynamics thinking that permeates the field.

FOUR DYNAMIC PROPERTIES

Dynamic properties are attributes of a model that specify the ways in which a model can change across time. They are mostly related to the *how* of theorizing, and, like most formalizations, their appropriateness in a model is determined by the phenomenon being studied. This point is important because it is a mistake to think some construct or mechanism conceptualized with a dynamic property in one model must be conceptualized with the same dynamic property in other models (e.g., individual skill levels, which are often properly conceptualized as static in theories of organizational phenomena with relatively short time frames [e.g., minutes, hours, days], might be conceptualized as dynamic when a longer time frame is considered [e.g., month, years]). The phenomenon to be explained, not the concept, drives the nature of the dynamics needed in a theory. Of course, one cannot theorize about dynamics without incorporating change across time. Such change requires an understanding that the past affects the future. A simple analog is that sampling with replacement is not a dynamic system, whereas sampling without replacement is. To understand how the influence of the past on the future can be

TABLE 4.1

Four Common Properties of Models With Dynamics

Dynamic property	Definition	Misinterpretation threats if ignored	Proposed modeling convention
Inertia	The conditions of Y persist until some force acts to change it absent some other force: $Y_t = Y_{t-1}$.	Past's relation to future is ignored; not understanding that factors determine rates of change continually.	Capitalize label of constructs with inertia; lowercase labels for constructs without inertia.
Feedback	A causal chain between factors with no end or origin.	Mistaking causes and consequences; missing compensatory effects and thus making Type III errors (wrong sign).	Use arrows to explicitly identify the loops and put signs on arrows. These signs help identify their type (reinforcing or balancing).
Asymmetric influence	ΔX can increase but not decrease Y (or vice versa).	Overextend the possible influence of a concept in a system; unbounded constructs can take on unrealistic values.	Bound causes (constructs point at other constructs) to only positive (or only negative) values; include signs on arrows.
Endogenous change	The factors (Xs) that change Y are part of Y and are structured into feedback loops.	Missing possible sources of changes. Making Type I, II, and III errors.	Include constructs involved in changes to constructs in feedback loops.

captured, we discuss inertia, the first of our four dynamic properties.

Inertia

In a theory, some of the constructs with the capacity to change have inertia. Constructs that exhibit inertia have the *property of conservation*, which is the notion that the state of the construct retains its condition over time until something changes it (Forrester, 1968). For example, the conservation of momentum in physics is about how an object in motion retains the same level of motion unless some force acts upon it (e.g., a rocket in space would continue at its current vector [i.e., speed and direction] until some other force, such as gravity or engine thrust, changes that vector). When some force does act upon it, inertia needs to be taken into account when determining the new level (i.e., value) of the construct given that force. In particular, a construct has inertia if (a) it retains its value or level when no force is acting on it and (b) the forces that act on it change it from the currently held value or level.

Inertia is a critical concept. In fact, fields often have their own name for it. In engineering, the property is referred to as *memory* because the current state of construct is retained over time. In physics, inertia is the property of *conservation*. Powers (1978) called concepts with inertia *dynamic constructs* because of their necessity in any dynamic system. Likewise, Forrester (1968) highlighted the importance of such constructs but used descriptive terms such as *stock* constructs (because the stock in an inventory has the property) or *level* constructs (because the constructs retain some equilibrium or baseline level, such as the level of a lake). We prefer the term *inertia* because it provides the intuition that is critical—prior conditions of a system are reflected in future conditions—and is unlikely to create confusion with specific domains such as the terms *conservation* or *memory* might.

A concept parallel to inertia can be found in the research stemming from work on groups and teams. Specifically, Marks, Mathieu, and Zaccaro (2001) implicitly spoke to the issue of inertia in their distinction between *states* and *processes*. States, they claimed, are properties of teams that persist over time and hence have inertia. Processes, on the other

hand, do not retain their level unless some force operates to maintain it. Unfortunately, the state/process distinction does not always track to the inertia/no inertia distinction because of timescale. For example, stress is easily conceptualized as a state, but depending on the timescale at which one wants to theorize about change, it may or may not have inertia. At the hourly timescale, stress will very much have inertia, and theorizing about change in stress that does not take into account prior levels is underspecified. At the monthly timescale, stress levels need not be conceptualized this way (i.e., a unit's level of stress the previous month is unrelated to stress in the next month). Similarly, a process is typically something without inertia when one thinks at a scale that exceeds the length of the process. If supervisory support is a set of activities that takes 2 hours, then outside of a 2-hour timescale, such events are independent. But within the 2-hour scale, the process would have inertia (once it is started, it should complete). People need to be explicit about whether constructs in their model have inertia or not, and timescale is critical to that decision.

Mitchell and James (2001) provided a number of examples of how, if one picks the wrong timescale, the subsequent investigation can be undermined because many changes, though important, are not permanent. For instance, in our ongoing stress example, one would expect the leaders' actions to reduce stress, but not instantaneously. James et al. (1982) discussed this in their concept of lag. For the dynamic theorist, the question is determining the rate of change one construct has on another and whether that rate is a function of the level of the construct or dichotomous (i.e., all or none).

The irony of inertia is that although it is key to understanding dynamics, it represents stability in a system. For example, an individual's level of self-efficacy or a group's level of collective efficacy, though possibly time-varying, is likely to remain at some level unless cues suggest it be changed. In addition, a construct that appears to have inertia may be better understood as a construct that is affected by other constructs that have inertia. For example, over a long time, scale stress may not have inertia, but the conditions that are stressors of the unit (e.g., individual, group, or organization) may tend to reoccur or have inertia. This would make it so that the level of stress reported across time periods was related, not because of inertia in the stress construct but because of inertia in the environmental conditions that caused stressors (e.g., an aggressive competitor).

In determining whether one should represent a construct as having inertia, a key notion is to think about the factors that might affect a construct and ask: Would other factors in the model determine the *level* of the construct or would they determine the direction and degree of *change* in the construct from whatever its current state is? Only constructs for which the latter is true are constructs with inertia. Another key notion is to think about trajectories of change in the construct. Is the property likely to maintain its value? Does it grow, cumulate, or decay? If yes, it likely has inertia. We would presume that leader support does not determine stress; rather, it decreases the current level of stress. Thus, stress (in this situation) should be modeled with inertia.

The criticality of specifying which constructs in one's model have inertia requires that the visual representation of such constructs differentiates them from constructs without the inertia property. Similar to the issue of multiple labels for the property, there are multiple conventions for representing such theories in graphical depictions of dynamic models. For example, system dynamics (e.g., Perlow & Repenning, 2009; Richardson, 1991) uses boxes exclusively for such constructs. Other, noninertia constructs are simply the construct label unadorned. Vancouver (e.g., Vancouver & Weinhardt, 2012) uses ovals for inertia constructs, boxes for other endogenous variables, and just the label for exogenous constructs, parameters, and constants. Engineers and cognitive scientists tend to put an arrow emerging from and then returning to constructs with inertia. We suggest a simpler representation technique: Capitalize only constructs that have inertia. This convention would not interfere with conventions that distinguish variables, represented as boxes, and constructs, presented by

ovals, common in structure modeling diagrams or make a model too busy with arrows.

In addition to the visual representation of inertia, we should consider the mathematical one. Mathematics has the attribute of universality and, when placed in a computational modeling platform (e.g., MATLAB, Vensim), will allow for workable simulations. Mathematical representations of dynamic phenomena have two flavors of time: discrete and continuous.[1] Discrete models represent the effects over time in discrete time steps. Thus, the level of a construct can take on different values each time step and might be expressed generically as a function of an array of xs (i.e., bold x) as follows:

$$y_t = f(\mathbf{x}_{t-1})$$

Verbally, this function would be stated as follows: y at Time t is a function of xs at Time t minus 1 (i.e., the previous time step). The $f()$ element in the equation represents "a function of" and the bold x signifies that it can be an array (i.e., a set of multiple x variables). This kind of theoretical specification is easily mapped to common methodological formalizations (e.g., multiple predictor variables tested in a multiple regression equation) as described earlier.

Yet, when constructs have inertia, an additional term is needed, which is the state of the y construct at the previous time. Specifically,

$$y_t = y_{t-1} + f(\mathbf{x}_{t-1})$$

With the addition of this term, $f(\mathbf{x}_{t-1})$ no longer determines the level of y but rather represents what determines the change in y. Verbally, it changes the specification of the model from "given this set of xs at Time $t-1$ we expect a certain value of y" to "given this set of xs at Time $t-1$ we expect the value of y to change by the results of the function of the array of x values." For this reason, another expression of the same equation is

$$\Delta y = f(\mathbf{x}_{t-1})$$

That is, the change in y, Δ, is some function of the xs. Indeed, the term on the right of the equals sign

---

[1] Discrete models are easier to represent mathematically, so we restrict our math to those types of theories. However, continuous models are not much more complicated. They simply need an integration function of the following kind: $y_t = y_0 + \int_0^t f(x)$. The key difference is that y at Time t is a function of its initial state, y_0, and the accumulation of the effect of x over the time period considered.

(i.e., the domain) of this last equation is often called the *rate* in dynamic theories because it represents the rate at which *y* is changing as a function of the previous levels of the *X* constructs. Whether one chooses to use discrete or continuous time, the theoretical specification must include an argument for why prior levels of *y* (i.e., y_{t-1}) should or should not be taken into account as well as how prior levels will be changed by the set of influencing constructs [i.e., $f(x_{t-1})$]. Also, note that one of the *x* inputs can also be y_{t-1} and the functions can be additive, multiplicative, or some other operation. Thus, one might have a model in which the effect of a construct *X* on the rate of change of a construct *Y* depends on the prior level of construct *Y*.

When inertia is added to a theoretical model, history matters, and the influence of an event can persist far after the event has completed. This persistence effect can be the source of misinterpreted findings from designs using lagged variables (e.g., the above example in which leader support is interpreted as an aggravator of stress). Moreover, if a construct has inertia, that opens the possibility that the level of that construct can continue to grow (or shrink) over time. For instance, it is well established in conflict research that negative affect can build over the course of a conflict. Part of the reason is because negative affect has inertia, but part of the reason is that negative affect leads those in conflict to act in ways that wind up further increasing the felt negative affect (Brett, Shapiro, & Lytle, 1998). Such evolution is called a *conflict spiral* because the level of negative affect escalates until something happens to abate it. Such escalation is made possible by inertia coupled with the next dynamic property—a circular influence structure that is termed a *feedback loop*.

Feedback Loops

A theory can specify causal structures that loop. In other words, changes to one construct will cause a subsequent chain of causal events that wind up further changing the level of that same construct in the future. Such a circular chain of causality is a feedback loop. Feedback loops tend to have two different varieties: self-reinforcing or self-correcting. The self-reinforcing structure is one in which the

arrows that constitute the causal chain have a net positive effect (e.g., stress leads to more errors, which increases stress). This could be a system in which all the arrows are positive or there is an even number of negative effect arrows (e.g., stress negatively influences cognitive processes, which negatively relates to the likelihood of a performance error, which increases stress). With the second variety—self-correcting structures—the number of negative influences in the loop is an odd number (e.g., stress motivates coping strategies, which mitigate stress).

Many theories in the social sciences recognize that feedback loops are needed to describe phenomena (e.g., Lindsley, Brass, & Thomas, 1995; Locke & Latham, 2004; Vancouver, 1996). Moreover, not considering feedback effects that are at play (e.g., reverse causality) is a kind of misspecification error that can undermine the interpretations of results (James et al., 1982; Vancouver, 2005). However, the implications of feedback loops in terms of conceptualizing and testing theories are rarely fully realized. For example, self-correcting and self-reinforcing feedback loops imply meaningfully different trajectories for the phenomena they represent. Self-correcting feedback structures will find an equilibrium point. As such, they can, on their own, describe phenomena. Positive feedback loops are inherently unstable because they imply infinite runaway growth (or decay). This means that if a model contains a positive feedback loop, there likely needs to be some kind of balancing, negative feedback process that will limit the positive feedback loop's effects. Absent this, the model will "blow up." This might be indicative of the kind of catastrophic change that can come from the underlying structural dynamics of a system (see Chapter 5, this volume). The capacity for such catastrophic change might also indicate a problem with the theory if such end states do not make sense given the phenomenon of interest, a problem we illustrate in a later example.

The notion of feedback in mathematical terms simply involves a small addition to the equations presented above and provides a simple way to understand what feedback means. Specifically, feedback occurs when y_{t-k}, where *k* represents some number of time steps, affects one or more of the xs in the $f(x_{t-1})$ term. This effect can occur via many mediators or with no mediators (e.g., the x_{t-1} is y_{t-1}). For example, increasing performance is presumed to reduce stress, and improving stress is presumed to help performance. Thus, if y is performance and x stress, then a previous level of performance, y_{t-k}, is somewhat determining x and thus y. Moreover, some previous level of stress, x_{t-k}, is somewhat determining y and thus x. In light of this, terms such as *antecedent* and *outcome* become largely meaningless in theories with feedback loops.

The father of general systems theory, von Bertalanffy, mathematically defined a system as one in which a state in the system was somewhat a function—a differential function to be exact—of that state's previous value (von Bertalanffy, 1950). All descriptions of feedback loops must include at least one construct with inertia (Forrester, 1968; Powers, 1978), whether conceptualized continuously (i.e., using a differential function) or discretely as we have done. Otherwise, no effect that occurred in an earlier time period would be retained to affect itself (or other constructs) at a later time period.

The issue of persistence over time makes determining timescale of particular importance, especially with respect to thinking about feedback. Feedback loops could be conceptualized as either cyclically recursive or nonrecursive[2] (James et al., 1982). We have been describing cyclically recursive models in which the sequence of influence is discernible. For example, stress (Y) at Time 1 leads to supervisory support (X) at Time 2, reducing stress at Time 3, possibly diminishing the need for supervisory support at Time 4 and so on. Cyclically recursive models are more amenable to prediction and control because the cause-and-effect cycles can be arranged into identifiable chains (James et al., 1982). In nonrecursive models the $X \rightarrow Y$ and $Y \rightarrow X$ causal links are rapid and indiscernible. James et al. gave the example of escalation in protestor violence (X) and police violence (Y) in response to situational factors such as the presence of riot gear

(A_1), the number of verbal obscenities (A_2), and so forth. Yet a closer inspection suggests that models would be recursive or nonrecursive depending on the timescale.

We suggest that nonrecursive models can be made into cyclically recursive models provided the timescale is short enough. Even in James et al.'s (1982) example of police and protestor violence, we presume that there is action and reaction at some timescale (as opposed to simultaneous action). The question for the theorist is whether changing a nonrecursive model to a cyclical one is actually helpful for understanding the phenomenon. In the above example of violence escalation, if the interest is in how certain antecedent conditions (riot gear, obscenities) incite the violence process, the specific dynamics of the X–Y feedback loop may be unimportant. One could model what starts, stops, speeds, or slows a nonrecursive loop, but because the links are simultaneous, one could not model the dynamics of the loop itself. If one were interested in the actions and reactions, perhaps the perceptual and interpretive processes, of people in crowds at these protests, finding an appropriate timescale so that the cyclical recursion could be modeled would likely be needed.

It is possible, even probable, that multiple constructs in a loop have inertia. This creates a special concern when representing a dynamic theory using discrete modeling because each time an effect is passed through a variable with inertia, it is delayed by one time step (i.e., the more time steps it takes for an effect to transgress the loop).[3] If the length of a time step is inappropriately specified, this can lead to a poorly represented phenomenon, at least in terms of the speed at which the processes play out. This adds a challenge in specifying the appropriate timescale for change in a phenomenon because the empirical data are often not available for knowing the timescale. Such knowledge is not needed prior to building a dynamic model. However, it will be a puzzle piece that should eventually be found, and predictions of the speed of effects from

---

[2]Nonrecursive in this case implies a process that loops back upon itself. It is yet another unfortunate case in American English of using a word for its own antonym (such as *acute*).
[3]In a continuous representation, the effect represents as beginning essentially instantaneously, but the time step is still important because it determines the amount of the effect that occurs given the rate specified in the model. Meanwhile, this rate can be a free parameter estimated from data.

a model cannot be assumed to be correct without this piece of the puzzle. Despite this challenge, a reason for representing theory is to highlight gaps in knowledge and assumptions. In the case of dynamic modeling, an assumption regarding the speed of processing will often be necessary early on in the model development and theory testing process. Thus, dynamic theories will often highlight gaps in knowledge regarding the rates of processes.

Finally, we have not mentioned how to depict feedback loops visually yet. The answer is straightforward: with arrows. That is, influences or signals from one construct that affect or are inputs to another construct should be represented with an arrow pointing at the affected or receiving construct. In the case of a direct feedback effect (e.g., the greater the size of the debt, the more quickly the debt increases given some interest rate), the arrow would point at the construct, which must have inertia, from which the arrow initiated. Generally, this would likely be rare because specifying the mechanisms with the system that cause change within the system (i.e., endogenous change) is a major purpose of the theory. However, there may be cases in which the process of endogenous change is not of much interest, but, as we note in the next section, needs to be included in the dynamic model to avoid a misspecification error (James et al., 1982). Importantly, the direct feedback case is different from the inertia property. Specifically, in the direct feedback case, y is both within (i.e., is one of the xs in) $f(x_{t-1})$ as well as outside of it. Or, more explicitly: $y_t = y_{t-1} + f(y_{t-1}, x_{t-1})$. This means one is specifying that the prior value of y affects the *rate of change* to the previous value of y. This is why we do not advocate the arrow pointing at self to represent inertia. Rather, the arrow pointing at self represents the special case of a feedback loop with no specified mediators (i.e., x variables).

Four other points need to be made when discussing arrows and feedback loops. First, because of the importance of the difference between positive and negative feedback loops, many advocate inclusion of the sign of each effect (i.e., for each arrow). That way it is easy to follow the arrows, count the number of negative signs, and determine the sign of the loop (i.e., even negative signs make a positive loop and uneven negative signs a negative loop; Richardson, 1991). We do not oppose this convention, but we would note that some functional relationships might not lend themselves to this monotonic representation (e.g., cyclical effect represented using a sine wave; stress's relationship to performance).

Second, the arrows in dynamic models represent the notion that the origin of the influence or signal affects the construct across the time scope represented by the model. Yet, some constructs with inertia may affect other parts of the system only at their introduction (e.g., construct Y has an initial value, y_0, that plays a role only at the start of the model). Vancouver (e.g., Vancouver, Weinhardt, & Vigo, 2014) uses a line with a dot to represent this relationship. We adopt that convention here (this is illustrated in a later example).

Third, we have been using the language "influence or signal" to describe what might be traversing an arrow in the last several paragraphs. This is because the common understanding of cause (i.e., influence) is often not appropriate for what one construct is doing to another construct over time, particularly if the "affected" construct does not have inertia. Consider, for example, the notion that one might experience distress when the level of stress experienced exceeds some threshold level. The threshold is not a cause of distress; only the stress is. However, the threshold value represents the level of stress where distress begins to emerge. In general, Forrester (1968) described policies (in organizations or other entries) in terms of actions that are initiated or stopped once some condition is met. The construct representing the condition is not thought of as a cause but rather a signal. Vancouver (2000) described in some detail how confusing the two led the authors of the TOTE model (test, operate, test, and exit—a simple, highly discrete description of a control system or policy; see Miller, Galanter, & Pribram, 1960) to draw some erroneous conclusions from their theory that disrupted psychology's view of goal systems for decades. That said, we do not advocate a special visual method for depicting the difference. Rather, we think the arrows should be thought of as representing the flow of information in the broad sense of information theory (Shannon, 1948).

Finally, and related to the above, we would recommend that constructs that one might hypothesize as playing a moderator role should point not at an arrow (i.e., path diagram convention) but rather at a construct that represents the presumed reason or location of the moderating effect. Partially this is because dynamic models will often be about explicating the processes that produce effects, and it is these that are affected by the moderator. More generally, this is because the arrows pointing at a construct indicate what terms go into the functional equation used to determine the value of the construct at every time point (especially if the model is computation and can be simulated). With regard to dynamic processes, many operations beyond multiplication, which is how moderation is generally operationalized, may be needed to properly represent a system. Creating special ways of depicting these equations and where the construct fits into each of them would be daunting (e.g., base vs. exponential in exponential term). Instead, we advocate the specification of the math so that the nature of the theorized effects the signals have is unambiguous. In fact, the math will become important and the nature of the functions a bit more complex when we consider the notion of asymmetric influence in the next section.

Asymmetric Influence

In conventional verbal or path model diagrams of a theory, a relationship of X causing Y implies symmetry of influence. That is, the notion is that as X goes up, Y goes up (down), and as X goes down, Y goes down (up) for relationships presumed to be positive (negative). This might be reasonable when X and Y are constructs that have reached some stable value via prior, but settled, processes in which the X variable led to the Y construct's value. Recall, this is a condition of testing causal models based on between-unit variances obtained from cross-sectional designs (James et al., 1982). However, in theorizing about dynamic processes, the notion that

some construct, X, might move another construct, Y, both higher and lower is difficult to conceptualize. Rather, what moves a construct up is likely different from what moves a construct down. This is what we mean by asymmetric influence.

Consider, for example, stressors that cause stress. Stressors above some level will increase stress. If a stressed system (stress has inertia so it can retain its level) were then to be in a condition of no stressors, stress would likely go down. However, the mechanism causing the level of stress to decrease is not the absence of stressors but rather coping with them. Coping is what decreases stress. Indeed, coping may be occurring when the stressors are occurring, and if sufficiently effective the coping may counter the effects of the stressors. If the stressors were completely balanced by the effects of coping, stress might stay relatively constant (i.e., maintain an equilibrium). If stressors exceed coping effects, stress rises, and if coping more than counters stressors, stress may decrease if it is not already nonexistent. The point is to illustrate that stressors affect stress in only one direction, and coping affects stress in only the other direction; both have asymmetric influence.[4]

Visual asymmetric effects are represented in system dynamic models by the direction of a special sort of arrow (i.e., double lined) that points either to or away from a construct with inertia, depending on whether the factors that determine the rate of change increase or decrease the level of the construct, respectively (see Appendix 4.1). Our preference is to allow the sign of the effect to signal the direction of the change (see Figure 4.2). In particular, when a construct points at a construct with inertia, the exogenous construct is represented as determining the rate of change to the endogenous construct. The sign determines the direction of that change provided the signs of the values of the exogenous construct are constant (e.g., preferably always positive). Indeed, mathematically, the key to representing asymmetric effects is via sign and bounding the cause to positive numbers. Thus, if

---

[4]As always, we note that the direction and symmetry of an effect depend on what the theorist means. It is conceivable that the resources used by the coping mechanism stress the system (e.g., "stress tests" of financial institutions relate to how coping with stressors affects a firm resources). Indeed, one could conceptualize a model in which coping is not the source of stress on a system but rather in which coping is engaged as a response to constructs that one might label stressors in such a model.

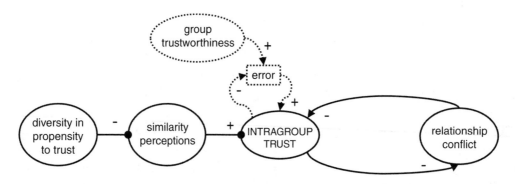

FIGURE 4.2.   A dynamic model of the processes possibly at play in the Ferguson and Peterson (2015) data. Dotted elements were added to create a working model.

x increases a variable and z decreases it, the equation might be $y_t = y_{t-1} + b_1 x_{t-1} - b_2 z_{t-1}$, where x and z are constrained to be 0 or positive (i.e., ≥ 0). Moreover, upper bounds are often recommended because the constructs represented are likely limited in the heights they can reach. In a later example this becomes a critical issue, and mathematical modelers often handle it with sigmoid functions (i.e., also called s-curves or ogive curves). In the example, we show how this might be represented in a simple way in dynamic, computational models.

The issue of asymmetric influence stems from the nature of change; that is, what causes something to change in one direction is often not the same thing that causes it to change in the other direction. The last element of dynamic theorizing is a function of the fact that things change, and feedback is a common feature of systems. Thus, if one is trying to understand some phenomenon that involves change and feedback loops, the change needs to be incorporated within the boundary of the model. That is, it must be endogenous to the model.

Endogenous Change

The notion of endogenous change is similar to the notion of self-contained functional equations in structural modeling (James et al., 1982). Self-containment means that all the relevant causes to some variable are included in the functional equation that represents how that cause obtains its value. In the case of a model of change, this requirement is specifically important when

considering feedback processes. In dynamic modeling endogenous change means that all feedback loops that can affect constructs in the model over the period of time modeled must be included in the model. It is the same as the dictum that any construct that might affect effects and other causes must be included in recursive (i.e., nonfeedback) models. Otherwise, the predictions of how a construct changes over time will be underspecified.

The inclination to include all relevant feedback loops in a model suggests that dynamic models will be hugely complex. In fact, dynamic models can get this way (e.g., Beer, 1966), and thus the tendency to be all-inclusive often needs to be actively tempered. Forrester (1968) may have put it best when he originally articulated the concept of endogenous change: "[Determine] the boundary, that encompasses the smallest number of components, within which the dynamic behavior under study is generated" (p. 4-2). The key is to separate the processes of interest from processes that might be active but of little interest to the point of the model. For example, one might be interested in the relationship between leader support and stress; in such a model one should assume that opponent processes that reduce stress independent of leader actions are engaged when a system is stressed (Muraven & Baumeister, 2000). The effects of these processes need to be represented, but because they are not central to the question at hand (e.g., what are the implications of coping behavior), they may not need to be unpacked. That is, they could be represented as a direct feedback loop, $f(y_{t-1})$, without intermediate X constructs.

Moreover, dynamic modeling is often used to vet theories of specific processes. The dynamic model is developed to determine if the processes *could* explain a phenomenon. An example of this type of model was provided by Vancouver, Li, Weinhardt, Steel, and Purl (2016). Specifically, they modeled luck, learning, and resource allocation processes related to job performance to assess various possible sources of positively skewed distributions in job performance observed in real-world data (O'Boyle & Aguinis, 2012). Via this type of modeling they were able to rule out the notion that distributions of stable exogenous individual differences could be responsible for the job performance distributions but retained the notion that positive feedback loop processes involving learning and resource allocation policies could be responsible. Similarly, in an example below we use a simple model to explore a dynamic theory of team trust. The model shows that underspecifying the feedback processes is a problem but that adding one more endogenous process might well correct the problem.

Limiting the model to be as simple as possible, but no simpler, is a critical skill in dynamic theorization. Often many factors affect a system, but not all have substantive influence on the theoretical question of interest. For example, oxygen is needed for any operation by a biological organism to function, but one can usually assume oxygen will be present in sufficient quantities (i.e., without dropping to dangerous levels) for most phenomena of interest to social scientists. Moreover, it might be that a construct thought relevant for explaining a phenomenon does not need to be represented in a dynamic model of that phenomenon. For example, Forrester's (1968) classic model of market growth (and decline) was designed to show how the processes internal (i.e., endogenous) to organizations can lead to their downfall via fewer customers, even when an infinite number of customers is assumed (Richardson, 2011).

We have now described four elements of dynamic processes that are frequently not a part of conventional theorizing but that are critical to any theory of change. Below we apply these notions to issues associated with multilevel phenomena and then discuss how the elements play out with a specific example.

MULTILEVEL DYNAMICS

One purpose of theory is to synthesize existing empirical work into coherent and evidence-based explanations for a phenomenon. Within the context of a particular investigation, theory must guide decisions about how to gather evidence about the nature of the variables under study. Taken together, the dynamic properties we have discussed open up several new avenues of investigation. Some of these avenues will refine the scope of the theories that are proposed. For instance, dynamics helps clarify an important aspect of omnibus context of *when* something happens (cf. Johns, 2006)—an issue that tends to be overlooked or minimized in many theories in the social and behavioral sciences. Specifications of *when* can be used as a boundary condition on theory (e.g., damage from relationship conflict cannot be fixed beyond some tipping point). Some new avenues of investigation can add depth to understanding of phenomena that already have some degree of temporal theorization. For instance, trust has been theorized to transform from being calculus-based to relationship-based as the relationship develops (Rousseau, Sitkin, Burt, & Camerer, 1998). It is possible to use our dynamic properties to explicitly model what is now only understood descriptively. But these are all instances of the broader capability that dynamics provides—a way to explain, predict, and control some phenomena over time. Dynamic properties make it possible to move beyond theorizing about average or settled relationships among concepts to theorizing about the variation that happens within and among them.

Given that this chapter is in a handbook on multilevel research, we want to highlight why it is particularly critical in multilevel theory to take dynamics into consideration. Multilevel theory is ripe for dynamic theorization because modeling how influence traverses levels necessitates the consideration of the time it takes for such influence to manifest at the different level. Moreover, because the levels exist simultaneously, there is also a strong reason to describe how feedback occurs between the levels. Yet, as several scholars have noted, most research about multilevel processes tests models of unidirectional and static influence chains (Cronin, Weingart, & Todorova, 2011; Kozlowski & Bell, 2003; McGrath, Arrow, & Berdahl, 2000). Building models that imply linear causality (i.e., no feedback loops) is a hard habit to break (Waller et al., 2016). Trying to incorporate the dynamic properties we have proposed provides an opportunity to sharpen theories of multilevel phenomena. Such dynamics can be incorporated into the contextual (properties of the higher level entity that affect lower level entities) and emergent (properties at the higher level that arise from the interaction among lower level entities) characterizations that are part of the language of multilevel models (Kozlowski, 2012). It is useful to reiterate and synthesize some of the lessons emerging from our earlier discussion into principles for use when constructing multilevel dynamic theory. These principles are aligned with the within-level issues discussed in the prior section, but they are tailored to multilevel analysis as a way to help researchers break from their linear chain habits.

> **Principle 1:** For any conceptual model, first identify which constructs do and do not have inertia.[5]

It is not simply that inertia is necessary for dynamics. Collectively, the inertial variables will determine the "state space" of the system—the possible ways in which the phenomenon may exist. This will create a natural boundary condition for the theory. For instance, in their study of conflict profiles, O'Neill, McLarnon, Hoffart, Woodley, and Allen (2015) hypothesized that although task, process, and relationship conflict could all rise and fall in their levels, certain combinations were implausible given the dynamics among the processes connecting these variables (e.g., one would not

find groups with high relationship and low process conflict because of their reciprocal influence). Because the constructs that have inertia are always in some form of existence, they are the foundation for the states into which a system can evolve.

A common source of inertial constructs in a multilevel system would be found in the contextual realm, which are typically thought of as "top down" (Kozlowski, 2012). Top-down constructs are argued to influence how lower level entities exist and interact (e.g., a group contextual property could be its diversity, its autonomy, or its task, among others) but may themselves change over the time frame the theory is presumed to span. Importantly, when they change, it is likely from their previous states, as opposed to some new value unrelated to a previous value. Compilational (e.g., the functional diversity requires specialization and coordination of roles) constructs are particularly likely to have inertia (Kozlowski & Klein, 2000).

Some contextual constructs are simply functions of the structural features of the collective (e.g., the level of demographic diversity; cf. Cronin et al., 2011), whereas others can be imposed by exogenous sources (e.g., a team is granted a level of autonomy by the organizational leadership). From a dynamic perspective, contextual constructs represent a source of inertia because they are often maintained by the conditions of the collective and thus are inclined toward stability over time. Absent some change process, a diverse group at Time 1 will be a diverse group at Time 2. Even if membership changes, it will change in relation to the prior conditions. Most often the inertia in a contextual factor comes from constancy in the properties of the level units that create it (e.g., in our example, the members possess stable demographic properties, but membership can change, albeit slowly).

Contextual features are not the only source of inertia in multilevel theory; emergence is as well. It is just that such inertia may take time to form. Emergent phenomena are typically thought of as "bottom up" (Kozlowski, 2012). Lower level elements interact to produce the higher level effects (e.g., disagreements among members in a team

---

[5]This is a reiteration of Forrester's oft-stated heuristic of "first identify the stocks."

cause team-level conflict to emerge). Such effects may also be compositional (e.g., the formation of a shared level of trust) or compilational (e.g., the splitting of the group into factions; Chan, 1998; Kozlowski & Klein, 2000). Yet for emergent constructs, one must think more carefully about the persistence of what emerges. The lower level process is the activity that produces the higher level construct, but the question is whether the influence of that construct will persist when the lower level activity stops. It is easy to imagine constructs where it does—team members who work to build trust with each other can stop their trust-building activity and have the level persist. Alternatively, there can be constructs where this does not happen; team effort might disappear the minute the team members stop trying. Finally, there can be constructs that emerge and fade. The feeling of being in conflict often persists beyond the momentary disagreements between team members that engendered the original experience of conflict, but these feelings may fade or diminish over time. The bottom line is that emergent phenomena require careful thought about the inertia of the higher level construct that emerges.

The determination of inertia among contextual and emergent factors also highlights the need to consider the appropriate timescale in which change can happen. Whereas some changes can be instantaneous (e.g., personnel changes to a team), others cannot be (e.g., the development of a transactive memory system in a team). The difference between a construct that has inertia, one that does not have inertia, or one that is constant may often come down to timescale. Decisions about inertia thus wind up requiring appropriate choices about timescale. Because inertial variables can change at different rates, aligning the timescale across variables will be key.

> **Principle 2:** For any conceptual model, identify how long it takes for inertial variables to change their levels and set the timescale boundary accordingly.

Fundamentally, when one is theorizing about how inertia can manifest in a multilevel system, one needs to ask of all the concepts: (a) How is the

level of the construct maintained over time? and (b) Can the construct continue to influence other aspects of the system even without maintenance of the level? With these two concerns it is critical to consider that the maintenance of and effect of an inertial variable's condition may cross levels. When considering how long it takes for an inertial variable's condition to change and how long it will naturally persist, one can make decisions more in terms of the focal constructs. Having identified the sources of inertia in a phenomenon, the next step is to think about feedback.

> **Principle 3:** Once the inertial variables have been identified and a timescale for the evolution of the system chosen, one must identify the reciprocal causality among the factors in the model.

Specifying feedback loops is essentially just entertaining the idea that there might be reverse causality in addition to the initial causality postulated. Or there might be a long but still looping causal chain. It is why this step tends to be a straightforward use of a well-honed skill—thinking about whether one factor influences another. What is critical is not resting until all hope of finding a feedback loop (or another feedback loop) is exhausted. Most things are related to themselves one way or another, plus another.

Then once loops are closed, one also needs to think about the linkage polarity to identify which are self-reinforcing and which are self-correcting. We get to this step in Principle 5. What can be tricky is that the loop may cross levels, so it necessitates thinking about emergence and contextual influence a bit differently.

Because dynamic theory characterizes influence over time, the way contextual and emergent processes manifest can be a bit different when making dynamic multilevel theory. Namely, once an emergent construct comes into existence, if it persists it could influence lower and upper level interactions much the way contextual constructs do. For example, once trust has emerged (bottom up) and been established in the group, the level of trust in that group acts as part of the context that affects ongoing interactions among group members (top down). Yet, as group trust affects the interaction among group members, such interaction may subsequently alter the level of group trust. Bottom-up and top-down processes can thus form feedback loops.

The feedback and processes determining higher and lower level constructs mean that the contextual/emergent distinction may not be as clear as one might assume. In a single time period these labels might clarify the direction of influence, but when time is added to the model, they lose their distinctiveness. Abandoning the need to keep contextual and emergent properties unidirectional allows for specification of a critical dynamic in multilevel systems—how many aspects of collective life happen to converge to a shared experience (i.e., compositional structures). This same feedback process could be used to explain how compilational structures emerge if one considers opposing polarity of influence in feedback structures. For example, as the contextual experience of demographic faultlines converges (+), it pushes apart the lower level elements (−) causing differentiation (c.f. Lau & Murnighan, 1998). Faction formation would be an example of such a process (Carton & Cummings, 2012). In Chapter 7 of this volume, Mathieu and Luciano provide a wealth of recommendations with respect to the articulation and study of emergence both within and across levels of analysis. They also explore the varied patterns of emergence that can be exhibited (e.g., growth, finding an equilibrium, dissipation, oscillation). The clear articulation of inertia and feedback will be critical for leveraging this work.

Many higher level factors in multilevel theory engage lower level processes when the factors come into existence. We mean that if the higher level factor exists, then the lower level processes necessarily operate. It therefore behooves researchers to consider whether higher-level constructs enact lower level endogenous process as a condition of their existence. With stress, for example, the level that is felt by an individual may change endogenously because of the individual's "psychological immune system," which is a process that is interindividual (and hence lower level). Yet, there is no way to uncouple that process from

stress—if stress exists, that process is engaged. This would be unlike anxiety, which could be modeled as a lower level process that affects stress but would not operate simply because stress has risen beyond some threshold. The point here is that once one has identified an upper level construct, it is critical to identify whether there are endogenous lower level change processes that must be part of the theory of how that upper level concept will persist over time.

> **Principle 4:** For each upper level construct, consider whether there are lower level processes that must operate on upper level constructs. If these processes can change the state of the upper level construct within the identified timescale, they must be included in the model.

Many concepts in the social sciences imply endogenous change processes at lower levels— essentially anything that grows or seeks an equilibrium level once it exists. To use a simple example, a colony of bacteria will grow because of mitosis (assuming appropriate food and other enabling conditions). To claim some factor affects this would have to be done with respect to that growth pattern. We might argue that if an organization exists, an organizational culture must exist, and therefore this culture will emerge from and be perpetuated by lower level processes. We imagine that although researchers understand intuitively that many attributes in the social sciences evolve on their own over time, there is scant reason to identify the endogenous change processes that affect the construct's state over time (Why would there be? Most research is static). But if a higher level concept always engages a lower level endogenous change process, we cannot understand how other factors affect that higher level construct without accounting for the evolution due to the endogenous change process.

Identifying what factors have endogenous change processes is again a question of boundary conditions. Timescale determines what kind of change would be detectable in the higher level construct. For example, in group learning (cf. Wilson, Goodman, & Cronin, 2007), there is a forgetting process in the individuals of the group. Such a process can affect retention depending on the length of time between the encoding of knowledge and its recall. The phenomenon being studied would determine which, if any, of the endogenous processes might need to be accounted for. For example, if one were studying group learning with respect to the refinement of common routines or instantiation into policy, the forgetting function might be less relevant.

The last point we want to make is relatively simple but important for multilevel theory, which is that what brings concepts into existence may not be what makes them go away. This is particularly important with emergence but can apply to a great many concepts across levels. Some lower level activity, such as trust violations, may cause a group-level concept, such as mistrust, to emerge or change. However, ceasing those violations may not cause the group-level concept to go away. Lessening the activity slows the growth but does not eliminate it. Alternately, organizational policies on compensation are widely understood to at best not upset people in the organization (Herzberg, 1974). This is an asymmetric top-down effect. Although this point is probably very easy to grasp, its implications are rarely a part of group or organization-level theory. This point is even more important when considering dynamics because of the implication on the polarity of the links in a feedback loop.

> **Principle 5:** Having identified all the influence links in a system, decide whether the influence represented is symmetric or asymmetric. Be clear about the polarity and the rationale for this in the theory and model.

Asymmetric influence may also help to explain how some lower level interaction patterns are more easily modified than others when there are changes to higher level attributes. For example, Hollenbeck, Ellis, Humphrey, Garza, and Ilgen (2011) showed that changing from a decentralized to a centralized decision structure was harder for command and control teams to manage than the reverse. The asymmetry in this case occurred because of the

variance in ease with which the team members could alter their interaction patterns given their prior experience. Centralized teams had no problem decentralizing, but decentralized teams had a real problem structuring their interactions to reap the efficiency benefits of a centralized structure. This kind of asymmetry requires explanation in terms of the lower level adaptation processes that come in response to the habits formed as a result of the higher level conditions. Such theory should not assume that all change is equally difficult.

Hollenbeck et al. (2011) pointed out that discovery of asymmetries like theirs is not possible with cross-sectional research. They stress the need for longitudinal research. We and others (Cronin et al., 2011; Hanges & Wang, 2012) agreed. Because the theoretical models guide the design and execution of investigations as well as the methodological tools brought to bear, in the last section we demonstrate how to apply the four dynamic properties to advance and refine thought on the appropriate means of theory testing. We also use this opportunity to illustrate the ability to keep the model simple. That is, much of the above discussion is designed to illustrate the opportunities that a dynamic approach to theorizing offers, particularly from a multilevel perspective, but we do not want to leave the impression that all these opportunities need to be realized in any particular dynamic theory.

NEW KINDS OF QUESTIONS, NEW KINDS OF ANALYSES

Having talked about some of the general uses of dynamics for multilevel theory, we think it also useful to demonstrate how to use the four properties to advance thinking in a more specific context. In this final section, we illustrate how one might use these new tools for theorizing to enrich the models that are offered and tested in the social sciences. We are going to use an example that used a very sophisticated empirical design and analytic (i.e., statistical) model recently published in a top journal. The model comes from a study on the effect of group-level diversity in trust propensity on group-level performance via intragroup trust

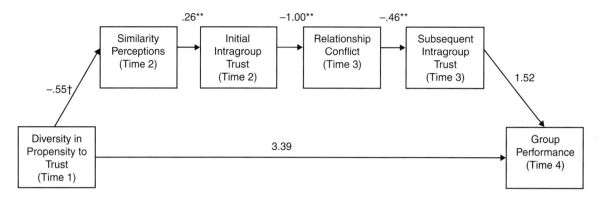

FIGURE 4.3. Four-stage mediation model of the effect of diversity in propensity to trust on group performance. Unstandardized regression coefficients are shown. Time 1 = prior to university entrance; Time 2 = after the first week of team interaction; Time 3 = end of term but before grades; Time 4 = grade on project was given. †p < .10. **p < .01. From "Sinking Slowly: Diversity in Propensity to Trust Predicts Downward Trust Spirals in Small Groups," by A. J. Ferguson and R. S. Peterson, 2015, *Journal of Applied Psychology, 100*, p. 1019. Copyright 2015 by the American Psychological Association.

(Ferguson & Peterson, 2015).[6] The analytic model is reproduced in Figure 4.3. The model is interesting in several ways. First, it includes at least one variable with inertia (i.e., intragroup trust) and a feedback loop (i.e., trust affects relationship conflict, which affects trust). Indeed, the study was designed to test a variant of a theory with a positive feedback loop thought to lead to a downward, reinforcing spiral of distrust (Zand, 1972). The variant was that diversity in propensity to trust, rather than or in addition to average level of propensity to trust, was thought to initiate the spiral. The significant coefficients noted in Figure 4.3 were used to interpret the validity of the theory and its predictions.

The interpretation of the above model is described as follows. People differ in how much they are willing to trust those they do not know (i.e., the variance in a group of the individual-level construct *trust propensity*). These variations in trust propensity determine the level of similarity perceived among team members by those on a new team (i.e., the greater the variation in individual trust propensity, the lower the level of perceived similarity within the team). This perception of similarity then determines an initial level of trust the team members have toward each other (i.e.,

intragroup trust). The level of trust inversely relates to relationship conflict (i.e., low trust leads to relationship conflict). Subsequent relationship conflict further decreases intergroup trust. Finally, intergroup distrust was presumed to diminish group performance, though we do not consider this last step in the model developed here, given that the interesting dynamics appear to occur before this final step.

As we think about the model through the lens of dynamics, the theory as described raises a question. In particular, it describes a positive feedback loop (i.e., trust decreases relationship conflict, and relationship conflict decreases trust), which might be better understood if the polarity of trust is switched (i.e., distrust increases conflict, which increases distrust). As noted above, positive feedback loops tend to lead to escalating processes (i.e., runaway behavior). Thus, it might be informative to explore the theory that Ferguson and Peterson (2015) described using the tools of the dynamic modeler (i.e., computational models and simulation). To guide this investigation, we constructed the model (solid lines and ovals in Figure 4.2) described by Ferguson and Peterson using the dynamic properties we have been discussing.

[6]We thank Amanda Ferguson and Randall Peterson for supporting and encouraging our use of their model as our exemplar for the limitations of nondynamic theorization.

One of the first things to note about the model is that we represent intragroup trust as having inertia. Hence, this construct's label is in all capitals to depict this property. Intragroup trust is depicted with inertia because it both retains its value and changes over time in the time frame simulated. Indeed, the Ferguson and Peterson (2015) investigation had as its centerpiece a presumed dynamic conceptualization of trust. Specifically, they conceptualized trust as something that evolves from a starting point (before there was team member interaction) and that can spiral upward or downward depending on the interaction patterns (i.e., relationship conflict) among group members.

We should also note that diversity in propensity to trust, similarity perceptions, and relationship conflict are not represented as constructs with inertia, which may seem odd given that the diversity in propensity to trust construct would be expected to retain its value over time. Moreover, the perception of a relatively stable attribute (i.e., similarity) likely has inertia and might even change over the time frame of the study (one semester) of the Ferguson and Peterson (2015) study. However, in the theory represented it plays no role beyond the initializing of the trust construct. In particular, the initializing of the trust construct, by the similarity perceptions, is represented by the dot at the end of the line from similarity perceptions to intragroup trust. As noted above, this means that the similarity variable determined the initial level of intragroup trust (see Figure 4.3 as well). Likewise, diversity of propensity to trust is connected to similarity perceptions to indicate it plays no role beyond the initial time step. Meanwhile, one might remember that Ferguson and Peterson measured propensity to trust in a data collection wave prior to the measurement of any of the other constructs in the model, but this is conceptually unimportant given propensity to trust is considered a stable individual difference variable.[7] Finally, we did not represent relationship conflict as a construct with inertia because it was not conceptualized this way in the theory. Arguably, this is reasonable

because it represents what is happening in a group behaviorally at any particular instance. That said, relationship conflict is conceivable as a construct with inertia because the conflict is retained in the minds and memories of the people experiencing it. This demonstrates that the conceptualization of a construct (e.g., as a behavior or a belief) must be clear when considering the dynamics.

In terms of feedback loops, one can see that a feedback loop is evident in the relationship between intragroup trust and relationship conflict and that it is a self-reinforcing feedback loop because the number of negative signs in the loop is even (Richardson, 1991). Note that this representation is different from the way Ferguson and Peterson (2015) depicted the model (Figure 4.3). This is because the Ferguson and Peterson depiction is useful for setting up the analysis and presenting the results from such analysis. Ours is meant to represent the conceptual space in a parsimonious way.

Before addressing the issues of asymmetric influences and endogenous change, we need to point out that the choices one makes about the structure of influence in a model, as well as how such influence persists (or not) over time, can be very complicated to imagine unaided by a computational model (Cronin, Gonzalez, & Sterman, 2009; Farrell & Lewandowsky, 2010). Operationalizing a theory computationally, therefore, helps substantially in assessing its validity. In this case, it will allow us to illustrate the relevance of the elements described above. Specifically, we operationalized the model in Figure 4.2 using the weights derived from the Ferguson and Peterson (2015) findings (see Figure 4.3). Specifically, the mean value for diversity of propensity to trust found in the Ferguson and Peterson study was 0.54 ($SD = 0.19$), so .50 was chosen as a default value and operationalized as a construct that could range from 0 to 1. Similarity perceptions were calculated by subtracting diversity in propensity to trust, weighted by −0.55, from 3.5 (i.e., similarity perceptions' midpoint on the scale). Likewise, intragroup trust was initiated at 0.26 times similarity perceptions. It was also changed at a rate

---

[7]It might be important methodologically because it might reduce measurement error due to common method bias (MacKenzie & Podsakoff, 2012).

determined by subtracting the value in relationship conflict weighted by 0.46. Finally, relationship conflict was its mean (i.e., 3) minus the value of intragroup trust.

To simulate the model described above, we set a 15-week time frame with 1-week time steps to represent a single semester, which was the time frame of the Ferguson and Peterson (2015) study. We used Vensim® PLE, available free for academics from http://www.Vensim.com (see Appendix 4.1 for the code used). As expected, the results highlighted a problem with the theory as specified. Specifically, the simulation led to an escalating drop in intragroup trust and an escalating rise in relationship conflict. This result was robust. That is, changing the weights or diversity of propensity to trust values changed the rate of this escalation but not the pattern. The result suggests that if the processes were accurately described, all groups would eventually devolve into a cauldron of conflict and mutual distrust.

A counterargument might be that a theoretical–methodological mismatch comes from how we have modeled trust and conflict. That is, we have allowed these parameters to change and exist in ways that do not fit with their real-life concepts. For example, intragroup trust cannot really drop below 0, and conflict could not increase to infinity. The modeler must take care to find functional forms for the constructs that are valid, and this extra step is often not part of how theorizing is typically done. We may think about measurement scales, but such scales are naturally bounded with floors and ceilings. When we simulate, such factors need to be built into the computational model. For example, one could weight that which is presumed to change the variable by the variable itself so that as it approaches 0, the effect of the change approaches 0. Likewise, one could weight that which changes the variable by the upper limit (e.g., 7) minus the variable so that as the variable approaches this upper limit, the effect of the change also approaches 0. It is through these functions that a sigmoid pattern is achieved (i.e., smaller changes at the high and low ends of

the construct).[8] That said, the bounded model also revealed a problem with the theory. In particular, intragroup trust always dropped to 0, even when diversity in propensity to trust was set to 0. The dynamics of the model, as thus far specified, simply forced trust to drop, which it does until it can drop no further.

The issues noted above for the variation of Zand's (1972) theory that Ferguson and Peterson (2015) sought to test are not unique to either the variation or Zand's theory. Most theories that include an uncontrolled positive feedback loop suffer from similar problems, and the field is replete with such models. To produce the realities they are meant to explain, these models require balancing negative feedback processes that moderate the positive feedback effect. Indeed, we believe adding such a process may fix that which ails the intragroup trust model.

In particular, the intragroup trust model assumes that initial propensities to trust, which in the Ferguson and Peterson (2015) study were obtained prior to the group members ever meeting, drives a process involved in determining intragroup trust and relationship conflict. Yet, another endogenous change process is also likely occurring during the time frame covered by the model. One of the primary determinants of trust is the trustworthiness of the targets (Mayer, Davis, & Schoorman, 1995). That is, group members have some level of trustworthiness aggregated to the group level in some way (e.g., average trustworthiness of members; trustworthiness of least trustworthy member), so we added this construct to the model. Second, we assumed that intragroup trust is moderated by the level of group trustworthiness. We therefore added a negative feedback loop (i.e., uneven negative effects in loop) in which group trustworthiness was compared with intragroup trust. Specifically, the difference between these signals represents an error in the team's trust of the group, which is used to "correct" the intragroup trust level (e.g., error = group trustworthiness − intragroup trust). This causes intragroup trust to approach

---

[8]In addition, the weight of effects often has to be reduced to avoid simulation errors or oscillating behavior. In particular, we reduced the weight of the effect of relationship conflict on intragroup trust by a factor of 10 (i.e., to 0.046) to obtain a well-behaved model.

the group's trustworthiness level. However, unlike relationship conflict, which can only asymmetrically reduce intragroup trust, error can take on both positive and negative values, though error is always "added" to intragroup trust. Meanwhile we rescaled intragroup trust to range from 0 to 1 by multiplying the two feedback inputs by intragroup trust and one minus intragroup trust. Finally, we set group trustworthiness to the midpoint (i.e., 0.5). We then ran two simulations: one with diversity in propensity to trust set to 0 and one where it was set to 1. The results of these simulations on intragroup trust over time are shown in Figure 4.4.

The results shown in Figure 4.4 and found in the model reveal several important points. First, they reveal a model of dynamic processes that are reasonable. That is, a group's trust for each other

likely differs initially as a function of initially relevant variables such as diversity in propensity to trust, but over time it becomes more of a function of the dynamic processes involved in learning the trustworthiness of the group. Second, the effects found in Ferguson and Peterson (2015) could be found if this model were accurately describing the processes involved. That is, diversity in propensity to trust is negatively related to similarity perceptions and to intragroup trust at Times 1 and 2, though these relationships disappear by Time 15 given the parameters on the model simulated. Moreover, the level of relationship conflict is negatively related to the degree to which intragroup trust falls over the course of the 15 weeks. This could be the negative effect captured in the −0.46 coefficient shown in Figure 4.3 given the nature of the

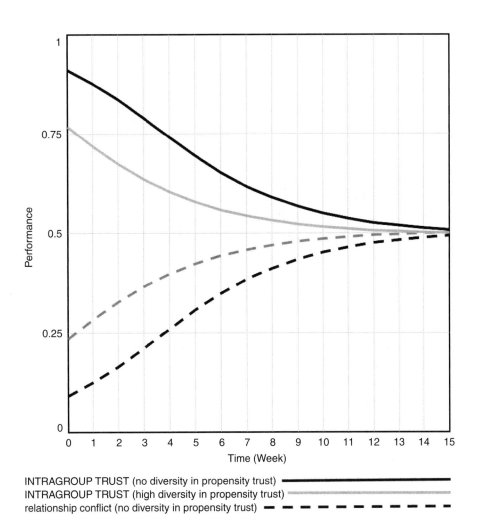

FIGURE 4.4.   Simulation results for final model in Figure 4.2.

analysis performed by Ferguson and Peterson (i.e., controlling for previous intragroup trust but not previous relationship conflict).

Yet, the model identifies some gaps to be filled because several assumptions are not considered (e.g., What is the typical trustworthiness of the groups?). Further, if the dynamics are correct, it implies a limit on the theory. That is, it only matters early on in a group's history. If the model had been tested under the condition of settled dynamics, as suggested by James et al. (1982), our simulation suggests that no effects would have been found because the only source of variance would be group trustworthiness. This can be inferred from Figure 4.4 because all lines converge on the group trustworthiness value, a value that was constant in our simulations.

In sum, because the results of dynamic processes are difficult to predict mentally (Cronin et al., 2009), we suggest first operationalizing those processes computationally (see Vancouver & Weinhardt, 2012, for a tutorial on the type of modeling used here). That is, computational models provide a test of the clarity of one's thinking about how the processes play out over time (Farrell & Lewandowsky, 2010). Moreover, when the math or logic of the computational model is included (e.g., see Appendix 4.2 for computational model of the trust example), the theory is precise and transparent (Adner, Pólos, Ryall, & Sorenson, 2009). In addition, a clear articulation of dynamics also should guide operationalization and methodological choices. That is, one can use the computational model to conduct experiments (Davis, Eisenhardt, & Bingham, 2007; Vancouver et al., 2016). In some cases, multiple computational models can be used to represent alternative theories that can be simulated and thus differentiated. For example, Vancouver and Scherbaum (2008) created a model of the self-regulation of behavior and another of the self-regulation of perceptions, placed the models in an experimental protocol to confirm the models made clearly different predictions, and then operationalized that protocol in an empirical study that produced a clear winner. Indeed, similar to theorizing dynamically, testing dynamic theories

requires a level of methodological sophistication not typical of organizational and applied psychology studies (DeShon, 2013; Hanges & Wang, 2012), though this state of the field appears to be changing and this handbook provides many examples of that methodological sophistication in operationalization (e.g., Chapters 17–24, this volume).

CONCLUSION

Dynamics are about change over time, but the point that Waller et al. (2016) made, and the problem that we sought to correct in this chapter, is that although scholars may want to incorporate more dynamics into their theories, old habits die hard. The field is in a kind of competency trap (Levinthal & March, 1993) where, because of well-developed skills using linear causal models, small refinements of this skill set are much more common than exploring new ways of modeling causality. As such, the field has continued to develop tools to address change over time. Examples include longitudinal analysis, growth models, multilevel modeling to examine observations nested in units, and the capacity to include time as a moderator, and more methods are being created all the time. Yet, if these are used only to develop and test linear causal models, the problems that dynamic causality creates for interpreting such models remain. Such a myopic approach limits the field's ability to explain, predict, and control the phenomena it is supposed to explain. We would say that the situation with respect to dynamics is much like that when the concept of levels of analysis first came into focus (cf. Rousseau, 1985). There was a lot of unintentional misspecification of conceptual models because of the failure to appreciate the concept of levels of analysis, and it took time and several papers to get researchers to understand the implications of the concept for theory, measurement, design, and interpretation.

To be sure, scientific understanding begins with descriptions of the key constructs and important classifications (i.e., taxonomies), followed by specifications of relationships among the constructs—both of which the science has been doing for some time. However, the next step in the scientific process is to specify how the constructs change (or do not change) over time within the unit of inquiry, preferably where the timescale is explicit. In this chapter, therefore, we sought to expand the kinds of models the field uses so that dynamics can be effectively incorporated and tested. We explained where dynamics can arise in the phenomena we study. We detailed some of the problems that occur when trying to force-fit superficial dynamic mindsets to real dynamic phenomena, even if one's observations are longitudinal and one's analytic method can model recursion. Finally, we provided guidance for how to incorporate such dynamism into multilevel theorization. We hope it moves us to better model phenomena in the social sciences as truly multilevel dynamic systems.

APPENDIX 4.1

Those in the field of system dynamics have their own conventions about how to model the four properties we have described. In Figure 4A.1 we have constructed a simple model demonstrating our four dynamic properties. There is a positive feedback loop (signified by the ball rolling down the hill) between X and Y (Y is the variable with inertia) and a negative, balancing (signified by the balanced scale) endogenous process. The flow-in and -out elements represent asymmetric influences. The flow-in elements are the factors that increase Y, and the flow-out elements are the factors that decrease it. Finally, the clouds represent infinity pools beyond the scope of the theory. That is, only X and Y, and Y on itself, are the endogenous changes represented in this model.

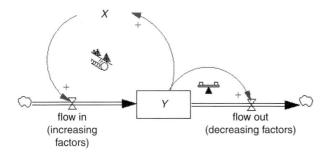

FIGURE 4A.1. Alternative representation of dynamic properties.

APPENDIX 4.2

Following is the Vensim code for the computational models presented in the chapter. This code can be found in the equation dialog boxes in Vensim models. That is, the code is not something that can be pasted into the software and run. Rather, within the Vensim software one can reproduce the models depicted in Figure 4.2 and then enter the equations below into their respective variables or constructs and accept the variables entered. Doing so should produce most of the arrows (Vensim conventions depart slightly from ours) and make the simulation ready to be run.

Initial Ferguson and Peterson (2015) model:

> diversity in propensity to trust = 0.5
> group trustworthiness = 0.5
> INTRAGROUP TRUST = INTEG(−0.46 ∗ relationship conflict, 0.26 ∗ similarity perceptions)
> relationship conflict = 3 − INTRAGROUP TRUST
> similarity perceptions = 3.5 − 0.55 ∗ diversity in propensity to trust

Revised model:

> diversity in propensity to trust = 0.5
> error = group trustworthiness − INTRAGROUP TRUST
> group trustworthiness = 0.5
> INTRAGROUP TRUST = INTEG((error − 0.01 ∗ relationship conflict) ∗ INTRAGROUP TRUST ∗ (1 − INTRAGROUP TRUST), 0.26 ∗ similarity perceptions)
> relationship conflict = 1 − 0.01 ∗ INTRAGROUP TRUST
> similarity perceptions = 3.5 − 0.55 ∗ diversity in propensity to trust

References

Adner, R., Pólos, L., Ryall, M., & Sorenson, O. (2009). The case for formal theory. *Academy of Management Review, 34*, 201–208. http://dx.doi.org/10.5465/AMR.2009.36982613

Ancona, D. G., Goodman, P. S., Lawrence, B. S., & Tushman, M. L. (2001). Time: A new research lens. *Academy of Management Review, 26,* 645–663.

Ancona, D. G., Okhuysen, G. A., & Perlow, L. A. (2001). Taking time to integrate temporal research. *Academy of Management Review, 26,* 512–529.

Beer, S. (1966). *Decision and control.* Chichester, England: Wiley.

Blount, S., & Janicik, G. A. (2001). When plans change: Examining how people evaluate timing changes in work organizations. *Academy of Management Review, 26,* 566–585.

Boulding, K. E. (1956). General systems theory—the skeleton of science. *Management Science, 2,* 197–208. http://dx.doi.org/10.1287/mnsc.2.3.197

Brett, J., Shapiro, D., & Lytle, A. (1998). Breaking the bonds of reciprocity in negotiations. *Academy of Management Journal, 41,* 410–424. http://dx.doi.org/10.5465/257081

Carton, A. M., & Cummings, J. N. (2012). A theory of subgroups in work teams. *Academy of Management Review, 37,* 441–470. http://dx.doi.org/10.5465/amr.2009.0322

Chan, D. (1998). Functional relations among constructs in the same content domain at different levels of analysis: A typology of composition models. *Journal of Applied Psychology, 83,* 234.

Cronin, M. A., Gonzalez, C., & Sterman, J. D. (2009). Why don't well-educated adults understand accumulation? A challenge to researchers, educators, and citizens. *Organizational Behavior and Human Decision Processes, 108,* 116–130. http://dx.doi.org/10.1016/j.obhdp.2008.03.003

Cronin, M. A., Weingart, L. R., & Todorova, G. (2011). Dynamics in groups: Are we there yet? *The Academy of Management Annals, 5,* 571–612. http://dx.doi.org/10.5465/19416520.2011.590297

Davis, J. P., Eisenhardt, K. M., & Bingham, C. B. (2007). Developing theory through simulation methods. *Academy of Management Review, 32,* 480–499. http://dx.doi.org/10.5465/AMR.2007.24351453

DeShon, R. P. (2013). Multivariate dynamics in organizational science. In S. W. J. Kozlowski (Ed.), *The Oxford handbook of organizational psychology* (pp. 117–142). New York, NY: Oxford University Press.

Farrell, S., & Lewandowsky, S. (2010). Computational models as aids to better reasoning in psychology. *Current Directions in Psychological Science, 19,* 329–335. http://dx.doi.org/10.1177/0963721410386677

Ferguson, A. J., & Peterson, R. S. (2015). Sinking slowly: Diversity in propensity to trust predicts downward trust spirals in small groups. *Journal of Applied Psychology, 100,* 1012–1024. http://dx.doi.org/10.1037/apl0000007

Forrester, J. W. (1968). Industrial dynamics—after the first decade. *Management Science, 14,* 398–415. http://dx.doi.org/10.1287/mnsc.14.7.398

Hamaker, E. L., & Wichers, M. (2017). No time like the present: Discovering the hidden dynamics in intensive longitudinal data. *Current Directions in Psychological Science, 26,* 10–15. http://dx.doi.org/10.1177/0963721416666518

Hanges, P., & Wang, M. (2012). Seeking the Holy Grail in organizational science: Uncovering causality through research design. In S. W. J. Kozlowski (Ed.), *The Oxford handbook of organizational psychology* (Vol. 1, pp. 79–116). New York, NY: Oxford University Press. http://dx.doi.org/10.1093/oxfordhb/9780199928309.013.0003

Herzberg, F. (1974). Motivation-hygiene profiles: Pinpointing what ails the organization. *Organizational Dynamics, 3,* 18–29. http://dx.doi.org/10.1016/0090-2616(74)90007-2

Hollenbeck, J. R., Ellis, A. P., Humphrey, S. E., Garza, A. S., & Ilgen, D. R. (2011). Asymmetry in structural adaptation: The differential impact of centralizing versus decentralizing team decision-making structures. *Organizational Behavior and Human Decision Processes, 114,* 64–74. http://dx.doi.org/10.1016/j.obhdp.2010.08.003

Humphrey, S. E., & Aime, F. (2014). Team microdynamics: Toward an organizing approach to teamwork. *The Academy of Management Annals, 8,* 443–503. http://dx.doi.org/10.5465/19416520.2014.904140

Huy, Q. N. (2001). Time, temporal capability, and planned change. *Academy of Management Review, 26,* 601–623. http://dx.doi.org/10.2307/3560244

James, L., Mulaik, S., & Brett, J. M. (1982). *Causal analysis: Assumptions, models, and data.* Beverly Hills, CA: Sage.

Johns, G. (2006). The essential impact of context on organizational behavior. *Academy of Management Review, 31,* 386–408. http://dx.doi.org/10.5465/AMR.2006.20208687

Kozlowski, S. (2012). Groups and teams in organizations. In A. B. Hollingshead & M. S. Poole (Eds.), *Research methods for studying groups and teams: A guide to approaches, tools, and technologies* (pp. 260–283). New York, NY: Routledge.

Kozlowski, S. W. J., & Bell, B. S. (2003). Work groups and teams in organizations. In D. K. Freedheim, *Handbook of psychology, Vol. 1. History of psychology.* Hoboken, NJ: Wiley & Sons. http://dx.doi.org/10.1002/0471264385.wei1214

Kozlowski, S. W. J., & Klein, K. J. (2000). A multilevel approach to theory and research in organizations: Contextual, temporal, and emergent processes. In K. J. Klein & S. W. J. Kozlowski (Eds.), *Multilevel* theory, research and methods in organizations: *Foundations, extensions, and new directions* (pp. 3–90). San Francisco, CA: Jossey-Bass.

Lau, D. C., & Murnighan, J. K. (1998). Demographic diversity and faultlines: The compositional dynamics of organizational groups. *Academy of Management Review, 23,* 325–340.

Lawrence, T. B., Winn, M. I., & Jennings, P. D. (2001). The temporal dynamics of institutionalization. *Academy of Management Review, 26,* 624–644.

Levinthal, D. A., & March, J. G. (1993). The myopia of learning. *Strategic Management Journal, 14*(S2), 95–112. http://dx.doi.org/10.1002/smj.4250141009

Lindsley, D. H., Brass, D. J., & Thomas, J. B. (1995). Efficacy-performing spirals: A multilevel perspective. *Academy of Management Review, 20,* 645–678.

Locke, E. A., & Latham, G. P. (2004). What should we do about motivation theory? Six recommendations for the twenty-first century. *Academy of Management Review, 29,* 388–403.

MacKenzie, S. B., & Podsakoff, P. M. (2012). Common method bias in marketing: Causes, mechanisms, and procedural remedies. *Journal of Retailing, 88,* 542–555. http://dx.doi.org/10.1016/j.jretai.2012.08.001

Marks, M. A., Mathieu, J. E., & Zaccaro, S. J. (2001). A temporally based framework and taxonomy of team processes. *Academy of Management Review, 26,* 356–376.

Mayer, R. C., Davis, J. H., & Schoorman, F. D. (1995). An integrative model of organizational trust. *Academy of Management Review, 20,* 709–734.

McGrath, J. E., Arrow, H., & Berdahl, J. L. (2000). The study of groups: Past, present, and future. *Personality and Social Psychology Review, 4,* 95–105. http://dx.doi.org/10.1207/S15327957PSPR0401_8

Miller, G. A., Galanter, E., & Pribram, K. H. (1960). *Plans and the structure of behavior.* New York, NY: Holt, Rinehart & Winston.

Mitchell, T. R., & James, L. R. (2001). Building better theory: Time and the specification of when things happen. *Academy of Management Review, 26,* 530–547.

Muraven, M., & Baumeister, R. F. (2000). Self-regulation and depletion of limited resources: Does self-control resemble a muscle? *Psychological Bulletin, 126,* 247–259. http://dx.doi.org/10.1037/0033-2909.126.2.247

Nahum-Shani, I., Henderson, M. M., Lim, S., & Vinokur, A. D. (2014). Supervisor support: Does supervisor support buffer or exacerbate the adverse effects of supervisor undermining? *Journal of Applied Psychology, 99,* 484–503. http://dx.doi.org/10.1037/a0035313

O'Boyle, E., Jr., & Aguinis, H. (2012). The best and the rest: Revisiting the norm of normality of individual performance. *Personnel Psychology, 65,* 79–119. http://dx.doi.org/10.1111/j.1744-6570.2011.01239.x

O'Neill, T. A., McLarnon, M. J., Hoffart, G. C., Woodley, H. J., & Allen, N. J. (2015). The structure and function of team conflict state profiles. *Journal of Management, 44,* 811–836. http://dx.doi.org/10.1177/0149206315581662

Perlow, L. A., & Repenning, N. P. (2009). The dynamics of silencing conflict. *Research in Organizational Behavior, 29,* 195–223. http://dx.doi.org/10.1016/j.riob.2009.06.007

Ployhart, R. E., & Vandenberg, R. J. (2010). Longitudinal research: The theory, design, and analysis of change. *Journal of Management, 36,* 94–120. http://dx.doi.org/10.1177/0149206309352110

Powers, W. T. (1978). Quantitative analysis of purposive systems: Some spadework at the foundations of scientific psychology. *Psychological Review, 85,* 417–435. http://dx.doi.org/10.1037/0033-295X.85.5.417

Richardson, G. P. (1991). System dynamics: Simulation for policy analysis from a feedback perspective. In P. A. Fishwick & P. A. Luker (Eds.), *Advances in simulation: Vol. 5. Qualitative simulation modeling and analysis* (pp. 144–169). New York, NY: Springer. http://dx.doi.org/10.1007/978-1-4613-9072-5_7

Richardson, G. P. (2011). Reflections on the foundations of system dynamics. *System Dynamics Review, 27,* 219–243. http://dx.doi.org/10.1002/sdr.462

Rousseau, D. M. (1985). Issues of level in organizational research: Multi-level and cross-level perspectives. *Research in Organizational Behavior, 7,* 1–37.

Rousseau, D. M., Sitkin, S. B., Burt, R. S., & Camerer, C. (1998). Not so different after all: A cross-discipline view of trust. *Academy of Management Review, 23,* 393–404. http://dx.doi.org/10.5465/AMR.1998.926617

Shannon, C. E. (1948, July & October). A mathematical theory of communication. *Bell System Technical Journal, 27,* 379–423, 623–656.

Sterman, J. D. (2000). *Business dynamics: Systems thinking and modeling for a complex world.* Boston, MA: Irwin McGraw-Hill.

Vancouver, J. B. (1996). Living systems theory as a paradigm for organizational behavior: Understanding humans, organizations, and social processes. *Behavioral Science, 41,* 165–204. http://dx.doi.org/10.1002/bs.3830410301

Vancouver, J. B. (2000). Self-regulation in organizational settings: A tale of two paradigms. In M. Boekaerts, P. R. Pintrich, & M. Zeidner, *Handbook of self-regulation* (pp. 303–341). San Diego, CA: Academic Press.

Vancouver, J. B. (2005). The depth of history and explanation as benefit and bane for psychological control theories. *Journal of Applied Psychology, 90,* 38–52. http://dx.doi.org/10.1037/0021-9010.90.1.38

Vancouver, J. B., Li, X., Weinhardt, J. M., Steel, P., & Purl, J. D. (2016). Using a computational model to understand possible sources of skews in distributions of job performance. *Personnel Psychology, 69,* 931–974. http://dx.doi.org/ 10.1111/peps.12141

Vancouver, J. B., & Scherbaum, C. A. (2008). Do we self-regulate actions or perceptions? A test of two computational models. *Computational & Mathematical Organization Theory, 14,* 1–22. http://dx.doi.org/10.1007/s10588-008-9021-7

Vancouver, J. B., & Weinhardt, J. M. (2012). Modeling the mind and the milieu: Computational modeling for micro-level organizational researchers. *Organizational Research Methods, 15,* 602–623. http://dx.doi.org/10.1177/1094428112449655

Vancouver, J. B., Weinhardt, J. M., & Vigo, R. (2014). Change one can believe in: Adding learning to computational models of self-regulation.

Organizational Behavior and Human Decision Processes, 124, 56–74. http://dx.doi.org/10.1016/ j.obhdp.2013.12.002

von Bertalanffy, L. (1950). An outline of general system theory. *The British Journal for the Philosophy of Science, 1,* 139–164.

Waller, M. J., Conte, J. M., Gibson, C. B., & Carpenter, M. A. (2001). The effect of individual perceptions of deadlines on team performance. *Academy of Management Review, 26,* 586–600.

Waller, M. J., Okhuysen, G. A., & Saghafian, M. (2016). Conceptualizing emergent states: A strategy to advance the study of group dynamics. *The Academy of Management Annals, 10,* 561–598.

Whetten, D. A. (1989). What constitutes a theoretical contribution. *Academy of Management Review, 14,* 490–495. http://dx.doi.org/10.2307/258554

Wilson, J. M., Goodman, P. S., & Cronin, M. A. (2007). Group learning. *Academy of Management Review, 32,* 1041–1059.

Zand, D. E. (1972). Trust and managerial problem solving. *Administrative Science Quarterly, 17,* 229–239.

## CHAPTER 5

THE MEANS ARE THE END: COMPLEXITY SCIENCE IN ORGANIZATIONAL RESEARCH

Juliet R. Aiken, Paul J. Hanges, and Tiancheng Chen

Many phenomena of interest to multilevel organizational researchers can be thought of as arising from the operation of complex adaptive systems. In this chapter, we describe various analytical methods that can be used to model and understand the behavior of complex adaptive systems. The methods we discuss are based on complexity science. Thus, we also explain what complexity science is and use complexity science to frame our discussion of research methods.

COMPLEXITY SCIENCE: BEYOND DETERMINISM AND REDUCTIONISM

Organizational researchers have traditionally taken a deterministic and reductionistic approach to understanding phenomena. *Determinism* is the belief that the present is completely a result of past events (Bishop, 2002). Scientific hypotheses consistent with determinism are expressed in the form "*X* causes *Y*." The most powerful research tool developed to establish causation is experimentation (Hanges & Wang, 2012). *Reductionism*, or more precisely, methodological reductionism, refers to the attempt to explain behavior operating at the level of an entire system by examining individual components of the system and identifying the interactions among these components (Kemeny & Oppenheim, 1956). In short, organizational researchers traditionally have expressed their explanations for some

phenomenon by drawing arrow-and-box diagrams in which various individual components (on the left of the diagram) combine to create the behavior (on the right of the diagram).

Both determinism and reductionism have served science well for many decades; however, they might also have hindered our progress, especially as we try to understand multilevel phenomena. Multilevel phenomena require scientists to think about interdependency, feedback loops, and codetermination of phenomena. In other words, *X* may cause *Y*, but *Y* can also cause *X*. When codetermination is embraced, both determinism and reductionism become a shaky ground on which to build an understanding of such phenomena (Hanges & Wang, 2012). Complexity science has emerged over the past 30 years, and this scientific approach holds promise in aiding researchers to think about and handle the challenges posed by multilevel phenomena.

Complexity science encompasses theories or trends that have been mentioned in our literature since the 1950s. For example, systems theory, nonlinear dynamical systems theory, network theory, synergetics, and complex adaptive systems theory are all incorporated into the broader term *complexity science* (Goldstein, 2008). This scientific approach is inherently about the emergence of system-wide behavior and the evolution of systems (Byrne, 1998; Friedenberg, 2009; Goldstein, 2008; Marion, 1999; Streufert, 1997; Vallacher, Read, & Nowak, 2002).

http://dx.doi.org/10.1037/0000115-006
The Handbook of Multilevel Theory, Measurement, and Analysis, S. E. Humphrey and J. M. LeBreton (Editors-in-Chief)

It focuses on how systems evolve and change over time (Eidelson, 1997; Hanges, Lord, Godfrey, & Raver, 2002; Schneider & Somers, 2006).

The basic unit of study in complexity science is the complex adaptive system (Uhl-Bien, Marion, & McKelvey, 2007). We turn our attention to what complex adaptive systems are in the next section of this chapter. However, as you read the next section, remember that the behavior of complex adaptive systems can be described as BOAR; that is, such systems lie between order (i.e., are completely engineered and deterministic) and randomness (i.e., are completely unpredictable). As a result, complex adaptive systems cannot be easily described, evolved, engineered, or predicted (DEEP; Page, 2010). Because such systems are DEEP, complexity science emphasizes prediction of patterns rather than discrete behaviors or outcomes of complex adaptive systems.

Complexity science provides a different scientific approach or conceptual lens that we can apply to multilevel systems. The key markers of complexity science, per our above discussion, are as follows:

1. Complexity science describes systems that are BOAR (Page, 2010). It is important to remember that not all multilevel interactions, outcomes, and studies are complex.
2. Complexity science is a useful framework for understanding the behavior of systems (Gilpin & Miller, 2013). In particular, it focuses on system *change*.
3. Complexity science focuses on patterns rather than discrete outcomes, as well as nonlinear rather than linear change (Gilpin & Miller, 2013).
4. Complexity science is useful for studying non-deterministic systems. It is not reductionist; rather, complexity science emphasizes that breaking a system into its components can destroy the phenomena you are trying to understand.
5. The basic unit of study in complexity science is the complex adaptive system.

WHAT ARE COMPLEX ADAPTIVE SYSTEMS?

Complex adaptive systems are self-contained, richly interconnected collections of elements (Eidelson, 1997; Page, 2010) that influence the behavior of

each other (Hanges et al., 2002; Vallacher & Nowak, 1994), and the joint interactivity of these elements result in the emergence of system-level behavior that is adaptive to some context or environment (Boyatzis, 2006; Fisher, 2009; Uhl-Bien et al., 2007). Such systems can be observed at multiple levels of analysis. For example, the brain can be conceptualized as a complex adaptive system. The brain (i.e., a self-contained system) comprises millions of neurons (i.e., elements) that are richly interconnected. Activity among a subset of neurons spreads across the brain to result in differential brain activation patterns that can be mapped using functional magnetic resonance imaging. Over time, the linkages among neurons positively activated with each other get stronger (Hebb, 1949). This change in wiring of the brain, also known as learning, causes different behavior to emerge at the system (i.e., brain) level of analysis. Indeed, consciousness (i.e., a system-level behavior) emerges from the operation of this richly interconnected and activated network of neurons. The triggering point that starts a subset of neurons to fire in the first place usually is, but does not have to be, some environmental input. Thus, changes in brain activation patterns in this neural network are adaptive to the environment.

Complex adaptive systems also operate at the social or group level. Individual ants, for example, are not intelligent and often will operate in a repetitive, mechanical manner. However, put these ants together in a colony in which the behaviors of interconnected ants are influenced by each other and amazing behavior emerges at the colony level of analysis. This emergent behavior is sufficiently flexible to potentially save the colony from threatening environmental occurrences. We see human organizations also behaving as complex adaptive systems. People (i.e., elements) are richly interconnected with other people in their group, department, and/or division. People within these clusters clearly influence each other. For example, people within an organization modify their behavior to be consistent with the values and informal norms of others in the organization. People also modify their behavior to be consistent with organizational policies, practices, and procedures put into place by people in leadership positions. At the level of the organization, organizational scholars talk about an emergent phenomenon known as organizational climate (Schneider, 1987; Schneider & Barbera, 2014; Schneider & Reichers, 1983; Schneider, White, & Paul, 1998). *Organizational climate* is defined as employees' shared interpretation of the organizational policies, practices, and procedures. Organizational climate needs to and eventually will change as the organization tries to adapt to its environment.

Not all multilevel systems are complex, however. Systems may have multiple elements, but these elements interact as a function of simple rules. Such systems are complicated to understand (because of the number of elements), but they are not necessarily complex. For example, a Boeing 737 plane has 367,000 parts, all of which form a complicated system. However, happily for the flying public, airplanes are not complex systems. They do not exhibit emergent properties, and the behavior of the plane is completely determined by the manipulation of individual elements. In short, not all systems are complex (Houchin & MacLean, 2005; Page, 2010), and research focusing on these kinds of systems does not need complexity science.

The key points to remember about complex adaptive systems are

1. Complex adaptive systems are characterized by rich interactions among diverse lower level units (Page, 2010).
2. The behavior of such systems lies BOAR (Page, 2010).
3. Not all systems comprising multiple elements are complex.

Complex adaptive systems are the unit of study in complexity science. Because complexity science is about emergence, the evolution of system behavior, and sensitivity to initial conditions, these characteristics are predicted to describe the behavior of complex adaptive systems. In the next section, we consider the first characteristic: emergence.

Characteristic 1: Emergence of System-Level Behavior
At first blush, complexity science may appear to be reductionist because it focuses our attention on how lower level elements drive upper-level

(i.e., system-wide) behavior (Hanges et al., 2002; Schneider & Somers, 2006). However, it is not reductionist because complexity science emphasizes the interactions and the influence among these lower level elements on each other, and these influences generate novel and interesting behaviors that emerge at the level of the system (Boyatzis, 2006; Eidelson, 1997). The creation of novel system-level behavior is called *emergence* (Schneider & Somers, 2006), which focuses on the gestalt of all the lower level elements working together. The system-level behavior is not easily predicted as a function of the lower level elements because it is not an additive function of those elements. Emergent system-level behavior is more than the sum of the behavior of lower level units.

Emergence is particularly important when one is interested in multilevel phenomena. One example is Houchin and MacLean's (2005) 4-year ethnographic study of the creation of a climate in a new public sector organization. As indicated earlier in this chapter, climate is defined as a shared concept. It emerges as a result of the interaction among employees and the joint influence that these interactions have on crafting a common conceptual framework for understanding the organization. Houchin and MacLean used an in-depth qualitative methodology known as ethnography to study how organizational climate develops and changes over time. These researchers found that the organizational climate that emerged in their studied organization was a compromise between the push of newly implemented organizational policies, practices, and procedures and the pull of employees' well-ingrained behaviors and expectations.

Another example illustrates what common emergent phenomena are when studying organizational phenomena. Lichtenstein (2000) conducted a series of weekly interviews with employees in a small entrepreneurial firm over a 9- to 12-month period. This organization was less than 7 years old, and its founder was still in charge. In large organizations, organizational climate usually is attributed to the goals, values, and beliefs of the founder (Schneider, 1987). However, due to the small size of this organization, all of the employees interacted and influenced the decisions of each other, and even the founder. The firm's strategy and structure (i.e., policies, practices, and procedures) emerged as a result of these interactions and not as a function of the founder's well thought-out and initial strategic plan.

The joint and richly interconnected behavior of the elements in a complex adaptive system will generate new system-level behavior. Although some of this system-level behavior is predictable from the behavior of the individual elements, the hallmark of complex adaptive systems is the potential for the emergence of completely surprising and unpredictable system-level behavior. That is, the system-level behavior cannot be completely understood by studying the behavior of individual elements. The complex adaptive system may start out behaving as expected or designed, but, over time, its behavior may evolve and the system actually may behave in a way that it was never intended to and may be completely undesired and harmful. In the next section, we discuss the evolution of complex adaptive systems and their unique pattern of behavioral change in response to pressures from its environment.

Characteristic 2: Evolution of System Behavior

Before we describe the evolution of a complex adaptive system's behavior, it is helpful to contextualize this discussion by using an example. Let's consider the context of the hotel industry and the different kinds of reputations and organizational climates that hotels may have with the general public. There are a variety of hotel climates possible, but for the sake of simplicity, let's assume that these various hotel climates can be placed along a hypothetical linear continuum that varies from "economical/ basic service" at one end to "luxury/individualized customer service" at the other. This linear continuum conceptualization of how people think about psychological and organizational phenomena is quite typical in the social sciences (see, e.g., Vallacher & Nowak, 1994). Figure 5.1A is our conceptualization of such a linear continuum representing hotel climates. As shown in this figure, the left side of continuum corresponds with an economical/basic service hotel climate, whereas

the right side of the continuum corresponds to the luxury/individualized customer service hotel climate. Hotels can be placed at different locations on this continuum as a function of their organizational climate. For example, perhaps the Motel 6 hotel chain might be located close to the left end of this continuum whereas the Four Seasons hotel chain might be located closer to the right side of the continuum. Both of these chains have found their niche market. Indeed, the perceptions of these hotels have become well established and entrenched with their customers over the years.

We can use this continuum conceptualization to explain how complex adaptive systems evolve. Let's assume we have some hotel (e.g., Hotel X) whose initial policies, practices, and procedures produced a climate that customers and employees would describe as similar to the Motel 6 climate. The ball in Figure 5.1 represents Hotel X's original location on the climate location. Now let's assume that the upper management of Hotel X decides that future growth requires a change in the hotel's policies, practices, and procedures, such that customers start to expect the hotel is more luxury/individualized service oriented. How would the Hotel X's climate evolve over time? Using the typically assumed linear continuum shown in Figure 5.1A, we see that the new hotel climate will evolve in a smooth and continuous manner over time because there is no resistance to this change.

However, this linear and continuous change in hotel climate is not consistent with the known organizational development literature. This literature confirms that the organizational climate does not change smoothly and continuously over time; rather, it probably evolves in a sudden and discontinuous manner (Gersick, 1991; Romanelli & Tushman, 1994). Indeed, some scholars have described that change in system-level phenomena has punctuated equilibriums. That is, for the majority of time, no change is seen. But dramatic change in the system-level phenomena occurs suddenly and quite dramatically over a short period. This is exactly the kind of change that complexity science predicts complex adaptive systems will have (e.g., Boyatzis, 2006; Eidelson, 1997; Styhre, 2002; Tsoukas & Hatch, 2001). To understand

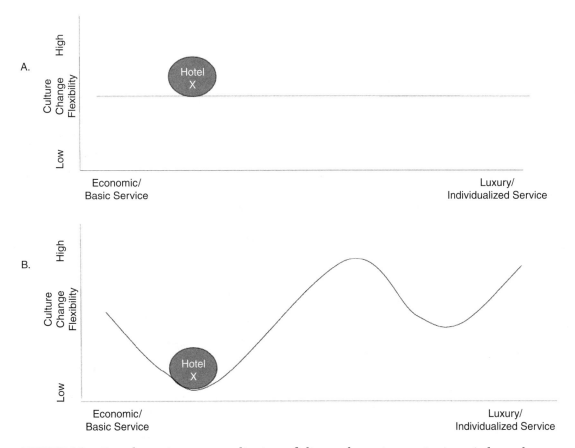

FIGURE 5.1. **Two alternative conceptualizations of climate change in organizations. A shows the typical social sciences perspective of change. B shows the new perspective of change from a complexity science perspective.**

why, we have to modify the typical social sciences assumption that perceptual continuums can be represented by linear surfaces.

Organizational climate arises from the interactions of employees inside and customers outside of the organization. The perceived climate of both the Motel 6 and Four Seasons hotel chains have been reinforced over the years, and these perceived climates are probably well established and entrenched in the mind of their employees and customers. Although employees' behavior occasionally may be inconsistent with the hotel's climate (e.g., Motel 6 providing more than basic service; Four Seasons failing to meet the needs of a customer), the climate does not immediately change. In other words, system-level phenomena have a certain stickiness to them, and they do not immediately change to evolutionary pressure.

Where does this stickiness come from? Complexity science points to interdependency, feed-back loops, and codetermination for an explanation. Organizational climates develop and change as a result of the rich interdependency among employees and even customers. Employees talk with each other to understand the behavioral implications of organizational policies, practices, and procedures. Eventually, a common understanding or climate is spread and shared among the employees. For climate to change then, it takes some employees to pay attention to and develop a new understanding regarding the meaning of changes to the organization. For the climate to change, this new understanding must spread through the company. However, the driving force for this new climate (i.e., adoptee group members) is matched by a counterforce by the employees holding onto the old climate (i.e., resistor group members) conceptualization. Feedback loops reinforcing the status quo climate and co-occurrence (i.e., new organizational policies [X] result in adoptee's climate perceptions [Y], but, simultaneously, resistors' climate perceptions [Y] result in resistance to new organizational policies [*X*]). The speed of change in organizational climate increases in a nonlinear manner as more resistor group members move to the adopter group, and the subsequent counterforce becomes weaker.

Complexity science represents the stickiness of organizational climate by introducing the concept of attractors. Attractors—in the mathematics of complexity science—capture the counterforces that act to stabilize system-level behavior. *Attractors* are gravitational sources that draw the current organization's climate perceptions to a particular location on the continuum. Similar to a golf ball's being drawn into a valley, attractors draw systems and perceptions about systems toward them (Byrne, 1998; Gilpin & Miller, 2013). To represent attractors, we modified the linear continuum shown in Figure 5.1A and introduced nonlinearity to this surface (see Figure 5.1B). As shown in the figure, the perceptual continuum has valleys and hills. The valleys represent locations of attractors (Eidelson, 1997) that pull psychological perception toward them. The hills, on the other hand, represent locations along the continuum that are unstable.[1] In Figure 5.1B, Hotel X has fallen into the valley closest to the economical/basic service end of the continuum. This figure implies that it is difficult for Hotel X to change its climate because the stickiness or gravitational pull of the original climate is strong.

Attractors differ in terms of their width and depth (Lord, 2008; Vallacher & Nowak, 1994). Wide attractors cover more space on the continuum. The width of an attractor represents the probability of falling into that valley. In Figure 5.1B, we show two attractors along the hotel climate continuum. One is at the economical/basic service end of the continuum, and the other attractor is at the luxury/individualized customer service end of the continuum. The valley representing the economical/basic service attractor covers more of the culture continuum than does the luxury/individualized customer service attractor. This implies that it is easier (i.e., higher probability) for a hotel to end up

with an economical/basic service climate perception than for that hotel to end up with a luxury/individualized customer service climate (i.e., lower probability).

Attractors also have depth. Deeper attractors represent stickier climates, and it is more difficult for a hotel to change its climate when in deep valleys. The middle of the Figure 5.1B climate continuum contains a hill, and this level of climate perception is believed to be unstable and easy to change. Organizations trying to develop a climate halfway between economical and luxury are unlikely to be successful in the long run. Of course, Figure 5.1B shows a simplified continuum, and the real continuum probably has more than two attractors (i.e., valleys) and probably requires more than a single continuum to fully capture the variety of possible organizational climates.

Hotel X can change its culture (i.e., it can move from one attractor to another). It will need lots of sustained improvements to overcome the gravitational counterforce generated by the depth and width of the economical/basic service attractor. Complexity science indicates that in the short run, no change in climate will be noticed. However, when sufficient pressure is applied over the long term (i.e., sustained and continuous changes to Hotel X's policies, practices, and procedures), the shift in the climate will be sudden and dramatic. This was illustrated by the aforementioned Lichtenstein's (2000) study with another system-level phenomenon: organizational culture. This new culture emerged after a crisis. Although the old culture persisted despite growing economic pressures, the new culture quickly emerged after the organization reached a crisis.

Although Figure 5.1B is useful to illustrate the attractor concept and the predicted behavior of a complex adaptive system, the reader should not interpret the figure as implying that the shape of the continuum is static. Rather, the landscape of this continuum is dynamic and can change as a result of new businesses entering the marketplace and/or

---

[1]This conceptualization of attractors in a perceptual continuum is similar to Einstein's (1920) interpretation of gravity's forces in his conceptualization of the space-time continuum. Objects with gravity, according to Einstein, bend the space-time continuum. Objects with greater mass (e.g., black holes) generate greater gravitational pull, and this is represented by saying that they substantially bend the space-time continuum.

old businesses changing their mission and their business strategy. For example, Airbnb changed the structure of the hotel landscape when the company capitalized on the sharing economy by allowing travelers to directly arrange for lodging with independent homeowners/apartment dwellers. Basically, Airbnb increased room availability across the nation, and existing hotels changed their business strategy to adapt to this new competitor. In the language of complexity science, Airbnb introduced a new attractor into Figure 5.1B's landscape. This new attractor not only created a new valley in the landscape but probably changed the depth and/or width of one or more of the already existing attractors. The change in the shape of the landscape is a result of the actions of other systems' (i.e., hotels) entering the marketplace— or by structural changes within a single system (i.e., Hotel X; Marion, 1999). For example, Uber changed the attractor landscape of the taxi industry, whereas Amazon.com changed and is still changing the landscape for various industries, ranging from books to groceries. Indeed, Amazon.com might be changing their landscape again by introducing bricks-and-mortar stores as part of their business strategy. Thus, the landscape of a complex adaptive system can almost be conceptualized as "dancing" over time (Page, 2010).

The prediction that complex adaptive systems evolve dramatically and discontinuously over time has been documented in a number of different studies. For example, Plowman et al. (2007) recounted the shift in the organizational mission and activities of a church. The church studied by these researchers was located in a wealthy area and historically had a wealthy congregation. The initial perturbation to this church occurred when one of its junior members (i.e., adopters) suggested that the church offer free breakfast to homeless individuals living nearby. This practice was adopted and continued over time. Soon, other nonprofit organizations started working with the church, and eventually, some new members who were less affluent than the original members started attending service. Gradually, the membership of the church started changing as older members (i.e., resistors) who were perhaps uncomfortable with the new members

or had different values left and were replaced by more of the new congregational members. Although the old culture persisted awhile, eventually the counterforce generated by the resistors diminished as they left and the church's culture changed. When culture did start changing, it was dramatic and sudden. Indeed, the church was soon known to have a unique culture in the area.

Another example comes from Chiles, Meyer, and Hench's (2004) description of the transformation of Branson, Missouri, from an isolated, untouched community whose natives scraped out their existence by farming rocky soil into a mecca of musical theaters. The transformation was started by the Reverend Harold Bell Wright's national best-selling novel, which described the area and its people. This book became an attractor, drawing the imagination of tourists and investors to the area. The influx of money into the region caused by this attractor generated new entrepreneurial effort. In complexity science terminology, the national attention to Branson caused by the book (i.e., attractor) created a valley in the landscape, and this attractor attracted tourists interested in outdoor activities. Over time, tourists began to demand nighttime entertainment, which attracted investors, who created new businesses (e.g., theaters) to meet this demand. The theaters and other businesses introduced a new attractor to the Branson economic landscape, and this new attractor turned out to be deeper than the original nature-oriented attractor once the word got out about the entertainment. Dramatically more tourists came to the town explicitly for the theaters. These tourists tended to spend more money than the original nature-oriented tourists. This spending resulted in the first real economic boom in the town around the 1950s and 1960. Consistent with complexity science, even though the number of tourists increased gradually over the years, the economic boom apparently occurred suddenly and dramatically.

Discontinuous change is actually seen at multiple levels of analysis and has been documented at the level of interpersonal perceptions (Hanges, Braverman, & Rentsch, 1991) and changes in perceptions of leaders (Foti, Knee, & Backert, 2008). In the next section, we discuss how multiple complex adaptive systems that start off identically can end up in completely different locations as a result of minor and apparently insignificant events. This is known in the literature as the butterfly effect.

Characteristic 3: Sensitivity to Initial Conditions

The behavior of complex adaptive systems is said to be sensitive to initial conditions. *Sensitivity to initial conditions* basically refers to the enhancement of information's influence as it spreads through a complex adaptive system. Remember that complex adaptive systems are made up of multiple, highly interconnected individuals who influence one another. In such systems, minor (almost ignorable) environmental events might generate minor changes in the behavior of a small subset of these individuals (i.e., adopters). Sometimes slight behavioral change among these adopters might spread through the entire system. As more people join the adopters, the influence and strength of this force for change becomes magnified. Indeed, as discussed in the previous section, the entire complex adaptive system could end up behaving in a completely different manner. The key point that we want to emphasize in this section is that small, imperceptible initial differences can have dramatic consequences for the behavior of the system in the long run (Hanges, 1987; Hanges et al., 1991, 2002; Plowman & Duchon, 2008; Schneider & Somers, 2006; Tsoukas & Hatch, 2001).

Many readers may recognize that this principle as the butterfly effect. For example, assume that two entrepreneurs working in the same industry have the same background (e.g., ethnic background, educational background) and the same content experiences and knowledge. Minor differences in the local economies (e.g., slight differences in tax policies, differential availability to markets and/or capital) where these entrepreneurs work can result in one entrepreneur's being successful and the other's being a failure.

This sensitivity to initial conditions was hinted at in the aforementioned Lichtenstein (2000) study. In that study, he compared three organizations that were facing similar crises. Lichtenstein chose these three organizations because they could be equated at

the beginning of the study. Specifically, they all were entrepreneurial organizations, less than 7 years old, and run by their founder/CEO. Each organization was on the verge of a transition in that they were introducing new products based on the vision of their CEO. These products were believed to expand each organization's bottom line as the organization moved into new markets. At the beginning of the study, each organization reported substantial tension created by financial losses caused by these new products. As discussed previously, one organization was able to successfully navigate this transition. However, the second organization failed and eventually had to be sold. The third organization handled the financial tension by downsizing and rededicating itself to its original customers. Thus, despite being matched at the beginning of the study and despite facing similar tensions, the three organizations ended up with dramatically different outcomes.

Of course, sensitivity to initial conditions can be seen wherever complex adaptive systems operate. In biology, for example, Freund et al.'s (2013) longitudinal study of genetically identical mice raised in the same enriched environment demonstrates this butterfly effect. These researchers found that observable individual differences among the mice emerged over time despite their identical genetic composition and identical environment. Freund et al. (2013) found that neuronal differences caused by slightly different environmental encounters built on each other. After 3 months, these mice demonstrated measurable and stable differences despite their identical genetic structure and the same environmental opportunities. Indeed, any parent of identical twins probably can relate to these findings.

The Freund et al. (2013) study demonstrates that interactions of lower level units (i.e., neural connections in mice brains) eventually changes the way mice interact with and learn from their environment. Trivial fluctuations in initial conditions can result in dramatic differences in end states due to feedback loops that either amplify or suppress emergent patterns of behavior. As such, some outcomes cannot be anticipated or predicted; they are unknowable until they occur (Schneider & Somers, 2006).

Feedback loops underlie why complex adaptive systems are sensitive to initial conditions. Two basic feedback loops important for complexity science are negative and positive feedback loops. *Negative feedback loops* act to dampen the effects of environmental interactions on a system. A classic example is the functioning of the integumentary biological system that helps the body regulate its temperature. Falling into a frozen lake will cause the temperature of a body to decrease. To prevent hypothermia, the body starts shivering in an attempt to increase glucose oxidation (i.e., glycolysis). On the other hand, walking in a desert will cause hyperthermia. The body activates sweat glands in an attempt to remove excess heat. Thus, the integumentary biological system acts as a negative feedback loop to minimize the influence of the environment on the system. In terms of organizational climate, negative feedback loops play a major role in the strengthening the counterforce to change that was discussed earlier.

Positive feedback loops amplify the effects of interactions and interventions in the system. A classic example is the beneficial consequences of compound interest rates on the value of investments and savings accounts. The growth rate of such accounts increases exponentially over time as the same interest rate is applied to increasingly larger account balances. Thus, compounding interest acts as a positive feedback loop on the investor's account balance. In terms of organizational climate change, positive feedback loops play a role in the growing strength of the forces for change over time. Together, negative and positive feedback loops work to drive slightly different systems to dramatically different end points, depending on the initial conditions of each system.

A variety of characteristics of complex adaptive systems can be studied, including emergence, discontinuous evolution of system behavior, and sensitivity to initial conditions. Some main points of those characteristics are summarized, as follows:

1. Emergence refers to situations in which the interactions among lower level elements generate new behavior at the higher level (Boyatzis, 2006; Eidelson, 1997; Schneider & Somers, 2006).
2. System-level emergent behaviors are more than the sum of the behavior of lower level units.

The rich interconnections among the lower level elements and their complex interactions have a nonlinear effect at the system level.

3. In complexity science, the change of system-level behavior of a complex adaptive system over time can be conceptualized as movement along a bumpy continuum or landscape. The valleys and hills of this landscape represent stable and unstable behavior of the system, respectively. The locations of stable system-level behavior along the continuum are called attractors.
4. Complexity science does not require the nature of the continuum/landscape to be constant over time. The shape of the landscape can change as a result of internal forces (e.g., structural changes within a complex adaptive system) and external forces (e.g., a new competitor—attractor— introduced into the market).
5. Complexity science indicates that changes in system-level phenomena occur dramatically and discontinuously. Complex adaptive systems initially resist change.
6. Sensitivity to initial conditions implies that small disturbances or events that affect the system can dramatically change the behavioral trajectory of a system over time. The effect of these disturbances may not be seen initially, but their effects are clearly evident over time.
7. The facilitation of or resistance to behavioral change can be explained by feedback loops. Positive feedback loops amplify the effects of small disturbances, whereas negative feedback loops attenuate the effects of small disturbances on system-level behavior.

These characteristics need to be empirically assessed before one can say that phenomena are produced by a complex adaptive system. Indeed, these aforementioned properties (e.g., emergence, discontinuous change, sensitivity to initial conditions) are essentially evidence, almost like fingerprints, that a complex adaptive system exists and underlie the phenomenon of interest. Chances are that you already may have been studying phenomena that truly result from complex dynamic systems without realizing it. In the next section of this chapter, we discuss the methods that have been developed to study complex dynamic systems.

THE RESEARCHER'S TOOLKIT: FINDING THE FINGERPRINTS OF COMPLEXITY

The characteristics of complex adaptive systems discussed earlier require multilevel researchers to add new tools in their methodological and analytical toolkit. When searching for evidence of complex adaptive systems, researchers need to use more longitudinal or repeated observation research designs than they have used traditionally. We are only able to detect changes in higher level phenomenon (e.g., discontinuous change, sensitivity to initial conditions) when we repeatedly measure phenomenon over time. Thus, unlike current research designs that typically measure phenomena at a one-time period (i.e., a single photograph) or, at most, two or three time periods common in current longitudinal research designs, we need to gather lots of measurements of the same behavior over time (DeShon, 2012; Kozlowski, Chao, Grand, Braun, & Kuljanin, 2013). Change and movement are detectable only when multiple photographs taken over time are flipped through (i.e., we need to view multiple frames to detect motion similar to watching a movie). Thus, the study of complex adaptive systems requires the collection of rich data. These data can be either qualitative or quantitative (e.g., big data). They may be collected on individuals over time, teams over time, or organizations over time.

Broadly construed, two types of methods can be used to investigate complex phenomena. The first approach to complexity research is labeled the *narrative* (Tsoukas & Hatch, 2001), or interpretive, approach (Poutanen, Siira, & Aula, 2016). This approach focuses on storytelling, subjectivity, and searching for meaning (Poutanen et al., 2016; Tsoukas & Hatch, 2001). Research conducted through this approach is contextualized and grounded in a historical, narrative account (Poutanen et al., 2016; Tsoukas & Hatch, 2001). The narrative or interpretive approach focuses on qualitative data and storytelling. The second approach to complexity research can be thought of as the *logico-scientific* (Tsoukas & Hatch, 2001), or objectivist, approach (Poutanen et al., 2016). This empirical approach is focused on uncovering the

"truth" and providing and testing good arguments grounded in solid theory (Poutanen et al., 2016; Tsoukas & Hatch, 2001). Research conducted through this approach is decontextualized and seeks to make universal generalizations (Poutanen et al., 2016; Tsoukas & Hatch, 2001). The logico-scientific or objectivist approach typically focuses on quantitative data and hypothesis testing.

Poutanen et al. (2016) provided an overview of a number of complexity research studies falling into these two broad categories. As they stated, many methods are needed to fully understand complex organizational phenomena. Consistent with this advice, we outline a number of qualitative and quantitative methods for investigating complex organizational phenomena. Research methods from both frameworks must be applied for complexity science in organizational psychology to progress. In the next section, we discuss both qualitative (e.g., interviews, observation) and quantitative (e.g., simulations, neural network analysis, social network analysis [SNA]) approaches to studying complex organizational phenomena.

Methods

Qualitative techniques. Qualitative data collection and analysis are perhaps currently the most common methods of research and analysis of complex adaptive systems at the organizational level of analysis. With the qualitative study of behavior produced by such systems, researchers dive into one or a few cases to obtain a narrative on the dynamic unfolding of change within those few instances. The detailed information obtained from this approach, as well as the grounded nature of this technique, is particularly useful for detecting emergence, discontinuous change, and sensitivity to initial conditions of complex adaptive systems. More specifically, qualitative techniques are extremely useful for specifying and documenting the initial conditions encountered by organizations at the beginning of a study. These techniques should also be useful for detecting any unanticipated discontinuous changes in behavior resulting from emergent organizational phenomena.

Although the narratives generated by qualitative analytic approaches vary somewhat in their components, many of these analyses use interviews and secondary sources (e.g., media) to gain an understanding of events and their context. All of these analyses tend to focus on providing narrative rather than numerical summaries of the insights gained. To avoid repeating information, we focus our discussion of qualitative data analysis on a few strategies that might be used when conducting qualitative studies on complex adaptive systems. As our discussion shows, qualitative data analysis techniques used by organizational researchers interested in complex adaptive systems blur the lines between research and practice, with the researcher's striving to simultaneously achieve both goals.

One method used previously is action research. Unlike traditional research methodology, action research starts with the assumption that the observer effect operates in all of research. The observer effect, first discussed in quantum physics, states that the process of observing a phenomenon or system necessarily changes that phenomenon or system. Action research therefore says that a researcher must become immersed in the system under investigation. Ethnography, as in Styhre's (2002) research on organizational change at a manufacturing production unit, is an example of action research.

Action research also can serve as a bridge between science and practice. For example, Jarvis, Gulati, McCririck, and Simpson (2013) conducted an ethnographic evaluation of a leadership training program using interviews, observations, guided conversations, and a 360-degree questionnaire administered before the program began and 6 months after the program. Jarvis et al. (2013) used these tools not only to evaluate the training but to reinforce the training and provide an additional intervention to deepen the learning coming out of the program, as well as to continually build stakeholder buy-in. In this way, research and practice were fully aligned, and research informed the shape of the training in real time as the evaluation unfolded.

In addition to bridging the gap between science and practice, when conducting a qualitative study of complex phenomena, it is acknowledged that always trying to eliminate the subjectivity in data may remove the richness of the obtained information. For example, through interviews and the analysis

of a video recording, Paraskevas (2006) studied the response of a hotel food chain to the crisis presented by a food poisoning outbreak. In those interviews, Paraskevas encouraged participants to provide their own first-person narrative perspective on events. By assembling, analyzing, and comparing those narratives, Paraskevas was able to obtain a richer holistic view of the crisis response, including perspective on the interconnectedness of seemingly unrelated events and actions.

Multilevel qualitative research of complex phenomena typically draws from a number of sources and multiple cases that are compared against one another (Brown & Eisenhardt, 1997). Research may include interviews (Brown & Eisenhardt, 1997; Chiles et al., 2004; Lichtenstein, 2000; Plowman et al., 2007; Shoham & Hasgall, 2005; Solansky, Beck, & Travis, 2014), surveys (Brown & Eisenhardt, 1997; Chiles et al., 2004), observational research (Brown & Eisenhardt, 1997; Chiles et al., 2004; Shoham & Hasgall, 2005; Solansky et al., 2014), business documents (e.g., plans, memos, reports, promotional materials, or e-mails; Chiles et al., 2004; Lichtenstein, 2000; Solansky et al., 2014), and external or archival data, such as data from the media, to understand the context within which the system operates (Brown & Eisenhardt, 1997; Chiles et al., 2004; Plowman et al., 2007). In other words, multilevel qualitative research on complex adaptive systems should be mixed method.

Qualitative multilevel research on complex phenomena may differ from traditional qualitative research in a few key ways. Research may be practiced in qualitative multilevel research designs, for example, through action research. Additionally, interviews used to inform complex organizational phenomena may fully embrace the subjectivity of each individual's experience. Qualitative multilevel research is multimethod, often including methods of archival data analysis that provide for a deeper understanding of the environment within which a given complex adaptive system operates. Next, we discuss quantitative techniques for gathering and analyzing data on complex phenomena.

Quantitative studies. Quantitative research methods also have been used when investigating complex phenomena. Although the narratives provided by qualitative approach may be more detailed and richer descriptions than typically provided using quantitative methods, the power of the quantitative methods is the precision with which patterns of behavior generated by complex adaptive systems can be measured and empirically verified. Traditional experiments, surveys, and archival studies can be conducted—with a twist—to productively study complex phenomena. For example, Foti et al. (2008) conducted an experiment in which cognitive networks were surveyed before and after participants watched videos of leaders. Likewise, Navarro, Curioso, Gomes, Arrieta, and Cortes (2013) collected and analyzed survey responses on work motivation over the course of 21 days. Lichtenstein, Carter, Dooley, and Gartner (2007) investigated dynamic patterns among the activities of new entrepreneurs using event histories and a panel survey. These researchers specifically focused on the temporal patterns of activities performed by new entrepreneurs.

As is demonstrated in the preceding examples, the twist to studying complex phenomena using traditional methods is surprisingly simple: Collect a large number of observations over time (Kozlowski et al., 2013) and investigate nonlinear fluctuations in those variables over time. As Navarro et al. (2013) have stated, in complex research, time is not just a variable. Instead, it provides context to help understand the observed behavior. As noted previously, each moment in time is not interchangeable in complex adaptive systems. An intervention today may yield drastically different results than an intervention several weeks from now. Each extra day of time required to implement the intervention may result in disproportionate changes in the success of that intervention.

Kozlowski et al. (2013) outlined a new quantitative research design paradigm that they have applied successfully to quantitatively study the emergence and evolution of system-level behavior. This paradigm starts with researchers' specifying a theory explicating the element-level processes that combine and interact to yield the system-level behavior. Once such a theory has been identified and the mechanisms specified, a computational model of the theory is created that allows researchers

to identify the unique behaviors resulting from a complex adaptive system that previously were unrecognized when the theory was presented and understood only verbally. Researchers have started following this recommendation, and studies using computer simulations to understand such rich and complex phenomena have started to appear. For example, Will (2016) developed a computer model demonstrating how leadership can emerge through interaction among multiple connected individuals. This modeling technique, called as *agent-based models*, has been helpful in explaining phenomena as wide ranging as the flocking behavior of birds to the rise and fall of ancient civilizations, behavior of financial markets, and organizational phenomena, such as emergent leadership (Macal & North, 2008). Simulations are particularly powerful for quantitative investigations of macrolevel phenomena (e.g., change of an organization). Simulations also are typically considered most effective and impactful when paired with studies of actual behavior.

The next stage of the Kozlowski et al. (2013) quantitative research design paradigm is to design human simulations that are consistent with the verbal theory and the computational model. Research participants are run through these simulations, and their behavior is repeatedly measured. The final stage of this new research paradigm is to use analytic techniques that can capture the dynamics of these data. Kozlowski et al. recommended the use of vector autoregressive models, which we discuss in a later section of this chapter. The central point of using such an analytic technique is that it verifies the agreement between the underlying theory, the computational simulations results, and the actual participant behavior.

Traditional survey, archival, and experimental research can be readily leveraged to study complex organizational phenomena. Any researcher interested in using these tools need to collect longitudinal data with many (e.g., 30 or more) observations of the same behavior over time. Additionally, these researchers need to consider time not only as a variable useful for predicting nonlinear changes and fluctuations but as part of the context surrounding and influencing the

TABLE 5.1

Two General Research Approaches to Investigating Complex Phenomena

Narrative/interpretive approach	Logico-scientific/objectivist
Focuses on storytelling, subjectivity, and search for meaning	Focuses on uncovering the "truth" and providing and testing good arguments grounded in solid theory
Qualitative data and storytelling	Quantitative data and hypothesis testing

observed fluctuations of the behavior of interest. In addition to investigating actual behavior, researchers interested in studying complex organizational phenomena may wish to use simulations to test theories of particularly macrolevel behavior.

Table 5.1 provides a summary of the qualitative and quantitative approaches used to study complex phenomena and Table 5.2 summarizes the various qualitative and quantitative techniques mentioned. In the next section, we discuss several possible quantitative analytic techniques for studying complex organizational phenomena. Our discussion only provides a sampling of the possible available techniques.

Analytic Techniques

Multilevel complex phenomena studied through quantitative methods may be analyzed a number of ways. In this section, we discuss four typical analytical techniques and review their usefulness with respect to analyzing complex multilevel phenomena in organizations specifically. These techniques are social network analysis, vector autoregressive models, cusp catastrophe modeling, and artificial neural networks.

TABLE 5.2

Summary of Research Techniques

Qualitative techniques	Quantitative techniques
Action research	Traditional longitudinal experiments
Interviews	Simulations
Surveys	Surveys
Observational research	Archival studies
Business documents	
External or archival data	

Interactions among lower level units: Social network analysis. As discussed earlier, complex adaptive systems are concerned with systems comprising interacting units that have influential relationships with each other (Page, 2010). Thus, one approach to studying such systems is to focus on the changing nature of the relationships among the lower level units of a system. However, we must move beyond the simple cause–effect conceptualization that currently is in favor in research (Hanges & Wang, 2012). The rich interconnections among units that influence each other imply that the effects of specific variables and actors are difficult to isolate. The influence of these units is felt through time and driven not only by an initiating behavior but by the current state of the system, prior actions, and ongoing interactions among the other units. Interventions occurring at one time may have no apparent effect, whereas the exact same intervention applied at a later time may dramatically change the system. Predictions of behavior and cause–effect relationship therefore are messy to do and to establish. In contrast, complexity science suggests that we need to focus on patterns of behavior rather than the behavior itself.

In the organizational literature, a focus on patterns can be seen in the work of Senge (2006) and his discussion of the fifth discipline. Senge used the term *the fifth discipline* to refer to *systems thinking*, which involves identifying patterns that repeat among the units in an organization as opposed to analyzing organizations as separate individuals or departments (e.g., HR department, manufacturing department) as the cause of or solution to a problem. Senge identified nine patterns (i.e., archetypes) that repeatedly occur within organizations, and the problems caused by these patterns can be solved only by working with the entire organizational system and not individual units/departments/components. Although the exact conditions that produce these patterns probably differ across organizations and situations, when viewed from a holistic perspective, the similarity in pattern and the similar consequences it has for the organizations is clear.

One such pattern identified by Senge (2006) was the *fixes that fail archetype*. In this pattern, an organization applies some solution to solve an existing problem. Although the fix is effective in the short term, it does not fix the problem in the long term. Indeed, the problem often gets worse in the long term because of the increasing number of side effects that emerge as a result of the short-term solution. For example, this pattern can be seen when local governments attempt to raise revenue by increasing taxes on certain products (e.g., cigarettes). In the short term, the revenue of the government increases. However, over time, the revenue will decrease and might stabilize at lower levels of revenue than before because fewer people are smoking as a result of the tax or more people are smuggling cigarettes from cheaper countries.

Another pattern is called the *tragedy of the commons* (Hardin, 2009). In this pattern, individuals acting in their own self-interest tend to exploit shared resources. The demand for the resources greatly outweighs the supply. Eventually, the resources become unavailable for everyone. For example, a few individuals acting in their own self-interest may decide that it is to their financial benefit to supplement their household budget by taking supplies (e.g., pens, paper) from their company. In the long run, however, these supplies are less available to everyone because the company, in an attempt to reduce the cost of supplies, place restrictions on who can access them. This pattern is seen repeatedly, from pollution to government regulations.

SNA is well suited to analyzing such patterns. For this analysis, information collected typically reflects ties between individuals in a group, teams within a department, departments within an organization, or branches/franchises within a multinational organization. The relationships being specified can reflect informal (i.e., friendship), influence, or communication relationships between these individuals, teams, departments, or branches/franchises (Aiken & Hanges, 2011). As discussed earlier, complex adaptive systems are self-contained, richly interconnected elements that interact to influence the behavior of each other. Thus, SNA maps the interrelationships among elements (e.g., people, teams, departments, branches/franchises) and specifies the nature (e.g., friendship, communication, influence) of these interrelationships to understand the emergent patterns between teams, departments, and organizations. This analysis produces quantitative measures describing properties of such systems. The most commonly used organizational applications of SNA are density (i.e., how richly interconnected the elements are) and centrality (i.e., the degree of hierarchical structure of the system).

SNA is inherently multilevel, using information about the interconnection among lower level elements to explain patterns emerging at the systems level. Thus, SNA is consistent with Senge's (2006) fifth discipline archetype argument in that it focuses our attention on the emergent patterns at the systems level, as opposed to unnecessarily focusing our attention on the individual elements. Consistent with this broader conceptualization of agents, recent network studies have begun to examine inter-team ties (e.g., Baldwin, Bedell, & Johnson, 1997; Hansen, Mors, & Løvås, 2005).

For example, if a researcher were interested in the consequences of different leadership styles on team effectiveness, SNA could identify the most influential person within a team via its centrality measure. SNA also can potentially identify moderators of this team leader's style by identifying team-level pattern differences among team members' relationships. Some team-level interconnection patterns might mitigate the leader's effectiveness, whereas others might enhance it. Indeed, consistent with the complex adaptive systems literature, emergent properties probably will be found after a certain SNA density level is achieved.

More recently, researchers have started to study and create unified *multinode networks*, which combine networks examining different types of elements/nodes. These nodes may differ in type (e.g., competencies, tasks, people) or in level of analysis (e.g., people, teams, departments). Multinode networks specify the interconnection between elements within a particular level of analysis (e.g., people) and between types/levels (e.g., the tasks performed by particular people, the competencies used to perform tasks, people's relationships to different organizations). For example, Marion, Christiansen, Klar, Schreiber, and Erdener (2016) recently created a multinode network in a study examining collective leadership in a school setting. Using both interview and network data, Marion et al. were able to simultaneously map relationships among people, tasks, and competencies in the school to understand emergent informal leadership patterns, emergent information flow patterns, and emergent clique behavioral patterns among school members. Furthermore, Marion et al. simulated different multinode networks by varying the degree of the input of the informal leadership pattern, information flow pattern, and emergent clique behavioral pattern (e.g., high, high, high; low, low, low; high, medium, low). Those simulated multinode networks then were used to predict organizational productivity capacity. They found that their multinode networks were able to better predict the organizational productivity capacity of the school's information network than single-node networks.

Researchers interested in complex adaptive systems may be particularly interested in how networks within and across nodes converge or diverge over time. Examples of convergence questions are whether individuals who are central at one element level (e.g., leader of a team) emerge over time to become central at a different element level (e.g., leader of a department). Another convergence question would be whether *boundary-spanners* (i.e., individuals with relationship to multiple teams) play a crucial role in enabling the entire network to coordinate behavioral responses to shocks from the environment. An example of a divergent question would be whether teams initially performing similar tasks will differentiate the nature of their tasks over time. These multinode networks can be used to model and test for an emergent

organizational system structure discussed in the complex adaptive systems literature.

The potential of SNA to answer questions regarding converging behavior of a dynamic system requires multiple measurements of such multinode networks over time. Not all traditional SNA computer programs are equipped to develop dynamic multinode networks, though. However, researchers interested in studying complex phenomena using SNA are recommended to investigate the shareware ORA-LITE package (Carley, 2018) developed out of Carnegie Mellon University. The role of time in social network studies is limited. These networks cannot be collected second by second. They may be particularly difficult to collect over a course of years. Perhaps given our current methodology, SNA is optimally suited to study dynamic phenomena that change on a daily, weekly, or monthly basis.

There are some disadvantages associated with SNA. The first is that missing data can be prevalent, thus disrupting the researcher's ability to accurately map existing networks. This disadvantage is likely compounded when networks are collected repeatedly over time. A second disadvantage is that repeated measurement of such networks may change the nature and behavior of the network itself. Similar to Heisenberg's (1927) uncertainty principle discussed in quantum physics and our earlier discussion of sensitivity to initial conditions, the very act of repeatedly measuring relationship networks probably changes the trajectory of those networks over time. Two individuals located in identical positions within the same network structure at time one may diverge into completely different locations in the network simply by repeatedly measuring the network of one of them. Perhaps the network of the person being repeatedly measured is less dynamic than the person not repeatedly assessed. Another disadvantage is that social network data are self-report. Self-report data may artificially inflate appearance of stability over time.

SNA holds substantial promise for quantitatively capturing the dynamics of the shifting interconnections and the developing hierarchical structure emerging from these interactions among the elements in a complex adaptive system. In the next section, we discuss how to analyze data showing how complex systems evolve and adapt to their environment over time.

Linear multilevel system change: Stochastic linear adaptive systems. As discussed earlier, the behavior of complex adaptive systems may converge if the system is under the influence of a single attractor. One analytic technique designed to empirically model the behavior of systems and a technique that was recommended explicitly by Kozlowski et al. (2013) is a kind of time-series analysis. More specifically, this approach is called *vector autoregressive (VAR) models*. Most of the applications in psychology and the business literature that have used such time-series models have used linear models.

A *linear dynamic system* is one that changes over time in a linear fashion. That is, the evolution of the system's behavior (*Y*) is driven by some basic mechanism (*X*). Linear change means that the same mechanism, *X*, is applied to the system repeatedly over time (DeShon, 2012). Linear dynamic models also are *time invariant*, that is, the magnitude of the underlying mechanism's (*X*) effect has on the system's behavior (*Y*) does not change, no matter how many times it is repeatedly applied.

When modeling a dynamic linear system, the researcher can use either a deterministic or a stochastic model. *Deterministic linear dynamic models* are ones in which the behavior of a system is influenced only by the mechanisms (X_1 and X_2) specified in the model. These models do not allow random error or mechanisms not specified in the model to influence the system's behavior. For example, in a deterministic model that specifies one dependent variable (i.e., *Y* = system behavior) and two mechanisms (X_1 and X_2), the system's behavior at some time in the future (e.g., time = *T* + 1) is only a function of the two specified mechanisms (X_1 and X_2).

In contrast, *stochastic linear dynamic models* are ones in which the behavior of a system is influenced by many mechanisms ($X_1, X_2, X_3, \ldots X_k$), but only some of these mechanisms (e.g., X_1 and X_2) are specified in the model. The unspecified mechanisms ($X_3, X_4, X_5, \ldots X_k$) still influence the system's behavior at some time in the future (*T* + 1), but the influences of these unspecified mechanisms are incorporated into the model as random error (ε).

Regardless of whether they are using deterministic or stochastic models, researchers try to capture two properties of the system's behavior. The first behavior, called *autocorrelation*, also known as serial correlation, refers to the influence of a variable (e.g., system behavior) at an earlier time (e.g., time *T*) on the behavior of that same system at some later time period (e.g., time *T* + 1). Figure 5.2 is a pictorial representation of several possible autocorrelational models. In Figure 5.2A, B, and C, we consider only five time periods of the system's behavior (*Y*). In Figure 5.2A, the system's behavior at each time period is not influenced by the system's prior behavior. This is an example of a system that does not have any autocorrelation.

We see autocorrelations in lots of psychological phenomena. For example, one common problem when conducting interviews is that the rating of a particular interviewee (e.g., interviewee 2) often is influenced by the rating of the immediately preceding interviewee (e.g., interviewee 1). In the interview literature, this is called a *contrast effect*, that is, the rating of one person is influenced by the people preceding that person. Autocorrelation measures the strength of the influence of the preceding interviewee on the subsequent

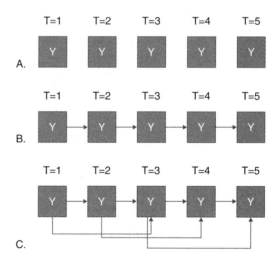

FIGURE 5.2. Three possible autocorrelation patterns. In this figure, *T* represents the time periods when system behavior (*Y*) is measured. A shows a system with no autocorrelation. B shows a system with an autocorrelation at lag = 1. C shows a system with an autocorrelation at lag = 2.

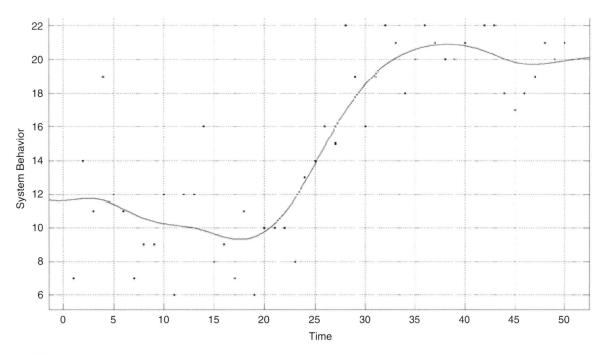

FIGURE 5.3.   Moving average example.

interviewee(s). If the rating of an interviewee is influenced only by the immediately preceding interviewee, we say we have a model with an autocorrelation at lag 1. Figure 5.2B is a pictorial representation of a model with an autocorrelation at lag 1. However, the rating of an interviewee can be influenced by many preceding interviewees, as shown in Figure 5.2C. For example, in Figure 5.2C, the behavior of Y at time 3 is influenced by the system's behavior at times 1 and 2. Thus, Figure 5.2C shows a 2-lag autocorrelation model.

The second property captured by researchers is whether the trend of the system's behavior is systematically changing over time. A *stationary time series* is one in which there is no systematic change in the mean behavior of a system (i.e., no trend) over time. However, the mean level of a system's behavior might change over time. If the behavior of a system systematically changes over time, the model is said to have a *moving average*. Figure 5.3 shows the trace line of some system's behavior over time (e.g., factory production levels). Notice that initially, the production of the factory was lower than the subsequent production level of the factor. This is an example of a moving average.

Seeing Figure 5.3, a researcher may ask, Why did the production level of the factory change over time?

The researcher may have a hypothesis that some mechanism (e.g., consumer demand) influenced the factory's production level. VAR models are used when we want to model the influence of one or more independent variables ($X_1, X_2, X_3, \ldots X_k$) on the behavior of one or more dependent variables ($Y_1, Y_2, Y_3, \ldots Y_k$). Figure 5.4 shows a VAR model in which factory productivity (Y) is tracked over five time periods. In this figure, we see that consumer demand (X) also is tracked over five time periods. To test the researcher's hypothesis that consumer demand is influencing factor production, we conducted a VAR model in which consumer demand (X) at time T influences subsequent factor production levels (Y) at time $T + 1$ (see arrow going from X to Y

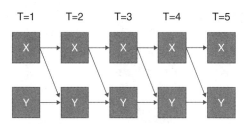

FIGURE 5.4.   Example of a vector autoregressive model in which factory productivity (Y) is a function of consumer demand (X) over time (T).

in Figure 5.4). The VAR analysis can be thought of as a regression analysis in which the autocorrelation of consumer demand and the autocorrelation of factory production levels are taken into account. The strength of X on Y can be thought of as the regression coefficients obtained from regression analysis. Given that we are modeling this phenomenon using a linear model, the strength of the regression weights is the same over time.

Schmidt and DeShon (2010) used a VAR model to examine the relationship between self-efficacy and performance within people. Classic motivation theory argues that self-efficacy should have a positive impact on subsequent performance (Bandura, 1997; Locke & Latham, 1990). Schmidt and DeShon measured participants' self-efficacy ratings and task performance scores for 50 or so time periods. Using VAR analysis, these researchers were able to show that contrary to classic motivation theory, Schmidt and DeShon found that performance at time T influenced subsequent self-efficacy, and not the other way around.

VAR models appear to be promising for modeling the dynamics and relationships of complex systems. However, linear VAR models are the most common models that have been applied in psychology and organizational sciences. These models probably are useful when a complex adaptive system is under the influence of a single dynamic attractor. However, what happens when the system is being pulled by two or more attractors? The system will exhibit discontinuous shifts that are not handled well by linear VAR models. In this next section, we discuss catastrophe models that are useful for studying discontinuous changes in complex adaptive systems.

Nonlinear multilevel system change: Cusp catastrophe modeling. *Catastrophe theory*, originally derived by Thom (1975), describes the behavior of a system as it evolves over time. Although this is exactly what VAR models do, the utility of catastrophe theory becomes apparent when the system is being influenced by two or more attractors. Repeated environmental pressure might push the system so that another attractor starts to influence its behavior. Thus, catastrophe theory can be used to model the discontinuous change of complex adap-

tive systems. Like the ball representing Hotel X's climate in Figure 5.1B, when the ball is at the apex of a hill on a nonlinear continuum/landscape, the system's behavior changes suddenly and discontinuously (Poston & Stewart, 1978). Thom identified seven different elementary catastrophe models that he hypothesized would explain the behavior of systems undergoing discontinuous change. These different models vary as a function of the number of predictors influencing the system, as well as the number of dependent measures assessing the system's behavior. An overview of Thom's catastrophe theory is shown in Table 5.3.

The majority of the empirical application of catastrophe theory in psychology and organizational behavior has focused on the *cusp model*, which is favored for various reasons. First, it is parsimonious comparing with the rest of the models, except the first one, and it can be described fairly quickly. Second, it is the first elementary catastrophe model that has specified statistical properties, such as probability distributions (Cobb, 1978, 1981). Moreover, it has been found useful in explaining competing attractors influence on a dynamic system.

In the cusp model, the behavior of the dynamic system (Y) is influenced by two independent variables. The first independent variable, denoted by α, is called the asymmetry parameter. The *asymmetry parameter* separates the two attractors, and changes along this parameter put pressure on

TABLE 5.3

Thom's (1975) Catastrophe Theory Taxonomy

Catastrophe model	No. of dependent variables	No. of independent variables
Fold	1	1
Cusp	1	2
Swallowtail	1	3
Butterfly	1	4
Hyperbolic umbolic (wave crest)	2	3
Elliptic umbolic (hair)	2	3
Parabolic umbolic (mushroom)	2	4

the system to change its behavior (Hanges et al., 1991). The second independent variable, denoted by β, is the bifurcation parameter. The *bifurcation parameter* affects the change pattern of the dynamic system when it switches from one attractor to the other. The cusp catastrophe model is useful for understanding the behavior of systems influenced by two attractors.

Cusp catastrophe modeling is inherently multilevel and cross level. Specifically, cusp catastrophe modeling uses individual observations over time to demonstrate emergent, catastrophic change at the system level. In cusp catastrophe modeling, hypotheses are tested regarding how lower level interactions lead to upper-level change. Thus, cusp catastrophe modeling ideally is suited to the study of complex multilevel phenomena, particularly with respect to modeling a bottom-up nonlinear change process.

We have discussed modeling change of a system's behavior with both linear and nonlinear models. However, how can we tell whether nonlinear dynamics are operating in the system generating our data? There are several indicators or fingerprints of a nonlinear dynamic system that can be tested for in a system's behavior. One of the easiest methods is for the researcher to look for what Gilmore (1981) has termed *catastrophe flags*, an approach that requires the researcher to look for characteristics signs or flags in the dependent variable's distribution. These signs correspond to specific predictions from the cusp catastrophe model regarding the behavior of the dependent variable. Something to look for in the trace line in the dependent variable are sudden discontinuous changes in the dependent variable. Another flag is whether the dependent variable exhibits bimodality for certain values of the asymmetry and bifurcation parameters. These are things that can hint that the dynamic nature of the system is more nonlinear than linear.[2]

So far, we have discussed analytic techniques for studying the shifting patterns of interactions among elements in a complex adaptive system and for modeling the evolution and change of system-level

behavior. In this next section, we discuss the last analytic tool that we cover in this chapter, namely, artificial neural networks.

Bottom-up emergence: Artificial neural networks. *Artificial neural networks* have been applied to model and further our understanding of emergent behavior produced by complex adaptive systems. The original work on these models focused on creating a computational model representing the activity of biological neurons (Somers, 1999). However, subsequent work has elaborated and expanded on these basic models so that neural networks provide computational models of various emergent psychological (e.g., schemas, learning) and organizational behavior (Bechtel & Abrahamsen, 2002; Scarborough, 1996; Scarborough & Somers, 2006).

At its most basic, neural networks model the relationships between variables. The easiest structure to use is to think of a basic neural network that has two input variables (X_1 and X_2) and one outcome variable (Y). The relationship between the two predictors and the dependent variable is specified according to the following equation:

$$Y = W_1 X_1 + W_2 X_2 + b_0.$$

In this equation, Y is a predicted value created by differentially weighting (W_1, W_2) the information of the two predictors (X_1, X_2). W_1 and W_2 are the weights assigned to the different input variables, and b_0 is a constant. Critical readers can see the similarity between this equation and ordinary regression analysis. Indeed, neural network analysis is a more general form of regression analysis (see, e.g., Aiken & Hanges, 2015). However, neural network analysis more general than ordinary least-squares regression because it handles more complex interconnections than traditional regression can handle.

Neural networks vary in their structure, shape, and function. Specifically, networks with different shapes are used for different purposes. In this article, we only discuss one kind of neural network. Specifically, we limit our discussion to the aforementioned feedforward neural network.

---

[2]Statistical techniques to estimate the parameters of the various catastrophe models have been proposed over the years. Some of the early researchers used ordinary least-squares regression analyses to empirically estimate these models (e.g., Guastello, 1995). Use of regression analysis for this purpose is controversial and has been criticized (Alexander, Herbert, DeShon, & Hanges, 1992).

To see how neural networks can model complex behavior, we have to consider a slightly more complex neural network: the feedforward neural network. *Feedforward neural networks* have predictor (i.e., input) and dependent (i.e., output) variables. The values of the input variables are measurable and can be directly input by the researcher. The output of the neural network (i.e., the dependent variable) also is directly observable and, indeed, is of interest to the researcher. However, feedforward neural networks can capture nonlinear behavior because of additional variables—the so-called hidden variables that are not measured by the researcher yet carry information about the complex interactions among the measured predictors. Figure 5.5 shows an example of a feedforward model. It is called *feedforward* because the information gets processed only in one direction: left to right. On the left of Figure 5.5 are the predictors and on the right is the dependent variable. Between these two layers of variables are the hidden (H_1 and H_2) variables. As shown by the arrows, the value of the hidden variables is a result of differential weighting of the input variables. Thus, similar to regression analysis, these hidden variables represent interaction terms. However, unlike interactions in regression analysis in which these terms are equally weighted combinations of the predictors, in neural network

models, the interactions can comprise dramatically different combinations of the predictors. Thus, the types of interactions that are considered and can be detected by neural networks are far more complex than considered in ordinary regression.

The preceding hypothetical example was merely a simple demonstration because we only had one neuron and two input variables presented. Now, imagine a network of five neurons connected to each other in a bidirectional relationship, each having two to three input variables that predicted them, and some of the input variables being connected to more than one neuron. It is a more complex situation because of the interdependency among the variables. Neural network analysis is capable of handling this interdependency of a complex adaptive system.

Neural network models have been applied successfully to validate tests (Scarborough, 1996), Marshall and English (2000) used neural networks to improve the prediction of child's risk of being abused and neglected. Collins and Clark (1993) used neural networks to predict workplace behavior. All of these models have used neural networks to capture statistical information about their data. For more information, see Hanges et al. (2002).

However, neural networks also can be created in a theory-oriented manner. There are many different

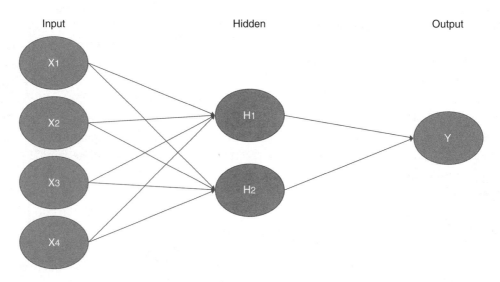

FIGURE 5.5. Example of a feedforward neural network. In this feedforward model, X_1, X_2, X_3, and X_4 represent different predictors of some dependent variable (Y). H_1 and H_2 represent hidden variables in this model.

neural networks. Hanges, Lord, and colleagues (Hanges, Dorfman, Shteynberg, & Bates, 2006; Hanges, Lord, & Dickson, 2000; Lord & Hall, 2003; Lord, Hanges, & Godfrey, 2003) have developed theory-based neural network models to understand leadership and decision-making behavior. Similarly, other researchers have developed neural network models of leadership perceptions (Wray, Palmer, & Bejou, 1994) and banking customer behaviors (Davies, Moutinho, & Curry, 1996). These models are multilevel in nature in that they discuss how information at the lower level of analysis can be combined to generate global, network-wide outcomes.

Neural network analysis is an appealing way of assessing nonlinear relationships among predictors and outcomes. Not only is it conceptually—at its base—similar to regression analysis (see, e.g., Aiken & Hanges, 2015), it is a powerful and simple way of leveraging existing data to study complex, nonlinear relationships. For readers with interest in neural network analysis, Hanges et al. (2002) provided a more thorough overview of how to conduct neural network analysis.

Complex multilevel data can be productively analyzed by SNA, VAR models, cusp catastrophe modeling, and artificial neural networks, as well as through narrative when using qualitative research. One challenge in conducting research on complex adaptive systems is the need for rich data. Because complexity science requires an immersive, rich analysis, research on complex adaptive systems tends to either zoom in on one organization or simulate larger systems and larger numbers of organizations. Thus, a key question in complexity science is how to link agent-based modeling and other simulations to the analysis of data collected from a real-world organization (see, e.g., Houchin & MacLean, 2005). Marion et al. (2016) demonstrated one productive way to make this connection. First, they collected data within an organization. Then, they worked from that data to run a simulation exploring how other outcomes might have emerged. The reverse may be practiced, as well. Specifically, researchers may run a simulation first and then test the theory again in a case study or on a smaller scale within an organization.

Complexity science requires researchers to step outside of their comfort zone in several ways:

1. Researchers must understand the environment in which a complex adaptive system operates, including the initial conditions of that system.
2. Researchers also must embrace the interconnectedness in the system, studying patterns and processes rather than discrete outcomes.
3. Researchers developing theories grounded in complexity science in organizational research should not think about only one level at a time while creating hypotheses.
4. Due to the independence within and between levels, researchers investigating complex organizational phenomena must keep the system level in mind while thinking through lower level interactions, and keep lower level units in mind while thinking through systemic change.
5. Complexity researchers must move past direct effects and consider how to test indirect and inconsistent effects within the system.
6. Perhaps most important, researchers in complex adaptive systems must fully embrace longitudinal research to reveal the nonlinear, catastrophic, emergent changes that complex adaptive systems undergo.

FINAL THOUGHTS: A CALL TO ARMS

A literature search on PsycINFO using the phrases "complexity science," "complexity theory," and "organizational" yielded only 146 articles, books, and book chapters. Given the small number of articles published in the organizational sciences that draw on complexity science, you may think that complexity science was only recently developed. That would be an incorrect conclusion to draw. Complexity science has been around for decades. It established a particularly powerful foothold in science in the 1980s with the formation of the Santa Fe Institute (Pascale, 1999). Although some researchers have investigated organizational phenomena through a complexity science perspective, as discussed in this chapter, and some practitioners have applied complexity science to their organizational change efforts (e.g., Beeson & Davis, 2000; Shaw, 1997), complexity science is still a fringe theory in the broader context of organizational behavior research. The Santa Fe Institute is perhaps the most well-known complexity research center in the United States. As a multidisciplinary research center, resident faculty members at that institute hold doctoral degrees in mathematics, physics, economics, energy and resources, survey methodology, biology, and evolutionary theory. No resident faculty members hold degrees in psychology or organizational behavior.

Why hasn't complexity science caught on in the organizational behavior and industrial and organizational (I/O) psychology literature? We believe that three key concerns have prevented the widespread implementation of complexity science in organizational research. We outline these concerns next and discuss how we, as a field, can overcome them. By doing so, we can expand our collective theoretical palate.

Statistical Challenges

Challenges maintaining and summarizing the kinds of rich data sets required by complexity research have likely dampened efforts to investigate complex phenomena. Specifically, for much of the 20th century, there simply was not a lot of high-powered statistical software available to most researchers. However, we have entered the era of big data. Many robust software packages exist that are well equipped to handle large databases and complex analyses, including analyses highlighted in this chapter. Thus, the software itself now exists for complexity research to thrive. However, the field of I/O psychology needs to implement more rigorous training to enable future I/O psychologists to leverage the software that is available to them. For example, introductory research courses can focus on teaching R (see https://www.r-project.org/contributors.html) or SAS, rather than SPSS. Additionally, upper-level courses should be offered to train students on complexity-specific analyses and the software that can be used to conduct such analyses (e.g., SNA in ORA-LITE [Carley, 2018]; catastrophe modeling in GEMCAT [Oliva, Desarbo, Day, & Jedidi, 1987]).

Community Challenges

Closely tied to the software challenge is the challenge of community and thus the opportunity to inspire new researchers to study complex phenomena. The complexity science research community in I/O psychology is fairly small. To date, the most systematic collaborations—even in book form—have focused on complexity leadership. The lack of a fully connected community in part drives challenges with training. Many graduate programs do not have anyone who studies complexity science in organizations, thus they may not be equipped to offer the kind of training needed to catalyze the next generation of complexity scientists. Two broad sets of actions can be taken to overcome this challenge. First, complexity researchers should come together as a community. Second, universities should leverage that community to provide cross-university training on complexity research and enable cross-university research projects between interested students and professors.

Discomfort

The final barrier to adoption of complexity science in organizational research may be the most challenging one to overcome: discomfort with complexity science itself. As we have discussed, complexity requires scientists to move away from strict determinism. For many scientists, breaking from determinism may be uncomfortable and difficult. As Schneider and Somers (2006) suggested, resistance to complexity science may be emotional, as well as intellectual. Because complexity science requires researchers to approach research itself from a different lens, complexity science may be intimidating or difficult for some to understand. Similarly, some budding researchers may be unsure how to apply complexity science in their research.

Because complexity science is so uncommonly applied in organizational research, many editors and reviewers may be unfamiliar with it. A lack of familiarity in editorial and review teams results in challenges publishing articles drawing on complexity science. Overcoming discomfort in the application of complexity science is again a challenge that can be solved primarily through training and the development of a robust community.

CONCLUSION

Complexity science is a useful tool. Like every tool, it is useful in solving some problems but not others. However, no tool is useful until you know how and when to apply it. Anyone interested in multilevel research needs to develop at least a conversational understanding of complexity science. Adding complexity science to your toolkit will give you the knowledge and skills you need to create and test theory you have never dreamed you could test. In our discussion, we have done our best to provide a high-level, easy-to-understand explanation of complexity science. We have provided a definition, key characteristics of complex adaptive systems, examples of complexity science in organizations, and a detailed discussion of some of the challenges and opportunities presented in research and analysis of complex adaptive systems. We have provided references and resources for further study for the interested reader. Finally, we have outlined a call for multilevel researchers to learn complexity science so that their own research streams can be enhanced.

References

Aiken, J. R., & Hanges, P. J. (2011). Research methodology for studying dynamic multi-team systems: Application of complexity science. In S. J. Zaccaro, M. A. Marks, & L. DeChurch (Eds.), *Multi-team systems: An organization form for dynamic and complex environments* (pp. 431–458). New York, NY: Routledge Academic.

Aiken, J. R., & Hanges, P. J. (2015). Teach an IO to Fish: Integrating data science into IO graduate education. *Industrial and Organizational Psychology: Perspectives on Science and Practice, 8,* 539–544. http://dx.doi.org/10.1017/iop.2015.80

Alexander, R. A., Herbert, G. R., DeShon, R. P., & Hanges, P. J. (1992). An examination of least-squares regression modeling of catastrophe theory. *Psychological Bulletin, 111,* 366–374. http://dx.doi.org/10.1037/0033-2909.111.2.366

Baldwin, T. T., Bedell, M. D., & Johnson, J. L. (1997). The social fabric of a team-based MBA program: Network effects on student satisfaction and performance. *Academy of Management Journal, 40,* 1369–1397. http://dx.doi.org/10.2307/257037

Bandura, A. (1997). *Self-efficacy: The exercise of control.* New York, NY: Freeman.

Bechtel, W., & Abrahamsen, A. (2002). *Connectionism and the mind: Parallel processing, dynamics, and evolution in networks* (2nd ed.). Malden, MA: Blackwell.

Beeson, I., & Davis, C. (2000). Emergence and accomplishment in organizational change. *Journal of Organizational Change Management, 13,* 178–189. http://dx.doi.org/10.1108/09534810010321508

Bishop, R. (2002). Deterministic and indeterministic descriptions. In H. Atmanspacher & R. Bishop (Eds.), *Between chance and choice: Interdisciplinary perspectives on determinism* (pp. 5–32). Charlottesville, VA: Imprint Academic.

Boyatzis, R. E. (2006). An overview of intentional change from a complexity perspective. *Journal of Management Development, 25,* 607–623. http://dx.doi.org/10.1108/02621710610678445

Brown, S. L., & Eisenhardt, K. M. (1997). The art of continuous change: Linking complexity theory and time-paced evolution in relentlessly shifting organizations. *Administrative Science Quarterly, 42,* 1–34. http://dx.doi.org/10.2307/2393807

Byrne, D. (1998). *Complexity theory and the social sciences: An introduction* (pp. 14–34). New York, NY: Routledge.

Carley, K. M. (2018). ORA-LITE (Version 8) [Software]. Retrieved from http://www.casos.cs.cmu.edu/projects/ora/software.php

Chiles, T. H., Meyer, A. D., & Hench, T. J. (2004). Organizational emergence: The origin and transformation of Branson, Missouri's musical theaters. *Organization Science, 15,* 499–519. http://dx.doi.org/10.1287/orsc.1040.0095

Cobb, L. (1978). Stochastic catastrophe models and multimodal distributions. *Behavioral Science, 23,* 360–374. http://dx.doi.org/10.1002/bs.3830230407

Cobb, L. (1981). Parameter estimation for the cusp catastrophe model. *Behavioral Science, 26,* 75–78. http://dx.doi.org/10.1002/bs.3830260107

Collins, J. M., & Clark, M. R. (1993). An application of the theory of neural computation to the prediction of workplace behavior: An illustration and assessment of network analysis. *Personnel Psychology, 46,* 503–524. http://dx.doi.org/10.1111/j.1744-6570.1993.tb00882.x

Davies, F., Moutinho, L., & Curry, B. (1996). ATM user attitudes: A neural network analysis. *Marketing Intelligence & Planning, 14,* 26–32. http://dx.doi.org/10.1108/02634509610110778

DeShon, R. P. (2012). Multivariate dynamics in organizational science. In S. W. J. Kozlowski (Ed.), *The Oxford handbook of organizational psychology* (Vol. 1, pp. 117–142). New York, NY: Oxford University Press.

Eidelson, R. J. (1997). Complex adaptive systems in the behavioral and social sciences. *Review of General Psychology, 1,* 42–71. http://dx.doi.org/10.1037/1089-2680.1.1.42

Einstein, A. (1920). *Relativity: The special and general theory* (R. W. Lawson, Trans.). New York, NY: Holt.

Fisher, L. (2009). *The perfect swarm: The science of complexity in everyday life.* New York, NY: Basic Books.

Foti, R. J., Knee, R. E., Jr., & Backert, R. S. G. (2008). Multi-level implications of framing leadership perceptions as a dynamic process. *Leadership Quarterly, 19,* 178–194. http://dx.doi.org/10.1016/j.leaqua.2008.01.007

Freund, J., Brandmaier, A. M., Lewejohann, L., Kirste, I., Kritzler, M., Krüger, A., . . . Kempermann, G. (2013). Emergence of individuality in genetically identical mice. *Science, 340,* 756–759. http://dx.doi.org/10.1126/science.1235294

Friedenberg, J. (2009). *Dynamical psychology: Complexity, self-organization and mind.* Litchfield, AZ: ISCE.

Gersick, C. J. (1991). Revolutionary change theories: A multilevel exploration of the punctuated equilibrium paradigm. *Academy of Management Review, 16,* 10–36. http://dx.doi.org/10.5465/AMR.1991.4278988

Gilmore, R. (1981). *Catastrophe theory for scientists and engineers.* New York, NY: Dover.

Gilpin, D. R., & Miller, N. K. (2013). Exploring complex organizational communities: Identity as emergent perceptions, boundaries, and relationships. *Communication Theory, 23,* 148–169. http://dx.doi.org/10.1111/comt.12008

Goldstein, J. (2008). Conceptual foundations of complexity science: Development and main constructs. In M. Uhl-Bien & R. Marion (Eds.), *Complexity leadership, part I: Conceptual foundations* (pp. 17–48). Charlotte, NC: Information Age.

Guastello, S. J. (1995). *Chaos, catastrophe, and human affairs: Applications of nonlinear dynamics to work, organizations, and social evolution.* Mahwah, NJ: Erlbaum.

Hanges, P. J. (1987). A catastrophe model of control theory's decision mechanism: The effects of goal difficulty, task difficulty, goal direction and task direction on goal commitment. *Dissertation Abstracts International, 48*(1-B), 294.

Hanges, P. J., Braverman, E. P., & Rentsch, J. R. (1991). Changes in raters' perceptions of subordinates: A catastrophe model. *Journal of Applied Psychology, 76,* 878–888. http://dx.doi.org/10.1037/0021-9010.76.6.878

Hanges, P. J., Dorfman, P. W., Shteynberg, G., & Bates, A. L. (2006). Culture and leadership: A connectionist information processing model. In W. H. Mobley & E. Weldon (Eds.), *Advances in global leadership* (Vol. 4, pp. 7–37). Bingley, England: Emerald Group.

Hanges, P. J., Lord, R. G., & Dickson, M. W. (2000). An information processing perspective on leadership and culture: A case for connectionist architecture. *Applied Psychology, 49,* 133–161. http://dx.doi.org/10.1111/1464-0597.00008

Hanges, P. J., Lord, R. G., Godfrey, E. G., & Raver, J. L. (2002). Modeling nonlinear relationships: Neural networks and catastrophe analysis. In S. Rogelberg (Ed.), *Handbook of research methods in industrial and organizational psychology* (pp. 431–455). Malden, MA: Blackwell.

Hanges, P. J., & Wang, M. (2012). Seeking the holy grail in organizational science: Uncovering causality through research design. In S. W. J. Kozlowski (Ed.), *The Oxford handbook of organizational psychology* (pp. 79–116). New York, NY: Oxford University Press. http://dx.doi.org/10.1093/oxfordhb/9780199928309.013.0003

Hansen, M. T., Mors, M. L., & Løvås, B. (2005). Knowledge sharing in organizations: Multiple networks, multiple phases. *Academy of Management Journal, 48,* 776–793. http://dx.doi.org/10.5465/AMJ.2005.18803922

Hardin, G. (2009). The tragedy of the commons. *Journal of Natural Resources Policy Research, 1,* 243–253. http://dx.doi.org/10.1080/19390450903037302

Hebb, D. O. (1949). *The organization of behavior.* New York, NY: Wiley.

Heisenberg, W. (1927). Uber den anschaulichen Inhalt der quantentheoretischen Kinematik und Mechanik [The physical content of quantum kinematics and mechanics]. *Zeitscrft Fuer Physik, 43,* 172–198.

Houchin, K., & MacLean, D. (2005). Complexity theory and strategic change: An empirically informed critique. *British Journal of Management, 16,* 149–166. http://dx.doi.org/10.1111/j.1467-8551.2005.00427.x

Jarvis, C., Gulati, A., McCririck, V., & Simpson, P. (2013). Leadership matters: Tensions in evaluating leadership development. *Advances in Developing Human Resources, 15,* 27–45. http://dx.doi.org/10.1177/1523422312467138

Kemeny, J., & Oppenheim, P. (1956). On reduction. *Philosophical Studies, 7,* 6–19. http://dx.doi.org/10.1007/BF02333288

Kozlowski, S. W. J., Chao, G. T., Grand, J. A., Braun, M. T., & Kuljanin, G. (2013). Advancing multilevel research design: Capturing the dynamics of emergence. *Organizational Research Methods, 16,* 581–615. http://dx.doi.org/10.1177/1094428113493119

Lichtenstein, B. B. (2000). Self-organized transitions: A pattern amid the chaos of transformative change. *Academy of Management Executive, 14,* 128–141.

Lichtenstein, B. B., Carter, N. M., Dooley, K. J., & Gartner, W. B. (2007). Complexity dynamics of nascent entrepreneurship. *Journal of Business*

Venturing, 22, 236–261. http://dx.doi.org/10.1016/j.jbusvent.2006.06.001

Locke, E. A., & Latham, G. P. (1990). Work motivation and satisfaction: Light at the end of the tunnel. *Psychological Science, 1,* 240–246. http://dx.doi.org/10.1111/j.1467-9280.1990.tb00207.x

Lord, R. G. (2008). Beyond transactional and transformational leadership: Can leaders still lead when they don't know what to do? In M. Uhl-Bien & R. Marion (Eds.), *Complexity leadership, part I: Conceptual foundations* (pp. 155–184). Charlotte, NC: Information Age.

Lord, R. G., & Hall, R. (2003). Identity, leadership categorization, and leadership schema. In D. V. Knippenberg & M. A. Hogg (Eds.), *Leadership and power: Identity processes in groups and organizations* (pp. 48–64). Thousand Oaks, CA: Sage. http://dx.doi.org/10.4135/9781446216170.n5

Lord, R. G., Hanges, P. J., & Godfrey, E. G. (2003). Integrating neural networks into decision making and motivational theory: Rethinking VIE theory. *Canadian Psychology/Psychologie canadienne, 44,* 21–38. http://dx.doi.org/10.1037/h0085815

Macal, C. M., & North, M. J. (2008, December). Agent-based modeling and simulation: ABMS examples. In *2008 Simulation Conference, WSC 2008, Winter* (pp. 101–112). http://dx.doi.org/10.1109/WSC.2008.4736060

Marion, R. (1999). *The edge of organization: Chaos and complexity theories of formal social systems.* Thousand Oaks, CA: Sage.

Marion, R., Christiansen, J., Klar, H. W., Schreiber, C., & Erdener, M. A. (2016). Informal leadership, interaction, cliques and productive capacity in organizations: A collective analysis. *Leadership Quarterly, 27,* 242–260. http://dx.doi.org/10.1016/j.leaqua.2016.01.003

Marshall, D. B., & English, D. J. (2000). Neural network modeling of risk assessment in child protective services. *Psychological Methods, 5,* 102–124. http://dx.doi.org/10.1037/1082-989X.5.1.102

Navarro, J., Curioso, F., Gomes, D., Arrieta, C., & Cortes, M. (2013). Fluctuations in work motivation: Tasks do not matter! *Nonlinear Dynamics, Psychology, and Life Sciences, 17,* 3–22.

Oliva, T., Desarbo, W., Day, D., & Jedidi, K. (1987). GEMCAT: A general multivariate methodology for estimating catastrophe models. *Behavioral Science, 32,* 121–137. http://dx.doi.org/10.1002/bs.3830320205

Page, S. E. (2010). *Diversity and complexity.* Princeton, NJ: Princeton University Press.

Paraskevas, A. (2006). Crisis management or crisis response system? A complexity science approach to organizational crises. *Management Decision, 44,* 892–907. http://dx.doi.org/10.1108/00251740610680587

Pascale, R. T. (1999). Surfing the edge of chaos. *Sloan Management Review, 40,* 83–94.

Plowman, D. A., Baker, L. T., Beck, T. E., Kulkarni, M., Solansky, T., & Travis, D. V. (2007). Radical change accidentally: The emergence and amplification of small change. *Academy of Management Journal, 50,* 515–543. http://dx.doi.org/10.5465/AMJ.2007.25525647

Plowman, D. A., & Duchon, D. (2008). Dispelling the myths about leadership: From cybernetics to emergence. In M. Uhl-Bien & R. Marion (Eds.), *Complexity leadership: Part 1: Conceptual foundations* (pp. 129–153). Charlotte, NC: Information Age.

Poston, T., & Stewart, I. (1978). *Catastrophe theory and its applications.* London, England: Pitman.

Poutanen, P., Siira, K., & Aula, P. (2016). Complexity and organizational communication: A quest for common ground. *Human Resource Development Review, 15,* 182–207. http://dx.doi.org/10.1177/1534484316639713

Romanelli, E., & Tushman, M. L. (1994). Organizational transformation as punctuated equilibrium: An empirical test. *Academy of Management Journal, 37,* 1141–1166. http://dx.doi.org/10.2307/256669

Scarborough, D. J. (1996). An evaluation of backpropagation neural network modeling as an alternative methodology for criterion validation of employee selection testing. *Dissertation Abstracts International: Section B. Sciences and Engineering, 56*(8-B), 4624.

Scarborough, D. J., & Somers, M. J. (2006). *Neural networks in organizational research: Applying pattern recognition to the analysis of organizational behavior.* Washington, DC: American Psychological Association. http://dx.doi.org/10.1037/11465-000

Schmidt, A. M., & DeShon, R. P. (2010). The moderating effects of performance ambiguity on the relationship between self-efficacy and performance. *Journal of Applied Psychology, 95,* 572–581. http://dx.doi.org/10.1037/a0018289

Schneider, B. (1987). The people make the place. *Personnel Psychology, 40,* 437–453. http://dx.doi.org/10.1111/j.1744-6570.1987.tb00609.x

Schneider, B., & Barbera, K. M. (2014). Introduction: The Oxford handbook of organizational climate and culture. In B. Schneider & K. M. Barbera (Eds.), *The Oxford handbook of organizational climate and culture* (pp. 3–22). New York, NY: Oxford University Press.

Schneider, B., & Reichers, A. E. (1983). On the etiology of climates. *Personnel Psychology, 36,* 19–39. http://dx.doi.org/10.1111/j.1744-6570.1983.tb00500.x

Schneider, B., White, S. S., & Paul, M. C. (1998). Linking service climate and customer perceptions of service quality: Test of a causal model. *Journal of Applied Psychology, 83*, 150–163. http://dx.doi.org/10.1037/0021-9010.83.2.150

Schneider, M., & Somers, M. (2006). Organizations as complex adaptive systems: Implications of complexity theory for research. *Leadership Quarterly, 17*, 351–365. http://dx.doi.org/10.1016/j.leaqua.2006.04.006

Senge, P. M. (2006). *The fifth discipline: The art and the practice of the learning organisations*. London, England: Random House Books.

Shaw, P. (1997). Intervening in the shadow systems of organizations: Consulting from a complexity perspective. *Journal of Organizational Change Management, 10*, 235–250. http://dx.doi.org/10.1108/09534819710171095

Shoham, S., & Hasgall, A. (2005). Knowledge workers as fractals in a complex adaptive organization. *Knowledge and Process Management, 12*, 225–236. http://dx.doi.org/10.1002/kpm.228

Solansky, S. T., Beck, T. E., & Travis, D. (2014). A complexity perspective of a meta-organization team: The role of destabilizing and stabilizing tensions. *Human Relations, 67*, 1007–1033. http://dx.doi.org/10.1177/0018726713516373

Somers, M. J. (1999). Application of two neural network paradigms to the study of voluntary employee turnover. *Journal of Applied Psychology, 84*, 177–185. http://dx.doi.org/10.1037/0021-9010.84.2.177

Streufert, S. (1997). Complexity: An integration of theories. *Journal of Applied Social Psychology, 27*, 2068–2095. http://dx.doi.org/10.1111/j.1559-1816.1997.tb01641.x

Styhre, A. (2002). Non-linear change in organizations: Organizational change management informed by complexity theory. *Leadership & Organization Development Journal, 23*, 343–351. http://dx.doi.org/10.1108/01437730210441300

Thom, R. (1975). *Structural stability and morphogenesis: An outline of a general theory of models*. Reading, MA: Benjamin.

Tsoukas, H., & Hatch, M. J. (2001). Complex thinking, complex practice: The case for a narrative approach to organizational complexity. *Human Relations, 54*, 979–1013. http://dx.doi.org/10.1177/0018726701548001

Uhl-Bien, M., Marion, R., & McKelvey, B. (2007). Complexity leadership theory: Shifting leadership from the industrial age to the knowledge era. *Leadership Quarterly, 18*, 298–318. http://dx.doi.org/10.1016/j.leaqua.2007.04.002

Vallacher, R., & Nowak, A. (Eds.). (1994). *Dynamical systems in social psychology*. New York, NY: Academic Press.

Vallacher, R. R., Read, S. J., & Nowak, A. (2002). The dynamical perspective in personality and social psychology. *Personality and Social Psychology Review, 6*, 264–273. http://dx.doi.org/10.1207/S15327957PSPR0604_01

Will, T. E. (2016). Flock leadership: Understanding and influencing emergent collective behavior. *Leadership Quarterly, 27*, 261–279. http://dx.doi.org/10.1016/j.leaqua.2016.01.002

Wray, B., Palmer, A., & Bejou, D. (1994). Using neural network analysis to evaluate buyer-seller relationships. *European Journal of Marketing, 28*(10), 32–48. http://dx.doi.org/10.1108/03090569410075777

CHAPTER 6

THE MISSING LEVELS OF MICROFOUNDATIONS: A CALL FOR BOTTOM-UP THEORY AND METHODS

Robert E. Ployhart and Jonathan L. Hendricks

Nearly all areas of the social sciences are concerned with the interplay between individuals and the collectives created by those individuals. How individual thought and action interrelate with collective thought and action is a question that spans philosophy to science and, within science, spans disciplines from economics, sociology, and psychology (von Bertalanffy, 1968). It comes as no surprise, then, that one of the enduring "Grand Challenges" facing the organizational sciences is understanding how intrafirm heterogeneity contributes to interfirm heterogeneity. Adam Smith (1776/1963) questioned the extent to which individuals contributed to the success of nations. Hall, Baird, and Geissler (1917) challenged applied psychologists to link psychological attributes to the outcomes of firms and society. Penrose (1959) pondered the likelihood of human capital's contribution to the "productive service" of firms. Despite having very different scholarly origins, these disciplines share a common assumption in that individual differences, and the manner in which members interact, are expected to contribute to differences in organizational-level processes and outcomes (e.g., Barney, 1991; Nahapiet & Ghoshal, 1998; Nyberg, Moliterno, Hale, & Lepak, 2014). After all, no organization exists without individuals because individuals comprise the collective that *is* the organization (Schneider, 1987; Weick, 1995).

There is little scientific debate about the interdependence between individuals and organizations. And this, paradoxically, is the problem. With few exceptions (e.g., research on top-management teams and strategic human capital resources), there is little critical examination of the extent to which individual differences and employee interactions contribute to firm-level differences in processes, performance, or competitive advantage. As we develop in this chapter, it has been far more convenient either to assume that individuals influence firms, or that they do not, than to explicitly specify the multilevel processes through which individuals relate to firm-level processes and outcomes (Felin, Foss, & Ployhart, 2015; Ployhart & Hale, 2014).

This chapter seeks to focus attention on what we believe has been an underappreciated and understudied topic in the organizational sciences: the specific mechanisms through which individuals (and interactions among individuals) contribute to firm-level process and outcome heterogeneity. We want to challenge researchers to consider explicitly how such a connection exists, by theoretically explicating the nature of bottom-up effects. We argue that this topic has not been sufficiently addressed in any scholarly area, including multilevel research in organizational behavior (OB), industrial and organizational psychology (I/O), and human resources (HR), strategic management research on

http://dx.doi.org/10.1037/0000115-007
The Handbook of Multilevel Theory, Measurement, and Analysis, S. E. Humphrey and J. M. LeBreton (Editors-in-Chief)

human capital resources, or research on strategic OB and the foundation of competitive advantage. We argue that although these areas are necessary for understanding the intrafirm determinants of firm-level heterogeneity, they currently do not provide a sufficient understanding because they lack explicit connection to the broader factor market (e.g., labor market) that firms compete in.

In making these arguments, we first briefly review the historical foundation that has come to frame the current micro–macro conversation. We focus special attention on research in microfoundations and strategic OB, and then critically examine the extent to which multilevel theory and methods have been incorporated into these research streams. It will be shown that most microfoundations and strategic OB research do not fully incorporate multilevel principles to the degree needed to connect with firm-level outcomes, such as competitive advantage. We then provide a general strategy to microfoundations research that integrates existing microfoundations and strategic OB research with multilevel principles. Our hope is this will help microfoundations researchers develop a better understanding of the bottom-up effects of individuals on organizational outcomes.

HISTORICAL FORCES THAT DIVIDE (BUT DON'T CONQUER)

There have historically been two fields of management that give privilege to either the individual or the collective (i.e., firms and organizations). One field, focused primarily on the characteristics and behaviors of individuals, comes from a scholarly tradition based within psychology. The other field, focused primarily on the characteristics and actions of firms, comes from a scholarly tradition based within economics and sociology. These traditions have come to be known as *micro* and *macro*, respectively (Hitt, Beamish, Jackson, & Mathieu, 2007;

Molloy, Ployhart, & Wright, 2011). Meso research represents a third type, but it is primarily based on small groups and smaller subunits within firms and thus tends to draw more heavily from psychology and OB (and to a lesser extent, sociology).[1]

Both micro and macro traditions have had reasonably well-defined problem spaces and thus a corresponding set of assumptions that has allowed each tradition to live within convenient theoretical boundaries. Figure 6.1 shows the major established empirical findings (solid arrows) and assumptions (dashed arrows) within the micro and macro disciplines. As the figure illustrates, both micro and macro research tend to be dominated by within-level research (individual/small group or firm, respectively). The micro literature tends to focus on the prediction of individual job performance (and small group performance) and assumes that individual performance behavior aggregates to influence firm performance. This *performance aggregation assumption* is essentially the focus of utility analysis (see Schneider, Smith, & Sipe, 2000). In contrast, the macro literature tends to examine whether resources (and, for our purposes, human capital resources) contribute to competitive advantage and firm performance (Crook, Todd, Combs, Woehr, & Ketchen, 2011).[2] However, it tends to rely on theory and assumptions that human capital resources emerge from individuals and interactions between individuals (e.g., Barney, 1991; Ployhart & Moliterno, 2011). The *human capital resource emergence assumption* enables strategy researchers to focus almost exclusively on firm-level relationships. For example, it is assumed that human capital resources contribute to competitive advantage because they are based on aggregation processes that are path dependent, socially complex, and causally ambiguous (Dierickx & Cool, 1989).

Figure 6.1 is clearly a stylized example in that it simplifies the nature of micro and macro research, and although there are studies that do test some

---

[1]Because micro and meso primarily originate within psychology and, to some extent, sociology, we frequently refer to them both as *micro* unless there is a need to be more specific.
[2]There is an important difference between firm performance and firm competitive advantage (Peteraf & Barney, 2003; Ployhart et al., 2014). Performance is an index based on market (e.g., customer satisfaction), financial (e.g., Tobin's q), or accounting (e.g., EBIT [earnings before interest and taxes]) metrics. Competitive advantage occurs when a firm generates above-average returns. Performance follows the logic that "more is better," whereas competitive advantage follows the logic of differentiation.

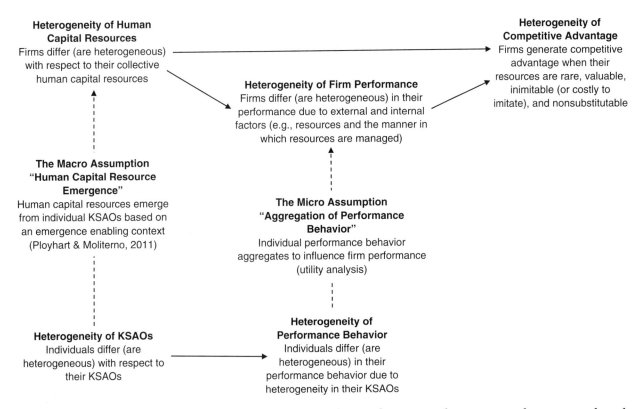

FIGURE 6.1.   Assumptions used to support inferences that firm performance and competitive advantage are shaped by individuals. Solid arrows indicate relationships reasonably well established in prior research. Dashed arrows indicate relationships generally assumed in prior research. The meso level is not shown to keep the figure simple. KSAO = knowledge, skills, abilities, and other characteristics.

of the assumptions, such research is the exception. That said, Figure 6.1 highlights the assumptions that are convenient for micro and macro scholars and enable the research machine in each discipline to hum along in a predictable manner. Indeed, all scientific disciplines make assumptions, and doing so is necessary to focus research attention in a manner that contributes to cumulative knowledge creation. For example, most micro/meso research assumes that the broader implications of individual and small group behavior have firm-level consequences— if not, then why should they be studied within organizational settings (Heath & Sitkin, 2001)? Alternatively, given the focus on competitive advantage and competitive environments, most macro research assumes that the firm level is the lowest needed to understand the determinants of firm performance (e.g., Winter, 2011).

However, problems arise when the prescriptions being generated from a body of research contradict known facts that exist in adjacent disciplines. The

problem with a bifurcated field of management is that the research literature fails to reflect organizational phenomena as they exist in nature (e.g., Johns, 2006). The phenomena we seek to understand, and the prescriptions we seek to offer, do not often conform to assumptions adopted in most management research. The nature of organizations is inherently multilevel, and thus any within-level research necessarily provides an incomplete picture of the role of talent in shaping organizational performance and competitive advantage (Simon, 1973). Therefore, as a field, we do not know much about how heterogeneity among individuals contributes to firm-level heterogeneity in performance and competitive advantage. We believe this is a profoundly disturbing conclusion.

One might expect that recognizing discrepancies caused by single-level thinking will lead management scholars to adopt a multilevel perspective to understand why and how the discrepancies exist. In the last few years there has been movement in this regard, most actively with the research on strategic human capital resources (Coff & Kryscynski, 2011; Nyberg & Wright, 2015; Ployhart & Hale, 2014; Wright, Coff, & Moliterno, 2014). But the challenge comes from trying to resolve discrepancies that span not only organizational levels but also distinct disciplines in the social sciences (e.g., psychology, economics, education, nursing, sociology). This is an exceedingly difficult endeavor because it requires revising the problem spaces, assumptions, and types of questions that one studies (Molloy et al., 2011). Reconciling multilevel *and* disciplinary divides requires a scholarly revolution that embraces a new framework, set of assumptions, and guiding principles.

The introduction of multilevel theory and methods can provide the spark capable of producing such a revolution. Multilevel concepts have appeared in various ways and in different literatures (e.g., Klein, Dansereau, & Hall, 1994; Rousseau, 1985; von Bertalanffy, 1968), but it was Klein and Kozlowski's (2000) book that offered the first integrated treatment of theory, methods, and analytics across levels. This book created a bridge that provided a blueprint for connecting micro and macro disciplines. In turn, this framework facilitated research trying to examine how micro cognition, affect, and behavior could shape higher level constructs and processes (e.g., team coordination, firm resources, performance).

The multilevel framework thus provides a mechanism for connecting micro and macro (Hitt et al., 2007). Rather than making convenient assumptions about cross-level linkages (or relying on theoretical arguments that remain untested), scholars have the theoretical, methodological, and analytical tools needed to challenge prior assumptions and start to explicitly examine cross-level linkages theoretically and empirically. Yet the multilevel frameworks have not had an even impact on micro–macro scholarship. As we show here, multilevel methods have been embraced by those trained in micro areas more than those trained in macro areas. Further, even those trained in the micro tradition tend not focus on bottom-up effects in their research. In the section that follows, we review two streams of research that seek to answer bottom-up questions

relating individuals and small groups to firm-level outcomes (performance and competitive advantage). One stream of research comes from strategic management and is known as *microfoundations* (Barney & Felin, 2013). This research identifies how the characteristics and behaviors of individuals and small groups shape firm outcomes and vice versa (Felin, Foss, & Ployhart, 2015; Ployhart & Hale, 2014). The second stream of research is known as STRategic Organizational BEhavior (STROBE) and has origins in I/O psychology and OB (Ployhart, 2015). STROBE examines how characteristics of individuals and small groups may shape organizational competitive advantage (e.g., do organizations that use team-based structures outperform those that do not?). Microfoundations research examines similar questions but with a more explicit focus on within-firm interactions among members (Felin et al., 2015). We show that even though both approaches seek to explain "bottom-up" processes, neither sufficiently incorporates multilevel principles into the theory, design, and analysis.

THE MEANING OF MICROFOUNDATIONS

The majority of research in strategic management treats the firm as the lowest level of interest (Aldrich, 2006). The theoretical foundation for strategic management research has been in economics, and hence the "higher order" factors examined in strategic management tend to be factor markets, industries, and competitive environments. Strategic management research certainly pays attention to within-firm characteristics, with top-management teams and human capital resources serving as obvious examples (Barney, 1991; Hambrick & Mason, 1984). Yet research in this tradition tends to place a more limited emphasis on phenomena occurring at levels lower within the firm (for illustrations in strategic HR, see Wright & Boswell, 2002). As a result, the nature and quality of human behavior within these lower levels has not been considered to be relevant to the questions of what determines firm performance and contributes to competitive advantage. Stated alternatively, any within-firm variability in the constructs of interest (e.g., individuals comprising a firm's human capital) is considered error variance, in a manner that within-condition variance is often treated as error variance in classic experiments assessed via analysis of variance.

The microfoundations "movement" is a reaction to ignoring within-firm variability. It represents a paradigmatic shift in which strategic management researchers give explicit focus to understanding within-firm causes for firm-level outcomes (Felin et al., 2015). Microfoundations rebuts the macro–micro view exemplified by collectivists such as Durkheim (1982), who focused on the influence of collective-level constructs such as rules, roles, and climate in determining outcomes at the same level. Collectivist arguments are built on the assumption that individuals are molded by their climate and culture, which washes out the impact of individual heterogeneity. Instead, microfoundations researchers share the opinion of Esser (1994), that causation begins at the bottom and thus emphasizes the role of individuals and interactions in determining macro outcomes (Felin & Foss, 2005).

A microfoundations emphasis is appealing because it provides the opportunity to generate theoretically driven and empirically testable insights into the lower level origins of organizational outcomes (Abell, Felin, & Foss, 2008; Felin & Foss, 2009). A limitation with purely collectivist (firm-level) research is the theoretical black box from which the causes of firm-level outcomes originate—a limitation that also prohibits actionable suggestions and insights (Abell et al., 2008; Barney & Felin, 2013). In contrast, microfoundations allow theoretical assumptions to be specified, hypothesized, and tested. For example, Grigoriou and Rothaermel (2014) found that organizational knowledge is a function of intraorganization knowledge networks, specifically between star performers and their colleagues. Their findings demonstrated the importance of star individuals as well as intrafirm interactions in generating organizational capabilities. Ultimately, microfoundations research allows researchers to more fully articulate *who*, *what*, *when*, and *how* human capital resources generate firm-level outcomes that include different types of performance and competitive advantage.

Thus, microfoundations provide a new perspective in identifying the drivers of organizational outcomes.

Rather than looking externally from the top-down (e.g., competitive environments, competitor actions), microfoundations advocates examining bottom-up processes from within the firm—specifically how intraorganization decisions and interactions affect the shaping of organizational capabilities over time (Barney & Felin, 2013). Explanations for firm capabilities thus can be found in psychological and sociological theories. For example, Kor and Mesko (2013) used arguments about social learning and integration to suggest that an organization's absorptive capacity is affected by the interactions within the top management team. Similar linkages have demonstrated how individual-level phenomena impact firm-level outcomes (Foss, 2011). On the surface, the microfoundations perspective provides a number of unique perspectives for future researchers to investigate. We review these perspectives in terms of defining microfoundations, identifying the focal interest on interactions within factor markets, and how microfoundations is similar to or different from strategic OB.

Definitions and Scope

The relatively recent interest in microfoundations has contributed to considerable breadth in developing both the definition and scope of microfoundations (Barney & Felin, 2013). Felin, Foss, Heimeriks, and Madsen (2012) provided a generic but broadly applicable definition: "In the simplest sense, a baseline micro-foundation for level N_t lies at level $N-1$ at time $t-1$, where the time dimension reflects a temporal ordering of relationships with phenomena at level $N-1$ predating phenomena at level N" (p. 1255). This is another way to say that microfoundations are defined in terms of organizational levels and that the causes of a higher level outcome exist at levels lower than the outcome and at time periods that precede the outcome. For example, a microfoundations perspective would propose that the cause of firm performance in 2015 is caused by within-firm determinants in 2014.

The high level of abstraction present in the definition of microfoundations allows great flexibility in defining microfoundation constructs. For example, microfoundation perspectives have been used in investigating interactions between consumers and firms (Jaanssen, 1993) as well as exploring individual characteristics and cognitions in shaping social networks (Tasselli, Kilduff, & Menges, 2015). Although the breadth of the definition provides a wide swath for researchers to explore microfoundations, the underlying assumption of microfoundations papers is that lower level phenomena provide a meaningful contribution to the formation of higher level phenomena. Furthermore, within the various types of within-firm resources, microfoundations give privilege to people. Foss (2011) suggested that microfoundations of strategic management are "foundations that are rooted in individual action and interaction" (p. 1414).

Given this assumption, the scope of micro-foundations research is focused on exploring the micro-macro link, where interactions and phenomena at a lower level provide the theoretical and empirical origins for higher level phenomena (Felin et al., 2015). For example, in management, microfoundations researchers have applied theories from psychology and sociology to explain why individual heterogeneity (Felin & Hesterly, 2007) and individual behavior and interactions (Barney & Felin, 2013) are sources of organizational outcomes. Thus, macro to macro relationships are understandably absent in an microfoundations analysis (Abell et al., 2008). Microfoundations researchers acknowledge that individual-level interactions are influenced by organizational-level factors (Coleman, 1990). However, microfoundations research emphasizes the micro-to-macro causal chain—the study of bottom-up influences on higher level outcomes. This is an important alternative to most existing within-level or cross-level research that emphasizes top-down effects (we discuss this in more detail shortly).

An additional feature in microfoundations research is the development and application of metatheory to link the micro to the macro (Humphrey & Aime, 2014). Just as constructs cannot be assumed to be isomorphic between levels (Kozlowski & Klein, 2000), microfoundations theories must be able to highlight the differences that exist between the

individual and collective levels (Barney & Felin, 2013). For example, Grigoriou and Rothaermel (2014) found that organizational knowledge stems not only from the knowledge possessed by employees and their behaviors but also by the "embeddedness" of individual relationships and interactions. The distinction between organizational and individual knowledge suggests that it is inaccurate to simply borrow psychological and sociological theories and apply them to a higher level of abstraction (Barney & Felin, 2013; Rousseau, 1985). Rather, firm outcomes necessitate an explanation of both individual- and collective-level theories. Thus, microfoundations focus on applying metatheories that encompass multiple levels, and thus a variety of theoretical frameworks from different disciplines may be used (Humphrey & Aime, 2014).

Emphasis on Interactions and Factor Markets

Microfoundations are concerned with intra-organization interactions and processes among employees that contribute to firm-level outcomes within competitive factor markets. Factor markets are where resources are exchanged. For example, the factor market for talent is the labor market. This cross-level perspective ensures that microfoundations are focused both on intrafirm interactions that affect firm-level outcomes, as well as factor markets that are external to the firm, to explain heterogeneity in firm competitive advantage.[3]

Interactions among people. Organizations are composed of individuals that are embedded within a unique social context. On one hand, the work organization context is just another form of context, such as families, social organizations, or schools and civic groups. On the other hand, the work organization creates a context that is unique from these other contexts because of the broader environment that surrounds organizations (e.g., competitive economic environment, legal and regulatory environment, cultural environment) and hence merits special consideration (Heath & Sitkin, 2001; Johns, 2006;

---

[3]It is worth noting that most microfoundations research follows the tradition of strategic management and emphasizes the study of competitive advantage over the study of firm performance.

Rousseau & Fried, 2001). Interactions between others within this organizational context shape affect, cognition, and behavior (Barsade, 2002; Lockwood & Kunda, 1997; Pearsall & Venkataramani, 2015), which ultimately shape and form the knowledge, skills, and abilities of the individuals (and groups) within that context (Ployhart & Moliterno, 2011). For example, Foss and Lindenberg (2013) argued that the way in which goals are framed to employees affects both firm-level motivation and the value created by the firm. Therefore, individual interactions are vital in explaining the microfoundations influences of firm heterogeneity.

Indeed, the microfoundations literature has taken a primary focus on understanding how interactions with others influence the isomorphism between the individual-level and the higher level manifestation of constructs (Ployhart & Moliterno, 2011). That is, the focus is the interaction between individuals, as well as the individuals themselves (Barney & Felin, 2013). For example, Overbeck, Correll, and Park (2005) found that although a team can have a large amount of aggregate ability, individual ability does not aggregate up to the team level when the team fails to sufficiently coordinate or communicate. Thus, interactions alter the manifestation of team, as well as firm, capabilities. Moreover, these interactions may have an impact on the emergence of seemingly unrelated firm outcomes. This was noted by Helfat and Peteraf (2015), who found that the dynamic capabilities of the organization emerged as a function of the social cognition of managers and interactions between managers. Although social cognition is distinct from the construct of dynamic capabilities, social interactions enhance the ability of the firm to overcome resistance to change and better align its strategic assets. Thus, firm-level outcomes are a function of both the members within the firm and the interactions among these members.

Factor markets. One of the areas in which microfoundations research differs from other approaches is the emphasis given to factor markets. Factor markets determine the external worth of an organizational resource (e.g., human capital resources, physical resources). As noted earlier, the factor market for talent is the relevant labor market from

which a firm competes for talent. It is not possible to estimate the worth or value of talent resources, or whether employees or the firm captures more value, without an explicit consideration of the broader factor market (Coff, 1999; Lepak, Smith, & Taylor, 2007). *Value capture* is the value that the organization appropriates for itself after distributing value to its various stakeholders (including the employees who created the value; Lepak et al., 2007). Value capture has a direct impact on competitive advantage because it determines the extent to which an organization captures the value that is created by its human capital resource pool (relative to competitors in the market for similar resources; Peteraf & Barney, 2003). Value creation is not enough to generate a competitive advantage because employees may be able to appropriate the value that they create (Coff, 1999). It is therefore critical to understand how value that is created is captured and distributed among stakeholders.

This means that factor markets are an essential element to understanding microfoundations because the factor market determines the value of the organization's human capital. For example, stars have been noted for their ability to generate disproportionate value for an organization (Nanda, Nohria, & Groysberg, 2009). However, stars are well known to the external market and are often able to appropriate more value than their peers who are not recognized as stars (Ravid, 1999). Thus, stars may not be a source of competitive advantage for an organization when they appropriate the value that they create—that is, stars are paid so much that any value they create for a firm is captured in their salary. However, there are instances in which a star fails to capture the value he or she creates. One instance in which this can occur is when a star's productivity is partially dependent on the other members of the star's team (Grigoriou & Rothaermel, 2014). In such instances, the complementarities that have been generated within the team both enhance the performance of the star and constrain the star's mobility because at least part of the star's performance is context dependent. Such a star will either not be seen as valuable to external competitors because he or she will be perceived to possess firm-specific, rather than generic, human capital, or the competitor will overpay to appropriate the star, which will generate performance losses for the competitor. This second instance was found by Groysberg, Lee, and Nanda (2008), who indicated that organizational performance can suffer as a result of star acquisition when star productivity declines after leaving his or her team members.

To summarize, microfoundations research is like most strategic management research in that it seeks to develop answers for when and why firms achieve competitive advantage. However, it differs from most strategic management research because it theorizes that the locus of value capture and competitive advantage resides among the interactions of members *within* the firm (rather than firm-level resources). The scope of microfoundations is focused on explicating the link from micro and macro. At its core, microfoundations is about the interaction among people and how these interactions create firm-level heterogeneity in competitive markets.

Strobe

Those trained in OB, HR, and I/O psychology may view work on microfoundations as new wine in old skins. On the surface, the study of microfoundations appears to be the study of groups, teams, culture, climate, and related classic topics. This criticism does have an element of truth when focusing on the "micro" part of microfoundations research—that is, the nature of employees and their interactions. Those of us in OB, HR, and I/O (i.e., micro and meso areas) are intimately familiar with small group processes, employee attitudes, team composition, knowledge-sharing among group members, and so on. This research is largely based on multilevel frameworks and gives considerable attention to inputs and processes that influence the emergence of higher level constructs from lower level constructs (Kozlowski & Klein, 2000). This micro–meso research is obviously relevant to microfoundations research, and thus it is easy to dismiss microfoundations as ignoring or reinventing research that has been ongoing for more than 100 years.

However, although giving extraordinary attention to the "inputs" of performance, micro research tends to give less attention to the nature of performance itself, particularly when firm-level performance is the focus. What makes microfoundations research unique is that it examines intrafirm member interactions within the context of firm-level characteristics, factor markets, and competitive environments. This broader context is something that is usually not considered explicitly in micro (or explicitly meso) research (see Cappelli & Sherer, 1991; Johns, 2006). Competitive advantage is not the same as job or even organizational performance (Ployhart & Hale, 2014; Ployhart, Nyberg, Reilly, & Maltarich, 2014). Performance may be an important precondition for competitive advantage, but competitive advantage is ultimately about differentiating the firm in a way that captures disproportionate value (Peteraf & Barney, 2003). Understanding the determinants of competitive advantage cannot occur without explicit consideration of competitors, competitive environments, and factor markets. As noted earlier, factor markets are the "arena" where resources are acquired, divested, or traded; labor markets are the most obvious example (Barney, 1986). Labor markets determine the value of resources based on basic laws of supply and demand. Thus, it is impossible to understand strategic choices, value, and competitive advantage without consideration of factor markets and competitive environments.

With this in mind, it becomes clear that existing micro and meso research do not overlap as much as many assume (for similar arguments, see Barney & Felin, 2013; Felin et al., 2015). Microfoundations research gives explicit attention to factor markets but little attention to multilevel processes that contribute to competitive advantage. Micro research gives more consideration to multilevel processes that lead to firm performance but essentially no attention to factor markets that are necessary for understanding competitive advantage. As a result, we actually don't know much about how traditionally micro and meso topics such as small group and team characteristics or employee attitudes, contribute to competitive advantage (Ployhart & Hale, 2014). Ployhart and Hale (2014) noted that there is considerable research linking collective employee attitudes, shared culture and climate, and even collective KSAOs (knowledge, skills, abilities, and other characteristics—i.e., human capital resources) to firm-level outcomes (e.g., productivity, sales) but

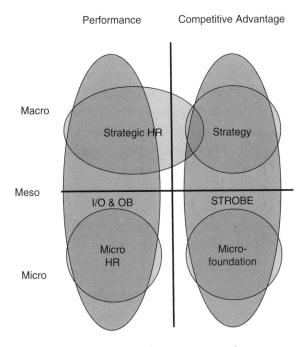

Performance   Competitive Advantage

Macro

Strategic HR   Strategy

Meso

I/O & OB   STROBE

Micro
HR

Micro-
foundation

Micro

FIGURE 6.2.   Scholarly domains across the micro, meso, and macro levels of analysis. Note that this figure is only a broad summary intended to identify the main themes and areas of focus in prior research. There are many examples of research that are exceptions to the summary shown below. HR = human resources; I/O = industrial and organizational psychology; OB = organizational behavior; STROBE = strategic organizational behavior. From "Strategic Organizational Behavior (STROBE): The Missing Voice in the Strategic Human Capital Conversation," by R. E. Ployhart, 2015, *Academy of Management Perspectives*, 29, p. 345. Copyright 2015 by Academy of Management. Adapted with permission.

not to competitive advantage. It was this observation that led to a complement to microfoundations research called STROBE (Ployhart, 2015; Ployhart & Hale, 2014). STROBE is a perspective that seeks to take traditionally micro topics and link them to firm-level competitive advantage.

Figure 6.2 provides an overview of different scholarly areas and is based on Ployhart (2015) and Ployhart et al. (2014). The circles and ellipses in the figure represent different scholarly domains: I/O, OB, HR, strategy, STROBE, and microfoundations. The vertical line represents different levels, macro (top), meso (middle), and micro (lowest). The horizontal line represents two firm outcomes: performance (e.g., productivity, sales) and competitive advantage (differentiation from competitors and generation of above-normal returns) (see Ployhart, 2015). Ellipses that span more than one quadrant are domains that address one or more levels, or both performance and competitive advantage. I/O and OB, micro HR and strategic HR, and STROBE deal with constructs at the micro, meso, and macro levels of analysis. In terms of outcomes, IO, OB, and micro HR focus mainly on performance. Strategic HR focuses primarily on performance but also considers competitive advantage. STROBE, microfoundations, and strategy focus on competitive advantage. Table 6.1 builds from these distinctions to offer more specific similarities and differences.

TABLE 6.1

Key Similarities and Differences Between Micro and Microfoundations Research

	Micro	Microfoundations
Phenomena of primary interest	Individuals, small groups, team processes, and collective manifestations of individuals within organizations	Interactions among individuals within competitive environments
Lowest level of interest	Individuals	Interactions among individuals
Outcomes of primary interest	Performance (individual or firm)	Competitive advantage
Scholarly discipline	Industrial and organizational psychology, organizational behavior, human resources	Strategic management, labor economics
Primary disciplinary foundation	Psychology	Economics, sociology
Secondary disciplinary foundation	Sociology	Psychology
Multilevel principles	Fundamentally part of theory and design	Rarely considered or recognized as a fundamental part of theory and design

Thus, when micro researchers are critical of microfoundations researchers, they are being selective because they are ignoring the fundamental importance of factor markets and competitive advantage. When microfoundations researchers are critical of OB, HR, and I/O researchers, they are focusing on the fact that micro research does not consider the broader macro competitive environment. Of course, the distinctions raised in Figure 6.2 and Table 6.1 are broad summaries, and there are exceptions to broad summary statements. For example, research on top-management teams often draws from psychological theory (Peterson, Smith, Martorana, & Owens, 2003), and some micro research draws from sociology (e.g., faultlines, relational demography; see Humphrey & Aime, 2014). But in general, the distinctions shown in Figure 6.2 and Table 6.1 tend to capture the majority of research in each area.

Identifying these distinctions is more than just an academic exercise. The purpose is not to carve up research settlements to be owned by different scholarly camps. The world does not need more silos. Rather, it is instructive to understand these differences in perception and focus because they help identify what work needs to be done moving forward. It is clear that the major task to advance the study of microfoundations is to more explicitly integrate the long tradition of scholarly micro research within the umbrella of strategic factor markets. In our opinion, basing this integration on a foundation of multilevel principles will be the fastest way to make it happen. However, the task is not a simple one because, in contrast to most multilevel research, the focus is not to identify top-down contextual effects but rather explicate bottom-up effects.

AN APPRAISAL OF MICROFOUNDATIONS FROM A MULTILEVEL LENS

The prior section defined the nature of microfoundations research and identified important distinctions from the adjacent scholarly domains of OB, HR, and I/O. We argued that one of the reasons micro scholars are dismissive of microfoundations research is because it does not conform to their way of thinking, particularly because it ignores multilevel principles. In this section, we consider this criticism

in more detail and evaluate the extent to which microfoundations research is consistent with a multilevel framework. For our purposes, we focus on the following elements of multilevel systems: emergence, multilevel principles, and time. We focus on these three areas because they are broadly fundamental to multilevel research and sufficiently highlight the key areas where microfoundations can benefit from multilevel frameworks.

Emergence

Emergence is fundamentally a theoretical question of how high-level collectives come to exist from lower level origins. Emergence usually takes a methodological tone (e.g., Bliese, 2000; Chan, 1998), but emergence is foremost a theoretical question (Kozlowski & Klein, 2000). Emergence has been considered in numerous areas, and there are many ways to conceptualize it (see an entire special issue devoted to this topic in *Managerial and Decision Economics*: "Emergent Nature of Organization, Markets and Wisdom of Crowds," 2012). However, because the framework developed by Kozlowski and Klein (2000) is the most common in the organizational literature, we adopt their approach and define an emergent phenomenon as one that "originates in the cognition, affect, behaviors, or other characteristics of individuals, is amplified by their interactions, and manifests as a higher-level, collective phenomenon" (p. 55). In the most fundamental manner, emergence occurs when individuals interact in ways that contribute to the formation of a new higher level construct. Remove the interaction between individuals, and emergence largely disappears (or at least changes in significant ways).

Kozlowski and Klein's (2000) framework was extremely influential because it pulled together many disparate views about emergence. In their framework, emergence exists on a continuum of composition to compilation. *Composition* forms of emergence occur where there is consensus or similarity among lower level observations. For example, when employees have similar perceptions about the climate in their organization, a firm-level climate construct emerges. *Compilation* forms of emergence occur when the lower-level observations are assembled in such a way that they complement each other, such as pieces in a puzzle. For example, cross-functional teams are assembled to complete tasks that are so complex, no one person has the necessary expertise to complete the team's task. Bliese (2000) took this logic a bit further and made the important observation that emergence is rarely purely composition or compilation but rather falls somewhere between the two idealized types (i.e., composition is a "fuzzy" process).

The micro and meso literatures take considerable effort in explicating the nature of emergence. For example, research on groups and teams describes a number of processes and types of team tasks that shape member interaction—and thus create different types of emergence (Kozlowski & Ilgen, 2006; Marks, Mathieu, & Zaccaro, 2001; Mathieu, Tannenbaum, Donsbach, & Alliger, 2014). Some of this work is making its way into the strategic human capital literature (e.g., Ployhart & Moliterno, 2011; Ployhart, Weekley, & Baughman, 2006). However, careful specification of emergence processes has not yet become widespread in the microfoundations literature—at least to the extent commonly adopted by micro researchers. This is an interesting disconnect because research focuses primarily on the *member interaction* itself as the focal construct. In contrast to the teams literature, microfoundations research gives less attention to how this *interaction construct* emerges from individual characteristics (e.g., composition or compilation), or how higher level (firm-level) constructs may emerge from these lower-level origins (e.g., human capital resources). The *predictor terrain* of microfoundations sits in the meso level (above individuals but below firms) and focuses on the bottom-up effects of member interactions on firm outcomes but tends to ignore how these interactions emerge and how they influence firm-level outcomes. This makes it difficult for microfoundations research to answer important questions about how those interactions contribute to firm heterogeneity and competitive advantage.

Principles of Multilevel Systems

Kozlowski and Klein (2000) also provided a framework for thinking about the core elements of multilevel systems (see also von Bertalanffy, 1968). For example, they pulled together concepts such as near decomposability, effect asymmetries, and bond strength as a means to develop core principles of multilevel systems. *Near decomposability* implies that levels that are interrelated cannot be truly disentangled, and thus there is always some misspecification in within-level research (Simon, 1973). *Effect asymmetries* recognize that top-down effects happen more quickly, and with greater consequence, than bottom-up effects. *Bond strength* refers to the fact that levels that are closely connected will be more highly interrelated, and so effects that happen at one level have increasingly weaker effects as the levels get farther apart. Taken together, these principles are essentially laws that govern multilevel systems.

Kozlowski and Klein (2000) also helped clarify three broad types of multilevel models. *Within-level* models are those in which the independent and dependent variables are both contained within the same level and are the dominant models in micro and macro research (see Figure 6.1). *Cross-level* models are those in which at least one of the independent variables is at a level different from the dependent variable. Usually, the cross-level model involves the dependent variable existing at a lower level. The cross-level model is the basic hierarchical linear model (HLM) and is the second most common type of model (after within-level models). Most cross-level models are "top-down" contextual models in which a higher level construct (e.g., climate) influences a lower level relationship or outcome (e.g., performance). *Homologous* models are rare and involve independent and dependent variables each existing at two or more levels.

Despite this prior development of multilevel models, microfoundations research does not typically provide an explicit consideration of these multilevel system principles. For example, Felin and Hesterly (2007) advanced a thoughtful examination of the microfoundations of knowledge and value creation. Although their conceptualization overlaps a great deal with multilevel principles such as effect asymmetries, the article does not give explicit consideration to multilevel issues as discussed here. Similarly, Coff and Kryscynski (2011) argued for the examination of microfoundations of competitive advantage but did not develop arguments detailing how these microfoundations may operate within and across levels. This neglect is despite the fact that many view microfoundations as being "embedded in a larger conversation related to multilevel theorizing and empirics" (Felin et al., 2015, p. 586). Yet there is not as strong of an explicit connection between microfoundations and multilevel principles as there could be. This may be explained by the fact that microfoundations research is (at present) primarily concerned with one specific type of multilevel relationship: a bottom-up effect whereby member interaction contributes to firm-level outcomes. As microfoundations research broadens, it will likely need to develop deeper connections with multilevel principles, especially as it expands to consider the emergence of higher level constructs from lower-level constructs.

Time

Any effect that produces change in an outcome does so over a period of time. Emergence occurs over time, top-down effects occur over time, and bottom-up effects occur over time (with bottom-up effects taking more time than top-down effects). Recent research on emergence has begun to consider the role of time in a much more substantive manner. For example, Kozlowski, Chao, Grand, Braun, and Kuljanin (2013, 2016) proposed that the emergence of team learning and team knowledge changes over time: Although the process is initially a compilation form of emergence because team members possess unique knowledge, the process becomes a composition form of emergence as information is shared to the rest of the team. In addition, they proposed a new quantitative research design using computational models and agent-based simulations specifically to enable researchers to more fully theoretically consider and empirically capture the dynamic emergent processes over time (Kozlowski et al., 2016). The micro and meso literatures may not always give careful specification to time, but much groups and teams research recognizes that time is critical for both emergence and the manifestation of team processes (e.g., Kozlowski & Ilgen, 2006; Marks et al., 2001).

Microfoundations research has recognized the importance of temporal issues in a broad manner. For example, Felin et al. (2012, 2015) highlighted the temporal separation of cause and effect and the fact that causes that influence outcomes at different levels necessarily operate over time (see also Abell et al., 2008). Felin and Hesterly (2007) discussed the spread and sharing of knowledge within firms, which implies a longitudinal process. In addition, Kehoe, Lepak, and Bentley (2018) highlighted how an individual star's external status influences later value capture. However, time has not generally been a prominent feature of microfoundations research (a concern raised with micro research as well; see an entire book edited by Shipp & Fried, 2014). The current lack of attention to time prevents researchers from having a better understanding about factors that influence competitive advantage, such as the dynamic nature of strategic factor markets, the development of isolating mechanisms, and the development of human capital resources.

IMPLICATIONS OF MULTILEVEL MICROFOUNDATIONS RESEARCH

The microfoundations movement is generating new insights into the intrafirm behavioral origins of value creation and competitive advantage, but it is often doing so without explicit consideration of multilevel principles even though the basic question of microfoundations research is one that crosses multiple levels (Felin et al., 2015). Perhaps this is not an issue in the short term because most strategic management research does not incorporate a multilevel perspective. We believe, however, that adopting multilevel principles into microfoundations must occur and will have two important implications: It will lead to new insights, and it will help to unite micro and macro.

New Multilevel Insights

How does a firm's competitive advantage emerge from member interactions? This simple question is as profound in its consequences as it is in the difficulty of answering it. Indeed, developing answers to this "bottom-up" question could have an enormous impact on multiple areas of science, such as how administrator–teacher interactions shape school-level outcomes or even how family member interactions shape family-level outcomes. The question considers how the interactions among people create different organizations, schools, and families. This is a difficult question, but it becomes more tractable by incorporating multilevel principles to guide the research process.

First, microfoundations research will benefit from explicit consideration and specification of emergence processes. Microfoundations research tends to give rich theoretical description to member interactions. Two excellent examples are studies by Felin and Hesterly (2007) and Foss and Lindenberg (2013); each study provides careful explication of member interactions and how those interactions may shape firm outcomes. Integrating these insights with theories of emergence would help further answer the question of how and why collective action emerges from these interactions. For example, competitive advantage should be more sustainable when the basis for that advantage is difficult or costly to imitate. Therefore, microfoundations processes based on compilation emergence models might contribute to competitive advantage more strongly than composition models because compilation emergence is based on interactions among different but complementary assets (Ployhart et al., 2014).

Second, microfoundations research should explicitly develop the linkages that lead from lower level origins to higher level constructs. Are these linkages reflective of homologous relationships or cross-level relationships? Are the cross-level relationships direct or mediated? Are the cross-level relationships due to emergence (higher level construct from lower-level origins) or relationships among entirely different constructs? It is not enough to provide careful explanations of the interactions within a firm; one must establish the conceptual path(s) through which these interactions contribute to higher level effects. If competitive advantage is about differentiation, then introducing multilevel principles could help better articulate the path(s) to differentiation. This may in turn help stimulate and direct research on STROBE and identify how micro–meso research leads to competitive advantage (Ployhart, 2015; Ployhart & Hale, 2014).

Third, incorporating multilevel principles into microfoundations research could help more effectively integrate it with existing micro–meso research (Hitt et al., 2007). Multilevel principles provide a common framework and language for thinking about organizational systems. As such, having a shared framework should facilitate theoretical integration because the framework creates a common understanding and requires adopting similar assumptions (Moliterno & Ployhart, 2016). A commonly accepted framework is lacking between micro–meso and macro approaches, which makes it difficult for these scholarly areas to communicate and disseminate findings from one area to the other (Molloy et al., 2011; Wright, Coff, & Moliterno, 2014). Multilevel principles necessarily encompass multiple levels and thus could provide an effective translation of findings across different areas. For example, perhaps multilevel principles can help establish agreement on the lowest level starting point—"the initial conditions"—of microfoundations and thus avoid the concerns about infinite regress (Barney & Felin, 2013; Felin et al., 2015).

Finally, the role of time in multilevel models, and particularly emergence, could enhance the theoretical precision of microfoundations research. Time is fundamental to microfoundations but has not been given sufficient theoretical attention (Felin et al., 2015). Yet bottom-up effects and emergence can only occur over time (Kozlowski & Chao, 2012; Kozlowski et al., 2013; Kozlowski & Klein, 2000). However, the role of time has been considered within strategic management in the form of path-dependency and time-compression diseconomies (e.g., Dierickx & Cool, 1989). This means there is a potential to link the strategic management view of path dependence with the micro–meso view of temporal effects on collective processes to develop new theory explaining temporal effects within microfoundations as a means to better understand competitive advantage. For example, it seems likely that, relative to emergence based on similarity (composition), compilation emergence will take more time to evolve because it is based on members with dissimilar characteristics (which in turn makes it harder to duplicate and thus contributes to competitive advantage).

Uniting Scholarly Disciplines
Overall, we believe there are only benefits to be gained from incorporating multilevel principles with

microfoundations scholarship. These benefits are likely to occur for micro, meso, and macro research. Multilevel principles may become a linchpin for connecting disparate scholarly areas because they provide a shared understanding, a way of comparing and contrasting assumptions, and a roadmap for key methodological and analytical concerns.

One example where this has already occurred is with strategic human capital resources (see Molloy & Ployhart, 2012; Ployhart, Nyberg, Reilly, & Maltarich, 2014). The strategic management perspective on human capital was adapted from Becker (1964) and similar labor economists who studied the role of education in wages and earnings. Within the macro level and scope of their theoretical frameworks, this adaptation made sense. However, some of the assumptions and predictions in strategic management and human capital theory were inconsistent with those found in micro scholarship within the HR and I/O psychology literatures (Ployhart, 2012). Introducing a multilevel model of human capital resource emergence thus contributed to greater fertilization of theories and findings across micro and macro literatures because the emergence model connected psychological and economic-sociological views of talent (Ployhart & Moliterno, 2011) and led to a methodological framework for studying them (Moliterno & Ployhart, 2016).

We envision similar opportunities for microfoundations research. If multilevel principles are introduced into this area, then the full contributions and insights from 100 years of micro and meso scholarship can be used to help inform the nature of microfoundations processes. Such insights include the nature of team processes and dynamics (Humphrey & Aime, 2014), models of emergence (Kozlowski & Klein, 2000) and methods relating to agreement, dispersion, aggregation, and non-independence (Bliese, 2000; LeBreton & Senter, 2008). At the same time, the full contributions and insights from decades of macro scholarship can be used to help inform how and when micro processes contribute to competitive advantage (i.e., STROBE) and different indices of firm performance (financial, operational, accounting-based, market). Both literatures are likely to change, but in ways that are more reflective of the real-world phenomena both seek to understand.

WHAT SHOULD RESEARCHERS DO DIFFERENTLY? A FRAMEWORK FOR CONDUCTING MULTILEVEL MICROFOUNDATIONS RESEARCH

It is one thing to talk about the possibilities of integrating microfoundations research with multilevel principles; it is another to do something about it. Microfoundations require different ways of thinking about theory, design, and analysis than other types of research, and there does not appear to be a process to conduct microfoundations research that is fully described in the extant literature. As a result, in this section we propose a framework and process for conducting multilevel microfoundations research. Exhibit 6.1 lays out a general approach for theorizing, designing, and analyzing multilevel microfoundations research, with a particular focus on explicating "bottom-up" effects.

Step 1. Theoretical Issues

Step 1 focuses entirely on theoretical issues that are frequently identified and addressed in "traditional" microfoundations research and are by far the most difficult issues to address. The challenge is that there is not much theoretical guidance on how to specifically conduct a study in which the "causal" variable exists at a level lower than the outcome variable (see Moliterno & Ployhart, 2016). On the other hand, this is the opportunity—the chance to make a significant contribution by developing such theory. So one should begin by drawing from the relevant theories as a means to conceptualize the dependent or outcome variable. This is always important but even more so in multilevel research because one needs to additionally specify the level at which the outcome theoretically exists (an issue distinct from measurement, as discussed subsequently) and the level(s) at which determinants or predictor variables are likely to exist.

An important challenge in developing the theoretical framework for microfoundations research often involves drawing theories from different disciplines. For example, many strategic management

---

EXHIBIT 6.1

Prescriptive Advice for Advancing a Multilevel Science of Microfoundations

---

1. Microfoundations theoretical issues
   a. Identify the relevant theories to be integrated (or used to develop new theory)
      i. Theories tend to be within level, so the researcher will need to develop theory that links theories across levels (see Step 2)
   b. Identify the outcome of interest
      i. Define the nature of the outcome (construct definition)
      ii. Clarify the level at which this outcome exists
   c. Specify theoretical and disciplinary assumptions, noting which are shared and which are inconsistent
   d. Identify the higher level, within-level, and lower level determinants or influences on the outcome
      i. Explicitly recognize the role of factor markets (extrafirm) in shaping the microfoundations processes (intrafirm)
2. Multilevel theoretical issues
   a. Specify the nature of the emergence process for the relevant constructs
   b. Specify the processes through which the various determinants influence the outcome variable
   c. Specify the nature of time and the role of temporal processes that are required to link constructs across levels
3. Design and measurement issues
   a. What is the level of measurement for each construct?
      i. Depending on the theory, aggregation, agreement, and dispersion indices are needed to empirically test emergence
   b. When is the timing of measurement for each construct?
   c. What steps will be taken to reduce concerns about endogeneity?
4. Analytical issues
   a. Estimation of emergence (consensus, agreement, dispersion, etc.)
   b. Ensure the statistical technique is consistent with the multilevel nature of the data
      i. Within level (regression or generalized linear model–based) if static; growth or change model if longitudinal
      ii. Cross level
         1. Top down (hierarchical linear model or random coefficient modeling)
         2. Bottom up (requires some form of emergence or upward mediated model)

Note. Data from Bliese (2000); Kozlowski and Klein (2000); Moliterno and Ployhart (2016); Molloy, Chadwick, Ployhart, and Golden (2011); Ployhart and Schneider (2005).

theories focus on firm-level competitive advantage, value creation, and value capture, as outcome variables, whereas many micro theories focus on operational performance at levels below the firm. Thus, it is not simply a task of integrating theories but a task of integrating disciplines that have developed theory for different types of dependent variables, at different levels, and have different assumptions. It is thus helpful to clearly identify these assumptions and see where they are aligned and misaligned. In doing so, one often identifies areas where the assumptions are completely contradictory to each other. For example, in the micro literature, one of the most robust findings is that general cognitive ability is the strongest predictor of job performance, and hence it is to every firm's benefit to use cognitive ability tests to hire applicants (Schmidt & Hunter, 1998). Yet cognitive ability is a generic KSAO in the sense

that it is applicable for all situations (and becomes more important as the complexity of the job increases). Consequently, when viewed from the perspective of strategic management, cognitive ability cannot be a source of competitive advantage precisely because, as a resource, it is transferrable to other firms who will receive the same benefits (all else equal; Ployhart, 2012). Thus, what is considered a "success" in one literature (the generalizability of cognitive ability) is considered a failure in another literature (the fact that cognitive ability is transferrable and cannot generate competitive advantage).

After identifying the relevant within-level theoretical arguments, one then needs to propose how the core theoretical arguments connect *across* levels. We cover the theorizing about explicating the theoretical issues of relationships across levels in Step 2, but it is important to first identify the core higher level, within level, and lower level determinants or influences on the outcome. In this regard, the most important outcome of interest is competitive advantage. This in turn means it becomes critical to explicitly theorize the role of factor markets in microfoundations (intrafirm) processes. The reason is because the value of resources, and the ability of resources to create value that is captured by the firm, is highly influenced by the nature of factor markets that exist beyond the firm's boundaries (see Barney, 1986; Coff, 1999). This is critical to understand because it is a point of departure from micro research. Simply put, we know almost nothing about the extent to which phenomena researched in the micro literature (e.g., satisfaction, cohesion, cognitive ability, personality) contribute to differentiating firms in a way that contributes to competitive advantage (Ployhart & Hale, 2014). Thus, one must consider how micro–meso phenomena are valued on the labor market.

Step 2. Multilevel Theoretical Issues

The suggestions developed in Step 1 focus on traditional microfoundations research, but the suggestions developed in Step 2 are new because the focus is on explicating the theoretical issues unique to multilevel theory and microfoundations research. This is where the multilevel framework is so critical: It clarifies the paths the theory may travel. One must first identify any constructs (if any) that are based on emergence processes. In instances in which an emergent construct is identified, it is imperative to theorize why emergence takes place and how it takes places (i.e., the processes). In our experience as reviewers, we frequently see studies that aggregate scores from the individual to unit level but provide no explanation or theoretical justification for why such aggregation is warranted. For example, is the aggregation due to the interdependence required by the task environment or to the nature of the specific construct in question? It is hard to simply accept empirical evidence of aggregation (e.g., intraclass correlation coefficients [ICC]) without a substantive understanding of what those numbers mean. Note that emergence issues may be relevant for predictors, outcomes, or any other variables in a study.

An issue that continues from Step 1 involves the explication of intervening mechanisms and

processes between constructs at different levels. Specifically, how do microfoundations such as coworker interactions or complementarities, contribute to firm-level performance or competitive advantage? This is an inherently bottom-up process, and consequently poses several significant challenges because there is little bottom-up theory on which to draw. For example, a question raised in STROBE is whether teams that are more effective and efficient in terms of their interactions contribute to firms that differentiate from competitors and create a competitive advantage (we do not mean top-management teams, but the lower level teams that comprise the soul of the organization). Figure 6.3 illustrates three approaches for conceptualizing this "bottom-up" microfoundations influence on firm-level competitive advantage (factor market influences are excluded for convenience). We use a general "teamwork" microfoundations construct as the lowest level determinant, purely as an illustration. Path 1 (solid arrow) posits that organizations with more effective teams create a new type of human capital resources (e.g., shared knowledge, collaboration), and this new resource contributes to competitive advantage (i.e., the "macro" assumption in Figure 6.1). Path 2 (dotted arrow) suggests that organizations with more effective teams show greater team performance, and this across-team performance aggregates to influence firm performance (i.e., the "micro" assumption in Figure 6.1). Path 3 (dashed arrow) proposes that organizations with more effective teams have spillover benefits on other teams and people (e.g., innovation, creativity, speed of knowledge diffusion, retention, contagion). Path 3 is the example closest to the logic underlying most microfoundations research. However, in each example, the theoretical argument is that effective teams do and cause "something" that connects the lower level to the firm level—this "something" needs to be theorized and measured.

Finally, researchers need to follow the guidance of microfoundations researchers (e.g., Felin et al., 2015) and consider the temporal issues underlying the levels and theoretical arguments. Recall that microfoundations researchers take Coleman's (1990) framework to propose that the determinant of the higher level outcome must temporally proceed that outcome. Multilevel principles bring this concept

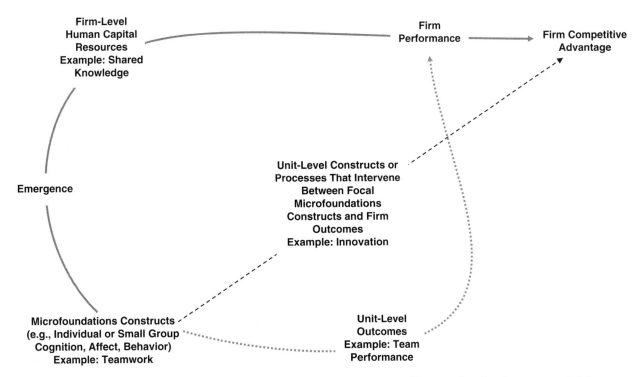

FIGURE 6.3. Pathways for operationalizing bottom-up microfoundation effects on firm-level outcomes. Solid arrow represents an indirect emergence process; dotted line represents an aggregation-through-performance outcomes process; dashed line represents a cross-level mediated process.

to life by identifying cross-level time asymmetries. Bottom-up effects tend to operate more slowly than top-down effects, so the question becomes how much time is necessary for microfoundations constructs to influence higher level constructs? For example, if teamwork becomes more effective and efficient, then when will the benefits of better teamwork be observed in firm performance or competitive advantage? Ultimately, the hypothesized path one proposes to link microfoundations and firm-level outcomes is likely to affect the amount of time required to locate significant effects.

Step 3. Design and Measurement Issues

The multilevel design and measurement issues are topics micro researchers have incorporated in their research for a long time, but these topics are just starting to be diffused into the strategic management literature. However, topics such as endogeneity are rarely considered in the micro literature but dominate within the macro literature (Wright et al., 2014). These methodological details have been discussed in great detail, and we do not want to belabor the issue

here (instead, see Bliese, 2000; LeBreton & Senter, 2008; and related chapters in this book). We instead summarize the key issues:

- The level of measurement for the construct needs to be specified (Kozlowski & Klein, 2000; Ployhart & Schneider, 2005). For example, a construct such as cohesion may be hypothesized to exist at the unit level, but the measures of that construct may be administered at the individual level (and the scores aggregated, as discussed shortly).

- If emergence is hypothesized, then indices that test the hypothesized form of emergence are necessary. These may involve ICC1, ICC2, agreement indices, or dispersion indices (see Bliese, 2000).

- The timing of measures needs to be addressed. If predictors must temporally precede outcomes and bottom-up effects operate fairly slowly, then it becomes necessary to justify and defend how much earlier the predictor measures must occur than the outcome measures. Unfortunately, as noted earlier, little is known about lags or how long it takes for bottom-up effects to occur, so the choice of measures is a bit exploratory. Therefore, it is good practice to try to over-measure whenever possible and to be sure to measure more frequently during the periods where the "action" is taking place, rather than relying on reoccurring measurement occasions (e.g., monthly) that may be too coarse (see Ployhart & Vandenberg, 2010).

- Endogeneity (i.e., correlation between predictor variables and residuals in a model) needs to be modeled or controlled. Endogeneity is a major concern in strategic management that is scarcely considered in micro research. This does not mean the problem is irrelevant in micro research, and micro scholarship would benefit from greater attention to this issue (Wright et al., 2014). Researchers can test for and attempt to control for endogeneity statistically, but is better if it can be addressed more directly as part of the measurement system or design. For example, controlling for prior measures of the higher level dependent variable can determine whether prior performance influences the lower level construct as well as the higher level outcome. Employing longitudinal designs further helps reduce endogeneity concerns. Usually one does not have complete control over the design, and so a combination of statistical and measurement corrections is the best one can hope for.

Step 4. Analytical Issues

Analytical issues tend to be the easiest to address because the theory and design largely dictate how the analysis should take place. The analytical choices for handling multilevel data have been expanding rapidly (see the chapters in this volume by Vandenberg & Richardson, Gavin & LeBreton, and Lang & Bliese), but most focus on variations of aggregation indices testing emergence (ICC1, ICC2, etc.), top-down models based on HLM, or temporal models (e.g., Lang & Bliese, 2009; see also their chapter in this volume). The appropriate model is dependent on the nature of the multilevel theorizing. Within-level theories can be tested by any number of the "classic" general linear model or mixed-effect model approaches (e.g., regression). Cross-level, top-down models, or longitudinal can

be tested with HLM or random coefficient modeling. But these models are of limited usefulness because they do not address the central question of how microfoundations produces "bottom-up" effects on firm-level outcomes. What is missing is a clear understanding of how to model bottom-up data in a manner that is not based on emergence processes. Moliterno and Ployhart (2016) discussed this issue in some detail and ultimately concluded that a combination of methodologies will be needed until the time comes when a full solution is possible.

Overall, the prescriptive advice offered in Exhibit 6.1 may seem daunting, but in reality, it is only a blending of common methods used in the either the micro or macro areas. The major points of departure are the need to precisely (a) specify the mechanisms through which bottom-up effects unfold, (b) determine the timing and duration of these effects, and (c) adopt models that sufficiently analyze those effects. On the downside, there is little guidance on how to address these points of departure. On the upside, this is an opportunity for scholars to tackle important questions that may generate significant new insights into the nature of microfoundations of competitive advantage. There is clearly much theoretical, methodological, and analytical work to be done.

CONCLUSION

We believe there is a bright future for micro-foundations, and it may contribute to a much-needed integration of theories and empirical findings across micro, meso, and macro levels. Incorporating multilevel principles and frameworks will be critical for making this integration tractable. Management research may have historically been within level, but organizations are hierarchical multilevel systems. To ignore multilevel principles is thus to ignore reality.

References

Abell, P., Felin, T., & Foss, N. (2008). Building micro-foundations for the routines, capabilities, and performance links. *Managerial and Decision Economics, 29,* 489–502. http://dx.doi.org/10.1002/mde.1413

Aldrich, H. E. (2006). *Organizations and environments.* Thousand Oaks, CA: Sage.

Barney, J. B. (1991). Firm resources and sustained competitive advantage. *Journal of Management, 17*, 99–120. http://dx.doi.org/10.1177/014920639101700108

Barney, J. B. (1986). Strategic factor markets: Expectations, luck, and business strategy. *Management Science, 32*, 1231–1241. http://dx.doi.org/10.1287/mnsc.32.10.1231

Barney, J. B., & Felin, T. (2013). What are microfoundations? *The Academy of Management Perspectives, 27*, 138–155.

Barsade, S. G. (2002). The ripple effect: Emotional contagion and its influence on group behavior. *Administrative Science Quarterly, 47*, 644–675. http://dx.doi.org/10.2307/3094912

Becker, G. S. (1964). *Human capital: A theoretical and empirical analysis with special reference to education.* Chicago, IL: University of Chicago Press.

Bliese, P. D. (2000). Within-group agreement, non-independence, and reliability: Implications for data aggregation and analysis. In K. J. Klein & S. W. J. Kozlowski (Eds.), *Multilevel theory, research, and methods in organizations: Foundations, extensions, and new directions* (pp. 349–381). San Francisco, CA: Jossey-Bass.

Cappelli, P., & Sherer, P. D. (1991). The missing role of context in OB. *Research in Organizational Behavior, 13*, 55–110.

Chan, D. (1998). Functional relations among constructs in the same content domain at different levels of analysis: A typology of composition models. *Journal of Applied Psychology, 83*, 234–246. http://dx.doi.org/10.1037/0021-9010.83.2.234

Coff, R. W. (1999). When competitive advantage doesn't lead to performance: The resource-based view and stakeholder bargaining power. *Organization Science, 10*, 119–133. http://dx.doi.org/10.1287/orsc.10.2.119

Coff, R. W., & Kryscynski, D. (2011). Drilling for microfoundations of human capital-based competitive advantages. *Journal of Management, 37*, 1429–1443. http://dx.doi.org/10.1177/0149206310397772

Coleman, J. S. (1990). *Foundations of social theory.* Cambridge, MA: Belknap.

Crook, T. R., Todd, S. Y., Combs, J. G., Woehr, D. J., & Ketchen, D. J., Jr. (2011). Does human capital matter? A meta-analysis of the relationship between human capital and firm performance. *Journal of Applied Psychology, 96*, 443–456. http://dx.doi.org/10.1037/a0022147

Dierickx, I., & Cool, K. (1989). Asset stock accumulation and sustainability of competitive advantage. *Management Science, 35*, 1504–1511. http://dx.doi.org/10.1287/mnsc.35.12.1504

Durkheim, E. (1982). *The rules of sociological method* (W. D. Halls, Trans.). London, England: Macmillan. http://dx.doi.org/10.1007/978-1-349-16939-9

Emergent nature of organization, markets and wisdom of crowds [Special issue]. (2012). *Managerial and Decision Economics, 33*, 283–452.

Esser, H. (1994). Explanatory sociology. *Soziologie, 3*, 177–190.

Felin, T., & Foss, N. J. (2005). Strategic organization: A field in search of micro-foundations. *Strategic Organization, 3*, 441–455. http://dx.doi.org/10.1177/1476127005055796

Felin, T., & Foss, N. J. (2009). Organizational routines and capabilities: Historical drift and a course-correction toward microfoundations. *Scandinavian Journal of Management, 25*, 157–167. http://dx.doi.org/10.1016/j.scaman.2009.02.003

Felin, T., Foss, N. J., Heimeriks, K. H., & Madsen, T. L. (2012). Microfoundations of routines and capabilities: Individuals, processes, and structure. *Journal of Management Studies, 49*, 1351–1374. http://dx.doi.org/10.1111/j.1467-6486.2012.01052.x

Felin, T., Foss, N. J., & Ployhart, R. E. (2015). The microfoundations movement in strategy and organization theory. *The Academy of Management Annals, 9*, 575–632. http://dx.doi.org/10.5465/19416520.2015.1007651

Felin, T., & Hesterly, W. S. (2007). The knowledge-based view, nested heterogeneity, and new value creation: Philosophical considerations on the locus of knowledge. *The Academy of Management Review, 32*, 195–218. http://dx.doi.org/10.5465/AMR.2007.23464020

Foss, N. J. (2011). Why micro-foundations for resource-based theory are needed and what they may look like. *Journal of Management, 37*, 1413–1428. http://dx.doi.org/10.1177/0149206310390218

Foss, N. J., & Lindenberg, S. (2013). Microfoundations for strategy: A goal-framing perspective on the drivers of value creation. *The Academy of Management Perspectives, 27*, 85–102. http://dx.doi.org/10.5465/amp.2012.0103

Grigoriou, K., & Rothaermel, F. T. (2014). Structural microfoundations of innovation: The role of relational stars. *Journal of Management, 40*, 586–615. http://dx.doi.org/10.1177/0149206313513612

Groysberg, B., Lee, L. E., & Nanda, A. (2008). Can they take it with them? The portability of star knowledge workers' performance. *Management Science, 54*, 1213–1230. http://dx.doi.org/10.1287/mnsc.1070.0809

Hall, G. S., Baird, J. W., & Geissler, L. R. (1917). Foreword. *Journal of Applied Psychology, 1*, 5–7. http://dx.doi.org/10.1037/h0065981

Hambrick, D. C., & Mason, P. A. (1984). Upper echelons: The organization as a reflection of its top managers. *The Academy of Management Review, 9*, 193–206.

Heath, C., & Sitkin, S. B. (2001). Big-B versus big-O: What is organizational about organizational behavior?

Journal of Organizational Behavior, 22, 43–58. http://dx.doi.org/10.1002/job.77

Helfat, C. E., & Peteraf, M. A. (2015). Managerial cognitive capabilities and the microfoundations of dynamic capabilities. *Strategic Management Journal, 36*, 831–850. http://dx.doi.org/10.1002/smj.2247

Hitt, M. A., Beamish, P. W., Jackson, S. E., & Mathieu, J. E. (2007). Building theoretical and empirical bridges across levels: Multilevel research in management. *Academy of Management Journal, 50*, 1385–1399. http://dx.doi.org/10.5465/AMJ.2007.28166219

Humphrey, S. E., & Aime, F. (2014). Team microdynamics: Toward an organizing approach to teamwork. *The Academy of Management Annals, 8*, 443–503.

Jaanssen, M. (1993). *Microfoundations: A critical inquiry.* London, England: Routledge.

Johns, G. (2006). The essential impact of content on organizational behavior. *The Academy of Management Review, 31*, 386–408. http://dx.doi.org/10.5465/AMR.2006.20208687

Kehoe, R. R., Lepak, D. P., & Bentley, F. S. (2018). Let's call a star a star: Task performance, external status, and exceptional contributors in organizations. *Journal of Management, 44*, 1848–1872.

Klein, K. J., Dansereau, F., & Hall, R. J. (1994). Levels issues in theory development, data collection, and analysis. *Academy of Management Review, 19*, 195–229.

Klein, K. J., & Kozlowski, S. W. J. (2000). *Multilevel theory, research and methods in organizations: Foundations, extensions, and new directions.* San Francisco, CA: Jossey-Bass.

Kor, Y. Y., & Mesko, A. (2013). Dynamic managerial capabilities: Configuration and orchestration of top executives' capabilities and the firm's dominant logic. *Strategic Management Journal, 34*, 233–244.

Kozlowski, S. W. J., & Chao, G. T. (2012). The dynamics of emergence: Cognition and cohesion in work teams. *Managerial & Decision Economics, 163*, 149–163.

Kozlowski, S. W. J., Chao, G. T., Grand, J. A., Braun, M. T., & Kuljanin, G. (2013). Advancing multilevel research design: Capturing the dynamics of emergence. *Organizational Research Methods, 16*, 581–615. http://dx.doi.org/10.1177/1094428113493119

Kozlowski, S. W. J., Chao, G. T., Grand, J. A., Braun, M. T., & Kuljanin, G. (2016). Capturing the multilevel dynamics of emergence: Computational modeling, simulation, and virtual experimentation. *Organizational Psychology Review, 6*, 3–33. http://dx.doi.org/10.1177/2041386614547955

Kozlowski, S. W. J., & Ilgen, D. R. (2006). Enhancing the effectiveness of work groups and teams. *Psychological Science in the Public Interest, 7*, 77–124. http://dx.doi.org/10.1111/j.1529-1006.2006.00030.x

Kozlowski, S. W. J., & Klein, K. J. (2000). A multilevel approach to theory and research in organizations: Contextual, temporal, and emergent processes. In K. J. Klein & S. W. J. Kozlowski (Eds.), *Multilevel theory, research, and methods in organizations: Foundations, extensions, and new directions* (pp. 3–90). San Francisco, CA: Jossey-Bass.

Lang, J. W., & Bliese, P. D. (2009). General mental ability and two types of adaptation to unforeseen change: Applying discontinuous growth models to the task-change paradigm. *Journal of Applied Psychology, 94*, 411–428. http://dx.doi.org/10.1037/a0013803

LeBreton, J. M., & Senter, J. L. (2008). Answers to 20 questions about interrater reliability and interrater agreement. *Organizational Research Methods, 11*, 815–852. http://dx.doi.org/10.1177/1094428106296642

Lepak, D. P., Smith, K. G., & Taylor, M. S. (2007). Value creation and value capture: A multilevel perspective. *The Academy of Management Review, 32*, 180–194. http://dx.doi.org/10.5465/AMR.2007.23464011

Lockwood, P., & Kunda, Z. (1997). Superstars and me: Predicting the impact of role models on the self. *Journal of Personality and Social Psychology, 73*, 91–103. http://dx.doi.org/10.1037/0022-3514.73.1.91

Marks, M. A., Mathieu, J. E., & Zaccaro, S. J. (2001). A temporally based framework and taxonomy of team processes. *Academy of Management Review, 26*, 356–376.

Mathieu, J. E., Tannenbaum, S. I., Donsbach, J. S., & Alliger, G. M. (2014). A review and integration of team composition models: Moving toward a dynamic and temporal framework. *Journal of Management, 40*, 130–160. http://dx.doi.org/10.1177/0149206313503014

Moliterno, T. P., & Ployhart, R. E. (2016). Multilevel models for strategy research: An idea whose time (still) has come. In G. B. Dagnino & C. Cinici (Eds.), *Research methods for strategic management* (pp. 51–77). New York, NY: Routledge.

Molloy, J. C., Chadwick, C., Ployhart, R. E., & Golden, S. J. (2011). Making intangibles "tangible" in tests of resource-based theory: A multidisciplinary construct validation approach. *Journal of Management, 37*, 1496–1518.

Molloy, J. C., & Ployhart, R. E. (2012). Construct clarity: Multidisciplinary considerations and an illustration using human capital. *Human Resource Management Review, 22*, 152–156. http://dx.doi.org/10.1016/j.hrmr.2011.11.010

Molloy, J. C., Ployhart, R. E., & Wright, P. M. (2011). The myth of "the" micro–macro divide: Bridging system-level and disciplinary divides. *Journal of Management, 37*, 581–609. http://dx.doi.org/10.1177/0149206310365000

Nahapiet, J., & Ghoshal, S. (1998). Social capital, intellectual capital, and the organizational advantage. *Academy of Management Review, 23,* 242–266.

Nanda, A., Nohria, N., & Groysberg, B. (2009). The risky business of hiring stars. *Harvard Business Review, 82,* 92–101.

Nyberg, A. J., Moliterno, T. P., Hale, D., & Lepak, D. P. (2014). Resource-based perspectives on unit-level human capital: A review and integration. *Journal of Management, 40,* 316–346. http://dx.doi.org/10.1177/0149206312458703

Nyberg, A. J., & Wright, P. M. (2015). 50 years of human capital research: Assessing what we know, exploring where we go. *The Academy of Management Perspectives, 29,* 287–295. http://dx.doi.org/10.5465/amp.2014.0113

Overbeck, J. R., Correll, J., & Park, B. (2005). Internal status sorting in groups: The problem of too many stars. *Research on Managing Groups and Teams, 7,* 169–199.

Pearsall, M. J., & Venkataramani, V. (2015). Overcoming asymmetric goals in teams: The interactive roles of team learning orientation and team identification. *Journal of Applied Psychology, 100,* 735–748. http://dx.doi.org/10.1037/a0038315

Penrose, E. T. (1959). *The theory of the growth of the firm.* New York, NY: Wiley.

Peteraf, M. A., & Barney, J. B. (2003). Unraveling the resource-based tangle. *Managerial and Decision Economics, 24,* 309–323. http://dx.doi.org/10.1002/mde.1126

Peterson, R. S., Smith, D. B., Martorana, P. V., & Owens, P. D. (2003). The impact of chief executive officer personality on top management team dynamics: One mechanism by which leadership affects organizational performance. *Journal of Applied Psychology, 88,* 795–808. http://dx.doi.org/10.1037/0021-9010.88.5.795

Ployhart, R. E. (2012). The psychology of competitive advantage: An adjacent possibility. *Industrial and Organizational Psychology: Perspectives on Science and Practice, 5,* 62–81. http://dx.doi.org/10.1111/j.1754-9434.2011.01407.x

Ployhart, R. E. (2015). *Strategic organizational behavior* (STROBE): The missing voice in the strategic human capital conversation. *The Academy of Management Perspectives, 29,* 342–356. http://dx.doi.org/10.5465/amp.2014.0145

Ployhart, R. E., & Hale, D., Jr. (2014). The fascinating psychological microfoundations of strategy and competitive advantage. *Annual Review of Organizational Psychology and Organizational Behavior, 1,* 145–172. http://dx.doi.org/10.1146/annurev-orgpsych-031413-091312

Ployhart, R. E., & Moliterno, T. P. (2011). Emergence of the human capital resource: A multilevel model. *The Academy of Management Review, 36,* 127–150. http://dx.doi.org/10.5465/amr.2009.0318

Ployhart, R. E., Nyberg, A. J., Reilly, G., & Maltarich, M. A. (2014). Human capital is dead; Long live human capital resources! *Journal of Management, 40,* 371–398. http://dx.doi.org/10.1177/0149206313512152

Ployhart, R. E., & Schneider, B. (2005). Multilevel selection and prediction: Theories, methods, and models. In A. Evers, O. Smit-Voskuyl, & N. Anderson (Eds.), *Handbook of personnel selection* (pp. 495–516). Chichester, England: Wiley.

Ployhart, R. E., & Vandenberg, R. J. (2010). Longitudinal research: The theory, design, and analysis of change. *Journal of Management, 36,* 94–120. http://dx.doi.org/10.1177/0149206309352110

Ployhart, R. E., Weekley, J. A., & Baughman, K. (2006). The structure and function of human capital emergence: A multilevel examination of the attraction–selection–attrition model. *Academy of Management Journal, 49,* 661–677. http://dx.doi.org/10.5465/AMJ.2006.22083023

Ravid, S. A. (1999). Information, blockbusters, and stars: A study of the film industry. *The Journal of Business, 72,* 463–492. http://dx.doi.org/10.1086/209624

Rousseau, D. M. (1985). Issues of level on organizational research. *Research in Organizational Behavior, 7,* 1–37.

Rousseau, D. M., & Fried, Y. (2001). Location, location, location: Contextualizing organizational research. *Journal of Organizational Behavior, 22,* 1–13. http://dx.doi.org/10.1002/job.78

Schmidt, F. L., & Hunter, J. E. (1998). The validity and utility of selection methods in personnel psychology: Practical and theoretical implications of 85 years of research findings. *Psychological Bulletin, 124,* 262–274. http://dx.doi.org/10.1037/0033-2909.124.2.262

Schneider, B. (1987). The people make the place. *Personnel Psychology, 40,* 437–453. http://dx.doi.org/10.1111/j.1744-6570.1987.tb00609.x

Schneider, B., Smith, D. B., & Sipe, W. P. (2000). Personnel selection psychology: Multilevel considerations. In K. J. Klein & S. W. J. Kozlowski (Eds.), *Multilevel theory, research, and methods in organizations: Foundations, extensions, and new directions* (pp. 91–120). San Francisco, CA: Jossey-Bass.

Shipp, A. J., & Fried, Y. (2014). *Time and work: Vol. 1. How time impacts individuals.* London, England: Psychology Press.

Simon, H. A. (1973). The organization of complex systems. In H. H. Pattee (Ed.), *Hierarchy theory* (pp. 1–27). New York, NY: Braziller.

Smith, A. (1963). *An inquiry into the nature and causes of the wealth of nations*. Homewood, IL: Irwin. (Original work published 1776)

Tasselli, S., Kilduff, M., & Menges, J. I. (2015). The microfoundations of organizational social networks: A review and an agenda for future research. *Journal of Management, 41*, 1361–1387. http://dx.doi.org/10.1177/0149206315573996

von Bertalanffy, L. (1968). *General systems theory.* New York, NY: Braziller.

Weick, K. E. (1995). *Sensemaking in organizations* (Vol. 3). Thousand Oaks, CA: Sage.

Winter, S. G. (2011). Problems at the foundation? Comments on Felin and Foss. *Journal of Institutional Economics, 7*, 257–277. http://dx.doi.org/10.1017/S1744137410000470

Wright, P. M., & Boswell, W. R. (2002). Desegregating HRM: A review and synthesis of micro and macro human resource management research. *Journal of Management, 28*, 247–276. http://dx.doi.org/10.1177/014920630202800302

Wright, P. M., Coff, R. W., & Moliterno, T. P. (2014). Strategic human capital: Crossing the great divide. *Journal of Management, 40*, 353–370. http://dx.doi.org/10.1177/0149206313518437

## CHAPTER 7

MULTILEVEL EMERGENCE IN WORK COLLECTIVES

John E. Mathieu and Margaret M. Luciano

With the benefit of hindsight, it is clear that the fields of applied psychology and organizational behavior, consistent with most areas in the social sciences, began a paradigm shift in the mid-1980s. Before that period, most research was single-level, such as examining individuals' perceptions, attitudes, and behaviors, or alternatively collective–organizational structures, climates, and outcomes. But the 1980s ushered in a new era within applied psychology that was denoted *meso-research* to emphasize that it sought to link variables across individual (micro) and higher (macro) levels of analysis such as groups or organizations (cf. James, Demaree, & Hater, 1980; Mossholder & Bedeian, 1983; Rousseau, 1985). House, Rousseau, and Thomas-Hunt (1995) defined meso theory and research as simultaneously spanning

> at least two levels of analysis wherein (a) one or more levels concern individual or group behavioral processes or variables, (b) one or more levels concern organizational processes or variables, and (c) the processes by which the levels of analysis are related are articulated in the form of bridging, or linking, propositions. (p. 73)

The central feature of meso thinking is that work collectives reside in nested arrangements. This paradigm has since evolved into a general multilevel framework whereby any focal phenomenon of interest may be influenced by factors above and below where it resides (Hitt, Beamish, Jackson, & Mathieu, 2007).

Rousseau (1985) provided a useful scaffold to guide multilevel research that suggests scholars need to consider the level of (a) theory, (b) measurement, and (c) analysis for the constructs included in their investigations. *Level of theory* refers to the focal level to which generalizations are designed to apply. "Level of measurement refers to the unit to which the data are directly attached . . . [whereas] the level of analysis is the unit—to which data are assigned for hypothesis testing and statistical analysis" (Rousseau, 1985, p. 4). The key point is that these three facets must, in one fashion or another, be aligned to minimize level-related confounds, or what are often referred to as fallacies of the wrong level.

Rousseau's (1985) framework helped guide the development of multilevel theory and research in the years that followed. Much of that first-generation work was scattered and inconsistent (Mathieu & Chen, 2011), however. Kozlowski and Klein (2000)

This work was conducted, in part, with support from the United States Army Research Institute (Contract: W911NF-15-1-0014; The Development of Construct Validation of Unobtrusive Dynamic Measures of Team Process and Emergent States). The opinions and positions expressed herein are, however, strictly those of the authors.

http://dx.doi.org/10.1037/0000115-008
The Handbook of Multilevel Theory, Measurement, and Analysis, S. E. Humphrey and J. M. LeBreton (Editors-in-Chief)

published an influential book that served to coalesce much of what was learned in the first decade and a half after Rousseau's chapter and outlined an agenda for future work. Now, another decade and half later, it is important to take stock of what has been learned since and of what challenges remain. Notably, one oft-mentioned conclusion concerning multilevel research is that we know far more about top-down relationships than we do about bottom-up relationships (cf. Hitt et al., 2007; Kozlowski & Klein, 2000; Mathieu & Chen, 2011; Rousseau, 2011). Indeed, Kozlowski, Chao, Grand, Braun, and Kuljanin (2013) submitted that "the vast majority of multilevel research is focused on top-down, cross-level effects, whereas emergence as a bottom-up process is largely neglected by quantitative investigators" (p. 582). They went on to suggest that

> there are two primary reasons for this
> state of affairs. First, when emergence
> is considered in multilevel research,
> it is primarily treated as part of mea-
> surement and construct validation for
> indicators that transcend levels (i.e.,
> constructs that are measured at a lower
> level but are aggregated to represent a
> higher level). Second, there are sub-
> stantial research ambiguities with
> respect to assessing and representing
> emergent phenomena. (Kozlowski
> et al., 2013, p. 582)

In short, although existing multilevel theory acknowledges the potential for top-down, bottom-up, and focal relationships, there is substantial ambiguity on what elements need to be articulated in theories of emergence and the implication of those elements for research methods associated with the study of work collectives.

Work collectives represent an important cross-roads where individual members connect with their organizations, and emergent variables are prominent in this area of theory and research. Work tasks and features of the embedding organizational context serve to shape the nature of dynamics that occur in work collectives. But work units are also cauldrons, where members' individual differences, preferences, actions, and reactions brew over time

to yield dynamics and outcomes that are difficult to understand. Accordingly, our main goal for this chapter is to advance a strategy for advancing and testing theories of emergent phenomena that integrates upward, focal, and downward influences on the emergence of phenomena over time in work collectives (e.g., teams, departments, organizations). We suggest that to appropriately advance and examine a dynamic theory, several elements need to be articulated: (a) the form of the construct, (b) the form of the emergence, and (c) the temporal theory that guides how that emergence occurs over time. All three elements must be aligned and articulated a priori because that in turn guides the empirical investigation (e.g., gathering appropriate measures, analyzing them accordingly, and what constitutes support for emergence). Failing to do so renders investigations open to alternative interpretations.

In the following section, we address the form of the construct by discussing the three common ways that emergent variables have been conceptualized and measured at a particular point in time: (a) averages, (b) variances, and (c) configurations. We then review existing theories of emergence and discuss how the three emergent variable forms may evolve and change over time. In addition, drawing from temporal theories including developmental, episodic, and event-based theories, and leveraging concepts from social network theory, we illustrate that emergent phenomena may evolve through different periods, such as formation, coalescing, transformation, and dissipating. The understanding of both the shape of the variables and how they change over time is important because emergence describes a change in form toward some particular arrangement. Stated differently, as different types of aggregate constructs develop into different forms that manifest differently over time, each of these elements and the alignment between them are critically important for appropriately advancing and testing theories of emergent phenomena.

Although our focus is on the dynamic properties of patterns of relationships that traverse levels of analysis, we also discuss the top-down influence of situational events, both external to the system and from within, as shocks that stimulate such dynamics. In addition, we discuss the bottom-up effects that can be revealed by adopting a network perspective. Finally, we discuss the key implications for research, as well as the methodological and analytic issues. Whereas our focus is on work collectives such as teams, units, or departments for expository purposes, the general principles may generalize to other units of inquiry (e.g., organizations, multiteam systems) and to other domains (e.g., volunteer organizations, political systems).

EMERGENT VARIABLES

Whereas top-down, multilevel investigations are frequent in the management and psychology literatures and represent a maturing science, progress concerning bottom-up influences are far less common. The challenge, to date, has been how best to represent the lower level influences at a higher level. In other words, in bottom-up relationships, the upper level variables (e.g., unit cohesion or performance) are criteria of lower level processes. The level of theory, therefore, is at the unit level of analysis, and therefore the level of analysis also needs to be the unit level. Yet the lower level phenomena are typically measured at the individual level and then aggregated in some fashion to an upper level of analysis (e.g., groups or organizations). To date, there have been essentially three ways in which lower level processes have been combined to represent higher level phenomena: (a) averages, (b) variances, and (c) configurations (Chan, 1998; Chen, Mathieu, & Bliese, 2004; Kozlowski & Klein, 2000).

Averages

The averages approach gathers lower level data and then uses the mean or other index of central tendency to represent a unit-level phenomenon. There are variations of this form of construct that differ in terms of their assumptions about the nature of the phenomena. For example, suppose that an investigator is interested in the impact of unit affect on unit performance over time. One way to represent affect would be to ask each unit member (perhaps via surveys or interviews) to report his or her personal affect and then to average those reports

to represent the unit's affect. If one conceives of unit affect as simply a by-product of individuals' personal feelings, then the individual reports can merely be summed or averaged as an *additive* (Chan, 1998) or *summary index* (Chen et al., 2004) construct. Alternatively, if one conceives of unit affect as a shared phenomenon whereby members experience a similar level of affect (e.g., affective tone; see George, 1990), then those individual reports would need to evidence homogeneity within units to warrant being averaged. This second example has been referred to as a *consensus* construct (Chan, 1998; Chen et al., 2004) and has the added requirement that different members need to exhibit the same patterns of affect. In both additive/summary index and consensus measures, the unit-level construct is thought to be an average of individual member's affect.

A third averaging approach has been referred to as a *referent-shift*–style measure whereby rather than asking respondents (typically members) to report how they personally feel, they are asked to report on the level of affect that they perceive to exist in the unit as a whole (e.g., Mason & Griffin, 2003). These types of constructs presume that there is a shared collective phenomenon to which all members are exposed. They differ from consensus constructs only in that the referent or target of assessment refers to the collective (e.g., unit) rather than a lower level (e.g., individual). As an aside, the term *referent-shift* is a bit of a misnomer and stems from psychologists "shifting" an individual-level construct to refer to higher level entities. At issue is that the referent of such measures needs to be aligned with the focal aggregate construct of interest, whether or not there is a lower level analog. For example, perceptions of unit coordination should be assessed with measures about the unit itself and are not derived from individual-level constructs. In any case, assuming respondents demonstrate sufficient homogeneity of responses on referent-shift (aligned) measures, their average scores are a good index of the collective property. Referent-shift measures place respondents in the role of key informants reporting on the existence and level of some collective phenomenon. They do not, however, reveal anything about how that collective state came about.

Variances

The variance approach for aggregating constructs suggests that some form of diversity within the unit represents a collective phenomenon. Harrison and Klein (2007) differentiated forms of variance in terms of *separation, variety,* and *disparity*. This differentiation relates to the degree, kind, or relative status of members regarding some construct of interest, respectively.

For example, "team mental models are team members' shared, organized understanding and mental representation of knowledge about key elements of the team's relevant environment" (Mohammed & Dumville, 2001, p. 90) and typically are indexed in terms of the correspondence of individuals' mental representations. Whether the scoring of shared mental models (SMMs) is done in terms of the variance between, or intercorrelations among, members' ratings of some stimulus materials (cf. Smith-Jentsch, Mathieu, & Kraiger, 2005), the resulting index is a separation-style score. At issue here is that the sharedness of mental models is not examined as a prerequisite for aggregating individuals' models to a "team model"—rather, the convergence index itself represents the extent to which individuals share a common knowledge structure. For example, Mathieu, Heffner, Goodwin, Cannon-Bowers, and Salas (2005) indexed the similarity of members SMMs using correlations between their ratings of task and team dimensions. However, the authors also categorized different configurations (i.e., patterns) of members' mental models relative to those of experts to represent different kinds of mental models—that is, variety, or differences in kind. Thus, the similarity of members' SMMs were used as an index of the extent to which they thought alike, and the categorizations of their mental models were used to classify the quality of those representations relative to normative models.

Disparity models represent a unique form of diversity that depends on both an individual's standing on a construct of interest and those of other unit members, such as his or her relative prestige, decision-making authority, or social power in a collective. The notion is that the gap between an extreme score and those of the rest of the unit captures a variable of interest, such as status or equity. Steiner (1972) advanced similar notions in terms of team task arrangements that constrain the team performance to be a function of the least or most competent member (i.e., disjunctive or conjunctive tasks, respectively). More generically in the multilevel literature, these are referred to as *frog pond*–style constructs, where the score that is used to represent a unit construct is the relative extreme in the collective, which itself depends on the distribution of scores in the unit. Chen et al. (2004) referred to this class of aggregate variables as *selected scores*. For example, one might conceive of indexing unit affect in terms of the most positive or negative member's feelings. Or emergent leadership might be indexed in terms of which member(s) exhibit the greatest number of leader behaviors over some period. Here again, however, a disparity-style score is a descriptive statistic of a unit property but does not reflect the processes that gave rise to such discrepancies.

Configurations

Configuration-style constructs refer to a pattern, profile, or other arrangement of lower level scores as representative of a higher level construct. Importantly, these configurations go beyond simple measures of central tendency or diversity and represent arrangements that cannot be adequately represented by means and variances. Kozlowski and Klein (2000) referred to these as *compilation*-style constructs. For example, one may envision that there exist subgroups in a unit, perhaps some who have received preferential treatment versus others who have not. Such "ingroup versus outgroup" dynamics could certainly generate positive affect among some members and negative affect among others. A simple mean or variance of unit members' individual affect scores would not reveal the critical divide that exists in the unit. Equally important, imagine asking members of an equally divided unit to report on the "average affect of the unit" (i.e., a referent shift measure). Members of both subgroups would likely report, and demonstrate high homogeneity of, "average" unit affect as they mentally balance the feelings of the in-group and out-group members. Those scores would not adequately represent how any individual member was feeling, nor a shared unit phenomenon, however.

Configuration or compilation constructs represent situations in which a nonuniform pattern of lower level scores constitute a higher level construct. For example, *transactive memory systems* refers to instances in which different unit members are responsible for different task demands (i.e., specialization), members know who to go to for different information and how to best coordinate their efforts. Thus, a well-functioning transactive memory system would be a combination of high *variety* (different members are responsible for different work), a high shared mental model of roles (members know who to go to for different information), and effective coordination (likely an additive composite of paired intermember exchanges). In another vein, unit tasks or work processes may put a greater premium on some members' efforts and interactions than others (cf. Humphrey & Aime, 2014). At issue is that relationships between different unit members are not uniform nor are they equally important for unit effectiveness.

Configural constructs suggest that traditional survey measurement scales may be limited in terms of how well they can reveal the underlying structure of relationships. Alternatively, social network techniques are well suited for revealing the structure or pattern of relationships between unit members, as well as between members and certain themes (e.g., planning activities, actions processes, boundary spanning) or tools (e.g., hardware or software use, physical tool use) to accomplish tasks (Crawford & LePine, 2013).

With a few notable exceptions, social network techniques saw relatively little consideration in the early days of meso-research. However, Brass (2000) noted that the network approach was not designed to confirm or refute scholars' a priori hypotheses concerning the presence of aggregate variables but rather reflects underlying patterns of relationships that may give rise to collective phenomena. Network analyses simultaneously can reveal individual (i.e., node) attributes, dyadic patterns of relationships, clique (i.e., subgroup formation), as well as represent the overall structure of a unit (e.g., density,

centralization). In so doing, network measurements and conceptions liberate investigators to consider how the pattern of relationships potentially evolve, solidify, transform, and dissipate over time (Borgatti & Foster, 2003). Notably, network analyses may be used in an exploratory fashion to distill groups and subgroups from a larger system on the basis of their patterns of interactions (Freeman, 1992). For example, Nelson (1989) used network analysis of organizational members' frequencies of contact to identify 84 groups within 20 organizations. They then illustrated significant differences in intra- versus extra-group conflict ties based on those groupings. In this fashion, network analyses can be used post hoc to address the unit problem in organizational research (Mathieu & Chen, 2011). Alternatively, network analyses may be used in conjunction with a priori designated units to model relationship patterns (e.g., Hansen, Mors, & Løvås, 2005).

For example, Kukenberger, D'Innocenzo, and Mathieu (2013) described how different patterns of a multiplex network of members' influences can be associated with different forms of shared leadership. Specifically, they advanced a 2 × 2 conception whereby (a) highly centralized networks focused on the same node (i.e., person) across dimensions reflect a *solo* leader (i.e., one member performs all leadership functions), (b) highly centralized networks focused on different nodes across dimensions reflect *distributed* leadership (i.e., different members lead different functions), (c) low centralized networks with high density across dimensions represent *collective* leadership (i.e., in which all members work together as leaders), and (d) low centralized networks with low density across dimensions reflects an *absence* of leadership (i.e., where no one is performing leadership functions).

In sum, different forms of aggregate measures represent collective constructs in different ways. Each has an underlying combination algorithm that is presumed to represent the collective construct. They are suitable for indexing a given state or process at any particular time, but they do not reflect the actual formation, change, or dissolution of a construct. As many others have previously chronicled, scholars typically index team dynamics once or twice in an investigation and use those measures to predict other variables of interest (Cronin, Weingart, & Todorova, 2011; Humphrey & Aime, 2014; Waller, Okhuysen, & Saghafian, 2016). Although such work is important and informative, it does not reveal anything about emergence.

EMERGENCE

The idea that collective dynamics evolve over time is as old as the study of work units themselves. Yet "there has been an enormous neglect of time in studies of groups in organizations, and that neglect

has had a number of negative consequences on our ability to understand and predict work group behaviors" (McGrath & Tschan, 2007, p. 3). "Most of the time, group performance involves cycles of behavior, sequences of acts, interactions among teammates, critical issues of timing synchronization among teammates, and critical temporal relations among different parts of the task" (McGrath & Tschan, 2007, p. 8). At issue, therefore, is the need to better understand the formation, influence, and dissipation of collective dynamics—or what is commonly referred to as the *emergence of collective variables*. Several conceptions and definitions of emergence have been proffered. Table 7.1 presents some of the notable sources and definitions.

TABLE 7.1

Emergence Definitions

Sources	Definitions of emergence
Ablowitz (1939, p. 2)	"There are levels of existence and there is a 'tendency of units of one kind in combination, to constitute units of a new kind, with more complex constitution and new qualities due to the new togetherness of the parts.'"
Morgeson and Hofmann (1999, p. 252)	"The structure of any given collective (e.g., a work team) can be viewed as a series of ongoing, events, and event cycles between the component parts (e.g., individuals). This structure, in turn, forms the basis for the eventual emergence of collective constructs."
Kozlowski and Klein (2000, p. 55)	"A phenomenon is emergent when it originates in the cognition, affect, behaviors, or other characteristics of individuals, is amplified by their interactions, and manifests as a higher level, collective phenomenon."
Marks, Mathieu, and Zaccaro (2001, p. 357)	"Emergent states have been defined as 'constructs that characterize properties of the team that are typically dynamic in nature and vary as a function of team.'"
Sawyer (2002, p. 20)	"Thus, an emergence theory that is both non-realist and non-reductionist requires simultaneous consideration of two directions of causation: emergence of the higher-level phenomenon from the lower level, and downward causation from the higher level to the lower level."
Cronin, Weingart, and Todorova (2011, p. 574)	"Emergence describes a process where a higher-level phenomenon comes into existence based on interaction among the lower-level elements. . . . Emergence often takes time to occur, and can continue to change over time."
Kozlowski (2012, p. 267)	"Emergence is the result of bottom–up processes whereby phenomenon and constructs that originate at a lower level of analysis, through social interaction and exchange, combine, coalesce, and manifest at a higher collective level of analysis."
Waller, Okhuysen, and Saghafian (2016, p. 565)	"Emergent team phenomena emanate from behaviors of group members, and include emergent states, behavioral patterns, and structures. In other words, emergent team phenomena may be (1) states such as collective cognition, affect, or other relatively enduring properties, (2) behavioral patterns such as conversational routines, conflict resolution, or feedback seeking, or (3) structures such as sub-groups or hierarchies."
Fulmer and Ostroff (2016, p. S122)	"First, emergent processes create a higher-level 'whole' that is formed from the individual 'parts' in the system. Second, some degree of interaction among the individual elements occurs, which fosters a convergence. Third, it is the interaction among the individual elements that allows a new pattern or form to emerge as a collective, higher level phenomenon. Finally, emergence is a dynamic process that occurs over time."

Emergent Constructs

Several underlying themes can be seen in the definitions in Table 7.1. First, there is an implied emergence form that lower level entities will "converge" or exhibit greater homogeneity over time. However, as detailed earlier, not all aggregate constructs would be expected to converge over time. The nature of the aggregate property—averages, diversity, or configurations—is what should be modeled. Accordingly, we submit that it is important to emphasize that emergence describes changes in form toward some particular arrangement. In other words, emergence of what—or toward what—is what is at issue.

For example, Figures 7.1 through 7.4 depict emergence of three forms of aggregate constructs. For sake of exposition, in all cases presume that, at origin, members of a unit are randomly distributed on some construct of interest. In the upper portions of Figures 7.1 through 7.3, we depict such an arrangement as a rectangular distribution, although we acknowledge that a normal (bell-shaped) distribution might be equally suitable. Figure 7.1 illustrates emergence toward an *average* construct, which exhibits a congealing or convergence around some level of interest. For example, using a consensus or referent-shift–style measure, members' perceptions of unit cohesion could be

converging around some point, whether that be low or high levels of cohesion, such as that shown in the lower portions of Figure 7.1. In sum, emergence of an average-style construct would be indicated by a reduction of variance over time.

In contrast, emergence of a *variance* type of construct would exhibit a different pattern over time. Variance-type constructs can emerge as patterns of separation or disparity (Harrison & Klein, 2007). For example, using a consensus-style measure in which each member rates his or her leader's behaviors, leader–member exchange relationships may exhibit a *separation* pattern over time (see left side of Figure 7.2). In other words, as a new leader interacts with his or her members, some may be treated favorably and others not (i.e., the leader may practice a classic in-group and out-group behavior style). If this happened to be proportional across the group, the leader's mean exchange score would remain at the midpoint, yet the variance around those scores would increase over time. In sum, the emergence of separation-style constructs will evidence an increase in variance over time.

Now consider the emergence of a single leader such as that shown in the right side of Figure 7.2. In this case, presume that we collect round-robin–style ratings in which each member rates the overall

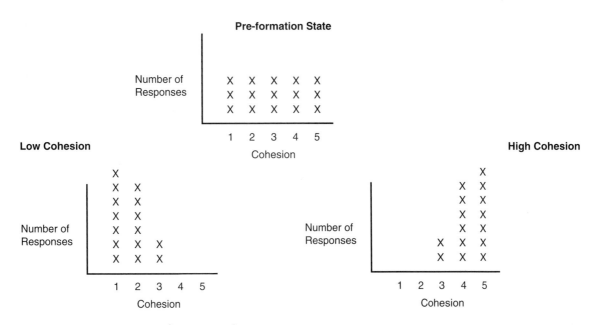

FIGURE 7.1.   Emergence of average-style constructs.

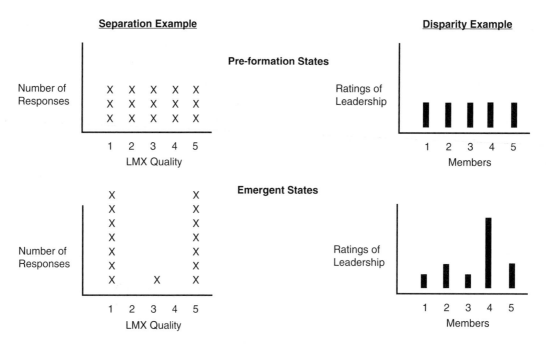

FIGURE 7.2.   Emergence of variance-style constructs. LMX = leader–member exchange.

leadership of all other members. This is a *disparity*-style variance-type construct in which one member's score on leadership behaviors are presumed to exceed those of others in the collective over time. Whereas, overall, the distribution of scores may not necessarily exhibit an increasing or decreasing mean or level of variability, the margin between that of an extreme member and others would increase over time. Notably, this pattern would also hold for

the emergence of an ostracism of a given member, only they would separate negatively from the pack on a likeability measures. In sum, the emergence of a disparity-style variance construct will evidence a particular pattern of an increasing margin between an extreme score and others in the unit over time, as aligned with the nature of the construct.

Figure 7.3 shows an example of a configural (shared leadership) construct, which is a more

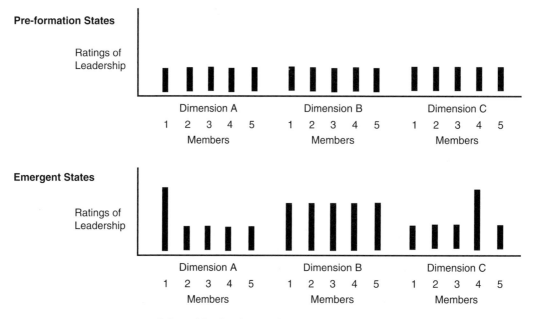

FIGURE 7.3.   Emergence of shared leadership–style construct.

complex form. For instance, again presume that members rate one another's leadership behaviors using a round-robin approach, but this time they do so on multiple dimensions (e.g., A, B, C). Figure 7.3 depicts an instance where Member 1 is rated as leading the "A" function, Member 4 is rated as leading the "C" function, and the "B" function is collectively led by all five members. This particular arrangement of leadership ratings would suggest a two thirds distributed design (with Members 1 and 4 leading A and C, respectively), and a one third collective form (in which all members contribute equally to the leadership of B; cf. D'Innocenzo, Mathieu, & Kukenberger, 2016). Notably, taking the average or variance indices of such ratings would not reveal this configural arrangement of shared leadership behaviors.

Configural-style constructs come in many other forms as well. For example, we are currently conducting research in which, in high-fidelity simulations, certain unit members should be coordinating their activities in a particular pattern in response to environmental events (Morgeson, Mitchell, & Liu, 2015). These patterns can be established, for example, via standard operating procedures or by military doctrine and rules of engagement. Once specified, however, these patterns of interaction can serve as a "target matrix," and observed members' behaviors can be gauged against

them. For example, as indexed using network-style measures, Figure 7.4 shows a target matrix of preferred interaction patterns in a multiteam system (MTS). MTSs are networks of interdependent teams working toward one or more common goals (Luciano, DeChurch, & Mathieu, 2018). The small circles represent component teams in the MTS (i.e., network nodes), and the circular loops associated with each depict their degree of *intrateam* coordination. The lines connecting the team nodes depict *interteam* relationships such as coordination behaviors (i.e., network ties). The thickness of the ties represents their relative strength with thicker lines representing stronger relations.

The upper panel of Figure 7.4 depicts a target matrix (i.e., an ideal pattern of MTS interactions in response to a particular event), and the series of observed interaction patterns over time are shown in the lower panel of the figure. Moving left to right across the lower panel, the pattern of MTS interactions is converging on the target matrix over time, as evidenced by the network patterns and quadratic assignment procedure correlations (Borgatti, Everett, & Johnson, 2013).

In sum, configural constructs may take on many forms that need to be articulated a priori or interpreted post hoc, to discern the pattern or extent to which they emerged over time. In other words, emergence cannot be modeled and understood in a

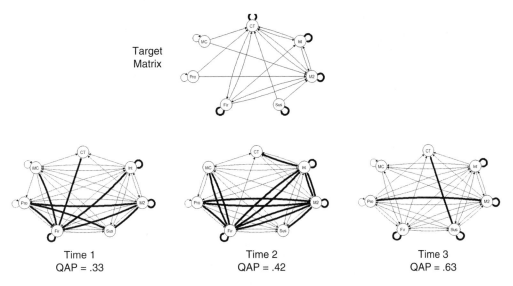

FIGURE 7.4. Emergence of a configural-style network construct. QAP = quadratic assignment procedure.

vacuum; one must specify the type of variable that one is anticipating to emerge, and its associated pattern of emergence over time, and then test it accordingly.

Emergence Origin

There is a second underlying theme concerning a question of origin in the emergence definitions presented in Table 7.1. Generally speaking, psychological theories of emergence are predicated on the notion that lower level entities combine to manifest a higher level construct (cf. Ablowitz, 1939; Cronin et al., 2011; Kozlowski & Klein, 2000; Waller et al., 2016). In other words, there is an atomistic approach whereby the collective property (e.g., unit cohesion) can be traced to the characteristics and interactions of constituent parts (i.e., members' attributes and interactions). In contrast, Morgeson and Hofmann (1999), and Marks, Mathieu, and Zaccaro (2001) advanced more holistic approaches and associated emergence with properties of the collective that evolve over time. Sawyer (2002) suggested that emergent properties might reflect bottom-up or top-down processes (or both)—a decidedly meso conception to which we subscribe.

A third theme in the emergence definitions is that it unfolds and develops over time. Accordingly, any understanding of emergence processes must explicitly incorporate a theory of time. Therefore, for our purposes, emergence can be defined as the movement of construct indicators over time, in reference to some construct structure of interest, as a function of multilevel forces. Although this definition may appear somewhat cumbersome, it details that (a) emergence is a multilevel phenomenon that can be a product of bottom-up, top-down, and/or level aligned forces; (b) different types of aggregate constructs will develop toward different structures or forms; and (c) emergence occurs over time. In what follows, we briefly consider different theories of emergence as a multilevel process and the temporal nature of emergent processes.

Theories of emergence. By and large, to date, studies of the dynamics of small collectives such as teams have modeled the influence of processes and states on later variables of interest. These designs typically measure a fully formulated state (e.g., empowerment) at one point in time and relate it to unit outcomes at some later point in time (for reviews, see Mathieu, Maynard, Rapp, & Gilson, 2008; Waller et al., 2016). There are relatively few longitudinal studies whereby unit-level predictors and outcomes are each measured over at least three occasions and linked in time-based modeling—and even fewer that explicitly model reciprocal relationships. For example, Mathieu, Kukenberger, D'Innocenzo, and Reilly (2015) sampled student teams competing in a business simulation over 10 weeks. They modeled the influence of team cohesion on later team performance, while also considering the reciprocal influence of team performance on later team cohesion levels. They employed the minimum requirement of three waves of data for a longitudinal study and were interested in the reciprocal influences associated with emergent *properties* (i.e., the state of cohesion at given times). However, they did not model the *processes* associated with the emergence of team cohesion over time.

Theories of emergence are about the *processes* associated with the formation, coalescing, transformation, and dissipating of collective dynamics over time. Current conceptions of emergence recognize the multilevel nature of the process—how emergence is a by-product of patterns of lower level interactions in a larger context (e.g., Fulmer & Ostroff, 2016; Kozlowski et al., 2013). Yet they tend to view the larger environment as an embedding context that places constraints or shapes those lower level processes. For example, Kozlowski and Chao (2012) submitted that individuals perceive and react to their environment. Notably, they argued

> These individual interactions within social units (e.g., teams, groups) have the potential to create shared perceptions that coalesce around a common understanding (i.e., homogeneous, composition emergence), distinctly different points of view that fragment the group (i.e., heterogeneous, compilation emergence), or very different interpretations

that vary across all the perceivers (i.e., no emergence, an individual property). (p. 339)

Similarly, Fulmer and Ostroff (2016) offered

Although social contexts are at a higher level of analysis, they are anchored in the cognitions, emotions, and normative behaviors of individual employees (Kozlowski & Klein, 2000). The fundamental theoretical basis rests on the assumption that there is some degree of convergence or consensus across individuals that creates a higher level property transcending individuals. (p. S122)

We do not limit our theory of emergence to bottom-up processes and submit that collective emergent processes may be a product of bottom-up, top-down, and focal level influences. That is, the upper level force may act not only as a context for lower level processes but may also serve to shape them over time.

Contextual features are not static entities and also may evolve over time. Moreover, collectives may act to select in which environments they operate and proactively shape elements of their environments (Tesluk & Mathieu, 1999). In other words, "emergent phenomena [are] unfolding in a proximal task- or social context that teams in part enact while also being embedded in a larger organization system or environmental context" (Kozlowski & Ilgen, 2006, p. 80). Thus, emergent collective properties may emanate from the unit or higher level rather than, or in addition to, patterns of members' interactions. For instance, as we write this chapter, the United States is going through a contentious transfer of power from the Obama to the Trump administrations. Movements, both supporting and protesting the incoming administration, have sprung up across the country. No doubt individual actors are working to organize such efforts and participants' actions. Yet there also can be no doubt that the primary driving force mobilizing these efforts stems from the change in power in the distal larger environment. That is,

environmental forces can also serve to generate the formation and nature of collective activities.

Environments are also nested in a traditional hierarchical sense. Organizational environments provide a larger context within which unit dynamics may operate (Fulmer & Ostroff, 2016; Kozlowski et al., 2013; Mathieu et al., 2008). For example, Morgeson et al. (2015) advanced a multilevel event-based conception of environmental influences. They argued that events can be defined in terms of their *strength* (i.e., novelty, disruptiveness, and criticality), *space* (i.e., origin and pervasiveness in the system), and *timing* (e.g., duration, timing, and variability). These features, then, necessitate the development and sustainability of different collective dynamics. Although more proximal to small units, their immediate task characteristics also have a significant role in shaping the processes and states that emerge. Steiner (1972) and McGrath (1984) advanced conceptions of task structures and requirements that influence work group processes. Moreover, group tasks may vary over time, and groups typically perform multiple tasks, both sequentially and simultaneously (Marks et al., 2001), which have serious implications for the allocations of resources and synchronicity of members' actions. Hinsz, Wallace, and Ladbury (2009) outlined how changing task conditions impose different information-processing and decision-making demands on work groups that require the groups to execute different actions over time. Consequently, different group processes emerge over time as circumstances warrant, and the group's responses and adaptability have implications for the necessity of future behaviors and associated states.

The coevolution of contextual forces and unit dynamics is a core feature of several theories. For example, Arrow, McGrath, and Berdahl (2000) submitted that

dynamical systems model the behavior of different levels of dynamical rules and variables—features of system operation that change, interdependently over time. Dynamical rules and variables can be classified into three categories that are demarcated by fuzzy boundaries.

Local dynamics refer to rules of activity for parts of the system, *global dynamics* refers to rules of activity for system-level properties that emerge out of local dynamics, and *contextual dynamics* refers to the impact of system-level parameters that affect the overall trajectory of global group dynamics over time whose values are determined in part by the group's embedding context. (pp. 40–41, emphasis added)

Drawing from Arrow et al. (2000), Kozlowski et al. (2013), Fulmer and Ostroff (2016), and others, we propose a general emergence framework such as that depicted in Figure 7.5. Like others, we are concerned with the processes that lead to the initial formation, coalescing, transformation, and dissipation of emergent properties over time. To be clear, there may well be any number of phases or processes that are presumed to unfold over time, and the process is not likely purely linear (e.g., a process that has dissipated can coalesce again). Yet for illustrative purposes, we outline the changing properties of the network across four periods: (a) preformation, (b) initial

formation, (c) coalescing, and (d) transforming in some manner, such as dissipating or fractionating. For example, let us consider the emergence of interpersonal based cohesion over time, as indicated by positive personal ties in Figure 7.5. At *preformation* of the unit, members have had no interactions with one another or the task and therefore have no basis for judging their cohesion. In real organizations, however, members may have worked on similar tasks in the past or with one another previously, so they may have some basis for anticipated levels of cohesion and begin closer to an initial-formation stage (Fulmer & Ostroff, 2016).

Early interactions during an *initial formation* phase will serve to begin the process of forming some level of cohesion. As shown in the figure, this may compile from a series of dyadic interactions to those of subgroups or the unit as a whole (Kozlowski, Gully, Nason, & Smith, 1999), largely depending on task characteristics. Early events (e.g., slow vs. high pace of activities, disruptions) may serve to dampen or amplify this process, and various interventions such as charter exercises (see Mathieu & Rapp, 2009) may facilitate the process. Collective states and task environments will

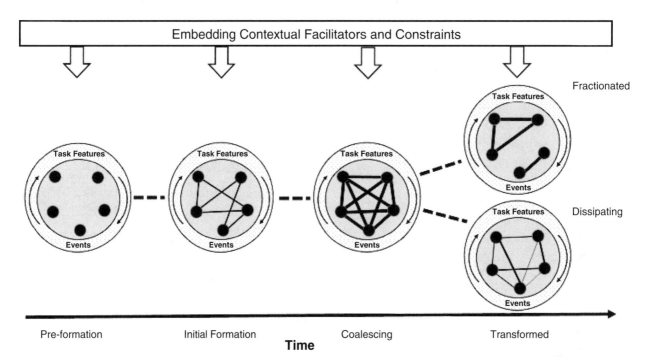

FIGURE 7.5. Example of emergence processes over time.

coevolve and perhaps lead to a *coalescing* phase in which cohesion ties are fully formed and complete. Cycling through a variety of episodes, perhaps with the aid of after-action reviews or debriefs (see Tannenbaum & Cerasoli, 2013), may play a role in these processes.

For illustrative purposes, in Figure 7.5 we have depicted two variations of a fourth, transforming stage of evolution. At issue is that various events, internal or external to the unit, may act as destabilizing forces and alter a fully formed emergent state. For example, perhaps a disagreement occurred between a pair of members, sparking alliance formation and a division, or *fractionation*, of the unit into subgroups. Fractionalization represents a change from one form to another. Zellmer-Bruhn (2003) found that team and task interruptions disrupted the equilibrium of a team and led to the enactment of new routines. Morgeson (2005) found that some situational events were disruptive enough to cause teams to reconsider their routines and to adopt new ones. Alternatively, perhaps the mission of a unit, such as a task force, loses its priority or importance. Although not formally disbanding, the unit may lose its salience to members, and the strengths of their ties may *dissipate* over time. Dissipation represents a deterioration or reversal from a formulated state to an earlier one. In both fractionalization and dissipation situations, however, the nature of the emergent state continues to evolve and change.

The overall point is that these collective dynamics, whether they are processes such as coordination and planning or states such as cohesion or shared cognitions, are volatile constructs subject to influence from members, as well as the proximal and distal environments. As shown, these dynamics unfold over time with a path dependence on earlier states. To reiterate, whereas the confluence of tasks, upward and downward influences, and dynamics are particularly salient in relatively small collectives such as teams or departments, they are not unique to them. Larger collectives such as strategic business units, organizations, and MTSs are all subject to similar forces.

A wide variety of factors may influence the emergence of different variables of interest. Fulmer and Ostroff (2016) reviewed the literature and distilled

the bases of four classes of emergent constructs: (a) cognition and learning, (b) perceptual, (c) attitudinal, and (d) affect. They outlined the potential impact of organizational structure and practices, leadership styles and behaviors, social processes and communication, and the distribution of members' individual attributes as salient predictors of the different forms. They concluded that there are some interesting trends in the literature, but far more research is warranted, especially in terms of predicting the emergence of collective affect. Furthermore, with few exceptions, the research that they reviewed focused on models of convergence—averages—with few investigations featuring variance or configuration-type constructs.

In sum, theories of emergence are about the processes that lead to states at different points in time. We and others have argued that these processes are by-products of multilevel forces from within, at, and above the level of the focal entities (e.g., teams, departments, organizations). And these processes unfold over time in a complex environment. Notably, although virtually all theories of emergence refer to temporal dynamics, rarely do they specify what is occurring over time to generate such changes. Importantly, time, in and of itself, is not a causal agent. However, events and processes that occur over time can be causal agents. Internal events are typically likened to developmental processes, whereas external events are mostly associated with cyclical task rhythms, shocks, or triggers from the environment. We turn now to such temporal dynamics associated with emergence.

Emergence over time. The phrase *emerges over time* is both a truism and valueless. Time is not a substantive variable per se but rather a surrogate for temporally related phenomena. Time comes in many forms and varieties that have different, yet related, implications for collectives (Ancona, Goodman, Lawrence, & Tushman, 2001). Several theories of temporal dynamics have been advanced over the years, including models of *development* (Kozlowski et al., 1999; Tuckman, 1965), *episodic* models (Marks et al., 2001; McGrath, 1991), and *event-based* models (Morgeson et al., 2015).

Developmental theories suggest that collectives go through a series of phases as members seek to understand their task environment and get to know one another. For instance, team development is described as "the path a [team] takes over its life-span toward the accomplishment of its main tasks" (Gersick, 1988, p. 9), and several models of such processes exist (e.g., Ancona & Chong, 1996; Gersick, 1988; Tuckman, 1965). Many of the developmental models assume that groups progress in a linear fashion from one stage to another, such as Tuckman's (1965; Tuckman & Jensen, 1977) stages of small group development. Tuckman's model includes four primary stages: forming, storming, norming, and performing, as well as adjourning.

In the *forming stage* of development, group members become familiar with each other and the task and work to establish a sense of stability and purpose. Thus, one might anticipate high information exchange between members but not necessarily the formation of team states such as cohesion. The following *storming phase* would suggest a divergence of members' opinions and perhaps heightened conflict levels as members debate their future course of action. In other words, high variance of opinions and low consensus would be expected. In the *norming phase*, one would anticipate that members' feelings and perceptions would begin to converge as they establish routinized work patterns and norms. The *performing stage* would suggest a pattern of activity associated with task accomplishment (e.g., McGrath, 1984), and the adjourning phase would suggest a dissipation of collective properties. In contrast, Gersick's (1988) punctuated equilibrium model would have its own predicted pattern of scores at the origination, midpoint, and near the end of a team lifecycle. At issue here is not the veracity of Tuckman's or Gersick's or any other developmental model but rather the fact that the temporal theory would predict different patterns or configurations of lower level (i.e., members') scores at different stages of development. Notably, developmental models are not limited to small collectives. For instance, Langley, Smallman, Tsoukas, and Van de Ven (2013) advanced a model of organizational change and development, whereas Huang and Knight (2017) proposed a developmental model of entrepreneurship and new venture creation.

Episodic models suggest that collectives perform different activities at different times, which may reoccur in a cyclical pattern. These approaches argue that units must execute different processes at different times, depending on task demands that recur in an episodic fashion (cf. Marks et al., 2001; McGrath, 1984). For instance, McGrath's time, interaction, and performance theory suggests that groups must simultaneously manage multiple bundles of activities over time. This suggests that different patterns of member activities would be anticipated at different times. Marks and her colleagues associated those different activities with performance episodes, which serve as demarcation points for recurring cycles of task accomplishment (Marks et al., 2001). Episodes are distinguishable periods of time over which performance accumulates and feedback is processed. They govern the rhythms of task performance for collectives and are distinguished by identifiable periods of action and transition periods between task accomplishments, as well as interpersonal processes which might be salient at any time. Rather than following a linear stage approach such as developmental models, for Marks et al. (2001),

> Episodes' durations stem largely from the nature of the tasks that teams perform and the technology that they employ, and from the manner in which members choose to complete work. Episodes are most easily identified by goals and goal accomplishment periods. (p. 359)

Episodic theories propose that collectives are doing different things at different times and therefore will exhibit ebbs and flows in their interaction patterns. Moreover, the emergence and quality of later exchanges will hinge, in part, on how well previous phases were performed. Therefore, the pattern of emergence is cyclical and exhibits a path dependence over time. In sum, cyclical theories of collective activity raise issues surrounding the pace and frequency of performance episodes. Researchers need to discern the most appropriate temporal "chunks" or units of time to consider. Aligning their research designs and analyses with such cycles represents both a challenge for researchers and an opportunity for new insights.

Event-based theories suggest that units are required to function differently in response to environmental triggers or conditions. Whereas episodic theories have a discernable rhythm to activities, event-based theories are typically less predictable. For example, Hinsz et al. (2009) outlined how changing task conditions impose different information-processing and decision-making demands on groups and require them to execute different types of actions over time. Consequently, different processes emerge over time as circumstances warrant, and the group's responses and adaptability have implications for the necessity of future behaviors and associated states. Morgeson et al. (2015) argued that such events may traverse levels of analysis and vary widely in terms of their impact and temporal parameters. These event features, then, necessitate the development and sustainability of different collective dynamics.

In sum, the value of articulating a temporal-based theory of emergence is that it focuses scholars' attention on critical periods of time where change of a certain type is presumed to operate. In other words, it is not sufficient to claim that a collective state will emerge or change over time. Scholars and practitioners alike need to know when a particular state is proposed to have formulated, what factors might facilitate or inhibit such formations, and why they develop (i.e., what are the processes by which they will emerge?). The answers to these questions guide the development of appropriate measurement protocols, research designs, and analytic tools for modeling emergent properties, as well as the nature and timing of interventions aimed at influencing them.

Research Implications

So far we have argued that scholars need to specify the type or form of emergent constructs in which they are interested and advance an associated temporal theory of emergence processes over time. Inherent in all theories of emergence is that collective constructs such as affective states, behaviors, and cognitions need to be indexed repeatedly over time for their emergent processes to be adequately

modeled and understood. Studying dynamic collective properties, especially ones that are presumed to emerge over time, requires sophisticated measurement, design, and analytic techniques (Luciano, Mathieu, Park, & Tannenbaum, 2018). It is not sufficient to simply call for "more longitudinal research" because without further guidance, such advice is too generic to be useful. Metaphorically, understanding collective dynamics is akin to following the plot line of a movie that emerges from the stringing together of various scenes of activity. In turn, those scenes emanate from a series of frames or snapshots of actions. Notably, the frames of activity are important because without valid and reliable indices of dynamic constructs at any given time, one cannot discern patterns that emerge and change over time. The fact that modeling dynamics requires measures that are both suitable for indexing collective properties at any given time (i.e., the frames or "statics"), as well of the sequencing of them over time, presents researchers with many challenges and decisions. It also necessitates a theory of unitization—that is, a sampling of temporal units that will enable the modeling of emergent processes. Accordingly, to study emergent collective processes, scholars need to gather a large number of measurements over time and to model them using sophisticated analytic techniques.

Measurement issues. Collective constructs subject to emergence can be measured using a variety of different techniques, and researchers should consider measurement alignment protocols (see Luciano, Mathieu, et al., 2018). To model emergent processes, however, a relatively high number of measurement occasions will be necessary. For example, Kozlowski et al. (2013) suggested that to model emergence, five, 10, or even 20 measurement periods may not be sufficient, and data should be gathered 30 or more times. Naturally, the frequency of measurement sampling would follow from the temporal theory and nature of the emergent processes and constructs in question, but these requirements go far beyond three waves of data.

Traditionally, organizational research of collective processes has been conducted using members' survey and interview responses and observations of their activities. *Multiitem survey instruments,* albeit short ones, remain a viable option for studying emergence but may well suffer from a variety of instrumentation and user biases over time. For example, the first author has studied crews conducting simulated Mars missions who remain in an analog spacecraft environment for weeks at a time. Participants are usually tolerant of end-of-day surveys and providing daily diary entries for research purposes in such contexts. In more traditional work environments, short surveys administered via cell phones using *experience sampling techniques* can minimize the biases associated with high-frequency administrations (Ballard, Tschan, & Waller, 2008). However, Carter, Carter, and DeChurch (2015) argued that

> if team members have not experienced sufficient interaction, as might be the case in initial phases of team development, they may find it difficult to accurately gauge emergent properties of their team. This inaccuracy in rating can result in measurement error and potentially inaccurate substantive conclusions. (p. 3)

Their analyses of two samples suggested that team members may not be able to accurately report the nature of emergent team states, particularly in early stages of the team. Thus, the analysis of collective emergence may be undermined by differential reliability and fidelity of survey measures over time.

Although it is perhaps viable to collect repeated multiitem survey measures for modeling emergence, the resulting scores are limited to testing average and variance-type constructs. Members' homogeneity or variance of responses can be calculated, per time, and modeled along with mean levels over time. As noted earlier, with the exception of perhaps identifying extreme scores within a collective distribution, traditional scale measures are not able to adequately represent various configural-style constructs. For those types of constructs, social network measures are far more suitable. Yet gathering traditional network measures at such a high frequency of administration may not be a viable option.

Experience sampling data generated from video coding provides an interesting way to bring to life the metaphor of collective dynamics as stringing together a series of frames. By layering in comparative case study methodology (Eisenhardt, 1989) researchers may explore in detail the process of emergence as well as when and why there are differences in the emergence process of the same construct. This approach could generate rich insights concerning the patterns of emergence combined with theory as to why changes occurred. However, it also necessitates a theory of unitization, is labor-intensive and potentially subject to biases (e.g., observational effects, subjective interpretations), and is perhaps best conceived of as part of a mixed-method methodology.

Qualitative techniques offer an alternative for better understanding emergent processes (Ballard et al., 2008; Kozlowski et al., 2013). Intensive case studies can provide a rich account and insights into collective emergent processes. For example, Liu and Maitlis (2014) performed a detailed analysis of five kinds of emotional dynamics, each associated with a different type of strategizing process, as expressed during 10 top management team meetings. Elsewhere, the second author spent 6 weeks in a hospital observing 394 patient handoffs from surgery to recovery and coding micro processes associated with handoff quality. There is no doubt that qualitative techniques are a valuable way to study emergent processes, but they are extremely time-intensive, subject to their own set of biases (e.g., observational effects, subjective interpretations), and require a large commitment on the part of researchers and an organization and unit members who are willing to deal with such intrusions.

New and emerging measurement technologies are capable of generating massive amounts of time-stamped "big data" that may be leveraged to index team dynamics. Indeed, George, Haas, and Pentland (2014) submitted that "evolving practices—using big data—can allow us to study entire organizations and workgroups in near-real time to predict individual and group behaviors, team social dynamics, coordination challenges, and performance outcomes" (p. 325). Specifically, we briefly outline two such measurement approaches: (a) computer-aided text (speech) analysis (CATA) and (b) wearable sensors.

The analysis of members' communications has been a mainstay of group's research from the dawn of the discipline. However, such analyses have typically been a painstaking endeavor involving recording communications, transcriptions, developing coding schemes, training coders, multiple revisions, and so forth (Fischer, McDonnell, & Orasanu, 2007). Certainly such a process yields a rich understanding of unit dynamics, but it is laborious and prone to unreliability. However, there have been recent developments in the area of linguistic analyses of text communications that converts text into substantive dimensions (Pollach, 2012).

Automated analyses of text materials are generally referred to as CATA in the social sciences. Quantitative-oriented forms of CATA can both count observed language use and be applied to derive latent construct meanings and use in context. For instance, Gibson and Zellmer-Bruhn (2001) used CATA techniques to examine the use of metaphors when describing teamwork. Members' communications of a variety of types (e.g., e-mails, text messages, or transcribed verbal communications) can be compiled and tagged in terms of source(s) and target(s) of the exchange, coded using CATA, and then scored as a collective or arranged in a time-based network arrangement. For example, members' individual positive or negative emotions could be scored from their written communications. These could be compiled as an additive index, or their homogeneity assessed (for consensus or referent-shift constructs) and their pattern of emergence could be modeled over time.

The past few years have seen the development of dedicated wearable sensor devices that are designed specifically for research purposes (Mukhopadhyay, 2015). For example, sociometric badges are small electronic devices that can be worn on a lanyard and provide infrared and Bluetooth measures of members' spatial propinquity and their body movements (Pentland, 2007). This particular brand of wearable sensor can also record raw audio or simply use audio streams to derive indices of members' speech activity, such as their intensity, relative talking time, and turn-taking patterns. The area of wearable sensors is advancing rapidly from sociometric badges, smart watches, and cell phone apps (Johnston et al., 2015) and beyond (Mukhopadhyay, 2015). These various devices generate streams of information that need to

be processed for use in behavioral research (Luciano, Mathieu, et al., 2018). Researchers will need to be cognizant of calibration issues, sampling rates and duration, timing and aggregation issues, and construct validity issues with regard to what exactly these indices convey in terms of collective dynamics. That said, the fact that these devices generate continuous time-stamped streams of information, often with relatively minimal intrusiveness, and can be configured to represent social network–style interactions offers great promise for the future and for the study of emergent processes.

Timing issues. The temporal theory guiding one's investigation of collective emergence proscribes a sampling frame for the timing of measurements (Ancona et al., 2001). For example, *developmental* theories suggest that collectives go through different stages or phases over their life cycles. The timing and duration of stages may not be, and are not likely to be, uniform across units. To adequately model the emergence of unit stages, however, one needs to collect data across time, when each unit is at different stages and transitioning between stages. This will not occur if one administers a survey (or any form of measurement) to all units at one point in time. Similarly, *episodic* theories suggest that collectives conduct transition processes such as interpreting feedback and formulating plans, after which they execute actions (Marks et al., 2001). Here again, simultaneously gathering measures about transition processes and action processes will result in a misalignment with one or the other process.

Rather than attempting to time measurements to align with the activation of an emergence process, an attractive alternative is to *gather data continually*. Continuous data streams enable modeling of the natural ebbs and flows of collective dynamics or sampling of instances from the continuous stream that correspond to certain developmental or episodic periods associated with emergence. The newer methods of measurements such as CATA and wearable sensors can yield massive amounts of ongoing streams of data. In these cases, the challenge becomes the development of automated scoring protocols and combination algorithms and determining the best aggregation durations.

Identifying meaningful units of time for continuous data is another challenge. Recall our movie metaphor. On one hand, one needs a sufficiently long interval for conversations to unfold or for behavioral patterns to reveal an underlying psychological state and yield reliable measures (i.e., frame rates). On the other hand, larger periods of time run the risk of obscuring meaningful differences and emergent processes that may develop quite quickly. Certainly, best practices would suggest that behaviors be recorded in as fine a grain as possible, which enables postprocessing options. Yet logistical concerns may make some options less viable than others (Luciano, Mathieu, et al., 2018). Ultimately, the temporal theory of the emergence process under investigation should guide such decisions.

In sum, the implications that collectives are doing different things at different times suggests at least two measurement strategies. First, researchers may attempt to synchronize the measurement of different constructs with when they are likely to be emerging, coalescing, or changing in one way or another. This is relatively easy to do in controlled laboratory investigations (e.g., Marks, DeChurch, Mathieu, Panzer, & Alonso, 2005) but much harder to accomplish in the field. Notably, this approach also requires an ipsative approach where each collective's progressions trigger measurement occasions that may not align across units. Yet the cross-unit consistency should be weighed against the value of better measurement alignment. The second option is to use continuous monitoring devices that generate time-stamped data. Although continuous data streams are an attractive option, they present many logistical, ethical, and cost issues (Luciano, Mathieu, et al., 2018). Privacy laws and individuals' willingness to be continuously monitored outside of laboratory environments are serious issues to contend with. Moreover, decisions concerning scoring protocols, combination algorithms, and temporal aggregation periods need to be addressed. Nevertheless, generating repeated measures of emergent states is necessary to model their emergent processes. In particular, social network–style measures, such as those illustrated in Figures 7.4 and 7.5, afford the opportunity to

model complex configural arrangements but impose even greater logistical demands. In any case, these measurement requirements must be fulfilled if scholars hope to study emergence.

Analytic issues. Traditional methods of assessing convergence and emergence around average- and variance-style aggregate constructs are well developed (cf. Cole, Bedeian, Hirschfeld, & Vogel, 2011; Estabrook, 2015; LeBreton & Senter, 2008; Tay, Woo, & Vermunt, 2014). In addition, techniques to simultaneously model nested and repeated measures data (i.e., mixed models) are mature and improving (e.g., Holcomb, Combs, Sirmon, & Sexton, 2010; Short, Ketchen, Bennett, & du Toit, 2006). Generally speaking, these techniques advance a multilevel mixed model where the lower level is a series of repeated measures and the upper level(s) index static or dynamic properties of the collectives. The lower level repeated measures need not be gathered uniformly across units, and multiple temporal codings can be used to represent a variety of different phenomena (Bliese, Adler, & Flynn, 2017).

For example, presume that we gather repeated observations of unit collective affect over time, and index them according to the type of construct we envision. Each measurement occasion can then be coded in terms of (a) when it was taken (i.e., clock time), (b) the period of evolution the collective was at (i.e., developmental stages), (c) whether the unit was in a transition or action phases (i.e., episodic models), and (d) the presence or absence of environmental circumstances (i.e., event-based models). Moreover, multiple temporal codes can be used to disentangle overlapping influences, such as discontinuous change models in concert with developmental models (see Bliese & Lang, 2016). Attributes of the collectives (e.g., unit composition) can be incorporated as second level between-unit characteristics, and those, in turn, perhaps nested in larger collectives (e.g., multiteam systems or organizations).

Although multilevel models provide powerful analytic techniques for modeling emergent processes, we clearly advocated the use of multidimensional dynamic social network measures for representing emergent constructs, especially for configural-type variables. Leenders, Contractor, and

DeChurch (2016) detailed a number of shortcomings of the use of aggregated survey measures to study dynamic collective properties. These include (a) underdeveloped theories of temporal relationships associated with emergence, (b) assumed homogeneity across members and their interactions, (c) the assumption that scores are homogeneous over (relatively long) time periods, and (d) the belief that repeated measurements of a construct capture unit dynamics. They proposed that relational events,

> defined as an interaction initiated by one team member to one or more other team members at a particular point in time, represent a more informative unit of investigation. . . . A relational event is minimally characterized by the time at which the interaction was initiated, the team member who initiated it, and the team member(s) who were the recipients. (Leenders et al., 2016, pp. 97–98)

Further, events can be classified along a number of dimensions, including their (a) contents or function (e.g., process, state, behavior), (b) modality (e.g., face-to-face exchanges, written communication, digitally mediated exchanges), (c) valence (i.e., positive, negative or neutral), and (d) strength (i.e., dichotomous or valued).

Relational events can also be used to represent multimode relationships. For example, Figure 7.6 depicts multiple forms of networks. The top disc represents a single-mode intermember interdependencies network driven by the positions that different members occupy. The nodes in this case are positions in a unit (e.g., surgeon, circulator nurse, and anesthesiologist). The second disc is a two-mode network that indexes the different tasks (hexagons) that members (circular nodes) perform. The third disc is a network of intermember relations, and the fourth is another two-mode network, this time crossing members with the tools (squares) that they may use. The bottom matrix depicts a multiplex intermember network of multiple functional relationships.

As depicted, network arrangements can represent a variety of collective constructs in multiple ways.

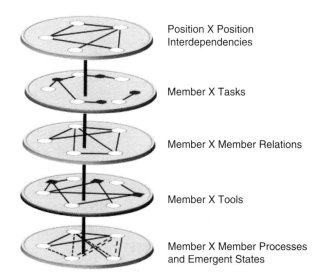

FIGURE 7.6. Emergence of multimode network structure.

Simple density measures (i.e., the number of possible connections that exist) are akin to average-style aggregate measures, and the consistency of linkages across nodes is akin to variance-style aggregate measures. However, the power of network methodologies is that they can represent complex configurations of relations, as associated with different emergent properties (e.g., highly centralize vs. fractionated). Social network analysis has the flexibility to index patterns of dyadic relationships, regions (i.e., cliques), or whole network features. As discussed earlier, this makes them particularly well suited for testing the emergence of different configural arrangements.

In some cases, network-derived indices can be incorporated into multilevel models. For example, presume that one collects a series of network measures of cohesion or members' leadership behaviors. Cohesion is an average-type construct, and the density of a unit networks could be modeled over time as an index of emergence. Alternatively, the relative node centrality of members' leadership scores over time would be an informative way to model the emergence of leadership in the unit—a variance (disparity)-style construct. Moreover, one could index the alignment of an observed pattern of behavior relative to a target matrix using quadratic assignment procedure correlations and model the emergence of configural-style constructs.

In other words, one can leverage social network measurement techniques and integrate them into more traditional multilevel modeling analyses.

There are also dedicated techniques for modeling dynamic social networks. For example, Leenders et al. (2016) described *sequential structure signatures*, which refer to hypothesized patterns of interactions over time. In other words, using time-ordered networks, the rate and extent to which a particular hypothesized configuration of relations emerges over time can be tested. For example, Klonek, Quera, Burba, and Kauffeld (2016) used sequential structure analyses to examine the emergence of different communication patterns during team meetings. Notably, they leveraged detailed observational codings of micro processes in their analyses, but the same approach could be applied with matrices formed from digital trace measures.

Social network analysis techniques are advancing rapidly. For example, Koujaku, Takigawa, Kudo, and Imai (2016) illustrated how network analyses can be used to identify and represent different forms of subgrouping that could be aligned with different configural constructs. Elsewhere, exponential random graph modeling (ERGM) enables scholars to specify sufficient statistics in the form "graph motifs," which are researchers' beliefs about the potential nature and interrelationships among actors (e.g., unit members). Sewell and Chen (2016) demonstrated how ERGM models can be used to model dynamic properties over time. Recent advancements have proposed multilevel exponential random graph modeling that are capable of simultaneously analyzing network that are nested in the traditional sense (cf. Slaughter & Koehly, 2016; Zappa & Lomi, 2015; Zappa & Robins, 2016). These too have been extended to model relationships over time (Carley, Columbus, & Landwehr, 2013).

CONCLUSION

Studying collective emergent processes is a demanding endeavor. To facilitate this process, we proposed an integrated strategy for advancing and testing theories about the emergence of collective phenomena over time. We argued that doing so requires scholars to articulate the *form(s) of the collective constructs* that they are interested in modeling (i.e., average, variance, or configural), which then specifies the *form of emergence* that is anticipated over time. In specifying how the construct may change over time (e.g., across time periods—preformation, initial formation, coalescing, transforming), it must be aligned with a *temporal theory* of interest (e.g., developmental, episodic, event-based). Notably, such processes may unfold at a given level of analysis, evidence upward influences, or be subject to downward influences over time. The form of the construct and emergence must be aligned with the temporal theory (or theories) and articulated a priori, which in turn guides the empirical investigation, including what constitutes support for emergence. Stated differently, it is not possible to model and understand emergence in a vacuum; one must specify the type of variable that one is anticipating to emerge and the associated pattern of emergence over time.

We then noted that there are measurement challenges that must be confronted. These include what type(s) of methods of measurement to use, how often to gather them, and when to gather them. We argued that network approaches are more flexible and offer many advantages over traditional survey and observation techniques but impose even greater logistical demands. Accordingly, we advocated some of the newer emerging measurement approaches such as CATA and wearable sensors that generate continuous streams of information but also noted that they engender additional considerations such as aggregation (over time) and indexing decisions. We then outlined some analytic approaches, including how to incorporate some network indices into traditional mixed-model multilevel analysis techniques, as well as some dedicated network analysis approaches, including sequential structure signatures and exponential random graph modeling.

Clearly, studying emergent collective phenomena is not for the faint- or lighthearted. However, with the combination of newer forms of measurement, network representations of collective properties, and advancements in longitudinal and multilevel network analyses, we may well be on the cusp of a new era. No doubt this will necessitate a refinement of existing theories and the developments of new conceptions, as well as extensions to additional levels of analysis and entities such as multiteam systems, communities of practices, organizational alliances, and nonwork collectives. By offering a strategy to identify and link the core elements of an emergent process over time, including bottom-up, top-down, and focal-level influences, with important measurement and analytic concerns, we hope to accelerate the coalescence of the literature on emergent phenomena.

References

Ablowitz, R. (1939). The theory of emergence. *Philosophy of Science, 6*, 1–16. http://dx.doi.org/10.1086/286529

Ancona, D., & Chong, C.-L. (1996). Entrainment: Pace, cycle, and rhythm in organizational behavior. *Research in Organizational Behavior, 18*, 251–284.

Ancona, D. G., Goodman, P. S., Lawrence, B. S., & Tushman, M. L. (2001). Time: A new research lens. *Academy of Management Review, 26*, 645–663.

Arrow, H., McGrath, J. E., & Berdahl, J. L. (2000). *Small groups as complex systems: Formation, coordination, development, and adaptation.* Thousand Oaks, CA: Sage.

Ballard, D. L., Tschan, F., & Waller, M. J. (2008). All in the timing: Considering time in multiple stages of group research. *Small Group Research, 39*, 328–351. http://dx.doi.org/10.1177/1046496408317036

Bliese, P. D., Adler, A. B., & Flynn, P. J. (2017). Transition processes: A review and synthesis integrating methods and theory. *Annual Review of Organizational Psychology and Organizational Behavior, 4*, 263–286. http://dx.doi.org/10.1146/annurev-orgpsych-032516-113213

Bliese, P. D., & Lang, J. W. (2016). Understanding relative and absolute change in discontinuous growth models: Coding alternatives and implications for hypothesis testing. *Organizational Research Methods, 19*, 562–592. http://dx.doi.org/10.1177/1094428116633502

Borgatti, S. P., Everett, M. G., & Johnson, J. C. (2013). *Analyzing social networks.* Thousand Oaks, CA: Sage.

Borgatti, S. P., & Foster, P. (2003). The network paradigm in organizational research: A review and typology. *Journal of Management, 29*, 991–1013. http://dx.doi.org/10.1016/S0149-2063(03)00087-4

Brass, D. J. (2000). Networks and frog ponds: Trends in multilevel research. In K. J. Klein & S. W. J. Kozlowski (Eds.), *Multilevel theory, research, and methods in organizations* (pp. 557–571). San Francisco, CA: Jossey-Bass.

Carley, K. M., Columbus, D., & Landwehr, P. (2013). *Automap user's guide.* Retrieved from Pittsburgh, PA: Novation.

Carter, N. T., Carter, D. R., & DeChurch, L. A. (2015). Implications of observability for the theory and measurement of emergent team phenomena. *Journal of Management, 44*, 1398–1425.

Chan, D. (1998). Functional relations among constructs in the same content domain at different levels of analysis: A typology of composition models. *Journal of Applied Psychology, 83*, 234–246. http://dx.doi.org/10.1037/0021-9010.83.2.234

Chen, G., Mathieu, J. E., & Bliese, P. D. (2004). A framework for conducting multilevel construct validation. In F. J. Dansereau & F. Yammarino (Eds.), *Research in multi-level issues: The many faces of multi-level issues* (Vol. 3, pp. 273–303). Oxford, England: Elsevier Science.

Cole, M. S., Bedeian, A. G., Hirschfeld, R. R., & Vogel, B. (2011). Dispersion-composition models in multilevel research: A data-analytic framework. *Organizational Research Methods, 14*, 718–734. http://dx.doi.org/10.1177/1094428110389078

Crawford, E. R., & LePine, J. A. (2013). A configural theory of team processes: Accounting for the structure of taskwork and teamwork. *Academy of Management Review, 38*, 32–48. http://dx.doi.org/10.5465/amr.2011.0206

Cronin, M. A., Weingart, L. R., & Todorova, G. (2011). Dynamics in groups: Are we there yet? *The Academy of Management Annals, 5*, 571–612. http://dx.doi.org/10.1080/19416520.2011.590297

D'Innocenzo, L., Mathieu, J. E., & Kukenberger, M. R. (2016). A meta-analysis of different forms of shared leadership–team performance relations. *Journal of Management, 42*, 1964–1991. http://dx.doi.org/10.1177/0149206314525205

Eisenhardt, K. M. (1989). Building theories from case study research. *Academy of Management Review, 14*, 532–550.

Estabrook, R. (2015). Evaluating measurement of dynamic constructs: Defining a measurement model of derivatives. *Psychological Methods, 20*, 117–141. http://dx.doi.org/10.1037/a0034523

Fischer, U., McDonnell, L., & Orasanu, J. (2007). Linguistic correlates of team performance: Toward a tool for monitoring team functioning during space missions. *Aviation, Space, and Environmental Medicine, 78*(Suppl.), B86–B95.

Freeman, L. C. (1992). The sociological concept of "group": An empirical test of two models. *American Journal of Sociology, 98*, 152–166. http://dx.doi.org/10.1086/229972

Fulmer, C. A., & Ostroff, C. (2016). Convergence and emergence in organizations: An integrative framework and review. *Journal of Organizational Behavior, 37*, S122–S145. http://dx.doi.org/10.1002/job.1987

George, G., Haas, M. R., & Pentland, A. (2014). Big data and management. *Academy of Management Journal, 57*, 321–326. http://dx.doi.org/10.5465/amj.2014.4002

George, J. M. (1990). Personality, affect, and behavior in groups. *Journal of Applied Psychology, 75*, 107–116. http://dx.doi.org/10.1037/0021-9010.75.2.107

Gersick, C. J. G. (1988). Time and transition in work teams: Toward a new model of group development. *Academy of Management Journal, 31*, 9–41. http://dx.doi.org/10.2307/256496

Gibson, C. B., & Zellmer-Bruhn, M. E. (2001). Metaphors and meaning: An intercultural analysis of the concept of teamwork. *Administrative Science Quarterly, 46*, 274–303. http://dx.doi.org/10.2307/2667088

Hansen, M. T., Mors, M. L., & Løvås, B. (2005). Knowledge sharing in organizations: Multiple networks, multiple phases. *Academy of Management Journal, 48*, 776–793. http://dx.doi.org/10.5465/AMJ.2005.18803922

Harrison, D. A., & Klein, K. J. (2007). What's the difference? Diversity constructs as separation, variety, or disparity in organizations. *Academy of Management Review, 32*, 1199–1228. http://dx.doi.org/10.5465/AMR.2007.26586096

Hinsz, V. B., Wallace, D. M., & Ladbury, J. L. (2009). Team performance in dynamic task environments. *International Review of Industrial and Organizational Psychology, 24*, 183–216.

Hitt, M. A., Beamish, P. W., Jackson, S. E., & Mathieu, J. E. (2007). Building theoretical and empirical bridges across levels: Multilevel research in management. *Academy of Management Journal, 50*, 1385–1399. http://dx.doi.org/10.5465/AMJ.2007.28166219

Holcomb, T. R., Combs, J. G., Sirmon, D. G., & Sexton, J. (2010). Modeling levels and time in entrepreneurship research: An illustration with growth strategies and post-IPO performance. *Organizational Research Methods, 13*, 348–389. http://dx.doi.org/10.1177/1094428109338401

House, R., Rousseau, D. M., & Thomas-Hunt, M. (1995). The meso paradigm: A framework for the integration of micro and macro organizational behavior. *Research in Organizational Behavior, 17*, 71–114.

Huang, L., & Knight, A. P. (2017). Resources and relationships in entrepreneurship: An exchange theory of the development and effects of the entrepreneur–investor relationship. *Academy of Management Review, 42*, 80–102. http://dx.doi.org/10.5465/amr.2014.0397

Humphrey, S. E., & Aime, F. (2014). Team microdynamics: Toward an organizing approach to teamwork. *Academy of Management Annals, 8*, 443–503. http://dx.doi.org/10.1080/19416520.2014.904140

James, L. R., Demaree, R. G., & Hater, J. J. (1980). A statistical rationale for relating situational variables and individual differences. *Organizational Behavior & Human Performance, 25*, 354–364. http://dx.doi.org/10.1016/0030-5073(80)90033-1

Johnston, M. J., King, D., Arora, S., Behar, N., Athanasiou, T., Sevdalis, N., & Darzi, A. (2015). Smartphones let surgeons know WhatsApp: An analysis of communication in emergency surgical teams. *American Journal of Surgery, 209*, 45–51. http://dx.doi.org/10.1016/j.amjsurg.2014.08.030

Klonek, F. E., Quera, V., Burba, M., & Kauffeld, S. (2016). Group interactions and time: Using sequential analysis to study group dynamics in project meetings. *Group Dynamics: Theory, Research, and Practice, 20*, 209–222. http://dx.doi.org/10.1037/gdn0000052

Koujaku, S., Takigawa, I., Kudo, M., & Imai, H. (2016). Dense core model for cohesive subgraph discovery. *Social Networks, 44*, 143–152. http://dx.doi.org/10.1016/j.socnet.2015.06.003

Kozlowski, S. W. (2012). Groups and teams in organizations: Studying the multilevel dynamics of emergence. In A. Hollingshead & M. S. Poole (Eds.), *Research methods for studying groups and teams: A guide to approaches, tools, and technologies* (pp. 260–283). New York, NY: Routledge.

Kozlowski, S. W., & Chao, G. T. (2012). The dynamics of emergence: Cognition and cohesion in work teams. *Managerial & Decision Economics, 33*, 335–354. http://dx.doi.org/10.1002/mde.2552

Kozlowski, S. W., Chao, G. T., Grand, J. A., Braun, M. T., & Kuljanin, G. (2013). Advancing multilevel research design: Capturing the dynamics of emergence. *Organizational Research Methods, 16*, 581–615. http://dx.doi.org/10.1177/1094428113493119

Kozlowski, S. W. J., Gully, S. M., Nason, E. R., & Smith, E. M. (1999). Developing adaptive teams: A theory of compilation and performance across levels and time. In D. R. Ilgen & E. D. Pulakos (Eds.), *The changing nature of work performance: Implications for staffing, personnel actions, and development* (pp. 240–292). San Francisco, CA: Jossey-Bass.

Kozlowski, S. W. J., & Ilgen, D. R. (2006). Enhancing the effectiveness of work groups and teams. *Psychological Science in the Public Interest, 7*, 77–124. http://dx.doi.org/10.1111/j.1529-1006.2006.00030.x

Kozlowski, S. W. J., & Klein, K. J. (2000). A multi-level approach to theory and research in organizations: Contextual, temporal, and emergent processes.

In K. J. Klein & S. W. J. Kozlowski (Eds.), *Multilevel theory, research, and methods in organizations* (pp. 3–90). San Francisco, CA: Jossey-Bass.

Kukenberger, M. R., D'Innocenzo, L., & Mathieu, J. E. (2013, April). *Compositional antecedents of a network measurement of collective, distributive leadership.* Paper presented at the Annual Meeting of Society for Industrial and Organizational Psychology, Houston, TX.

Langley, A., Smallman, C., Tsoukas, H., & Van de Ven, A. H. (2013). Process studies of change in organization and management: Unveiling temporality, activity, and flow. *Academy of Management Journal, 56*, 1–13. http://dx.doi.org/10.5465/amj.2013.4001

LeBreton, J. M., & Senter, J. L. (2008). Answers to 20 questions about interrater reliability and interrater agreement. *Organizational Research Methods, 11*, 815–852. http://dx.doi.org/10.1177/1094428106296642

Leenders, R. T. A., Contractor, N. S., & DeChurch, L. A. (2016). Once upon a time: Understanding team processes as relational event networks. *Organizational Psychology Review, 6*, 92–115. http://dx.doi.org/10.1177/2041386615578312

Liu, F., & Maitlis, S. (2014). Emotional dynamics and strategizing processes: A study of strategic conversations in top team meetings. *Journal of Management Studies, 51*, 202–234. http://dx.doi.org/10.1111/j.1467-6486.2012.01087.x

Luciano, M. M., DeChurch, L. A., & Mathieu, J. E. (2018). Multiteam systems: A structural framework and meso-theory of system functioning. *Journal of Management, 44*, 1065–1096. http://dx.doi.org/10.1177/0149206315601184

Luciano, M. M., Mathieu, J. E., Park, S., & Tannenbaum, S. I. (2018). A fitting approach to construct and measurement alignment: The role of big data in advancing dynamic theories. *Organizational Research Methods, 21*, 592–632. http://dx.doi.org/10.1177/1094428117728372

Marks, M. A., DeChurch, L. A., Mathieu, J. E., Panzer, F. J., & Alonso, A. (2005). Teamwork in multiteam systems. *Journal of Applied Psychology, 90*, 964–971. http://dx.doi.org/10.1037/0021-9010.90.5.964

Marks, M. A., Mathieu, J. E., & Zaccaro, S. J. (2001). A temporally based framework and taxonomy of team processes. *Academy of Management Review, 26*, 356–376.

Mason, C. M., & Griffin, M. A. (2003). Group absenteeism and positive affective tone: A longitudinal study. *Journal of Organizational Behavior, 24*, 667–687. http://dx.doi.org/10.1002/job.210

Mathieu, J., Maynard, M. T., Rapp, T., & Gilson, L. (2008). Team effectiveness 1997–2007: A review of recent advancements and a glimpse into the future. *Journal of Management, 34*, 410–476. http://dx.doi.org/10.1177/0149206308316061

Mathieu, J. E., & Chen, G. (2011). The etiology of the multilevel paradigm in management research. *Journal of Management, 37*, 610–641. http://dx.doi.org/10.1177/0149206310364663

Mathieu, J. E., Heffner, T. S., Goodwin, G. F., Cannon-Bowers, J. A., & Salas, E. (2005). Scaling the quality of teammates' mental models: Equifinality and normative comparisons. *Journal of Organizational Behavior, 26*, 37–56. http://dx.doi.org/10.1002/job.296

Mathieu, J. E., Kukenberger, M. R., D'Innocenzo, L., & Reilly, G. (2015). Modeling reciprocal team cohesion-performance relationships, as impacted by shared leadership and members' competence. *Journal of Applied Psychology, 100*, 713–734. http://dx.doi.org/10.1037/a0038898

Mathieu, J. E., & Rapp, T. L. (2009). Laying the foundation for successful team performance trajectories: The roles of team charters and performance strategies. *Journal of Applied Psychology, 94*, 90–103. http://dx.doi.org/10.1037/a0013257

McGrath, J. E. (1984). *Groups: Interaction and performance.* Englewood Cliffs, NJ: Prentice Hall.

McGrath, J. E. (1991). Time, interaction, and performance (TIP): A theory of groups. *Small Group Research, 22*, 147–174. http://dx.doi.org/10.1177/1046496491222001

McGrath, J. E., & Tschan, F. (2007). Temporal matters in the study of work groups in organizations. *The Psychologist-Manager Journal, 10*, 3–12. http://dx.doi.org/10.1080/10887150709336609

Mohammed, S., & Dumville, B. C. (2001). Team mental models in a team knowledge framework: Expanding theory and measurement across disciplinary boundaries. *Journal of Organizational Behavior, 22*, 89–106. http://dx.doi.org/10.1002/job.86

Morgeson, F. P. (2005). The external leadership of self-managing teams: Intervening in the context of novel and disruptive events. *Journal of Applied Psychology, 90*, 497–508. http://dx.doi.org/10.1037/0021-9010.90.3.497

Morgeson, F. P., & Hofmann, D. A. (1999). The structure and function of collective constructs: Implications for multilevel research and theory development. *Academy of Management Review, 24*, 249–265.

Morgeson, F. P., Mitchell, T. R., & Liu, D. (2015). Event system theory: An event-oriented approach to the organizational sciences. *Academy of Management Review, 40*, 515–537. http://dx.doi.org/10.5465/amr.2012.0099

Mossholder, K. W., & Bedeian, A. G. (1983). Cross-level inference and organizational research: Perspectives on interpretation and application. *Academy of Management Review, 8*, 547–558.

Mukhopadhyay, S. C. (2015). Wearable sensors for human activity monitoring: A review. *IEEE Sensors Journal, 15*, 1321–1330. http://dx.doi.org/10.1109/JSEN.2014.2370945

Nelson, R. E. (1989). The strength of strong ties: Social networks and intergroup conflict in organizations. *Academy of Management Journal, 32*, 377–401. http://dx.doi.org/10.2307/256367

Pentland, A. (2007). Automatic mapping and modeling of human networks. *Physica A, 378*, 59–67. http://dx.doi.org/10.1016/j.physa.2006.11.046

Pollach, I. (2012). Taming textual data: The contribution of corpus linguistics to computer-aided text analysis. *Organizational Research Methods, 15*, 263–287. http://dx.doi.org/10.1177/1094428111417451

Rousseau, D. M. (1985). Issues of level in organizational research: Multi-level and cross-level perspectives. *Research in Organizational Behavior, 7*, 1–37.

Rousseau, D. M. (2011). Reinforcing the micro/macro bridge: Organizational thinking and pluralistic vehicles. *Journal of Management, 37*, 429–442.

Sawyer, R. K. (2002). Emergence in psychology: Lessons from the history of non-reductionist science. *Human Development, 45*, 2–28. http://dx.doi.org/10.1159/000048148

Sewell, D. K., & Chen, Y. (2016). Latent space models for dynamic networks with weighted edges. *Social Networks, 44*, 105–116. http://dx.doi.org/10.1016/j.socnet.2015.07.005

Short, J. C., Ketchen, D. J., Jr., Bennett, N., & du Toit, M. (2006). An examination of firm, industry, and time effects on performance using random coefficients modeling. *Organizational Research Methods, 9*, 259–284. http://dx.doi.org/10.1177/1094428106287572

Slaughter, A. J., & Koehly, L. M. (2016). Multilevel models for social networks: Hierarchical Bayesian approaches to exponential random graph modeling. *Social Networks, 44*, 334–345. http://dx.doi.org/10.1016/j.socnet.2015.11.002

Smith-Jentsch, K. A., Mathieu, J. E., & Kraiger, K. (2005). Investigating linear and interactive effects of shared mental models on safety and efficiency in a field setting. *Journal of Applied Psychology, 90*, 523–535. http://dx.doi.org/10.1037/0021-9010.90.3.523

Steiner, I. D. (1972). *Group processes and productivity*. New York, NY: Academic Press.

Tannenbaum, S. I., & Cerasoli, C. P. (2013). Do team and individual debriefs enhance performance? A meta-analysis. *Human Factors, 55*, 231–245. http://dx.doi.org/10.1177/0018720812448394

Tay, L., Woo, S. E., & Vermunt, J. K. (2014). A conceptual and methodological framework for psychometric isomorphism: Validation of multilevel construct measures. *Organizational Research Methods, 17*, 77–106. http://dx.doi.org/10.1177/1094428113517008

Tesluk, P. E., & Mathieu, J. E. (1999). Overcoming roadblocks to effectiveness: Incorporating management of performance barriers into models of work group effectiveness. *Journal of Applied Psychology, 84*, 200–217. http://dx.doi.org/10.1037/0021-9010.84.2.200

Tuckman, B. W. (1965). Developmental sequence in small groups. *Psychological Bulletin, 63*, 384–399. http://dx.doi.org/10.1037/h0022100

Tuckman, B. W., & Jensen, M. A. C. (1977). Stages of small-group development revisited. *Group & Organization Studies, 2*, 419–427. http://dx.doi.org/10.1177/105960117700200404

Waller, M. J., Okhuysen, G. A., & Saghafian, M. (2016). Conceptualizing emergent states: A strategy to advance the study of group dynamics. *The Academy of Management Annals, 10*, 561–598. http://dx.doi.org/10.1080/19416520.2016.1120958

Zappa, P., & Lomi, A. (2015). The analysis of multilevel networks in organizations: Models and empirical tests. *Organizational Research Methods, 18*, 542–569. http://dx.doi.org/10.1177/1094428115579225

Zappa, P., & Robins, G. (2016). Organizational learning across multi-level networks. *Social Networks, 44*, 295–306. http://dx.doi.org/10.1016/j.socnet.2015.03.003

Zellmer-Bruhn, M. E. (2003). Interruptive events and team knowledge acquisition. *Management Science, 49*, 514–528. http://dx.doi.org/10.1287/mnsc.49.4.514.14423

## CHAPTER 8

MULTILEVEL THOUGHTS ON SOCIAL NETWORKS

Daniel J. Brass and Stephen P. Borgatti

In this chapter, we present a social network perspective as a lens for promoting multilevel research. We begin by noting how the relational focus inherent in social networks adds the possibility of incorporating interpersonal, intergroup, and interorganizational measures and analyses to our traditional multilevel thinking. We provide guidelines organized around questions of entitivity, aggregation, designating network boundaries, isomorphisms, and the content and context of networks. We present a practical guide to which researchers might look to explain variance in phenomena of interest by focusing on multilevel social networks.

Before discussing the role of multilevel research in social network theory and analysis, let us begin with some basic assumptions about multilevel research. Most of us in the organizational sciences begin by selecting a dependent variable to predict, such as individual or organizational performance. Or perhaps we choose to focus on an independent variable, such as network centrality, and consider how it might affect a variety of dependent variables. This is largely based on personal interest. We then attempt to identify independent variables that may be related to our dependent variable, or vice versa. In the process, we encounter variables that may or may not be at the same level of analysis. Individual performance seems to be affected by group performance, and vice versa. Indeed, individuals are

nested within groups, groups within organizations, organizations within industries, and so on. If we are to explain the variance in our dependent variable of interest, it might be necessary to look beyond the individual in explaining individual performance, beyond the group in explaining group performance, and so forth.

Faced with a labeling issue of what to call this type of research, we agree to refer to it as *cross-level research* and, consequently, are forced to confront issues surrounding the appropriate ways to measure constructs at different levels of analysis, questions of isomorphism, and accusations of anthropomorphism (Hitt, Beamish, Jackson, & Mathieu, 2007; Rousseau, 1985). As we progress, we develop advanced statistical techniques and nomenclature and eventually devote volumes and conferences to discuss multilevel research. All this is to the benefit of explaining our dependent variable of interest, the greatest benefit being an awareness of where to look for important constructs and independent variables. We expand our research possibilities and consequent insights by having developed both easily recognizable labels for levels of analysis and multilevel models that focus our awareness.

A typical model for promoting multilevel research and providing a guide for "where to look" is presented in Figure 8.1. The *X* represents the independent variables; *Y* represents the dependent

http://dx.doi.org/10.1037/0000115-009
The Handbook of Multilevel Theory, Measurement, and Analysis, S. E. Humphrey and J. M. LeBreton (Editors-in-Chief)

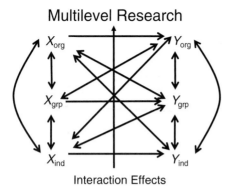

Multilevel Research

Interaction Effects

FIGURE 8.1. Template for assessing multilevel relationships. grp = group; ind = individual; org = organizational; X = independent variables; Y = dependent variables.

variables; and ind, grp, and org designate the commonly accepted levels of analysis: individual, group, and organizational, respectively. Arrows indicate possible relationships, most going both directions, noting bottom-up and top-down effects, as well as possible construct isomorphisms (constructs at different levels of analysis that have the same meaning). The middle arrow from bottom to top alerts researchers to consider moderation effects. Longitudinal paths over multiple time periods can be included by simply adding additional columns of X and Y variables. Figure 8.1 can also be used to trace sequential series of variables and arrows. For example, Coleman's (1990) famous "bathtub" model suggests that higher level constructs affect lower level constructs, which in turn affect other lower level constructs that affect higher level constructs (i.e., $X_{grp} \rightarrow X_{ind} \rightarrow Y_{ind} \rightarrow Y_{grp}$). Frameworks such as Figure 8.1 can be usefully applied by noting where prior research has occurred and suggesting areas for future exploration.

LOOKING FOR ENTITIES

It is important to note that the individual, group, and organizational levels of analysis do not represent an exhaustive list of possible levels. They are easily recognized by organizational researchers because they correspond to organizations' formally designated structures. However, we could just as easily argue that individuals are nested within dyads, dyads within

triads, triads within groups of four, and so on. Indeed, common experience notes the importance of couples, and Simmel (1950) and subsequently Krackhardt (1998) focused on the importance of triads and the fundamental differences between dyads and triads.

Weick (1979) suggested that the key transitions in size (and possible corresponding levels of analysis) are two, three, four, seven, and nine. The dyad represents interdependence, reciprocation, and accommodation—processes absent when considering a single individual. The triad produces the possibility of a two-against-one alliance and issues of control and cooperation. The triad is less vulnerable to defection than the dyad; if one person leaves, a social unit of two still remains. However, an alliance of two is not sufficient to gain control in a group of four. A seven-person group creates the possibility of two dyads and a triad with the dyads taking control if they align. A group of nine allows a coalition to form within a triad and coalitions between a pair of triads. Weick's focus is on cooperation and control, and he suggested that much can be learned about much larger organizations through the study of small numbers. Statistically, social network analysis often considers dyadic relationships as cross-nested within the two actors involved, and in ego network research it is standard to regard ties as nested within the respondent (ego), who in turn may be nested within a group or organization.

We do not mean to complicate multilevel research unnecessarily but only to note that the typical reliance on individual, group, and organizational levels of analysis does not preclude additional levels as justified by particular research questions. Designating levels is ultimately a question of social entitivity. Does the social unit represent an entity requiring measurement of properties that are not simply the sum of the parts? The question has stimulated and frustrated group researchers for years: What constitutes a group? Shaw (1976) evaluated many variations of definitions of groups and concluded that it is a matter of cognition and perception. The only basis of attributing entitivity to a social unit (and subsequently designating it as a level of analysis) is our perception of it. We cognitively group objects, or social units in our case, based on proximity in physical or psychological space, similarity on one or more attributes, and the extent to which they form a pattern that is perceived as the best possible figure in relation to the ground. Most important is common fate: Do the people occupy in the same place at the same time, move together, and share the same outcome? Do we perceive them as behaving as one entity? Do they perceive themselves as an entity? Of course, this emphasis on perception raises the possibility of misperception by the researcher, the participants, or both. But even our physical environment (nonsocial entitivity) and attempts to measure it scientifically are limited by our awareness and perception.

Questions of entitivity are seldom addressed but easily answered when considering legally formed organizations and formally designated groups within organizations. As depicted in Figure 8.1, researchers can consider how one level affects another and debate proper measurement and aggregation/disaggregation methods. Whether constructs are considered metaphors or aggregate realities, these frameworks such as Figure 8.1 can usefully generate questions of "what micro can learn from macro," and vice versa. These questions and debates change substantially when we consider multilevel social network theory and analysis.

LOOKING FOR NETWORKS OF RELATIONSHIPS

Social network analysis begins with the assumption that actors are embedded in a complex network of relationships with other actors. A *social network* is typically defined as a set of nodes and a set of ties representing some relationship, or absence of a relationship, between the nodes. In the case of social networks, the nodes represent social entities; most commonly, we consider individuals, groups, and organization as nodes, or actors, in the network. But, as just mentioned, dyads, triads, or even the network itself could be considered entities if they satisfy the noted criteria. An implicit assumption is that networks can be nested within networks, allowing for overlapping entities. A dyad can be nested within a triad that is nested within a group. Adding levels of analysis, where levels correspond to entities, necessarily complicates any

attempts at comprehensive reviews, but researchers can easily focus on a particular entity justified by their research question. Questions of entitivity are not exclusive features of social network analysis; they apply to traditional analyses as well. Rather, the distinguishing feature of social network analysis is the focus on the connections among the actors: The connections are of equal or more importance than the actors. Actors can be connected on the basis of (a) similarities (same location, membership in the same group, or similar attributes such as gender), (b) social relations (kinship, roles, affective relations such as friendship, or cognitive relations such as "knows about"), (c) interactions (talks with, gives advice to, forms an alliance with), or (d) flows (e.g., information; Borgatti, Mehra, Brass, & Labianca, 2009; see Figure 8.2). Although the particular content of the connections represented by the ties is limited only by the researcher's interest, typically studied are flows of information (communication, advice), expressions of affect (friendship), or formal connections such as interorganizational alliances. Ties may also be used to represent physical proximity or affiliations in groups, such as CEOs who sit on the same boards of directors (e.g., Mizruchi, 1996). We refer to a focal actor in a network as *ego;* the other actors with whom ego has direct relationships are called *alters*.

Social network theory does not easily fit our traditional notions of levels of analysis and the entitivity of actors because the unit of observation is the ties among the actors rather than the actors themselves. The focus is on the link, and the unit of measurement is the relationship rather than, or in addition to, the actor. This does not preclude an individual, group, or organizational level of observation in network studies. For example, network studies often combine individual-level data such as gender or personality with relational data (cf. Brass, 1985; Mehra, Kilduff, & Brass, 2001). However, the distinguishing feature of network studies is the measurement of connections.

As illustrated in the preceding examples, the designation of a connection can vary depending on one's research question, and the measurement can be based on observations, interviews, archival or "physical" data, or respondents' reports.

Types of Ties

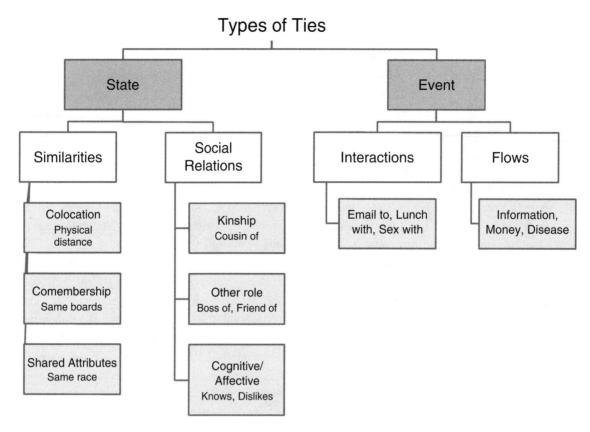

FIGURE 8.2.   Network content.

Researchers may sometimes wish to distinguish between perceived and "actual" networks. For example, Krackhardt and Porter (1985) argued that perceived connections between employees who quit an organization and those who stayed were a more appropriate predictor of "stayers'" satisfaction than actual connections. In addition, Kilduff and Krackhardt (1994) showed that audience perceptions of connections to high-status others were a better predictor of perceived performance than actual connections (actual being measured as reciprocated agreement between specified respondents). Thus, cognitive representations of networks, or networks as "prisms" as well as "pipes," have been the focus of network studies (Podolny, 2001).

The practical question of whether to measure actual or perceived networks is best answered by the research question. Questions that focus on the motivated actions or feelings of actors may be best addressed by their perceptions of the network. Actors may feel included or isolated based on their perceived connections, and issues of status

and influence are often contingent on perceptions of others' connections. On the other hand, actual connections are more important when studying the spread of disease, the benefits of the flow of information or money, or the workflow structure in an organization.

Typical social science research data are entered into a case-by-variable data matrix for analysis. For example, each case or respondent is represented by a row in the matrix, and the columns represent variables that are measured. Each cell represents the value of the variable for the respondent. However, social network data describe relationships and are typically entered into an actor-by-actor matrix in which each cell represents the presence or absence of a relationship (or the valued data describing the relationship) between the two actors. Filling the cells in an actor-by-actor social network is routine when archival data are used (e.g., e-mail logs) or when observation is possible.

However, the designation of relationships imposes some practical problems for researchers when relying on actors' responses to questions such as, "Whom do you consider to be a friend?" Does a relationship exist if Mary says she is a friend of Jane but Jane does not designate Mary as a friend? Similar questions arise when considering "valued" network data, rather than binary data that simply indicate the presence or absence of a tie. For example, researchers may ask respondents to indicate on a Likert-type scale how close the friendship tie is, or how frequently ego communicates with an alter. However, as evident from Figure 8.2, not all relationships are considered symmetric, and social network analysis can handle asymmetric or directional ties as well. For example, Jack may go to Bob for advice or money, but Bob does not seek advice or money from Jack. When respondents' values differ, the researcher must decide whether to retain the different values when calculating measures, or whether to use the minimum, maximum, or some average to represent the value of the relationship. Answers, of course, depend on one's research question and theoretical justification.

Although a researcher might begin a longitudinal study by noting that none of the actors are linked initially, the commonsense idea of a network (if not the technical graph-theoretic definition) implies more than one link. Indeed, the added value of the network perspective, the unique contribution, is that it goes beyond the dyad and provides a way of considering the structural arrangement of many actors and the paths of connections (Borgatti, Everett, & Johnson, 2013; Brass, 2012). As Wellman (1988) noted, "It is not assumed that network members engage only in multiple duets with separate alters" (p. 20). Indeed, it might be said that the triad is the basic building block of networks (Krackhardt, 1998; Simmel, 1950). The focus is on the relationships *among* the dyadic relationships (i.e., the network). Typically, a minimum of two links connecting three actors is implicitly assumed in order to have a network worth studying and to establish such notions as indirect linkages or paths.

An extensive variety of network measures have been developed over the years (see Brass, 2012, for a glossary, or Borgatti, Everett, & Freeman, 2002), as social network researchers have examined how the pattern of connections among the actors affects various outcomes. Such measures are often referred

to as *structural*, as they represent the structure or configuration of relationships. These structural measures can be further classified as *point* measures when they describe an actor's position within a network and *whole network* measures when they describe the configuration of the entire network (or some subnetwork within it). In addition, a set of *ego network* measures have been developed to characterize a focal actor's pattern of direct ties in the absence of, or regardless of, indirect extended ties. An ego network contains only the focal actor ego's direct ties to alters and any ties between the alters. An ego network may be extracted from whole network data but more typically is constructed based on information obtained from the focal actor (see Perry, Pescosolido, & Borgatti, 2017, for a more detailed explanation of ego network measures).

Network measures can, and likely should, be added to traditional nonnetwork measures when attempting to answer research questions. Although they are not meant to be a substitute for properties of actors as individuals, they do force attention to the question of treating actors as if they were isolated entities. Just as multilevel discussion focuses our attention away from single levels of analysis, network research focuses our attention away from treating actors as if they exist in isolation of other actors.

Although the social network approach has an inherently multilevel perspective (actors are embedded within networks), it does not easily correspond to our traditional notions of level of analysis. Actors can be said to be nested/embedded within the network, but the network itself is not necessarily considered an entity. In some cases, the networks we study correspond to some formal or natural group with boundaries as in the traditional case of groups, organizations, or industries. In other cases, they may not. Nevertheless, the network is considered the primary context that provides opportunities and constraints for the actors.

The network focus on relationships provides a different and additional solution to the question of where to look. It seems appropriate to add the interpersonal, intergroup, and interorganizational levels of analysis in the traditional model depicted in Figure 8.1 (see, e.g., Phelps, Heidl, & Wadhwa, 2012). A quick review of the literature shows where researchers have "looked." Several researchers have shown how interpersonal relationships affect individual outcomes (cf. Brass, 1984; Burt, 1992), and studies have shown how individual characteristics can affect interpersonal relationships (Mehra et al., 2001). Among others, Hansen (1999) and Reagans, Zuckerman, and McEvily (2004) have investigated interpersonal relationships and group outcomes, whereas Tsai and Ghoshal (1998) and Tsai (2001) have shown that intergroup relationships affect group outcomes. In addition, there are many studies of interorganizational relationships and organizational outcomes (cf. Gulati, 1995; Uzzi, 1997).

However, adding interpersonal, intergroup, and interorganizational levels of analysis to a typical model such as Figure 8.1 quickly becomes burdened with too many crossing arrows. Trying to visually represent it becomes a personally time-consuming and frustrating exercise. Adding to the complexity is the possibility of considering a network as an entity and the possibility of networks nested within networks (see Moliterno & Mahony, 2011, for an extended discussion). Yet, given a dependent variable of interest, researchers would be advised to consider how interpersonal, intergroup, and interorganizational relationships might add additional explanatory variance. Although the level of measurement is the relationship, the practical, least confusing, and most easily communicated solution when speaking of networks of relationships is to identify them by noting the actors involved. Thus, we can speak of networks of individuals, groups, organizations, and so on. Although it promotes easy communication, this nomenclature does not adequately address our questions of entitivity and subsequently our designation of levels of analysis and where to look.

To address entitivity, we note that the basic building blocks can be between two individuals, two groups, or two organizations. These dyadic building blocks are combined to form triads, groups of four or more, as in the Weick example. From a multilevel perspective, researchers might investigate any number considered to be an entity in the network. Depending on our interest and research question, we might study, for example, interaction patterns among couples or triads as well as individuals,

noting in each case that the entity is embedded within a larger network. Of course, social network researchers might investigate triads within groups, for instance, without necessarily treating the possible triads as entities. As an example, Granovetter's (1973) well-known "strength of weak ties" theory was illustrated through analyses of triads without consideration of whether the various possible triads represented entities. As previously noted, entitivity is a matter of perception. Social networks are often touted for their ability to integrate micro and macro approaches (Wellman, 1988); they provide the opportunity to simultaneously investigate the whole and the parts (Ibarra, Kilduff, & Tsai, 2005). The dyadic relationships are used to compose the network; they are the parts that form the whole.

AGGREGATION

Multilevel analysis typically includes considerable discussion concerning how measurement of lower level constructs aggregate to higher level measures (Bliese, 2000; Kozlowski & Klein, 2000). For network analysis, it is important to note the distinction between point or position in the network measures and whole network measures. A point measure, such as the centrality of an actor, can be calculated (based on the entire configuration of the network) and assigned to each particular actor in the network. Such measures indicate the position of the actor within the network. Whole network measures describe the entire network, or some specified subgroup, such as the part of the network that corresponds to a given department or location. For example, the density of the network is calculated as the number of actual ties among the actors in the network divided by the total number of possible ties. Density is a property of the entire network.

Some whole network measures, such as density and average degree centrality (average number of ties to each actor in the network), are the result of aggregating node-level or tie-level measures. Other whole network measures, such as centralization, are normalized standard deviations of node-level centrality. *Centralization* refers to the difference between the centrality scores of the most central actor and those of other actors in a network. A network is maximally decentralized when all actors in the network have the same centrality score. Still other network measures such as *core-peripheriness* cannot be computed by averaging lower level scores. Core-peripheriness is a measure of the extent to which a network is structured such that core members connect to everyone, whereas peripheral members connect only to core members and not to other members of the periphery. It is purely a whole-network-level concept and measure. In each case, such measures would be considered "configural," in Kozlowski and Klein's (2000) terminology. Configural unit properties are the result of the pattern, distribution, or variability of ties within the unit.

Some confusion may arise because some point measures, such as betweenness centrality, are the result of the configuration of nodes and ties within the entire network, even though these point measures are assigned to individual actors and typically thought of as actor-level properties. For example, using the actor in the network to designate our level of analysis (as previously noted for ease of communication), the point measure is considered to be at the level of analysis of the actor. Thus, for our purposes, individual actor centrality is designated as the individual level of analysis and group centrality as the group level. If the network boundaries correspond to our traditionally noted entities (e.g., group, organization), the whole network measures are considered to be at the group, or organizational, level of analysis. Thus, for example, considering how an actor's centrality within a densely connected network or group might affect individual performance would be designated as a cross-level analysis (the point centrality measure is at the individual level and the whole network density measure is at the group level).

Related to aggregation are questions of composition: How does the lower level construct relate to the same construct at a higher level? Network constructs such as actor centrality mean the same thing and are measured the same way regardless of whether the ties are between, for example, individuals, groups, or organizations. Although several different measures of centrality have been developed, the concepts are the same across levels of analysis (Brass, Galaskiewicz, Greve, & Tsai,

2004). Betweenness centrality refers to an actor being along the shortest paths in the network, and this is so regardless of what kinds of actors compose the network. Although some point measures may be aggregated to characterize a network, such whole network properties should not be confused with point measures. For example, the average centrality of individual actors within a group network does not represent the centrality of the group within a network of other groups. The centrality of a group is a point measure representing the group's position within a network of groups and is dependent on measuring group-to-group connections.

A more fundamental and practical question concerns the difference between individual ties and group ties. For example, Breiger (1974) noted that when two people interact, they not only represent themselves but also may represent any formal or informal group/organization of which they are a member. Following Breiger, individual interaction can sometimes be assumed to also represent group interaction. As a practical question of measurement, is any interaction between two members of different groups (organizations, ethnic groups, genders) considered interaction between different groups? As the argument goes, groups don't talk to each other, individuals do. However, sometimes groups enter into formal agreements that are independent of the particular individuals involved, such as when organizations form alliances. In other cases, individuals interact as representatives of their organizations, as when the U.S. ambassador to Israel interacts with his counterpart on official business.

However, it is not clear how individual interaction should be combined to measure group interactions. For example, a researcher might combine all the interpersonal links of members of a group and treat them as examples of intergroup relationships. Coupled with this individual–group duality approach, the researcher might also assume that the individuals within the group share information (or whatever resource might be flowing through the network) within the group. For example, CEOs who sit on the same boards of directors are assumed to exchange some information that is subsequently diffused through their respective organizations and affects organization outcomes (e.g., Galaskiewicz & Burt,

1991). These assumptions are typically not directly tested (Zaheer & Soda, 2009).

While the Breiger (1974) arguments concerning the "duality of persons and groups" provide a convenient compositional model for moving across levels of analysis, it is not clear that individual interaction always represents group or organizational interaction, or that individuals are even aware of all the possible groups and organizations of which the person they are talking with is a member. The assumption that people are not able to distinguish between, for example, communications that represent the individual and communications that represent the group is also doubtful. When an individual is speaking for a group or organization, the interaction might be quite different from when the person is speaking as a friend. Although personal, informal relationships might provide avenues for group negotiations, for example, problems may occur when personal communication is misconstrued as official group communication. The distinction may be in the eye of the receiver, but it is likely that group interactions (i.e., communication representing the groups) may affect interpersonal relationships, and vice versa. Equally questionable is the assumption that anything flowing to or from an individual of a group is shared within the group. We suggest avoiding aggregation issues by collecting relationship data clearly identified as individual, group, or organizational. For example, Tsai and Ghoshal (1998) asked respondents to identify group relationships when building intergroup networks.

LOOKING FOR BOUNDARIES

Social network measures have been developed to tap concepts associated with dyads, triads, groups, and larger networks. Some measures describe an actor's position within the network, such as betweenness centrality. Such measures assigned to individual actors are inherently multilevel because they can be calculated only with knowledge of the entire structure and that actor's location in that structure. Another example is eigenvector centrality, in which an actor's centrality is proportional to the sum of the eigenvector centralities of its network neighbors. Actors also can be clustered into groups

or cliques based on their relationships within the network. Thus, it is possible to study the effects of whole network characteristics (e.g., core-periphery structure) on group (e.g., clique formation) and individual (e.g., centrality) characteristics. Combining measures at different levels, researchers might ask how individual centrality within the group interacts with the centralization of the group to affect important outcomes such as individual power. Although possible, such analyses have rarely been undertaken (see Sasidharan, Santhanam, Brass, & Sambamurthy, 2012, for an exception).

In each case, whether assigning measures to describe the actor's position in the network or describing the entire network, a practical issue involves establishing the network boundary. If it is indeed a small world, bounding the network for research purposes is an important, if seldom addressed, issue. Depending on the research question, what is the appropriate membership of the network? This involves specifying the number of different types of networks (i.e., types of tie) to include, as well as the number of links removed from ego (indirect links) that should be considered. Both decisions have conceptual and methodological implications when considering levels of analysis.

Formal boundaries have traditionally been used to designate different entities and different levels of analysis, and from a social network perspective these boundaries can be used to designate actors in the network and interpersonal, intergroup, or interorganizational relationships. Despite the social network focus on relationships, actors must be designated and consideration must be given to whether they represent entities, as in the traditional case of multilevel analyses. However, the practical question remains as to where to bound the network. If actors are embedded in networks that affect their behavior, it is important to identify the network even if it is not typically considered an entity in and of itself (Laumann, Marsden, & Prensky, 1992).

Organizational researchers have been relatively silent on the network boundary issue of how many links (direct and indirect) to include, as the network extends well beyond ego's direct ties. The importance of this boundary specification is emphasized by

Brass's (1984) finding that an individual's centrality within departments was positively related to power and promotions, whereas individual centrality within the entire organization produced a negative finding. The appropriate number of links has recently garnered renewed attention with the publication of Burt's (2007) findings. In investigating structural holes and performance, he found that indirect ties extending beyond ego's local direct-tie network did not significantly add to the explained variance in individual performance. The findings justify his use of data focusing on ego's local, direct-tie network (ego network data) but are thus far limited to the analysis of structural holes. Structural holes exist in an actor's network to the extent that the actor is connected to others who are not themselves connected. For example, Burt's findings are obviously unrelated to contagion studies in which, for example, your friend buys the same computer brand as his friend, and you, in turn, follow suit. Although information may decay or become distorted as it travels through long paths, it may nevertheless affect behavior, as in the case of widely disseminated rumors. Likewise, culture can be thought of as information that is contagiously spread through a number of long paths. In addition, several research findings document the importance of third-party ties (two steps removed from ego): Bian (1997) in finding jobs; Gargiulo (1993) in gaining two-step leverage; Labianca, Brass, and Gray (1998) in perceptions of conflict; and Bowler and Brass (2006) in organizational citizenship behavior. In sum, there is evidence for both a local and the more extended network approach, and it is likely that debate will ensue and continue. Including the appropriate number of links is likely a function of the research question and the mechanism involved in the flow, but assuredly researchers will need to attend to and justify their boundaries more explicitly in the future.

Identifying the domain of possible types of relationships (network content) is equally important, as actors are embedded in different types of networks and one network may be thought of as embedded in another network (see Borgatti & Halgin, 2011, for an extended discussion of network content). For example, Burt (1983) noted that people tend to organize their relationships around four categories: friendship, acquaintance, work, and kinship. Types of networks (the content of the relationships) are also sometimes classified as informal versus formal, or instrumental versus expressive (Ibarra, 1992). For example, Grosser, Lopez-Kidwell, and Labianca (2010) found that negative gossip was primarily transmitted through expressive friendship ties, whereas positive gossip flowed through instrumental ties. However, different types of relationships often tend to overlap, and it is sometimes difficult to exclusively separate ties on the basis of content.

Conceptually, the issue is whether one type of tie may be appropriated for a different use (expressive ties are appropriated for instrumental purposes), or whether some types of ties (e.g., friendship) normatively include a variety of different interactions. For example, friendship and workplace ties are often used to sell Girl Scout cookies. Does this mean that friendship ties are appropriated for use as financial or economic ties? Or does this merely indicate that friendship relationships are leveraged for selling cookies, just as they are for a number of interactions such as picking me up at the airport or watering my plants? Indeed, Granovetter's (1985) critique of economics argued that economic transactions are embedded in, and are affected by, networks of interpersonal relationships (see also Uzzi, 1997). These transactions occur within the context of broader relationships. Referring to Figure 8.2, we note that networks of interactions, for example, may be subsumed under networks of relationships. Granovetter (1973) distinguished between strong and weak ties on the basis of time, emotional intensity, intimacy, and reciprocal services (family and close friends). Strong ties have more frequent exposure, are more motivated to help, and are more influential than weak tie acquaintances. However, the strength of weak ties is their ability to provide diverse, nonredundant information that may be more useful than strong ties in finding jobs.

Some research (e.g., Podolny & Baron, 1997) suggests different outcomes from different types of networks. For example, it is unlikely that negative ties can be appropriated for positive use. *Negative ties* are defined as "enduring, recurring set of negative judgments, feelings and behavioral intentions toward another person" (Labianca & Brass, 2006, p. 597). Centrality in a conflict network will certainly lead to different results than centrality in a friendship network. In practice, researchers must be aware of network content and look to different types of networks to more fully explain variance in their dependent variable of interest. Network content (i.e., the "type" of network) is an important consideration when looking for multilevel isomorphisms.

LOOKING FOR ISOMORPHISMS

Multilevel theory has shed new light on issues of isomorphism: whether constructs mean the same thing across level of analysis (construct isomorphism) and whether relationships are the same at different levels of analysis (relationship isomorphism). As Moliterno and Mahony (2011) noted, "a multilevel model in general should be able to specify whether, and how, a particular construct manifests similarly across levels of analysis" (p. 448). From a practical point of view, this multilevel criterion is often viewed as "what micro can learn from macro," or vice versa. That is, researchers often garner ideas and adapt constructs from one level of analysis for application at a different level. When researchers take care to avoid the possibility of anthropomorphizing, it can be a useful metaphorical process of thinking about how organizations are like individuals, or vice versa, and how constructs at one level of analysis might have equivalent constructs at a different level of analysis, or how causal relationships at one level of analysis might be replicated at another level. Because of the abstract nature of nodes, ties, and networks, we note that network concepts and measures have been applied across a wide range of research topics and levels of analysis.

Network measures themselves can obviously be applied to any kind of nodes and ties, whether they are neurons, persons, or organizations. At the measurement level, they mean the same thing: Degree centrality always means the number of ties for a node. Such measures were developed to represent concepts such as centrality that can be applied across a wide range of relationship content or contexts. But the consequences of this varies by

content and context. Clearly, centrality (although measured the same and meant to represent the same concept—being at the center of the network) means different things for different kinds of ties. As previously noted, degree centrality in the friendship network (number of friendship ties) is clearly different from degree centrality in the enemy network (number of enemies). In addition, the content of ties tends to differ across levels of analysis such that organizations are not exactly friends and persons tend not to engage in trade agreements. Even for the same kind of tie and same kind of node, there are other major contextual differences. Being central in a friendship network in high school is different from being central in a friendship network at church. Thus, even when network measures and concepts are invariant across level of analysis, the extent to which they are isomorphic is largely dependent on the content of the ties and the context in which the network occurs.

Another way to approach this is in terms of functionality. Suppose information is flowing through organizational ties and through person-level ties. Nodes with a high degree (number of ties) can be expected to have a higher probability of receiving information than low-degree nodes. So here there is isomorphism. But the type and consequences of the information may be very different. Another example of a functional isomorphism can be drawn from Granovetter (1973). He took as a theoretical premise that strong ties create a certain kind of weak transitivity, namely, that if A and B have a strong tie, and B and C have a strong tie, then A and C will likely have at least a weak tie. As just noted, he defined strong ties in terms of time spent together, emotional intensity, intimacy, and reciprocal services. What if his theory is to be applied to organizations? Should we look for semantic analogues of time, intensity, and so on? The functional answer is yes, but whatever we find must pass one criterion: The strong tie analogue must exhibit weak transitivity. If it doesn't, it cannot play the role of a strong tie.

The same cautions are in order when looking for relationship isomorphisms. Although it is tempting to note that a relationship between network density and innovation was found at both the individual level of analysis (Obstfeld, 2005) and the organizational level of analysis (Ahuja, 2000), we note several key differences in content and context. Although both Obstfeld and Ahuja used the same network measure and concept, Ahuja's network was composed of organizational joint ventures in the chemical industry with the number of organizational patents as a measure of innovation. Obstfeld's individual-level network was a combination of different contents (discuss important matters, communicate to get work done, be influential in getting new projects approved, socialize informally, and turn to for advice) and his dependent variable was role involvement in designated innovation projects in the automobile industry. One could force the isomorphism and argue that the density/innovation relationship is robust across different network content and context (and different dependent variables). Or one could note the differences but recognize the metaphorical usefulness of looking for density–innovation relationships at different levels of analysis. As a practical guideline, we see value in thinking about how relationships at one level of analysis might be translated to different levels.

Individuals are not organizations, and strategic alliances are not interpersonal interactions. Perhaps we should be looking for differences rather than similarities. Differences denote complementary areas to explore. What do macro network researchers do differently from micro network researchers, and vice versa? Such questions may indicate fruitful areas if micro were metaphorically "like" macro, and vice versa. They may also denote where the discontinuities between individual and group or organizational levels of analysis exist.

LOOKING FOR CROSS-LEVEL EFFECTS

Most existing organizational network research involves a single level of analysis. For example, Brass (1984) noted how individual centrality was related to individual influence, Tsai and Ghoshal (1998) found that group centrality was related to group value creation, and Ahuja (2000) noted how organizational structural holes were related to organizational innovation. Although Brass (1984)

calculated separate measures of individual actor's centrality within their workgroups, departments, and the entire organization, no whole network measures of groups or the organization were included, nor were any group networks measured. One of the few examples of cross-level network analysis is the study by Sasidharan et al. (2012). The authors found that central actors within centralized groups benefited most from the introduction of a new Enterprise computer system. Thus, there remain many opportunities for cross-level organizational network research.

As a practical technique for generating such research, one can simply look to marry point network measures typically assigned to actors with whole network measures assigned to our traditional organizational entities such as groups or organizations. Thus, one might ask how actor centrality within densely connected groups affects individual satisfaction and performance. In addition, one could investigate point network measures at different levels of analysis. For example, how does individual centrality combine with group centrality to affect individual influence? Do central actors in less central groups wield more influence than peripheral actors in highly central groups? These examples combine network measures at different levels of analysis, but network measures can also easily be combined with traditional measures to investigate organizational phenomena. For example, do central groups in organizations with participative cultures perform better than central groups in nonparticipative organizations? Do high self-monitors (a personality trait) in densely connected groups perform more organizational citizenship behaviors than high self-monitors in a sparsely connected group?

CONCLUSION

As a practical guide to multilevel network research, we have chosen to focus on where researchers might look to explain variance in important outcomes. Our focus has been on patterns of relationships, questions of entitivity, exploration of content and context in looking for isomorphisms, and network boundaries. In the process, we hope that we have generated some previously overlooked questions and stimulated some fruitful thought. Ultimately, our goal is to promote both social network research and multilevel research in the hope of more inclusive and more comprehensive investigation of multilevel phenomena.

References

Ahuja, G. (2000). Collaboration networks, structural holes, and innovation: A longitudinal study. *Administrative Science Quarterly, 45*, 425–455. http://dx.doi.org/10.2307/2667105

Bian, Y. (1997). Bringing strong ties back in: Indirect ties, network bridges, and job searches in China. *American Sociological Review, 62*, 366–385. http://dx.doi.org/10.2307/2657311

Bliese, P. D. (2000). Within-group agreement, non-independence, and reliability: Implications for data aggregation and analysis. In K. J. Klein & S. W. J. Kozlowski (Eds.), *Multilevel theory, research, and methods in organizations, foundations, extensions, and new directions* (pp. 349–381). San Francisco, CA: Jossey-Bass.

Borgatti, S. P., Everett, M. G., & Freeman, L. (2002). *UCINET for Windows: Software for social network analysis*. Harvard, MA: Analytic Technologies.

Borgatti, S. P., Everett, M. G., & Johnson, J. C. (2013). *Analyzing social networks*. London, England: Sage.

Borgatti, S. P., & Halgin, D. S. (2011). On network theory. *Organization Science, 22*, 1168–1181. http://dx.doi.org/10.1287/orsc.1100.0641

Borgatti, S. P., Mehra, A., Brass, D. J., & Labianca, G. (2009). Network analysis in the social sciences. *Science, 323*, 892–895. http://dx.doi.org/10.1126/science.1165821

Bowler, W. M., & Brass, D. J. (2006). Relational correlates of interpersonal citizenship behavior: A social network perspective. *Journal of Applied Psychology, 91*, 70–82. http://dx.doi.org/10.1037/0021-9010.91.1.70

Brass, D. J. (1984). Being in the right place: A structural analysis of individual influence in an organization. *Administrative Science Quarterly, 29*, 518–539. http://dx.doi.org/10.2307/2392937

Brass, D. J. (1985). Men's and women's networks: A study of interaction patterns and influence in an organization. *Academy of Management Journal, 28*, 327–343. http://dx.doi.org/10.2307/256204

Brass, D. J. (2012). A social network perspective on organizational psychology. In S. W. J. Kozlowski (Ed.), *The Oxford handbook of organizational psychology* (Vol. 1, pp. 667–695). New York, NY: Oxford University Press. http://dx.doi.org/10.1093/oxfordhb/9780199928309.013.0021

Brass, D. J., Galaskiewicz, J., Greve, H. R., & Tsai, W. (2004). Taking stock of networks and organizations: A multilevel perspective. *Academy of Management Journal, 47*, 795–817.

Breiger, R. L. (1974). The duality of persons and groups. *Social Forces, 53*, 181–190.

Burt, R. S. (1983). Distinguishing relational content. In R. S. Burt & M. J. Minor (Eds.), *Applied network analysis: A methodological introduction* (pp. 35–74). Beverly Hills, CA: Sage.

Burt, R. S. (1992). *Structural holes: The social structure of competition*. Cambridge, MA: Harvard University Press.

Burt, R. S. (2007). Second-hand brokerage: Evidence on the importance of local structure on managers, bankers, and analysts. *Academy of Management Journal, 50*, 119–145. http://dx.doi.org/10.5465/AMJ.2007.24162082

Coleman, J. S. (1990). *Foundations of social theory*. Cambridge, MA: Harvard University Press.

Galaskiewicz, J., & Burt, R. S. (1991). Interorganizational contagion in corporate philanthropy. *Administrative Science Quarterly, 36*, 88–105. http://dx.doi.org/10.2307/2393431

Gargiulo, M. (1993). Two-step leverage: Managing constraint in organizational politics. *Administrative Science Quarterly, 38*, 1–19. http://dx.doi.org/10.2307/2393252

Granovetter, M. (1973). The strength of weak ties. *American Journal of Sociology, 78*, 1360–1380. http://dx.doi.org/10.1086/225469

Granovetter, M. (1985). Economic action and social structure: The problem of embeddedness. *American Journal of Sociology, 91*, 481–510. http://dx.doi.org/10.1086/228311

Grosser, T. J., Lopez-Kidwell, V., & Labianca, G. (2010). A social network analysis of positive and negative gossip in organizational life. *Group and Organization Management, 35*, 177–212. http://doi.org/10.1177/1059601109360391

Gulati, R. (1995). Social structure and alliance formation patterns: A longitudinal analysis. *Administrative Science Quarterly, 40*, 619–652. http://dx.doi.org/10.2307/2393756

Hansen, M. T. (1999). The search-transfer problem: The role of weak ties in sharing knowledge across organization subunits. *Administrative Science Quarterly, 44*, 82–111. http://dx.doi.org/10.2307/2667032

Hitt, M. A., Beamish, P. W., Jackson, S. E., & Mathieu, J. E. (2007). Building theoretical and empirical bridges across levels: Multilevel research in management. *Academy of Management Journal, 50*, 1385–1399. http://dx.doi.org/10.5465/AMJ.2007.28166219

Ibarra, H. (1992). Homophily and differential returns: Sex differences in network structure and access in an advertising firm. *Administrative Science Quarterly, 37*, 422–447. http://dx.doi.org/10.2307/2393451

Ibarra, H., Kilduff, M., & Tsai, W. (2005). Zooming in and out: Connecting individuals and collectivities at the frontiers of organizational network research. *Organization Science, 16*, 359–371. http://dx.doi.org/10.1287/orsc.1050.0129

Kilduff, M., & Krackhardt, D. (1994). Bringing the individual back in: A structural analysis of the internal market for reputation in organizations. *Academy of Management Journal, 37*, 87–108. http://dx.doi.org/10.2307/256771

Kozlowski, S. W. J., & Klein, K. J. (2000). A multilevel approach to theory and research in organizations: Contextual, temporal, and emergent processes. In K. J. Klein & S. W. J. Kozlowski (Eds.), *Multilevel theory, research, and methods in organizations: Foundations, extensions, and new directions* (pp. 3–90). San Francisco, CA: Jossey-Bass.

Krackhardt, D. (1998). Simmelian ties: Super strong and sticky. In R. M. Kramer & M. A. Neale (Eds.), *Power and influence in organizations* (pp. 21–38). Thousand Oaks, CA: Sage. http://dx.doi.org/10.4135/9781483345291.n2

Krackhardt, D., & Porter, L. W. (1985). When friends leave: A structural analysis of the relationship between turnover and stayers' attitudes. *Administrative Science Quarterly, 30*, 242–261. http://dx.doi.org/10.2307/2393107

Labianca, G., & Brass, D. J. (2006). Exploring the social ledger: Negative relationships and negative asymmetry in social networks in organizations. *Academy of Management Review, 31*, 596–614. http://dx.doi.org/10.5465/AMR.2006.21318920

Labianca, G., Brass, D. J., & Gray, B. (1998). Social networks and perceptions of intergroup conflict: The role of negative relationships and third parties. *Academy of Management Journal, 41*, 55–67. http://dx.doi.org/10.2307/256897

Laumann, E. O., Marsden, P. V., & Prensky, D. (1992). The boundary specification problem in social network analysis. In L. C. Freeman, D. R. White, & A. K. Romney (Eds.), *Research methods in social network analysis* (pp. 61–86). New Brunswick, NJ: Transaction.

Mehra, A., Kilduff, M., & Brass, D. J. (2001). The social networks of high and low self-monitors: Implications for workplace performance. *Administrative Science Quarterly, 46*, 121–146. http://dx.doi.org/10.2307/2667127

Mizruchi, M. (1996). What do interlocks do? An analysis, critique, and assessment of research on interlocking directorates. In J. Hagan & K. S. Cook (Eds.), *Annual review of sociology* (Vol. 22, pp. 271–298). Palo Alto, CA: Annual Reviews.

Moliterno, T. P., & Mahony, D. M. (2011). Network theory of organizations: A multilevel approach. *Journal of Management, 37*, 443–467. http://dx.doi.org/10.1177/0149206310371692

Obstfeld, D. (2005). Social networks, the *tertius lungens* orientation, and involvement in innovation. *Administrative Science Quarterly, 50*, 100–130. http://dx.doi.org/10.2189/asqu.2005.50.1.100

Perry, B. L., Pescosolido, B. A., & Borgatti, S. P. (2017). *Egocentric network analysis: Foundations, methods, and models.* Cambridge, England: Cambridge University Press.

Phelps, C., Heidl, R., & Wadhwa, A. (2012). Knowledge, networks, and knowledge networks: A review and research agenda. *Journal of Management, 38*, 1115–1166. http://dx.doi.org/10.1177/0149206311432640

Podolny, J. M. (2001). Networks as the pipes and prisms of the market. *American Journal of Sociology, 107*, 33–60. http://dx.doi.org/10.1086/323038

Podolny, J. M., & Baron, J. N. (1997). Resources and relationships: Social networks and mobility in the workplace. *American Sociological Review, 62*, 673–693. http://dx.doi.org/10.2307/2657354

Reagans, R., Zuckerman, E., & McEvily, B. (2004). How to make the team: Social networks vs. demography as criteria for designing effective teams. *Administrative Science Quarterly, 49*, 101–133.

Rousseau, D. M. (1985). Issues of level in organizational research: Multi-level and cross-level perspectives. In L. L. Cummings & B. M. Staw (Eds.), *Research in organizational behavior* (pp. 1–37). Greenwich, CT: JAI Press.

Sasidharan, S., Santhanam, R., Brass, D. J., & Sambamurthy, V. (2012). The effects of social network structure on Enterprise system success: A longitudinal multilevel analysis. *Information Systems Research, 23*, 658–678.

Shaw, M. E. (1976). *Group dynamics.* New York, NY: McGraw-Hill.

Simmel, G. (1950). *The sociology of Georg Simmel.* New York, NY: Free Press.

Tsai, W. (2001). Knowledge transfer in intraorganizational networks: Effects of network position and absorptive capacity on business unit innovation and performance.

Academy of Management Journal, 44, 996–1004. http://dx.doi.org/10.2307/3069443

Tsai, W., & Ghoshal, S. (1998). Social capital and value creation: The role of intrafirm networks. *Academy of Management Journal, 41,* 464–476. http://dx.doi.org/10.2307/257085

Uzzi, B. (1997). Social structure and competition in interfirm networks: The paradox of embeddedness. *Administrative Science Quarterly, 42,* 35–67. http://dx.doi.org/10.2307/2393808

Weick, K. E. (1979). *The social psychology of organizing* (2nd ed.). San Francisco, CA: McGraw-Hill.

Wellman, B. (1988). Structural analysis: From method and metaphor to theory and substance. In B. Wellman & S. D. Berkowitz (Eds.), *Social structures: A network approach* (pp. 19–61). New York, NY: Cambridge University Press.

Zaheer, A., & Soda, G. (2009). Network evolution: The origins of structural holes. *Administrative Science Quarterly, 54,* 1–31.

## CHAPTER 9

CONCEPTUAL FOUNDATIONS OF MULTILEVEL SOCIAL NETWORKS

Srikanth Paruchuri, Martin C. Goossen, and Corey Phelps

As research on social networks has grown exponentially over the past few decades (Borgatti & Halgin, 2011), social network theory has become an important theoretical paradigm in many social sciences disciplines and beyond (Borgatti, Mehra, Brass, & Labianca, 2009). Within organizational research, social network theory has been used to understand and explain a wide range of managerial and organizational phenomena, including individual creativity, ethical behavior, career mobility, technology adoption and organizational innovation, profitability, and market-entry choices (see Brass, Galaskiewicz, Greve, & Tsai, 2004, for a review). A core insight from network research is that social actors, whether individuals or collectives (e.g., work teams or organizations), are connected via social relationships, and the qualities and patterning of these ties influence actor behavior and outcomes, and the evolution of the ties and networks themselves (Brass et al., 2004).

A primary reason for the growth of social network research is that the tools of network analysis can be applied to phenomena at any level of analysis, including individuals, groups, business units, firms, industries, and countries (Wasserman & Faust, 1994). As long as the analyst can conceptualize the phenomenon of interest as a *network*—a system of nodes in which some nodes are connected to other nodes by a particular type of relationship—then the tools of network analysis and social network theory

may be brought to bear. Although this conceptual and methodological flexibility has contributed to a rapid increase in social network research within different levels of analysis, research across levels of analysis is almost nonexistent.

This lacuna is surprising given the multilevel, embedded nature of organizational networks. Nodes in organizational social networks can be individuals or collectives, such as teams, departments, divisions, subsidiaries, and organizations. These nodes represent nested systems because organizations are multilevel systems of relationships (Hitt, Beamish, Jackson, & Mathieu, 2007). Nodes at lower levels of analysis are, at least partially, nested in higher level collectives, and these collectives are themselves networks of nodes at lower levels of analysis (Harary & Batell, 1981). For example, individuals are nested in teams, which can vary in the pattern of social ties among their members. Teams are nested in organizational units, such as departments, which consist of teams that are professionally connected to one another. Organizations themselves are embedded in networks of interorganizational relationships, such as strategic alliances, which can vary in the connectedness of organizational members. Despite their inherent multilevel nature, most research has ignored this aspect of organizational social networks and how it may influence phenomena of interest (Lomi, Robins, & Tranmer, 2016).

http://dx.doi.org/10.1037/0000115-010
The Handbook of Multilevel Theory, Measurement, and Analysis, S. E. Humphrey and J. M. LeBreton (Editors-in-Chief)

Consider, for instance, research on creativity and innovation. For years, scholars have studied how the characteristics and configurations of people's social ties affect their creativity, how an organizational subunit's relationships with other units influence its ability to innovate, and how a firm's inter-organizational alliances affect its innovation performance (Phelps, Heidl, & Wadhwa, 2012). Although this research has shown that networks matter for creativity and innovation at each level of analysis, it has not investigated potential cross-level effects. For example, research has yet to examine how relationships among individuals or units within organizations moderate or mediate the influence of interorganizational relationships on organizational innovation or how interorganizational ties impact individual and team-level creativity.

The preoccupation of network research on single-level of analysis has two important implications for social network theory. First, most research has assumed a high degree of theoretical isomorphism across levels, particularly from the interpersonal level on up. Studies of intra- and interorganizational networks typically have used causal explanations from interpersonal network research and implicitly have assumed these explanations hold for networks of social collectives (Phelps et al., 2012; Sorenson & Rogan, 2014). For example, drawing on Coleman's (1988) research that showed that individual trustworthiness increases when everyone in the network knows everyone else because opportunistic behavior is more visible and readily sanctioned, alliance researchers have argued that dense alliance networks, in which a firm's partners also are directly allied, will produce trust among alliance partners (and their personnel) much like closure in an interpersonal network generates trust (e.g., Ahuja, 2000). Although the assumption of homology across levels simplifies theorizing, it is unclear if and why specific social network structures or positions should lead to similar outcomes at different levels of analysis. Empirical investigations and validation of such fundamental assumptions have been largely absent.

Second, network research typically has treated collectives, including organizational divisions, subsidiaries, and entire organizations, as simple,

unitary actors rather than the large, internally complex, and geographically distributed collectives they are. Although anthropomorphizing social collectives may be theoretically and empirically appropriate for some research purposes (see King, Felin, & Whetten, 2010), the extent to which doing so is appropriate is a matter for theory and empirics to discern. Future research must examine the extent to which causal explanations generated from interpersonal network research are isomorphic to the intra- and interorganizational levels when the actors at these levels are social collectives. For example, to what extent is it valid to claim (theoretically) that because three large organizations maintain partnerships with each other their respective employees are more likely to trust one another? The validity of claims about how interorganizational network structure affects trust between organizations is likely to depend on the pattern and quality of social ties among the members of the organizations. Moreover, such a simplification implicitly assumes that networks at different levels operate independently and effects are not dependent on higher or lower level network structures. This assumption, however, is unlikely to hold because prior studies have shown that network structures at different levels influence each other (Zappa & Lomi, 2016) and the effects of network structure at one level depend on network structures at other levels (Paruchuri, 2010).

Investigating the effect of networks at a single level can result in an incomplete and inaccurate understanding of social networks and their influence on particular phenomena when the joint or contingent effects of networks at other levels are ignored. Failure to adopt a multilevel perspective when there are cross-level effects results in a theoretically impoverished understanding of the phenomena and can lead to misspecified models for estimation and biased and invalid inferences. Recognizing the multilevel nature of social networks and incorporating this multilevel perspective into our theorizing and analytics can help us in specifying and testing more accurate models and generate a better understanding of the integrated influence of social networks at different levels. Because organizational networks are a multilevel phenomenon and ignoring their multilevel nature presents important limitations to understanding them, they require a multilevel theory. Despite repeated calls for such theory (e.g., Brass et al., 2004; Moliterno & Mahony, 2011; Phelps et al., 2012), little attention has been paid to multilevel network theory and modeling (Lomi et al., 2016).

In this chapter, we address these limitations by drawing on and extending the nascent research on multilevel networks. We briefly introduce foundational social network concepts and then define multilevel social networks, clarifying what constitutes multilevel social networks. We then present multilevel network constructs, with special emphasis on understanding constructs at higher level(s) than the individual. Next, we present a framework of multilevel network models and explain how social networks at different levels influence one another, and how networks at different levels jointly influence other phenomena. To clarify the concept of multilevel social networks, we compare and contrast our approach with other conceptualizations of multilevel networks. We end by discussing recommendations for future research on multilevel networks.

A BRIEF INTRODUCTION TO SOCIAL NETWORKS

A *social network* is a bounded system of social actors connected to one another via a type of social relationship (Wasserman & Faust, 1994). The actors (or "nodes") can be individuals or collectives of individuals (e.g., teams, organizational units, organizations), and the relationships can be of great variety (e.g., advice-seeking, work collaboration, alliance), have positive or negative valence (e.g., friends vs. enemies), be directed (e.g., when you seek advice from someone) or undirected (e.g., when two people collaborate on a project), and may be weighted (to capture the strength or intensity of ties) or unweighted (to reflect the presence/absence of ties). Figure 9.1 provides an example. This interpersonal friendship network consists of five nodes (i.e., individuals A, B, C, D, and E) with different pairs of nodes connected by friendship ties (i.e., AB, AC, CD, BE, and AE). That is, A is friends with B, C and E; B

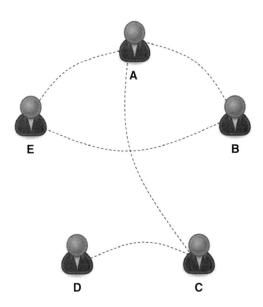

FIGURE 9.1.   Example of a social network.

is friends with A and E; C is friends with A and D; D is friends with C; and E is friends with A and B.

Social networks can be conceptualized in any setting in which there are social actors and ties among them. For instance, we can represent nurses in a surgical ward as nodes in a network and their collaborations in a surgery as a tie. When we observe all collaborations among all nurses in a department across all surgeries in a day, we can produce the social network represented in Figure 9.1. Alternatively, the nodes in Figure 9.1 could represent firms in an industry, and the ties could indicate strategic alliances among them.

Social network researchers use the term *ego* to refer to a focal actor and *alters* to indicate those connected to the focal actor. For example, when considering actor A in Figure 9.1 as the focal actor of interest, actor A is called ego and actors B, C and E are called alters. A pair of actors connected by a tie is a *dyad*. When a single type of tie connects a dyad, the tie is *uniplex*. When multiple types of ties connect a dyad, the relationship is *multiplex*. For example, Figure 9.2 shows a set of actors connected by work collaboration ties (indicated by dashed lines) and by friendship ties (indicated by solid lines). The figure shows that some pairs of actors (i.e., AB and BE) are connected by collaboration and friendship ties (signifying multiplex relationships), whereas other pairs are connected by uniplex ties

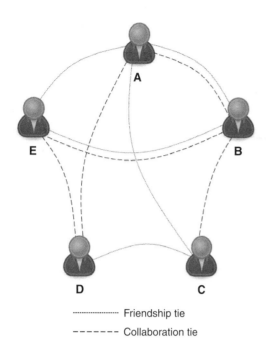

FIGURE 9.2.   Example of a multiplex network.

- - - - - - - - - - Friendship tie

- - - - - - Collaboration tie

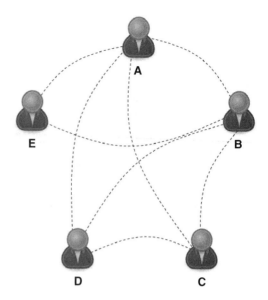

FIGURE 9.3.   Example of a denser social network.

of collaboration (i.e., AD and DE) or friendship (i.e., AC, AE, and CD).

Network scholars differentiate relational properties of social ties from social network structure. Relational properties are dyad specific, such as the strength or multiplexity of a tie, whereas *network structure* refers to the pattern of ties across a bounded set of actors. Within the domain of network structure, network researchers distinguish among an actor's position within a network, the structure of ties among an actor's alters (i.e., ego network structure), and the pattern of ties among all actors in a network (i.e., whole network structure). An example of a measure of an actor's position in a network is its *degree centrality*, which is defined as the number of alters connected to ego. In the social network example depicted in Figure 9.1, the degree centrality of actor A is 3, whereas actors B, C, and E have a degree centrality of 2, and actor D has a degree centrality of 1. An often examined indicator of ego network structure is *structural holes*, defined as the extent to which an actor's alters are not connected to one another (Burt, 1992). In Figure 9.1, because A is connected to actors B, C, and E and no ties exist between B and C and C and E, actor A spans two structural holes (i.e., between B and C, and C and E). A basic

measure of whole network structure is *density*, which represents the ratio of ties that exist among all actors in a network relative to all possible ties. Comparing the networks in Figures 9.1 and 9.3, the network in Figure 9.3 has a density of 0.8 (or 80%), whereas the network in Figure 9.1 has a density of 0.5 (or 50%).

Multilevel Social Networks

The networks just described are *single-level social networks* because, although each network consists of multiple actors, these nodes are of a single type and exist at a single level, and are connected by one or more types of ties specific to that level. Following prior research (Carley, 1991; Iacobucci & Wasserman, 1990; Lomi et al., 2016; Moliterno & Mahony, 2011), we define a *multilevel social network* as consisting of nodes that (a) exist at two or more levels (e.g., individuals and organizations), where the lower level nodes are, at least partially, hierarchically nested within higher level nodes; and (b) are connected by distinct ties at each level (e.g., individuals are connected by work collaborations and organizations are connected by alliances).

Another defining feature of multilevel social networks is the potential for cross-level effects. The nested nature of lower level actors in higher level collectives, such as individuals in teams, can create interdependencies among the lower level actors that affect the formation of ties among them (Hitt et al., 2007). For example, membership in the same team creates interdependencies among team members because teamwork requires coordination, leading to an increased likelihood of social ties among team members (Hitt et al., 2007). Ties at higher levels of analysis also can create interdependencies across actors at lower levels (Zappa & Robins, 2016). For example, the creation of a contractual alliance between two organizations establishes a need for members of the partnered organizations to coordinate their activities and cooperate to execute the alliance agreement, resulting in interpersonal ties that span organizational boundaries (Sorenson & Rogan, 2014). Ties at lower levels can influence the formation and functioning of ties at higher levels, such as when the presence of interpersonal relationships among members of two organizations helps to establish a formal interorganizational relationship between them (Berends, Van Burg, & Van Raaij, 2011).

Using this conceptualization of multilevel social networks, we now present and explain different constructs used in multilevel social network studies. Although our multilevel framework allows for many levels of analysis, we limit our discussion to two levels: lower level and higher level nodes. For ease of exposition, we equate lower level nodes to individual persons and higher level nodes to collectives (e.g., teams, classes, projects, organizations).

Lower Level Node Constructs

Network constructs related to lower level nodes, such as individuals, consist of all actor-specific social network metrics, including measures of network position and ego network structure. As mentioned previously, an example of a node-level construct is degree centrality.

Higher Level Node Constructs

Just like lower level nodes, such as individuals, higher level collectives (e.g., teams, projects, classes, departments, organizations) can be treated as unitary actors in a network in which ties connect them to one another. Consequently, actor-specific network measures, such as degree centrality,

apply just as with lower level nodes. Higher level constructs are *global* when their measurement does not rely on observations of lower level actor characteristics and pertains instead to the relatively objective, descriptive, and observable characteristics of the unit that originate at the unit level (Kozlowski & Klein, 2000).

However, constructs related to higher level collectives also can emerge from lower level phenomena. Kozlowski and Klein (2000) identified two ways higher level constructs emerge from lower level actors (e.g., individuals): composition and compilation. We build on each approach to describe the relationship between lower and higher level node constructs in the context of multilevel social networks.

Constructs based on shared lower level node properties. Higher level node characteristics are derived from the shared properties of lower level nodes and their interactions. The typical construct based on shared unit properties involves the aggregation of lower level data to form the measure of the higher level construct. Such multilevel measurement models often are *composition models* of emergence (e.g., Chan, 1998; Kozlowski & Klein, 2000). This approach assumes the lower level phenomenon is isomorphic with the higher level phenomenon—the constructs at the two levels reference the same conceptual content, have the same meaning, and share similar nomological networks (albeit at different levels of analysis). This approach allows the analyst to aggregate lower level observations to measure the construct at the higher level of analysis (Kozlowski & Klein, 2000). When observations about the construct at the lower level of analysis are shared and homogenous (i.e., converge), they can be aggregated to reflect the collective-level construct. For example, employees' perceptions of their work environments (i.e., psychological climate) may be aggregated to measure the higher level construct of organizational climate (Chan, 1998; James, Demaree, & Wolf, 1984). Few social network constructs are derived from models that assume shared unit properties (Krackhardt, 1987).

Constructs based on the configuration of lower level properties. In contrast to *composition* models, *compilation models* of higher level emergence are based on the principle that the higher level construct results from the configuration of lower level observations. Although configural unit properties originate at the individual level, they are not assumed to coalesce and converge among the members of a collective. Configural properties characterize patterns, distribution, and/or variability among individuals' contributions to the higher level phenomenon.

Applied to a theory of multilevel networks, a configural property of a higher level node could be a network structural measure of the whole network that consists of the lower level nodes, such as the density of ties among the lower level nodes or a measure of the distribution (e.g., minimum, maximum, variance, or standard deviation) of network properties at lower level nodes.

Joint-Level Constructs

Unlike constructs from traditional, nonnetwork multilevel studies, a distinct set of constructs exist within the realm of multilevel social networks. These constructs are joint level and consist of nodes and ties at different levels, as well cross-level ties. Joint-level constructs can be measured by flattening the network by ignoring the distinctions between the levels of nodes and ties. Consider the following example: Two universities are connected by a formal contractual collaboration to deliver a joint degree program and by a professor who is affiliated by employment with both universities. The universities represent higher level actors, and the contractual relationship between them represents a higher level tie, whereas the employment relationship between the professor and the two universities represents cross-level ties, which often are referred to as affiliation ties (e.g., Lazega, Jourda, Mounier, & Stofer, 2008). One could flatten this multilevel network by treating the three nodes and the ties that connect them as a single-level network. Given this flattened, one-level network, we could use the single-level network framework to compute network measures, such as the degree centrality of each actor, as described earlier. Because these measures incorporate nodes and ties at different levels, we call such constructs *joint-level constructs*. For other examples of joint-level constructs, see

Brennecke and Rank (2016) and Wang, Robins, Pattison, and Lazega (2016).

CLASSES OF MULTILEVEL SOCIAL NETWORKS

An important advantage of our conceptualization of multilevel networks in this chapter is its generality. This conceptualization can accommodate diverse situations of varying complexity. To illustrate, we elaborate on six classes of multilevel networks, which are increasing in their complexity. For ease of understanding, we present these multilevel networks with only two levels but note that they can be extended to include three or more levels.

We distinguish among these classes of multilevel networks by examining three contingencies, as presented in Table 9.1. The first contingency concerns the extent of nesting: Does each lower level node have one or more cross-level ties (Lazega, Mounier, Jourda, & Stofer, 2006)? An example is whether children in a school are affiliated with one or more classrooms. If all children attend only one classroom (i.e., there is a one-to-one mapping between children and classrooms), then the network is *fully nested*. If a child is affiliated with more than one classroom, then the network is *cross-nested*. The second contingency focuses on whether lower level ties are limited to other lower level nodes nested within the same higher order collective: Do lower level nodes maintain ties only with other lower level nodes connected to the same higher level node? An example of this contingency is whether individual employees affiliated with one organization collaborate with individual employees affiliated with a different organization. If nurses of a surgical department collaborate only with other nurses from the same department, the network consists solely of *within-unit* ties and is a within-unit network. If these nurses collaborate with nurses from other departments, the network is *cross-unit*. The last contingency focuses on whether ties among nodes at each level or across levels are uniplex or multiplex. If only one type of tie is considered at both levels, the network is *uniplex*. If multiple types of ties are considered at either level, the network is *multiplex*. We combine these different types of networks to form six classes of multilevel networks.

TABLE 9.1

Types of Multilevel Networks

Multilevel network class	Are lower level units completely nested in a higher level unit?	Are lower level units nested in a higher level unit allowed to form ties to lower level units nested in another higher level unit?	Are the considered ties uniplex or multiplex?	Illustrative example
I. Fully nested within-unit uniplex network	Yes	No	Uniplex	Students belong to only one classroom, and they collaborate only with students in their classroom; classrooms, as nodes in a network, also are connected by teacher friendship ties.
II. Fully nested cross-unit uniplex network	Yes	Yes	Uniplex	Students belong to only one classroom, but they also could collaborate with students from other classrooms; classrooms, as nodes in a network, also are connected by teacher friendship ties.
III. Cross-nested cross-unit uniplex network	No	Yes	Uniplex	Students may affiliate with different classrooms, and they could collaborate with students from any classroom; classrooms, as nodes in a network, also are connected by teacher friendship ties.
IV. Fully nested within-unit multiplex network	Yes	No	Multiplex	Similar to multilevel network Class I, but students also can have friendship ties and teachers also can have collaboration ties, so both levels have friendship and collaboration ties.
V. Fully nested cross-unit multiplex network	Yes	Yes	Multiplex	Similar to multilevel network Class II, but students also can have friendship ties and teachers also can have collaboration ties, and students' ties may cut across classrooms.
VI. Cross-nested cross-unit multiplex network	No	Yes	Multiplex	Similar to multilevel network Class III, but students also can have friendship ties and teachers also can have collaboration ties.

Class I: Fully Nested Within-Unit Uniplex Networks

The first class of multilevel networks are the simplest. In this class of multilevel networks, (a) each lower level node is nested in only one higher level node, (b) each lower level node can form ties with only those lower level nodes nested in the same higher level node, and (c) the nodes at each level are connected with only one type of tie (e.g., friendship, collaboration, alliance, information-sharing), even if such ties are distinct at different levels and cross-levels. This class of multilevel network consists of "networks of networks."

An illustration is presented in Figure 9.4. In this figure, the lower level nodes might represent individuals (e.g., children) and higher level nodes define a social collective (e.g., classrooms). This class defines a setting in which each lower level unit or node (e.g., children) may be affiliated only with a single higher level unit or node (e.g., classroom). In this class of multilevel networks, only one type of tie

is possible at each level (e.g., study collaborations among children).

Class II: Fully Nested Cross-Unit Uniplex Networks

To derive the second class of multilevel social networks, we remove the restriction that lower level nodes only have ties within the same higher level node. For example, employees (lower level nodes) affiliated with different organizations (higher level nodes), may, under a Class II multilevel social network, collaborate with employees of other organizations, as depicted in Figure 9.5. For another example, students (lower level nodes) affiliated with different classrooms (higher level nodes) may be friends with one another.

Class III: Cross-Nested Cross-Unit Uniplex Networks

To derive the third class of multilevel networks, we remove the restriction that each lower level node

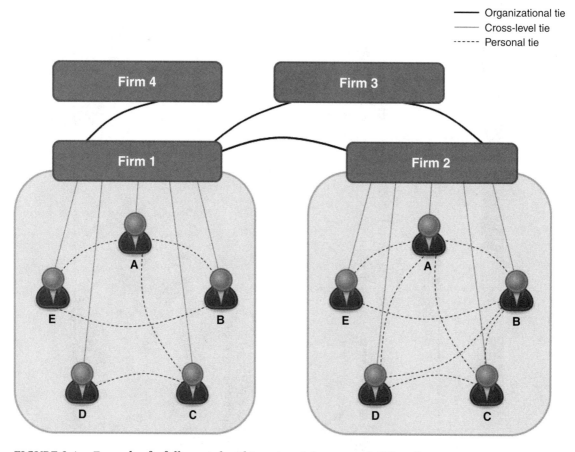

FIGURE 9.4.   Example of a fully nested within-unit uniplex network (Class I).

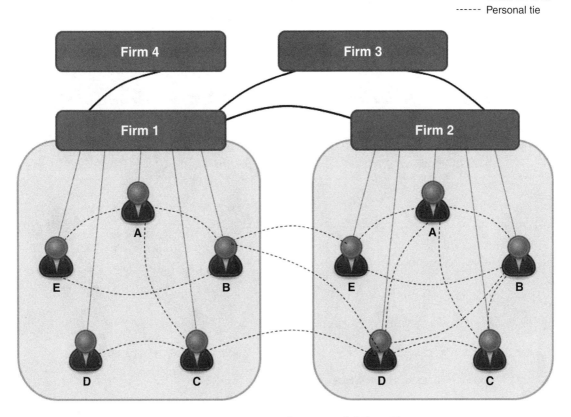

FIGURE 9.5.   Example of a fully nested cross-unit uniplex network (Class II).

be connected to only one higher level node. For example, a nurse (lower level node) may be affiliated with multiple departments (higher level nodes) and collaborate with nurses affiliated with her own and other departments, as depicted in Figure 9.6. For another example, students (lower level nodes) may be affiliated with multiple classrooms and have friends within each classroom and other classrooms.

Class IV: Fully Nested Within-Unit Multiplex Networks

The next three classes of multilevel networks are derived from the first three classes by easing the restriction that within each level and across levels there is only a single type of tie. For example, as shown in Figure 9.7, a Class IV network is simply a Class I network that contains multiple types of ties. Multiplexity may occur at the lower level (e.g., nurses collaborate and also are friends), at the higher level (e.g., departmental collaboration ties and interdepartmental membership ties), or at both levels.

Class V: Fully Nested Cross-Unit Multiplex Networks

The fifth class of multilevel networks corresponds to Class II multilevel networks but again removes the restriction that only a single type of network tie is allowed within and between levels (see Figure 9.8). Continuing with the example of nurses, in this class of multilevel networks, nurses are nested within each department, but ties among nurses may consist of collaboration and friendship ties within or across departments.

Class VI: Cross-Nested Cross-Unit Multiplex Networks

The sixth class of multilevel social networks corresponds to a Class III network but also removes the restriction of a single type of network tie (see Figure 9.9). For example, nurses may be affiliated with multiple departments in a hospital, and the ties among nurses may consist of collaboration and friendship ties within or across departments.

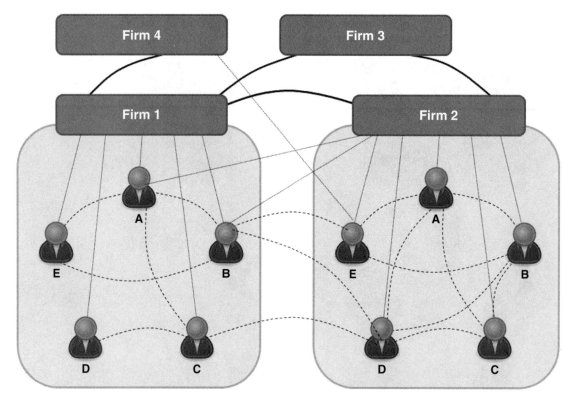

FIGURE 9.6.   Example of a cross-nested cross-unit uniplex network (Class III).

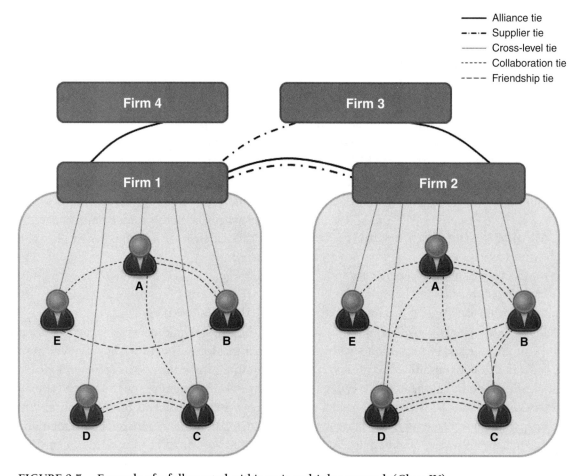

FIGURE 9.7.   Example of a fully nested within-unit multiplex network (Class IV).

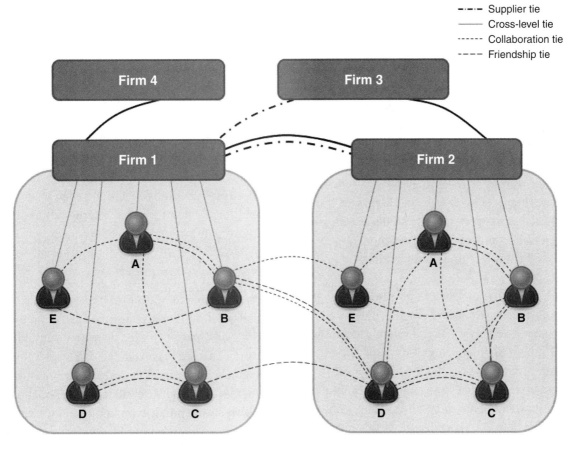

FIGURE 9.8. Example of a fully nested cross-unit multiplex network (Class V).

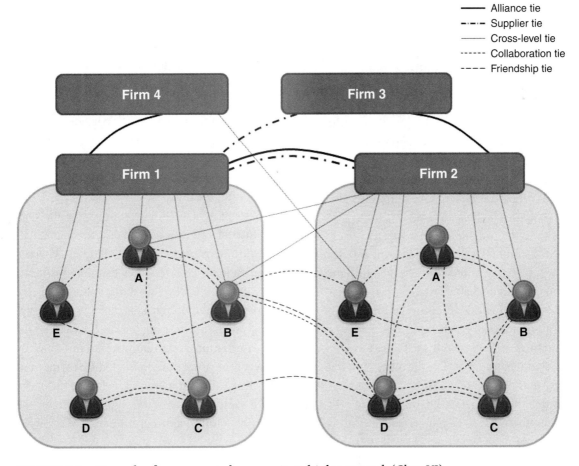

FIGURE 9.9. Example of a cross-nested cross-unit multiplex network (Class VI).

MULTILEVEL SOCIAL NETWORK MODELS

Given the nascence and complexity of multilevel social networks, most research has examined Class I and, to a lesser degree, Class II multilevel networks, although exceptions exist (see the example of Berends et al., 2011, discussed in the Cross-Level Direct Effects Models section that follows). To comprehensively address multilevel social network models, we build on Kozlowski and Klein's (2000) discussion of cross-level models. We discuss cross-level direct-effect models, cross-level moderator models, and cross-level frog-pond models.

Cross-Level Direct-Effects Models

Cross-level direct-effect models describe how a variable at one level directly affects a variable at another level. Although Kozlowski and Klein (2000) limited their attention to discussing how higher level constructs may influence lower level constructs, both top-down and bottom-up effects are possible in multilevel networks. An example of this model is provided in a study by Berends et al. (2011). We first describe their study and then interpret it as a cross-level direct-effects multilevel network model.

An illustrative study.   Berends et al. (2011) described the development of a new material for the aerospace industry as an outcome of interactions among individuals and organizations. That study examined the interactions of scientists and organizations that collaborated in developing the new material. Using a qualitative approach based on interviews and various types of archival data, the authors described how the formation and termination of interorganizational relationships affected interpersonal ties, and vice versa.

Regarding tie formation, Berends et al. (2011) described the mutual influence of interorganizational and interpersonal relationships. On the one hand, the formation of an alliance between two organizations could engender communication and collaboration between their employees. Through such activities, scientists built social ties across organizational boundaries. On the other hand, social ties among scientists working at different organizations could lead to the formation of research and development (R&D) alliances between firms by

identifying opportunities for value-creating interfirm collaboration.

Berends et al. (2011) also showed how interorganizational ties change because of changes in boundary-spanning interpersonal relationships. When scientists changed how they collaborate, for instance, by inviting more collaborators from other organizations, the interorganizational relationships adapted to facilitate such changes. Berends et al. showed how the termination of an interorganizational tie produced a downward cross-level influence on the dissolution of interpersonal collaborations.

Interpretation as a multilevel network model. Berends et al. (2011) investigated a Class V multilevel network: a fully nested cross-unit multiplex network. That study considered two levels of nodes: individuals (lower level nodes) and organizations (higher level nodes). The interorganizational ties considered were purely contractual and were put in place to share knowledge while protecting ownership rights. Cross-level ties between individuals and organizations reflected employment relationships, and the ties among individuals were multiplex because they included both work collaboration and friendship. Scientists were employed by only one organization, so the lower level nodes were fully nested within a single higher level node. Employees collaborated within and across organizations, so ties were cross-unit. Berends et al. considered multiplex ties among lower level nodes (i.e., work-collaboration and friendship), even though they considered uniplex ties between organizations and between individuals and organizations.

Berends et al. (2011) examined the influences and interactions among different levels of networks. The authors argued that the individual-level and organizational-level ties they examined, although very different, codeveloped over time as the actors pursued a common purpose, namely, innovation. The study found that higher level network dynamics (i.e., formation and dissolution of an alliance between organizations) affected tie formation and dissolution at a lower level (i.e., formation and dissolution of ties among individuals). The study also found a direct influence of a lower level network (i.e., presence of a friendship tie between individuals) on tie formation at a higher level (i.e., interorganizational alliances).

Other studies. Although Berends et al. (2011) used qualitative data and methods, other studies have used quantitative methods to examine cross-level direct-effects models. For example, Wang, Robins, Pattison, and Lazega (2013) and Zappa and Lomi (2015) used multilevel exponential random graph models to investigate multilevel networks. Those studies examined the dissolution of ties at different levels in multilevel social networks and showed how to quantitatively explore cross-level direct-effects multilevel models.

Cross-Level Moderator Models

Cross-level moderator models are appropriate for situations in which a researcher hypothesizes that a construct at one level moderates the strength or direction of the relationship between constructs residing at another level. Typically, these models describe how a higher level construct (e.g., team cohesion) moderates the relationship between two lower level constructs (e.g., the relationship between employee personality and the likelihood employees would engage in acts of workplace deviance). In multilevel network models, network constructs exist at different levels and can appear as predictor, moderator, or dependent variables.

An illustrative study. The study by Paruchuri (2010) is an example of a cross-level moderator model of multilevel networks. It examined how inter- and intraorganizational networks jointly affected knowledge sourcing by inventors. Paruchuri described how the extent to which an inventor's knowledge is used by colleagues is influenced by his or her centrality in the intraorganizational inventor network and how this influence is conditioned by the organization's position in the interorganizational alliance network. The knowledge that inventors use depends significantly on their social ties: Connections to colleagues make them aware of new knowledge and allow them to learn and acquire this knowledge (Singh, 2005). The more collaborative ties an inventor has with other inventors in the firm, the more the inventor can communicate his or her

knowledge and have it used by others. Paruchuri argued that the firm's position in the interorganizational R&D alliance network moderates this relationship. R&D alliances facilitate knowledge spillovers between firms. A firm's centrality in the R&D alliance network increases the knowledge spillovers it receives, which allows inventors to access more, diverse, and novel technologies to be used in their innovations. Paruchuri found the effect of inventor centrality on the diffusion of the inventor's knowledge to other inventors weakens as his or her firm becomes more central in the industry R&D alliance network.

Interpretation as a multilevel network model. The network described in the Paruchuri (2010) study is a Class I multilevel network: a fully nested within-unit uniplex network. That study considered two levels of nodes: individual inventors (lower level nodes) and organizations (higher level nodes). The interorganizational ties were contractual R&D collaborations, which allowed firms to share knowledge. Cross-level ties between inventors and organizations reflected employment relationships, and the ties among individuals were collaboration ties. Inventors were employed by only one organization, so the lower level nodes were fully nested within a single higher level node. Cross-unit ties did not exist because inventors were theorized to collaborate only within their firms. Paruchuri considered only uniplex ties: collaboration ties among inventors, alliances among firms, and cross-level employment relationships between inventors and firms.

From a multilevel network model perspective, the Paruchuri (2010) study examined how the influence of a lower level node property (i.e., inventor network centrality) on another lower level node property (i.e., use of inventor knowledge by colleagues) was moderated by a higher level node property (i.e., firm R&D alliance network centrality).

Cross-Level Frog-Pond Models

Cross-level frog-pond models consider how a lower level node's relative standing within a higher level unit influences the outcomes associated with the lower level nodes (Kozlowski & Klein, 2000). The term *frog-pond* captures the comparison between a focal actor (i.e., the frog) on a particular measure and the aggregation of the measure, such as the average, at the level of a higher order collective (i.e., the pond; Klein, Dansereau, & Hall, 1994). A cross-level frog-pond model examines how the effect on a lower level actor depends on the relative standing of the lower level actor to all others in a higher level unit, such as the education of an actor relative to the average education of all others in the group. Although an individual may have only a moderate education, such as a high school diploma, compared with the average education of his or her team, the individual may be highly educated. Frog-pond models are cross-level models because they incorporate both unit- and network-level components. This type of model also has been called a heterogeneous, parts, and individual-within-group model (Dansereau, Yammarino, & Kohles, 1999; Klein et al., 1994).

An illustrative study. Although none of the extant literature uses the frog-pond multilevel network model perfectly, two studies have come rather close. First, Bizzi (2013) examined the dark side of structural holes by looking at how individual outcomes are dependent on actor brokerage and the group-level mean in structural holes, that is, the average of span of structural holes of all individuals in the group. Following the cross-level frog-pond model, he created a variable that measured how an individual's span of structural holes is vis-à-vis that group-level mean. He then used that mean to predict outcomes at the individual level, such as individual job satisfaction and job performance. Similarly, Lazega et al. (2008) identified "big fish" and "small fish" among the scientists in cancer research laboratories by using their social network centrality. Cancer researchers were classified as "big fish" when they had an above-median in-degree and out-degree centrality in the advice network. That relative standing in the community influenced the impact factor of their publications and that effect.

Interpretation as a multilevel network model.
The network described by Bizzi (2013) was a Class II multilevel network: a fully nested cross-unit uniplex network. That study considered two levels of

nodes: individual employees (lower level nodes) and groups (higher level nodes). In the ties, cross-level ties between individuals and groups considered were affiliation, and the ties considered among individuals were information-sharing ties.

In nesting (our first criterion for multilevel network classification), because employees were affiliated with only one group, the lower level nodes (i.e., employees) were nested within a single higher level node (i.e., group). In cross-unit ties (the second element for multilevel network classification), each employee of a group was theorized to share information with other employees of the same group and employees affiliated with other groups. Last, in type of ties (the third criterion for multilevel network classification), Bizzi (2013) considered only one type of tie for each aspect (the information-sharing tie among lower level nodes and affiliation ties at cross-level; no type of ties was considered at the higher level nodes level). It was a study of only uniplex ties.

Although the Bizzi (2013) study was similar to the frog-pond concept, it did not meet the precise description proposed by Kozlowski and Klein (2000) because Bizzi did not assess the interaction of individual brokerage with team-level brokerage.

The network described by Lazega et al. (2008) also was a Class II multilevel, fully nested cross-unit uniplex network. That study simultaneously looked at the interpersonal and interorganizational levels. The interpersonal network consisted of French cancer scientists and the advice ties among them observed through a survey among all those scientists that asked about technological, managerial, and financial advice. The interorganizational network contained the cancer laboratories and the connections among them, as indicated by each laboratory director asked about sharing technological resources, joint research programs, and conference invitations. That network was fully nested because scientists in the study were linked to a single R&D laboratory. Because they often had advice ties outside of their own lab, those linkages crossed organizational boundaries and formed a cross-unit network. Although both the interpersonal and interorganizational networks contained various types of ties, that is, a multiplex network, they were collapsed into a single type resulting in a uniplex network. Social comparison took place because scientists varied by their centrality.

Although the Lazega et al. (2008) study used the frog-pond model, it did not fully meet the definition of Kozlowski and Klein (2000): Lazega et al. (2008) classified scientists by comparing individual centralities to that of the entire industry and not specifically their laboratory and, relatedly, also observed a higher level network of interorganizational ties, which was not part of the Kozlowski and Klein (2000) model.

WHAT ARE *NOT* MULTILEVEL NETWORK MODELS?

To further define the conceptual space of multilevel social networks, we contrast our conceptualization with other network research that has used the multilevel moniker but does not accord with our view. Although we draw on examples from the management and organizational literature, the issues we identify extend to other disciplines.

Not all multilevel models qualify as multilevel network models. We discuss two popular multilevel models to illustrate the additional requirements of multilevel network models: microfoundation models (Felin & Foss, 2005; Felin, Foss, Heimeriks, & Madsen, 2012; Foss & Pedersen, 2016) and Coleman's boat model (Coleman, 1990). Both models are based on the argument that a higher level phenomenon is explained by a lower level process.

Microfoundation Models

A *microfoundation model* seeks to explain higher order, collective phenomena using the aggregation of lower order, individual-level factors (Barney & Felin, 2013). An example of a microfoundation model is Nerkar and Paruchuri (2005). That study focused on the dynamics of inventor networks within firms to explain the evolution of firm-level R&D capabilities. Although that study linked network dynamics among collaborations of individual inventors with a higher level unit property (firm R&D capability), it did not constitute a multilevel social network model because it did not consider networks at both lower and higher level nodes and cross-level ties connecting the two.

Coleman Boat Models

Coleman's boat model, depicted in Figure 9.10, is a well-known multilevel sociological model (Coleman, 1990). This model describes how actions/events at one level lead to consequences at that level via processes at a lower level. An illustration of this model is a study of the effects of a merger on firm R&D. Paruchuri and Eisenman (2012) investigated the influence of a merger on firm innovation activities. They argued that interfirm mergers created anxiety among individual inventors within the firms due to potential structural, procedural, and cultural changes. They posited that the anxiety caused by a merger would lead inventors in the merged firms to increasingly collaborate with more central inventors and avoid collaborating with those who connect

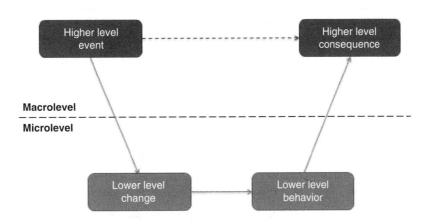

FIGURE 9.10. Example of Coleman's boat model (Coleman, 1990) for multilevel processes.

otherwise unconnected groups of inventors. This lower level network dynamic altered the merged firm's rate and direction of innovation. Because social network properties appeared only at the lower level, it was not a multilevel network model.

An illustration of a Coleman's boat model (Coleman, 1990) that is a multilevel network model is a study by Goossen (2014). He theorized that a firm's formation of interorganizational ties would influence interpersonal, intrafirm networks by shaping the flow of knowledge through them, thereby influencing individual innovation performance. These individual innovation outcomes then would aggregate to form firm-level innovation outcomes.

FUTURE RESEARCH AGENDA

Multilevel network research is in its infancy and provides substantial opportunities for scholars to enrich our understanding of organizational phenomena. In this section, we identify a few of these research opportunities, as displayed in Table 9.2.

Direct-Effects Research

Direct-effects multilevel network research examines how network structures at two (or more) levels interact and coevolve (Hitt et al., 2007). In this vein, scholars could examine how lower level networks adapt their structural and relational characteristics to changes in higher level networks, and vice versa. Researchers also could explore how networks at two (or more) levels evolve through mutual interactions.

To explore the effects of higher level networks on lower level networks, research could use the first class of multilevel network models, which use a strict hierarchical view of multilevel networks (Harary & Batell, 1981; Watts, Dodds, & Newman, 2002) and examine how lower level ego networks change in response to changes in network characteristics of the higher level collective in which they are nested. For example, individuals are likely to form new ties or terminate old ones when their firms initiate or terminate alliances with other firms (Berends et al., 2011).

Studies also could be informed by the second and third classes of multilevel networks.

Research could examine how changes in higher level networks enable lower level actors to form boundary-spanning ties with lower level actors affiliated with other higher level nodes or develop affiliations with other higher level actors. Research also could explore which lower level actors are more likely to form such ties. For example, research could examine which inventors from two recently allied firms are likely to develop collaborative interpersonal ties. Likewise, scholars could build on Berends et al. (2011) and investigate the impact of the termination or restructuring of interorganizational ties on lower level boundary-spanning relationships, such as the network properties of individuals whose ties survive such a termination or restructuring.

Although we have focused only on two levels, research could examine three or more levels. For example, researchers could explore how a firm's network position influences the interactions among its business units and how these interactions shape the interactions among individuals within and across business units.

Taking a different perspective, researchers also could investigate bottom-up processes: how network properties of lower level actors affect network properties of higher level actors. For example, research could investigate whether and when the formation of boundary-spanning ties between individuals working in different organizations lead to the firms' forming an alliance. Similarly, research could explore how changes in lower level boundary-spanning ties influence the termination or restructuring of higher level ties.

Joint-Effects Research

Research could explore how network properties at higher and lower levels jointly influence various organizational phenomena. For example, research could investigate how interfirm ties and intrafirm networks interact to influence the knowledge outcomes of intrafirm units and how interfirm ties and interpersonal networks influence individual outcomes. Researchers have explored questions in this vein (Lazega et al., 2008; Moliterno & Mahony, 2011; Paruchuri, 2010; Payne, Moore, Griffis, & Autry, 2011; Rothaermel & Hess, 2007).

TABLE 9.2

Directions for Future Research

Type	Topic	Examples
Direct-effects research—bottom up	How lower level social networks influence the structure of higher level social networks	▪ Does the lack of information-sharing ties among individuals lead to organizations' developing more informational ties to other organizations? ▪ How does termination of friendship ties among employees in two business units affect the business unit collaboration?
Direct-effects research—top down	How higher level social networks influence the structure of lower level social networks	▪ Are individuals more likely to develop cross-unit ties when their organization has few external connections? ▪ How do interfirm alliances influence the number shared, cross-nested employees?
Direct-effects research—dynamics	How higher level and lower level networks mutually evolve over time	▪ Do higher level and lower level networks follow similar or opposing trends in network density?
Joint-effects research—interaction	How a higher/lower level network influences the relationship between a lower/higher level network and another, nonnetwork concept	▪ Does brokerage in a higher level network strengthen the effect of brokerage on performance in a lower level network? ▪ Does density of the lower level network among nurses weaken the effect of a central position in a hospital's higher level network?
Joint-effects research—configuration	How the combination of two different network structures at different levels affect another, nonnetwork concept	▪ Is a combination of higher level network brokerage and lower level network closure preferred for consulting teams? ▪ Are certain types of combinations of higher level and lower level network structures complementary?
Joint-effects research—dynamics	How the evolution in a higher/lower level network influences the relationships between a lower/higher level network and another, nonnetwork concept	▪ How does a gradual worsening of trust between political parties influence the relationship between politicians and their support for each other's resolutions?
Methodological—HLM	Multilevel regressions allow for estimating joint effects in a variety of settings	▪ How does the centrality of schools—connected via teachers jointly with the centrality of pupils through friendships—influence pupils' performance?
Methodological—MERGM	ERGM for multilevel networks	▪ What network mechanisms (e.g., brokerage and closure) drive tie formation at different levels?
Methodological—qualitative	In-depth multilevel case studies	▪ What are the mechanisms explaining the direct-effect and joint-effect multilevel relationships?
Methodological—simulation	Simulations allow for modeling and observing dynamics over time	▪ How do friendship ties among employees within and between firms influence organizational learning in the presence/absence of contractual agreements that allow full/partial information-sharing?

Note. ERGM = exponential random graph models; HLM = hierarchical linear models; MERGM = multilevel exponential random graph models.

One potential area for future research relates the effects of network structures at multiple levels jointly to a nonnetwork property, such as power, creativity, or performance. The recent increase in multilevel research may be driven by a theoretical perspective, but it often is chosen because of the advancements in multilevel methods, like hierarchical linear modeling. However, many of these methods require the dependent variable to be measured at the lowest unit of analysis, but certain dimensions of the dependent variable do not exist at the lowest unit of analysis, like new product introductions. Such cases may require investigation of a multilevel network effect by having a higher level node characteristic interact with a lower level network characteristic.

Units and Levels of Analysis

Although organizational phenomena typically are affected by more than two levels (Gupta, Tesluk, & Taylor, 2007), most multilevel network research has dealt with the individual and organizational levels. Alternative levels, such as teams, business units, or regions, have not received much attention. However, the selection of levels often is ambiguous, and many studies could have used alternative levels. Because it is the role of theory, whether inductively or deductively derived, to identify the relevant levels of analysis for a particular phenomenon (Rousseau, 1985), we encourage future research to integrate theories to increase the levels of analysis investigated. For example, prior treatments of multilevel research have emphasized the importance of the mesolevel in understanding organizational phenomena (House, Rousseau, & Thomas-Hunt, 1995; Klein & Kozlowski, 2000). Although the mesolevel is key to understanding how and when micro- and macrolevels interact, the investigation of all three in network research is exceedingly rare.

Methodological Opportunities

Research on multilevel networks often uses a quantitative approach, which is consistent with the quantitative nature of social networks, in general. This approach comes with constraints, however, in the topics and processes that can be investigated. Quantitative methods initially were developed to

examine network structure and not for network evolution. Although new methods have been introduced to assess network evolution (Snijders, 2011), process research is still lagging. In addition, multilevel methods like random coefficient regression provide several constraints, including the dependent variable's being at the lowest level in the hierarchy.

There are opportunities for multilevel network research to use alternative research methods. First, qualitative and mixed-method research provides a good approach to explore issues about which we lack sufficient understanding or for which other methods are not available. For example, Berends et al. (2011) and Liebeskind, Oliver, Zucker, and Brewer (1996) have provided examples of how qualitative research can contribute to understanding multilevel networks. Besides relying on interviews, future research also could use archival data to reconstruct networks. Yin (2013, p. 50) described how an embedded case study involves multiple units of analysis, which is useful for such a multilevel investigation. Many of the common packages for qualitative data analysis (e.g., NVivo [QSR International, 2018], QDA Miner [Provalis Research, 2018], MAXQDA [Verbi, 2018], Dedoose ["Full Qualitative and Mixed Methods Support," 2018]) nowadays support the coding of connections and networks, and allow for multilevel coding and categories.

Second, future research could use simulation methods to explore the dynamics of multilevel networks. Although simulations have been used to model specifications at a single level (e.g., Fang, Lee, & Schilling, 2010; Lazer & Friedman, 2007; Zhao & Anand, 2013), multilevel networks studies have used them to assess network evolution (Zappa & Lomi, 2015). Multilevel network simulations are easily facilitated by software packages, such as hergm (within the R environment; Schweinberger, Handcock, & Luna, 2018) or MPNet (Schweinberger & Luna, 2018; Wang, Robins, Pattison, & Koskinen, 2014). We see opportunities for using simulations techniques to assess topics key to multilevel networks. For example, such a study could improve our understanding of knowledge diffusion by simulating both the interorganizational and intraorganizational diffusion processes.

CONCLUSION

In this chapter, we contributed to the conceptual development of multilevel social network theory. We explained how extant single-level network research typically makes questionable assumptions about the isomorphism of causal mechanisms across levels and the independence of cross-level effects, which can lead to biased results and incorrect inferences. To address these limitations, we introduced multilevel social networks and explained how they differ from other related concepts in the social networks literature. We developed a typology of multilevel social networks and discussed their implications for different cause-and-effect relationships. To promote research in this area, we explained important multilevel network constructs and models, and proposed an agenda to guide future research.

References

Ahuja, G. (2000). Collaboration networks, structural holes, and innovation: A longitudinal study. *Administrative Science Quarterly, 45,* 425–455. http://dx.doi.org/10.2307/2667105

Barney, J., & Felin, T. (2013). What are microfoundations? *Academy of Management Perspectives, 27,* 138–155. http://dx.doi.org/10.5465/amp.2012.0107

Berends, H., Van Burg, E., & Van Raaij, E. M. (2011). Contacts and contracts: Cross-level network dynamics in the development of an aircraft material. *Organization Science, 22,* 940–960. http://dx.doi.org/10.1287/orsc.1100.0578

Bizzi, L. (2013). The dark side of structural holes a multilevel investigation. *Journal of Management, 39,* 1554–1578. http://dx.doi.org/10.1177/0149206312471385

Borgatti, S. P., & Halgin, D. S. (2011). On network theory. *Organization Science, 22,* 1168–1181. http://dx.doi.org/10.1287/orsc.1100.0641

Borgatti, S. P., Mehra, A., Brass, D. J., & Labianca, G. (2009). Network analysis in the social sciences. *Science, 323,* 892–895. http://dx.doi.org/10.1126/science.1165821

Brass, D. J., Galaskiewicz, J., Greve, H. R., & Tsai, W. (2004). Taking stock of networks and organizations: A multilevel perspective. *Academy of Management Journal, 47,* 795–817. http://dx.doi.org/10.2307/20159624

Brennecke, J., & Rank, O. N. (2016). The interplay between formal project memberships and informal advice seeking in knowledge-intensive firms: A multilevel network approach. *Social Networks, 44,* 307–318. http://dx.doi.org/10.1016/j.socnet.2015.02.004

Burt, R. S. (1992). *Structural holes: The social structure of competition.* Cambridge, MA: Harvard University Press.

Carley, K. (1991). A theory of group stability. *American Sociological Review, 56,* 331–354. http://dx.doi.org/10.2307/2096108

Chan, D. (1998). Functional relations among constructs in the same content domain at different levels of analysis: A typology of composition models. *Journal of Applied Psychology, 83,* 234–246. http://dx.doi.org/10.1037/0021-9010.83.2.234

Coleman, J. S. (1988). Social capital in the creation of human capital. *American Journal of Sociology, 94,* S95–S120.

Coleman, J. S. (1990). *Foundations of social theory.* Cambridge, MA: Harvard University Press.

Dansereau, F., Yammarino, F. J., & Kohles, J. C. (1999). Multiple levels of analysis from a longitudinal perspective: Some implications for theory building. *Academy of Management Review, 24,* 346–357. http://dx.doi.org/10.5465/AMR.1999.1893940

Fang, C., Lee, J., & Schilling, M. A. (2010). Balancing exploration and exploitation through structural design: The isolation of subgroups and organizational learning. *Organization Science, 21,* 625–642. http://dx.doi.org/10.1287/orsc.1090.0468

Felin, T., & Foss, N. J. (2005). Strategic organization: A field in search of micro-foundations. *Strategic Organization, 3,* 441–455. http://dx.doi.org/10.1177/1476127005055796

Felin, T., Foss, N. J., Heimeriks, K. H., & Madsen, T. L. (2012). Microfoundations of routines and capabilities: Individuals, processes, and structure. *Journal of Management Studies, 49,* 1351–1374. http://dx.doi.org/10.1111/j.1467-6486.2012.01052.x

Foss, N. J., & Pedersen, T. (2016). Microfoundations in strategy research. *Strategic Management Journal, 37,* E22–E34. http://dx.doi.org/10.1002/smj.2362

Full qualitative and mixed methods support. (2018). [Dedoose: Qualitative data analysis software]. Retrieved from https://www.dedoose.com/home/features

Goossen, M. C. (2014). *Intraorganizational networks, Interorganizational collaboration and firm innovation* [doctoral dissertation]. Retrieved from https://pastel.archives-ouvertes.fr/tel-01360523

Gupta, A. K., Tesluk, P. E., & Taylor, M. S. (2007). Innovation at and across multiple levels of analysis. *Organization Science, 18,* 885–897. http://dx.doi.org/10.1287/orsc.1070.0337

Harary, F., & Batell, M. F. (1981). What is a system? *Social Networks, 3,* 29–40. http://dx.doi.org/10.1016/0378-8733(81)90003-4

Hitt, M. A., Beamish, P. W., Jackson, S. E., & Mathieu, J. E. (2007). Building theoretical and empirical bridges across levels: Multilevel research in management. *Academy of Management Journal, 50,* 1385–1399. http://dx.doi.org/10.5465/AMJ.2007.28166219

House, R., Rousseau, D. M., & Thomas-Hunt, M. (1995). The meso paradigm: A framework for the integration of micro and macro organizational behavior. In L. L. Cummings & B. M. Staw (Eds.), *Research in organizational behavior: An annual series of analytical essays and critical reviews* (Vol. 17, pp. 71–114). Greenwich, CT: JAI Press.

Iacobucci, D., & Wasserman, S. (1990). Social networks with two sets of actors. *Psychometrika, 55,* 707–720. http://dx.doi.org/10.1007/BF02294618

James, L. R., Demaree, R. G., & Wolf, G. (1984). Estimating within-group interrater reliability with and without response bias. *Journal of Applied Psychology, 69,* 85–98. http://dx.doi.org/10.1037/0021-9010.69.1.85

King, B. G., Felin, T., & Whetten, D. A. (2010). Perspective—Finding the organization in organizational theory: A meta-theory of the organization as a social actor. *Organization Science, 21,* 290–305. http://dx.doi.org/10.1287/orsc.1090.0443

Klein, K. J., Dansereau, F., & Hall, R. J. (1994). Levels issues in theory development, data collection, and analysis. *Academy of Management Review, 19,* 195–229.

Klein, K. J., & Kozlowski, S. W. (2000). From micro to meso: Critical steps in conceptualizing and conducting multilevel research. *Organizational Research Methods, 3,* 211–236. http://dx.doi.org/10.1177/109442810033001

Kozlowski, S. W., & Klein, K. J. (2000). A multilevel approach to theory and research in organizations: Contextual, temporal, and emergent processes. In K. J. Klein & S. W. Kozlowski (Eds.), *Multilevel theory, research and methods in organizations: Foundations, extensions, and new directions* (pp. 3–90). San Francisco, CA: Jossey-Bass.

Krackhardt, D. (1987). Cognitive social structures. *Social Networks, 9,* 109–134. http://dx.doi.org/10.1016/0378-8733(87)90009-8

Lazega, E., Jourda, M.-T., Mounier, L., & Stofer, R. (2008). Catching up with big fish in the big pond? Multi-level network analysis through linked design. *Social Networks, 30,* 159–176. http://dx.doi.org/10.1016/j.socnet.2008.02.001

Lazega, E., Mounier, L., Jourda, M.-T., & Stofer, R. (2006). Organizational vs. personal social capital in scientists' performance: A multi-level network study of elite French cancer researchers (1996–1998). *Scientometrics, 67,* 27–44. http://dx.doi.org/10.1007/s11192-006-0049-5

Lazer, D., & Friedman, A. (2007). The network structure of exploration and exploitation. *Administrative Science Quarterly, 52,* 667–694. http://dx.doi.org/10.2189/asqu.52.4.667

Liebeskind, J. P., Oliver, A. L., Zucker, L., & Brewer, M. (1996). Social networks, learning, and flexibility: Sourcing scientific knowledge in new biotechnology firms. *Organization Science, 7,* 428–443. http://dx.doi.org/10.1287/orsc.7.4.428

Lomi, A., Robins, G., & Tranmer, M. (2016). Introduction to multilevel social networks. *Social Networks, 44,* 266–268. http://dx.doi.org/10.1016/j.socnet.2015.10.006

Moliterno, T. P., & Mahony, D. M. (2011). Network theory of organization: A multilevel approach. *Journal of Management, 37,* 443–467. http://dx.doi.org/10.1177/0149206310371692

Nerkar, A., & Paruchuri, S. (2005). Evolution of R&D capabilities: The role of knowledge networks within a firm. *Management Science, 51,* 771–785. http://dx.doi.org/10.1287/mnsc.1040.0354

Paruchuri, S. (2010). Intraorganizational networks, interorganizational networks, and the impact of central inventors: A longitudinal study of pharmaceutical firms. *Organization Science, 21,* 63–80. http://dx.doi.org/10.1287/orsc.1080.0414

Paruchuri, S., & Eisenman, M. (2012). Microfoundations of firm R&D capabilities: A study of inventor networks in a merger. *Journal of Management Studies, 49,* 1509–1535. http://dx.doi.org/10.1111/j.1467-6486.2012.01066.x

Payne, G. T., Moore, C. B., Griffis, S. E., & Autry, C. W. (2011). Multilevel challenges and opportunities in social capital research. *Journal of Management, 37,* 491–520. http://dx.doi.org/10.1177/0149206310372413

Phelps, C., Heidl, R., & Wadhwa, A. (2012). Knowledge, networks, and knowledge networks: A review and research agenda. *Journal of Management, 38,* 1115–1166. http://dx.doi.org/10.1177/0149206311432640

Provalis Research. (2018). QDA Miner [Qualitative data analysis software]. Retrieved from https://provalisresearch.com/products/qualitative-data-analysis-software

QSR International. (2018). NVivo [Qualitative data analysis software]. Retrieved from http://www.qsrinternational.com/nvivo/what-is-nvivo

Rothaermel, F. T., & Hess, A. M. (2007). Building dynamic capabilities: Innovation driven by individual-, firm-, and network-level effects. *Organization Science, 18,* 898–921. http://dx.doi.org/10.1287/orsc.1070.0291

Rousseau, D. M. (1985). Issues of level in organizational research: Multi-level and cross-level perspectives. In L. L. Cummings & B. M. Staw (Eds.), *Research in organizational behavior: An annual series of analytical essays and critical reviews* (Vol. 7, pp. 1–37). Greenwich, CT: JAI Press.

Schweinberger, M., Handcock, M. S., & Luna, P. (2018). Package "hergm." Retrieved from https://cran.r-project.org/web/packages/hergm/hergm.pdf

Schweinberger, M., & Luna, P. (2018). hergm: Hierarchical exponential–family random graph models. *Journal of Statistical Software, 85*, 1–39. http://dx.doi.org/10.18637/jss.v085.i01

Singh, J. (2005). Collaborative networks as determinants of knowledge diffusion patterns. *Management Science, 51*, 756–770. http://dx.doi.org/10.1287/mnsc.1040.0349

Snijders, T. A. B. (2011). Statistical models for social networks. *Annual Review of Sociology, 37*, 131–153. http://dx.doi.org/10.1146/annurev.soc.012809.102709

Sorenson, O., & Rogan, M. (2014). (When) do organizations have social capital? *Annual Review of Sociology, 40*, 261–280. http://dx.doi.org/10.1146/annurev-soc-071913-043222

Verbi. (2018). What is MAXQDA? [Qualitative data analysis software]. Retrieved from https://www.maxqda.com/what-is-maxqda

Wang, P., Robins, G., Pattison, P., & Koskinen, J. H. (2014). *MPNet: Program for the simulation and estimation of (p*) exponential random graph models for multilevel networks*. Melbourne, Australia: Melbourne School of Psychological Sciences, The University of Melbourne. Retrieved from https://static1.squarespace.com/static/57a1436215d5dbbcd2031828/t/581ac475e58c62432be83acf/1478149242644/MPNetManual.pdf

Wang, P., Robins, G., Pattison, P., & Lazega, E. (2013). Exponential random graph models for multilevel networks. *Social Networks, 35*, 96–115. http://dx.doi.org/10.1016/j.socnet.2013.01.004

Wang, P., Robins, G., Pattison, P., & Lazega, E. (2016). Social selection models for multilevel networks. *Social Networks, 44*, 346–362. http://dx.doi.org/10.1016/j.socnet.2014.12.003

Wasserman, S., & Faust, K. (1994). *Social network analysis: Methods and applications*. Cambridge, England: Cambridge University Press. http://dx.doi.org/10.1017/CBO9780511815478

Watts, D. J., Dodds, P. S., & Newman, M. E. J. (2002). Identity and search in social networks. *Science, 296*, 1302–1305. http://dx.doi.org/10.1126/science.1070120

Yin, R. K. (2013). *Case study research: Design and methods* (5th ed.). Thousand Oaks, CA: Sage.

Zappa, P., & Lomi, A. (2015). The analysis of multilevel networks in organizations models and empirical tests. *Organizational Research Methods, 18*, 542–569. http://dx.doi.org/10.1177/1094428115579225

Zappa, P., & Lomi, A. (2016). Knowledge sharing in organizations: A multilevel network analysis. In E. Lazega & T. A. B. Snijders (Eds.), *Multilevel network analysis for the social sciences* (pp. 333–353). Cham, Switzerland: Springer. http://dx.doi.org/10.1007/978-3-319-24520-1_14

Zappa, P., & Robins, G. (2016). Organizational learning across multi-level networks. *Social Networks, 44*, 295–306. http://dx.doi.org/10.1016/j.socnet.2015.03.003

Zhao, Z. J., & Anand, J. (2013). Beyond boundary spanners: The "collective bridge" as an efficient interunit structure for transferring collective knowledge. *Strategic Management Journal, 34*, 1513–1530. http://dx.doi.org/10.1002/smj.2080

## PART II

MULTILEVEL MEASUREMENT AND DESIGN

CHAPTER 10

INTRODUCTION TO DATA COLLECTION IN MULTILEVEL RESEARCH

Le Zhou, Yifan Song, Valeria Alterman, Yihao Liu, and Mo Wang

Multilevel research has gained tremendous popularity in organizational psychology in the past 3 decades. In multilevel research, researchers are interested in phenomena that span across two or more levels in a hierarchically nested system (Kozlowski & Klein, 2000). A considerable volume of literature has discussed levels of analysis issues in organizational research. Nevertheless, the majority of this literature has focused on theory development and data analyses, with relatively few articles, chapters, or books specifically devoted to data collection issues in multilevel research. In a notable exception, Klein, Dansereau, and Hall (1994) discussed how assumptions about levels of analysis can influence data collection choices, especially how the level of measurement should be aligned with the level of theory. Klein and Kozlowski (2000) also provided some recommendations for sampling, mostly focusing on the issue of range restriction (i.e., whether there is sufficient variance at the level of analysis of theoretical interest and whether there is sufficient within-unit homogeneity to support aggregating lower level responses to a higher level). Although these existing recommendations are informative, they have not paid sufficient attention to some important issues that researchers should take into consideration while planning and executing data collection in multilevel research, such as sampling strategies and data collection

logistics. Thus, an updated review on planning and conducting data collection in multilevel research is needed, which is the goal of this chapter.

Two types of nested structures are commonly seen in data collected for multilevel research. We differentiate these two types to provide more specific recommendations later, although we do not consider these two types of studies to be mutually exclusive. Specifically, as illustrated in Figure 10.1, one type of multilevel research collects repeated observations from the same individuals or units over time. In this type of research, the higher level (i.e., Level 2) study units are individuals or units, and the lower level (i.e., Level 1) study units are repeated measurements taken on those individuals or units. For example, researchers may be interested in (a) whether two within-person level variables are related (e.g., whether within-person commuting stressor is related to within-person commuting strain; Zhou et al., 2017), (b) whether a within-person relationship between two within-person level variables varies across individuals due to stable, between-person differences (e.g., whether the within-person relationship between commuting stressor and strain varies across individuals with different commuting means efficacy beliefs; Zhou et al., 2017), (c) whether between-person differences predict the pattern of changes in a variable over time (e.g., whether general mental ability predicts

Le Zhou's work on this manuscript was partly supported by research grant 1533151 from the National Science Foundation.
http://dx.doi.org/10.1037/0000115-011
The Handbook of Multilevel Theory, Measurement, and Analysis, S. E. Humphrey and J. M. LeBreton (Editors-in-Chief)

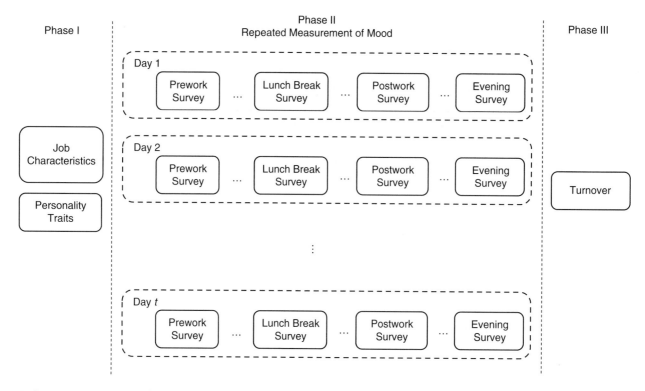

FIGURE 10.1. Events/observations nested within individuals collected over a period of *t* days.

changes in career success indicators; Judge, Klinger, & Simon, 2010); and (d) whether the pattern of changes in a variable is associated with longer term person-level outcomes (e.g., whether the fluctuation of newcomer socialization tactics is related to newcomer socialization outcomes; Song, Liu, Shi, & Wang, 2017). As illustrated in Figure 10.1, to answer these questions, researchers can (a) in Phase I, measure time-invariant factors, such as between-person individual differences (e.g., Judge et al., 2010; Zhou et al., 2017)[1]; (b) in Phase II, repeatedly measure the same variables from the same individuals or units over time; and (c) in Phase III, measure distal outcome variables after the repeated measurements conclude (e.g., socialization outcomes; Song et al., 2017).

Another type of multilevel research collects data from individuals or smaller units nested within

larger units (e.g., dyads nested in teams, multiteam systems nested in organizations, schools nested in countries). Some of these larger units are units within an organization (e.g., work groups/teams, departments, classrooms; see Figure 10.2). For example, researchers may be interested in examining whether an employee's political skill in a work unit is related to his or her relationship with the leader of the unit and whether this relationship varies across organizational units that differ in leader's tendency to endorse political behaviors (Shi, Johnson, Liu, & Wang, 2013). Some studies collect data from individuals or smaller organizational units nested in much larger clusters (e.g., industries, socioeconomic classes, occupations, countries). For example, researchers may be interested in examining whether relationships between variables differ across societies and whether societal cultural values can explain

[1]In this example, it is assumed that the time-invariant factors are theorized as independent variables (i.e., causes) and the repeated measured variables are theorized as dependent variables in causal hypotheses. Therefore, measuring these time-invariant factors in Phase I helps set up temporal precedence of the independent variables to the dependent variables so that when the other causal inference conditions are satisfied (i.e., associations between the variances in predictor and outcome variables, and ruling out alternative explanations; Popper, 1959), causal inference could be drawn later. It should be noted that other temporal relationships among variables can exist (Mitchell & James, 2001). Therefore, we are not suggesting that all multilevel studies with repeated measurements should measure time-invariant factors first. When measurement occurs should be informed by the specific theory to be tested (Mitchell & James, 2001).

Time 1 Data Collection   Time 2 Data Collection   ...   Time *t* Data Collection

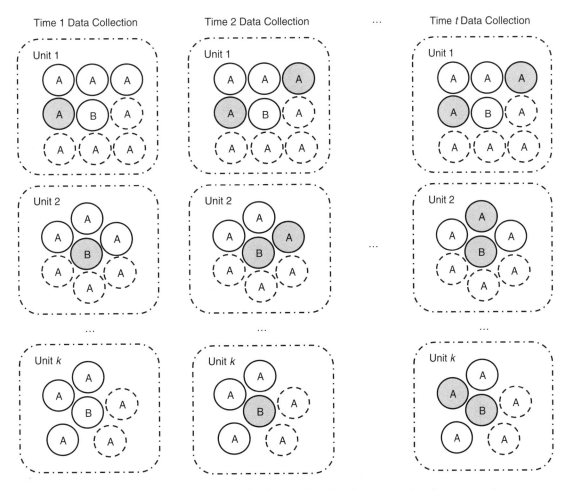

FIGURE 10.2. Collecting data from individuals nested within *k* organizational units at *t* time points. A = individuals who are direct reports to individuals denoted as B; dashed circles = individuals not sampled; shadowed circles = nonresponse; solid circles = individuals sampled.

the between-society differences (van de Vijver & Matsumoto, 2011). In this type of multilevel research, the higher level (i.e., Level 2) study units are the larger units, whereas the lower level (i.e., Level 1) study units are individuals or smaller units nested within the larger units. Sometimes time is not the main focus in this type of multilevel research, and thus there are not any repeated measurements. However, it is possible for a multilevel study to measure the same individuals or units repeatedly over time and to study smaller units nested within larger units. In this case, there are three or more levels of analysis: the repeated measurements (i.e., Level 1), smaller units (i.e., Level 2), and larger units (i.e., Level 3).

In the following sections, we first discuss common issues in multilevel research, including

sample size, sampling strategies, and responses quality. We then discuss issues specific to research with repeated measurements (e.g., data collection tools used in this type of research), research studying smaller units nested in larger units (e.g., informant and referent), and cross-culture research (e.g., data collection logistics). Our recommendations (summarized in Table 10.1) are based on our review of recent developments in the literature. We do not attempt to elaborate on every possible issue in collecting data in multilevel research because some of these issues are covered in detail in other chapters in this handbook or in other resources. For example, readers can refer to Chapter 11 for more details on measurement of multilevel constructs and to Chapter 14 for more technical details of power analysis.

Summary of Recommendations

TABLE 10.1

Data collection concern	Common issues	Repeated measurements	Individuals and units nested within larger units	Cross-cultural
Sample size	• Use power analysis tools for multilevel models • Consider ICC, both Level 2 and Level 1 sample sizes • Conduct different power analyses for different effects (e.g., fixed effects vs. variances) • Assess costs of large Level 1 and/or Level 2 samples	• Longer study period and/or higher frequency of data collection can cause participant fatigue and/or tech failure		• Sample cultures systematically when resources are adequate • Use purposive sampling strategy to sample cultures when resources are limited
Sampling strategy	• Define population, and decide whether both Level 1 and Level 2 sampling designs are needed • Consider different sampling designs, including non-probability sampling (e.g., convenience sampling) and probability sampling (e.g., simple random sampling, stratified random sampling) • Consider use adaptive sampling to study rare events, individuals, or units	• Decide the duration of the entire study based on the phenomenon of interest • Choose a sampling schedule (e.g., interval-, signal-, or event-contingent, or a combination) based on the feature of the phenomenon and research questions • Be aware of the pros and cons of different sampling intervals and frequencies	• Define the Level 2 and Level 1 boundaries clearly when the organizational structure is complex	
Informant and referent			• Consider who should be the informants: individuals or records • Consider what referent to use in the measures: individual ("I am") or unit ("My group") • Choose the informant and the referent based on the nature of constructs	

Data collection tools and logistics	• Choose the data collection tools based on the pros and cons of different tools and research design		• Manage geographically distributed data collection using employee roster and online tools • Follow a comprehensive approach in translating measurement tools • Evaluate the measurement equivalence of surveys with original and translated languages • Measure and/or minimize various cultural differences in response styles: social desirable responding, acquiescent response style, and extreme response style
Response quality	• Consider the mechanism of missing data, and document participants' unit membership change or turnover • Be aware that participants' conceptualization, understanding, and/or sensitivity to events that may change over time	• Keep surveys short to avoid low-quality data but be cautious about using extremely brief scale and examine its psychometric properties before data collection • Provide clear survey instructions regarding the temporal context of the questions • Consider the impact of participants' job attitudes on their likelihood to respond • Incorporate some social interactions with participants but not too many to avoid demand characteristics • Consider the impact of social pressure and social desirability, minimize the impact of shared responding environment, if unwanted, measure social desirability directly, if needed • Consider the sensitivity of the topic of the questionnaire, assure participant confidentiality, embed auxiliary scales, if needed • Be aware of the impact of long survey and social loafing on careless responding, embed bogus items, use post hoc detectors • Use access control and authentication mechanism to reduce unwanted responses	
Examples	• Schneider, Salvaggio, and Subirats (2002) • Chudoba, Wynn, Lu, and Watson-Manheim (2005)	• Bono, Glomb, Shen, Kim, and Koch (2013) • Lanaj, Johnson, and Lee (2016)	• Atwater, Wang, Smither, and Fleenor (2009) • Mueller, Hattrup, Spiess, and Lin-Hi (2012)

Note. The recommendations for columns 3–5 should be taken into consideration along with the recommendations from column 2 (i.e., the common issues). ICC = intraclass correlation.

COMMON ISSUES

Sample Size

As in any other kind of research using statistical tests, multilevel researchers need to know before data collection how large the sample size should be to achieve sufficient statistical power to detect the effects of theoretical interest. Multiple factors together decide the required sample size, including d (effect size of the parameter of theoretical interest), α (probability of Type I error), as well as statistical power (1 − probability of Type II error). Traditional power analysis methods for single-level models are not directly applicable to multilevel models because the lower level observations in multilevel models (e.g., within-person repeated observations) do not satisfy the assumption of independence.

In particular, researchers need to consider several issues specific to multilevel models. First, given that Level 1 observations are nested within Level 2, the intraclass correlation (ICC) must be taken into consideration when estimating statistical power for multilevel models. ICC is the ratio of the Level 2 variances to the total variance, which is a unit-weighted sum of the Level 1 and Level 2 variances. In power analyses, because a priori estimation of variances is difficult, ICC values often are estimated using values reported in previous research (Scherbaum & Ferreter, 2009). Second, researchers need to consider both Level 2 and Level 1 sample sizes (e.g., how many individuals and how many within-person observations per person to sample, how many companies and how many departments within each company to sample). In general, a small Level 2 sample size will result in low statistical power for detecting effects of Level 2 variables on Level 1 outcomes (Mathieu, Aguinis, Culpepper, & Chen, 2012; Scherbaum & Ferreter, 2009). A small Level 2 sample size also can result in low statistical power for detecting the cross-level moderating effect of Level 2 variables on the random slopes between Level 1 variables (Mathieu et al., 2012). A small Level 1 sample size can lead to inadequate power for detecting Level 1 effects (Snijders, 2005). Third, for a given sample, the statistical power of detecting different effects in the same multilevel model, such as fixed effects, variance components, and

cross-level interactions, can vary (Scherbaum & Ferreter, 2009). Therefore, to determine the optimal sample size, researchers may need to conduct multiple computations for different effects in the model.

Based on these considerations, there are some general recommendations for planning Level 1 and/or Level 2 sample sizes. For instance, if the research question focuses on Level 1 relationships, there should be a premium on the average number of Level 1 observations per Level 2 unit. If the research question focuses on Level 2 relationships, there should be a premium on Level 2 sample size (Raudenbush & Liu, 2000). If the research question focuses on cross-level interactions, Mathieu et al. (2012) recommended that the average Level 1 sample size should have "a relative premium of about 3:2 as compared to the Level 2 sample size" (p. 959). In addition, efforts have been made to advance knowledge from general rules of thumb (Kreft & de Leeuw, 1998) to a priori power analysis for multilevel models. Several programs are available for computing statistical power or required sample sizes for multilevel models, including Power IN Two-level designs (PINT; Snijders & Bosker, 1993), Optimal Design (Raudenbush, Spybrook, Liu, & Congdon, 2005), and codes for R (provided by Mathieu et al., 2012).

Researchers also should be aware that although statistical power is improved by increasing sample size at Level 1 and/or Level 2, larger sample size usually comes at some costs. For example, in repeated measurements of the same individuals using experience sampling method (ESM), responding to multiple surveys a day or wearing certain devices can discourage individuals from participating (Dimotakis, Ilies, & Judge, 2013). As a result, to motivate participation in ESM studies, researchers may have to compensate participants. Therefore, financial costs of ESM studies can be high to obtain adequate Level 2 sample size (i.e., to have an adequate number of participants). In addition, in studies using repeated measurements, although a longer study period or more frequent sampling can increase Level 1 sample size, it also may result in participant fatigue and higher risk of technological failure of data collection tools (Dimotakis et al., 2013).

Sampling Strategies

Sampling strategy is closely related to biases in the estimates obtained later in statistical analyses. The basic idea of sampling and estimation is that

> the variable of interest is measured on every unit in the sample without error, so that errors in the estimates occur only because just part of the population is included in the sample. Such errors are referred to as *sampling errors*. (Thompson, 2012, p. 5)

Statistics commonly used in organizational research often are based on the assumption that only sampling errors exist in a data set (e.g., using simple averages as estimates of population means). Nonsampling errors also may occur, which can result in biased estimates, such as when a group of targeted individuals are not included in the actual sample due to unavailability at the time of data collection or for other more deliberate reasons (e.g., refusing to answer part of or a whole questionnaire). Although it is difficult to discover and remove all nonsampling errors, researchers should carefully plan their sampling strategies and choose the appropriate estimation methods accordingly (Thompson, 2012).

More specifically in multilevel research, because units at two different levels are studied, researchers may need to plan for sampling strategies at both the higher level (also called primary study units) and the lower level (also called secondary study units). It is possible that the size of the primary study units (e.g., number of U.S. states) or the secondary study units (e.g., number of members per team) is reasonably small. When the size of the primary study units is small, all of the primary study units can be included, and sampling design only concerns sampling the secondary study units. When the size of the secondary study units is small, sampling design only concerns sampling the primary study units, and then all of the secondary units in each sampled primary unit will be studied. Sometimes it is not possible to study all primary and secondary units. For example, there potentially could be a large number of individuals in a defined population, and there are endless moments within individuals when their affective states can manifest. In this case,

multistage sampling designs need to be implemented. In the first stage, primary study units are sampled. In the second stage, either the same number of secondary study units is sampled from each primary study unit, or a sampling probability proportional to the primary study unit size can be used for each primary study unit (Crano & Brewer, 2014; Thompson, 2012).

Sampling: Level 2 study units. Sampling Level 2 study units in multilevel research is similar to sampling study units in single-level studies. Specifically, researchers first need to define which population they are interested in and then select a suitable sampling strategy. In general, sampling strategies include probability sampling designs and nonprobability sampling designs (Thompson, 2012). In organizational research, nonprobability sampling has been more popular than probability sampling methods because there are fewer logistic constraints when using nonprobability sampling methods (Landers & Behrend, 2015). One of the most popular nonprobability sampling designs in organizational research is *convenience sampling*, in which the sample is drawn from an available and convenient population. For example, researchers may have access to employees of a specific organization, which is considered a convenient population. In the sampling process, researchers simply include employees from this organization who are available and willing to participate to form a sample of convenience (e.g., Bono, Foldes, Vinson, & Muros, 2007; Ilies, Dimotakis, & Watson, 2010; Wang, Liao, Zhan, & Shi, 2011). Despite the popularity of convenience sampling in organizational research, Ployhart and Vandenberg (2010) suggested that "whenever possible, . . . try to avoid convenience samples" (p. 103) because it often is unknown whether assumptions of the estimation methods have been satisfied in the convenience sampling process.

Under probability sampling, researchers can use simple random sampling or stratified random sampling. *Simple random sampling* is a sampling design in which n distinct study units (e.g., individuals) are selected from the N units that are known to exist in the population (e.g., all workers in the service industry). The sample is composed in a way that each study unit has an equal probability of being selected from the population (Thompson, 2012). Simple random sampling design also assures that each possible sample of *n* units have the same probability of being selected from the population as any other samples of size *n*. Stratified sampling can be used when researchers want to ensure the sample spans across the full spectrum of the population. In *stratified random sampling*, researchers first partition the population (e.g., all universities in the United States) based on certain criteria (e.g., geographical location, ranking, number of faculty members) before conducting simple random sampling within each stratum. It is assumed that units within the same stratum are homogenous (Thompson, 2012). Sample size of each stratum is proportional to the size of the stratum out of the whole population. Thus, summing the sample sizes of all strata together should equal the desired total sample size. In the case that some strata are too small, the number of units per stratum to be chosen can be disproportional to its relative size, and the estimation procedure needs to take the unequal probabilities across strata into consideration (Boehnke, Lietz, Schreier, & Wilhelm, 2011).

Sampling: Level 1 study units.   Sometimes researchers choose to study all secondary units (e.g., all team members; Zhang & Peterson, 2011) in each sampled primary unit. In this case, only one step of sampling is needed (i.e., sampling the primary units). This approach usually is preferred for small groups and teams research because having data collected from the entire team can ensure better measurement quality, especially when the team-level measures have to be aggregated from individual-level responses (see an example in Koopmann, Lanaj, Wang, Zhou, & Shi, 2016; see further discussions about aggregation in Chan, 1998; LeBreton & Senter, 2008). Sometimes it is not possible to study all secondary units when the primary units have a large number of lower level units (e.g., the primary units as large-size corporations containing hundreds of employees), which requires researchers to plan Level 1 sampling strategy.

Ideally, researchers should consider using probability sampling strategies (simple or stratified

random sampling) to sample Level 1 study units or justify why nonprobability sampling strategies are appropriate. However, in organizational psychology research, the common practice is to use convenience sampling without much consideration of the implications of sampling design on estimation results. When convenience sampling is used, researchers sample Level 1 study units (e.g., within-person experiences, individuals, or organizational units) that are easier to access during data collection (e.g., Atwater, Wang, Smither, & Fleenor, 2009; G. Chen, Kirkman, Kim, Farh, & Tangirala, 2010; X. P. Chen, Liu, & Portnoy, 2012; Mueller, Hattrup, Spiess, & Lin-Hi, 2012). Although this practice is sometimes questioned, some researchers have argued that when the purpose of a study is to test the efficacy of a theory instead of to generalize an estimate to the population, using convenience sampling at the lower level can still generate meaningful findings under certain conditions (e.g., Boehnke et al., 2011). For example, in cross-culture comparative research, Boehnke et al. (2011) argued that when researchers can show individuals conveniently sampled from each culture (i.e., the lower level samples from each higher level unit) are "comparable across cultures and typical of the culture from which they originate" (p. 124), the lower level convenience samples still can offer meaningful information about cross-culture differences.

Sampling: Adaptive strategies.   Multilevel research also may target individuals or units that have relatively low representations in the general populations (e.g., patients with certain types of rare diseases, start-ups that specialize in certain products). Some multilevel studies examine changes in individuals or units before and after rare events (e.g., major life events, organizational changes, new government policies). In such situations, adaptive sampling strategies can be used. *Adaptive sampling* refers to sampling designs in which the procedures for selecting the study units depend on the obtained values on the variable of interest, which often is used to increase the effectiveness of sampling effort in research involving rare cases or situations (Thompson, 2012). Given that researchers cannot always know accurately when and where the rare cases occur in advance, an adaptive sampling procedure can help researchers adjust the scope of study units sampled. For instance, assume a researcher is interested in employees' work–life balance before and after voluntary turnover. Because the researcher is unable to know which employees will voluntarily leave their jobs before data collection starts, the researcher can begin the study by sampling employees across the whole organization and follow them repeatedly for some time. If, after a short period of data collection and a preliminary inspection of the data, the researcher learns that among all the sampled employees those from the sales department have a higher rate of voluntary turnover, the researcher may start to oversample employees from the sales department. By adapting the sampling design, the researcher is able to increase the likelihood that the final sample will include a sufficient number of "rare case" participants (e.g., those participants who elect to voluntarily leave the organization). Failing to adopt an adaptive sampling strategy, this study can be underpowered due to the low base rate of the phenomenon of interest. When using adaptive sampling, researchers should choose the appropriate estimator in statistical analyses to account for unknown or unequal probabilities of being sampled. For example, when adaptive cluster sampling design is used, modified versions—instead of the original versions of Hansen–Hurwitz estimator and Horvitz–Thompson estimator—should be used. This is because the original versions of these two estimators require knowing the inclusion probabilities of each study unit in the final sample, which is not satisfied in adaptive cluster sampling design (Thompson, 2012).

Response Quality

Survey length. Because longer surveys require more effort and attention from participants, even highly motivated participants may feel exhausted or impatient and thus provide low-quality responses when the survey is overly long (Meade & Craig, 2012) given that participants' attention tend to wane over the course of long surveys (Baer, Ballenger, Berry, & Wetter, 1997). Therefore, researchers ought to try to keep the surveys short to increase response

quality, especially for studies that ask the same questions repeatedly over time (Dimotakis et al., 2013). Nevertheless, using single-item or very brief scales to keep surveys short also may raise concerns because very brief scales may not sufficiently cover the construct space. In terms of how many items are adequate for surveys used in multilevel research, there are no conclusive recommendations so far. Although some researchers have argued that a well-chosen, single item should be sufficient as long as evidence on its face and content validity can be provided (e.g., Fisher & To, 2012), other researchers have suggested that a minimum of three items should be used for measuring each construct (e.g., Shrout & Lane, 2011). Our recommendation is that researchers need to review existing studies using the same brief scale or conduct pilot studies to determine whether there is sufficient evidence about the psychometric properties of the brief scale (e.g., see Riza, Ganzach, & Liu, 2016, for justifications of using a single-item scale of job satisfaction; see van Hooff, Geurts, Kompier, & Taris, 2007, for justifications of using a single-item scale of fatigue).

Survey instructions. Survey instructions also can impact response quality. For instance, it has been documented that retrospective responses usually suffer from biases (e.g., Stone, Broderick, Shiffman, & Schwartz, 2004; Stone et al., 1998). Retrospective responses may reveal less about what has happened but capture more of the typical reactions of the individual based on individuals' personality or their general knowledge (Robinson & Clore, 2002). Particularly in multilevel research with repeated measurements, to obtain high-quality responses and minimize retrospective bias, researchers should provide participants with clear instructions regarding the time window assessed. For example, because affective states often fluctuate from day to day or even within a day, researchers should clearly instruct participants to rate their affective states "right now" if the purpose is to capture momentary affective states.

Participants' motivation to respond. According to Rogelberg, Luong, Sederburg, and Cristol (2000), individuals who do not complete surveys, denoted *noncompliants*, tend to have higher turnover intentions, less organizational commitment, and less job satisfaction compared with those employees who do comply with the survey requests. In addition, individuals who are skeptical or hold negative attitudes concerning how their responses will be used by the organization also are less likely to comply (Rogelberg et al., 2000). Therefore, researchers need to be aware of, and consider the potential influence from, individuals' job attitudes on their likelihood to comply. Researchers can take some proactive actions to motivate participants' compliance, such as assuring the confidentiality of their responses and explaining organizations' commitment to making improvements based on research results. Providing monetary incentives may help receive more responses in certain survey settings (Musch & Reips, 2000). In addition to taking proactive measures, after data collection ends, if researchers detect systematic differences between the respondents and noncompliants (e.g., differences in job attitudes; Rogelberg et al., 2000) or differences across Level 2 units in the ratio of respondents to noncompliants, statistical procedures can be taken to account for these systematic differences (e.g., Hirschfeld, Cole, Bernerth, & Rizzuto, 2013).

Social interaction between researchers and participants.   According to Dillman, Smyth, and Christian (2009), social interaction between the researcher and the participants can promote the response quality because participants tend to follow the prosocial social norm to cooperate with the researcher and follow the survey instructions when they interact with researchers in person. When using online surveys or mobile devices to collect data, the level of social contact between the researcher and the participants is lower compared with handing out paper-and-pencil surveys in person and thus may result in participants' decreased personal accountability for the response quality. Therefore, to increase the response quality, researchers can design data collection in a way that involves some social interactions with participants, even when using online surveys or mobile devices. For example, researchers can introduce the plan of the study to the participants in person at the beginning of the research (e.g., Lanaj,

Johnson, & Lee, 2016). However, when participants interact too well with the researcher and are aware of what the researcher is trying to investigate, they may provide distorted responses and thus lower response quality (i.e., demand characteristics; McCambridge, de Bruin, & Witton, 2012).

Social pressure and social desirability.   The shared data collection environment (e.g., employees responding to surveys in a conference room; patients responding to surveys in a doctor's waiting room) can introduce unwanted biases to responses because as participants may feel peer pressure to respond in a certain manner if other respondents are around them (Shadish, Cook, & Campbell, 2002). Some data collection practices can minimize such potential biases due to shared social environment. For example, instead of sampling from one organization, researchers can survey individuals or work units from similar branches or organizations that are in different locations. As such, social pressure due to sharing the same work space may be alleviated.

Respondents also may be motivated to respond in a biased manner because they believe their employers expect them to behave in a certain way. Individuals even may feel that the only way to avoid ruining their reputation in the company is to not participate at all. Highlighting the importance of research to respondents may dissuade them from not responding and encourage them to answer questions truly (Rogelberg et al., 2000). For example, researchers may tell individuals that honest responses will help contribute to both improving scientific knowledge and understanding what is going on in their work settings. However, when respondents exercise social desirability, it does not always result in unusable responses and sometimes may inform the theory at hand (Zerbe & Paulhus, 1987). A more systematic way of knowing the respondents' motivation in answering surveys is to include special items or scales in surveys to help screen for biased responses (e.g., biases from social desirability, Paulhus, 2002). This approach requires researchers to have expected the need for including such scales in their surveys.

Topic of the questionnaire.   Another issue that can result in nonresponses is the survey content.

A questionnaire that mostly asks respondents to report sensitive information (e.g., affection toward coworkers, supervisors' abusive behaviors, company's unethical conduct) and lacks confidentiality can demotivate employees to respond. This is especially true in smaller work groups because aggregated results from such surveys still can be easily traced back to the individual employees surveyed. Refraining from collecting identifiers can ensure protection of confidentiality when the topic of the questionnaire is sensitive. When collecting repeated measurements or ratings about the same individuals from different sources, researchers can assign unique codes to participants to signal confidentiality and explain to them that the code-identifier matching document is stored in a safe physical space or in a password-protected computer (Crano & Brewer, 2014). Another measure to take when planning surveys of sensitive topic is to embed auxiliary scales, such as social desirability and justice sensitivity scales, in the survey. Assuming that participants who do not respond to certain questions at least respond to these auxiliary scales, researchers can compare characteristics of the respondents and noncompliants. Anonymity is not without any concern. Respondents may feel less accountable for their responses when anonymity is assured, which may result in careless responses (Meade & Craig, 2012).

Careless responses. Careless responding may increase as the survey length increases or the repeated measurement continues. For instance, participants may select the same option for consecutive items or respond in a random fashion, both of which will impact data quality. Meade and Craig (2012) recommended including bogus items to identify potential careless responses and screen poor quality data. If no a priori actions were taken, other indices can be examined after data collection, such as response time, outlier analysis, consistency indices, and response patterns (e.g., Meade & Craig, 2012). When more than one individuals from the same unit is invited to fill out surveys simultaneously, careless responses also may occur due to *social loafing* (i.e., the tendency for individuals to make fewer efforts when working collectively than when working individually; Karau & Williams, 1993). To reduce the impact from social loafing, researchers can emphasize to participants that each of their individual responses will have an impact on the findings and that their responses cannot be replaced by their coworkers' responses.

Unwanted responses. Sometimes the data can be contaminated by unwanted responses from participants not in the defined population, especially in studies using online surveys that allow survey links to be forwarded to other individuals not targeted in the sampling process (Stanton & Rogelberg, 2001). Access control (i.e., controlling who has access to the surveys) and authentication (i.e., verification of the identity of the actual respondents) can decrease unwanted responses. For instance, use of the organization's intranet can help preclude responses from individuals outside the organization (Gilmore, Kormann, & Rubin, 1999). Researchers also can use respondent identifiers or passwords (Schmidt, 2000). In addition, researchers also may receive unwanted duplicate responses from the same participants either by accident or on purpose. To avoid these unwanted responses, researchers can emphasize the need for one and only one response from each respondent at each measurement time point in the instructions and implement mechanisms to eliminate repeated access to the surveys from the same respondents within the same time period (e.g., inspecting Internet protocol [IP] addresses; Stanton & Rogelberg, 2001).

Researchers who follow all the aforementioned recommendations may still face missing responses in the data. The missing pattern can be more complicated in multilevel studies than single-level studies. For example, as illustrated in Figure 10.2, the responses of targeted individuals in the sample may be missing for all the study surveys (e.g., person B in Unit 2 in Figure 10.2) or may be missing for only some of the surveys (e.g., person B in Unit *k* in Figure 10.2). Therefore, in addition to the previously mentioned data collection stage considerations, researchers still may need to handle missing data at the analysis stage (see the discussion on missing data analyses in Newman, 2014; Reips, Buchanan, Krantz, & McGrawn, 2011; Schafer & Graham, 2002).

ISSUES IN MULTILEVEL RESEARCH WITH REPEATED MEASUREMENTS

Multilevel research with repeated measurements ranges from studies that measure participants' affective states once every 200 milliseconds (e.g., Gabriel & Diefendorff, 2015) to longitudinal panel studies that survey newcomers once every 2 weeks (e.g., Kammeyer-Mueller, Wanberg, Rubenstein, & Song, 2013). When there is a relatively short time interval between measurements (e.g., a few hours or a day), the most popular method used to collect data is ESM (Beal, 2011, 2015), which also is known as ecological momentary assessment (Beal & Weiss, 2003), everyday experience methods (Reis & Gable, 2000), and daily diary methods (Bolger, Davis, & Rafaeli, 2003). In this section, we discuss data collection issues in multilevel research using ESM design and other panel designs.

Schedule of Sampling Level 1 Study Units

In multilevel research with repeated measurements from the same individuals or units, it often is not possible to include all lower level units (e.g., affective states and team processes at every point of time) because these states or processes are continuous. Thus, researchers need to decide how to sample the Level 1 study units after deciding which Level 2 study units to sample. First, researchers need to decide the duration (i.e., starting and ending points) of the entire study. For some phenomenon, this decision can be based on existing research. For example, newcomer research showed that the first 90 to 100 days is the key to newcomer adjustment (Kammeyer-Mueller et al., 2013). Thus, newcomer studies can start from when the newcomers enter the organization and end at about 90 days after newcomers' entry. If there is no prior research to guide this decision, researchers need to carefully study the phenomenon before data collection starts. In addition to considering the duration of the entire study, researchers also need to consider how to

design the schedule of the repeated measurements. There are four recommended ways to design the repeated measurement schedule: interval-, signal-, or event-contingent reporting, and combinations of these schedules (Bolger et al., 2003; Shiffman, 2014).

Interval-contingent reporting requires participants to report at predetermined fixed intervals. For example, in ESM studies, participants' responses may be due at 9:00 a.m., 12:00 p.m., and 3:00 p.m. of each day during the study. In newcomer research, participants' responses may be due every other Friday. Given that the times for reporting are specified, it can be conducted without repeated signaling to participants. Nevertheless, according to Fisher and To (2012), participants' compliance can be improved if signals (e.g., e-mails or text messages) are used as reminders in the interval-contingent reporting schedule. When using interval-contingent reporting, researchers need to consider the pros and cons of different lengths of intervals. Longer intervals can reduce interruptions to participants' ongoing life or work activities (Bolger et al., 2003). However, it may obscure natural cycles or rhythms of events, or result in retrospective memory bias in responses (e.g., Redelmeier & Kahneman, 1996). Shorter intervals may be able to capture a complete and detailed picture of participants' experience throughout the study period (Dimotakis et al., 2013). It may, however, result in survey fatigue and high signal-to-noise ratio in responses (Bolger et al., 2003). Therefore, researchers should carefully select the intervals of reporting based on the research phenomenon. Specifically, as recommended in the literature (Bolger et al., 2003; Dimotakis et al., 2013; Ployhart & Vandenberg, 2010), three important questions need to be considered: (a) What time lag is acceptable between the actual experience and the measurement? (b) What time frame is optimal to capture the dynamic processes that are of interest? and (c) What are the sample and context constraints (e.g., any objective limits on time and frequency of measurement)?[2]

---

[2]The current chapter does not discuss how to collect data to test other more sophisticated theories about time (e.g., endogenous change, inertia, and equilibrium in variables, delayed effects, cyclical relationships between variables). This is mainly because there have not been many more precise theories that explicate time-related elements in the organizational psychology field. Interested readers can refer to Mitchell and James (2001), as well as Chapter 4 of this book, to see how to theorize time. As a first step toward testing process-oriented theories, some researchers have recently recommended the collection of intensive longitudinal data (see Kozlowski, Chao, Grand, Braun, & Kuljanin, 2013; Wang, Zhou, & Zhang, 2016).

Signal-contingent reporting uses signaling devices to provide fixed or random signals to prompt participants to respond (e.g., signals from mobile phones and tablets). This approach can capture participants' immediate experiences with minimal retrospective memory bias if participants respond shortly after the signal reminder. It also can be used to collect representative samples of the individuals' experiences when the signals are provided randomly (Fisher & To, 2012). However, one potential limitation of the random signal approach is that the measures may become intrusive and burdensome (Bolger et al., 2003).

Event-contingent reporting requires participants to respond when specific events occur (Wheeler & Reis, 1991). Because the responses largely depend on the occurrence of the events, researchers should provide participants with a clear definition of the onset of the events (Sadikaj, Moskowitz, & Zuroff, 2011). Otherwise, participants may not reliably identify events of interest to the researchers and thus provide inaccurate responses. For example, when studying alcohol abuse, researchers need to provide accurate information on how much alcohol consumption should be considered as an alcohol abuse event to ensure each participant has the same criterion to initiate reporting. But event-contingent reporting does not necessarily need to be initiated by participants themselves. Researchers can develop programs that are able to automatically detect the event (e.g., smoking; Ali et al., 2012) and signal participants to start reporting when the event is detected. Researchers also can combine two or more of the abovementioned sampling schedules. For example, event-contingent reporting and interval-contingent reporting can be combined to compare responses following a specific event with responses without the specific events (e.g., Mohr et al., 2001).

Data Collection Tools

A variety of data collection tools have been used in multilevel research with repeated measurements. We discuss both the conventional methods (i.e., paper-and-pencil surveys and phone interviews) and newer methods (i.e., online surveys, mobile devices or applications, ambulatory measures, wearable sensors, and physiological markers).

Conventional methods. When using paper-and-pencil surveys, participants usually receive a packet containing surveys for each measurement time point along with instructions on when and how to respond to the surveys (e.g., Wang et al., 2013). One disadvantage of a paper-and-pencil survey is that it is difficult for researchers to know whether there was timely compliance among participants (Fisher & To, 2012). Research shows that late responding can be common in studies using paper-and-pencil surveys (Stone & Broderick, 2009). Alternatively, researchers may opt to use telephone interviews to collect data across multiple time points based on the Level 1 sampling schedule for their research questions. However, telephone interviews have been criticized for being too time-consuming and requiring participants' access to phones (Eatough, Shockley, & Yu, 2016).

Online surveys. Online surveys have become a popular method to collect repeated observations from the same individuals or units over time. Data collection via online surveys typically is accomplished by sending reminder e-mails to participants that include links to the online survey (e.g., Lanaj et al., 2016). One advantage of this approach is that the data can be time stamped such that researchers are able to monitor participants' patterns of compliance with data collection protocols (Eatough et al., 2016). In addition, some online survey platforms (e.g., Qualtrics, https://www.qualtrics.com; SurveyMonkey, https://www.surveymonkey.com; PsychData, https://www.psychdata.com/default.asp) also allow researchers to construct more sophisticated surveys. For example, researchers might make the display of future questions (e.g., What is your current Undergraduate Grade Point Average) contingent on responses to previous questions (e.g., Are you currently enrolled in 2-year or 4-year College/University?). Researchers also can use online survey platforms to present questions (or blocks of questions) in a randomized manner or present some form of visual stimulus (e.g., images; videos) before collecting the criteria of interest (e.g., response times to the stimulus; accuracy in discriminating characteristics of the stimulus), which are particularly beneficial in multilevel research, including experimental or quasi-experimental design elements. However, online surveys require participants to have reliable access to the Internet, and potential differences in participants' Internet speeds may create differences in their survey experiences (Kulikowski & Potasz-Kulikowska, 2016). Another concern is that organizations (or rather, some leaders/managers) may not be supportive of employees visiting survey websites during their time at work (Eatough et al., 2016). In addition, when online surveys are sent to participants' cell phones, participants may fail to respond to some signals and miss the survey window if the signals are not easy to notice (e.g., when the smartphone is in vibrate setting). Online surveys also may result in limited clarity and control regarding how and who actually responded to the surveys (e.g., two or more participants appearing as one; Nosek, Banaji, & Greenwald, 2002). Researchers should build in survey access control and response verification mechanisms to minimize influence from unwanted responses (see our discussion in the section Unwanted Responses).

Mobile devices or applications. Mobile devices, such as programmable personal digital assistants (e.g., Purdue Momentary Assessment Tool; Weiss, Beal, Lucy, & MacDermid, 2004) and smartphones with preprogrammed applications (Expimetrics, https://app.expimetrics.com), also are used in repeated measurements. Mobile devices allow studies to provide response signals, present survey items, and record responses all through the same device (Le, Choi, & Beal, 2006). Similar to online surveys, one advantage of this approach is that it enables the recording of the time stamps of the actual responses, which can help researchers to monitor and verify the extent to which participants were complying with study protocols (e.g., Song, Foo, & Uy, 2008). The diverse functions of mobile devices also enable researchers to collect various forms of real-time data from the participants, including images and voices. In addition, tools (e.g., SurveySignal, http://www.surveysignal.com, and SurveyPocket, http://www.surveypocket.com) have been designed to initiate the survey automati-

cally and transmit the responses wirelessly to the researchers' secure computer server after an initial setup procedure (Beal, 2015), which makes it possible to collect a large number of observations. However, similar to online surveys, some of these devices or applications also require participants to have reliable access to the Internet.

Ambulatory measures, wearable sensors, and physiological markers. *Ambulatory measures* refer to measures that are adapted for collecting data from participants while they are walking or moving in their natural environment (e.g., home, commute, workplace); such assessment systems have become popular recently in multilevel research with repeated measurements (Eatough et al., 2016). There are several physiological indices that can be recorded by ambulatory measures used in organizational studies. For example, blood pressure has been used to reflect individuals' reaction to stressors (e.g., McEwen, 1998) and negative events (e.g., Bono, Glomb, Shen, Kim, & Koch, 2013). Heart rate also is used because it is associated with poor self-regulatory strength and emotional regulation capacity (Appelhans & Luecken, 2006). Wearable ambulatory monitors that can be used to measure blood pressure and heart rate include arm-cuff and wristwatch-style digital monitors of blood pressure (see Eatough et al., 2016, for a detailed summary). In addition to blood pressure and heart rate, ESM studies also have used ambulatory methods to measure sleep quality/quantity (e.g., Berkman, Buxton, Ertel, & Okechukwu, 2010; Pereira & Elfering, 2014). Wristwatchlike devices that monitor sleep are available, as well (Ancoli-Israel et al., 2003). Multilevel research also has used neuroendocrine markers (e.g., cortisol). The measurement of these markers usually is conducted through saliva or urine sampling. Consequently, this method usually has many requirements for participants to follow to allow the biological sample collection process (Kivlighan et al., 2004), which may cause huge burdens for participants and result in low compliance.

Despite that using the abovementioned measures can allow the inclusion of objective data in the studies, these measures also have drawbacks. For example, participants have to wear certain devices during the entire duration of the assessment windows, which may increase their inconvenience and decrease their willingness to participate. In addition, the inspection, filtering, analysis, and interpretation of data from these measures can be complex, especially when the data are continuous rather than discrete (e.g., blood pressure; Ilies et al., 2010; interested readers can refer to Wang et al., 2016, for more discussion on analyzing dynamic data). Furthermore, the cost of the relevant devices also can be a concern for some researchers.

Response Quality

Turnover. When collecting repeated observations from individuals working in the same organization, researchers may need to pay particular attention to the mechanism of missing data in the data collection process. For example, participants may switch to a different work unit within the organization halfway through the study. These different work units may have different work contexts (e.g., different work climates). In this case, observed changes in the participants could be attributed to time and/or different work contexts. We suggest researchers document this change in organizational unit membership in the data collection stage and carefully handle these cases in the data analyses stage. For example, some participants may leave the organization between two measurement points. Turnover research has suggested that there are systematic differences across employees who stay, who voluntarily leave, or involuntarily leave (e.g., differences in job satisfaction; Hom, Lee, Shaw, & Hausknecht, 2017). Therefore, it is important for researchers to collect information about turnover and examine whether the results are different when individuals who left the organizations are included versus excluded in the analyses. Furthermore, when repeated measurements are collected from organizational units, researchers also can examine turnover rates at the unit level because they may signal some important between-unit differences in a particular organization. For example, if a group of employees has a significantly different turnover rate than another

group, it may point to some structural issues that differ between these organizational units included in the same sample (e.g., differences in management and leadership quality; Hausknecht & Trevor, 2011).

Changes in subjective interpretation of the scale. Some concerns have been raised about whether participants would adapt their interpretation of the scale or response strategies simply due to being exposed to the same questions repeatedly. Participants receiving repeated assessment may have a different understanding of the surveyed events over time. For example, participants may have an enhanced understanding of the surveyed events or become more sensitive to the targeted events. Using justice as an example, if participants have not formed justice evaluations before the study, they may construct their responses to justice-related questions on the spot each time they are surveyed and gradually develop their justice evaluation systems (Barsky, Kaplan, & Beal, 2011). As such, it is not clear whether participants' responses reflect the same constructs as defined by the researchers. However, Thomas and Diener (1990) found that participants' accuracy in recalling moods did not change after reporting their mood four times a day for 3 weeks, which suggested that participants' sensitivity to certain psychological states (e.g., mood) can remain the same at least throughout the study. It also is possible that the repeated assessments may change participants' conceptualization of the domain of interest. For example, a study focusing on intimacy may repeatedly measure certain types of intimacy indicators; as a result, the participants may become increasingly conscious of these indicators while less sensitized to other types of intimacy (Bolger et al., 2003). However, no research has provided solid evidence to support this concern. To summarize, there are potential concerns regarding participants' attrition, resistance, and habituation due to repeated assessment by the same questions. However, to date, research focused on elucidating these concerns is sorely lacking from the extant literature. Thus, future research is needed to better understand the strengths and weaknesses associated with the use of repeated measures designs.

ISSUES IN STUDYING SMALLER ORGANIZATIONAL UNITS NESTED IN LARGER UNITS

Sampling Strategies

In research involving organizational units nested within each other, before deciding the sampling plans, researchers should pay attention to whether individuals or smaller units are working exclusively for only one larger work unit (as illustrated in the example in Figure 10.2). It is possible that individuals or smaller units operate in more than one department, report to multiple supervisors in charge of different projects, or rotate among several teams in different locations (e.g., Chudoba, Wynn, Lu, & Watson-Manheim, 2005).

For example, a researcher may have access to employees working in a large organization with a matrix structure (e.g., functional areas fully crossed with product divisions), where each smallest group is supervised by both a functional area manager and a product division manager. When these complicated structures and reporting relationships exist, researchers need to clearly define the boundaries of Level 2 and Level 1 study units and clarify the sampling strategies accordingly. For example, if the researcher is interested in comparing groups across different divisions, the researcher can focus either on a particular functional area or study all functional areas. When only one functional area is included in the research, groups are nested under different divisions (and division managers). When more than one functional area is included, groups are not only nested under divisions, which is the grouping variable of theoretical interest, but also nested under functional areas. In this case, if there are systematic differences across the functional areas (i.e., a grouping variable not of theoretical interest), such as differences in sampling strategies (random sampling vs. snowball sampling) and/or response rates, these differences should be taken into consideration in the data analyses stage.

Sometimes the organizational structure is highly organic and project based such that the same employees may have multiple team memberships and not all employees are fully crossed with all team memberships. In this situation, even when all team members and team leaders are sampled and participated in the study, raters (e.g., team leaders) and ratees (e.g., team members) still may not be fully crossed or nested (called ill-structured measurement designs in Putka, Le, McCloy, & Diaz, 2008). When analyzing interrater reliability, conventional interrater reliability estimators (e.g., ICC) can be biased if applied to ill-structured measurement designs, and alternative estimators should be used (see Putka et al., 2008).

Informant and Referent

When planning research that involves study units at different organizational levels (e.g., individuals and teams), researchers also need to consider who should be the informants that provide the data (e.g., human resources [HR] managers, team leaders, or HR records) and what referent (e.g., "I am" or "my group") to use in the measures. We recommend researchers make decisions about informants and referents based on the conceptualization of the specific construct. There are three broad categories of constructs in multilevel studies examining lower level units nested in larger units: (a) individual-level constructs, (b) constructs that originate from and manifest at the unit level, and (c) constructs that originate from the individual level but manifest as unit-level properties (Chan, 1998; Kozlowski & Klein, 2000).

First, to measure an individual-level construct, the referent should be the individual. Informants who respond to measures of individual-level constructs can be individuals, managers, or existing records. When the constructs to be measured can be observed by managers and when managers' ratings are aligned with the conceptualization (e.g., *individual task performance*, defined as individuals' behaviors that fulfill in-role job responsibilities), researchers can use managers as the informants. The number of managers often is smaller than the number of individuals included as Level 1 study units. As such, researchers need to take into consideration the nested structure of the ratings (i.e., ratings from the same managers are nested within the managers) in data analyses. However, when the constructs describe internal perceptions and psychological states of individuals (e.g., perceived aggression toward an individual, psychological climate), individuals themselves should be the informants. The number of informants then is the same as the number of individual-level study unit to be sampled. When the individual-level constructs are observable demographic characteristics (e.g., organizational tenure) or objective records (e.g., salary), data also can be obtained from companies' HR records.

Second, when measuring constructs that originate from and manifest at the unit level (i.e., *global unit properties*; Kozlowski & Klein, 2000), the informants are sources that have subject matter knowledge about the unit and the referent is the unit. The number of informants can be one or more, depending on how many informants are needed to provide sufficient coverage of the subject matter. For example, to measure the size of a team as indicated by the number of team members, the informants can be the company's records that document the organizational structure or the manager who oversees the team. One informant probably is sufficient to provide the accurate values of the team sizes. To measure the strategy of a firm, the informants can be the top executives, given that the top management team as a collective designs and oversees the strategy of the firm.

Third, different informants and referents are used to measure unit-level constructs that originate from the individual level, depending on the composition or compilation models (Chan, 1998; Kozlowski & Klein, 2000). Specifically, when a unit-level construct is conceptualized by the *additive model* to indicate the average or sum of individual unit members' properties, the referent is the individual unit member and the informants can be the unit members, unit managers, or existing records. For example, in teams that have an additive task structure, task performance of individual team members as reported by themselves, observed by their managers, or recorded by the production system can be used to measure team performance. Averages or totals of the individual team members' performance are indicators of team performance (Steiner, 1972). When a unit-level construct is conceptualized by

the *direct consensus model* (i.e., a shared unit property; Kozlowski & Klein, 2000), the referent is the individual and the informants should be the individuals. A core component of direct consensus model is the consensus among members of a given unit. Therefore, using unit managers or existing records as informants would not allow researchers to assess consensus among the members. When a unit-level construct is conceptualized by the *referent-shift model*, which also is a shared unit property, the referent should be the unit (e.g., "this group," "all members of this group") and the informants should be the individual members of the unit to assess consensus among unit members. When a unit-level construct is conceptualized by the *dispersion model* (i.e., a type of configural unit property; Kozlowski & Klein, 2000), the referent can be either the individual or the unit, whereas the informants can be individual unit members, unit managers, or existing records. When differences among unit members in their individual attributes are of interest, the referent can be the individual (e.g., variety in individual knowledge domain, separation in individual's preference, disparity in individual income; see further discussion in Harrison & Klein, 2007). Information about these individual attributes can be provided by the individuals (e.g., personal values and beliefs), their managers (if the attributes are observable, e.g., gender), or the existing records (e.g., organizational tenure). When differences among unit members in how they see the unit are of interest, the referent can be the unit and the informants are the individuals (e.g., a measure of climate strength; Schneider, Salvaggio, & Subirats, 2002). When the *process model* is used to conceptualize a configural unit property, the informants and the referents depend on the specific process studied (see Kozlowski & Klein, 2000; see Kozlowski et al., 2013, for discussions on how to theorize and test process-oriented models). In terms of the number of informants, when the individuals are used as the informants, a *higher coverage rate* (i.e., number of informants who provide responses divided by the total number of individuals actually in a unit) allows more accurate measures of the unit-level construct (assuming there is no other bias except sampling bias).

ISSUES IN STUDYING INDIVIDUALS FROM DIFFERENT CULTURES

In this section, we use cross-cultural research to illustrate the issues involved in collecting multilevel data from much larger clusters that span across different countries or cultural regions (e.g., X. P. Chen et al., 2012). We do not consider this type of research to be a unique category conceptually distinctive from other multilevel studies involving individuals or units nested in larger units. We highlight these issues in this section based on the consideration that cultural differences and geographical distance may require special attention to logistics issues.

Sampling Strategies

In organization studies, one of the most extensive efforts on cross-cultural research so far is the GLOBE project led by House and colleagues (House, Hanges, Javidan, Dorfman, & Gupta, 2004), which surveyed managers from more than 900 organizations in 62 nations. Despite that the GLOBE project is an excellent example for cross-cultural research, a considerable number of existing studies have taken a convenience sampling approach (Boehnke et al., 2011) in which they simply compared a limited number of countries (e.g., two countries) with a multigroup design (e.g., Schaubroeck, Lam, & Xie, 2000; Shao & Skarlicki, 2014). This is not a limitation when the purpose of the research is to compare those specific countries. However, when generalizability is of interest and the focal variable at the culture level is continuous in nature, cross-cultural studies that adopt a multilevel design that systematically sample cultures would be more ideal than a multigroup design (e.g., Atwater et al., 2009; G. Chen et al., 2010; Mueller et al., 2012).

However, resources often are limited and do not allow researchers to access and sample randomly from all countries or cultures. Therefore, researchers need to use a purposive sampling strategy when selecting Level 2 study units to maximize statistical power (Boehnke et al., 2011). In this case, sampling can be guided by considering the *cultural zone* (i.e., a region of countries that share similar cultural values and belief systems; Inglehart & Welzel, 2005).

Samples that cover various cultural zones can capture more differences (thus, larger variances at Level 2) in the culture-related variables of interest compared with samples that only cover cultures from the same cultural zone (see Gupta & Hanges, 2004, for a systematic review on culture zones). Several cultural zone classification systems can be used. For example, Inglehart and Welzel (2005) summarized and distinguished nine cultural zones based on multiple cultural value dimensions, including Confucian, Protestant Europe, Orthodox, Catholic Europe, English Speaking, South Asia, Islamic, Africa, and Latin America. Similarly, Schwartz (2008) categorized countries in the world into eight distinct cultural zones. A purposive sampling would include cultures from at least two different cultural zones based on these classifications. As for which specific cultural zones to sample from, researchers could make decisions based either on their accessibility to data and/or the specific research questions. For example, researchers for a study on cultural differences in religious beliefs may want to spread its sampling into multiple cultural zones with different religious beliefs (e.g., Catholic Europe, Islamic, Confucian).

Data Collection Logistics

Managing geographically distributed data collection. In cross-cultural research, researchers often need to collect data from geographically distributed locations, the management of which can be challenging. We offer recommendations based on practices reported in the literature. First, in cross-cultural research collecting data from employees working in multiple branches or subsidiaries of the same company managed by the same HR system, it is desirable to first understand the organizational structure and obtain a roster from the HR department. Researchers then can systematically select employees based on their formal reporting relationships. Researchers also can solicit help from the HR department to systematically distribute information about the study and recruit participants (e.g., Mueller et al., 2012). Second, in cross-cultural research collecting data from individuals located in different cultures and not formally affiliated with one another through shared organizational membership, researchers can consider recruiting participants through web-based tools or online market place, such as Amazon Mechanical Turk (https://www.mturk.com; e.g., Buhrmester, Kwang, & Gosling, 2011; Paolacci & Chandler, 2014). In these online survey platforms, researchers may be allowed to set up filters to manage which countries to collect data from, the criteria for eligible participants (e.g., age, gender, or language), and how many participants to survey from each country. Compared with paper-and-pencil based surveys, these online surveys can help reduce costs associated with survey distribution and data entry. However, researchers should be aware that issues associated with online surveys still apply here (see the discussion in the Online Surveys section). In addition, researchers may have less control over the sampling process when the platform provider is unable to verify demographics of the users (i.e., survey respondents) and/or does not allow the researchers to randomly sample from the users. In addition, a *snowball approach*, which asks participants already recruited to further contact other members of the same population who may be willing to participate in the study, is another alternative approach to collect and manage cross-cultural data collection, especially when the populations are difficult to reach by researchers themselves (e.g., substance users in certain countries; Boehnke et al., 2011).

Translation and measurement equivalence of survey tools.   Translating measurement tools may be one of the most common issues researchers have to resolve when conducting research in different language contexts. Brislin's (1970) translation and back-translation procedures have emerged as the golden standard in survey translation. Recent research has suggested a more comprehensive approach to the translation of measurement tools. In particular, Hambleton and colleagues developed the International Test Commission Guidelines for Test Adaptation (Hambleton, 1994; Hambleton, Merenda, & Spielberger, 2005) to provide systematic guidance on carrying out survey translation and adaptation. Their recommendations were summarized into five general categories: general translation questions

(e.g., "Does the item have the same or highly similar meaning in the two languages?"), item format and appearance (e.g., "Is the item format, including physical layout, the same in the two language versions?"), grammar and phrasing (e.g., "Are there any grammatical clues that might make this item easier or harder in the target language version?"), passages and other item-relevant stimulus materials (e.g., "Does the passage depict any individual or groups in a stereotypic fashion through occupation, emotion, situation, or otherwise?"), and cultural relevance and specificity (e.g., "Have terms in the item in one language been suitably adapted to the cultural environment of the second language version?"). Research including participants from diverse language backgrounds is encouraged to follow these guidelines.

It is worth noting that the ultimate goal of survey translations is to achieve measurement equivalence across different languages using a common measure. *Measurement equivalence* is defined as the level of comparability of measurement outcomes across different samples (e.g., samples speaking different languages; for a review, see van de Vijver & Leung, 2011). Measurement equivalence is important for cross-culture research because it ensures that the observed mean score differences (or lack thereof) can be meaningfully attributed to between-culture differences (or lack thereof) versus being driven by problematic measurement across cultures. In general, measurement equivalence can be evaluated in two approaches: (a) the item-based approach in which item response theory is used to examine measurement equivalence/differences at the item level and (b) the structural equation modeling-based approach in which confirmatory factor analysis is used to examine measurement equivalence/differences at the scale level (for reviews and more technical details for establishing measurement equivalence, see Raju, Laffitte, & Byrne, 2002; Tay, Meade, & Cao, 2015; Vandenberg & Lance, 2000; Wang & Russell, 2005).

Response Quality

Differences in response styles.   Data collected from different cultures may be influenced by systematic, between-culture differences in response styles due to different culture values. This issue also may exist in data collected from different occupations or industries. These response style differences can lead to systematic biases in measurement and even misinterpretations of research findings concerning cultural differences (for a review, see Johnson, Shavitt, & Holbrook, 2011). We discuss three most commonly studied response styles and how to minimize potential biases brought by these response styles.

Socially desirable responding (SDR) refers to a tendency for respondents to systematically portray themselves in a more favorable manner when answering survey questions (Paulhus, 1991). Research generally has found that individuals in collectivist cultures (e.g., Asian cultures) tend to have greater SDR than individuals in individualist cultures (e.g., Western cultures; Bernardi, 2006). However, some researchers have argued that the exact associations between cultural values and SDR depend on the specific type of SDR of theoretical concern. For example, Lalwani, Shrum, and Chiu (2009) distinguished *self-deceptive enhancement* (i.e., the tendency to describe oneself in an inflated way) and *impression management* (i.e., the tendency to describe oneself in a socially normative way) as two distinct types of SDR. They found that individualism was associated only with self-deceptive enhancement, whereas collectivism was associated only with impression management. We recommend two practices. First, researchers can measure SDR as a substantive variable and then include it either as a control or a study variable in data analyses (e.g., Lalwani et al., 2009). Several well-established measures of SDR are available, such as the Paulhus Deception Scale (Paulhus, 1991) and Marlowe–Crowne Social Desirability Scale (Crowne & Marlowe, 1960). Second, SDR can be reduced effectively by allowing greater privacy and anonymity to participants' responses (e.g., Himmelfarb & Lickteig, 1982).

Acquiescent response style (ARS) is known as individuals' tendency to agree rather than disagree on response scales (Smith, 2004) and can be captured by the ratio of participants' responses as "agree" and "strongly agree" out of all survey responses. Similar to SDR, ARS also has been found to be higher in participants from collectivistic cultures than individualistic cultures (e.g., Harzing, 2006; van Herk, Poortinga, & Verhallen, 2004). One common practice to reduce ARS is including a mixed set of positively worded and reserve-worded items in the survey questionnaire. However, there has been unresolved controversy about the effectiveness of this practice (e.g., Wong, Rindfleisch, & Burroughs, 2003). In addition, ARS can be detected by comparing the proportion of participants who agree with one statement with the proportion of participants who disagree with the other, with a larger discrepancy between the two proportions indicating a higher level of ARS.

Extreme response style (ERS) is known as individuals' tendency to consistently use the extreme ends of response scales when answering survey items with multiple anchors (Clarke, 2001). ERS can be quantified by counting the proportion of survey items on which participants select an extreme response option (e.g., *strongly agree* or *strongly disagree*) out of the total number of items (e.g., Harzing, 2006). Research has shown that samples from Western cultures tend to respond with greater ERS than samples from East Asian cultures but less so compared with samples from South Asian cultures (e.g., Dolnicar & Grün, 2007; Harzing, 2006). Harzing (2006) also found that samples from southern European and Latino countries demonstrated more ERS than those from other regions of Europe. Thus, as with other response styles reviewed earlier, individuals from different cultures may have different propensities in ERS (e.g., Harzing, 2006), which may introduce systematic measurement confounds into the substantial empirical findings if not handled properly (Johnson et al., 2011). To detect ERS, recent research has suggested using a latent approach (e.g., structural equation modeling, Cheung & Rensvold, 2000; item response theory, de Jong, Steenkamp, Fox, & Baumgartner, 2008) in evaluating the presence of ERS without requiring explicit measures of ERS. This latent approach is particularly promising for cross-cultural researching using archival data sets when measures on ERS may not be available.

OTHER ISSUES

Other Forms of Data

Network data. *Network data* indicate the relationships (e.g., friendship ties, communication ties, or trust ties) between nodes. These nodes can be individual workers, organizations, or communities. When collecting network data for multilevel studies, researchers need to pay attention to two specific issues. First, researchers should define the boundary of the networks, including both the actors and the ties they will study, and then apply appropriate sampling strategies (Wasserman & Faust, 1994). Researchers either can identify the boundary based on clearly defined membership (e.g., membership of individual workers in each work unit; e.g., Venkataramani, Zhou, Wang, Liao, & Shi, 2016) or define boundaries based on the relations studied (e.g., those who publish in certain journals are identified as academics working on a certain topic; Guimerà, Uzzi, Spiro, & Amaral, 2005). In organizational research involving small work groups and teams, it is possible to recruit all members of each network to participate in a study (e.g., Venkataramani et al., 2016). When it is not possible to study all members of the network, both probability sampling strategies and chain methods (e.g., snowball sampling) can be used (see Wasserman & Faust, 1994, for a review). Second, response rate of the network data not only affects statistical power of hypotheses testing but also the extent to which data collected accurately reflect the actual network. Therefore, when the size of the network is reasonably small, researchers should try to achieve high response and thus coverage rates.

Archival data. As recommended in recent literature (e.g., Beal, 2015), organizational researchers can complement primary data collection efforts with archival data. Without requesting responses from participants to survey questionnaires, archival data can come from organizations records (e.g., entry and exit of organizational members), public records (e.g., collaboration networks among researchers based on publications; Guimerà et al., 2005), or digital traces (e.g., e-mails, activities in social media, and database usage history; e.g., Landers, Brusso,

Cavanaugh, & Collmus, 2016). If the same users repeatedly access the same platforms (e.g., a Web-based application), repeated observations from the same individuals or units often are stored (i.e., as in multilevel research with repeated measurements). If users accessing the platforms (e.g., company e-mail server) are nested within organizational units, data similar to those collected in multilevel research with individuals or units nested in larger units are available. It also is possible that data from individuals or organizational units in different cultures who access the same websites (e.g., Facebook) are available, which is similar to cross-culture data discussed previously. Therefore, the same aforementioned concerns may apply to archival data, as well as primary data collection. Although these data often are collected without any prespecified research element, researchers should still understand how the data were generated. For example, it is possible that users can customize settings of the applications to block certain data from being recorded, which can result in systematic sampling bias. Real-time data storage also may be limited by Internet connection stability. In addition, some psychological mechanisms may not be captured in the archival data (e.g., psychological states or personality traits), which may require researchers to combine both primary data collection and data obtained from archival records in the same research.

Data Collection Ethics

All the data collection practices discussed earlier, as well as managing collected data, should be conducted based on careful considerations of legal and ethical issues. For example, researchers may need to learn about different institutional review board policies relevant for each participating organization and country. In addition, when measurements from multiple sources and/or multiple time points are collected, privacy of participants' responses should be protected, despite the need to link data across different measurement occasions. When using newer forms of data (e.g., digital traces in social media), researchers also may need to be aware of intellectual property and cybersecurity regulations (see discussions in Landers et al., 2016) to avoid controversial practices (e.g., Kramer, Guillory,

& Hancock, 2014). The American Psychological Association (APA; 2010) provides specific guidance on ethics in data collection, which also is relevant for multilevel research.

CONCLUSION

This chapter reviewed data collection issues in multilevel research, which specifically focuses on sample size, sampling strategies, data collection tools and logistics, and response quality. We provided recommendations mainly based on recent advancements in the research method literature or studies recently published in organizational research journals. Due to space limitations, we did not focus on technical details of each practice and how to align different design choices with data analyses techniques. Nevertheless, we hope researchers consider some of the materials offered here in future multilevel research to improve the quality of their data and findings.

References

Ali, A. A., Hossain, S. M., Hovsepian, K., Rahman, M., Plarre, K., & Kumar, S. (2012). mPuff: Automated detection of cigarette smoking puffs from respiration measurements. *2012 ACM/IEEE 11th International Conference on Information Processing in Sensor Networks (IPSN)*, 269–280. http://dx.doi.org/10.1109/IPSN.2012.6920942

American Psychological Association. (2010). *Ethical principles of psychologists and code of conduct (2002, Amended June 1, 2010)*. Retrieved from http://www.apa.org/ethics/code/index.aspx

Ancoli-Israel, S., Cole, R., Alessi, C., Chambers, M., Moorcroft, W., & Pollak, C. P. (2003). The role of actigraphy in the study of sleep and circadian rhythms. *Sleep, 26*, 342–392. http://dx.doi.org/10.1093/sleep/26.3.342

Appelhans, B. M., & Luecken, L. J. (2006). Heart rate variability as an index of regulated emotion responding. *Review of General Psychology, 10*, 229–240. http://dx.doi.org/10.1037/1089-2680.10.3.229

Atwater, L., Wang, M., Smither, J. W., & Fleenor, J. W. (2009). Are cultural characteristics associated with the relationship between self and others' ratings of leadership? *Journal of Applied Psychology, 94*, 876–886. http://dx.doi.org/10.1037/a0014561

Baer, R. A., Ballenger, J., Berry, D. T., & Wetter, M. W. (1997). Detection of random responding on the MMPI-A. *Journal of Personality Assessment, 68*, 139–151. http://dx.doi.org/10.1207/s15327752jpa6801_11

Barsky, A., Kaplan, S. A., & Beal, D. J. (2011). Just feelings? The role of affect in the formation of organizational fairness judgments. *Journal of Management, 37*, 248–279. http://dx.doi.org/10.1177/0149206310376325

Beal, D. J. (2011). Industrial/organizational psychology. In M. R. Mehl & T. A. Conner (Eds.), *Handbook of research methods for studying daily life* (pp. 601–619). New York, NY: Guilford Press.

Beal, D. J. (2015). ESM 2.0: State of the art and future potential of experience sampling methods in organizational research. *Annual Review of Organizational Psychology and Organizational Behavior, 2*, 383–407. http://dx.doi.org/10.1146/annurev-orgpsych-032414-111335

Beal, D. J., & Weiss, H. M. (2003). Methods of ecological momentary assessment in organizational research. *Organizational Research Methods, 6*, 440–464. http://dx.doi.org/10.1177/1094428103257361

Berkman, L. F., Buxton, O., Ertel, K., & Okechukwu, C. (2010). Managers' practices related to work-family balance predict employee cardiovascular risk and sleep duration in extended care settings. *Journal of Occupational Health Psychology, 15*, 316–329. http://dx.doi.org/10.1037/a0019721

Bernardi, R. A. (2006). Associations between Hofstede's cultural constructs and social desirability response bias. *Journal of Business Ethics, 65*, 43–53. http://dx.doi.org/10.1007/s10551-005-5353-0

Boehnke, K., Lietz, P., Schreier, M., & Wilhelm, A. (2011). Sampling: The selection of cases for culturally comparative psychological research. In D. Matsumoto & F. J. R. van de Vijver (Eds.), *Cross-cultural research methods in psychology* (pp. 101–129). New York, NY: Cambridge University Press.

Bolger, N., Davis, A., & Rafaeli, E. (2003). Diary methods: Capturing life as it is lived. *Annual Review of Psychology, 54*, 579–616. http://dx.doi.org/10.1146/annurev.psych.54.101601.145030

Bono, J. E., Foldes, H. J., Vinson, G., & Muros, J. P. (2007). Workplace emotions: The role of supervision and leadership. *Journal of Applied Psychology, 92*, 1357–1367. http://dx.doi.org/10.1037/0021-9010.92.5.1357

Bono, J. E., Glomb, T. M., Shen, W., Kim, E., & Koch, A. J. (2013). Building positive resources: Effects of positive events and positive reflection on work stress and health. *Academy of Management Journal, 56*, 1601–1627. http://dx.doi.org/10.5465/amj.2011.0272

Brislin, R. W. (1970). Back-translation for cross-cultural research. *Journal of Cross-Cultural Psychology, 1*, 185–216. http://dx.doi.org/10.1177/135910457000100301

Buhrmester, M., Kwang, T., & Gosling, S. D. (2011). Amazon's Mechanical Turk: A new source of inexpensive, yet high-quality, data? *Perspectives on Psychological Science, 6*, 3–5. http://dx.doi.org/10.1177/1745691610393980

Chan, D. (1998). Functional relations among constructs in the same content domain at different levels of analysis: A typology of composition models. *Journal of Applied Psychology, 83*, 234–246. http://dx.doi.org/10.1037/0021-9010.83.2.234

Chen, G., Kirkman, B. L., Kim, K., Farh, C. I., & Tangirala, S. (2010). When does cross-cultural motivation enhance expatriate effectiveness? A multilevel investigation of the moderating roles of subsidiary support and cultural distance. *Academy of Management Journal, 53*, 1110–1130. http://dx.doi.org/10.5465/AMJ.2010.54533217

Chen, X. P., Liu, D., & Portnoy, R. (2012). A multilevel investigation of motivational cultural intelligence, organizational diversity climate, and cultural sales: Evidence from U.S. real estate firms. *Journal of Applied Psychology, 97*, 93–106. http://dx.doi.org/10.1037/a0024697

Cheung, G. W., & Rensvold, R. B. (2000). Assessing extreme and acquiescence response sets in cross-cultural research using structural equations modeling. *Journal of Cross-Cultural Psychology, 31*, 187–212. http://dx.doi.org/10.1177/0022022100031002003

Chudoba, K. M., Wynn, E., Lu, M., & Watson-Manheim, M. B. (2005). How virtual are we? Measuring virtuality and understanding its impact in a global organization. *Information Systems Journal, 15*, 279–306. http://dx.doi.org/10.1111/j.1365-2575.2005.00200.x

Clarke, I., III. (2001). Extreme response style in cross-cultural research. *International Marketing Review, 18*, 301–324. http://dx.doi.org/10.1108/02651330110396488

Crano, W. D., & Brewer, M. B. (2014). *Principles and methods of social research* (3rd ed.). Mahwah, NJ: Erlbaum.

Crowne, D. P., & Marlowe, D. (1960). A new scale of social desirability independent of psychopathology. *Journal of Consulting Psychology, 24*, 349–354. http://dx.doi.org/10.1037/h0047358

de Jong, M. G., Steenkamp, J. B. E., Fox, J. P., & Baumgartner, H. (2008). Using item response theory to measure extreme response style in marketing research: A global investigation. *Journal of Marketing Research, 45*, 104–115. http://dx.doi.org/10.1509/jmkr.45.1.104

Dillman, D. A., Smyth, J. D., & Christian, L. M. (2009). *Internet, mail, and mixed-mode surveys: The tailored design method* (3rd ed.). Hoboken, NJ: Wiley.

Dimotakis, N., Ilies, R., & Judge, T. A. (2013). Experience sampling methodology. In J. M. Cortina & R. S. Landis (Eds.), *Modern research methods for the study of behavior in organizations* (pp. 319–348). New York, NY: Routledge.

Dolnicar, S., & Grün, B. (2007). Cross-cultural differences in survey response patterns. *International Marketing Review, 24*, 127–143. http://dx.doi.org/10.1108/02651330710741785

Eatough, E., Shockley, K., & Yu, P. (2016). A review of ambulatory health data collection methods for employee experience sampling research. *Applied Psychology, 65*, 322–354. http://dx.doi.org/10.1111/apps.12068

Fisher, C. D., & To, M. L. (2012). Using experience sampling methodology in organizational behavior. *Journal of Organizational Behavior, 33*, 865–877. http://dx.doi.org/10.1002/job.1803

Gabriel, A. S., & Diefendorff, J. M. (2015). Emotional labor dynamics: A momentary approach. *Academy of Management Journal, 58*, 1804–1825. http://dx.doi.org/10.5465/amj.2013.1135

Gilmore, C., Kormann, D., & Rubin, A. D. (1999). Secure remote access to an Internet Web server. *IEEE Network, 13*, 31–37. http://dx.doi.org/10.1109/65.806985

Guimerà, R., Uzzi, B., Spiro, J., & Amaral, L. A. N. (2005). Team assembly mechanisms determine collaboration network structure and team performance. *Science, 308*, 697–702. http://dx.doi.org/10.1126/science.1106340

Gupta, V., & Hanges, P. (2004). Regional and climate clustering of societal cultures. In R. House, P. Hanges, M. Javidan, P. Dorfman, & V. Gupta (Eds.), *Culture, leadership, and organizations: The GLOBE study of 62 societies* (pp. 178–218). Thousand Oaks, CA: Sage.

Hambleton, R. K. (1994). Guidelines for adapting educational and psychological tests: A progress report. *European Journal of Psychological Assessment, 10*, 229–240.

Hambleton, R. K., Merenda, P. F., & Spielberger, C. (Eds.). (2005). *Adapting educational and psychological tests for cross-cultural assessment*. Mahwah, NJ: Erlbaum.

Harrison, D. A., & Klein, K. J. (2007). What's the difference? Diversity constructs as separation, variety, or disparity in organizations. *Academy of Management Review, 32*, 1199–1228. http://dx.doi.org/10.5465/AMR.2007.26586096

Harzing, A. W. (2006). Response styles in cross-national survey research: A 26-country study. *International*

Journal of Cross Cultural Management, 6, 243–266. http://dx.doi.org/10.1177/1470595806066332

Hausknecht, J. P., & Trevor, C. O. (2011). Collective turnover at the group, unit, and organizational levels: Evidence, issues, and implications. *Journal of Management, 37,* 352–388. http://dx.doi.org/10.1177/0149206310383910

Himmelfarb, S., & Lickteig, C. (1982). Social desirability and the randomized response technique. *Journal of Personality and Social Psychology, 43,* 710–717. http://dx.doi.org/10.1037/0022-3514.43.4.710

Hirschfeld, R. R., Cole, M. S., Bernerth, J. B., & Rizzuto, T. E. (2013). Voluntary survey completion among team members: Implications of noncompliance and missing data for multilevel research. *Journal of Applied Psychology, 98,* 454–468. http://dx.doi.org/10.1037/a0031909

Hom, P. W., Lee, T. W., Shaw, J. D., & Hausknecht, J. P. (2017). One hundred years of employee turnover theory and research. *Journal of Applied Psychology, 102,* 530–545. http://dx.doi.org/10.1037/apl0000103

House, R. J., Hanges, P. J., Javidan, M., Dorfman, P. W., & Gupta, V. (2004). *Leadership, culture and organizations: The GLOBE study of 62 societies.* Thousand Oaks, CA: Sage.

Ilies, R., Dimotakis, N., & Watson, D. (2010). Mood, blood pressure, and heart rate at work: An experience-sampling study. *Journal of Occupational Health Psychology, 15,* 120–130. http://dx.doi.org/10.1037/a0018350

Inglehart, R., & Welzel, C. (2005). *Modernization, cultural change, and democracy: The human development sequence.* Cambridge, England: Cambridge University Press. http://dx.doi.org/10.1017/CBO9780511790881

Johnson, T. P., Shavitt, S., & Holbrook, A. L. (2011). Survey response styles across cultures. In D. Matsumoto & F. J. R. van de Vijver (Eds.), *Cross-cultural research methods in psychology* (pp. 130–175). New York, NY: Cambridge University Press.

Judge, T. A., Klinger, R. L., & Simon, L. S. (2010). Time is on my side: Time, general mental ability, human capital, and extrinsic career success. *Journal of Applied Psychology, 95,* 92–107. http://dx.doi.org/10.1037/a0017594

Kammeyer-Mueller, J., Wanberg, C., Rubenstein, A., & Song, Z. (2013). Support, undermining, and newcomer socialization: Fitting in during the first 90 days. *Academy of Management Journal, 56,* 1104–1124. http://dx.doi.org/10.5465/amj.2010.0791

Karau, S. J., & Williams, K. D. (1993). Social loafing: A meta-analytic review and theoretical integration. *Journal of Personality and Social Psychology, 65,* 681–706. http://dx.doi.org/10.1037/0022-3514.65.4.681

Kivlighan, K. T., Granger, D. A., Schwartz, E. B., Nelson, V., Curran, M., & Shirtcliff, E. A. (2004). Quantifying blood leakage into the oral mucosa and its effects on the measurement of cortisol, dehydroepiandrosterone, and testosterone in saliva. *Hormones and Behavior, 46,* 39–46. http://dx.doi.org/10.1016/j.yhbeh.2004.01.006

Klein, K. J., Dansereau, F., & Hall, R. J. (1994). Levels issues in theory development, data collection, and analysis. *Academy of Management Review, 19,* 195–229.

Klein, K. J., & Kozlowski, S. W. (2000). From micro to meso: Critical steps in conceptualizing and conducting multilevel research. *Organizational Research Methods, 3,* 211–236. http://dx.doi.org/10.1177/109442810033001

Koopmann, J., Lanaj, K., Wang, M., Zhou, L., & Shi, J. (2016). Nonlinear effects of team tenure on team psychological safety climate and climate strength: Implications for average team member performance. *Journal of Applied Psychology, 101,* 940–957. http://dx.doi.org/10.1037/apl0000097

Kozlowski, S. W. J., Chao, G. T., Grand, J. A., Braun, M. T., & Kuljanin, G. (2013). Advancing multilevel research design: Capturing the dynamics of emergence. *Organizational Research Methods, 16,* 581–615. http://dx.doi.org/10.1177/1094428113493119

Kozlowski, S. W. J., & Klein, K. J. (2000). A multilevel approach to theory and research in organizations: Contextual, temporal, and emergent processes. In K. J. Klein & S. W. J. Kozlowski (Eds.), *Multilevel theory, research, and methods in organizations: Foundations, extensions, and new directions* (pp. 3–90). San Francisco, CA: Jossey-Bass.

Kramer, A. D. I., Guillory, J. E., & Hancock, J. T. (2014). Experimental evidence of massive-scale emotional contagion through social networks. *Proceedings of the National Academy of Sciences of the United States of America, 111,* 8788–8790. http://dx.doi.org/10.1073/pnas.1320040111 (Editorial Expression of Concern published 2014, *Proceedings of the National Academy of Sciences of the United States of America, 111,* p. 10779. http://dx.doi.org/10.1073/pnas.1412469111)

Kreft, I., & de Leeuw, J. (1998). *Introducing multilevel modeling.* London, England: Sage. http://dx.doi.org/10.4135/9781849209366

Kulikowski, K., & Potasz-Kulikowska, K. (2016). Can we measure working memory via the Internet? The reliability and factorial validity of an online n-back task. *Polish Psychological Bulletin, 47,* 51–61. http://dx.doi.org/10.1515/ppb-2016-0006

Lalwani, A. K., Shrum, L. J., & Chiu, C. Y. (2009). Motivated response styles: The role of cultural values, regulatory focus, and self-consciousness in socially desirable responding. *Journal of Personality and Social Psychology, 96,* 870–882. http://dx.doi.org/10.1037/a0014622

Lanaj, K., Johnson, R. E., & Lee, S. M. (2016). Benefits of transformational behaviors for leaders: A daily investigation of leader behaviors and need fulfillment. *Journal of Applied Psychology*, *101*, 237–251. http://dx.doi.org/10.1037/apl0000052

Landers, R. N., & Behrend, T. S. (2015). An inconvenient truth: Arbitrary distinctions between organizational, Mechanical Turk, and other convenience samples. *Industrial and Organizational Psychology: Perspectives on Science and Practice*, *8*, 142–164. http://dx.doi.org/10.1017/iop.2015.13

Landers, R. N., Brusso, R. C., Cavanaugh, K. J., & Collmus, A. B. (2016). A primer on theory-driven Web scraping: Automatic extraction of big data from the Internet for use in psychological research. *Psychological Methods*, *21*, 475–492. http://dx.doi.org/10.1037/met0000081

Le, B., Choi, H. N., & Beal, D. J. (2006). Pocket-sized psychology studies: Exploring daily diary software for palm pilots. *Behavior Research Methods*, *38*, 325–332. http://dx.doi.org/10.3758/BF03192784

LeBreton, J. M., & Senter, J. L. (2008). Answers to 20 questions about interrater reliability and interrater agreement. *Organizational Research Methods*, *11*, 815–852. http://dx.doi.org/10.1177/1094428106296642

Mathieu, J. E., Aguinis, H., Culpepper, S. A., & Chen, G. (2012). Understanding and estimating the power to detect cross-level interaction effects in multilevel modeling. *Journal of Applied Psychology*, *97*, 951–966. http://dx.doi.org/10.1037/a0028380

McCambridge, J., de Bruin, M., & Witton, J. (2012). The effects of demand characteristics on research participant behaviours in non-laboratory settings: A systematic review. *PLoS One*, *7*, e39116. http://dx.doi.org/10.1371/journal.pone.0039116

McEwen, B. S. (1998). Stress, adaptation, and disease. Allostasis and allostatic load. *Annals of the New York Academy of Sciences*, *840*, 33–44. http://dx.doi.org/10.1111/j.1749-6632.1998.tb09546.x

Meade, A. W., & Craig, S. B. (2012). Identifying careless responses in survey data. *Psychological Methods*, *17*, 437–455. http://dx.doi.org/10.1037/a0028085

Mitchell, T. R., & James, L. R. (2001). Building better theory: Time and the specification of when things happen. *Academy of Management Review*, *26*, 530–547.

Mohr, C. D., Armeli, S., Tennen, H., Carney, M. A., Affleck, G., & Hromi, A. (2001). Daily interpersonal experiences, context, and alcohol consumption: Crying in your beer and toasting good times. *Journal of Personality and Social Psychology*, *80*, 489–500. http://dx.doi.org/10.1037/0022-3514.80.3.489

Mueller, K., Hattrup, K., Spiess, S. O., & Lin-Hi, N. (2012). The effects of corporate social responsibility on employees' affective commitment: A cross-cultural investigation. *Journal of Applied Psychology*, *97*, 1186–1200. http://dx.doi.org/10.1037/a0030204

Musch, J., & Reips, U. D. (2000). A brief history of Web experimenting. In M. H. Birnbaum (Ed.), *Psychological experimentation on the Internet* (pp. 61–87). San Diego, CA: Academic Press. http://dx.doi.org/10.1016/B978-012099980-4/50004-6

Newman, D. A. (2014). Missing data: Five practical guidelines. *Organizational Research Methods*, *17*, 372–411. http://dx.doi.org/10.1177/1094428114548590

Nosek, B. A., Banaji, M. R., & Greenwald, A. G. (2002). E-Research: Ethics, security, design, and control in psychological research on the Internet. *Journal of Social Issues*, *58*, 161–176. http://dx.doi.org/10.1111/1540-4560.00254

Paolacci, G., & Chandler, J. (2014). Inside the Turk: Understanding Mechanical Turk as a participant pool. *Current Directions in Psychological Science*, *23*, 184–188. http://dx.doi.org/10.1177/0963721414531598

Paulhus, D. L. (1991). Measurement and control of response bias. In J. P. Robinson & P. R. Shaver (Eds.), *Measures of personality and social psychological attitudes* (pp. 17–59). San Diego, CA: Academic Press. http://dx.doi.org/10.1016/B978-0-12-590241-0.50006-X

Paulhus, D. L. (2002). Socially desirable responding: The evolution of a construct. In H. I. Braun, D. N. Jackson, D. E. Wiley, H. I. Braun, D. N. Jackson, & D. E. Wiley (Eds.), *The role of constructs in psychological and educational measurement* (pp. 49–69). Mahwah, NJ: Erlbaum.

Pereira, D., & Elfering, A. (2014). Social stressors at work, sleep quality and psychosomatic health complaints—A longitudinal ambulatory field study. *Stress & Health*, *30*, 43–52. http://dx.doi.org/10.1002/smi.2494

Ployhart, R. E., & Vandenberg, R. J. (2010). Longitudinal research: The theory, design, and analysis of change. *Journal of Management*, *36*, 94–120. http://dx.doi.org/10.1177/0149206309352110

Popper, K. (1959). *The logic of scientific discovery*. New York, NY: Basic Books.

Putka, D. J., Le, H., McCloy, R. A., & Diaz, T. (2008). Ill-structured measurement designs in organizational research: Implications for estimating interrater reliability. *Journal of Applied Psychology*, *93*, 959–981. http://dx.doi.org/10.1037/0021-9010.93.5.959

Raju, N. S., Laffitte, L. J., & Byrne, B. M. (2002). Measurement equivalence: A comparison of methods based on confirmatory factor analysis and item response theory. *Journal of Applied Psychology*, *87*, 517–529. http://dx.doi.org/10.1037/0021-9010.87.3.517

Raudenbush, S. W., & Liu, X. (2000). Statistical power and optimal design for multisite randomized trials. *Psychological Methods, 5,* 199–213. http://dx.doi.org/10.1037/1082-989X.5.2.199

Raudenbush, S. W., Spybrook, J., Liu, X., & Congdon, R. (2005). Optimal Design for Longitudinal and Multilevel Research (Version 1.55) [Computer software]. Chicago, IL: University of Chicago Press.

Redelmeier, D. A., & Kahneman, D. (1996). Patients' memories of painful medical treatments: Real-time and retrospective evaluations of two minimally invasive procedures. *Pain, 66,* 3–8. http://dx.doi.org/10.1016/0304-3959(96)02994-6

Reips, U. D., Buchanan, T., Krantz, J. H., & McGrawn, K. (2011). Methodological challenges in the use of the Internet for scientific research: Ten solutions and recommendations. *Studia Psychologica, 11,* 5–18.

Reis, H. T., & Gable, S. L. (2000). Event-sampling and other methods for studying everyday experience. In H. T. Reis & C. M. Judd (Eds.), *Handbook of research methods in social and personality psychology* (pp. 190–222). New York, NY: Cambridge University Press.

Riza, S. D., Ganzach, Y., & Liu, Y. (2016). Time and job satisfaction: A longitudinal study of the differential roles of age and tenure. *Journal of Management.* Advance online publication. http://dx.doi.org/10.1177/0149206315624962

Robinson, M. D., & Clore, G. L. (2002). Belief and feeling: Evidence for an accessibility model of emotional self-report. *Psychological Bulletin, 128,* 934–960. http://dx.doi.org/10.1037/0033-2909.128.6.934

Rogelberg, S. G., Luong, A., Sederburg, M. E., & Cristol, D. S. (2000). Employee attitude surveys: Examining the attitudes of noncompliant employees. *Journal of Applied Psychology, 85,* 284–293. http://dx.doi.org/10.1037/0021-9010.85.2.284

Sadikaj, G., Moskowitz, D. S., & Zuroff, D. C. (2011). Attachment-related affective dynamics: Differential reactivity to others' interpersonal behavior. *Journal of Personality and Social Psychology, 100,* 905–917. http://dx.doi.org/10.1037/a0022875

Schafer, J. L., & Graham, J. W. (2002). Missing data: Our view of the state of the art. *Psychological Methods, 7,* 147–177. http://dx.doi.org/10.1037/1082-989X.7.2.147

Schaubroeck, J., Lam, S. S., & Xie, J. L. (2000). Collective efficacy versus self-efficacy in coping responses to stressors and control: A cross-cultural study. *Journal of Applied Psychology, 85,* 512–525. http://dx.doi.org/10.1037/0021-9010.85.4.512

Scherbaum, C. A., & Ferreter, J. M. (2009). Estimating statistical power and required sample sizes for organizational research using multilevel modeling.

Organizational Research Methods, 12, 347–367. http://dx.doi.org/10.1177/1094428107308906

Schmidt, W. C. (2000). The server side of psychology Web experiments. In M. H. Birnbaum (Ed.), *Psychological experimentation on the Internet* (pp. 285–310). San Diego, CA: Academic Press. http://dx.doi.org/10.1016/B978-012099980-4/50013-7

Schneider, B., Salvaggio, A. N., & Subirats, M. (2002). Climate strength: A new direction for climate research. *Journal of Applied Psychology, 87,* 220–229. http://dx.doi.org/10.1037/0021-9010.87.2.220

Schwartz, S. H. (2008). *Cultural value orientations: Nature and implications of national differences.* Moscow, Russia: State University Higher School of Economics Press.

Shadish, W. R., Cook, T. D., & Campbell, D. T. (2002). *Experimental and quasi-experimental designs for generalized causal inference.* Boston, MA: Houghton Mifflin.

Shao, R., & Skarlicki, D. P. (2014). Service employees' reactions to mistreatment by customers: A comparison between North America and East Asia. *Personnel Psychology, 67,* 23–59. http://dx.doi.org/10.1111/peps.12021

Shi, J., Johnson, R. E., Liu, Y., & Wang, M. (2013). Linking subordinate political skill to supervisor dependence and reward recommendations: A moderated mediation model. *Journal of Applied Psychology, 98,* 374–384. http://dx.doi.org/10.1037/a0031129

Shiffman, S. (2014). Conceptualizing analyses of ecological momentary assessment data. *Nicotine & Tobacco Research, 16*(Suppl. 2), S76–S87. http://dx.doi.org/10.1093/ntr/ntt195

Shrout, P. E., & Lane, S. P. (2011). Psychometrics. In M. R. Mehl & T. A. Conner (Eds.), *Handbook of research methods for studying daily life* (pp. 302–320). New York, NY: Guilford Press.

Smith, P. B. (2004). Acquiescent response bias as an aspect of cultural communication style. *Journal of Cross-Cultural Psychology, 35,* 50–61. http://dx.doi.org/10.1177/0022022103260380

Snijders, T. A. (2005). Power and sample size in multilevel linear models. In B. S. Everitt & D. C. Howell (Eds.), *Encyclopedia of statistics in behavioral science* (Vol. 3, pp. 1570–1573). London, England: Wiley. http://dx.doi.org/10.1002/0470013192.bsa492

Snijders, T. A., & Bosker, R. J. (1993). Standard errors and sample sizes for two-level research. *Journal of Educational and Behavioral Statistics, 18,* 237–259. http://dx.doi.org/10.3102/10769986018003237

Song, Y., Liu, Y., Shi, J., & Wang, M. (2017). Use of proactive socialization tactics and socialization outcomes: A latent growth modeling approach to understanding newcomer socialization process. *Academy of Management Discoveries, 3,* 42–63.

Song, Z., Foo, M. D., & Uy, M. A. (2008). Mood spillover and crossover among dual-earner couples: A cell phone event sampling study. *Journal of Applied Psychology, 93*, 443–452. http://dx.doi.org/10.1037/0021-9010.93.2.443

Stanton, J. M., & Rogelberg, S. G. (2001). Using Internet/Intranet Web pages to collect organizational research data. *Organizational Research Methods, 4*, 200–217. http://dx.doi.org/10.1177/109442810143002

Steiner, I. D. (1972). *Group process and productivity.* New York, NY: Academic Press.

Stone, A. A., & Broderick, J. E. (2009). Protocol compliance in real-time data collection studies. In R. F. Belli, F. P. Stafford, & D. F. Alwin (Eds.), *Calendar and time diary methods in life course research* (pp. 243–256). Thousand Oaks, CA: Sage. http://dx.doi.org/10.4135/9781412990295.d22

Stone, A. A., Broderick, J. E., Shiffman, S. S., & Schwartz, J. E. (2004). Understanding recall of weekly pain from a momentary assessment perspective: Absolute agreement, between- and within-person consistency, and judged change in weekly pain. *Pain, 107*, 61–69. http://dx.doi.org/10.1016/j.pain.2003.09.020

Stone, A. A., Schwartz, J. E., Neale, J. M., Shiffman, S., Marco, C. A., Hickcox, M., . . . Cruise, L. J. (1998). A comparison of coping assessed by ecological momentary assessment and retrospective recall. *Journal of Personality and Social Psychology, 74*, 1670–1680. http://dx.doi.org/10.1037/0022-3514.74.6.1670

Tay, L., Meade, A. W., & Cao, M. (2015). An overview and practical guide to IRT measurement equivalence analysis. *Organizational Research Methods, 18*, 3–46. http://dx.doi.org/10.1177/1094428114553062

Thomas, D. L., & Diener, E. (1990). Memory accuracy in the recall of emotions. *Journal of Personality and Social Psychology, 59*, 291–297. http://dx.doi.org/10.1037/0022-3514.59.2.291

Thompson, S. K. (2012). *Sampling* (3rd ed.). Hoboken, NJ: Wiley. http://dx.doi.org/10.1002/9781118162934

Vandenberg, R. J., & Lance, C. E. (2000). A review and synthesis of the measurement invariance literature: Suggestions, practices, and recommendations for organizational research. *Organizational Research Methods, 3*, 4–70. http://dx.doi.org/10.1177/109442810031002

van de Vijver, F. J. R., & Leung, K. (2011). Equivalence and bias: A review of concepts, models, and data analytic procedures. In D. Matsumoto & F. J. R. van de Vijver (Eds.), *Cross-cultural research methods in psychology* (pp. 17–45). New York, NY: Cambridge University Press.

van de Vijver, F. J. R., & Matsumoto, D. (2011). Introduction to the methodological issues associated with

cross-cultural research. In D. Matsumoto & F. J. R. van de Vijver (Eds.), *Cross-cultural research methods in psychology* (pp. 1–14). New York, NY: Cambridge University Press.

van Herk, H., Poortinga, Y. H., & Verhallen, T. M. (2004). Response styles in rating scales evidence of method bias in data from six EU countries. *Journal of Cross-Cultural Psychology, 35*, 346–360. http://dx.doi.org/10.1177/0022022104264126

van Hooff, M. L. M., Geurts, S. A. E., Kompier, M. A. J., & Taris, T. W. (2007). "How fatigued do you currently feel?" Convergent and discriminant validity of a single-item fatigue measure. *Journal of Occupational Health, 49*, 224–234. http://dx.doi.org/10.1539/joh.49.224

Venkataramani, V., Zhou, L., Wang, M., Liao, H., & Shi, J. (2016). Social networks and employee voice: The influence of team members' and team leaders' social network positions on employee voice. *Organizational Behavior and Human Decision Processes, 132*, 37–48. http://dx.doi.org/10.1016/j.obhdp.2015.12.001

Wang, M., Liao, H., Zhan, Y., & Shi, J. (2011). Daily customer mistreatment and employee sabotage against customers: Examining emotion and resource perspectives. *Academy of Management Journal, 54*, 312–334. http://dx.doi.org/10.5465/AMJ.2011.60263093

Wang, M., Liu, S., Liao, H., Gong, Y., Kammeyer-Mueller, J., & Shi, J. (2013). Can't get it out of my mind: Employee rumination after customer mistreatment and negative mood in the next morning. *Journal of Applied Psychology, 98*, 989–1004. http://dx.doi.org/10.1037/a0033656

Wang, M., & Russell, S. S. (2005). Measurement equivalence of the Job Descriptive Index across Chinese and American workers: Results from confirmatory factor analysis and item response theory. *Educational and Psychological Measurement, 65*, 709–732. http://dx.doi.org/10.1177/0013164404272494

Wang, M., Zhou, L., & Zhang, Z. (2016). Dynamic modeling. *Annual Review of Organizational Psychology and Organizational Behavior, 3*, 241–266. http://dx.doi.org/10.1146/annurev-orgpsych-041015-062553

Wasserman, S., & Faust, K. (1994). *Social network analysis: Methods and applications.* New York, NY: Cambridge University Press. http://dx.doi.org/10.1017/CBO9780511815478

Weiss, H., Beal, D. J., Lucy, S. L., & MacDermid, S. M. (2004). *Constructing EMA studies with PMAT: The Purdue Momentary Assessment Tool user's manual.* West Lafayette, IN: Purdue University Military Family Research Institute.

Wheeler, L., & Reis, H. T. (1991). Self-recording of everyday life events: Origins, types, and uses. *Journal of*

Personality, 59, 339–354. http://dx.doi.org/10.1111/j.1467-6494.1991.tb00252.x

Wong, N., Rindfleisch, A., & Burroughs, J. E. (2003). Do reverse-worded items confound measures in cross-cultural consumer research? The case of the material values scale. *Journal of Consumer Research, 30*, 72–91. http://dx.doi.org/10.1086/374697

Zerbe, W. J., & Paulhus, D. L. (1987). Socially desirable responding in organizational behavior: A reconception. *Academy of Management Review, 12*, 250–264.

Zhang, Z., & Peterson, S. J. (2011). Advice networks in teams: The role of transformational leadership and members' core self-evaluations. *Journal of Applied Psychology, 96*, 1004–1017. http://dx.doi.org/10.1037/a0023254

Zhou, L., Wang, M., Chang, D., Liu, S., Zhan, Y., & Shi, J. (2017). Commuting stress process and self-regulation at work: Moderating roles of daily task significance, family interference with work, and commuting means efficacy. *Personnel Psychology, 70*, 891–922.

## CHAPTER 11

CONSTRUCT VALIDATION IN MULTILEVEL STUDIES

Andrew T. Jebb, Louis Tay, Vincent Ng, and Sang Woo

In this chapter, we provide an overview of the concepts and procedures involved in construct validation in multilevel studies. We identify four classes of constructs that vary with respect to (a) the level on which they are measured (e.g., the individual level or the group level) and (b) the level on which they reside (i.e., what level of units the attribute describes). The first section defines these construct classes and then describes construct validation for the first two, as they require techniques that are similar to validation practices at the individual level. The remainder of the chapter discusses construct validation for the two remaining construct classes, those that emerge from interactions among individual-level units (i.e., emergent constructs). The fact that these constructs rely on aggregating lower level measurements requires added validity evidence. This evidence is needed to (a) justify aggregation (interrater agreement), (b) show adequate reliability of the group-level measures (intraclass correlations), and (c) demonstrate that factor structure is preserved at the higher level (psychometric isomorphism). Subsequently, we outline nomological network approaches to validity for when the higher level maintains similar relations to the lower level (i.e., homology) and when it does not. We provide detailed explanations the methodology, offer current reviews of literatures, give empirical examples, and provide software code in Appendix 11.1 to conduct the analyses.

Constructs are the currency of everyday language (Churchland, 1981) and formal scientific research (Podsakoff, Mackenzie, & Podsakoff, 2016). In the organizational sciences, many constructs create the foundation of our inquiry. Developing new explanatory constructs—or elaborating on old ones—is the essence of scientific progress and enhances our understanding of the world (Cronbach & Meehl, 1955). Although debates continue on the degree to which constructs are "real" (c.f. Borsboom, Mellenbergh, & van Heerden, 2003), a general consensus across authors (Cronbach & Meehl, 1955; Edwards & Bagozzi, 2000; Ghiselli, 1964; Nunnally & Bernstein, 1994; Tay, Woo, & Vermunt, 2014) has been reached: Constructs are hypothetical abstractions that organize covarying phenomena in the real world.

For a given construct, we can refer to its level of analysis in two different ways: (a) the level on which it is measured and (b) the level on which the construct resides (i.e., what units are described by the attribute in question). For example, traditionally constructs in the organizational sciences are both measured and reside on one level, the level of the *individual*. Individual self-efficacy is measured by directly administering surveys to individuals, which are also the units described by this construct (Chen, Gully, & Eden, 2001). For these constructs, researchers ensure the validity of measurement by following rigorous standards of scale development

http://dx.doi.org/10.1037/0000115-012
The Handbook of Multilevel Theory, Measurement, and Analysis, S. E. Humphrey and J. M. LeBreton (Editors-in-Chief)

(Clark & Watson, 1995; DeVellis, 1991; Furr, 2011; Hinkin, 1998; Tay & Jebb, 2017). Subsequent construct validation then takes place within the paradigm of testing *nomological networks* (Cronbach & Meehl, 1955), which subsumes convergent and discriminant validity (Campbell & Fiske, 1959; Carlson & Herdman, 2012) and criterion-related validity (Binning & Barrett, 1989; Cronbach & Meehl, 1955).

Construct validation at the individual level only is well understood in organizational research, but it is insufficient to cover all constructs one might want to measure. Because organizations are structured hierarchically into teams, departments, and organizations (Kozlowski & Klein, 2000), many constructs involve levels of analysis that go beyond the individual. The emergence of the *multilevel paradigm* (Mathieu & Chen, 2011) has given researchers the opportunity to study these other constructs, but they also require additional validation techniques. As opposed to constructs operating solely on the individual level, constructs in multilevel analyses vary in the levels on which they (a) are measured and (b) reside. In the following section, we identify four other classes of constructs that invoke other levels of analysis and thus beget different approaches to construct validation.

VALIDATING CONSTRUCTS IN MULTILEVEL STUDIES

Class 1: Temporally Nested Constructs

A first class of constructs found in multilevel contexts are *temporally nested* constructs. When multiple levels of analysis are being considered, the first thing that usually comes to mind is individuals being nested in teams, departments, or organizations— levels which can all be viewed as going "above" the individual. By contrast, temporally nested constructs go "below" by looking at the same individual (or group) repeatedly *over time*. Within-unit observations are inherently longitudinal, as the time dimension allows changes within groups or individuals to emerge. Examples of temporally nested constructs are plentiful in organizational research

because of the increasing use of growth modeling (Bliese & Ployhart, 2002; Chan, 1998a). In fact, most individual-level measures can be simply repurposed as measures of temporally nested constructs. For instance, within-person strain has been measured using the same individual-level measure over multiple time periods (Fuller et al., 2003). This has been the case for many other constructs, including surface acting (Beal, Trougakos, Weiss, & Dalal, 2013), job satisfaction (Chen, Ployhart, Thomas, Anderson, & Bliese, 2011), core self-evaluations (Wu & Griffin, 2012), organizational citizenship behaviors (Eby, Butts, Hoffman, & Sauer, 2015), and affect (Beal et al., 2013).

Like regular individual-level data, demonstrating validity for temporally nested measures first requires calculating an index of reliability at each time point, or the extent to which observed scores are repeatable across measurements (Furr & Bacharach, 2013; Nunnally & Bernstein, 1994). When the measure consists of multiple items, reliability can be estimated using the internal consistency of the measure at each time point. For instance, Ng, Feldman, and Lam (2010) investigated longitudinal relationships between psychological contract breach and affective commitment. They reported that Cronbach's alpha was $\alpha = 97$ for contract breach and $\alpha = .94$ for affective commitment for each time point. Similarly, Wang (2007) showed that reliability ranged from $\alpha = .86$ to $\alpha = .92$ across five waves of psychological well-being measures. In addition to internal consistency reliability, an alternative index is test–retest reliability, which is especially useful for single-item measures. For example, LeBlanc and Kelloway (2002) used test–retest reliability for a measure of risk for violence across a period of a month, $r = .92$, $p < .01$. If test–retest reliability is very low, this may be because the measure is unreliable or for reasons other than unreliability that can be reasoned through (e.g., construct scores changed because there was too much time between measurements).

In addition to reliability, there are other ways of demonstrating validity of a temporally nested construct. This is especially needed for measures that have not been rigorously validated at the standard individual level. In these cases, one can apply the nomological network paradigm in much the same way as at the individual level described above. For instance, Wu and Griffin (2012) used a measure of core self-evaluations from past archival data. Because there was no measure in the data specifically for this construct, the authors used six items with relevant content that they subsequently submitted to validation through nomological relations. Specifically, they examined convergent validity with an established measure of core self-evaluations (Judge, Erez, Bono, & Thoresen, 2003) in a sample of 310 undergraduates and found an acceptable association of *r* = .70. Similarly, Lucas, Diener, and Suh (1996) measured different well-being constructs using a variety of different methods (e.g., self-report and informant report at multiple time points). Analyzing these correlations within the multitrait, multimethod matrix framework (Campbell & Fiske, 1959), the authors found compelling evidence for discriminant validity of various well-being measures (e.g., life satisfaction, self-esteem, negative affect, positive affect).

One last component of validity for temporally nested measures (in addition to reliability and nomological networks) is what Ployhart and Vandenberg (2010) referred to as *longitudinal validity*. This entails that the frame of reference individuals use when responding to items remains the same across time. If not, then measurement (i.e., longitudinal validity) is compromised. One method for providing evidence for longitudinal validity is to test for *measurement invariance*—that the factor structure of the measure does not change as a function of when measurement occurs (or else the measured construct potentially changes as well). There are different grades of measurement invariance based on different levels of strictness (e.g., configural invariance and metric invariance), and the degree of invariance may depend, in part, on the time lag between measurements. Guidelines for testing measurement invariance can be readily found (Bashkov & Finney, 2013; Cheung & Lau, 2012; Raju, Laffitte, & Byrne, 2002; Tay, Meade, & Cao, 2015; Vandenberg & Lance, 2000), and practical examples in actual research are also numerous (Boyce, Wood, Daly, & Sedikides, 2015; Eby et al., 2015; Ritter, Matthews, Ford, & Henderson, 2016).

Class 2: Constructs Completely at the Group Level

A second class of constructs found in multilevel analysis comprises both those that reside at the group level and those that are measured at the group level. An example of this construct type is *group size* (Carter & Mossholder, 2015; Vidyarthi et al., 2016). Whether it be the size of a team, department, or organization, this construct is measured directly from groups (by a simple count of individuals within groups) and only describes a property of groups. Other examples include group performance when the measures of success are assessing the group as a collective whole rather than being aggregated from individual performance scores (e.g., Chen et al., 2002), group region (Brickson, 2005), and organizational age (Brickson, 2005). In past discussions of multilevel modeling, constructs of this class have been referred to as "aggregate properties" (Chen, Mathieu, & Bliese, 2005) or "global unit properties" (Kozlowski & Klein, 2000).

The class of constructs that are both measured and reside at the group level can be viewed as analogous to the constructs, described in the introduction, that are measured and reside solely at the individual level (e.g., individual self-efficacy). However, there are two important features of this new class. First, constructs both measured and residing at the group level are often represented by single-indicator measures rather than by multiple indicators (e.g., Brickson, 2005). Second, these constructs tend to be less abstract and more objective (e.g., group size or age) and are thus often measured with little measurement error.

These characteristics makes for a more convenient validation process for researchers. When there are single-indicator measures, reliability estimates cannot be calculated, with the exception of test–retest reliability. However, reliability estimates are usually unnecessary (including test–retest), because in most cases one can safely assume that reliability is above the acceptable standards due to low measurement error. This aligns with how this construct type is treated within academic literatures, in which reliability estimates are rarely provided. Moreover, this class of group-level constructs is often "operationally defined" (Cronbach & Meehl,

1955, p. 232), that is, when the construct is *defined* by the measure itself (i.e., its operationalization) rather than as an overarching theoretical concept. Group size is an example of an operationally defined measure, as the construct simply *is* the number of individuals within the group. Inferences from operationally defined measures are off the hook from construct validation (Cronbach & Meehl, 1955), as they are a priori valid by nature. Finally, if reasonable doubts about validity remain, then the validation process for inferences from this construct class "amounts to a traditional construct validation process restricted only to an aggregate level" (Chen, Mathieu, & Bliese, 2005, p. 285). Thus, researchers can test nomological network relations to assess whether expected relations are supported.

Class 3: Constructs Measured From Individuals but Residing in Groups

In the third class of constructs found in multilevel analyses, the constructs are measured at the individual level but describe attributes of groups. For instance, team diversity or team cohesion are operationalized using measurements from individuals (e.g., gender, ethnicity, team cohesion perceptions; Harrison, Price, & Bell, 1998; O'Reilly, Caldwell, & Barnett, 1989). They cannot, however, be conceived at the individual level, because "individual diversity" or "individual cohesion" are nonsensical. Instead, the constructs reside at the group level because groups are the units that they necessarily describe. Unlike the aforementioned two classes of constructs, this type of construct is an example of *emergence*, in which higher level phenomena manifest, or "emerge," from interactions taking place on a lower level. Emergence is a central concept in multilevel measurement and analysis (Bliese, 2000; Chan, 1998b; Kozlowski & Klein, 2000). Emergent constructs also require more sophisticated validation procedures because *more than one level of analysis* is at play. Perhaps the most significant additional aspect is the specification of the construct's *composition model*, or the theoretical account of how the lower level attributes combine to produce higher level phenomenon. Construct validation practices for these emergent constructs are similar to the final construct class, multilevel constructs, and the

two are described together in the remainder of the chapter.

Class 4: Multilevel Constructs

The last class of constructs in multilevel analyses we discuss are *multilevel constructs*. Like the class just described, multilevel constructs emerge from interactions among individuals and are therefore measured at the individual level only. However, they reside at both the individual and group level simultaneously because the construct describes properties of both units. For instance, job satisfaction is measured from individuals, but one also can aggregate these scores and discuss organizational-level job satisfaction as exerting effects above and beyond those found at the individual level (Oh, Kim, & Van Iddekinge, 2015). Having simultaneous effects from multiple levels characterizes other multilevel constructs, such as propensity to trust (Ferguson & Peterson, 2015), personality traits such as emotional stability and extraversion (Oh et al., 2015), servant leadership (Chen, Kirkman, Kanfer, Allen, & Rosen, 2007; Liden, Wayne, Zhao, & Henderson, 2008), and abusive supervision (Farh & Chen, 2014).

Despite the intuitive appeal of multilevel constructs, their properties pose unique practical challenges to measurement. For instance, like other emergent constructs, higher level measurements are created by aggregating scores at the individual level. But how should this aggregation be carried out? Under what conditions is constructing an aggregate appropriate, and when is it not? How can we be sure that the aggregated measure has validity? And how are we supposed to think about a higher level construct theoretically—that is, what is the substantive meaning of an aggregate construct?

This complex set of issues means (a) that researchers must ensure that their measurements capture their target theoretical constructs and (b) that these constructs are clearly articulated. The remainder of the chapter describes validation approaches for multilevel constructs (and those in Class 3). We draw on the work by Chen, Mathieu, and Bliese (2005), who proposed a general framework of multilevel construct validation composed of five steps to be followed in order: (a) construct definition, (b) articulation of the nature of the aggregate construct, (c) psychometric properties of construct across levels of analysis, (d) construct variability between units, and (e) construct function across levels of analysis. This framework is highly useful, and we build upon this prior work. The primary substance of the chapter is an involved discussion of four complementary approaches to construct validation for emergent constructs: (a) *score similarity*, (b) *psychometric isomorphism*, (c) *nomological networks with homology*, and (d) *nomological networks without homology*. These approaches are presented in detail and include descriptions of statistical methods and their logic, cutoff criteria used for decision making, and empirical demonstrations. Prior to these sections, however, we discuss two core issues of multilevel measurement so that the present chapter can be used on its own without relying on other sources (e.g., Chen, Mathieu, & Bliese, 2005; Kozlowski & Klein, 2000). These two preceding topics are (a) the importance and development of construct definitions and (b) the theory and history of composition models.

CONSTRUCT DEFINITIONS

The basis for accurate construct measurement is a clear definition of what the target construct *is*. This point was strongly argued by Ryan and Deci (2006), who noted the unique challenge of fields that use colloquial terms: "Science requires specification of terms in exacting ways, especially in a field like ours where terms often have multiple lay meanings" (p. 1580). In the Chen, Mathieu, and Bliese (2005) framework, "construct definition" is Step 1, which includes determining "what the focal construct is, what it includes and excludes, whether it is unidimensional or multidimensional, whether its basis is formative or summative, and what its underlying nature is" (p. 279). This is no different from the initial stage of measurement at the individual level (Clark & Watson, 1995; Hinkin, 1998), as these principles apply to *all* constructs, not merely multilevel ones.

Unfortunately, the importance of this step is all too frequently overlooked. Podsakoff et al. (2016) discussed the continued lack of conceptual clarity within the organizational sciences and the numerous problems it creates. These problems include needless construct proliferation; fuzzy or undefined boundaries among constructs; a susceptibility to improper, inadequate, or contaminated measures; unclear tests of discriminant validity; ambiguity when testing an assumed nomological network; and inhibited scientific communication and progress (see Podsakoff et al., 2016, pp. 166–167). For multilevel constructs, offering clear definitions is more difficult because they involve greater degrees of abstraction. The group-level units (e.g., teams, departments, and organizations) are more abstract than concrete individuals, and this is reflected in the degree of conceptual fuzziness in group-level constructs; it is far easier to conceive of an individual's motivation than an entire team's. Moreover, given that multilevel relationships are estimated less frequently than single-level relationships, errors stemming from improper definitions are less likely to be corrected (Ioannidis, 2012; Stroebe, Postmes, & Spears, 2012). Measures of constructs at the group level may be used only once in the specific context of a lone study. By contrast, individual-level measures are used repeatedly in a wide variety of contexts, leading to scale refinements and the detection of errors.

In sum, the importance of clear construct definitions carries weight for measurement at all levels of analysis but may be especially challenging for constructs that involve higher levels in multilevel models. Given the need for clear definitions, there are several strategies for maintaining concept clarity. First, scholars can (a) continue to emphasize the importance of clear definitions and (b) require them as a nonnegotiable first step. Second, researchers can consult the many resources available that give concrete guidance in forming accurate construct definitions (Johnson, Rosen, Chang, Djurdjevic, & Taing, 2012; Locke, 2012; Mackenzie, 2003; Molloy & Ployhart, 2012; Podsakoff et al., 2016; Slaney & Garcia, 2015). For instance, Podsakoff et al. (2016) propose four stages of constructing good definitions: (a) identify potential attributes by collecting a representative set of definitions; (b) organize the attributes by theme, and identify those that are necessary, sufficient, or common across themes;

(c) develop a working definition of the concept; and (d) refine the conceptual definition (e.g., identify remaining ambiguities, minimize jargon, and solicit feedback from peers). Locke (2012) offers some complementary advice, including (a) grounding the concept in concrete reality (i.e., the phenomenon it manifests in the real world), (b) clearly distinguishing the concept from related concepts, and (c) not assuming that previous definitions are good ones ("often they are not"; p. 148).

MODELS OF EMERGENCE

Like many disciplines, research in the organizational sciences usually occurs at the individual level, where the properties of units can be measured directly using self- and other report. By contrast, constructs at higher, more abstract levels of analysis (e.g., team and organization), are often operationalized by aggregating lower level scores (construct Classes 3 and 4 above). The specific methods for aggregation are given by *composition models* (Chan, 1998b), theoretical models that specify how higher level constructs emerge from lower level phenomenon. In other words, composition models are models of emergence that imply how data should be aggregated to form the target construct (Kozlowski & Klein, 2000). Although composition models are technically *theoretical* models of emergence, they are so strongly tied to operationalization that it sometimes seems that they instead refer to specific ways for aggregating data (e.g., "collective efficacy was *measured* [emphasis added] using referent-shift composition models in the three samples"; Chen, Mathieu, & Bliese, 2005, p. 296). Strong arguments could be made for viewing composition models as *both* theoretical and operational models of the mapping from lower level to higher level constructs. In either case, composition models are crucial because they answer the question, "How do we measure a higher level construct?" Every construct in Class 3 (measured at individual, residing at group) and 4 (multilevel) have a model of composition. As such, these models are the bridge from multilevel theory to measurement.

In the Chen, Mathieu, and Bliese (2005) framework, specifying a composition model is Step 2 in multilevel construct validation (i.e., "articulating the nature of the construct"). However, this should not be taken to mean that a construct's composition model is something an analyst freely chooses or "selects"; rather, it is already determined by the theoretical nature of the construct. In this way, specifying a composition model can—and perhaps should—be viewed as an aspect of Step 1: construct definition. That is, part of defining a multilevel or Class 3 construct is to state how the phenomenon emerges from lower level interactions, and this requires no less consideration than other parts of construct definition (James, 1982).

Prior Composition Model Taxonomies

It is also important to discuss the slightly different ways in which organizational scholars have used and extended the concept of composition models. In the first typology made by Chan (1998b), composition models were described as specifying the "functional relationships" between constructs across levels. The phrase "functional relationship" can be understood as a mapping of the "transformation across levels" (Chan, 1998b, p. 234), or put more simply, how emergence happens. Thus, composition models were originally conceived as theoretical models of emergence, or how higher level constructs were "composed" out of their lower level counterparts. Accordingly, Chan's (1998b) framework focused only on when the higher level constructs came from the interaction of lower level units (called *elemental composition*). It included five types: (a) additive, (b) direct consensus, (c) referent-shift, (d) dispersion, and (e) process composition models.

Shortly after this typology, Kozlowski and Klein (2000) introduced the distinction between composition and compilation models, two "qualitatively distinct types" of emergence (p. 16). Composition models were redefined to be cases of emergence in which the higher level construct was "essentially the same as its constituent elements" (i.e., the lower level construct; p. 16). Composition models represented cases of cross-level *isomorphism*, or when the higher level construct has the same meaning as its lower level counterpart. In real data, composition is fully realized when all individual-level units have the same score within their groups;

in this case, the group-level mean will have the same value as all of its constituent elements, and the two can be treated as identical with respect to their substantive meaning. By contrast, *compilation* models represent cases of emergence in which the lower level construct is qualitatively different in meaning than the higher level construct (i.e., nonisomorphism). In real data, compilation is realized when there is variation within groups and the group-level and. individual-level scores differ.

Composition and compilation can be seen as opposing poles on the isomorphism continuum. They are also *idealized*, or purely theoretical, forms of emergence. In real applications, emergence is not likely to be characterized by either total homogeneity or total heterogeneity. This led Bliese (2000) to extend Kozlowski and Klein (2000) by introducing "fuzzy" composition models, in which both similarities and differences exist across the constructs at different levels (called "partial isomorphism"). Similarities exist because higher level scores depend on lower level scores, and differences are a function of other higher level factors that only influence the higher level construct (Bliese, 2000).

Finally, in the validation framework of Chen, Mathieu, and Bliese (2005), the term "composition model" was used in the original sense of Chan (1998b). No explicit reference to compilation models was made, and a focus is placed on composition models as ways of operationalizing higher level constructs. The authors added "selected score" and "aggregate properties" to the typology and describe fuzzy vs. pure composition as well.

Synthesizing Past Frameworks

In the literature on multilevel analysis, Chan (1998b), Kozlowski and Klein (2000), and Chen, Mathieu, and Bliese (2005) have all posited typologies of composition models (for a good comparison of these, see Table 2 in Chen, Mathieu, & Bliese, 2005). Although each framework uses slightly different terminology, their content is highly similar. In total, there have been eight composition models proposed: (a) aggregate properties, (b) selected score, (c) additive, (d) dispersion, (e) direct consensus, (f) referent-shift, (g) dispersion, and (h) process. We summarize them in Table 11.1, while more

extensive descriptions can be found in Chan (1998b, pp. 235–242), Chen, Mathieu, and Bliese (2005, pp. 279–287), and Kozlowski and Klein (2000, pp. 65–74). In Table 11.1, group-level performance is repeated as a substantive example for all the composition models. This was done to highlight the fact that the same construct can be conceived as emerging in different ways, depending on the context. For instance, group-level performance can be additive when it is conceptualized as the sum total of individual performance (e.g., group performance as the summed sales of individuals). Alternatively, the same group-level construct follows a referent-shift composition model when it is conceived as the average of individuals' reports of their perception of the group's performance.

It should also be noted that, although these models represent the major types of composition, other types may be possible. For instance, Sinha, Janardhanan, Greer, Conlon, and Edwards (2016) recently studied *skewed* team conflict, defined as "when there is a critical mass (majority bloc) of team members with certain conflict perceptions and a small proportion of members with the opposing perception" (p. 1046). This construct was operationalized by a measure of within-group using the following formula:

$$\text{Skew} = \frac{1}{N} \sum_{i=1}^{N} \left[\frac{x_i - \bar{X}}{SD} \right]^3. \quad (11.1)$$

Thus, as organizational theory advances, more specific forms of composition may become evident. However, the number of composition models is finite, and its major forms have been identified and summarized in Table 11.1.

COMPOSITION MODELS AND CONSTRUCT VALIDATION

The early portions of this chapter described four classes of constructs that differed with respect to (a) the level on which they were measured and (b) the level on which they reside (i.e., what units they describe). We then devoted a space to discussing previous work on composition models because they are one of the most important aspects

TABLE 11.1

Composition Models for Emergent Constructs With Descriptions and Examples

Model	Form of emergence	Typical operationalization	Examples
Selected score	Construct emerges from a single lower level unit of unique importance.	Score of a specific lower level unit	Group performance determined by the worst or best performer; group communication as the value for a group leader
Additive	Construct emerges as some combination of lower level scores in which consensus is not required.	Within-group sum or average	Group performance as the sum total sales of its members; group creativity defined as the sum creativity of its members
Dispersion	Construct emerges as the variability of within-group units.	The group standard deviation, variance, or range	Group performance when performance is determined by the variation in individual performance; member gender diversity as the standard deviation of a gender variable
Direct consensus	Construct emerges as the consensus of lower level responses. Measurement items reference the lower level only.	Within-group agreement or average	Group performance as indexed by shared perceptions of the individuals' own performance; group affect as the similarity in affect of individuals
Referent-shift	Construct emerges as the consensus regarding a group-level property. Measurement items directly reference higher level property.	Within-group agreement or average	Group performance as indexed by the shared perceptions of group members of the team's performance; trust in supervisor as indexed by within-group agreement of trust
Process	Only when lower level and higher level constructs are *processes* that occur over time. The higher level process is assumed to be analogous to the lower level process.	No standard single measure; parameters of process are compared across levels	Group performance as the process of (a) determining performance goals and (b) maintaining across levels
Skewness	Construct emerges as a pattern of within-group variation in which the majority have similar scores in a range of the distribution but others have significantly different scores.	Within-group skewness	Group skewed performance; group skewed justice perceptions

of conducting validation for Class 3 and Class 4 constructs (multilevel constructs). This is because a construct's particular composition model *determines the type of empirical validation strategy required.* Each composition model (e.g., direct consensus, dispersion) contains assumptions about emergence that must be empirically verified. For instance, referent-shift composition assumes that there is a single global property that is perceived by individuals. In the selected score model, the assumption is that a single member of the group holds a uniquely important role in the system and that the higher level construct

emerges as that individual's score (e.g., the worst or best performer). In the following sections, we describe three approaches necessary for multilevel construct validation noted by Tay et al. (2014). These are (a) *reliability* and *agreement*, both demonstrating the consistency of scores within groups; (b) *psychometric isomorphism*, which shows that the factor structure of a construct remains constant across levels; and (c) *nomological network* and *homology*, which establish validity by verifying expected empirical relations. Each of these approaches tests different assumptions and are differentially applicable to the composition models. More specifically, we can divide composition models into two camps: (a) direct consensus and referent-shift models, which require all three approaches to be met for construct validity; and (b) the remaining models (i.e., additive, dispersion, and selected score), which can only demonstrate validity by testing a nomological network (Cronbach & Meehl, 1955; what Chan [1998b] calls the "validity of the index"). Construct validity of the latter is evidenced when relationship expected through theory matches the observed empirical relations. As seen, the demands of direct consensus and referent-shift are the most stringent. These types of models contain the most assumptions that must be empirically tested.

RELIABILITY OF SCORES

In multilevel analyses, an important distinction can be made between two kinds of reliability. The first is *psychometric reliability*, which is reliability in the classic sense (i.e., the repeatability of results). The second is *aggregate reliability*, or the extent to which within-group scores are similar enough to justify aggregation. The goal here is to evaluate within-group score similarity for purposes of data aggregation, and this is only applicable to direct consensus and referent-shift composition models.

Psychometric Reliability

When possible, researchers should examine more traditional forms of psychometric reliability (i.e., those typically used for individual-level measures). Unlike aggregate reliability, psychometric reliability applies to every model of emergence. The two most common forms of psychometric reliability are *internal consistency* reliability and *test–retest* reliability. For internal consistency, Cronbach's alpha can be calculated from aggregated indicator scores; similarly, omega (i.e., the amount of variance explained by a latent variable; McDonald, 1999) can be calculated from aggregated indicator scores using a confirmatory factor analytic model. For test–retest reliability, aggregated scores at the higher level can be examined over multiple occasions to determine the extent they display rank-order stability.

Aggregate Reliability

When is similarity assumed? In cases where emergence occurs through direct consensus or referent-shift composition, a crucial step in multilevel construct validation is demonstrating that scores within groups are similar. This is because these two composition models conceive the higher level construct as being made up of a consensus among group members. Therefore, to justify this assumption, one must demonstrate statistically that there is sufficient similarity within groups. Other models do not rely on the assumption that within-group scores are similar. For instance, in dispersion composition, the emergent higher level construct is conceived as the variation among lower level scores; any operational measure, such as the range or standard deviation, does not assume similarity across group members. In fact, *low similarity* across group members (i.e., high variance) is substantively interesting. Similarly, the selected score model views the higher level construct as emerging from the score of a single group member that is uniquely important (e.g., the ability of a team as determined by its weakest performer). In this case, similarity of within-group scores is simply irrelevant to this particular model of emergence. In the rest of this section, we explain common indices for demonstrating score similarity, their computation and statistical rationale, and recommendations for *how much* similarity is required (i.e., cutoff value conventions).

Similarity indices: IRA and IRR. In multilevel construct validation, the two most commonly used indices of similarity are *interrater agreement* (IRA) and *interrater reliability* (IRR; LeBreton & Senter, 2008). Although the names of these statistics seem to imply raters providing explicit ratings on some phenomenon (e.g., employee performance), a more general framing is that these statistics show the extent to which observations within a set are similar— that is, "agreeing" in terms of their value. Within a multilevel context, each lower level unit may be conceptualized as a "rater," each higher level unit as its "target," and its score, its "rating." Estimates of IRR or IRA provide information about the extent to which lower level units (e.g., raters) are substitutable (James, 1982) in either an absolute or relative sense.

In IRA, similarity is defined in terms of the *absolute* value of scores (i.e., to what degree are the scores furnished by two raters of a single target equivalent to one another). Estimates of IRA are typically based (in part) on the degree of within-group variability in observed scores (James, Demaree, & Wolf, 1984; LeBreton & Senter, 2008). In contrast, IRR is defined in terms of the relative consistency with which lower level units (e.g., raters) can discriminate between higher level units (e.g., groups). Estimates of IRR are typically based on some form of correlation coefficient (LeBreton & Senter, 2008; Schmidt, Viswesvaran, & Ones, 2000). Consequently, bivariate Pearson product-moment correlations are rarely used in multilevel research (LeBreton & Senter, 2008). Rather, *intraclass correlation coefficients* (ICCs) are used to index reliability, with the most commonly used ICC being derived from a one-way random effects ANOVA. This particular ICC is technically a function of both IRA and IRA (i.e., absolute and relative similarity; LeBreton & Senter, 2008). In the following sections, we describe the indices that are most commonly used in organizational research. For a more expansive review of IRA and IRR measures, see LeBreton and Senter (2008).

Interrater agreement.   The most common measure of similarity in multilevel research is IRA (James et al., 1984; LeBreton & Senter, 2008), and the most common measures of IRA are r_{WG} for single items and $r_{WG(J)}$ for multiple items (James et al., 1984; James, Demaree, & Wolf, 1993). The computation of r_{WG} is straightforward:

$$r_{WG} = 1 - \frac{S_X^2}{S_E^2}. \qquad (11.2)$$

Here, the numerator is simply the observed variance of the group, which indexes the (dis)similarity among observed scores. The r_{WG} statistic assumes that there is a single "true score" value, so that all the observed variation within the group is error. The denominator is the expected variance when there is absolutely *no* agreement among group members. This is the expected variance associated with a complete lack of agreement (i.e., completely random responding). As a result, the denominator will almost always be larger in magnitude than the numerator, and this

ratio grows smaller with more similarity. To provide a more intuitive index, this ratio is subtracted from 1 so that higher values indicate more agreement. Values of r_{WG} generally range between 0 and 1, 1 being the case when the observed variance is zero (i.e., every group member has the same score), and 0 being the case when the observed variance equals the variance expected under random responding. It is possible that a computed r_{WG} value exceeds the bounds of 0–1. See LeBreton and Senter (2008, pp. 827–828) and LeBreton, James, and Lindell (2005) for guidance in these cases.

Cutoff recommendations.   To justify aggregation using r_{WG}, a minimum cutoff score of $r_{WG} = .70$ has been conventionally used (LeBreton & Senter, 2008). The first use of this criterion was in George (1990) and was based on personal communication with the creator of r_{WG}, L. James (LeBreton & Senter, 2008). More recently, LeBreton and Senter (2008) constructed a more extensive system of cutoff criteria made up of the following categories: .00–.30 as a "lack of agreement," .31–.50 as "weak agreement," .51–.70 as "moderate agreement," .71–.90 as "strong agreement," and .91–1.00 as "very strong agreement." However, the authors noted the limitations of applying discrete cutoffs to continuous measures of evidence. When cutoffs are applied mechanistically and insensitive to context, research progress can be undermined. As articulated by Sir Ronald Fisher (1956): "No scientific worker has a fixed level of significance at which from year to year, and in all circumstances, he rejects hypotheses" (p. 42). Similarly, no multilevel researcher should have a fixed level of IRA (or IRR) that he or she applies in all their research regardless of context. Applying cutoffs too rigidly leads to a couple of problems: discounting of important results that might fail to reach an arbitrary statistical threshold and the proliferation of questionable research practices aimed at exceeding that threshold (John, Loewenstein, & Prelec, 2012; Simmons, Nelson, & Simonsohn, 2011). A better way is to make a case-by-case decision as to what IRA or IRR estimate is acceptable for the given context. This decision should be informed by previous research rather than being bound to it. More discussion of IRA cutoffs can be found in LeBreton and Senter (2008).

Choosing an appropriate null distribution. As can be seen, r_{WG} has many appealing statistical properties: It is a computationally simple and conceptually intuitive. However, there is a catch to using r_{WG} as an index of similarity. Although the numerator, the observed variance, can be easily calculated from the sample data, the denominator is a hypothetical quantity that must be deduced from theory. Specifically, deriving this quantity requires the researcher to answer the following question: What would the variance be if there was a total lack of agreement among group members (i.e., totally random responding)? Or, stated another way, how would the pattern of responses be *distributed* if there was no higher level construct influencing the individual-level responses? Traditionally, operationalizing this variance has proceeded under the assumption that a totally random response process would follow a *uniform distribution* (LeBreton, Burgess, Kaiser, Atchley, & James, 2003). Under this model, the probability of observing any one response is exactly the same as all the others, giving the distribution its characteristic rectangular shape.

Driving the use of this model is the idea that the most appropriate model of random responding is when all response categories are equally likely. However, the flaw with this logic is that there are a number of well-documented *response biases* that influence individuals' responses in a systematic way, even in the absence of any higher level constructs (Furnham, 1986; Furnham & Henderson, 1982). In other words, even if there is no common higher level construct among individuals (e.g., shared organizational mood or climate), certain response options are still more likely than others. Examples of relevant response biases include the *central tendency bias*, when individuals tend to select options closer to the middle of scales, and *positive response bias*, when individuals tend to select positive response options (e.g., "agree," or "yes"). Because of these common biases, the uniform distribution is generally not a good model of random responding, and because it has the largest variance of any probability distribution with the same support, it can inflate the r_{WG} estimate. As a result, LeBreton and Senter (2008, p. 830) called for *a moratorium* on the default use of the uniform distribution in organizational research.

Given that the uniform distribution is an often inappropriate model, methodologists within the field of applied psychology have offered recommendations for various alternatives. In their original article, James et al. (1984) stated that researchers, in addition to using the uniform distribution, should use several distributions in order to accommodate the possibility of different response biases. These alternative models included the *triangular distribution* to model central tendency bias, as well as distributions with skew to model leniency and severity biases (see James et al., 1984). Ultimately, the shape of the distribution should correspond to the patterns dictated by expected response biases. However, these may not be fully known with certainty, which motivates the use of multiple different models and examining their convergence. To promote the use of these alternative models, LeBreton and Senter (2008, Table 2) provided expected variance values for different distributions that correspond to various scale lengths and response biases.

Reporting results from several models. One final issue is reporting. If multiple distributions are used for r_{WG}, then how should the final results be reported? We repeat and elaborate on the guidance given by LeBreton and Senter (2008). Once a set of candidate distributions are chosen, the researcher can calculate r_{WG} for each group. If the entire set of values is not unreasonably large, one can simply report all the estimates (e.g., 3 distributions × 6 groups = 18 estimates). However, if there are several multilevel constructs being aggregated across many groups, the number of estimates can rise very quickly, growing multiplicatively (e.g., 3 distributions × 3 constructs × 20 groups = 180 estimates). Under these conditions, the analyst can take advantage of the fact that the r_{WG} estimates for a given model form their own distribution that can be described just like any type of sample data. For example, the arithmetic mean of the r_{WG} estimates can serve as a point estimate of these values—or the median, if the values are skewed. Point estimates should always be accompanied by measures of dispersion, or variability, to indicate how consistent the set of estimates is within a given model. We recommend that analysts report the range (i.e., minimum and maximum), because it provides the estimated lower and upper bounds of agreement within each model. The range can be supplemented by the standard deviation, mean absolute deviation, or robust estimators in the case of skewness (e.g., the median absolute deviation from the median). As LeBreton and Senter (2008) suggested, an analyst can also provide the percentage of estimates that fall above a prespecified cutoff or a full plot of the estimates, such as a histogram or kernel density plot. In any case, these descriptive statistics should provide a thoughtful summary of the set of r_{WG} estimates under each model.

Summary of IRA. The r_{WG} statistic is a measure of IRA that has been used extensively for demonstrating similarity of within-group responses to justify the assumptions of direct consensus and referent-shift composition. Suggested cutoff values were described above, as was the importance of selecting an appropriate model of random responding (or multiple models when response biases are not fully known). LeBreton and Senter (2008) reviewed additional measures of IRA, such as Schmidt and Hunter's (1989) within-group standard deviation (SD_X) and standard error (SE_M), average deviation indices (AD; Burke, Finkelstein, & Dusig, 1999) and the a_{WG} (Brown & Hauenstein, 2005). In this chapter, we have chosen to focus primarily on r_{WG}, as it is the most common index used in multilevel research and can be used on its own to justify certain composition models. For more information regarding these other statistics, see the discussion by LeBreton and Senter (2008, pp. 818–825), as well as the original sources just listed.

Interrater reliability. Reliability is a core psychometric property of any measurement instrument, referring to the extent to which it produces observed scores that are repeatable (i.e., the proportion of variation due to true scores; Furr & Bacharach, 2013; Nunnally & Bernstein, 1994). In multilevel measurement, indices of IRR are used to (a) provide a reliability estimate of the higher-level construct and (b) demonstrate similarity within groups to justify aggregation. As noted earlier, reliability in multilevel measurement is indexed by ICCs, which are mixed measures of both agreement and reliability (i.e., IRA and IRR; LeBreton & Senter, 2008).

The ICC(1) and the ICC(2). There are two general types of the ICC used in multilevel modeling:

the ICC(1) and the ICC(2). Both the ICC(1) and the ICC(2) are well suited for multilevel research because they presume that the lower level units (e.g., raters and individuals) are nested inside higher level units (e.g., groups). These statistics are based upon the variance decomposition from a one-way random-effects ANOVA. Here, the factor is a categorical variable that codes group membership, and its effect is considered random because the groups are considered to be randomly sampled from a larger population of groups. The total observed variance of the outcome variable is partitioned into two components: (a) the variance *between groups* (*MSB*, mean-square between) and (b) the variance that exists *within groups* (*MSW*, mean-square within). The formula for the ICC(1) is

$$ICC(1) = \frac{MSB - MSW}{MSB + [(K-1) \times MSW]}. \quad (11.3)$$

The ICC(1) may be interpreted as the proportion of total variance in a lower level outcome variable (e.g., individual-level job satisfaction) that is attributable to the lower level units being nesting within higher level units (e.g., employees nested within work teams; Bliese, 2000). If this value is large enough, then there is sufficient between-group variance to include higher level predictors (e.g., team cohesion; Chen, Mathieu, & Bliese, 2005; Kahn, 2011). It should *not* be used to justify aggregation or as a measure of reliability at the group level (James, 1982).

By contrast, the ICC(2) may be used as the reliability estimate of a higher level measure (LeBreton & Senter, 2008). The ICC(2) is also computed from a one-way random effects ANOVA table as

$$ICC(2) = \frac{MSB - MSW}{MSB}. \quad (11.4)$$

The ICC(2) statistic is interpretable as an index of the stability, or reliability, of the group means.

Cutoff recommendations. When using the ICC(1) to justify higher level predictors, we repeat the advice given by a number of other resources (e.g., Chen, Mathieu, & Bliese, 2005; Kahn, 2011; LeBreton & Senter, 2008). The ICC(1) can be thought of as an effect size that describes the amount of variance explained, similar to the R^2 statistic from a regression model. These values do not have to be very large to be practically significant. Experts in methodology have noted that values as low .01 can be considered small but consequential effects (Cohen, 1992; LeBreton & Senter, 2008). Larger values also justify the inclusion of higher level predictors, though smaller values might preclude them.

As stated, the purpose of the ICC(2) in multilevel models is as a reliability estimate to show that group means are reliable indicators of the higher level construct. The minimally acceptable reliability should depend on the research context. When the stakes are high, a large ICC(2) value might better serve the goals of the analysis. However, for general research purposes, a commonly used minimum reliability is .70 (Lance, Butts, & Michels, 2006). It should also be noted that both ICCs are a function of IRR (relative similarity) as well as IRA (absolute similarity), and high values can only be obtained when both IRR and IRA are high. Conversely, this means that a *low* ICC can be a function of (a) low IRA, (b) low IRR, or (c) both (LeBreton et al., 2003). When this is the case, one should investigate the source of the discrepancy (see LeBreton & Senter, 2008).

FACTORIAL VALIDITY

Apart from establishing reliability, factorial validity is also crucial to construct validity. The most important aspect of factorial validity is *factor structure*, which refers to the relationships between items and latent variables (i.e., the number of latent variables and the pattern of item loadings; Furr, 2011; Tay et al., 2014). In multilevel construct validation, factor structure is an important concern when higher level measures are made from multiple items (just as with multi-item measures at the individual level). When only a single item is aggregated, however, examination of factor structure is impossible because there is only one factor and one loading.

There are two forms of factorial validity: (a) *psychometric isomorphism*, which analyzes the factor structure at multiple levels; and (b) *single-level analysis of factor structure*. The first, psychometric isomorphism, occurs when one needs to demonstrate that a particular factor structure is consistent across

levels (only for Class 4, multilevel constructs). Psychometric isomorphism is only pertinent for two types of emergence models that posit similar content between levels: direct consensus and referent-shift consensus. However, constructs that emerge in other ways (e.g., additive and dispersion) also require tests of factor structure when their measures contain multiple indicators. These cases are much less common, but when they occur, a conventional single-level analysis of factor structure can be applied to the aggregate higher level scores. Typically, one will expect a one-factor model, which can be formally compared to models with more than one factor.

Psychometric Isomorphism

When we have multilevel constructs emerging from a direct consensus or referent-shift model, one assumes that there is a degree of similarity between the lower level and higher level constructs. To justify this must assumption, one must demonstrate psychometric isomorphism, "a construct validation technique when we posit multilevel constructs which have similar content across levels" (Tay et al., 2014, p. 98). In referent-shift and direct consensus composition, an assumption is that the meaning, or content, of the lower level scores is maintained at the higher level. Psychometrically, this requires showing that the factor structure is also preserved across levels, and psychometric isomorphism is just a test of this assumption.

Psychometric isomorphism can be better understood by an analogy to measurement validation at the individual level. In this simpler case, part of the validation process is ensuring that each item strongly relates to only one latent variable and that the number of latent variables is as expected. These criteria are tested using exploratory and confirmatory factor analytic models. Psychometric isomorphism merely adapts this procedure for testing across levels. It seeks to show (a) that the number of underlying factors, or latent variables, remains consistent across levels (called *configural isomorphism*); and (b) that the magnitude of the item loadings is also consistent across levels (called *metric isomorphism*). The terms *configural* and *metric* are borrowed from the measurement invariance literature (Vandenberg & Lance, 2000), as psychometric isomorphism is also related to measurement invariance. In measurement invariance, one wants to show that the internal structure of the instrument is consistent across different groups (e.g., racial groups or clusters of responses at different time points). If the internal structure is consistent, then one can safely draw inferences about the similarities or differences between the groups. Thus, one can think of traditional measurement invariance as occurring "horizontally" (i.e., at the same level but across groups) and psychometric isomorphism as another type of invariance that occurs "vertically" (i.e., across levels of analysis). In fact, psychometric isomorphism has also been referred to as "measurement equivalence isomorphism" (Tay et al., 2014, p. 79).

Configural isomorphism.   The first component of psychometric isomorphism is configural isomorphism, which means that the number of factors and the pattern of zero/nonzero loadings (simple structure) remain the same across levels. Just as with measurement invariance, psychometric isomorphism is not a binary state but may be present in degrees. The strictest form of configural isomorphism is *strong* configural isomorphism, which occurs when there is total correspondence in the factor structure across levels (i.e., when both the number of factors and pattern of loadings are fully replicated). When strong configural isomorphism is found between constructs, the meaning of the higher level construct and its relationships with other variables can be interpreted just as at the lower level.

Following strong configural isomorphism is *weak* configural isomorphism. Weak configural isomorphism occurs when the number of factors is preserved but the pattern of loadings is not replicated. If only weak configural isomorphism is present, then the meaning of the construct may or may not be preserved. This is because interpreting a factor depends on the content of its items. When its items are different, then its meaning might also differ. Researchers who come across weak configural isomorphism should carefully examine the loading pattern to see whether factor meanings are preserved.

Finally, the weakest type of configural isomorphism is called *partial* configural isomorphism. Partial configural isomorphism occurs when some, but not all, of the factors are reproduced at the higher level. When only partial configural isomorphism exists, the higher level and lower level constructs are not equivalent because their underlying structure is fundamentally different. In this case, the higher level construct must be given a new definition and interpretation from its lower level counterpart.

Metric isomorphism.   Configural isomorphism describes the extent to which a factor structure is preserved across levels. It is the most fundamental form of psychometric isomorphism. However, if one demonstrates configural isomorphism, one can go on to test for *metric isomorphism*, a more stringent version of psychometric isomorphism in which the *magnitudes* of the factor loadings are also replicated across levels. There are two types of metric isomorphism: *strong* and *weak*. Strong metric isomorphism describes cases when the magnitudes of the loadings are exactly the same. This is the strongest form of psychometric isomorphism one can show, as both the entire factor structure and loading magnitudes are equal. By contrast, weak metric isomorphism occurs when merely the *rank ordering* of factor loadings is equivalent between levels.

Procedures for Psychometric Isomorphism Tests

The various degrees of psychometric isomorphism are tested using latent variable modeling, which identifies and compares the psychometric properties of measures situated at different levels of analysis. Tay et al. (2014) described two distinct approaches for testing psychometric isomorphism, *separate* vs. *simultaneous* estimation, which differ in how they estimate the parameters of the measurement models. Separate estimation involves ignoring the nested structure of the data and separately estimating factor structures at the different levels. That is, measurement models are fitted separately to the raw individual-level data and to the aggregated group-level data. However, Muthén (1994), as well as others (e.g., Pornprasertmanit, Lee, & Preacher, 2014), have voiced significant concerns about ignoring the nesting of observations within groups. Analyzing the individual-level data this way results in biased parameter estimates, incorrect standard errors, and an overstated lack of model fit (Muthén, 1994; Pornprasertmanit et al., 2014). Conversely, analyzing the aggregated data in isolation results in similar biases because the covariance matrix aggregated within the sample is a biased estimate of the group-level population covariance matrix (Dyer, Hanges, & Hall, 2005). For these reasons, separate estimation is not generally recommended, though there may be instances when it can be useful (see Tay et al., 2014, p. 88).

In contrast to separate estimation, simultaneous estimation explicitly models the nested structure of the data. This approach utilizes *multilevel factor analytic modeling* (see Dyer et al., 2005, for an accessible introduction, and Muthén, 1994, for a more technical treatment). In this modeling framework, the different forms of psychometric isomorphism can be tested by comparing models that vary the factor structure (for configural isomorphism) and loading magnitudes (for metric isomorphism). More specific guidance on model comparison procedures (e.g., the type and number of fit indices) can be found in Tay et al. (2014, pp. 88–91).

As an illustrative example, we simulated multilevel data based on the Conscientiousness and Sportsmanship factors of Podsakoff, MacKenzie, Moorman, and Fetter's (1990) organizational citizenship behavior (OCB) scale. The data were generated

using the software package Latent Gold 4.5 and consisted of 100 groups with 10 individuals each. (Data and syntax are available by request from the first author.) As a first step, we conducted a preliminary factor analyses to ensure that the lower level factor structure aligned with what was expected. We conducted this analysis on the raw covariance matrix, ignoring the nested structure (which is acceptable in this preliminary stage; Tay et al., 2014). The two-factor model (CFI = .999, TLI = .998, RMSEA = .013, SRMR$_{within}$ = .01) was superior to a one-factor model (CFI = .689, TLI = .60, RMSEA = .019, SRMR$_{within}$ = .162), which confirmed our measurement model. All model results from this section are displayed in Table 11.2. We then tested for strong configural isomorphism, or that the entire factor structure holds across levels. To do this, one must specify and compare models with varying numbers of factors. In our case, we fit four models to the data with the group means used for the higher level scores. Two models represented strong configural isomorphism by fixing the number of factors and loading patterns (i.e., zero vs. nonzero) to be exactly the same at both levels. However, one model posited a single factor (Model 1-1), while the other, two factors (Model 2-2). The other two models

TABLE 11.2

Model Fit Statistics for Tests of Psychometric Isomorphism

Step	No. of factors	LL	BIC	CAIC	CFI	Npar	RMSEA	SRMR	TLI
Initial factor structure									
Individual level	1	−16808.7202	33824.6731	33854.6731	0.689	30	0.190	0.162	0.600
Individual level	2	−16181.7274	32577.5953	32608.5953	0.999	31	0.013	0.010	0.998
Configural isomorphism									
Configural	1-1	−16542.2723	33360.8548	33400.8548	0.515	40	0.196	0.145	0.376
Nonconfigural	1-2	−16502.7804	33295.6866	33337.6866	0.677	42	0.161	0.145	0.579
Nonconfigural	2-1	−16107.5238	32498.2656	32539.2656	0.979	41	0.041	0.041	0.973
Strong Configural	2-2	−16080.3253	32450.7763	32492.7763	0.997	42	0.015	0.022	0.996
Metric isomorphism									
Strong metric	2-2	−16100.6025	32456.7919	32408.5963	0.998	37	0.014	0.022	0.997

Note. For column showing number of factors, the individual level is listed first, and the group level follows. BIC = Bayesian information criterion; CAIC = consistent Akaike information criterion; CFI = confirmatory fit index; LL = log likelihood; Npar = number of parameters; RMSEA = root mean square error of approximation; SRMR = standardized root mean square residual (within); TLI = Tucker–Lewis index.

were nonconfigural and had different combinations of factors per level (Models 1-2 and 2-1). Model comparisons showed that the strong configural model with two factors provided the best fit to the data (Model 2-2: CFI = .997, TLI = .996, RMSEA = .015, SRMR$_{within}$ = .022).

If strong configural isomorphism is present, one can then move on to tests of metric isomorphism (i.e., that the magnitude of loadings is similar across levels). Weak metric isomorphism is found when the rank ordering of loadings is preserved, and one tests this by simply calculating rank-order correlations between the loadings at the different levels. Tentative advice is that correlations must be at least $r = .50$ to demonstrate weak metric isomorphism (Tay et al., 2014). For our data, we computed the rank-order correlation between item loadings for both the Conscientiousness and Sportsmanship factors across levels (five loadings and thus observations for each). We found that weak metric isomorphism held, but just for the first factor: $r = .89$ and $r = -.12$, respectively. (No significance tests are necessary here.) If the analyst discovers that weak metric isomorphism is present for one or more factors, he or she can move to test for strong metric isomorphism. This is done by fitting another multilevel factor model in which the loadings across levels are constrained to be *exactly equal*. A superior fit of this model over another model with factor loadings not constrained to equality across levels (i.e., the strong configural model) demonstrates strong metric isomorphism. We fit a final model to our data that fixed the magnitude of the higher level loadings for Conscientiousness to be the same as the lower level. (We continued to freely estimate the Sportsmanship loadings because weak metric isomorphism did not hold for this factor.) Comparing this model to the strong configural model (our previous candidate) showed that strong metric isomorphism was supported (CFI = .998, TLI = .997, RMSEA = .014, SRMR$_{within}$ = .022).

VALIDITY THROUGH THE NOMOLOGICAL NETWORKS AND HOMOLOGY

The concept of the nomological network has been a cornerstone of construct validation ever since its introduction by Cronbach and Meehl (1955). The nomological network is the irreducible "system of laws" that describes theoretical relations between a construct and other constructs. This network is established deductively through theory and inductively through empirical investigation. Once part of the network becomes defined, it produces testable predictions for how a measure will relate to measures of other constructs (Cronbach & Meehl, 1955, p. 290). Testing these empirical predictions amounts to a validity test of the inference that scores from the measure represents the target construct—assuming that the relations described by the nomological network are correct.

Showing validity requires that a measure exhibits empirical relations that are consistent with its construct's predefined nomological network, and this empirical process extends to measurement at all levels of analysis. At the individual level, testing the nomological network has been described as a critical part of scale development after a measure has been constructed (Hinkin, 1998). It is no less important for multilevel contexts, as individual-level validation practices are paralleled by Chen, Mathieu, and Bliese's (2005) Step 5 ("construct function across levels of analysis"), where one examines the construct's "relationships with other constructs at various levels of analysis" (p. 292). In the previous two sections of this chapter, we reviewed empirical techniques for validating the assumptions of the direct consensus and referent shift composition models: similarity indices (i.e., interrater reliability) and psychometric isomorphism. In the current section, we discuss the approach to multilevel validation based on nomological network relations.

NOMOLOGICAL NETWORK AND MODELS OF HOMOLOGY

In order for the nomological network to aid in construct validation, part of the network must be defined a priori (Cronbach & Meehl, 1955). If no part of the nomological network has been determined beforehand, then it is difficult for predictions to be made. As discussed earlier, multilevel constructs are (a) more abstract than individual-level constructs and (b) investigated with less frequency. These two factors typically lead to the nomological networks of multilevel constructs being less known and tested. However, one benefit is that, depending on the composition model, a higher level construct can "borrow" a portion, or the majority, of its nomological network from the lower level. This borrowing is possible when there is *homology* (Kozlowski & Klein, 2000), defined as when a higher level construct and its lower level counterpart maintain similar relationships to other constructs (Chen, Bliese, & Mathieu, 2005). The underlying logic is that "isomorphic constructs that maintain greater similarity in meaning across levels are more likely to have homologous (i.e., similar) relationships across levels" (Chen, Mathieu, & Bliese, 2005, p. 292). Thus, preserved meanings lead to preserved associations. For instance, under the direct consensus and referent-shift composition models, the construct meaning and factor structure may be preserved across levels, producing similarity in nomological network relations. By contrast, other composition models, such as dispersion and selected score, will likely have more nomological network differences.

Homology is an aid for specifying the nomological network of a multilevel construct. However, homology cannot simply be assumed; it must be empirically tested, and this requires that a *model* of homology be specified. In their paper, Chen, Bliese, and Mathieu (2005) present four models of homology: (a) metaphoric, (b) proportional, (c) identical, and (d) hybrid. These models vary with respect to (a) their degree of homology and (b) how theoretically specific they are. *Metaphoric* models are the most prevalent and require the least amount of knowledge regarding construct relationships. In this case, homology is present, but metaphoric models are totally agnostic with regard to its strength. Statistically, metaphoric models only require that corresponding statistical relationships *exist* across levels. This is tested by comparing the pattern of significant relations among constructs at different levels. An example of a metaphoric model is organizational personality, which is expected to operate in a similar way at the group level as at the individual level (Oh et al., 2015; Stewart, 2003) Metaphoric theories may pass into other, more specific, types of homology as they develop theoretically.

After the metaphoric model, two stronger models of homology are the *proportional* and *identical* models. These models go beyond the simple presence of relationships by examining relationship *magnitude*. Proportion models state that the strengths of relationships may differ across levels but will remain proportional (i.e., equal when multiplied by a certain value). For instance, safety climate at the group level shows proportionally stronger associations to past safety accidents than at the individual level (Beus, Muñoz, Arthur, & Payne, 2013). By contrast, in the identical model, the magnitudes of relationships are identical across levels. For example, there is some evidence for identical relations between individual and group-level efficacy with respect to regulation, reflection, and flexibility/cooperation (Gröschke, 2013).

Finally, a multilevel construct can also have a combination of different types of homology relations within its nomological network. For instance, the relationships for individual-level performance and group performance could be metaphoric with respect to certain variables, proportional for others, and identical still for others. This would be an example of *hybrid* homology, which combines two or more of the aforementioned homology models. Also, one could argue that one very important model of homology has been left out: cases in which no homology is expected (i.e., no similarity). If empirical relations differ markedly across levels, this does not mean that the multilevel measures are necessarily invalid. The multilevel construct may simply have a different substantive meaning or psychometric properties across levels, which may produce these observed differences. In summary, homologies are important because

> if researchers find that relationships are homologous across levels of analysis, it adds to the parsimony and breadth of theories. In contrast, should relationships prove not to be homologous across levels, it signals a boundary condition and a need to refine theories and to better understand how the processes operate at each distinct level. (Chen, Bliese, & Mathieu, 2005, p. 376)

More specific implications for each homology type can be found in the Chen, Bliese, and Mathieu (2005) article.

Techniques for Homology Testing

Statistical tests of homology can use different methods, such as within and between analysis (WABA), multilevel structural equation modeling, and random coefficient modeling (RCM; Chen, Mathieu, & Bliese, 2005). In this chapter, we review the RCM approach detailed by Chen, Bliese, and Mathieu (2005, pp. 385–398) and originally described by Widaman (2000). The RCM approach is advantageous because it can be applied to many composition models and has a relatively straightforward implementation. The other statistical approaches are limited to certain types of composition and are more challenging to implement (see Chen, Bliese, & Mathieu, 2005).

Metaphoric homology.   Metaphoric theories require only that presence of relationships is preserved across levels (magnitude is irrelevant). Testing this model is accomplished by fitting two separate regression models, one at the individual level and the other at the group level. The number of significant relationships across the two models are tallied and compared. If the pattern holds, then this validates a metaphoric model. The group-level model is a weighted least squares regression conducted on the aggregated data. The observations are weighted by the sample size of each group to account for the fact that larger groups are estimated with more precision. We will refer to this as Model 1. The individual-level model, on the other hand, requires a multilevel model in order to avoid violating the assumption of independence among observations (which might otherwise result in biased significance tests for the coefficients). We refer to this model as Model MLM. To illustrate a test of metaphoric homology, we simulated data related to the previous OCB example and examined associations between OCBs and agreeableness and job satisfaction. We simulated data from 22 organizations with random numbers of individuals between 80 and 120. We used the software package R because of its flexibility in multilevel and regression modeling (Culpepper & Aguinis, 2011). The syntax for replicating the analysis can be found in Appendix 11.1.

We fit both models to the data and compared their patterns of significance. In Model MLM (individual level), both coefficients were significant: $b_1 = .40$, $SE = .02$, $p < .001$ for agreeableness and $b_2 = .52$, $SE = .02$, $p < .001$ for satisfaction. In Model 1 (group level), by contrast, neither coefficient was significant, $b_1 = .32$, $SE = .21$, $p = .14$ and $b_2 = .35$, $SE = .20$, $p = .10$, respectively. However, statistical power at the group level was much lower than at the individual level because of far fewer observations (22 vs. 2,234). This is a frequent issue when testing metaphoric homology, and researchers have recommend relaxing the group-level alpha level as a solution (Chen, Bliese, & Mathieu, 2005). In our data, the group-level effect sizes were $b_1 = .32$ and $b_2 = .35$. To reach a more desirable level of power, we calculated what alpha level would allow for a power of .70. Using the sample size and estimated slopes in the calculation led to alpha levels $\alpha = .30$ and $\alpha = .26$ for the two respective effects. After adopting these conventions, both group-level effects were statistically significant, in support of metaphoric homology. When relaxing the alpha level in other cases, we recommend that researchers not be held to any single decision rule but that they critically assess metaphoric homology based on (a) the group-level sample size, (b) the observed effect sizes, and (c) what is reasonable in terms of power and alpha (e.g., power between .60 and 80 and alpha perhaps no greater than $\alpha = .40$). R code for these power calculations is included in the syntax to Appendix 11.1.

Proportional and identical homology.   If metaphoric homology is shown, the analyst can then proceed to test the stricter proportional model. In proportional homology, the relationship sizes at the higher level are a multiplicative factor of those at the lower level (i.e., proportional). Furnishing evidence for this specific model requires additional steps. Specifically, one fits another model to the group-level data and then compares it to the first model of the group-level data that was used in the metaphoric test (i.e., Model 1, the regular weighted least squares regression). This second model, Model 2, is also a weighted least squares regression model but a restricted version; it constrains the size of the associations to be proportional across levels. Its form is

$$Y_i = b_0 + c(b_1 \times X_{1i} + b_2 \times X_{2i}) + \epsilon. \qquad (11.5)$$

Note that this is just a standard regression model with two predictors. However, there are two crucial differences. First, the coefficients are fixed to be the estimates from Model MLM, the individual level model used in the previous test for metaphoric homology (in our example, $b_1 = .40$ and $b_2 = .52$). Second, Model 2 includes an additional parameter, c, which allows the coefficients to vary by a constant multiplicative factor. After this model is estimated, it is compared to Model 1 using an F test, the equation for which is

$$F_i = \frac{SSE_{M2} - SSE_{M1}/(k_{M1} - k_{M2})}{SSE_{M1}/(N - k_{M1})}. \qquad (11.6)$$

A nonsignificant F statistic indicates that neither model is a significant improvement over the other. When this is the case, the proportional model is selected because it is the more parsimonious of the two (i.e., has fewer free parameters). Note that to test proportional homology (as well as identical homology), the only statistical models that need to be estimated are at the higher level; no further models for the lower level are needed. Using the same example data, we estimated Model 2 and compared it to Model 1. The F test was nonsignificant, $F = .02$, $p = .98$, indicating that a proportional model of homology provided a better fit. The estimate of the c parameter was $c = .72$, $p = .02$, meaning that the higher level associations are smaller in magnitude by a factor of .72 than those at the lower level.

Finally, if one finds that proportional homology is supported, then one can test for the strictest form, identical homology. This is done by using one final model, Model 3, which constrains the relationships to be identical in magnitude across levels. The mathematical form of Model 3 is just like the proportional model, Model 2, in Equation 11.5 but with the scaling factor removed. Thus, no parameters are estimated in Model 3. An F test (Equation 11.6) is then used to compare the two models, and identical homology is supported if the test is also nonsignificant.

Extending our example one final time, the F test comparing Model 3 with Model 2 was indeed nonsignificant, $F = .96$, $p = .34$, which appeared to support identical homology. However, the actual values of the regression coefficients told a much different story. The estimates of Model MLM (lower level model) were $b_1 = .40$ and $b_2 = .52$, whereas the estimates from Model 1 were $b_1 = .32$ and $b_2 = .35$. These are clearly not "identical." In fact, we knew that identical homology was not correct because the data had been simulated from a proportional model. What was the problem? This example was deliberately chosen to demonstrate a very common pitfall when testing homology: the low power of the F tests. This is very common because, although there may be many individuals, the number of higher level groups is usually quite small. In order to compensate for this low power, some researchers have suggested adopting a more relaxed alpha level, just as in metaphoric homology (e.g., $\alpha = .20$; Chen, Bliese, & Mathieu, 2005). However, in our data, we would have needed to set alpha to $\alpha = .68$ for the final F test to reach the recommended power standard of .80 (Cohen, 1992). Moreover, a failure to reject the null when testing either proportional or identical homology (i.e., when F tests are used) is an error in favor of the more *complex* model, which harms parsimony. Thus, if researchers do not properly consider the issue of power, then the most complex model and *least* parsimonious conclusion (identical homology) could be chosen every time—regardless of what the true underlying homology is.

The lesson here is that one should not blindly accept the results of significance tests, because they have many well-known shortcomings (Cohen, 1994; Rozeboom, 1960). A better solution is to supplement the F tests with a critical *examination of the coefficients* (i.e., effect sizes). This involves comparing the estimates Model MLM and Model 1 to see what model of homology they imply. (In our analysis, these estimates were $b_1 = .40$ and $b_2 = .52$ compared to $b_1 = .32$ and $b_2 = .35$.) If metaphoric homology is supported, one can go on to test for proportional homology by (a) conducting an F test and (b) multiplying the coefficients of Model MLM by the estimated c parameter (in our data, $c = .72$) to determine if they become equal to the coefficients at the higher level (Model 1). When we did this, we found that the relationships became approximately the same in magnitude ($b_1 = .29$ and $b_2 = .38$ versus $b_1 = .32$ and $b_2 = .35$), which indicated proportionality and validated the properties our data were simulated to have. If proportional homology is supported, one can more accurately test for identical homology by (a) conducting an F test and then (b) visually examining the size of the coefficients to see if they are the same (or else the nonsignificant test may be merely an artifact of low power).

Although proportional and identical homology are the most common, there is a final model worth reviewing: the hybrid homology model. Because this kind of homology is a combination of the other homology types, one must look at the relationships across levels on a case-by-case basis (i.e., a variable-by-variable basis rather than omnibus F tests of whole models). For metaphoric homology, one can simply determine if a particular relationship is statistically significant across levels. By contrast, proportional homology cannot be examined on an individual basis. For identical homology, we suggest the approach offered by Chen, Bliese, and Mathieu (2005, pp. 390–393). First, one takes the original group-level data and subtracts the values that were fitted, or predicted, from Model 3 (the model representing identical homology). This creates a new dependent variable that is made up of the residuals if identical homology were true. (For instance, if identical homology were perfectly true, then all these residuals would be zero.) Then, this new variable is regressed on the same set of group-level predictors. The estimated coefficients of this model represent the *deviations* from identical homology, and any significant effect indicates that it is nonidentical across levels.

Final Thoughts on the Nomological Network

Construct validity through the nomological network is a matter of testing theoretically expected relationships against real data. When homology across levels is posited, part of the nomological network for one level becomes "filled out" by the network occurring at the other level. In this chapter, we reviewed recent work on tests for homology. However, what about when a multilevel construct is not believed to have any homology? In these cases, showing nomological network validity at higher levels can only be demonstrated by the standard approach: testing whether observed empirical relations match what is expected by theory (Cronbach & Meehl, 1955). This means that, for a number of higher level constructs, the only approach to validation is to simply examine its relations with other measures.

CONCLUSION

Multilevel theories are nuanced and provide understanding of organizational events and structures. However, multilevel analysis also requires an elaboration on construct theory, measurement principles, and empirical validation. Collected volumes are necessary to tabulate the ever-changing landscape of multilevel research. In this chapter, we have provided conceptual and empirical guidance on construct validation in multilevel analyses. This guidance has ranged from various theoretical issues, such as elaborating on construct definitions and how compositions models are to be understood, to empirical tests of reliability, factorial validity, and nomological network validity. This information represents a summary of current thinking on the topic and provides a working framework for practical researchers.

It is apparent that multilevel research will continue to evolve over time. However, as work accumulates, developments have a way of reaching an asymptote. For instance, although researchers may uncover other models of composition to describe multilevel phenomena, it is hard to imagine that many more will become prevalent. Moreover, different types of validity and brands of validation evidence (e.g., factorial, score similarity) will remain core components despite any refinements that may come. Thus, despite the possibility of new insights and methodology (e.g., estimation procedures for homology or psychometric isomorphism), certain aspects are simply foundational to multilevel research. It is these aspects that comprise the current chapter and inform multilevel practice across contemporary scientific disciplines.

APPENDIX 11.1: R CODE FOR SIMULATING DATA AND CONDUCTING HOMOLOGY TESTS

```
#######Load Packages#######
library(lme4)
library(MASS)
library(pwr)


#######Generate Data#######
#1.) Group-Level
mu<-c(3.5,4,3)#specify means
covmx<-matrix(data = c(1,.32,.39,.32,1,.07,.39,.07,1),
    nrow = 3,ncol = 3)#specify covariance matrix
set.seed(5299)
gdata<-mvrnorm(22,mu,covmx,empirical=TRUE)#s
    imulate data
gdata<-data.frame(gdata)#remake as data frame
colnames(gdata)<-c("OCB","Agree","JSAT")#rename
    variables
cor(gdata)#confirm correlations match parameters

#2.) Individual-Level
set.seed(5299)
groupN<-sample(80:120,22,replace=T)#get Ns per
    group
groups<-rep(1:22,times=groupN)
covmx<-matrix(data=c(1,.45,.56,.45,1,.10,.56,.10,1),
    nrow=3,ncol=3)#specify covariance matrix
set.seed(5299)
idata<-mvrnorm(sum(groupN),mu,covmx,
    empirical=T)#simulate data
idata<-cbind(idata,groups)#add group coding column
    to data matrix
idata<-data.frame(idata)#remake as data frame
colnames(idata)<-c("OCB","Agree","JSAT","Group")
    #rename variables
cor(idata)#confirm correlations match parameters

#######Test 1: Metaphoric Homology#######
:#1.) Model MLM is a multilevel model for the
    nested individual-level data
ModelMLM<-lmer(OCB~Agree+JSAT+(1+Agree+
    JSAT|Group),data=idata)

#2.) Model 1 is a standard weighted least squares
    regression for the group-level data
Model1<-lm(OCB~Agree+JSAT,data=gdata,weights=
    groupN)

#3.) Examine whether pattern of significance
    converges across models
summary(ModelMLM)$coefficients
summary(Model1)$coefficients
#Determine appropriate alpha level (Here, we specified
    our desired power and got a reasonable #alpha)
pwr.r.test(n = 22,r = .35,sig.level=NULL,power=.70)


#######Test 2: Proportional Homology#######
#1.) Store coefficients from Model MLM
params<-summary(ModelMLM)$coefficients[,1]

#2.) Model 2 is a standard weighted least squares
    regression with the parameters fixed to
#Model MLM and a proportionality parameter
Model2<-lm(OCB~I(params[2]*Agree+params[3]*
    JSAT),data=gdata,weights=groupN)
c<-summary(Model2)$coefficients[2]#proportionality
    parameter

#3.) Compare Model 2 with Model 1 using F-test
#Retrieve SSE and specify number of parameters
    in Model 1
SSE1<-deviance(Model1)
k1<-3
#Retrieve SSE and specify number of parameters
    in Model 2
SSE2<-deviance(Model2)
k2<-1
#Retrieve total N
N<-nobs(Model1)
#Calculate F-statistic
Fstat1<-((SSE2-SSE1)/(k1-k2))/(SSE1/(N-k1))
#Evaluate whether F-statistic is significant
#(non-significance means we accept proportional
    model)
pf(q=Fstat1,df1=(k1-k2),df2=(N-k1),lower.tail=
    FALSE)
#Informally compare coefficients to see if proportional
    (ignore intercept)
params*c#Model MLM (individual level)
summary(Model1)$coefficients[,1]#Model 1
    (group level)
```

#######Test 3: Identical Homology#######
#1.) Model 3 is a weighted least squares regression with all parameters fixed to
#Model MLM and no proportionality parameter
Model3<-lm(OCB~offset(params[2]*Agree)+ offset(params[3]*JSAT),data=gdata,weights= groupN)

#2.) Compare Model 3 with Model 2 using F-test
#Retrieve SSE and specify number of parameters in Model 3
SSE3<-deviance(Model3)
k3<-0
#Calculate F-statistic
Fstat2<-((SSE3-SSE2)/(k2-k3))/(SSE2/(N-k2))
#Evaluate whether F-statistic is significant (non-significance means we accept identical model))
pf(q=Fstat2,df1=(k2-k3),df2=(N-k2),lower. tail=FALSE)
#Informally compare coefficients to see if identical (ignore intercept)
summary(ModelMLM)$coefficients
summary(Model1)$coefficients

References

Bashkov, B. M., & Finney, S. J. (2013). Applying longitudinal mean and covariance structures (LMACS) analysis to assess construct stability over two time points: An example using psychological entitlement. *Measurement and Evaluation in Counseling and Development, 46,* 289–314. http://dx.doi.org/10.1177/0748175613497038

Beal, D. J., Trougakos, J. P., Weiss, H. M., & Dalal, R. S. (2013). Affect spin and the emotion regulation process at work. *Journal of Applied Psychology, 98,* 593–605. http://dx.doi.org/10.1037/a0032559

Beus, J. M., Muñoz, G. J., Arthur, W., Jr., & Payne, S. C. (2013, August). *A multilevel construct validation of safety climate.* Paper presented at the 2013 Academy of Management Meeting, Orlando, FL.

Binning, J. F., & Barrett, G. V. (1989). Validity of personnel decisions: A conceptual analysis of the inferential and evidentiary bases. *Journal of Applied Psychology, 74,* 478–494. http://dx.doi.org/10.1037/0021-9010.74.3.478

Bliese, P. D. (2000). Within-group agreement, non-independence, and reliability: Implications for data aggregation and analysis. In K. J. Klein & S. W. Kozlowski (Eds.), *Multilevel theory, research, and methods in organizations* (pp. 349–381). San Francisco, CA: Jossey-Bass.

Bliese, P., & Ployhart, R. E. (2002). Growth modeling using random coefficient models: Model building, testing, and illustrations. *Organizational Research Methods, 5,* 362–387. http://dx.doi.org/10.1177/109442802237116

Borsboom, D., Mellenbergh, G. J., & van Heerden, J. (2003). The theoretical status of latent variables. *Psychological Review, 110,* 203–219. http://dx.doi.org/10.1037/0033-295X.110.2.203

Boyce, C. J., Wood, A. M., Daly, M., & Sedikides, C. (2015). Personality change following unemployment. *Journal of Applied Psychology, 100,* 991–1011. http://dx.doi.org/10.1037/a0038647

Brickson, S. L. (2005). Organizational identity orientation: Forging a link between organizational identity and organizations' relations with stakeholders. *Administrative Science Quarterly, 50,* 576–609. http://dx.doi.org/10.2189/asqu.50.4.576

Brown, R. D., & Hauenstein, N. (2005). Interrater agreement reconsidered: An alternative to the r_{wg} indices. *Organizational Research Methods, 8,* 165–184. http://dx.doi.org/10.1177/1094428105275376

Burke, M. J., Finkelstein, L. M., & Dusig, M. S. (1999). On average deviation indices for estimating interrater agreement. *Organizational Research Methods, 2,* 49–68. http://dx.doi.org/10.1177/109442819921004

Campbell, D. T., & Fiske, D. W. (1959). Convergent and discriminant validation by the multitrait-multimethod matrix. *Psychological Bulletin, 56,* 81–105. http://dx.doi.org/10.1037/h0046016

Carlson, K. D., & Herdman, A. O. (2012). Understanding the impact of convergent validity on research results. *Organizational Research Methods, 15,* 17–32. http://dx.doi.org/10.1177/1094428110392383

Carter, M. Z., & Mossholder, K. W. (2015). Are we on the same page? The performance effects of congruence between supervisor and group trust. *Journal of Applied Psychology, 100,* 1349–1363. http://dx.doi.org/10.1037/a0038798

Chan, D. (1998a). The conceptualization and analysis of change over time: An integrative approach incorporating longitudinal mean and covariance structures analysis (LMACS) and multiple indicator latent growth modeling (MLGM). *Organizational Research Methods, 1,* 421–483. http://dx.doi.org/10.1177/109442819814004

Chan, D. (1998b). Functional relations among constructs in the same content domain at different levels of analysis: A typology of composition models. *Journal of Applied Psychology, 83,* 234–246. http://dx.doi.org/10.1037/0021-9010.83.2.234

Chen, G., Bliese, P. D., & Mathieu, J. E. (2005). Conceptual framework and statistical procedures for delineating and testing multilevel theories of homology.

Organizational Research Methods, 8, 375–409. http://dx.doi.org/10.1177/1094428105280056

Chen, G., Bliese, P. D., Payne, S. C., Zaccaro, S. J., Simsarian Webber, S., Mathieu, J. E., & Born, D. H. (2002). Simultaneous examination of the antecedents and consequences of efficacy beliefs at multiple levels of analysis. *Human Performance, 15,* 381–409. http://dx.doi.org/10.1207/S15327043HUP1504_05

Chen, G., Gully, S. M., & Eden, D. (2001). Validation of a new general self-efficacy scale. *Organizational Research Methods, 4,* 62–83. http://dx.doi.org/10.1177/109442810141004

Chen, G., Kirkman, B. L., Kanfer, R., Allen, D., & Rosen, B. (2007). A multilevel study of leadership, empowerment, and performance in teams. *Journal of Applied Psychology, 92,* 331–346. http://dx.doi.org/10.1037/0021-9010.92.2.331

Chen, G., Mathieu, J. E., & Bliese, P. D. (2005). A framework for conducting multilevel construct validation. In F. J. Yammarino & F. Dansereau (Eds.), *Multi-level issues in organizational behavior and processes* (pp. 273–303). Bingley, England: Emerald Group.

Chen, G., Ployhart, R. E., Thomas, H. C., Anderson, N., & Bliese, P. D. (2011). The power of momentum: A new model of dynamic relationships between job satisfaction change and turnover intentions. *Academy of Management Journal, 54,* 159–181. http://dx.doi.org/10.5465/AMJ.2011.59215089

Cheung, G. W., & Lau, R. S. (2012). A direct comparison approach for testing measurement invariance. *Organizational Research Methods, 15,* 167–198. http://dx.doi.org/10.1177/1094428111421987

Churchland, P. M. (1981). Eliminative materialism and the propositional attitudes. *The Journal of Philosophy, 78,* 67–90.

Clark, L. A., & Watson, D. (1995). Constructing validity: Basic issues in objective scale development. *Psychological Assessment, 7,* 309–319. http://dx.doi.org/10.1037/1040-3590.7.3.309

Cohen, J. (1992). A power primer. *Psychological Bulletin, 112,* 155–159. http://dx.doi.org/10.1037/0033-2909.112.1.155

Cohen, J. (1994). The earth is round (*p* < .05). *American Psychologist, 49,* 997–1003. http://dx.doi.org/10.1037/0003-066X.49.12.997

Cronbach, L. J., & Meehl, P. E. (1955). Construct validity in psychological tests. *Psychological Bulletin, 52,* 281–302. http://dx.doi.org/10.1037/h0040957

Culpepper, S. A., & Aguinis, H. (2011). R is for revolution: A cutting-edge, free, open source statistical package. *Organizational Research Methods, 14,* 735–740. http://dx.doi.org/10.1177/1094428109355485

DeVellis, R. F. (1991). *Scale development: Theory and applications.* Newbury Park, CA: Sage.

Dyer, N. G., Hanges, P. J., & Hall, R. J. (2005). Applying multilevel confirmatory factor analysis techniques to the study of leadership. *The Leadership Quarterly, 16,* 149–167. http://dx.doi.org/10.1016/j.leaqua.2004.09.009

Eby, L. T., Butts, M. M., Hoffman, B. J., & Sauer, J. B. (2015). Cross-lagged relations between mentoring received from supervisors and employee OCBs: Disentangling causal direction and identifying boundary conditions. *Journal of Applied Psychology, 100,* 1275–1285. http://dx.doi.org/10.1037/a0038628

Edwards, J. R., & Bagozzi, R. P. (2000). On the nature and direction of relationships between constructs and measures. *Psychological Methods, 5,* 155–174. http://dx.doi.org/10.1037/1082-989X.5.2.155

Farh, C. I. C., & Chen, Z. (2014). Beyond the individual victim: Multilevel consequences of abusive supervision in teams. *Journal of Applied Psychology, 99,* 1074–1095. http://dx.doi.org/10.1037/a0037636

Ferguson, A. J., & Peterson, R. S. (2015). Sinking slowly: Diversity in propensity to trust predicts downward trust spirals in small groups. *Journal of Applied Psychology, 100,* 1012–1024. http://dx.doi.org/10.1037/apl0000007

Fisher, R. A. (1956). *Statistical methods and scientific inference.* Edinburgh, Scotland: Oliver and Boyd.

Fuller, J. A., Stanton, J. M., Fisher, G. G., Spitzmüller, C., Russell, S. S., & Smith, P. C. (2003). A lengthy look at the daily grind: Time series analysis of events, mood, stress, and satisfaction. *Journal of Applied Psychology, 88,* 1019–1033. http://dx.doi.org/10.1037/0021-9010.88.6.1019

Furnham, A. (1986). Response bias, social desirability and dissimulation. *Personality and Individual Differences, 7,* 385–400. http://dx.doi.org/10.1016/0191-8869(86)90014-0

Furnham, A., & Henderson, M. (1982). The good, the bad and the mad: Response bias in self-report measures. *Personality and Individual Differences, 3,* 311–320. http://dx.doi.org/10.1016/0191-8869(82)90051-4

Furr, R. M. (2011). *Scale construction and psychometrics for personality and social psychology.* London, England: Sage. http://dx.doi.org/10.4135/9781446287866

Furr, R. M., & Bacharach, V. R. (2013). *Psychometrics: An introduction* (2nd ed.). Thousand Oaks, CA: Sage.

George, J. M. (1990). Personality, affect, and behavior in groups. *Journal of Applied Psychology, 75,* 107–116. http://dx.doi.org/10.1037/0021-9010.75.2.107

Ghiselli, E. E. (1964). *Theory of psychological measurement.* New York, NY: McGraw-Hill.

Gröschke, D. (2013). Group competence: Empirical insights for the management of groups in dynamic and complex situations. *Organizational Cultures:*

An International Journal, 12, 11–22. http://dx.doi.org/ 10.18848/2327-8013/CGP/v12i04/50891

Harrison, D. A., Price, K. H., & Bell, M. P. (1998). Beyond relational demography: Time and the effects of surface- and deep-level diversity on work group cohesion. *Academy of Management Journal, 41,* 96–107.

Hinkin, T. R. (1998). A brief tutorial on the development of measures for use in survey questionnaires. *Organizational Research Methods, 1,* 104–121. http://dx.doi.org/10.1177/109442819800100106

Ioannidis, J. P. (2012). Why science is not necessarily self-correcting. *Perspectives on Psychological Science, 7,* 645–654. http://dx.doi.org/10.1177/1745691612464056

James, L. R. (1982). Aggregation bias in estimates of perceptual agreement. *Journal of Applied Psychology, 67,* 219–229. http://dx.doi.org/10.1037/ 0021-9010.67.2.219

James, L. R., Demaree, R. G., & Wolf, G. (1984). Estimating within-group interrater reliability with and without response bias. *Journal of Applied Psychology, 69,* 85–98. http://dx.doi.org/10.1037/0021-9010.69.1.85

James, L. R., Demaree, R. G., & Wolf, G. (1993). r_{wg}: An assessment of within-group interrater agreement. *Journal of Applied Psychology, 78,* 306–309. http://dx.doi.org/10.1037/0021-9010.78.2.306

John, L. K., Loewenstein, G., & Prelec, D. (2012). Measuring the prevalence of questionable research practices with incentives for truth telling. *Psychological Science, 23,* 524–532. http://dx.doi.org/10.1177/ 0956797611430953

Johnson, R. E., Rosen, C. C., Chang, C. H. D., Djurdjevic, E., & Taing, M. U. (2012). Recommendations for improving the construct clarity of higher-order multidimensional constructs. *Human Resource Management Review, 22,* 62–72. http://dx.doi.org/10.1016/ j.hrmr.2011.11.006

Judge, T. A., Erez, A., Bono, J. E., & Thoresen, C. J. (2003). The core self-evaluations scale: Development of a measure. *Personnel Psychology, 56,* 303–331. http://dx.doi.org/10.1111/j.1744-6570.2003.tb00152.x

Kahn, J. H. (2011). Multilevel modeling: Overview and applications to research in counseling psychology. *Journal of Counseling Psychology, 58,* 257–271. http://dx.doi.org/10.1037/a0022680

Kozlowski, S. W., & Klein, K. J. (2000). A multilevel approach to theory and research in organizations: Contextual, temporal, and emergent processes. In K. J. Klein & S. W. Kozlowski (Eds.), *Multilevel theory, research, and methods in organizations* (pp. 3–90). San Francisco, CA: Jossey-Bass.

Lance, C. E., Butts, M. M., & Michels, L. C. (2006). The sources of four commonly reported cutoff criteria: What did they really say? *Organizational Research*

Methods, 9, 202–220. http://dx.doi.org/10.1177/ 1094428105284919

LeBlanc, M. M., & Kelloway, E. K. (2002). Predictors and outcomes of workplace violence and aggression. *Journal of Applied Psychology, 87,* 444–453. http:// dx.doi.org/10.1037/0021-9010.87.3.444

LeBreton, J. M., James, L. R., & Lindell, M. K. (2005). Recent issues regarding r_{WG}, r_{WG}, $r_{WG(J)}$, and $r_{WG(J)}$. *Organizational Research Methods, 8,* 128–138. http://dx.doi.org/10.1177/1094428104272181

LeBreton, J. M., Burgess, J. R. D., Kaiser, R. B., Atchley, E. K., & James, L. R. (2003). The restriction of variance hypothesis and interrater reliability and agreement: Are ratings from multiple sources really dissimilar? *Organizational Research Methods, 6,* 80–128. http://dx.doi.org/10.1177/1094428102239427

LeBreton, J. M., & Senter, J. L. (2008). Answers to 20 questions about interrater reliability and interrater agreement. *Organizational Research Methods, 11,* 815–852. http://dx.doi.org/10.1177/1094428106296642

Liden, R. C., Wayne, S. J., Zhao, H., & Henderson, D. (2008). Servant leadership: Development of a multidimensional measure and multi-level assessment. *The Leadership Quarterly, 19,* 161–177. http://dx.doi.org/10.1016/j.leaqua.2008.01.006

Locke, E. A. (2012). Construct validity vs. concept validity. *Human Resource Management Review, 22,* 146–148. http://dx.doi.org/10.1016/j.hrmr.2011.11.008

Lucas, R. E., Diener, E., & Suh, E. (1996). Discriminant validity of well-being measures. *Journal of Personality and Social Psychology, 71,* 616–628. http://dx.doi.org/ 10.1037/0022-3514.71.3.616

MacKenzie, S. B. (2003). The dangers of poor construct conceptualization. *Journal of the Academy of Marketing Science, 31,* 323–326. http://dx.doi.org/10.1177/ 0092070303031003011

Mathieu, J. E., & Chen, G. (2011). The etiology of the multilevel paradigm in management research. *Journal of Management, 37,* 610–641. http://dx.doi.org/ 10.1177/0149206310364663

McDonald, R. P. (1999). *Test theory: A unified treatment.* Mahwah, NJ: Lawrence Erlbaum.

Molloy, J. C., & Ployhart, R. E. (2012). Construct clarity: Multidisciplinary considerations and an illustration using human capital. *Human Resource Management Review, 22,* 152–156. http://dx.doi.org/10.1016/ j.hrmr.2011.11.010

Muthén, B. (1994). Multilevel covariance structure analysis. *Sociological Methodology, 22,* 376–398. http://dx.doi.org/10.1177/0049124194022003006

Ng, T. W. H., Feldman, D. C., & Lam, S. S. K. (2010). Psychological contract breaches, organizational commitment, and innovation-related behaviors:

A latent growth modeling approach. *Journal of Applied Psychology*, 95, 744–751. http://dx.doi.org/10.1037/a0018804

Nunnally, J., & Bernstein, I. (1994). *Psychometric theory* (3rd ed.). New York: McGraw-Hill.

Oh, I.-S., Kim, S., & Van Iddekinge, C. H. (2015). Taking it to another level: Do personality-based human capital resources matter to firm performance? *Journal of Applied Psychology*, 100, 935–947. http://dx.doi.org/10.1037/a0039052

O'Reilly, C. A., III, Caldwell, D. F., & Barnett, W. P. (1989). Work group demography, social integration, and turnover. *Administrative Science Quarterly*, 34, 21–37. http://dx.doi.org/10.2307/2392984

Ployhart, R. E., & Vandenberg, R. J. (2010). Longitudinal research: The theory, design, and analysis of change. *Journal of Management*, 36, 94–120. http://dx.doi.org/10.1177/0149206309352110

Podsakoff, P. M., MacKenzie, S. B., Moorman, R. H., & Fetter, R. (1990). Transformational leader behaviors and their effects on followers' trust in leader, satisfaction, and organizational citizenship behaviors. *The Leadership Quarterly*, 1, 107–142. http://dx.doi.org/10.1016/1048-9843(90)90009-7

Podsakoff, P. M., Mackenzie, S. B., & Podsakoff, N. P. (2016). Recommendations for creating better concept definitions in the organizational, behavioral, and social sciences. *Organizational Research Methods*, 19, 159–203. http://dx.doi.org/10.1177/1094428115624965

Pornprasertmanit, S., Lee, J., & Preacher, K. J. (2014). Ignoring clustering in confirmatory factor analysis: Some consequences for model fit and standardized parameter estimates. *Multivariate Behavioral Research*, 49, 518–543. http://dx.doi.org/10.1080/00273171.2014.933762

Raju, N. S., Laffitte, L. J., & Byrne, B. M. (2002). Measurement equivalence: A comparison of methods based on confirmatory factor analysis and item response theory. *Journal of Applied Psychology*, 87, 517–529. http://dx.doi.org/10.1037/0021-9010.87.3.517

Ritter, K.-J., Matthews, R. A., Ford, M. T., & Henderson, A. A. (2016). Understanding role stressors and job satisfaction over time using adaptation theory. *Journal of Applied Psychology*, 101, 1655–1669. http://dx.doi.org/10.1037/apl0000152

Rozeboom, W. W. (1960). The fallacy of the null-hypothesis significance test. *Psychological Bulletin*, 57, 416–428. http://dx.doi.org/10.1037/h0042040

Ryan, R. M., & Deci, E. L. (2006). Self-regulation and the problem of human autonomy: Does psychology need choice, self-determination, and will? *Journal of Personality*, 74, 1557–1586. http://dx.doi.org/10.1111/j.1467-6494.2006.00420.x

Schmidt, F. L., & Hunter, J. E. (1989). Interrater reliability coefficients cannot be computed when only one stimulus is rated. *Journal of Applied Psychology*, 74, 368–370. http://dx.doi.org/10.1037/0021-9010.74.2.368

Schmidt, F. L., Viswesvaran, C., & Ones, D. S. (2000). Reliability is not validity and validity is not reliability. *Personnel Psychology*, 53, 901–912. http://dx.doi.org/10.1111/j.1744-6570.2000.tb02422.x

Simmons, J. P., Nelson, L. D., & Simonsohn, U. (2011). False-positive psychology: Undisclosed flexibility in data collection and analysis allows presenting anything as significant. *Psychological Science*, 22, 1359–1366. http://dx.doi.org/10.1177/0956797611417632

Sinha, R., Janardhanan, N. S., Greer, L. L., Conlon, D. E., & Edwards, J. R. (2016). Skewed task conflicts in teams: What happens when a few members see more conflict than the rest? *Journal of Applied Psychology*, 101, 1045–1055. http://dx.doi.org/10.1037/apl0000059

Slaney, K. L., & Garcia, D. A. (2015). Constructing psychological objects: The rhetoric of constructs. *Journal of Theoretical and Philosophical Psychology*, 35, 244–259. http://dx.doi.org/10.1037/teo0000025

Stewart, G. L. (2003). Toward an understanding of the multilevel role of personality in teams. In M. R. Barrick & A. M. Ryan (Eds.), *Personality and work: Reconsidering the role of personality in organizations* (pp. 183–204). San Francisco, CA: Jossey-Bass.

Stroebe, W., Postmes, T., & Spears, R. (2012). Scientific misconduct and the myth of self-correction in science. *Perspectives on Psychological Science*, 7, 670–688. http://dx.doi.org/10.1177/1745691612460687

Tay, L., & Jebb, A. T. (2017). Scale development. In S. Rogelberg (Ed.), *Encyclopedia of industrial and organizational psychology* (2nd ed.; pp. 1379–1384). Thousand Oaks, CA: Sage.

Tay, L., Meade, A. W., & Cao, M. (2015). An overview and practical guide to IRT measurement equivalence analysis. *Organizational Research Methods*, 18, 3–46. http://dx.doi.org/10.1177/1094428114553062

Tay, L., Woo, S. E., & Vermunt, J. K. (2014). A conceptual and methodological framework for psychometric isomorphism: Validation of multilevel construct measures. *Organizational Research Methods*, 17, 77–106. http://dx.doi.org/10.1177/1094428113517008

Vandenberg, R. J., & Lance, C. E. (2000). A review and synthesis of the measurement invariance literature: Suggestions, practices, and recommendations for organizational research. *Organizational Research Methods*, 3, 4–70. http://dx.doi.org/10.1177/109442810031002

Vidyarthi, P. R., Singh, S., Erdogan, B., Chaudhry, A., Posthuma, R., & Anand, S. (2016). Individual deals within teams: Investigating the role of relative i-deals for employee performance. *Journal of Applied Psychology, 101,* 1536–1552. http://dx.doi.org/10.1037/apl0000145

Wang, M. (2007). Profiling retirees in the retirement transition and adjustment process: Examining the longitudinal change patterns of retirees' psychological well-being. *Journal of Applied Psychology, 92,* 455–474. http://dx.doi.org/10.1037/0021-9010.92.2.455

Widaman, K. F. (2000). Testing cross-group and cross-time constraints on parameters using the general linear model. In T. D. Little, K. U. Schnabel, & J. Baumert (Eds.), *Modeling longitudinal and multilevel data: Practical issues, applied approaches, and specific examples* (pp. 163–186). Mahwah, NJ: Lawrence Erlbaum.

Wu, C.-H., & Griffin, M. A. (2012). Longitudinal relationships between core self-evaluations and job satisfaction. *Journal of Applied Psychology, 97,* 331–342. http://dx.doi.org/10.1037/a0025673

## CHAPTER 12

MULTILEVEL MEASUREMENT: AGREEMENT, RELIABILITY, AND NONINDEPENDENCE

Dina V. Krasikova and James M. LeBreton

Across the social sciences, but especially in the organizational sciences, researchers have begun paying greater attention to phenomena, processes, and relationships that frequently span multiple hierarchical levels (Aguinis, Pierce, Bosco, & Muslin, 2009). Addressing research questions about such phenomena, relationships, and processes naturally requires collecting multilevel data and analyzing these data using techniques that account for their hierarchical structures. The latter, in turn, requires that researchers assess a degree of nonindependence in the data obtained at the lower level of analysis (Bliese, 2000) and, conditional on one's theory, may require that lower level data are aggregated to represent higher level constructs (Chan, 1998). Whether researchers are interested in the assessment of nonindependence, aggregation of the lower level scores, or even determining the amounts of score dispersion within higher level units (Smith-Crowe, Burke, Kouchaki, & Signal, 2013), they need to examine a degree of consensus or consistency (Kozlowski & Hattrup, 1992) in their data. This is especially true when data are provided by multiple observers (e.g., employees nested within work groups, students nested within classrooms, romantic partners nested within couples). When multiple observers/raters provide the data on the focal constructs of interest, researchers may wish to estimate the extent to which the data provided by the observers/raters are similar to one using estimates of interrater agreement or interrater reliability (LeBreton, Burgess, Kaiser, Atchley, & James, 2003).

The purpose of this chapter is threefold. First, we provide a comprehensive overview of agreement and reliability indices and their applications in a multilevel context. Second, we integrate classic work and newer developments in the interrater agreement/reliability domain, with the result being a user-friendly guide to the application of agreement and reliability indices within multilevel contexts. We hope that this guide, supplemented with illustrative examples included in Appendices 12.1–12.3, will help researchers identify, compute, and properly interpret agreement and reliability indices that best fit the purpose of their studies. Finally, we discuss the use of agreement and reliability indices in a novel context, estimation of interrater agreement in dyads, where their application is less straightforward and warrants a more focused discussion.

The chapter is organized as follows. After clarifying the definitional boundaries between interrater agreement and interrater reliability, we discuss three common applications of agreement and reliability indices in multilevel contexts: assessment of nonindependence, estimation of within-unit agreement, and assessment of reliability of unit means. For each of these applications, we discuss their meaning in a multilevel context and review relevant agreement and reliability indices. We then proceed with a discussion of agreement and

http://dx.doi.org/10.1037/0000115-013
The Handbook of Multilevel Theory, Measurement, and Analysis, S. E. Humphrey and J. M. LeBreton (Editors-in-Chief)

reliability issues in dyadic studies and conclude the chapter with a step-by-step guidance on the choice and application of agreement and reliability indices.

ON THE MEANING OF AGREEMENT AND RELIABILITY IN MULTILEVEL CONTEXTS

Within the context of multilevel research, the concepts of interrater agreement and interrater reliability refer to the extent to which ratings furnished by multiple judges (e.g., students) nested or clustered within some higher level structure (e.g., classrooms) are similar to one another. However, interrater agreement and reliability differ from one another in how similarity is defined.

Interrater agreement assesses the extent to which ratings of one or multiple targets provided by multiple judges are similar in terms of their absolute values, and thus, the extent to which judges may be conceptualized as interchangeable with one another (James, Demaree, & Wolf, 1984; Kozlowski & Hattrup, 1992; LeBreton & Senter, 2008). Thus, complete agreement will be achieved if all judges provide identical ratings of a given target or multiple targets. Consider, for example, 10 employees asked to rate their common supervisor's leadership effectiveness on a 5-point scale ranging from 1 (*not effective at all*) to 5 (*very effective*). Perfect interrater agreement is manifested when all employees provide their supervisor with identical ratings (e.g., 5, 5, 5, 5, 5, 5, 5, 5, 5, 5). If one or more employees provide ratings that differ from the ratings of their peers, then there is a lack of perfect interrater agreement (e.g., 1, 1, 2, 2, 3, 3, 4, 4, 5, 5).

Whereas interrater agreement defines rater similarity in terms of "absolute consensus," *interrater reliability* defines rater similarity in terms of the consistency in the rank ordering of targets (e.g., teachers) based on the ratings (e.g., teacher effectiveness scores) that are furnished by multiple judges of those targets (e.g., students; James et al., 1984; Kozlowski & Hattrup, 1992; LeBreton et al., 2003; LeBreton & Senter, 2008). Consider, for example, two students who were asked to rate five teachers on their effectiveness using a 5-point scale ranging from 1 (not effective at all) to 5 (very effective). Imagine that Student 1 gave the following set of ratings to Teachers 1–5, respectively: 5, 5, 5, 4, and 4,

and Student 2 gave a different set of ratings to the same teachers: 2, 2, 2, 1, and 1. In this example, we observe perfect interrater reliability because the relative rank orders of ratings of different targets (teachers) are identical across the judges (students), with the first three scores being higher than the remaining two for both judges. Also, it should be noted that interrater agreement in this example is low (Student 1 views the teachers as effective and Student 2 views them as not effective), which suggests that high interrater reliability does not automatically imply high interrater agreement. These examples are intentionally oversimplified to help illustrate differences between interrater agreement and reliability and show that one does not necessarily imply the other. In reality, differences among the patterns of scores provided by judges are rarely as clear-cut as in our example; hence, there is a need for indices that would quantify the degree of agreement and reliability across judges in different analytic situations.

We now turn to the discussion of uses of interrater agreement and reliability indices in multilevel studies. Below, we focus on three common applications of these indices: (a) assessment of nonindependence, (b) estimation of within-unit agreement, and (c) estimation of between-unit reliability of means. Table 12.1 summarizes the information presented in the chapter into a user-friendly guide to help researchers navigate through the multitude of interrater agreement and reliability indices and select the best index based on the analytic purpose and specifics of their studies.

NONINDEPENDENCE IN MULTILEVEL CONTEXTS

One common use of agreement/reliability indices in multilevel contexts involves the assessment of the extent to which there is nonindependence among the lower level units due to their membership within higher level units. Observations collected from the lower level units nested within higher level units (e.g., individuals nested within teams, teams nested within departments, departments nested within organizations, organizations nested within industries) are often not independent of one another.

TABLE 12.1

Guidelines on the Use of Indices of Interrater Agreement and Reliability in Multilevel Research

Purpose	Index	Conditions for use	Interpretation	Notes and cautions
To assess nonindependence among the ratings of multiple targets furnished by multiple judges nested within higher level units and determine whether multilevel modeling should be used instead of a single-level regression	ICC(1), also referred to as $\rho\alpha$, and $\rho\beta$	• Multiple targets are rated by multiple judges. • Targets are rated using a single item or multiple items.	Even small ICC(1)s indicate nonignorable nonindependence.	It is important that researchers compute both $\rho\alpha$ or $\rho\beta$ for a comprehensive assessment of nonindependence. If only $\rho\alpha$ or $\rho\beta$ is used, researchers may mistakenly conclude that judges' ratings are independent.
To assess agreement among ratings of a single target furnished by multiple judges and justify the aggregation of these ratings to form an indicator of a unit-level construct	r_{WG}, $AD_{M(J)}$, or $AD_{Md(J)}$	• Single target is rated by multiple judges. • The target is rated using a single item. • The target has a single true score. • No inadmissible values are expected.	Higher values of r_{WG} and lower values of AD indicate within-group agreement and may be used to justify aggregation in composition models that require within-group agreement (e.g., direct consensus model; referent-shift consensus model). Lower values indicate a lack of agreement.	Choosing between the r_{WG} and AD indices: r_{WG} and $r_{WG(J)}$ • are standardized metrics that allow to compare agreement across scales with a different number of response options • require modeling a null distribution $AD_{M(J)}$, $AD_{Md(J)}$, $AD_{M(J)}$, $AD_{Md(J)}$ • assess agreement using the original scale as a metric • do not require modeling null distributions
	$r_{WG(J)}$, $AD_{M(J)}$ or $AD_{Md(J)}$	• Single target is rated by multiple judges. • The target is rated using multiple items. • The target has a single true score. • No inadmissible values are expected.		
	$r^\star_{WG\_IndexD}$	• Single target is rated by multiple judges. • The target is rated using a single item. • The target has a single true score. • A regular r_{WG} may take on an inadmissible value.		Choosing between Index C and Index D: • $r^\star_{WG(J)\_IndexC}$ is more intuitively interpretable. • $r^\star_{WG(J)\_IndexD}$ is recommended when maximum disagreement is expected and in dyadic studies
	$r^\star_{WG(J)\_IndexC}$ or $r^\star_{WG(J)\_IndexD}$	• Single target is rated by multiple judges. • The target is rated using multiple items. • The target has a single true score.	Negative values indicate (a) improper specification of null distribution, (b) nontrivial subgroup differences, or (c) sampling error.	
	r_{WGp}	• A regular $r_{WG(J)}$ may take on an inadmissible value. • Single target is rated by multiple judges. • The target is rated using a single item. • The target has multiple true scores.		
	$r_{WGp(J)}$	• A regular r_{WG} may take on an inadmissible value. • Single target is rated by multiple judges. • The target is rated using multiple items. • The target has multiple true scores. • A regular $r_{WG(J)}$ may take on an inadmissible value.		
To assess the amount of dispersion	SD	• Single target is rated by multiple judges. • The target is rated using a single item or multiple items.	Indicates dispersion using SD as a unit.	
To assess reliability of unit means	ICC(K), also referred to as ICC(2)	• When judges' ratings are averaged to form indicators of higher level constructs, the reliability of these aggregated scores should be determined before they are used in a multilevel model.	Higher values indicate higher reliability.	Typically used in conjunction with some form of r_{WG}. When an r_{WG} indicates the level of agreement sufficient for aggregation, ICC(K) or ICC(2) is computed to examine the reliability of these aggregated scores across level units.

Nonindependence implies that some linkages exist among the lower level units because of the group membership and associated with it common fate, local history effects, social interaction, or colocation of the lower level units (Kenny & Judd, 1986). As a result, observations obtained from the lower level units nested within one group (or another higher level unit) may be more similar to each other than to observations obtained from the units nested within other groups.

Take, for example, a simple two-level multilevel model in which individuals (e.g., children) are nested within groups (e.g., classrooms), for which we are interested in understanding predictors of performance (e.g., student grades). Within a two-level model, we are able to partition the variance in performance into a component that represents within-group variance in individual-level performance (σ^2) and the between-group variance in individual-level performance (τ_{00}). Nonindependence exists when the between-group variance is nontrivial (i.e., when $\tau_{00} > 0$). Indeed, one of the first steps in most multilevel analyses is to establish the necessity of a multilevel analysis by estimating the degree of nonindependence in the dependent variables of interest (Hofmann, Griffin, & Gavin, 2000; Raudenbush & Bryk, 2002; see also Chapter 17, this volume). Failing to account for nonindependence may lead to increased Type I or Type II error rates. Thus, when nonindependence is detected, multilevel modeling is recommended over a single-level regression (Bliese & Hanges, 2004; Kreft & de Leeuw, 2002).

Within the typical multilevel study, nonindependence has been assessed using an intraclass correlation coefficient, referred to as ICC(1) (Bartko, 1976; Bliese, 2000; LeBreton & Senter, 2008; McGraw & Wong, 1996) or ρ_α (Aguinis & Culpepper, 2015). ICC(1) (or, ρ_α) indicates the extent to which the variability in judges' ratings is due to their nesting within units and is calculated as a ratio of between-unit variance in judges' ratings across targets over the total amount of variance in ratings. Greater values of ICC(1), or ρ_α, computed for the outcome variables (Bliese, 2000) imply nonindependence and necessitate the use of multilevel modeling. In addition to obtaining ICC(1) or ρ_α, it is recommended that researchers also assess non-

independence in the lower level observations that is due to the group differences in slopes using a newly developed index: ρ_β (Aguinis & Culpepper, 2015). The portion of variance in the lower level ratings that is due to the slope differences is not captured by ICC(1) or ρ_α. Thus, the sole reliance on ICC(1) or ρ_α may result in a misleading conclusion that lower level observations are independent. This implies that both ICC(1) and ρ_β should be computed on the outcome variables for a more comprehensive and accurate assessment of nonindependence. This also suggests that, when at least one of the indices indicates nonindependence, researchers should choose multilevel modeling over single-level regressions (Aguinis & Culpepper, 2015). ICC(1) or ρ_α and ρ_β are computed and interpreted as follows.

Estimating Nonindependence With ICC(1) or ρ_α

In multilevel studies, ICC(1) (Bartko, 1976; Bliese, 2000; James, 1982; LeBreton & Senter, 2008; McGraw & Wong, 1996) or ρ_α (Aguinis & Culpepper, 2015) is used when researchers are interested in estimating nonindependence in judges' ratings due to their unit membership (Hofmann, Griffin, & Gavin, 2000). Essentially, ICC(1) indexes the degree of similarity in judges' ratings over multiple targets or units and provides information about the extent to which judges' ratings are influenced by their nesting within a common target or unit. For example, nine employees nested within three teams are asked to rate their engagement in organizational citizenship behaviors (OCB). These employees' ratings are likely nonindependent. Ratings furnished by employees nested within the same team may be more similar to each other than to the ratings provided by employees in the other teams because of the group norms with regards to OCB, common socialization practices, and leadership influences within the group. ICC(1) computed based on scores provided by these nine employees would furnish a single estimate of nonindependence, indicating the extent to which employee ratings are driven by between-group factors versus within-group differences.

To assess the extent to which the nesting of judges within targets has resulted in the judges' ratings being nonindependent, we first partition the overall variance in the ratings into between-group and within-group components. Next, we assess the extent to which the between-group component contributes to the overall variance. If the proportion of total variance that is between-group variance is zero, then the ratings are independent. If this proportion is nonzero, then the ratings are nonindependent. Variance components are obtained from a one-way random effects ANOVA model that treats ratings as the dependent variable and groups as the "treatment" variable. These variance components can then be used to compute ICC(1) (Bliese, 2000; Hofmann, 1997; Raudenbush & Bryk, 2002):

$$ICC(1) = \tau_{00}/(\tau_{00} + \sigma^2).\qquad(12.1)$$

ICC(1) is interpreted as a proportion of variance in ratings that is due to the judges' nesting within groups. If ICC(1) exceeds zero (as small as .05 [LeBreton & Senter, 2008], or even smaller [Kreft & de Leeuw, 2002]), that indicates that nonindependence among the judges' ratings is likely nonignorable and multilevel modeling should be used to account for it.

Equation 12.1 is used to compute ICC(1) in two-level models. Its extension to models with three and more levels is straightforward. With the addition of each extra level, total variance in the lower level ratings obtains an extra variance component that is due to the nesting of Level 2 units (e.g., work groups) within Level 3 units (e.g., departments), Level 4 units (organizations), and so on. These variance components can then be used to compute ICC(1) for each level to assess similarity in the ratings furnished by judges at each lower level that is due to their nesting within the higher level units (Aguinis, Gottfredson, & Culpepper, 2013; Snijders & Bosker, 2012). For example, in a three-level model (e.g., employees are nested within teams, and teams are nested within departments), similarity among employee ratings that is due to their membership within departments can be assessed using a variant of the ICC(1) computed as

$$ICC = \varphi_{00}/(\varphi_{00} + \tau_{00} + \sigma^2),\qquad(12.2)$$

where φ_{00} is the variance in the judges' ratings that resides between departments. A nonzero ICC(1) would indicate the need to explicitly model nesting within Level 3 (or higher level) units, whereas an ICC(1) approaching zero would allow the researcher to collapse a three-level model into a two-level model.

Interpreting ICC(1)

When it comes to interpreting ICC(1) and assessing nonindependence, even small amounts of between-unit variance may be meaningful. LeBreton and Senter (2008) indicated that an ICC(1) as small as .05 may indicate nonignorable nonindependence. Kreft and de Leeuw (2002) referred to Barcikowski (1981) to demonstrate that even smaller ICC(1) may result in the increasingly inflated alpha levels with the increasing number of judges per unit. For example, an ICC(1) of .01 in a traditional linear model may result in the inflated alphas of .06, .08, .11, and .17 when the number of judges per unit is 10, 25, 50 and 100, respectively. An ICC(1) of .05 is shown to result in even higher alphas of .11, .19, .30 and .43 when the number of judges per unit is 10, 25, 50 and 100, respectively. ICC(1)'s greater than .05 result in even more inflated alphas. This example illustrates that ignoring nonindependence in the presence of ICC(1) exceeding .01, especially with a large number of judges per unit, may result in the increased probability of a Type I error. Thus, we suggest that researchers adopt a more conservative ICC(1) = .01 as evidence of nonignorable nonindependence, especially when the number of judges per unit in their sample is large ($\geq$ 10).[1]

Estimating Nonindependence With ρ_β

As discussed above, only estimating ICC(1) or ρ_α may be insufficient for detecting the effect of nesting of judges within groups, especially if the effect is related to between-group differences in slopes. Aguinis and Culpepper (2015) demonstrated that ICC(1), which they labeled ρ_α, is a function of only

---

[1]In this chapter, we summarize the guidelines offered in the literature acknowledging that the cutoff scores proposed for indices of interrater agreement and reliability (as well as many other cutoffs) are somewhat arbitrary and should not be blindly applied without considering the specifics of a given study and a research question at hand.

one aspect of the variability in lower level ratings: the variability that is due to group mean differences. (Note: Within a regression framework, group mean differences are manifested as differences in the "intercepts" of the regression equations.) Thus, this statistic ignores another important aspect of variability: the variability in ratings that is associated with group differences in regression slopes. These authors noted that sole reliance on ρ_α may lead to a misleading conclusion of nonindependence among the lower level observations with the subsequent use of a single-level regression instead of a multilevel model. Thus, these authors recommended that, in addition to computing ρ_α, researchers also compute ICC(beta), or ρ_β, to estimate the proportion of variance in ratings that is due to the differences in group slopes. ICC(beta) is computed as

$$\text{ICC(beta)} = \frac{tr\left[\mathbf{T}\dfrac{\mathbf{X}'_C \mathbf{X}_C}{N-1}\right]}{S^2}, \qquad (12.3)$$

where tr refers to a matrix trace, $\mathbf{X}_C$ is a matrix of group-mean-centered predictors for all groups and judges nested within groups, $\mathbf{X}'_C\mathbf{X}_C$ is the group-mean-centered sums of squared predictors across groups, $\dfrac{\mathbf{X}'_C\mathbf{X}_C}{N-1}$ is the average within-group relationship among predictors over groups, $\mathbf{T}$ is the variance–covariance matrix of the random effects, and S^2 is the total variance in lower level ratings (i.e., within variance + between variance). Thus, $tr\left[\mathbf{T}\dfrac{\mathbf{X}'_C\mathbf{X}_C}{N-1}\right]$ can be interpreted as the amount of the within-group variance that is due to the slope differences. Aguinis and Culpepper (2015) developed a freely available R code that can be used to compute ICC(beta).

WITHIN-UNIT AGREEMENT

Another common use of interrater agreement indices in multilevel contexts involves establishing agreement to justify aggregation of data collected at a lower level (e.g., individual perceptions of a work environment) to represent constructs that emerge and function at a higher level (e.g., organizational climate). In multilevel studies, constructs at the higher level of analysis capture properties of the corresponding higher level units (e.g., dyadic social exchange relationship quality, group affective tone, organizational climate). Depending on the level where these higher level unit properties originate and manifest themselves, they can be of three types: global, shared, and configural (Kozlowski & Klein, 2000).

Global unit properties have their origin and are manifest directly at the unit level (e.g., dyad colocation or group size). Because these properties tend to be descriptive and directly observable, they are typically measured directly at the unit level and do not require tests of interrater agreement and reliability. Unlike global unit properties, *shared* and *configural* unit properties originate in the characteristics of the lower level units and through interactions among them emerge as properties of the higher level units. Because shared and configural unit properties cannot be measured directly at the higher level, they are typically assessed at the level of origin with the subsequent aggregation of the lower level scores to form indicators of the higher level unit properties. Indices of interrater agreement and reliability are often used to help to determine whether such aggregation is appropriate.

Shared unit properties "emerge as a consensual, collective aspect of the unit as a whole" (Kozlowski & Klein, 2000, p. 30) and thus require that lower level unit properties are sufficiently similar for them to converge into a shared collective property. This model of emergence via bottom-up processing is referred to as a *composition* model and often necessitates the existence of consensus among the lower level units. Such consensus typically assumes one of two forms: direct consensus or referent-shift consensus (Chan, 1998). *Direct consensus* composition models imply that lower level units have similar properties (e.g., perceptions, attitudes, beliefs) that, when aggregated, will represent an isomorphic construct at the unit level. For example, when group members experience similar emotions, their individual affective states can be aggregated to represent a group-level affective tone (George, 1990). *Referent-shift consensus* implies that lower level units provide consensual assessments of a common referent (e.g., their group, leader, entire organization) and, when aggregated, these convergent assessments will represent an isomorphic construct representing this referent's collectively attributed quality. For example, when all group members provide converging ratings of their team's potency, their individual assessments can be aggregated to represent an emergent quality of potency at the team level.

Although both direct and referent-shift consensus models share the requirement that scores obtained from lower level units converge and agree with one another, they differ in how questions are presented to the lower level units. Direct consensus models use questions that are framed in a manner that asks lower level units to evaluate some self-referential characteristic (i.e., data are collected from participants residing at a lower level in the hierarchy using questions in which participants are asked about themselves). For example, students may be asked to rate their positive and negative affectivity, employees may be asked to rate their self-efficacy for performing some task, or individuals in couples therapy might be asked to rate their level of marital satisfaction. In contrast, as the name implies, referent-shift consensus models use questions that shift the framing of items away from the lower level units to ask about characteristics of higher level units. For example, students might be asked to rate the emotional tone of their *classrooms*, employees may be asked to furnish perceptions of their *teams'* efficacy, or individuals in couples therapy might be asked to rate the overall level of harmony in their *family*.

Both direct consensus and referent-shift consensus models hinge on the assumption of agreement among the lower level units. Thus, when researchers are interested in the assessment of shared unit properties, they should evaluate the degree of consensus among the lower level units before they can aggregate their scores to obtain indicators of shared unit properties. Agreement among the lower level ratings with the purpose of aggregating them to represent shared unit properties is typically assessed using r_{WG} indices (James et al., 1984; LeBreton & Senter, 2008).

Historically, indices of interrater agreement have been used in composition multilevel measurement models based on consensus properties; more recently, researchers have begun using IRA indices when studying *configural unit properties*. These properties originate at the lower level and manifest at the higher level, but, unlike shared properties, they do not imply convergence among the lower level observations (Kozlowski & Klein, 2000). Instead, configural unit properties emerge through a process of compilation, when the lower level properties add up (nonuniformly and, frequently, nonlinearly) to form a higher level configural property. Given that configural properties capture the within-group dispersion of the lower level properties (e.g., a bimodal pattern of leader–member exchange [LMX] dispersion within a group; LeBreton, James, & Lindell, 2005; Li & Liao, 2014), no similarity among the lower level units is expected, and no interrater agreement is needed before these configural constructs are incorporated in a multilevel model. However, interrater agreement indices may still be used in such multilevel studies to provide information about the amounts of dispersion among the lower level units. Among the interrater agreement indices, standard deviation and variance have been most commonly used to assess the amounts of dispersion (cf. Erdogan & Bauer, 2010; LeBreton & Senter, 2008; Liden, Erdogan, Wayne, & Sparrowe, 2006; Nishii & Mayer, 2009; Schneider, Salvaggio, & Subirats, 2002). The interested reader is also encouraged to read Chapter 11, this volume, which also discusses issues related to within-unit agreement and data aggregation.

Estimating Within-Unit Agreement Using r_{WG} Indices

There are multiple variants of r_{WG} indices to be used in different contexts. Although the methodological underpinnings of all r_{WG} indices are similar, these indices are computed differently and are applied in different analytic situations.

Single-item r_{WG} index. The most basic *single-item* r_{WG} index (James et al., 1984; James, Demaree, & Wolf, 1993) estimates interrater agreement when K judges (e.g., team members) rate a single target (e.g., team climate) on a single item using an approximately interval scale of measurement and it is reasonable to assume that the target has a single true score. This r_{WG} is computed as follows:

$$r_{WG} = 1 - \frac{s_X^2}{\sigma_E^2}, \quad (12.4)$$

where s_X^2 is the observed variance on item X, and σ_E^2 is a theoretical "null variance" that represents the variability one would expect to see on this same item if judges were to randomly respond to the item. s_X^2 is computed from the ratings furnished by the judges, and σ_E^2 is determined based on the distribution of ratings expected if there were no systematic agreement among the judges and their responses were due to random error (James et al., 1984, 1993). When judges are in complete agreement and give identical ratings to the target, $s_X^2 = 0$, leading to $r_{WG} = 1$ indicating perfect interrater agreement. When judges have a complete lack of agreement, their ratings are expected to be random noise (i.e., their ratings are not affected by the properties of the common target). In this case, $s_X^2 \approx \sigma_E^2$ and r_{WG} approaches 0, indicating a complete lack of agreement. In general, larger r_{WG} can be obtained if observed variance is substantially smaller than expected variance, suggesting that r_{WG} can be *interpreted* as "the proportional reduction in error variance" (LeBreton & Senter, 2008, p. 835) due to the systematic similarity in judges' ratings of a common target.

A distribution of expected variance, referred to as a *null distribution*, may take different forms depending on whether judges' random ratings can be considered uniformly distributed across response options on a given scale (resulting in a uniform or rectangular distribution) or nonuniformly distributed due to a response bias (resulting in a triangular or skewed distributions). For example, it is possible that judges' ratings may be largely random noise but that their random responses were manifested after first being influenced by some systematic response bias (e.g., a leniency bias). Given that r_{WG} depends on expected variance, computing σ_E^2 using an inaccurate null distribution may result in values that are underestimated, overestimated, or even inadmissible (< 0 or > 1). Thus, it is critical that researchers carefully select a null distribution that

would most accurately reflect a distribution of scores under condition of no agreement among the judges. We discuss the choice of null distributions and computations of expected variance below in the section on null distributions.

Multi-item $r_{WG(J)}$ index and its variants. A *multi-item r_{WG} index* or $r_{WG(J)}$ (James et al., 1984, 1993) estimates interrater agreement when K judges rate a single target on J essentially parallel items using an approximately interval scale of measurement and the target has a single true score. $r_{WG(J)}$ is computed as follows:

$$r_{WG(J)} = \frac{J\left(1 - \frac{\overline{s}_{Xj}^2}{\sigma_E^2}\right)}{J\left(1 - \frac{s_{\overline{X}j}^2}{\sigma_E^2}\right) + \left(\frac{s_{\overline{X}j}^2}{\sigma_E^2}\right)}, \quad (12.5)$$

where $\overline{s}_{Xj}^2$ is the average observed variance across J essentially parallel items. Expected variance σ_E^2 is obtained as discussed above and shown below in the section on null distributions. As LeBreton et al. (2005) noted, the $r_{WG(J)}$ index is essentially the Spearman–Brown prophesy equation applied to the single-item r_{WG} statistic, with the correction factor being the number of items, J.

Although r_{WG} and $r_{WG(J)}$ range between 0 and 1, sometimes they take on inadmissible values. This occurs when the observed variance exceeds expected variance under conditions of no agreement among the judges. LeBreton et al. (2005) noted three situations where one might obtain such out-of-range values. One situation was noted above and occurs when the researcher has selected an incorrect null distribution (e.g., a heavily skewed null distribution is used when a uniform null distribution would capture judges' random responding more accurately).

A second situation in which one might observe out-of-range values involves the judges' ratings conforming to a bimodal or multimodal distribution. For example, one half of the ratings might fall on the lowest end of the scale (e.g., 1 on a 5-point scale) and another half on the highest end of the scale (e.g., 5 on a 5-point scale). When judges' ratings form two distal modes, it indicates systematic disagreement and results in a large amount of observed variance that will likely exceed expected variance and result in a negative value of r_{WG}. Multimodal distributions might be suggestive of an underlying measurement model that contains two or more "true scores" on the target. For example, mentors working with multiple protégés may develop "ingroups" and "outgroups" among their protégés. In this case, protégés from the ingroup might have a decidedly different relationship with their mentor compared with their outgroup counterparts. In such circumstances, LeBreton et al. (2005) recommended using a different estimate of r_{WG}, one that is based upon a pooled within-groups observed variance (see also LeBreton & Senter, 2008). We discuss this statistic later in the chapter.

The final situation where one might observe out-of-range values is when targets are rated by very few raters. For example, consider a situation where a single leader (target) is rated by five subordinates (judges) on a single item using a 5-point scale. These subordinates assign the leader scores of 1, 2, 3, 4, and 5. The observed variance on these ratings is 2.14. The null variance that is to be expected when raters respond randomly to a 5-point scale is estimated to be 2.00 (see Table 2 in LeBreton & Senter, 2008). Thus, estimating r_{WG} using a uniform null distribution would yield a negative estimate of agreement. LeBreton et al. (2005) suggested that when the negative r_{WG} values were relatively small in magnitude, they could simply be reset to zero. Alternatively, Lindell and colleagues (Lindell & Brandt, 1997; Lindell, Brandt, & Whitney, 1999) proposed two variations of r_{WG} that are allowed to assume out-of-range values.

The first variation—referred to as Index C— eliminates the Spearman–Brown correction for multiple items built into Equation 12.5 and simply averages item variances to obtain observed variance across items (Lindell et al., 1999):

$$r^*_{WG(J)\_IndexC} = 1 - \frac{\overline{s}^2_{XJ}}{\sigma^2_E}, \qquad (12.6)$$

where $\overline{s}^2_{Xj}$ is the average of the observed variances on each of the J essentially parallel items and σ^2_E is computed based on the expected null distribution.

It should be noted that Equation 12.6 will reduce to Equation 12.4, when $J = 1$.

Another variation—referred to as Index D— explicitly models extreme disagreement among the judges by substituting σ^2_E, variance expected under no agreement among the judges, with σ^2_{MV}, variance expected under maximum disagreement among the judges (Lindell et al., 1999):

$$r^*_{WG(J)\_IndexD} = 1 - \frac{\overline{s}^2_{XJ}}{\sigma^2_{MV}}, \qquad (12.7)$$

where σ^2_{MV} refers to the variance in the maximum dissensus distribution, in which judges' scores are equally distributed between the lower (X_L) and the upper (X_U) ends of the scale. σ^2_{MV} is computed as $.5(X^2_U + X^2_L) - [.5(X_U + X_L)]^2$ (Lindell et al., 1999). A single-item version of this index is

$$r^*_{WG\_IndexD} = 1 - \frac{s^2_X}{\sigma^2_{MV}}. \qquad (12.8)$$

The difference between the two indices is that $r^*_{WG(J)\_IndexC}$ ranges between −1 and +1, and $r^*_{WG(J)\_IndexD}$ ranges between 0 and +1 (with a cautionary note that the lower boundary of $r^*_{WG(J)\_IndexD}$ may be below 0 when the scale has more than 5 response options). Lindell et al. (1999) recommended $r^*_{WG(J)\_IndexC}$ because of its intuitive interpretability, where −1 indicates complete systematic disagreement, 0 indicates lack of agreement or random response, and 1 indicates complete systematic agreement among the judges. However, we would like to note that $r^*_{WG(J)\_IndexD}$ may be also useful is some specific cases when extreme disagreement among the judges could be a concern. Below, we discuss one such case that involves estimating agreement in dyadic models where the number of judges (K) is equal to 2.

Using r_{WGp} and $r_{WGp(J)}$ to estimate agreement with multiple true scores. All variations of r_{WG} discussed above are designed for use in situations when the target has a single true score (e.g., team members rate their team's potency and this team is expected to have one true potency score estimated using the average of the members' ratings). It is also possible that the target has multiple true scores (e.g., employees rate their LMX with the leader, and this leader can be expected to have two true LMX scores: one from their ingroup members and one from their outgroup members; LeBreton & Senter, 2008). When there is a theoretical reason to assume that a target may have multiple true scores, each provided by a separate subgroup (e.g., ingroup vs. outgroup members), it is recommended that researchers use two other variants of r_{WG}: r_{WGp} (a single-item estimate of interrater agreement) and $r_{WGp(J)}$ (its multi-item extension; LeBreton et al., 2005; LeBreton & Senter, 2008). The reason why a special type of r_{WG} is needed when multiple true scores are expected is that multiple true scores imply disagreement between the subgroups of judges and may result in inadmissible values of r_{WG} and $r_{WG(J)}$, a problem r_{WGp} and $r_{WGp(J)}$ are specifically designed to address. The key difference between these two indices and the original r_{WG} and $r_{WG(J)}$ is that instead of using observed variance among the judges' ratings, r_{WGp} and $r_{WGp(J)}$ are computed using variance first estimated for each subgroup separately and then pooled into a single estimate of observed variance.

A single-item r_{WGp} estimates interrater agreement when K judges rate a single target on a single item using an approximately interval scale of measurement and there is a theoretical reason to believe that the target has multiple true scores. This r_{WGp} is computed as follows (LeBreton et al., 2005):

$$r_{WGp} = 1 - \frac{s_{X,\sigma}^2}{\sigma_E^2}.\qquad(12.9)$$

In this equation, σ_E^2 is expected variance, and $s_{X,\tau}^2$ is pooled variance across subgroups computed as the weighted average of the subgroup's variances $(n_A/N)S_A^2 + (n_B/N)S_B^2$, where n_A and n_B are the number of ratings in Subgroup A and Subgroup B, respectively, S_A^2 and S_B^2 are subgroup variances, and N is the total number of ratings across both subgroups.

A multi-item $r_{WGp(J)}$ estimates interrater agreement when K judges rate a single target on multiple items using an approximately interval scale of measurement and there is a theoretical reason to believe that the target has multiple true scores. The multi-item $r_{WGp(J)}$ is a straightforward extension of a single-item r_{WGp} (LeBreton & Senter, 2008):

$$r_{WGp(J)} = \frac{J\left(1 - \frac{\overline{s}_{X,\sigma(j)}^2}{\sigma_E^2}\right)}{J\left(1 - \frac{\overline{s}_{X,\sigma(j)}^2}{\sigma_E^2}\right) + \left(\frac{\overline{s}_{X,\sigma(j)}^2}{\sigma_E^2}\right)},\qquad(12.10)$$

where $\overline{s}_{X,\sigma(j)}^2$ is the average of the pooled variances across the J items and σ_E^2 has the same meaning as above.

Several caveats are needed with respect to r_{WGp} and $r_{WGp\,(J)}$. First, whether a target has a single or multiple true scores should be determined based on theoretical considerations a priori, before an interrater agreement index is computed. Such theoretical frameworks—for example, LMX theory (Graen & Uhl-Bien, 1995), a theory of subgroups (Carton & Cummings, 2012), a dispersion theory of team efficacy (DeRue, Hollenbeck, Ilgen, & Feltz, 2010), or a framework distinguishing among forms of diversity (Harrison & Klein, 2007)—may provide grounds for determining whether a target has multiple true scores. Second, subgroups that will be used to compute a pooled variance estimate should be identified before the data are inspected and analyzed to avoid capitalizing on chance (LeBreton et al., 2005). Finally, r_{WGp} and $r_{WGp(J)}$ require homogeneity of error variances across the subgroups. If this assumption is violated, pooled variance cannot be computed, and separate r_{WG} or $r_{WG\,(J)}$ should be obtained for the subgroups (LeBreton et al., 2005).

Interpreting r_{WG} indices. The r_{WG} indices can be interpreted as the proportional reduction in error variance due to the agreement among the judges. Thus, a value of r_{WG} indicates a proportion of variance in the ratings that can be attributed to the agreement among the judges. For example, an $r_{WG} = .70$ means that 70% of variance in the ratings is due to the judges' agreement and the remaining 30% is error variance. LeBreton and Senter (2008) proposed a set of cutoffs for different levels of agreement: 0.00–0.30 (lack of agreement), 0.31–0.50 (weak agreement), 0.51–0.70 (moderate agreement), 0.71–0.90 (strong agreement), and 0.91–1.00 (very strong agreement). We once again caution against the unconditional reliance on these cutoffs. For example, an $r_{WG} = .70$ may indicate meaningful agreement in one context (e.g., with a newly develop scale) but indicate insufficient agreement in other contexts (e.g., with the use of a well-validated and widely used scale). Thus, it is critical that researchers interpret inter-rater agreement within the context of their studies.

Choosing null distributions to estimate r_{WG} indices. To compute any variant of r_{WG}, researchers need to calculate variance expected under condition of no agreement among the judges: σ_E^2. Expected variance cannot be derived from the ratings furnished by the judges and should be determined based on the distribution of ratings expected when judges respond at random (i.e., null distribution). Given that the choice of a null distribution affects the resultant value of an r_{WG} index, it is strongly recommended that researchers carefully select null distributions to compute σ_E^2 based on theoretical considerations or prior empirical evidence. It is also recommended that multiple relevant null distributions are used to compute r_{WG} to avoid under- or overestimating interrater agreement that may occur when a wrong distribution is chosen (James et al., 1984; LeBreton & Senter, 2008).

The most intuitive and popular option has been a uniform or rectangular null distribution, in which the proportion of judges endorsing each response option on a scale is the same. For example, for a 5-point scale, the proportions would be .2, .2, .2, .2, and .2 for anchor 1 (e.g., *strongly disagree*), 2 (e.g., *disagree*), 3 (e.g., *neither disagree nor agree*), 4 (e.g., *agree*), and 5 (e.g., *strongly agree*), respectively. Because of its intuitive interpretability, simplicity, and a readily available equation that can be used to compute σ_E^2 for discrete response scales, a uniform distribution has been more popular among researchers than its alternatives (LeBreton & Senter, 2008). Using a uniform null distribution, σ_E^2 is computed as

$$\sigma_E^2 = \left(A^2 - 1\right)/12, \qquad (12.11)$$

where A is a number of anchors in a discrete response scale.

However, a uniform distribution implies that scale anchors are equally likely to be selected by judges, which is not always true when judges

respond at random. In some situations, judges may prefer some response options over others due to factors other than high interrater agreement. For example, response sets (e.g., social desirability, leniency bias, severity bias, central tendency bias) may result in the nonuniform distributions even when judges do not agree with one another. For example, a central tendency bias is associated with the higher proportions of judges who prefer anchors in the middle of scale, and thus is likely to result in a triangular distribution. Thus, it is strongly recommended that researchers do not rely solely on the uniform null distributions when computing r_{WG} but instead carefully select null distributions that more accurately reflect random responding in the context of their studies (James et al., 1984; LeBreton & Senter, 2008). Researchers may want to consider the specifics of their sample and scales to determine whether response biases are possible, ponder the nature of phenomena under examination, consult with the underlying theory, and rely on the empirical evidence from prior studies in order to determine the extent to which response biases may influence judges' ratings.

Once researchers have identified appropriate null distributions, they can compute σ_E^2 following steps outlined and illustrated in Table 12.2. At Step 1, values of scale anchors (a_i) are recorded. At Step 2, proportions (p_i) of responses per anchor are identified based on the chosen null distribution. At Step 3, the expected value of the chosen null distribution is computed as

$$E(X) = \sum a_i p_i, \qquad (12.12)$$

where a_i are scale anchors and p_i are proportions assigned to each anchor. At Step 4, the expected variance is computed as

$$\sigma_E^2 = \sum \left[(a_i - E(X))^2 p_i\right], \qquad (12.13)$$

where $E(X)$, a_i, and p_i have the same meaning as above.

The example in Table 12.2 shows a 5-point scale with anchors 1, 2, 3, 4, and 5, and the corresponding proportions per anchor for a slightly

TABLE 12.2

Computing Expected Error Variance for r_{WG} on Discrete Response Scales: Steps and Illustration

Step 1: Record anchor values for a discrete response scale (a_i): E.g., a 5-point scale	a_1 1	a_2 2	a_3 3	a_4 4	a_5 5
Step 2: Record proportions of responses per anchor (p_i) E.g., a slightly skewed null distribution	p_1 .05	p_2 .15	p_3 .20	p_4 .35	p_5 .25
Step 3: Compute $E(X)$ as shown in Equation 12.12:	a_1*p_1 .05	a_2*p_2 .30	a_3*p_3 .60 $E(X)=3.6$	a_4*p_4 1.4	a_5*p_1 1.25
Step 4: Compute σ_E^2 as shown in Equation 12.13:	$[a_1-E(X)]^2$ .34	$[a_2-E(X)]^2$ .38	$[a_3-E(X)]^2$ .07 $\sigma_E^2=1.34$	$[a_4-E(X)]^2$ .06	$[a_5-E(X)]^2$ .49

skewed null distribution: .05, .15, .20, .35, and .25 (LeBreton & Senter, 2008). The resultant expected error variance is 1.34. The same steps can be taken to compute variance for any null distribution of ratings obtained using a discrete scale. Researchers can adjust the number of anchors depending on the scale they use and change proportions at Step 2 depending on what null distribution they consider relevant. The latter can be found in Table 12.3 that contains proportions per anchor for the most frequently used 5-point and 7-point scales taken from LeBreton and Senter (2008) and Smith-Crowe et al. (2013); see their Table 2). If researchers wish to obtain proportions of judges endorsing each response option for scales with a different number of anchors (e.g., 6, 8, 9, 10, and 11), we refer them to LeBreton and Senter (2008).

Estimating Within-Unit Agreement Using Average Deviation Indices

Average deviation (AD) indices were proposed as an alternative to r_{WG} (Burke & Dunlap, 2002; Burke, Finkelstein, & Dusig, 1999). The key departures from r_{WG} are the following. First, AD eliminates the need to explicitly model a null distribution, which is the major difficulty in computing r_{WG}. Second, AD has a practical advantage over r_{WG}

by allowing to interpret agreement in the units of the original scale.

Variants of AD indices. Multiple versions of AD have been proposed. The most basic version of $AD_{M(j)}$ estimates interrater agreement as the average deviation from the scale mean (M) among K judges rating a single target on a single item (j) using an approximately interval scale of measurement:

$$AD_{M(j)} = \frac{\left(\sum_{k=1}^{K}\left|X_{jk}-\bar{X}_J\right|\right)}{K}, \qquad (12.14)$$

where X_{jk} is the rating of item j furnished by judge k, and $\bar{X}_J$ is the item mean over the K judges.

AD can also be estimated around the scale median (Md), yielding a more robust test of interrater agreement:

$$AD_{Md(j)} = \frac{\left(\sum_{k=1}^{K}\left|X_{jk}-MD_j\right|\right)}{K}. \qquad (12.15)$$

The multi-item versions of $AD_{M(j)}$ and $AD_{Md(j)}$, respectively, are

$$AD_{M(J)} = \frac{\sum_{j=1}^{J}AD_{M(J)}}{J} \qquad (12.16)$$

TABLE 12.3

Proportions of Judges per Scale Anchor for Different Null Distributions and Commonly Used Response Scales

Distribution	Proportion of judges per scale anchor						
	1	2	3	4	5	6	7
5-point scale							
Slight skew	.05	.15	.20	.35	.25		
Moderate skew	.00	.10	.15	.40	.35		
Heavy skew	.00	.00	.10	.40	.50		
Triangular	.11	.22	.34	.22	.11		
Moderate bimodal	.00	.50	.00	.50	.00		
Extreme bimodal	.50	.00	.00	.00	.50		
Normal	.07	.24	.38	.24	.07		
Uniform	.20	.20	.20	.20	.20		
7-point scale							
Slight skew	.05	.05	.10	.15	.15	.30	.20
Moderate skew	.00	.05	.10	.10	.15	.35	.25
Heavy skew	.00	.00	.05	.10	.15	.30	.40
Triangular	.05	.10	.20	.30	.20	.10	.05
Moderate bimodal	.00	.50	.00	.00	.00	.50	.00
Extreme bimodal	.50	.00	.00	.00	.00	.00	.50
Normal	.02	.08	.20	.40	.20	.08	.02
Uniform	.14	.14	.14	.14	.14	.14	.14

Note. From "Answers to 20 Questions About Interrater Reliability and Interrater Agreement," by J. M. LeBreton and J. L. Senter, 2008, *Organizational Research Methods*, *11*, pp. 832–833; and "Assessing Interrater Agreement via the Average Deviation Index Given a Variety of Theoretical and Methodological Problems," by K. Smith-Crowe, M. J. Burke, M. Kouchaki, and S. M. Signal, 2013, *Organizational Research Methods, 16*, p. 134. Copyright 2008 and 2013 by Sage Publications. Adapted with permission.

$$AD_{M(J)} = \frac{\sum_{j=1}^{J} AD_{Md(J)}}{J}, \qquad (12.17)$$

where *J* is the number of scale items.

Interpreting *AD* indices. *AD* indices indicate agreement using the original scale as a metric. Thus, the values of an *AD* index that would constitute

meaningful agreement should be determined for each scale specifically in the context of a given study. Nonetheless, there is a set of cutoff scores proposed by Burke and Dunlap (2002) to facilitate the interpretation of *AD* indices. These authors suggested the cutoffs of 0.8, 1.2, 1.5, and 1.8 for acceptable interrater agreement on the 5-, 7-, 9-, and 11-point item scales, respectively.[2]

Estimating Within-Unit Dispersion Using Standard Deviation (*SD*)

SD was also proposed (Schmidt & Hunter, 1989), albeit criticized (Kozlowski & Hattrup, 1992; Roberson, Sturman, & Simons, 2007), as an index of interrater agreement. However, *SD* (or, *SD* squared) could be a useful measure of dispersion as it estimates the spread of ratings around the mean. *SD* is computed as follows:

$$SD_X = \sqrt{\sum_{k=1}^{K} \frac{(X_k - \bar{X})^2}{K - 1}}, \qquad (12.18)$$

where is the *k*th judge's rating on item *X*, and $\bar{X}$ is the average rating across the *K* judges.

Similarities and Differences Among the Indices of Interrater Agreement

All interrater agreement indices essentially capture deviations of the individual judges' scores from the mean (or median) and thus can be expected to provide converging estimates of (dis)agreement among the judges. However, there are some differences among these indices that make them differentially applicable across analytic situations.

The key feature of *SD* that distinguishes it from r_{WG} and *AD* is that *SD* captures the dispersion of judges' ratings around the mean. However, it captures only one aspect of dispersion—its amount—and provides no information about its pattern or configuration (e.g., skew or the presence of modes). Given its focus on the deviations from the mean, *SD* appears to be better suited for testing

[2]In addition, both single- and multiitem variants of r_{WG} and *AD* can be tested for significance. Smith-Crowe, Burke, Cohen, and Doveh (2014) provide critical values for r_{WG}, $r_{WG(J)}$, $AD_{Md(J)}$ and $AD_{Md(J)}$ computed using a different number of judges (5, 10, 30, and 100), scale anchors (4, 5, and 7), and null distributions.

dispersion composition models (Chan, 1998) and examining amounts (not patterns) of dispersion rather than assessing interrater agreement per se (LeBreton & Senter, 2008). If researchers are interested in interrater agreement, r_{WG} or AD would be more suitable options.

Further, both r_{WG} and AD assess interrater agreement and tend to be highly correlated (Burke et al., 1999; LeBreton & Senter, 2008). Thus, selecting a specific index of agreement is often a matter of personal choice. The key differences between these two families of agreement indices are the following. First, r_{WG} requires that researchers specify a null distribution of no agreement, whereas AD is free of this requirement. The second difference is scaling and interpretation. r_{WG} ranges between 0 and 1, with 0 indicating lack of agreement and 1 indicating complete agreement. The AD indices estimate agreement in the metric of the original scale. Thus, r_{WG} furnishes and estimate of agreement on a finite scale and may be interpreted as a proportional reduction in error variance. The AD indices, on the other hand, provide estimates of dispersion or deviation in the metric of the original response scale.

RELIABILITY OF UNIT-LEVEL MEANS

After averaging scores supplied by members nested in different higher level units (e.g., employees in work groups, students in classrooms, soldiers in platoons) to represent shared unit properties (e.g., work group affective tone, school-level social climate, platoon-level deployment readiness), researchers may want to estimate the extent to which the unit level means reliably discriminate between units (e.g., groups). If unit means do not appear to be reliable indicators of true unit scores and do not reliably discriminate between units, they cannot be used as indicators of shared unit properties and included as group-level variables in multilevel models.

To estimate the reliability of unit means when each target is rated by a separate set of K judges, ICC(K) (LeBreton & Senter, 2008; McGraw & Wong, 1996), also referred to as ICC(2) (Bartko, 1976; James, 1982; Bliese, 2000), is used. For Unit g, reliability of this unit's mean can be computed as

follows (Raudenbush & Bryk, 2002; McGraw & Wong, 1996):

$$\text{ICC}(2)_g = \tau_{00}/(\tau_{00} + \sigma^2/k_g), \qquad (12.19)$$

where $\text{ICC}(2)_g$ is reliability of mean for Unit g and k_g is the number of judges in the unit. By averaging $\text{ICC}(2)_g$ estimates across G units, an overall index of unit-level mean reliability can be obtained to assess the extent to which estimated unit means are reliable indicators of true means (Raudenbush & Bryk, 2002). Variance components for computing ICC(2) are obtained from a one-way random effects ANOVA model in which judges' ratings are the dependent variable and groups are the "treatment" variable.

Now, we turn to one agreement-related issue that has not been considered before: the use of interrater agreement indices in dyadic models.

LOOKING AHEAD: SOME SUGGESTIONS FOR THE ESTIMATION OF AGREEMENT IN DYADS

Dyadic models, a special case of multilevel models, have become increasingly popular among researchers interested in phenomena that involve interdependence, relationships, or exchanges among two parties (e.g., LMX, interpersonal trust, and knowledge sharing) and thus can be considered fundamentally dyadic (Gooty & Yammarino, 2011; Krasikova & LeBreton, 2012; see also Chapter 18, this volume). A number of research questions (e.g., examining convergence in mentor–protégé perceptions of cooperation, spouse–spouse perceptions of relationship conflict, patient–therapist perception of therapy effectiveness) may require estimating agreement among dyad members' ratings. In organizational research, for example, LMX scholars have long been interested in the degree of convergence among leader and follower ratings of LMX and typically assessed it using the Pearson product-moment correlation coefficient r (e.g., Gerstner & Day, 1997; Sin, Nahrgang, & Morgeson, 2009). In other areas of organizational research, researchers interested in the convergence between dyad members' characteristics, beliefs, and perceptions used polynomial regression (Edwards & Parry, 1993) to model the effects of dyadic (in)congruence on the outcomes (e.g., Zhang et al., 2012).

Although *r* and polynomial regression provide meaningful information about similarity among dyad members' ratings, neither are sufficient to estimate the degree of within-dyad agreement. Correlation coefficients only estimate similarity in the relative rank orders of ratings provided by dyad members and thus are not suitable for gauging interrater agreement. Polynomial regression allows assessing congruence among the ratings furnished by dyad members, but unlike interrater agreement indices (e.g., r_{WG}), it does not yield a single index of similarity among judges' ratings. Thus, if researchers want to obtain a single index of interrater agreement or wish to assess similarity among dyad members on the outcome variable, polynomial regression will be of little help. This suggests the need for an interrater agreement index that can be used in dyadic studies.

Interrater Agreement in Dyads: Challenges

The greatest challenge associated with the use of r_{WG} and $r_{WG(J)}$ in their most traditional form in dyadic studies is that dyads necessarily include two members. This means that the number of judges providing ratings for a r_{WG} or $r_{WG(J)}$ in a dyadic context is 2. With the small number of judges, especially as small as $K = 2$, observed variance in the ratings is frequently equal to or exceeds expected error variance, resulting in the zero or inadmissible values of r_{WG} and $r_{WG(J)}$. Although an r_{WG} of 0 is admissible and can be simply interpreted as the lack of agreement, when $K = 2$ it may overestimate disagreement (i.e., within-dyad agreement will be attenuated).

To illustrate this point, we computed r_{WG} and $r_{WG(J)}$ using a uniform null distribution for dyads with different levels of agreement and two scales with the different number of response options: a 5-point scale and a 7-point scale (see Table 12.4). Dyad members' ratings falling on the two neighboring anchors on a scale (e.g., one dyad member endorsed Option 1 [*strongly disagree*] and another dyad member endorsed Option 2 [*disagree on a single item or all items in a scale*]) are labeled "adjacent." This condition constitutes the highest level of agreement next to perfect agreement indicated by the identical

ratings provided by both dyad members (e.g., both dyad members endorse Option 1: [*strongly disagree*]. Dyad members' ratings separated by 1 point (e.g., 1 and 3), 2 points (e.g., 1 and 4), and so on, are referred to as ratings that are 1 point apart, 2 points apart, and so on, in Table 12.4. The highest level of disagreement occurs when dyad members are 3 points apart on a 5-point scale and 5 points apart on a 7-point scale (i.e., 1 and 7).

As seen from the first panel of Table 12.4, when dyad members provide ratings that are only one point apart on a 5-point scale (e.g., one dyad member endorses 1 [*strongly disagree*], and another member endorses 3 [*neither disagree nor agree*]), it yields an $r_{WG} = 0$, with the use of a uniform distribution. This r_{WG} misleadingly indicates complete disagreement when dyad members are in fact far away from lacking agreement (i.e., their ratings are only 1 point apart). Further, if dyad members provide ratings that are 2 points apart on a 5-point scale (e.g., 1 [*strongly disagree*] and 4 [*agree*]), it yields an $r_{WG} = -1.25$ (inadmissible), with the use of a uniform distribution. As seen in the table, $r_{WG(J)}$ behaves similarly by yielding admissible values only when dyad member's ratings are either adjacent or 1 point apart. In all other cases, it results in inadmissible and uninterpretable values. Overall, the pattern of results in the first panel of Table 12.4 demonstrates that, when used in dyadic studies, r_{WG} and $r_{WG(J)}$ computed based on the uniform null distributions may indicate complete lack of agreement, even when the actual levels of agreement are quite high, and these indices will often assume inadmissible values as the discrepancy between the dyad members' ratings increases. This suggests that r_{WG} and $r_{WG(J)}$ computed using a uniform null distribution are inappropriate for use in dyadic studies.

Interrater Agreement in Dyads: Solutions

One solution is to reset negative values of r_{WG} and $r_{WG(J)}$ to zero and interpret them as a complete lack of agreement among judges. LeBreton et al. (2005) proposed this approach to dealing with inadmissible r_{WG} values under the assumption that these values result from sampling error. However, in dyads, inadmissible values are encountered too often, result from the small number of judges rather than

TABLE 12.4

Comparison of r_{WG} Indices Used to Estimate Interrater Agreement in Dyads

Dyad members' ratings are:	r_{WG}						$r_{WG(J)}$					
	5-point scale			7-point scale			5-point scale			7-point scale		
	s_X^2	σ_E^2	r_{WG}	s_X^2	σ_E^2	r_{WG}	$\bar{s}_{Xj}^2$	σ_E^2	$r_{WG(J)}$	$\bar{s}_{Xj}^2$	σ_E^2	$r_{WG(J)}$
Uniform null distribution												
adjacent	0.50	2.00	0.75	0.50	4.00	0.88	0.50	2.00	0.94	0.50	4.00	0.97
1 point apart	2.00	2.00	0.00	2.00	4.00	0.50	2.00	2.00	0.00	2.00	4.00	0.83
2 points apart	4.50	2.00	−1.25	4.50	4.00	−0.13	4.50	2.00	**1.56**	4.50	4.00	−1.25
3 points apart	8.00	2.00	−3.00	8.00	4.00	−1.00	8.00	2.00	**1.36**	8.00	4.00	**1.67**
4 points apart				12.50	4.00	−2.13				12.50	4.00	**1.42**
5 points apart				18.00	4.00	−3.50				18.00	4.00	**1.35**
Moderate bimodal null distribution												
adjacent	0.50	1.00	0.50	0.50	4.00	0.88	0.50	1.00	0.83	0.50	4.00	0.97
1 point apart	2.00	1.00	−1.00	2.00	4.00	0.50	2.00	1.00	**1.67**	2.00	4.00	0.83
2 points apart	4.50	1.00	−3.50	4.50	4.00	−0.13	4.50	1.00	**1.35**	4.50	4.00	−1.25
3 points apart	8.00	1.00	−7.00	8.00	4.00	−1.00	8.00	1.00	**1.30**	8.00	4.00	**1.67**
4 points apart				12.50	4.00	−2.13				12.50	4.00	**1.42**
5 points apart				18.00	4.00	−3.50				18.00	4.00	**1.35**
Extreme bimodal null distribution												
adjacent	0.50	4.00	0.88	0.50	9.00	0.94	0.50	4.00	0.97	0.50	9.00	0.99
1 point apart	2.00	4.00	0.50	2.00	9.00	0.78	2.00	4.00	0.83	2.00	9.00	0.95
2 points apart	4.50	4.00	−0.13	4.50	9.00	0.50	4.50	4.00	−1.25	4.50	9.00	0.83
3 points apart	8.00	4.00	−1.00	8.00	9.00	0.11	8.00	4.00	**1.67**	8.00	9.00	0.38
4 points apart				12.50	9.00	−0.39				12.50	9.00	**3.50**
5 points apart				18.00	9.00	−1.00				18.00	9.00	**1.67**

	$r_{WG\_IndexD}^*$						$r_{WG(J)\_IndexD}^*$					
	5-point scale			7-point scale			5-point scale			7-point scale		
	s_X^2	σ_{MV}^2	r_{WG}^*	s_X^2	σ_{MV}^2	r_{WG}^*	$\bar{s}_{Xj}^2$	σ_{MV}^2	$r_{WG(J)}^*$	$\bar{s}_{Xj}^2$	σ_{MV}^2	$r_{WG(J)}^*$
Maximum dissensus null distribution												
adjacent	0.50	4.00	0.88	0.50	9.00	0.94	0.50	4.00	0.88	0.50	9.00	0.94
1 point apart	2.00	4.00	0.50	2.00	9.00	0.78	2.00	4.00	0.50	2.00	9.00	0.78
2 points apart	4.50	4.00	−0.13	4.50	9.00	0.50	4.50	4.00	−0.13	4.50	9.00	0.50
3 points apart	8.00	4.00	−1.00	8.00	9.00	0.11	8.00	4.00	−1.00	8.00	9.00	0.11
4 points apart				12.50	9.00	−0.39				12.50	9.00	−0.39
5 points apart				18.00	9.00	−1.00				18.00	9.00	−1.00

Note. s_X^2, $\bar{s}_{Xj}^2$, and $\bar{s}_{Xj}^2$ are observed variances used to compute their respective variants of r_{WG}; σ_E^2 is expected variance based on a uniform, moderate bimodal, or extreme bimodal null distribution; and σ_{MV}^2 is expected variance based on a maximum dissensus null distribution. Boldfaced entries are inadmissible values of the r_{WG} indices.

sampling error, and, as shown in Table 12.4, occur even with small amounts of disagreement. Thus, resetting all inadmissible values to zero will result in the overestimated levels of disagreement. That is, most dyads in a sample, even those with small disagreement, will end up with $r_{WG} = 0$.

Another solution is to use bimodal null distributions to compute expected variance in dyads. Bimodal null distributions should more accurately reflect random responding by dyad members because two responses that are at least 1 point apart will necessarily form a bimodal distribution. To test this solution, we computed of r_{WG} and $r_{WG(J)}$ based on the moderate bimodal and extreme bimodal null distributions. Proportions for both bimodal distributions used to compute σ_E^2 are provided in Table 12.3. As shown in Table 12.4, moderate bimodal null distributions tend to result in the zero or inadmissible values of r_{WG} and $r_{WG(J)}$ even with small amounts of disagreement (when ratings are at least 1 point apart on a 5-point scale and at least 2 points apart on a 7-point scale). Extreme bimodal null distributions also take on inadmissible values with moderate amounts of disagreement (i.e., ratings are 2 points apart) on a 5-point scale. However, on a 7-point scale, they yield inadmissible values only with large (ratings are 4 points apart) and maximal (ratings are 5 points apart) amounts of disagreement. Thus, r_{WG} and $r_{WG(J)}$ computed based on extreme bimodal null distributions appear a more suitable candidate for use in the dyadic contexts compared to uniform and moderate bimodal null distributions.

An alternative solution is to estimate Lindell et al.'s (1999) $r_{WG\_IndexD}^*$ and $r_{WG(J)\_IndexD}^*$ (see Equations 12.7 and 12.8) comparing the dyad members' (i.e., judges') observed variance to the variance expected under maximum dissensus among the judges (σ_{MV}^2). The last panel in Table 12.4 provides $r_{WG\_IndexD}^*$ and $r_{WG(J)\_IndexD}^*$ indices computed for our example. Just like r_{WG} and $r_{WG(J)}$ computed on extreme bimodal null distributions, $r_{WG\_IndexD}^*$ and $r_{WG(J)\_IndexD}^*$ result in fewer inadmissible values compared to uniform and moderate bimodal null distributions. $r_{WG\_IndexD}^*$ and $rr_{WG(J)\_IndexD}^*$ yield inadmissible (i.e., negative) values only with large amounts of disagreement (e.g., ratings that are 4 or

5 points apart on a 7-point scale). Further, a single-item $r_{WG\_IndexD}^*$ performs similarly to a single-item r_{WG} computed based on the extreme bimodal null distribution on both 5- and 7-point scales. However, a multi-item $r_{WG(J)\_IndexD}^*$ seems to perform better than a multi-item r_{WG} computed based on the extreme bimodal null distribution. Inadmissible values yielded by $r_{WG(J)\_IndexD}^*$ (−0.13 and −1.00 for a 5-point scale and −0.39 and −1.00 for a 7-point scale) are substantially smaller than inadmissible values yielded by $r_{WG(J)}$ computed based on the extreme null distribution (−.1.25 and 1.67, respectively, for a 5-point scale, and 3.50 and 1.67, respectively, for a 7-point scale). Thus, a multi-item $r_{WG(J)\_IndexD}^*$ appears to be the best candidate for use in the dyadic contexts among other multi-item variants of r_{WG}. Among the single-item variants of r_{WG}, both $r_{WG\_IndexD}^*$ and r_{WG} computed based on the extreme null distribution appear to be suitable candidates for use in dyadic studies.

Interrater Agreement in Dyads: Recommendations

Based on all of the above, we recommend the following with regard to the use of r_{WG} indices in dyadic studies. First, we do *not* recommend that researchers interested in assessing agreement within dyads (a) blindly reset negative r_{WG}'s to zero and interpret them as indicators of complete disagreement, or (b) compute r_{WG} and $r_{WG(J)}$ using uniform or moderate bimodal null distributions. Instead, we recommend that researchers estimate agreement using extreme bimodal and maximum dissensus distributions. More specifically, when dyad members furnish ratings using a *single*-item scale, we suggest researchers use $r_{WG\_IndexD}^*$ or r_{WG} computed based on the extreme null distribution to estimate agreement. However, when dyad members furnish ratings using a *multi*-item scale, we recommend that researchers use $r_{WG(J)\_IndexD}^*$ as a measure of interrater agreement.

Further, if any of these recommended indices result in inadmissible values, it will most likely indicate extreme disagreement. We suggest that researchers examine those dyads with extreme disagreement more closely to decide whether the level of disagreement between dyad members is sufficient to reset the negative values to 0 and interpret them as maximal disagreement.

Our final recommendation is to use scales with a larger number of response options (e.g., 7-point scales) when researchers are interested in estimating interrater agreement in dyads. The last two panels in Table 12.4 show that a 5-point scale yields inadmissible values for all four recommended indices (i.e., r_{WG} and $r_{WG(J)}$ computed based on the extreme bimodal null distribution, $r^*_{WG\_IndexD}$, and $r^*_{WG(J)\_IndexD}$) even with moderate amounts of disagreement. A 7-point scale, however, yields inadmissible values only with large levels of disagreement. Thus, we recommend that researcher use scales with a greater number of anchors when they are interested in estimating interrater agreement in dyads.

GUIDELINES ON THE ESTIMATION OF AGREEMENT AND RELIABILITY IN MULTILEVEL STUDIES

Table 12.1 presents a summary of guidelines regarding the application of interrater agreement and reliability indices in multilevel studies. These guidelines are distilled from the detailed discussions of each index provided in the corresponding sections of this chapter. Table 12.1 is thus intended to provide a big-picture overview and a user-friendly summary of decisions to be made by researchers when deciding which agreement or reliability index, if any, should be used in their studies.

To choose the most appropriate interrater agreement or reliability index for their study, researchers first need to determine the purpose this index will serve: to gauge the amounts of nonindependence and determine whether the use of multilevel modeling is warranted, to assess agreement and justify aggregation, assess amounts of dispersion, or examine reliability of unit means (see the first column of Table 12.1). Each purpose is served by a separate set of indices (see the second column of Table 12.1). The choice among indices serving the same purpose is determined by the specifics of an analytic context in which interrater agreement and reliability needs to be assessed (see the third column of Table 12.1). The remaining two columns summarize interpretation guidelines (the fourth column)

and contain some explanatory or cautionary notes related to the application of specific indices (the last column).

As seen in the table, when researchers are concerned with the amounts of nonindependence among judges' ratings because of the judges' nesting within higher level units, ICC(1) (also referred to as ρ_α) and ρ_β should be used. The former evaluates nonindependence because of the differences in group means, whereas the latter evaluates nonindependence because of differences in slopes. Taken together, these two indices allow for a comprehensive assessment of nonindependence and thus prevent researchers from wrongfully concluding that the grouping effect can be ignored and their data can be analyzed using a single-level regression.

When researchers want to assess agreement and justify aggregation, they should use some variant of an r_{WG} index or an *AD* index. The choice among the variants of r_{WG} and *AD* depends on the number of items in a scale used to rate a target (single item vs. multiple items), the presence of a single or multiple true scores, and the possibility of inadmissible values. When both r_{WG} or *AD* can be used, researchers should choose between the two depending on whether they look for a standardized metric of agreement (the purpose served best by r_{WG}) or want to measure agreement using the original scale as a metric (the purpose served by an *AD* index). Researchers should also consider whether they can model a null distribution, a condition required by r_{WG} but not by the *AD* indices.

When researchers aggregate judges' ratings to form an indicator of a higher level construct (using a direct consensus or a referent-shift consensus model), the reliability of these aggregated scores should be assessed before they can be used as a unit-level variable in a multilevel model. This purpose is served by ICC(K), also referred to as ICC(2), indicating how reliably these aggregated ratings distinguish between groups.

CONCLUSION

With the growing interest in studying multilevel phenomena and processes in behavioral research, indices of agreement and reliability have become increasingly popular. Given that these indices have a number of uses and appear in multiple variants designed for different analytic contexts, we thought an integrative discussion about these indices might be useful to researchers. This chapter provided such a discussion with a particular focus on the differences among indices of agreement and reliability, and their use in the assessments of nonindependence, within-unit agreement and the reliability of unit-level means in multilevel studies.

It is our hope this chapter will facilitate the use of agreement and reliability indices in social sciences and help researchers select, compute, and properly interpret nonindependence, within-unit agreement, and the reliability of unit-level means. We also hope that our recommendations for estimating interrater agreement in dyads will help answer previously unanswered research questions about convergence in dyad members' assessments of dyadic phenomena. In addition, we hope that the illustrative example included in our appendices serves to further clarify these concepts, their statistical estimation, and their substantive interpretation.

APPENDIX 12.1: OVERVIEW OF ILLUSTRATIVE EXAMPLES

DESCRIPTION OF THE DATA

The data used in our illustrative examples were those that were analyzed in a special issue of *Leadership Quarterly* in 2002. This special issue was coedited by Paul Bliese, Ronald Halverson, and Chester Schriesheim (Bliese, Halverson, & Schriesheim, 2002). The data frame is made up of 2,042 soldiers nested within 49 unique army companies (COMPID). The focal variables for our illustration include scales scores for hostility (HOSTILE) and leadership climate (LEAD). In addition, we will be examining the 11 items that compose the leadership climate scale score (LEAD01–LEAD11).

RESEARCH QUESTIONS

Question 1: Are the soldiers' ratings of hostility nonindependent because of the nesting of soldiers within army companies?

Question 2: Is there sufficient within-group (i.e., within army company) agreement to justify aggregating the soldiers' perceptions of leadership climate to the company level?

Question 3: At the company level, do the mean leadership climate ratings reliably discriminate between groups (i.e., between army companies)?

APPENDIX 12.2: ILLUSTRATIVE EXAMPLES USING R: RESULTS AND INTERPRETATIONS

Question 1: Are the soldiers' ratings of hostility nonindependent because of the nesting of soldiers within army companies?

This research question is addressed by estimating and interpreting the ICC(1). For our illustration, we estimated the ICC(1) using two different approaches.

The first approach computed the variance components using the *aov* function and then plugged these variance components in the *ICC1* function. The *aov* function estimates the variance components for the ICC(1) using a least-squares estimator and is generally best suited for balanced designs (i.e., designs where there are an identical number of Level 1 units (soldiers) nested in each of the Level 2 units (companies).

The *aov* function requires the user to specify the dependent variable (HOSTILE) and the grouping variable (COMPID), along with the data frame (lq2002) and a statement concerning the treatment of any missing data. Applying the *ICC1* function to the variance components obtained with the *aov* function yielded an ICC(1) estimate of .05400494, indicating that ~5% of the variance in soldiers' hostility ratings is attributed to their nesting within army companies. Thus, there is evidence that the soldiers' ratings of hostility are nonindependent.

The second approach computed the variance components using the *lme* function that is part of the *nlme* package. This function estimates variance

Number of Soldiers Nested in Army Companies

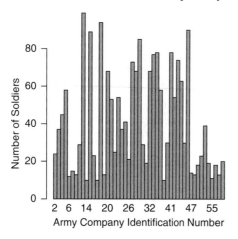

FIGURE 12A.1.   Barplot illustrating unbalanced data.

components using either maximum likelihood or restricted maximum likelihood (the default) and is better suited for unbalanced data. As illustrated with our *barplot* (Figure 12A.1), there is strong evidence that the data are unbalanced. Thus, it is probably safer to use the *lme* function to estimate variance components and then manually compute the ICC(1) value using these variance components.

Similar to the *aov* function, the *lme* function requires the user to specify the dependent variable (HOSTILE) and the grouping variable (COMPID), along with the data frame (lq2002) and a statement concerning the treatment of any missing data. In addition, the user is required to specify (a) the structural equation for the fixed regression, which in our simple null model is a fixed intercept (i.e., ~1), and (b) the structural equation for the random regression, which in our simple null model is a random intercept (i.e., random = ~1). We saved the results of this analysis to a new object denoted model.1b. We then applied the *VarCorr* function to this object to obtain our variance components. The between-groups variance is labeled "(intercept)" in the R output; the within-groups variance is labeled "residual."

We manually estimated the ICC(1):

$$ICC1.model.1b = .0594961/(.0594961 + 1.0166930)$$

$$= 0.05528406.$$

Although this estimate is similar to the estimate obtained via *aov*, it is slightly different. However, the substantive interpretation is the same: roughly 5% of the variance in soldiers' ratings of hostility is attributed to their nesting within different army companies (i.e., the data appear to be nonindependent).

Question 2: Is there sufficient within-group (i.e., within army company) agreement to justify aggregating the soldiers' perceptions of leadership climate to the company level?

This research question is addressed by estimating and interpreting estimates of within-group agreement. For our illustration, we estimated the single-item r_{WG} index for the first leadership climate item (LEAD01). We also estimated the multi-item $r_{WG(j)}$ index for the 11-item leadership climate scale.

rwg.   To estimate within-group agreement for a single item, we used the *rwg* function, which is part of the *multilevel package*. The *rwg* function requires the user to specify the dependent variable (LEAD01) and the grouping variable (COMPID). In addition, the user must specify the random response null variance. For our illustration, we estimated r_{WG} based on both a uniform null distribution and a slightly skewed null distribution. The latter allows us to estimate the levels of within-group agreement in the presence of a response bias (e.g., leniency bias). For a 5-point scale, the expected variance based on a uniform null response distribution is 2.00; the expected variance based on a slightly skewed null distribution was set to 1.34 (see Table 2 in LeBreton & Senter, 2008, for variance estimates based on other scales or response biases, or use the protocols presented in this chapter for estimating your null variance).

Based upon a uniform null response distribution, the results indicated, on average, that there was only modest agreement within army companies with a mean r_{WG} of 0.42. Examining a frequency distribution of these r_{WG} values (remember, r_{WG} is computed separately for each of the 49 army companies), reveals that the majority of r_{WG} values fell in the .40 to .50 range.

Not surprisingly, the mean estimate dropped to 0.17 when estimating agreement under the condition that a slight leniency bias may have restricted the variance in soldier ratings.

It is also possible to test the statistical significance of r_{WG} values using the *rwg.sim* function in the *multilevel* package. This function requires the user to specify a group size (we used 42, the average group size), the number of response categories (5, in our example), and the number of simulations to replicate (10,000). The resulting output consists of a distribution of simulated r_{WG} values. To test for statistical significance, one simply compares observed r_{WG} values to some a priori specified percentile (e.g., 95th). It is important to note that because this is a simulated distribution, specific cutoffs for specific percentiles may differ slightly from user to user.

$r_{WG(J)}$. To estimate multiitem, within-group agreement (i.e., agreement over the 11 items comprising the leadership climate scale), we used the *rwgj* function, which is also part of the *multilevel package*. The *rwgj* function requires the user to specify the items composing the leadership scale. These items are denoted LEAD01 through LEAD11 in the data frame and are located in Columns 3 through 13 in the data frame. Rather than list the 11 items, we used a notational shortcut to specify the 11 items using matrix notation: lq2002[,c(3:13)]. The user is also required to specify the grouping variable (COMPID) and the random response null variance. Again, we estimated $r_{WG(J)}$ using null variances based on both uniform and slightly skewed distributions.

Unlike the results for the single-item estimates of agreement, the multi-item estimates based on $r_{WG(J)}$ revealed (on average) relatively strong agreement within army companies. The mean $r_{WG(J)}$ based on a uniform null response distribution was .87. However, the estimate based upon a slightly skewed null response distribution was much lower at .41.

It is also possible to test the statistical significance of the multiitem $r_{WG(J)}$ estimates using the *rwg.j.sim* function included in the *multilevel* package.

Summary. Overall, there was mixed supported for the aggregation of soldier-level climate perceptions to the group level. If one could safely assume that the soldiers' data were free from

response biases (e.g., if soldiers were assured of confidentiality and that the results would be used solely for research purposes), then the results from the $r_{WG(J)}$ analyses suggest that data may be safely aggregated to the company level. Specifically, the average $r_{WG(J)}$ was .87, with a range from .77 to .94. In contrast, if there was reason to believe that the soldiers responses might have been influenced by a pervasive leniency bias, then the results are less encouraging. Although one group obtained a maximum $r_{WG(J)}$ of .88 (indicating strong agreement), at least one group had a $r_{WG(J)}$ estimate of 0.00. This variability between groups in their levels of agreement may suggest that there are varying degrees of "climate strength" (cf. Schneider et al., 2002).

Question 3: At the company level, do the mean leadership climate ratings reliably discriminate between groups (i.e., between army companies)?

Our final research question is addressed by estimating and interpreting the ICC(2). For our illustration, we estimated ICC(2) for the overall leadership climate scale score (LEAD), and again illustrated this process using the *aov* and *lme* functions in R.

The first approach computed the variance components using the *aov* function and then plugged these variance components in the *ICC2* function. As noted above, the *aov* function estimates the variance components for the ICC(2) using a least-squares estimator and is generally best suited for balanced designs (i.e., designs in which there are an identical number of Level 1 units (soldiers) nested in each of the Level 2 units (companies).

The *aov* function requires the user to specify the variable of interest (LEAD) and the grouping variable (COMPID), along with the data frame (lq2002) and a statement concerning the treatment of any missing data. Applying the *ICC1* and *ICC2* function to the variance components obtained with the *aov* function yielded an ICC(1) estimate of 0.08795622 and an ICC(2) value of 0.8007544.

The ICC(1) value indicates that ratings from individual soldiers are highly unreliable, but the ICC(2) value indicates that group means (i.e., mean LEAD scores aggregated over soldiers, nested within different army companies) reliably and effectively discriminate between groups.

The second approach computed the variance components using the *lme* function that is part of the *nlme* package. As noted above, this function estimates variance components using either maximum likelihood or restricted maximum likelihood (the default) and is better suited for unbalanced data.

Similar to the *aov* function, the *lme* function requires the user to specify the dependent variable (LEAD) and the grouping variable (COMPID), along with the data frame (lq2002) and a statement concerning the treatment of any missing data. In addition, the user is required to specify (a) the structural equation for the fixed regression, which in our simple null model is a fixed intercept (i.e., ~1), and (b) the structural equation for the random regression, which in our simple null model is a random intercept (i.e., random = ~1). We saved the results of this analysis to a new object, denoted model.2b. We then applied the *VarCorr* function to this object to obtain our variance components. The between-groups variance is labeled "(intercept)" in the R output; the within-groups variance is labeled "residual."

We manually estimated the ICC(1) and ICC(2):

$$ICC1.model.2b = 0.07434663 \Big/ \left(\begin{array}{c} 0.07434663 \\ + 0.61513752 \end{array} \right)$$

$$= 0.1078294.$$

$$ICC1.model.2b = 0.07434663 \Big/ \left(\begin{array}{c} 0.07434663 \\ + 0.61513752/42 \end{array} \right)$$

$$= 0.8354233.$$

Although both estimates are similar to what was obtained using *aov*, they are not identical. Nevertheless, the substantive interpretations are the same. The ICC(1) value indicates that ratings from individual soldiers are highly unreliable, but the ICC(2) value indicates that group means (i.e., mean LEAD scores aggregated over soldiers, nested within different army

companies) reliably and effectively discriminate between groups.

APPENDIX 12.3: ILLUSTRATIVE EXAMPLES USING R: COMPLETE ANNOTATED SYNTAX

```
# R Code for Krasikova & LeBreton
###########################################
#####STEP 1: Loading Packages & Data#####
###########################################

# Install the multilevel package
install.packages("multilevel")

# Load the multilevel package into the library of
  active resources
library(multilevel)

# Load the lq2002 dataframe
### Note: This dataframe contains the data used in
  a special issue of Leadership Quarterly (Vol 13)
  published in 2002
data(lq2002, package="multilevel")

# List the names of the variables included in the
  lq2002 data frame
names(lq2002)

# Examine the structure of the dataframe
str(lq2002)

# Note: The COMPID variable is the grouping
  variable
### This variable is a nominal variable that simply
  identifies the Army Company to which soldiers
  were assigned (i.e., nested)
### COMPID should be treated as a nominal/
  categorical variable, but it is currently classified as
  an integer variable
class(lq2002$COMPID)

### We will reclassify this variable by overwriting in
  the dataframe
lq2002$COMPID=as.factor(lq2002$COMPID)
class(lq2002$COMPID)
```

```
###########################################
#####STEP 2: Estimating Non-Independence#####
###########################################

# Estimation of Non-Independence via ICC(1)
### We will treat HOSTILE as our dependent variable
### Using the aov function: regress the DV
    (HOSTILE) onto the grouping variable (COMPID)
### aov works best if you have a balanced design
    (same number of L1 units nested in each L2 unit)
model.1a<-aov(HOSTILE~COMPID,data=lq2002,
    na.action=na.omit)
summary(model.1a)
### now simply apply the ICC1 function to the
    model.1a output
ICC1(model.1a)
```

```
### With unbalanced designs, it is probably better
    to estimate a "Null" Model using the lme function
    from the nlme package
### The nlme package is automatically loaded when
    using multilevel
### Otherwise use: install.packages("nlme")
### Followed by: library("nlme")
### The data are unbalanced
counts=table(lq2002$COMPID)
barplot(counts, main="# of Soldiers Nested in Army
    Companies",
xlab = "Army Company Identification Number",
ylab = "# of Soldiers")
model.1b=(lme(HOSTILE~1,random=~1|COMPID,
    data=lq2002,na.action=na.omit))
```

```
### Obtain the variance components from this
    model
VarCorr(model.1b)
```

```
### Manually compute the ICC(1)
ICC1.model.1b=.0594961/(.0594961+1.0166930);
    ICC.model.1b
```

```
###########################################
###STEP 3: Estimating Within-Group Agreement###
###########################################

# Estimation of Within-Group Agreement using rwg
    and rwgj functions
```

```
### We are interested in whether soldiers nested
    in Army companies agree in their perceptions of
    leadership climate
names(lq2002)
### We will estimate the single item rwg for the first
    leadership climate item
### We will estimate rwg using both a uniform null
    distribution and a slightly skewed distribution
rwg.lead01.un = rwg(lq2002$LEAD01,
    lq2002$COMPID,ranvar=2.00)
rwg.lead01.ss=rwg(lq2002$LEAD01,
    lq2002$COMPID, ranvar=1.34)
summary(rwg.lead01.un); summary(rwg.lead01.ss)
hist(rwg.lead01.un$rwg,
xlab = "Estimate of rwg",
ylab = "Frequency")
```

```
### We can test whether the observed rwg=.4234 is
    statistically significantly different from zero
### Need to specify a group size for the simulation;
    so we selected 42 (the mean group size)
rwg.lead01.sim = rwg.sim(gsize=42,
    nresp=5,nrep=10000)
quantile(rwg.lead01.sim,c(.90,.95,.99))
```

```
### We will estimate the multi-item rwgj across the
    11 leadership climate items
rwgj.lead.un=rwg.j(lq2002[,c(3:13)],
    lq2002$COMPID,ranvar=2.00)
rwgj.lead.ss=rwg.j(lq2002[,c(3:13)],
    lq2002$COMPID,ranvar=1.34)
summary(rwgj.lead.un); summary(rwgj.lead.ss)
rwgj.lead.sim=rwg.j.sim(gsize=42, nitems=11,nresp
    =5,itemcors=cor(lq2002[,3:13]),nrep=10000)
quantile(rwgj.lead.sim,c(.90,.95,.99))
```

```
# The multilevel package also contains functions that
    allow users to compute other measures of agreement
### ad.m can be used to compute the Average Devia-
    tion index (Burke, Finkelstein, & Dusig, 1999)
### awg can be used to estimate the agreement
    within group index (Brown & Hauenstein, 2005)
### rgr.agree can be used to compute agreement
    using a random group resampling procedure
    (Bliese & Halverson, 2002)
### rwg.j.lindell can be used to compute agreement
    using the r*wgj statistic (Lindell, Brandt, &
    Whitney, 1999)
```

```
##############################################
###STEP 3: Estimating Reliability of Group Means###
##############################################
```

```
# Estimation of the ICC2; stability or reliability of
    group means
### We will treat LEAD (the scale score for the
    11 leadership climate items) as our L1 variable
### Using the aov function: regress the DV (LEAD)
    onto the grouping variable (COMPID)
### As noted above, aov works best if you have a
    balanced design (same number of L1 units nested
    in each L2 unit)
model.2a<-aov(LEAD~COMPID,data=lq2002,
    na.action=na.omit)
summary(model.2a)
### now simply apply the ICC1 & ICC2 functions
    to the model.2a output
ICC1(model.2a)
ICC2(model.2a)
### As noted above, with unbalanced designs it is
    probably better to estimate a "Null" Model using
    the lme function ### The data are unbalanced
model.2b=(lme(LEAD~1,random=~1|COMPID,
    data=lq2002,na.action=na.omit))
```

```
### Obtain the variance components from this model
VarCorr(model.2b)
```

```
### Manually compute the ICC(1)
ICC1.model.2b=0.07434663/
    (0.07434663+0.61513752); ICC.model.2b
```

```
### Manually compute the ICC(2)
### Note: Need to specify the number of raters/
    group to estimate the ICC(2); we will use the
    mean of 42 raters
ICC2.model.2b=0.07434663/
    (0.07434663+0.61513752/42); ICC2.model.2b
```

References

Aguinis, H., & Culpepper, S. A. (2015). An expanded decision-making procedure for examining cross-level interaction effects with multilevel modeling. *Organizational Research Methods, 18*, 155–176. http://dx.doi.org/10.1177/1094428114563618

Aguinis, H., Gottfredson, R. K., & Culpepper, S. A. (2013). Best-practice recommendations for estimating cross-level interaction effects using multilevel modeling. *Journal of Management, 39*, 1490–1528. http://dx.doi.org/10.1177/0149206313478188

Aguinis, H., Pierce, C. A., Bosco, F. A., & Muslin, I. S. (2009). First decade of *Organizational Research Methods*: Trends in design, measurement, and data-analysis topics. *Organizational Research Methods, 12*, 69–112. http://dx.doi.org/10.1177/1094428108322641

Barcikowski, R. S. (1981). Statistical power with group mean as the unit of analysis. *Journal of Educational and Behavioral Statistics, 6*, 267–285. http://dx.doi.org/10.3102/10769986006003267

Bartko, J. J. (1976). On various intraclass correlation reliability coefficients. *Psychological Bulletin, 83*, 762–765. http://dx.doi.org/10.1037/0033-2909.83.5.762

Bliese, P. D. (2000). Within-group agreement, nonindependence, and reliability: Implications for data aggregation and analysis. In K. J. Klein & S. W. J. Kozlowski (Eds.), *Multilevel theory, research, and methods in organizations: Foundations, extensions, and new directions* (pp. 349–381). San Francisco, CA: Jossey-Bass.

Bliese, P. D., & Halverson, R. R. (2002). Using random group resampling in multilevel research: An example of the buffering effects of leadership climate. *The Leadership Quarterly, 13*, 53–68.

Bliese, P. D., Halverson, R. R., & Schriesheim, C. A. (2002). Benchmarking multilevel methods in leadership: The articles, the model, and the data set. *The Leadership Quarterly, 13*, 3–14. http://dx.doi.org/10.1016/S1048-9843(01)00104-7

Bliese, P. D., & Hanges, P. J. (2004). Being both too liberal and too conservative: The perils of treating grouped data as though they were independent. *Organizational Research Methods, 7*, 400–417. http://dx.doi.org/10.1177/1094428104268542

Brown, R. D., & Hauenstein, N. M. (2005). Interrater agreement reconsidered: An alternative to the r_{wg} indices. *Organizational Research Methods, 8*, 165–184.

Burke, M. J., & Dunlap, W. P. (2002). Estimating interrater agreement with the average deviation index: A user's guide. *Organizational Research Methods, 5*, 159–172. http://dx.doi.org/10.1177/1094428102005002002

Burke, M. J., Finkelstein, L. M., & Dusig, M. S. (1999). On average deviation indices for estimating interrater agreement. *Organizational Research Methods, 2*, 49–68. http://dx.doi.org/10.1177/109442819921004

Carton, A. M., & Cummings, J. N. (2012). A theory of subgroups in work teams. *Academy of Management Review, 37*, 441–470. http://dx.doi.org/10.5465/amr.2009.0322

Chan, D. (1998). Functional relations among constructs in the same content domain at different levels of analysis: A typology of composition models. *Journal of Applied Psychology, 83,* 234–246. http://dx.doi.org/10.1037/0021-9010.83.2.234

DeRue, D. S., Hollenbeck, J., Ilgen, D., & Feltz, D. (2010). Efficacy dispersion in teams: Moving beyond agreement and aggregation. *Personnel Psychology, 63,* 1–40. http://dx.doi.org/10.1111/j.1744-6570.2009.01161.x

Edwards, J. R., & Parry, M. E. (1993). On the use of polynomial regression equations as an alternative to difference scores in organizational research. *Academy of Management Journal, 36,* 1577–1613. http://dx.doi.org/10.5465/256822

Erdogan, B., & Bauer, T. N. (2010). Differentiated leader–member exchanges: The buffering role of justice climate. *Journal of Applied Psychology, 95,* 1104–1120. http://dx.doi.org/10.1037/a0020578

George, J. M. (1990). Personality, affect, and behavior in groups. *Journal of Applied Psychology, 75,* 107–116. http://dx.doi.org/10.1037/0021-9010.75.2.107

Gerstner, C. R., & Day, D. V. (1997). Meta-analytic review of leader–member exchange theory: Correlates and construct issues. *Journal of Applied Psychology, 82,* 827–844. http://dx.doi.org/10.1037/0021-9010.82.6.827

Gooty, J., & Yammarino, F. J. (2011). Dyads in organizational research: Conceptual issues and multilevel analyses. *Organizational Research Methods, 14,* 456–483. http://dx.doi.org/10.1177/1094428109358271

Graen, G. B., & Uhl-Bien, M. (1995). Relationship-based approach to leadership: Development of leader–member exchange (LMX) theory of leadership over 25 years: Applying a multi-level multi-domain perspective. *The Leadership Quarterly, 6,* 219–247. http://dx.doi.org/10.1016/1048-9843(95)90036-5

Harrison, D. A., & Klein, K. J. (2007). What's the difference? Diversity constructs as separation, variety, or disparity in organizations. *Academy of Management Review, 32,* 1199–1228. http://dx.doi.org/10.5465/AMR.2007.26586096

Hofmann, D. A., Griffin, M. A., & Gavin, M. B. (2000). The application of hierarchical linear modeling to organizational research. In K. J. Klein & S. W. J. Kozlowski (Eds.), *Multilevel theory, research, and methods in organizations: Foundations, extensions, and new directions* (pp. 467–511). San Francisco, CA: Jossey-Bass.

Hofmann, D. A. (1997). An overview of the logic and rationale of hierarchical linear models. *Journal of Management, 23,* 723–744. http://dx.doi.org/10.1177/014920639702300602

James, L. R. (1982). Aggregation bias in estimates of perceptual agreement. *Journal of Applied Psychology, 67,* 219–229. http://dx.doi.org/10.1037/0021-9010.67.2.219

James, L. R., Demaree, R. G., & Wolf, G. (1984). Estimating within-group interrater reliability with and without response bias. *Journal of Applied Psychology, 69,* 85–98. http://dx.doi.org/10.1037/0021-9010.69.1.85

James, L. R., Demaree, R. G., & Wolf, G. (1993). r_{wg}: An assessment of within-group interrater agreement. *Journal of Applied Psychology, 78,* 306–309. http://dx.doi.org/10.1037/0021-9010.78.2.306

Kenny, D. A., & Judd, C. M. (1986). Consequences of violating the independence assumption in analysis of variance. *Psychological Bulletin, 99,* 422–431. http://dx.doi.org/10.1037/0033-2909.99.3.422

Kozlowski, S. W., & Hattrup, K. (1992). A disagreement about within-group agreement: Disentangling issues of consistency versus consensus. *Journal of Applied Psychology, 77,* 161–167. http://dx.doi.org/10.1037/0021-9010.77.2.161

Kozlowski, S. W., & Klein, K. J. (2000). A multilevel approach to theory and research in organizations: Contextual, temporal, and emergent processes. In K. J. Klein & S. W. J. Kozlowski (Eds.), *Multilevel theory, research, and methods in organizations: Foundations, extensions, and new directions* (pp. 3–90). San Francisco, CA: Jossey-Bass.

Krasikova, D. V., & LeBreton, J. M. (2012). Just the two of us: Misalignment of theory and methods in examining dyadic phenomena. *Journal of Applied Psychology, 97,* 739–757. http://dx.doi.org/10.1037/a0027962

Kreft, I., & de Leeuw, J. (2002). *Introducing multilevel modeling.* Thousand Oaks, CA: Sage.

LeBreton, J. M., Burgess, J. R., Kaiser, R. B., Atchley, E. K., & James, L. R. (2003). The restriction of variance hypothesis and interrater reliability and agreement: Are ratings from multiple sources really dissimilar? *Organizational Research Methods, 6,* 80–128. http://dx.doi.org/10.1177/1094428102239427

LeBreton, J. M., James, L. R., & Lindell, M. K. (2005). Recent issues regarding r_{WG}, r_{WG}, $r_{WG(J)}$, and $r_{WG*(J)}$. *Organizational Research Methods, 8,* 128–138. http://dx.doi.org/10.1177/1094428104272181

LeBreton, J. M., & Senter, J. L. (2008). Answers to 20 questions about interrater reliability and interrater agreement. *Organizational Research Methods, 11,* 815–852. http://dx.doi.org/10.1177/1094428106296642

Li, A. N., & Liao, H. (2014). How do leader–member exchange quality and differentiation affect performance in teams? An integrated multilevel dual process model. *Journal of Applied Psychology, 99,* 847–866. http://dx.doi.org/10.1037/a0037233

Liden, R. C., Erdogan, B., Wayne, S. J., & Sparrowe, R. T. (2006). Leader-member exchange, differentiation, and task interdependence: Implications for individual and group performance. *Journal of Organizational Behavior, 27,* 723–746. http://dx.doi.org/10.1002/job.409

Lindell, M. K., & Brandt, C. J. (1997). Measuring interrater agreement for ratings of a single target. *Applied Psychological Measurement, 21,* 271–278. http://dx.doi.org/10.1177/01466216970213006

Lindell, M. K., Brandt, C. J., & Whitney, D. J. (1999). A revised index of interrater agreement for multi-item ratings of a single target. *Applied Psychological Measurement, 23,* 127–135. http://dx.doi.org/10.1177/01466219922031257

McGraw, K. O., & Wong, S. P. (1996). Forming inferences about some intraclass correlation coefficients. *Psychological Methods, 1,* 30–46. http://dx.doi.org/10.1037/1082-989X.1.1.30

Nishii, L. H., & Mayer, D. M. (2009). Do inclusive leaders help to reduce turnover in diverse groups? The moderating role of leader–member exchange in the diversity to turnover relationship. *Journal of Applied Psychology, 94,* 1412–1426. http://dx.doi.org/10.1037/a0017190

Raudenbush, S. W., & Bryk, A. S. (2002). *Hierarchical linear models: Applications and data analysis methods* (2nd ed.). Thousand Oaks, CA: Sage.

Roberson, Q. M., Sturman, M. C., & Simons, T. L. (2007). Does the measure of dispersion matter in multilevel research? A comparison of the relative performance of dispersion indexes. *Organizational Research Methods, 10,* 564–588. http://dx.doi.org/10.1177/1094428106294746

Schmidt, F. L., & Hunter, J. E. (1989). Interrater reliability coefficients cannot be computed when only one stimulus is rated. *Journal of Applied Psychology, 74,* 368–370. http://dx.doi.org/10.1037/0021-9010.74.2.368

Schneider, B., Salvaggio, A. N., & Subirats, M. (2002). Climate strength: A new direction for climate research. *Journal of Applied Psychology, 87,* 220–229. http://dx.doi.org/10.1037/0021-9010.87.2.220

Sin, H.-P., Nahrgang, J. D., & Morgeson, F. P. (2009). Understanding why they don't see eye to eye: An examination of leader–member exchange (LMX) agreement. *Journal of Applied Psychology, 94,* 1048–1057. http://dx.doi.org/10.1037/a0014827

Smith-Crowe, K., Burke, M. J., Cohen, A., & Doveh, E. (2014). Statistical significance criteria for the r_{WG} and average deviation interrater agreement indices. *Journal of Applied Psychology, 99,* 239–261. http://dx.doi.org/10.1037/a0034556

Smith-Crowe, K., Burke, M. J., Kouchaki, M., & Signal, S. M. (2013). Assessing interrater agreement via the average deviation index given a variety of theoretical and methodological problems. *Organizational Research Methods, 16,* 127–151. http://dx.doi.org/10.1177/1094428112465898

Snijders, T. A., & Bosker, R. J. (2012). *Multilevel analysis.* London, England: Sage.

Zhang, Z., Wang, M. O., & Shi, J. (2012). Leader–follower congruence in proactive personality and work outcomes: The mediating role of leader–member exchange. *Academy of Management Journal, 55,* 111–130. http://dx.doi.org/10.5465/amj.2009.0865

LOOKING WITHIN: AN EXAMINATION, COMBINATION, AND EXTENSION OF WITHIN-PERSON METHODS ACROSS MULTIPLE LEVELS OF ANALYSIS

Daniel J. Beal and Allison S. Gabriel

Over the past 20 years, there has been a rapid increase in intraindividual studies in the social and behavioral sciences. Indeed, recent searches of the literature for studies utilizing a suite of intraindividual methods—from daily diaries to experience sampling methodology (ESM)—indicate that over 300 studies have been published using this methodological approach, with more than half of these studies emerging in just the last 6 years alone (Clarivate Analytics, 2018). In part, the increase of intraindividual research has come about due to the fact that the methods are becoming increasingly more user-friendly (e.g., ESM and diary studies can be implemented using online survey platforms; smartphone apps are being created) and more analytic resources and approaches are being developed to help scholars analyze the complex data structures that intraindividual methods yield (e.g., multilevel moderated mediation with M*plus* and R; discontinuous growth modeling; lagged panel analyses). Additionally, the increase in this approach has coincided with growing awareness that many of the theories that we use in the social sciences have dynamic components that need to be properly addressed. For example, within management and applied psychology, severally commonly applied theories—from affective events theory (Weiss & Cropanzano, 1996) and episodic views of performance (Beal, Weiss, Barros, & MacDermid, 2005; Morgeson, Mitchell, & Liu, 2015) to social exchange theory

(Blau, 1964; Cropanzano & Mitchell, 2005) and theories highlighting dynamic exchanges between interaction partners (Andersson & Pearson, 1999; Groth & Grandey, 2012)—all have dynamic underpinnings, meaning that, in general, person-level assessments of constructs implied by these theories may be missing the empirical mark.

In light of the ease of implementation of and the theoretical necessity for intraindividual research, scholars have implemented a variety of methodological approaches, including daily diaries, ESM, and, more recently, continuous rating assessments (CRAs). The goal of each approach is to provide insight into day-to-day, event-to-event, and even moment-to-moment fluctuations in attitudes, emotions, and experiences of individuals. However, although each approach has its merits, little work has considered the ways in which the approaches can be used in tandem; that is, while reviews of the various intraindividual approaches exist (e.g., Beal, 2015; Gabriel, Diefendorff, Bennett, & Sloan, 2017; Ohly, Sonnentag, Niessen, & Zapf, 2010), they are often viewed as occurring in isolation from one another. This is interesting, given that scholars have argued that multilevel research should integrate what is occurring across various levels of analysis. Bliese, Chan, and Ployhart (2007; see also Chen, Bliese, & Mathieu, 2005) encouraged scholars to focus on homology, or the consideration of how effects may change as researchers move across levels. Although

http://dx.doi.org/10.1037/0000115-014
The Handbook of Multilevel Theory, Measurement, and Analysis, S. E. Humphrey and J. M. LeBreton (Editors-in-Chief)

this has led some scholars to consider how effects change at the person- and event-level of analysis (e.g., Gabriel, Diefendorff, Chandler, Moran, & Greguras, 2014), we contend that this consideration likely applies to moving across various temporal levels embedded within various intraindividual techniques. That is, as researchers move across lower levels of analysis, important insights about temporal patterns can be gained, in addition to knowledge about how constructs may emerge at various time points.

Our goal in the current chapter is to highlight how methods to examine intraindividual phenomena can be used separately or in tandem to achieve this understanding. This chapter first explores the space surrounding the within-person level of analysis as it relates to different descriptions of immediate, lived experiences of individuals (e.g., Weiss & Rupp, 2011). Then, we describe an integrative, programmatic method for linking these approaches. Finally, we move these methods to a higher level of analysis, describing how insights gained at the within-person level can inform emergent models at the individual level of analysis and identifying some of the potential hurdles such models might encounter. Importantly, the purpose of this chapter is not to just provide an overview—or how-to guide—for conducting research with intraindividual approaches (for reviews achieving this objective to gain familiarity with the approaches, see Beal, 2015; Beal & Weiss, 2003; Dimotakis, Ilies, & Judge, 2013; Fisher & To, 2012; Gabriel et al., 2017; Ohly et al., 2010). Rather, we aim to present an overview of the ways in which scholars using intraindividual methods can implement these approaches collaboratively to delve deeper into theoretical questions of interest. Thus, having a preliminary understanding of what ESM and CRA methods represent will prove fruitful for interpreting the current chapter.

TEMPORAL LEVELS OF FIVE WITHIN-PERSON METHODS

Across the five approaches to within-person designs we describe below, there are three unifying characteristics highlighted by Beal (2015): (a) measuring an event or experience occurring in the *natural*

environment, (b) assessing constructs and/or events close to their actual occurrence capturing the *immediacy of the experience*, and (c) ensuring *representative sampling* of individuals' experiences. The first point captures events in the environment as opposed to being constrained by laboratory contexts (although we note that one method, CRA, can occur in experimental settings); this helps enhance the ecological validity of the constructs being captured. The second point helps in eliminating retrospective biases (Robinson & Clore, 2002) by capturing experiences closer to the time that they are actually occurring, as opposed to asking participants to recall or mentally aggregate over extended time frames. The last point focuses on the fact that, when assessing events and/or constructs repeatedly over several hours, days, and weeks, researchers can help ensure that they are getting a fairly accurate representation of the lived experience of individuals (Beal, Trougakos, Weiss, & Dalal, 2013; Weiss & Rupp, 2011). Thus, although there are nuances in the intraindividual approaches outlined below, all five aim at achieving these three points. Instead, the primary differences across the five approaches is the time referent, or level of aggregation, being considered.

The *daily ESM* approach involves using ESM methods to capture constructs that are recalled across an entire day. As such, for scholars who are perhaps unclear of the pacing of the construct(s) being studied (i.e., it is unclear how quickly or how long it takes a process to unfold), having participants reflect upon the entire workday can prove fruitful. With this approach, organizational researchers might ask employees to recall their level of performance on various tasks throughout the day (e.g., Gabriel, Diefendorff, & Erickson, 2011), the types and level of various emotion-regulation strategies used during interactions (e.g., Judge, Woolf, & Hurst, 2009; Wagner, Barnes, & Scott, 2014), the various demands experienced over the course of the day (e.g., Rodell & Judge, 2009), or ratings of the behaviors exhibited by others at work, including coworkers and supervisors (e.g., Barnes, Lucianetti, Bhave, & Christian, 2015; Matta, Erol-Korkmaz, Johnson, & Biçaksiz, 2014). In studying social interactions outside of the workplace, spouses could be asked to recall their interactions with each other over the course of a day, reflecting on partner responsiveness and intimacy during discussions with each other (e.g., Laurenceau, Barrett, & Rovine, 2005), or children being asked to report on peer harassment that occurred while at school on a given day (e.g., Nishina & Juvonen, 2005).

As an example from organizational research, Yang and Diefendorff (2009) assessed the daily relationships between counterproductive work behaviors targeted toward the organization and individuals, negative emotions, and various situational antecedents, such as ambiguity and both supervisor and coworker interpersonal (in)justice. As part of their ESM procedure, participants were administered a survey at the end of each workday online at 4:00 p.m. and were asked to complete the survey prior to leaving work. Each item that was part of the ESM survey was adapted to be assessed on a daily basis. For instance, regarding customer interpersonal injustice, participants responded to items such as: "Regarding your customers' behavior *today*, to what extent did your customers treat you with respect?" (Yang & Diefendorff, 2009, p. 271; italics added for emphasis). As another example of a daily approach, in a dyadic ESM study focusing on performance and work engagement, Bakker and Xanthopoulou (2009) had coworker pairs each complete a survey at the end of the workday, with items focusing on mental aggregations over the entire day. For instance, items focusing on engagement reflected how engaged employees were over the entire workday (e.g., "*Today*, I felt strong and vigorous while working"), as were performance items (e.g., "*Today*, I fulfilled all the requirements of my job"; Bakker & Xanthopoulou, 2009, p. 1565; italics added for emphasis). Of course, the daily ESM approach implicitly allows for a great likelihood of recall bias to enter into the evaluations being made compared to the other approaches described in detail below (e.g., reflecting on engagement over the entire workday makes it unclear how engagement in the morning and afternoon is being mentally weighted or recalled). Nonetheless, this approach provides researchers with the opportunity to understand how phenomena of interest change from one day to the next.

Unlike the daily approach that focuses on aggregations of experiences over an entire day, the *episodic approach* shifts down a temporal level, assessing briefer periods of time and further reducing the amount of mental aggregation that study participants are required to make. For example, researchers who use ESM with a signal-contingent approach—that is, an approach in which participants respond to a survey when they are signaled to do so (e.g., by a survey being e-mailed at a planned and/or random time)—may ask study participants to respond to survey items since the last time they were surveyed (e.g., "since the last beep"), over a specific period of time (e.g., "over the last 2 hours"), or in reference to a specific event (e.g., "during the last social interaction"; "during the last task you completed"). Conversely, researchers can also use an event-contingent approach, which asks study participants to complete ESM surveys only when a particular event happens to them (e.g., when women are in a social interaction in which they decided to disclose or hide their pregnancy [Jones, 2017]; when an e-mail is received after hours [Butts, Becker, & Boswell, 2015]; when experiencing a particular issue and/or occurrence associated with an eating or psychological disorder [Berg et al., 2013]). This latter approach places a heavy burden on research participants, requiring them to remember to complete a survey shortly after the occurrence of the event of interest to the researchers.

Theoretically, *episodes* in this approach refer to subjective divisions of an individual's daily experience. Beal and colleagues (Beal et al., 2005; Beal & Weiss, 2003) have discussed this idea extensively; to summarize, an episode refers to the natural manner in which individuals chunk their ongoing experiences into coherent, goal-relevant segments. Typically, these segments allow for key features of the episode to be encoded more effectively and help impart meaning to what would otherwise be a continuous stream of information (Barker, 1968; Swallow, Zacks, & Abrams, 2009). Ideally, survey items using this approach would be framed around specific, identifiable episodes in an individual's day. This means that researchers need to think carefully about issues concerning the identifiability of particular types of episodes and how quickly the phenomenon of interest will unfold in the time frame being assessed (Gabriel et al., 2017; Monge, 1990). For instance, if researchers are examining mentor–mentee interactions and have fairly short time frames being assessed with their episodic approach, it is possible that an interaction between a mentor and his or her protégé may not even occur during the specified time frame, making the measurement inaccurate and invalid. Importantly, this issue of time is one that affects all ESM and intraindividual approaches and has been the focus of theorizing by Monge (1990) and others (e.g., George & Jones, 2000; Mitchell & James, 2001; Ployhart & Vandenberg, 2010), who have lamented that scholars who wish to assess research questions associated with dynamics and time need to carefully select the time frame being referenced in the construct assessments (as an example, see Methot, Lepak, Shipp, & Boswell, 2017).

Several examples of an episodic approach to ESM exist. Within the organizational sciences, Benedetti, Diefendorff, Gabriel, and Chandler (2015) were interested in how employees experienced different types of motivation at work. Specifically, Benedetti et al. (2015) assessed participants' motivation for pursuing *their last work-related task* five times a day for 10 workdays; these surveys were administered via PalmPilots using the Purdue Momentary Assessment Tool (Weiss, Beal, Lucy, & MacDermid, 2004) to randomly signal participants throughout the workday at semirandom times that were at least 75 minutes apart. The motivation items were prefaced with instructions asking participants to think about the last work-related task they had completed. Participants then rated the extent to which the task was pursued because it was enjoyable and interesting (i.e., intrinsic motivation) versus it being because their supervisor asked them to complete it or the situation demanded it (i.e., extrinsic motivation). These instructions helped participants reflect back on one salient performance episode. In another recent example, Butts et al. (2015) asked participants to complete surveys in the evening after they received work-related e-mail, stating: "Complete the survey based upon the most recent electronic communication received from work after working hours" (p. 773). Importantly,

if participants did not experience such an event, they were further instructed to not provide any data. All survey items were asked in referent to the e-mail event; for instance, participants assessed the affective tone of the e-mail, how long it took them to respond to the e-mail, and how they felt affectively after reading the e-mail. As a final example, Beal and colleagues (2013) sought to break down an episode into smaller chunks, asking a sample of restaurant employees to complete surveys before and after a mealtime rush.

A blend of the daily and episodic ESM approaches would be the *day reconstruction method* (DRM; Kahneman, Krueger, Schkade, Schwarz, & Stone, 2004) or a variant of that approach. According to Kahneman et al. (2004), this method takes components of episodic ESM in that it has participants think about particular salient events. However, participants in a DRM study, rather than being surveyed after the event or several times throughout the day, are asked to write down and rebuild specific events that happened throughout the workday at a later time, which minimizes the interruptions associated with ESM. For instance, participants would first write down a description of an event (e.g., what occurred or who was involved) and recall feelings experienced during the event; as stated by Kahneman et al., "the goal is to provide an accurate picture of the experience associated with activities [e.g., commuting] and circumstances [e.g., a job with time pressure]" (p. 1776). Thus, a well-executed DRM study should help people relive what occurred to them, reducing biases typically associated with recalling information. As the DRM asks for a more specific reconstruction of daily experiences, it in many ways blends daily and episodic approaches. The key distinction between the DRM as originally described by Kahneman and colleagues and any ESM variant is that only a single day is reconstructed for each participant.

Despite the necessarily limited range of experiences captured per person, Kahneman et al. (2004) suggested that the DRM still provides a representative range of situations and experiences by allowing for larger samples of individuals with less burden of participation. Finally, although not recommended by Kahneman et al., it is possible to blend the DRM with daily ESM. This approach would—at the end of each day of the multiday study—ask people to reconstruct their experiences by walking through and rating each episode sequentially. The goal with this method would be to obtain a more precise and continuous recall and judgment of a day's events relative to simply asking people to mentally summarize, as is typically the case in daily ESM studies.

As an example of this hybrid approach, Bakker, Demerouti, Oerlemans, and Sonnentag (2013) examined workaholism and recovery experiences. Bakker et al. had participants for 9 workdays each evening before going to bed select activities from a list that they engaged in during the evening, indicating how long they spent on each activity and their happiness associated with each activity. Likewise, Oerlemans and Bakker (2014) had participants for 2 workweeks complete a survey in the morning in which they reconstructed the time they spent on off-job activities after they left work the previous day. Participants were asked to rebuild their postwork time in chronological order and then report on their current level of recovery. As noted by Oerlemans and Bakker, using DRM helped facilitate "access to encoded momentary experiences" that occurred the prior evening, reducing recall biases (p. 306).

If a random sampling of an individual's day-to-day experiences are desired rather than experiences surrounding a particular event or time frame, another measurement approach can be used, which we refer to as *momentary ESM*. This approach, which reflects the original form of experience sampling methods (Csikszentmihalyi, Larson, & Prescott, 1977), focuses on assessing key constructs "in the moment" as participants respond to survey signals. For instance, using the signal-contingent approach, when participants are sent an ESM survey, they may be asked questions in which they respond about emotions and cognitions "right now" or "at the present moment." For instance, in the Benedetti et al. (2015) study noted above, the researchers were also interested in assessing job satisfaction and vitality at the present moment. Accordingly, items such as "*at this moment*, I am satisfied with my job" and "*at this moment*, I feel alive and vital" were asked when participants were signaled (Benedetti et al., 2015,

p. 41, italics added for emphasis). Other researchers have taken this approach, with Gabriel et al. (2014) assessing perceptions of person–organization and person–job fit perceptions at the survey signal, and Beal and colleagues (2013) assessing the extent to which restaurant employees currently felt fatigued.

Whereas diaries and ESM approaches often are focused on mentally aggregating experiences over weeks, days, hours, and/or specific events (e.g., Beal, 2015; Ohly et al., 2010), our final approach—continuous rating assessments (CRAs)—can be viewed as the *continuous approach*, focusing on capturing unfolding dynamics *within* a specific event (Gabriel, Diefendorff, Bennett, & Sloan, 2017; Ruef & Levenson, 2007). More specifically, theories and constructs assessed with diaries and ESM assessments—such as emotions (e.g., Beal, Trougakos, Weiss, & Green, 2006; Scott & Barnes, 2011), social exchange relationships (e.g., Rosen, Koopman, Gabriel, & Johnson, 2016), job stressors and demands (e.g., Dimotakis, Scott, & Koopman, 2011; Sonnentag & Zijlstra, 2006), social support (Eisenberger, Taylor, Gable, Hilmert, & Lieberman, 2007; Siewert, Antoniw, Kubiak, & Weber, 2011), and marital communication and intimacy (Laurenceau et al., 2005)—often are presumed to ebb and flow over the course of a day or an event. Stated differently, in a given interaction between a person and his or her environment, he or she may have moment-to-moment fluctuations in mood, perceptions, and/or feelings of stress contingent upon changes continuously experienced over time. Thus, although ESM methods capture change that occurs between events or day to day, these approaches miss the changes and trajectories of constructs that occur within an event as it dynamically unfolds over time.

As reviewed by Gabriel et al. (2017; see also Ruef & Levenson, 2007), CRA is a within-person methodological approach that can better capture changes in constructs within a salient event. To do this, CRA captures moment-to-moment variations by asking individuals to continuously assess their feelings and cognitions as an event is unfolding; this event can either be happening to the participant for the first time during the ratings (i.e., online or in vivo ratings) or during a cued recall of an event. These ratings are collected via a handheld or computerized rating dial that allows participants to adjust their ratings as much or as little as possible in order to accurately reflect their current level of a given construct. Moreover, as evidenced in research conducted in social psychology (e.g., Mauss, Levenson, McCarter, Wilhelm, & Gross, 2005; Mauss et al., 2011), self-reported CRAs can also be combined with other dynamic assessments such as physiological markers of arousal (e.g., galvanic skin response, heart rate, eye tracking, facial coding technology). Importantly, CRA can be a valuable tool for better addressing time-related issues over relatively short periods of time, such as better understanding the rate of change of constructs, as well as the permanence of change, magnitude of change, and the lag of change that occurs (see Monge, 1990, for a review).

Original work on CRA emerged in marital research (e.g., Gottman & Levenson, 1985; Levenson & Gottman, 1983; see Ruef & Levenson, 2007, for a review). Within this line of work, researchers wanted to allow marital interactions to naturally unfold, versus stopping the natural conversation at random points to collect spouses' assessments of affect and other psychological constructs (i.e., the "talk-table" approach; Gottman et al., 1976). As highlighted by Ruef and Levenson (2007), switching to CRA in marital research led to a much less intrusive measurement approach and enhanced external validity given that there were fewer interruptions being made in the natural conversation. In the organizational sciences, there are two studies that have used CRA. Naidoo and Lord (2008) used online CRA to assess perceptions of leader charisma. In this study, Naidoo and Lord manipulated the level of imagery being expressed in audio recordings of actors reciting the inaugural address of U.S. president Franklin Delano Roosevelt. As participants were listening to the presidential speech, they moved a mouse on a computer connected to a CRA scale, where 0 corresponded to not at all charismatic and 100 corresponded to extremely charismatic. In another example, Gabriel and Diefendorff (2015) put participants in a call-center simulation in which they were exposed to a hostile customer caller. Using cued-recall CRA, after going through the difficult customer call, participants listened back to

the call and provided separate continuous ratings using a computer program of their felt emotions during the call, as well as their use of two emotion-regulation strategies—surface acting and deep acting (Grandey, 2000)—in a counterbalanced order. Ratings were collected every 200 milliseconds and aggregated to create 1-second averages for analyses. In addition, third-party raters who were blind to the study hypotheses and condition listened back to the call and provided continuous ratings of how positive or negative the vocal tone of the participant was. As such, CRA not only captures emotions and cognitions associated with an event, but dynamic assessments of performance-related constructs as well.

Conceptual Similarities and Differences Among the Five Methods

Ultimately, our goal in this chapter is to initially outline the ways various within-person data collection methods connect (see also Gabriel et al., 2017). Doing so will provide a more complete picture of how a particular experience or set of experiences unfold, from the most immediate reactions and fluctuations to the more aggregate progression of daily life. However, before we link these different methods together, or discuss how one might go about doing so, it will be helpful to consider some of the central similarities and differences of the five methods that largely relate to the timing of the approaches in assessing phenomena of interest. As described above, each approach to exploring within-person variability focuses on a different timing or pacing of relevant constructs, with the fastest pacing occurring with CRA, followed by momentary ESM, episodic ESM, DRM, and daily approaches. However, beyond this surface-level difference are more fundamental elements of what each method tries to capture.

We have summarized these elements in Table 13.1 and framed them around three common research goals that within-person researchers strive to achieve: (a) capturing a representative sample of an individual's varying experiences, (b) mapping patterns of change in these experiences, and (c) linking one stream of experiences to another. We split the latter category into a goal to link intraindividual experiences

---

TABLE 13.1

Capacity of Five Categories of Within-Person Methods to Achieve a Set of Conceptual Within-Person Research Goals

Within-person research goal	CRA	Momentary ESM	Episodic ESM	DRM	Daily ESM
Representative sample of an individual's experiences	−	+++	+	+	+
Comprehensive account of dynamics	+++	+	++	++	++
Capacity to link sequential experiences (within days)	+++	++	+++	++	−
Capacity to link sequential experiences (across days)	−	+	++	−	+++

Note. A minus suggests that the method is relatively ineffective at achieving the conceptual goal, whereas pluses indicate relative effectiveness (which increases as pluses increase) at achieving the conceptual goal. CRA = continuous rating assessments; DRM = day reconstruction method; ESM = experience sampling methodology.

within days versus a goal to link experiences across days based on the current state of the intraindividual literature. That is, many studies now seem focused on linking immediate, within-day experiences together (e.g., Beal et al., 2013; Gabriel et al., 2014; Rosen et al., 2016; Trougakos, Beal, Cheng, Hideg, & Zweig, 2015), whereas others focus on linking aggregate daily experiences or experiences lagged across the natural break of each day (e.g., Beal & Ghandour, 2011; Foo, Uy, & Baron, 2009; Scott & Barnes, 2011; Wang et al., 2013).

Representativeness. When we consider representativeness in intraindividual research, we are focusing on the extent to which researchers are capturing the lived experiences of individuals in a variety of contexts (e.g., Weiss & Rupp, 2011). This is often why researchers ensure that their survey period spans several days and weeks, with surveys administered at different times: It is assumed that individuals' experiences change from day to day and from event to event, and researchers are aiming to capture an accurate reflection of what happens to individuals across time. As such, if researchers were to only survey at a particular time of day (e.g., the end of the day), or on a particular day of the week (e.g., Monday or Friday), they would run the risk of missing out on both typical events (e.g., what happens to most people on a typical day), and, on the other end of the continuum, extreme or atypical events.

If we examine the first row of Table 13.1—the goal of capturing a representative sample of an individual's

experiences—the least effective approach is continuous rating assessment. This should come as no surprise: The purpose of CRA is to take an in-depth look into a particular event in isolation, rather than obtaining a representative sample of experiences across several days. In contrast, the other varieties of ESM and diary designs are capable of accomplishing the goal of representativeness to varying degrees. This also should come as no surprise, as ESM methods were derived in large part as a way of introducing ecological validity into an area of social research that often relied on experiments that were unlikely to capture experiences as they were lived (Csikszentmihalyi & Larson, 1987; cf. Aronson & Carlsmith, 1968). Interestingly, it is difficult to determine the extent to which the DRM accomplishes this goal. On one hand, it samples a single day from each participant, leaving glaring holes in a variety of experiences each of us have over even a few days' time. On the other hand, samples for DRM studies are typically large, so they may achieve a representative sample of experiences across people rather than within. The downside, however, is that despite a potentially large range of experiences across people, individual antecedents and consequences of those experiences will be limited to what occurred on a single day.

Of the ESM permutations, there are differences in their capacity to gain a representative sample of experiences. Daily ESM studies, which emphasize mental aggregations of states experienced during the day (e.g., "To what extent have you been satisfied with your job today?"), as well as episodic

ESM studies (e.g., "To what extent have you been satisfied with your job since the last survey?"), are somewhat limited in providing a representative depiction, as the variability of experiences that occurs within a day or episode is funneled into a single score. As a result, these methods cannot capitalize on within-day or within-episode variance to obtain a full picture of one's life as it is lived. That said, these methods have their merits. First, it is unlikely that unusual states within a day or episode would not be reflected in some aggregation of those states. For example, suppose that an employee experiences typical levels of job satisfaction throughout most of the day but in the afternoon receives news suggesting that a promotion is likely. The influence of this pivotal event is likely to be borne out in the day's assessment of job satisfaction. Capturing this peak level of job satisfaction helps the entire sample of daily ratings become more representative of the full range of job satisfaction that one might experience (cf. Fredrickson, 2000). The same process would be true for episodic ESM, but perhaps to an even greater extent, as aggregations represent only single episodes within a day rather than the entire day. We should note, however, that the process governing which states are reflected in an individual's episodic or daily report is a question for which answers are only at an early stage (e.g., Miron-Shatz, 2009). As a result, elements of experience that color one's daily or episodic reports may help increase their representativeness, but these elements may also decrease it. An additional question that future research must address is the predictive validity of different levels of aggregate responses: There may be differences between immediate satisfaction aggregated to the day and one rating of daily satisfaction, but if both approaches are related like outcomes of interest are, then these details may not matter. In contrast, if these approaches are differentially predictive, then understanding the respective patterns of prediction may be pivotal.

That said, the method that best accomplishes the goal of representativeness is the original momentary ESM described by Czikszentmihalyi and colleagues (e.g., Csikszentmihalyi & Graef, 1980; Csikszentmihalyi et al., 1977), given that this method features the reporting of immediate states randomly sampled throughout the day. As such, it is unlikely to capture a biased set of experiences that would occur only if a certain type of event were sampled or if surveys were only administered at a particular time. Yet, it is interesting to note that the approach to ensure a representative range of experiences has not been discussed in great detail. Most ESM discussion (e.g., Beal & Weiss, 2003; Bolger, Davis, & Rafaeli, 2003; Csikszentmihalyi & Larson, 1987) provides descriptive accounts of what researchers typically do when conducting ESM, rather than suggesting a theoretically driven rationale for study design choices.

By identifying the key elements of ESM, Beal (2015) provided a foundation from which such a theoretically driven approach might be established. With respect to representative sampling, the goal in determining the sampling strategy, in terms of signals per day and total duration of the study, should lie in an assessment of how the experience under examination changes over time. If the experience (e.g., states of happiness) fluctuates greatly over brief periods of time, then a brief period of time could produce a representative sample of an individual's experiences. The focus on variability of the experience in question and the capacity to obtain representative samples from potentially small sets of experiences has been emphasized most ardently in the qualitative methods literature (e.g., Glaser & Strauss, 1967; Gobo, 2004), and we suspect that this type of discussion is clearly applicable to ESM as well. As an example, consider a state such as boredom. Although there may be a number of different forms of boredom, it seems fair to suggest that, relative to states of anger or happiness, boredom may not exhibit a tremendous degree of variability over time within a particular individual. As a result, obtaining a representative sample of boredom states would likely require far fewer instances of boredom than would be necessary to obtain an equally representative sample of anger or happiness states.

Dynamics. As displayed in second row of Table 13.1, researchers also may have a goal of determining what, if any, pattern of change exists in a given variable. In longitudinal panel designs, where change is examined over a longer period of time but with relatively few periods of observation, latent growth models often provide an estimate of the overall pattern of change. In intensive repeated measures designs such as ESM or CRA, patterns of change tend to be much less stable and far more complex. Beal and Weiss (2003) and Beal (2015) discussed how anticipated patterns might be examined using trends, cycles, and autoregressive effects, while Beal and Ghandour (2011) provided a substantive example using daily positive and negative affect. Perhaps the most important factor to consider when evaluating the extent to which a given method can accurately and comprehensively map the dynamic patterns of a conceptual variable is the level of aggregation for the variable.

Take, as an example, affective states. When construed as an immediate state, it is likely to fluctuate a great deal over potentially very brief periods of time. Gabriel and Diefendorff (2015) demonstrated this very effectively using CRA to map affective states during customer interactions lasting less than 5 minutes. Indeed, at the most immediate level of aggregation, CRA is by far the best equipped to examine dynamic patterns of volatile variables, and it can be used to help researchers understand—perhaps in an exploratory manner—the rate at which a construct of interest changes within an event. Yet, affective state is a good example of a variable that has been successfully conceptualized at numerous levels of aggregation. For example, key events are known to give rise to episodically experienced emotion (Russell & Feldman Barrett, 1999; Weiss & Cropanzano, 1996), and describing the key features of such episodes allows for a meaningful and predictive level of aggregation (e.g., Beal et al., 2006). To the extent that emotion episodes are experienced in a patterned manner over time, episodic ESM, DRM, or combinations are the most appropriate way in which to capture such a pattern. Similarly, numerous papers have relied on daily aggregation of affective state (i.e., asking people to report on their affective experience for the day) and have shown that this level of aggregation also reliably predicts other constructs similarly assessed at the daily level (e.g., Judge, Scott, & Ilies, 2006; Sonnentag & Zijlstra, 2006). This approach also has demonstrated reliable dynamic patterns of affect (e.g., Beal & Ghandour,

2011; Benedetti et al., 2015) and other relevant constructs (e.g., Rosen et al., 2016).

The final method that could be used to capture dynamic patterns of a conceptual variable is momentary ESM. This approach has both advantages and disadvantages. For example, it is the only approach capturing immediate states that has the capacity to examine longer term dynamic patterns (i.e., across days). CRA captures dynamics of immediate states as well, but necessarily does so over a very brief period of time. The issue that arises for momentary ESM, however, is that the random dispersion of observations throughout the day makes it difficult to understand the continuity of a particular dynamic state. Continuing with affective state as the example, a momentary ESM study might capture a high level of anxiety at 10:03 a.m., and a similarly high level of anxiety reported at the next signal occurring at 12:53 p.m. This second high point for anxiety could reflect the continuation of the previous state, or it could represent the peak of an entirely new state that emerged during the intervening survey period. Because momentary ESM cannot assess the true variability of the continuous stream of immediate affective experience, it may not provide a completely accurate description of its dynamic patterns. Ironically, neither episodic approaches, DRM, nor daily approaches suffer from this dilemma, as they are focused on more aggregate forms of affective experience. That is, episodic ESM, DRM, and daily ESM provide reasonably good depictions of the dynamics of episodically experienced states and daily states. However, they would provide fairly poor depictions of the dynamics of immediately experienced states, but of course that is not the goal of these methods.

Linking within days. Perhaps one of the most common goals of researchers using some form of within-person design is to connect one conceptual variable with another one within the same day. Too often, this goal is implemented using a concurrent within-person correlational analysis strategy. Although there are conditions under which concurrent relations might be feasible or preferable, if causal inferences are sought, this approach is certainly suboptimal (Edwards, 2008). That is, even if multiple assessments of constructs are taken across several days, if the researchers analyze relationships assessed at the same point in time, the same issues associated with common method bias and correctly specified causal order still plague DRM and ESM assessments. Instead, researchers should be pursuing these goals using lagged effects with appropriate temporal controls (Beal, 2015; Beal & Weiss, 2003). Although this sounds easy enough, the details of this approach need to be carefully considered when an ESM study is being designed. In particular, one must consider the pacing of changes not only in both conceptual variables separately but also in how they fluctuate together. For example, if someone is interested in how task autonomy predicts feelings of psychological vitality, one must consider not only the dynamic properties of both variables separately (perhaps autonomy fluctuates on a daily basis, while vitality fluctuates on more of a momentary basis) but also what measurement approach would be best to capture their covariation. When possible, it is usually advantageous to measure all variables at the fastest pace—there might be less within-person variation in the less dynamic construct, but it is likely a worthwhile endeavor to demonstrate this characteristic empirically.

Interestingly, researchers are beginning to pay more attention to linking constructs within days in ESM research. For example, Rosen et al. (2016) studied the relation between incivility and depletion. Specifically, using an episodic approach, the researchers assessed exposure to incivility in the morning (i.e., Time 1) and related it to a concurrent assessment of depletion (i.e., Time 1). Rosen and colleagues then sought to link depletion to subsequent acts of incivility toward others later in the workday (i.e., Time 2). By doing so, the authors were able to examine more downstream consequences of incivility and subsequent depletion that occurred within the same workday. Likewise, Koopman, Lanaj, and Scott (2016) assessed how engaging in organizational citizenship behaviors in the morning predicted increased positive affect and decreased work-goal progress in the afternoon, allowing them to delve into the "bright" and "dark" sides associated with engaging in citizenship behaviors throughout the workday. As a final example, using a CRA approach researchers can

also connect constructs within a single episode. For instance, Gabriel and Diefendorff (2015) used a series of lagged variables to examine the causal relationships among felt emotions, emotion regulation, and ratings of emotional performance (i.e., vocal tone). As such, even the most micro of intraindividual approaches can be used to link constructs together across multiple time points.

As these examples demonstrate, both CRA and episodic ESM are effective at capturing the connections between a day's events, experiences, and behaviors. Clearly, daily ESM cannot serve this role, as it necessarily aggregates within-day experiences. Momentary ESM does have the capacity to link experiences within days, but as this method's momentary emphasis cannot provide a depiction of the continuous stream of experience within a given day, there is again the possibility that momentary states will be more difficult to connect with prior or subsequent momentary states. As episodically framed items are designed to capture the essence of what was experienced (at least from a subjective point of view), this approach likely represents a better option for the purpose of linking experiences within days. Although the DRM also holds this advantage, it has an additional disadvantage. Specifically, as reports of within-day experiences are solicited at the same time, this method seems particularly likely to be subject to consistency and other forms of mono method bias (see Podsakoff, MacKenzie, Lee, & Podsakoff, 2003).

Linking across days. Beyond assessing constructs within a day, researchers are further examining how constructs captured via ESM may spill over across days. For instance, it may be that a construct captured in the evening spills over to predict a work-related attitude the next workday. When this is being considered, it is likely the case that episodic or daily ESM approaches would best lend themselves to these questions, as researchers need to carefully consider when certain experiences may happen; using a momentary approach could miss key events (e.g., a negative or positive interaction at home after work; Butts et al., 2015). CRA and DRM—given their focus on single events and single days—are unlikely to fit questions tied to linking constructs across days. Of course, alterations of DRM that extend across multiple days (e.g., Bakker et al., 2013) would be less subject to these issues and would potentially be effective for this goal.

Areas of research that are seeing an increase in designs that link experiences across days include research at the work–family interface. For example, in the study previously described by Butts et al. (2015), the researchers not only assessed experiences with after-hours e-mail as they happened but also linked these evaluations to important outcomes the next workday, including perceptions of work–family conflict. In research related to workplace recovery, Sonnentag, Binnewies, and Mojza (2008) had participants evaluate different types of recovery experiences (e.g., psychological detachment, relaxation, and mastery experiences) they had in the evening after work and linked these experiences to sleep quality and affect the next morning.

Linking Information Across Within-Person Methods

Although each intraindividual design associated with ESM and/or CRA can be viewed as either/or, we argue—as do Gabriel et al. (2017)—that the methods should be viewed in a more integrated manner to help researchers not only to better understand how relationships change depending on the level of analysis but also to better understand complex phenomena of interest. Gabriel et al. (2017) suggested that researchers may be able to, for instance, start with ESM research to identify the prevalence of a type of event and then use CRA to better unpack the dynamics that may or may not occur within that event. However, as we describe below, it is likely that researchers can move back and forth across the various methods.

Proposal for an integrative, programmatic approach. In our collective experience, it is clear that many research efforts may not follow a programmatic, phenomenon-based developmental process. Instead, we often conduct one or more studies in an attempt to answer a specific practical question, to clarify a particular theoretical ambiguity, or to combine two or more theoretical accounts of similar effects or sets of effects. There is nothing wrong with these approaches, yet they do not often lend themselves to a detailed account of how a particular process

operates across a broad and representative range of contexts, particularly contexts that are temporal in nature. They are geared more toward filling in particular, but perhaps idiosyncratic, sections of a much larger canvas—each effort provides a piece of the picture, but little sense of the whole can be made until a great many pieces have been added. This approach is certainly germane to within-person organizational research as much as it is to more macro areas of research, but we feel that the suite of methods described here have the potential to be linked in a programmatic way that builds understanding in a more coherent fashion.

To accomplish this goal, we will be using an example of an aspiring social science researcher who would like to understand more about the immediate experiences of positive self-conscious emotion and its links to how discriminatory behaviors are interpreted by low-status individuals, or literally: pride and prejudice. Although one approach would be to examine trait levels of pride and global perceptions of discrimination, our researcher believes that the manner in which these two constructs connect on an immediate, dynamic, and within-person basis is likely to yield greater insights. As neither construct is well understood through a within-person lens, an initial exploratory investigation seems warranted.

Step 1: Exploration of temporal properties. Given that most scientific efforts in the psychological and organizational sciences are based at the levels of the individual, the group, or the organization (Kozlowski & Klein, 2000), it is at least understandable, if not predictable, that the dynamic properties of within-person phenomena will not be easily specified at the earliest phases of study design. For organizational researchers in particular, tackling a within-person topic will often require some initial exploration. Although it might seem reasonable to start this exploration at the lowest level of aggregation possible (e.g., using CRA), we argue instead that starting at higher levels of aggregation is likely more useful. As we just stated, this field is not intimately familiar with intraindividual processes and dynamics, and so mapping out the most immediate and momentary instances of a given construct may not be wise. More importantly, a more aggregated approach can provide information relevant to the baseline frequency of a particular experience, state, or behavior, with the modest assumption that the occurrence of most focal constructs will be memorable enough within the day on which they occur.

As an example, consider the construct of pride being examined by our trusty novice to within-person approaches. Pride, as it is based in specific contexts of socially valued events characterized by personal responsibility (Tracy, Shariff, & Cheng, 2010), may not have a noticeable regular occurrence for many people (perhaps excepting hubristic individuals; see Tracy & Robins, 2007). Of course, given the human tendencies toward self-enhancement and self-serving attributions, we might also reasonably expect at least modest levels of pride on a regular basis. Not knowing what to expect, it might be advisable for our researcher to begin her efforts with the version of the DRM that blends with daily ESM. As the DRM is typically more intensive than other ESM surveys, the duration of the study might be reasonably limited to a week. This approach carries with it several advantages to an initial mapping of the dynamic and substantive properties of pride experiences. First, as an emotional experience, it is likely to have episodic properties that would be captured better by the DRM than daily ESM alone. At the same time, if pride experiences carried forward into the next day (or longer), including a daily ESM component would facilitate detection of such lagged effects. Another advantage of combining approaches is that an initial mapping of dynamic patterns (even within-day) would be feasible using the time-sequenced aspects of the DRM (Kahneman et al., 2004). Although Table 13.1 suggests that neither of these methods are particularly well suited for the goal of obtaining a representative sampling of experiences, as we noted earlier, the combination of the two methods might offset their respective shortcomings here and be an effective way to address this goal.

This approach might also be useful for exploring the dynamic properties of prejudice experienced by low-status individuals. Again, it is unclear how often instances of prejudice might be perceived (though research suggests that both perceived and objective discrimination is quite common for minorities and stigmatized groups; Leslie, King, Bradley, & Hebl, 2008), so starting at a broader level and attempting to summarize the frequency of occasions is advisable. A number of other organizational scholars have suggested that—at least for the field of organizational research and likely beyond—there is a need to include this initial attempt at uncovering dynamics (George & Jones, 2000; Mitchell & James, 2001) before meaningful and temporally informed theory can be applied. We echo this, but we recognize that running a study of this complexity for no purpose other than documenting temporal features of the phenomena being examined is unlikely to be met with open arms from researchers who have too many pragmatic concerns and resource limitations to invest such effort. Indeed, one of the reasons why the combined DRM/daily ESM approach is useful is that it allows researchers to go beyond simple documentation of temporal properties to examine substantive questions concerning how two or more dynamic variables are linked together.

We are aware, however, that this sort of initial study is unlikely to provide definitive evidence either for highly accurate within-day temporal properties or for evidence of causal order. With respect to accurate within-day temporal properties, this approach relies on the DRM and the recall of the day's episodes along with their qualities and durations. Diener and Tay (2014) pointed out that when the DRM approach is compared with momentary ESM approaches, the DRM is estimated to be only modestly related to temporally matched scores on ESM, and they go further to suggest that "the size of these estimates will lead investigators to use ESM where this is feasible" (p. 258). Furthermore, as we have noted earlier, attempts to link two or more variables within days using the DRM is likely to contain substantial amounts of method variance. As people are asked to recount the episodes of their day and then rate, for example, feelings of pride as well as experiences of prejudice, then any implicit narrative, transient mood state, or desire to be consistent in their responses will serve to obscure the true connection between these variables.

Step 2: Informed application of within-person design. As these issues suggest, researchers should not stop with an initial combined DRM/daily ESM study. Instead, they should treat the information gleaned as suggestive of the temporal properties and potential links between two or more within-person constructs of interest. With this information in hand, researchers should be better able to select the most appropriate within-person design for the next study. As Step 1 provides only information aggregated to the episodic level, then it seems unlikely that a CRA study would follow. As we suggest below, however, incorporating this method into a programmatic effort is likely essential to a full understanding of many within-person phenomena, and it is the centerpiece of the third step described below. At this point, however, if the phenomena under investigation revealed substantial or likely variation at the within-day level, then either the episodic ESM or momentary ESM approaches would be likely candidates for a second study.

A consideration of the advantages of these two designs taken from Table 13.1 reveals under what circumstances one might select episodic or momentary ESM. Although both methods are somewhat effective for each research goal, a concise summary suggests that if obtaining a representative sampling of experiences is paramount, the clear choice would be a momentary ESM design. For all other research goals described in the table, however, episodic ESM holds a slight advantage. The primary reason for this advantage is the capacity of episodic ESM to capture the continuity of an experience both within and across days. Momentary ESM, with its emphasis on snapshots of immediate states, has the potential to mischaracterize this continuity.

For example, let's say that Step 1 revealed to our novice researcher that pride experiences ranged from frequencies of multiple times per day to once every few days, whereas experiences of prejudicial treatment from higher status individuals occurred multiple times per day for all of the low-status participants. Despite the slightly slower pacing of pride experiences, an episodic ESM approach is well matched to both variables. A well-designed episodic ESM study would carefully consider the possible or likely episodic structure of the sample's day. If the sample is relatively homogenous with respect to prominent daily activities (e.g., they all hold the same type of jobs from the same organization), then it might be possible to identify common episodes that form the basis of the within-day sampling regimen (e.g., mealtime rushes for wait staff; Beal et al., 2013). If there is greater heterogeneity of daily activities, then one might resort to more typical daily temporal structures. For example, the first survey might be completed midmorning and refer to activities involved in waking up, preparing for the day, and arrival at school or work. The second survey could be completed prior to lunch and cover activities since the midmorning survey. A third survey might occur midafternoon, covering the postlunch period of time, and a final survey could be completed at the end of the day, summarizing experiences since the midafternoon survey. Although these surveys are not necessarily aligned with the subjectively experienced episodes of each individual, targeting a sample's collective activity structure can provide a reasonable degree of overlap with episodic structures likely experienced by many individuals. Still, another option would be to use an event-contingent approach focused on particular episodes of interest, such as the experience of pride or perceptions of prejudicial behavior from others. Creative combinations are also possible, such as the blending of signal-contingent and event-contingent approaches (e.g., participants are instructed to complete a survey each time they perceive prejudicial treatment while also completing scheduled or signaled surveys to capture episodic experiences of pride).

Regardless of the approach taken, items would ask participants to summarize over the intervening episode or period of time, allowing lagged or cross-lagged effects to be more readily detected using appropriate modeling choices (Beal, 2015). This approach could provide reasonable answers, for example, to questions such as whether the prior experience of pride buffers subsequent perceptions of prejudicial behavior, or whether prior perceptions of prejudicial behavior limit the extent to which pride is subsequently experienced. This capacity to link separate episodes of two or more variables while controlling or examining dynamic patterns of the modeled variables is a key strength of the episodic ESM approach.

One possibility that we have yet to consider in Step 2 is what to do if the initial step was suggestive of a slower within-person process that occurred more on a day-to-day basis than on a within-day basis. In many ways, this discovery would place the researchers at an advantage, as Step 1 happened to be well suited to the dynamics that were identified. Indeed, one might reasonably ask whether our researcher should stop with Step 1. Although doing so certainly seems ideal for minimizing an effort-to-reward ratio, we suspect that the concerns with this approach noted earlier limit the theoretical contribution from Step 1 to the point that it would be difficult to reach the bar currently set by many journals. In which case, what should be the next step? Our answer involves adding at least two components of increased precision and rigor to the initial daily ESM design. One component would be to provide a better match to the discovered time course. Specifically, the initial combined DRM/daily ESM design is likely to have extended only for a few days. As we noted above, the DRM places an increased burden on participants and typically demands a larger sample size. Trade-offs in study design therefore suggest that such a design would be difficult to sustain over long periods of time. If, however, the initial study suggests a longer time frame for the dynamics of the variables under investigation, then using just a daily ESM design would enable researchers to extend the duration of the study, allowing for a more comprehensive examination of temporal patterns.

The second component would be to include an experimental manipulation that would strengthen causal inferences implied in Step 1. Although experimental manipulations are rare in ESM research, a recent review of this literature recommended their implementation (Beal, 2015). In many ways, this approach reflects an ideal combination of field and lab studies: ESM provides the representative, naturalistic context of in situ experiences, and the inclusion of within- or between-person manipulations provide an increased level of rigor absent from field work. Such manipulations could be implemented outside of the ESM survey (e.g., employees begin ESM either in a pretest–posttest training group or in a control group) or as a

part of the ESM survey (e.g., framing of items or inclusion of manipulated instructions). Together, the inclusion of a time frame well matched to the variables of interest along with the inclusion of one or more manipulated independent variables would generate a particularly potent and rigorous study.

Step 3: Isolating and dissecting crucial episodes. The episodic approach outlined above, particularly when it is preceded by an initial temporal exploration of the relevant variables, provides a robust examination of within-person dynamics. It is often difficult to delve more deeply within an episode, however, particularly when intervening mechanisms (i.e., mediators) are likely important but occur quickly either after the experience of the predictor variable or immediately prior to the criterion variable. Such mechanisms are quite common, as cognitive or affective reactions often follow an event of interest very rapidly (e.g., Sander, Grandjean, & Scherer, 2005). Behavioral responses to these reactions also are often close to immediate. Thus, a comprehensive mapping of an entire event–interpretation–action process might transpire over the course of seconds or minutes.

Clearly, none of the ESM approaches (or DRM) are capable of describing processes of this sort, yet our lives are replete with experiences just like this. Indeed, scholars have begun to try and tease apart events, their immediate reactions (e.g., depletion), and subsequent behaviors (e.g., Rosen et al., 2016), but these designs often involve an assumption of which part of the process is occurring faster or slower than the other (i.e., assuming that a particular timing of an ESM survey is appropriate). For instance, in the Gabriel and Diefendorff (2015) study referred to previously, participants were put through a call center simulation in which they were exposed to a hostile customer; this context was chosen to build on past emotional labor research that had focused on incivility in an experimental context (e.g., Rupp & Spencer, 2006), but could not properly test the dynamics of the event. By assessing the felt emotions in response to incivility, the regulatory response participants had to the incivility (i.e., how much participants regulated their emotions), and their performance (i.e., third-party ratings of vocal tone), mapping the event–interpretation–action process was possible. Indeed, using a cross-lagged panel design, Gabriel and Diefendorff were able to temporally separate and identify which processes came first (e.g., felt emotions always → emotion regulation, but not vice versa). In their review of CRA, Gabriel et al. (2017) further provide several examples and applications of CRA, from examining the unfolding dynamics of performance feedback exchanges, to understanding how job applicants experience recruitment information as they are being exposed to it. Again, all of these instances involve a deep dive into one singular, salient episode for employees.

In the case of assessing experiences associated with pride and prejudice, CRA could help glean several insights not fully captured with the various ESM or DRM approaches. For example, when the possibility that pride might influence perceptions of prejudice is examined, participants could be exposed to a manipulation of pride (vs. neutral or other affective state) and then placed in a carefully crafted simulation in which another participant (confederate) engages in subtle (or perhaps not-so-subtle) forms of discrimination. Participants would provide continuous ratings on one or more dimensions of their experience (e.g., perceptions of fair treatment, current affective state, current levels of task, or other forms of motivation).

Importantly, this analysis provides information about multiple specific behaviors or events that occur within a single episode that would be difficult to obtain from the aggregate reports of episodic ESM. Gabriel et al. (2017) referred to these shorter instances as microevents within a larger event, meaning that even within one single episode, different microevents may unfold that give way to important temporal dynamics. Likewise, scholars in social psychology have used CRA to assess how specific emotions—such as anger or happiness—occur when participants are exposed to stimuli such as images or short videos (e.g., Mauss et al., 2005). Again, the goal in Step 3 is to dissect broader episodes into microevents that can aid understanding in both (a) why constructs vary momentarily and (b) how processes interrelate within a given event.

MOVING TO THE BETWEEN-PERSON LEVEL

Although the aforementioned discussion focuses largely on how to move across several sublevels within the microlevel of analysis, there is room to consider how our understanding of temporal dynamics may coalesce and shape person-level attitudes and behaviors. An exhaustive discussion of every possibility is beyond the scope of this chapter, but we detail some ways that researchers can integrate within- and between-person research to create a more informative story.

Composition and Compilation Models

As was true with early efforts to specify multilevel structure and function (Kozlowski & Klein, 2000), particular care should be taken to consider how within-person states, perceptions, and behaviors emerge at higher levels of analysis (e.g., homologous versus differential effects at higher levels of analysis). Unfortunately, the within-person literature has paid fairly little attention to such issues (see Gabriel et al., 2014, as an exception). For instance, concepts such as composition and compilation—commonly used in the multilevel literature focusing on groups and teams—are scarcely mentioned in the within-person literature. In part this is likely due to the lack of connection between these two multilevel areas of research (i.e., terms developed in one area may not easily transfer to another), but the larger issue is that focused consideration of what these concepts mean is rare in the within-person literature. To be clear, and from a within-person perspective, composition models would suggest that momentary or episodic states, perceptions, and behaviors function in a similar way (i.e., homologously, isomorphically) when they emerge at the person level of analysis. As a result, individual-level constructs comprise one of several potential aggregations of states measured at the immediate, episodic, or daily level; that is, a composition model specifying the emergence of conscientiousness at the individual level might consist of the average of conscientious behaviors measured over repeated episodes for a given individual over several days (cf. Fleeson, 2001).

Chan (1998) described a number of possible composition models for group-level phenomena that emerge from properties of individuals, and

Kozlowski and Klein (2000) clarified and expanded upon many of these more specific forms. These models apply equally well to the within-person domain, though the implications of their tenets differ in interesting ways. For example, an *additive model* would suggest that the higher level (i.e., the individual level) is a simple sum or average of the lower level parts (i.e., relatively immediate states, perceptions, and behaviors), regardless of the variance of those parts. In contrast, a *direct consensus model* requires evidence of relatively homogeneous lower level parts as justification for aggregation. Thus, someone who varied greatly in terms of conscientious behavior from day to day or event to event could not be described by his or her average level of conscientiousness under a direct consensus composition model, given that evidence of stability, perhaps using ICCs or agreement indices, would need to be provided first, and these statistics would likely indicate that researchers should not engage in aggregation. However, such an individual could be described by an average level of conscientiousness if an additive model were put forth.

Chan's (1998) *referent-shift model* has an interesting translation as a composition model for within-person properties. In this case, it implies that individuals repeatedly describe a particular emergent property of themselves over time. That is, rather than asking a number of people whether their group acts in a conscientious manner, it might instead entail asking an individual about his or her level of conscientiousness repeatedly over time. One implication of this model for within-person phenomena is that it will clearly shift the bulk of the variance away from the moment-to-moment variations of the target characteristic and toward the more enduring and stable features of the evaluated self (Kahneman & Riis, 2005; Robinson & Clore, 2002). The interesting question that arises from considering this model is whether it is the recalled, stable features of identity that best characterize an emergent individual-level property, or whether it is best characterized not only by what is typical but also by the vagaries, peaks, and rock bottom of lived experience (e.g., "peak and end" information; Fredrickson & Kahneman, 1993).

To the extent that deviations from the prototypical states, perceptions, and behaviors are of interest as phenomena that emerge at the individual level, Kozlowski and Klein (2000) would argue that such complex aggregations are better considered compilation models, as they capture something distinct from the immediate experience itself. For example, *dispersion models* shift the emphasis away from stable averages of life's experiences and toward the amount of variation that occurs around one's average experience (something unlikely to be imparted by a self-report of one particular experience). Although within-person research examining this sort of compositional model is scarce, there are examples. For instance, Beal and his colleagues (Beal & Ghandour, 2011; Beal et al., 2013) have examined the concept of *affect spin*, which is a way of capturing variability in affective state. Likewise, Scott and colleagues have begun to consider within-person variation as a meaningful construct at the between-person level of analysis, examining variables such as emotional labor variability (e.g., Scott, Barnes, & Wagner, 2012) and daily variability in justice (Matta, Scott, Colquitt, Koopman, & Passantino, 2017).

Finally, *process-oriented compilation models* emphasize complex connections among parts of the whole that produce emergent properties. For within-person phenomena, this model would refer to connections among states, perceptions, and behaviors over time. For example, Glomb, Beal, Yang, and Bhave (2014) examined negative emotional inertia as a factor in understanding how workers react to negative events. In this case, negative emotional inertia was specified as the autoregression of negative affect (i.e., on immediately prior negative affect). As such, it represents a complex connection between two consecutively experienced states. Such models have been discussed in more detail by Wang, Hamaker, and Bergeman (2012) and in the emotions literature, in particular (e.g., Kuppens, Oravecz, & Tuerlinckx, 2010).

Emergent Properties as Perceptual Versus Mathematical Aggregations

Thus far, we have discussed details and considerations in situations when researchers might wish to aggregate within-person phenomena to the between-person level. However, we have not considered whether such an effort would be either reasonable or advisable. As an example, let's again consider the personality trait of conscientiousness. At the within-person level, there is now ample evidence that within-person fluctuations in conscientiousness are substantial in terms of both frequency and magnitude (Fleeson, 2001, 2004). As a result, we can meaningfully ask about the antecedents and consequences of more immediate conscientious behavior. Moreover, we now have a second viable means to assess conscientiousness as a trait. The first method, of course, would be through a traditional personality questionnaire; the second method, however, would be one of several potential aggregations of the within-person conscientiousness states along the lines of the composition and compilation models outlined above. Given the discussion earlier in the chapter about the meaning of within-person phenomena captured immediately, episodically, or daily, it should by now be clear that these two methods could produce fairly distinct estimates of personality, with the first reflecting the use of semantic memory in constructing stable self-perceptions or self-evaluations, and the second reflecting a prespecified mathematical aggregation of multiple, temporally dispersed self-perceptions of personality derived primarily from episodic memories obtained close to the experienced conscientious behavior. Research has supported the notion that these two estimates of personality are strongly correlated but empirically distinct constructs (Fleeson & Gallagher, 2009; uncorrected meta-analytic rs between .42 and .56 [.48 for conscientiousness specifically]). Moreover, other aggregations, such as variability in conscientious behavior, provide even more distinct descriptions of personality.

Statistical considerations.   Although the conceptual connections of these elements of personality to other constructs seem like exciting new ground to explore, there are a number of more pragmatic considerations. For example, most multilevel models examining within-person states use cluster-mean centering (i.e., within-person centering) for within-person predictor variables such as

conscientious behavior. The interpretation at this level of analysis would therefore reflect how changes in an individual's conscientious behavior relative to his or her typical level of conscientiousness (i.e., conscientious behavior across all days of the study) predict an outcome variable of interest (e.g., ratings of performance). To examine the effects at a higher level of analysis would therefore require adding the means (or other aggregations of conscientiousness) into the model as a person-level predictor variable. Furthermore, given the likely statistical dependence of means with other aggregations (e.g., variance and skewness), the means would likely need to be incorporated alongside other aggregates at the between-person level of analysis. For example, examining whether variability in conscientiousness predicted average levels of performance for individuals in a sample would require first controlling for average levels of conscientiousness. The reason for this step is that, particularly when using scales such as the ubiquitous Likert-type scale, higher or lower average scores are likely to reduce variance due to the upper and lower boundaries of the scale (Beal & Dawson, 2007). Thus, without first considering the influence of average conscientiousness, one might interpret conscientiousness variability as having predictive validity, even though this validity is potentially due to the average level of conscientiousness.

In addition, the aggregation of repeatedly measured states often carries with it differences in the psychometric properties of the measures used, particularly as they compare to the best examples of measures used for assessing traits (e.g., measures of the Big Five or other such perceptual aggregations of individual differences). Specifically, because ESM or CRA methods are assessed repeatedly, it is difficult to require participants to respond to lengthy, broad-domain measures without creating undue burden—and consequent problems with data quality. This dilemma seems to have been handled in ESM studies in several ways, but broadly there are two approaches: Assess a narrower domain of the construct of interest, or use only a few items to assess a broad domain. The first approach allows researchers to use scales that will often achieve acceptable levels of internal consistency reliability, but the cost is that the full domain of the construct cannot be captured. In these cases the onus is on the researchers to provide evidence that the narrower domain assessed is not overstated in its relevance to the full domain of the trait-level construct. Consequently, ESM studies taking this approach will have a more targeted focus in their research goals and conclusions.

The implications of the second approach depend, at least in part, on the viability of assessing broad domains with a small number of items. In some cases, broad overall assessments can still achieve acceptable levels of reliability with only a few items (e.g., job satisfaction; Ilies & Judge, 2002; Judge & Ilies, 2004). In other cases—particularly when a higher order construct composed of multiple subdomains is being assessed—the result is relatively poor reliability estimates for the brief scales that are used (e.g., Fleeson & Gallagher, 2009). More importantly, it is sometimes unclear to what extent the scales that are revised for use in ESM reflect the structure and validity of the original, trait-level construct. That is, if a new scale is used, often the psychometric properties of the scale are defended only by the inclusion of coefficient alpha, and it is unclear even whether this alpha reflects the nested nature of the observations (i.e., internal consistency based on total variance vs. just within-person variance). Although it is perhaps true that undertaking and reporting a separate validation effort for considerably shortened scales is unlikely to be seen as a contribution worthy of publication in our more prestigious journals, one should at a minimum report the results of an appropriate multilevel confirmatory factor model along with a comparison to published models of trait measures.

Conceptual considerations. Putting aside issues related to statistical modeling, we'd like to return to the potential of this analysis to increase our understanding of personality and other variables that have stable interindividual components (e.g., job or life satisfaction). Assuming that reasonably reliable and valid measures can be created for assessing episodic or statelike analogues, we suggest that whereas standard measures of personality or other similarly stable constructs

reflect what Kahneman and Riis (2005) referred to as the "remembering self," episodes or personality states assessed repeatedly across a representative period of time and aggregated to the level of the individual reflect what Kahneman and Riis referred to as the "experiencing self." For instance, in the world of work and organizations, the differences between these two reflections might be fairly important. Methodologically, it seems plausible that indices of the experienced and evaluated selves vary in terms of the common method biases that might be present. For example, linking indices of the experienced self to other, more evaluative constructs (e.g., job satisfaction) might be less likely to be influenced by consistency motifs or implicit theories that might otherwise inflate these effects (cf. Podsakoff et al., 2003). In contrast, indices based on experiences might be more likely to be influenced by dispositional affectivity or the stable aspects of transient mood states. Specifically, to the extent that each report of conscientious behavior is influenced consistently by negative or positive mood, the aggregation of these experienced personality states will reflect elements of trait affectivity. Indices of the evaluated self might also be influenced these factors, but the nature of this influence will be less systematic, as one's current or dispositional mood is only influencing a single response (i.e., to the global self-report of personality). To the extent that moods vary, this influence will be less systematically tied to affective dispositions.

More substantively, the difference between assessments of the experienced self and the evaluated self could reveal widely varying effects on outcomes of interest to a wide array of disciplines. Although the specification of a theory to determine the nature and magnitude of such differences is beyond the purview of this chapter, an existing and well-documented distinction in organizational psychology might provide a good starting point. Specifically, as discussed by Weiss and Cropanzano (1996), affect-driven and judgment-driven behaviors in response to particular affective events seem to fit as differential outcomes of the experienced and evaluated self, respectively. Affect-driven behaviors are work-relevant actions that are determined primarily by immediate affective states, which more closely correspond to the experienced self. However, judgment-driven behaviors likely take more time to develop (i.e., may unfold at a differential rate) and are a function of work attitudes generated by the aforementioned affective reactions and accumulated (and often more stable) beliefs. As stated by Weiss and Cropanzano (1996), judgment-driven behaviors "are the consequences of decision processes where one's evaluation of one's job is part of the decision matrix" (p. 13). Although affective events theory (AET) represents only one conceptual basis on which one might expect differences between the experienced and evaluated selves, it is quite possible that many such differences exist across the psychological and organizational sciences. The analysis of within-person processes and their aggregation to the between-person level makes it clear that researchers have, up to now, been firmly rooted in only the evaluated self. We look forward to discovering the extent to which a consideration of both perspectives can inform our theories and our findings.

CONCLUSION

Over the course of this chapter, we have provided an integrated overview of several intraindividual methodologies as a means to illustrate not only what different types of empirical questions they address but also how they can be utilized in tandem. Specifically, by using several intraindividual methods to delve into a phenomenon of interest, we posit that researchers can gain a more complete understanding of the lived experience of employees on a day-to-day basis and how these day-to-day experiences may culminate in meaningful, between-person characteristics. As scholars continue to increasingly employee these methods, we hope that they consider using them conjointly and in a more programmatic manner.

References

Andersson, L. M., & Pearson, C. M. (1999). Tit for tat? The spiraling effect of incivility in the workplace. *Academy of Management Journal, 24,* 452–471.

Aronson, E., & Carlsmith, J. M. (1968). Experimentation in social psychology. In G. Lindzey & E. Aronson (Eds.), *Handbook of social psychology* (Vol. 2, pp. 1–79). Reading, MA: Addison-Wesley.

Bakker, A. B., Demerouti, E., Oerlemans, W., & Sonnentag, S. (2013). Workaholism and daily recovery: A day reconstruction study of leisure activities. *Journal of Organizational Behavior, 34,* 87–107. http://dx.doi.org/10.1002/job.1796

Bakker, A. B., & Xanthopoulou, D. (2009). The crossover of daily work engagement: Test of an actor–partner interdependence model. *Journal of Applied Psychology, 94,* 1562–1571. http://dx.doi.org/10.1037/a0017525

Barker, R. G. (1968). *Ecological psychology: Concepts and methods for studying the environment of human behavior.* Stanford, CA: Stanford University Press.

Barnes, C., Lucianetti, L., Bhave, D., & Christian, M. (2015). "You wouldn't like me when I'm sleepy": Leaders' sleep, daily abusive supervision, and work unit engagement. *Academy of Management Journal, 58,* 1419–1437. http://dx.doi.org/10.5465/amj.2013.1063

Beal, D. J. (2015). ESM 2.0: State of the art and future potential of experience sampling methods in organizational research. *Annual Review of Organizational Psychology and Organizational Behavior, 2,* 383–407. http://dx.doi.org/10.1146/annurev-orgpsych-032414-111335

Beal, D. J., & Dawson, J. F. (2007). On the use of Likert-type scales in multilevel data influence on aggregate variables. *Organizational Research Methods, 10,* 657–672. http://dx.doi.org/10.1177/1094428106295492

Beal, D. J., & Ghandour, L. (2011). Stability, change, and the stability of change in daily workplace affect. *Journal of Organizational Behavior, 32,* 526–546. http://dx.doi.org/10.1002/job.713

Beal, D. J., Trougakos, J. P., Weiss, H. M., & Dalal, R. S. (2013). Affect spin and the emotion regulation process at work. *Journal of Applied Psychology, 98,* 593–605. http://dx.doi.org/10.1037/a0032559

Beal, D. J., Trougakos, J. P., Weiss, H. M., & Green, S. G. (2006). Episodic processes in emotional labor: Perceptions of affective delivery and regulation strategies. *Journal of Applied Psychology, 91,* 1053–1065. http://dx.doi.org/10.1037/0021-9010.91.5.1053

Beal, D. J., & Weiss, H. M. (2003). Methods of ecological momentary assessment in organizational research. *Organizational Research Methods, 6,* 440–464. http://dx.doi.org/10.1177/1094428103257361

Beal, D. J., Weiss, H. M., Barros, E., & MacDermid, S. M. (2005). An episodic process model of affective influences on performance. *Journal of Applied Psychology, 90,* 1054–1068. http://dx.doi.org/10.1037/0021-9010.90.6.1054

Benedetti, A. A., Diefendorff, J. M., Gabriel, A. S., & Chandler, M. M. (2015). The effects of intrinsic and extrinsic sources of motivation on well-being depend on time of day: The moderating effects of workday accumulation. *Journal of Vocational Behavior, 88,* 38–46. http://dx.doi.org/10.1016/j.jvb.2015.02.009

Berg, K. C., Crosby, R. D., Cao, L., Peterson, C. B., Engel, S. G., Mitchell, J. E., & Wonderlich, S. A. (2013). Facets of negative affect prior to and following binge-only, purge-only, and binge/purge events in women with bulimia nervosa. *Journal of Abnormal Psychology, 122,* 111–118. http://dx.doi.org/10.1037/a0029703

Blau, P. M. (1964). *Exchange and power in social life.* New York, NY: Wiley.

Bliese, P., Chan, D., & Ployhart, R. E. (2007). Multilevel methods: Future directions in measurement, longitudinal analyses, and nonnormal outcomes. *Organizational Research Methods, 10,* 551–563. http://dx.doi.org/10.1177/1094428107301102

Bolger, N., Davis, A., & Rafaeli, E. (2003). Diary methods: Capturing life as it is lived. *Annual Review of Psychology, 54,* 579–616. http://dx.doi.org/10.1146/annurev.psych.54.101601.145030

Butts, M. M., Becker, W. J., & Boswell, W. R. (2015). Hot buttons and time sinks: The effects of electronic communication during nonwork time on emotions and work–nonwork conflict. *Academy of Management Journal, 58,* 763–788. http://dx.doi.org/10.5465/amj.2014.0170

Chan, D. (1998). Functional relations among constructs in the same content domain at different levels of analysis: A typology of composition models. *Journal of Applied Psychology, 83,* 234–246. http://dx.doi.org/10.1037/0021-9010.83.2.234

Chen, G., Bliese, P., & Mathieu, J. (2005). Conceptual framework and statistical procedures for delineating and testing multilevel theories of homology. *Organizational Research Methods, 8,* 375–409. http://dx.doi.org/10.1177/1094428105280056

Clarivate Analytics. (2018, April 20). Retrieved from the University of Arizona's subscription-based *Web of Science* database.

Cropanzano, R., & Mitchell, M. S. (2005). Social exchange theory: An interdisciplinary review. *Journal of Management, 31,* 874–900. http://dx.doi.org/10.1177/0149206305279602

Csikszentmihalyi, M., & Graef, R. (1980). The experience of freedom in daily life. *American Journal of Community Psychology, 8,* 401–414. http://dx.doi.org/10.1007/BF00912853

Csikszentmihalyi, M., & Larson, R. (1987). Validity and reliability of the experience-sampling method. *Journal of Nervous and Mental Disease, 175,* 526–536. http://dx.doi.org/10.1097/00005053-198709000-00004

Csikszentmihalyi, M., Larson, R., & Prescott, S. (1977). The ecology of adolescent activity and experience. *Journal of Youth and Adolescence, 6,* 281–294. http://dx.doi.org/10.1007/BF02138940

Diener, E., & Tay, L. (2014). Review of the day reconstruction method (DRM). *Social Indicators Research, 116,* 255–267. http://dx.doi.org/10.1007/s11205-013-0279-x

Dimotakis, N., Ilies, R., & Judge, T. A. (2013). Experience sampling methodology. In J. M. Cortina & R. S. Landis (Eds.), *Modern research methods for the study of behavior in organizations* (pp. 319–348). New York, NY: Routledge.

Dimotakis, N., Scott, B. A., & Koopman, J. (2011). An experience sampling investigation of workplace interactions, affective states, and employee well-being. *Journal of Organizational Behavior, 32,* 572–588. http://dx.doi.org/10.1002/job.722

Edwards, J. R. (2008). To prosper organizational psychology should . . . overcome methodological barriers to progress. *Journal of Organizational Behavior, 29,* 469–491. http://dx.doi.org/10.1002/job.529

Eisenberger, N. I., Taylor, S. E., Gable, S. L., Hilmert, C. J., & Lieberman, M. D. (2007). Neural pathways link social support to attenuated neuroendocrine stress responses. *Neuroimage, 35,* 1601–1612.

Fisher, C. D., & To, M. L. (2012). Using experience sampling methodology in organizational behavior. *Journal of Organizational Behavior, 33,* 865–877. http://dx.doi.org/10.1002/job.1803

Fleeson, W. (2001). Toward a structure- and process-integrated view of personality: Traits as density distribution of states. *Journal of Personality and Social Psychology, 80,* 1011–1027. http://dx.doi.org/10.1037/0022-3514.80.6.1011

Fleeson, W. (2004). Moving personality beyond the person-situation debate: The challenge and the opportunity of within-person variability. *Current Directions in Psychological Science, 13,* 83–87. http://dx.doi.org/10.1111/j.0963-7214.2004.00280.x

Fleeson, W., & Gallagher, P. (2009). The implications of Big Five standing for the distribution of trait manifestation in behavior: Fifteen experience-sampling studies and a meta-analysis. *Journal of Personality and Social Psychology, 97,* 1097–1114. http://dx.doi.org/10.1037/a0016786

Foo, M.-D., Uy, M. A., & Baron, R. A. (2009). How do feelings influence effort? An empirical study of entrepreneurs' affect and venture effort. *Journal of Applied Psychology, 94,* 1086–1094. http://dx.doi.org/10.1037/a0015599

Fredrickson, B. L. (2000). Extracting meaning from past affective experiences: The importance of peaks, ends, and specific emotions. *Cognition and Emotion, 14,* 577–606. http://dx.doi.org/10.1080/026999300402808

Fredrickson, B. L., & Kahneman, D. (1993). Duration neglect in retrospective evaluations of affective episodes. *Journal of Personality and Social Psychology, 65,* 45–55. http://dx.doi.org/10.1037/0022-3514.65.1.45

Gabriel, A. S., & Diefendorff, J. M. (2015). Emotional labor dynamics: A momentary approach. *Academy of Management Journal, 58,* 1804–1825. http://dx.doi.org/10.5465/amj.2013.1135

Gabriel, A. S., Diefendorff, J. M., Bennett, A. A., & Sloan, M. D. (2017). It's about time: The promise of continuous rating assessments for the organizational sciences. *Organizational Research Methods, 20,* 32–60. http://dx.doi.org/10.1177/1094428116673721

Gabriel, A. S., Diefendorff, J. M., Chandler, M. M., Moran, C. M., & Greguras, G. J. (2014). The dynamic relationships of work affect and job satisfaction with perceptions of fit. *Personnel Psychology, 67,* 389–420. http://dx.doi.org/10.1111/peps.12042

Gabriel, A. S., Diefendorff, J. M., & Erickson, R. J. (2011). The relations of daily task accomplishment satisfaction with changes in affect: A multilevel study in nurses. *Journal of Applied Psychology, 96,* 1095–1104. http://dx.doi.org/10.1037/a0023937

George, J. M., & Jones, G. R. (2000). The role of time in theory and theory building. *Journal of Management, 26,* 657–684. http://dx.doi.org/10.1177/014920630002600404

Glaser, B. G., & Strauss, A. L. (1967). *The discovery of grounded theory: Strategies for qualitative research.* Hawthorne, NY: Aldine de Gruyter.

Glomb, T. M., Beal, D. J., Yang, T., & Bhave, D. P. (2014, May). *Staying power: Emotional inertia as a moderator of event-affect relationships.* Paper presented at the 29th Annual Conference of the Society of Industrial and Organizational Psychology, Honolulu, HI.

Gobo, G. (2004). Sampling, representativeness, and generalizability. In C. Seale, G. Gobo, J. F. Gubrium, & D. Silverman (Eds.), *Qualitative health research* (pp. 435–455). Thousand Oaks, CA: Sage.

Gottman, J., Notarius, C., Markman, H., Bank, S., Yoppi, B., & Rubin, M. E. (1976). Behavior exchange theory and marital decision making. *Journal of Personality and Social Psychology, 34,* 14–23. http://dx.doi.org/10.1037/0022-3514.34.1.14

Gottman, J. M., & Levenson, R. W. (1985). A valid procedure for obtaining self-report of affect in marital interaction. *Journal of Consulting and Clinical Psychology, 53,* 151–160. http://dx.doi.org/10.1037/0022-006X.53.2.151

Grandey, A. A. (2000). Emotion regulation in the workplace: A new way to conceptualize emotional labor. *Journal of Occupational Health Psychology, 5,* 95–110. http://dx.doi.org/10.1037/1076-8998.5.1.95

Groth, M., & Grandey, A. (2012). From bad to worse: Negative exchange spirals in employee–customer service interactions. *Organizational Psychology Review, 2,* 208–233. http://dx.doi.org/10.1177/2041386612441735

Ilies, R., & Judge, T. A. (2002). Understanding the dynamic relationships among personality, mood, and job satisfaction: A field experience sampling study. *Organizational Behavior and Human Decision Processes, 89,* 1119–1139. http://dx.doi.org/10.1016/S0749-5978(02)00018-3

Jones, K. P. (2017). To tell or not to tell? Examining the role of discrimination in the pregnancy disclosure process at work. *Journal of Occupational Health Psychology, 22,* 239–250. http://dx.doi.org/10.1037/ocp0000030

Judge, T. A., & Ilies, R. (2004). Affect and job satisfaction: A study of their relationship at work and at home. *Journal of Applied Psychology, 89,* 661–673. http://dx.doi.org/10.1037/0021-9010.89.4.661

Judge, T. A., Scott, B. A., & Ilies, R. (2006). Hostility, job attitudes, and workplace deviance: Test of a multilevel model. *Journal of Applied Psychology, 91,* 126–138. http://dx.doi.org/10.1037/0021-9010.91.1.126

Judge, T. A., Woolf, E. F., & Hurst, C. (2009). Is emotional labor more difficult for some than for others? A multilevel, experience-sampling study. *Personnel Psychology, 62,* 57–88. http://dx.doi.org/10.1111/j.1744-6570.2008.01129.x

Kahneman, D., Krueger, A. B., Schkade, D. A., Schwarz, N., & Stone, A. A. (2004). A survey method for characterizing daily life experience: The day reconstruction method. *Science, 306,* 1776–1780. http://dx.doi.org/10.1126/science.1103572

Kahneman, D., & Riis, J. (2005). Living and thinking about it: Two perspectives on life. In N. Baylis, F. A. Huppert, & B. Keverne (Eds.), *The science of well-being* (pp. 284–304). New York, NY: Oxford Press. http://dx.doi.org/10.1093/acprof:oso/9780198567523.003.0011

Koopman, J., Lanaj, K., & Scott, B. A. (2016). Integrating the bright and dark sides of OCB: A daily investigation of the benefits and costs of helping others. *Academy of Management Journal, 59,* 414–435. http://dx.doi.org/10.5465/amj.2014.0262

Kozlowski, S. W. J., & Klein, K. J. (2000). A multilevel approach to theory and research in organizations: Contextual, temporal, and emergent processes. In K. Klein & S. W. J. Kowzlowski (Eds.), *Multilevel theory, research, and methods in organizations: Foundations, extensions, and new directions* (pp. 3–90). San Francisco, CA: Jossey-Bass.

Kuppens, P., Oravecz, Z., & Tuerlinckx, F. (2010). Feelings change: Accounting for individual differences in the temporal dynamics of affect. *Journal of Personality and*

Social Psychology, 99, 1042–1060. http://dx.doi.org/10.1037/a0020962

Laurenceau, J.-P., Barrett, L. F., & Rovine, M. J. (2005). The interpersonal process model of intimacy in marriage: A daily-diary and multilevel modeling approach. *Journal of Family Psychology, 19,* 314–323. http://dx.doi.org/10.1037/0893-3200.19.2.314

Leslie, L. M., King, E. B., Bradley, J. C., & Hebl, M. R. (2008). Triangulation across methodologies: All signs point to persistent stereotyping and discrimination in organizations. *Industrial and Organizational Psychology: Perspectives on Science and Practice, 1,* 399–404. http://dx.doi.org/10.1111/j.1754-9434.2008.00073.x

Levenson, R. W., & Gottman, J. M. (1983). Marital interaction: Physiological linkage and affective exchange. *Journal of Personality and Social Psychology, 45,* 587–597. http://dx.doi.org/10.1037/0022-3514.45.3.587

Matta, F. K., Erol-Korkmaz, H. T., Johnson, R. E., & Biçaksiz, P. (2014). Significant work events and counterproductive behavior: The role of fairness, emotions, and emotion regulation. *Journal of Organizational Behavior, 35,* 920–944. http://dx.doi.org/10.1002/job.1934

Matta, F. K., Scott, B. A., Colquitt, J. A., Koopman, J., & Passantino, L. G. (2017). Is consistently unfair better than sporadically fair? An investigation of justice variability and stress. *Academy of Management Journal, 60,* 743–770. http://dx.doi.org/10.5465/amj.2014.0455

Mauss, I. B., Levenson, R. W., McCarter, L., Wilhelm, F. H., & Gross, J. J. (2005). The tie that binds? Coherence among emotion experience, behavior, and physiology. *Emotion, 5,* 175–190. http://dx.doi.org/10.1037/1528-3542.5.2.175

Mauss, I. B., Shallcross, A. J., Troy, A. S., John, O. P., Ferrer, E., Wilhelm, F. H., & Gross, J. J. (2011). Don't hide your happiness! Positive emotion dissociation, social connectedness, and psychological functioning. *Journal of Personality and Social Psychology, 100,* 738–748. http://dx.doi.org/10.1037/a0022410

Methot, J. R., Lepak, D., Shipp, A. J., & Boswell, W. R. (2017). Good citizen interrupted: Calibrating a temporal theory of citizenship behavior. *Academy of Management Review, 42,* 10–31. http://dx.doi.org/10.5465/amr.2014.0415

Miron-Shatz, T. (2009). Evaluating multiepisode events: Boundary conditions for the peak-end rule. *Emotion, 9,* 206–213. http://dx.doi.org/10.1037/a0015295

Mitchell, T. R., & James, L. R. (2001). Building better theory: Time and the specification of when things happen. *Academy of Management Review, 26,* 530–547.

Monge, P. R. (1990). Theoretical and analytical issues in studying organizational processes. *Organization Science, 1,* 406–430. http://dx.doi.org/10.1287/orsc.1.4.406

Morgeson, F. P., Mitchell, T. R., & Liu, D. (2015). Event system theory: An event-oriented approach to the organizational science. *Academy of Management Review, 40,* 515–537. http://dx.doi.org/10.5465/amr.2012.0099

Naidoo, L. J., & Lord, R. G. (2008). Speech imagery and perceptions of charisma: The mediating role of positive affect. *The Leadership Quarterly, 19,* 283–296. http://dx.doi.org/10.1016/j.leaqua.2008.03.010

Nishina, A., & Juvonen, J. (2005). Daily reports of witnessing and experiencing peer harassment in middle school. *Child Development, 76,* 435–450. http://dx.doi.org/10.1111/j.1467-8624.2005.00855.x

Oerlemans, W. G., & Bakker, A. B. (2014). Burnout and daily recovery: A day reconstruction study. *Journal of Occupational Health Psychology, 19,* 303–314. http://dx.doi.org/10.1037/a0036904

Ohly, S., Sonnentag, S., Niessen, C., & Zapf, D. (2010). Diary studies in organizational research: An introduction and some practical recommendations. *Journal of Personnel Psychology, 9,* 79–93. http://dx.doi.org/10.1027/1866-5888/a000009

Ployhart, R. E., & Vandenberg, R. J. (2010). Longitudinal research: The theory, design, and analysis of change. *Journal of Management, 36,* 94–120. http://dx.doi.org/10.1177/0149206309352110

Podsakoff, P. M., MacKenzie, S. B., Lee, J.-Y., & Podsakoff, N. P. (2003). Common method biases in behavioral research: A critical review of the literature and recommended remedies. *Journal of Applied Psychology, 88,* 879–903. http://dx.doi.org/10.1037/0021-9010.88.5.879

Robinson, M. D., & Clore, G. L. (2002). Belief and feeling: Evidence for an accessibility model of emotional self-report. *Psychological Bulletin, 128,* 934–960. http://dx.doi.org/10.1037/0033-2909.128.6.934

Rodell, J. B., & Judge, T. A. (2009). Can "good" stressors spark "bad" behaviors? The mediating role of emotions in links of challenge and hindrance stressors with citizenship and counterproductive behaviors. *Journal of Applied Psychology, 94,* 1438–1451. http://dx.doi.org/10.1037/a0016752

Rosen, C. C., Koopman, J., Gabriel, A. S., & Johnson, R. E. (2016). Who strikes back? A daily investigation of when and why incivility begets incivility. *Journal of Applied Psychology, 101,* 1620–1634. http://dx.doi.org/10.1037/apl0000140

Ruef, A. M., & Levenson, R. W. (2007). Continuous measurement of emotion. In J. A. Coan & J. B. Allen (Eds.), *Handbook of emotion elicitation and assessment* (pp. 286–297). New York, NY: Oxford University Press.

Rupp, D. E., & Spencer, S. (2006). When customers lash out: The effects of customer interactional injustice on emotional labor and the mediating role of discrete emotions. *Journal of Applied Psychology, 91*, 971–978. http://dx.doi.org/10.1037/0021-9010.91.4.971

Russell, J. A., & Feldman Barrett, L. (1999). Core affect, prototypical emotional episodes, and other things called emotion: Dissecting the elephant. *Journal of Personality and Social Psychology, 76*, 805–819. http://dx.doi.org/10.1037/0022-3514.76.5.805

Sander, D., Grandjean, D., & Scherer, K. R. (2005). A systems approach to appraisal mechanisms in emotion. *Neural networks, 18*, 317–352. http://dx.doi.org/10.1016/j.neunet.2005.03.001

Scott, B. A., & Barnes, C. M. (2011). A multilevel investigation of emotional labor, affect, withdrawal, and gender. *Academy of Management Journal, 54*, 116–136. http://dx.doi.org/10.5465/AMJ.2011.59215086

Scott, B. A., Barnes, C. M., & Wagner, D. T. (2012). Chameleonic or consistent? A multilevel investigation of emotional labor variability and self-monitoring. *Academy of Management Journal, 55*, 905–926. http://dx.doi.org/10.5465/amj.2010.1050

Siewert, K., Antoniw, K., Kubiak, T., & Weber, H. (2011). The more the better? The relationship between mismatches in social support and subjective well-being in daily life. *Journal of Health Psychology, 16*, 621–631. http://dx.doi.org/10.1177/1359105310385366

Sonnentag, S., Binnewies, C., & Mojza, E. J. (2008). "Did you have a nice evening?" A day-level study on recovery experiences, sleep, and affect. *Journal of Applied Psychology, 93*, 674–684. http://dx.doi.org/10.1037/0021-9010.93.3.674

Sonnentag, S., & Zijlstra, F. R. H. (2006). Job characteristics and off-job activities as predictors of need for recovery, well-being, and fatigue. *Journal of Applied Psychology, 91*, 330–350. http://dx.doi.org/10.1037/0021-9010.91.2.330

Swallow, K. M., Zacks, J. M., & Abrams, R. A. (2009). Event boundaries in perception affect memory encoding and updating. *Journal of Experimental Psychology: General, 138*, 236–257. http://dx.doi.org/10.1037/a0015631

Tracy, J. L., & Robins, R. W. (2007). The psychological structure of pride: A tale of two facets. *Journal of Personality and Social Psychology, 92*, 506–525. http://dx.doi.org/10.1037/0022-3514.92.3.506

Tracy, J. L., Shariff, A. F., & Cheng, J. T. (2010). A naturalist's view of pride. *Emotion Review, 2*, 163–177. http://dx.doi.org/10.1177/1754073909354627

Trougakos, J. P., Beal, D. J., Cheng, B. H., Hideg, I., & Zweig, D. (2015). Too drained to help: A resource depletion perspective on daily interpersonal citizenship behaviors. *Journal of Applied Psychology, 100*, 227–236. http://dx.doi.org/10.1037/a0038082

Wagner, D. T., Barnes, C. M., & Scott, B. A. (2014). Driving it home: How workplace emotional labor harms employee home life. *Personnel Psychology, 67*, 487–516. http://dx.doi.org/10.1111/peps.12044

Wang, L. P., Hamaker, E., & Bergeman, C. S. (2012). Investigating inter-individual differences in short-term intraindividual variability. *Psychological Methods, 17*, 567–581. http://dx.doi.org/10.1037/a0029317

Wang, M., Liu, S., Liao, H., Gong, Y., Kammeyer-Mueller, J., & Shi, J. (2013). Can't get it out of my mind: Employee rumination after customer mistreatment and negative mood in the next morning. *Journal of Applied Psychology, 98*, 989–1004. http://dx.doi.org/10.1037/a0033656

Weiss, H. M., Beal, D. J., Lucy, S. L., & MacDermid, S. M. (2004). *Constructing EMA studies with PMAT: The Purdue momentary assessment tool user's manual.* West Lafayette, IN: Purdue University.

Weiss, H. M., & Cropanzano, R. (1996). Affective events theory: A theoretical discussion of the structure, causes, and consequences of affective experiences at work. *Research in Organizational Behavior, 18*, 1–74.

Weiss, H. M., & Rupp, D. E. (2011). Experiencing work: An essay on a person-centric work psychology. *Industrial and Organizational Psychology: Perspectives on Science and Practice, 4*, 83–97. http://dx.doi.org/10.1111/j.1754-9434.2010.01302.x

Yang, J., & Diefendorff, J. M. (2009). The relations of daily counterproductive workplace behavior with emotions, situational antecedents, and personality moderators: A diary study in Hong Kong. *Personnel Psychology, 62*, 259–295. http://dx.doi.org/10.1111/j.1744-6570.2009.01138.x

## CHAPTER 14

POWER ANALYSIS FOR MULTILEVEL RESEARCH

Charles A. Scherbaum and Erik Pesner

Despite the prevalence of multilevel organizational research, many of the decisions involved in the design and evaluation of multilevel research remain challenging for researchers (Aguinis, Gottfredson, & Culpepper, 2013; Bliese, Chan, & Ployhart, 2007; LaHuis, Hartman, Hakoyama, & Clark, 2014). One of those decisions is how to estimate statistical power and necessary sample sizes. For many researchers, multilevel statistical power is an area that is not well understood. It is also an area where current practice is not as rigorous as it could be (Mathieu, Aguinis, Culpepper, & Chen, 2012; Scherbaum & Ferreter, 2009).

For single-level studies, statistical power is a relatively straightforward concept, and guidelines for computing and reporting statistical power are well developed (e.g., J. Cohen, 1988). However, statistical power for multilevel research is inherently more complex because it involves a larger number of factors at multiple levels of analysis (Mathieu & Chen, 2011). Best practices recommendations for power analyses for multilevel organizational research and accessible tools to estimate statistical power are only relatively recent developments (e.g., Aguinis et al., 2013; Mathieu et al., 2012; Scherbaum & Ferreter, 2009).

In this chapter, we cover the growing and diverse literatures on the approaches to computing statistical power in multilevel organizational

research. In reviewing these approaches and literatures, our focus is on estimating statistical power for tests of fixed effects, cross-level interactions and variance components in two-level models because these are the primary effects of interest in multilevel organizational research (Aguinis et al., 2013; Mathieu et al., 2012; Scherbaum & Ferreter, 2009). In the remainder of this chapter, we review the current state of statistical power estimation in organizational research; describe the factors playing a role in multilevel statistical power; and outline the methods used to estimate statistical power for fixed effects, cross-level interactions, and variance components.

MULTILEVEL POWER ANALYSIS IN THE ORGANIZATIONAL RESEARCH

Multilevel analyses are commonly used in organizational research because they are well suited for nested data that cross hierarchically differentiated or conceptually distinct levels of analyses, which are characteristic of many organizational phenomena (Bliese, 2000; Chan, 2011; Davison, Kwak, Seo, & Choi, 2002; Kozlowski & Klein, 2000). For nested, or nonindependent data (i.e., data that share a common source of variance), multilevel analysis provides greater accuracy in parameter estimation through the simultaneous specification of both within-level

http://dx.doi.org/10.1037/0000115-015
The Handbook of Multilevel Theory, Measurement, and Analysis, S. E. Humphrey and J. M. LeBreton (Editors-in-Chief)

and between-level error structures (Aguinis et al., 2013; Raudenbush, 1988; Raudenbush & Bryk, 2002; Mathieu et al., 2012).

In a demonstration of the growing prevalence of multilevel organizational research, Mathieu and colleagues (2012) provided a systematic review of every article published in the *Journal of Applied Psychology* between the years 2000 and 2010. These authors reported that the number of articles reporting multilevel research grew from an average of three articles published each year between 2000 and 2002 to an average of 13 articles each year between 2008 and 2010 (Mathieu et al., 2012). We provided a continuation of this investigation by reviewing every article published in the *Journal of Applied Psychology* between January 2010 and December 2015. We found that 139 of the 535 articles (i.e., roughly 26%) published during this 6-year span reported multilevel research. In other words, during these 6 years there was an average of 23 articles reporting multilevel research in the *Journal of Applied Psychology* each year. The increasing prevalence of multilevel methods is not limited to the *Journal of Applied Psychology*. For example, Aguinis, Pierce, Bosco, and Muslin (2009) found that multilevel analyses were the third most commonly used analysis approach in *Organizational Research Methods* between 1998 and 2007.

Despite the popularity and prevalence of multi-level organizational research, there are numerous methodological and analytical choices that are challenging for researchers, and guidance on these issues is only a recent development (e.g., Aguinis et al., 2013; LaHuis et al., 2014). One area that especially stands out as a challenge for researchers is the estimation of statistical power and necessary sample sizes in multilevel research.

Statistical power is the probability of detecting an effect when it does exist. Under the logic of null hypothesis significance testing, statistical power can be described as the overlap between a sampling distribution of a population parameter under the null hypothesis and a sampling distribution under an alternative hypothesis. The degree of overlap between the alternative distribution and the null distribution is the probability of a Type II error (i.e., failing to reject the null hypothesis when it is false),

which is represented by β. Statistical power is the area under the alternative distribution that does not overlap with the null distribution (i.e., $1.0 - \beta$). In other words, it is the probability of correctly rejecting a false null hypothesis.

Despite the consensus regarding the importance of statistical power for making statistical inferences in organizational research, power analyses are rarely reported for single-level organizational research designs (Aguinis & Vandenberg, 2014; Aguinis, Beaty, Boik, & Pierce, 2005; Austin, Boyle, & Lualhati, 1998; Austin, Scherbaum, & Mahlman, 2002; Mone, Mueller, & Mauland, 1996). It appears that power analyses for multilevel organizational research are reported even less frequently. Of the 139 articles published in the *Journal of Applied Psychology* between 2010 and 2015 that reported multilevel research, only three reported the statistical power of their effects or the power analysis used to determine the minimum sample sizes required for their studies. Although the majority of these researchers did not mention statistical power in their articles, several of them raised the concern about statistical power when noting that small sample sizes were a potential limitation in their studies (e.g., Harman, Ellington, Surface, & Thompson, 2015; Todorova, Bear, & Weingart, 2014; Venkataramani, Richter, & Clarke, 2014; Yakovleva, Reilly, & Werko, 2010). Mathieu et al. (2012) reported a similar pattern in earlier *Journal of Applied Psychology* articles, noting that several authors listed statistical power as a potential limitation of their research studies.

Given that the literature on multilevel power analysis is highly technical and often published in sources unfamiliar to most organizational researchers, it is not surprising that multilevel power analysis is rarely conducted or reported in organizational research. Nevertheless, the underutilization of statistical power analyses in multilevel research is concerning (Aguinis et al., 2013; Cunningham & Johnson, 2016; Mathieu et al., 2012; McNeish & Stapleton, 2016; Scherbaum & Ferreter, 2009; Zhan, 2013).

A number of scholars have called for the widespread adoption of a more a directed mindset and rigorous approach toward conducting and reporting statistical power analysis for multilevel research (e.g., Mathieu et al., 2012; Scherbaum & Ferreter, 2009). In other disciplines, these types of power analysis are becoming a requirement (e.g., Institute of Education Sciences, 2016). The current chapter is meant to echo this notion and build on the recent work aimed at helping researchers conduct these analyses. The following sections of this chapter first outline the analytical foundation of multilevel models; then the factors that impact multilevel statistical power and; finally, the methods used to estimate statistical power for fixed effects, cross-level interactions, and variance components.

OVERVIEW OF MULTILEVEL ANALYSES

To understand the estimation of statistical power in multilevel research, it is necessary to briefly describe the underlying equations in multilevel analyses. For the purposes of this chapter, we focus on two-level models given that they are most frequently used in multilevel organizational research. A basic Level 1 model with one predictor can be expressed as follows:

$$Y_{ij} = \beta_{0j} + \beta_{1j}X_{ij} + r_{ij}, \tag{14.1}$$

where Y_{ij} is the score on the outcome for the ith person in group j, β_{0j} is the intercept for group j, β_{1j} is the slope for group j, X_{ij} is the value on the predictor for the ith person in group j, and r_{ij} is the Level 1 error term for person i in group j. The models at Level 2 with one predictor can be expressed as follows:

$$\beta_{0j} = \gamma_{00} + \gamma_{01}W_j + u_{0j} \tag{14.2}$$

$$\beta_{1j} = \gamma_{00} + \gamma_{11}W_j + u_{1j}, \tag{14.3}$$

where γ_{00} and γ_{10} are the Level 2 intercepts, W_j is the value on the Level 2 predictor for members of group j, γ_{01} and γ_{11} are the Level 2 slopes, and u_{0j} and u_{1j} are the Level 2 error terms. The full model that combines Equations 14.1, 14.2, and 14.3 takes the following form:

$$Y_{1j} = \gamma_{00} + \gamma_{01}W_j + \gamma_{10}X_{ij} + \gamma_{11}W_jX_{ij} + u_{0j} + u_{1j}X_{ij} + r_{ij}, \tag{14.4}$$

where the first term represents the grand mean, the second term represents the fixed effect in the

intercept, the third term represents the effect of the Level 1 predictor, and the fourth term represents the cross-level interaction. The remaining three terms represent the random effects. Each parameter in this model is estimated with an associated standard error. These standard error terms are used to perform statistical significance tests for each parameter. The parameters for the fixed effects and cross-level interactions are evaluated with a t test and the parameters for the random effects are tested with a chi-square.

FACTORS THAT IMPACT STATISTICAL POWER IN MULTILEVEL RESEARCH

One of the primary complexities in estimating statistical power for multilevel organizational research concerns the number of factors involved (Mathieu & Chen, 2011). This is because the applicable factors may depend on the specific effects that a researcher is investigating (Mathieu et al., 2012). As is the case with single-level research, statistical power is impacted by the chosen value (e.g., $p < .05$) for the probability of making a Type I error (i.e., rejecting the null hypothesis when it is true; α). In multilevel research, as with single-level research, there is a relationship between α and β. For example, as the value of α increases (e.g., .05 to .10), the value of β decreases and, correspondingly, statistical power is increased. Although single-level and multilevel research share several other factors in common, they differ in fundamental respects, and each factor warrants special consideration. To estimate statistical power using the formula and tools described in this chapter, it will be necessary to compute or estimate values for each of the factors reviewed here. A priori power calculations require a researcher to estimate these values from the results of previous research, results of a pilot study, use rules of thumb, or compute them from existing data. The quality of the statistical power estimates will be only as high as the quality of the estimates for the factors in the equation.

Although not discussed as a separate factor, the standard errors for each parameter in a multilevel model (e.g., γ_{00}, γ_{10}, γ_{01}, γ_{11}, u_{0j}, and μ_{1j}) play an important role in multilevel power analysis and are impacted by the factors that are discussed in this chapter. As is described, the accuracy of the standard errors can be impacted by a number of factors as well as the interactions between them (Maas & Hox, 2004, 2005). In the context of multilevel power analysis, the accuracy of the standard error estimates is important to consider because standard errors that are positively or negatively biased may lead to overestimates or underestimates of statistical power. To date, most of the work on computing multilevel statistical power has focused on how various factors impact the standard error, which in turn impacts statistical power (Scherbaum & Ferreter, 2009; Snijders & Bosker, 1993).

Sample Size

Sample size is a key determinant in single-level power estimation. The same is true for multilevel power estimation. In the latter case, there are multiple sample sizes to consider. More specifically, there is a sample size to consider at each level of a multilevel model and a total sample. For example, in a two-level model of the impact of leader characteristics (Level 2) on the relationships between employee engagement and organizational citizenship behaviors (Level 1), there are different sample sizes for each level in the model. At Level 2, we might have $J = 20$ leaders. At Level 1, we might collect data from $n = 10$ subordinates nested in each of the $J = 20$ leaders. Thus (with a perfectly balanced design), our Level 1 sample size is simply the product $n \times J$ or $10 \times 20 = 200$. Finally, we can combine the Level 1 sample size with the Level 2 sample size to obtain total, combined sample size of 220.

In single-level designs, the estimation of statistical power is a monotonic function of the sample size when the other factors are held constant. In multilevel analyses, power is not a monotonic function of the sample sizes at either level when holding the other factors constant. In other words, simply increasing the sample size at Level 1 or increasing the sample sizes at Level 1 and Level 2 simultaneously may have only a minimal impact on power. In this respect, estimating power is a problem of optimization

because one must determine the range of sample sizes at each level of analysis to obtain the desired level of statistical power.

Most of the simulation research to date has found that increasing the sample size at the highest level of analysis (e.g., sampling more groups) does more to raise statistical power than increasing the sample size at the lower level of analysis (i.e., sampling more people in the groups; e.g., Kreft, 1996; Snijders & Bosker, 1993). For example, the simulation studies of Bassiri (1988), Browne and Draper (2000), Kim (1990), and Mok (1995) found that increasing the sample size at Level 2 had a greater impact on increasing power for fixed effects than increasing the sample size at Level 1. Likewise, the Bassiri (1988) and van der Leeden and Busing (1994) simulation studies concluded that an increase in the sample size at Level 2 had a greater impact on the statistical power than an increase in the sample size at Level 1 for tests of cross-level interactions. More recently, Spybrook, Kelcey, and Dong (2016) came to a similar conclusion about the importance of the higher level sample size in cross-level interactions. In contrast, the findings of Mathieu et al. (2012) indicate that sample sizes at both Level 1 and Level 2 are important, but the Level 1 sample size was relatively more important in determining the statistical power of tests of cross-level interactions. The difference in the conclusions of Mathieu et al. compared with the previous research is that the latter modeled a larger number of factors and tested slightly different models with their centering approach compared with Spybrook et al. (2016). These differences may have led to the reversal in the relative importance of the Level 1 and Level 2 sample sizes. However, additional research is needed to test this speculation. Afshartous (1995), Busing (1993), and van der Leeden and Busing (1994) have found that sample sizes less than 30 at Level 2 led to an underestimation of the standard errors for the Level 2 variance components and an overestimation of statistical power, whereas Maas and Hox (2004, 2005) found a similar pattern for Level 2 sample sizes of both 30 and 50.

This simulation research has led to the establishment of rules of thumb to help guide choices about the necessary sample sizes in multi-level research. For example, Kreft (1996) suggested a minimum of 30 groups with 30 individuals in those groups for each type of effect in multilevel research (see also Busing, 1993, and van der Leeden & Busing, 1994, for a similar recommendation). Hox (1998) advocated an even larger sample size, with a minimum of 50 groups and 20 individuals in each group. We agree with Mathieu et al. (2012) that although these rules of thumb are helpful, they do not eliminate the need to conduct a multilevel power analysis. As Mathieu et al. noted, a number of factors were not included in those simulations, which could impact conclusions about statistical power and sample sizes. Moreover, the rules of thumb from different authors and simulation research often disagree, which can leave a researcher confused and uncertain as to which rule to follow. From a more practical perspective, the rules of thumb indicate sample sizes that are far beyond what is typically seen in many areas of research. For example, 30 groups with 30 people in each group leads to a total sample size of over 900. However, Mathieu et al.'s review of articles published in the *Journal of Applied Psychology* found that the median Level 1 sample size was 5 and the median Level 2 sample size was 51 (i.e., total sample size close to 250). For research designs with these more typical sample size constraints it is necessary to directly estimate statistical power in order to understand and interpret the likelihood of detecting an effect that exists.

Intraclass Correlation

When data are hierarchically nested, the data gathered from the individuals within a group are often not statistically independent. In these cases, data provided by an individual in the group is to some degree redundant with the data provided by the other individuals in the group. In other words, the group in which an individual resides can account for variance in the individual-level data. The degree to which these group differences can account for the total variance impacts statistical power in multilevel research. An intraclass correlation coefficient (ICC) is a statistic often used to index these relationships.

The ICC is the ratio of the between group variability to the total variability. For a given fixed effect or cross-level interaction, the ICC can be expressed as

$$\rho = \tau/(\tau + \sigma^2), \qquad (14.5)$$

where ρ is the ICC, τ is the between-group variance for a given Level 2 effect (e.g., fixed effect, cross-level interaction), and σ^2 is the Level 1 residual variance. Thus, this ICC represents the between-group variance divided by the total variance. As Bliese (2000) and LeBreton and Senter (2008) have noted, this formulation of the ICC in multilevel modeling is equivalent to the ICC(1) from Bartko (1976) and ICC(1,1) from Shrout and Fleiss (1979). The discussion of ICCs in this chapter assume the ICC(1) formulation unless otherwise noted. Although not reviewed in detail here, it is important to note that there has been recent work developing alternative ICC formulations. Aguinis and Culpepper (2015) reported on a new ICC, called ICC_{beta}, for use in the context of cross-level interactions. This ICC was designed to better assess how much of the variance in the lower level outcome variable can be attributed to differences in the higher level slopes. Aguinis and Culpepper (2015) presented a simulation demonstrating the value of this ICC for examining cross-level interactions.

There are several types of models available in multilevel modeling (e.g., regression with means as outcomes model, intercepts and slopes as outcomes model; Raudenbush & Bryk, 2002). Often, the modeling process involves building from the simpler models (e.g., a one-way random effect analysis of variance model) to the more complex models (e.g., intercepts and slopes as outcomes model). Consequently, one can obtain several values of τ and σ^2 that could be used to compute the ICC (see Chapter 12, this volume; LaHuis et al., 2014). The ICC that is used in the statistical power computations should be computed using τ and σ^2 from the model being studied. For example, if a researcher is interested in computing the ICC for model testing a cross-level interaction, the ICC should use τ and σ^2 from the intercepts and slopes as outcomes model used to test the cross-level interaction.

An ICC can range in value from 0.0 to +1.0. Larger values indicate a stronger relationship between the data collected from individuals within the same group (i.e., a greater degree of dependence). In these cases, the between-group variance at the higher level of analysis accounts for a relatively larger proportion of the total variance. Larger values for the ICC can increase the power to detect effects at Level 2 (Mathieu et al., 2012; Raudenbush & Liu, 2000). Conversely, smaller values indicate that the group level of analysis accounts for less of the total variation in the data. In these cases, the power to detect a Level 1 effect is increased (Mathieu et al., 2012; Raudenbush & Liu, 2000) and multilevel analyses may not be required (Aguinis et al., 2013; Raudenbush, 1997; Reise & Duan, 2003).

There are a variety of estimates for the typical ICC values found in the literature (see Chapter 12, this volume). Snijders and Bosker (1999), Bliese (2000), and Peugh (2010) have suggested that ICC values typically range between .05 and .20. In their review of multilevel research published in the *Journal of Applied Psychology*, Mathieu et al. (2012) found ICC values ranging from .00 to .39. Hedges and Hedberg (2007) suggest that ICC values between .10 and .25 have been reported in educational research. In considering the possible values for an ICC, Bliese noted that values above .30 are possible, but likely not the norm in organizational research. Considering the various estimates offered in the past, Mathieu et al. suggested that ICC values between .15 and .30 are reasonable estimates for computing multilevel statistical power.

Model Parameter

The parameter of interest in a multilevel analysis needs to be taken into account when considering statistical power (e.g., γ_{00}, γ_{10}, γ_{01}, γ_{11}, τ_{00}, and τ_{11}); specifically, for a given sample size and ICC, the statistical power for the parameters for simple fixed effects, variance components, and cross-level interactions will differ. On the basis of the existing simulation research, statistical power is generally higher for simple fixed effect (e.g., γ_{00}, γ_{10}, and γ_{01})

and variance components (e.g., τ_{00} and τ_{11}) than for cross-level interactions (e.g., γ_{11}).

In addition to the type of parameter, the magnitude of the chosen parameter is important to consider when estimating statistical power. As is true with single-level research, larger effects generally have larger statistical power than smaller effects at any given sample size. Mathieu et al. (2012) reported a mean value for the cross-level interaction parameter of .11 (i.e., γ_{11}; labeled as γ_{1w} in Mathieu et al.'s Table 1). They found values ranging from −.06 to .48 in the articles reporting multilevel research in the *Journal of Applied Psychology* between 2000 and 2010. Mathieu et al. also reported a mean value of .11 for the fixed effect of the Level 2 predictor (i.e., γ_{01}; labeled as γ_{0w} in Mathieu et al.'s Table 1). They found values ranging from −.23 to .56 in the articles reporting multilevel research in the *Journal of Applied Psychology* between 2000 and 2010.

As noted by Mathieu et al. (2012) and others (Snijders, 2005; Snijders & Bosker, 1993), estimating the value of model parameters for multilevel power analysis is challenging. Estimating or computing the values of these parameters is challenging because there is limited guidance in the form of rules of thumb to use when making these estimates (Mathieu et al., 2012; Raudenbush & Liu, 2000).

Other Factors

Several other factors have the potential to impact statistical power in multilevel research. One of them is the use of *covariates* at Level 1 (e.g., Raudenbush, 1997). Covariates have the potential to reduce the between-group variance and correspondingly shift the optimal allocation of sample size at each level. The use of covariates can impact the optimal allocation of the sample such that a smaller Level 2 sample size and larger Level 1 sample size is preferable (Reise & Duan, 2003). Given that cost of sampling Level 2 units is typically greater than sampling Level 1 units, the use of covariates may provide organizational researchers a practical way to increase statistical power in their multilevel research designs.

Measurement error is another factor that is rarely considered in the estimation of statistical power (Mathieu et al., 2012). Measurement error can lead to larger standard errors, which in turn result in lower statistical power. In their simulation study, Mathieu et al. (2012) found that the reliability of scores on the Level 1 outcome, Level 1 predictor, and Level 2 predictor were statistically significant factors in determining multilevel statistical power. However, the magnitude of those effects was small. Nevertheless, the reliability estimates of the predictors and criteria should be considered when making judgments about the anticipated level of statistical power that can be achieved in a research study as well as the level of power that was actually achieved once the study has been completed.

Although specific guidance for researchers to use when considering the impact of measurement reliability on multilevel statistical power estimates is limited, the results of Mathieu et al.'s (2012) simulation allow for a few general recommendations. Their results make clear that measurement error had a small but meaningful impact on multilevel statistical power compared with the other factors they consider (e.g., sample sizes). Thus, when considering strategies to increase multilevel statistical power, strategies focused on increasing reliability (e.g., replacing measures with lower reliability with those showing higher reliability) is likely to be less effective compared to other strategies such as increasing the sample sizes. However, Mathieu et al.'s simulation used reliability estimates that are only in the range of what would be considered acceptable (i.e., reliability ≥.80). The impact of measurement reliability on multilevel statistical power estimates could be greater when considering reliability estimates below .80. If a researcher must use a measure or measures with reliability estimates that are lower than .80, increasing the sample sizes at one or more levels of the research design would be advisable to minimize the impact of the unreliability on the estimate of statistical power. Also, it is likely that measurement error compounds. that use Using multiple measures with lower reliability will have a larger impact than a single measure with low reliability. Therefore, the degree to which a researcher may need to compensate for low reliability with larger samples will vary with the total amount of measurement error across the measures. Additional research is clearly needed to explore these possibilities and provide more specific

guidance on the role of measurement error in multilevel power estimates.

A third factor that can impact statistical power and required sample sizes in multilevel research is the *estimation method*. At this point, however, there is little specific advice that can be offered regarding this factor (Reise & Duan, 2003). The simulation work that does exist suggests that the two primary estimation procedures, restricted maximum likelihood and full maximum likelihood, work equally well. The computations discussed in the subsequent sections assume the use of the restricted maximum likelihood estimation procedure given that it is the more commonly used of the two methods.

It is also important to take into account the centering of the predictors. In multilevel analysis, variables can be either grand mean or group mean centered to represent deviations from the overall mean or deviations from the mean of the given group (Hofmann & Gavin, 1998). Centering of variables at Level 1 and Level 2 is a common practice in multilevel research. It is recommended for use depending on the specific research question (Enders & Tofighi, 2007). The centering of predictors can lead to less ambiguous interpretations about the nature of cross-level interactions by disentangling the between-group and within-group variance at Level 1 in the interaction with the Level 2 predictor (Mathieu et al., 2012). Disentangling the within- and between-group variance at Level 1 can impact the value of the ICC, which can in turn affect multilevel statistical power.

Interactions Among the Factors

Although the impact of each factor has been discussed separately, they can also have interactive effects on multilevel statistical power. For example, Maas and Hox (2004, 2005) examined the accuracy of the standard errors for fixed effects. They found that Level 2 sample sizes less than 30 led to standard errors that were too small under a moderate to large ICC, but the bias was less extreme under a small ICC. Mathieu et al. (2012) found interactions between the Level 1 and Level 2 sample sizes, between the size of the cross-level interaction and the Level 2 sample size, between the size of the cross-level interaction and the Level 2 sample size, and between the size of the cross-level interaction and standard deviation of the slopes. Currently, these interactive effects are not well understood. Most tools for estimating multilevel statistical power acknowledge these interactive effects and present power under a range of different combinations of the factors that affect statistical power.

ESTIMATING STATISTICAL POWER

In single-level research, the approach for estimating power is fairly direct. One just needs to know or estimate the Type I error rate, the effect size, and the sample size. These three pieces of information allow one to directly compute the power. Multilevel power analysis generally takes a less direct approach. As previously noted, the strategy often taken uses the standard error to estimate multilevel statistical power and is based on the work of Snijders and Bosker (1993). The standard errors are used because they can be easily translated into statistical power using the normal approximation for the distribution of the coefficient that is being estimated (Snijders & Bosker, 1993). In multilevel analyses, the parameters for the simple fixed effects and cross-level interactions are examined using a t test composed of the value of the parameter divided by its standard error. Thus, maximizing power can be achieved through minimizing the standard error. On the basis of the t test, Snijders and Bosker (1993, 1999) derived a formula that can be used to determine the maximum value of the standard error for a coefficient that will achieve a given level of power for a particular two-tailed level of α and effect size:

$$\text{Standard Error} \leq \frac{\text{Effect Size}}{z_{1-\alpha/2} + z_{1-\beta}}, \quad (14.6)$$

where $Z_{1-\alpha/2}$ is the z-score associated with the chosen level of a Type I error for a two-tailed test and $Z_{1-\beta}$ is the z-score associated with the desired level of statistical power. Raudenbush and Liu (2000) offered a standardized effect size that can be used in multilevel statistical power calculations:

$$\ddot{a} = \frac{\tilde{a}_{xx}}{\sqrt{\hat{o}_{xx}^2 + \sigma^2}}, \quad (14.7)$$

where γ_{xx} is the parameter of interest, $\hat{o}_{xx}^2$ is the variance component for the parameter of interest, and σ^2 is the lower level variance component. Raudenbush and Liu suggested that $\delta = 0.20$ is a small effect size, $\delta = 0.50$ is a medium effect size, and $\delta = 0.80$ is a large effect size.

Considering a two-level model for a fixed effect of the difference between an experimental and treatment group, if α were set to 0.05 ($Z_{1-\alpha/2} = 1.96$), the desired level of power was 0.90 ($Z_{1-\beta} = 1.29$), and a medium size effect was of interest ($\delta = 0.50$), the standard errors would need to be less than or equal to $0.15 \left(\text{i.e.,} \frac{0.50}{1.29 + 1.96} \right)$. This formula can also be manipulated so that the level of power ($Z_{1-\beta}$) is determined from the effect size, the level of α, and the standard errors:

$$Z_{1-\beta} \leq \frac{\text{Effect Size}}{\text{Standard Error}} - Z_{1-\alpha/2}. \quad (14.8)$$

Considering a two-level model for a cross-level interaction, if α were set to .05 ($Z_{1-\alpha/2} = 1.96$), a small effect size ($\delta = 0.20$), and the standard error of 0.23, $Z_{1-\beta}$ would be -1.09 $\left(\text{i.e.,} \left(\frac{0.20}{0.23} \right) - 1.96 \right)$ and the statistical power is estimated to be approximately 0.14.

For most situations, determining the desired standard error is relatively straightforward. The difficulty arises when determining the allocation of sample sizes at Level 1 and Level 2 that produce the desired standard errors at a given ICC or range of ICCs. Snijders (2001) even suggested that at best this process is educated guesswork. However, in many situations there are constraints (e.g., work groups have a fixed number of members, or there are a fixed number of work groups) that limit the possible sample sizes at either level. In a multilevel context, maximum power and minimal or desired standard errors are not simple linear functions of the sample size at either level. It is recommended that one compute the standard errors for a variety of Level 1 and Level 2 sample size combinations because sample size choices can then be made that maximize a variety of criteria (e.g., desired power, practicality).

In this chapter, we present the equations for estimating multilevel power for balanced designs (i.e., equal numbers of Level 1 units nested in each Level 2 unit). Although different equations may be used to estimate power in unbalanced designs, a number of authors have suggested that it is acceptable to use the equations for balanced designs and simply substitute the average Level 1 sample size (or minimum Level 1 sample size) into the estimation equations (Longford, 1993; Mathieu et al., 2012; Raudenbush & Bryk, 2002; Scherbaum & Ferreter, 2009; Snijders & Bosker, 1999).

Fixed Effects

Approximate multilevel power computations for simple fixed effects have received the most attention and development in the literature (Scherbaum & Ferreter, 2009). To reiterate the logic of this approach, one first estimates the variance for the parameter of interest, and then one estimates the values of the Level 1 and Level 2 sample sizes needed to achieve a minimal or desired value for the standard error given the variance. The standard error can then be used in Equation 14.8 to estimate the statistical power. The statistical power for tests of γ_{00} are not typically the primary focus of organizational researchers and are thus not considered here; instead, our focus is on the equations for estimating the standard errors for γ_{01}. Raudenbush (1997) described the equation for estimating the variance for the fixed effects of the slope term in the Level 2 equation predicting Level 1 intercepts (i.e., γ_{01} in Equation 14.4) as follows:

$$var(\gamma_{01}) = \frac{4(\tau_{00} + \sigma^2/n)}{J}. \qquad (14.9)$$

This formula can be rewritten as (see Raudenbush et al., 2011; Spybrook et al., 2011)

$$var(\gamma_{01}) = \frac{4(\rho + (1-\rho)/n)}{J}. \qquad (14.10)$$

The standard error of γ_{01} is computed by taking the square root of $var(\gamma_{01})$,

$$S.E.(\gamma_{01}) = \sqrt{var(\gamma_{01})}, \qquad (14.11)$$

where τ_{00} is the variance of the Level 2 intercept term, σ^2 is the Level 1 variance, ρ is the ICC (see Equation 14.5), J is the Level 2 sample size, and n is the Level 1 sample size (i.e., minimum or average within-group sample size with unbalanced designs). The computation of the ICC should be based on the values of τ and σ^2 for the model being studied. For fixed effects models, these values typically come from the regression with means as outcomes model or the intercepts and slopes as outcomes model (Raudenbush & Bryk, 2002).

To understand the estimation of statistical power for a fixed effect (i.e., γ_{01}), consider as an example a research study examining the impact of a leader development program (Level 2) on the performance of employees reporting to a leader (Level 1). A medium effect size (e.g., $\delta = 0.50$) is the minimum effect of interest for the researcher. A two-tailed α of .05 is used in the statistical tests. On the basis of previous research in the leadership development literature, the researcher estimates the ICC to be $\rho = 0.25$. Given the size of the organization and the leader development budget, the researcher believes $J = 20$ leaders will be available, with 10 participating in the development program and the other 10 serving as a control group. The researcher plans to sample 10 employees reporting to each leader. Plugging these values into Equation 14.10 and Equation 14.11 yields an estimated standard error of 0.254 for γ_{01}

$$\left(\text{i.e., } \sqrt{\frac{4\left(0.25 + \frac{(1-0.25)}{10}\right)}{20}}\right).$$ Using these values

in Equation 14.8 produces a value of 0.00 for $Z_{1-\beta}$ $\left(\text{i.e., } \left(\frac{0.50}{0.254}\right) - 1.96\right)$. The statistical power is the probability associated with this Z-score, and in this case the probability associated with a Z of 0.00 is 0.50, which is a modest level of statistical power.

The researcher may want to increase the power to a value above 0.80. In this example, he or she can increase the number of leaders (i.e., Level 2) or increase the number of employees sampled from each leader (i.e., Level 1). To illustrate the impact of changing the number of leaders or the number of subordinates nested within leaders, Figure 14.1 displays power curves for various sample sizes at

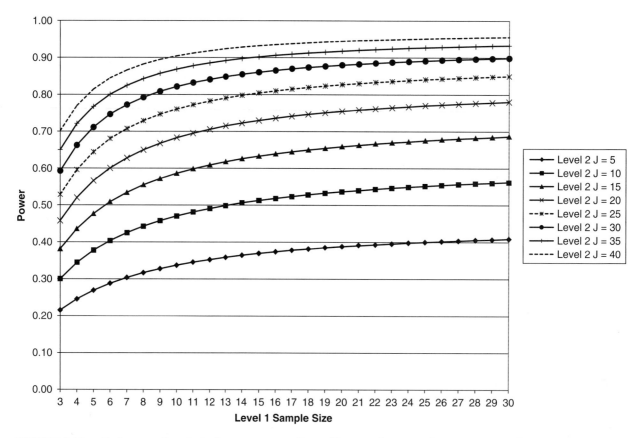

FIGURE 14.1.   Estimates of statistical power at a medium effect size for γ_{01} under varying sample sizes at Level 1 and Level 2.

Level 1 and Level 2 for a medium effect size (i.e., $\delta = 0.50$). This figure was created using Microsoft Excel, the data from the example, Equation 14.10, Equation 14.11, and Equation 14.8. As can be seen in the figure, increasing the sample size at Level 2 has a much greater impact on statistical power for this effect than increasing the sample size at Level 1. For example, if the sample size at Level 2 is $J = 20$ leaders, and the sample size at Level 1 is $n = 10$ employees (per leader), the estimate of the statistical power is 0.50. If one were to increase the number of employees to $n = 20$ (per leader), the estimate of statistical power is only 0.55. Thus, doubling the sample size at Level 1 increases power by 10%. In contrast, if a researcher retains $n = 10$ subordinates per leader, but doubles the number of leaders to $J = 40$, power increases to 0.79, which is a 58% increase in power (see also Figure 14.1).

Much of the work on multilevel power originally comes from the literature on multistage sampling (e.g., Cochran, 1977). In multistage sampling, the

cost associated sampling units at each stage is a major consideration. The cost of sampling units at different levels can be substantially different, with higher level units being more expensive to sample than lower-level unit. In multistage studies, researchers seek to optimize the allocation of sample sizes at each level, given the total project budget and the cost of sampling from each level. This is a similar question faced by multilevel researchers. Cost considerations have been integrated into the formulas for estimating multilevel statistical power (see Raudenbush, 1997, or Snijders, 2001).

In the multistage sampling literature, the relationship between the cost of sampling at each level and the total cost is expressed as follows:

$$\text{Total budget} = CJ + cnJ, \qquad (14.12)$$

where C is the cost of sampling a Level 2 unit, J is the sample size at Level 2, c is the cost of sampling a Level 1 unit, and n is the sample size at Level 1. For example, if the total budget is $100,000, sampling a leader costs $10,000, and sampling an employee costs $1,000, a researcher could allocate samples ranging from one extreme of $J = 9$ leaders and $n = 1$ employee nested within each leader to the other extreme of $J = 1$ leader and $n = 90$ employees nested within this single leader.

To estimate the *optimal* sample size at Level 1 given the sampling costs,

$$n_{optimal} = \sqrt{\frac{\sigma^2}{\tau_{00}}} * \sqrt{\frac{C}{c}}. \qquad (14.13)$$

The optional sample size at Level 2 can be computed as

$$J_{optimal} = \frac{T}{(n_{optimal} \times c) + C}, \qquad (14.14)$$

where T is the total budget. For our scenario (setting $\sigma^2 = 0.75$ and $\tau_{00} = 0.25$) we obtain $n_{optimal} = 1.83$

$\left(\text{i.e., } \sqrt{\frac{0.25}{0.75}} \times \sqrt{\frac{\$10,000}{\$1,000}} \right)$ and $J_{optimal} = 8.45$

$\left(\text{i.e., } \frac{\$100,000}{(1.83 * \$1,000) + \%10,000} \right)$; rounding these

values to the nearest whole number yields optimal sample sizes of $J = 8$ leaders and $n = 2$ subordinates (per leader).

One can then use these values with Equations 14.10, 14.11, and 14.8 to estimate the statistical power. If we assume a medium effect size (e.g., $\delta = 0.50$), a two-tailed α of 0.05, and $\rho = 0.25$., we can plug these values and our optional sample sizes into Equation 14.10, and Equation 14.11 yields an estimated standard error of 0.559 for γ_{01}

$\left(\text{i.e., } \sqrt{\left(\frac{4\left(0.25 + \frac{(1-0.25)}{2} \right)}{8} \right)} \right)$. Using these

values in Equation 14.8 produces a value of -1.07 for $Z_1 - \beta$ $\left(\text{i.e., } \left(\frac{0.50}{0.559} \right) - 1.96 \right)$ and an estimated statistical power is 0.14. Thus, in this particular cost optimization scenario, we are unable to achieve a satisfactory level of statistical power. Our inability to obtain acceptable power is driven by the extreme cost associated with obtaining data from leaders (i.e., $C = \$10,000$/leader) relative to our overall

budge (i.e., $T = \$100,000$). Thus, faced with this scenario, we might strive to identify mechanisms for lower the costs of data collection or securing more funding for the collection of additional data.

For example, holding all other parameters constant, if we were able to lower the cost of data collection to $2,500/leader and $250/subordinate, we would obtain new optimal sample sizes of approximately $n = 2$ subordinates per leader

$\left(\text{i.e., } \sqrt{\frac{0.25}{0.75}} \times \sqrt{\frac{\$2,500}{\$250}} \right)$ and $J = 34$ leaders

$\left(\text{i.e., } \frac{\$100,000}{(1.83 * \$250) + \$2,500} \right)$. Using these new

values in Equation 14.10 and Equation 14.11 yields an estimated standard error of 0.271 for γ_{01}

$\left(\text{i.e., } \sqrt{\left(\frac{4\left(0.25 + \frac{(1-0.25)}{2} \right)}{34} \right)} \right)$. Using these values

in Equation 14.8 produces a value of -0.115 for $Z_{1-\beta}$ $\left(\text{i.e., } \left(\frac{0.50}{0.271} \right) - 1.96 \right)$ and an estimated statistical of 0.45, which represents a 214% increase in statistical power.

Cross-Level Interactions

Estimating the statistical power of cross-level interactions is much more complicated than estimating the power of simple fixed effects (Mathieu et al., 2012; Scherbaum & Ferreter, 2009; Spybrook et al., 2016). With the exception of the work of Mathieu et al. (2012) and Spybrook et al. (2016), the majority of the literature on the statistical power of cross-level interactions is conceptual (e.g., Hox, 2002; Kreft & de Leeuw, 1998; Snijders & Bosker, 1999). As Snijders (2005) noted, there are no clear formulae for some general cases of complex multilevel models. Computationally, the primary difficulty is estimating the standard errors. Snijders and Bosker's (1993) derivation of formulas for estimating the statistical power of cross-level interactions requires more than 30 equations in matrix algebra. In their formulation, a large number of factors must be estimated, including the means, variances, and covariances for the predictor variables at both levels, the sample sizes at each level, and the variances and covariances for the random effects. These values are notoriously difficult to estimate a priori.

Although Mathieu et al. (2012) did not provide the specific formula they used to estimate the power of cross-level interactions, they did present an approach to estimate statistical power for cross-level interactions. Their approach incorporates many of the same factors as Snijders and Bosker (1993) but explicitly considers the magnitude of the cross-level interaction and the direct effects of the Level 1 and Level 2 predictors. Most recently, Spybrook et al. (2016) presented formulas for cross-level interactions in two- and three-level models in the context of cluster randomized experimental studies with Level 1 and Level 2 covariates. Given that these designs are not common in organizational research, we do not review these formulas in detail.

VARIANCE COMPONENTS

Much less research has focused on the statistical power for tests involving the variance components. These estimates are a function of the sample size, the variables at both levels of analysis, and the variance estimates themselves (M. Cohen, 1998; Khuri, 2000). Most of this work has focused on the estimates for the standard errors for the variance components of the Level 2 intercept term (τ_{00}). Estimates for the standard errors for the variance component in the Level 2 slope term (τ_{11}) are much more complex and not well documented. As Snijders and Bosker (1999) noted, there is no simple or well-developed approach to estimating the standard errors for this parameter. Despite the interest in this parameter, there is little guidance that can be provided at this point.

Longford (1993) derived estimates for the variance of τ_{00}, as well as for σ^2. Longford's equation for the variance of τ_{00} can be rewritten as follows:

$$\text{var}(\tau_{00}) = \frac{2\sigma^4}{nJ}\left(\frac{1}{n-1} + 2\left(\frac{\tau_{00}}{\sigma^2}\right) + n\left(\frac{\tau_{00}}{\sigma^2}\right)^2\right),$$ (14.15)

where J is the sample size at Level 2, n is the sample size at Level 1, σ^2 is the within-group variance, σ^4 is the standard deviation raised to the 4th power, and τ_{00} is the between-group variance for

the intercept term. When using these formulas, one will need to take the square root of σ^2 to determine σ for the purpose of computing σ^4. The standard error is computed by taking the square root of the variance:

$$S.E.(\tau_{00}) = \sqrt{\text{var}(\tau_{00})}.$$ (14.16)

Longford's formula for the Level 1 variance component is as follows:

$$\text{var}(\sigma^2) = \frac{2\sigma^4}{nJ - J},$$ (14.17)

where J, n, σ^2, and σ^4 are the same as above. The standard error is computed by taking the square root of the variance:

$$S.E.(\sigma^2) = \sqrt{\text{var}(\sigma^2)}.$$ (14.18)

Continuing with a leader development example, the organization may want to know whether there is already systematic variability between leaders in employee performance before implementing a development program. The organization is interested only in determining whether a at least a medium sized effect exists (i.e., $\delta = .50$) and can provide access to a maximum of 20 leaders. There is an average of five employees per leader. The researcher estimates the ICC to be 0.078 and the value of τ_{00} to be 0.16. The formula for the ICC (see Equation 14.5) can be rearranged to solve for σ^2 $\left(\text{i.e., } \hat{\sigma}^2 = \frac{\hat{o}_{00} - (\hat{o}_{00} \times \tilde{n})}{p}\right)$. Using the provided values, σ^2 equals 1.9 $\left(\text{i.e., } \sigma^2 = \frac{0.16 - (0.16 \times 0.078)}{0.078}\right)$ and σ equals 1.38. By substituting these values into Equation 14.15 and Equation 14.16, the standard error of the variance component of the Level 2 intercept is estimated to be 0.18 $\left(\text{i.e., } \sqrt{\frac{2 \times 1.38^4}{20*5}\left(\frac{1}{5-1} + 2\left(\frac{0.16}{1.90}\right) + 5\left(\frac{0.16}{1.90}\right)^2\right)}\right)$. Substituting this value into Equation 14.8 with a value of $\delta = 0.50$ for the effect size and 1.96 for $Z_{1-\alpha/2}$, results in a value of $Z_{1-\beta} = 0.80$ $\left(\text{i.e., } \left(\frac{0.50}{0.18}\right) - 1.96\right)$ and an estimated statistical power of 0.78.

M. Cohen (1998) presented an approach to integrate the cost of sampling and the total budget into the computation of the optimal sample sizes for variance components. To compute the optimal sample size at Level 1 for the variance of τ_{00},

$$n_{optimal} = \frac{1}{2w} + \sqrt{2\left(\frac{C}{c}\right) * \frac{1}{w} + \frac{1}{4w^2}}, \quad (14.19)$$

where $w = \tau_{00} / \sigma^2$. This result can be substituted into Equation 14.14 to determine the optimal sample size at Level 2. These sample sizes can be substituted into Equation 14.15 to determine the variance and subsequently the standard errors for the Level 2 variance component for the intercept from Equation 14.16. The sample sizes can be substituted into Equations 14.17 and 14.18 for variance of the Level 1 variance component. These standard errors can then be substituted into Equation 14.8 to estimate the statistical power.

Assuming the leadership development program has a budget of $50,000, sampling a leader costs $1,000, sampling an employee costs $200, $\sigma^2 = 1.90$ and $\tau_{00} = 0.16$, we obtain $n_{optimal} = 77.28$

$$\left(\text{i.e., } \frac{1}{2\left(\frac{0.16}{1.90}\right)} + \sqrt{2\left(\frac{\$1,000}{\$200}\right) \times \frac{1}{\left(\frac{0.16}{1.90}\right)} + \frac{1}{4\left(\frac{0.16}{1.90}\right)^4}} \right) \text{ and}$$

$J_{optimal} = 3.04 \left(\text{i.e., } \frac{\$50,000}{(77.28 * \$200) + \$1,000} \right);$

rounding these values to the nearest whole number yields optimal sample sizes of $n = 77$ subordinates (per leader) and $J = 3$ leaders.

One can then use these values with Equations 14.15, 14.16, and 14.8 to estimate the statistical power. If we assume a medium effect size (e.g., $\delta = 0.50$) and a two-tailed α of .05, we can plug these values and the optional sample sizes into Equation 14.15 and Equation 14.16, which yields an estimated standard error of 0.15 for τ_{00}

$$\left(\text{i.e., } \sqrt{\frac{2 * 1.38^4}{77 * 3}\left(\frac{1}{77-1} + 2\left(\frac{0.16}{0.73}\right) + 77\left(\frac{0.16}{0.73}\right)^2\right)} \right). \text{ Using these}$$

values in Equation 14.8 produces a value of 1.37 for $Z_{1-\beta} \left(\text{i.e., } \left(\frac{0.50}{0.15}\right) - 1.96 \right)$ and an estimated statistical power of 0.913.

RESOURCES FOR ESTIMATING MULTILEVEL STATISTICAL POWER

There are several resources currently available for computing estimates of multilevel statistical power. The resources vary primarily in the research designs for which they are best suited and the types of effects that can be estimated. We review several of the most widely accessible resources that are currently available. This is likely to be an evolving area with new resources being developed and existing resources being refined. In the following section, we provide an example of using each resource. A summary of the programs and the effects they are best suited for are presented in Table 14.1.

Optimal Design

Raudenbush and colleagues (Raudenbush et al., 2011; Spybrook et al., 2011) have developed a program called *Optimal Design* that estimates power for fixed effects using the ICC, effect size, the Type I error rate, and sample sizes at higher and lower levels for intervention studies using a wide variety of cluster-randomized, multisite, and repeated measures designs. The program offers the user a good deal of flexibility with a minimum number of required inputs. The program is structured such that the user can manipulate one factor at a time to examine the impact of that factor alone on

TABLE 14.1

Multilevel Power Estimation Programs

Program	Fixed effects	Cross-level interactions
Optimal Design	X	
Scherbaum and Ferreter's Excel Program	X	
PowerUp!	X	X
PINT	X	X
Multilevel power tool		X

Note. PINT = Power in Two Levels.

statistical power. The results are presented graphically as power curves, which are helpful for understanding how power could be impacted by particular changes in sample sizes, effect sizes, and the ICC. The program is user friendly, comes with extensive documentation on the software, and covers the underlying power formulas used in the software. The Optimal Design program and user manual are available for download at https://sites.google.com/site/optimaldesignsoftware/home.

To use the program, the researcher needs to select the type of research design (e.g., cluster randomized design) and the type of power curve to display (e.g., power vs. Level 2 sample size). The user then clicks on icons related to the lower level sample size (n), the higher level sample size (J), the Type I error rate (α), the effect size (δ), and the ICC to enter the desired values. With the values of the parameters selected, the program plots the power curves.

Scherbaum and Ferreter's Excel Program

Scherbaum and Ferreter (2009) developed a program in Microsoft Excel to compute the multilevel statistical power of simple fixed effects. The program requires the user to input the ICC, the Level 1 variance, the Level 2 variance of the intercept term, and the effect size. The user can then enter a range of Level 1 and Level 2 sample sizes in order to understand their impact on statistical power. The results are presented graphically as power curves, which is helpful for understanding how statistical power could be impacted by particular changes in sample sizes, effect sizes, and the ICC. The Excel program is available by emailing the first author at charles.scherbaum@baruch.cuny.edu.

To use the program, the researcher needs to enter the Level 1 variance (σ^2), the Level 2 variance (τ_{00}), the effect size (δ), the Level 1 sample size (n), and Level 2 sample size (J). If the researcher has an estimate of the ICC, this value can be entered instead of the Level 1 and Level 2 variance components. With the values of the parameters entered, the worksheet produces power curves based on the provided parameters.

PowerUp!

Spybrook and colleagues (Dong & Maynard, 2013; Dong, Kelcey, Spybrook, & Maynard, 2016) developed a Microsoft Excel program called *PowerUp!*

that estimates the minimal detectable effects and required sample sizes for simple fixed effects and cross-level interactions in two-, three-, or four-level models for several different types of experimental designs. The program does not compute statistical power directly, but the higher level sample sizes and effect sizes needed to achieve a desired level of statistical power. Depending on the calculation selected, the required inputs include the ICC, the sample sizes at the higher and lower levels, the number of variables at each level, the Type I error rate, the desired level of power, and the minimum effect size of interest. The program also allows inputs-related experimental designs (e.g., retention rate in each condition). The output of the program is either the sample size required at the higher level or analysis or the minimum effect size needed to achieve a given level of statistical power. The PowerUp! is available for download at http://www.causalevaluation.org/. There is also an online version of PowerUp! using R (see https://www.r-project.org/) that can be used to consider the impact of cost constraints.

The Excel program can guide the user through the choices about the research designs and provides the opportunity to input the required parameters. The specific parameters required will vary on the basis of the selected research design and selected output of either the calculation for minimum effect size or required sample size. However, the basic input for all options includes the lower level sample size (n), the Type I error rate (α), the number of tails in the statistical test, the ICC, the proportion of the sample randomized to the treatment, and the number of covariates at each level. Depending on the calculation selected, the higher level sample size (J) or the minimum desired effect size (δ) can be entered and, depending on the calculation selected, the higher level sample size (J) or the minimum effect size (δ) needed to achieve the given level of statistical power is computed.

Power in Two Levels

Snijders, Bosker, and colleagues (Snijders & Bosker, 1993; Snijders, Bosker, & Guldemond, 1996) developed a Windows-based program called Power in Two Levels (PINT). This program estimates the standard errors of simple fixed effects and cross-level interactions for a variety of complex two-level models. The major difficultly in using this program is that it requires the user to input a large number of estimated parameters, including

- the number of Level 1 variables,
- the number of Level 1 variables with fixed effects only,
- the number of Level 2 variables,
- the means of the Level 2 predictor variables,
- the variances and covariances for the Level 2 predictors,
- the variances and covariances for the Level 1 predictors,
- the minimum and maximum sample size at Level 2,
- the total cost, and
- the relative cost of sampling a Level 2 unit compared to a Level 1 unit.

For example, if the cost of a Level 2 unit is $10,000 and the cost of a Level 1 unit is $1,000, the relative cost is 10.

The results are generated in an output file, which includes the parameters used in the calculations and the value of the standard error for each parameter in the model for varying sample sizes and costs. These values can then be used with Equation 14.8 to compute the estimated statistical power. An extensive user manual and the formulas used by the program are presented in Snijders and Bosker (1993) and Snijders (2001, 2005). The program guides the user through a series of windows to input the required values. This program is ideal for multilevel models that include several Level 1 or Level 2 variables or any complex multilevel model. The PINT program and user manual are available for download for at https://www.stats.ox.ac.uk/~snijders/multilevel.htm.

Multilevel Power Tool

Mathieu et al. (2012) developed a program in R called the *Multilevel Power Tool* that can be used to estimate the multilevel statistical power of cross-level interactions. The program requires the user to input a number of estimates including

- the average Level 1 sample size (n),
- the Level 2 sample size (J),

- the ICC for the Level 1 predictor,
- the variance components for Level 2,
- the variance component for Level 1,
- the Level 1 effect of the predictor,
- the direct cross-level effect of the Level 2 predictor,
- the between group interaction effect obtained between the means on the Level 1 predictor and Level 2 predictor,
- the intercept of the Level 2 intercept term, and
- the cross-level interaction effect.

The output of the program is the estimate of the statistical power for the cross-level interaction based on the inputs provided. The Multilevel Power Tool program in R is available for download at http://hermanaguinis.com/crosslevel.html. A web-based version using a graphic interface is available at https://aguinis.shinyapps.io/ml_power/.

EXAMPLE USES OF THE RESOURCES FOR ESTIMATING MULTILEVEL STATISTICAL POWER

In this section, we provide an example of using each program. We demonstrate the use of Optimal Design, the Excel worksheets from Scherbaum and Ferreter (2009), and PowerUp! for the multilevel statistical power of fixed effects in an experimental design as these programs are best suited for these effects and designs. We demonstrate the use of PINT and the Multilevel Power Tool in the context of a cross-level interaction in a nonexperimental research design as these programs are well equipped for these effects and designs.

Fixed Effects

An organization is interested in determining whether moving to a pay for performance compensation strategy will improve employee productivity. The organization wishes to conduct a pilot test of the pay-for-performance system to evaluate its effectiveness before implementing the system in the entire organization. Given concerns about diffusion of treatment, the organization randomly assigns entire organizational units to remain on the current compensation plan or participate in the new pay-for-performance plan. All employees in the unit participated in the assigned plan. Given the level and nature of randomization, this example can be considered a cluster randomized design. In this research study, there are 20 organizational unit participating in the pilot study with 10 units assigned to each condition, each unit contains an average of 30 employees, a Type I error rate of 0.05 will be used, the organization is interested in at least a medium effect size ($\delta = 0.50$), and the ICC is estimated to be 0.15. The researcher will use these inputs to estimate of statistical power for the test of the fixed effect associated with the compensation strategy (γ_{01}).

Using the Optimal Design program, we select the option for cluster randomized trials and the power versus Level 2 sample chart. We input the values for the ICC, effect size, Level 1 sample size, Level 2 sample size, and Type I error rate. Using the graph produced by these inputs, we can see that the estimate of statistical power is approximately 0.80 for the test of the fixed effect for the intervention (γ_{01}) at a Level 2 sample size of 20. Thus, given the estimated parameters the researcher should have a reasonable level of power to test the fixed effect associated with the compensation system.

Using the Scherbaum and Ferreter (2009) spreadsheet, we input the values for the ICC, effect size, Level 1 sample size, Level 2 sample size and z-score for the Type I error rate (1.96). Using the graph produced by these inputs, we can see that the estimate of statistical power is approximately 0.75 for the test of the fixed effect for the intervention (γ_{01}) at a Level 2 sample size of 20. Thus, given the estimated parameters the researcher should have a reasonable level of power to test the fixed effect associated with the compensation system.

Using the PowerUp! program, we selected the cluster-randomized assignment research design and Model 3.1, which is the appropriate option for a two-level model. Using the worksheet for the required sample sizes and using the parameters in Appendix 14.1, the program indicated the required Level 2 sample size to achieve a statistical power of 0.78 for the test of the fixed effect for the intervention (γ_{01}) is 22 organizational units.

Given the parameters that were entered into these programs, each produced similar estimates of the multilevel statistical power or the Level 2

sample sizes for the test of the fixed effect for the intervention (γ_{01}). Thus, each is a reasonable choice for estimating multilevel statistical power for a fixed effect. The choice among the programs could be driven by the desire for graphical versus numerical output and the flexibility to create different graphs of the factors impacting statistical power.

Cross-Level Interactions

A researcher is conducting a nonexperimental study examining how leader characteristics can moderate the relationship between employee engagement and employee organizational citizenship behaviors. In particular, the researcher is interested in the cross-level interaction involving leader charisma (Level 2) on the relationships between employee engagement and organizational citizenship behaviors (Level 1). The estimated values of the needed inputs for PINT and the Multilevel Power Tool are presented in Appendix 14.2 and Appendix 14.3. The researcher will use these inputs to estimate statistical power for the test of the cross-level interaction associated with the leader's charisma (γ_{11}). It is important to note that the input into these programs is different, so the results may not be directly comparable. The major difference is that PINT requires the means of the Level 2 predictor variables and the variance and covariance of all of the predictor variables and the Multilevel Power Tool requires the estimates of the coefficients for the predictor variables. Thus, the choice between these two programs may be driven by the availability of either set of information.

Using the PINT program, we enter the parameters in Appendix 14.2 into the interface. First, the program asks for the number of Level 1 predictors, the number of Level 1 predictors with fixed effects, the number of Level 2 predictors and the location of where the output files will be saved. On the basis of the number of predictors at Level 1 and Level 2, the program will adjust the subsequent input to capture the means, variances, and covariance for all of the variables. For this example, the program will ask for the means and variances of the one Level 1 variable and the one 2-level variable. The program will not ask for the covariance given the single variable at each level. However, the program would ask for this information if there were more variables at either level.

On the following screens, the program asks the user to input the mean of the Level 2 predictors, the value of the within-groups variance components (σ^2) and covariance. The program asks the user whether budget constraints should be used or whether all possible sample size combinations should be used. If the user chooses to look at all possible combinations, the program will ask for the maximum Level 2 sample size, the maximum Level 1 sample size, the minimum Level 1 sample size, and the size of the increments to report on the changes in the Level 1 and Level 2 sample size. If the user decides to select budget constraints, the program asks for the total budget, the relative costs of a Level 2 unit compared with a Level 1 unit, the minimum and maximum Level 2 sample sizes, as well as the size of the increments to report on the changes in the Level 1 and Level 2 sample size. Once the choice about the use of budget constraint has been entered, the program asks the user whether the standard errors should be computed, the input file saved only, or if the program should quit. When the user selects to compute the standard errors, the program will create the output file with the results and the program will close.

Using the parameters in Appendix 14.2, the PINT program produced the values for the standard error under several model parameters, shown in Table 14.2. These standard errors can then be used with Equation 14.8 to estimate the statistical power. Using these values of the standard error with a medium effect size ($\delta = .20$) and a Type I error rate of 0.05 in Equation 14.8 produces the statistical power estimates presented in Table 14.3. Using these values in Table 14.3, the researcher can see that statistical power of the test of the cross-level interaction will generally be low. In this case, increasing the Level 2 sample size or increasing the Level 1 sample size within a Level 2 sample size will have a positive impact on power.

Using the Multilevel Power Tool, we entered the parameter in Appendix 14.3 into the web-based interface. The interface is a single screen and the user can run the simulation after inputting the values. The program indicated that the statistical power for the test of the cross-level interaction (γ_{11}) is 0.359. Given this is a low level of power,

the impact of adding additional leaders (Level 2) or additional employees (Level 1) will be positive. If the researcher could add 10 additional leaders to the study, the statistical power would increase to 0.588. If the researcher could add 10 additional employees reporting to each leader to the study, the statistical power would increase to 0.560. In this case, increasing either the Level 1 or Level 2 sample size could increase power to about the same degree. The researcher could examine the various combinations of the two sample sizes to determine the most feasible increase in the sample sizes to produce the highest level of statistical power.

One interesting point is that with similar inputs, the PINT program and Multilevel Power Tool produce different estimates of the statistical power with the Multilevel Power Tool producing lower estimates than the PINT program. The difference in the two programs is likely driven by the difference in the inputs for the predictors. Also, the calculations of power for the PINT program explicitly requires an estimate of the effect size (via Equation 14.8). Given that the equations for the Multilevel Power Tool were not included in Mathieu et al. (2012), the role of an effect size in the calculation is not clear. Given these differences in the estimates, future research is clearly needed to compare these programs more directly and systematically.

CONCLUSION

Given the pervasiveness of multilevel analyses in organizational research and the increasing accessibility of tools for conducting multilevel power analysis, the incorporation of multilevel power analysis into our practices of designing and reporting organizational research is needed (e.g., Aguinis et al., 2013; Mathieu et al., 2012; Scherbaum & Ferreter, 2009). The rules that apply to single-level power analysis do not necessarily apply to multilevel research and cannot be used as a substitute. The goals of this chapter were to acquaint researchers with the basic aspects of power analyses in the most commonly encountered multilevel context and to familiarize researchers with the primary approaches and available tools for computing multilevel power.

TABLE 14.2

Standard Errors From Example Power in Two Levels Analysis

Total sample size ($N \times n$)	Level 1 sample size (N)	Level 2 sample size (n)	SE of γ_{00} (const.)	SE of γ_{10} (group)	SE of τ_{11} (random)	SE of γ_{10} (cross-L)
60	10	6	0.305	0.123	0.380	0.153
66	11	6	0.290	0.117	0.362	0.146
72	12	6	0.278	0.112	0.347	0.139
78	13	6	0.267	0.107	0.333	0.134
84	14	6	0.257	0.104	0.321	0.129
90	15	6	0.249	0.100	0.310	0.125
96	16	6	0.241	0.097	0.300	0.121
102	17	6	0.234	0.094	0.291	0.117
108	18	6	0.227	0.091	0.283	0.114
114	19	6	0.221	0.089	0.275	0.111
120	20	6	0.215	0.087	0.269	0.108
80	10	8	0.265	0.106	0.348	0.140
88	11	8	0.252	0.101	0.332	0.134
96	12	8	0.241	0.097	0.318	0.128
104	13	8	0.232	0.093	0.306	0.123
112	14	8	0.224	0.090	0.294	0.118
120	15	8	0.216	0.087	0.284	0.114
128	16	8	0.209	0.084	0.275	0.111
136	17	8	0.203	0.082	0.267	0.107
144	18	8	0.197	0.079	0.260	0.104
152	19	8	0.192	0.077	0.253	0.102
160	20	8	0.187	0.075	0.246	0.099
100	10	10	0.237	0.095	0.328	0.132
110	11	10	0.226	0.091	0.313	0.126
120	12	10	0.217	0.087	0.299	0.120
130	13	10	0.208	0.084	0.288	0.116
140	14	10	0.200	0.081	0.277	0.112
150	15	10	0.194	0.078	0.268	0.108
160	16	10	0.187	0.075	0.259	0.104
170	17	10	0.182	0.073	0.252	0.101
180	18	10	0.177	0.071	0.245	0.098
190	19	10	0.172	0.069	0.238	0.096
200	20	10	0.168	0.067	0.232	0.093

<h2>TABLE 14.3</h2>

Estimated Statistical Power From Example Power in Two Levels Analysis

Total sample size ($N \times n$)	Level 1 sample size (N)	Level 2 sample size (n)	Z-score for the Type I error rate ($Z_{1-\alpha/2}$)	Effect size (δ)	Z-score for the Type II error rate $Z_{1-\beta}$	Estimated statistical power
60	10	6	1.96	0.2	−0.651	0.258
66	11	6	1.96	0.2	−0.587	0.279
72	12	6	1.96	0.2	−0.526	0.300
78	13	6	1.96	0.2	−0.467	0.320
84	14	6	1.96	0.2	−0.411	0.341
90	15	6	1.96	0.2	−0.356	0.361
96	16	6	1.96	0.2	−0.304	0.381
102	17	6	1.96	0.2	−0.253	0.400
108	18	6	1.96	0.2	−0.203	0.419
114	19	6	1.96	0.2	−0.155	0.438
120	20	6	1.96	0.2	−0.108	0.457
80	10	8	1.96	0.2	−0.533	0.297
88	11	8	1.96	0.2	−0.463	0.322
96	12	8	1.96	0.2	−0.397	0.346
104	13	8	1.96	0.2	−0.333	0.370
112	14	8	1.96	0.2	−0.271	0.393
120	15	8	1.96	0.2	−0.212	0.416
128	16	8	1.96	0.2	−0.155	0.439
136	17	8	1.96	0.2	−0.099	0.461
144	18	8	1.96	0.2	−0.045	0.482
152	19	8	1.96	0.2	0.007	0.503
160	20	8	1.96	0.2	0.059	0.523
100	10	10	1.96	0.2	−0.445	0.328
110	11	10	1.96	0.2	−0.371	0.355
120	12	10	1.96	0.2	−0.300	0.382
130	13	10	1.96	0.2	−0.232	0.408
140	14	10	1.96	0.2	−0.167	0.434
150	15	10	1.96	0.2	−0.104	0.459
160	16	10	1.96	0.2	−0.043	0.483
170	17	10	1.96	0.2	0.016	0.506
180	18	10	1.96	0.2	0.073	0.529
190	19	10	1.96	0.2	0.129	0.551
200	20	10	1.96	0.2	0.183	0.573

APPENDIX 14.1: PARAMETERS USED IN THE POWERUP! EXAMPLE

Parameter	Value	Label in program
Effect size (δ)	0.5	MRES = MDES
Type I error rate (α)	0.05	Alpha level (α)
Number of tails	2	Two-tailed or one-tailed test?
Desired level of power ($1 - \beta$)	0.75	Power ($1 - \beta$)
ICC	0.15	Rho (ICC)
Average Level 1 sample size (n)	30	n (average cluster size)
Proportion of Level 2 sample retained in the analysis (%)	100	Sample retention rate: Level 2 units
Proportion of Level 1 sample retained in the analysis (%)	100	Sample retention rate: Level 1 units
Proportion of the sample in the experimental condition	0.5	P
Proportion of variance in Level 1 outcome explained by Level 1 covariates	0	R_1^2
Proportion of variance in Level 2 outcome explained by Level 2 covariates	0	R_2^2
Number of Level 2 covariates	0	g^*

Note. ICC = intraclass correlation; MDES = minimum detectable effect size; MRES = minimum relevant effect size.

APPENDIX 14.2: PARAMETERS USED IN THE POWER IN TWO LEVELS EXAMPLE

Parameter	Value	Label in program
Number of Level 1 variables	1	Number of level 1 vars
Number of Level 1 variables with fixed effects only	0	Number of these with fixed effects only
Number of Level 2 variables	1	Number of level 2 vars
Means of the Level 2 predictor variable	2.3	Mean of Level 2 variables
Variance of the Level 1 predictor variable		Within group covariance matrix
Covariances of the Level 1 predictor variables		Within group covariance matrix
Variances of the Level 2 predictor variables	0.89	Between group covariance matrix
Covariances of the Level 2 predictor variables	—	Between group covariance matrix
Variance of the Level 1 variance component	0.79	Level 1 residual variance
Variance of the Level 2 variance component in the intercept term	0.002	Level 2 random effect covariance matrix
Variance of the Level 2 variance component in the slope term	0.076	Level 2 random effect covariance matrix
Covariances of the Level 2 variance components	0.005	Level 2 random effect covariance matrix
Relative cost of a Level 2 unit to a Level 1 unit		Cost parameter
Total budget		Total budget
Minimum Level 1 sample size	6	Minimum group size
Maximum Level 1 sample size	10	Maximum group size
Maximum Level 2 sample size	20	Maximum number of groups
Level 2 sample size increment	2	Step size

APPENDIX 14.3: PARAMETERS USED IN THE MULTILEVEL POWER TOOL EXAMPLE

Parameter	Value	Label in program
Average Level 1 sample size (n)	10	Average Level 1 sample size (n_i)
Level 2 sample size (J)	20	Level 2 sample size (n_j)
ICC for the Level 1 predictor	0.15	ICC1 for X (ρ_x)
Intercept in the Level 2 intercept term (γ_{00})	0.02	Level 1 intercept (γ_{00})
Direct effect of the Level 1 predictor on the outcome (γ_{01})	0.4	Direct cross-level effect of average X_j on Y ($\gamma_{0\bar{x}}$)
Direct cross-level effect of the Level 2 predictor on the outcome (γ_{02})	0.04	Direct cross-level effect of W on Y (γ_{0w})
Between-group interaction effect of the Level 2 and Level 1 predictor on the outcome	0.16	Between-group interaction effect between W and $\bar{X}$ (γ_{0xw})
Intercept in the Level 2 slope term (γ_{10})	0.38	Level 1 effect of X on Y (γ_{10})
Level 2 the cross-level interaction effect (γ_{11})	0.18	Cross-level interaction effect (γ_{1w})
Variance components for the Level 2 intercept (τ_{00})	0.002	Variance component for intercept (τ_{00})
Variance components for the Level 2 slope (τ_{11})	0.076	Variance of Level 1 slopes (τ_{11})
Variance component for Level 1 (σ^2)	0.79	Variance component for residual, within variance (σ^2)
Type I error rate	0.05	Type I error rate
Number of replications	1,000	Number of replications
Seed for random number generator	818	Set seed for random number generator

Note. ICC = intraclass correlation.

References

Afshartous, D. (1995, April). *Determination of sample size for multilevel model design.* Paper presented at the Annual Meeting of the American Educational Research Association, San Francisco, CA.

Aguinis, H., Beaty, J. C., Boik, R. J., & Pierce, C. A. (2005). Effect size and power in assessing moderating effects of categorical variables using multiple regression: A 30-year review. *Journal of Applied Psychology, 90,* 94–107. http://dx.doi.org/10.1037/0021-9010.90.1.94

Aguinis, H., & Culpepper, S. A. (2015). An expanded decision making procedure for examining cross-level interaction effects with multilevel modeling. *Organizational Research Methods, 18,* 155–176. http://dx.doi.org/10.1177/1094428114563618

Aguinis, H., Gottfredson, R. K., & Culpepper, S. A. (2013). Best-practice recommendations for estimating cross-level interaction effects using multilevel modeling. *Journal of Management, 39,* 1490–1528. http://dx.doi.org/10.1177/0149206313478188

Aguinis, H., Pierce, C. A., Bosco, F. A., & Muslin, I. S. (2009). First decade of *Organizational Research Methods*: Trends in design, measurement, and data-analysis topics. *Organizational Research Methods, 12,* 69–112.

Aguinis, H., & Vandenberg, R. J. (2014). An ounce of prevention is worth a pound of cure: Improving research quality before data collection. *Annual Review of Organizational Psychology and Organizational Behavior, 1,* 569–595. http://dx.doi.org/10.1146/annurev-orgpsych-031413-091231

Austin, J. T., Boyle, K. A., & Lualhati, J. C. (1998). Statistical conclusion validity for organizational science researchers: A review. *Organizational ResearchMethods, 1,* 164–208. http://dx.doi.org/10.1177/109442819812002

Austin, J. T., Scherbaum, C. A., & Mahlman, R. A. (2002). History of research methods in industrial and organizational psychology: Measurement, design, analysis. In S. G. Rogelberg (Ed.), *Handbook of research methods in industrial and organizational psychology* (pp. 3–33). Malden, MA: Blackwell.

Bartko, J. J. (1976). On various intraclass correlation reliability coefficients. *Psychological Bulletin, 83,* 762–765. http://dx.doi.org/10.1037/0033-2909.83.5.762

Bassiri, D. (1988). *Large and small sample properties of maximum likelihood estimates for hierarchical linear models* (Unpublished doctoral dissertation). Michigan State University, East Lansing.

Bliese, P. D. (2000). Within-group agreement, non-independence, and reliability: Implications for data aggregation and analysis. In K. J. Klein & S. W. J. Kozlowski (Eds.), *Multilevel theory, research, and methods in organizations: Foundations, extensions, and new directions* (pp. 349–381). San Francisco, CA: Jossey-Bass.

Bliese, P. D., Chan, D., & Ployhart, R. E. (2007). Multilevel methods: Future directions in measurement, longitudinal analyses, and nonnormal outcomes. *Organizational Research Methods, 10*, 551–563. http://dx.doi.org/10.1177/1094428107301102

Browne, W. J., & Draper, D. (2000). Implementation and performance issues in the Bayesian and likelihood fitting of multilevel models. *Computational Statistics, 15*, 391–420. http://dx.doi.org/10.1007/s001800000041

Busing, F. (1993). *Distribution characteristics of variance estimates in two-level models.* Unpublished manuscript, Leiden University, Leiden, the Netherlands.

Chan, D. (2011). Advances in analytical strategies. In S. Zedeck (Ed.), *APA handbook of industrial and organizational psychology* (Vol. 1, pp. 85–113). Washington, DC: American Psychological Association.

Cochran, W. G. (1977). *Sampling techniques* (3rd ed.). New York, NY: Wiley.

Cohen, J. (1988). *Statistical power analysis for the behavioral sciences* (2nd ed.). Hillsdale, NJ: Erlbaum.

Cohen, M. (1998). Determining sample sizes for surveys with data analyzed by hierarchical linear models. *Journal of Official Statistics, 14*, 267–275.

Cunningham, T. D., & Johnson, R. E. (2016). Design effects for sample size computation in three-level designs. *Statistical Methods in Medical Research, 25*, 505–519. http://dx.doi.org/10.1177/0962280212460443

Davison, M. L., Kwak, N., Seo, Y. S., & Choi, J. (2002). Using hierarchical linear models to examine moderator effects: Person-by-organization interaction. *Organizational Research Methods, 5*, 231–254. http://dx.doi.org/10.1177/1094428102005003003

Dong, N., Kelcey, B., Spybrook, J., & Maynard, R. A. (2016). PowerUp! moderator: A tool for calculating statistical power and minimum detectable effect size of the moderator effects in cluster randomized trials (Version 1.05) [Computer software]. Available from http://www.causalevaluation.org/

Dong, N., & Maynard, R. A. (2013). PowerUp!: A tool for calculating minimum detectable effect sizes and minimum required sample sizes for experimental and quasi-experimental design studies. *Journal of Research on Educational Effectiveness, 6*, 24–67. http://dx.doi.org/10.1080/19345747.2012.673143

Enders, C. K., & Tofighi, D. (2007). Centering predictor variables in cross-sectional multilevel models: A new look at an old issue. *Psychological Methods, 12*, 121–138. http://dx.doi.org/10.1037/1082-989X.12.2.121

Harman, R. P., Ellington, J. K., Surface, E. A., & Thompson, L. F. (2015). Exploring qualitative training reactions: Individual and contextual influences on trainee commenting. *Journal of Applied Psychology, 100*, 894–916. http://dx.doi.org/10.1037/a0038380

Hedges, L. V., & Hedberg, E. C. (2007). Intraclass correlation values for planning group-randomized trials in education. *Educational Evaluation and Policy Analysis, 29*, 60–87. http://dx.doi.org/10.3102/0162373707299706

Hofmann, D. A., & Gavin, M. B. (1998). Centering decisions in hierarchical linear models: Implications for research in organizations. *Journal of Management, 24*, 623–641. http://dx.doi.org/10.1177/014920639802400504

Hox, J. J. (1998). Multilevel modeling: When and why. I. Balderjahn, R. Mathar, & M. Schader (Eds.), *Classification, data analysis, and data highways* (pp. 147–154). New York, NY: Springer-Verlag.

Hox, J. J. (2002). *Multilevel analysis: Techniques and applications.* Mahwah, NJ: Erlbaum.

Institute of Education Sciences. (2016). *Research grants request for applications for awards beginning in fiscal year 2017* (Report No. *CFDA Number 84.305A*). Washington, DC: U.S. Department of Education.

Khuri, A. I. (2000). Designs for variance components estimation: Past and present. *International Statistical Review, 68*, 311–322. http://dx.doi.org/10.1111/j.1751-5823.2000.tb00333.x

Kim, K. S. (1990). *Multilevel data analysis: A comparison of analytical alternatives* (Unpublished doctoral dissertation). University of California, Los Angeles.

Kozlowski, S. W., & Klein, K. J. (2000). A multilevel approach to theory and research in organizations: Contextual, temporal, and emergent processes. In K. Klein & S. Kozlowski (Eds.), *Multilevel theory, research, and methods in organizations: Foundations, extensions, and new directions* (pp. 3–90). San Francisco, CA: Jossey-Bass.

Kreft, I. (1996). *Are multilevel techniques necessary? An overview including simulation studies.* Unpublished manuscript, California State University, Los Angeles.

Kreft, I., & de Leeuw, J. (1998). *Introducing multilevel modeling.* Thousand Oaks, CA: Sage. http://dx.doi.org/10.4135/9781849209366

LeBreton, J. M., & Senter, J. L. (2008). Answers to 20 questions about interrater reliability and inter-rater agreement. *Organizational Research Methods, 11*, 815–852. http://dx.doi.org/10.1177/1094428106296642

LaHuis, D. M., Hartman, M. J., Hakoyama, S., & Clark, P. C. (2014). Explained variance measures for multilevel models. *Organizational Research Methods, 17*, 433–451. http://dx.doi.org/10.1177/1094428114541701

Longford, N. T. (1993). *Random coefficients models.* New York, NY: Oxford University Press.

Maas, C. J. M., & Hox, J. J. (2004). Robustness issues in multilevel regression analysis. *Statistica Neerlandica, 58*, 127–137. http://dx.doi.org/10.1046/j.0039-0402.2003.00252.x

Maas, C. J. M., & Hox, J. J. (2005). Sufficient sample sizes for multilevel modeling. *Methodology: European Journal of Research Methods for the Behavioral and Social Sciences, 1*, 86–92. http://dx.doi.org/10.1027/1614-2241.1.3.86

Mathieu, J. E., Aguinis, H., Culpepper, S. A., & Chen, G. (2012). Understanding and estimating the power to detect cross-level interaction effects in multilevel modeling. *Journal of Applied Psychology, 97*, 951–966. http://dx.doi.org/10.1037/a0028380

Mathieu, J. E., & Chen, G. (2011). The etiology of the multilevel paradigm in management research. *Journal of Management, 37*, 610–641. http://dx.doi.org/10.1177/0149206310364663

McNeish, D. M., & Stapleton, L. M. (2016). The effect of small sample size on two-level model estimates: A review and illustration. *Educational Psychology Review, 28*, 295–315.

Mok, M. (1995). Sample size requirements for 2-level designs in educational research. *Multilevel Modelling Newsletter, 7*, 11–15.

Mone, M. A., Mueller, G. C., & Mauland, W. (1996). The perceptions and usage of statistical power in applied psychology and management research. *Personnel Psychology, 49*, 103–120. http://dx.doi.org/10.1111/j.1744-6570.1996.tb01793.x

Peugh, J. L. (2010). A practical guide to multilevel modeling. *Journal of School Psychology, 48*, 85–112. http://dx.doi.org/10.1016/j.jsp.2009.09.002

Raudenbush, S. W. (1988). Educational applications of hierarchical linear models: A review. *Journal of Educational Statistics, 13*, 85–116. http://dx.doi.org/10.3102/10769986013002085

Raudenbush, S. W. (1997). Statistical analysis and optimal design for cluster randomized trials. *Psychological Methods, 2*, 173–185. http://dx.doi.org/10.1037/1082-989X.2.2.173

Raudenbush, S. W., & Bryk, A. S. (2002). *Hierarchical linear models: Applications and data analysis methods* (2nd ed.). Thousand Oaks, CA: Sage.

Raudenbush, S. W., & Liu, X. (2000). Statistical power and optimal design for multisite randomized trials. *Psychological Methods, 5*, 199–213. http://dx.doi.org/10.1037/1082-989X.5.2.199

Raudenbush, S. W., Spybrook, J., Congdon, R., Liu, X. F., Martinez, A., & Bloom, H. (2011). Optimal Design software for multi-level and longitudinal research (Version 3.01) [Computer software]. Available from http://www.wtgrantfoundation.org

Reise, S. P., & Duan, N. (2003). Design issues in multilevel studies. In S. P. Reise & N. Duan (Eds.), *Multilevel modeling: Methodological advances, issues, and applications* (pp. 285–298). Mahwah, NJ: Erlbaum.

Scherbaum, C. A., & Ferreter, J. M. (2009). Estimating statistical power and required sample sizes for organizational research using multilevel modeling. *Organizational Research Methods, 12*, 347–367. http://dx.doi.org/10.1177/1094428107308906

Shrout, P. E., & Fleiss, J. L. (1979). Intraclass correlations: Uses in assessing rater reliability. *Psychological Bulletin, 86*, 420–428. http://dx.doi.org/10.1037/0033-2909.86.2.420

Snijders, T. A. (2001). Sampling. In A. H. Leyand & H. Goldstein (Eds.), *Multilevel modeling of health statistics* (pp. 159–174). New York, NY: Wiley.

Snijders, T. A. (2005). Power and sample size in multilevel modeling. In B. S. Everitt & D. C. Howell (Eds.), *Encyclopedia of statistics in behavioral science* (Vol. 3, pp. 1570–1573). Chichester, England: Wiley.

Snijders, T. A., & Bosker, R. J. (1993). Standard errors and sample sizes for two-level research. *Journal of Educational Statistics, 18*, 237–259. http://dx.doi.org/10.3102/10769986018003237

Snijders, T. A., & Bosker, R. J. (1999). *Multilevel analysis: An introduction to basic and advanced multilevel modeling.* Thousand Oaks, CA: Sage.

Snijders, T. A., Bosker, R. J., & Guldemond, H. (1996). *PINT user's manual* (Version 1.6). Gröningen/Enschede, the Netherlands: KIP software. Retrieved from https://www.kip.com/software.php

Spybrook, J., Bloom, H., Congdon, R., Hill, C., Martinez, A., & Raudenbush, S. (2011). *Optimal Design plus empirical evidence: Documentation for the Optimal Design software* (Version 3.0) [Computer software]. Chicago: University of Chicago.

Spybrook, J., Kelcey, B., & Dong, N. (2016). Power for detecting treatment by moderator effects in two- and three-level cluster randomized trials. *Journal of Educational and Behavioral Statistics, 41*, 605–627. http://dx.doi.org/10.3102/1076998616655442

Todorova, G., Bear, J. B., & Weingart, L. R. (2014). Can conflict be energizing? A study of task conflict, positive emotions, and job satisfaction. *Journal of Applied Psychology, 99*, 451–467. http://dx.doi.org/10.1037/a0035134

van der Leeden, R., & Busing, F. (1994). *First iteration versus IGLS/RIGLS estimates in two-level models: A Monte Carlo study with ML3* (Preprint PRM 94-03). Leiden, the Netherlands: Leiden University.

Venkataramani, V., Richter, A. W., & Clarke, R. (2014). Creative benefits from well-connected leaders: Leader social network ties as facilitators of employee radical creativity. *Journal of Applied Psychology, 99,* 966–975. http://dx.doi.org/10.1037/a0037088

Yakovleva, M., Reilly, R. R., & Werko, R. (2010). Why do we trust? Moving beyond individual to dyadic perceptions. *Journal of Applied Psychology, 95,* 79–91. http://dx.doi.org/10.1037/a0017102

Zhan, G. (2013). Statistical power in international business research: Study levels and data types. *International Business Review, 22,* 678–686. http://dx.doi.org/10.1016/j.ibusrev.2012.10.004

## CHAPTER 15

EXPLAINED VARIANCE MEASURES FOR MULTILEVEL MODELS

David M. LaHuis, Caitlin E. Blackmore, and Kinsey B. Bryant-Lees

An important aspect of reporting results from multilevel analyses is to describe the magnitude of effects observed. In general, reporting effect sizes is important because they are useful in theory building (Aguinis et al., 2010) and communicating results to others from different professions (Thompson, 2002). In multilevel research, reporting effects sizes is especially important because some of the relationships examined may have low power (Mathieu, Aguinis, Culpepper, & Chen, 2012).

Explained variance (R^2) is the most commonly reported effect size in multilevel modeling. However, because there are multiple variance components in most multilevel models, there are multiple estimates of explained variance that could be computed. For example, in a basic model containing one Level 1 predictor, one Level 2 predictor, and a cross-level interaction, there are potentially three variance components (e.g., within-group variance, intercept variance, and slope variance) that a researcher can explain. There are a number of explained variance measures for multilevel models, but there has been little agreement in terms of what should be reported. For example, LaHuis, Hartman, Hakoyama, and Clark (2014) reported that roughly 40% of multilevel studies in top organizational journals failed to report any metric summarizing explained variance. This lack of reporting was probably a function of some known issues with some of the measures (e.g., they can result in negative explained variance estimates)

and the fact that, until recently, the accuracy of these measures was unknown.

In this chapter, we describe several multilevel effect size measures and recent simulation research comparing their efficacy. We limit our discussion to multilevel models with continuous outcomes because they are the most common. Explained variance measures for generalized linear mixed models are treated in Nakagawa and Schielzeth (2013). We begin with a comparison of how variance is partitioned in ordinary least squares (OLS) regression and multilevel models. Next, we present a running empirical example of a two-level study that is used to demonstrate how each measure can be calculated and interpreted. We then address how explained variance can be calculated for multilevel growth curve models. We conclude the chapter by reviewing recent simulation research on explained variance measures and present several recommendations for the use of effect size measures in multilevel models.

PARTITIONING VARIANCE IN ORDINARY LEAST SQUARES REGRESSION

Many of the multilevel explained variance measures are based on the R^2 typically calculated in OLS regression. In OLS, partitioning variance in the outcome into explained and unexplained variance is relatively straightforward. Predicted scores for each

http://dx.doi.org/10.1037/0000115-016
The Handbook of Multilevel Theory, Measurement, and Analysis, S. E. Humphrey and J. M. LeBreton (Editors-in-Chief)

individual case can be computed using the regression coefficients and predictor values. The variance of these predicted scores (var [$\hat{Y}$]) reflects explained variance in the outcome. Similarly, the variance of the residuals reflects unexplained variance (σ^2). Thus, R^2 can be expressed as a ratio of explained variance to total variance (var[Y]):

$$R^2(\text{OLS}) = \frac{\text{var}(\hat{Y})}{\text{var}(Y)} \qquad (15.1)$$

or as 1 minus the ratio of unexplained variance to total variance:

$$R^2(\text{OLS}) = 1 - \frac{\sigma^2}{\text{var}(Y)}. \qquad (15.2)$$

PARTITIONING VARIANCE IN MULTILEVEL MODELS

To illustrate the partitioning of variance in multilevel models, we begin describing a basic two-level multilevel model that includes two Level 1 predictors ($X1$, $X2$), one Level 2 predictor (Z), and a cross-level interaction ($X1 \times Z$) predicting a Level 1 outcome (Y). This model can be expressed using equations at different levels:

Level 1:

$$Y_{ij} = \beta_{0j} + \beta_{1j}(X1_{ij}) + \beta_{2j}(X2_{ij}) + r_{ij} \qquad (15.3)$$

Level 2:

$$\beta_{0j} = \gamma_{00} + \gamma_{00}(Z) + \mu_{0j} \qquad (15.4)$$

$$\beta_{1j} = \gamma_{10} + \gamma_{11}(Z) + \mu_{1j} \qquad (15.5)$$

$$\beta_{2j} = \gamma_{20} + \mu_{2j}. \qquad (15.6)$$

In these equations, β_{0j} is the intercept and β_{1j} and β_{2j} are the regression slopes predicting Y_{ij} using $X1_{ij}$, and $X2_{ij}$, respectively. The Level 1 error is r_{ij}, and its variance (σ^2) represents within-group variance not explained by the model. The subscripts i and j refer to the Level 1 and 2 units, respectively. Z is a Level 2

predictor, the γs are Level 2 regression coefficients, and U_{0j}, U_{1j}, and U_{2j} represent Level 2 errors. These errors have a variance/covariance matrix denoted as T. Thus, the variances of U_{0j}, U_{1j}, and U_{2j} are referred to as τ_{00}, τ_{11}, and τ_{22}, respectively.

A general way of expressing multilevel models with p Level 1 predictors and q Level 2 predictors is

$$Y_{ij} = \gamma_{00} + \sum_{h=1}^{p}\gamma_{h0}X_{hij} + \sum_{k=1}^{q}\gamma_{0k}Z_{kj} + \sum_{k=1}^{q}\sum_{h=1}^{p}\gamma_{hk}Z_{kj}X_{hij}$$

$$+ U_{0j} + \sum_{h=1}^{p}U_{hj}X_{hij} + r_{ij}. \qquad (15.7)$$

In Equation 15.7, h ranges from 1 to p and is used to indicate a specific Level 1 predictor. The subscript k has the same meaning for Level 2 predictors. This equation assumes that the Level 1 predictors X_{hij} do not correlate with the Level 2 predictors Z_{kj}. There is a maximum of $p + 1$ random parameters, but there may be fewer if researchers specify random slopes for a subset of Level 1 predictors. The first four terms contain the fixed part of the model and contribute to the prediction of the outcome. The last three terms contain the random part of the model. It is common to allow the intercept and slopes to covary. A positive covariance between a random intercept and random slope means that groups with higher intercept values have stronger within-group effects, whereas a negative covariance suggests groups with higher intercept values have weaker within-group effects.

Partitioning variance in multilevel models is complicated by the presence of multiple error variance components and the potential for those errors to correlate. As with OLS, predicted scores for each case can be computed using the fixed regression coefficients and the corresponding values for the predictors (i.e., using the first four terms of Equation 15.7). We denote those predicted scores as $\hat{Y}_{ij}$ and their variance as var($\hat{Y}_{ij}$). This can be combined with the error variance terms to partition variance in multilevel models. As Snijders and Bosker (2012) showed, the variance partitioning for a random intercept model can be expressed as

$$\text{var}(Y_{ij}) = \text{var}(\hat{Y}_{ij}) + \tau_{00} + \sigma^2, \qquad (15.8)$$

where var(Y_{ij}) is the observed variance of the outcome and the other terms are defined as before. The presence of random slopes complicates the partitioning of variance because they introduce the possibility of correlations among the Level 2 error terms. Snijders and Bosker showed that with random slopes variance in Y can be partitioned as follows:

$$\text{var}\left(Y_{ij}\right) = \text{var}\left(\hat{Y}_{ij}\right) + \tau_{00} + 2\mu'_{X(q)}T_{10} + \mu'_{X(q)}T_{11}\mu_{X(q)}$$
$$+ \text{trace}\left(T_{11}\sum{}_{X(p)}\right) + \sigma^2\text{trace}\left(T_{11}\sum{}_{X(p)}\right),$$
$$(15.9)$$

where $\mu_{X(q)}$ is a vector of Level 1 predictor means, T_{10} is a vector of intercept-slope covariances, and T_{11} is the covariance matrix of random slopes. The term *trace*($T_{11}\Sigma_{X(p)}$) represents the contribution of the random slopes to the variance in Y_{ij}, and it is the sum of the diagonals of the resulting matrix when the slope covariance matrix T_{11} is postmultiplied by the covariance matrix of predictors with random slopes. When all the Level 1 predictors are grand mean centered, $\mu_{X(q)}$ is a vector of zeros and Equation 15.9 simplifies to

$$\text{var}\left(Y_{ij}\right) = \text{var}\left(\hat{Y}_{ij}\right) + \tau_{00} + trace\left(T_{11}\sum{}_{X(p)}\right) + \sigma^2.$$
$$(15.10)$$

AN EMPIRICAL EXAMPLE

As an empirical example, we analyzed data provided in the multilevel package (Bliese, 2016) for the open source statistical program R. These data were first reported in Bliese and Halverson (1996) and were used for demonstration purposes by Bliese (2002). The data consisted of four variables: (a) work group cohesion (W.Cohes), (b) leadership climate perceptions (W.Lead), (c) well-being, and (d) work hours (W.Hours). There were 7,382 cases nested within 99 groups. Appendix 15.1 describes the process of using R to compute the various effect size measures.

Our proposed model consisted of individuals' W.Hours, W.Lead, and W.Cohes as Level 1 predictors of individuals' WB. G.Hours, G.Lead, G.Cohes were included as Level 2 predictors. In addition, we specified a cross-level interaction between

group-level work hours and individuals' leadership climate perceptions. The Level 1 variables were group mean centered. The equations for this model were as follows:

$$WB = \beta_{0j} + \beta_{1j}(\text{W.Hours}) + \beta_{2j}(\text{W.Lead})$$
$$+ \beta_{3j}(\text{W.Cohes}) + r_{ij} \qquad (15.11)$$

$$\beta_{0j} = \gamma_{00} + \gamma_{01}(\text{G.Hours}) + \gamma_{02}(\text{G.Lead})$$
$$+ \gamma_{03}(\text{G.Cohes}) + u_{0j} \qquad (15.12)$$

$$\beta_{1j} = \gamma_{10} \qquad (15.13)$$

$$\beta_{2j} = \gamma_{20} + \gamma_{21}(\text{G.Hours}) + u_{2j} \qquad (15.14)$$

$$\beta_{3j} = \gamma_{30}. \qquad (15.15)$$

The proposed model has three variance components—τ_{00}, τ_{11}, and σ^2—that can be used in calculating estimates of explained variance in WB. Several explained variance measures for multilevel models compute explained variance using reduction in variance components; that is, we can assess how much τ_{00}, τ_{11}, and σ^2 decrease when predictors are added. This is similar to the conception of the OLS R^2 in Equation 15.2. Alternatively, we can partition the variance in well-being into explained and unexplained variance and calculate an R^2 similar to the OLS R^2 in Equation 15.1. In the following sections, we describe both approaches. As typical with multilevel models, we estimated several simpler models building up to the proposed model.

R^2 MEASURES BASED ON REDUCTION IN VARIANCE COMPONENTS

Some of the earliest explained variance measures for multilevel models were based on the reduction of unexplained variance when predictors are added to a model (Bryk & Raudenbush, 1992; Raudenbush & Bryk, 2002). These approximate R^2 values can be calculated by first estimating the null model to determine σ^2 and τ_{00}. Next, residual σ^2 and τ_{00} are computed from a full model with predictors added.

The explained variance at each level can be calculated using these formulas:

$$R_1^2\,(\text{approx.}) = \frac{\sigma_{null}^2 - \sigma_{full}^2}{\sigma_{null}^2} \qquad (15.16)$$

$$R_2^2\,(\text{approx.}) = \frac{\tau_{00\,null} - \tau_{00\,full}}{\tau_{00\,null}}. \qquad (15.17)$$

For the well-being example, we estimated a model with no predictors (Model 0) to obtain the initial variance components. As shown in Table 15.1, σ_{null}^2 was 0.790 and τ_{00NULL} was 0.036. We then estimated Model 1, which consisted of W.Hours, W.Lead, and W.Cohes as Level 1 predictors of well-being. As shown in Table 15.1, W.Hours ($\gamma = -0.03$, $p < .05$), W.Lead ($\gamma = 0.47$, $p < .05$), and W.Cohes ($\gamma = 0.08$, $p < .05$) all significantly predicted well-being. The Level 1 error variance (σ_{M1}^2) for Model 1 was 0.643. Thus, R_1^2 (approx.) equaled

$$R_1^2\,(\text{approx.}) = \frac{0.790 - 0.643}{0.790} = .19. \qquad (15.18)$$

This suggests that W.Hours and W.Lead perceptions explain 19% of the Level 1 variance in well-being.

TABLE 15.1

Parameter Estimates From the Well-Being Example

Parameter	0	1	2	3
			Model	
γ_{00}	2.77	2.77	3.53	3.55
$\gamma_{W.Hours}$		−0.03*	−0.03*	−0.02*
$\gamma_{W.Lead}$		0.47*	0.47*	−0.07
$\gamma_{W.Cohes}$		0.08*	0.08*	0.08*
$\gamma_{G:Hours}$			−0.14*	−0.14*
$\gamma_{G:Lead}$			0.25*	0.25*
$\gamma_{G:Cohes}$			0.04	0.04
$\gamma_{G:Hours \times Lead}$				0.05*
τ_{00}	0.04	0.04	0.01	0.01
τ_{11}				0.00
τ_{01}				0.00
σ^2	0.79	0.64	0.64	0.64

Note. G:Cohes, G:Hours, G:Hours × Lead, and G:Lead = group-level measures of these constructs (i.e., group means); W.Cohes, W.Hours, and W.Lead = individual-level measures of these constructs (i.e., group-mean centered).

At Level 2, the intercept variance for Model 1 (τ_{00M1}) was .038, resulting in an R_2^2 (approx.) of

$$R_2^2\,(\text{approx.}) = \frac{0.036 - 0.038}{0.036} = -.06. \qquad (15.19)$$

This negative value occurs because R_2^2 (approx.) does not consider the interplay between Level 1 and Level 2 variances. As shown by Snijders and Bosker (2012), the variance of the group means in Y (Y_j) is

$$\text{var}(Y_j) = \tau_{00} + \frac{\sigma^2}{n_j}. \qquad (15.20)$$

Thus, when group-mean–centered predictors are added, the Level 1 error variance is reduced; however, the variance in the group means is unchanged, and the τ_{00} must increase to make Equation 15.20 hold.

In Model 2, we added Level 2 predictors. As shown in Table 15.1, only group cohesion was the only nonsignificant predictor of well-being. The intercept variance (τ_{00M2}) was .010, and the Level 1 variance (σ_{M2}^2 remained 0.643. Thus, there was no change in R_1^2 (approx.). The R_2^2 (approx.) for Model 2 was .73, suggesting that 73% of the Level 2 variance could be explained by the Level 2 predictors.

Finally, we tested the full proposed model (Model 3). This model included a random slope for leadership climate and a cross-level interaction between W.Lead and W.Hours. As noted above, the presence of random slopes complicates the partitioning of variance. Although this can be somewhat mitigated by grand-mean-centering the Level 1 predictors, we followed LaHuis et al.'s (2014) recommendation that researchers calculate R_1^2 (approx.) and R_2^2 (approx.) by using a model without random slopes.

Results from Model 3 are presented in Table 15.1. The cross-level interaction was statistically significant ($\gamma = 05.$, $p = .09$). However, as shown in Table 15.2, there was no change in R_1^2 (approx.) and a small increase in R_2^2 (approx.). This highlights the need for researchers to consider effect size measures when reporting multilevel analyses.

R_1^2 (approx.) and R_2^2 (approx.) are intuitive and straightforward to interpret; however, they ignore the interplay between Level 1 and Level 2 variances

TABLE 15.2

Explained Variance Estimates for
the Well-Being Example

Model	R_1^2 (approx.)	R_2^2 (approx.)	R^2 (S&B)	R^2 (MVP)
1	.19	−.06	.17	.18
2	.19	.72	.21	.21
3	.19	.73	.21	.21

Note. MVP = multilevel variance partitioning;
S&B = Snijders & Bosker.

in determining between-group variance. This can lead to negative estimates, because adding Level 1 predictors may cause τ_{00} to increase to balance out the decrease in σ^2. Snijders and Bosker (1994) developed an alternative measure that does consider the combination of Level 1 and Level 2 variances. They proposed a Level 1 measure that uses both σ^2 and τ_{00} and reflects the total amount of explained variance:

$$R^2(\text{S\&B}) = 1 - \frac{\tau_{00|\text{full}} + \sigma^2_{\text{full}}}{\tau_{00|\text{null}} + \sigma^2_{\text{null}}}. \quad (15.21)$$

Population values for R^2(Snijders & Bosker [S&B]) cannot be negative; however, sample estimates may be negative when the model is misspecified.

Neither the R^2(approx.) nor R^2(S&B) consider directly the effects of random slopes; thus, they are appropriate for random-intercept models. Although Snijders and Bosker (1994) presented an equation for an R^2 measure for random slope models, they noted that, in practice, residual slope variances contribute little to predicting the outcome. As such, researchers can simply calculate R^2 by estimating a random-intercept model and using Equation 15.21.

We calculated R^2(S&B) for all three models that were estimated. For Model 1, R^2(S&B) equaled

$$R^2(\text{S\&B}) = 1 - \frac{0.643 + 0.038}{0.790 + 0.036} = .17. \quad (15.22)$$

R^2(S&B) indicates the amount of total variance that can be explained. Thus, the .17 suggests that 17% of the total variance in well-being can be

explained by the three Level 1 predictors. Because R^2(S&B) considers both the Level 1 and Level 2 variance components, the slight increase in intercept variance from Model 0 to Model 1 does not produce a negative estimate.

In Model 2, R^2(S&B) equaled .21. The change in R^2(S&B) was .04, suggesting that the addition of the Level 2 variables explained an additional 4% of the total variance in well-being. Finally, the R^2(S&B) for Model 3 was .21. Again, this suggests that the cross-level interaction had a small effect size.

R^2 MEASURES BASED ON MULTILEVEL PARTITIONING OF VARIANCE

Nakagawa and Schielzeth (2013) proposed measures for general linear mixed models that are based on the full partitioning of variance for multilevel models. For the linear model, the variance is partitioned as described by Snijders and Bosker (2012). An R^2 measure based on the multilevel variance partitioning R^2(MVP) can be calculated using the equation

$$R^2(\text{MVP}) = \frac{\text{var}(\hat{Y}_{ij})}{\text{var}(\hat{Y}_{ij}) + \tau_{00} + \sigma^2}. \quad (15.23)$$

Put simply, R^2(MVP) is the ratio of predicted score variance to the sum of predicted score variance and Level 1 and Level 2 variances.

Nakagawa and Schielzeth (2013) did not address random-slope models; however, incorporating random slopes in the partitioning of variance in Y_{ij} can be done using Equation 15.9. The explained variance measure for models with random slopes can be calculated using this formula:

$$R^2(\text{MVP}) = \frac{\text{var}(\hat{Y}_{ij})}{\text{var}(\hat{Y}_{ij}) + \tau_{00} + 2\mu'_{x(q)}T_{10} + \mu'_{x(q)}T_{11}\mu_{x(q)} + \text{trace}(T_{11}\sum_{x(p)}) + \sigma^2}. \quad (15.24)$$

As with R^2(S&B), R^2(MVP) is a total explained variance measure.

To calculate R^2(MVP), we first calculated the amount of variance in well-being that could be explained by the predictors. For Model 1, a predictor score for each case was calculated using the fixed effects and the case's score on each individual predictor:

$$\hat{Y}_{ij} = 2.77 + -0.03\left(W.hrs_{ij}\right) + .47\left(W.lead_{ij}\right)$$
$$+ .08\left(W.cohes_{ij}\right). \quad (15.25)$$

The variance of the $\hat{Y}_{ij}$ was .145. Thus, $R^2(MVP)$ was

$$R^2(MVP) = \frac{0.145}{0.145 + 0.038 + 0.643} = .18. \quad (15.26)$$

This suggests that 18% of the total variance in well-being can be explained by the Level 1 predictors.

For Model 2, $R^2(MVP)$ equaled .21, which suggests that the Level 2 predictors explained an additional 3% of the total variance in well-being. The significance of the change in $R^2(MVP)$ can be assessed by calculating a likelihood ratio test that compares the deviance ($-2 *$ log likelihood from estimating the model) from a simpler model with that from a more complicated model. The difference between the two is distributed as a chi-square with degrees of freedom equal to the differences in estimated parameters. To assess the significance of the change in $R^2(MVP)$ from Model 1 to Model 2, we subtracted the Model 2 deviance (17,758) from the Model 1 deviance (17,797), resulting in a chi-square of 38.33. Because Model 1 had 6 degrees of freedom and Model 2 had 9 degrees of freedom, this chi-square had 3 degrees of freedom and was statistically significant, $\chi^2(3) = 38.33$, $p < .01$. This indicated that Model 2 explained significantly more variance than Model 1.

We calculated $R^2(MVP)$ for Model 3 using Equation 15.24. The variance of the $\hat{Y}_{ij}$ was .171, τ_{00M3} equaled .010, and the Level 1 variance (σ^2_{M3}) was 0.638. Because the means of the Level 1 predictors were 0, the term $2\mu'_{X(q)}T_{10} + \mu'_{X(q)}T_{11}\mu_{X(q)}$ equaled 0. The sum of the slope variances equaled .005; thus,

$$R^2(MVP) = \frac{0.171}{0.171 + 0.010 + 0.638 + 0.005} = .21.$$
$$(15.27)$$

As with $R^2(S\&B)$, adding the cross-level interaction did not increase $R^2(MVP)$. Thus, although statistically significant, the interaction between group work hours and leadership climate had a very small effect size.

MULTILEVEL GROWTH CURVE MODELS

Multilevel random coefficient modeling provides a flexible framework for analyzing repeated measures in that they can be used to assess how a variable changes (grows) over time. Using multirandom coefficient modeling, these growth curve models can be applied to unbalanced data (when individuals do not have measurements for each occasion), model various time functions, and incorporate additional levels (Bliese & Ployhart, 2002). Growth curve models often necessitate more complicated residual covariance structures because occasions closer in time may be more related than those that are more distant. These more complicated covariance structures typically affect the standard errors of fixed effects but not the fixed effects estimates themselves. Thus, similar to random slopes, complicated residual covariance structures will likely not have a large impact on estimates of explained variance.

To help illustrate calculating explained variance for growth curve analyses, we use a fixed-occasion example with three time points; specifically, we reanalyzed the data from Bliese and Ployhart (2002) assessing changes in job satisfaction. The data were obtained from the multilevel package in R (see https://www.r-project.org/) and contain 495 respondents from the U.S. Army. We omitted cases with missing data, resulting in a data set with 344 individuals, each with three measurement occasions (6 months apart). We calculated how much variance in job satisfaction could be explained by age, gender, and time in unit using several different residual covariance structures. For simplicity, we do not consider the process for considering which error structure is appropriate. The process of specifying the random part of the model is ultimately a balance of choosing the simplest model that adequately fits the data. We refer interested readers to Snijders and Bosker's (2012) Chapter 15 and Bliese and Ployhart (2002) for model-building strategies.

For fixed-occasion designs, it is helpful to think about the variance–covariance matrix for scores across occasions. For example, the present data are completely balanced with three occasions at which job satisfaction is measured, and each individual has a score at all three time points. The variance–covariance matrix for these occasions equals

$$\sum(Y) = \begin{pmatrix} .99 & .50 & .30 \\ .50 & .86 & .46 \\ .30 & .46 & .76 \end{pmatrix}. \qquad (15.28)$$

The diagonals of this matrix represent the variance of job satisfaction at each time point, and the off-diagonals are the covariances. The initial goal of specifying growth curve models is to find a function for time and a covariance structure for residuals that produces a residual covariance matrix that approximates the one in Equation 15.28. Once this is accomplished, predictors can be added to determine how much of the variance in the outcome can be explained.

In the following paragraphs we consider three types of residual covariance structures. These structures were chosen because they reflect a range of complexity. We begin with the least complex (most restrictive) and progress to the most complex.

Compound Symmetry

The *compound symmetry model* is defined by a residual covariance matrix in which all the variances are equal across time points and all covariances between different occasions have the same value. To be specific, the residual variance–covariance matrix equals

$$\sum(Y') = \begin{pmatrix} \tau_{00}+\sigma^2 & \tau_{00} & \tau_{00} \\ \tau_{00} & \tau_{00}+\sigma^2 & \tau_{00} \\ \tau_{00} & \tau_{00} & \tau_{00}+\sigma^2 \end{pmatrix}. \qquad (15.29)$$

For the job satisfaction example, the compound symmetry model is a random-intercept model with time (coded as 0,1,2) as a predictor. The Level 1

TABLE 15.3

Parameter Estimates From the Job Satisfaction Example

Parameter	CS0	CS1	FAC0	FAC1	UC0	UC1
γ_{00}	3.20	2.56	3.20	2.56	3.20	2.62
γ_{Time}	0.04	0.04	0.04	0.04	0.04	0.04
γ_{Age}		0.03*		0.03*		0.03*
γ_{Gender}		-0.15		-0.13		-0.15
γ_{Time_Unit}		0.00		0.01		.00
τ_{00}	0.42	0.40	0.14	0.14	0.44	0.40
$\sigma^2 Time\ 1$	0.45	0.45	0.73	0.71	0.56	0.55
$\sigma^2 Time\ 2$	0.45	0.45	0.73	0.71	0.44	0.41
$\sigma^2 Time\ 3$	0.45	0.45	0.73	0.71	0.33	0.36

Note. CS0 = the compound-symmetry model with only time as a predictor; CS1 = the compound-symmetry model with external predictors; FAC0 = the first-order autocorrelation model with only time as a predictor; FAC1 = the first-order autocorrelation model with external predictors; UC0 and UC1 = the unconstrained models without and with external predictors, respectively.

variance is constant across time points. Results for this model (CS0) are presented in Table 15.3. There was a statistically significant effect of time, which suggests that job satisfaction changed over time. The Level 1 and 2 variances were .35 and. 42, respectively. This produces the following variance–covariance matrix:

$$\sum(Y'_{CS0}) = \begin{pmatrix} .87 & .42 & .42 \\ .42 & .87 & .42 \\ .42 & .42 & .87 \end{pmatrix}. \qquad (15.30)$$

This is the same model that underlies the general random-intercept model described previously and is specified by having time as a predictor. When this model is used for repeated measures, the multilevel explained variance measures can be used without alteration.

To demonstrate the general approach to calculating explained variance for repeated measures analyses, we estimated a model where age, gender, and tenure predicted job satisfaction. The results are presented in Table 15.3. Only age ($\gamma=0.03, p<.01$)

was statistically significant. The residual covariance matrix equaled

$$\sum (Y'_{CS1}) = \begin{pmatrix} .84 & .39 & .39 \\ .39 & .84 & .39 \\ .39 & .39 & .84 \end{pmatrix}. \qquad (15.31)$$

Snijders and Bosker (2012) described calculating an explained variance measure by comparing the sum of the diagonals of the residual covariance matrices for the models with and without predictors. For example, the sum of the diagonals is 2.52 for the matrix in Equation 15.29 and 2.61 for the matrix in Equation 15.28. R^2 can be calculated as follows:

$$R^2(\text{S\&B}) = 1 - \frac{\text{trace}\left(\sum Y'_{CS1}\right)}{\text{trace}\left(\sum Y'_{CS0}\right)} = 1 - \frac{.84 + .84 + .84}{.87 + .87 + .87}$$

$$= 1 - \frac{2.52}{2.61} = .03. \qquad (15.32)$$

Thus, according to R^2(S&B) the predictors explain 3% of the variance in job satisfaction. Alternatively, one could calculate R^2 using the partitioning of variance from the model with predictors. We calculated the variance of predicted scores at each time point using the process defined above and computed their variance–covariance matrix ($\sum \hat{Y}_{CS1}$). Thus,

$$R^2(\text{MVP}) = \frac{\text{trace}\left(\sum \hat{Y}_{CS1}\right)}{\text{trace}\left(\sum \hat{Y}_{CS1}\right) + \text{trace}\left(\sum Y'_{CS1}\right)}$$

$$= \frac{.035 + .035 + .035}{.035 + .035 + .035 + .841 + .841 + .841}$$

$$= \frac{.10}{2.61} = .04. \qquad (15.33)$$

As with the well-being example, R^2(S&B) and R^2(MVP) produced similar explained variance estimates.

First-Order Autocorrelation

In the first-order autocorrelation model, the variances are fixed over time, but the correlations between occasions vary in a structured manner;

specifically, the correlation between occasion s and occasion t is ρ^{t-s}. Thus, the correlation between job satisfaction at Occasions 1 and 2 is ρ, and the correlation between Occasions 1 and 3 is ρ^2. This allows for occasions closer together in time to be more closely related. For the job satisfaction data, the variance–covariance matrix of job satisfaction for the first-order autocorrelation model with no explanatory predictors (FAC0) is

$$\sum (Y'_{FAC0}) = \begin{pmatrix} 0.87 & 0.48 & 0.30 \\ 0.48 & 0.87 & 0.48 \\ 0.30 & 0.48 & 0.87 \end{pmatrix}. \qquad (15.34)$$

When age, gender, and time in unit are added as predictors (FAC1), the variance–covariance matrix of residuals is

$$\sum (Y'_{FAC1}) = \begin{pmatrix} 0.84 & 0.45 & 0.28 \\ 0.45 & 0.84 & 0.45 \\ 0.28 & 0.45 & 0.84 \end{pmatrix}. \qquad (15.35)$$

Following Equation 15.32,

$$R^2(\text{S\&B}) = 1 - \frac{0.84 + 0.84 + 0.84}{0.87 + 0.87 + 0.87}$$

$$= 1 - \frac{2.52}{2.61} = .03. \qquad (15.36)$$

We also calculated R^2(MVP) using Equation 15.33. The variance of predicted job satisfaction scores was .03; thus,

$$R^2(\text{MVP}) = \frac{0.03 + 0.03 + 0.03}{0.03 + 0.03 + 0.03 + 0.84 + 0.84 + 0.84}$$

$$= \frac{0.10}{2.61} = .04. \qquad (15.37)$$

This suggests that the variables explained 3% of the variance in job satisfaction according to R^2(S&B), and 4% according to R^2(MVP).

Unconstrained

In the unconstrained model, both the residual variances and covariances are allowed to vary across occasions. This is the most complex covariance structure because it is fully saturated (there are no degrees of freedom). For the job satisfaction data, the variance–covariance matrix for the baseline model was

$$\sum(Y'_{UC0}) = \begin{pmatrix} .99 & .50 & .30 \\ .50 & .86 & .46 \\ .30 & .46 & .76 \end{pmatrix}. \quad (15.38)$$

When age, gender, and time in unit are added as the predictors, the resulting residual covariance matrix equals

$$\sum(Y'_{UC1}) = \begin{pmatrix} .95 & .46 & .28 \\ .46 & .82 & .44 \\ .28 & .44 & .76 \end{pmatrix}. \quad (15.39)$$

Inserting the relevant values from Equations 15.36 and 15.37 into Equation 15.32 produces

$$R^2(S\&B) = 1 - \frac{.95 + .82 + .76}{.99 + .86 + .76} = 1 - \frac{2.52}{2.61} = .03. \quad (15.40)$$

We also calculated variance for predicted scores on the basis of the fixed effects for each time point. As with the other models, this equaled .03. Thus,

$$R^2(MVP) = \frac{.03 + .03 + .03}{.03 + .03 + .03 + .94 + .82 + .76}$$
$$= \frac{.09}{2.61} = .03. \quad (15.41)$$

Both measures suggested that 3% of the variance in job satisfaction could be explained by age, gender, and time in unit.

Growth Curve Model Summary

As expected, the explained variance estimates were similar across all three residual variance–covariance structures that we considered. The complex error structures do not have a large effect on the fixed effects estimates and therefore have little impact on the partitioning of variance. This is similar to

the argument that researchers would obtain similar explained variance estimates with and without random slopes because their variance contributes little to the prediction of the outcome. However, as with random-slope variance, incorporating complicated error structures into the calculation of explained variance is straightforward.

ACCURACY OF MULTILEVEL R^2 MEASURES

LaHuis et al. (2014) evaluated the accuracy of the existing measures of explained variance for multilevel models by conducting two sets of Monte Carlo simulations: one using a random intercept model and one using a random slope model. For each set of simulations, the authors manipulated the number of groups, the average group size, the intraclass correlation in the outcome, and the amount of explained variance. The choice of values for each condition was informed by a comprehensive review of the extant multilevel articles in the organizational literature.

On the basis of their results, LaHuis et al. (2014) concluded that R_1^2(approx.), R^2(S&B), R^2(OLS), and R^2(MVP) were all acceptable choices for calculating explained variance in multilevel models. Differences in efficiency and levels of bias among these measures were trivial and did not appear to be greatly influenced by the number of groups, group size, amount of explained variance at each level, amount of between-group variance in the outcome, or centering choice: R^2(OLS), and R^2(MVP) did not produce negative effect size values, and R_1^2(approx.) and R^2(S&B) rarely produced negative effect size values (< 1%). Therefore, decisions concerning which measure to use may be resolved by the nature of the research question and personal preference. Although R_1^2(approx.) and R^2(S&B) produce easily interpretable values reflecting a comparison of variance components between models, researchers should be aware that missing data in the Level 1 predictors may produce unequal model sample sizes. Alternatively, R^2(MVP) produces an internally consistent partitioning of variance from a single multilevel model. Although the process of calculating R^2(MVP) is slightly more involved, LaHuis et al. provided an R function that will produce each measure.

The presence of random slopes complicates estimating explained variance in multilevel models. LaHuis et al. (2014) found that incorporating substantial random-slope variance biased both R_1^2(approx.) and R_2^2(approx.). Therefore, they recommended using random-intercept models to calculate R_1^2(approx.) and R_2^2(approx.) when there are random slopes.

R_2^2(approx.) did not perform well under any of the conditions; it was the least precise and most biased of all measures evaluated, and it frequently produced negative effect size values (8%–51%). Therefore, LaHuis et al. (2014) discouraged its use. Researchers who wish to report level-specific explained variance can report R_1^2(approx.) for Level 1 explained variance, but there does not appear to be an acceptable option for reporting Level 2 explained variance. As a substitute to R_2^2(approx.), the authors recommended that researchers use the change in total variance produced by adding Level 2 predictors, which provides an estimate of the variance explained by these predictors.

LaHuis et al. (2014) also stressed the importance of evaluating whether different results are obtained by analyzing the data using group-mean centering versus grand-mean centering. Grand-mean-centering a variable that has different within- and between-group effects may result in biased estimates when using OLS and multilevel modeling approaches. Therefore, group-mean centering should be used with the group mean added as a Level 2 predictor in these cases. Finally, if researchers wish to report explained variance in multilevel models with R^2(OLS), they will still need to calculate significance levels and confidence intervals with multilevel modeling because the OLS-based standard errors will be biased.

CONCLUSION AND RECOMMENDATIONS

On the basis of the Monte Carlo simulation research, as well as our experience with these measures, we make several recommendations. First, we strongly encourage researchers to include some estimate of explained variance when reporting results from a multilevel analysis. Our preference is for R^2(MVP) because we believe it to be the closest analog to R^2(OLS) and it is based on a single model. R_1^2(approx.) and R^2(S&B) share good estimation

properties but require multiple models to be estimated. Second, we recommend that researchers group-mean-center the predictors and reintroduce the group mean as a Level 2 variable. This results in a clearer partitioning of the variance and provides unbiased estimates of the within- and between-group effects. From an explained variance perspective, group-mean centering allows researchers to test hypotheses about which variables affect the outcome at Level 2.

We recommend that researchers use changes in R^2 to indicate the magnitude of cross-level interactions. Because the scaling of the cross-level interactions depends on the size of the slope that is varying, it can be difficult to interpret the size of the effect. The significance of the change in R^2 can be evaluated with the statistical significance of the newly added parameter. If more than one parameter is added, then the statistical significance of the change in R^2 can be tested using the likelihood ratio test between the simpler and more complicated model. It is important to note that using the likelihood ratio test for assessing the significance of fixed effects is appropriate only when full maximum likelihood estimation is used (Hox, 2002).

Finally, although specifying growth curve models often involves more complicated covariance structures for the residuals, the calculation of explained variance for these models is relatively simple. The more complicated structures will likely have little impact on explained variance estimates, and researchers will obtain similar values with and without incorporating them in computing explained variance. However, because calculating explained variance for these models is straightforward, we recommend that researchers base explained variance estimates on the error structure that provides the best fit to the data.

APPENDIX 15.1: ESTIMATION DETAILS

The R script can be downloaded from https://app.box.com/v/EffectSizeFunction. We first downloaded the file and then sourced the script for the multilevel effect size function:

source ('~/Downloads/
multilevel_effect_size_function.r').

This allowed us to use the multilevel effect size function on lmer objects. For example, we estimated Model 1 using the lmer function:

$$m1 = lmer(WBEING \sim W.HRS + W.LEAD + W.COHES + (1|GRP), data = bh1996).$$

It is important to note that the effect size function assumes that the grand means for all Level 1 predictors are 0. Next, we estimated the multilevel R^2s using the sourced multilevel effect size function:

$$multilevel.effect.size(m1).$$

This returns values for R_1^2(approx.), R_2^2(approx.), R^2(S&B), and R^2(MVP).

For the growth curve analyses, we used the lme function in the nlme package. This allowed us to estimate more complicated covariance structures. As an example, we estimated the unconstrained model with no predictors:

$$uco0 = m4univ = lme(JSAT \sim TIME, random$$
$$= \sim 1| SUBNUM, correlation = corSymm(),$$
$$weights = varIdent(form = \sim 1| TIME),$$
$$data = univclean).$$

The residual covariance matrix can be obtained using the getVarCov function:

$$uco0.ecov = getVarCov(uco0, type = 'marginal')\$'1'.$$

We the summed the diagonals of this matrix:

$$uco0.evar = sum(diag[uco0.ecov]).$$

We followed the same procedure for the model with explanatory predictors (uco1) to obtain uco1.evar. These were used to calculate explained variance. For example,

$$R^2(S\&B) = 1 - \frac{uco1.evar}{uco0.evar}.$$

R^2(MVP) was calculated using uco1.evar and the variance of predicted scores based on the fixed effects from the model with explanatory predictors.

References

Aguinis, H., Werner, S., Lanza Abbott, J., Angert, C., Park, J. H., & Kohlhausen, D. (2010). Customer-centric science: Reporting significant research results with rigor, relevance, and practical impact in mind. *Organizational Research Methods, 13,* 515–539. http://dx.doi.org/10.1177/1094428109333339

Bliese, P. D. (2002). Multilevel random coefficient modeling in organizational research: Examples using SAS and S-PLUS. In N. Schmitt (Series Ed.) and F. Drasgow, N. Schmitt, F. Drasgow (Volume Eds.), *Measuring and analyzing behavior in organizations: Advances in measurement and data analysis.* (pp. 401–445). San Francisco, CA: Jossey-Bass.

Bliese, P. D. (2016). Multilevel: Multilevel functions. R package version 2.6. Retrieved from https:// CRAN.R-project.org/package=multilevel

Bliese, P. D., & Halverson, R. R. (1996). Individual and nomothetic models of job stress: An examination of work hours, cohesion, and well-being. *Journal of Applied Social Psychology, 26,* 1171–1189. http://dx.doi.org/10.1111/j.1559-1816.1996. tb02291.x

Bliese, P. D., & Ployhart, R. E. (2002). Growth modeling using random coefficient models: Model building, testing, and illustrations. *Organizational Research Methods, 5,* 362–387. http://dx.doi.org/10.1177/ 109442802237116

Bryk, A. S., & Raudenbush, S. W. (1992). *Hierarchical linear models: Applications and data analysis methods.* Newbury Park, CA: Sage.

Hox, J. J. (2002). *Multilevel analysis: Techniques and applications.* Mahwah, NJ: Erlbaum.

LaHuis, D. M., Hartman, M. J., Hakoyama, S., & Clark, P. C. (2014). Explained variance measures for multilevel models. *Organizational Research Methods, 17,* 433–451. http://dx.doi.org/10.1177/ 1094428114541701

Mathieu, J. E., Aguinis, H., Culpepper, S. A., & Chen, G. (2012). Understanding and estimating the power to detect cross-level interaction effects in multilevel modeling. *Journal of Applied Psychology, 97,* 951–966. http://dx.doi.org/10.1037/a0028380

Nakagawa, S., & Schielzeth, H. (2013). A general and simple method for obtaining R2 from generalized linear mixed-effects models. *Methods in Ecology and*

Evolution, 4, 133–142. http://dx.doi.org/10.1111/
j.2041-210x.2012.00261.x

Raudenbush, S. W., & Bryk, A. S. (2002). *Hierarchical
linear models: Applications and data analysis methods*
(2nd ed.). Thousand Oaks, CA: Sage.

Snijders, T. A. B., & Bosker, R. J. (1994). Modeled variance
in two-level models. *Sociological Methods &
Research, 22,* 342–363. http://dx.doi.org/10.1177/
0049124194022003004

Snijders, T. A. B., & Bosker, R. J. (2012). *Multilevel
analysis: An introduction to basic and advanced
multilevel modeling* (2nd ed.). Los Angeles,
CA: Sage.

Thompson, B. (2002). "Statistical," "practical," and
"clinical": How many kinds of significance do
counselors need to consider? *Journal of Counseling
& Development, 80,* 64–71. http://dx.doi.org/10.1002/
j.1556-6678.2002.tb00167.x

## CHAPTER 16

MISSING DATA IN MULTILEVEL RESEARCH

Simon Grund, Oliver Lüdtke, and Alexander Robitzsch

Multilevel data are often incomplete, for example, when participants refuse to answer some items in a questionnaire or drop out of a study that involves multiple measurement occasions. Even though there is a consensus that current state-of-the-art procedures for statistical analyses with missing data should be preferred (e.g., Allison, 2001; Enders, 2010; Little & Rubin, 2002; Newman, 2014; Schafer & Graham, 2002), simpler methods such as listwise deletion (LD) prevail and are still widely applied in research practice (Jeličić, Phelps, & Lerner, 2009; Nicholson, Deboeck, & Howard, 2017; Peugh & Enders, 2004). This is problematic because these methods can distort parameter estimates and statistical inference. In this chapter, we provide a general introduction to the problem of missing data in multilevel research, and we present two principled methods for handling incomplete data: multiple imputation (MI) and maximum likelihood (ML) estimation. We discuss how these procedures can be used to address missing data in multilevel research, and we consider their commonalities as well as their individual strengths and weaknesses. A brief computer simulation study is used to illustrate the statistical behavior of the parameter estimates obtained from these methods. Finally, we illustrate their application in a data analysis example and provide the syntax files and computer code needed to reproduce our results.

EXAMPLE: JOB SATISFACTION AND LEADERSHIP STYLE

To provide an illustration of the ideas presented here, we adopt a running example in which we examine the relationships between job satisfaction and several work-related variables. For the purpose of this chapter, we regard the multilevel structure as cross-sectional, for example, with employees at Level 1 nested within work groups at Level 2. The example is based on the data from Klein et al. (2000). The study features a sample of 750 employees from 50 work groups with measures of job satisfaction (SAT), negative leadership style (LS), workload (WL), and cohesion (COH). We altered the data set slightly by (a) transforming workload into a categorical variable (high vs. low) and (b) treating cohesion as a *global* variable that was directly assessed at Level 2 (e.g., a supervisor rating). We investigated the relationships between employees' job satisfaction and negative leadership style, workload, and cohesion using a multilevel random intercept model (Snijders & Bosker, 2012). In the hierarchical notation of Raudenbush and Bryk (2002), the Level 1 equation of the model reads

$$SAT_{ij} = \beta_{0j} + \beta_{1j}\left(LS_{ij} - \overline{LS}_{\cdot j}\right) + \beta_{2j}WL_{ij} + r_{ij}$$

$$(16.1)$$

http://dx.doi.org/10.1037/0000115-017
The Handbook of Multilevel Theory, Measurement, and Analysis, S. E. Humphrey and J. M. LeBreton (Editors-in-Chief)

with Level 2 equations

$$\beta_{0j} = \gamma_{00} + \gamma_{01}\overline{LS}_{\cdot j} + \gamma_{02}COH_j + u_{0j}$$

$$\beta_{1j} = \gamma_{10}$$

$$\beta_{2j} = \gamma_{20}. \qquad (16.2)$$

Here, SAT_{ij} denotes the job satisfaction of an employee i in group j. The ratings on leadership style were subjected to group-mean centering, where LS_{ij} denotes employees' individual ratings of leadership style, and $\overline{LS}_{\cdot j}$ denotes the average rating in group j. Finally, WL_{ij} denotes employees' workload, and COH_j denotes a work group's cohesion (e.g., a supervisor rating). The random intercept, u_{0j} and the residuals, r_{ij} were each assumed to follow a normal distribution with mean zero and variances τ_0^2 and σ^2, respectively. In the remainder of this chapter, we will express this model with a combined notation (e.g., Snijders & Bosker, 2012)

$$SAT_{ij} = \gamma_{00} + \gamma_{10}\left(LS_{ij} - \overline{LS}_{\cdot j}\right) + \gamma_{01}\overline{LS}_{\cdot j}$$
$$+ \gamma_{20}WL_{ij} + \gamma_{02}COH_j + u_{0j} + r_{ij}. \quad (16.3)$$

In this chapter, we focus on multilevel models in which only the intercept varies across groups. Longitudinal research designs as well as multilevel models with additional random effects (e.g., random slopes) are considered in the Discussion section.

MISSING DATA IN MULTILEVEL RESEARCH

It is well known that simpler methods of dealing with missing data (e.g., LD) can severely compromise statistical decision making (e.g., Enders, 2010; Little & Rubin, 2002). For example, when analyses are based on only the complete cases, then parameter estimates can be biased (i.e., the estimates may systematically differ from the "true" values that hold in the population) when data are missing in a systematic manner (e.g., see Schafer & Graham, 2002). However, even when data are missing in an unsystematic manner, inferences based on LD are often inefficient (i.e., low statistical power) due to the reduction in sample size and because potentially useful information about the missing data is being ignored (e.g., Newman, 2014).

Therefore, the common goals of the "principled" methods for handling missing data (e.g., ML and MI) are to (a) provide unbiased estimates for the statistical parameters of interest, (b) acknowledge the uncertainty that is due to missing data, and (c) make full use of the data in order to limit the loss of efficiency. However, before we devote ourselves to explaining these methods, it will be useful to first establish a formal framework for discussing the missing data problems and the challenges that can arise in multilevel research. In the following section, we discuss (a) possible mechanisms that can lead to missing data and (b) different patterns of missing data that can occur in multilevel data.

Missing Data Mechanisms

Rubin (1976) considered three broad classes of missing data mechanisms. We assume that there is a hypothetical complete data set, $\mathbf{Y}$, which can be decomposed into an observed part, $\mathbf{Y}_{obs}$, and an unobserved part, $\mathbf{Y}_{mis}$, where an indicator matrix, $\mathbf{R}$, denotes which elements are observed and which ones are missing. Rubin defined data to be missing at random (MAR) when the probability of observing data, $P(\mathbf{R})$, is independent of the missing data given the observed data, that is, $P(\mathbf{R}|\mathbf{Y}) = P(\mathbf{R}|\mathbf{Y}_{obs})$. In other words, under MAR, no link remains between the chance of observing data and the data themselves (i.e., they occur at random) once the observed data are taken into account. A special case of this scenario occurs when the probability of missing data is completely independent of the data, that is, $P(\mathbf{R}|\mathbf{Y}) = P(\mathbf{R})$, which is referred to as missing *completely* at random (MCAR). By contrast, when the probability of missing data is related to the unobserved data, that is, $P(\mathbf{R}|\mathbf{Y}) = P(\mathbf{R}|\mathbf{Y}_{obs},\mathbf{Y}_{mis})$, it is more difficult to infer from incomplete data and strong assumptions must be made about the missing data mechanism (see Carpenter & Kenward, 2013; Enders, 2011). This is referred to as missing *not* at random (MNAR).

The meaning of these mechanisms can be subtle, and they are best explained in an example (see also Enders, 2010). Consider the simple scenario illustrated in Figure 16.1, where negative leadership style is associated with lower job satisfaction, and

Without job satisfaction   **With job satisfaction**

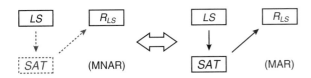

FIGURE 16.1.   Example of systematic data loss and the effects of ignoring possible causes of missing data. *LS* = leadership style; MAR = missing at random; MNAR = missing not at random; R_{LS} = indicator for missing values in leadership style; *SAT* = job satisfaction.

ratings on leadership style are missing (R_{LS}) as a function of job satisfaction, say, because employees with low job satisfaction were less willing to answer questions about their supervisors (single-headed arrows). In this scenario, larger values of leadership style would be more likely to be missing (double-headed arrow), rendering statements about this variable misleading as long as they do not take the missing data mechanism into account (left panel). For example, the estimated mean of leadership style may be well below the "true" mean because larger values have a higher chance of being missing. However, with job satisfaction taken into account, these ties are broken (right panel): Given the values of job satisfaction, the scores of leadership style are now MAR, allowing us to estimate the *conditional* mean of leadership style given job satisfaction (e.g., using linear regression) and to make statements about the overall mean on this basis (see also Carpenter & Kenward, 2013).

The notion of missing data mechanisms allows us to identify conditions under which a missing data treatment may yield more or less accurate results in some model of interest. For example, LD generally provides unbiased estimates for a model of interest only under MCAR (see also Newman, 2014). In addition, LD may provide unbiased results in some very specific scenarios in which data are MAR or MNAR (e.g., Galati & Seaton, 2016; Little, 1992). However, because the assertion of specific missing data mechanisms requires untestable assumptions to be made, LD should be avoided in favor of procedures that make full use of the data and that are applicable under a more general set of

assumptions (e.g., ML and MI; see also Schafer & Graham, 2002). Both ML and MI provide unbiased results under MAR. In such a case, the exact mechanism need not be known and may even be different from individual to individual as long as the observed data are sufficient to "break the link" between the unobserved data and the probability that they are missing (Carpenter & Kenward, 2013). To make this assumption more plausible, it is often recommended that auxiliary variables be included in the treatment of missing data. Such variables are not part of the model of interest but are related to the probability of missing data or the variables with missing data themselves (Collins, Schafer, & Kam, 2001; Enders, 2008; Graham, 2003). Including such variables is beneficial because (a) they make the MAR assumption more plausible, and (b) if they are related to the variables of interest, they provide information about the missing values and improve statistical power (Collins et al., 2001).

Patterns of Missing Data

For the treatment of missing data, it can also be useful to distinguish different *patterns* of missing data. Such a distinction may help researchers to identify problems with the data and navigate choices regarding the missing data treatment. In accordance with Newman (2014), we distinguish three basic patterns: *item*, *construct*, and *unit* nonresponse. Item nonresponse denotes cases in which participants fail to answer a single item on a questionnaire (e.g., an item concerning salary from a questionnaire for assessing job satisfaction). By contrast, construct and unit nonresponse, respectively, denote cases in which all items pertaining to a certain construct or even a participant's entire questionnaire may be missing (e.g., because a participant was absent on the day the company conducted a survey). In the present chapter, we focus on item nonresponse, although construct nonresponse can often be addressed by applying similar methods (see also Gottschall, West, & Enders, 2012). Unit nonresponse can be more complicated to deal with and is often addressed by employing survey weights (e.g., Särndal, Swensson, & Wretman, 2003).

In multilevel research, item, construct, and unit nonresponse can occur at different levels of the sample (see also van Buuren, 2011). According to Kozlowski and Klein (2000), we may again distinguish three different patterns of missing data. Data can be missing (a) at Level 1, (b) in *global* variables at Level 2, or (c) in *shared* variables at Level 2. Missing data at Level 1 refer to the lowest level of the sample (e.g., missing data from employees). Global variables refer to variables that are directly assessed at Level 2 (e.g., missing data in supervisor rating), whereas shared variables denote variables that are assessed at Level 1 and then aggregated at Level 2 (e.g., a group average based on incomplete data collected from employees). Because missing data both at Level 1 and in shared variables at Level 2 originate at Level 1, they can usually be addressed by the same methods. Missing data in global variables sometimes require additional considerations but can be treated with similar tools. Additional patterns of missing data are possible (e.g., incomplete data about group membership), but these will not be our focus in the present chapter (Goldstein, 2011; for a discussion, see Hill & Goldstein, 1998).

For example, consider Table 16.1. In the first group of employees, only a single response to the workload variable is missing (Level 1, item missing). In the second group, the ratings on leadership style

are missing for all employees (Level 1, item missing), and the group mean is missing as a result (shared Level 2, item missing). In the third group, one employee did not respond to any items (Level 1, unit missing). In that group, the group mean might be calculated from the observed values, but it will be subject to uncertainty and possible bias because the underlying items are incomplete (shared Level 2, item missing). In addition, the cohesion score is missing for all employees in that group (global Level 2, item missing). Finally, the last employee could not be assigned to a group with sufficient certainty.

METHODS FOR HANDLING MISSING DATA

In this section, we consider two general procedures that are currently regarded as principled methods for handling missing data (e.g., Schafer & Graham, 2002). First, we consider MI. We elaborate on different approaches to multilevel MI, and we discuss potential challenges when specifying imputation models for multilevel data. As a second procedure, we consider the estimation of multilevel models by ML. Finally, we provide a comparison of the two procedures from a practical point of view.

Multiple Imputation

The basic idea in MI is to replace missing values with an "informed guess" obtained from the observed data and a statistical model (the imputation model). A schematic representation of this process is displayed in Figure 16.2. Multiple imputation generates several (M) replacements for the missing data by drawing from a predictive distribution of the missing data, given the observed data and the parameters of the imputation model. The M data sets are then analyzed separately, yielding M sets of parameter estimates (i.e., $\hat{Q}_1, \ldots, \hat{Q}_M$), and these are combined into a set of final parameter estimates (i.e., $\hat{Q}_{MI}$) and inferences using the rules outlined by Rubin (1987).

When performing MI, the imputation model must be chosen in such a way that it "matches" the model of interest, that is, it must be specified in such a way that it preserves the relationships among variables and the relevant features of the analysis model (Meng, 1994; Schafer, 2003). For example, if the model of interest is a regression model with

TABLE 16.1

Hypothetical Example of a Pattern of Missing Data in a Multilevel Sample

Case	Group	SAT_{ij}	LS_{ij}	WL_{ij}	COH_j	$\overline{LS}_{.j}$
1	1	2.3	?	High	3.8	?
2	1	1.7	?	Low	3.8	?
3	1	1.7	?	High	3.8	?
4	2	1.8	2.3	Low	?	2.2
5	2	1.4	2.1	High	?	2.2
6	2	?	?	?	?	2.2
7	3	3.4	1.2	Low	2.7	1.4
8	3	2.8	1.8	?	2.7	1.4
9	3	3.1	1.2	Low	2.7	1.4
10	?	2.1	2.3	High	?	?

Note. Missing observations are indicated by question marks. *COH* = cohesion; *LS* = leadership style; *SAT* = job satisfaction; *WL* = workload.

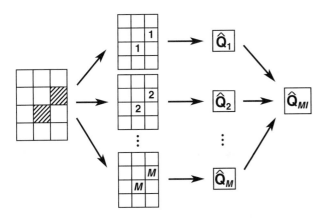

FIGURE 16.2. Schematic representation of multiple imputation (MI) and the analysis of multiply imputed data sets. $\hat{Q}$ = estimator of the parameter of interest.

an interaction effect, then the imputation model must also include the interaction; otherwise, it will be more difficult to detect the interaction effect in subsequent analyses (Enders, Baraldi, & Cham, 2014). In multilevel research, it is important for the imputation model to incorporate the multilevel structure of the data. In the following, we review different strategies for accommodating the multilevel structure during MI, including ad hoc strategies on the basis of single-level MI. We consider two broad approaches to MI: joint modeling and the fully conditional specification of MI. In the joint modeling approach, a single statistical model is

specified for all incomplete variables simultaneously. In the fully conditional specification, each variable is imputed in turn using a sequence of models (for a discussion, see Carpenter & Kenward, 2013). Finally, we discuss strategies for analyzing multiply imputed data sets and pooling their results.

Strategies based on single-level multiple imputation. Perhaps the simplest approach to multilevel MI is to ignore the multilevel structure of the data and employ single-level MI. With this strategy, the multilevel structure is disregarded altogether. Not surprisingly, it has been shown that single-level MI can lead to biased estimates in subsequent multilevel analyses (Black, Harel, & McCoach, 2011; Enders, Mistler, & Keller, 2016; Taljaard, Donner, & Klar, 2008). Lüdtke, Robitzsch, and Grund (2017) demonstrated that single-level MI tends to underestimate the intraclass correlation (ICC; also known as the ICC(1)) of variables with missing data and may either under- or overestimate within- and between-group effects in multilevel random intercept models. Figure 16.3 shows the expected bias in the ICC of a variable Y relative to its true value (i.e., in percent) and for different numbers of individuals per group (n), different values of the ICC of Y and an auxiliary variable X, and different amounts of missing data (25%, 50%). As can be seen, single-level MI tends to underestimate the true ICC. For example, in the

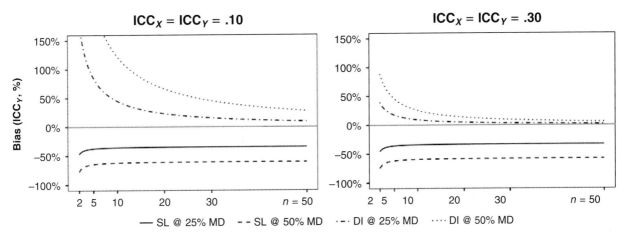

FIGURE 16.3. Expected bias for the estimator of the ICC of a variable of interest (Y) under single-level MI (SL) and the dummy-indicator approach (DI). It is assumed that all groups contain the same number of individuals (n) and the same proportion of missing data (MD) in Y. ICC$_X$ = intraclass correlation of an auxiliary variable; ICC$_Y$ = intraclass correlation of the variable of interest.

scenario with $n = 5$ individuals per group and 25% missing data, single-level MI is expected to yield an estimate of only .062 when the true ICC is .100 and of only .191 when the true ICC is .300. In either case, the true ICC is underestimated by approximately 37%.

To remedy this situation, it has been suggested that the multilevel structure be represented by a number of dummy indicator variables (i.e., the DI approach; e.g., Graham, 2009). This strategy effectively estimates a separate group mean for each group by estimating the imputation model conditional on group membership, thus incorporating group differences during MI (see also Enders et al., 2016). For example, the differences in job satisfaction between the 50 work groups in our running example can be represented in a regression model by the intercept and an additional 49 dummy variables (with one group selected as a reference group). The performance of this strategy depends on the situation in which it is applied. As demonstrated by Drechsler (2015), the DI approach tends to overestimate the ICC of variables with missing data but yields approximately unbiased estimates of the regression coefficients in a multilevel analysis model when missing data are restricted to the dependent variable (see also Andridge, 2011). However, because the DI approach exaggerates the variance between groups, it provides only a biased estimate of the between-group effect if missing values occur in explanatory variables (Lüdtke et al., 2017). As shown in Figure 16.3, the DI approach tends to overestimate the true ICC. The bias is particularly strong when the true ICC is small and there are only a few individuals per group. For example, with $n = 5$ individuals per group and 25% missing data, the DI strategy is expected to yield an estimate of around .186 when the true ICC is .100 and of around .353 when the true ICC is .300. This corresponds to overestimations of the ICC by approximately 86% and 18%, respectively.

Joint modeling. To accommodate the nested structure of multilevel data, it has been recommended that MI be performed by using mixed-effects models (e.g., Enders et al., 2016; Lüdtke et al., 2017; Yucel, 2008). In the joint modeling approach to multilevel MI, a single model is specified for all variables with and without missing data, and imputations are generated from this model for all variables simultaneously.[1] The joint model can be regarded as a multivariate extension of univariate multilevel models; that is, it addresses multiple dependent variables simultaneously. The model reads

$$\mathbf{y}_{1ij} = \boldsymbol{\gamma}_1 + \mathbf{u}_{1j} + \mathbf{r}_{1ij} \qquad \text{(Level 1)}$$

$$\mathbf{y}_{2j} = \boldsymbol{\gamma}_2 + \mathbf{u}_{2j}, \qquad \text{(Level 2)} \qquad (16.4)$$

where $\mathbf{y}_{1ij}$ denotes a vector of responses for individual i in group j with fixed intercepts $\boldsymbol{\gamma}_1$, random intercepts $\mathbf{u}_{1j}$, and residuals $\mathbf{r}_{ij}$. Similarly, $\mathbf{y}_{2j}$ denotes a vector of responses for group j (i.e., global variables) with fixed intercepts $\boldsymbol{\gamma}_2$ and residuals $\mathbf{u}_{2j}$. The random effects and residuals at Level 2 ($\mathbf{u}_{1j}, \mathbf{u}_{2j}$) are assumed to jointly follow a multivariate normal distribution with mean zero and covariance matrix $\boldsymbol{\Psi}$. The residuals at Level 2 follow a multivariate normal distribution with mean zero and covariance matrix $\boldsymbol{\Sigma}$. The joint model was originally developed by Schafer and Yucel (2002) to treat missing data at Level 1 and has since been extended to address missing data in categorical variables and variables at Level 2 (Asparouhov & Muthén, 2010; Carpenter & Kenward, 2013; Goldstein, Carpenter, Kenward, & Levin, 2009).

To illustrate how the joint model accommodates the multilevel structure, consider our running example and the illustration in Figure 16.4. The model of interest is a random intercept model that includes variables assessed at Levels 1 and 2 as well as relations between job satisfaction and leadership style both within and between groups (Equation 16.3). The joint model includes all variables as dependent variables in a multivariate random intercept model (Figure 16.4). For each variable at Level 1, the model includes a random

[1]The joint model can be expressed in a more general way, which allows fully observed variables to be included as predictor variables on the right-hand side of the model. However, in the present chapter, we consider only the "empty" specification of the model because it is easy to specify and widely applicable in the context of multilevel random intercept models (Enders et al., 2016; for a discussion, see Grund, Lüdtke, & Robitzsch, 2016b).

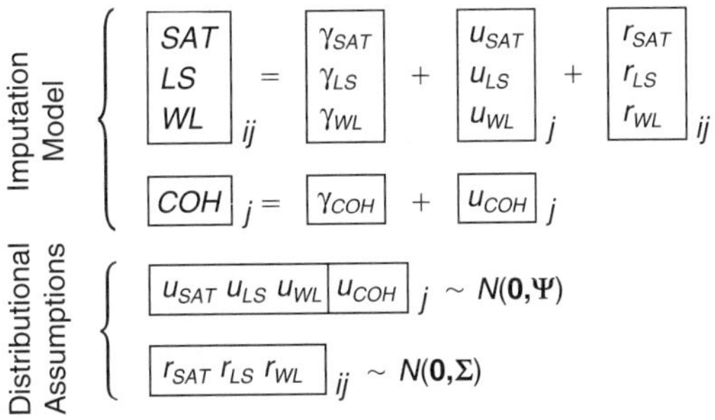

FIGURE 16.4. Schematic representation of the joint imputation model and its distributional assumptions in the running example. *COH* = cohesion; *LS* = leadership style; *SAT* = job satisfaction; *WL* = workload.

intercept $\mathbf{u}_{1j} = (u_{SAT,j}, u_{LS,j}, u_{WL,j})$, representing the components of these variables that vary between groups, and a residual term $\mathbf{r}_{1ij} = (r_{SAT,ij}, r_{LS,ij}, r_{WL,ij})$, representing the differences within groups. For cohesion, which was assessed directly at Level 2, the model includes a residual term $\mathbf{u}_{2j} = (u_{COH,j})$. The critical point in this model is that it assumes that the random effects and residuals at Level 2 (i.e., global and shared variables) may be correlated ($\mathbf{\Psi}$) and that the residuals at Level 1 may be correlated as well ($\mathbf{\Sigma}$). This illustrates that the joint model indeed "matches" the multilevel structure because it allows the user to differentiate between (a) the within- and between-group components that can be present in variables at Level 1 and (b) the relations between variables within and between groups. The joint model (or variants thereof) is implemented in the packages pan (Schafer & Zhao, 2016) and jomo (Quartagno & Carpenter, 2016) for the statistical software R as well as in the standalone software packages SAS (Mistler, 2013), M*plus* (Asparouhov & Muthén, 2010), and REALCOM (Carpenter, Goldstein, & Kenward, 2011).

Fully conditional specification. As an alternative to the joint model, the joint distribution of the variables with missing data can be approximated by imputing one variable at a time using a sequence of univariate models. To address multivariate patterns of missing data, the procedure iterates back and forth between variables with missing data, conditioning on the other variables in the data set (or a subset of them). This approach is referred to as the fully

conditional specification of MI (FCS; van Buuren, Brand, Groothuis-Oudshoorn, & Rubin, 2006). Specifically, for a set of variables at Levels 1 and 2, a sequence of conditional imputation models can be specified as follows:

$$y_{1ijp} = \mathbf{y}_{1j(-p)}\mathbf{\gamma}_p + u_{jp} + r_{ijp} \qquad \text{(Level 1)}$$

$$y_{2jq} = \mathbf{y}_{j(-q)}\mathbf{\gamma}_q + u_{jq}, \qquad \text{(Level 2)} \quad (16.5)$$

where y_{1ijp} is the *p*-th variable with missing data at Level 1, and $\mathbf{y}_{ij-(p)}$ is a set of predictors for that variable that may include any variable other than y_{1ijp}. Similarly, y_{2jq} is the *q*-th variable with missing data at Level 2 (i.e., a global variable), and $\mathbf{y}_{j-(q)}$ is a set of predictor variables that may include any other variable at Level 2 (i.e., global variables) as well as the between-group components of any variable at Level 1. The random intercepts u_{jp} as well as the residuals r_{ijp} and u_{jq} in each model are each assumed to follow independent normal distributions (see also van Buuren, 2011). To address multiple variables with missing data, the FCS algorithm arranges them in a sequence and visits one variable at a time, generating imputations from the imputation model assigned to each variable. Once a variable has been completed in this manner, it can be used as a predictor in any of the other imputation models. After each variable has been visited, the sequence is repeated, and new imputations are generated until the algorithm converges, yielding the first of multiple imputations.

The sequential nature of the FCS algorithm requires some rethinking. In contrast to the joint model, the FCS algorithm allows different predictors to be selected for each target variable, and conversely, all target variables can act as predictors in any other target's imputation model. Moreover, in order to preserve the relationships between variables, it is in fact *required* that the imputation model for each target variable is conditioned on the other variables. To incorporate relationships between variables at Level 2, the group means of the variables at Level 1 must be calculated and included as predictors. In addition, the group means must be updated once new imputations for the underlying variables have been obtained; this process of updating the group means is known as *passive* imputation (e.g., Royston, 2005).

To illustrate multilevel FCS, consider our running example and the illustration in Figure 16.5. Missing data in job satisfaction, leadership style, and workload can be imputed by applying separate multilevel models, where the model for workload should be appropriate for binary categorical data (e.g., a logistic multilevel model). Cohesion can be imputed by using a regression model at Level 2. To preserve the relationships between the variables within and between groups, all variables are included as predictor variables in the other variables' imputation models, and the group means are updated and included by using passive imputation. The FCS and similar approaches for multilevel data are implemented in the package mice (van Buuren & Groothuis-Oudshoorn, 2011) for the statistical software R as well as in the standalone software packages M*plus* (Asparouhov & Muthén, 2010) and Blimp (Keller & Enders, 2018).

Incomplete categorical variables. There are several options for treating missing values in categorical and ordinal variables. The first option is to treat categorical variables as continuous for the purpose of MI and to round the resulting values to comply with the original categories in that variable. For

example, imputations for ordinal data may be rounded using 0.5, 1.5, and so forth as thresholds; for binary data, adaptive rounding can be applied, which uses the mean of the imputed values to adjust the threshold accordingly (see Carpenter & Kenward, 2013). Adaptive rounding has been shown to perform well for binary missing data (Bernaards, Belin, & Schafer, 2007), but also MI without rounding appears to work well for binary and (some) ordinal variables (Schafer, 1997; W. Wu, Jia, & Enders, 2015). Finally, it is possible to impute categorical and ordinal variables using a latent variable approach. In this approach, imputations are generated for a set of underlying latent variables that represent the relative probability of being assigned to a given category. Based on the latent scores, the assignment to a category can then be simulated by using an appropriate link function (e.g., a probit link for latent normal variables; see Carpenter & Kenward, 2013). For a variable with C categories, this approach introduces $C-1$ latent variables that represent the possible contrasts between categories (Carpenter & Kenward, 2013; see also Goldstein et al., 2009). For binary variables, this is equivalent to generating imputations from a generalized linear mixed-effects model (e.g., a logistic or probit model). These procedures, too, appear to work well for both

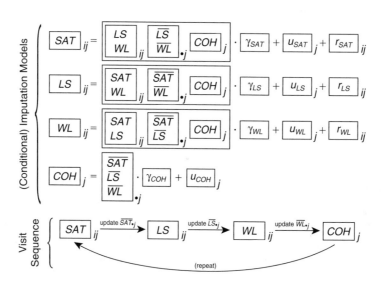

FIGURE 16.5. Schematic representation of the sampling steps in the fully conditional specification of multilevel multiple imputation in the running example. *COH* = cohesion; *LS* = leadership style; *SAT* = job satisfaction; *WL* = workload.

binary and polytomous data (Demirtas, 2009; W. Wu et al., 2015; see also Enders et al., 2016).

Analyzing multiply imputed data. The idea underlying MI is to generate plausible replacements for each missing value, thus transforming a data set with "missing data" into a data set with "complete data." This process is repeated M times (hence, the qualifier "multiple"), yielding M completed versions of the original data (see Figure 16.2). Once the set of M data sets has been obtained, the model of interest must be fit separately to each data set, yielding M estimates of some parameter of interest, say $\hat{Q}_m$ (e.g., regression coefficients; $m = 1, \ldots, M$), and M estimates of the sampling variance of that estimate, $\hat{V}_m$ (e.g., squared standard errors). According to Rubin (1987), the combined point estimate is the average of the individual estimates

$$\hat{Q}_{MI} = \frac{1}{M} \sum_{m=1}^{M} \hat{Q}_m. \qquad (16.6)$$

The combined estimate of the sampling variance of the estimator incorporates two different sources of uncertainty:

$$\hat{V}_{MI} = \hat{W} + \left(1 + \frac{1}{M}\right)\hat{B}, \qquad (16.7)$$

where $\hat{W}$ denotes the sampling variance *within* imputations, that is, the average of the individual variance estimates

$$\hat{W} = \frac{1}{M} \sum_{m=1}^{M} \hat{V}_m, \qquad (16.8)$$

and $\hat{B}$ denotes the sampling variance *between* imputations, that is, the variance of the point estimates across data sets:

$$\hat{B} = \frac{1}{M-1} \sum_{m=1}^{M} \left(\hat{Q}_m - \hat{Q}_{MI}\right)^2. \qquad (16.9)$$

Using the combined point and variance estimates, standard hypothesis tests can be carried out on the basis of a Student's *t* distribution with v degrees of freedom. Rubin (1987) recommended calculating the degrees of freedom as follows:

$$v = (M-1)\left[1 + \frac{1}{\text{RIV}}\right]^2, \qquad (16.10)$$

where the expression

$$\text{RIV} = \frac{\hat{W}}{(1 + 1/M)\hat{B}}, \qquad (16.11)$$

denotes the relative increase in the sampling variance of the estimator that is due to missing data (see also Barnard & Rubin, 1999). In addition, several alternative formulas have been proposed for more complex hypotheses that may involve several parameters simultaneously, for example, when testing the overall effect of categorical explanatory variables or when testing for random slopes using a likelihood-ratio test (see Appendix 16.1; see also Reiter & Raghunathan, 2007).

The general idea behind Rubin's rules is to approximate the sampling distribution of $\hat{Q}$ that would be obtained with infinite M but based on only a small number of imputations. Naturally, the larger the number that is chosen for M, the better the approximation becomes, which raises the question of "How many are needed?" Traditionally, $M = 5$ imputations have been recommended (Rubin, 1987), but more can be necessary when the amount of missing data increases or the model of interest becomes more complex (Bodner, 2008; Graham, Olchowski, & Gilreath, 2007). This is especially important because most software packages for multilevel MI generate $M = 5$ imputations by default. In our experience, $M = 20$ imputations are usually sufficient for estimating and testing the parameters in most applications of multilevel models. However, when large portions of the data are missing (say more than 50%) or complex hypotheses that involve multiple parameters are being tested, we recommend generating 50 to 100 imputed data sets (see also Bodner, 2008; Raghunathan, 2015).

Maximum Likelihood

The general principle behind ML estimation is that the values of the parameters in a statistical model can be chosen in such a way that the likelihood of the data becomes maximal. When the data contain missing values, it is often possible to estimate the model directly using only the observed data. This procedure is often referred to as *direct* or *full information* ML. Using ML, the likelihood is evaluated on a case-by-case basis; that is, cases with incomplete records contribute to the likelihood only to the extent to which they have data (Little & Rubin, 2002). The ML estimates of the parameters in a model of interest are consistent when the data are MAR or MCAR; that is, missing data occur in an unsystematic fashion when the variables in the model are taken into account (Little & Rubin, 2002).

The main principle by which ML "deals" with missing data is that it imposes distributional assumptions on incomplete variables. For this reason, common multilevel software packages often handle missing values only in the dependent variable of the model (e.g., HLM, SAS), where such assumptions are already in place, but cases with missing values in explanatory variables are discarded because no distributional assumptions have been made for them. To circumvent this restriction, it has been suggested that researchers adopt the framework of *structural equation modeling* (SEM), which allows the user to introduce distributional assumptions for all variables by defining them as endogenous (i.e., dependent) variables in a single analysis model (e.g., Allison, 2012; Enders, 2010). For example, in the statistical software M*plus*, this is achieved by including the variances and covariances of the explanatory variables in the modeling statement. Using this strategy, it is often possible to prevent the software from discarding these cases and to apply the ML principle to both the dependent and explanatory variables in a model of interest. Furthermore, this perspective offers the possibility of including auxiliary variables that may improve the plausibility of the MAR assumption and the accuracy of estimates under ML (Enders, 2008; Graham, 2003). Software that supports ML for multilevel models from the perspective of SEM includes the standalone software packages M*plus* (Muthén & Muthén, 2012), Latent GOLD (Vermunt & Magidson, 2016), gllamm (Rabe-Hesketh, Skrondal, & Pickles, 2004), and xxM (Mehta, 2013).

As an alternative to direct ML, estimates of the parameters in a multilevel model can be obtained from a two-stage procedure by first estimating a covariance matrix within and between groups on the basis of the observed data; in the second stage, the parameters of interest are derived from the variances and covariances estimated in the first stage (Yuan & Bentler, 2000). Conceptually, two-stage ML is similar to the perspective taken in SEM. We will not consider this approach further, but using two-stage ML can offer advantages when working with nonnormal variables and because auxiliary variables are easily incorporated into the estimation procedure (Savalei & Bentler, 2009; Yuan, Yang-Wallentin, & Bentler, 2012).

Comparison of Maximum Likelihood and Multiple Imputation

From a theoretical point of view, ML and MI are not vastly different, and the two can be expected to yield similar results when they operate under similar assumptions (Schafer & Graham, 2002). However, from a practical point of view, the differences can be substantial. Fitting models using ML is often easy, provided that a software package that supports the estimation of the model of interest can be found. Furthermore, because ML does not separate the treatment of missing data from the analysis, the missing data model is always consistent with the analysis model; that is, the two models are always based on the same set of assumptions (Allison, 2012). However, integrating the treatment of missing data and the estimation of the analysis model into a single step also has disadvantages. First, the distributional assumptions needed for the treatment of missing data now also enter the analysis model even though they might not have originally been part of it. Second, auxiliary variables must be incorporated directly into the model of interest, thus making the analysis model more complex (Graham, 2003). In applications with only a few well-behaved variables, this is usually not a problem; but in practice, it can become problematic, for example, when the inclusion of auxiliary variables leads to a mix of continuous and categorical variables at both Levels 1 and 2. Such models are difficult for the user to specify, and a given software package might not even fully support it, forcing the user to alter the model or make decisions he or she would not have made otherwise.

Conducting MI, on the other hand, is more complicated at first glance. First, an imputation model that is consistent with the model of interest must be chosen. Then, the user must specify the number of imputations and the number of iterations for which the sampling procedure should run. Finally, he or she must ensure that the algorithm has converged before any analyses can be carried out (see also Allison, 2012). Once the imputations have been generated, the user must fit the analysis model to each of the imputed data sets and combine their results into a final set of parameter estimates and inferences. Especially for inexperienced users, performing MI can be a daunting task. On the other hand, modern procedures for multilevel MI are powerful and very flexible in accommodating a variety of models. In addition, many software packages for multilevel MI automatize at least some of these steps. Finally, the separation between the treatment of missing data and the analysis phase makes it straightforward to handle a variety of variables and to include auxiliary variables without altering the model of interest.

SIMULATION

Next, we report the results from a computer simulation study. This study was intended to illustrate the general performance of ML and MI in a controlled setting. We conducted this study with two models of interest in mind. The first model of interest (Model 1) was the model from our running example:

$$SAT_{ij} = \gamma_{00} + \gamma_{10}\left(LS_{ij} - \overline{LS}_{\cdot j}\right) + \gamma_{01}\overline{LS}_{\cdot j}$$
$$+ \gamma_{20}WL_{ij} + \tilde{a}_{02}COH_j + u_{0j} + r_{ij}.$$

$$(16.3, \text{revisited})$$

This represents the standard formulation of multilevel models in which the observed group means represent the shared perception of leadership style among members of the same group.

The second model of interest (Model 2) is also known as the "multilevel latent covariate model" (Lüdtke et al., 2008) and differs from the first

model in that it uses the true, unobserved group means or between-group components to represent the shared perception of individuals in each group. The model reads

$$SAT_{ij} = \gamma_{00} + \gamma_{10}LS_{W,ij} + \gamma_{01}LS_{B,j} + \gamma_{20}WL_{ij}$$
$$+ \gamma_{02}COH_j + u_{0j} + r_{ij}, \qquad (16.12)$$

where $LS_{W,ij}$ and $LS_{B,j}$ denote the within- and between-group components of leadership style (Asparouhov & Muthén, 2006; Lüdtke et al., 2008). Formulating the model in terms of the true within- and between-group components can be beneficial because it corrects for the fact that the group mean is calculated from a finite number of observations and thus provides only an unreliable measure of the true between-group component (see Croon & van Veldhoven, 2007; Raudenbush & Bryk, 2002). In the organizational literature, the reliability of the group mean is also known as the ICC(2), and it expresses the extent to which differences between the observed group means reflect true differences between groups (Bliese, 2000; see also LeBreton & Senter, 2008). It is a matter of debate in the multilevel literature which formulation of the model of interest is more appropriate. For example, it can be argued that the formulation in Model 2 is appropriate if the shared perception among individuals is of primary interest (e.g., ratings of team climate, leadership effectiveness), whereas Model 1 may be appropriate if the variation within groups is itself of interest or if the observed group mean is simply regarded as a summary measure (e.g., gender ratio, socioeconomic status; for further discussion, see Lüdtke et al., 2008). However, the main motivation for including these two approaches to modeling between-group effects in the present chapter was that their distinction is important for the treatment of missing data under ML (see below).

In the simulation study, the samples were generated from either Model 1 (the "standard" model) or Model 2 (the "latent covariate" model) in order to allow for a comparison between conditions in which one of the two models is the "true" model. The parameters of the simulation were loosely based on the data from Klein et al. (2000). The samples consisted of $G = 50$ groups of size $n = 10$. All variables were standardized across groups with mean zero and unit total variance. For the ratings on leadership style and job satisfaction, we assumed ICCs of .10 and .20, respectively. In addition, we assumed that negative leadership style was correlated with cohesion at the group level ($r = -.15$). For the two workload categories (high vs. low), we generated a standard normal variable with an ICC of .20, and we used 0.38 as a breaking point to dichotomize that variable, resulting in 35% and 65% of individuals with high and low workloads, respectively. For simplicity, we assumed that workload was uncorrelated with the other explanatory variables. Finally, we assumed the following fixed effects in the data-generating model: $\gamma_{00} = 0$ (intercept), $\gamma_{10} = -.20$ and $\gamma_{01} = -.70$ (leadership style), $\gamma_{20} = -.30$ (workload), and $\gamma_{02} = .10$ (cohesion). The variance components τ_0^2 and σ^2 then followed. We induced missing values in cohesion completely at random (5%) and in leadership style (15%) and workload (10%) on the basis of job satisfaction (lower job satisfaction corresponded with a greater chance of missing data). Finally, we induced missing values in job satisfaction completely at random (10%).

Using this procedure, we generated 5,000 data sets from both Models 1 and 2. In each data set, we carried out MI using both joint modeling (using jomo; Quartagno & Carpenter, 2016) and FCS (using mice; van Buuren & Groothuis-Oudshoorn, 2011) in the statistical software R. Afterwards, we fitted the respective model of interest using M*plus* 7 (Muthén & Muthén, 2012). We also used M*plus* to estimate the model with ML, and we addressed missing data in explanatory variables by specifying distributional assumptions for these variables. In the context of Model 2, applying ML is relatively easy because M*plus* already imposes the necessary distributional assumptions when decomposing leadership style into its within- and between-group components. The distributional assumptions for the remaining variables can be added by defining them as endogenous variables at Level 1 or Level 2,

respectively.[2] On the other hand, in the context of Model 1, missing data in explanatory variables pose a greater challenge when estimating the model using ML. We consider two strategies for this case, neither of which is completely satisfying. In the first strategy (ML1), distributional assumptions are specified as before by defining explanatory variables as endogenous variables at Levels 1 and 2, respectively. However, this strategy unintentionally adopts the within- and between-group decomposition for leadership style (as in Model 2), thus correcting between-group effects that did not require correction. As a second option (ML2), the group means of leadership style can be calculated beforehand from the observed data, and distributional assumptions can be imposed only on the within-group deviations of leadership style. In this specification, the group means are consistent with the analysis model, but the between-group effects of leadership style may be biased if values are missing in a systematic manner (similar to LD).

In Table 16.2, we included the mean estimates of the three procedures for the two models of interest as well as the coverage of the 95% confidence interval. Ideally, the mean estimates should be close to the true values in the data-generating model, and the coverage rates should be close to 95%. In the context of Model 2, both MI and ML yielded parameter estimates that were very close to the true values, and coverage rates were close to the nominal value of 95%. However, the between-group effect of leadership style (γ_{01}) was slightly too large under ML, which may be attributed to the small sample size at Level 2 (Lüdtke et al., 2008). In the context of Model 1, the parameter estimates obtained from MI were again close to the true values, but the between-group effect of leadership style (γ_{01}) was slightly underestimated. Under ML, specifying leadership style as an endogenous variable (ML1), and thus adopting the within- and between-group decomposition, led to severe bias in the between-group regression coefficients. By contrast, when the group means were calculated beforehand

---

[2]Using ML, it was also not straightforward to accommodate both (a) the multilevel structure of the variables and (b) the fact that workload is categorical. Therefore, we treated workload as a continuous variable. Although this may be acceptable for a dichotomous variable with similar frequencies in both categories, it will lead to problems when explanatory variables have multiple categories or some categories occur much more frequently than others.

TABLE 16.2

Mean Estimates (and Coverage Rates for the 95% Confidence Interval) for the Two Models of Interest for Multiple Imputation and Maximum Likelihood

| | Model 1 | | | | | Model 2 | | | |
	True	JM	FCS	ML1	ML2	True	JM	FCS	ML1
γ_{00}	0.000	0.003	0.002	0.004	0.011	0.000	0.001	0.000	0.001
		(95.0)	(95.0)	(96.1)	(94.1)		(94.8)	(94.3)	(95.1)
γ_{10}	−0.200	−0.202	−0.200	−0.203	−0.200	−0.200	−0.201	−0.200	−0.200
		(94.7)	(94.7)	(94.9)	(94.7)		(93.8)	(94.0)	(94.3)
γ_{01}	−0.700	−0.648	−0.660	−1.215	−0.633	−0.700	−0.708	−0.714	−0.803
		(94.6)	(94.5)	(91.8)	(90.5)		(95.4)	(95.1)	(96.1)
γ_{20}	−0.300	−0.301	−0.300	−0.302	−0.303	−0.300	−0.298	−0.297	−0.299
		(94.8)	(95.0)	(94.9)	(94.8)		(94.9)	(94.9)	(94.9)
γ_{02}	0.100	0.102	0.102	0.067	0.105	0.100	0.098	0.099	0.095
		(94.3)	(93.8)	(95.5)	(92.7)		(95.0)	(94.4)	(95.4)
τ_0^2	0.083	0.085	0.082	0.035	0.081	0.088	0.079	0.078	0.069
		(95.4)	(94.0)	(91.9)	(91.5)		(95.0)	(93.9)	(92.3)
σ^2	0.751	0.747	0.747	0.746	0.749	0.790	0.786	0.786	0.786
		(94.1)	(94.1)	(94.1)	(94.3)		(94.6)	(94.5)	(94.8)

Note. FCS = fully conditional specification of multiple imputation; γ_{00} = intercept; γ_{10} = within-group effect of leadership style; γ_{01} = between-group effect of leadership style; γ_{20} = effect of workload; γ_{02} = effect of cohesion; JM = joint modeling of multiple imputation; ML1 = maximum likelihood with true within- and between-group components for leadership style; ML2 = maximum likelihood with group means for leadership style calculated from the observed data; σ^2 = residual variance; τ_0^2 = intercept variance.

from the observed data (ML2), thus treating only the within-group deviations as endogenous, the group-level effect of leadership style (γ_{01}) was only slightly underestimated. The coverage rates were relatively close to the nominal value of 95% for most parameters but tended to be slightly smaller under ML, especially when the group means were calculated from the observed data (ML2).

In conclusion, both ML and MI provided accurate results when their assumptions were met and when these assumptions were consistent with the model of interest. These requirements were more easily fulfilled in the context of Model 2, in which case both MI and ML yielded reasonable parameter estimates. However, in the context of Model 1, the results were more diverse. Under ML, following the usual advice to treat explanatory variables as endogenous can lead to an unwanted "shift" in the analysis model; in the present case, this resulted in parameter estimates that were severely distorted. When the group means were calculated beforehand, we observed only little

bias. However, this approach slightly overestimated the precision of the parameter estimates because it ignored the fact that group means were calculated from incomplete records. Under MI, estimates were accurate, and the confidence intervals showed good coverage properties, providing the most reasonable approximation to the true parameters overall.

EXAMPLE APPLICATION

In this section, we apply the missing data methods to our running example. The running example is based on the data from Klein et al. (2000) and essentially mimics the conditions in our simulation study except that the example data set contains *un*standardized variables instead. Missing values were induced in the data set in the same way as in the simulation study. As a result, 21.9% of the employees had missing values on at least one variable; these were distributed across job satisfaction (9.2%), leadership style (12.3%), workload (11.5%), and cohesion (4.0%).

The data set is included in the R package mitml (Grund, Robitzsch, & Lüdtke, 2016). The model of interest was the "standard" multilevel model in Equation 16.3 (Model 1). We applied MI using the joint model implemented in the jomo package in R, and we estimated the model of interest using the lme4 package (Bates, Maechler, Bolker, & Walker, 2016). To assist with the analyses, we used the mitml package, which provides a wrapper function for the jomo package as well as tools for analyzing multiply imputed data sets (see also Grund et al., 2016b). For ML estimation, we used M*plus*, where we calculated the group means of leadership style from the observed records (as in ML1) and adopted the within- and between-group decomposition for the remaining variables (as in ML2). The computer code and the M*plus* syntax file are provided in Appendix 16.2.

To set up the imputation model using jomo and mitml, two formulas that denoted the imputation model for variables at Levels 1 and 2, respectively, had to be specified (see Equation 16.4 and Figure 16.4). In accordance with the "empty" specification of the model, all variables were treated as target variables, and no predictor variables were specified except for a "one" for the intercept. We generated $M = 100$ imputations in this manner. The number of iterations for the algorithm was chosen in such a way that convergence could be established by inspecting convergence criteria (e.g., Gelman & Rubin, 1992) and diagnostic plots for the parameters of the imputation model (Grund et al., 2016b; see also Schafer & Olsen, 1998). After running MI, the model of interest was fitted to each of the imputed data sets using lme4, and the parameter estimates were pooled by employing Rubin's rules in order to obtain a final set of parameter estimates and inferences. The results obtained from ML and MI are presented in Table 16.3. The two analyses suggested that negative leadership style had a relatively strong impact on employees' job satisfaction when employees' workload and the work group's cohesion were taken into account. Under MI, for any one-unit change in the leadership style ratings within groups (Level 1), the expected change in job satisfaction was $-.532$ ($p < .001$). Between groups, a one-unit change in the shared perception of leadership style ratings (Level 2) was associated with an expected change in job satisfaction of -1.566 ($p < .001$).

TABLE 16.3

Estimates for the Parameters in the Model of Interest Obtained From Maximum Likelihood and Multiple Imputation in the Running Example

Parameter	M*plus* (ML2)		jomo (MI)			
	Est.	SE	Est.	SE	RIV	FMI
Intercept (γ_{00})	0.291***	0.136	0.257†**	0.140	0.167	0.143
Level 1						
Leadership style (γ_{10})	−0.526***	0.091	−0.532***	0.092	0.341	0.255
Workload (γ_{20})	−0.863***	0.197	−0.842***	0.195	0.259	0.206
Level 2						
Leadership style (γ_{01})	−1.491***	0.319	−1.566***	0.349	0.237	0.192
Cohesion (γ_{02})	0.237***	0.088	0.243***	0.091	0.075	0.070
Level 2 residual variance (τ_0^2)	0.268***	0.128	0.286***			
Level 1 residual variance (σ^2)	4.940***	0.283	4.962***			

Note. ML2 = maximum likelihood with group means for leadership style calculated from the observed data; MI = multiple imputation; Est. = estimate; SE = standard error; RIV = relative increase in variance; FMI = fraction of missing information; γ_{00} = intercept; γ_{10} = within-group effect of leadership style; γ_{20} = effect of workload; γ_{01} = between-group effect of leadership style; γ_{02} = effect of cohesion; τ_0^2 = intercept variance; s_2 = residual variance.
†$p < .10$. *$p < .05$. **$p < .01$. ***$p < .001$ (two-tailed).

Furthermore, there was a negative effect of high (vs. low) workload (-0.842, $p < .001$) on job satisfaction and a positive effect of cohesion (0.243, $p = 0.007$). The results obtained from ML were virtually identical. Perhaps the largest difference between the two procedures was the standard error for the between-group effect of leadership style, which might reflect the slightly too narrow confidence intervals under ML observed in the simulation study.

In addition, we also investigated whether the within-group effect of leadership style *varied* across groups, that is, whether there was significant variance in the slope of leadership style. To this end, we fitted an alternative model that contained a random slope for within-group effect of leadership style. The alternative model was compared with the model of interest using the D_3 statistic (Meng & Rubin, 1992), which can be interpreted as a pooled LRT for multiply imputed data sets (Appendix 16.1). The D_3 statistic suggested that there was not enough evidence to conclude that the effect of leadership style truly varied across groups, $F(2,3707.9) = 2.621$ ($p = .071$). Therefore, the alternative model was rejected in favor of the model of interest.[3] Furthermore, we were interested in whether the effect of leadership style was larger between than within groups. For this purpose, we used the D_1 statistic, which allowed us to test the difference between the two coefficients against zero by specifying it as a linear constraint (Appendix 16.1; see also Kreft, de Leeuw, & Aiken, 1995). The D_1 statistic suggested that the two parameters were significantly different from one another, $F(1,2471.3) = 8.253$ ($p = .004$), that is, the between-group effect (-1.57) was significantly larger than the within-group effect (-0.53).

DISCUSSION

In this chapter, we provided an introduction to multilevel modeling with missing data. In particular, we looked at two principled methods for handling missing data: MI and estimation by ML. The general ideas behind ML and MI are not vastly different, and both may be regarded as state-of-the-art procedures for handling missing data (Schafer & Graham, 2002). The differences between the two methods are most often of a practical nature. Although the two procedures tend to give the same answers if they are based on similar assumptions, carrying out a given task is often easier with one procedure than the other. For example, ML is very easy to incorporate into one's regular workflow because the missing data treatment is performed during the estimation of the model of interest (see also Allison, 2012). On the other hand, addressing missing values and including auxiliary variables may prove to be challenging depending on where the missing data occur and how complex the model becomes once all factors are taken into account, for example, if categorical variables contain missing data or between-group effects are represented by observed group means. By contrast, MI allows for the very flexible modeling of different types of variables and including auxiliary variables is straightforward. On the other hand, performing MI and analyzing multiple data sets can be challenging, especially for less experienced users or when nonstandard analyses and hypothesis tests are required. That being said, although we clearly see ML as the easier-to-use alternative (see Allison, 2012; Enders, 2010), we tend to favor MI for its flexibility and because it separates the imputation from the analysis phase (see Carpenter & Kenward, 2013; Schafer & Graham, 2002; see also Grund, Lüdtke, & Robitzsch, 2018).

As in every introduction to these or similar procedures, it is not possible to give all possible research scenarios the attention they deserve. In this chapter, we restricted our discussion to cross-sectional multilevel models with a single level of clustering, that is, individuals nested within some higher-level collective. In principle, the procedures discussed here generalize naturally to models with additional levels of clustering, for example, three-level models (Goldstein, 2011; Keller, 2015; Yucel, 2008), models with cross-classified random effects (Goldstein, 2011; Hill & Goldstein, 1998), or models with multiple memberships (Goldstein,

---

[3]Note that, because the imputation model did not include random slopes, it did not "match" the alternative model. For this reason, the hypothesis test was not completely trustworthy and was included here only for the purpose of illustration.

2011; Yucel, Ding, Uludag, & Tomaskovic-Devey, 2008). However, these procedures are not widely available in standard software, and more research is needed to evaluate their performance in realistic research scenarios.

Another topic that we did not discuss explicitly is the treatment of missing data in longitudinal research designs (e.g., repeated measurements, diary studies, experience sampling, ecological momentary assessment). This topic is particularly interesting, however, because multilevel models are frequently used to analyze longitudinal data. Fortunately, many of the ideas presented here can also be applied to longitudinal data (see also Black, Harel, & Matthews, 2013; Newman, 2003). For example, assume that a researcher is interested in estimating a growth curve model with missing data in the dependent variable that should be treated using MI. It is then useful to distinguish studies in which the longitudinal design is balanced or unbalanced with respect to time, that is, whether all participants were measured at the same or a different set of time points (see W. Wu, West, & Taylor, 2009). If all participants were measured on the same set of time points, then the longitudinal data structure can be expressed in a wide data format, and single-level MI can be used to treat the missing values in the dependent variable (for a two-stage ML procedure, see Yuan et al., 2012). However, if participants were measured at potentially different or unbalanced time points, then procedures based on mixed-effects models for multilevel MI may be more appropriate (see Equation 16.4). However, even though the model by Schafer and Yucel (2002) was developed explicitly with applications to longitudinal data in mind, the model lacks the flexibility to incorporate some covariance structures at Level 1 that are commonly used in longitudinal analysis models (see Pinheiro & Bates, 2000). Similar problems may be observed when ML is used to estimate growth curve models because it is difficult to establish a homogeneous covariance structure for this type of data (W. Wu et al., 2009).

Even though there has been a substantial amount of interest in missing data methods for multilevel data in recent years, some questions still provide challenges for the future. One such example is the treatment of missing data in multilevel models with random slopes or in models with nonlinear and interaction effects. For example, it has been shown that current implementations of MI are not perfectly suited for handling missing data in explanatory variables in multilevel models with random slopes (e.g., Enders et al., 2016; Gottfredson, Sterba, & Jackson, 2017; Grund, Lüdtke, & Robitzsch, 2016a; see also von Hippel, 2009). Similar problems may occur under ML but have yet to be discussed more thoroughly in the applied missing data literature (however, see Enders et al., 2014). In order to make sure that imputations are consistent with the model of interest, it has been argued that the substantive analysis model should be taken into account during MI (Bartlett, Seaman, White, & Carpenter, 2015; Carpenter & Kenward, 2013). Several authors have proposed procedures that incorporate these ideas using rejection sampling or a Metropolis–Hastings algorithm for multilevel MI, but these procedures are not yet available in standard software (Erler et al., 2016; Goldstein, Carpenter, & Browne, 2014; L. Wu, 2010). Similar procedures have been proposed in the context of ML, where the likelihood function in a multilevel model can be factored into separate components that refer to the model of interest and additional models for explanatory variables with missing data (Ibrahim, Chen, & Lipsitz, 2001; Stubbendick & Ibrahim, 2003).

To sum up, missing data are an ever-present problem in research practice. We believe that ML and MI provide powerful tools for the treatment of missing data in multilevel research. The two procedures both come with their own strengths and weaknesses, and one may be preferred over the other for a specific missing data problem. At the end of the day, however, they are more similar than they are different, and both offer a substantial improvement over approaches such as LD in terms of generality, theoretical foundation, accuracy of parameter estimates, and statistical power. In the present chapter, we provided an introduction to these methods, and we offered guidance on how to apply them in multilevel research. The treatment of missing data is not without its challenges, and there remain many open (and interesting) questions for the future.

However, we believe that these methods are a valuable addition to the researcher's toolbox, which, if applied correctly, can improve the quality of the conclusions we draw from our data and that of our research altogether. We hope that this chapter will promote the adoption of MI and ML and will encourage researchers to use these procedures in their own research projects.

APPENDIX 16.1: MULTIPARAMETER HYPOTHESIS TESTS IN MULTIPLE IMPUTATION

In research practice, statistical hypotheses often involve multiple parameters simultaneously (e.g., linear constraints, comparisons of nested models). In analyses with complete data, multiparameter hypothesis tests are often performed using the Wald test or likelihood-ratio test (LRT). To pool a series of Wald tests on the basis of a series of parameter vectors, $\hat{Q}_m$, and covariance matrices, $\hat{V}_m$, Li, Raghunathan, and Rubin (1991) proposed that researchers should use the test statistic

$$D_1 = \frac{\left(\hat{Q}_{MI} - Q_0\right)^T \hat{W}^{-1} \left(\hat{Q}_{MI} - Q_0\right)}{K(1 + \mathrm{ARIV}_1)}, \quad (16A.1)$$

where $\hat{Q}_{MI}$ and $\hat{W}$ are the average estimates of the parameter vector and its covariance matrix (see Equations 16.6 and 16.8), Q_0 contains the hypothesized values of the parameters under the null hypothesis, and ARIV_1 is an estimate of the average relative increase in variance (ARIV) due to nonresponse across parameters (see Enders, 2010). The D_1 statistic can be used in a similar manner as Rubin's rules (1987), that is, it can be used to test a set of parameters (or a linear transformation thereof) that have an approximately normal sampling distribution (e.g., regression coefficients).

It is sometimes difficult to calculate D_1, for example, because estimates of the covariance matrix are unavailable. As an alternative, Li, Meng, Raghunathan, and Rubin (1991) proposed that a set of Wald-like test statistics, D_m, be pooled as follows:

$$D_2 = \frac{\bar{D}K^{-1} + (M+1)(M-1)^{-1}\mathrm{ARIV}_2}{1 + \mathrm{ARIV}_2}, \quad (16A.2)$$

where $\bar{D}$ is the average of the D_m, and ARIV_2 is an alternative estimate of the ARIV. The D_2 statistic can be used for any quantity that follows a χ^2-distribution, for example, a Wald test of a set of regression coefficients (or a linear transformation thereof) or an LRT comparing two nested models (see also Snijders & Bosker, 2012).

As a third option, Meng and Rubin (1992) proposed a test statistic for pooling a series of LRTs as follows:

$$D_3 = \frac{\tilde{L}}{K(1 + \mathrm{ARIV}_3)}, \quad (16A.3)$$

where the ARIV_3 is another estimate of the average relative increase in variance, which includes (a) the average LRT statistic evaluated at the *actual* parameter estimates and (b) the average LRT statistic evaluated at the *average* parameter estimates for the two models ($\tilde{L}$). This test statistic can be used in the same manner as the LRT, for example, for comparing two nested statistical models (see above).

In general, D_1 and D_3 tend to be the more reliable procedures and should be used when possible. However, because software implementations of D_1 and D_3 are sometimes not available, D_2 may be an interesting alternative given its ease of application. Even though D_2 was optimized to work with a small number of imputations ($M = 3$), results from D_2 tend to be much more robust when more imputations (say, $M \geq 20$) are used (Grund, Lüdtke, & Robitzsch, 2016c; Licht, 2010). Care should be taken when large portions of the data are missing (say, more than 50%) because D_2 and (to a lesser extent) D_3 tend to be less robust in these cases.

APPENDIX 16.2: COMPUTER CODE FOR THE EXAMPLE APPLICATION

Printed below is the computer code used for multilevel MI in the data analysis example.
```
# *** Description of the 'leadership' data set:
#
# GRPID: indicator for work groups
# JOBSAT: job satisfaction (Level 1)
```

```
# NEGLEAD: ratings on negative leadership
    style (Level 1)
# WLOAD: workload (Level 1, "low" vs. "high")
# COHES: group cohesion (Level 2)

# Multiple imputation is performed with an "empty"
    joint model using jomo. The
# model of interest is fit using lme4, and the mitml
    package is used for pooling
# tests and parameters.

library(lme4)
library(mitml)

# set up random number generator
set.seed(1234)

# load data
data(leadership)

# *** Imputation phase:
#
# set up "empty" model
fml <- list(NEGLEAD + JOBSAT + WLOAD ~ 1
    + (1|GRPID),    # Level 1 model
    COHES ~ 1)    # Level 2 model

# impute
imp <- jomoImpute(leadership, formula=fml,
    n.burn=5000, n.iter=500, m=100)

# assess convergence
summary(imp)    # convergence criteria ("Rhat")
plot(imp)    # diagnostic plots

# create list of completed data sets
implist <- mitmlComplete(imp, print="all")

# *** Analysis phase:
#

# apply group-mean centering
implist <- within(implist,{
    G.NEGLEAD <- clusterMeans(NEGLEAD,GRPID)
    I.NEGLEAD <- NEGLEAD - G.NEGLEAD
})
```

```
# fit model of interest and pool parameter estimates
fit <- with(implist, lmer(JOBSAT ~ I.NEGLEAD +
    G.NEGLEAD + WLOAD + COHES + (1|GRPID)))
testEstimates(fit, var.comp=TRUE)

# test for random slope of leadership style (using D3)
fit2 <- with(implist, lmer(JOBSAT ~ I.NEGLEAD +
    G.NEGLEAD + WLOAD + COHES +
    (1+I.NEGLEAD|GRPID)))
anova(fit, fit2)

# test for contextual effect of leadership style
    (using D1)
context <- "G.NEGLEAD - I.NEGLEAD"
testConstraints(fit, constraint=context)
```

Printed below is the M*plus* syntax that was used for
    ML estimation of the model of interest.

```
DATA:
file = leadership.dat;

VARIABLE:
names = GRPID JOBSAT COHES NEGLEAD
    WLOAD;
usevariables = JOBSAT COHES NEGLEAD WLOAD
    NEGLEADM;
within = NEGLEAD;
between = COHES NEGLEADM;
cluster = GRPID;
missing = all (-99);

DEFINE:
NEGLEADM = cluster_mean (NEGLEAD);
    ! calculate group means from the observed data
center NEGLEAD (groupmean);    ! group-mean
    centering

ANALYSIS:
type = twolevel;
estimator = ml;

MODEL:
%within%
JOBSAT on NEGLEAD
    WLOAD (1);   ! restrict effect of workload to be
    equal at both levels
NEGLEAD with WLOAD;   ! explanatory variables
    as endogenous, allow covariances
```

%between%
JOBSAT on NEGLEADM COHES
   WLOAD (1);   ! restrict effect of workload to be
   equal at both levels
NEGLEADM with COHES;   ! explanatory
   variables as endogenous, allow covariances
NEGLEADM with WLOAD;
COHES with WLOAD;

References

Allison, P. D. (2001). *Missing data*. Thousand Oaks, CA: Sage.

Allison, P. D. (2012). Handling missing data by maximum likelihood. In *Proceedings of the SAS Global Forum*. Retrieved from http://support.sas.com/resources/papers/proceedings12/312-2012.pdf

Andridge, R. R. (2011). Quantifying the impact of fixed effects modeling of clusters in multiple imputation for cluster randomized trials. *Biometrical Journal, 53*, 57–74. http://dx.doi.org/10.1002/bimj.201000140

Asparouhov, T., & Muthén, B. O. (2006). *Constructing covariates in multilevel regression* (Mplus Web Notes No. 11). Retrieved from https://www.statmodel.com/download/webnotes/webnote11.pdf

Asparouhov, T., & Muthén, B. O. (2010). *Multiple imputation with* Mplus (Technical Appendix). Retrieved from http://statmodel.com/download/Imputations7.pdf

Barnard, J., & Rubin, D. B. (1999). Miscellanea: Small-sample degrees of freedom with multiple imputation. *Biometrika, 86*, 948–955. http://dx.doi.org/10.1093/biomet/86.4.948

Bartlett, J. W., Seaman, S. R., White, I. R., & Carpenter, J. R., for the Alzheimer's Disease Neuroimaging Initiative. (2015). Multiple imputation of covariates by fully conditional specification: Accommodating the substantive model. *Statistical Methods in Medical Research, 24*, 462–487. http://dx.doi.org/10.1177/0962280214521348

Bates, D., Maechler, M., Bolker, B., & Walker, S. (2016). Lme4: Linear mixed-effects models using 'Eigen' and S4 (Version 1.1–12). [Website.] Retrieved from http://CRAN.R-project.org/package=lme4

Bernaards, C. A., Belin, T. R., & Schafer, J. L. (2007). Robustness of a multivariate normal approximation for imputation of incomplete binary data. *Statistics in Medicine, 26*, 1368–1382. http://dx.doi.org/10.1002/sim.2619

Black, A. C., Harel, O., & Matthews, G. (2013). Techniques for analyzing intensive longitudinal data with missing values. In M. R. Mehl & T. S. Connor (Eds.), *Handbook of research methods for studying daily life* (pp. 339–356). New York, NY: Guilford Press.

Black, A. C., Harel, O., & McCoach, D. B. (2011). Missing data techniques for multilevel data: Implications of model misspecification. *Journal of Applied Statistics, 38*, 1845–1865. http://dx.doi.org/10.1080/02664763.2010.529882

Bliese, P. D. (2000). Within-group agreement, non-independence, and reliability: Implications for data aggregation and analysis. In K. J. Klein & S. W. J. Kozlowski (Eds.), *Multilevel theory, research, and methods in organizations: Foundations, extensions, and new directions* (pp. 3–90). San Francisco, CA: Jossey-Bass.

Bodner, T. E. (2008). What improves with increased missing data imputations? *Structural Equation Modeling, 15*, 651–675. http://dx.doi.org/10.1080/10705510802339072

Carpenter, J. R., & Kenward, M. G. (2013). *Multiple imputation and its application*. Hoboken, NJ: Wiley. http://dx.doi.org/10.1002/9781119942283

Carpenter, J. R., Goldstein, H., & Kenward, M. G. (2011). REALCOM-IMPUTE software for multilevel multiple imputation with mixed response types. *Journal of Statistical Software, 45*, 1–14. http://dx.doi.org/10.18637/jss.v045.i05

Collins, L. M., Schafer, J. L., & Kam, C.-M. (2001). A comparison of inclusive and restrictive strategies in modern missing data procedures. *Psychological Methods, 6*, 330–351. http://dx.doi.org/10.1037/1082-989X.6.4.330

Croon, M. A., & van Veldhoven, M. J. P. M. (2007). Predicting group-level outcome variables from variables measured at the individual level: A latent variable multilevel model. *Psychological Methods, 12*, 45–57. http://dx.doi.org/10.1037/1082-989X.12.1.45

Demirtas, H. (2009). Rounding strategies for multiply imputed binary data. *Biometrical Journal, 51*, 677–688. http://dx.doi.org/10.1002/bimj.200900018

Drechsler, J. (2015). Multiple imputation of multilevel missing data—Rigor versus simplicity. *Journal of Educational and Behavioral Statistics, 40*, 69–95. http://dx.doi.org/10.3102/1076998614563393

Enders, C. K. (2008). A note on the use of missing auxiliary variables in full information maximum likelihood-based structural equation models. *Structural Equation Modeling, 15*, 434–448. http://dx.doi.org/10.1080/10705510802154307

Enders, C. K. (2010). *Applied missing data analysis*. New York, NY: Guilford Press.

Enders, C. K. (2011). Missing not at random models for latent growth curve analyses. *Psychological Methods, 16*, 1–16. http://dx.doi.org/10.1037/a0022640

Enders, C. K., Baraldi, A. N., & Cham, H. (2014). Estimating interaction effects with incomplete predictor variables. *Psychological Methods, 19*, 39–55. http://dx.doi.org/10.1037/a0035314

Enders, C. K., Mistler, S. A., & Keller, B. T. (2016). Multilevel multiple imputation: A review and evaluation of joint modeling and chained equations imputation. *Psychological Methods, 21,* 222–240. http://dx.doi.org/10.1037/met0000063

Erler, N. S., Rizopoulos, D., van Rosmalen, J., Jaddoe, V. W. V., Franco, O. H., & Lesaffre, E. M. E. H. (2016). Dealing with missing covariates in epidemiologic studies: A comparison between multiple imputation and a full Bayesian approach. *Statistics in Medicine, 35,* 2955–2974. http://dx.doi.org/10.1002/sim.6944

Galati, J. C., & Seaton, K. A. (2016). MCAR is not necessary for the complete cases to constitute a simple random subsample of the target sample. *Statistical Methods in Medical Research, 25,* 1527–1534. http://dx.doi.org/10.1177/0962280213490360

Gelman, A., & Rubin, D. B. (1992). Inference from iterative simulation using multiple sequences. *Statistical Science, 7,* 457–472. http://dx.doi.org/10.1214/ss/1177011136

Goldstein, H. (2011). *Multilevel statistical models* (4th ed.). Hoboken, NJ: Wiley.

Goldstein, H., Carpenter, J. R., & Browne, W. J. (2014). Fitting multilevel multivariate models with missing data in responses and covariates that may include interactions and non-linear terms. *Journal of the Royal Statistical Society. Series A (Statistics in Society), 177,* 553–564. http://dx.doi.org/10.1111/rssa.12022

Goldstein, H., Carpenter, J. R., Kenward, M. G., & Levin, K. A. (2009). Multilevel models with multivariate mixed response types. *Statistical Modelling, 9,* 173–197. http://dx.doi.org/10.1177/1471082X0800900301

Gottfredson, N. C., Sterba, S. K., & Jackson, K. M. (2017). Explicating the conditions under which multilevel multiple imputation mitigates bias resulting from random coefficient-dependent missing longitudinal data. *Prevention Science, 18,* 12–19. http://dx.doi.org/10.1007/s11121-016-0735-3

Gottschall, A. C., West, S. G., & Enders, C. K. (2012). A comparison of item-level and scale-level multiple imputation for questionnaire batteries. *Multivariate Behavioral Research, 47,* 1–25. http://dx.doi.org/10.1080/00273171.2012.640589

Graham, J. W. (2003). Adding missing-data-relevant variables to FIML-based structural equation models. *Structural Equation Modeling: A Multidisciplinary Journal, 10,* 80–100. http://dx.doi.org/10.1207/S15328007SEM1001_4

Graham, J. W. (2009). Missing data analysis: Making it work in the real world. *Annual Review of Psychology, 60,* 549–576. http://dx.doi.org/10.1146/annurev.psych.58.110405.085530

Graham, J. W., Olchowski, A. E., & Gilreath, T. D. (2007). How many imputations are really needed? Some practical clarifications of multiple imputation theory. *Prevention Science, 8,* 206–213. http://dx.doi.org/10.1007/s11121-007-0070-9

Grund, S., Lüdtke, O., & Robitzsch, A. (2016a). Multiple imputation of missing covariate values in multilevel models with random slopes: A cautionary note. *Behavior Research Methods, 48,* 640–649. http://dx.doi.org/10.3758/s13428-015-0590-3

Grund, S., Lüdtke, O., & Robitzsch, A. (2016b). Multiple imputation of multilevel missing data: An introduction to the R package pan. *SAGE Open, 6*(4), 1–17. http://dx.doi.org/10.1177/2158244016668220

Grund, S., Lüdtke, O., & Robitzsch, A. (2016c). Pooling ANOVA results from multiply imputed datasets: A simulation study. *Methodology: European Journal of Research Methods for the Behavioral and Social Sciences, 12,* 75–88. http://dx.doi.org/10.1027/1614-2241/a000111

Grund, S., Lüdtke, O., & Robitzsch, A. (2018). Multiple imputation of missing data for multilevel models: Simulations and recommendations. *Organizational Research Methods, 21,* 111–149. http://dx.doi.org/10.1177/1094428117703686

Grund, S., Robitzsch, A., & Lüdtke, O. (2016). Mitml: Tools for multiple imputation in multilevel modeling (Version 0.3–2). Retrieved from http://CRAN.R-project.org/package=mitml

Hill, P. W., & Goldstein, H. (1998). Multilevel modeling of educational data with cross-classification and missing identification for units. *Journal of Educational and Behavioral Statistics, 23,* 117–128. http://dx.doi.org/10.3102/10769986023002117

Ibrahim, J. G., Chen, M.-H., & Lipsitz, S. R. (2001). Missing responses in generalised linear mixed models when the missing data mechanism is nonignorable. *Biometrika, 88,* 551–564. http://dx.doi.org/10.1093/biomet/88.2.551

Jeličić, H., Phelps, E., & Lerner, R. M. (2009). Use of missing data methods in longitudinal studies: The persistence of bad practices in developmental psychology. *Developmental Psychology, 45,* 1195–1199. http://dx.doi.org/10.1037/a0015665

Keller, B. T. (2015). *Three-level multiple imputation: A fully conditional specification approach* (Master's thesis). Arizona State University. Retrieved from https://repository.asu.edu/attachments/162109/content/Keller_asu_0010N_15391.pdf

Keller, B. T., & Enders, C. K. (2018). *Blimp user's guide (Version 1.1)*. Retrieved from http://www.appliedmissingdata.com/blimpuserguide-5.pdf

Klein, K. J., Bliese, P. D., Kozlowski, S. W. J., Dansereau, F., Gavin, M. B., Griffin, M. A., . . . Bligh, M. C. (2000). Multilevel analytical techniques: Commonalities, differences, and continuing questions. In K. J. Klein & S. W. J. Kozlowski (Eds.), *Multilevel theory, research, and methods in organizations: Foundations, extensions, and new directions* (pp. 512–553). San Francisco, CA: Jossey-Bass.

Kozlowski, S. W. J., & Klein, K. J. (2000). A multilevel approach to theory and research in organizations: Contextual, temporal, and emergent processes. In K. J. Klein & S. W. J. Kozlowski (Eds.), *Multilevel theory, research, and methods in organizations: Foundations, extensions, and new directions* (pp. 3–90). San Francisco, CA: Jossey-Bass.

Kreft, I. G. G., de Leeuw, J., & Aiken, L. S. (1995). The effect of different forms of centering in hierarchical linear models. *Multivariate Behavioral Research, 30,* 1–21. http://dx.doi.org/10.1207/s15327906mbr3001_1

LeBreton, J. M., & Senter, J. L. (2008). Answers to 20 questions about interrater reliability and interrater agreement. *Organizational Research Methods, 11,* 815–852. http://dx.doi.org/10.1177/1094428106296642

Li, K.-H., Meng, X.-L., Raghunathan, T. E., & Rubin, D. B. (1991). Significance levels from repeated *p*-values with multiply-imputed data. *Statistica Sinica, 1,* 65–92. Retrieved from http://www.stat.sinica.edu.tw/statistica//j1n1/j1n15/j1n15.htm

Li, K.-H., Raghunathan, T. E., & Rubin, D. B. (1991). Large-sample significance levels from multiply imputed data using moment-based statistics and an *F* reference distribution. *Journal of the American Statistical Association, 86,* 1065–1073. http://dx.doi.org/10.1080/01621459.1991.10475152

Licht, C. (2010). *New methods for generating significance levels from multiply-imputed data* (Doctoral dissertation). Universität Bamberg. Retrieved from http://d-nb.info/101104966X/34

Little, R. J. A. (1992). Regression with missing *X*'s: A review. *Journal of the American Statistical Association, 87,* 1227–1237. http://dx.doi.org/10.1080/01621459.1992.10476282

Little, R. J. A., & Rubin, D. B. (2002). *Statistical analysis with missing data* (2nd ed.). Hoboken, NJ: Wiley. http://dx.doi.org/10.1002/9781119013563

Lüdtke, O., Marsh, H. W., Robitzsch, A., Trautwein, U., Asparouhov, T., & Muthén, B. (2008). The multilevel latent covariate model: A new, more reliable approach to group-level effects in contextual studies. *Psychological Methods, 13,* 203–229. http://dx.doi.org/10.1037/a0012869

Lüdtke, O., Robitzsch, A., & Grund, S. (2017). Multiple imputation of missing data in multilevel designs: A comparison of different strategies. *Psychological Methods, 22,* 141–165. http://dx.doi.org/10.1037/met0000096

Mehta, P. D. (2013). xxM (Version 0.6.0). Retrieved from http://xxm.times.uh.edu

Meng, X.-L. (1994). Multiple-imputation inferences with uncongenial sources of input. *Statistical Science, 9,* 538–558. http://dx.doi.org/10.1214/ss/1177010269

Meng, X.-L., & Rubin, D. B. (1992). Performing likelihood ratio tests with multiply-imputed data sets. *Biometrika, 79,* 103–111. http://dx.doi.org/10.1093/biomet/79.1.103

Mistler, S. A. (2013). A SAS® macro for computing pooled likelihood ratio tests with multiply imputed data. [Paper 440–2013] In *Proceedings of the SAS Global Forum.* Retrieved from http://support.sas.com/resources/papers/proceedings13/440-2013.pdf

Muthén, L. K., & Muthén, B. O. (2012). *Mplus user's guide* (7th ed.). Los Angeles, CA: Muthén & Muthén. Retrieved from https://www.statmodel.com/download/usersguide/Mplus%20user%20guide%20Ver_7_r3_web.pdf

Newman, D. A. (2003). Longitudinal modeling with randomly and systematically missing data: A simulation of ad hoc, maximum likelihood, and multiple imputation techniques. *Organizational Research Methods, 6,* 328–362. http://dx.doi.org/10.1177/1094428103254673

Newman, D. A. (2014). Missing data: Five practical guidelines. *Organizational Research Methods, 17,* 372–411. http://dx.doi.org/10.1177/1094428114548590

Nicholson, J. S., Deboeck, P. R., & Howard, W. (2017). Attrition in developmental psychology: A review of modern missing data reporting and practices. *International Journal of Behavioral Development, 41,* 143–153. http://dx.doi.org/10.1177/0165025415618275

Peugh, J. L., & Enders, C. K. (2004). Missing data in educational research: A review of reporting practices and suggestions for improvement. *Review of Educational Research, 74,* 525–556. http://dx.doi.org/10.3102/00346543074004525

Pinheiro, J., & Bates, D. M. (2000). *Mixed-effects models in S and S-PLUS.* New York, NY: Springer.

Quartagno, M., & Carpenter, J. R. (2016). Jomo: Multilevel joint modelling multiple imputation (Version 2.3–1). Retrieved from http://CRAN.R-project.org/package=jomo

Rabe-Hesketh, S., Skrondal, A., & Pickles, A. (2004). Generalized multilevel structural equation modeling. *Psychometrika, 69,* 167–190. http://dx.doi.org/10.1007/BF02295939

Raghunathan, T. E. (2015). *Missing data analysis in practice.* Boca Raton, FL: CRC Press.

Raudenbush, S. W., & Bryk, A. S. (2002). *Hierarchical linear models: Applications and data analysis methods* (2nd ed.). Thousand Oaks, CA: Sage.

Reiter, J. P., & Raghunathan, T. E. (2007). The multiple adaptations of multiple imputation. *Journal of the*

American Statistical Association, 102, 1462–1471. http://dx.doi.org/10.1198/016214507000000932

Royston, P. (2005). Multiple imputation of missing values: Update. *The Stata Journal, 5,* 188–201. Retrieved from https://www.stata-journal.com/sjpdf.html?articlenum=st0067_1

Rubin, D. B. (1976). Inference and missing data. *Biometrika, 63,* 581–592. http://dx.doi.org/10.1093/biomet/63.3.581

Rubin, D. B. (1987). *Multiple imputation for nonresponse in surveys.* Hoboken, NJ: Wiley. http://dx.doi.org/10.1002/9780470316696

Särndal, C.-E., Swensson, B., & Wretman, J. (2003). *Model assisted survey sampling.* New York, NY: Springer.

Savalei, V., & Bentler, P. M. (2009). A two-stage approach to missing data: Theory and application to auxiliary variables. *Structural Equation Modeling: A Multidisciplinary Journal, 16,* 477–497. http://dx.doi.org/10.1080/10705510903008238

Schafer, J. L. (1997). *Analysis of incomplete multivariate data.* Boca Raton, FL: CRC Press. http://dx.doi.org/10.1201/9781439821862

Schafer, J. L. (2003). Multiple imputation in multivariate problems when the imputation and analysis models differ. *Statistica Neerlandica, 57,* 19–35. http://dx.doi.org/10.1111/1467-9574.00218

Schafer, J. L., & Graham, J. W. (2002). Missing data: Our view of the state of the art. *Psychological Methods, 7,* 147–177. http://dx.doi.org/10.1037/1082-989X.7.2.147

Schafer, J. L., & Olsen, M. K. (1998). Multiple imputation for multivariate missing-data problems: A data analyst's perspective. *Multivariate Behavioral Research, 33,* 545–571. http://dx.doi.org/10.1207/s15327906mbr3304_5

Schafer, J. L., & Yucel, R. M. (2002). Computational strategies for multivariate linear mixed-effects models with missing values. *Journal of Computational and Graphical Statistics, 11,* 437–457. http://dx.doi.org/10.1198/106186002760180608

Schafer, J. L., & Zhao, J. H. (2016). Pan: Multiple imputation for multivariate panel or clustered data (Version 1.4). Retrieved from http://CRAN.R-project.org/package=pan

Snijders, T. A. B., & Bosker, R. J. (2012). *Multilevel analysis: An introduction to basic and advanced multilevel modeling.* Thousand Oaks, CA: Sage.

Stubbendick, A. L., & Ibrahim, J. G. (2003). Maximum likelihood methods for nonignorable missing responses and covariates in random effects models. *Biometrics, 59,* 1140–1150. http://dx.doi.org/10.1111/j.0006-341X.2003.00131.x

Taljaard, M., Donner, A., & Klar, N. (2008). Imputation strategies for missing continuous outcomes in cluster randomized trials. *Biometrical Journal, 50,* 329–345. http://dx.doi.org/10.1002/bimj.200710423

van Buuren, S. (2011). Multiple imputation of multilevel data. In J. J. Hox (Ed.), *Handbook of advanced multilevel analysis* (pp. 173–196). New York, NY: Routledge.

van Buuren, S., & Groothuis-Oudshoorn, K. (2011). mice: Multivariate imputation by chained equations in R. *Journal of Statistical Software, 45,* 1–67. http://dx.doi.org/10.18637/jss.v045.i03

van Buuren, S., Brand, J. P. L., Groothuis-Oudshoorn, C. G. M., & Rubin, D. B. (2006). Fully conditional specification in multivariate imputation. *Journal of Statistical Computation and Simulation, 76,* 1049–1064. http://dx.doi.org/10.1080/10629360600810434

Vermunt, J. K., & Magidson, J. (2016). Upgrade Manual for Latent GOLD 5.1. Belmont, MA: Statistical Innovations Inc. Retrieved from http://www.statisticalinnovations.com/wp-content/uploads/UpgradeManual5.1.pdf

von Hippel, P. T. (2009). How to impute interactions, squares, and other transformed variables. *Sociological Methodology, 39,* 265–291. http://dx.doi.org/10.1111/j.1467-9531.2009.01215.x

Wu, L. (2010). *Mixed effects models for complex data.* Boca Raton, FL: CRC Press.

Wu, W., Jia, F., & Enders, C. (2015). A comparison of imputation strategies for ordinal missing data on Likert scale variables. *Multivariate Behavioral Research, 50,* 484–503. http://dx.doi.org/10.1080/00273171.2015.1022644

Wu, W., West, S. G., & Taylor, A. B. (2009). Evaluating model fit for growth curve models: Integration of fit indices from SEM and MLM frameworks. *Psychological Methods, 14,* 183–201. http://dx.doi.org/10.1037/a0015858

Yuan, K.-H., & Bentler, P. M. (2000). Three likelihood-based methods for mean and covariance structure analysis with nonnormal missing data. *Sociological Methodology, 30,* 165–200. http://dx.doi.org/10.1111/0081-1750.00078

Yuan, K.-H., Yang-Wallentin, F., & Bentler, P. M. (2012). ML versus MI for missing data with violation of distribution conditions. *Sociological Methods & Research, 41,* 598–629. http://dx.doi.org/10.1177/0049124112460373

Yucel, R. M. (2008). Multiple imputation inference for multivariate multilevel continuous data with ignorable non-response. *Philosophical Transactions of the Royal Society A: Mathematical, Physical and Engineering Sciences, 366,* 2389–2403. http://dx.doi.org/10.1098/rsta.2008.0038

Yucel, R. M., Ding, H., Uludag, A. K., & Tomaskovic-Devey, D. (2008). Multiple imputation in multiple classification and multiple-membership structures. In *Proceedings of the Section on Bayesian Statistical Science of the American Statistical Association.* 4006–4013. Retrieved from https://ww2.amstat.org/sections/srms/Proceedings/y2008/Files/302707.pdf

## Part III

MULTILEVEL ANALYSIS

## CHAPTER 17

A PRIMER ON MULTILEVEL (RANDOM COEFFICIENT) REGRESSION MODELING

Levi K. Shiverdecker and James M. LeBreton

Hierarchical nesting is a fundamental property woven into the fabric of existence itself: from the microscopic organelles nested within our cells to the Milky Way galaxy nested within an infinitely expanding universe. Residing at a level somewhere in between, social scientists find themselves pondering questions relating to both hierarchical and temporal nesting. For example, clinical psychologists may want to investigate the efficacy of therapy for clients nested within different therapists. Similarly, organizational psychologists may want to examine the moderating role of a group-level phenomenon (e.g., team cohesion) on the relationship between person-level variables (e.g., employee-level burnout and employee-level turnover). Alternatively, developmental psychologists might wish to investigate within-person trends (e.g., growth and/or decline in cognitive abilities) across the lifespan. These hierarchically and temporally nested structures may be thought of as *multilevel* structures because they span multiple conceptual levels (e.g., repeated observations nested in persons nested in groups). The first part of this handbook focuses on issues related to multilevel constructs and multilevel theories. The second part of this handbook focuses on issues related to multilevel measurement and multilevel design. The third section of the handbook transitions to discussing various multilevel analytic tools and issues. The purpose of the current chapter

is to provide the reader with a basic grounding in the classic multilevel regression (MLR) model.

To effectively tackle the analyses for research questions involving nested data structures, particular statistical analytic techniques must be employed to ensure that the subsequent results are unbiased and as consistent as possible to the true population parameters. Specifically, MLR has been, and continues to be, one of the most popular data analytic techniques used to test multilevel research questions and hypotheses. MLR is sometimes referred to by other names including hierarchical linear modeling, random coefficients regression (RCR), mixed effects modeling, mixed determinants modeling, or most commonly, multilevel modeling (MLM). We elected to use the MLR label rather than MLM in order to distinguish this approach to multilevel analysis from the other approaches presented in this handbook.

The onset of this chapter provides a brief introduction to MLR using an illustrative example that will be the focal example utilized for the subsequent sections of the chapter. The introduction to our illustrative example and the MLR analytic framework will be followed by a description of why MLR is necessary for nested data by examining how alternative methods may be inappropriate and how MLR circumvents the shortcomings of these alternatives. The chapter progresses into a step-by-step introduction to a model building/comparison

http://dx.doi.org/10.1037/0000115-018
The Handbook of Multilevel Theory, Measurement, and Analysis, S. E. Humphrey and J. M. LeBreton (Editors-in-Chief)

approach for using MLR analyses for hierarchically nested data.

Caveat. The models described in this chapter are applicable only when the dependent variable is measured at the lowest level (Level 1) in the nested structure. Independent variables may be measured at either the lower or at higher levels (Level 1, Level 2, etc.).

ILLUSTRATIVE EXAMPLE

One way to initially conceptualize MLR is to imagine taking a single-level research question and testing that research question across multiple samples. For the remainder of our chapter, we will rely on an illustrative example where we initially wish to test the hypothesis that there is a positive linear relationship between employees' levels of trait aggression (AGG; James & LeBreton, 2010, 2012) and their subsequent levels of counterproductive workplace behaviors (CWBs; e.g., harassment, lying, theft, sabotage; Bennett & Robinson, 2000). We generated a data set corresponding to data from 600 employees uniquely nested in 60 different

teams. To simplify our presentation, the data are balanced with 10 employees assigned to each of the 60 teams.

We begin by regressing CWBs onto AGG using the data from the first 10 employees nested in Group 1. We repeat this analysis for each of the remaining groups, leading to 60 independent estimates of the regression coefficients (i.e., intercept and slope). Figures 17.1 through 17.4 provide a summary of the results for the first four groups. Table 17.1 contains the regression weights and R^2 estimates for each of the 60 groups and Figure 17.5 provides a visual representation of the 60 separate regressions superimposed on a single graph. Appendix 17.1 contains a copy of the R code used to generate all of the analyses and figures presented in this chapter. A brief review of Table 17.1 and Figures 17.1 through 17.5 reveals that there is substantial variability in the results across these 60 groups. For example, when trait AGG is zero (i.e., the minimum score on our survey), the predicted levels of employees' CWB (i.e., intercept coefficients) varies across the groups ranging from –0.37 to 3.15. Similarly, the strength of the relationship varies

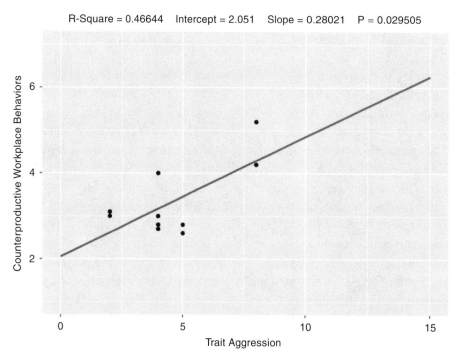

R-Square = 0.46644   Intercept = 2.051   Slope = 0.28021   P = 0.029505

FIGURE 17.1.   Simple linear regression of counterproductive workplace behaviors onto trait aggression using data for the 10 employees nested in Group 1.

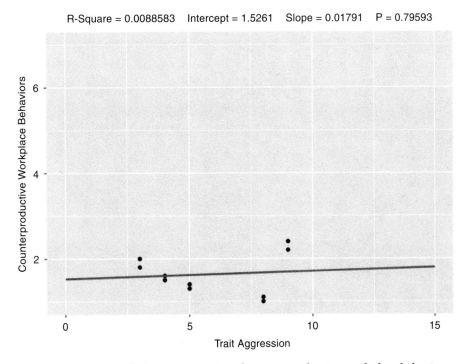

R-Square = 0.0088583   Intercept = 1.5261   Slope = 0.01791   P = 0.79593

FIGURE 17.2.   Simple linear regression of counterproductive workplace behaviors onto trait aggression using data for the 10 employees nested in Group 2.

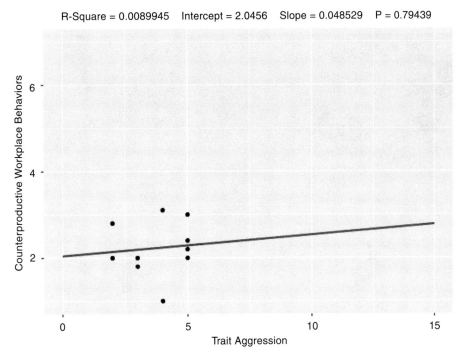

R-Square = 0.0089945   Intercept = 2.0456   Slope = 0.048529   P = 0.79439

FIGURE 17.3.   Simple linear regression of counterproductive workplace behaviors onto trait aggression using data for the 10 employees nested in Group 3.

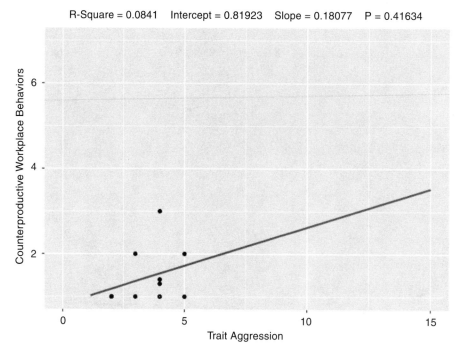

R-Square = 0.0841   Intercept = 0.81923   Slope = 0.18077   P = 0.41634

FIGURE 17.4.   Simple linear regression of counterproductive workplace behaviors onto trait aggression using data for the 10 employees nested in Group 4.

TABLE 17.1

Results of Simple Linear Regression Analyses Repeated for the 60 Groups

Group	Intercept	Slope	R^2
1	2.051041667	0.280208333	0.4664359014
2	1.526119403	0.017910448	0.0088583358
3	2.045588235	0.048529412	0.0089944992
4	0.819230769	0.180769231	0.0840995184
5	1.906250000	−0.006250000	0.0009360599
6	1.441791045	0.011194030	0.0030809256
7	1.352941176	−0.011764706	0.0008650519
8	0.991428571	0.042857143	0.2008928571
9	2.685294118	−0.132352941	0.1153681812
10	1.072727273	0.403030303	0.6802415013
11	−0.065753425	0.526027397	0.6173426667
12	1.686363636	−0.022727273	0.0025826446
13	3.050000000	−0.316666667	0.2103729604
14	0.733644860	0.192990654	0.5455519520
15	0.144927536	0.585507246	0.2992724286
16	−0.370000000	0.450000000	0.3806390977
17	1.968421053	0.456578947	0.4242980577
18	1.180000000	0.075000000	0.1785714286
19	0.881250000	0.218750000	0.2734375000
20	6.250000000	−1.150000000	0.4467905405
21	0.600000000	0.200000000	0.5977011494

TABLE 17.1

Results of Simple Linear Regression Analyses Repeated for the 60 Groups (*Continued*)

Group	Intercept	Slope	R^2
22	1.471698113	0.037735849	0.0314465409
23	2.764705882	−0.376470588	0.8366013072
24	−0.600000000	0.550000000	0.8897058824
25	1.375852273	0.076988636	0.1862018782
26	2.718518519	−0.237037037	0.3108682453
27	2.023076923	−0.053846154	0.0088066139
28	1.200000000	0.200000000	0.1397849462
29	1.127777778	0.138888889	0.0964506173
30	1.267924528	0.109433962	0.1823899371
31	0.719230769	0.219230769	0.2431158336
32	1.626415094	−0.015094340	0.0058055152
33	1.157142857	0.328571429	0.1420515575
34	1.925000000	−0.025000000	0.0125000000
35	0.978378378	0.237837838	0.2198501022
36	1.448648649	−0.035135135	0.0496474736
37	0.727058824	0.270588235	0.4227941176
38	1.360000000	0.080000000	0.0421052632
39	3.100000000	−0.212500000	0.1619955157
40	1.066666667	−0.008333333	0.0104166667
41	1.672727273	−0.018181818	0.0014204545
42	0.873913043	0.082608696	0.0421926134
43	0.695652174	0.313043478	0.2860295740
44	0.991304348	0.026086957	0.0489130435
45	2.900000000	−0.550000000	0.7438524590
46	0.813235294	0.704411765	0.5582152954
47	3.145454545	−0.345454545	0.2369543814
48	0.900000000	0.250000000	0.3409090909
49	1.337096774	0.111290323	0.2666330645
50	1.561194030	0.216417910	0.2120310609
51	2.884210526	−0.273684211	0.2928308425
52	1.610000000	0.150000000	0.0757575758
53	0.561111111	0.181944444	0.7696896304
54	1.854022989	0.101149425	0.0519168820
55	0.542718447	0.190291262	0.7698057250
56	0.908108108	0.216216216	0.3931203931
57	1.849411765	0.094117647	0.1742919390
58	0.003030303	0.453030303	0.2730418476
59	1.305000000	0.075000000	0.0546116505
60	−0.088888889	0.459259259	0.8043523750

across the groups with slopes ranging from −0.55 (and an R^2 of 0.00) to 0.70 (and an R^2 of 0.84).

Now, obviously, much of the variability is driven by sampling error. After all, we are conducting regression analyses using the samples size of $N = 10$. However, we also suspect that some of the variance may be attributed to differences in the social relationships that have formed within these groups. Specifically, we hypothesize that scores on a measure of group cohesiveness (COH) might be negatively related to CWBs even after controlling for employee-level AGG. Essentially, we predict that employees working in a highly cohesive group will be less likely to engage in CWBs than those working in fragmented or uncohesive groups. In addition, we hypothesize that the variability in slopes observed in

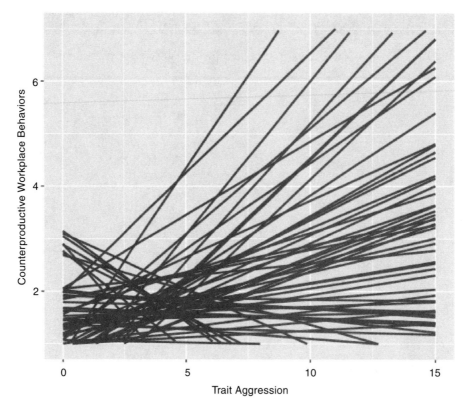

FIGURE 17.5. Simple linear regression of counterproductive workplace behaviors onto trait aggression for each of the 60 groups.

Figure 17.5 may also be related to COH. Specifically, we hypothesize weaker (positive) relationships between CWBs and AGG for highly cohesive groups, but this (positive) relationship will grow stronger as teams become less cohesive. Conceptually, we are trying to use a group-level variable (COH) to explain some of the between-groups variability in the regression coefficients (see Table 17.1 and Figure 17.5).

Stated formally, we plan to test the following hypotheses:

1. There is a positive relationship between individual-level trait AGG and individual-level CWBs.
2. There is a negative relationship between group-level COH and individual-level CWBs.
3. Group-level COH will moderate the strength of the relationship between individual-level trait AGG and individual-level CWBs, such that the relationship will become weaker as group-level COH increases.

For this example, we will assume that cohesion is operationalized as the shared perception among employees nested in work groups. It is presumed that the cohesion data were collected at the individual level and aggregated (i.e., averaged) to the group level after establishing that sufficient agreement among employees existed within the work groups (see Chapter 12, this volume; also cf. James, Demaree, & Wolf, 1984; 1993; LeBreton & Senter, 2008). The remainder of this chapter discusses how a researcher could use our sample data to test the above hypotheses. Like other treatments of MLR, we first explain the necessity of MLR for testing these hypotheses and then adopt a model-building procedure to formally test our hypotheses.

NONINDEPENDENCE AND MULTILEVEL REGRESSION

One might speculate whether it is necessary to use more complicated multilevel techniques when it appears that simpler techniques (e.g., ordinary least squares [OLS] regression or analysis of covariance [ANCOVA]) may be suited for testing hypotheses such as those noted earlier in the chapter. For example, we could test a regression model that includes a term representing AGG, a term representing COH, and a term representing the cross-product of AGG with COH (AGG * COH). Alternatively, we could simply add the group-level cohesion scores to the data in Table 17.1 and then use those scores to predict the regression coefficients. That is, we could examine whether the variability in COH overlaps with the variability in intercepts (β_0) and slopes (β_1). At first blush, either of these strategies seems to be a reasonable approach to testing our hypotheses. However, as we will see, these approaches fail to properly account for the fact that employees are nested within groups.

OLS is a very powerful, simple, and effective estimation procedure. For example, when errors (a) have a mean of zero, (b) are identically distributed, and (c) are uncorrelated with one another, the OLS estimates are said to be "BLUE"—the Best Linear Unbiased Estimates (Cohen, Cohen, West,

& Aiken, 2003; Myers, 1990). If the errors are also normally distributed, the OLS estimates are said to be "MVUE"—the minimum variance unbiased estimates (Cohen et al., 2003; Myers, 1990). Unfortunately, when data are nested, the errors are frequently nonindependent. This nonindependence is visually depicted in Figure 17.6, which contains an analysis of the data from the first two groups in our example. When we separately estimate regression lines for each group, we see that Group 1 (thin dashed line) has a very steep slope, whereas Group 2 (thin dot-dash line) is flatter. However, if we ignored group membership and simply analyzed the data from all 20 employees, we would obtain a common regression line (thick solid line). The fact that these data are nonindependent is easily observed when considering the implications of using the common regression line to predict CWBs using AGG scores. Essentially, using the common line will tend to underestimate the predicted scores for employees working in Group 1 and overestimate the predicted scores for employees working in Group 2. The problem of nonindependence may also be

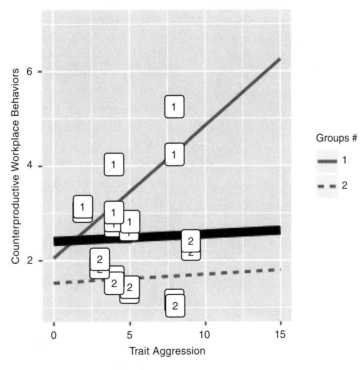

FIGURE 17.6. Simple linear regression of counterproductive workplace behaviors onto trait aggression using data from the first two groups.

observed by comparing the equations that would be tested using OLS to the equation that we will eventually test using MLR.

Single-Level Regression Approach

To illustrate the differences between the single-level OLS approach and the MLR approach we will examine the equations that each approach would use for testing a common "main effects" model. The OLS approach essentially relies on an analysis of covariance (James & Williams, 2000; Kreft & de Leeuw, 1998; Raudenbush & Bryk, 2002):

$$CWB_{ij} = \beta_0 + \beta_1(AGG_{ij}) + \beta_2(COH_j) + e_{ij}, \quad (17.1)$$

where $i = 1$ to n_j Level-1 units (e.g., employees; children) nested within the $j = 1$ to J Level-2 units (e.g., teams; classrooms). Thus, in our example, AGG_{ij} refers to the trait aggression score for the ith employee working in the jth group and COH_j refers to the cohesion score for group j, which is computed as the mean taken over the n_j employees nested in that group. The βs represent unstandardized regression coefficients and e_{ij} represent the unique error for employee i nested in group j.

To summarize, the OLS approach is represented by Equation 17.1 and consists of our outcome variable, a single (fixed) intercept coefficient, two fixed slope coefficients, and a single error term. As we will see, reliance on a single error term is problematic because we are unable to properly model potential dependencies in the data attributed to the nesting of the Level-1 units within the Level-2 units. As a result, estimates of error variance may be biased, resulting in biased standard errors and tests of statistical significance. To address this issue, the MLR approach attempts to disentangle or partition the error variance into variance that resides at the individual level (i.e., within-group variance) and variance that resides at the group level (i.e., between-group variance).

Multilevel Regression Approach

The main effects model using MLR is a bit different (Hox, 2010; Kreft & de Leeuw, 1998; Raudenbush & Bryk, 2002):

$$\text{Level 1: } CWB_{ij} = \beta_{0j} + \beta_{1j}(AGG_{ij}) + r_{ij} \quad (17.2)$$

$$\text{Level 2: } \beta_{0j} = \gamma_{00} + \gamma_{01}(COH_j) + U_{0j} \quad (17.3)$$

$$\beta_{1j} = \gamma_{10}, \quad (17.4)$$

where β represent Level-1 *random* regression coefficients (i.e., coefficients that may vary across groups), γ represent the Level-2 *fixed* regression coefficients (i.e., coefficients that are invariant across groups), r_{ij} is the Level-1 random effect, and U_{0j} is the Level-2 random effect. Substituting the Level-2 equations into the Level-1 equations, we obtain the mixed equation

$$CWB_{1j} = [\gamma_{00} + \gamma_{01}(COH_j) + U_{0j}]$$
$$+ [\gamma_{10}(AGG_{ij})] + r_{ij}. \quad (17.5)$$

Returning to Equation 17.5, the elements in the first set of brackets provide information about the unique intercept for group j (i.e., β_{0j}). This intercept is a function of (a) a fixed intercept coefficient (γ_{00}) representing a common or pooled intercept applied to all individuals in all groups, (b) the effect of group j's score on COH_j (γ_{01}), and (c) a unique effect (i.e., error) that is applied to only the members of group j (U_{0j}). Because each group will have a unique, group-level effect (i.e., each group has a different score on U_{0j}), the variability in these group-level scores represents the between-groups variability in intercepts (i.e., the extent that groups assume different intercept values, even after modeling COH_j and AGG_{ij}).

The elements in the second bracket provide information about the unique slope for group j (i.e., β_{1j}). In the "main effects only" model, the unique slope for group j isn't really unique, but instead is fixed to common value across all groups: γ_{10}. Later in the chapter, we illustrate how it is possible to estimate separate group-level slopes. To further the comparison with OLS, Equation 17.5 may be rewritten as

$$CWB_{ij} = \gamma_{00} + \gamma_{10}(AGG_{ij}) + \gamma_{01}(COH_j)$$
$$+ U_{0j} + r_{ij}. \quad (17.6)$$

Comparison of Equations 17.1 and 17.6 reveals the similarities and differences between these approaches. In terms of similarities, both approaches furnish estimates of three (fixed) regression coefficients. These coefficients represent (a) a fixed intercept (i.e., β_0 for OLS; γ_{00} for MLR), (b) a fixed slope representing the strength of the relationship between CWB and AGG (i.e., β_1 for OLS; γ_{10} for MLR), and (c) a fixed slope representing the cross-level effect of COH on CWB (i.e., β_2 for OLS; γ_{01} for MLR).

The fundamental difference is found in the error terms. The OLS approach contains a single error term (i.e., e_{ij}), whereas the MLR approach includes two error terms—one that is unique to the employee (i.e., r_{ij}) and one that is applied to all of the employees nested within a common group (i.e., U_{0j}). Thus, the MLR approach partitions errors into a component that resides within groups (i.e., r_{ij}) and a component that resides between groups (i.e., U_{0j}). By appropriately partitioning these errors, we are able to obtain unbiased estimates of the standard errors and thus unbiased tests of statistical significance (Bliese & Hanges, 2004; Raudenbush & Bryk, 2002).

We now turn to a detailed, step-by-step tutorial on how researchers may go about building and testing models within an MLR framework. To facilitate our tutorial, we will analyze and interpret data corresponding to the illustrative example presented earlier in the chapter.

MULTILEVEL REGRESSION: A MODEL-BUILDING APPROACH

With a basic grasp of the tenets underlying MLR in place, we now turn to our illustrative example and our tutorial on MLR. Our tutorial adopts a model-building/model comparison perspective (Aguinis & Culpepper, 2015; Bliese & Ployhart, 2002; Hofmann, 1997; Hofmann, Griffin, & Gavin, 2000) and is structured as follows. First, for each model, we provide a general introduction/overview of the structural equations to be tested. Next, we discuss the interpretation of the regression coefficients and variance components associated with each model. Finally, we test each model using our illustrative example data, and provide a brief interpretation of the results.

Model 1: Null Model or the Unconditional ANOVA Model

Overview. Researchers with nested data are encouraged to test the extent to which their

data may violate the independence assumption underlying the use of OLS. This is accomplished by conducting a simple, one-way ANOVA on the dependent variable (e.g., CWB_{ij}), where we treat group membership as a "grouping" variable or factor in a one-way random effects ANOVA. The Null model is so named because it does not include any Level-1 or Level-2 predictor variables. As we illustrate, the Null model partitions the variance in the outcome or dependent variable into a component that resides within groups and a separate component that resides between groups. If the nesting of Level-1 units (e.g., employees) within Level-2 units (e.g., groups or teams) violates the independence assumption, we would expect to see that group membership explains a nontrivial amount of variance in our dependent variable. Using the notation of Raudenbush and Bryk (2002), the Null model may be presented as

$$\text{Level 1: } CWB_{ij} = \beta_{0j} + r_{ij} \qquad (17.7a)$$

$$\text{Level 2: } \beta_{0j} = \gamma_{00} + U_{0j}, \qquad (17.8a)$$

where, β_{0j} = the mean CWB score for group j, γ_{00} = grand mean score on CWB based on data from all individuals in all groups, r_{ij} = Level-1 residual for person i in group j (i.e., the deviation between a person's CWB score and his or her group's mean), and U_{0j} = Level-2 residual for group j (i.e., the deviation between the mean for group j and the grand mean). Substituting Equation 17.8 into Equation 17.7 yields the "mixed" equation:

$$\text{Mixed: } CWB_{ij} = \gamma_{00} + U_{0j} + r_{ij}. \qquad (17.9a)$$

This equation states that the CWB score for person i nested in group j is a function of (a) a common or grand mean, (b) the extent to which their group mean deviates from the grand mean, and (c) the extent to which their individual score deviates from the group mean.

Raudenbush and Bryk (2002) noted that Equation 17.8 represents a one-way random effects ANOVA model because "the group effects are construed as random" (p. 24). And the total variance (VAR) in CWBs may be partitioned thusly:

$$\text{VAR}(\text{CWB}_{ij}) = \text{VAR}(\gamma_{00} + U_{0j} + r_{ij}) \quad (17.10a)$$

$$\text{VAR}(\text{CWB}_{ij}) = \text{VAR}(\gamma_{00}) + \text{VAR}(U_{0j}) + \text{VAR}(r_{ij}). \quad (17.10b)$$

Because the grand mean is a constant (i.e., it has no variance), it drops out of the equation:

$$\text{VAR}(\text{CWB}_{ij}) = \text{VAR}(U_{0j} + r_{ij}). \quad (17.11)$$

And, assuming that the data meet requisite assumptions concerning the independence of Level-1 and Level-2 errors (see Raudenbush & Bryk, 2002):

$$\text{VAR}(\text{CWB}_{ij}) = \tau_{00} + \sigma^2, \quad (17.12a)$$

where τ_{00} = the variance in CWB scores that resides between groups (i.e., the variance in U_{0j}) and σ^2 = to the variance in CWB scores that resides within groups (i.e., the variance in r_{ij}). If you are like us, the first time you see these equations, you may have a difficult time making the connection between the MLR notation and the basic ANOVA model that is purportedly being tested using Equations 17.7a–17.9a). However, the connection becomes clearer with a slightly different representation of these equations.

Alternative notation. First, we will replace CWB_{ij} with the more commonly used Y_{ij} and rewrite Equations 17.7 and 17.8 using a conventional ANOVA notation:

$$\text{Level 1: } Y_{ij} = \bar{Y}_j + r_{ij} \quad (17.7b)$$

$$\text{Level 2: } \bar{Y}_j = \bar{\bar{Y}} + U_{0j}, \quad (17.8b)$$

where, $\bar{Y}_j$ = the mean outcome score for group j, $\bar{\bar{Y}}$ = grand mean score on the outcome based on scores from all individuals in all groups, r_{ij} = Level-1 residual for person i in group j (i.e., the deviation between a person's outcome score and his or her group's mean; $(Y_{ij} - \bar{Y}_j)$), and U_{0j} = Level-2 residual for group j (i.e., the deviation between the mean for group j and the grand mean; $(\bar{Y}_j - \bar{\bar{Y}})$. Substituting

Equation 17.8a into Equation 17.7a yields the "mixed" equation:

$$\text{Mixed: } Y_{ij} = \bar{\bar{Y}} + U_{0j} + r_{ij}, \quad (17.9b)$$

which is equivalent to

$$\text{Mixed: } Y_{ij} = \bar{\bar{Y}} + (\bar{Y}_j - \bar{\bar{Y}}) + (Y_{ij} - \bar{Y}_j). \quad (17.9b2)$$

The first step in estimating the variance in Y_{ij} is to compute the sum of squared deviations between Y_{ij} and the grand mean, $\bar{\bar{Y}}$:

$$\sum(Y_{ij} - \bar{\bar{Y}})^2 = \sum([\bar{\bar{Y}} + (\bar{Y}_j - \bar{\bar{Y}}) + (Y_{ij} - \bar{Y}_j) - \bar{\bar{Y}}])^2 \quad (17.9b3)$$

$$\sum(Y_{ij} - \bar{\bar{Y}})^2 = \sum(\bar{Y}_j - \bar{\bar{Y}})^2 + \sum(Y_{ij} - \bar{Y}_j)^2. \quad (17.9b4)$$

We then divide these sums by the appropriate degrees of freedom to obtain estimates of means squares and eventually variance components:

$$\frac{\sum(Y_{ij} - \bar{\bar{Y}})^2}{N-1} = \frac{\sum(\bar{Y}_j - \bar{\bar{Y}})^2}{J-1} + \frac{\sum(Y_{ij} - \bar{Y}_j)^2}{N-J} \quad (17.9b4)$$

$$\text{VAR}(Y_{ij}) = \tau_{00} + \sigma^2. \quad (17.12b)$$

Interpreting the regression coefficients. Another way to approach the interpretation of the multilevel notation is to consider the meaning of the regression coefficients presented in Equations 17.7a through 17.9a. Equation 17.7a is simply stating that, absent any other information about the i individuals nested in group j, the best "estimate" for each person's outcome scores (i.e., CWB_{ij}) will be the mean CWB score for group j (β_{0j} in Equation 17.7a and $\bar{Y}_j$ in Equation 17.7b). The group mean will be an imperfect estimate of the individual scores, and this imperfection is manifested as error (r_{ij}). Equation 17.8a is simply stating that, absent any other information about the j groups, the best "estimate" for each group mean (denoted β_{0j} in Equation 17.8a and $\bar{Y}_j$ in Equation 17.8b) is the grand mean (denoted γ_{00} in Equation 17.8a and $\bar{\bar{Y}}$ in Equation 17.8b). The grand mean will be an imperfect estimate of the group means and this imperfection is manifested as error (U_{0j}).

Variance decomposition and interpretation. The variance components computed from the Null model allow us to estimate the proportion of variance in CWBs that resides between and within groups. This variance ratio will enable us to determine if the nesting of Level-1 units within Level-2 units has resulted in a violation of the independence assumption. Formally, this variance ratio is defined as the intraclass correlation obtained from a one-way random effects ANOVA (Bliese, 2000; James, 1982; Raudenbush & Bryk, 2002):

$$ICC(1) = \frac{\tau_{00}}{\tau_{00} + \sigma^2}. \qquad (17.13)$$

Returning to our original hypotheses, we are hoping to predict a portion of the within-groups (i.e., employee-level) variance in CWBs using our employee-level predictor (AGG) and we are hoping to predict some of the variability in group-level intercepts and slopes using our group-level predictor (COH). Thus, it is important that we establish that the variance in CWBs exists both within and between groups. In other words, if there is no meaningful within-group variance in CWBs, it is unlikely that AGG will emerge as a significant predictor of CWBs. Likewise, if CWB scores do not vary between groups, it is unlikely that COH will emerge as a significant predictor of CWBs.

Model 1: Illustrative example. Appendix 17.1 contains the R code used to analyze the data in our illustrative example (R Development Core Team, 2017). The opening lines of Appendix 17.1 address data management issues and the installation of the R packages we use in our data analysis. For most of our analyses, we use pre-defined functions that are part of the *multilevel* package and the *nlme* package. Specifically, we rely heavily on the linear mixed effects (*lme*) function that we use to test the Null model presented in Equations 17.7 and 17.8. The *lme* function requires the user to identify the outcome variable,

specify which effects will be treated as fixed and which will be treated as random, and to specify the grouping (nesting) variable corresponding to those random effects.

Fixed effects refer to the effects in Equations 17.7a and 17.8a that do not vary and reside at Level 2. In our example, the fixed effects are represented using γ. In contrast, the random effects are the effects that are allowed to vary across groups (e.g., U_{0j}) and within groups (e.g., r_{ij}). The R code to estimate the Null model is

```
Null.Model = lme(CWB~1, random =
    ~1|GROUP, data = mlr)
```

The above code accomplishes the following:

- It creates a new "object" in the R environment called Null.Model. And it assigns to this new object the results of the *lme* function.
- The first argument needed for the *lme* function is the name of our outcome variable, CWB, which is regressed on our mixed effects model. This regression is denoted by ~.
- The second argument identifies the fixed component of the mixed effects regression. In the case of the Null model, we have a single fixed effect (i.e., the grand mean of CWB). Referring back to Equation 17.8a, we see that this grand mean is represented by the fixed regression coefficient, γ_{00}. Readers familiar with the matrix algebra representation of multiple regression may recall that it is necessary to append a vector of "1s" to the matrix of predictor variables in order to estimate the intercept. Thus, R uses the number "1" to represent intercepts.

The third argument identifies the random component of the mixed effects regression. Here we set this component equal to the regression of CWBs onto random intercepts. In addition, it is necessary to identify the grouping variable for which unique intercepts are estimated. In our case, this is simply the group identifier variable. Thus, the random component is given by using the syntax "random=~1|GROUP".

Finally, we identify the dataframe we are analyzing. In our case, our data are stored in a file called mlr (consistent with our chapter title, multilevel regression) thus the final argument for the *lme* function is simply "data=mlr".

Essentially, the above code runs the Null model and saves the output to a new object called Null. Model. To see a summary of the results we simply apply the *summary* function to the Null.Model. We present a portion of this output here:

summary(Null.Model)

Random effects:
 Formula: ~1 | GROUP

	(Intercept)	Residual
StdDev:	0.50181	0.7770552

Fixed effects: CWB ~ 1

	Value	Std.Error	DF
(Intercept)	1.858667	0.07213353	540

	t-value	p-value
(Intercept)	25.76703	0

Number of Observations: 600
Number of Groups: 60

The above output includes information about the single fixed effect that we estimated—the grand mean on CWBs ($\gamma_{00} = 1.86$); this number is statistically significantly different from zero (which may or may not have substantive meaning, depending on the specific research questions being addressed). We interpret this coefficient as indicating that, on average, employees engaged in limited acts of CWB (i.e., a 1.86 is a relatively low average given a 7-point Likert-type scale). In addition, information is presented about the random effects. Specifically, τ_{00} (i.e., the variance in intercepts/the variance in CWBs residing between groups) and σ^2 (i.e., the variance within groups). Unfortunately, this information is presented as standard deviations rather than variance components. Thus, one either needs to manually convert these estimates to variance components by squaring them or apply the *VarCorr* function to the Null.Model object.

VarCorr(Null.Model)

GROUP = pdLogChol(1)

	Variance	StdDev
(Intercept)	0.2518133	0.5018100
Residual	0.6038148	0.7770552

We can use these variance components to compute the ICC(1) using Equation 17.13. Here we see that approximately 29% of the variance in CWBs resides between groups (i.e., .2518133/(.2518133 + .6038148) = 0.2943023), and thus 71% of the variance resides within groups. LeBreton and Senter (2008) noted that ICC(1) values of .05 or larger may be interpreted as indicative of practically significant nesting effects. In addition, we can test whether the between-groups variability is statistically significantly different from zero by comparing the Null model to a model that constrains the intercepts to be fixed. This is accomplished by estimating the fixed regression using the *gls* function in R and then comparing the overall fit of the two models using the *anova* function with a likelihood ratio test.

Null.Model.2 = gls(CWB~1, data=mlr)
anova(Null.Model, Null.Model.2)

	Model df	AIC	BIC	logLik	Test
Null.Model	1	3	1507.031	1520.217	
Null.Model.2	2	2	1614.235	1623.025	

	Model df	L.Ratio	p-value
Null.Model	−750.5154		
Null.Model.2	−805.1175	1 vs 2 109.2041	< .0001

The above results indicate that constraining the intercepts to be equal results in a statistically worse-fitting model. Stated alternatively, the variance in intercepts that was estimated as part of the Null model is statistically significantly different from zero—or simply stated, there is significant between-groups variance in CWB scores. Overall, we conclude that there is sufficient between-groups variance to warrant adopting MLR to test our hypotheses.

Model 2: Random Coefficient Regression Model

Overview. After establishing that the CWB scores vary both within and between groups, we may begin adding predictors to our model to try and explain some of this variability. This new model is denoted the random coefficient regression (RCR) model. We typically proceed by adding lower level predictors into the model before adding in the higher level predictors. Hypothesis 1 states that individual-level AGG will be positively related to individual-level CWBs. Thus, we will proceed by including AGG scores as a Level-1 predictor of CWBs. However, before adding these variables to our model, there are two important decisions that must be made.

First, we must decide how to "scale" the Level-1 predictor, AGG. Although our measure of AGG has a meaningful zero point, many measures used in the social sciences do not. A meaningful zero point is important because it allows for a meaningful interpretation of intercepts. To provide scales with a meaningful zero point, researchers typically center scores around a mean—either a grand mean or the group mean. Grand mean centering yields results that are identical to using the raw data (with the exception of the intercepts, because one is simply adding or subtracting the same constant value from every score; Hofmann & Gavin, 1998; Kreft & de Leeuw, 1998; Raudenbush & Bryk, 2002). Thus, the variance does not change nor does the covariance between a grand mean-centered variable and the other variables in the analysis. In contrast, group mean centering (also referred to as centering within context; Zhang, Zyphur, & Preacher, 2009) will typically yield results that differ from both the raw data and the grand mean-centered data. In the case of Hypothesis 1, we are interested in the individual-level effect of AGG and thus we want to purge any possible group-level effect from our data. This is accomplished by centering each of the AGG_{ij} scores around their respective group means, $\overline{AGG_j}$. To verify that we have eliminated all between-group differences in aggression by group mean-centering the scores, we can run a one-way ANOVA on the centered scores or simply request a summary of group means on the centered scores. The ANOVA returns an F-value of 1 and the summary of group means reveals that each group now has a mean of zero; thus, because all groups have identical group means, one can verify that there is no between-groups variability in the group mean-centered AGG scores.

Second, we must decide which regression coefficients to treat as random. Looking ahead, we see that Hypothesis 2 is essentially a "main effect" hypothesis suggesting that fewer CWBs will be observed as group COH scores increase. This main effect is manifested as variability in Level-1 intercepts. Thus, we will continue to treat the Level-1 intercepts as random and allow these intercepts to vary between groups. In addition, Hypothesis 3 represents a cross-level moderation hypothesis; it states that the strength of the relationship between AGG and CWB (i.e., Level-1 slope) will vary as a function of group COH (i.e., Level-2 variable). The strength of the AGG→CWB relationship is manifested in the Level-1 slope coefficients. Thus, if we wish to establish that COH explains variance in the Level-1 relationship, we must also treat the Level-1 slopes as random.

With those decisions made, we may specify the structural equations for the random coefficient regression model:

$$\text{Level 1: } CWB_{ij} = \beta_{0j} + \beta_{1j}\left(AGG_{ij} - \overline{AGG_j}\right) + r_{ij}$$
(17.14)

$$\text{Level 2: } \beta_{0j} = \gamma_{00} + U_{0j} \tag{17.15a}$$

$$\beta_{0j} = \gamma_{10} + U_{1j}, \tag{17.15b}$$

where β_{0j} = unique intercept for group j, β_{1j} = the unique slope for group j, γ_{00} = the average or fixed intercept (pooled within groups), γ_{10} = the average or fixed slope (pooled within groups), r_{ij} = Level-1 residual for individual i in group j, U_{0j} = Level-2 intercept residual for group j (i.e., the difference between the fixed intercept and the unique intercept assigned to group j), U_{1j} = the Level-2 slope residual for group j (i.e., the difference between the fixed slope and the unique slope assigned to group j).

As can be seen, there are two major differences between the Null model and the RCR model. First, a Level-1 predictor and its corresponding β_{1j} coefficient are introduced in the Level-1 equation. Thus, we have added the β_{1j} coefficients as a second, Level-2 outcome variable. This model is somewhat similar to the traditional OLS regression; however, both the intercept and slope are allowed to vary across groups. This model is called the random coefficient regression model because we are allowing the intercept and slope coefficients to vary across groups.

Interpreting the regression coefficients. Whereas the Null model consists of a single fixed effect (fixed intercept), the RCR model consists of two fixed effects: a fixed intercept and a fixed slope. In the Null model, γ_{00} is interpreted as the grand mean of CWB; however, in the RCR model the intercept takes on a new meaning: it is interpreted as a common (or pooled within-groups) intercept. Our fixed slope, γ_{10}, is interpreted as a common (or pooled within-groups) slope –; it represents the (average) relationship between individual-level trait aggression and individual-level CWBs. Remember, by group mean centering AGG (i.e., removing the between-group variance) we obtain a pure estimate of the (individual-level) covariance between AGG and CWBs. Thus, we test Hypothesis 1 by examining the significance of γ_{10}. In addition to these two fixed coefficients, separate intercepts (β_{0j}) and slopes (β_{1j}) are also estimated for each group.

Variance decomposition and interpretation. Whereas the Null model consisted of two random effects corresponding to the Level-1 error variance (i.e., within-groups variance in CWB) and the Level-2 error variance (i.e., between-groups variance in CWB), the RCR model consists of four random effects: σ^2, τ_{00}, τ_{11}, *and* τ_{01}.

Variance within groups. First, we obtain an estimate of the variance in r_{ij} (i.e., σ^2). This variance component is now interpreted as the *residual* within-group variance in CWBs (i.e., the within-groups variance in CWBs that exists *after* adding centered AGG scores as a Level-1 predictor variable). We can compare the estimate obtained for σ^2 from the RCR model with the one obtained from the Null model, to determine how much of the within-groups variance in CWBs was accounted for by our Level-1 predictor. Specifically, we can compute an effect size that is interpreted as a proportional reduction in error (see Chapter 15 for additional information about estimating effect sizes in MLR):

$$\text{pseudo-}R^2 = \frac{\sigma^2_{ANOVA} - \sigma^2_{RCR}}{\sigma^2_{ANOVA}}. \qquad (17.16)$$

Variance in Level-1 intercepts. Second, we obtain an estimate of the variance in U_{0j}, denoted τ_{00}. This variance component is now interpreted as the variance in the Level-1 intercepts across groups. Recall that Hypothesis 2 states COH will explain variance in CWBs. Because COH is a variable that resides between groups, it is only able to predict the portion of variance in CWBs that resides between groups. Thus, we want to confirm that there is statistically significant variance in intercepts. This is accomplished by testing two nested models: one where group-level intercepts are fixed to a common value, the other where they are allowed to take on unique values.

Variance in Level-1 slopes. Third, because we decided to treat the Level-1 predictor (i.e., $AGG_{ij} - \overline{AGG_j}$) as a random effect, we also obtained an estimate of the variance in U_{1j}, denoted τ_{11}. This variance component is interpreted as the variance in group-level slopes. Recall that Hypothesis 3 states COH will moderate the strength of the Level-1 relationship between AGG and CWBs. Because COH is a variable that resides between groups, it is only able to predict variance in slopes that reside between groups. Thus, we want to confirm that there is statistically significant variance in slopes. Again, this is accomplished by testing two nested models: one where group-level slopes are fixed to a common value, and the other where they are allowed to take on unique values.

However, Aguinis and Culpepper (2015) noted several problems with relying solely on the test of nested models. Specifically, they noted that (a) the likelihood ratio test used to test for significant variance in slopes is asymptotically too conservative and (b) it is possible to conclude that there is statistically significant variance in slopes when the magnitude of slope variance is practically nonsignificant/trivial. To address these concerns, Aguinis and Culpepper offered a new intraclass correlation: ICC_β. This new statistic provides an effect size representing the proportion of "within-group outcome variance attributed to slope differences" (p. 162). Thus, the ICC_β provides an effect size for Model 2 (i.e., the RCR model) that is akin to the ICC(1) effect size estimated for Model 1 (i.e., the Null model). One important implication of Aguinis and Culpepper's new statistic is that researchers interested in testing cross-level *interactions* are encouraged to include the estimation of ICC_β in their model testing process, even if the ICC(1) does not suggest practically significant nesting effects. As Aguinis and Culpepper noted,

> We suggest that researchers contemplating the use of multilevel [regression], as well as those who suspect nonindependence in their data structure, expand the decision criteria for using such data analytic approach to include both types of intraclass correlations. Continued use of [ICC(1)] as the sole decision criteria may lead to inappropriate use of data analytic approaches that require independence across observations and also lead to opportunity cost in terms of testing precise and specific cross-level interaction effect hypotheses. (p. 170)

We concur and encourage researchers, especially those testing cross-level interactions, to estimate both types of ICCs.

Covariance between Level-1 intercepts and slopes. Finally, because we allowed both intercepts and slopes to vary, we obtain an estimate of the covariance between U_{0j} and U_{1j}, denoted τ_{01}. This final variance component is interpreted as the covariance between group-level intercepts and group-level slopes. Although this covariance is not of particular interest in the current study, the covariance between intercepts and slopes is frequently of interest in longitudinal studies examining growth/decline over time.

Model 2: Illustrative example. The test of Hypothesis 1, which is organic to the RCR model, is the significance test for the Level-2 fixed effect γ_{10}. The γ_{10} coefficient is the mean (pooled within-groups) slope coefficient across all groups. A significant γ_{10} coefficient tells us that, on average across all groups, the slope describing the individual relationship between CWB and AGG is significantly different from zero. The significance of the γ_{10} parameter tells us that there is a significant individual-level relationship between CWB and AGG; however, this significance test does not provide information about the magnitude of the relationship, which may be estimated using Equation 17.16. Before using the

RCR Model to test our example hypotheses, we will recap the three important pieces of information that this specific model provides:

- An estimate and significance test for Level-2 intercept and slope variance; along with effect size estimates for slope variation (i.e., ICC_β),
- An estimate for the Level-1 relationships (direct test of H1), and
- A pseudo-R^2 to evaluate the magnitude of the Level-1 relationships.

Prior to specifying the RCR model, we will first compute group-mean centered scores on our measure of trait aggression and add these scores to our data frame. To accomplish this process, we use the *aggregate* function to compute group means and save these values into a new data frame. We then use the *rename* function to simply assign meaningful names to the variables, followed by the *merge* function to combine the two data frames. Finally, we compute a new variable by subtracting group means from raw scores and saving the centered scores as a new variable in our data frame.

```
AGG.Aggregated=aggregate(mlr[,c(2)],
    list(mlr$GROUP), mean, na.rm=T)
AGG.Aggregated=rename(AGG.Aggregated,
    replace=c("Group.1"="GROUP",
    "x"="AGG.GroupMean"))
mlr=merge(mlr,AGG.Aggregated,by="GROUP")
mlr$AGG.Group=mlr$AGG-mlr$AGG.
    GroupMean
```

Now that we have properly scaled our measure of trait aggression (AGG), we can write and execute the R code to test the RCR model:

```
RCR.Model=lme(CWB~1+AGG.Group,
    random=~1+AGG.Group|GROUP,data=mlr)
```

The above code accomplishes the following:

- It creates a new "object" in the R environment called RCR.Model, and it assigns to this new object the results of the linear mixed effects (*lme*) function.
- The first argument needed for the *lme* function is the name of our outcome variable, CWB, which is to be regressed on our mixed effects model. This regression is denoted by ~ .

- The second argument identifies the fixed component of the mixed effects regression. In the case of the RCR model, we have two fixed effects (i.e., a fixed intercept and a fixed slope for the group-mean centered aggression scores; see Equations 17.15a and 17.15b).
- The third argument identifies the random component of the mixed effects regression. Here we set this component equal to the regression of CWBs onto both random intercepts and slopes (see Equation 17.14). In addition, we also must identify the grouping variable. Thus, the random component is given by using the syntax random = ~1+AGG.Group|GROUP.
- Finally, we identify our dataframe using data=mlr.

After running the above code, we can request a summary of the results and apply the *VarCorr* function to the RCR.Model and compare the results to the *VarCorr* function applied to our original Null.Model. These variance components are used to compute the pseudo-R^2 statistics.

summary(RCR.Model)

Linear mixed-effects model fit by REML
 Data: mlr
AIC	BIC	logLik
1427.714	1454.075	–707.8569

Random effects:
 Formula: ~1 + AGG.Group | GROUP
 Structure: General positive-definite, Log-Cholesky parametrization

	StdDev	Corr
(Intercept)	0.5137365	(Intr)
AGG.Group	0.1414664	0.751
Residual	0.6947630	

Fixed effects: CWB ~ 1 + AGG.Group

	Value	Std.Error	DF
(Intercept)	1.858667	0.07213353	539
AGG.Group	0.107824	0.02484711	539

	t-value	p-value
(Intercept)	25.767026	0
AGG.Group	4.339498	0

Correlation:
	(Intr)
AGG.Group	0.508

Standardized Within-Group Residuals:
Min	Q1	Med
–2.9409451	–0.6694657	–0.1675953

Q3	Max
0.5779086	3.8372834

Number of Observations: 600
Number of Groups: 60

VarCorr(RCR.Model)

GROUP = pdLogChol(1 + AGG.Group)
	Variance	StdDev	Corr
(Intercept)	0.26392523	0.5137365	(Intr)
AGG.Group	0.02001274	0.1414664	0.751
Residual	0.48269566	0.6947630	

Starting with the direct test of Hypothesis 1, the fixed effect for the Level-1 relationship between CWB and group-mean centered AGG (γ_{10}) is significant and positive; $\gamma_{10} = 0.11$, $p < .05$. This significant fixed effect provides support for Hypothesis 1 and is interpreted as "for every unit increase in individual-level aggression, CWB scores are predicted to increase by .11 units." Next, we compute a pseudo-R^2 to investigate the magnitude of this relationship by plugging the appropriate variance components into Equation 17.16.

VarCorr(Null.Model) #displays variance/covariance of parameters from ANOVA

GROUP = pdLogChol(1)
	Variance	StdDev
(Intercept)	0.2518133	0.5018100
Residual	0.6038148	0.7770552

VarCorr(RCR.Model) #displays variance/covariance of parameters from RCR

GROUP = pdLogChol(1 + AGG.Group)
	Variance	StdDev	Corr
(Intercept)	0.26392523	0.5137365	(Intr)
AGG.Group	0.02001274	0.1414664	0.751
Residual	0.48269566	0.6947630	

The estimate of the within-groups variance in CWBs from the Null model (i.e., σ^2_{NULL}) is 0.60. The estimate of the residual within-groups variance in CWBs, after controlling for group-mean centered AGG (i.e., σ^2_{RCR}) is 0.48. Therefore, using Equation 17.16, the pseudo-R^2 for the relationship between CWB and AGG is approximately 0.20, suggesting that group-mean centered AGG accounts for roughly 20% of the within-group variance in CWB. Thus, not only was our predictor statistically significantly related to the outcome, but it appeared to explain a practically meaningful proportion of the within-groups variance in CWBs. At this point, if we had additional Level-1 predictors (e.g., age, sex, other personality traits), we could add them into the Level-1 equation and try to explain even more of the within-groups variance in CWBs.

Our next two hypotheses require that we have significant variance in both intercepts (Hypothesis 2) and slopes (Hypothesis 3). It is possible to conduct a significance test on the variance estimates in the RCR.Model output by comparing the RCR.Model to a model that constrains the intercept and slope to assumed fixed values (i.e., sets the variance in intercepts = 0 and the variance in slopes = 0). First, we use *gls* to estimate a model with both fixed intercept and fixed slope:

RCR.Model.2=gls(CWB~1+AGG.Group,data=mlr)

Next we use *lme* to estimate a model with random intercepts, but with a fixed slope and compare this to the prior model with fixed intercept and fixed slope.

RCR.Model.3=lme(CWB~1+AGG.Group, random=~1|GROUP,data=mlr) anova(RCR.Model.2,RCR.Model.3)

Model	df	AIC	BIC	logLik	Test
RCR.Model.2	1	3	1587.21	1600.390	
RCR.Model.3	2	4	1465.15	1482.724	

Model	df	L.Ratio	p-value
RCR.Model.2		790.6048	
RCR.Model.3		–728.5749	1 vs 2 124.0599 < .0001

The results indicate that the random intercepts model (RCR.Model.3) is a better fit to the data; thus,

there is statistically significant variance in intercepts. We can repeat this process by comparing RCR. Model.3 (i.e., random intercepts and a fixed slope) to the original RCR.Model (i.e., random intercepts and random slopes).

anova(RCR.Model.3,RCR.Model)

Abbreviated R Output:

Model	df	AIC	BIC	logLik	Test
RCR.Model.3	1	4	1465.150	1482.724	
RCR.Model.	2	6	1427.714	1454.075	

Model	df	L.Ratio	p-value
RCR.Model.3		–728.5749	
RCR.Model.		–707.8569	1 vs 2 41.43588 < .0001

Results confirm there is also statistically significant variance in slopes. Stated alternatively, there is significant between-groups variance in both intercepts ($\tau_{00} = 0.26$, $p < .0001$) and slopes ($\tau_{11} = 0.02$, $p < .0001$). Consequently, we are justified in moving forward with our model-building/comparison approach to test Hypotheses 2 and 3. In addition, we could estimate the ICC_β using the *iccbeta* package in R. Unfortunately, this package relies on a different package (*lme4*) and a different function (*lmer*) for estimating the variance components used to estimate ICC_β Introducing and explaining this alternative package and the accompanying functions is beyond the scope of the current chapter. However, the interested reader is directed to Aguinis and Culpepper (2015) for an excellent discussion underlying the use and interpretation of ICC_β. Hopefully, the *iccbeta* package will be updated to allow output from the *lme* function that is part of the *nlme* package.

Model 3: Intercepts-as-Outcomes Model

Overview. Hypothesis 2 proposes that our Level-2 predictor, COH, will explain a portion of the between-groups variance in CWBs. This test is manifested as a cross-level direct or main effect in our third model, the Intercepts-as-Outcomes (IAO) model:

Level 1: $CWB_{ij} = \beta_{0j} + \beta_{1j}\left(AGG_{ij} - \overline{AGG_j}\right) + r_{ij}$

(17.14, revisited)

Level 2: $\beta_{0j} = \gamma_{00} + \gamma_{01}(COH_j) + U_{0j}$ (17.17a)

$$\beta_{0j} = \gamma_{10} + U_{1j},$$ (17.17b)

where β_{0j} = unique intercept for group j, β_{1j} = the unique slope for group j, γ_{00} = the average or fixed intercept (pooled within-groups), γ_{10} = the average or fixed (pooled within-groups) slope corresponding to the group-mean centered aggression scores, γ_{01} = fixed slope corresponding to the effect of group-level COH, r_{ij} = Level-1 residual for individual i in group j, U_{0j} = Level-2 intercept residual for group j (i.e., the difference between the fixed intercept and the unique intercept assigned to group j), U_{1j} = the Level-2 slope residual for group j (i.e., the difference between the fixed slope and the unique slope assigned to group j). The IAO model is similar to the RCR model. The primary difference is the introduction of a Level-2 predictor (COH_j) in the Level-2 intercept equation (17.17a). There are two important consequences that occur when we introduce a Level-2 predictor of β_{0j}. Adding COH to the Level-2 intercept equation (a) changes the interpretation of τ_{00} and (b) introduces a new fixed effect (γ_{01}) into the Level-2 intercept equation.

Interpreting the regression coefficients. Our IAO model consists of three fixed effects: a fixed intercept and two fixed slopes. The fixed intercept, γ_{00}, is still interpreted as a common (or pooled within-groups) intercept. Our fixed slope, γ_{10}, is interpreted as a common (or pooled within-groups) slope— it represents the (average) relationship between individual-level trait aggression and individual-level CWBs. The final fixed effect, γ_{01}, is interpreted as a common (or pooled within-groups) slope—it represents the (average) relationship between group-level cohesion scores and (the between-groups portion of) individual-level CWBs.

Variance decomposition and interpretation.

Variance within groups. This model will continue to generate an estimate of within-groups residual error variance (i.e., the within-groups variance in CWBs that exists after including group-mean centered trait aggression scores in the model). Because we have not made any changes to the Level-1 equation, the σ^2 estimate from the IAO model is typically

the same as what was observed in the RCR model. However, it is possible for these estimates to change slightly.

Variance in Level-1 intercepts. In contrast, our estimate of the variance in U_{0j}, denoted τ_{00}, typically will change when compared to the estimate that was obtained using the RCR model. This variance component is now interpreted as the residual variance in the Level-1 intercepts that remains after including COH in the model. It is possible to use the variance components from the RCR and IAO models to obtain a pseudo-R^2 for our Level-2 predictor (again, we encourage readers to refer to Chapter 15 for additional information about estimating effect sizes in MLR). Although there are several options for estimating effect sizes, we opted to compute a pseudo-R^2 using the τ_{00} estimate from the RCR model and the τ_{00} estimate from the IAO model:

Level-2 intercept model pseudo-R^2

$$= \frac{\tau_{00(RCR)} - \tau_{00(IAO)}}{\tau_{00(RCR)}}.$$ (17.18)

Finally, we can also test whether the remaining variance in intercepts is statistically significant by comparing two nested models: one where group-level intercepts are fixed to a common value, and the other where they are allowed to take on unique values. If τ_{00} from the IAO model is statistically significant, we could try to explain this residual between-groups variance in intercepts by adding in additional group-level variables (e.g., group size, group age).

Variance in Level-1 slopes. Because we continued to treat the Level-1 predictor (i.e., $AGG_{ij} - \overline{AGG_j}$) as a random effect, we also obtain an estimate of the variance in U_{1j}, denoted τ_{11}. This variance component is interpreted as the variance in group-level slopes. Recall that Hypothesis 3 states COH will moderate the strength of the Level-1 relationship between AGG and CWBs. Thus, we want to confirm that there is statistically significant variance in slopes across groups. Again, this is accomplished by comparing two nested models: one where group-level slopes are fixed to a common value, the other where the group-level slopes are allowed to take on unique values.

Covariance between Level-1 intercepts and slopes. Finally, because we allowed both intercepts and slopes to vary, we will continue to obtain an estimate of the covariance between U_{0j} and U_{1j}, denoted τ_{01}. This final variance component is interpreted as the covariance between group-level intercepts and group-level slopes.

Model 3: Illustrative example. The test of Hypothesis 2 is furnished by the significance test on the fixed regression weight, γ_{01}. We specify the IAO model in R:

IAO.Model=lme(CWB~1+AGG.Group+COH, random=~1+AGG.Group|GROUP,data=mlr)

The above code simply augments the fixed portion of the mixed regression by requesting a slope coefficient for the COH variable. After requesting a summary of the results, we find that there is a significant main effect of COH on CWB ($\gamma_{01} = -0.61$, $p < .05$), suggesting that for every unit increase in group-level cohesion scores, CWBs decrease by .61 units. Thus, as groups become more cohesive, individuals within those groups are (on average) less likely to engage in CWBs.

summary(IAO.Model)

Linear mixed-effects model fit by REML
Data: mlr

AIC	BIC	logLik
1409.822	1440.565	−697.9109

Random effects:
Formula: ~1 + AGG.Group | GROUP
Structure: General positive-definite, Log-Cholesky parametrization

	StdDev	Corr
(Intercept)	0.3754431	(Intr)
AGG.Group	0.1426068	0.63
Residual	0.6950287	

Fixed effects: CWB~ 1 + AGG.Group + COH

	Value	Std.Error	DF
(Intercept)	5.237037	0.6025813	539
AGG.Group	0.107299	0.0251456	539
COH	−0.613264	0.1089084	58

	t-value	p-value
(Intercept)	8.691006	0
AGG.Group	4.267102	0
COH	−5.631011	0

We obtain estimates of the variance components using the *VarCorr* function and compare the between-groups variance in intercepts from the RCR model to the residual between-groups variance in intercepts from the IAO model.

VarCorr(RCR.Model)

GROUP = pdLogChol(1 + AGG.Group)

	Variance	StdDev	Corr
(Intercept)	0.26392523	0.5137365	(Intr)
AGG.Group	0.02001274	0.1414664	0.751
Residual	0.48269566	0.6947630	

VarCorr(IAO.Model)

GROUP = pdLogChol(1 + AGG.Group)

	Variance	StdDev	Corr
(Intercept)	0.14095753	0.3754431	(Intr)
AGG.Group	0.02033669	0.1426068	0.63
Residual	0.48306484	0.6950287	

Specifically, we estimate a pseudo-R^2 using Equation 17.18 and obtain a value of .46 (i.e., $[0.26{-}0.14]/0.26 = .46$), which indicates that by adding COH to the model, we were able to explain roughly 46% of the between-groups variance in intercepts. It is possible to test whether the remaining variance in intercepts is statistically significant by comparing a model that constrains the intercepts to be fixed to a model that frees them to vary. First, we use *gls* to estimate a model with both fixed intercept and fixed slope:

IAO.Model.2=gls(CWB~1+AGG.Group+COH, data=mlr)

Next, we use *lme* to estimate a model with random intercepts, but with fixed slopes:

IAO.Model.3=lme(CWB~1+AGG.Group+COH, random=~1|GROUP,data=mlr)

Comparing the fit of these models indicates that even after including our significant predictor (COH), the remaining (i.e., residual) variance in intercepts is statistically significant. Thus, if we had additional predictors of group intercepts, we could attempt to predict some of the remaining variance by including those predictors in Equation 17.17a.

anova(IAO.Model.2,IAO.Model.3)

Model df		AIC	BIC	logLik	Test
IAO.Model.2	1	4	1488.774	1506.341	
IAO.Model.3	2	5	1437.808	1459.767	

Model df		L.Ratio	p-value
IAO.Model.2	−740.3869		
IAO.Model.3	−713.9038	1 vs 2 52.96621	< .0001

Finally, we can compare the fit of IAO.Model.3 to the original IAO.Model to confirm that the variance in slopes continues to be significant, and thus we are justified in moving forward to test our third and final hypothesis. Not surprisingly, the variance in slopes is statistically significant. Thus, we will proceed to test Hypothesis 3, which states that COH will help to explain some of the variance in slopes (i.e., group-level COH will moderate the strength of the relationship between employee-level AGG and employee-level CWB).

anova(IAO.Model.3,IAO.Model)

Model df		AIC	BIC	logLik	Test
IAO.Model.3	1	5	1437.808	1459.767	
IAO.Model.	2	7	1409.822	1440.565	

Model df		L.Ratio	p-value
IAO.Model.3	−713.9038		
IAO.Model	−697.9109	1 vs 2 31.98579	< .0001

Model 4: Slopes-as-Outcomes Model

Overview. Hypothesis 3 proposes that our Level-2 variable, COH, will moderate the relationship between our Level-1 variables, AGG and CWB. This test is manifested as a cross-level interaction in our fourth model, the Slopes-as-Outcomes (SAO) model:

$$\text{Level 1: } CWB_{ij} = \beta_{0j} + \beta_{1j}\left(AGG_{ij} - \overline{AGG_j}\right) + r_{ij}$$

$$(17.14, \text{revisited})$$

$$\text{Level 2: } \beta_{0j} = \gamma_{00} + \gamma_{01}\left(COH_j\right) + U_{0j} \quad (17.17a)$$

$$\beta_{1j} = \gamma_{10} + \gamma_{11}\left(COH_j\right) + U_{1j}, \quad (17.19)$$

where β_{0j} = unique intercept for group j, β_{1j} = the unique slope for group j, γ_{00} = the average or fixed intercept (pooled within-groups), γ_{10} = the average or fixed (pooled within-groups) slope corresponding to the group-mean centered aggression scores, γ_{01} = the fixed slope corresponding to the effect of group-level COH, γ_{11} = fixed slope corresponding to the relationship of group-level COH to the Level-1 slopes (β_{1j}), r_{ij} = Level-1 residual for individual i in group j, U_{0j} = Level-2 intercept residual for group j (i.e., the difference between the fixed intercept and the unique intercept assigned to group j), U_{1j} = the Level-2 slope residual for group j (i.e., the difference between the fixed slope and the unique slope assigned to group j). The SAO model is similar to the IAO model. The primary difference is the introduction of a Level-2 predictor (COH_j) in the Level-2 slope equation (17.19). There are two important consequences that occur when we introduce a Level-2 predictor of β_{1j}. Adding COH to the Level-2 slope equation (a) changes the interpretation of τ_{11}, and (b) introduces a new fixed effect parameter (γ_{11}).

Interpreting the regression coefficients. Our SAO model consists of four fixed effects: a fixed intercept and three fixed slopes. The fixed intercept, γ_{00}, is still interpreted as a common (or pooled within-groups) intercept. Our fixed slope, γ_{10}, is interpreted as a common (or pooled within-groups) slope—it represents the (average) relationship between individual-level trait aggression (AGG) and individual-level CWBs. The fixed slope, γ_{01}, is interpreted as a fixed slope representing the (average) relationship between group-level cohesion scores and the between-groups portion of individual-level CWBs. Finally, γ_{11}, is interpreted as a fixed slope representing the relationship between group-level cohesion scores and the Level-1 slopes (β_{1j}). If γ_{11} is positive, it indicates that as COH increases (i.e., groups become more cohesive), the bivariate relationship between employee-level AGG and CWB also increases. If γ_{11} is negative, it indicates that as COH increases (i.e., groups become more cohesive), the relationship between individual-level AGG and CWB decreases. Based on Hypothesis 3, we are hoping to see a significant negative γ_{11} coefficient.

Variance decomposition and interpretation.

Variance within groups. This model will continue to generate an estimate of within-groups residual error variance (i.e., the within-groups variance in CWBs that exists after including group-mean centered AGG scores in the model). Because we have not made any changes to the Level-1 equation, the σ^2 estimate from the SAO model is typically the same as what was observed in the RCR and IAO models. However, it is possible for these estimates to change slightly.

Variance in Level-1 intercepts. Similarly, our estimate of the variance in U_{0j}, denoted τ_{00}, is unlikely to change dramatically from what was observed in the IAO model, because we have not modified Equation 17.17a. This variance component is still interpreted as the residual variance in the Level-1 intercepts that remains after including COH in the model.

Variance in Level-1 slopes. In contrast, our estimate of the variance in U_{1j}, denoted τ_{11}, takes on new meaning in the SAO model. Specifically, this variance component is interpreted as the *residual* variance in group-level slopes that remains after including COH_j as a predictor of slopes (see Equation 17.19). It is possible to use the variance components from the IAO and SAO models to obtain a pseudo-R^2 for our Level-2 predictor. For our estimate of pseudo-R^2, we rely on the τ_{11} estimate from the IAO model and the τ_{11} estimate from the SAO model:

Level-2 intercept model pseudo-R^2

$$= \frac{\tau_{11(IAO)} - \tau_{11(SAO)}}{\tau_{11(IAO)}}. \qquad (17.20)$$

This coefficient is interpreted as an effect size, representing the proportion of variance in slopes that is explained using group-level COH scores. Finally, we can also test whether the remaining variance in slopes is statistically significant by comparing two nested models, one where group-

level slopes are fixed to a common value the other where they are allowed to take on unique values. If the residual variance, τ_{11}, from the SAO model is statistically significant, we could try to explain this variance by adding in additional group-level variables (e.g., group size, group structure, group age) as predictors of Level-1 slopes.

Covariance between Level-1 intercepts and slopes. Finally, because we allowed both intercepts and slopes to vary, we will continue to obtain an estimate of the covariance between U_{0j} and U_{1j}, denoted τ_{01}. This final variance component is interpreted as the covariance between group-level intercepts and group-level slopes.

Model 4: Illustrative example. The test of Hypothesis 3 is furnished by the significance test on the fixed regression weight, γ_{11}. We specify the SAO model in R:

```
SAO.Model=lme(CWB~1+AGG.Group+COH+
    AGG.Group:COH,random=~1+AGG.
    Group|GROUP,data=mlr)
```

The above code simply augments the fixed portion of the mixed regression by including a cross-product term between employee-level (group-mean centered) aggression and group-level cohesion. In R, cross-products between specific variables are specified using a colon (:) rather than an asterisk (*), which is more commonly used in other software packages. After requesting a summary of the results, we find that COH is a significant moderator of the relationships between individual-level AGG and CWB ($\gamma_{11} = -0.17$, $p < .05$). Specifically, for every unit increase in group-level cohesion scores, the group-level relationships (i.e., β_{1j}) are predicted to decrease by .17 units. This significant cross-level interaction is visually depicted in Figure 17.7.

```
summary(SAO.Model)
```

Linear mixed-effects model fit by REML
Data: mlr

AIC	BIC	logLik
1405.847	1440.969	–694.9234

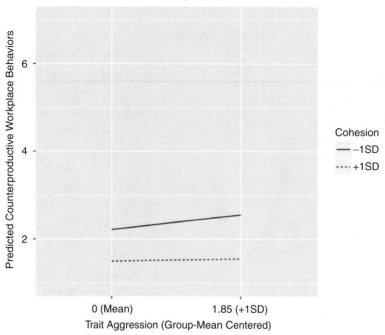

FIGURE 17.7. Cross-level moderating effect of group-level cohesion on the individual-level relationship between counterproductive workplace behaviors and trait aggression.

Random effects:

Formula: ~1 + AGG.Group | GROUP

Structure: General positive-definite,
    Log-Cholesky parametrization

	StdDev	Corr
(Intercept)	0.3701347	(Intr)
AGG.Group	0.1209911	0.601
Residual	0.6945231	

Fixed effects: CWB ~1 + AGG.Group + COH +
    AGG.Group:COH

	Value	Std.Error	DF
(Intercept)	6.002650	0.6461452	538
AGG.Group	1.020849	0.2761603	538
COH	−0.752243	0.1168581	58
AGG.Group:COH	−0.165673	0.0499978	538

	t-value	p-value
(Intercept)	9.289939	0e+00
AGG.Group	3.696583	2e-04
COH	−6.437237	0e+00
AGG.Group:COH	−3.313596	1e-03

We obtain estimates of the variance components using the *VarCorr* function and compare the between-groups variance in slopes from the IAO model to the residual between-groups variance in slopes from the SAO model:

VarCorr(IAO.Model)

GROUP = pdLogChol(1 + AGG.Group)

	Variance	StdDev	Corr
(Intercept)	0.14095753	0.3754431	(Intr)
AGG.Group	0.02033669	0.1426068	0.63
Residual	0.48306484	0.6950287	

VarCorr(SAO.Model)

GROUP = pdLogChol(1 + AGG.Group)

	Variance	StdDev	Corr
(Intercept)	0.13699971	0.3701347	(Intr)
AGG.Group	0.01463884	0.1209911	0.601
Residual	0.48236236	0.6945231	

Specifically, we estimate a pseudo-R^2 using Equation 17.20 and obtain a value of 0.28

(i.e., [0.020–0.014]/0.020 = .28), which indicates that by adding COH to the model, we were able to explain roughly 28% of the between-groups variance in slopes. It is possible to test whether the remaining variance in slopes is statistically significant by comparing a model that constrains the slopes to be fixed to a model that allows them to vary. Recall that the residual variance in intercepts from the IAO model was statistically significant. Thus, we will continue to model intercepts as random while testing whether significant variance remains in slopes:

SAO.Model.2=lme(CWB~1+AGG.Group+COH+
   AGG.Group:COH,random=~1|GROUP,data=mlr)

We then compare the fit of the original SAO model (random intercepts and random slopes) with the above model (random intercepts and fixed slope):

anova(SAO.Model.2, SAO.Model)

Model	df	AIC	BIC	logLik	Test
SAO.Model.2	1	6	1422.043	1448.384	
SAO.Model	2	8	1405.847	1440.969	

Model	df	L.Ratio	p-value
SAO.Model.2	–705.0212		
SAO.Model	–694.9234	1 vs 2 20.19572	< .0001

The results indicate that the remaining (i.e., residual) variance in slopes is statistically significant. Thus, if we had additional predictors of group slopes, we could attempt to predict the remaining variance by including those predictors in Equation 17.19 (and, as a main effect in Equation 17.17a, too).

EXPANDING THE MODEL-BUILDING/ COMPARISON APPROACH TO MULTILEVEL REGRESSION

A disclaimer is in order after walking the reader through the process of developing and comparing a series of models in our quest to test three example hypotheses. The hypotheses and models that we tested were extremely simple. However, after mastering the basics of MLR, the reader will be better positioned to articulate and test more sophisticated models. For example, consider how

you would update the four basic models (Null, RCR, IAO, SAO) to test a few additional hypotheses:

- Hypothesis 4: Employee sex will moderate the strength of the relationship between employee aggression and counterproductive workplace behaviors, such that the strength of the relationship will be stronger for male employees than for female employees.
- Hypothesis 5: Group size will moderate the strength of the relationship between group cohesion and counterproductive workplace behaviors, such that the negative effect will become stronger as group size gets smaller.

Essentially, Hypothesis 4 is adding an additional Level-1 predictor of CWBs and treating it as a moderator variable for the Level-1 relationship, and Hypothesis 5 is adding an additional Level-2 predictor of CWBs and treating it as a moderator variable of the Level-2 relationship. These seem like simple enough hypotheses, but how would one go about using the model-building approach to test these hypotheses?

We encourage you to take a few minutes to think through (and write down) the model equations and the R code that would be required to test these additional hypotheses. Did you come up with something along the lines of the following?

Null Model

$$\text{Level 1: } CWB_{ij} = \beta_{0j} + r_{ij}$$

$$\text{Level 2: } B_{0j} = \gamma_{00} + U_{0j}$$

The Null model doesn't change from what was presented in the chapter. Thus, the Null model would have a single fixed effect (γ_{00}) and two random effects corresponding to the variance in CWBs that reside within (σ^2) and between groups (τ_{00}).

RCR Model

In contrast, the RCR model becomes appreciably more complex. Specifically, we have added employee sex to the Level-1 equation, along with the cross-product between sex and aggression. In addition, for each of these additional terms, we had to decide whether to treat them as random or fixed (or both).

In our case, we elected to treat each of them as both fixed and random (hence the separate error terms for each of the Level-2 equations):

Level 1: $CWB_{ij} = \beta_{0j} + \beta_{1j}\left(AGG_{ij} - \overline{AGG_j}\right)$
$+ \beta_{2j}\left(SEX_{ij}\right)$
$+ \beta_{3j}\left(AGG_{ij} - \overline{AGG_j}\right)*\left(SEX_{ij}\right) + r_{ij}$

Level 2: $\beta_{0j} = \gamma_{00} + U_{0j}$
$\beta_{1j} = \gamma_{10} + U_{1j}$
$\beta_{2j} = \gamma_{20} + U_{2j}$
$\beta_{3j} = \gamma_{30} + U_{3j}.$

The test of Hypothesis 4 is provided by a test on the significance of γ_{30}. If this coefficient was significant, then we would likely want to estimate the proportion of Level-1 variance that is attributed to the interaction effect. This effect size would be computed by comparing the σ^2 from the above RCR model to the σ^2 obtained from a main effects model. Formally, we could estimate the effect size for the interaction between two Level-1 variables as

Level 1 pseudo-$R^2 = \dfrac{\sigma^2_{MainEffects} - \sigma^2_{MainEffects+Cross-Product}}{\sigma^2_{MainEffects}}.$

To properly specify this RCR model, we need to know which effects to treat as fixed and which to treat as random. In the above equation, there are four fixed effects corresponding to the Level-2 γ coefficients. In addition, the above equations indicate that random effects are to be estimated for each of the predictors. Thus, there are four random effects corresponding to the variability in intercepts (τ_{00}), the slopes for aggression (τ_{11}), the slopes for sex (τ_{22}), and the slopes for the cross-product terms (τ_{33}). And, there is a Level-1 random effect corresponding to the within-groups variance (σ^2). Finally, the four random coefficients from the Level-1 equations are also allowed to covary with one another, resulting in six additional covariance terms (i.e., $\tau_{01}, \tau_{02}, \tau_{03}, \tau_{12}, \tau_{13}, \tau_{23}$).

Thus, moving from our original RCR model to a model that includes an additional Level-1 variable and its cross-product with our original Level-1

variable yields a substantially more complex model. Adding to this complexity would be decisions concerning how to scale sex (e.g., dummy codes, effect codes, group or grand-mean centered). We do not delve into the various interpretations of different centering strategies; rather, we direct the reader to other sources that are specifically focused on scaling/centering of predictors (Hofmann & Gavin, 1998; Raudenbush & Bryk, 2002). Whereas our original RCR model contained two fixed effects and four random effects, our revised RCR model now contains four fixed effects and 11 random effects. The R code for this revised RCR model would look something like:

```
RCR.Model = lme(CWB~1+AGG.Group+
    SEX+AGG.Group:SEX,random=~1+AGG.
    Group+SEX+AGG.Group:SEX|GROUP,
    data=mlr)
```

IAO Model

To test Hypothesis 5, we will need to also revise the IAO model. Specifically, we have added group size to the Level-2 equation predicting intercepts, along with the cross-product between group size and cohesion:

Level 1: $CWB_{ij} = \beta_{0j} + \beta_{1j}\left(AGG_{ij} - \overline{AGG_j}\right)$
$+ \beta_{2j}\left(SEX_{ij}\right)$
$+ \beta_{3j}\left(AGG_{ij} - \overline{AGG_j}\right)*\left(SEX_{ij}\right) + r_{ij}$

Level 2: $\beta_{0j} = \gamma_{00} + \gamma_{01}\left(COH_j\right) + \gamma_{02}\left(SIZE_j\right)$
$+ \gamma_{03}\left(COH_j\right)*\left(SIZE_j\right) + U_{0j}$
$\beta_{1j} = \gamma_{10} + U_{1j}$
$\beta_{2j} = \gamma_{20} + U_{2j}$
$\beta_{3j} = \gamma_{30} + U_{3j}.$

The test of Hypothesis 5 is provided by a test on the significance of γ_{03}. If this coefficient were significant, we would need to estimate the proportion of intercept variance that is attributed to this interaction effect. This effect size would be computed by comparing the τ_{00} from the above IAO model with the τ_{00} obtained from a main effects model. Formally, we could estimate the effect size for the interaction between two Level-2 variables as

$$\text{Level 2 pseudo-}R^2 = \frac{\tau_{00(MainEffects)} - \tau_{00(MainEffects+Cross-Product)}}{\tau_{00(MainEffects)}}.$$

To properly specify this IAO model, we need to know which effects to treat as fixed and which to treat as random. In the above equation, there are seven fixed effects corresponding to the Level-2 γ coefficients. In addition, the above equations indicate that random effects are to be estimated for each of the predictors. Thus, we will continue to have the 11 random effects that were estimated in our revised RCR model.

The R code for this revised IAO model would look something like:

IAO.Model = lme(CWB~1+AGG.Group+SEX+
AGG.Group:SEX+COH+SIZE+COH:SIZE,
random=~1+AGG.Group+SEX+AGG.Group:
SEX|GROUP, data=mlr)

Finally, in order to test our original Hypothesis 3, we would specify the SAO model by adding COH as a Level-2 predictor of slope coefficients representing the regression of CWBs onto aggression:

Level 1: $CWB_{ij} = \beta_{0j} + \beta_{1j}\left(AGG_{ij} - \overline{AGG_j}\right)$

$$+ \beta_{2j}\left(SEX_{ij}\right)$$

$$+ \beta_{3j}\left(AGG_{ij} - \overline{AGG_j}\right)*\left(SEX_{ij}\right) + r_{ij}$$

Level 2: $\beta_{0j} = \gamma_{00} + \gamma_{01}\left(COH_j\right) + \gamma_{02}\left(SIZE_j\right)$

$$+ \gamma_{03}\left(COH_j\right)*\left(SIZE_j\right) + U_{0j}$$

$$\beta_{1j} = \gamma_{10} + \gamma_{11}\left(COH_j\right) + U_{1j}$$

$$\beta_{2j} = \gamma_{20} + U_{2j}$$

$$\beta_{3j} = \gamma_{30} + U_{3j}.$$

Thus, we need to estimate a final, eighth, fixed effect (γ_{11}). This is accomplished in R:

SAO.Model = lme(CWB~1+AGG.Group+SEX+
AGG.Group:SEX+COH+SIZE+COH:SIZE+
COH:AGG.Group,random=~1+AGG.Group+
SEX+AGG.Group:SEX|GROUP,data=mlr)

MULTILEVEL (RANDOM COEFFICIENT) REGRESSION MODELS: CONCLUDING COMMENTS

Given the ubiquitous nature of nested data structures, we hope that our chapter provides researchers with an initial (albeit basic) introduction to how MLR models may be used to test hypotheses using data conforming to a nested or multilevel structure. Table 17.2 provides a brief summary of our model-building/comparison approach using MLR. In addition to our basic introduction (and the other helpful chapters in this handbook), we encourage readers to explore issues including (a) implications for the scaling and centering of data (e.g., Hofmann & Gavin, 1998; Raudenbush & Bryk, 2002 [especially Chapters 2 and 5]; Zhang, Zyphur, & Preacher, 2009), (b) extensions of the MLR model to longitudinal applications (i.e., temporal nesting of repeated Level-1 observations within Level-2 units; Bliese & Ployhart, 2002; Bryk & Raudenbush, 1987; Raudenbush & Bryk, 2002), (c) strategies for testing hypotheses involving multilevel mediation (see Chapter 20; also Bauer, Preacher, & Gil, 2006; Preacher, Zyphur, & Zhang, 2010; Zhang et al., 2009), (d) issues associated with the analysis of dyadic data (i.e., individuals nested in couples or pairs; see Chapter 18; also Atkins, 2005; Kenny, Kashy, & Cook, 2006; Krasikova & LeBreton, 2012; Lyons & Sayer, 2005), and (e) how to avoid fallacies of inference when interpreting the results from a multilevel analysis (Firebaugh, 1978; Greenland, 2002; James, 1982; Mossholder & Bedeian, 1983; Ostroff, 1993).

Finally, just like the traditional, single-level OLS regression model carries with it certain underlying assumptions, so too does the more complicated MLR model (Hox, 2010; Raudenbush & Bryk, 2002; Snijders & Bosker, 2012). One's data and theory should be closely examined to determine whether these assumptions are likely met or violated:

- The Level-1 residuals (r_{ij}) have a mean of zero, are normally and independently distributed, and have a constant (homoscedastic) variance (σ^2).
- The Level-1 residuals are uncorrelated with the Level-1 predictors.
- The Level-1 residuals are uncorrelated with the Level-2 residuals (U_{0j}, U_{1j}, etc.).

TABLE 17.2

Multilevel Regression: A Model Comparison Approach

Model	Specific steps	Associated equations	What to look for
1. Null	A. Estimate Null model with fixed and random intercepts	Level 1: $CWB_{ij} = \beta_{0j} + r_{ij}$ Level 2: $\beta_{0j} = \gamma_{00} + U_{0j}$	
	B. Estimate variance components		τ_{00}: variance in Level-1 outcome variable that resides between Level-2 units. σ^2: variance in Level-1 outcome variable that resides within Level-2 units.
	C. Compute and interpret ICC(1)	$ICC(1) = \dfrac{\tau_{00}}{\tau_{00} + \sigma^2}$	Interpreted as the proportion of variance in Level-1 outcome variable that is attributed to the nesting of Level-1 units in Level-2 units.
	D. Estimate alternative model with fixed intercept	Level 1: $CWB_{ij} = \beta_{0j} + r_{ij}$ Level 2: $\beta_{0j} = \gamma_{00}$	
	E. Test for significant variance in intercepts by comparing fit of the Null model (Step A) and the alternative model (Step D)		If the less restrictive model (Step A) is better fitting, then there is significant variance in Level-1 outcome scores across Level-2 units.
2. RCR	A. Add Level-1 predictor variables and estimate the RCR model with fixed and random intercepts and slopes	Level 1: $CWB_{ij} = \beta_{0j} + \beta_{1j}(AGG_{ij} - \overline{AGG}_j) + r_{ij}$ Level 2: $\beta_{0j} = \gamma_{00} + U_{0j}$ $\beta_{1j} = \gamma_{10} + U_{1j}$	
	B. Estimate variance components for RCR		τ_{00}: variance in intercepts τ_{11}: variance in slopes τ_{01}: covariance between intercepts and slopes σ^2: residual variance in Level-1 outcome (variable that exists after including Level-1 predictor variables in the model)
	C. Compute and interpret ICC_β	ICC_β (See Aguinis & Culpepper, 2015, for equations or use the *iccbeta* package in R to estimate this intraclass correlation.)	Interpreted as the proportion of variance in Level-1 outcome variable that is attributed to group slope differences. This statistic is especially important if researchers have hypotheses about cross-level interactions/moderators.
	D. Interpret fixed coefficients		γ_{00}: pooled or average intercept γ_{10}: pooled or average slope (effect of Level-1 predictor on Level-1 outcome)
	E. Compute and interpret pseudo-R^2	$\text{pseudo-}R^2 = \dfrac{\sigma^2_{Null} - \sigma^2_{RCR}}{\sigma^2_{Null}}$	Interpreted as the proportion of Level-1 outcome variance that may be explained using the Level-1 predictor variable.
	F. Estimate alternative model with fixed intercept and fixed slope	Level 1: $CWB_{ij} = \beta_{0j} + \beta_{1j}(AGG_{ij} - \overline{AGG}_j) + r_{ij}$ Level 2: $\beta_{0j} = \gamma_{00}$ $\beta_{1j} = \gamma_{10}$	
	G. Estimate alternative model with random intercept and fixed slope.	Level 1: $CWB_{ij} = \beta_{0j} + \beta_{1j}(AGG_{ij} - \overline{AGG}_j) + r_{ij}$ Level 2: $\beta_{0j} = \gamma_{00} + U_{0j}$ $\beta_{1j} = \gamma_{10}$	

TABLE 17.2

Multilevel Regression: A Model Comparison Approach (*Continued*)

Model	Specific steps	Associated equations	What to look for
	H. Test for significant variance in intercepts by comparing fit of models from Steps F and G.		If the model from Step G is a better-fitting model than the one from Step F, then there is significant variance in intercepts. Note: this result is typically consistent with the results of Step E from the previous Null model testing sequence.
	I. Test for significant variance in slopes by comparing fit of models from Steps A and F.		If the model from Step A is a better-fitting the one from Step G, then there is significant variance in slopes.
3. IAO	A. Add Level-2 predictors of intercepts and estimate IAO model with fixed and random intercepts and slopes.	Level 1: $CWB_{ij} = \beta_{0j} + \beta_{1j}(AGG_{ij} - \overline{AGG}_j) + r_{ij}$ Level 2: $\beta_{0j} = \gamma_{00} + \gamma_{01}(COH_j) + U_{0j}$ $\beta_{1j} = \gamma_{10} + U_{1j}$	
	B. Estimate variance components for IAO		τ_{00}: residual variance in intercepts that exists after including Level-2 predictor variable in the model τ_{11}: variance in slopes τ_{01}: covariance between intercepts and slopes σ^2: residual variance in Level-1 outcome variable that exists after including Level-1 predictor variables in the model.
	C. Interpret fixed coefficients	$\gamma_{00}; \gamma_{10}; \gamma_{01}$	γ_{00}: fixed (pooled) intercept γ_{10}: fixed (pooled) slope (relationship between Level-1 predictor variable and Level-1 outcome variable) γ_{01}: fixed slope (relationship between Level-2 predictor variable on the Level-1 outcome variable)
	D. Compute and interpret pseudo-R^2	$\text{pseudo-}R^2 = \dfrac{\tau_{00(RCR)} - \tau_{00(IAO)}}{\tau_{00(RCR)}}$	Interpreted as the proportion of intercept variance that may be explained using the Level-2 predictor variable.
	E. Estimate alternative model with fixed intercept and fixed slope.	Level 1: $CWB_{ij} = \beta_{0j} + \beta_{1j}(AGG_{ij} - \overline{AGG}_j) + r_{ij}$ Level 2: $\beta_{0j} = \gamma_{00} + \gamma_{01}(COH_j)$ $\beta_{1j} = \gamma_{10}$	
	F. Estimate alternative model with random intercept and fixed slope.	Level 1: $CWB_{ij} = \beta_{0j} + \beta_{1j}(AGG_{ij} - \overline{AGG}_j) + r_{ij}$ Level 2: $\beta_{0j} = \gamma_{00} + \gamma_{01}(COH_j) + U_{0j}$ $\beta_{1j} = \gamma_{10}$	
	G. Test for significant residual variance in intercepts by comparing fit of models from Steps E and F.		If the model from Step E is the better-fitting model, that suggests the Level-2 predictor has explained all of the meaningful variance in intercepts. If the model from Step F is the better-fitting model, which suggests there is still significant variance in intercepts (could add additional Level-2 predictors to try and explain this variance).

(*continues*)

TABLE 17.2

Multilevel Regression: A Model Comparison Approach (*Continued*)

Model	Specific steps	Associated equations	What to look for
	H. Test for significant variance in slopes by comparing fit of models from Steps A and F.		If the model from Step A is the better-fitting model, that suggests there is significant variance in slopes, and it makes sense to proceed with tests of potential cross-level moderators.
4. SAO	A. Add level-2 predictors of slopes and estimate SAO model with fixed and random intercepts and slopes.	Level 1: $CWB_{ij} = \beta_{0j} + \beta_{1j}(AGG_{ij} - \overline{AGG}_j) + r_{ij}$ Level 2: $\beta_{0j} = \gamma_{00} + \gamma_{01}(COH_j) + U_{0j}$ $\beta_{1j} = \gamma_{10} + \gamma_{11}(COH_j) + U_{1j}$	
	B. Estimate variance components for SAO		τ_{00}: residual variance in intercepts that exists after including Level-2 predictor variable in the model τ_{11}: residual variance in slopes that exists after including Level-2 predictor variable in the model τ_{01}: covariance between intercepts and slopes σ^2: residual variance in Level-1 outcome variable that exists after including Level-1 predictor variables in the model.
	C. Interpret fixed coefficients		γ_{00}: fixed (pooled) intercept γ_{10}: fixed (pooled) slope (relationship between Level-1 predictor variable and Level-1 outcome variable) γ_{01}: fixed slope (relationship between Level-2 predictor variable on the Level-1 outcome variable) γ_{11}: fixed slope (relationship between the Level-2 predictor variable and the relationship between the Level-1 predictor and outcome variables)
	D. Compute and interpret pseudo-R^2	$\text{pseudo-}R^2 = \dfrac{\tau_{11(IAO)} - \tau_{11(SAO)}}{\tau_{11(IAO)}}$	Interpreted as the proportion of slope variance that may be explained using the Level-2 predictor variable.
	E. Estimate alternative model with fixed slope.	Level 1: $CWB_{ij} = \beta_{0j} + \beta_{1j}(AGG_{ij} - \overline{AGG}_j) + r_{ij}$ Level 2: $\beta_{0j} = \gamma_{00} + \gamma_{01}(COH_j) + U_{0j}$ $\beta_{1j} = \gamma_{10} + \gamma_{11}(COH_j)$	
	F. Test for significant residual variance in slopes by comparing fit of models from Steps A and E.		If the model from Step E is the better-fitting model, which suggests the Level-2 predictor has explained all of the meaningful variance in slopes. If the model from Step A is the better-fitting model, that suggests there is still significant variance in slopes.
	G. Test for significant variance in slopes by comparing fit of models from Steps A and F.		If the model from Step A is the better fitting model, then that suggests there is significant variance in slopes and it makes sense to proceed with test of potential cross-level moderators.
	H. Graph cross-level moderators		

Note. AGG = aggression; COH = cohesiveness; CWB = counterproductive workplace behaviors; IAO = Intercepts-as-Outcomes; ICC = intraclass correlation; RCR = random coefficients regression; SAO = Slopes-as-Outcomes.

- The Level-2 residuals each have a mean of zero, follow a multivariate normal distribution, and are independent among Level-2 groups.
- The Level-2 residuals are uncorrelated with the Level-2 predictors.

APPENDIX 17.1: ANNOTATED R CODE

```
# Code corresponding to:
# Shiverdecker, L. K., & LeBreton, J. M. (2018).
    Multilevel (random coefficient) regression
    modeling.
# In S. E. Humphrey & J. M. LeBreton
    (Eds.), Handbook of multilevel theory,
    measurement, and
# analysis (Chapter 17). Washington, DC:
    American Psychological Association.

# Step 1: Read in Data File for Multilevel
    Regression Examples (mlr.csv)
mlr <- read.csv("mlr.csv", header=T, sep=",")

# Step 2: Install packages and load into working
    library of tools
install.packages("multilevel"); library(multilevel)
install.packages("ggplot2"); library(ggplot2)
install.packages("data.table"); library(data.table)
install.packages("plyr"); library(plyr)

# Step 3: Create function to plot figures 1:4
ggplotRegression <- function (fit) {
require(ggplot2)
ggplot(fit$model, aes_string(x =
    names(fit$model)[2], y = names(fit$model)
    [1])) + geom_point() + xlim(0,15) +
    ylim(1,7)+
stat_smooth(method = "lm", se=FALSE, col =
    "red", fullrange=T) +
labs(title = paste("R-Square =
    ",signif(summary(fit)$r.squared, 5),
    "Intercept =",signif(fit$coef[[1]],5),
    "Slope =",signif(fit$coef[[2]], 5),
    "P =",signif(summary(fit)$coef[2,4], 5)))+
labs(x="Trait Aggression", y="Counterproductive
    Workplace Behaviors") }
```

```
#Step 4: Plot Figures
###Create Subsets of Data Used in Figures 1–4
    (note: mlr dataframe was already sorted by
    GROUP variable)
group1 <- lm(CWB~AGG,data=mlr[01:10,])
group2 <- lm(CWB~AGG,data=mlr[11:20,])
group3 <- lm(CWB~AGG,data=mlr[21:30,])
group4 <- lm(CWB~AGG,data=mlr[31:40,])
group1234 = lm(CWB~AGG,data=mlr[01:40,])

###Generate Figures 1–4
ggplotRegression(group1)
ggplotRegression(group2)
ggplotRegression(group3)
ggplotRegression(group4)
ggplotRegression(group1234)

###Generate Figure 5
all.groups=ggplot(mlr,aes(x=AGG,y=CWB,grou
    p=GROUP))+ xlim(0,15) + ylim(1,7)+stat_
    smooth(method = "lm", se=FALSE,
    fullrange=T) + labs(x="Trait Aggression",
    y="Counterproductive Workplace
    Behaviors")
all.groups

###Figure 6
groups12=ggplot(mlr[1:20,],aes(y = CWB, x
    = AGG)) + geom_point(size = 3, alpha
    = .8) + geom_smooth(method="lm",
    fullrange=T, se= F, size = 1, aes(linetype
    = as.factor(GROUP), group = GROUP))
    + geom_smooth(method = "lm",size =
    3, colour = 'black', se = F, fullrange=T)
    + xlim(0,15) + ylim(1,7)+ labs(x="Trait
    Aggression", y="Counterproductive
    Workplace Behaviors", linetype="Group #")+
    geom_label(aes(label =GROUP),color='blue')
groups12

#Step 5: Generate the Coefficients in Table 1
set.seed(1)
dat <- data.table(x=mlr$AGG, y=mlr$CWB,
    grp=mlr$GROUP)
OLS = dat[,list(intercept=coef(lm
    (y~x))[1], coef=coef(lm(y~x))
    [2],rsq=summary(lm(y~x))$r.squared)
```

```
,by=grp]
OLS
min(OLS[,2]); max(OLS[,2])
min(OLS[,3]); max(OLS[,3])
min(OLS[,4]); max(OLS[,4])

# Step 6: Multilevel Regression Models
###Null Model(One-Way Random Effects
    ANOVA)
# CWB~1, Regressing CWB onto a fixed
    intercept
# random=~1 Regressing CWB onto random
    intercepts
# |GROUP, Identifies the level 2 variable named
    as "group"
# data=mlr Identifies the data set where "CWB"
    and "group" are located
Null.Model = lme(CWB~1, random=~1|GROUP,
    data=mlr)
summary(Null.Model)

#Estimating the ICCs from the Null Model
VarCorr(Null.Model)
Null.ICC=GmeanRel(Null.Model)
names(Null.ICC) #returns the names of the
    variables in the object "Null.ICC"
Null.ICC$ICC #returns the value of the ICC
    variable in the Null.ICC object which is the
    ICC(1)
Null.ICC$MeanRel #returns the 60 ICC(2)
    values corresponding to each group
    intercept
#Note: values identical b/c all groups are the
    exact same size . . . so sigma^2/nj is the same
    for all groups.
mean(Null.ICC$MeanRel) #estimates the mean
    across the groups which is the ICC(2) or
    ICC(k) [where k = 60]

Null.Model.2=gls(CWB~1, data=mlr)
    #Estimating Null Model with Fixed
    Intercepts
logLik(Null.Model.2)*–2 #Manually estimating
    –2*loglikelihood of Null Models
logLik(Null.Model)*–2
–2*(–805.1175)—2*(–750.5154) #Manually
    estimating the difference in likelihood ratios
```

```
anova(Null.Model, Null.Model.2) #Manually
    comparing fixed vs. fixed + random
    intercepts
summary(Null.Model) #Displaying summary of
    Null.Model
VarCorr(Null.Model) #Displaying the variance/
    covariance matrix

### Grand Mean Center the Level 1 Predictor
    (NOTE: Not used in this chapter; included
    only for illustrative purposes)
mean(mlr$AGG)
mlr$AGG.Grand=mlr$AGG-4.035167
# Aggregate employee-level trait aggression
    scores to the group level
AGG.Aggregated=aggregate(mlr[,c(2)],
    list(mlr$GROUP), mean, na.rm=T)
names(AGG.Aggregated)
AGG.Aggregated=rename(AGG.Aggregated,
    replace=c("Group.1"="GROUP",
    "x"="AGG.GroupMean")) #renames
    specific variables
names(AGG.Aggregated)
mlr=merge(mlr,AGG.Aggregated,by="GROUP")
names(mlr)

### Group Mean Center the Level 1 Predictor
mlr$AGG.Group=mlr$AGG-mlr$AGG.
    GroupMean
names(mlr)

#Random Coefficient Regression Model
# CWB~1+AGG.group regressing CWB onto
    fixed effect for intercept
# random=~1+AGG.group regressing CWB onto
    random intercepts and slopes (AGG.group)
# |GROUP, identifying the level 2 (grouping)
    variable
# data=mlr name of data file

RCR.Model=lme(CWB~1+AGG.Group,
    random=~1+AGG.Group|GROUP,data=mlr)
summary(RCR.Model)
VarCorr(Null.Model) #displays variance/
    covariance of parameters from ANOVA
VarCorr(RCR.Model) #displays variance/
    covariance of parameters from RCR
```

```
#Estimating the ICC_beta from the RCR Model
###NOTE: As of August 9, 2017 the icc_beta
    package was not available for version 3.4.0
    of R

#Use gls to estimate model with fixed intercept
    and fixed slope
RCR.Model.2=gls(CWB~1+AGG.
    Group,data=mlr)

#Use lme to estimate a model with random
    intercept and fixed slope
RCR.Model.3=lme(CWB~1+AGG.Group,
    random=~1|GROUP,data=mlr)
#Test if RCR.Model.3 is a better fit to the data
    than RCR.Model.2
anova(RCR.Model.2,RCR.Model.3)

#Test if RCR.Model (Random Intercepts &
    Slopes) is a better fit to the data than RCR.
    Model.3
anova(RCR.Model.3,RCR.Model)

#Intercepts-as-Outcomes Model
#Adding Cohesion as a level 2 predictor
IAO.Model=lme(CWB~1+AGG.
    Group+COH,random=~1+AGG.
    Group|GROUP,data=mlr)
summary(IAO.Model)
VarCorr(RCR.Model)
VarCorr(IAO.Model)

#Use gls to estimate model with fixed intercept
    and fixed slopes
IAO.Model.2=gls(CWB~1+AGG.
    Group+COH,data=mlr)

#Use lme to estimate a model with random
    intercept and fixed slopes
IAO.Model.3=lme(CWB~1+AGG.Group+COH,
    random=~1|GROUP,data=mlr)

#Test if IAO.Model.2 (Fixed Intercept & Slopes)
    is a better fit than IAO.Model.3 (Random
    Intercepts & Fixed Slopes)
anova(IAO.Model.2,IAO.Model.3)
```

```
#Test if IAO.Model3 (Random Intercepts &
    Fixed Slopes) is a better fit original IAO.
    Model (Random Intercepts & Slopes)
anova(IAO.Model.3,IAO.Model)

#Slopes-as-Outcomes Model
#Testing the cross-level moderating effect of L2
    cohesion on the relationship
###between L1 CWBs and L1 group-mean
    centered aggression scores
#Cross-Product Effect is denoted using ":"
#helping~1+AGG.Group+COH + AGG.
    Group:COH, Fixed coef. for intercept,
    aggression, cohesion, cross-product
#random=~1+AGG.Group Random coefficients
    for intercept and aggression
#|GROUP Name of level 2 grouping variable
    "GROUP"
#data=mlr Data containing variables in SAO

SAO.Model=lme(CWB~1+AGG.
    Group+COH+AGG.
    Group:COH,random=~1+AGG.
    Group|GROUP,data=mlr)
summary(SAO.Model)

#Request variance components to estimate
    quasi-R2 for slope variance
VarCorr(IAO.Model)
VarCorr(SAO.Model)
SAO.Rsq=(0.02033669–0.01463884)/
    0.02033669
SAO.Rsq

#Test whether the remaining variance in slopes is
    significant
SAO.Model.2=lme(CWB~1+AGG.
    Group+COH+AGG.Group:COH,random=
    ~1|GROUP,data=mlr)
anova(SAO.Model.2, SAO.Model)

# Step 7: Plotting the Cross-Level Interaction
    (Figure 7)
#Descriptive statistics for cross-level moderator
mean(mlr$COH)
sd(mlr$COH)
```

```
#manual estimation of moderator values at +1
    and −1 sd
5.508833 − 0.4758722; 5.508833 + 0.4758722

mean(mlr$AGG.Group) #estimating mean of
    trait aggression
sd(mlr$AGG.Group) # obtaining sd of trait
    aggression

#creating a new data frame with high-low
    values for (AGG.Group (M; +1SD),
    COH(-1SD; +1SD))
inter.data=data.frame(AGG.
    Group=c(0.0000,0.0000, 1.835865,
    1.835865),
COH=c(5.032961,5.984705,5.032961,5.984705))
inter.data #displaying the data frame

#adding a new variable called "predicted" to
    this new data frame using the 'predict'
    function
inter.data$predicted=predict(SAO.Model,inter.
    data,level=0)
inter.data #confirming new variable added to
    data frame

#plotting the cross-level interaction (Option 1:
    Use the 'interaction.plot' function)
interaction.plot(inter.data$AGG.Group,inter.
    data$COH,inter.data$predicted)
interaction.plot(inter.data$AGG.Group,inter.
    data$COH,inter.data$predicted,
    ylab="Counterproductive Work Behaviors",
    xlab="Aggression (Group-Mean Centered)",
    trace.label="Cohesion")
###cleaning up the plot
inter.data$AGG.Group2=c("0 (Mean)","0
    (Mean)","1.85 (+1SD)","1.85 (+1SD)")
inter.data$COH2=c("-1SD","+1SD",
    "-1SD","+1SD")
inter.data
interaction.plot(inter.data$AGG.Group2,inter.
    data$COH2,inter.data$predicted,
    ylab="Counterproductive Work Behaviors",
    xlab="Aggression (Group-Mean Centered)",
    trace.label="Cohesion")
#plotting the cross-level interaction (Option 2:
    Use the 'ggplot' function)
```

```
ggplot(inter.data,aes(x=AGG.Group2,
    y=predicted,group=COH2)) +
geom_line(aes(linetype=factor(COH2)))+ #
    Graph separate lines for high and low levels
    of cohesion
labs(title="Cross-Level Moderating Effect
    of Cohesion", x="Trait Aggression
    (Group-Mean Centered)", y="Predicted
    Counterproductive Work Behaviors")+
scale_linetype_discrete(name="Cohesion")+
ylim(1,7)

#Step 8: Concluding Examples
####SEX as level-1 moderator of cwb-agg
####SIZE as level-2 moderator of cwb-coh

#Specification of Null Model
Null.Model = lme(CWB~1, random=~1|GROUP,
    data=mlr)

#Specification of RCR
RCR.Model = lme(CWB~1+AGG.
    Group+SEX+AGG.Group:SEX,
random=~1+AGG.Group+SEX+AGG.
    Group:SEX|GROUP, data=mlr)

#Specification of IAO
IAO.Model = lme(CWB~1+AGG.
    Group+SEX+AGG.
    Group:SEX+COH+SIZE+COH:SIZE,
    random=~1+AGG.Group+SEX+AGG.
    Group:SEX|GROUP, data=mlr)
#Specification of SAO
SAO.Model = lme(CWB~1+AGG.
    Group+SEX+AGG.Group:SEX+COH
    +SIZE+COH:SIZE+COH:AGG.Group,
    random=~1+AGG.Group+SEX+AGG.
    Group:SEX|GROUP, data=mlr)
```

References

Aguinis, H., & Culpepper, S. A. (2015). An expanded decision-making procedure for examining cross-level interaction effects with multilevel modeling. *Organizational Research Methods, 18*, 155–176. http://dx.doi.org/10.1177/1094428114563618

Atkins, D. C. (2005). Using multilevel models to analyze couple and family treatment data: Basic and advanced issues. *Journal of Family Psychology, 19*, 98–110. http://dx.doi.org/10.1037/0893-3200.19.1.98

Bauer, D. J., Preacher, K. J., & Gil, K. M. (2006). Conceptualizing and testing random indirect effects and moderated mediation in multilevel models: New procedures and recommendations. *Psychological Methods, 11*, 142–163. http://dx.doi.org/10.1037/1082-989X.11.2.142

Bennett, R. J., & Robinson, S. L. (2000). Development of a measure of workplace deviance. *Journal of Applied Psychology, 85*, 349–360. http://dx.doi.org/10.1037/0021-9010.85.3.349

Bliese, P. D. (2000). Within-group agreement, nonindependence, and reliability: Implications for data aggregation and analysis. In K. J. Klein & S. W. Kozlowski (Eds.), *Multilevel theory, research, and methods in organizations* (pp. 349–381). San Francisco, CA: Jossey-Bass.

Bliese, P. D., & Hanges, P. J. (2004). Being both too liberal and too conservative: The perils of treating grouped data as though they were independent. *Organizational Research Methods, 7*, 400–417. http://dx.doi.org/10.1177/1094428104268542

Bliese, P. D., & Ployhart, R. E. (2002). Growth modeling using random coefficient models: Model building, testing, and illustrations. *Organizational Research Methods, 5*, 362–387. http://dx.doi.org/10.1177/109442802237116

Bryk, A. S., & Raudenbush, S. W. (1987). Application of hierarchical linear models to assessing change. *Psychological Bulletin, 101*, 147–158. http://dx.doi.org/10.1037/0033-2909.101.1.147

Cohen, J., Cohen, P., West, S. G., & Aiken, L. S. (2003). *Applied multiple regression/correlation analysis for the behavioral sciences* (3rd ed.). New York, NY: Routledge (Lawrence Erlbaum Associates).

Firebaugh, G. (1978). A rule for inferring individual-level relationships from aggregate data. *American Sociological Review, 43*, 557–572. http://dx.doi.org/10.2307/2094779

Greenland, S. (2002). A review of multilevel theory for ecologic analyses. *Statistics in Medicine, 21*, 389–395. http://dx.doi.org/10.1002/sim.1024

Hofmann, D. A. (1997). An overview of the logic and rationale of hierarchical linear models. *Journal of Management, 23*, 723–744. http://dx.doi.org/10.1177/014920639702300602

Hofmann, D. A., & Gavin, M. B. (1998). Centering decisions in hierarchical linear models: Implications for research in organizations. *Journal of Management, 24*, 623–641. http://dx.doi.org/10.1177/014920639802400504

Hofmann, D. A., Griffin, M. A., & Gavin, M. B. (2000). The application of hierarchical linear modeling to organizational research. In K. J. Klein & S. W. J. Kozlowski (Eds.), *Multilevel theory, research, and methods in organizations* (pp. 467–511). San Francisco, CA: Jossey-Bass.

Hox, J. J. (2010). *Multilevel analysis: Techniques and applications* (2nd ed.). In G. A. Marcoulides (Ed.), *Quantitative Methodology Series*. New York, NY: Routledge.

James, L. R. (1982). Aggregation bias in estimates of perceptual agreement. *Journal of Applied Psychology, 67*, 219–229. http://dx.doi.org/10.1037/0021-9010.67.2.219

James, L. R., Demaree, R. G., & Wolf, G. (1984). Estimating within-group interrater reliability with and without response bias. *Journal of Applied Psychology, 69*, 85–98. http://dx.doi.org/10.1037/0021-9010.69.1.85

James, L. R., Demaree, R. G., & Wolf, G. (1993). r_{wg}: An assessment of within-group interrater agreement. *Journal of Applied Psychology, 78*, 306–309. http://dx.doi.org/10.1037/0021-9010.78.2.306

James, L. R., & LeBreton, J. M. (2010). Assessing aggression using conditional reasoning. *Current Directions in Psychological Science, 19*, 30–35. http://dx.doi.org/10.1177/0963721409359279

James, L. R., & LeBreton, J. M. (2012). *Assessing the implicit personality through conditional reasoning.* Washington, DC: American Psychological Association. http://dx.doi.org/10.1037/13095-000

James, L. R., & Williams, L. J. (2000). The cross-level operator in regression, ANCOVA, and contextual analysis. In K. J. Klein & S. W. J. Kozlowski (Eds.), *Multilevel theory, research, and methods in organizations* (pp. 382–424). San Francisco, CA: Jossey-Bass.

Kenny, D. A., Kashy, D. A., & Cook, W. L. (2006). *Dyadic data analysis.* New York, NY: Guilford Press.

Krasikova, D. V., & LeBreton, J. M. (2012). Just the two of us: Misalignment of theory and methods in examining dyadic phenomena. *Journal of Applied Psychology, 97*, 739–757. http://dx.doi.org/10.1037/a0027962

Kreft, I., & de Leeuw, J. (1998). *Introducing multilevel modeling.* Thousand Oaks, CA: Sage. http://dx.doi.org/10.4135/9781849209366

LeBreton, J. M., & Senter, J. L. (2008). Answers to 20 questions about interrater reliability and interrater agreement. *Organizational Research Methods, 11*, 815–852. http://dx.doi.org/10.1177/1094428106296642

Lyons, K. S., & Sayer, A. G. (2005). Longitudinal dyad models in family research. *Journal of Marriage and Family, 67*, 1048–1060. http://dx.doi.org/10.1111/j.1741-3737.2005.00193.x

Mossholder, K. W., & Bedeian, A. G. (1983). Cross-level inference and organizational research: Perspectives on interpretation and application. *The Academy of Management Review, 8,* 547–558. http://dx.doi.org/10.2307/258256

Myers, R. H. (1990). *Classical and modern regression with applications* (2nd ed.). Belmont, CA: Duxbury Press.

Ostroff, C. (1993). Comparing correlations based on individual-level and aggregated data. *Journal of Applied Psychology, 78,* 569–582. http://dx.doi.org/10.1037/0021-9010.78.4.569

Preacher, K. J., Zyphur, M. J., & Zhang, Z. (2010). A general multilevel SEM framework for assessing multilevel mediation. *Psychological Methods, 15,* 209–233. http://dx.doi.org/10.1037/a0020141

R Development Core Team. (2017). *The R Project for Statistical Computing.* Vienna, Austria. Retrieved from http://www.R-project.org

Raudenbush, S. W., & Bryk, A. S. (2002). *Hierarchical linear models: Applications and data analysis methods* (2nd ed.). Thousand Oaks, CA: Sage.

Snijders, T. A. B., & Bosker, R. J. (2012). *Multilevel analysis: An introduction to basic and advanced multilevel modeling* (2nd ed.). Washington, DC: Sage.

Zhang, Z., Zyphur, M. J., & Preacher, K. J. (2009). Testing multilevel mediation using hierarchical linear models: Problems and solutions. *Organizational Research Methods, 12,* 695–719. http://dx.doi.org/10.1177/1094428108327450

CHAPTER 18

DYADIC DATA ANALYSIS

Andrew P. Knight and Stephen E. Humphrey

A manager and an employee meet to discuss
a performance evaluation. A therapist greets a
client and begins their weekly session. A recruiter
conducts a series of one-on-one interviews with
prospective employees. A worker shares a meal with
a colleague with whom he hopes to partner on a new
project. At the end of the day, the partner goes home
and shares the interaction with her spouse over
dinner. The spouse, in turn, recounts the meeting
she had earlier that day with their son's teacher. As
these examples illustrate, many human experiences
transpire between two people—in a dyad.

Reflecting the ubiquity of dyadic experiences,
many prominent theories of human behavior
feature the dyad as a foundational unit of analysis.
Exchange theories, for example, explain the flow
of resources between, at the most basic level, two
parties (Blau, 1964; Emerson, 1976; Homans,
1958). Conceptualizations of the process of social
construction, such as through sensemaking and
sense giving, often diagnose the reciprocal dyadic
interactions through which events are labeled and
interpreted (Weick, 1995). Theories of interpersonal
and romantic relationships offer explanations of
the development and trajectory of connections
between two people (e.g., Byrne, 1971; Finkel,
Simpson, & Eastwick, 2017; Newcomb, 1961).
Relatedly, conceptualizations of interpersonal
perception unpack the factors that underlie one
person's view of another (Kenny, 1994). Within

organizations, theories about roles and coordination
rest upon dyadic connections between organizational
subsystems (e.g., Katz & Kahn, 1978). And Weick's
(1979) impactful theory of organizing treats the
continuous reconstitution of organizations as
composed of dyadic building blocks—double
interacts between two people.

Although the dyad is the foundation of many
prominent theories in the social sciences, the dyad
has not historically been a focal level of analysis
in empirical research (Krasikova & LeBreton,
2012). In research on human behavior within
organizations, for example, researchers have
eschewed dyadic investigations due, in part, to a
prevailing emphasis on individual (e.g., satisfaction,
performance), group (e.g., cohesion, performance),
and organizational (e.g., effectiveness) outcomes
as the most meaningful phenomena to explain.
The historical dearth of investigations using dyadic
methods may also stem from the challenges of
using the nuanced research methods needed to
conduct dyadic research—both in data collection
and data analysis. Research on diversity is an
instructive example. Although many studies of
diversity in organizations are grounded in social
psychological theories of dyadic similarity-attraction
(Williams & O'Reilly, 1998), researchers have most
commonly examined aggregate diversity effects at
the individual (e.g., Tsui, Egan, & O'Reilly, 1992) or
group (e.g., van Knippenberg & Schippers, 2007)

http://dx.doi.org/10.1037/0000115-019
The Handbook of Multilevel Theory, Measurement, and Analysis, S. E. Humphrey and J. M. LeBreton (Editors-in-Chief)

levels of analysis. As multilevel theorists have long admonished, misalignment of theory, method, and analysis can obscure or distort the substantive conclusions that researchers draw from empirical investigations (Klein, Dansereau, & Hall, 1994).

Spurred by these concerns, in recent years, there has been burgeoning interest in dyadic data analysis. Scholars have used dyadic data analysis to study a wide range of phenomena, such as emotion (Eisenkraft & Elfenbein, 2010), deference (Joshi & Knight, 2015), helping behavior (van der Vegt, Bunderson, & Oosterhof, 2006), rivalry (Kilduff, Elfenbein, & Staw, 2010), interpersonal harming (Lam, van der Vegt, Walter, & Huang, 2011), the formation of work-related network ties (Casciaro & Lobo, 2008), and trust (Jones & Shah, 2016)—to name just a few topics recently studied. This burgeoning interest stems first from a growing recognition that there are substantively interesting criterion variables at the dyad level and, further, that understanding dyadic processes can unpack the interpersonal mechanisms that might precede the emergence of higher level individual, group, and organizational phenomena (e.g., Gooty & Yammarino, 2011; Krasikova & LeBreton, 2012; Liden, Anand, & Vidyarthi, 2016; Tse & Ashkanasy, 2015). Second, the growing use of dyadic data analysis reflects organizational researchers' increasing familiarity with and access to the methodological and statistical tools needed to conduct a dyadic investigation (e.g., Gonzalez & Griffin, 2012; Kenny & Kashy, 2011; Kenny, Kashy, & Cook, 2006; Krasikova & LeBreton, 2012).

The purpose of this chapter is to provide researchers with an entry point to dyadic data analysis. Recognizing the diversity of methods used across different literatures that are grounded in different substantive research traditions, our objective is not to provide a comprehensive review of the vast range of methods that are available. Readers interested in a more comprehensive treatment should consult Kenny, Kashy, and Cook's (2006) accessible and informative book on the topic. Instead, our goal in this chapter is to expose researchers to core concepts and a basic theoretical framework that can guide a research effort targeting the dyad level. To help researchers apply these methods to their own

questions, we describe several exemplar publications that use dyadic data analysis. To illustrate the nuances of dyadic data analysis, we describe in detail one specific model—the social relations model (SRM)—and present a step-by-step empirical example to delineate the basic steps of a dyadic analysis. As part of this illustrative application, we provide new software code for estimating the SRM using multilevel modeling in R and describe how to interpret the output of the analysis.

We first describe the scope of this chapter, which focuses on a tradition of dyadic data analysis with roots in social psychology. Next, we define and explain a broad framework underlying a dyadic analysis. We then review several exemplar papers, highlighting the unique insights that can be gained from this approach. In a deep dive into a specific dyadic approach, we then discuss issues of statistical estimation, software, and the interpretation of results. We conclude by addressing alternative techniques and areas on the frontiers of dyadic data analysis.

FOUNDATIONS OF MODELING DYADIC PHENOMENA

In the social sciences, there are two main analytical traditions that focus on dyadic phenomena. The first, which is perhaps best known to researchers who examine phenomena at a more macro level, is social network analysis (Borgatti, Mehra, Brass, & Labianca, 2009; Wasserman & Faust, 1994). With deep roots in sociology, and to a lesser extent social psychology, researchers have used social network analysis to shed light on a broad range of topics—at both the micro level (e.g., creativity, leadership, power, and influence) and macro level (e.g., syndication, strategic alliances) (Brass, Galaskiewicz, Greve, & Tsai, 2004; Burt, Kilduff, & Tasselli, 2013). The dyad—the connection (e.g., relationship, communication frequency) between two entities (e.g., people, firms)—is the basic building block in social network analysis. But the dyad is not generally the core focus within social network analysis. Reflecting its roots in sociology, the focus of most social network research is social structure—either understanding how different patterns of ties emerge or on how different patterns of ties provide constraints or opportunities (e.g., production of social capital). Although there are branches of social network analysis that feature dyadic ties more prominently (e.g., Snijders, van de Bunt, & Steglich, 2010), the dyadic tie is typically used as an input to some aggregation function in network analysis (e.g., centrality, density, network closure).

The second tradition—which we feature in this chapter—is the modeling of interpersonal perceptions and relationships developed by Kenny and his colleagues (Kenny, 1994; Kenny & Albright, 1987; Kenny et al., 2006; Kenny & La Voie, 1984; Kenny & Zaccaro, 1983; Malloy & Kenny, 1986; Warner, Kenny, & Stoto, 1979). This tradition is especially prevalent in research examining phenomena at a more micro level, such as in the study of families and the development of romantic relationships (e.g., Finkel & Eastwick, 2008). Kenny's paradigm for dyadic data analysis offers significant potential for researchers whose work rests upon dyadic theoretical mechanisms. With its roots in social psychology, this tradition developed initially as an analysis of variance (ANOVA)-based approach, focused on identifying, estimating, and explaining different sources of variance in individuals' interactions with others (e.g., Kenny, 1994). In the decades since its initial development, however, the paradigm has matured and now affords researchers tremendous flexibility, offering a range of models that can be estimated with structural equation modeling (e.g., Cook, 1994; Olsen & Kenny, 2006), multilevel modeling (e.g., Kenny & Kashy, 2011; Snijders & Kenny, 1999), and Bayesian modeling (e.g., Lüdtke, Robitzsch, Kenny, & Trautwein, 2013). The approach has also become practically accessible to researchers across all major statistical platforms (e.g., R, SAS, SPSS, Stata).

We focus in this chapter specifically on this second research tradition. We do so for three reasons. First, a heavy focus of social network analysis is modeling social structure, rather than dyadic interactions and behavior. Second, other chapters in this handbook familiarize readers with the core principles and ideas of social network analysis. Third, Kenny and his colleagues' framework for conceptualizing and modeling

interpersonal behavior allows scholars to test and refine theories that a network approach is less well-equipped to answer. To provide researchers with an introduction to a relatively newer and less familiar approach, we bound our focus to dyadic data analysis focused on interpersonal perception and relationships.

Conceptualization of Sources of Variance in Interpersonal Perception and Behavior

As an introduction to dyadic data analysis, we first describe an overarching way of conceptualizing sources of variance in interpersonal perception and behavior, using a running example to explain these sources. Imagine two groups of five people each (Group 1: Alex, Brianna, Carl, Diane, and Emily; Group 2: Frank, Gary, Heidi, Ingrid, and James) who interact with one another in a brainstorming exercise. At the end of the exercise, the group members rate how much they trust each other. This design, which is common in dyadic research, is called a round robin design—each member of the group rates every other member of the group on some attribute or provides a rating of his or her relationship with each other member. Although a full round robin design is not essential for conducting a dyadic study—and, indeed, Kenny et al. (2006) described several other research designs—a round robin design offers the most flexibility and potential for estimating the drivers of dyadic interpersonal perceptions, relationships, or behaviors.

Conceptually, there are three primary levels of analysis in this framework: the group level, the individual level, and the dyad level (Snijders & Kenny, 1999). The group level reflects contextual effects that lead the members of one group to interact with or perceive one another in a way that, on average, differs from the members of another group. For example, consider a scenario in which Group 1 brainstorms face-to-face and Group 2 brainstorms virtually. The face-to-face interactions might lead the members of Group 1 to report trusting one another more, on average, than the members of Group 2 report trusting one another.

The individual level reflects the consistent ways that people interact with or perceive one another.

Note that this consistency is across partners in a given situation, not necessarily across time or across situations. In a dyadic framework, there are two kinds of individual-level tendencies, referred to as the actor (or perceiver) effect and the partner (or target) effect. The actor effect reflects how people tend to view or behave with others, in general; it is "the tendency for a person to exhibit a consistent level of response across all interaction partners" (Kenny et al., 2006, p. 192). For example, Alex may tend to be very trusting, reporting high levels of trust with each other member of his group. Diane, on the other hand, may not be so trusting—her ratings of her teammates may be uniformly low. This difference between Alex and Diane is captured by variance in the actor effect. The partner effect in a dyadic framework describes how individuals tend to be viewed or rated by others, in general; that is, "the degree to which multiple partners respond in a similar way to a particular individual" (Kenny, Mohr, & Levesque, 2001, p. 129). In this example, all members of Group 1 may report relatively high trust with Emily, but relatively low trust with Diane. Whereas Emily is viewed as very trustworthy by her teammates, Diane is viewed as very untrustworthy. This difference is captured by variance in the partner effect.

Finally, the dyad level (or the relational level) reflects idiosyncratic ways that a given actor views or behaves with a given partner. The dyad effect "is the unique way in which a person behaves with a particular partner" (Kenny et al., 2001, p. 130); that is, it is one person's rating of another after accounting for the actor's general tendency in viewing others and the partner's general tendency in being viewed by others. The dyad effect is a form of residual that remains after controlling for group level, individual-level actor, and individual-level partner effects. For example, Alex may especially trust Carl, and vice versa, because Alex and Carl are both vocal and passionate fans of a given sports team.

As we have described it so far, dyadic data analysis may seem identical to the typical multilevel model with which organizational researchers are highly familiar. However, the prototypical multilevel model in the social sciences reflects a "Russian

dolls" model of nesting, in which individuals are perfectly nested within groups and groups are perfectly nested within organizations (e.g., Klein et al., 1994). What makes a dyadic analysis with round robin data unique is that dyadic ratings are cross-nested (Snijders & Kenny, 1999); actors and partners are nested within one another. Rather than viewing this as a nuisance factor, dyadic models leverage cross-nesting to capture nuances of interpersonal perceptions and relationships. Cross-nesting enables examining, for example, how symmetric an interpersonal process is.

Kenny and colleagues' framework describes two kinds of symmetry—dyadic reciprocity and generalized reciprocity. Dyadic reciprocity reflects the degree to which a given actor's perception is linked to a given partner's perception, controlling for each person's individual tendencies. Generalized reciprocity, in contrast, reflects the degree to which actor effects (i.e., people's stable tendencies in viewing others) are linked to partner effects (i.e., people's stable tendencies in being viewed by others). The difference between dyadic and generalized reciprocity is subtle, but important. Applied to our running example, dyadic reciprocity addresses the question of whether, if Alex especially trusts Carl, does Carl also especially trust Alex? Generalized reciprocity, in contrast, addresses the question of whether group members who tend to report trusting most others also tend to be trusted by most others. Generalized reciprocity is the covariance between individual actor and partner effects.

The group, individual, and dyad levels of analysis described above underlie a myriad of specific models for dyadic data analysis (for details, see Gonzalez & Griffin, 2012; Kenny et al., 2006). Which specific model a researcher adopts should be driven by the overarching research question, the associated research design, and the availability of data. Some research designs preclude estimating some of the effects described above. For example, estimating an actor (perceiver) effect requires that each person rates (i.e., perceives or evaluates) multiple other partners (targets); estimating a partner (target) effect requires that each person is rated by multiple other actors (perceivers); and estimating a dyad or relational effect requires that each person rates and is rated by others (i.e., participants serve as both actors and partners). As noted above, the round robin design in which each person rates each other person in the group provides the most flexibility examining dyadic phenomena. Because of its comprehensiveness and flexibility, we focus our empirical illustration in this chapter on this design.

Exemplar Applications of Dyadic Data Analysis

To highlight the potential value of using dyadic data analysis, we describe in detail three recent exemplar publications that used the SRM. These examples provide a sample of the kinds of questions that dyadic analysis can help answer, as well illustrate the unique insights that can stem from a dyadic analysis.

Eisenkraft and Elfenbein (2010) provided a unique application of dyadic data analysis for studying the origins of affective experiences in organizations. Building from theories of individual differences, they postulated that there were systematic and idiosyncratic differences in how people make *others* feel—what they referred to as "affective presence." That is, some people are hypothesized to elicit positive feelings in their partners during interpersonal interactions, while other people are hypothesized to elicit negative feelings in their interaction partners. In contrast to most research on individual differences, which focuses on how an individual's traits *influence his or her own behavior*, Eisenkraft and Elfenbein's research examined how an individual's traits *influence the attitudes or behaviors of others*. Note that affective presence is, to use the language introduced above, a partner effect—it is the way that a person's characteristics systematically influence the responses of others. Eisenkraft and Elfenbein studied affective presence using a round robin research design, in which 239 MBA students who were organized into 48 teams rated their positive and negative affect during interactions with each of their fellow teammates. Results derived from a social relations analysis revealed that individuals' feelings during interpersonal interactions were shaped by their own trait affectivity, but also by the affective presence of their partners. Eisenkraft and Elfenbein

found that affective presence was as powerful in explaining a person's feelings as was the person's own trait affectivity. Their findings underscore the value of a dyadic approach in theory development, research design, and data analysis for explicating how both people's stable individual differences—the actor's trait affectivity and the partner's affective presence—influence the emotional experiences that unfold during interpersonal interactions.

Erez, Schilpzand, Leavitt, Woolum, and Judge (2015) provided a second, and related, exemplar application of dyadic data analysis. The authors used a dyadic lens to consider how individual differences influence actors' appraisals of their interaction partners' performance, as well as actors' behavior towards their partners. Erez et al. postulated that introverted people are especially sensitive to the interpersonal characteristics of others when forming perceptions of them, relying heavily on others' interpersonal personality traits like agreeableness and extraversion to form their judgments. Note that Erez et al.'s arguments focused inherently on a *dyadic* or relational effect—that one actor's perception of another *depends on* the attributes of both the actor and the partner. The way that a partner's characteristics (i.e., agreeableness, extraversion) influence an actor's perceptions depends on the actor's own characteristics (i.e., introversion). Said differently, the relationship between a partner's personality and an actor's perception of and behavior towards that partner is moderated by the actor's personality. Erez et al. used two studies—one survey-based and the second experimental—to examine their conceptual model. In the survey-based study, 207 graduate students were organized into teams of four to five members; within each team, participants provided round robin ratings of one another. Social relations analyses and multilevel modeling supported the idea that an actor's perception of a partner is a function of the interaction between the actor's personality and the partner's personality. Introverted individuals' perceptions were more strongly influenced (negatively) by a partner's extraversion and agreeableness. Erez et al.'s findings illustrate the value, both theoretical and empirical, of a dyadic perspective for examining interpersonal perception.

A third exemplar application of dyadic data analysis is Joshi and Knight's (2015) study of dyadic deference in multidisciplinary research groups. Using a dyadic perspective, the authors built and tested a theoretical model to explain the dyadic drivers, above and beyond any individual drivers, of interpersonal deference—the act of yielding to the preferences or perspectives of another. The authors used the SRM with round robin survey data from 619 members of 55 multidisciplinary research groups to examine the degree to which deference is a function not just of one person's attributes, but of the interaction of the attributes (e.g., gender, education) of the person receiving deference and of the person conferring deference. Joshi and Knight's (2015) analysis showed that, in addition to any individual-level drivers of deference (i.e., actor and partner effects), the degree of alignment between two interaction partners' attributes (e.g., similarity) shapes deference. Furthermore, the authors' findings highlighted how a dyadic approach can yield unique insights into interpersonal processes. The results of the social relations analysis—and, specifically, the reciprocity correlations—showed that perceiving competence is a fundamentally different interpersonal process than perceiving social closeness or affinity with another. Perceiving competence is an asymmetric process at the individual level ($r = -0.20$)—those who are viewed as highly competent tend to view their teammates as being lower in competence. Perceiving social affinity, on the other hand, is a symmetric process at the individual level ($r = 0.39$)—those who are viewed as being friends tend to also view their teammates as friends. At the dyad-level, however, both of these processes are symmetric—dyadic reciprocity correlations were positive for both perceptions of competence ($r = 0.14$) and feelings of social affinity ($r = 0.56$). These insights into the symmetry and asymmetry of interpersonal dynamics are unique strengths of a dyadic approach; studying status at the individual level would obscure these important differences in social perceptions.

As these examples illustrate, dyadic data analysis can provide new insights into enduring areas of inquiry in the social sciences. Dyadic data analysis offers researchers at least three unique benefits. First, and with respect to *theory*, dyadic data analysis affords the opportunity to align the level of methods and analysis with the theory that underlies a prediction, thus avoiding fallacies of inference (Krasikova & LeBreton, 2012). Of course, this benefit is only realized if the theory underlying a prediction is indeed about a dyadic phenomenon. Second, and with respect to *statistical analysis*, dyadic data analysis offers the ability to account for the multiple sources of nonindependence and the cross-nested nature of interpersonal interactions. Failing to account for these nuances when analyzing dyadic data can result in biased parameter estimates and flawed conclusions. Third, and with respect to *understanding*, dyadic data analysis can offer insights into a phenomenon that are unavailable if a researcher focuses instead on an individual or group level of analysis. For example, and as shown by both Eisenkraft and Elfenbein (2010) and Erez et al. (2015), a dyadic approach facilitates examining specifically which element (actor, partner, dyad) of an interpersonal interaction is driving variance in perceptions or behaviors. Dyadic data analysis can help answer the question of whether an interpersonal phenomenon is something that is elicited by a person, something that is in the eye of the beholder, or something that is dependent on the interaction of two people. A dyadic approach can also, as shown by Joshi and Knight (2015), provide unique insights into the symmetry of interpersonal processes that are not available from other approaches. For example, do those who give advice to others also tend to receive advice from others? If one worker gives advice to her colleague, does that specific colleague reciprocate and also give advice? Answering such questions necessitates a dyadic approach, which separates the individual (actor and partner) and relational effects, and also models reciprocity. These unique elements help refine old theories and enable the development of new insights into interpersonal dynamics in organizations.

AN EMPIRICAL ILLUSTRATION OF THE SOCIAL RELATIONS MODEL

To further illustrate the value of dyadic data analysis for organizational research, and to provide a step-by-step guide for doing such an analysis, we examine the concept of *trust*—the willingness of one person to be vulnerable to another (Rousseau, Sitkin, Burt, & Camerer, 1998)—within work teams. Trust is multidimensional, comprising both cognitive and affective components (McAllister, 1995). The cognitive dimension of trust in work teams reflects one person's belief that a team member can contribute to the work of the group. The affective dimension reflects one person's belief that another team member genuinely cares for him or her. Importantly, scholars commonly conceptualize trust as a relational phenomenon that is shaped by individual characteristics of a trustor (i.e., actor or perceiver) and a trustee (i.e., partner or target), as well as aspects of the relationship between the two (i.e., dyadic relationship) (cf. Mayer, Davis, & Schoorman, 1995; Schoorman, Mayer, & Davis, 2007). The relational nature of trust invites the use of dyadic data analysis (Jones & Shah, 2016).

Our illustration uses survey data from 432 students, organized into 108 four-person teams, that were instructed to complete a creative task. Due to missing data on some of the predictor variables included in this illustrative analysis, the sample used below comprised 108 groups, 414 unique individuals, and 1,190 directed dyads (i.e., actor ratings of a given partner).[1] The teams were asked to, in a 60-minute work period, develop and execute a creative idea for a poster to recruit volunteers to participate in a campus blood drive. Before beginning this interdependent task, participants first completed a survey that assessed individual characteristics and team members' familiarity with one another. After completing the team task and delivering their blood drive poster, participants completed a second survey that assessed elements of team dynamics and team members' perceptions of one another.

For this example, we examined the degree to which trust between team members is a function of two characteristics—gender (−1 = Female, 1 = Male) and self-reported social skills. These characteristics were assessed on the survey that participants completed prior to working on the

poster with their teammates. Social skills—reflecting participants' ability to take others' perspective, read others' intentions, and adjust their behavior—was measured using a 7-item scale ($\alpha = 0.81$; Ferris, Witt, & Hochwarter, 2001). A sample item is "I find it easy to put myself in the position of others."

The criterion variables that we examined were team members' cognitive and affective trust of their teammates. In the survey administered after the group task, participants responded to items from McAllister (1995), assessing their perceptions of their teammates. Data were collected using a round robin design, with each person rating each other member of the team. Three items measured the cognitive dimension of trust (e.g., "I can rely on this person not to make my job more difficult by careless work," $\alpha = 0.75$) and three items measured the affective dimension of trust (e.g., "If I share my problems with this person, I know [s]he would respond constructively and caringly," $\alpha = 0.87$).

Analytical Approach

We illustrate how to conduct a social relations analysis using random coefficient modeling (variously called hierarchical linear modeling and, more generally, multilevel modeling)—a type of analysis that is already familiar to many social science researchers. Although Kenny and his colleagues initially developed the SRM as an ANOVA-based model, Snijders and Kenny (1999) showed how the parameters of the SRM can be estimated using multilevel modeling. The unit of observation for criterion variables in the SRM is the directed dyadic relationship, which describes the perception or relationship from one person, the actor (i), to another person, the partner (j). An actor's perception of a given partner can result from characteristics of the group the two are in (i.e., the group effect), individual-level actor characteristics (i.e., the actor effect), individual-level partner characteristics (i.e., the partner effect), and, dyad-level characteristics (i.e., the relational or dyad effect, which is conditional on the unique pairing of a given actor with a given partner).

[1]As the purpose of this chapter is not to test and evaluate formal theory, but rather to provide an illustration of how one goes about using the SRM, we did not attempt to impute missing data (for guidance on imputing missing data, see Grund, Lüdtke, & Robitzsch, 2016).

Variance in directed dyadic ratings by actors of their partners can thus stem from differences across groups (i.e., group variance), differences across individual actors (i.e., actor variance), differences across individual partners (i.e., partner variance), and differences across dyads (i.e., relational or dyad variance). The SRM is therefore a multilevel model, in which directed dyadic outcomes are nested within individuals, which are nested within groups (Kenny et al., 2006; Snijders & Kenny, 1999). However, as noted above, the SRM estimates the cross-nested nature of the dyadic perceptions or relationships by specifying the covariance between dyad members' relational effects and the covariance between actor effects and partner effects.

A multilevel modeling approach to fitting the SRM has several advantages compared with the ANOVA-based estimation methods initially developed by Kenny. Snijders and Kenny (1999) noted three strengths, in particular, of the multilevel modeling approach:

> The multilevel formulation of the SRM allows straightforwardly for the inclusion of covariates, for missing data on the dependent variable (provided that the data are missing by design or at random), and the estimation of specialized models (e.g., equal actor and partner variance). (p. 476)

A multilevel modeling approach also easily handles unequal group sizes (Kenny, 1996). These strengths, combined with researchers' growing familiarity with multilevel modeling, make it an attractive option for estimating the SRM. Kenny et al. (2006) provided the code used to run the SRM as a multilevel model using various software packages (e.g., MLWIN, SAS) in an online supplement. In this chapter, we introduce a new option for researchers seeking to estimate the SRM using multilevel modeling—the lme function in the nlme package (Pinheiro, Bates, DebRoy, Sarkar, & R Core Team, 2016) in the software environment R. Below we describe our approach and in Appendix 18.1 provide the code needed to estimate the SRM using multilevel modeling in R.

Data Preparation

As a first step, a researcher must prepare a data set at the dyad level with a few key identifiers. Each observation in the data set (i.e., each row) contains one group member's rating of another group member. This structure captures the fact that the data set comprises directed dyadic ratings—there is one row for A's rating of B and a separate row for B's rating of A. Note that this mandates having a distinct criterion rating from each member of the dyad; it is not appropriate to assign a single criterion value to both observations. Table 18.1 provides a subset of the data set used in this illustration—showing one way to prepare data for a dyadic analysis. Several variables in the data set indicate the nested and interdependent nature of the observations. Unique identifiers indicate the team (group_id), rater (act_id), ratee (part_id), and dyad (dyad_id) to which a given observation belongs. Further, the data set includes two sets of dummy variables—a1 to a4 and p1 to p4—that are needed to estimate the SRM using multilevel modeling and the clever approach described by Snijders and Kenny (1999) for circumventing the limitations regarding cross-nesting in many multilevel modeling software packages. These dummy variables range from 1 to k, where k is the size of the largest group in the data set; in this empirical example, the largest group has four members. One set of the dummies identifies the rater or actor (i.e., "a") and the second set identifies the ratee or partner (i.e., "p") for a given directed dyadic observation.

In addition to these identifiers, Table 18.1 also illustrates how dyadic data sets may include covariates across multiple levels of analysis. Table 18.1 only contains a subset of the covariates used in the illustration; however, what is shown reflects the general structure of how covariates can be included in an analysis. At the team level, for example, the data set contains the mean rating of team members' social skills (ss_x). At the individual level, there are values for the social skills of the trustor (act_ss) and of the trustee (part_ss). At the dyad level, there is a variable indicating the absolute value of the difference between the trustor and the trustee's social skills (absdif_ss). Also at the dyad level,

TABLE 18.1

Sample Portion of Data Set Used in Empirical Illustration

group_id	act_id	part_id	dyad_id	a1	a2	a3	a4	p1	p2	p3	p4	ss_x	act_ss	part_ss	absdif_ss	trust_cog
1	1	2	1	1	0	0	0	0	1	0	0	4.18	4.00	4.40	0.40	5.33
1	1	3	2	1	0	0	0	0	0	1	0	4.18	4.00	3.50	0.50	4.67
1	1	4	3	1	0	0	0	0	0	0	1	4.18	4.00	4.80	0.80	4.67
1	2	1	1	0	1	0	0	1	0	0	0	4.18	4.40	4.00	0.40	7.00
1	2	3	4	0	1	0	0	0	0	1	0	4.18	4.40	3.50	0.90	5.33
1	2	4	5	0	1	0	0	0	0	0	1	4.18	4.40	4.80	0.40	4.67
1	3	1	2	0	0	1	0	1	0	0	0	4.18	3.50	4.00	0.50	7.00
1	3	2	4	0	0	1	0	0	1	0	0	4.18	3.50	4.40	0.90	6.00
1	3	4	6	0	0	1	0	0	0	0	1	4.18	3.50	4.80	1.30	5.33
1	4	1	3	0	0	0	1	1	0	0	0	4.18	4.80	4.00	0.80	6.33
1	4	2	5	0	0	0	1	0	1	0	0	4.18	4.80	4.40	0.40	7.00
1	4	3	6	0	0	0	1	0	0	1	0	4.18	4.80	3.50	1.30	4.67
2	5	6	7	1	0	0	0	0	1	0	0	2.83	3.50	3.10	0.40	6.00
2	5	7	8	1	0	0	0	0	0	1	0	2.83	3.50	2.10	1.40	6.00
2	5	8	9	1	0	0	0	0	0	0	1	2.83	3.50	2.60	0.90	6.00
2	6	5	7	0	1	0	0	1	0	0	0	2.83	3.10	3.50	0.40	4.33
2	6	7	10	0	1	0	0	0	0	1	0	2.83	3.10	2.10	1.00	6.00
2	6	8	11	0	1	0	0	0	0	0	1	2.83	3.10	2.60	0.50	6.00
2	7	5	8	0	0	1	0	1	0	0	0	2.83	2.10	3.50	1.40	4.00
2	7	6	10	0	0	1	0	0	1	0	0	2.83	2.10	3.10	1.00	6.00
2	7	8	12	0	0	1	0	0	0	0	1	2.83	2.10	2.60	0.50	6.00
2	8	5	9	0	0	0	1	1	0	0	0	2.83	2.60	3.50	0.90	6.00
2	8	6	11	0	0	0	1	0	1	0	0	2.83	2.60	3.10	0.50	4.33
2	8	7	12	0	0	0	1	0	0	1	0	2.83	2.60	2.10	0.50	6.00

there is the directed dyadic rating of the cognitive dimension of how much one person trusts the other (trust_cog). This—the directed dyad level—is the lowest level of analysis in a round robin design. All other values are, in some way, repeated across rows, because the actor in one row is the partner in a different row. The identifier variables described above instruct the software on how to handle this interdependence in accordance with the SRM.

Null Models: Variance Decomposition of Cognitive and Affective Trust

The next step in a social relations analysis is to conduct a variance decomposition of the focal directed dyadic ratings, which estimates how much a given rating is attributable to characteristics of groups, actors, partners, and relationships. This variance decomposition is analogous to the first step of any other multilevel analysis, in which a researcher first examines intraclass correlations or changes in model fit indices to determine whether there is meaningful variation in intercepts or slopes at different levels of analysis. The variance decomposition for a social relations analysis entails fitting a null model—a model without fixed effect covariates—to the data. This null model is presented below:

$$Y_{ijk} = \mu + G_k + A_{ik} + P_{jk} + E_{ijk}, \qquad (18.1)$$

where Y_{ijk} is actor i's trust of partner j in group k, μ is an overall intercept term, G_k is the random group effect for group k, A_{ik} is the random actor effect for actor i, P_{jk} is the random partner effect for partner j, and E_{ijk} is the random relational effect that reflects the unique way that actor i rated partner j. To estimate the SRM, it is necessary to specify the structure of the variance-covariance matrix for these random effects. Note that the relational component in Equation 18.1 reflects a combination of both the true relational effect and random error (i.e., residual). Unless there are multiple measures of the focal criterion variable, these effects are confounded (i.e., it is not possible to separate the true relational effect from the residual or error; Kenny, 1994).

Per our prior discussion, the model estimates the variance of the group effects (σ_G^2), the individual

actor effects (σ_A^2), the individual partner effects (σ_P^2), and the relational effects (σ_E^2). As above, without multiple measures of the focal criterion variable, it is not possible to separate relational variance from residual, or error, variance. The covariances among all random effect terms except for two are fixed to zero. The two that are estimated reflect the model's assumption of two forms of reciprocity. The model estimates the covariance between actor effects and partner effects, which is the generalized reciprocity term (σ_{AP}). And the model estimates the covariance between the relational effects for the members of a given dyad (i.e., E_{ijk} and E_{jik}), which is the dyadic reciprocity term ($\sigma_{E_{ijk},E_{jik}}$). The results of the null model thus provide the parameter estimates needed to parse the variance in a given directed dyadic rating.

Figure 18.1 provides annotated code and output for the null model for cognitive trust. Additional code, including expanded commentary, is available in Appendix 18.1 and online (http://apknight.org/pdsrm-example.R). Note that the raw output of R's lme function contains standard deviations and correlations, rather than variances and covariances, for the random effects. Standard error estimates are not provided by lme for these random effects parameters because these are only asymptotically valid and, accordingly, should only be used with large sample sizes (see Singer, 1998, p. 351). Even without standard errors and tests of whether these parameters significantly differ from zero, however, the variance partitioning enables examining the relative contribution that group, actor, partner, and dyad characteristics make to trust ratings.

Table 18.2 shows the conversion of the raw output from lme into variance-covariance parameter estimates and, then, into variance component percentages and reciprocity correlations. To convert the standard deviations into variance parameters, square the standard deviation parameter. To convert the correlations into covariance parameters, multiply the correlation estimate by the product of the standard deviations of its elements. Computing variance component percentages requires two additional steps. First, sum the variance parameter estimates for group, actor, partner, and dyad—this provides the sum total

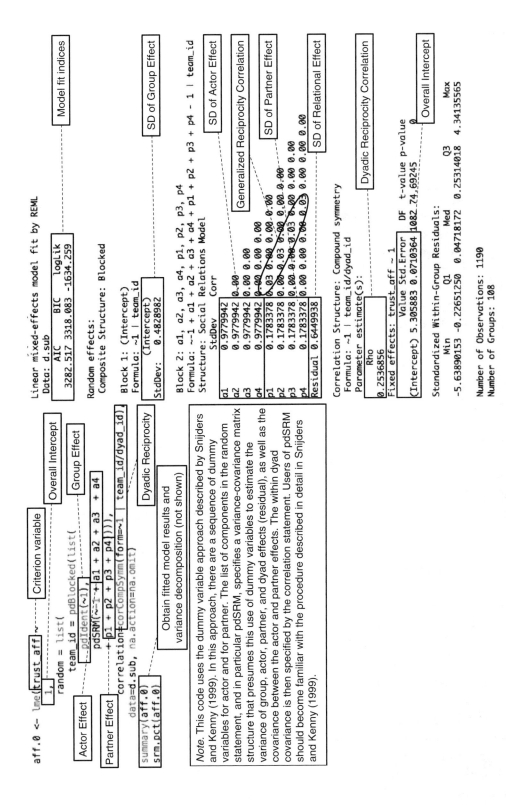

FIGURE 18.1. Explanation of code and output for estimating the social relations model using the lme function in the nlme package in R.

TABLE 18.2

Results of Variance Decomposition Analysis for Cognitive Trust and Affective Trust

	Cognitive trust			Affective trust		
	Output from lme (standard deviation)	**Variance parameter**	**Variance percentage**	**Output from lme (standard deviation)**	**Variance parameter**	**Variance percentage**
Team-level (σ_G^2)	0.46	0.21	15.35	0.48	0.23	14.24
Individual-level, Actor (σ_A^2)	0.90	0.81	59.41	0.98	0.96	58.41
Individual-level, Partner (σ_P^2)	0.15	0.02	1.57	0.18	0.03	1.94
Dyad-level (σ_E^2)	0.57	0.32	23.67	0.64	0.42	25.41
	Output from lme (correlation)	**Covariance estimate**	**Reciprocity correlation**	**Output from lme (correlation)**	**Covariance estimate**	**Reciprocity correlation**
Generalized reciprocity ($\sigma_{A,P}$)	−0.31	−0.04	−0.31	0.03	0.01	0.03
Dyadic reciprocity ($\sigma_{E_{ijk},E_{jik}}$)	0.14	0.04	0.14	0.25	0.11	0.25

Note. N = 1,190 directed dyadic ratings from 414 individuals nested in 108 groups.

variance (Snijders & Kenny, 1999). Then, divide each of these values by the sum total to compute the portion of total variance accounted for by group, actor, partner, and dyad, respectively. The helper function srm.pct, included in the pdSRM code linked above, can be used to easily perform these transformations and covert the raw output from lme into variance percentages and reciprocity correlations.

Given that these values represent the portion of variance in a directed dyadic rating attributable to each source, one could use traditional approaches for interpreting them as effect sizes (see LeBreton & Senter, 2008). As Table 18.2 shows, for both cognitive trust (59%) and affective trust (58%) a substantial portion of the variance in directed dyadic ratings is attributable to the trustor (i.e., actor effect). The variance partitioning indicates that some individuals tend to be relatively more trusting of others, in general, whereas other individuals tend to be relatively less trusting of others, in general. In contrast, the partner effect contributes relatively little to perceptions of cognitive (2%) and affective (2%) trust. The results of the null model suggest that the phenomenon of trust—at least early on in

the life of a relationship (Jones & Shah, 2016)—is heavily in the eye of the beholder, not the beholden.

In addition to decomposing the variance into group, actor, partner, and relational components, the results of the null model indicate the degree to which ratings are symmetric or reciprocal. As described above, generalized reciprocity is a form of reciprocity at the individual level, measuring the degree to which the individual tendencies of actors align with the individual tendencies of partners. In this example, generalized reciprocity describes how much a person who tends to trust others is, himself or herself, similarly trusted by others. Table 18.2 provides the generalized reciprocity correlation, which reflects the association between the actor effect and the partner effect. For cognitive trust this value is −0.31, which indicates that those who tend to trust others' abilities tend to be trusted slightly less by their teammates. As Table 18.2 shows, the generalized reciprocity correlation for affective trust is very small, but positive: 0.03. Changing to the dyad level, Table 18.2 also shows the estimate of dyadic reciprocity—both as a correlation and as a covariance parameter. Note that in the SRM, the variance of the dyad members is fixed to be equivalent through the specification of a compound symmetric structure. Accordingly, for the covariance between E_{ijk} and E_{jik}, the components have equal variance. The dyadic reciprocity correlation is 0.14 for cognitive trust and 0.25 for affective trust. These values indicate that, within a dyad, if an actor trusts a partner, that specific partner is likely to also trust the actor.

The results illustrate the value of considering reciprocity for understanding interpersonal relationships and perception in work teams. As other research using dyadic data analysis has shown (e.g., Joshi & Knight, 2015), the basic properties of interpersonal processes reflecting competence may be strikingly different from those reflecting warmth. For the example of trust, we observe that reciprocity at the individual level (i.e., generalized reciprocity) is negative for the cognitive dimension, but positive for the affective dimension. Perceiving competence seems to be an asymmetric interpersonal process, such that those who are viewed by their teammates as highly competent tend to view their teammates as lower in competence. In contrast, perceiving warmth seems to be a symmetric interpersonal process—those who are viewed as caring tend to view others also as caring. Once individual tendencies are controlled, however, ratings of trust are symmetric for both the cognitive and affective dimensions; that is, dyadic reciprocity is positive for both. Within a given dyad, people tend to reciprocate their beliefs about trust.

Prediction Models: Examination of Covariates at Multiple Levels of Analysis

Although the variance decomposition and reciprocity correlations are interesting and shed light on the nature of an interpersonal process, many researchers may wish to test hypotheses about covariates—that is, about why scores on outcome variables (e.g., trust, relationship satisfaction, work–family conflict) vary across teams, actors, partners, and dyads. In the next step of our illustration, we include two common types of covariates—one categorical and one continuous—at multiple levels of analysis to show how to estimate and interpret

the results of analyses with predictor variables. In predicting cognitive and affective trust, we examine the role of social skills and gender, organizing our discussion of these covariates by level of analysis.

The prediction models for both cognitive and affective trust may be specified using the following equation:

$$\begin{aligned} Y_{ijk} = \mu &+ G_k + A_{ik} + P_{jk} + E_{ijk} + \beta_{TSS} \text{TeamSocialSkills}_k \\ &+ \beta_{TGD} \text{TeamPctMale}_k + \beta_{ActSS} \text{SocialSkills}_{ik} \\ &+ \beta_{ActMale} \text{Male}_{ik} + \beta_{PartSS} \text{SocialSkills}_{jk} \\ &+ \beta_{PartMale} \text{Male}_{jk} + \beta_{DydMale} \left(\text{Male}_{ik} \times \text{Male}_{jk} \right) \\ &+ \beta_{DydSS} \left(\left| \text{SocialSkills}_{ik} - \text{SocialSkills}_{jk} \right| \right), \quad (18.2) \end{aligned}$$

where, again, Y_{ijk} is actor i's trust of partner j in group k and μ is an overall intercept term.

In contrast to Equation 18.1, however, the overall intercept and the group (G_k), actor (A_{ik}), partner (P_{jk}), and relational (E_{ijk}) effects in Equation 18.2 are now conditional upon the included fixed effect covariates. Each of these covariates is explained in greater detail below.

When using multilevel modeling to estimate the SRM—and, especially, when testing hypotheses about covariates—it is common to present the results in the format illustrated by Table 18.3, in addition to the variance decomposition results provided in Table 18.2. Note that Models 1 and 3 of Table 18.3 are the results of the null models described above for cognitive and affective trust, respectively. Reflecting the fact that these models lack covariates, there are no fixed effect coefficients in Models 1 and 3, other than the intercept. For reporting in Table 18.3, the standard deviations and correlations for the random effects included in the raw output from lme have been transformed into variances and covariances. Given that the raw output of different multilevel modeling functions (e.g., R's lme, SAS's PROC MIXED) contain different kinds of estimates, researchers should specify what values they report (e.g., variance, standard deviation).[2]

[2]It is useful to note other differences in the output from lme compared with, for example, the output from SAS PROC MIXED. In PROC MIXED, the two terms for the dyadic component—the residual and the dyadic covariance—are independent components, such that the total dyadic variance is the sum of the two. In the output from lme, the residual term reflects the sum of the unique dyadic variance and the dyadic covariance. So, the residual term output by lme is equal to the sum of the two SAS components.

TABLE 18.3

Results of Dyadic Data Analysis Using the Social Relations Model

| | Cognitive trust | | | | Affective trust | | | |
| | Model 1 | | Model 2 | | Model 3 | | Model 4 | |
	Est.	SE	Est.	SE	Est.	SE	Est.	SE
Fixed effects								
Intercept	5.52	0.06	5.54	0.07	5.31	0.07	5.32	0.07
Team % male			−0.28	0.28			−0.09	0.31
Team social skills			−0.13	0.16			−0.06	0.18
Actor gender			−0.06	0.06			0.00	0.06
Actor social skills			0.18	0.06**			0.19	0.07**
Partner gender			−0.05	0.02*			−0.08	0.03**
Partner social skills			0.06	0.02*			0.05	0.03+
Actor gender × Partner gender			0.05	0.02*			0.09	0.03**
Absolute Difference in Social Skills			−0.01	0.03			−0.03	0.04
Random effects								
Team	0.21		0.20		0.23		0.24	
Actor	0.81		0.79		0.96		0.94	
Partner	0.02		0.02		0.03		0.03	
Dyad	0.32		0.32		0.42		0.40	
Generalized reciprocity	−0.04		−0.04		0.01		0.01	
Dyadic reciprocity	0.04		0.04		0.11		0.09	
Model fit								
Log Likelihood	−1,503.98		−1,507.61		−1,634.26		−1,636.02	
AIC	3,021.95		3,045.21		3,282.52		3,302.03	

Note. Fixed effects entries are unstandardized coefficients (Est.) and standard errors (SE). Random effects entries are variance and covariance parameter estimates. $N = 1,190$ directed dyadic ratings from 414 individuals nested in 108 groups. AIC = Akaike information criterion.
$^+p < .10$, $^*p < .05$, $^{**}p < .01$, two-tailed.

Models 2 and 4 of Table 18.3 include covariates predicting cognitive and affective trust, respectively. In entering these covariates into our analyses, we first grand mean centered any continuous variables, which is important given that the intercept terms in these multilevel models are substantively interesting (Hofmann & Gavin, 1998). In lme's raw output, the results for fixed effect covariates are listed directly beneath the header for "Fixed Effects." In the null model results depicted in Figure 18.1, there is only the Intercept term listed here; for the prediction models, there would be additional covariates, listed one per line beneath the Intercept term.

Starting at the highest level of analysis, we observed in the null model results discussed above that groups in this sample vary meaningfully in how much members tend to trust one another. For both affective and cognitive trust, the members of some groups trust one another more than do the members of other groups. To examine whether social skills and gender can help explain this variance, we created two group-level variables that represent group composition with respect to gender and social skills. For gender, we computed the percentage of group members who are male ($TeamPctMale_k$) and for social skills we computed the average (mean) of group members' social skills ($TeamSocialSkills_k$). As Table 18.3 shows, neither of these team-level covariates helps to explain why trust is higher in some groups than others. Gender composition has a nonsignificant relationship with cognitive ($\beta_{TGD} = -0.28$, n.s.) and affective

($\beta_{TGD} = -0.09$, n.s.) trust, as does average social skills (cognitive trust: $\beta_{TSS} = -0.13$, n.s.; affective trust: $\beta_{TSS} = -0.06$, n.s.). Note that these parameter estimates are conditional upon the inclusion of other effects in the model. That is, the percentage of men in a team does not provide statistically significant incremental prediction above and beyond actor, partner, and relational effects.

Next, at the individual level of analysis there are two sets of covariates to consider—characteristics of the actor and characteristics of the partner. Models 2 and 4 of Table 18.2 include both the actor's gender and social skills, as well as the partner's gender and social skills as covariates of trust. With respect to actor characteristics, actor social skills is significantly positively related to cognitive trust ($\beta_{ActSS} = 0.18$, $p < .01$) and affective trust ($\beta_{ActSS} = 0.19$, $p < .01$), holding constant the other effects in the model. This positive coefficient indicates that those who are higher in social skills tend to be more trusting of others, in general, than those who are lower in social skills. Across their partners, actors higher in social skills report higher cognitive and affective trust than do actors lower in social skills. Second, with respect to partner characteristics, both gender and partner social skills help explain who tends to be trusted by team members. The results in Table 18.3 show that men are trusted relatively less than are

women for cognitive ($\beta_{PartMale} = -0.05$, $p < .05$) and affective ($\beta_{PartMale} = -0.08$, $p < .01$) trust. Additionally, partner social skills has a positive relationship with trust: team members who are higher in social skills are trusted more by their teammates than are team members lower in social skills (cognitive: $\beta_{PartSS} = 0.06$, $p < .05$; affective: $\beta_{PartSS} = 0.05$, $p < .10$).

Finally, at the dyad level of analysis, Models 2 and 4 present two different ways of examining dyadic effects. With respect to gender, the interaction term between actor gender and partner gender sheds light on specifically who tends to trust whom in teams (cognitive: $\beta_{DydMale} = 0.05$, $p < .05$; $\beta_{DydMale} = 0.09$, $p < .01$). As shown in Figure 18.2, the gender effect for cognitive and affective trust is driven by women tending to report more trust of other women than of men; the effect is particularly strong for the affective dimension of trust. Note that an alternative approach for examining the role of gender would be to include a variable indicating whether dyad members are either the same or different genders. This approach could be appropriate for testing hypotheses motivated by a similarity-attraction or social identity mechanism, but offers a less nuanced view of dyadic effects (as it would show a muted effect of similarity—the average of the female-female and male-male relationships—rather than the unique effect of the female-female relationships).

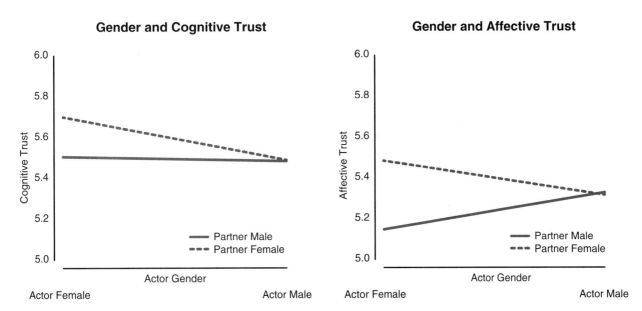

FIGURE 18.2. Plots of interaction between actor gender and partner gender predicting trust.

We illustrate this type of approach with the continuous variable social skills. In this case, we computed the absolute value of the difference between an actor's and a partner's social skills (i.e., $|SocialSkills_{ik} - SocialSkills_{jk}|$). The coefficients for this variable in Table 18.2, which are both nonsignificant (cognitive: $\beta_{DydSS} = -0.01$, n.s; affective: $\beta_{DydSS} = -0.03$, n.s.), reflect the degree to which separation between an actor and a partner on this attribute relates to trust between the two, accounting for their individual tendencies to trust and be trusted.

In addition to the statistical significance of fixed effect covariates, researchers often wish to communicate how important the covariates are for explaining the group, actor, partner, and relational effects. Scholars have suggested a number of different approaches for calculating the variance explained by predictors at different levels of analysis in multilevel models (e.g., Hox, 2002; Singer, 1998; Snijders & Bosker, 1999). These scholars also noted, however, that there are potential problems with estimates of variance explained that are derived from comparing the size of the variance parameter estimates across models with and without covariates. One possible approach for circumventing these challenges, which might be particularly appropriate given the complexity of the SRM, is a Bayesian framework for multilevel modeling. Gelman and Pardoe (2006) provided detailed information about how to implement such an approach.

How Valuable Is the Complexity of Dyadic Data Analysis?

To illustrate the unique benefits of dyadic data analysis, we reanalyzed the data described above using an approach focused on the individual level of analysis. Specifically, we approached the data set with a focus on why some individuals might be trusted more than others (i.e., on perceptions of individual trustworthiness). This focus on why some are trusted more than others targets one of the sources of variance that we described above—the partner effect that reflects individual partners' tendencies to elicit relatively homogeneous reactions from actors. As a first step in taking this individual-level approach, we examined whether teammates tended to agree with one another in their

ratings of a given person and whether teammates' average ratings of a person varied (i.e., whether there is consensus in views of trustworthiness). To do so, we computed two versions of the intraclass correlation and the $r_{wg(j)}$ metric (Bliese, 2000). These calculations showed significant nonindependence in team members' ratings of a focal person on their team for cognitive trust [ICC(1) = 0.17, $p < .01$] and for affective trust [ICC(1) = 0.15, $p < .01$]. Reflecting the small size of the groups in this data set, however, the mean ratings of a given individual were low in reliability for both cognitive [ICC(2) = 0.37] and affective [ICC(2) = 0.35] trust. Group members did tend to agree with one another in their ratings of trust in a focal team member, as shown in measures of inter-rater agreement for cognitive (Average $r_{wg(j)}$ = 0.81) and affective (Average $r_{wg(j)}$ = 0.77) trust.

Given these values, we proceeded to aggregate team members' ratings of one another, computing the mean of team members' ratings of trust with a given person, for each person on the team. We then fit a set of multilevel models for cognitive and affective trust that focused on the individual level of analysis; we also included a random intercept for team to account for potential team-level nonindependence. The results of these models, presented in Table 18.4, show few significant effects of gender or social skills on perceptions of trustworthiness at either the team level or the individual level. In contrast to the dyadic analysis, which depicted gender and social skills relating to trust in nuanced ways, the individual-level analysis showed only that men are less likely than women to be trusted on the affective dimension ($\beta = -0.08$, $p < .01$).

It is important to note that the insights drawn from this individual-level analysis are fundamentally different from those derived from the dyadic analysis. In part this reflects the fact that the kinds of questions that researchers have the flexibility to ask at the dyad level differ from those that a researcher targeting the individual level might ask. The dyadic analyses unpacked the main effect of gender found in the individual-level analysis and revealed that men received lower trust ratings because women tended to rate other women more highly in trust. By separating the variance in an

TABLE 18.4

Results of Individual-Level Analysis Using Traditional Multilevel Modeling

	Cognitive trust				Affective trust			
	Model 1		Model 2		Model 3		Model 4	
	B	SE	B	SE	B	SE	B	SE
Fixed effects								
Intercept	5.52	0.06	5.53	0.06	5.31	0.07	5.33	0.07
Team % male			−0.42	0.25			−0.01	0.29
Team social skills			0.12	0.15			0.16	0.17
Gender			−0.03	0.03			−0.08	0.03**
Social skills			−0.001	0.03			−0.01	0.04
Random effects								
Team	0.37		0.36		0.48		0.48	
Residual	0.26		0.26		0.31		0.31	
Model fit								
Deviance	819.30		814.20		896.20		889.80	
AIC	829.00		845.00		905.70		919.60	

Note. N = 414 individuals nested in 108 groups. Random effects are variance estimates. B = unstandardized regression weight; SE = standard error for B.
$^{†}p < .10$, $^{*}p < .05$, $^{**}p < .01$, two-tailed.

interpersonal perception or relationship into the constituent parts of the interacting individuals, a dyadic approach offers the flexibility to test effects at multiple levels of analysis. The individual-level analysis that we report here focuses only on one portion of the pattern of variance—the partner—examined by the dyadic analysis. As the dyadic variance decomposition revealed, the partner component is actually the least impactful driver of trust in early relationships. Actor tendencies and relational effects have a far greater impact on ratings of trust. This ability to tease apart effects is constrained in an aggregate analysis. Whether this is a limitation, though, depends on a researcher's question and the theoretical perspectives that inform the investigation. As with any form of multilevel research, theory must come first.

ALTERNATIVE APPROACHES FOR ANALYZING DYADIC DATA

We have illustrated above—both through a discussion of published research and an empirical illustration—one type of dyadic data analysis that

is useful for understanding the nature and drivers of interpersonal perception and relationships. This chapter has, however, just scratched the surface, and researchers have several other alternatives for analyzing dyadic data. Some of these alternatives reflect software differences that would provide the same substantive results and insights as those that we reported. Other alternatives, however, reflect different statistical approaches that are grounded in different assumptions about the drivers of dyadic phenomena. Using these alternatives would yield results that would likely mirror the results above in some ways, but could also differ in some ways.

Before describing these alternatives, we first underscore a key assumption underlying the social psychological approach that we have illustrated above, which is that dyadic interactions are independent. That is, the model presumes that the variance in an interpersonal perception or relationship is due to the group, the actor, the partner, and the dyad—not to other combinations of interactions, such as triadic effects or some other structure of connections among individuals. In some research contexts, however, this assumption may not be tenable—at least on the surface. For example, two employees who interact with a shared boss also probably interact with each another. Any conversations and interactions about their boss open the door to effects that are not modeled by the SRM, such as the possibility that one employee's relationship with the boss influences her perception of her coworker. Kenny and colleagues (2006) noted that they have found little evidence that triadic effects bias the insights from the SRM. However, it is important for researchers using the SRM—or, really, any of the models in this same family—to consider whether variance in a given interpersonal perception or behavior could be due to effects other than the group, the actor, the partner, and the dyad.

Software Alternatives

We illustrated how to estimate the SRM using multilevel modeling, which offers flexibility, easily addresses missing data, and accommodates unbalanced group sizes (Snijders & Kenny, 1999). As mentioned above, Kenny et al. (2006) provided code for estimating the SRM using a range of software platforms, including SAS, SPSS, and MLwiN. In this chapter, we showed a new method for estimating the SRM in the free and open-source software environment R using the lme function of the multilevel modeling package nlme. One alternative to using lme to estimate the SRM using R is the R2MLwiN package (Zhang, Parker, Charlton, Leckie, & Browne, 2016) and the code provided by Snijders and Kenny (1999) for MLwiN. This approach, however, would require a license for MLwiN, which will be called by R. Stata users could take a similar approach, using the runmlwin command in Stata (Leckie & Charlton, 2012) to call MLwiN; this would also require an MLwiN license.

Beyond using multilevel modeling, there are other alternatives for researchers interested in conducting dyadic data analysis in R. If a researcher wishes to use ANOVA or SEM to conduct dyadic data analysis, there are several options available within R. The TripleR package (Schönbrodt, Back, & Schmukle, 2015) enables estimating the SRM using an ANOVA-based approach. The fSRM package (Schönbrodt, Stas, & Loeys, 2016) provides tools for fitting the SRM with roles using a SEM-based approach. Additionally, Kenny and colleagues have developed

a web-based suite of R applications for conducting several different kinds of dyadic data analyses (Kenny, 2016). With options in R proliferating and many preexisting options in other software environments, there is no shortage of options for conducting dyadic data analysis, making the technique increasingly accessible for organizational researchers.

Alternative Statistical Models

Although we do not intend this chapter to provide a comprehensive accounting of techniques for dyadic data analysis, we highlight here two alternative models that may be particularly useful for researchers who have collected dichotomous and/or longitudinal data on interpersonal perceptions or relationships. Because the SRM and its derivatives grew out of an ANOVA-based framework, they are less attractive options for analyzing such data. Instead, models that grew out of the social networks tradition could offer more flexibility and the potential to model structural effects alongside dyadic effects.

First, for data that are dichotomous and at a single point in time, the *p*2 model is an option that, conceptually, aligns well with the SRM (van Duijn, Snijders, & Zijlstra, 2004; Zijlstra, van Duijn, & Snijders, 2006). Like the SRM, *p*2 partitions a directed dyadic, binary outcome into group-level, individual-level, and dyad-level components. However, reflecting roots in a social networks tradition, the model is a probabilistic one, in which the drivers of a relationship are examined as influencing the likelihood that it matches one of four possibilities (i.e., 0,0; 1,0; 0,1; 1,1). The model is estimated using a Bayesian Markov Chain Monte Carlo algorithm and is implemented in freely available software.

Second, researchers have only recently begun to tackle dynamics using the SRM (see, Jones & Shah, 2016; Nestler, Geukes, Hutteman, & Back, 2017). For a more flexible approach to modeling dyadic data that are longitudinal and for research questions regarding how relationships change over time, researchers might consider dynamic stochastic actor-based modeling (Snijders et al., 2010). These models use Bayesian Markov Chain Monte Carlo algorithms to fit a range of flexible models and test hypotheses regarding the interplay of actor states and interpersonal relationships over time. The RSiena package in R can be used to fit these models (Ripley, Boitmanis, & Snijders, 2013).

CONCLUSION

Many core theories in the social sciences rely on assumptions about dyadic perceptions, interactions, or relationships (Krasikova & LeBreton, 2012). Yet dyadic dynamics have often been overlooked in social science research, with focusing instead on individual-level, group-level, and organizational-level processes and outcomes. In this chapter, we described approaches to data analysis that are uniquely focused on the dyad, offering researchers the ability to test theories of interpersonal dynamics at the appropriate level (or levels) of analysis.

APPENDIX 18.1

The code below was used to produce the results included in the chapter for cognitive trust. There are two models below—a null model and a prediction model. An expanded version of this code, with detailed annotations and comments that explain what each of the lines of code mean is available at http://apknight.org/pdsrm-example.R.

Before running the models below, you must input a set of specialized functions. To do so, run the following command, which loads a structure for the social relations model

source("http://apknight.org/pdSRM.R")

This is a null social relations model, which provides the parameters needed to conduct a variance decomposition

```
cog.0 <-
lme(trust_cog ~
    1,
    random = list(
        team_id = pdBlocked(list(
            pdIdent(~1),
            pdSRM(~-1
                + a1 + a2 + a3 + a4
                + p1 + p2 + p3 + p4)))),
    correlation = corCompSymm(form = ~1 | team_id/dyad_id),
    data = d.sub, na.action=na.omit)
```

summary(cog.0)

The results of this summary statement are

Linear mixed-effects model fit by REML
Data: d.sub

AIC	BIC	logLik
3021.952	3057.518	−1503.976

Random effects:
Composite Structure: Blocked

Block 1: (Intercept)
Formula: ~1 | team_id
   (Intercept)
StdDev: 0.4564505

Block 2: a1, a2, a3, a4, p1, p2, p3, p4
Formula: ~−1 + a1 + a2 + a3 + a4 + p1 + p2 + p3 + p4 | team_id
Structure: Social Relations Model

	StdDev	Corr						
a1	0.8978951							
a2	0.8978951	0.000						
a3	0.8978951	0.000	0.000					
a4	0.8978951	0.000	0.000	0.000				
p1	0.1459404	−0.311	0.000	0.000	0.000			
p2	0.1459404	0.000	−0.311	0.000	0.000	0.000		
p3	0.1459404	0.000	0.000	−0.311	0.000	0.000	0.000	
p4	0.1459404	0.000	0.000	0.000	−0.311	0.000	0.000	0.000

Residual 0.5668108

Correlation Structure: Compound symmetry
Formula: ~1 | team_id/dyad_id
Parameter estimate(s):
  Rho
0.1379389
Fixed effects: trust_cog ~ 1

	Value	Std.Error	DF	t-value	p-value
(Intercept)	5.520423	0.06377217	1082	86.56477	0

Standardized Within-Group Residuals:

Min	Q1	Med	Q3	Max
−6.6440216	−0.2198626	0.0502427	0.2611959	4.4251627

Number of Observations: 1190
Number of Groups: 108

END summary STATEMENT RESULTS

srm.pct(aff.0)

The results of this srm.pct statement are

	variances.and.covariances	percents.and.correlations
Group	0.208	15.352
Actor	0.806	59.406
Partner	0.021	1.569
Dyad	0.321	23.673
Generalized Reciprocity	−0.041	−0.311
Dyadic Reciprocity	0.044	0.138

END srm.pct STATEMENT RESULTS

This is a model that includes fixed effects parameters to predict the group, actor, partner, and dyadic variance

```
cog.1 <- lme(trust_cog ~
        gender_pct_grd + social_skills_x_grd
        + act_gender + act_social_skills_grd
        + part_gender + part_social_skills_grd
        + act_gender*part_gender + absdif_social_skills_grd

        ,
        random = list(
            team_id = pdBlocked(list(
                pdIdent(~1),
                pdSRM(~-1 + a1 + a2 + a3 + a4
                + p1 + p2 + p3 + p4)))),
                correlation=corCompSymm(form=~1 | team_id/dyad_id),
            data=d, na.action=na.omit)

summary(cog.1)
```

The results of this summary statement are

Linear mixed-effects model fit by REML
 Data: d.sub
   AIC   BIC   logLik
 3045.212   3121.324   −1507.606

Random effects:
 Composite Structure: Blocked

 Block 1: (Intercept)
 Formula: ~1 | team_id
     (Intercept)
 StdDev: 0.4525179

 Block 2: a1, a2, a3, a4, p1, p2, p3, p4
 Formula: ~ −1 + a1 + a2 + a3 + a4 + p1 + p2 + p3 + p4 | team_id
 Structure: Social Relations Model

	StdDev	Corr						
a1	0.8887494							
a2	0.8887494	0.000						
a3	0.8887494	0.000	0.000					
a4	0.8887494	0.000	0.000	0.000				
p1	0.1462831	−0.355	0.000	0.000	0.000			
p2	0.1462831	0.000	−0.355	0.000	0.000	0.000		
p3	0.1462831	0.000	0.000	−0.355	0.000	0.000	0.000	
p4	0.1462831	0.000	0.000	0.000	−0.355	0.000	0.000	0.000

 Residual 0.5628685
 Correlation Structure: Compound symmetry
 Formula: ~1 | team_id/dyad_id

Parameter estimate(s):
 Rho
0.1257927

Fixed effects: trust_cog ~ 1 + gender_pct_grd + social_skills_x_grd + act_gender + act_social_skills_grd + part_gender + part_social_skills_grd + act_gender * part_gender + absdif_social_skills_grd

	Value	Std.Error	DF	t-value	p-value
(Intercept)	5.544265	0.06513712	1076	85.11683	0.0000
gender_pct_grd	−0.276140	0.27638097	105	−0.99913	0.3200
social_skills_x_grd	−0.128293	0.15933052	105	−0.80520	0.4225
act_gender	−0.058049	0.05810358	1076	−0.99906	0.3180
act_social_skills_grd	0.184720	0.06129098	1076	3.01382	0.0026
part_gender	−0.050029	0.02410284	1076	−2.07565	0.0382
part_social_skills_grd	0.057971	0.02489518	1076	2.32860	0.0201
absdif_social_skills_grd	−0.010907	0.03031094	1076	−0.35984	0.7190
act_gender:part_gender	0.047186	0.02265628	1076	2.08271	0.0375

 Correlation:

	(Intr)	gndr__	scl___	act_gn	act___	prt_gn	prt___	abs___
gender_pct_grd	0.118							
social_skills_x_grd	0.006	−0.016						
act_gender	−0.239	−0.422	0.006					
act_social_skills_grd	0.000	0.015	−0.399	−0.009				
part_gender	−0.103	−0.180	0.004	0.051	−0.002			
part_social_skills_grd	0.000	0.008	−0.173	−0.002	0.031	−0.015		
absdif_social_skills_grd	−0.003	−0.016	0.012	0.008	−0.008	0.026	−0.033	
act_gender:part_gender	0.002	−0.032	0.004	−0.076	0.004	−0.186	0.010	−0.009

Standardized Within-Group Residuals:

Min	Q1	Med	Q3	Max
−6.61434986	−0.23963132	0.03880915	0.28392874	4.32217245

Number of Observations: 1190
Number of Groups: 108

References

Blau, P. M. (1964). *Exchange and power in social life*. New York, NY: Wiley.

Bliese, P. D. (2000). Within-group agreement, non-independence, and reliability: Implications for data aggregation and analysis. In K. J. Klein & S. W. J. Kozlowski (Eds.), *Multilevel theory, research, and methods in organizations: Foundations, extensions, and new directions* (pp. 349–381). San Francisco, CA: Jossey-Bass.

Borgatti, S. P., Mehra, A., Brass, D. J., & Labianca, G. (2009). Network analysis in the social sciences. *Science, 323,* 892–895. http://dx.doi.org/10.1126/science.1165821

Brass, D. J., Galaskiewicz, J., Greve, H. R., & Tsai, W. (2004). Taking stock of networks and organizations: A multi-level perspective. *Academy of Management Journal, 47,* 795–817. http://dx.doi.org/10.5465/20159624

Burt, R. S., Kilduff, M., & Tasselli, S. (2013). Social network analysis: Foundations and frontiers on advantage. *Annual Review of Psychology, 64,* 527–547. http://dx.doi.org/10.1146/annurev-psych-113011-143828

Byrne, D. (1971). *The attraction paradigm*. New York, NY: Academic Press.

Casciaro, T., & Lobo, M. S. (2008). When competence is irrelevant: The role of interpersonal affect in task-related ties. *Administrative Science Quarterly, 53,* 655–684. http://dx.doi.org/10.2189/asqu.53.4.655

Cook, W. L. (1994). A structural equation model of dyadic relationships within the family system. *Journal of Consulting and Clinical Psychology, 62*, 500–509. http://dx.doi.org/10.1037/0022-006X.62.3.500

Eisenkraft, N., & Elfenbein, H. A. (2010). The way you make me feel: Evidence for individual differences in affective presence. *Psychological Science, 21*, 505–510. http://dx.doi.org/10.1177/0956797610364117

Emerson, R. M. (1976). Social exchange theory. *Annual Review of Sociology, 2*, 335–362. http://dx.doi.org/10.1146/annurev.so.02.080176.002003

Erez, A., Schilpzand, P., Leavitt, K., Woolum, A. H., & Judge, T. A. (2015). Inherently relational: Interactions between peers' and individuals' personalities impact reward giving and appraisal of individual performance. *Academy of Management Journal, 58*, 1761–1784. http://dx.doi.org/10.5465/amj.2011.0214

Ferris, G. R., Witt, L. A., & Hochwarter, W. A. (2001). Interaction of social skill and general mental ability on job performance and salary. *Journal of Applied Psychology, 86*, 1075–1082. http://dx.doi.org/10.1037/0021-9010.86.6.1075

Finkel, E. J., & Eastwick, P. W. (2008). Speed-dating. *Current Directions in Psychological Science, 17*, 193–197. http://dx.doi.org/10.1111/j.1467-8721.2008.00573.x

Finkel, E. J., Simpson, J. A., & Eastwick, P. W. (2017). The psychology of close relationships: Fourteen core principles. *Annual Review of Psychology, 68*, 383–411. http://dx.doi.org/10.1146/annurev-psych-010416-044038

Gelman, A., & Pardoe, I. (2006). Bayesian measures of explained variance and pooling in multilevel (hierarchical) models. *Technometrics, 48*, 241–251. http://dx.doi.org/10.1198/004017005000000517

Gonzalez, R., & Griffin, D. (2012). Dyadic data analysis. In H. Cooper, P. M. Camic, D. L. Long, A. T. Panter, D. Rindskopf, & K. J. Sher (Eds.), *APA handbook of research methods in psychology, Vol 3: Data analysis and research publication* (Vol. 3, pp. 439–450). Washington, DC: American Psychological Association. http://dx.doi.org/10.1037/13621-022

Gooty, J., & Yammarino, F. J. (2011). Dyads in organizational research: Conceptual issues and multilevel analyses. *Organizational Research Methods, 14*, 456–483. http://dx.doi.org/10.1177/1094428109358271

Grund, S., Lüdtke, O., & Robitzsch, A. (2016). Multiple imputation of missing covariate values in multilevel models with random slopes: A cautionary note. *Behavior Research Methods, 48*, 640–649. http://dx.doi.org/10.3758/s13428-015-0590-3

Hofmann, D. A., & Gavin, M. B. (1998). Centering decisions in hierarchical linear models: Implications for research in organizations. *Journal of Management, 24*, 623–641. http://dx.doi.org/10.1177/014920639802400504

Homans, G. C. (1958). Social behavior as exchange. *American Journal of Sociology, 63*, 597–606. http://dx.doi.org/10.1086/222355

Hox, J. (2002). *Multilevel analysis: Techniques and applications.* Mahwah, NJ: Lawrence Erlbaum.

Jones, S. L., & Shah, P. P. (2016). Diagnosing the locus of trust: A temporal perspective for trustor, trustee, and dyadic influences on perceived trustworthiness. *Journal of Applied Psychology, 101*, 392–414. http://dx.doi.org/10.1037/apl0000041

Joshi, A., & Knight, A. P. (2015). Who defers to whom and why? Dual pathways linking demographic differences and dyadic deference to team effectiveness. *Academy of Management Journal, 58*, 59–84. http://dx.doi.org/10.5465/amj.2013.0718

Katz, D., & Kahn, R. L. (1978). *The social psychology of organizations.* New York, NY: Wiley.

Kenny, D. A. (1994). *Interpersonal perception: A social relations analysis.* New York, NY: Guilford Press.

Kenny, D. A. (1996). Models of non-independence in dyadic research. *Journal of Social and Personal Relationships, 13*, 279–294. http://dx.doi.org/10.1177/0265407596132007

Kenny, D. A. (2016). *DyadR: Web programs for dyadic data analysis.* Retrieved from http://davidakenny.net/DyadR/DyadR.htm

Kenny, D. A., & Albright, L. (1987). Accuracy in interpersonal perception: A social relations analysis. *Psychological Bulletin, 102*, 390–402. http://dx.doi.org/10.1037/0033-2909.102.3.390

Kenny, D. A., & Kashy, D. A. (2011). Dyadic data analysis using multilevel modeling. In J. Hox & J. K. Roberts (Eds.), *Handbook of advanced multilevel analysis* (pp. 344–360). New York, NY: Routledge.

Kenny, D. A., Kashy, D. A., & Cook, W. L. (2006). *Dyadic data analysis.* New York, NY: Guilford Press.

Kenny, D. A., & La Voie, L. (1984). The social relations model. In L. Berkowitz (Ed.), *Advances in experimental social psychology* (Vol. 18, pp. 142–182). Orlando, FL: Academic Press.

Kenny, D. A., Mohr, C. D., & Levesque, M. J. (2001). A social relations variance partitioning of dyadic behavior. *Psychological Bulletin, 127*, 128–141. http://dx.doi.org/10.1037/0033-2909.127.1.128

Kenny, D. A., & Zaccaro, S. J. (1983). An estimate of variance due to traits in leadership. *Journal of Applied Psychology, 68*, 678–685. http://dx.doi.org/10.1037/0021-9010.68.4.678

Kilduff, G. J., Elfenbein, H. A., & Staw, B. M. (2010). The psychology of rivalry: A relationally dependent analysis of competition. *Academy of Management*

Journal, 53, 943–969. http://dx.doi.org/10.5465/
AMJ.2010.54533171

Klein, K. J., Dansereau, F., & Hall, R. J. (1994). Levels
issues in theory development, data collection, and
analysis. *Academy of Management Review, 19,*
195–229.

Krasikova, D. V., & LeBreton, J. M. (2012). Just the two
of us: Misalignment of theory and methods in
examining dyadic phenomena. *Journal of Applied
Psychology, 97,* 739–757. http://dx.doi.org/10.1037/
a0027962

Lam, C. K., van der Vegt, G. S., Walter, F., & Huang, X.
(2011). Harming high performers: A social comparison perspective on interpersonal harming in work
teams. *Journal of Applied Psychology, 96,* 588–601.
http://dx.doi.org/10.1037/a0021882

LeBreton, J. M., & Senter, J. L. (2008). Answers to 20 questions about interrater reliability and interrater agreement. *Organizational Research Methods, 11,* 815–852.
http://dx.doi.org/10.1177/1094428106296642

Leckie, G., & Charlton, C. (2012). runmlwin?: A
program to run the MLwiN multilevel modeling
software from within Stata. *Journal of Statistical
Software, 52,* 1–40. http://dx.doi.org/10.18637/
jss.v052.i11

Liden, R. C., Anand, S., & Vidyarthi, P. (2016). Dyadic
relationships. *Annual Review of Organizational
Psychology and Organizational Behavior, 3,*
139–166. http://dx.doi.org/10.1146/annurev-
orgpsych-041015-062452

Lüdtke, O., Robitzsch, A., Kenny, D. A., & Trautwein, U.
(2013). A general and flexible approach to estimating
the social relations model using Bayesian methods.
Psychological Methods, 18, 101–119. http://dx.doi.org/
10.1037/a0029252

Malloy, T. E., & Kenny, D. A. (1986). The social relations
model: An integrative method for personality
research. *Journal of Personality, 54,* 199–225. http://
dx.doi.org/10.1111/j.1467-6494.1986.tb00393.x

Mayer, R. C., Davis, J. H., & Schoorman, F. D. (1995). An
integrative model of organizational trust. *Academy of
Management Review, 20,* 709–734. http://dx.doi.org/
10.2307/258792

McAllister, D. J. (1995). Affect- and cognition-based trust
as foundations for interpersonal cooperation in organizations. *Academy of Management Journal, 38,* 24–59.

Nestler, S., Geukes, K., Hutteman, R., & Back, M. D.
(2017). Tackling longitudinal round-robin data:
A social relations growth model. *Psychometrika,
82,* 1162–1181. http://dx.doi.org/10.1007/
s11336-016-9546-5

Newcomb, T. M. (1961). *The acquaintance process.*
New York, NY: Holt, Rinehart & Winston.
http://dx.doi.org/10.1037/13156-000

Olsen, J. A., & Kenny, D. A. (2006). Structural equation
modeling with interchangeable dyads. *Psychological
Methods, 11,* 127–141. http://dx.doi.org/10.1037/
1082-989X.11.2.127

Pinheiro, J. C., Bates, D. M., DebRoy, S. S., Sarkar, D., &
R Core Team. (2016). *nlme: Linear and nonlinear mixed
effects models.* R package version 3.1-137. Retrieved
from https://cran.r-project.org/web/packages/nlme/
citation.html

Ripley, R., Boitmanis, K., & Snijders, T. A. (2013). *RSiena:
Siena—Simulation Investigation for Empirical Network
Analysis.* Retrieved from https://cran.r-project.org/
web/packages/RSiena/citation.html

Rousseau, D. M., Sitkin, S. B., Burt, R. S., & Camerer, C.
(1998). Not so different after all: A cross-discipline
view of trust. *Academy of Management Review, 23,*
393–404. http://dx.doi.org/10.5465/AMR.1998.926617

Schönbrodt, F. D., Back, M. D., & Schmukle, S. C. (2015).
*TripleR: Social relation model (SRM) analyses for single
or multiple groups.* R package version 1.5.3. Retrieved
from http://cran.r-project.org/package=TripleR/
index.html

Schönbrodt, F. D., Stas, L., & Loeys, T. (2016). *TripleR:
Social Relation Model (SRM) analyses for single or
multiple groups.* R package version 1.5.3. Retrieved
from http://cran.r-project.org/package=TripleR/
index.html

Schoorman, F. D., Mayer, R. C., & Davis, J. H. (2007).
An integrative model of organizational trust:
Past, present, and future. *Academy of Management
Review, 32,* 344–354. http://dx.doi.org/10.5465/
AMR.2007.24348410

Singer, J. D. (1998). Using SAS PROC MIXED to fit multilevel models, hierarchical models, and individual
growth models. *Journal of Educational and Behavioral
Statistics, 23,* 323–355. http://dx.doi.org/10.3102/
10769986023004323

Snijders, T. A. B., & Bosker, R. J. (1999). *Multilevel
analysis.* London, England: Sage.

Snijders, T. A. B., & Kenny, D. A. (1999). The social
relations model for family data: A multilevel approach.
Personal Relationships, 6, 471–486. http://dx.doi.org/
10.1111/j.1475-6811.1999.tb00204.x

Snijders, T. A. B., van de Bunt, G. G., & Steglich, C. E. G.
(2010). Introduction to stochastic actor-based models
for network dynamics. *Social Networks, 32,* 44–60.
http://dx.doi.org/10.1016/j.socnet.2009.02.004

Tse, H. H. M., & Ashkanasy, N. M. (2015). The dyadic
level of conceptualization and analysis: A missing link
in multilevel OB research? *Journal of Organizational
Behavior, 36,* 1176–1180. http://dx.doi.org/10.1002/
job.2010

Tsui, A. S., Egan, T. D., & O'Reilly III, C. A. (1992). Being
different: Relational demography and organizational
attachment. *Administrative Science Quarterly, 37,*
549–579. http://dx.doi.org/10.2307/2393472

van der Vegt, G. S., Bunderson, J. S., & Oosterhof, A. (2006). Expertness diversity and interpersonal helping in teams: Why those who need the most help end up getting the least. *Academy of Management Journal, 49*, 877–893. http://dx.doi.org/10.5465/AMJ.2006.22798169

van Duijn, M. A. J., Snijders, T. A. B., & Zijlstra, B. J. H. (2004). p_2: A random effects model with covariates for directed graphs. *Statistica Neerlandica, 58*, 234–254. http://dx.doi.org/10.1046/j.0039-0402.2003.00258.x

van Knippenberg, D., & Schippers, M. C. (2007). Work group diversity. *Annual Review of Psychology, 58*, 515–541. http://dx.doi.org/10.1146/annurev.psych.58.110405.085546

Warner, R. M., Kenny, D. A., & Stoto, M. (1979). A new round robin analysis of variance for social interaction data. *Journal of Personality and Social Psychology, 37*, 1742–1757. http://dx.doi.org/10.1037/0022-3514.37.10.1742

Wasserman, S., & Faust, K. (1994). *Social network analysis: Methods and applications*. Cambridge, England: Cambridge University Press. http://dx.doi.org/10.1017/CBO9780511815478

Weick, K. E. (1979). *The social psychology of organizing* (2nd ed.). Reading, MA: Addison-Wesley.

Weick, K. E. (1995). *Sensemaking in organizations*. Thousand Oaks, CA: Sage.

Williams, K. Y., & O'Reilly, C. A. (1998). Demography and diversity in organizations: A review of 40 years of research. In B. M. Staw (Ed.), *Research in organizational behavior* (Vol. 20, pp. 77–140). Greenwich, CT: JAI Press.

Zhang, Z., Parker, R. M. A., Charlton, C. M. J., Leckie, G., & Browne, W. J. (2016). R2MLwiN?: A package to run MLwiN from within R. *Journal of Statistical Software, VV*(II), 1–46.

Zijlstra, B. J. H., van Duijn, M. A. J., & Snijders, T. A. B. (2006). The multilevel p2 model: A random effects model for the analysis of multiple social networks. *Methodology; European Journal of Research Methods and Social Sciences, 2*, 42–47. http://dx.doi.org/10.1027/1614-2241.2.1.42

## CHAPTER 19

A PRIMER ON MULTILEVEL STRUCTURAL MODELING: USER-FRIENDLY GUIDELINES

Robert J. Vandenberg and Hettie A. Richardson

We were invited by the volume's editors to contribute a "nuts 'n' bolts" chapter on how to conduct multilevel structural equation modeling (MLSEM).[1] To fulfill this mandate, we present a model-testing process, beginning with an example of a null model (no predictors) and ending with a test of a conceptual framework that includes covariates at both Level 1 (a.k.a., the within level) and Level 2 (a.k.a., the between level). Before explaining this process and presenting the conceptual framework, we briefly describe why researchers might consider using MLSEM analysis rather than the traditional non–structural equation modeling (SEM) approach. Embedded within the latter is an explanation of why the MLSEM examples in this chapter were all analyzed using the M*plus* software package (L. K. Muthén & Muthén, 1998–2015).[2] We note that, whereas each example's complete syntax is in the body of this chapter, M*plus* output is quite extensive. To facilitate use of this chapter as a learning tool, we include within it excerpts from M*plus* output that are most necessary for interpreting the primary outcomes for each example. Complete M*plus* (.inp) syntax and output (.out) files, as well as the data used in the examples, may be downloaded at http://pubs.apa.org/books/supp/humphrey/.

WHY MLSEM?

Given the complexities associated with SEM in general, and perhaps the need to learn a statistical package (i.e., M*plus*), readers may question the value in employing MLSEM relative to alternative multilevel analysis options. As noted in Heck and Thomas (2015; cf. Mehta & Neale, 2005), there are two primary advantages to using SEM (regardless of the specific form of analysis); they are (a) incorporation of latent variables and (b) adjustment of the latent variables and the estimated relationships between them for measurement error. Non-SEM multilevel-analytical procedures have neither of these advantages. Assuming a validated multi-item measure (e.g., job satisfaction, perceived organizational support) is used to represent a construct in a multilevel framework, the common practice in the non-SEM approach is to compute the mean across items and to use this value to represent the construct in subsequent analyses. As is well documented, this practice inappropriately assumes that the mean is a perfect representation of the underlying construct and has no measurement error. It is also common to report the reliability coefficient in non-SEM multilevel studies. Ironically, use of such a statistic indicates that, contrary to

---

[1] A "nuts 'n' bolts" perspective is exactly what we provide. It is, therefore, assumed that the reader has an understanding of the principles underlying CFA and SEM, as we will not be reviewing those principles here. It is also assumed that the reader possesses an understanding of the random coefficients modeling (non-SEM) approach to multilevel analyses.

[2] All uses of the term M*plus* from this point forward are credited to L. K. Muthén and B. O. Muthén (1998–2015).

http://dx.doi.org/10.1037/0000115-020
The Handbook of Multilevel Theory, Measurement, and Analysis, S. E. Humphrey and J. M. LeBreton (Editors-in-Chief)

what is assumed during the analyses, the referenced measure is indeed imperfect. As a side note, Cronbach's coefficient alpha, which is frequently computed as the index of reliability, is inferior in many respects to the composite reliability index that can be computed within SEM (for a succinct explanation from an unknown blog author, see http://zencaroline.blogspot.com.au/2007/06/composite-reliability.html).

Imperfect measurement is not inconsequential. The greater the imperfection, the greater is the likelihood of attenuating observed relationships among measures representing one's constructs of interest. This concern is salient across levels in a multilevel analysis. The confirmatory factor analysis (CFA) aspect of general SEM attempts to accommodate a measure's imperfection. Specifically, the researcher hypothesizes that a latent factor (unobserved variable) accounts for the variances and covariances among a set of items (observed or manifest variables) representing a given construct and, that the latter item set is not accounted for by any other latent factor that may be specified (Bollen, 1989; Heck & Thomas, 2015). For present purposes, two of the more important outcomes of the CFA are the factor loadings (lambda values) and error-uniqueness terms (theta-delta or theta-epsilon values) for each item representing a given construct. The latent variables and associations between them are adjusted for measurement error through these values. To illustrate, a standardized lambda is the unique correlation of an item with its underlying latent variable. Squaring the standardized lambda quantifies the item's unique reliability as it pertains to its relationship with its latent variable. Subtracting the squared lambda value from one and multiplying that difference with the item's variance produces the error-uniqueness term for the item (i.e., the amount of total variance due to unreliability).

The term *unique* in the last few sentences above is important. Namely, items representing the same underlying construct are likely to each have different lambda values and, consequently, different error-uniqueness terms. Put another way, how reliably they represent the underlying construct varies from item to item. Items exhibiting this kind of variation

are often referred to as a congeneric item set because both the factor loadings (lambdas) and the error-uniqueness terms are unique to each item, even though they presumably operationalize the same construct. Accounting for this variation is essentially the adjustment for error within each latent variable. As such, when estimating the parameters representing the hypothesized relationships among the latent variables, the parameter estimates will be disattenuated from measurement error (Bollen, 1989; Heck & Thomas, 2015).

When only using the mean across an item set to represent a multi-item measure in a multilevel analysis, the researcher is inadvertently assuming there is tau equivalence among items; that is, the items have the same degree of association with the underlying construct and the same error-uniqueness terms. This assumption rarely reflects the real world and, as such, the more realistic assumptions allowed in SEM is one of the reasons a multilevel researcher may want to consider an MLSEM approach. The congeneric nature of the item set also underlies our assertion that computing the composite reliability index may be a better alternative than computing Cronbach's coefficient alpha as the index of reliability. As is the case when averaging values across items, coefficient alpha assumes tau equivalence among items. Again, tau equivalence is not a realistic characterization of how items relate to their underlying construct. The composite reliability index is more credible, however, because its calculation takes into consideration the variability among the factor loadings and error-uniqueness terms for the set of items operationalizing a given construct. Therefore, even if a researcher will eventually apply a non-SEM analysis to his/her multilevel model (i.e., use means to represent constructs), we recommend reporting the composite reliability index instead of Cronbach's coefficient alpha.

Assuming the potential value of MLSEM is now apparent, readers might further wonder why they should use M*plus* (i.e., as opposed to another statistical package) to conduct MLSEM. The simplest answer is convenience and functionality. Initially, we primarily used hierarchical linear modeling (HLM) (Raudenbush & Bryk, 2002) for multilevel analyses. Given that our multilevel "needs" were quite simple in those days, using observed, nonlatent variables, and limiting the number of outcome variables to one seemed sufficient.[3]

As our familiarity with multilevel modeling expanded, it became apparent how useful M*plus* would be for employing latent variables instead of means to operationalize underlying constructs. Further, M*plus* allows researchers to build rather complex models including a mix of latent and observed-only variables, as well as address mediation hypotheses and other less straightforward conceptual expectations.

M*plus* is certainly not the only SEM package to offer multilevel functionality. Although we do not use either, both EQS (http://www.mvsoft.com/eqs60.htm) and LISREL (http://www.ssicentral.com/lisrel/index.html#overview) have MLSEM functionality. Our personal preference for M*plus* should not be interpreted as an endorsement of M*plus* over EQS or LISREL, or as an indication that M*plus* is inherently superior. We have never compared the MLSEM functionality of the various packages, and it is our understanding that they should be equivalent. Rather, our use of M*plus* is driven by the fact that we have completed the learning curve process for using it, and it fully meets our multilevel needs. As such, we have had little incentive to invest time in mastering other statistical packages.

Given that neither author is an R user, we reached out to Professor Paul Bliese (University of South Carolina) via email and asked him whether MLSEM is supported in R. He was uncertain as to the answer, so he in turn reached out to Professor Jonas Lang (University of Ghent). The following is the actual email transcript from Professor Lang (personal communication, January 26, 2017):

> Open Mx http://openmx.ssri.psu.edu/ is an R package which is now also on CRAN and is basically capable of doing many things that Mplus can do including multilevel SEM. However, it is painful to use it for more complex models. The user interface is very matrix based (a bit like early versions of Lisrel).
>
> * * *
>
> https://github.com/OpenMx/OpenMx/blob/master/inst/models/nightly/MultilevelStateSpaceEx5.R
> http://psychological-research.org/R/OpenMx-ML-SEM_3-univariate-ri-rs.html
> * * *Basic Multilevel Modeling SEM is possible with standard SEM packages that support multi group SEM using the basic Muthen Method from 1994.
> * * * http://stats.stackexchange.com/questions/10996/r-package-for-multilevel-structural-equation-modeling
> http://smr.sagepub.com/content/22/3/376.short
>
> There is a new xxM package that seems to do it. I have not looked into it. http://xxm.times.uh.edu/
>
> The best hope for an easy to use Mplus-like R interface for the future is the lavaan package by my Ugent colleague Yves Roseel. Lavaan is the most frequently used SEM package and easy to use. However, the current version does not support multilevel SEM. I talked to Yves in September and he said that he is working on a multilevel module and is planning to release something in 2017.
>
> * * *Some multilevel CFA models can be fit in lmer (typically somewhat simplified). A good strategy is typically to look at examples/documentation for the GLLAMM package in Stata that uses an integrative SEM/mixed modeling approach and see what can be implemented in R. There is now a new package called mediation which implements the most state of the art multilevel mediation approach (Imai et al.) using lmer.
>
> * * *
>
> The latest version of the Bayesian package MCMCglmm has a path function which can fit a lot of multilevel SEM models. However, MCMCglmm comes from a

---

[3]Incidentally, M*plus* provides very similar estimates (within a 1,000th decimal point) to HLM for simple observed variable, single-outcome models.

451

biology tradition so it is sometimes hard to translate what they do into the typical psychology thinking and the documentation does not yet include examples.

We visited each of the links provided by Professor Lang and reviewed the documentation with one question in mind. Namely, could we evaluate the conceptual model anchoring the examples in the current chapter using any of the R packages? While the xxM R package showed the greatest promise in our opinion, the answer was "no" in all cases. Even Professor Lang in a later email told us "I still do multilevel SEM with Mplus but use R for everything else and I look forward to making the switch for multilevel SEM, too! Jonas" (personal communication, January 26, 2017).

To summarize, there were two goals to this first section. Goal 1 was to provide a rationale for why a researcher might want to consider a MLSEM approach over a non-SEM approach in testing a multilevel model. The primary reason is to account for measurement error when estimating the latent variables and conceptual paths between them. Goal 2 was to explain our use of M*plus* and make readers aware of other commercial and free-ware packages. Our use as stated is one of convenience and functionality. Of course, when the variables under consideration are all observed (i.e., they are not multi-item measures of some underlying construct), almost any of the multilevel packages *may* suffice. "May" is stressed to emphasize that we have not made any direct comparisons across packages. We turn now to the conceptual model which is the basis for the examples used throughout this chapter and then to a step-by-step guide to the actual empirical illustrations.

CONCEPTUAL BASIS FOR THE EXAMPLES

As should be the case with all data collection efforts, it is assumed there is a conceptual framework driving one's activities. Further, it is the researcher's goal to *eventually* test this framework as it represents a set of focal hypotheses critical to achieving support for

the underlying theory. For purposes of the current chapter, the frameworks we will *build up to* testing are presented in Figures 19.1 and 19.2.

Emphasis on *eventually* and *build up to* denotes that the researcher does not jump to testing the full model immediately after completing data collection. Rather, some assumptions need to be examined first. It is only after meeting these assumptions that the full model may be evaluated. Two important initial steps are (a) testing the measurement model of the latent variables (completing a multilevel CFA [MLCFA]) before placing directional arrows between constructs; and (b) justifying the aggregation of the higher level variables (e.g., group perceptions of transformational leadership [TL] and group climate of high involvement work processes [HIWP]—in the present example, see the large arrows pointing upward) from the within (i.e., within group) level to the between (i.e., between group) level using similarity indices (LeBreton & Senter, 2008). A complete explanation of these assumptions is given in subsequent sections.

The model in Figure 19.1[4] is based on the second author's dissertation (Richardson, 2001) and one of the publications to emerge from that dissertation (Richardson & Vandenberg, 2005). Definitions of the constructs shown in Figure 19.1 and sample items from the utilized measures are presented in Table 19.1. At the within level (i.e., Level 1), the model includes two key constructs. *TL* is a perceived set of behaviors via which leaders seek to increase follower awareness of task outcomes, activate the followers' higher order needs, and stimulate followers to act in the interests of the unit or organization (Podsakoff, MacKenzie, Moorman, & Fetter, 1990). HIWP is believed to result from organizational practices and/or leader behaviors, and reflects perceptions that employees experience four attributes at work: (a) *power* to act and make decisions, (b) *information* to make accurate decisions, (c) *knowledge* needed to use power effectively, and (d) *rewards* for doing so (Lawler, 1996).

In the present model, an individual employee's perceptions of HIWP can be thought of as a psychological climate that is based on his/her personal beliefs

---

[4]Variables in all figures represented by ellipses are latent variables, each with an underlying measurement model consisting of a set of observed/manifest variables. The manifest variables are not shown in Figures 19.1 and 19.2 to reduce visual complexity. Variable labels encased in rectangles are observed variables only.

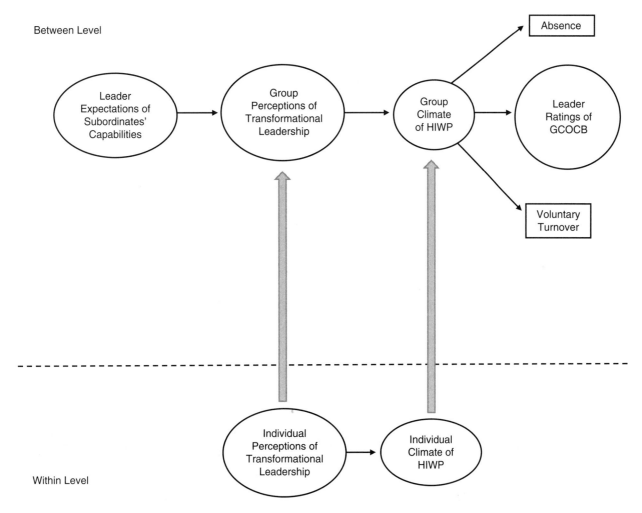

FIGURE 19.1.   Hypothetical conceptual framework. GCOCB = Group Collective Organizational Citizenship
Behavior; HIWP = high involvement work processes.

about features of the work setting to which he/she
attaches meaning (Schneider & Reichers, 1983). As is
the case with any individual psychological climate, an
employee's perceptions about HIWP serve as a frame
of reference for guiding his/her individual behaviors
(Zohar, 1980), although we do not consider individual
behaviors in the present model. Because leadership
by an immediate supervisor is a key filter through
which employees experience organizational practices
and interpret the work environment (Kozlowski &
Doherty, 1989), the theoretical expectation is that an
individual employee's perceptions of his or her leader's
ambient treatment of group members in general
(i.e., TL) will be positively associated with his/her
individual perceptions of HIWP.

At the between level (i.e., Level 2), the proposed
model draws on principles of self-fulfilling prophecy

(Eden, 1990) to suggest that the group leader's
perceptions of whether group members are capable
of operating effectively in a HIWP context (i.e.,
leader expectations [LE] and signaling of those
expectations) should be positively associated with
TL behaviors as perceived by the collective group,
which in turn should be positively associated
with the group climate for HIWP. Because they are
collective (i.e., as opposed to individual as is the
case at Level 1), these two variables reflect meanings that are shared among employees within a
work group, and they emerge when interpretations
across employees converge in similar or agreed-
upon perceptions. This definition implies that,
even though any one employee may not personally experience the attributes of the climate, the
group as a whole tends to perceive the attributes

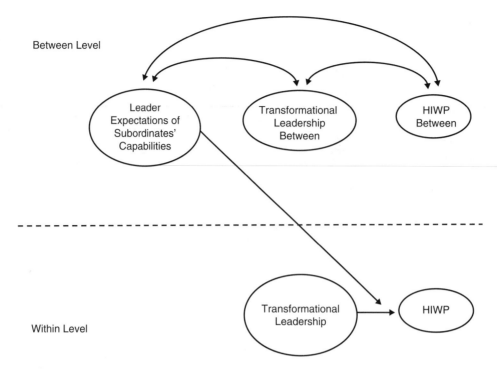

FIGURE 19.2.   Hypothetical conceptual framework with random slope vector and controlling for nonindependence. HIWP = high involvement work processes.

TABLE 19.1

Summary Constructs and Definitions, With Sample Items

Construct name (level)	Rating source	Construct definition and explanation (number of items in measure*)	Sample items
Leader expectations of subordinates' capabilities (between, Level 2)	Leaders	Leader beliefs that his/her employees, as a group, are capable of performing in the ways required by involvement (5 items reduced to 2 parcels and one single item as indicators)	"I believe my subordinates have good decision-making abilities."
Individual perceptions of transformational leadership (within, Level 1)	Individual group members	Individual employee perceptions about how group members as a whole are treated by the leader; comprised of four dimensions: ■ Individualized support (3 items combined into 1 parcel) ■ High performance expectations (3 items combined into 1 parcel) ■ Role modeling (3 items combined into 1 parcel) ■ Confidence in followers (3 items combined into 1 parcel)	■ "My supervisor behaves in a manner that is thoughtful of the needs of my work unit." ■ "My supervisor will not settle for second best from members of my work unit." ■ "My supervisor leads by example." ■ "My supervisor shows members of my work unit that he/she strongly believes in their abilities."

TABLE 19.1

Summary Constructs and Definitions, With Sample Items (*Continued*)

Construct name (level)	Rating source	Construct definition and explanation (number of items in measure)	Sample items
Group perceptions of transformational leadership (between, Level 2)	Individual group members nested within groups/leaders	Collective, group-level perceptions about how group members as a whole are treated by the leader; isomorphic to the individual-level construct; created by averaging individual group member ratings within work groups (12 items total combined into 4 dimension-based parcels, as described above)	Items are identical to those used for the within-level transformational leadership behavior construct
Individual psychological climate of high involvement work processes (within, Level 1)	Individual group members	Individual employee perceptions that members within his/her group experience four attributes (dimensions): ▪ Power to act and make decisions (2 items combined into 1 parcel) ▪ Information about business results and goals (2 items combined into 1 parcel) ▪ Rewards tied to performance and growth (2 items combined into 1 parcel) ▪ Knowledge of work and business (2 items combined into 1 parcel)	▪ "My work unit has enough freedom over how we do our jobs." ▪ "Management communicates a clear organizational mission and how each unit contributes to achieving that mission." ▪ "There is a strong link between how well members of my work unit perform their jobs and the likelihood of their receiving recognition and praise." ▪ "Members of my work unit have had sufficient job-related training."
Group climate of high involvement work processes (between, Level 2)	Individual group members nested within groups/leaders	Collective, group-level perceptions that employees within that group experience the four involvement climate attributes (dimensions); isomorphic to the individual-level; created by averaging the individual ratings within work groups (8 items total combined into 4 dimension-based parcels, as described above)	Items are identical to those used for the within-level high involvement work processes construct
Absence rate (between, Level 2)	Archival records	Annual rate of absenteeism averaged for the work group (1 calculated item)	Average number of employees on work group payroll, total number of workdays for the year, the number of worker-days lost through absence
Group Collective Organizational Citizenship Behavior (between, Level 2)	Leaders	Discretionary, extra-role behavior that is not explicitly linked to a given job and is focused on improving the work group or organization; demonstrated on average across work-group employees (5 items reduced to 2 parcels and one single item as indicators)	"My subordinates make suggestions to improve work procedures."
Voluntary turnover rate (between, Level 2)	Archival records	Annual rate of turnover averaged for the work group (1 calculated item)	Average number of employees on work group payroll, total number of workdays for the year, the number of worker-days lost through voluntary separations

Note. Items comprising each construct were combined into "parcels" of two or more items averaged together (Hall, Snell, & Foust, 1999). When constructs were comprised of multiple underlying dimensions (i.e., the transformational leadership and high involvement work processes constructs), parcels were created by averaging the items within dimensions such that each latent indicator parcel reflected a single dimension. Otherwise, parcels were created by randomly combining items. Note that parceling is not required for multilevel confirmatory factor analysis or multilevel structural equation modeling. We used parceling only as a means of simplifying a complex model and reducing the number of parameters to be estimated.

as part of the work environment and is likely to behave accordingly. As such, a group climate for HIWP should be negatively associated with *absence* and *voluntary turnover rates* for the group and positively associated with the leader's rating of the *Group's Collective Organizational Citizenship Behavior* (GCOCB; that is, the extent to which the group as a whole engages in discretionary behaviors intended to improve the work group or organization).

Reserving a more complete explanation for a later section, the framework in Figure 19.2 depicts a cross-level interaction hypothesis. Namely, we expect the slope of the relationship from TL to HIWP to vary across groups (random vector of slope coefficients) as a function of LE. We include this model because testing Figure 19.1 involves only the random vector of intercepts. Further, we illustrate with Figure 19.2 how a researcher may control for nonindependence among observations when conceptual interest only resides at the within or individual level.

As suggested by the description above, the model presented in Figure 19.1 is at multiple levels in that it reflects individuals (Level 1) nested within workgroups (Level 2) that are directly supervised by given leader (also Level 2). The MLCFA and MLSEM techniques that we present below, however, are applicable to many other types and degrees of multilevel nesting. For instance, our data could be modeled with a third level, indicating that the workgroups are further nested within organizations. Scholars working in other areas might wish to model children (Level 1) nested in classrooms (Level 2), or perhaps neighborhoods (Level 1) nested within cities or municipalities (Level 2). In turn, these could be respectively nested within schools (Level 3) and school districts (Level 4), and in counties (Level 3) and states (Level 4). Repeated observations (Level 1) could likewise be nested in individuals (Level 2), such as when researchers monitor within-patient variation in symptoms in response to medication, therapy, or other intervention. Such a design would also allow scholars to investigate whether there is within-person fluctuation in emotion despite person-level tendencies to experience characteristic positive or negative affect across time and situations.

In a similar vein, temporal observation periods can be nested within one another such that hourly observations (Level 1) could be nested within days (Level 2), which are nested in weeks, months, and years (Levels 3, 4, and 5, respectively). Heck and Thomas (2015) presented excellent examples of three-level models using both non-SEM and MLSEM analyses.

In the present case, data were collected across 167 work groups, with data for each group coming from five randomly sampled members for a total sample size of 835 individuals. There are three unique features to the model in Figure 19.1. The first is that TL and HIWP are the only variables in the model collected at the level of individual group members (i.e., Level 1) and aggregated up to the group level (i.e., Level 2). Second, the observed variables/items operationalizing the LE and GCOCB latent variables were completed by only the 167 group leaders (none of whom were one of the five group members who responded to the TL and HIWP items). The third unique feature is that the absence and turnover data were taken from archival records. In other words, the data to test Figure 19.1 came from three different sources.

The forthcoming material is guided by Raudenbush and Bryk's (2002) principles of estimation and hypothesis testing (see Chapter 1), and by Heck and Thomas (2015). In general, one starts with a null model and eventually builds toward testing the full conceptual model. Our null model starts by addressing whether for TL and HIWP there is significant variability at the between level (groups in the current case) and whether aggregation is justified, which is determined by calculating ICC(1) and ICC(2) values. Assuming the latter yields positive outcomes, we move to the hypothesis testing phase. This phase begins by using MLCFA to test the expectation that the measurement model for the latent variables at both levels combined is adequate. If this expectation is supported, it is then appropriate to evaluate the hypotheses represented by the directional arrows in Figure 19.1. The major difference between what is currently presented and that which is in Raudenbush and Bryk's book is our use of SEM and their use of non-SEM analytic procedures.

Our model is consistent, however, with material presented in Heck and Thomas.

AGGREGATION ASSUMPTIONS

As noted by Raudenbush and Bryk (2002), point estimation procedures are undertaken to determine whether there is significant between-level variance on the variables that are aggregated to Level 2 (the group level in our data). The presumption is that there is a very low probability of finding significant associations of the aggregated collective (i.e., group-level) variables to or from other variables at the between level if between-group differences on the aggregated variables are statistically nonsignificant. Within a non-SEM context, these differences are

commonly evaluated using an analysis of variance (ANOVA) approach. As illustrated in Figure 19.3, the SEM analogy to the latter is a MLCFA of the aggregated variables. The underlying logic of MLCFA is based on the following equation:

$$y_{ci} = \tau + \lambda\eta_{ci} + \varepsilon_{ci}, \qquad (19.1)$$

where y = the vector of items/observed variables operationalizing some construct, τ (tau) = the vector of intercepts/means, λ (lambda) = the vector of factor loadings, η (eta) = the relevant latent factor, and ε (epsilon) = the vector of item residuals/uniqueness. Critically important in Equation 19.1 is the subscript "ci". This subscript denotes that the individual responses, "i", on the observed variables are no

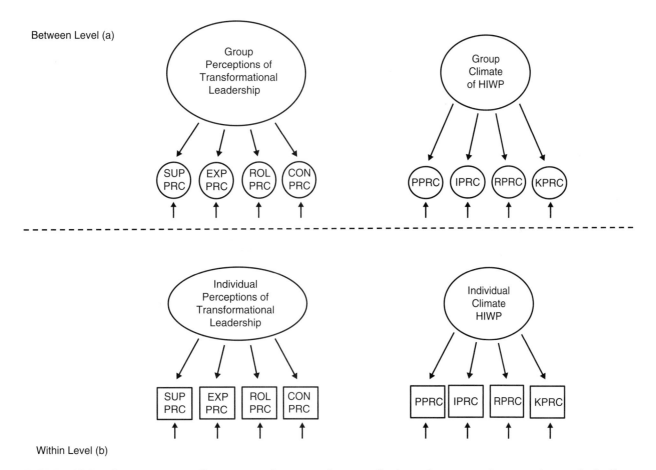

FIGURE 19.3.   Aggregation justification. Based on prior theoretically derived operationalizations (i.e., Podsakoff et al., 1990; Vandenberg et al., 1999), transformational leadership and high involvement work processes (HIWP) are each comprised of four underlying dimensions (at both levels) created by averaging the items measuring each of those dimensions. SUPPRC = parcel of individualized support items; EXPPRC = parcel of exhibiting high performance expectations items; ROLPRC = parcel of role modeling items; CONPRC = parcel of confidence in followers' items; PPRC = parcel of power items; IPRC = parcel of information items; RPRC = parcel of rewards items; KPRC = parcel of knowledge items (see also Table 19.2).

longer independent (i.e., totally idiosyncratic), but the responses are now also conditional on belonging to some cluster, "c" (groups in the current case). It is beyond our scope to provide the technical logic underlying the following statement, but excellent treatments are provided by B. O. Muthén (1994), and B. O. Muthén and Satorra (1995). Namely, what Equation 19.1 ultimately means is that there is a measurement model at the within-group level (i.e., Level 1) representing only that part of the responses due to the individual, "i", and a separate measurement model at the between-group level (i.e., Level 2) representing that part of the responses due to belonging to a specific cluster/group, "c". Therefore, Equation 19.1 may be expanded to reflect the following:

$$y_{ci} = \tau + \Lambda_B \eta_{Bc} + \varepsilon_{Bc} + \Lambda_W \eta_{Wci} + \varepsilon_{Wci}, \quad (19.2)$$

where y_{ci} = the vector of responses for the ith person in the cth cluster; τ = the vector of intercepts; Λ_B (lambda between) and Λ_W (lambda within) = matrices of factor loadings; η_{Bc} = the latent between factor varying randomly among/between clusters; η_{Wci} = the latent within factor varying randomly over individuals in clusters; and ε_{Bc} and ε_{Wci} = between and within residuals/uniqueness, respectively.

Taking a more pragmatic perspective to Figure 19.3, the preceding indicates that the responses and corresponding latent variable at the within level (Level 1) are based on all 835 individuals in the present sample, independent of the groups to which they belong. Similarly, the observed variables and corresponding latent variable at the between level (Level 2) are based on the 167 groups independent of the 835 individuals belonging to those groups. In short, we like to say that the within level is that part due to what "I" as an individual contribute to the responses uninfluenced by the fact that I belong to some cluster or group. In turn, the between level is that part due to what "we" collectively contribute. The observed variables for TL and HIWP at the between level are the 167 group intercepts or taus (τ). They are encased in circles or ellipses because they are themselves latent variables derived from the measurement model at the within level (Heck & Thomas, 2015; Mehta & Neale, 2005; B. O. Muthén, 1994; B. O. Muthén & Satorra, 1995).

Of importance is the statistical significance of the variance of the latent variable, η_{Bc}. If it is statistically significant, the assumption of between-group differences on the aggregated variable has been satisfied.

The following M*plus* syntax provides this evaluation for the TL within and between latent variables. A summary key to the latent construct and observed/manifest indicator labels used in this and all other syntax in this chapter is presented in Table 19.2.

TABLE 19.2

Key to Construct, Variable, and Item Labels as Used in Syntax and Output

Full latent construct and observed variable names	Latent construct labels	Manifest indicator and observed variable labels*
Leader expectations of subordinates' capabilities (between, Level 2)	LE	SUBPRC1 SUBPRC2 EXPSUB5
Individual perceptions of transformational leadership (within, Level 1)	TRANSIND	SUPPRC1 EXPPRC1 ROLPRC1 CONFPRC1
Group perceptions of transformational leadership (between, Level 2)	TRANSBET	SUPPRC1 EXPPRC1 ROLPRC1 CONFPRC1
Individual psychological climate of high involvement work processes (within, Level 1)	HIWPIND	PPRC1 IPRC1 RPRC1 KPRC1
Group climate of high involvement work processes (between, Level 2)	HIWPBET	PPRC1 IPRC1 RPRC1 KPRC1
Absence rate (between, Level 2)		ABSRATE
Group Collective Organizational Citizenship Behavior (between, Level 2)	GROUPOCB	OCBPRC1 OCBPRC2 OCBPRC3
Voluntary turnover rate (between, Level 2)		VOLRATE
Group identification (clustering variable)		GID

Note. *The letters "PRC" indicate a parcel of two or more manifest items.

Title: One-Way CFA - Transformational Leaders—
Figure 19.3a

DATA: FILE IS
C:\Users\rvandenb\Dropbox\Projects\CARMA\
    MLSEM\Data\demo2txtchapt.dat;

Variable: Names are GID SUBPRC1 SUBPRC2
    EXPSUB5 SUPPRC1 EXPPRC1 ROLPRC1
    CONFPRC1 PPRC2 IPRC1 RPRC1 KPRC1
    OCBPRC1 OCBPRC2 OCBPRC3 ABSRATE
    VOLRATE;

Usevariables are GID SUPPRC1 EXPPRC1
ROLPRC1 CONFPRC1;

Cluster is GID;
ANALYSIS: TYPE = TWOLEVEL;
MODEL:
%WITHIN%
TransInd by SUPPRC1 EXPPRC1 ROLPRC1
    CONFPRC1;
TransInd (MSWTr);

%BETWEEN%
TransBet by SUPPRC1 EXPPRC1 ROLPRC1
    CONFPRC1;
TransBet (MSBTr);

Model Constraint:

New (ICC1BR ICC2 ICC2A);
ICC1BR = MSBTr / (MSBTr +MSWTr);
!Based on BrykandRaudenbusch, eq. 4.6, p.71
ICC2 = MSBTr / (MSBTr +(MSWTr/5));
!Based on BrykandRaudenbusch, eq. 4.7, p.72
ICC2a = (5 ∗ ICC1BR)/(1 +(4 ∗ ICC1BR));
!Based on Bliese, eq. 1 on p. 357

Output: Sampstat Residual Tech1 CINT
    Stand(STDYX);

All M*plus* analyses require a "Title:" command
followed by some user specified designation for a
particular run. The "Data: File is" command is likewise required, and it instructs M*plus* where the data
file is located. The location in this example is obviously in the first author's Dropbox cloud under a
number of subfolders. The "demo2txtchapt.dat" is a
tab-delimited text file in which each column is a
variable and each row is an individual respondent.

Data in our shop are typically entered in either SPSS or
EXCEL. However, any data management system associated with any of the major statistical software packages will suffice. Before exporting an M*plus* readable
file, we will undertake data integrity checks such as
detecting out of range values, evaluating skewness and
kurtosis, and most importantly, evaluating whether
missing values are missing at random, or missing not a
random. The current example had no missing data, but
if there had been, we would have used 99999 for each
missing data point (i.e., because this value would not
match any valid responses for items in the data set).
M*plus* accepts text (e.g., .dat; .txt) or csv files. Further,
whereas the current example is a raw data file, M*plus*
also accepts files of variance-covariance matrices,
means, and other types. If a file has an unusual format
to it, one can use the "format" command to instruct
M*plus* as to the proper structure.

The "Variable: Names are" command provides
the labels for each column of variables in the data
file. Therefore, the first column is labeled GID
(Group IDentification number), the second column
SUBPRC1 (the first item parcel for leader expectations of subordinates' capabilities), and so forth. The
"Usevariables are . . ." line instructs M*plus* that only
those five variables will be used in the immediate
analyses. "GID" is our label for the first column—
it could have been labeled anything. The five individuals in the first group all have values of "1" in
this column. Those in the second group have values
of "2", and so forth until the five individuals in the
167th group all have values of "167" in this column.
The other four variables are the labels for the four
TL observed variables as shown in Figure 19.3a. The
"Cluster is" line instructs M*plus* to use GID as the
variable around which to create the between-group
variables. Therefore, everyone with a GID of "1"
is treated as one cluster, and those with a GID of
"2" as another cluster, etc. "ANALYSIS: TYPE =
TWOLEVEL" instructs M*plus* that a multilevel
analysis is forthcoming. Specifically, it evokes the
algorithm to estimate the random vector of intercepts to be used in the multilevel framework defined
in the MODEL statement. The "ANALYSIS: TYPE =
TWOLEVEL" line needs an additional specification
to also estimate the random vector of slopes, which
we provide when we test Figure 19.2.

The "MODEL:" command is required in that M*plus* expects the syntax operationalizing the primary analyses to follow it. That operationalization in the current case is to define measurement models at the within (Level 1) and between (Level 2) levels. Any syntax under the "%WITHIN%" command is executed on the variance/covariance matrix of the individuals disattenuated from their respective groups, and the syntax following "%BETWEEN%" is executed on variance/covariance matrix of the cluster/groups. Under "%WITHIN%", the "TransInd by SUPPRC1 EXPPRC1 ROLPRC1 CONFPRC1" line instructs M*plus* to create a latent variable called TransInd (this is a user provided label, i.e., referencing TL at the individual level in this case) and define its measurement model using the four manifest variables following the "by" command. The first observed variable is selected by default in M*plus* as the referent indicator. Similarly, the "TransBet by SUPPRC1 EXPPRC1 ROLPRC1 CONFPRC1" line under "%BETWEEN%" creates the latent variable titled TransBet (TL at the between level; again, a user-provided label) using the manifest variables following the "by" command to define its measurement model.

Two cautionary notes are warranted. First, the names of the latent variables at both levels must differ from one another—hence, our use of "Ind" in one and "Bet" in the other. Second, given that the labels are identical for the manifest variables following the two "by" commands, a person could falsely conclude that the same observed variables are being used at both levels. Recall, however, that it is the variance/covariance matrix of the 835 individual scores disattenuated from their respective groups analyzed at the within level. In contrast, it is the variance/covariance matrix among the 167 cluster/group-level intercepts/tau values used at the between level.

The syntax as described above is enough to compute and test whether the variance of the latent variable at the between level, η_{Bc}, is statistically significant. However, we have built into our syntax an extra feature that also derives the ICC(1) and ICC(2) values for the latent variable. As LeBreton and Senter (2008) noted, these are two of the more important justifications for aggregation among the many available alternatives. The relevant syntax starts with the command lines "TransInd (MSWTr)" and "TransBet (MSBTr)". Within M*plus*, anytime a variable name (observed, or latent—as in the current case) is specified on its own (i.e., not within brackets), it alerts M*plus* that you are going to do something with the variance of that variable. In the present example, these commands are respectively instructing M*plus* to internally label the variance of the TL latent variable at the individual level using "MSWTr" and to use "MSBTr" to internally label the variance of the TL latent variable at the between level.

A valuable feature in M*plus* is the ability to define and execute equations using "Model Constraint." As specified in the syntax above, it is used to define and execute the ICC(1) (ICC1BR) and ICC(2) equations from Raudenbush and Bryk (2002), and the ICC(2) equation (ICC2A) from Bliese (2000). Locations in the original sources for the specific equations are noted in lines beginning with "!" in the syntax above. The current equations are an adaptation of their ANOVA point estimation procedure to a SEM framework. The values 5 and 4 in the syntax are either the average per group sample size (5), or that average minus 1 (4). Although the groups in the current sample all comprised the same number of respondents, uneven per group sample sizes are likely more typical. When groups vary in size, the average per group sample size or "*s*" is calculated using the following equation:

$$s = \left[n^2 - \sum_{c=1}^{C} n_c^2 \right] [n(C-1)]^{-1}, \quad (19.3)$$

where C is the number of clusters, n is the total sample size, and n_c is the number of individuals in a cluster. M*plus* automatically computes s in cases where the per cluster sample sizes are uneven. This convention is important to know, as it impacts the calculation of the ICC values and thus the relevant syntax must be run twice. The first time uses arbitrary values in the ICC equations where the 4 and 5 values are now. The sole reason for this first run is to obtain the value of s. The second run of the syntax substitutes "*s-1*" where the values of 4 appear above, and s where a 5 appears. This second run, therefore, would contain the appropriate values of ICC for the latent variable.

The final line to highlight is the "Output:" command. As shown in the M*plus* user's guide, there are many output options available. Illustrated in the current example are sample statistics (Sampstat), confidence intervals (CINT), and standardized results (Stand(STDYX)). Selected output for TL in Figure 19.3a is as follows (complete output is available online at http://pubs.apa.org/books/supp/humphrey/):

Estimated Intraclass Correlations for the Y Variables

SUPPRC1 0.539 EXPPRC1 0.458 ROLPRC1 0.526
   CONFPRC1 0.542

Chi-Square Test of Model Fit

   Value 15.248*
   Degrees of Freedom 4
   P-Value 0.0042
   RMSEA (Root Mean Square Error Of
      Approximation)

   Estimate 0.058

   CFI/TLI

   CFI 0.994
   TLI 0.982

SRMR (Standardized Root Mean Square Residual)

   Value for Within 0.008
   Value for Between 0.001

Within Level (unstandardized)

   TRANSIND BY
   SUPPRC1 1.000 0.000 999.000 999.000
   EXPPRC1 0.999 0.034 29.630 0.000
   ROLPRC1 0.988 0.035 27.980 0.000
   CONFPRC1 0.960 0.037 25.786 0.000

Between Level (unstandardized)

   TRANSBET BY
   SUPPRC1 1.000 0.000 999.000 999.000
   EXPPRC1 0.911 0.020 45.946 0.000
   ROLPRC1 0.962 0.023 41.056 0.000
   CONFPRC1 0.979 0.027 35.859 0.000

Variances

   TRANSBET 0.573 0.061 9.350 0.000
   New/Additional Parameters
   ICC1BR 0.603 0.044 13.588 0.000

ICC2 0.884 0.019 46.353 0.000
ICC2A 0.884 0.019 46.353 0.000

The above is a very small part of the total output provided in M*plus*. Starting with the first two lines ("Estimated Intraclass . . ."), we see that M*plus* calculated ICC(1) values for the observed/manifest variables operationalizing the TL latent variable. Contrast these results with the last four lines ("New/Additional . . ."), where the "MODEL CONSTRAINT" feature was used to compute the ICC(1) and ICC(2) values for the TL latent variable itself. In general, an ICC(1) value is the percentage of variance in the variable attributable to cluster (groups in the current case) membership (Bliese, 2000; LeBreton & Senter, 2008). Therefore, and for example, 54% of variance in the "SUPPRC1" observed/manifest variable is due to group membership. Additionally, 60% of the TL latent variable (ICC1BR) is also due to group membership. The ICC(2) value, in contrast, roughly means that the groups can be reliably differentiated in terms of the variable of interest (Bliese, 2000; LeBreton & Senter, 2008), which is currently the TL latent variable. Even though calculated slightly differently, the ICC(2) (Raudenbush & Bryk, 2002) and ICC2A (Bliese, 2000) values are identical, as they should be. Following each of the TL latent variable's ICC values are the standard error of the estimate (e.g., .044 for ICC1BR), the t-value (e.g., .602 ÷ .044 = 13.588), and the level of significance or alpha level for that t-value (e.g., .0000). The following quote succinctly summarizes how to interpret the values:

> ICC(1) and ICC(2) values are often used to assess whether aggregation to the group level is appropriate. Statistically significant ICC(1) values suggest dependence in the data structure, indicating that individual-level analyses would be inappropriate, whereas high ICC(2) values indicate reliable between-group differences, supporting aggregation to the group level. For a group-level construct to be reliable, it should yield significant ICC(1) and acceptable ICC(2) values.

As such, the higher ICC(1) and ICC(2), the larger the extent to which the construct is shared by group members and the more reliable the resulting group construct. (van Mierlo, Vermunt, & Rutte, 2009, p. 374)

Therefore, by all benchmarks, the TL latent variable in the present data satisfies the standards for aggregation. Additionally, as indicated by the "Variances" line above, the between-level variance of the TL latent variable is statistically significant (Raudenbush & Bryk, 2002). In short, aggregation is justified, and with the significant variance, we can be reasonably confident that, if there are associations among the between-level constructs, those associations will be statistically significant.

We are aware that there are many more forms of interrater agreement and reliability beyond the ICC values (see Bliese, 2000; LeBreton & Senter, 2008; van Mierlo et al., 2009). The interested reader should consult the latter sources and an article by Biemann, Cole, and Voelpel (2012) for further information. Indeed, Biemann and Cole (2014) developed an excellent Excel tool that is free to download, and may be used to calculate within group agreement (r_{wg}) and ICC values. It may be found at http://www.sbuweb.tcu.edu/mcole/docs/Tool%20for%20Computing%20IRA%20and%20IRR%20Estimates_v1.5.zip. Bliese has likewise created a package for assessing a variety of within-group agreement and reliability indices (available at https://cran.r-project.org/web/packages/multilevel/index.html). SPSS code for estimating ICC and r_{wg} values can be found in LeBreton and Senter (2008).

With respect to the other output provided above, we leave interpretation to the reader. In short, the model fit indices should be strong, indicating that the measurement models at both levels of the MLCFA provide adequate fit to the data. Further, the factor loadings should be strong and statistically significant.

In terms of the HIWP latent variable (Figure 19.3b), its selected syntax is as follows:

Title: One-Way CFA—High Involvement Work
    Processes—Figure 19.3b

DATA: FILE IS
C:\Users\rvandenb\Dropbox\Projects\CARMA\
    MLSEM\Data\demo2txtchapt.dat;

Variable: Names are GID SUBPRC1 SUBPRC2
    EXPSUB5 SUPPRC1 EXPPRC1 ROLPRC1
    CONFPRC1 PPRC2 IPRC1 RPRC1 KPRC1
    OCBPRC1 OCBPRC2 OCBPRC3 ABSRATE
    VOLRATE;

Usevariables are GID PPRC2 IPRC1 RPRC1 KPRC1;
Cluster is GID;
ANALYSIS: TYPE = TWOLEVEL;
MODEL:
%WITHIN%
HIWPInd by PPRC2 IPRC1 RPRC1 KPRC1;
HIWPInd (MSWhiwp);
%BETWEEN%
HIWPBet by PPRC2 IPRC1 RPRC1 KPRC1;
HIWPBet (MSBhiwp);

Model Constraint:
New (ICC1BRHI ICC2HI ICC2AHI);
ICC1BRHI = MSBhiwp / (MSBhiwp +MSWhiwp);
ICC2HI = MSBhiwp / (MSBhiwp +(MSWhiwp/5));
ICC2aHI = (5 ∗ ICC1BRhi) / (1+(4 ∗ ICC1BRHi));

Without belaboring the issue, the output for the HIWP latent variable was similar to that observed above for the TL latent variable. ICC1BR was .55, and both ICC(2) values were .86. Additionally, the variance of the between-level HIWP was .52 and highly statistically significant. Therefore, the conclusions here are identical to those drawn for the TL latent variable in terms of aggregation justification and the significance of the variance of the between-level latent variable.

In summary, the purpose of this first section was to illustrate the SEM equivalent to Raudenbush and Bryk's (2002) principles of point estimation. Indeed, as noted in Heck and Thomas (2015), the MLCFA models are referred to as the "null models" and serve the same function as the null model in non-SEM multilevel analyses. Although the illustrations above treat each latent variable independently, we normally would have undertaken the analyses with both variables in the same model. Although keeping them independent simplified the current explanation, the reality is that the TL and HIWP variables are related to one another. Therefore, the impact of that interrelationship needs accounting for when calculating the point estimates. In that case, Figure 19.3 would be modified by dropping the (a) and (b), and including double-headed curved arrows between the latent variables at both the within and between levels. The curved arrows denote that the covariance among the latent variables at both levels should be estimated in addition to the other parameters. When we did this with the current variables, the absolute values of the estimates changed by .01 (at the most), but none of our inferences changed with respect to the justifications for aggregation or the significance of the variance of the between-level latent variables. As a reminder, the syntax and output for all of the analyses may be found at http://pubs.apa.org/books/supp/humphrey/. We turn next to hypothesis testing.

HYPOTHESIS TESTING

As noted previously, the goal is to test the path model in Figure 19.1, since those paths presumably represent some set of conceptually justified hypotheses. Following the recommendations of Anderson and Gerbing (1988), however, it is most prudent to first test the viability of the measurement model representing the latent variables before restricting the relationships between them to specific paths. The full measurement model in the current case is presented in Figure 19.4. As illustrated, the full measurement model not only includes the two aggregated TL and HIWP latent variables, but also the LE and GCOCB latent variables. Recall that the LE and GCOCB measures were completed only by the 167 group leaders. For this reason, the LE and GCOCB measures are treated as latent variables only at the between level.

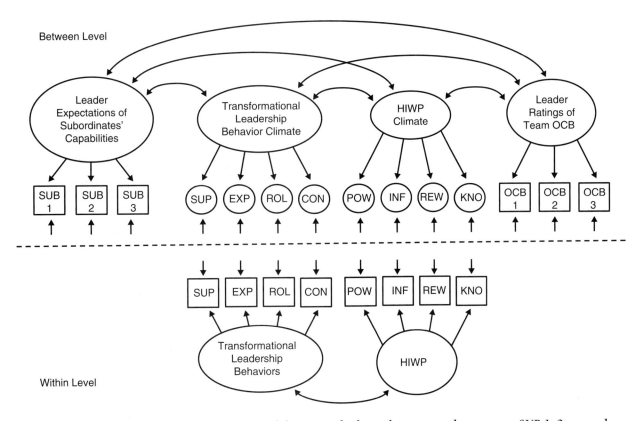

FIGURE 19.4. Test of the full measurement model. HIWP = high involvement work processes; SUB 1–3 = parcels of items measuring leader expectations of subordinates' capabilities; SUP = individualized support; EXP = exhibiting high performance expectations; ROL = role modeling; CON = confidence in followers; POW = power; INF = information; REW = rewards; KNO = knowledge; OCB 1–3 = Organizational Citizenship Behaviors.

The syntax to evaluate the full measurement model in Figure 19.4 is as follows:

Title: One-Way CFA—Full Measurement Model—Figure 19.4

DATA: FILE IS
C:\Users\rvandenb\Dropbox\Projects\CARMA\
    MLSEM\Data\demo2txtchapt.dat;

Variable: Names are GID SUBPRC1 SUBPRC2
    EXPSUB5 SUPPRC1 EXPPRC1 ROLPRC1
    CONFPRC1 PPRC2 IPRC1 RPRC1 KPRC1
    OCBPRC1 OCBPRC2 OCBPRC3 ABSRATE
    VOLRATE;

Usevariables are GID SUPPRC1 EXPPRC1
    ROLPRC1 CONFPRC1 PPRC2 IPRC1 RPRC1
    KPRC1 SUBPRC1 SUBPRC2 EXPSUB5
    OCBPRC1 OCBPRC2 OCBPRC3;

Between = SUBPRC1 SUBPRC2 EXPSUB5 OCBPRC1
    OCBPRC2 OCBPRC3;

Cluster is GID;

ANALYSIS: TYPE = TWOLEVEL;

MODEL:
%WITHIN%
TransInd by SUPPRC1 EXPPRC1 ROLPRC1
    CONFPRC1;
TransInd (MSWTr);
HIWPInd by PPRC2 IPRC1 RPRC1 KPRC1;
HIWPInd (MSWhiwp);

%BETWEEN%
TransBet by SUPPRC1 EXPPRC1 ROLPRC1
    CONFPRC1;
TransBet (MSBTr);
HIWPBet by PPRC2 IPRC1 RPRC1 KPRC1;
HIWPBet (MSBhiwp);
LE by SUBPRC1 SUBPRC2 EXPSUB5;
GroupOCB by OCBPRC1 OCBPRC2 OCBPRC3;

Model Constraint:

New (ICC1BRTr ICC1BRHI ICC2TR ICC2HI
    ICC2ATr ICC2AHI);
ICC1BRTr = MSBtr / (MSBtr +MSWtr);
ICC2TR = MSBtr / (MSBtr +(MSWtr/5));
ICC2aTR = (5 * ICC1BRTr) / (1 +(4 * ICC1BRTR));

ICC1BRHI = MSBhiwp / (MSBhiwp +MSWhiwp);

ICC2HI = MSBhiwp / (MSBhiwp +(MSWhiwp / 5));
ICC2aHI = (5 * ICC1BRhi) / (1 +(4 * ICC1BRHi));

Output: Sampstat Residual Tech1 CINT
    Stand(STDYX);

As explained previously, the "Usevariables are . . ." command instructs Mplus to use the listed variables in any forthcoming "MODEL" specification. In the current case, the variables to be used are the cluster variable (GID) and all the manifest/observed variables for the six latent variables in Figure 19.4. A new command not used in previous examples is "Between =". This line instructs Mplus that the manifest variables following the equal sign reside only at the between level. Without this restriction, Mplus would attempt to partition the within portion of the variance-covariance matrix for these variables from the between portion. Doing so would cause a fatal error, however, because these variables only exist at the between level. Similarly, there may be cases where variables only reside at the within level (i.e., gender, age, education, etc.). In those cases, one would use the "Within =" command.

There are three other general differences between this syntax and previous examples. The first is that the measurement models for all latent variables are specified simultaneously. The second difference is that there are the two additional measurement models under the "%BETWEEN%" command—one for the LE latent variable and the other for the GCOCB latent variable. The third difference is that the syntax for calculating the ICC(1) and ICC(2) values has been expanded so that they are simultaneously estimated for the two aggregated latent variables, TL and HIWP. ICCs cannot be calculated for the LE and GCOCB latent variables because these variables reside only at the between level. Per Raudenbush and Bryk (2002), however, we should examine the variance of these latent variables. As stated above, the probability of finding significant associations among the between variables are greatly lowered if the variance of a between variable is small and perhaps statistically nonsignificant.

Selected output for the model in Figure 19.4 is as follows (again, full output is available at http://pubs.apa.org/books/supp/humphrey/):

Estimated Intraclass Correlations for the Y Variables

SUPPRC1 0.541 EXPPRC1 0.462 ROLPRC1 0.527 CONFPRC1 0.544
PPRC2 0.440 IPRC1 0.399 RPRC1 0.436 KPRC1 0.451

MODEL FIT INFORMATION

Chi-Square Test of Model Fit

Value 362.970*
Degrees of Freedom 90
P-Value 0.0000
Scaling Correction Factor 0.7428
for MLR

RMSEA (Root Mean Square Error Of Approximation)

Estimate 0.060

CFI/TLI

CFI 0.957
TLI 0.944

SRMR (Standardized Root Mean Square Residual)

Value for Within 0.035
Value for Between 0.051

MODEL RESULTS

Two-Tailed
Estimate S.E. Est./S.E. P-Value

Within Level (Unstandardized)

TRANSIND BY
SUPPRC1 1.000 0.000 999.000 999.000
EXPPRC1 0.998 0.032 30.759 0.000
ROLPRC1 0.978 0.036 27.355 0.000
CONFPRC1 0.944 0.039 24.301 0.000

HIWPIND BY
PPRC2 1.000 0.000 999.000 999.000
IPRC1 1.144 0.058 19.881 0.000
RPRC1 1.037 0.046 22.504 0.000
KPRC1 0.854 0.044 19.286 0.000

Between Level (Unstandardized)

TRANSBET BY
SUPPRC1 1.000 0.000 999.000 999.000
EXPPRC1 0.914 0.020 45.278 0.000
ROLPRC1 0.967 0.024 40.074 0.000
CONFPRC1 0.988 0.028 34.963 0.000

HIWPBET BY
PPRC2 1.000 0.000 999.000 999.000
IPRC1 0.913 0.041 22.120 0.000
RPRC1 0.951 0.033 29.121 0.000
KPRC1 0.900 0.038 23.478 0.000

LE BY
SUBPRC1 1.000 0.000 999.000 999.000
SUBPRC2 1.254 0.094 13.385 0.000
EXPSUB5 1.477 0.101 14.635 0.000

GROUPOCB BY
OCBPRC1 1.000 0.000 999.000 999.000
OCBPRC2 1.206 0.141 8.530 0.000
OCBPRC3 1.449 0.202 7.186 0.000

Variances
TRANSBET 0.583 0.062 9.338 0.000
HIWPBET 0.520 0.057 9.199 0.000
LE 0.541 0.078 6.960 0.000
GROUPOCB 0.301 0.055 5.484 0.000

New/Additional Parameters
ICC1BRTR 0.605 0.046 13.292 0.000
ICC1BRHI 0.551 0.046 12.034 0.000
ICC2TR 0.884 0.019 45.455 0.000
ICC2HI 0.860 0.022 38.580 0.000
ICC2ATR 0.884 0.019 45.455 0.000
ICC2AHI 0.860 0.022 38.580 0.000

Evaluating the overall fit indices first, those familiar with SEM procedures would conclude that this model fits the data quite well; that is, as specified, the variance-covariance matrices reproduced at the within and between levels of the model in Figure 19.4 closely fit the observed variance-covariance matrices at those levels. Also, all the manifest variables at both levels possess strong and statistically significant factor loadings (unstandardized) to their respective latent variables. Evaluating the "Variances" indicates that there is statistically significant between cluster/group variance for all latent variables including the LE and GCOCB latent variables. Finally, the ICC(1) and ICC(2) values for the two aggregated variables remained relatively unchanged even with the greatly expanded model in Figure 19.4 (i.e., relative to the models in Figure 19.3). In summary, the measurement model in Figure 19.4 fits the data quite well, and the justifications for aggregation remained unchanged.

Before proceeding with the tests of Figures 19.1 and 19.2, we would like to address a likely question the reader may have at this point. Namely, why not simply begin with the test of Figure 19.4, and skip the tests of Figure 19.3, because the conclusions, particularly those for aggregation, are the same? We have two responses. The first is to ease the explanation of a complex topic by splitting it into smaller "bites." The second response, though, is the process outlined in the chapter up to this point represents our modus operandi. Assume for a moment that we started with Figure 19.4 (or even Figure 19.1) and obtained unacceptable overall fit indices. Because we leapt so far forward in the analyses, we would have no clue at this point what aspects of the model in Figure 19.4 (or Figure 19.1) contribute to the poor fit. We would have to work backward to deconstruct the findings and uncover the underlying factors. To be frank, this backward approach risks evolving into post hoc attempts to fix undesirable outcomes. By using a stepped, forward or building-block approach as applied in this chapter, any potential problems can be identified early. Although it will not always be possible, perhaps the problem can be dealt with using a reasonable, conceptually driven approach, leaving the conceptual integrity of the model under examination relatively intact. In the end, this choice is a personal preference; however, it is one that is backed by nearly 57 years of the authors' combined experience in SEM procedures.

Now that all the assumptions have been evaluated and met, and the full measurement model has been supported, we can move to Anderson and Gerbing's (1988) second step—the test of the SEM path model. The following *Mplus* syntax (selected) is relevant to testing Figure 19.1.

Title: One-Way CFA—Test of Conceptual Model—
    Figure 19.1

DATA: FILE IS
C:\Users\rvandenb\Dropbox\Projects\CARMA\
    MLSEM\Data\demo2txtchapt.dat;

Variable: Names are GID SUBPRC1 SUBPRC2
    EXPSUB5 SUPPRC1 EXPPRC1 ROLPRC1
    CONFPRC1 PPRC2 IPRC1 RPRC1 KPRC1
    OCBPRC1 OCBPRC2 OCBPRC3 ABSRATE
    VOLRATE;

Usevariables are GID SUPPRC1 EXPPRC1
    ROLPRC1 CONFPRC1 PPRC2 IPRC1 RPRC1
    KPRC1 SUBPRC1 SUBPRC2 EXPSUB5
    OCBPRC1 OCBPRC2 OCBPRC3 ABSRATE
    VOLRATE;

Between = SUBPRC1 SUBPRC2 EXPSUB5 OCBPRC1
    OCBPRC2 OCBPRC3 ABSRATE VOLRATE;

Cluster is GID;

ANALYSIS: TYPE = TWOLEVEL;
MODEL:
%WITHIN%
TransInd by SUPPRC1 EXPPRC1 ROLPRC1
    CONFPRC1;
TransInd;
HIWPInd by PPRC2 IPRC1 RPRC1 KPRC1;
HIWPInd;

HIWPInd on TransInd;

%BETWEEN%
TransBet by SUPPRC1 EXPPRC1 ROLPRC1
    CONFPRC1;
TransBet;
HIWPBet by PPRC2 IPRC1 RPRC1 KPRC1;
HIWPBet;
ExptLdr by SUBPRC1 SUBPRC2 EXPSUB5;
OCBGroup by OCBPRC1 OCBPRC2 OCBPRC3;
TransBet on ExptLdr (p1);
HIWPBet on TransBet (p2);
OCBGroup on HIWPBet (p3);
ABSRATE on HIWPBet (p4);
VOLRATE on HIWPBet (p5);

Model Constraint:
New (ExpHIW TranOCB ExpOCB TranAbs ExpAbs
    TranVol ExpVol);
ExpHIW = p1 * p2;

TranOCB = p2 * p3;
ExpOCB = p1 * p2 * p3;
TranAbs = p2 * p4;
ExpAbs = p1 * p2 * p4;
TranVol = p2 * p5;
ExpVol = p1 * p2 * p5;

!See pg 603 of Ver. 7 User's Manual. It explains that the MLR uses a sandwich estimator
!to compute the standard errors to deal with data that are nonnormal.
!Also go to http://www.statmodel.com/discussion/ messages/11/9365.html?1333847195

Output: Sampstat Residual Tech1 CINT Stand(STDYX);

There are three general differences between the syntax above and that covered previously. The first is the inclusion of two archival measures, "ABSRATE" and "VOLRATE," respectively representing group absences and voluntary turnover collected for some period after the attitudinal measures were administered. These are at the group level only and, therefore, are specified as only between-level variables. Further, because they are observed variables, they are encased in rectangles. The second difference is the multiple uses of the "on" command (e.g., as in the line "HIWPInd on TransInd (p2);"). This command regresses HIWP onto TL at the within level, and therefore, represents the single-headed arrow from TL to high involvement work processes in Figure 19.1.

The third general difference is the "Model Constraint:" feature, which is now specified to test indirect effects. For the following illustration, we are making the untenable assumption that there is a strong conceptual underpinning for every possible mediating effect at the between level in Figure 19.1. The reader is referred to LeBreton, Wu, and Bing (2009) for an explanation of why mediating/ indirect effects require strong conceptual underpinnings, and why one should not test indirect effects simply for the sake of doing so. Our illustration is unrealistic, therefore, because we probably would have only one or two conceptually anchored media- tion hypotheses. Our point, however, is to illus- trate how one would test different combinations.

The illustration begins with the line "TransBet on ExptLdr (p1);". Besides instructing M*plus* to regress the TransBet (group perceptions of TL) latent variable onto the ExptLdr (LE—leader expecta- tions) latent variable, it is also instructing M*plus* to internally label that path coefficient p1 by using the "(p1);" command. The label is user specified, and we could have just as easily identified it using any other unique name of our choosing. There are similar labels given to all the other path coefficients at the between level.

Turning to the commands following the "Model Constraint:" line, the first is a set of new variable names, one for each of the tested indi- rect effects. The label "ExpHIW", for example, refers to the presumed mediation effect of leader expectations on the climate for high involve- ment work processes through group perceptions of TL. Therefore, the first three letters represent the starting variable in the mediation chain and the last three letters reflect the last variable in the chain. Again, these are all user specified labels, and the logic underlying them is our preference. The next set of lines operationalizes the tests for mediation. For example, "ExpHIW = p1 * p2;", instructs M*plus* to multiply the path labeled p1 (LE to group perceptions of TL) with the path labeled p2 (group perceptions of TL to group climate for HIWP). The latter is based on the convention that indirect effects are defined as the product of the $X \rightarrow M$ path and the $M \rightarrow Y$ path (LeBreton et al., 2009). The other presumed medi- ation effects are similarly operationalized in subse- quent command lines.

Before turning to the results, there is a need to briefly address how M*plus* accounts for the nonnor- mality of product terms. It is beyond our purview to enter the full debate on whether bootstrapping is superior to the Sobel test. Of the two approaches, bootstrapping appears to be applied most frequently in the organizational sciences because of some presumed defects with respect to the Sobel test's ability to deal with nonnormality. However, as Koopman, Howe, and Hollenbeck (2015) noted recently, the preference for bootstrapping is based largely on statistical and methodological myth and urban legend. Through a series of well-conducted simulations, Koopman et al.

demonstrate that the Sobel test performs quite effectively, and that there are indeed more issues with bootstrapping than previously known. M*plus* does have bootstrapping capabilities for almost any estimated parameter if that is one's preference. Nonetheless, we went with the default procedure in M*plus* which uses an MLR (maximum likelihood robust) estimation procedure for dealing with the nonnormality inherent in product terms. This procedure is like a Sobel test. In the syntax above, there are references to the M*plus* user manual and to a URL at the M*plus* website which explain the test. To facilitate understanding, we highly recommend having MacKinnon's (2008) book available when viewing the explanation. Due to the Koopman et al. study and these other resources, we are confident that the MLR procedure adequately deals with the nonnormality underlying the product terms.

The following is selected output from the test of Figure 19.1.

Chi-Square Test of Model Fit

Value 437.336*
Degrees of Freedom 117
P-Value 0.0000
Scaling Correction Factor 0.8318
for MLR

RMSEA (Root Mean Square Error Of Approximation)

Estimate 0.057

CFI/TLI

CFI 0.949
TLI 0.936

SRMR (Standardized Root Mean Square Residual)

Value for Within 0.035
Value for Between 0.089

MODEL RESULTS
Two-Tailed
Estimate S.E. Est./S.E. P-Value

Within Level
HIWPIND ON
TRANSIND 0.797 0.053 14.977 0.000
Between Level

TRANSBET ON
EXPTLDR 0.594 0.090 6.611 0.000

HIWPBET ON
TRANSBET 0.794 0.055 14.439 0.000

OCBGROUP ON
HIWPBET 0.455 0.089 5.086 0.000

ABSRATE ON
HIWPBET −1.759 0.391 −4.502 0.000

VOLRATE ON
HIWPBET −6.232 1.378 −4.522 0.000

New/Additional Parameters
EXPHIW 0.472 0.079 6.000 0.000
TRANOCB 0.362 0.077 4.717 0.000
EXPOCB 0.215 0.060 3.558 0.000
TRANABS −1.397 0.325 −4.300 0.000
EXPABS −0.830 0.235 −3.526 0.000
TRANVOL −4.950 1.109 −4.464 0.000
EXPVOL −2.940 0.814 −3.611 0.000

The model fit indices suggest a relatively strong fitting model to the data. Further, all the direct paths illustrated in Figure 19.1 are statistically significant and directionally consistent with conceptual expectations. For example, the stronger the group climate for HIWP, the lower the rates of voluntary turnover (−6.232) and absence (−1.759) within a group. Most interesting, though, are the results following the "New/Additional Parameters" line. If there had been strong conceptual anchors for each of the mediating relationships, every one of them is statistically significant and directionally consistent. For example, leader expectations had a statistically significant negative indirect effect (−.830) on group absences through both aggregated collective variables (i.e., TL and HIWP).

All the examples to this point have incorporated only the random vector of intercepts. Therefore, the last example for this chapter is the test of Figure 19.2, which includes a cross-level interaction hypothesis claiming that the slope of the relationship from TL to HIWP within each group is dependent upon the strength of leader expectations—the more positive the expectations, the stronger the slope. A random vector of slopes is required to test this hypothesis. An additional purpose for evaluating Figure 19.2 is as follows. Assume for a moment that a researcher is only interested in testing hypotheses at the within/individual level. Although there is no conceptual interest or need to evaluate the associations among the between-level aspects of the variables, it is known or suspected that the observations are clustered and, consequently, nonindependent. As such, there remains a statistical need to control for the nonindependence. This need is captured in Figure 19.2 by specifying the TL and HIWP latent variables at the between level. The term "climate" has been removed from the latent variable labels because in this context there is no conceptual reason for using it. The specification in Figure 19.2 simply illustrates the desire to remove the nonindependence among the observations, while testing the association from TL to HIWP at the individual level of analysis. While Figure 19.2 includes a cross-level interaction for illustration purposes, controlling for nonindependence would be the same even if there was not a cross-level interaction hypothesis. It should be noted that in non-SEM multilevel analyses, where mean values are used to represent the variables, those variables would simply be group-mean centered to account for the nonindependence. We contend, however, that the approach illustrated via Figure 19.2 is the simplest when variables are latent.

The syntax required to test the model in Figure 19.2 is as follows:

Title: Multilevel Test of Figure 19.2

DATA: FILE IS
C:\Users\rvandenb\Dropbox\Projects\CARMA\
    MLSEM\Data\demo2txtchapt.dat;

Variable: Names are GID SUBPRC1 SUBPRC2
    EXPSUB5 SUPPRC1 EXPPRC1 ROLPRC1
    CONFPRC1 PPRC2 IPRC1 RPRC1 KPRC1
    OCBPRC1 OCBPRC2 OCBPRC3 ABSRATE
    VOLRATE;

Usevariables are GID SUPPRC1 EXPPRC1
    ROLPRC1 CONFPRC1 PPRC2 IPRC1 RPRC1
    KPRC1 SUBPRC1 SUBPRC2 EXPSUB5;

Between = SUBPRC1 SUBPRC2 EXPSUB5;

Cluster is GID;

ANALYSIS: TYPE = TWOLEVEL Random;
ALGORITHM=INTEGRATION EM;
MITERATIONS = 2000;
Integration = 10;
processors = 4;

MODEL:
%WITHIN%
TransInd by SUPPRC1 EXPPRC1 ROLPRC1
    CONFPRC1;
TransInd;
HIWPInd by PPRC2 IPRC1 RPRC1 KPRC1;
HIWPInd;
HIWPInd on TransInd;

TrantoHI | HIWPInd on TransInd;

%BETWEEN%
TransBet by SUPPRC1 EXPPRC1 ROLPRC1
    CONFPRC1;
TransBet;
HIWPBet by PPRC2 IPRC1 RPRC1 KPRC1;
HIWPBet;
ExptLdr by SUBPRC1 SUBPRC2 EXPSUB5;

TrantoHI on ExptLdr;

Output: Sampstat Residual Tech1 CINT
    Stand(STDYX);

Starting with the five command lines within the "ANALYSIS: . . ." array, the "Random . . .", "ALGORITHM=INTEGRATION EM;", "MITERATIONS = 2000;", and "Integration = 10;" lines are a set that is needed to estimate the random vector of slopes in a latent variable setting. Explanations of each and the various options available within each command are explained in the M*plus* user's guide as well as at the M*plus* website, www.statmodel.com. In brief, "ALGORITHM= INTEGRATION EM;" instructs M*plus* to use expectation maximization (EM) for the numerical integration calculations. Normally, "MITERATIONS = 2000;" does not need to be written out, as the default number of 500 iterations for the EM algorithm is adequate. In our case, though, the first run of the model in Figure 19.2 did not converge on a final solution, and the resulting output suggested increasing the number of iterations. We found a final solution by changing the iterations to 2000. The "Integration = 10;" command instructs M*plus* to use 10 integration points per dimension. The "processors = 4;" command is a feature that is available for all M*plus* modeling procedures. Namely, the computer on which the syntax for Figure 19.2 was executed had four core processors. This command instructs M*plus* to use all four for the execution of the syntax. If a computer had 12 core processors, for example, this value would be changed to 12.

xscommand is required to create the random vector of slopes/coefficients and to internally label that vector TrantoHI. Once again, the label is user specified and, therefore, could have been called any unique name. This command executes the regression of HIWP onto TL as many times as there are clusters. In the current case, TrantoHI would contain 167 slopes, one each per group. Above this line is the command "HIWPInd on TransInd;". By default, this regression is not in the output at the within/individual level when only the random vector for the slopes is created. To obtain this regression across all observations, it is thus necessary to separately include this command line, even though it appears in the command to create the random vector of slopes.

There are two aspects of the "%Between%" syntax to highlight. The first is "TrantoHI on ExptLdr;". This executes the cross-level interaction. In the current case, it is the test of the hypothesis that the relationship between TL and HIWP within each group is dependent upon the group leaders' expectations that a group can operate in a HIWP environment. The second aspect of this syntax to highlight is that while the measurement models for the TL and HIWP latent variables at the between level are estimated, there are no paths between them. By specifying them in this manner, we control for the nonindependence among the observations, while testing the hypothesized association between TL and HIWP at the within/individual level.

With respect to the output, two values are worth noting. First, the hypothesis regarding the association from TL to HIWP at the within/individual level is supported (.24, $t = 2.76$, $p < .006$); however, the

cross-level interaction hypothesis is not supported ($-.25$, $t = -1.319$, $p < 0.187$). The absence of support is not surprising given that the variance of the random vector of slopes was statistically nonsignificant and, as such, there were no between-group statistical differences in the slopes. The remaining output with respect to the measurement models at both levels had values equivalent those obtained in all previous tests.

In closing this chapter, we would like to make the reader aware of two other features that make M*plus* an attractive alternative to testing multilevel models. First, we are personally unaware of any studies in which the random vector of slopes was used as a predictor of some outcome. Although researchers tend to use it as an outcome of some variable at the between level, that does not have to be the case. Therefore, we modified the syntax for Figure 19.2 by (a) reintroducing absence as a variable at the between level, (b) removing the path from leader expectations to the TL-to-HIWP vector of slopes, and (c) specifying a path from that vector to absence. That is, group level absence was treated as a function of the strength of the slopes between TL and HIWP within each group. From our perspective, this is not an unreasonable expectation. The model converged on a solution. As was the case with Figure 19.2, the TL to HIWP association at the within/individual level was positive and statistically significant, but the slopes-to-absence hypothesis was statistically nonsignificant. Simply stated, our point is that unlike other multilevel modeling software packages, M*plus* permits flexibility in the roles (exogenous, endogenous, mediation, etc.) the variables may have in the specified conceptual frameworks.

The second feature worth noting is that, although our charge was to create a "nuts 'n' bolts" chapter on SEM multilevel modeling, we could have easily made this a chapter into one on taking a non-SEM approach to multilevel modeling using M*plus*. In each of the examples, we would have simply used observed variables instead of latent variables—used the means of the multi-item variables. Again, our key point is that M*plus* provides a great deal of flexibility relative to most other multilevel software packages—the type of flexibility needed to address hypotheses within complex conceptual frameworks.

It seems that most other multilevel packages are very limited in their capacities and, therefore, are best suited for simple frameworks.

Finally, the current database did not contain a third level into which the groups could be nested. Therefore, it was not possible to illustrate a MLSEM using three levels. However, three-level MLSEM may be undertaken using M*plus*. Starting on page 174, Heck and Thomas (2015) provided numerous examples of this. Further, the database for their examples and the corresponding syntax may be downloaded at www.routledge.com/9781848725522. There are three extensions that would need to be added to the two-level syntax used in this chapter to estimate models at three levels. First, assume that the current groups were nested within 30 companies and there was a column in the database labeled "compcode." All individuals belonging to the groups from Company 1 would have a "1" in that column. All individuals in the groups from Company 2 would have a "2" in that column, and this would continue until all individuals belonging to Company 30 had a "30" in that column. Therefore, the "CLUSTER =" command would be changed to "CLUSTER = compcode GID" in all of the examples above. The highest level variable (e.g., compcode) must be listed first. The second extension to the current syntax would be "ANALYSIS: Type = threelevel;", instead of "twolevel." This instructs M*plus* that a three-level multilevel analysis is forthcoming. The third extension would occur within the "MODEL" commands. There would now be two "%Between%" subcommands—one for compcode, "%Between compcode%", and one for GID, "%Between GID%". "%Within%" would remain the same. As was the case in the two-level examples for this chapter, the syntax defining the model at each level would be specified under these subcommands. As currently programmed, M*plus* is not capable of analyzing anything above three levels. Although we have not used it, according to its website, LISREL can also analyze up to three levels.

CONCLUSION

We hope the material in this chapter provides a sufficient foundation for the reader to start using MLSEM, if his or her research questions lend themselves toward a latent variable approach. As stated, there are some clear advantages of this analytical framework over the non-SEM approaches. Consistent with the latter approaches, however, statistical power is an issue, particularly given that latent variable analyses in general are asymptotic. Therefore, researchers need to give substantial thought to the sample sizes required for and available at each level, with our general advice being to maximize them at all levels. The authors also know that using excellent operationalizations of the focal constructs is imperative. Excellent means that at a minimum the measure has been frequently used in research with suitable empirical evidence supporting its validity. This is not the place to use "new" or "newish" measures where the validity of each has not been well established. Further, it denotes that the measure is appropriate for testing multilevel hypotheses. For example, the referent for the items should focus respondents on the target entity addressed in a level (Chan, 1998). Finally, begin the MLSEM process using the technique outlined in this chapter. Jumping to analysis of the full model will in high probability lead to disappointing or at least ambiguous outcomes.

References

Anderson, J. C., & Gerbing, D. W. (1988). Structural equation modeling in practice: A review and recommended two-step approach. *Psychological Bulletin, 103*, 411–423. http://dx.doi.org/10.1037/0033-2909.103.3.411

Biemann, T., & Cole, M. S. (2014). *An Excel 2007 tool for computing interrater agreement (IRA) & interrater reliability (IRR)*. Retrieved from http://www.sbuweb.tcu.edu/mscole/articles.html

Biemann, T., Cole, M. S., & Voelpel, S. (2012). Within-group agreement: On the use (and misuse) of r_{wg} and $r_{wg(j)}$ in leadership research and some best practice guidelines. *The Leadership Quarterly, 23*, 66–80. http://dx.doi.org/10.1016/j.leaqua.2011.11.006

Bliese, P. D. (2000). Within-group agreement, nonindependence, and reliability: Implications for data aggregation and analysis. In K. J. Klein & S. W. J. Kozlowski (Eds.), *Multilevel theory, research, and methods in organizations: Foundations, extensions, and new directions* (pp. 349–381). San Francisco, CA: Jossey-Bass.

Bollen, K. (1989). *Structural equations with latent variables*. New York, NY: Wiley. http://dx.doi.org/10.1002/9781118619179

Chan, D. (1998). Functional relations among constructs in the same content domain at different levels of analysis: A typology of composition models. *Journal of Applied Psychology, 83,* 234–246. http://dx.doi.org/10.1037/0021-9010.83.2.234

Eden, D. (1990). *Pygmalion in management: Productivity as a self-fulfilling prophecy.* Lexington, MA: Lexington Books.

Hall, R. J., Snell, A. F., & Foust, M. S. (1999). Item parceling strategies in SEM: Investigating the subtle effects of unmodeled secondary constructs. *Organizational Research Methods, 2,* 233–256. http://dx.doi.org/10.1177/109442819923002

Heck, R. H., & Thomas, S. L. (2015). *An introduction to multilevel modeling techniques: MLM and SEM approaches using Mplus.* New York, NY: Routledge.

Koopman, J., Howe, M., & Hollenbeck, J. R. (2015). Pulling the Sobel test up by its bootstraps. In C. E. Lance & R. J. Vandenberg (Eds.), *More statistical and methodological myths and urban legends* (pp. 224–244). New York, NY: Routledge.

Kozlowski, S. W., & Doherty, M. L. (1989). Integration of climate and leadership: Examination of a neglected issue. *Journal of Applied Psychology, 74,* 546–553. http://dx.doi.org/10.1037/0021-9010.74.4.546

Lawler, E. E., III. (1996). *From the ground up: Six principles for building the new logic corporation.* San Francisco, CA: Jossey-Bass.

LeBreton, J. M., & Senter, J. L. (2008). Answers to 20 questions about interrater reliability and inter-rater agreement. *Organizational Research Methods, 11,* 815–852. http://dx.doi.org/10.1177/1094428106296642

LeBreton, J. M., Wu, J., & Bing, M. N. (2009). The truth(s) on testing for mediation in the social and organizational sciences. In C. E. Lance & R. J. Vandenberg (Eds.), *Statistical and methodological myths and urban legends: Received doctrine, verity, and fable in the organizational and social sciences* (pp. 107–141). New York, NY: Routledge.

MacKinnon, D. P. (2008). *An introduction to statistical mediation analysis.* New York, NY: Lawrence Erlbaum.

Mehta, P. D., & Neale, M. C. (2005). People are variables too: Multilevel structural equations modeling. *Psychological Methods, 10,* 259–284. http://dx.doi.org/10.1037/1082-989X.10.3.259

Muthén, B. O. (1994). Multilevel covariance structure analysis. *Sociological Methods & Research, 22,* 376–398. http://dx.doi.org/10.1177/0049124194022003006

Muthén, B. O., & Satorra, A. (1995). Complex sample data in structural equation modeling. *Sociological Methodology, 25,* 267–316. http://dx.doi.org/10.2307/271070

Muthén, L. K., & Muthén, B. O. (1998–2015). *Mplus user's guide* (7th ed.) [Software user guide]. Los Angeles, CA: Muthén & Muthén.

Podsakoff, P. M., MacKenzie, S. B., Moorman, R. H., & Fetter, R. (1990). Transformational leader behaviors and their effects on followers' trust in leader, satisfaction, and organizational citizenship behaviors. *The Leadership Quarterly, 1,* 107–142. http://dx.doi.org/10.1016/1048-9843(90)90009-7

Raudenbush, S. W., & Bryk, A. S. (2002). *Hierarchical linear models: Application and data analysis methods* (2nd ed.). Thousand Oaks, CA: Sage.

Richardson, H. A. (2001). *Exploring the mechanisms through which high-involvement work processes result in group-level performance outcomes* (Unpublished doctoral dissertation), University of Georgia, Athens.

Richardson, H. A., & Vandenberg, R. J. (2005). Integrating managerial perceptions and transformational leadership into a work-unit level model of employee involvement. *Journal of Organizational Behavior, 26,* 561–589. http://dx.doi.org/10.1002/job.329

Schneider, B., & Reichers, A. (1983). On the etiology of climates. *Personnel Psychology, 36,* 19–39. http://dx.doi.org/10.1111/j.1744-6570.1983.tb00500.x

Vandenberg, R. J., Richardson, H. A., & Eastman, L. J. (1999). The impact of high involvement work processes on organizational effectiveness: A second-order latent variable approach. *Group & Organization Management, 24,* 300–339. http://dx.doi.org/10.1177/1059601199243004

van Mierlo, H., Vermunt, J. K., & Rutte, C. G. (2009). Composing group-level constructs from individual-level survey data. *Organizational Research Methods, 12,* 368–392. http://dx.doi.org/10.1177/1094428107309322

Zohar, D. (1980). Safety climate in industrial organizations: Theoretical and applied implications. *Journal of Applied Psychology, 65,* 96–102. http://dx.doi.org/10.1037/0021-9010.65.1.96

MODERATED MEDIATION IN MULTILEVEL STRUCTURAL EQUATION MODELS: DECOMPOSING EFFECTS OF RACE ON MATH ACHIEVEMENT WITHIN VERSUS BETWEEN HIGH SCHOOLS IN THE UNITED STATES

Michael J. Zyphur, Zhen Zhang, Kristopher J. Preacher, and Laura J. Bird

At roughly similar times in the 1980s, social scientists formalized what have become enduring interests in multilevel modeling (e.g., Raudenbush & Bryk, 1986) and moderation and mediation (e.g., Baron & Kenny, 1986). Today, moderation and mediation models have been synthesized so that these effects can be combined and estimated in a wide variety of cases (Edwards & Lambert, 2007; Preacher, Rucker, & Hayes, 2007), including with latent variables and latent interactions (Cheung & Lau, 2015; Sardeshmukh & Vandenberg, 2016). In the multilevel arena, approaches now exist that allow assessing multilevel mediation (e.g., Preacher, Zyphur, & Zhang, 2010; Preacher, Zhang, & Zyphur, 2011) and multilevel moderation with latent variables (e.g., Preacher, Zhang, & Zyphur, 2016).

What remains to be offered, however, is a synthesis of these interests in a way that allows estimating moderation and mediation at multiple levels of analysis. Our chapter addresses this by first describing the logic of moderated mediation, including how to formalize it as a structural equation model (SEM). We then extend this logic to multilevel SEM (MSEM) to estimate level-specific moderated mediation. Our approach allows the typical random

coefficient prediction method for estimating cross-level moderation with random slopes (as outcomes), but our approach can also use a latent moderated structural equations (LMS) approach to estimate moderation, which requires latent variable interactions (see Preacher et al., 2016).

To avoid the high-dimensional numerical integration that often accompanies these interactions, we describe a Bayesian *plausible values* approach that multiply-imputes latent variable scores in the first step, then allowing researchers to form product terms as if they were observed to estimate moderated effects in a second step. This approach can be used for any model wherein latent interactions or power polynomials otherwise require numerical integration, and therefore, it is also applicable in single-level models (e.g., Sardeshmukh & Vandenberg, 2016). In the context of MSEM, our plausible values approach has the benefit of comparatively fast estimation while still allowing higher level product terms to be treated as if they were measured with error (e.g., unlike Leite & Zuo, 2011).

We offer a worked example using the well-known High School and Beyond (HS&B) data set (e.g., Raudenbush & Bryk, 1986, 2002), with

http://dx.doi.org/10.1037/0000115-021
The Handbook of Multilevel Theory, Measurement, and Analysis, S. E. Humphrey and J. M. LeBreton (Editors-in-Chief)

7,185 students nested in 160 schools. The HS&B data and M*plus* program code for all models that we estimate can be downloaded from quantpsy.org. With these additional materials, the reader can estimate the models that we specify and modify them to experiment with multilevel moderated mediation.

To help the reader keep track of the parameters in our models, we use familiar mediation notation (as in Baron & Kenny, 1986), with regression coefficients as follows: *a* is the first path in a mediation relationship, *b* is the second path in a mediation relationship, *c* is the total effect of a predictor on an ultimate outcome without controlling for a mediator, and *c′* is the direct effect of a predictor on an ultimate outcome while controlling for a mediator. Furthermore, where appropriate, we use subscripts that indicate the outcome variable and the predictor variables associated with a regression coefficient. We illustrate this notation next but recommend that the unfamiliar reader first consult primary texts such as Baron and Kenny (1986), MacKinnon (2008), Preacher and Hayes (2004), Preacher et al. (2007), and Hayes (2013).

Our models estimate some effects of being Black in the United States. Given long-running racism and racial segregation in the United States (Bonilla-Silva, 2006), and because race is social and relational (see Lucal, 1996; Smedley & Smedley, 2005; Tsui, Egan, & O'Reilly, 1992), we treat individuals' self-identification as being Black or non-Black as indicating an important racial categorization in society—it matters. To be clear, as with feminist approaches to sex or gender (Haraway, 2006), our use of these terms and this categorization for our analyses is not meant to reify or otherwise reproduce racism. Instead, by showing negative effects of identifying as Black on math achievement both directly and indirectly via socioeconomic status (SES) within and between schools, our goal is to show racial inequalities so that they can be taken seriously and addressed.

In our Discussion section, we describe the benefits of our MSEM approach. They include an improved ability to conceptually reason and hypothesize about multilevel moderated mediation effects. Furthermore, the flexibility of MSEM allows random intercepts and random slopes that can be used as predictors, outcomes, indicators, mediators, or moderators at higher levels of analysis. With this expanded toolbox, researchers can better conduct research that addresses worldly problems of concern, such as racism.

MODERATED MEDIATION

To preface our discussion of multilevel moderated mediation, we first introduce basic concepts associated with moderation and mediation. We then treat moderated mediation in a single-level SEM framework and offer an empirical example using the HS&B data set.

Moderation

Moderation refers to an interaction or a conditional effect, wherein the effect of a predictor variable *x* on an outcome variable *y* varies across the levels of another predictor *w* (Cohen, Cohen, West, & Aiken, 2013). This kind of effect is usually modeled by forming a product term *xw* among the two predictor variables as follows (see a conceptual model of this effect in Figure 20.1a; see a more statistically accurate depiction in Figure 20.1b):

$$y_i = v_y + c_{yx}x_i + c_{yw}w_i + c_{yxw}x_iw_i + \varepsilon_{y,i}, \qquad (20.1)$$

wherein *i* is a unit of observation (e.g., an individual student); *v* is an intercept; each *c* is a regression coefficient; and ε is a residual. The conditional nature of the effects can be shown by rearranging Equation 20.1, which we do to illustrate the example of *x*'s effect on *y* across varying levels of *w*:

$$y_i = \left(v_y + c_{yw}w_i\right) + \left(c_{yx} + c_{yxw}w_i\right)x_i + \varepsilon_{y,i}. \qquad (20.2)$$

Here, the first parenthetical term is a *simple intercept*, which equals the expected value of *y* when *w* takes on a specific value; whereas the second parenthetical term is a *simple slope* of *x*, which equals the expected value of *y* when *w* takes on a specific value (Preacher et al., 2007). To test for moderation, researchers typically examine the statistical significance of c_{yxw}, which is sensible because only if $c_{yxw} \neq 0$ will the coefficient on *x* in Equation 20.2 detectably deviate from c_x. Furthermore, the statistical significance of

A

B

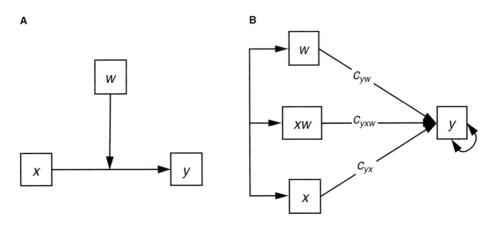

FIGURE 20.1. (a) A conceptual diagram of a moderation model. (b) A path diagram of a moderation model, wherein covariances among predictors are accounted for when deriving coefficients rather than explicitly estimated.

a given simple slope can be computed for any given value of w, or it can be computed continuously across a range of observed w values. All this is typically done on the basis of the standard error (*SE*) of c_{yxw} as computed under normal theory.

Mediation

By the term *mediation* we mean an indirect effect, such as the effect of x on y that is carried by a mediator m (Cohen et al., 2013). This kind of effect can be shown in equations for y and m as follows (see Figure 20.2):

$$m_i = \nu_m + a_{mx}x_i + \varepsilon_{m,i} \qquad (20.3)$$

$$y_i = \nu_y + b_{ym}m_i + c'_{yx}x_i + \varepsilon_{y,i} \qquad (20.4)$$

so that with substitution the indirect effect of x is shown to be a product term as follows:

$$y_i = \nu_y + b_{ym}\left(\nu_m + a_{mx}x_i + \varepsilon_{m,i}\right) + c'_{yx}x_i + \varepsilon_{y,i}, \qquad (20.5)$$

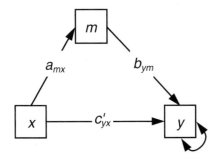

FIGURE 20.2. Path diagram of a mediation model.

which can be rearranged to show a traditional regression model structure as follows:

$$y_i = \left(\nu_y + b_{ym}\nu_m\right) + \left(a_{mx}b_{ym} + c'_{yx}\right)x_i + b_{ym}\varepsilon_{m,i} + \varepsilon_{y,i}, \qquad (20.6)$$

wherein the first parenthetical term is an intercept; the second parenthetical term is the total effect of x, composed of an indirect effect $a_{mx}b_{ym}$ and a direct effect c'_{yx}; and the term $b_{ym}\varepsilon_{m,i}$ is the direct effect of m that is independent of x. To test for mediation, researchers often modify traditional tests of statistical significance by estimating a confidence interval (CI) around $a_{mx}b_{ym}$—although the literature on mediation has historically distinguished between *partial* and *full* mediation (e.g., Baron & Kenny, 1986), we do not reproduce this distinction here and instead focus on indirect effects. Because estimates of such effects are not normally distributed, normal theory does not apply, and therefore, bootstrapping, Monte Carlo, or Bayes procedures are typically used (e.g., Preacher & Hayes, 2008; Preacher & Selig, 2012; Wang & Preacher, 2015; Yuan & MacKinnon, 2009).

Moderated Mediation

The term *moderated mediation* refers to the dependence of an indirect effect on at least one moderator variable w, such that indirect effects are made conditional on values of a moderator (or moderators). Many specifications produce moderated mediation (Hayes, 2013), but a general type can be shown by combining the logic of Equations 20.1, 20.3, and 20.4 as follows (see Figures 20.3a and 20.3b; see Model 59 in Hayes, 2018):

$$m_i = \nu_m + a_{mx}x_i + a_{mw}w_i + a_{mxw}x_iw_i + \varepsilon_{m,i} \qquad (20.7)$$

$$y_i = \nu_y + b_{ym}m_i + b_{ymw}m_iw_i + c'_{yx}x_i + c'_{yw}w_i$$
$$+ c'_{yxw}x_iw_i + \varepsilon_{y,i}, \qquad (20.8)$$

such that w moderates the effects of x on m and m on y (i.e., the "first stage" and "second stage" moderated mediation from Edwards & Lambert, 2007), and w moderates the direct effect of x on y (i.e., the traditional form of moderation). The effects involved in this model can be shown by substitution as follows:

$$y_i = \nu_y + b_{ym}\left(\nu_m + a_{mx}x_i + a_{mw}w_i + a_{mxw}x_iw_i + \varepsilon_{m,i}\right)$$
$$+ b_{ymw}\left(\nu_m + a_{mx}x_i + a_{mw}w_i + a_{mxw}x_iw_i + \varepsilon_{m,i}\right)w_i$$
$$+ c'_{yx}x_i + c'_{yw}w_i + c'_{yxw}x_iw_i + \varepsilon_{y,i}, \qquad (20.9)$$

which can be rearranged as follows:

$$y_i = \left[\nu_y + b_{ym}\nu_m + \left(\begin{array}{c} b_{ymw}\nu_m + a_{mw}b_{ym} \\ + a_{mw}b_{ymw}w_i + c'_{yw} \end{array}\right)w_i\right]$$
$$+ \left[(a_{mx} + a_{mxw}w_i)(b_{ym} + b_{ymw}w_i) + (c'_{yx} + c'_{yxw}w_i)\right]x_i$$
$$+ \left(b_{ym} + b_{ymw}w_i\right)\varepsilon_{m,i} + \varepsilon_{y,i}, \qquad (20.10)$$

which has a similar interpretation as Equation 20.6, such that the first bracketed term is the simple intercept of y, which includes indirect and direct

effects of w; the second bracketed term is the total effect of x, which is composed of first the indirect effect $(a_{mx} + a_{mxw}w_i)(b_{ym} + b_{ymw}w_i)$ and then the direct effect $(c'_{yx} + c'_{yxw}w_i)$; the first parenthetical term on the third line is the direct effect of m, which is moderated by w; and the final term is the residual of y.

For the uninitiated reader to fluently understand moderated mediation in Equation 20.10, some explanation is in order. Focusing on the effect of x in the second bracketed term, the moderation coefficients are a_{mxw} and b_{ymw}. Both of these are multiplied by w so that when both coefficients are equal to zero, moderation is not present and Equation 20.10 is more like Equation 20.6 because the indirect effect of x reduces to $a_{mx}b_{ym}$. However, if $a_{mxw} \neq 0$ and/or $b_{ymw} \neq 0$, moderation is present. Specifically, a_{mxw} allows for moderation of the path linking the independent variable and the mediator (i.e., the a_{mx} path) and b_{ymw} allows for moderation of the path linking the mediator and the dependent variable (i.e., the b_{ym} path). But because b_{ym} is part of the indirect effects involving paths a_{mx} and a_{mxw}, both of these paths can be moderated by w when multiplied by b_{ymw}.

As the reader may intuit, there are many ways to specify moderated mediation (see Hayes, 2013, 2015, 2018). Instead of describing the many cases that are possible, we want to offer a general model structure for understanding moderated mediation that can be extended to the multilevel case. We now do this with a general SEM specification (e.g., Edwards & Lambert,

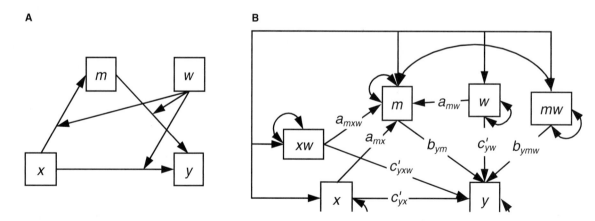

FIGURE 20.3.   (a) A conceptual diagram of our single-level moderated mediation model. (b) A path diagram of our single-level moderated mediation model, wherein predictor covariances are explicitly estimated, including a covariance among m and mw. Path coefficients are labeled as in our equations, with a terms indicating initial paths in a mediation/indirect effects equation, b terms indicating second paths in a mediation/indirect effects equation, and c' paths indicating direct effects.

2007; Hayes & Preacher, 2013). Here, and in our multilevel models, we use variants and simplifications of the model in Muthén and Asparouhov (2008) as implemented in M*plus* (see Muthén & Muthén, 2016; see also Preacher et al., 2010, 2016).

A General Structural Equation Model Specification and Estimation

To begin, we show an "all y" SEM specification as follows:

$$\mathbf{y}_i = \mathbf{v} + \mathbf{\Lambda}\mathbf{\eta}_i + \mathbf{\varepsilon}_i \qquad (20.11)$$

$$\mathbf{\eta}_i = \mathbf{\alpha} + \mathbf{B}\mathbf{\eta}_i + \mathbf{\zeta}_i, \qquad (20.12)$$

wherein $\mathbf{y}_i$ is a vector of observed scores on the dependent variables (often called *observed indicators*); $\mathbf{v}$ is a vector of intercepts capturing the mean structure of the data; $\mathbf{\Lambda}$ is a matrix of factor loadings representing the strength and direction of relationships among latent variables and their observed indicators; $\mathbf{\varepsilon}_i$ is a vector of residuals with covariance matrix $\mathbf{\Theta}$ (typically with unrestricted diagonal elements, i.e., estimated variances); $\mathbf{\eta}_i$ is typically a vector of latent variables that are believed to cause the covariance structure of observed indicators, but it may also be used to reflect the actual observed variables if $\mathbf{\Lambda}$ contains unities that link each observed variable with a single latent variable and elements in $\mathbf{v}$ and $\mathbf{\Theta}$ are fixed at zero; $\mathbf{\alpha}$ is a vector of intercepts or means corresponding to a latent variable mean structure (typically restricted to zero); $\mathbf{B}$ is a matrix of regression coefficients often used to model causal effects among latent variables; and $\mathbf{\zeta}_i$ is a matrix of residuals with covariance matrix $\mathbf{\Psi}$ (typically with unrestricted diagonal elements, i.e., variances). In the case of latent interactions, $\mathbf{\eta}_i$ can be used to stack products of latent variables so that all observed, latent, and product-term variables can be understood as existing in $\mathbf{\eta}_i$—this is useful for concision, reducing the complexity of our equations (for more technical treatments, see Klein & Moosbrugger, 2000; Klein & Muthén, 2007; Preacher et al., 2016).

The result is that in Equations 20.11 and 20.12, all moderation, mediation, and moderated mediation effects are either contained in $\mathbf{B}$, or they can be constructed from elements in $\mathbf{B}$. For example, Equations 20.7 and 20.8 can be shown in the form of Equations 20.11 and 20.12 as follows:

$$\mathbf{y}_i = \begin{bmatrix} m_i \\ y_i \\ x_i \\ w_i \\ xw_i \\ mw_i \end{bmatrix} = \mathbf{v} + \mathbf{\Lambda}\mathbf{\eta}_i + \mathbf{\varepsilon}_i$$

$$= \begin{bmatrix} 0 \\ 0 \\ 0 \\ 0 \\ 0 \\ 0 \end{bmatrix} + \begin{bmatrix} 1 & 0 & 0 & 0 & 0 & 0 \\ 0 & 1 & 0 & 0 & 0 & 0 \\ 0 & 0 & 1 & 0 & 0 & 0 \\ 0 & 0 & 0 & 1 & 0 & 0 \\ 0 & 0 & 0 & 0 & 1 & 0 \\ 0 & 0 & 0 & 0 & 0 & 1 \end{bmatrix} \begin{bmatrix} \eta_m \\ \eta_y \\ \eta_x \\ \eta_w \\ \eta_{xw} \\ \eta_{mw} \end{bmatrix} + \begin{bmatrix} 0 \\ 0 \\ 0 \\ 0 \\ 0 \\ 0 \end{bmatrix}$$

$$(20.13)$$

and

$$\mathbf{\eta}_i = \begin{bmatrix} \eta_m \\ \eta_y \\ \eta_x \\ \eta_w \\ \eta_{xw} \\ \eta_{mw} \end{bmatrix} = \mathbf{\alpha} + \mathbf{B}\mathbf{\eta}_i + \mathbf{\zeta}_i$$

$$= \begin{bmatrix} v_m \\ v_y \\ \alpha_x \\ \alpha_w \\ \alpha_{xw} \\ \alpha_{mw} \end{bmatrix} + \begin{bmatrix} 0 & 0 & a_{mx} & a_{mw} & a_{mxw} & 0 \\ b_{ym} & 0 & c'_{yx} & c'_{yw} & c'_{yxw} & b_{ymw} \\ 0 & 0 & 0 & 0 & 0 & 0 \\ 0 & 0 & 0 & 0 & 0 & 0 \\ 0 & 0 & 0 & 0 & 0 & 0 \\ 0 & 0 & 0 & 0 & 0 & 0 \end{bmatrix} \begin{bmatrix} \eta_m \\ \eta_y \\ \eta_x \\ \eta_w \\ \eta_{xw} \\ \eta_{mw} \end{bmatrix}$$

$$+ \begin{bmatrix} \varepsilon_{m,i} \\ \varepsilon_{y,i} \\ \zeta_{x,i} \\ \zeta_{w,i} \\ \zeta_{xw,i} \\ \zeta_{mw,i} \end{bmatrix}. \qquad (20.14)$$

Here, by constraining the values of $\mathbf{v}$, $\boldsymbol{\Lambda}$, and $\boldsymbol{\varepsilon}_i$, Equation 20.13 equates the terms in $\boldsymbol{\eta}_i$ to the observed variables in $\mathbf{y}_i$. Furthermore, the constraints imposed in Equation 20.14 result in any variables that are both predictors of the same outcome and are not related in $\mathbf{B}$ having an unrestricted relationship in $\boldsymbol{\Psi}$. Given this ordering of variables in $\boldsymbol{\eta}_i$, for example, the matrix $\boldsymbol{\Psi}$ might be shown as

$$\boldsymbol{\Psi} = \begin{bmatrix} \psi_{m,m} & & & & & \\ 0 & \psi_{y,y} & & & & \\ 0 & 0 & \psi_{x,x} & & & \\ 0 & 0 & \psi_{x,w} & \psi_{w,w} & & \\ 0 & 0 & \psi_{x,xw} & \psi_{w,xw} & \psi_{xw,xw} & \\ \psi_{m,mw} & 0 & \psi_{x,mw} & \psi_{w,mw} & \psi_{xw,mw} & \psi_{mw,mw} \end{bmatrix},$$

(20.15)

wherein the diagonal elements are variances or residual variances, and off-diagonal elements are covariances or residual covariances.

Estimation can be accomplished with a variety of tools. SEM is typically estimated with maximum likelihood, which may be robust to nonnormality and the nonindependence of observations (as in Muthén & Muthén, 2016). However, Bayesian approaches are also possible (see Muthén & Asparouhov, 2012). In all cases, estimators of uncertainty such as CIs for indirect effects should not be based on normal theory.

Single-Level Moderated Mediation: Race in High School and Beyond

Using SEM, any combination of parameters can be estimated and used to examine moderated mediation (e.g., using Mplus features such as "model indirect" and "model constraint"; Muthén & Muthén, 2016). To show this, we use the HS&B data (see online Mplus files in "Single.Level. Modmed.zip"). For illustrative purposes, we treat the data as single-level and use a sandwich estimator to adjust SEs for nonindependence (with "Type=Complex" and "Cluster=school" in Mplus). To derive all CIs reported in the following text, we use a Monte Carlo approach that allows estimating CIs in the presence of clustered data

(which presents difficulty for more common nonparametric bootstrapping; see Preacher & Selig, 2012; online Mplus files in "MonteCarlo. CI.zip"). Throughout, when SEs conform to normal theory, we present p-values rather than CIs. We would not normally recommend a single-level approach for these data, but working with this example allows us to contrast single-level results with the multilevel results we present later.

The variables we use are: *student math achievement*, with higher scores implying greater achievement on a standardized test; *student SES*, with higher scores meaning higher parental income, education, occupational attainment, and education-related possessions such as books; *student race*, wherein 1 = Black and 0 = other; and *student gender*, wherein 0 = male and 1 = female. More details about the variables can be found in the publication on the HS&B data by National Opinion Research Center (1980).

We estimate a model wherein math achievement y is a function of SES m and race x, with SES m also being a function of race x. This model allows estimating some effects of being Black in the United States, which can negatively affect math achievement directly and indirectly via SES (Altonji & Blank, 1999; Bertrand & Mullainathan, 2004; Bonilla-Silva, 2006; Steele & Aronson, 1995). Similar negative effects are known in the epidemiology literature, pointing to negative effects of being Black in the United States on health and other outcomes both directly and via SES (Navarro, 1990; Ren, Amick, & Williams, 1999). Furthermore, this is a sensible model in terms of causality because we assume that changes in student math achievement cannot influence parental SES and that changes in math achievement or parental SES cannot influence individual race.

We allow gender w to moderate all relationships (as in Equations 20.7–20.10, 20.13, and 20.14). This moderator is sensitive to different forms of race-based differences for Black men versus Black women (see Galinsky, Hall, & Cuddy, 2013; Hall, Hall, & Perry, 2016; Thomas, Witherspoon, & Speight, 2008; Tomaskovic-Devey, 1993; Wingfield, 2007). Because of such gender differences, the direct and indirect effects of race may differ for males versus females, and any direct effect of SES may differ. As with race, changes in other study variables cannot influence gender.

Table 20.1 displays model parameters. On the basis of Equation 20.10, we can define multiple effects that will be of interest. These are specified under "model constraint" in the M*plus* input and shown in Table 20.2. To understand their construction, we formally define them and explain their substantive meaning. Although w is categorical, our logic also works for continuous moderators by choosing relevant values of w (e.g., 1 standard deviation above and below the mean) to make comparisons like those we describe.

First, we define the indirect effect for females, which is the simple slope of the indirect effect when the moderator gender = 1 (i.e., $w = 1$). This is

$$\left(a_{mx} + a_{mxw}w_i\right)\left(b_{ym} + b_{ymw}w_i\right) = \left(a_{mx} + a_{mxw}\right)\left(b_{ym} + b_{ymw}\right), \quad (20.16)$$

which is the indirect effect of race on math achievement via SES for females and is -1.255 with 95% CI $[-1.634, -.867]$, indicating that Black females have

TABLE 20.1

Single-Level Moderated Mediation Model Parameters

Parameter	Estimate	Standard error	*p* value
SES parameters			
v_m (SES intercept)	.192	—	—
a_{mx} (race→SES)	−.505	.064	<.001
a_{mw} (gender→SES)	−.117	.039	.002
a_{mxw} (race*gender→SES)	.061	.078	.432
Math achievement parameters			
v_y (MA intercept)	14.31	—	—
b_{ym} (SES→MA)	2.515	.211	<.001
b_{ymw} (SES*gender→MA)	.312	.261	.232
c'_{yx} (race→MA)	−3.012	.368	<.001
c'_{yw} (gender→MA)	−1.466	.251	<.001
c'_{yxw} (race*gender→MA)	.318	.481	.509

Note. MA = math achievement; SES = socioeconomic status.

TABLE 20.2

Single-Level Moderated Mediation Model's Further Calculated Parameters

Parameter name	Lower 2.5%	Estimate	Upper 97.5%	Standard error	*p* value
Female					
Indirect race effect	−1.634	−1.255	−.867	—	—
Direct race effect	—	−2.694	—	.412	<.001
Total race effect	−4.926	−3.949	−2.947	—	—
SES effect	—	2.827	—	.173	<.001
Male					
Indirect race effect	−1.604	−1.27	−.954	—	—
Direct race effect	—	−3.012	—	.368	<.001
Total race effect	−5.117	−4.282	−3.432	—	—
SES effect	—	2.515	—	.211	<.001
Difference in effects (male–female)					
Indirect race effect	−0.444	−.015	.397	—	—
Direct race effect	—	−.318	—	.481	.509
Total race effect	−1.396	−.333	.719	—	—
SES effect (b_{ymw})	—	−.312	—	.261	.232

Note. Where parameters involve products of coefficients, confidence intervals are generated by Monte Carlo using parameter estimates and their asymptotic covariance matrix with 10,000 draws. SES = socioeconomic status.

lower math achievement due to the effect of their race on their SES. The equivalent conditional indirect effect for males is when gender = 0 (i.e., $w = 0$) or

$$(a_{mx} + a_{mxw}w_i)(b_{ym} + b_{ymw}w_i) = a_{mx}b_{ym}, \quad (20.17)$$

which defines the indirect effect of race on math achievement via SES for males and is –1.27 with 95% CI [–1.604, –.954], indicating that Black males have lower math achievement due to the effect of their race on their SES. In turn, the difference in the indirect effects for men versus women is defined as follows:

$$a_{mx}b_{ym} - (a_{mx} + a_{mxw})(b_{ym} + b_{ymw})$$
$$= -(a_{mx}b_{ymw} + a_{mxw}b_{ym} + a_{mxw}b_{ymw}). \quad (20.18)$$

This difference is interpreted as the moderating effect of gender on the indirect effect of race on math achievement via SES while holding the direct effect of race constant. This difference is –.015 with 95% CI [–.444, .397], indicating no statistically significant difference between males and females in the indirect effect of race on math achievement via SES—although the point estimate of –.015 means the indirect effect of race appears to be slightly more negative for males, the CI centering almost on zero.

Comparing the direct effects of race on math achievement shows a similar pattern. For females ($w = 1$) this effect is

$$c'_{yx} + c'_{yxw}w_i = c'_{yx} + c'_{yxw}, \quad (20.19)$$

which describes the direct effect of race on math achievement for females and is –2.694 ($p < .001$), indicating that Black females have lower math achievement. The effect for males ($w = 0$) is

$$c'_{yx} + c'_{yxw}w_i = c'_{yx}, \quad (20.20)$$

which describes the direct effect of race on math achievement for males and is –3.012 ($p < .001$), indicating that Black males have lower math achievement. In turn, the difference in male versus female direct effects is

$$c'_{yx} - (c'_{yx} + c'_{yxw}) = -c'_{yxw}. \quad (20.21)$$

This difference is interpreted as the conditional interaction between race and gender (because SES

is controlled for) and is –.318 ($p = .509$), indicating no statistically significant difference between males and females in the direct effect of race on math achievement.

For total effects, the same logic applies, so that the effect for females ($w = 1$) is

$$(a_{mx} + a_{mxw}w_i)(b_{ym} + b_{ymw}w_i) + (c'_{yx} + c'_{yxw}w_i)$$
$$= (a_{mx} + a_{mxw})(b_{ym} + b_{ymw}) + (c'_{yx} + c'_{yxw}), \quad (20.22)$$

which is the overall effect of race on math achievement for females and is –3.949 with 95% CI [–4.926, –2.947], indicating that for females, race has an overall negative effect on math achievement. For males ($w = 0$) this is

$$(a_{mx} + a_{mxw}w_i)(b_{ym} + b_{ymw}w_i) + (c'_{yx} + c'_{yxw}w_i)$$
$$= a_{mx}b_{ym} + c'_{yx}, \quad (20.23)$$

which describes the overall effect of race on math achievement for males and is –4.282 with 95% CI [–5.117, –3.432], indicating that for males race has an overall negative effect on math achievement. In turn, the difference in these effects for males versus females is

$$a_{mx}b_{ym} + c'_{yx} - [(a_{mx} + a_{mxw})(b_{ym} + b_{ymw}) + (c'_{yx} + c'_{yxw})]$$
$$= -(a_{mx}b_{ymw} + a_{mxw}b_{ym} + a_{mxw}b_{ymw} + c'_{yxw}). \quad (20.24)$$

This difference is interpreted as the moderating effect of gender on the effect of race on math achievement. This difference is –.333 with 95% CI [–1.396, .719], indicating no statistically significant difference between males and females in the overall effect of race on math achievement.

The direct effect of SES can also be estimated. For females ($w = 1$), this is

$$b_{ym} + b_{ymw}w_i = b_{ym} + b_{ymw}, \quad (20.25)$$

which describes the effect of SES on math achievement for females while holding race constant. This effect is 2.827 ($p < .001$), indicating that higher SES for females leads to higher math achievement. The same effect for males ($w = 0$) is

$$b_{ym} + b_{ymw}w_i = b_{ym}, \quad (20.26)$$

which describes the effect of SES on math achievement for males while holding race constant. This effect is 2.515 ($p < .001$), indicating that higher SES for males leads to higher math achievement. In turn, their difference is simply

$$b_{ym} - (b_{ym} + b_{ymw}) = -b_{ymw}, \qquad (20.27)$$

which describes the moderating effect of gender on the effect of SES on math achievement while holding race constant. This is $-.312$ ($p = .232$), indicating no statistically significant difference between males and females in the effect of SES on math achievement while holding race constant.

Overall, the pattern of results for race is consistent with the long-running history of racism in the United States. The effects of being Black on math achievement are negative, both indirectly via SES and directly. This is predictable given the substantial literature on racism and its effects both generally (e.g., Bonilla-Silva, 2006) and on standardized test scores specifically (e.g., Steele & Aronson, 1995). However, contrary to what some research may suggest (e.g., Galinsky et al., 2013), we find no moderating effect of gender, even when testing direct effects of SES.

MULTILEVEL MODERATED MEDIATION IN MULTILEVEL STRUCTURAL EQUATION MODELS

Unfortunately, these models and analyses are insensitive to the clustering in our data except that they adjust *SE*s. When children are nested in schools or data are otherwise grouped, different variances and effects are mixed: between group and within group (Cronbach, 1976; Cronbach & Snow, 1977; Cronbach & Webb, 1975; Preacher et al., 2010, 2016; Zhang, Zyphur, & Preacher, 2009). Between-group variances and effects are related to group means, whereas within-group variances and effects are related to deviations away from the means (as in analysis of variance [ANOVA]). In turn, when analyzing data and making inferences, within-group terms represent individuals (e.g., students) and between-group terms represent groups (e.g., schools). To motivate this style of representation, we first justify it as follows.

Motivating the Study of Race Between and Within Schools

Our position (e.g., Preacher et al., 2010, 2011, 2016; Zhang et al., 2009) is that by ignoring clustering, single-level analyses create "uninterpretable blends" of variances and effects that are attributable to different kinds of things—students versus schools (Cronbach, 1976, p. 9.20). Furthermore, differences in the magnitudes of these terms across levels of analysis "occur with considerable regularity" (Raudenbush & Bryk, 2002, p. 140), and these differences have critical implications for substantive interventions that might be designed to target entire groups (e.g., schools) versus the individuals residing within them. The job of the data scientist who endeavors to inform intervention or policy planning is to decompose variances and effects so that inferences about different kinds of entities can be unambiguously made in light of the clustered structure of a data set.

Despite the long recognition of the need to decompose level-specific effects (e.g., Dansereau & Yammarino, 2000), there is some debate regarding this point, especially for mediation and moderation analyses (e.g., Pituch & Stapleton, 2012; Tofighi & Thoemmes, 2014). Therefore, we clarify our views and then connect them to the case of multilevel moderated mediation to study race in the HS&B data. First, consider a data set with information from students in a single school $j = 1$ and a simple bivariate model:

$$y_{i1} = v + \beta x_{i1} + \varepsilon_{i1}. \qquad (20.28)$$

Here, β is the effect of x on y for all students in school $j = 1$. As with all single-level regression models, we and most other researchers would refer to β as an individual-level effect. However, what researchers mean is that β is a within-school effect, which becomes clear by rewriting Equation 20.28 in terms of variances, covariances, and means as follows:

$$y_{i1} = \mu_y + \frac{\sigma_{xy}}{\sigma_x^2}(x_{i1} - \mu_x) + \varepsilon_{i1}, \qquad (20.29)$$

wherein μ terms are means, σ_{xy} is x-y covariance, and σ_x^2 is the variance of x.

As Equation 20.29 shows, group means play no part in deriving β in single-level analyses—the means for *y* and *x* could be changed by any value and β would be unchanged. Also, statistical inference with *SE*s is a function of ε_{i1}, which is a within-school term. In turn, so-called *individual-level* analyses with data from a single group estimate within-group effects, meaning that when researchers make inferences about individuals, they have all along been making within-group inferences (i.e., inferences about individuals that are always relative to the mean of the group). Therefore, consistent with typical regression practices, we recommend using within-group terms to make inferences about individuals.

To further illustrate this point, consider the HS&B data with *N* students in *J* schools. To make inferences about students, any confounding "unobserved heterogeneity" associated with schools should be controlled. This kind of "fixed-effects" model—in econometrics terms—can be constructed by creating *J*-1 indicator variables (e.g., dummy codes) in a vector z_j as follows:

$$y_{ij} = v + \beta x_{ij} + \delta'_j z_j + \varepsilon_{ij}. \qquad (20.30)$$

Here, the effect of school membership is accounted for by the coefficients in the vector δ_j and the effect of *x* on *y* for students is still β, which is a within-group term, as is ε_{ij} (which is used for statistical inference with *SE*s). Furthermore, by accounting for the "school effects" δ_j, what is really occurring is that the school means are being entirely accounted for, which is to say that δ_j is accounting for all between-school variance, which is associated with schools—to emphasize, in this kind of fixed-effects model, there is no remaining between-school variance that can be accounted for with any additional predictors. In other words, when attempting to make inferences about individuals while controlling for group effects, researchers focus on within-group variance to make inferences about individuals and control for between-group variance to model the effect of groups, as is done when "within-group centering" data by eliminating group means (Preacher et al., 2010).

Moreover, to motivate inferences about groups by using between-group variances and effects, consider

an experiment wherein researchers randomly assign participants to a control group $x_{j=1}$ or an experimental group $x_{j=2}$. To make an inference about the effect of interest, researchers must model the effect of group membership, which can be shown as follows:

$$y_{ij} = v + \beta x_j + \varepsilon_{ij}, \qquad (20.31)$$

wherein the model now reflects terms for an individual *i* and a group *j*, with *x* coding for group membership. Here, the effect of interest is β, which in an ANOVA framework is well known as a between-group effect, capturing the difference between the two group means. Here, researchers do not substantively care about ε_{ij} because this within-group term is typically regarded as being due to individual or subject-specific effects.

In all these cases—typical regression models, fixed-effects regression controlling for group effects, and ANOVA—researchers always make inferences about individuals using within-group variances or effects that model deviations away from group means, and inferences are made about groups using between-group variances or effects that model group means. Therefore, in all our models we decompose the between- and within-group parts of any observed variables measured at the "individual" level, so accurate inferences can be made about the appropriate kinds of things that are being assessed (e.g., students, schools, communities). Such decomposition of level-specific effects has long been recommended in the literature (e.g., Cronbach, 1976; Cronbach & Webb, 1975; Dansereau & Yammarino, 2000; Kozlowski & Klein, 2000), but this work is often overlooked.

For studying race, separating student versus school effects is key because different processes can influence students within schools versus schools as wholes (Benner & Graham, 2013), especially because schools are typically defined by local environments such as neighborhoods. Although Black students in a school may experience individualized forms of racism as noted previously (motivating a focus on within-school effects), there is evidence that collective "institutional" racism has profound effects. For example, formal and informal segregationist agendas in the United States drove Black individuals into poor and blighted neighborhoods (Massey &

Denton, 1993; Seitles, 1998; Williams & Collins, 2001)—an infamous example is the design of low bridge overpasses to keep Black bus passengers from crossing into upper-class White neighborhoods (Caro, 1974). In addition to being excluded from important social capital, institutional racism has had profound effects, including poorer nutrition, education, and employment rates, as well as community problems that make life unstable, stressful, and emotionally hard (Seaton & Yip, 2009; Umaña-Taylor, 2016; Williams, 1999; Williams & Williams-Morris, 2000).

In turn, institutional racism causes covariance between racial composition, such as the proportion of Black students in a school, and the collective testing outcomes at a school. This effect may operate directly, but it can also function indirectly through collective SES, which further reflects the problems of poorer neighborhoods and schools (e.g., Pickett & Pearl, 2001). As a moderator, gender composition could influence these effects because of the different ways that Black males and females are collectively treated (Hall et al., 2016; Wingfield, 2007).

Therefore, it is reasonable to decompose the between- versus within-school parts of observed variables to examine collective versus individual effects of race. To do so, we now introduce multilevel approaches to moderation, mediation, and moderated mediation.

Multilevel Moderation

To understand MSEM for the purposes of multilevel moderated mediation analyses, we begin by extending moderation, mediation, and moderated mediation models from Equations 20.1, 20.3, 20.4, 20.7, and 20.8 to the multilevel case. In these models, observed variables such as y will typically reflect within- and between-group components when data are clustered or otherwise nested. These components can be decomposed as follows:

$$y_{ij} = y_{Bj} + y_{Wij}, \qquad (20.32)$$

wherein a B subscript indicates a between-group part (e.g., a school mean, sometimes referred to as a *random intercept*) and a W subscript indicates a within-group part (e.g., a student's relative standing after subtracting the school mean).

In turn, the moderation model in Equation 20.1 can be reformulated by decomposing the B and W parts of all relevant variables as follows (for concision, we omit random slopes as regression coefficients that vary across groups, which are possible in our MSEM approach):

$$y_{Bj} = \nu_{By} + c_{Byx}x_{Bj} + c_{Byw}w_{Bj} + c_{Byxw}x_{Bj}w_{Bj} + \varepsilon_{By,j} \qquad (20.33)$$

$$y_{Wij} = c_{Wyx}x_{Wij} + c_{Wyw}w_{Wij} + c_{Wyxw}x_{Wij}w_{Wij} + \varepsilon_{Wy,ij}, \qquad (20.34)$$

wherein all terms are as before, but B terms denote between-school variables or effects and W terms denote within-school variables or effects. Notice that the intercept for y in Equation 20.33 is a B term, which is consistent with our arguments related to Equations 20.28 to 20.31. Notice also that the product terms $x_{Bj}w_{Bj}$ and $x_{Wij}w_{Wij}$ are not $(xw)_{Bj}$ and $(xw)_{Wij}$, because the latter implies first multiplying x and w and then decomposing the B and W parts of the product term, which is not the same as multiplying the B and W components (Preacher et al., 2016).

The point of Equations 20.33 and 20.34 is that the B coefficients can be used to make inferences about groups (e.g., schools), and the W coefficients can be used to make inferences about individuals, who are by design nested in the groups. The moderation effects c_{Byxw} and c_{Wyxw} have the same interpretation as previously, except they apply to moderation of B and W effects—similar operations as in Equation 20.2 can define B and W moderation (Preacher et al., 2016).

Multilevel Mediation

The same is true for the mediation model in Equations 20.3 and 20.4, which in a multilevel framework would be

$$m_{Bj} = \nu_{Bm} + a_{Bmx}x_{Bj} + \varepsilon_{Bm,j} \qquad (20.35)$$

$$y_{Bj} = \nu_{By} + b_{Bym}m_{Bj} + c'_{Byx}x_{Bj} + \varepsilon_{By,j} \qquad (20.36)$$

$$m_{Wij} = a_{Wmx}x_{Wij} + \varepsilon_{Wm,ij} \qquad (20.37)$$

$$y_{Wij} = b_{Wym}m_{Wij} + c'_{Wyx}x_{Wij} + \varepsilon_{Wy,ij}, \qquad (20.38)$$

wherein all terms are as before and with similar interpretations, except the B parts apply to groups (e.g., schools) and the W parts apply to individuals, who are nested within groups. Furthermore, the same logic of mediation exists, with B and W indirect effects being $a_{Bmx}b_{Bym}$ and $a_{Wmx}b_{Wym}$, respectively—the reader can perform the same operations as in Equations 20.5 and 20.6 for both B and W mediation (Preacher et al., 2010).

Multilevel Moderated Mediation

Multilevel moderated mediation implies the same straightforward extension to the B and W case, so that Equations 20.7 and 20.8 become (again, for concision, we omit random slopes)

$$m_{Bj} = \nu_{Bm} + a_{Bmx}x_{Bj} + a_{Bmw}w_{Bj} + a_{Bmxw}x_{Bj}w_{Bj} + \varepsilon_{Bm,j} \tag{20.39}$$

$$y_{Bj} = \nu_{By} + b_{Bym}m_{Bj} + b_{Bymw}m_{Bj}w_{Bj} + c'_{Byx}x_{Bj}$$
$$+ c'_{Byw}w_{Bj} + c'_{Byxw}x_{Bj}w_{Bj} + \varepsilon_{By,j} \tag{20.40}$$

$$m_{Wij} = a_{Wmx}x_{Wij} + a_{Wmw}w_{Wij} + a_{Wmxw}x_{Wij}w_{Wij} + \varepsilon_{Wm,ij} \tag{20.41}$$

$$y_{Wij} = b_{Wym}m_{Wij} + b_{Wymw}m_{Wij}w_{Wij} + c'_{Wyx}x_{Wij}$$
$$+ c'_{Wyw}w_{Wij} + c'_{Wyxw}x_{Wij}w_{Wij} + \varepsilon_{Wy,ij}, \tag{20.42}$$

wherein moderated mediation has the same familiar form, except with separate B and W parts to allow inference to groups and individuals. In turn, the same operations we used to explain moderated mediation after Equation 20.8 apply to Equations 20.39 to 20.42, with B indirect and direct effects for groups as $(a_{Bmx} + a_{Bmxw}w_{Bj})(b_{Bym} + b_{Bymw}w_{Bj})$ and $(c'_{Byx} + c'_{Byxw}w_{Bj})$, respectively, and W indirect and direct effects for individuals as $(a_{Wmx} + a_{Wmxw}w_{Wij})(b_{Wym} + b_{Wymw}w_{Wij})$ and $(c'_{Wyx} + c'_{Wyxw}w_{Wij})$, respectively. Here, the reader can apply the same logic as with single-level analyses, keeping in mind that B effects apply to groups and W effects apply to individuals.

A General Multilevel Structural Equation Model Specification and Estimation

To estimate terms in Equations 20.33 to 20.42 with B and W moderated mediation parameters that mirror those in Equations 20.16 to 20.27 (and Table 20.1 and 20.2), we extend the SEM in Equations 20.11 to 20.15 to the multilevel case.

We do this succinctly as follows, but we note that the interested reader can consult complementary treatments in Preacher et al. (2010, 2011, 2016):

$$\mathbf{y}_{ij} = \Lambda\boldsymbol{\eta}_{ij} \tag{20.43}$$

$$\boldsymbol{\eta}_{ij} = \boldsymbol{\alpha}_j + \mathbf{B}_j\boldsymbol{\eta}_{ij} + \boldsymbol{\zeta}_{ij} \tag{20.44}$$

$$\boldsymbol{\eta}_j = \boldsymbol{\mu} + \boldsymbol{\beta}\boldsymbol{\eta}_j + \boldsymbol{\zeta}_j, \tag{20.45}$$

wherein the meaning of terms differs from Equations 20.11 to 20.15.

In Equation 20.43, $\mathbf{y}_{ij}$ is a vector of observed variables; Λ is a matrix indicating whether variables vary within groups, between groups, or both; and $\boldsymbol{\eta}_{ij}$ is a vector of latent variables that vary either within or between groups. For example, Equation 20.32 can be formulated as Equation 20.43 to clarify its meaning as follows:

$$y_{ij} = \Lambda\boldsymbol{\eta}_{ij} = \begin{bmatrix} 1 & 1 \end{bmatrix}\begin{bmatrix} y_{Bj} \\ y_{Wij} \end{bmatrix} = y_{Bj} + y_{Wij}, \tag{20.46}$$

wherein the two elements in Λ for y_{ij} indicate that it has W and B parts, contained in $\boldsymbol{\eta}_{ij}$.

In turn, Equation 20.44 contains the B part of observed variables in an intercept vector $\boldsymbol{\alpha}_j$ (again, these are sometimes referred to as *random intercepts*), the W effects among the W parts of observed variables in a matrix $\mathbf{B}_j$, and W residuals in a vector $\boldsymbol{\zeta}_{ij}$. In other words, the W structural model is in $\mathbf{B}_j$, and therefore, $\mathbf{B}_j$ will contain W moderated mediation terms, such as those in Equations 20.41 and 20.42.

Alternatively, Equation 20.44 contains B model parts as follows: $\boldsymbol{\eta}_j$ contains all B variables of interest from $\boldsymbol{\eta}_{ij}$, but this is done by stacking the B intercepts in $\boldsymbol{\alpha}_j$ as well as any random slopes from $\mathbf{B}_j$; $\boldsymbol{\mu}$ is a vector of intercepts or grand means; $\boldsymbol{\beta}$ is a matrix of B effects; and $\boldsymbol{\zeta}_j$ is a vector of B residuals. In other words, the B structural model is in $\boldsymbol{\beta}$, and therefore, $\boldsymbol{\beta}$ will contain B moderated mediation terms, such as those in Equations 20.39 and 20.40.

Hopefully, by now the reader can infer that multilevel moderated mediation merely requires applying familiar single-level concepts to the W and B model parts in Equations 20.44 and 20.45. However, before proceeding, there are a few caveats to mention. First, MSEM allows for more flexibility than we can cover here, such as random slopes (e.g., for *W* effects in $\mathbf{B}_j$, which would be stacked in $\boldsymbol{\eta}_j$). Such slopes allow cross-level interactions, which may be a useful complement to the multilevel moderated mediation we examine here. The interested reader can easily pursue this using our logic and that in Preacher et al. (2010, 2016), which discusses special issues related to the use of random slopes and cross-level interactions.

Second, because the *B* and *W* parts of an observed variable are latent, they must be estimated. This estimation can be done by calculating school averages, but as in most multilevel models (e.g., Raudenbush & Bryk, 2002), MSEM does this using an empirical Bayes approach to account for sampling error. However, in some cases, this may be unwarranted, and researchers may prefer to compute group means for *B* parts as if they were observed (see Lüdtke et al., 2008; Lüdtke, Marsh, Robitzsch, & Trautwein, 2011; Marsh et al., 2009; Preacher et al., 2016). For HS&B data, both individuals and schools were randomly sampled, and therefore, empirical Bayes estimation is warranted.

Third, in Equations 20.33 and 20.34, we noted that $x_{Bj}w_{Bj}$ and $x_{Wij}w_{Wij}$ are not $(xw)_{Bj}$ and $(xw)_{Wij}$. The implication for moderated mediation in MSEM is that the reader cannot simply compute observed product terms for interacting variables such as $x_{ij}w_{ij}$ and then specify these in $\mathbf{y}_{ij}$ from Equation 20.43. The reason is that MSEM decomposes the *W* and *B* parts of observed variables to account for uncertainty associated with sampling error (as implied by Equation 20.46).

To estimate *W* and *B* moderation requires computing product terms for latent *B* and *W* variables separately, as in $x_{Bj}w_{Bj}$ and $x_{Wij}w_{Wij}$ (Preacher et al., 2016). This is done in M*plus* by putting a latent variable "behind" a set of *B* and *W* parts of observed variables and then forming product terms as latent variable interactions—which Preacher et al. (2016) specified in their online supplemental material. Figure 20.4 shows this, wherein the interacting *B* and *W* parts of observed variables are treated as latent, with the variances of their *B* and *W* parts fixed to .01 to facilitate convergence (as in Preacher et al., 2016). This allows estimating the

product terms required for multilevel moderation of various kinds.

Fourth, the recommended approach to latent interactions from Preacher et al. (2016) uses LMS, which is implemented in M*plus* (see Klein & Moosbrugger, 2000; Klein & Muthén, 2007). However, this approach can encounter serious difficulties with convergence in the case of high-dimensional numerical integration. For example, the model in Figure 20.4 using the HS&B data was not estimable with adequate dimensions of numerical integration, and we could not achieve convergence using the "Integration=Montecarlo" approach to this integration as shown in Preacher et al.'s (2016) online supplemental material (the reader is invited to experiment with the M*plus* input in "Multilevel. ModMed.zip"). This is because our model has many latent variables (i.e., three *B* terms, three *W* terms, as well as their associated latent product terms), which is not surprising when combining the approaches of Preacher et al. (2016) with that of Preacher et al. (2010). Such complexity is to be expected with multilevel moderated mediation (consider multilevel versions of Hayes, 2018, which could even include many random slopes of *W* model parts). Indeed, such complexity is to be expected even in the single-level case of moderated mediation with latent variables.

Therefore, to avoid numerical integration, we use a Bayesian plausible values approach to latent variable interactions in M*plus* (see Asparouhov & Muthén, 2010a, 2010b, 2010c). This approach uses Bayesian estimation with default "diffuse" or "uninformative" prior probabilities to approximate maximum-likelihood estimation (see Muthén & Asparouhov, 2012). The key to this estimation is that it allows generating a Bayesian analog of factor scores for latent variables by sampling from their posterior distribution some number of times (20 in our case; see Mislevy et al., 1992, and Von Davier, Gonzalez, & Mislevy, 2009). Interestingly, this is equivalent to a multiple imputation method with latent variables treated as missing data, which overcomes the need for estimating latent variables and their interactions directly, which requires computationally difficult numerical integration.

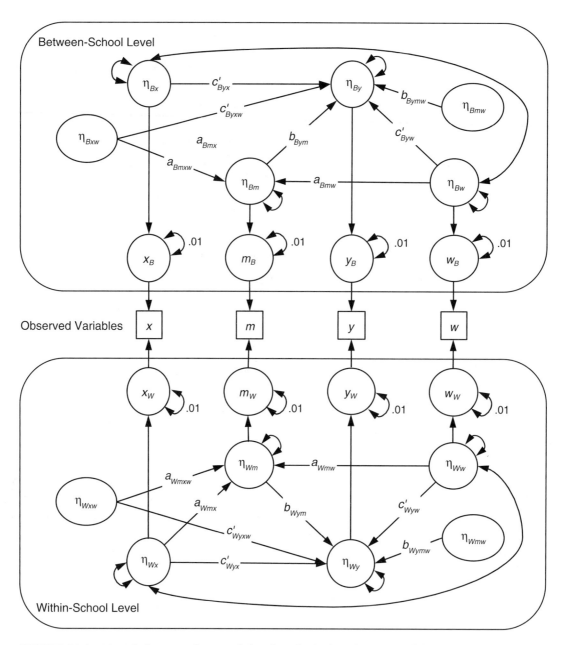

FIGURE 20.4.   A path diagram of our multilevel moderated mediation model.

Although research on multiple imputation shows that interactions or nonlinear effects should be used for imputing observed data (e.g., Bartlett et al., 2015; Seaman, Bartlett, & White, 2012; von Hippel, 2009), including in the multilevel case (Goldstein, Carpenter, & Browne, 2014), our approach imputes missing unobserved variables rather than observed variables, and therefore, our method should capture some of the interaction and nonlinear patterns that are a function of the observed, nonmissing data. In the multilevel case, we expect that latent W and B scores can be accurately estimated even without including latent products in the model—although there are conditions for this being the case, including having no missing data (or few missing data) along observed variables (for insight, see the previous citations). After generating the plausible values in a first step, a maximum likelihood procedure is used to estimate parameters and compute model fit in a second step (Asparouhov & Muthén, 2010a, 2010b; Enders, 2010), with estimates averaged across the plausible values and *SE*s adjusted for the uncertainty they indicate (as in Rubin, 1987; Schafer, 1997).

Our approach has two steps. Step 1: Plausible values are generated in M*plus* by estimating the model of interest without latent interactions, using a Bayes estimator with default diffuse/uninformative prior probability distributions (see M*plus* files in "Multilevel.ModMed.Plausible.Values.zip"). Step 2: A model is estimated using plausible values as if they were multiple imputations (e.g., Rubin, 1987; Schafer, 1997), using a typical maximum-likelihood based approach, with product terms computed for the plausible values to approximate latent interactions (see Figure 20.5). This allows treating all *B* and *W* model parts as if they were observed, with uncertainty in latent variable values treated as variation across the multiple imputations (i.e., differences in the plausible values). To capture

this uncertainty we use 20 imputations, which is a common number for multiple imputations (e.g., Rubin, 1987; Schafer, 1997). As the reader can grasp by experimenting with the full multilevel model and the two-step plausible values approach, the latter drastically simplifies the estimation of models involving latent interactions.

Fifth, and finally, because testing mediation with indirect effects cannot use *SE*s derived from normal theory, alternative approaches are recommended that we previously described. In the multilevel case with latent interactions, the situation is also complicated (see Zyphur, Zammuto, & Zhang, 2016). Therefore, we use a Monte Carlo approach wherein parameter estimates and their asymptotic covariance matrix are used to generate 10,000 estimates of effects (as in Zyphur et al., 2016; see online M*plus* files in "MonteCarlo.CI.zip"), which are then used to estimate CIs empirically.

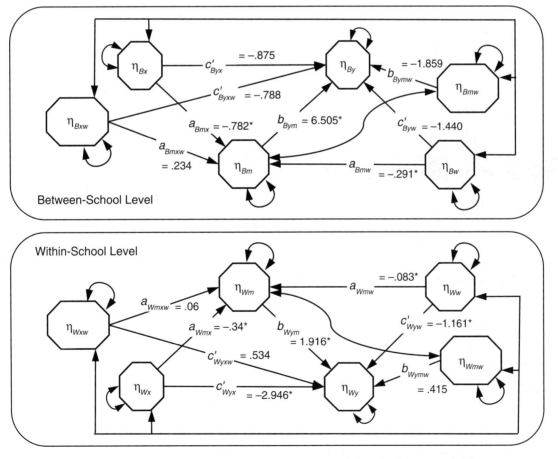

FIGURE 20.5. A path diagram of our multilevel mediation model with all latent variables as plausible values (i.e., multiply imputed), which we represent as octagons.

Between- and Within-School Race in High School and Beyond

Tables 20.3 and 20.4 display B and W model parameters, respectively (see also Figure 20.5). On the basis of Equation 20.10, B and W moderated mediation effects can be defined for Equations 20.16 to 20.27 (as applied to Equations 20.39–20.42). These are specified under "model constraint" in our online M*plus* files and shown in Tables 20.5 and 20.6 for B and W parameters, respectively. Because of the many results that exist in these tables, we summarize them for the sake of concision as follows.

The first thing to observe is that the W effects for students follow the same pattern as the single-level results—the direct and indirect effects of race have CIs that do not contain zero, and there is no moderation by gender. This similarity is expected because single-level analyses allow W parameters to dominate when there are many more units of observation at the W level compared with the B level and when W variances are larger than B variances (Preacher et al., 2010, 2016). For findings on the effects of race, the implication is that for any given student, being Black in the United States is harmful for math achievement directly and by having a negative effect on SES—again, both effects are

TABLE 20.3

Within-Level Moderated Mediation Model Parameters

Parameter	Estimate	Standard error	*p* value
SES effects			
a_{Wmx} (race→SES)	−.34	.037	<.001
a_{Wmw} (gender→SES)	−.083	.018	<.001
a_{Wmxw} (race*gender→SES)	.06	.068	.377
Math achievement effects			
b_{Wym} (SES→MA)	1.916	.118	<.001
b_{Wymw} (SES*gender→MA)	.415	.277	.134
c'_{Wyx} (race→MA)	−2.946	.259	<.001
c'_{Wyw} (gender→MA)	−1.161	.183	<.001
c'_{Wyxw} (race*gender→MA)	.534	.514	.299

Note. MA = math achievement; SES = socioeconomic status.

TABLE 20.4

Between-Level Moderated Mediation Model Parameters

Parameter	Estimate	Standard error	*p* value
SES effects			
v_{Bm} (SES intercept)	.324	—	—
a_{Bmx} (race→SES)	−.782	.222	<.001
a_{Bmw} (gender→SES)	−.291	.166	<.001
a_{Bmxw} (race*gender→SES)	.234	.39	.149
Math achievement effects			
v_{By} (MA intercept)	13.761	—	—
b_{Bym} (SES→MA)	6.505	.99	<.001
b_{Bymw} (SES*gender→MA)	−1.859	1.46	.203
c'_{Byx} (race→MA)	−.875	1.279	.494
c'_{Byw} (gender→MA)	−1.440	1.085	.184
c'_{Byxw} (race*gender→MA)	−.788	2.105	.708

Note. MA = math achievement; SES = socioeconomic status.

consistent with the long-running history of racism in the United States. However, gender seems to make little difference in these effects (although Table 20.3 shows that gender does have a sizable effect on math achievement, though this effect is smaller than the effect of race).

The B effects for schools, however, tell a different story. The upper panel of Table 20.6 shows results for all-female schools. The indirect effect of race on math achievement via SES for a school is −2.553 when comparing a school of Black females versus a school of non-Black females (with a CI not containing zero). However, the direct effect of race on math achievement for a school is −1.664 when comparing a school of Black females versus a school of non-Black females (with a CI containing zero). We have two important notes regarding this result. First, because variables often have distinctive meanings, varying measurement metrics and different reliabilities at W versus B levels (Bliese, 2000; Kozlowski & Klein, 2000), their path coefficients and the associated indirect effects are not readily comparable across levels. For example, the B indirect effect of −2.553 is not directly comparable to the same W indirect effect of −.652 because the units of analysis are different. This said, at each level, the same variable's direct

TABLE 20.5

TABLE 20.5

Within-Level Moderated Mediation Model's Further Calculated Parameters

Parameter name	Lower 2.5%	Estimate	Upper 97.5%	Standard error	*p* value
Female					
Indirect race effect	−1.06	−0.652	−.305	—	—
Direct race effect	—	−2.412	—	.507	<.001
Total race effect	−4.218	−3.064	−1.915	—	—
SES effect	—	2.332	—	.300	<.001
Male					
Indirect race effect	−.824	−.651	−.497	—	—
Direct race effect	—	−2.946	—	.259	<.001
Total race effect	−4.164	−3.597	−3.032	—	—
SES effect	—	1.916	—	.118	<.001
Difference in effects (male–female)					
Indirect race effect	−.319	.001	.367	—	—
Direct race effect	—	−.534	—	.514	.299
Total race effect	−1.563	−.533	.476	—	—
SES effect (b_{Wymw})	—	.415	—	.277	.134

Note. Where parameters involve products of coefficients, confidence intervals are generated by Monte Carlo using parameter estimates and their asymptotic covariance matrix with 10,000 draws. SES = socioeconomic status.

TABLE 20.6

Between-Level Moderated Mediation Model's Further Calculated Parameters

Parameter name	Lower 2.5%	Estimate	Upper 97.5%	Standard error	*p* value
Female					
Indirect race effect	−4.145	−2.553	−.893	—	—
Direct race effect	—	−1.664	—	1.105	.132
Total race effect	−6.512	−4.217	−1.475	—	—
SES effect	—	4.646	—	.713	<.001
Male					
Indirect race effect	−7.357	−5.077	−2.913	—	—
Direct race effect	—	−.875	—	1.279	.494
Total race effect	−8.452	−5.953	−3.151	—	—
SES effect	—	6.505	—	.99	<.001
Difference in effects (male–female)					
Indirect race effect	−5.907	−2.524	.704	—	—
Direct race effect	—	.788	—	2.105	.708
Total race effect	−6.09	−1.736	2.698	—	—
SES effect (b_{Bymw})	—	−1.859	—	1.46	.203

Note. Where parameters involve products of coefficients, confidence intervals are generated by Monte Carlo using parameter estimates and their asymptotic covariance matrix with 10,000 draws. SES = socioeconomic status.

and indirect effects can be compared and the relative magnitude of these effects can be informative (e.g., the *W* direct effect for females is –2.412 and the *W* indirect effect is –.652). Also, the level-specific ratios of direct versus indirect effects are not influenced by measurement metrics and can be compared across *B* and *W* levels. Second, we used theoretically extreme values for the *B*-level moderator's high versus low conditions (i.e., a school's gender composition can be 100% female or 100% male). We similarly used extreme values for the school-level race variable such that a school can be 100% Black or 100% non-Black. Using extreme values helps our interpretation of the conditional indirect effects given the categorical predictor and moderator variables. When a continuous moderator is examined, the more conventional approach is to use one level-specific standard deviation above and below its level-specific mean to calculate indirect effects at *B* and *W* levels. Overall, these findings show that for all-female schools, school-level race appears to influence school-level math achievement via school-level SES. This finding might be driven by neighborhood-level and school-level variables related to poverty. However, there is no direct effect of school-level race on school-level math achievement.

The same pattern of findings holds for Black males in all-male schools. As shown in the middle panel of Table 20.6, the indirect effect of school-level race on school-level math achievement via school-level SES for a school consisting solely of Black males is –5.077 when comparing a school of Black males versus a school of non-Black males (with a CI not containing zero). However, the direct effect yields a different conclusion, namely that the effect of school-level race on school-level math achievement for a school composed solely of Black males is –.875 when compared with a school of non-Black males (with a CI including zero). Therefore, again, for an entire male-only school, the effect of race appears to operate only indirectly via SES. Comparing the all-male school versus all-female school conditions, the difference in indirect effects has a confidence interval including zero (i.e., [–5.907, .704]). Therefore, school-level gender does not moderate the indirect effect of race on math achievement via school-level SES.

In sum, these results indicate that being a Black student in the United States has negative effects on math achievement, both directly and indirectly via SES, with the direct effects being stronger than those via SES. However, for schools as wholes, this is not the case. Consistent with centuries of institutional racism and other forms of injustice that cause a correlation between race and SES at the neighborhood and community levels (Bonilla-Silva, 2006), lower test scores for all-Black schools (regardless of gender) appear to be entirely due to SES. The implication is that, at the school level, the poverty and socioeconomic exclusion associated with racial differences may explain the effect of race on a school's math achievement. Overall, to address differences in test scores, the United States—like other countries—must do more to create racial equality by reducing the relationship between racial categories and important outcomes and socioeconomic resources.

DISCUSSION

We have described a novel approach for investigating multilevel moderated mediation using MSEM. Both conceptually and by example, we explored just one of the many possibilities for estimating these models, including a novel plausible values approach that avoids numerical integration—which would have otherwise derailed our analyses. Future work can explore specific cases that include random slopes and variables that vary only at the between-groups levels of analysis (see thorough treatments in Preacher et al., 2010, 2016). In all cases, the between- and within-groups parts of observed variables can be used to make inferences to higher versus lower level entities.

Our plausible values approach can be used for any model wherein latent interactions or power polynomials would otherwise require numerical integration and observed data provide adequate information to estimate latent standings. Therefore, this might be useful for single-level models that rely on LMS or other computationally intensive methods (e.g., Sardeshmukh & Vandenberg, 2016). Our plausible values approach has the benefit of allowing comparatively fast estimation when the number of multiple imputations is not overly large, but it does require various conditions being met that we will explore in a future paper. However, we do offer a word of caution when using asymptotic (co)variances of parameter estimates to compute CIs with a Monte Carlo procedure, as we use here. Because these covariances are meant to be asymptotic with similar estimation assumptions as a maximum likelihood estimator, researchers may be motivated to produce many multiple imputations, perhaps 1,000 or 10,000. For the purpose of our example and to make our online supplemental materials easier to download, we limited the number of imputations to 20, which is common in the multiple imputation and plausible values literatures (e.g., Mislevy et al., 1992; Rubin, 1987; Schafer, 1997; Von Davier et al., 2009).

Beyond concerns regarding the number of imputations, there are additional limitations with our approach and inferences that should be recognized. First, our data are from 1979 and therefore may no longer be a good representation of the United States in various ways, including the Black and non-Black composition of schools. Second, related to this composition, the inferences we make at the school level are based on some extrapolations from our data (i.e., theoretically extreme values for school-level race and school-level gender). Although there are schools in our sample and in the United States wherein students are almost all Black or all non-Black (indeed, the overall trend of this segregation is getting worse rather than better in public schools; see Frankenberg & Lee, 2002), no schools in our sample were composed of all-Black males or all-Black females. Therefore, our inferences regarding moderated mediation warrant some caution at the school level because they cannot be clearly mapped onto observed ranges in the data (this is a general problem for interpreting and reporting effects that involve moderation; see Hayes, 2013; Hayes & Preacher, 2013).

In conclusion, whether estimating multilevel moderated mediation or other effects, we hope that we have shown the potential power of statistical modeling to produce images of people and society that can motivate practical action. In terms of race, it is clear that the United States and other nations have a long way to go before justice or equality will be realized, and therefore, additional steps should be taken to eliminate racial inequalities. In our view, this should be the goal of statistical analyses: to motivate changes that make a difference.

References

Altonji, J. G., & Blank, R. M. (1999). Race and gender in the labor market. In O. Ashenfelter & D. Card (Eds.), *Handbook of labor economics* (3rd ed., pp. 3143–3259). New York, NY: Elsevier.

Asparouhov, T., & Muthén, B. (2010a). *Chi-square statistics with multiple imputation* (Version 2). Retrieved from https://www.statmodel.com/download/MI7.pdf

Asparouhov, T., & Muthén, B. (2010b). Multiple imputation with M*plus*. Retrieved from https://www.statmodel.com/download/Imputations7.pdf

Asparouhov, T., & Muthén, B. (2010c). Plausible values for latent variables using M*plus*. Retrieved from http://www.statmodel.com/download/Plausible.pdf

Baron, R. M., & Kenny, D. A. (1986). The moderator–mediator variable distinction in social psychological research: Conceptual, strategic, and statistical considerations. *Journal of Personality and Social Psychology, 51*, 1173–1182. http://dx.doi.org/10.1037/0022-3514.51.6.1173

Bartlett, J. W., Seaman, S. R., White, I. R., & Carpenter, J. R. (2015). Multiple imputation of covariates by fully conditional specification: Accommodating the substantive model. *Statistical Methods in Medical Research, 24*, 462–487. http://dx.doi.org/10.1177/0962280214521348

Benner, A. D., & Graham, S. (2013). The antecedents and consequences of racial/ethnic discrimination during adolescence: Does the source of discrimination matter? *Developmental Psychology, 49*, 1602–1613. http://dx.doi.org/10.1037/a0030557

Bertrand, M., & Mullainathan, S. (2004). Are Emily and Greg more employable than Lakisha and Jamal? A field experiment on labor market discrimination. *The American Economic Review, 94*, 991–1013. http://dx.doi.org/10.1257/0002828042002561

Bliese, P. D. (2000). Within-group agreement, non-independence, and reliability: Implications for data aggregation and analysis. In K. J. Klein & S. W. Kozlowski (Eds.), *Multilevel theory, research, and methods in organizations* (pp. 349–381). San Francisco, CA: Jossey-Bass.

Bonilla-Silva, E. (2006). *Racism without racists: Color-blind racism and the persistence of racial inequality in the United States*. Lanham, MD: Rowman & Littlefield.

Caro, R. A. (1974). *The power broker: Robert Moses and the fall of New York.* New York, NY: Random House.

Cheung, G. W., & Lau, R. S. (2015). Accuracy of parameter estimates and confidence intervals in moderated mediation models: A comparison of regression and latent moderated structural equations. *Organizational Research Methods, 20,* 746–769. http://dx.doi.org/10.1177/1094428115595869

Cohen, J., Cohen, P., West, S. G., & Aiken, L. S. (2013). *Applied multiple regression/correlation analysis for the behavioral sciences.* New York, NY: Routledge.

Cronbach, L. J. (1976). *Research on classrooms and schools: Formulation of questions, design, and analysis.* Stanford, CA: Stanford University Evaluation Consortium.

Cronbach, L. J., & Snow, R. (1977). *Aptitudes and instructional methods: A handbook for research on interactions.* New York, NY: Irvington.

Cronbach, L. J., & Webb, N. (1975). Between-class and within-class effects in a reported aptitude * treatment interaction: Reanalysis of a study by G. L. Anderson. *Journal of Educational Psychology, 67,* 717–724. http://dx.doi.org/10.1037/0022-0663.67.6.717

Dansereau, F., & Yammarino, F. J. (2000). Within and between analysis: The variant paradigm as an underlying approach to theory building and testing. In K. J. Klein & S. W. J. Kozlowski (Eds.), *Multilevel theory, research, and methods in organizations: Foundations, extensions, and new directions* (pp. 425–466). San Francisco, CA: Jossey-Bass.

Edwards, J. R., & Lambert, L. S. (2007). Methods for integrating moderation and mediation: a general analytical framework using moderated path analysis. *Psychological methods, 12,* 1–22. http://dx.doi.org/10.1037/1082-989X.12.1.1

Enders, C. K. (2010). *Applied missing data analysis.* New York, NY: Guilford Press.

Frankenberg, E., & Lee, C. (2002). *Race in American public schools: Rapidly resegregating school districts.* Retrieved from: http://files.eric.ed.gov/fulltext/ED468063.pdf

Galinsky, A. D., Hall, E. V., & Cuddy, A. J. (2013). Gendered races: Implications for interracial marriage, leadership selection, and athletic participation. *Psychological Science, 24,* 498–506. http://dx.doi.org/10.1177/0956797612457783

Goldstein, H., Carpenter, J. R., & Browne, W. J. (2014). Fitting multilevel multivariate models with missing data in responses and covariates that may include interactions and non-linear terms. *Journal of the Royal Statistical Society: Series A. Statistics in Society, 177,* 553–564. http://dx.doi.org/10.1111/rssa.12022

Hall, A. V., Hall, E. V., & Perry, J. L. (2016). Black and blue: Exploring racial bias and law enforcement in the killings of unarmed black male civilians. *American Psychologist, 71,* 175–186. http://dx.doi.org/10.1037/a0040109

Haraway, D. (2006). A cyborg manifesto: Science, technology, and socialist-feminism in the late 20th century. In J. Weiss, J. Nolan, J. Hunsinger, & P. Trifonis (Eds.), *The international handbook of virtual learning environments* (pp. 117–158). Amsterdam, Netherlands: Springer. http://dx.doi.org/10.1007/978-1-4020-3803-7_4

Hayes, A. F. (2013). *Introduction to mediation, moderation, and conditional process analysis: A regression-based approach.* New York, NY: Guilford Press.

Hayes, A. F. (2015). An index and test of linear moderated mediation. *Multivariate Behavioral Research, 50,* 1–22. http://dx.doi.org/10.1080/00273171.2014.962683

Hayes, A. F. (2018). *Model templates for PROCESS for SPSS and SAS.* Retrieved from http://docplayer.net/408084-Model-templates-for-process-for-spss-and-sas-c-2013-2015-andrew-f-hayes-and-the-guilford-press-model-1-conceptual-diagram-statistical-diagram.html

Hayes, A. F., & Preacher, K. J. (2013). Conditional process modeling: Using structural equation modeling to examine contingent causal processes. In G. R. Hancock & R. O. Mueller (Eds.), *Structural equation modeling: A second course* (2nd ed., pp. 219–266). Charlotte, NC: Information Age.

Klein, A. G., & Moosbrugger, H. (2000). Maximum likelihood estimation of latent interaction effects with the LMS method. *Psychometrika, 65,* 457–474. http://dx.doi.org/10.1007/BF02296338

Klein, A. G., & Muthén, B. O. (2007). Quasi-maximum likelihood estimation of structural equation models with multiple interaction and quadratic effects. *Multivariate Behavioral Research, 42,* 647–673. http://dx.doi.org/10.1080/00273170701710205

Kozlowski, S. W. J., & Klein, K. J. (2000). A multilevel approach to theory and research in organizations: Contextual, temporal, and emergent processes. In K. J. Klein & S. W. J. Kozlowski (Eds.), *Multilevel theory, research, and methods in organizations: Foundations, extensions, and new directions* (pp. 3–90). San Francisco, CA: Jossey-Bass.

Leite, W. L., & Zuo, Y. (2011). Modeling latent interactions at level 2 in multilevel structural equation models: An evaluation of mean-centered and residual-centered unconstrained approaches. *Structural Equation Modeling, 18,* 449–464. http://dx.doi.org/10.1080/10705511.2011.582400

Lucal, B. (1996). Oppression and privilege: Toward a relational conceptualization of race. *Teaching Sociology, 24,* 245–255. http://dx.doi.org/10.2307/1318739

Lüdtke, O., Marsh, H. W., Robitzsch, A., & Trautwein, U. (2011). A 2 × 2 taxonomy of multilevel latent contextual models: Accuracy-bias trade-offs in full and partial error correction models. *Psychological Methods, 16*, 444–467. http://dx.doi.org/10.1037/a0024376

Lüdtke, O., Marsh, H. W., Robitzsch, A., Trautwein, U., Asparouhov, T., & Muthén, B. (2008). The multi-level latent covariate model: A new, more reliable approach to group-level effects in contextual studies. *Psychological Methods, 13*, 203–229. http://dx.doi.org/10.1037/a0012869

MacKinnon, D. P. (2008). *Introduction to statistical mediation analysis.* Mahwah, NJ: Taylor & Francis.

Marsh, H. W., Lüdtke, O., Robitzsch, A., Trautwein, U., Asparouhov, T., Muthén, B., & Nagengast, B. (2009). Doubly-latent models of school contextual effects: Integrating multilevel and structural equation approaches to control measurement and sampling error. *Multivariate Behavioral Research, 44*, 764–802. http://dx.doi.org/10.1080/00273170903333665

Massey, D. S., & Denton, N. A. (1993). *American apartheid: Segregation and the making of the underclass.* Cambridge, MA: Harvard University Press.

Mislevy, R. J., Johnson, E. G., & Muraki, E. (1992). Scaling procedures in NAEP. *Journal of Educational Statistics, 17*, 131–154.

Muthén, B. O., & Asparouhov, T. (2008). Growth mixture modeling: Analysis with non-Gaussian random effects. In G. Fitzmaurice, M. Davidian, G. Verbeke, & G. Molenberghs (Eds.), *Longitudinal data analysis* (pp. 143–165). Boca Raton, FL: Chapman & Hall/CRC.

Muthén, B., & Asparouhov, T. (2012). Bayesian structural equation modeling: A more flexible representation of substantive theory. *Psychological Methods, 17*, 313–335. http://dx.doi.org/10.1037/a0026802

Muthén, L. K., & Muthén, B. O. (2016). Mplus *user's guide* (7th ed.). Los Angeles, CA: Author.

National Opinion Research Center. (1980). *High School and Beyond information for users: Base year (1980) data.* Chicago, IL: National Opinion Research Center.

Navarro, V. (1990). Race or class versus race and class: Mortality differentials in the United States. *The Lancet, 336*, 1238–1240. http://dx.doi.org/10.1016/0140-6736(90)92846-A

Pickett, K. E., & Pearl, M. (2001). Multilevel analyses of neighbourhood socioeconomic context and health outcomes: A critical review. *Journal of Epidemiology and Community Health, 55*, 111–122. http://dx.doi.org/10.1136/jech.55.2.111

Pituch, K. A., & Stapleton, L. M. (2012). Distinguishing between cross- and cluster-level mediation processes in the cluster randomized trial. *Sociological Methods & Research, 41*, 630–670. http://dx.doi.org/10.1177/0049124112460380

Preacher, K. J., & Hayes, A. F. (2004). SPSS and SAS procedures for estimating indirect effects in simple mediation models. *Behavior Research Methods, Instruments & Computers, 36*, 717–731. http://dx.doi.org/10.3758/BF03206553

Preacher, K. J., & Hayes, A. F. (2008). Asymptotic and resampling strategies for assessing and comparing indirect effects in multiple mediator models. *Behavior Research Methods, 40*, 879–891. http://dx.doi.org/10.3758/BRM.40.3.879

Preacher, K. J., Rucker, D. D., & Hayes, A. F. (2007). Addressing moderated mediation hypotheses: Theory, methods, and prescriptions. *Multivariate Behavioral Research, 42*, 185–227. http://dx.doi.org/10.1080/00273170701341316

Preacher, K. J., & Selig, J. P. (2012). Advantages of Monte Carlo confidence intervals for indirect effects. *Communication Methods and Measures, 6*, 77–98. http://dx.doi.org/10.1080/19312458.2012.679848

Preacher, K. J., Zhang, Z., & Zyphur, M. J. (2011). Alternative methods for assessing mediation in multilevel data: The advantages of multilevel SEM. *Structural Equation Modeling, 18*, 161–182. http://dx.doi.org/10.1080/10705511.2011.557329

Preacher, K. J., Zhang, Z., & Zyphur, M. J. (2016). Multilevel structural equation models for assessing moderation within and across levels of analysis. *Psychological Methods, 21*, 189–205. http://dx.doi.org/10.1037/met0000052

Preacher, K. J., Zyphur, M. J., & Zhang, Z. (2010). A general multilevel SEM framework for assessing multilevel mediation. *Psychological Methods, 15*, 209–233. http://dx.doi.org/10.1037/a0020141

Raudenbush, S., & Bryk, A. S. (1986). A hierarchical model for studying school effects. *Sociology of Education, 59*, 1–17. http://dx.doi.org/10.2307/2112482

Raudenbush, S. W., & Bryk, A. S. (2002). *Hierarchical linear models: Applications and data analysis methods.* New York, NY: Sage.

Ren, X. S., Amick, B. C., & Williams, D. R. (1999). Racial/ethnic disparities in health: The interplay between discrimination and socioeconomic status. *Ethnicity & Disease, 9*, 151–165.

Rubin, D. B. (1987). *Multiple imputation for nonresponse in surveys.* New York, NY: Wiley. http://dx.doi.org/10.1002/9780470316696

Sardeshmukh, S. R., & Vandenberg, R. J. (2016). Integrating moderation and mediation: A structural equation modeling approach. *Organizational Research Methods, 20*, 721–745. http://dx.doi.org/10.1177/1094428115621609

Schafer, J. L. (1997). *Analysis of incomplete multivariate data*. London, England: Chapman & Hall. http://dx.doi.org/10.1201/9781439821862

Seaman, S. R., Bartlett, J. W., & White, I. R. (2012). Multiple imputation of missing covariates with non-linear effects and interactions: An evaluation of statistical methods. *BMC Medical Research Methodology, 12*, 46. http://dx.doi.org/10.1186/1471-2288-12-46

Seaton, E. K., & Yip, T. (2009). School and neighborhood contexts, perceptions of racial discrimination, and psychological well-being among African American adolescents. *Journal of Youth and Adolescence, 38*, 153–163. http://dx.doi.org/10.1007/s10964-008-9356-x

Seitles, M. (1998). The perpetuation of residential racial segregation in America: Historical discrimination, modern forms of exclusion, and inclusionary remedies. *Journal of Land Use & Environmental Law, 14*, 89–124.

Smedley, A., & Smedley, B. D. (2005). Race as biology is fiction, racism as a social problem is real: Anthropological and historical perspectives on the social construction of race. *American Psychologist, 60*, 16–26. http://dx.doi.org/10.1037/0003-066X.60.1.16

Steele, C. M., & Aronson, J. (1995). Stereotype threat and the intellectual test performance of African Americans. *Journal of Personality and Social Psychology, 69*, 797–811. http://dx.doi.org/10.1037/0022-3514.69.5.797

Thomas, A. J., Witherspoon, K. M., & Speight, S. L. (2008). Gendered racism, psychological distress, and coping styles of African American women. *Cultural Diversity and Ethnic Minority Psychology, 14*, 307–314. http://dx.doi.org/10.1037/1099-9809.14.4.307

Tofighi, D., & Thoemmes, F. (2014). Single-level and multilevel mediation analysis. *The Journal of Early Adolescence, 34*, 93–119. http://dx.doi.org/10.1177/0272431613511331

Tomaskovic-Devey, D. (1993). *Gender & racial inequality at work: The sources and consequences of job segregation*. Ithaca, NY: Cornell University Press.

Tsui, A. S., Egan, T. D., & O'Reilly, C. A. (1992). Being different: Relational demography and organizational attachment. *Administrative Science Quarterly, 37*, 549–579. http://dx.doi.org/10.2307/2393472

Umaña-Taylor, A. J. (2016). A post-racial society in which ethnic-racial discrimination still exists and has significant consequences for youths' adjustment. *Current Directions in Psychological Science, 25*, 111–118. http://dx.doi.org/10.1177/0963721415627858

Von Davier, M., Gonzalez, E., & Mislevy, R. (2009). What are plausible values and why are they useful. *IERI monograph series, 2*, 9–36.

von Hippel, P. T. (2009). How to impute interactions, squares, and other transformed variables. *Sociological Methodology, 39*, 265–291. http://dx.doi.org/10.1111/j.1467-9531.2009.01215.x

Wang, L., & Preacher, K. J. (2015). Moderated mediation analysis using Bayesian methods. *Structural Equation Modeling, 22*, 249–263. http://dx.doi.org/10.1080/10705511.2014.935256

Williams, D. R. (1999). Race, socioeconomic status, and health. The added effects of racism and discrimination. *Annals of the New York Academy of Sciences, 896*, 173–188. http://dx.doi.org/10.1111/j.1749-6632.1999.tb08114.x

Williams, D. R., & Collins, C. (2001). Racial residential segregation: A fundamental cause of racial disparities in health. *Public Health Reports, 116*, 404–416. http://dx.doi.org/10.1016/S0033-3549(04)50068-7

Williams, D. R., & Williams-Morris, R. (2000). Racism and mental health: The African American experience. *Ethnicity & Health, 5*, 243–268. http://dx.doi.org/10.1080/713667453

Wingfield, A. H. (2007). The modern mammy and the angry Black man: African American professionals' experiences with gendered racism in the workplace. *Race, Gender, & Class, 14*, 196–212.

Yuan, Y., & MacKinnon, D. P. (2009). Bayesian mediation analysis. *Psychological Methods, 14*, 301–322. http://dx.doi.org/10.1037/a0016972

Zhang, Z., Zyphur, M. J., & Preacher, K. J. (2009). Testing multilevel mediation using hierarchical linear models: Problems and solutions. *Organizational Research Methods, 12*, 695–719. http://dx.doi.org/10.1177/1094428108327450

Zyphur, M. J., Zammuto, R. F., & Zhang, Z. (2016). Multilevel latent polynomial regression for modeling (in)congruence across organizational groups: The case of organizational culture research. *Organizational Research Methods, 19*, 53–79. http://dx.doi.org/10.1177/1094428115588570

ANYTHING BUT NORMAL: THE CHALLENGES, SOLUTIONS, AND PRACTICAL CONSIDERATIONS OF ANALYZING NONNORMAL MULTILEVEL DATA

Miles A. Zachary, Curt B. Moore, and Gary A. Ballinger

Scholars are often interested in examining multilevel phenomena in which the outcome of interest is not normally distributed. For example, researchers in organizational behavior and applied psychology concerned with deviant employee behavior may seek to understand how factors at the individual, group, and/or organizational level affect the propensity of an employee to engage in deviant behavior (e.g., Dineen, Lewicki, & Tomlinson, 2006), the severity of deviant behaviors (e.g., Wang, Liao, Zhan, & Shi, 2011), or the number of incidences of workplace aggression (e.g., Dietz, Robinson, Folger, Baron, & Schulz, 2003). Similarly, scholars in strategic management and entrepreneurship interested in firm entry into new markets may consider how factors at different levels of analysis influence the likelihood of the decision to enter a particular market (e.g., Rose & Ito, 2008). Scholars in developmental psychology may study specific factors associated with grade retention and promotion for children using independent variables at the school and individual level (Huang, 2014). Researchers in clinical psychology often look at treatments and factors that operate at multiple levels in investigating behaviors of addicts, using abstinence as a binary dependent variable measured over time (Feingold, Oliveto, Schottenfeld, & Kosten, 2002). In each of these cases, the outcome variable

of interest is reflected by data that are inherently nonnormal. Thus, scholars should test hypotheses about these outcomes using models that assume that the data are produced by some distribution other than a normal, or Gaussian, distribution.

The fact that many outcome variables in the social sciences are not normally distributed introduces challenges to common multilevel analytical techniques. Multilevel analysis techniques such as random coefficient modeling (also commonly referred to as *hierarchical linear modeling* or *mixed-effects regression*) and multilevel structural equations modeling have become increasingly popular tools for analyzing hierarchical or nested data. Although these techniques often rely on maximum likelihood estimation procedures that are robust to violations of the assumptions of traditional least-squares maximization, such as independence of error terms, they make implicit assumptions about (a) the probability distribution that produces the response variable (i.e., Y) and (b) the relationship between the expected value of the response variable (i.e., $E(Y)$) and the linear predictor (i.e., the linear combination of explanatory variables—$X_1, X_2, \ldots X_k$). In particular, most applications assume that the residuals are normally distributed (i.e., $r_{ij} \sim$ normal $(0, \sigma^2)$) and the response variable is related to the

http://dx.doi.org/10.1037/0000115-022
The Handbook of Multilevel Theory, Measurement, and Analysis, S. E. Humphrey and J. M. LeBreton (Editors-in-Chief)

linear predictor through an identity link function (i.e., $g(\mu) = \eta = \mu$). The failure of scholars to address these assumptions minimizes analytical precision and obfuscates interpretation (Ballinger, 2004; Gardner, Mulvey, & Shaw, 1995; Harrison, 2002).

Despite these challenges, tools for analyzing nonnormal multilevel data are becoming more accessible to organizational scholars as statistical software packages have become simpler to use and have added more and more functionality. For one, generalized linear mixed modeling offers researchers the ability to examine multilevel relationships that are characterized by nonnormal response variables with greater precision and more direct interpretation. This is accomplished by allowing the research to specify both the distribution from which the data are produced (e.g., Gaussian, Poisson, negative binomial, gamma) and the relationship between the expected value of the response variable and the linear predictor (e.g., identity, logit, probit, complementary log-log, power). Unfortunately, although generalized linear mixed models (GLMMs) are well suited for analyzing nonnormal multilevel data, adoption has been limited and slow to progress. This limited adoption of these models may be driven by (a) researchers' uncertainty about how best to structure data, (b) how to properly specify GLMMs, and (c) how to properly identify and interpret the parameter estimates of interest (i.e., how to correctly test research hypotheses).

Our objective in this chapter is to create a greater awareness of the challenges and solutions to nonnormal multilevel data analysis, as well as to provide guidance on practical applications. In the first section, we review the primary challenges to analyzing nonnormal multilevel data using traditional multilevel data analysis techniques, including violations of the assumption of normality, range limitations, and variability (or lack thereof) in the dependent variable. In the second section, we introduce the GLMM and discuss its statistical components. In the third section, we develop a sequence of model-building steps for constructing and evaluating GLMMs, then demonstrate their application by considering and testing several basic hypotheses using example data drawn from a sample of 2,820 firms listed on New York, NASDAQ,

and Canadian stock exchanges. In the final section, we conclude by discussing some of the tradeoffs to using GLMMs, as well as ways in which scholars can leverage GLMMs to examine important research questions in the social sciences.

THE CHALLENGES OF NONNORMAL RESPONSE VARIABLES

We couch our discussion in this section of our chapter within the context of the organizational sciences. However, the points that are observed in this section are applicable to the social sciences more generally. In the past several decades, organizational scholars have shifted away from exclusively focusing on "micro" and "macro" subfields (Tosi, 1992) toward an integrated, multilevel approach to understanding organizational phenomena (Hitt, Beamish, Jackson, & Mathieu, 2007; Mathieu & Chen, 2011). Analysis of these questions would involve testing the impact of factors that exist at the individual and firm units of analysis on outcomes at the individual and firm unit of analysis. This emergence of cross-level research has required the application of more mixed models that can take into account the nonindependence of observations made from respondents at the individual unit of analysis (e.g., board members), as well as the cross-level aspects of using individual-level responses to predict group (or firm) level outcomes.

Another consequence of the current paradigm shift is that many of the response variables of interest to organizational and psychological researchers (particularly individual and organizational performance, specific behaviors or outcomes like abstinence or grade promotions, job turnover, network centrality, etc.) are not, by their nature, normally distributed (Aguinis & O'Boyle, 2014; Aguinis, O'Boyle, Gonzalez-Mulé, & Joo, 2016; Freeman, 1978–1979; Harrison, 2002). This suggests that many of the traditional means of mixed-effects regression by which we examine multilevel organizational data may no longer be appropriate. In particular, our increasing interest in nonnormal outcomes presents analytical challenges related to issues such as heteroskedastic variance, restriction of range in the outcome variable(s), and situations in which the variance of the outcome variable is dependent on the mean level of the outcome variable.

Heteroskedastic (Nonconstant) Variance

An assumption in many traditional multilevel analytical techniques is that data are produced by a normal distribution with residuals having within-level means of zero and constant variance. When the assumption of normality is violated by data produced by a nonnormal distribution, the corresponding variance for values of the response variable may be nonconstant (McCullagh & Nelder, 1989; Pindyck & Rubinfeld, 1998). *Nonconstant variance*, or *heteroscedasticity*, occurs when the error variance is not equal across the range of response variable values. In other words, the dispersion of error—the difference between actual (Y) and predicted $(\hat{Y})$ values of the response variable—varies across different values of the response variable. For example, heteroscedasticity may occur when examining the relationship between annual sales growth and firm age. Differences in sales basis (i.e., sales in the prior year) between younger and older firms is likely to influence growth in sales such that the variance in sales growth among younger firms is higher than the variance in sales growth among older firms.

Although heteroscedasticity does not bias model estimates, it does bias variance estimates or standard errors. A *standard error* is the standard deviation of an estimate of a regression coefficient and reflects how well the model estimates the "true" value of a coefficient. Standard errors are used to calculate test statistics such as the t statistic and z statistic, which when compared with a standard normal value determine the stability of the coefficient (i.e., statistical significance). An upward or downward biasing of standard errors obscures the reliability of confidence intervals and hypothesis tests. In particular, when the value of a standard error is biased such that it is lower than it should otherwise be, the test statistic is inflated and the p value is smaller, potentially leading to a *Type I error*, or incorrect rejection of the null hypothesis. Conversely, when the value of a standard error is biased such that it is higher than it should otherwise be, the test statistic is deflated and the p value is larger, increasing the possibility

of a *Type II* error, or a failure to reject the null hypothesis. In either case, nonconstant errors caused by nonnormal data increase the likelihood of misinterpreting the statistical significance of a regression coefficient.

Range Limitations

Using traditional multilevel modeling techniques to analyze nonnormal data is also often complicated by variance restrictions on the dependent variable. In theory, a truly continuous normal distribution is capable of producing values that range from $-\infty$ to $+\infty$. The assumption of normality of data in traditional multilevel techniques extends to the possible values generated in the regression process. In other words, traditional multilevel techniques assume that any predicted value is theoretically possible given that the predicted value is assumed to be produced by a normal distribution. This can be a problem, however, because nonnormal data are often restricted to a certain set of possible values. Such data are commonly referred to as *limited range dependent variables* (e.g., Harrison, 2002). For example, binary data can only exist as a 0 or 1, and count data is always positive (e.g., 0, 1, 2, . . . n). Consequently, relying on traditional multilevel techniques, the regression coefficients and independent variables may often combine to produce predictions that fall outside the possible range (Gardner et al., 1995) and thus are difficult (if not impossible) to interpret (McCullagh & Nelder, 1989).

Transformation Problems

A common "solution" to the problem of nonnormality is for researchers to transform the response variable before data analysis or using some form of aggregation to shift the distribution of their response variables to approximately normal. For example, when the sample distribution of a response variable is positively skewed (i.e., most of the observations are observed to the left of the mean), a researcher may attempt to shift the distribution by taking the square root or natural log of the response variable. Conversely, when the sample distribution of a response variable is negatively skewed (i.e., most of the observations are observed to the right of the mean), a researcher may attempt to shift the distribution by squaring or cubing the response variable. However, transformations are often sensitive to misspecification issues and do not necessarily result in efficient and unbiased parameter estimates (Buntin & Zaslavsky, 2004; Duan, 1983; Gardner et al., 1995; Harrison, 2002). Furthermore, transformation of the response variable often obscures interpretation, particularly when it comes to communicating effect sizes. For example, consider the complexities facing an author who is seeking to provide a meaningful, substantive interpretation of a variable that is a significant linear predictor of a criterion when that criterion may have been subjected to a square root inverse transformation. Researchers who transform a response variable must either report the effect size in terms of the transformation, which often may not make much practical sense, or they have to convert the predicted effect size back into the terms of interest, which often produces an effect size that is not particularly meaningful.

Proper Modeling of Nonnormal Outcomes

Together, these issues suggest that attempting to use traditional multilevel techniques to analyze response variables that are not normally distributed is inappropriate and is likely to affect the results and interpretation of the analysis. So, common sense would dictate that one should use a model that expresses the response variable in terms that theoretically match its values. Gardner and colleagues (1995) expressed this sentiment well: "One should consider regression models that fit the natural features of the data" (p. 394). However, to date, there has been scant treatment of how to best to fit a model to the features of such data, especially within the context of multilevel models. To address this gap, we discuss and demonstrate how multilevel models may be extended using the generalized linear model developed by McCullagh and Nelder (1989). As we illustrate, this model is able to account for nonnormality, accommodate range limitations, and avoid the troubles arising from transforming response variables. In the next section, we (a) introduce the theory behind generalized linear models, (b) briefly review the different types of response variables that may be assessed using these models, (c) discuss the core components of generalized linear models,

(d) extend the basic generalized linear model to accommodate multilevel research questions using a GLMM, and (e) explain how to fit and interpret GLMMs.

SOLUTIONS FOR ADDRESSING NONNORMAL RESPONSE VARIABLES

Generalized linear models represent a class of statistical techniques that include a number of commonly used models designated as special cases of general linear models. Among these special cases, the general linear model is perhaps the best-known subset of models, which include regression analysis, analysis of variance (ANOVA), and analysis of covariance (ANCOVA). Traditional multilevel models, such as random coefficient modeling (also known as *hierarchical linear models* or *mixed models*), are generalizations or extensions of the basic general linear model. However, another special case includes models for response variables other than continuous-normal, such as logit/probit regression, Poisson regression, log-linear models, generalized estimating equations, and GLMMs. These models are more efficient techniques for analyzing nonnormal data, but determining which one to use depends on several basic factors largely centering on characteristics of the response variable. In fact, a researcher can specify any one of these models by understanding the properties of their response variable of interest. Accordingly, we briefly review the types of response variables before discussing the components of generalized linear models.

Types of Response Variables
Binary variables. *Binary variables* are nominal variables that reflect discrete observations that occur in terms of one of two possible states, such as "yes" or "no," "success" or "failure," and "win" or "lose." These variables are often coded as "1" or "0" in a data set according to whether the event has occurred or not. As such, one common approach to modeling binary data is to model the probability of the event occurring. Because the probability of an event p occurring is limited to a value between 0 and 1, binary data are often modeled using a Bernoulli probability distribution. Binary response

variables are common in management and applied psychology research when a researcher wants to model the occurrence of a specific event, such as job turnover (e.g., Felps et al., 2009; Lee, Mitchell, Sablynski, Burton, & Holtom, 2004), director exit (e.g., Marcel & Cowen, 2014), employee layoffs (e.g., Ndofor, Vanevenhoven, & Barker, 2013), and firm bankruptcy (e.g., Xia, Dawley, Jiang, Ma, & Boal, 2016).

Proportional variables. A *proportional variable* is a special type of binary variable in which individuals in a group are exposed to the same treatment condition but record one of two different responses. When *n* individuals are exposed to a particular treatment, *f* individuals are observed to respond one way, and *n − f* are observed to respond in another way. For example, in a series of field experiments in which employees are observed in organizations with varying degrees of abusive supervision, a researcher may record the decision of *f* employees to leave the organization while *n − f* remain in each organization. The probability that an employee will leave is therefore modeled as a function of the level of abusive supervision. Like binary variables, proportional variables are produced by a probability distribution other than normal and so are often modeled using a Bernoulli distribution.

Rate variables. A *rate variable* is a special case of proportional variables. In some instances, the value of a variable may be proportional to the size or scope of the object of the measurement. The scaling of a proportional variable results in a rate, which can make it easier to compare values across subgroupings. For example, a researcher interested in examining the differences in employee theft between male and female employees may have data on the number of instances of theft in an organization by both males and females. However, it may be important to factor in differences in the proportion of males and females in the sample. Thus, the researcher could calculate the instances of employee theft for males and females across a stable base number of observations (i.e., # of instances of theft in males/100 males; # of instances of theft in females/100 females). This establishes a rate of theft that can easily be compared between subgroupings of males and females. Unlike

proportional variables, rate variables result in values greater than 1, so they cannot be modeled using a Bernoulli distribution. Instead, such data can often be modeled using the Poisson distribution.

Count variables. *Count variables* are measurements in which the value indicates the discretized amount of something or the number of times an event occurs, such as the number of tasks completed, the number of firm acquisitions, and the number of franchise units. For example, the rate of firm innovation has often been measured using annual patent counts (e.g., Ahuja, 2000; Ahuja & Katila, 2001; Sorensen & Stuart, 2000; Wadhwa & Kotha, 2006). Other important examples of counted variables that may be used as dependent variables are indicators of network centrality, such as degree or betweenness (Freeman, 1978–1979). One of the more important characteristics of count variables is that they are limited to nonnegative values (i.e., $y \geq 0$), and so exist in terms of $0, 1, 2, 3, \ldots n$. As a result, it is incorrect to assume that count variables are produced by a normal distribution. Instead, researchers often model count data using either a Poisson or negative binomial distribution.

Ordinal variables. *Ordinal variables* refer to categorical variables in which the categories are ordered in some meaningful way. However, unlike continuous variables, which are separated by scalar differences (e.g., a value of 2 is twice as large as 1), the differences between ordinal variables are not constant. For example, in the widely used Positive and Negative Affect Schedule (Watson, Clark, & Tellegen, 1988, p. 1070), respondents are asked to specify to what extent they experience a particular emotion over a specific time frame. The anchors are *very slightly or not at all, a little, moderately, quite a bit,* and *extremely*. In this case, there is certainly an order to the responses, but one should not treat the differences between responses as scalar. To analyze ordinal data, scholars often model the data using a Poisson distribution or even a binomial distribution in certain special cases.

Continuous variables. *Continuous variables* are variables that are not necessarily restricted to a particular range of values. Although in theory this suggests that the values of a continuous variable could range from −∞ to +∞, researchers accept a variable to be continuous if it can take on any value between two particular values. However, continuous variables may be difficult to obtain for several reasons. First, most instruments used to measure a given variable are not precise enough to report an exact value. For example, analytical balances used to weigh fine amounts of substances often report weight in grams to only the 10,000th decimal place. In this case, the instrument measuring the weight of a substance can only report a value of weight to a certain extent. Second, phenomena bounded by physical limitations may restrict seemingly continuous values to a particular range. For instance, although researchers often treat temperature as a continuous variable, the laws of physics suggest that temperature can only fall to −273.15 degrees Celsius, a theoretical temperature commonly referred to as *absolute zero*. So, it is somewhat incorrect to assume that temperature can range from −∞ to +∞. That being said, continuous response models are often considered in terms of approximations rather than precise values. As such, examples in management and applied psychology often include variables in which the theoretical values have significant range, such as employee salaries and measures of firm performance.

Although continuous variables can be produced under conditions of normality, not all continuous variable data are normal. Determining whether continuous data are normally distributed or not is a matter of theory and/or empirical analysis. As we suggested, if the process that generates the continuous variable is not likely to be normal in theory, it is unlikely to be normally distributed. For example, recent research on "star performers" suggested that work or job performance is not necessarily a normally distributed phenomenon (Aguinis & O'Boyle, 2014). So, it would seem inappropriate to assume that performance data would be naturally produced by a normal distribution. In cases in which a continuous variable could be assumed to be produced by a normal distribution, a researcher could examine whether the data collected in their sample deviate strongly

from a normal distribution using tests such as the Shapiro-Wilks test or by examining the data in a histogram. This is less of a concern so long as the residuals are normally distributed. However, nonnormality becomes a much bigger issue when the residuals are not normally distributed.

Constructing a Generalized Linear Model

Generalized linear models consist of three primary components: (a) a family distribution component[1] that specifies the conditional distribution of the outcome variable (e.g., Gaussian [normal], binomial, gamma, Poisson), (b) a linear predictor that denotes the model regressors and assumes the form of a weighted linear combination of the regressors, and (c) a link function that relates the linear predictor to the response variable. Next, we consider each of these components individually and discuss how best to specify them.

Family distribution component. The *family distribution component* of a generalized linear model specifies the conditional probability distribution of the response variable $Y|X$. Sometimes referred to as a *noise* or *error model*, the family distribution component answers the question of how error is introduced to the prediction through the link function. In other words, specifying the appropriate probability distribution can help explain the pattern of differences between the observed values and the predicted values. The expressed probability distribution is integrated into the model through "the calculation of the covariance matrix [of the regression coefficients] by multiplying the components against an $N \times N$ matrix ($\mathbf{W}$) with a value W_i on the diagonal that is determined by the variance function" (Ballinger, 2004, p. 132), where N is the number of observations in the sample, and W_i is a specified weighting used in the iteratively reweighted least squares estimation procedure. Moreover, the family distribution component specifies the form of the dispersion or scale parameter (ϕ), which relates the population variance to model estimates. Specifically, these components integrate into

---

[1]The family distribution component is often referred to as the *random component*. However, because this chapter is focused on generalized linear mixed modeling, which contains both fixed and random effects, we chose to rename it the *family distribution* component to avoid confusion.

the calculation of the covariance matrix of the regression model coefficients accordingly:

$$\text{Cov}(\hat{\boldsymbol{\beta}}) = \phi(X^{T}\hat{W}X)^{-1}. \qquad (21.1)$$

Specifying the appropriate family distribution is therefore important because misspecification can lead to biased error calculations and incorrect statistical inferences (Gardner et al., 1995).

In generalized linear models, a researcher can specify any distribution that belongs to the exponential family of distributions that describe a class of distributions, including normal or Gaussian, binomial, Poisson, negative binomial, and gamma distributions. Exponential distributions take on the general form

$$f(y;\theta,\phi) = \exp\left[\frac{y\theta - b(\theta)}{a(\phi)} + c(y,\phi)\right], \qquad (21.2)$$

where, $a(\cdot)$, $b(\cdot)$, and $c(\cdot)$ are specific functions, y are independent observations of Y, θ is the canonical parameter, and ϕ is the dispersion or scale parameter. The canonical parameter determines the shape of the distribution of Y, whereas the dispersion parameter determines variance from the mean of the distribution. In the exponential distribution equation, the $b(\cdot)$ function is of particular importance because its first- and second-order derivative specifies the mean value (i.e., $b'(\theta) = E(y)$) and the variance (i.e., $a(\phi) \cdot b''(\theta) = Var(y)$) of the distribution, respectively. For example, in the normal distribution, it is assumed that $\theta = \mu$, $\phi = \sigma^2$, $a(\phi) = \phi$, $b(\theta) = \theta^2/2$, and $c(y,\phi) = -[y^2/\phi + \log(2\pi\phi)/2]$, which come together in the general form

$$f(y,\mu,\sigma^2) = \left[\frac{y\mu - \frac{\mu^2}{2}}{\sigma^2} - \frac{y^2}{2\sigma^2} - \frac{1}{2}\log(2\pi\sigma^2)\right], \qquad (21.3)$$

where y are independent observations of Y, μ is the expected value of Y, and σ^2 is the variance in Y. Conversely, the Poisson distribution, which is another special case within the exponential distribution family, assumes that $\theta = \log(\mu)$, $a(\phi) = 1$, $b(\theta) = \exp(\theta)$, and $c(y,\phi) = -\log(y!)$. When

substituted into the exponential distribution, the general form becomes

$$f(y,\mu) = \exp[y\theta - \exp(\theta) - \log(y!)], \qquad (21.4)$$

where y are independent observations of $Y|X$, μ is the expected value of $Y|X$, and $y!$ is the factorial of $Y|X$ (e.g., $4! = 4 \times 3 \times 2 \times 1 = 24$). Although a complete explanation of each exponential distribution and its components is beyond the scope of this chapter, we outline the components and canonical link functions (covered in greater detail later) of the most common exponential distributions in Table 21.1.

Determining which distribution to specify as the family distribution component of a generalized linear model depends on the type of response variable being modeled. To be sure, it can be difficult to understand the exact covariance structure describing a data set (Horton & Lipsitz, 1999). Fortunately, generalized linear modeling is typically robust to somewhat imprecise error distribution specification (Gardner et al., 1995). This is especially the case when the model incorporates the correlation between observations (compensating for repeated observation), such as in generalized estimating equations (Zeger & Liang, 1986) or generalized linear mixed modeling (Breslow & Clayton, 1993). However, researchers should make their best effort to correctly specify a distribution corresponding to the response variables to efficiently estimate regression coefficients (McCullagh & Nelder, 1989). To do so, the research should consider the type of response variable in question and which distribution might reasonably produce such data. For example, if the response variable is binary, the researcher should specify the binomial distribution, which produces data with a range of 0 to 1. Conversely, if the response variable is a count variable, a researcher should consider either the Poisson or negative binomial distribution, depending on the level of dispersion. In cases in which the mean is approximately equivalent to the variance, Poisson is ideal, but in cases in which dispersion is higher, the negative binomial is preferable (Gardner et al., 1995). Overall, the specification of the family distribution component of a generalized linear model should reflect the response data being analyzed.

TABLE 21.1

Properties of Common Distributions

	Normal	Poisson	Negative binomial	Binomial	Gamma
$a(\phi)$	σ^2	1	1	1	v^{-1}
$b(\cdot)$	$\sigma^2/2$	e^θ	$-\dfrac{\log(1-e^\theta)}{k}$	$n\log(1+e^\theta)$	$-\log(-\theta)$
$c(y;\phi)$	$-\dfrac{1}{2}\left[\dfrac{y^2}{\phi}+\log(2\pi\phi)\right]$	$-\log y!$		$\log\dbinom{n}{y}$	$v\log(vy)-\log y-\log\Gamma(v)$
$\mu(\theta)=E(Y;\theta)$	θ	e^θ	$-\dfrac{e^\theta}{(-1+e^\theta)k}$	$\dfrac{n\cdot e^\theta}{(1+e^\theta)}$	$-\dfrac{1}{\theta}$
Canonical $g(\cdot)$	identity	log	$\log\left(\dfrac{k\mu}{1+k\mu}\right)$	logit	$-\dfrac{1}{\mu}$
$V(\mu)$	σ^2	μ	$\mu+k\mu^2$	$np(1-p)$	μ^2
$\mathrm{Var}(y)$	σ^2	μ	$\mu+k\mu^2$	$n\mu(1-\mu)$	μ^2/v

Linear predictor. The *linear predictor* ($X\boldsymbol{\beta}$), also commonly referred to as the *systematic component*, refers to the linear combination of explanatory variables ($X_1, X_2, \ldots X_p$) in the model. A linear predictor has the same purpose in generalized linear models as it does in a general linear model. In a regression, the linear predictor is characterized by (a) the design matrix X containing the observed values on the $p-1$ independent variables that are obtained from n observations and (b) the vector of p parameters ($\boldsymbol{\beta}$):

$$X_{n\times p}=\begin{bmatrix} 1 & X_{11} & \cdots & X_{1(p-1)} \\ 1 & X_{21} & & \\ \vdots & & \ddots & \\ 1 & X_{n1} & & X_{n(p-1)} \end{bmatrix} \quad (21.5)$$

$$\boldsymbol{\beta}_{p\times 1}=\begin{bmatrix} \beta_0 \\ \beta_1 \\ \vdots \\ \beta_{p-1} \end{bmatrix}, \quad (21.6)$$

where p is the number of parameters to be estimated, and n is the number of observations in the sample. Thus, the generalized linear model suggests that a specified function of the mean of response variable y is a function of the linear predictor $\eta = X\boldsymbol{\beta}$.

Link function. The *link function* $g(\cdot)$ is a function that specifies the relationship between the random component and the linear predictor by relating the expected value of a response variable Y to the predictor variables $X_1, X_2, \ldots X_p$. In particular, the link function transforms the mean of the distribution rather than transforming the response variable values themselves. This is an important distinction between generalized linear modeling and traditional linear modeling using transformed response variables, and it is one of the features that makes the generalized linear model so useful for analyzing nonnormal data.

There are a number of link functions from which to choose in the generalized linear modeling, including identity, log, logit/probit, complementary log-log, and power. The most basic link function is the *identity link*, which relates the mean of the distribution directly to the linear predictor (i.e., $\eta = g(E(Y)) = g(\mu)$). This is most commonly used when constructing a linear regression model or an ANOVA/ANCOVA in which a normal distribution is assumed to produce the response variable. Another important link function is the *logit link*, which is typically the default link function for data produced by a Bernoulli distribution. The logit link function relates the mean of the Bernoulli distribution (π) to the linear predictor as the log odds of the mean (i.e., $\eta = \text{logit}(\pi) = \ln[\pi/(1 - \pi)]$). For count variables, for which the Poisson distribution is the appropriate random component, the traditional link function is a log link. The log link function relates the mean of the Poisson distribution to the linear predictor as the natural logarithm of the mean (i.e., $\eta = \ln(\mu)$). The resulting regression coefficients in a Poisson model represent the expected change in the natural log of the mean of the response variable a one-unit change in the covariate (Gardner et al., 1995; McCullagh & Nelder, 1989). In similar cases using logit, probit, or log link functions, the regression coefficients should be exponentiated before being interpreted (Ballinger, 2004), which can be accomplished by calculating the inverse of the natural log of the regression coefficient thus:

$$EXP(b_n) = e^{b_n}. \qquad (21.7)$$

The appropriateness of a link function depends on the particular distribution specified in the family distribution component, so researchers should choose carefully. The *natural* or *canonical link function* is the link function that leads to the desired statistical properties of the generalized linear model given the specified distribution. As a result, the canonical link is often the default for special cases of the generalized linear model. For example, a *logistic regression* is simply a generalized linear model in which a binomial distribution is specified as the random component, a mixed linear combina-

tion of continuous and noncontinuous explanatory variables are specified as the linear predictor, and a logit link function is used to relate the mean of the binomial distribution to the linear predictor. Another common generalized linear model is a *Poisson regression*, which reflects a Poisson distribution as the random component, a mixed linear combination of explanatory variables as the linear predictor, and a log link function that relates the mean of the Poisson distribution to the linear predictor. In many cases, a researcher can rely on the canonical link as the appropriate link function once the appropriate probability distribution has been identified. We provide a more complete list of these special cases of generalized linear models and their related components in Table 21.2.

The value of the link function also extends to the estimation of generalized linear models as the likelihood equation simplifies as a result of the link function. As a result, the standard error estimates are more efficient and unbiased, which means that researchers are less likely to commit a Type I or Type II error when interpreting the statistical significance of the test statistic. Evaluating the regression coefficient can be more difficult because it must be interpreted consistent with the link transformation. For example, specifying an identity link function in a Poisson model estimates coefficients that can be interpreted as the rate difference. However, when specifying the log link function (which is the canonical link function for a Poisson model), the estimated coefficients should be interpreted as the log difference of the expected response. That being said, interpretation is easier once a regression

TABLE 21.2

The Component Properties of Common Generalized Linear Models

Model	Family distribution component	Systematic component	Link function (canonical)	Types of response variables
Linear regression	Normal (Gaussian)	Continuous	Identity	Continuous
Logistic regression	Binomial	Mixed	Logit	Binomial/proportional
Loglinear regression	Poisson	Categorical	Log	Count
Poisson regression	Poisson	Mixed	Log	Count
Negative binomial regression	Negative binomial	Mixed	Generalized log	Count

coefficient has been exponentiated. For instance, in a Poisson model predicting the relationship between firm age and the number of franchised locations, a regression coefficient of $b_{AGE} = 0.10$ should first be exponentiated as EXP $(b_{AGE}) = e^{0.10} = 1.11$. This can then be interpreted as an 11% increase in the number of franchised locations for each unit change in firm age.

It should be noted that the link function also places some constraints on the model. Specifically, generalized linear models are subject to a stricter relationship between the mean of the distribution and the variance of the response variable. For example, a generalized linear model that specifies a Poisson distribution and uses the canonical log link function assumes that the variance of Y is equal to the mean μ. This assumption is fairly rigid and suggests that if the mean and variance of the response variable Y are not equal (or very close), the data are overdispersed or underdispersed. *Overdispersion* refers to the situation in which there is greater variance in a particular variable than would otherwise be expected given the specified distribution. Alternatively, *underdispersion* describes the opposite situation in which there is less variance in a particular variable than would otherwise be expected given the specified distribution. Dispersion issues are problematic because they can result in biased standard errors, thus affecting the calculation of test statistics and significance levels. Such issues are likely more prevalent in multilevel data because the variance may be biased by unobserved subgroup effects. The most common solution is to use a negative binomial specification, which produces less biased estimates and narrower confidence intervals. However, other modifications can also be made to compensate for these issues. A simple solution might be to specify a robust variance estimator in place of the default estimator in maximum likelihood (Hilbe, 1998). Similarly, a researcher may choose to make a customized adjustment by overriding the default scale parameter and specify the actual variance in the response variable. Such adjustments alter the likelihood estimation to what is known as a *quasi-likelihood estimation*, which is similar yet more flexible than maximum likelihood estimation (Wedderburn, 1974).

Extending to Generalized Linear Mixed Models

To this point, our focus has been on explaining the theory and specific components of generalized linear modeling as a means of analyzing response variables that are not produced by a normal distribution with a mean of 0 and constant variance of 1. However, as discussed in the first section of this chapter, organizational scholars are often interested in explaining nonnormal response variables that are subject to grouping effects. This is a problem because one of the most critical assumptions of generalized linear modeling is the independence of observations (Breslow, 1996). Shared characteristics of observations belonging to some higher level group (e.g., work teams, organizations, strategic groups, industries) often result in pooled residuals because unobserved higher level factors are biasing the observational responses. Likewise, nonindependence may also emerge as a problem in longitudinal data, where repeated observations are likely to be correlated within a respondent. Failure to account for correlation among responses because of grouping effects and/or autocorrelation can result in estimates of the regression parameters that are not efficient and may lead to incorrect inferences about regression parameters because the variance can be "incorrect" when the correlation between respondents is substantial (Diggle, Heagerty, Liang, & Zeger, 2002).

Fortunately, generalized linear models can be extended to accommodate this assumption. These extended models are often referred to as *generalized linear mixed models*; the *mixed* moniker added because they include both fixed effects (i.e., population-average effects) and random effects (i.e., subgroup-specific effects). The GLMM takes the form

$$y = X\beta + Z\gamma + \varepsilon, \tag{21.8}$$

where y is an $N \times 1$ vector related to the outcome variable, X is an $N \times p$ matrix of p predictor variables, β is a $p \times 1$ vector of the fixed-effects regression coefficients, Z is the $N \times q$ matrix for the q random effects, γ is a $q \times 1$ vector of random effects, and ε is an $N \times 1$ vector of residuals, which correspond to y left unexplained by the model. As in other multilevel models, GLMMs can also be framed in terms of a two-level equation set for the ith observation within the jth cluster:

$$L1: Y_{ij} = \beta_{0j} + \beta_{1j}X + r_{ij}$$

$$L2: \beta_{0j} = \gamma_{00} + u_{0j}$$

$$L2: \beta_{1j} = \gamma_{10} + u_{1j}, \qquad (21.9)$$

where β_{0j} is the Level 1 intercept coefficient of Y_{ij} for cluster j, β_{0j} is the Level 1 slope coefficient for cluster j, r_{ij} is the Level 1 random effect, γ_{00} and γ_{10} are Level 2 fixed effects, and u_{0j} and u_{0j} are Level 2 random effects. The two-level equations can be simplified into a single mixed-effects equation by substituting the Level 2 equations into their respective β coefficients thus:

$$Y_{ij} = \gamma_{00} + u_{0j} + (\gamma_{10} + u_{1j})X + r_{ij}. \qquad (21.10)$$

Several components of the GLLM are the same as in the more basic generalized linear model. The specification of the distribution in the family distribution component should be the same for models extended to include mixed effects. Similarly, the link function $g(\cdot)$ has the same purpose of relating the response variable Y to the linear predictor η. However, the linear predictor itself is different. Indeed, what makes GLMMs different is the addition of the random effects $Z\gamma$ to the linear predictor. As a result, the linear predictor takes the general form

$$\eta = X\beta + Z\gamma. \qquad (21.11)$$

And thus:

$$g(\mu) = g[E(Y)] = \eta, \qquad (21.12)$$

where the linearized function of μ is equivalent to the linearized function of the expected value of Y, which is equal to the linear predictor η. Specified as a single mixed-effects equation, a GLMM can be defined thus:

$$\eta_{ij} \equiv g[E(Y_{ij})] = \gamma_{00} + u_{0j} + (\gamma_{10} + u_{1j})X + r_{ij}, \qquad (21.13)$$

where the linear predictor η_{ij} is defined as the linearized function of the conditional expectation

of Y_{ij} given the fixed and random effects specified in the model. In both cases, an important distinction between traditional multilevel models and GLMMs is how the link function relates the expected value of an outcome (i.e., $E[Y_{ij}]$) to the linear predictor (i.e., η_{ij}), which is necessary when assuming that the specified outcome variable of interest is produced by a process other than a normal distribution (McCullagh & Nelder, 1989).

The number of rows in the design matrix Z is fixed to the number of observations n in a sample; however, the number of columns will change according to the random effects being examined. For intercept-only random-effects models, the number of rows in the design matrix Z is equal to q, which is the number of random groupings. The columns contain only 1s and 0s that are used to identify to which grouping the observations belong. For example, a sample of 100 individuals in five work teams would have a design matrix Z with 100×5 dimensions with each of the five columns using 0s and 1s to assign each individual into their corresponding work team:

$$Z_{100\times5} = \begin{bmatrix} 1_{1j} & 0_{1j} & 0_{1j} & 0_{1j} & 0_{1j} \\ 0_{2j} & 0_{2j} & 0_{2j} & 1_{2j} & 0_{2j} \\ \vdots & \vdots & \vdots & \vdots & \vdots \\ 0_{100j} & 1_{100j} & 0_{100j} & 0_{100j} & 0_{100j} \end{bmatrix}. \qquad (21.14)$$

If a random slope is added to an intercept-only random-effects model, the number of columns doubles. The additional columns will also only contain 1s and 0s to denote group membership. So, in the same example, the design matrix Z would now have 100×10 dimensions. One can see that as the number of groupings increases, the computational burden increases proportionately.

As for the random parameters γ, it is tempting to assume they will be estimated similar to the fixed parameters β. However, these parameters are not directly estimated but rather represent deviations from the fixed parameters, which reflect the mean value of the fixed effect. Indeed, it is assumed that the random effects γ are normally distributed, with a mean of zero and a variance of G, which is the variance–covariance matrix of the random effects. For an intercept-only mixed model, G is a 1×1 matrix with a value of σ^2, which represents the variance component of the random intercept. However, for a model that includes both random intercept and random slope parameters, G is a 2×2 matrix that has the form

$$\mathbf{G}_{2\times 2} = \begin{bmatrix} \sigma^2_{int} & \sigma^2_{int,slope} \\ \sigma^2_{int,slope} & \sigma^2_{slope} \end{bmatrix}, \quad (21.15)$$

where, σ^2_{int} and σ^2_{slope} are the variances of the random intercept and slope, respectively, and the $\sigma^2_{int,slope}$ is the covariance between the random intercept and slope. The nature of the covariances in the G matrix depends on how the parameters are specified and any constraints placed on these parameters. For instance, if the random effects are assumed to be independent of each other, the covariance between the random intercept and slope would be 0 (i.e., $\sigma^2_{int,slope} = 0$).

Like generalized linear models, several special cases of GLLMs can similarly be evaluated. Perhaps the most basic is simply a *traditional mixed-effects linear regression*:

$$g[E(Y_{ij})] = \eta_{ij}$$
$$= \gamma_{00} + u_{0j} + (\gamma_{10} + u_{1j})X + r_{ij}, Y \sim \text{normal}, \quad (21.16)$$

where the identity link function $g(\cdot)$ directly relates the mean μ to the linear predictor η. In this case, the fixed-effects coefficients and variance components can be interpreted the same as in a traditional mixed-effects linear regression. The random coefficients are not directly estimated in a mixed model but can often be predicted after model fitting. Another special case of a GLMM is the *mixed-effects logistic regression*:

$$\text{logit}[E(Y_{ij})] = \eta_{ij}$$
$$= \gamma_{00} + u_{0j} + (\gamma_{10} + u_{1j})X + r_{ij},$$
$$Y \sim \text{Bernoulli}, \quad (21.17)$$

where the logit link function $\text{logit}(\mu) = \ln[\mu/(1 - \mu)]$ relates the log odds of the mean μ to the linear

predictor η. As with traditional logistic regression, the fixed-effects coefficients should be interpreted as the log odds of returning a response value of 1, and the random effects must be predicted after fitting the model. Last, a *mixed-effects Poisson regression* is yet another special case of a GLMM. The mixed-effects Poisson regression is modeled as

$$\ln[E(Y_{ij})] = \eta_{ij}$$
$$= \gamma_{00} + u_{0j} + (\gamma_{10} + u_{1j})X + r_{ij}, Y \sim \text{Poisson}, \quad (21.18)$$

where the log link function $\ln(\mu)$ relates the natural log of the mean μ to the linear predictor η. The fixed-effects coefficients are interpreted in terms of the expected log count, which is the same as for traditional Poisson regression. As in the previous cases, the random-effects coefficients are not estimated directly and should be calculated following model fitting.

To help better understand the logic behind GLMMs, as well as to help readers understand how to interpret the output from such models with an eye toward testing hypotheses, we demonstrate the practical application of these with a couple of examples in the next section.

PRACTICAL APPLICATIONS

GLMMs offer researchers a range of analytical options for modeling nonnormal response variables without the problems or complications presented by traditional multilevel techniques. However, using GLMMs typically requires incremental model building and successive evaluations of model fit and fit improvement. Although generalized linear mixed modeling is decades old, there is currently a lack of guidance on how a researcher should approach building and testing such models. To help address this, we draw on the model building and specification processes for generalized estimating equations from Ballinger (2004) and multilevel models from Hofmann (1997) and Bliese and colleagues (e.g., Bliese, 2002; Bliese & Ployhart, 2002) to create a sequence of steps for constructing and testing a generalized linear mixed model. Table 21.3 provides an outline

Model-building steps	**What to interpret**
I. Determine fixed-effects model	
A. Specify the linear predictor η	Significance test of model parameters
B. Specify the family distribution	Significance test of model parameters
C. Specify the link function $g(\cdot)$	Significance test of model parameters
II. Test for intercept variance	
A. Specify the clustering variable	
B. Specify the null model with random intercept-only for clustering variable	Intraclass correlation coefficient
C. Compare models with and without a random intercept	Difference in log-likelihood statistic
III. Determine mixed-effects model	
A. Introduce random intercepts into the fixed-effects model	Significance test of model parameters Difference in log-likelihood statistic
B. Introduce random slopes into the fixed-effects model	Significance test of model parameters Difference in log-likelihood statistic
IV. Predicting intercept or slope variance	
A. Introduce predictors of random intercepts or slopes	Significance test of model parameters Difference in log-likelihood statistic

TABLE 21.3

Basic Generalized Linear Mixed Model-Building Sequence

of these steps and which model components should be interpreted.

As a demonstration of the process of constructing and interpreting GLMMs, we provide two examples using data drawn from a sample of 2,820 publicly traded firms listed on New York, NASDAQ, and Canadian stock exchanges. The first example demonstrates the process of modeling a binary response variable (i.e., high-tech industry membership), whereas the second example explores the process of modeling a count response variable (i.e., patent counts). We model these two examples using SAS 9.4 and include the corresponding syntax. In these examples, the steps (e.g., Step 1A) refer to the model building sequence in Table 21.3. Appendix 21.1 includes a detailed explanation of the SAS commands used in the two examples as well.

Example 1: Multilevel Binary Outcome Data

In this first example, we test the following hypotheses:

- H1: Firm-level research and development (R & D) expenditures are positively associated

with being in technology-intensive (i.e., high-tech) industries.
- H2: Stock exchange-level acquisition investments are positively associated with technology-intensive industries after controlling for firm-level R & D expenditures.
- H3: Stock-exchange level acquisition investments positively moderate the relationships between firm-level R & D expenditures—high-tech industry classification relationships.

Step 1: Specification of the fixed-effects model. The first step in constructing a GLMM is to determine the fixed-effects portion of the model. This begins by first specifying the linear predictor η (Step 1A). As discussed previously, the linear predictor is the linear equation of explanatory variables that are hypothesized to be related to the response variable (i.e., $\eta = X_1 + X_2 \ldots + X_n$). The researcher must also specify the family distribution that presumably produced the data (Step 1B) and the link function (Step 1C), which linearizes the data by relating the mean of the distribution to the linear predictor. Evaluating the fixed-effects model includes interpreting the regression coefficients and their statistical significance, as well as assessing overall model fit. Commonly reported fit statistics might include log likelihood, a Wald χ^2, Akaike's information criterion, or Bayesian information criterion.

For this example, we want to test first the hypothesis that firm-level R & D expenditures (Level-1 IV: *rd_exp*) are significantly related to membership in technology-intensive (DV: *hightech*) industries (Step 1A), while controlling for gross acquisition expenses (IV: *g_acq*). The response variable, *high-tech industry membership*, is measured using a dichotomous scale (i.e., 1 for member in a high-tech industry, 0 otherwise); thus, the response variable is not normally distributed but rather binomial. Using PROC Logistic in SAS, the family distribution is automatically specified as a binomial distribution (Step 1B) with a logit link function (Step 1C). The fixed-effects model would be specified using PROC Logistic in SAS as follows:

```
PROC Logistic data=SASUSER.HighTech_GLMM;
MODEL hightech = rd_exp g_acq /solution
   ODDSRATIO;
run;
```

Step 2: Test for intercept variance. The second step of our analysis starts by specifying a classification variable that corresponds to the clustering effect, which allows the intercept to vary between identified subgroups. Our sample includes firms listed on the NASDAQ, New York, and Canadian stock exchanges. Previous research has suggested that high-tech firms are more likely to list on the U.S. NASDAQ exchange (Moore, Bell, Filatotchev, & Rasheed, 2012). Therefore, we expect within-group (i.e., within-stock exchange) correlations to create clustered data (Step 2A) when predicting high-tech industry classification (DV: *hightech*). Neither the ordinary least squares nor the logistic model accounts for error covariance among firms on the same stock exchange. To assess whether there is significant intercept variation between groups (i.e., stock exchanges in this example), we specify a null model (i.e., an unconditional means model) that only includes a random intercept (i.e., no other variables are included in the model) for the stock exchange listing of the firm (*exchg*), with an indepen-

dent error covariance structure using the PROC GLIMMIX command (generalized linear mixed effects) in SAS, and compute the intraclass correlation coefficient (ICC; Step 2B). The ICC = .1774 with a 95% confidence interval of 0.114–0.265, indicating 17.74% of the variance in the High-Tech Industry DV is significantly related to the stock exchange of the firm.

We can compare and assess model fit between the logistic model without a random intercept (the fixed-effects model from Step 1) to the intercept-only mixed-effects model using a chi-squared test based on the difference in log likelihood of each model (Step 2C). The results of the likelihood ratio test indicate rejection of the null hypothesis of no difference between models ($\Delta - 2LL = 54.08$, $p < .001$). Thus, we conclude there is significant intercept variation regarding high-tech industry classification across the three stock exchanges, and the random intercept model is a better fit. In addition, the results from Model 1 in Table 21.4 indicate a variance component estimate of 0.710 with a standard error of 0.185, further indicating significant variability between stock exchanges. The unconditional means/null model is estimated in SAS as follows:

```
PROC GLIMMIX data = SASUSER.HighTech_
   GLMM COVTEST;
CLASS exchg;
MODEL hightech=/solution link=logit dist =
   binomial ODDSRATIO;
RANDOM INTERCEPT /SUBJECT=exchg
   TYPE=VC;
run;
```

Step 3: Determine the mixed-effects model. When significant intercept variance is found between groups, the third step introduces random effects into the fixed-effects model, which results in a mixed-effects model. First, we assess whether there is significant variance in the intercepts (Step 3A). In this example, we test whether R & D expenditure (IV: *rd_exp*) is a significant predictor of high-tech industry (DV: *hightech*), coupled with a random intercept for stock exchange (*exchg*). In support of H1, the results of Model 2 in Table 21.4 indicate R & D expenditure (odds ratio = 1.09,

Analysis of Binomial Outcome Example

Fixed effects	Model 1	Model 2	Model 3	Model 4	Model 5
Intercept	0.75**	1.44**	1.14**	1.03**	1.05**
R & D investment (R&D)		1.09**	1.10**	1.04**	1.06**
Stock exchange average net income (NI)				1.07**	1.10**
R&D * NI					1.14*
Random effects (exchange)					
Intercept error variance	0.71	0.09	0.115	0.19	0.04
	(0.19)	(0.03)	(0.05)	(0.07)	(0.01)
Slope error variance			0.13	0.29	0.50
			(0.09)	(0.10)	(0.23)
−2LL	−696.60**	−708.56**	−718.16**	−722.40**	−856.20**
Δ in −2LL		−11.96**	−9.60*	−13.84**	−133.80**

Note. Standard errors are in parentheses. LL = log-likelihood.
*$p < .05$. **$p < .01$.

$p < .001$) is a significant predictor of high-tech industry membership. The addition of the R & D expenses predictor and random intercept ($\tau_{intercept} = 0.089$) significantly improves model fit ($\Delta - 2LL = -11.96, p < .01$). The random intercept model is estimated in SAS as follows:

```
PROC GLIMMIX data=SASUSER.HighTech_
    GLMM COVTEST;
CLASS exchg;
MODEL hightech = rd_exp/solution link=logit
    dist = binomial ODDSRATIO;
RANDOM INTERCEPT /SUBJECT=exchg
    TYPE=VC;
run;
```

In Step 3A, we first tested a model that consists of a Level 1 predictor (or predictors) and a random intercept for the clustering variable. Step 3B expands the random intercept model to include a random slope into the fixed-effects model. In further support of H1, Model 3 in Table 21.4 still finds that R & D expenditure (odds ratio = 1.09, $p < .001$) is a significant predictor of high-tech industry membership. The addition of the random slope ($\tau_{slope} = 0.133$) significantly improves model fit ($\Delta \chi^2 = -9.60$, $p < .05$). The random slope model is estimated in SAS as follows:

```
PROC GLIMMIX data=SASUSER.HighTech_
    GLMM COVTEST;
CLASS exchg;
MODEL hightech = rd_exp/solution link=
    logit dist = binomial ODDSRATIO;
RANDOM INTERCEPT rd_exp/SUBJECT=
    exchg TYPE=VC;
run;
```

Finally, we introduce a group-level (i.e., Level 2) predictor variable into the model with the Level 1 R & D expenditures (IV: *rd_exp*) predictor and random slope to text H2. In this example, we add the stock exchange's average acquisition investments (IV: *g_acq*) as the Level 2 predictor into the model, which also includes a random slope for R & D expenditures. In support of H2, the results indicate that stock exchange's average acquisition investments (odds ratio = 1.07, $p < .01$) are significant predictors of high-tech industry membership (DV: *hightech*), while controlling for firm-level R & D expenditures (odds ratio = 1.04, $p < .01$). Furthermore, the additional Level 2 variable (IV: *g_acq*) significantly improves model fit ($\Delta - 2LL = -9.60, p < .05$). The variance component of the intercept ($\tau_{intercept} = 0.185$) and the slope ($\tau_{slope} = 0.287$) suggest significant variation in intercepts and slopes across stock exchanges. The random slope model with Level 2 slope effect is estimated in SAS as follows:

```
PROC GLIMMIX data=SASUSER.HighTech_
    GLMM COVTEST;
CLASS exchg;
MODEL hightech = rd_exp g_acq/solution
    link=logit dist = binomial ODDSRATIO;
RANDOM INTERCEPT rd_exp /SUBJECT=
    exchg TYPE=VC;
run;
```

Step 4: Determine predictors of random slopes.
In Step 4, we determine whether the variance in the slopes across groups (i.e., stock exchanges) is significantly related to our Level 2 predictor by introducing the cross-level interaction term: R & D expenditures (IV: rd_exp) × stock exchange average acquisition investments (IV: g_acq). The results suggest average stock exchange acquisition investments are a significant, positive moderator of the relationship between R & D expenses and high-tech industry (odds ratio = 1.14, $p < .05$) and significantly improves model fit ($\Delta - 2LL = -133.80$, $p < .001$). Moreover, the variance components of the intercept ($\tau_{intercept} = 0.038$) and slope ($\tau_{slope} = 0.503$) show considerable variation. The cross-level interaction model is specified in SAS as follows:

```
PROC GLIMMIX data=SASUSER.HighTech_
    GLMM COVTEST;
CLASS exchg;
MODEL hightech = rd_exp g_acq rd_exp*g_
    acq/solution link=logit dist = binomial
    ODDSRATIO;
RANDOM INTERCEPT /SUBJECT=exchg
    TYPE=VC;
run;
```

Example 2: Multilevel Count Outcome Data

For this second example, we want to test the following hypotheses:

- H1: Firm-level intangible assets are positively associated with a firm's number of patents.

- H2: Industry-level munificence is positively related to a firm's number of patents after controlling for firm-level intangible assets.
- H3: Industry-level munificence positively moderates the firm-level intangible assets—number of patents relationships.

Step 1: Specification of the fixed-effects model.
For this example, we are interested in examining firm-level intangible assets and industry-level munificence linear predictors of patent counts (Step 1A). A normal distribution would likely include negative patent counts and account poorly for the left truncated distribution of the response variable. Consequently, a Poisson distribution, in which the variance is expected to equal the mean, or a negative binomial distribution, when low values of the data (e.g., zero) are inflated, are designed for dependent variables that represent counts. An analysis of the observed distribution seems to indicate that zero values are overdispersed (see Figure 21.1), and as a result, we use the negative binomial distribution (Step 1B). The canonical link function for both distributions is the log function (Step 1C).

Step 2: Test for intercept variance. For this example, we expect the data will be clustered on the basis of industry classification (two-digit SIC codes; Step 2A). Using PROC GLIMMIX in SAS, we construct a null model that only includes a random intercept for two-digit SIC codes (*sic2*), which produces an ICC = 13.81%. (Step 2B). It is important to note that calculating the ICC in negative binomial models is not as straightforward as in other multilevel models. Unlike linear and logit/probit mixed-effects models, negative binomial mixed-effects models do not produce the typical residual variance estimates commonly used to calculate ICCs (cf. Raudenbush & Bryk, 2002). Instead, unexplained between-group variance is captured by the dispersion parameter α (Tseloni & Pease, 2003), which is estimated in the process of fitting the model. This is typically reported in natural log form, so researchers should be careful to exponentiate, if necessary. Thus, the ICC can be calculated by the following formula:

$$ICC = \frac{\hat{o}_{00}}{\hat{o}_{00} + \hat{a}}, \qquad (21.19)$$

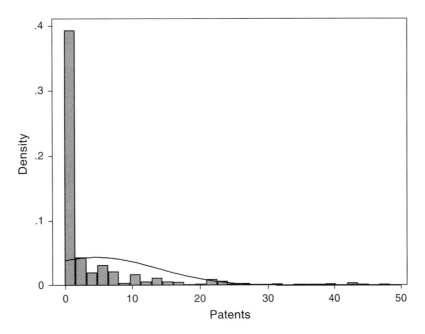

FIGURE 21.1. Histogram of patent counts.

where τ_{00} represents the random intercept variance, and α represents the estimated dispersion or residual Level 1 variance.

In addition, the random intercept improves model fit significantly compared with a Poisson regression without a random intercept ($\chi^2 = 570.88$, $p < .001$; Step 3C). The SAS code is as follows:

```
PROC GLIMMIX data=SASUSER.PATENT_
    GLMM COVTEST;
CLASS sic2;
MODEL patents = /solution link=log
    distribution=negbinomial;
RANDOM INTERCEPT /SUBJECT=sic2
    TYPE=VC;
run;
```

Step 3: Determine mixed-effects models. Next, we introduce our Level 1 predictor to analyze the relationship between patent counts (DV: *patents*) and intangible assets (IV: *intan_assets*) and also include a random intercept (Step 3A). In support of H1, Model 2 from Table 21.5 indicates intangible assets are positively related to patent counts ($\beta = 1.09$, $p < .001$) and improved model fit ($\Delta - 2LL = -1,031.85$, $p < .001$). The SAS code is as follows:

```
PROC GLIMMIX data=SASUSER.PATENT_
    GLMM COVTEST;
CLASS sic2;
MODEL patents = intan_assets/solution link=log
    distribution = negbinomial;
RANDOM INTERCEPT /SUBJECT=sic2
    TYPE=VC;
run;
```

Model 3 from Table 21.5 introduces a random slope to Model 2 (Step 3B). In further support of H1, the results reported for Model 3 in Table 21.5 indicate a significantly positive relationship between intangible assets and patent counts ($\beta = 1.10$, $p < .001$) and improved model fit ($\Delta - 2LL = -78.61$, $p < .01$). The SAS code for Model 3 is as follows:

```
PROC GLIMMIX data=SASUSER.PATENT_
    GLMM COVTEST;
CLASS sic2;
MODEL patents = intan_assets/solution link=log
    distribution = negbinomial;
RANDOM INTERCEPT intan_assets/SUBJECT=
    sic2 TYPE=VC;
run;
```

Next, we introduce a group-level (i.e., Level 2) predictor variable into the model with the Level 1

		TABLE 21.5			

Analysis of Count Outcome Example

Fixed effects	Model 1	Model 2	Model 3	Model 4	Model 5
Intercept	4.45**	4.15**	3.07**	2.96**	2.93**
Intangible assets (IA)		1.09**	1.10**	2.17**	2.22**
Industry munificence (IM)				1.45**	1.06**
IA * IM					1.41*
Random effects (exchange)					
Intercept error variance	0.37	0.75	0.42	0.62	0.04
	(0.10)	(0.34)	(0.12)	(0.18)	(0.01)
Slope error variance			1.01	1.35	0.50
			(0.31)	(0.42)	(0.23)
−2LL	−5870.86**	−6902.71**	6981.32**	−7011.92**	−7153.87**
Δ in −2LL		−1031.85**	−78.61**	−30.60**	−141.95**

Note. Standard errors are in parentheses. LL = log-likelihood.
*p < .05. **p < .01.

intangible assets expenditures (IV: *intan_assets*) predictor and random slope to text H2. In this example, we add industry munificence (IV: *ind_mun*) as the Level 2 predictor into the model, which also includes a random slope. In support of H2, the results of Model 4 in Table 21.5 indicate industry munificence ($\beta = 1.45$, $p < .001$) is significantly related to patent counts and improves model fit ($\Delta - 2LL = -30.60$, $p < .01$). The SAS code for Model 4 is as follows:

```
PROC GLIMMIX data = SASUSER.PATENT_
    GLMM COVTEST;
CLASS sic2;
MODEL patents=intan_assets ind_mun/solution
    link=log distribution=negbinomial;
RANDOM INTERCEPT intan_assets/SUBJECT=
    sic2 TYPE=VC;
run;
```

Step 4: Determine predictors of random slopes. In Step 4, we determine whether the variance in the slopes across groups (i.e., two-digit SIC codes) is significantly related to our Level 2 predictor by introducing the cross-level interaction term: intangible assets (IV: *intan_assets*) × industry munificence (IV: *ind_mun*). The results from Model 5 in Table 21.5 suggest industry munificence

is a significant, positive moderator of the relationship between intangible assets and patent counts ($\beta = 1.41$, $p < .05$) and significantly improves model fit ($\Delta - 2LL = -141.95$, $p < .001$). The SAS code for Model 5 is as follows:

```
PROC GLIMMIX data=SASUSER.PATENT_
    GLMM COVTEST;
CLASS sic2;
MODEL patents = intan_assets ind_mun
    intang_assets*ind_mun /solution link=log
    distribution=negbinomial;
RANDOM INTERCEPT intan_assets/SUBJECT=
    sic2 TYPE=VC;
run;
```

CONCLUSION

The purpose of this chapter has been to provide an introduction to GLMMs and how they can be used to overcome common yet significant problems related to inappropriately modeling nonnormal multilevel data. Recent advances in the functionality of statistical software packages that are frequently used by researchers in psychology, organizational behavior, and strategy (e.g., SAS, SPSS, Stata) have made the application of mixed models to multilevel data much easier. This has increased our ability to ask and answer a wider array of questions and test more nuanced theoretical questions. GLMMs offer researchers the ability to examine a variety of nonnormal multilevel organizational phenomena while remaining true to the form of the distribution that produced the sampled data. To help increase awareness and provide greater accessibility to generalized linear mixed modeling, we also presented several examples of how such models can be applied to examine nonnormal multilevel data in practice. Finally, we outlined a step-by-step process for building and testing GLMMs that we hope provides some practical guidance to future researchers. Our goal is to help scholars better understand how to use these methods and thereby encourage the collection and analysis of multilevel studies of nonnormal phenomena.

Generalized linear mixed modeling offers researchers several important advantages. Primarily, the correct use of GLMMs allows for the modeling of nonnormal clustered data, enabling researchers to make stronger inferences about regression results because these approaches avoid potential biases and the lack of efficiency in estimation that is offered by less sophisticated approaches. Being able to model data using an approach that matches distribution assumptions in the data allows researchers to communicate results and effect sizes in ways that make our work more useful to practitioners as well. The ability to use these approaches in clustered data, be it multilevel data or longitudinal data, also allows researchers to use all available data better and to more carefully isolate causal relationships by mitigating the harmful biases introduced by nonindependence of observations.

Despite its advantages, generalized linear mixed modeling should be approached with some caution. First, as discussed in greater detail earlier, the fixed- and random-effect estimates are sensitive to the model specifications. As our examples demonstrate, differences in family distribution and link function specifications can produce different regression coefficients and effect sizes as well as change the statistical significance of the coefficients themselves. This sensitivity suggests that scholars should be careful to correctly specify the family distribution,

link function, linear predictor, and covariance structure appropriately to minimize such biases.

Although it is not a limitation, it should be noted that GLMMs may be more difficult to fit than traditional mixed-model approaches. Unlike traditional linear mixed models, which can fit the log-likelihood function directly, generalized linear mixed modeling requires an iterative estimation process. Earlier integration methods for solving the log-likelihood equation in GLMMs included penalized quasi-likelihood and marginal quasi-likelihood (Breslow & Clayton, 1993) but were limited by biased estimates in smaller samples (Rodríguez & Goldman, 1995) and the inability to compare models using likelihood-ratio tests. Fortunately, as computers have advanced, more efficient estimation procedures have become available, including Gauss-Hermite quadrature (and variations) and Laplacian approximation. That being said, most GLMMs are quite complex (particularly when specifying an unstructured covariance structure) and so can be quite time consuming and computationally intensive. One possible solution is to reduce the number of quadrature points (the default is often seven points), but this should be tested against higher numbers of points for robustness. Overall, a researcher should consider the natural trade-offs between speed and accuracy of analysis when augmenting default estimation procedures.

The added flexibility of mixed-effects models like GLMMs may have trouble converging using certain data. Most mixed models rely on the Newton-Raphson algorithm to maximize the log-likelihood function, which uses a gradient vector and second derivative Hessian matrix in its calculation. This procedure fails to converge when the Hessian calculation becomes unstable and is often the result of a ridge in the log-likelihood function, which makes a unique solution impossible. A ridge is commonly caused by two possible issues. First, if observations in the data are not sufficiently repeated (meaning there are multiple unique observations within a given subgroup), the random parameters will be confounded with the overall model errors and unable to achieve convergence. Second, convergence may fail if the random variance components are near zero. Many software packages that default to the Newton-Raphson algorithm switch between alternative maximizing procedures if convergence is not achieved within a certain number of iterations, but this may not solve the issue. If this is the case, a researcher may consider using the expectation-maximization algorithm (Dempster, Laird, & Rubin, 1977) to refine the starting values, which may help maximize the log-likelihood equation more efficiently. Many other diagnostic tools are still becoming available and should be explored if and when a model consistently fails to converge.

Altogether, we see GLMMs as particularly valuable to organizational researchers because so often organizational phenomena are not only explained by factors at multiple levels of analysis but also are not produced by a normal distribution process. By generalizing the traditional linear mixed-effects model to allow for the specification of the family distribution and link components, users can be more confident in their estimations and interpretations of the results. We believe that increased use of this method can help advance organizational research by allowing scholars to examine more unique data without compromising the benefits of this diversity, perhaps enabling future researchers to discover new and important relationships that have been overlooked as a result of improper treatment of nonnormal multilevel data.

APPENDIX 21.1: EXPLANATION OF SAS SYNTAX FROM EXAMPLES

Example 1: SAS Code for Multilevel Binary Outcome Data

```
PROC GLIMMIX data=SASUSER.HighTech_
    GLMM COVTEST;
CLASS exchg;
MODEL hightech = rd_exp g_acq rd_exp*g_acq/
    solution link=logit dist = binomial
    ODDSRATIO;
RANDOM INTERCEPT /SUBJECT=exchg
    TYPE=VC;
run;
```

Explanation of SAS Syntax:

PROC GLIMMIX ← invokes the Generalized Linear Mixed Model procedure
data = SASUSER.HighTech_GLMM ← specifies the input datafile
COVTEST; ← requests z-tests for covariance (random) effects

CLASS exchg; ← denotes our classification variable
MODEL hightech = rd_exp g_acq rd_exp*g_acq ← describes the fixed-effects model as IVs = DVs, including the cross-level interaction between R & D expenditures (rd_exp) and gross acquisition expenses (g_acq)
/solution ← requests fixed-effects significance tests
link = logit ← specifies the link function
dist = binomial ← specifies the distribution for the response variable
ODDSRATIO; ← requests parameter estimates to be reported as Odds Ratios

RANDOM ← indicates random effects will be specified
INTERCEPT ← specifies the Intercept as a Random effect
/SUBJECT=exchg ← indicates the level of the Random effects
TYPE=VC; ← specifies variance components as the covariance structure
run; ← every PROC command must end with a RUN command

Example 2: SAS Code for Multilevel Count Outcome Data

```
PROC GLIMMIX data=SASUSER.PATENT_
    GLMM COVTEST;
CLASS sic2;
MODEL patents = intan_assets ind_mun
    intang_assets*ind_mun /solution link=log
    dist=negbinomial;
RANDOM INTERCEPT intan_assets/
    SUBJECT=sic2 TYPE=VC;
run;
```

Explanation of SAS Syntax:

PROC GLIMMIX ← invokes the Generalized Linear Mixed Model procedure

data=SASUSER.PATENT_GLMM ← specifies the input datafile

COVTEST; ← requests z-tests for covariance (random) effects

CLASS sic2; ← denotes our classification variable

MODEL patents = intan_assets ind_mun ← describes the fixed-effects model as IVs = DVs, intang_assets*ind_mun including the cross-level interaction between intangible assets (*intan_assets*) and industry munificence (*ind_mun*)

/solution ← requests fixed-effects significance tests

link=log ← specifies the link function

dist=negbinomial; ← specifies the distribution for the response variable

RANDOM ← indicates random effects will be specified

INTERCEPT intan_assets ← specifies the Intercept and Intangible Assets (*intan_assets*) as Random effects

/SUBJECT = sic2 ← indicates the level of the Random effects

TYPE=VC; ← specifies the covariance structure as variance components

run; ← every PROC command must end with a RUN command

References

Aguinis, H., & O'Boyle, E., Jr. (2014). Star performers in twenty-first century organizations. *Personnel Psychology, 67*, 313–350. http://dx.doi.org/10.1111/peps.12054

Aguinis, H., O'Boyle, E., Jr., Gonzalez-Mulé, E., & Joo, H. (2016). Cumulative advantages: Conductors and insulators of heavy-tailed productivity distributions and productivity stars. *Personnel Psychology, 69*, 3–66. http://dx.doi.org/10.1111/peps.12095

Ahuja, G. (2000). Collaboration networks, structural holes, and innovation: A longitudinal study. *Administrative Science Quarterly, 45*, 425–455. http://dx.doi.org/10.2307/2667105

Ahuja, G., & Katila, R. (2001). Technological acquisitions and the innovation performance of acquiring firms: A longitudinal study. *Strategic Management Journal, 22*, 197–220. http://dx.doi.org/10.1002/smj.157

Ballinger, G. A. (2004). Using generalized estimating equations for longitudinal data analysis. *Organizational Research Methods, 7*, 127–150. http://dx.doi.org/10.1177/1094428104263672

Bliese, P. D. (2002). Multilevel random coefficient modeling in organizational research: Examples using SAS and S-PLUS. In F. Drasgow & N. Schmitt (Eds.), *Measuring and analyzing behavior in organizations: Advances in measurement and data analysis* (pp. 401–445). San Francisco, CA: Jossey-Bass.

Bliese, P. D., & Ployhart, R. E. (2002). Growth modeling using random coefficient models: Model building, testing, and illustrations. *Organizational Research Methods, 5*, 362–387. http://dx.doi.org/10.1177/109442802237116

Breslow, N. E. (1996). Generalized linear models: Checking assumptions and strengthening conclusions. *Statistica Applicata, 8*, 23–41.

Breslow, N. E., & Clayton, D. G. (1993). Approximate interference in generalized linear mixed models. *Journal of the American Statistical Association, 88*, 9–25.

Buntin, M. B., & Zaslavsky, A. M. (2004). Too much ado about two-part models and transformation? Comparing methods of modeling Medicare expenditures. *Journal of Health Economics, 23*, 525–542. http://dx.doi.org/10.1016/j.jhealeco.2003.10.005

Dempster, A. P., Laird, N. M., & Rubin, D. B. (1977). Maximum likelihood from incomplete data via the EM algorithm. *Journal of the Royal Statistical Society: Series B. Statistical Methodology, 39*, 1–38.

Dietz, J., Robinson, S. L., Folger, R., Baron, R. A., & Schulz, M. (2003). The impact of community violence and an organization's procedural justice climate on workplace aggression. *Academy of Management Journal, 46*, 317–326. http://dx.doi.org/10.5465/30040625

Diggle, P. J., Heagerty, P., Liang, K. Y., & Zeger, S. L. (2002). *Analysis of longitudinal data* (2nd ed.). Oxford, England: Oxford University Press.

Dineen, B. R., Lewicki, R. J., & Tomlinson, E. C. (2006). Supervisory guidance and behavioral integrity: Relationships with employee citizenship and deviant behavior. *Journal of Applied Psychology, 91*, 622–635. http://dx.doi.org/10.1037/0021-9010.91.3.622

Duan, N. (1983). Smearing estimate: A nonparametric retransformation method. *Journal of the American Statistical Association, 78*, 605–610. http://dx.doi.org/10.1080/01621459.1983.10478017

Feingold, A., Oliveto, A., Schottenfeld, R., & Kosten, T. R. (2002). Utility of crossover designs in clinical trials: Efficacy of desipramine vs. placebo in opioid-dependent cocaine abusers. *The American Journal on Addictions, 11,* 111–123. http://dx.doi.org/10.1080/10550490290087884

Felps, W., Mitchell, T. R., Hekman, D. R., Lee, T. W., Holtom, B. C., & Harman, W. S. (2009). Turnover contagion: How coworkers' job embeddedness and job search behaviors influence quitting. *Academy of Management Journal, 52,* 545–561. http://dx.doi.org/10.5465/AMJ.2009.41331075

Freeman, L. C. (1978–1979). Centrality in social networks conceptual clarification. *Social Networks, 1,* 215–239. http://dx.doi.org/10.1016/0378-8733(78)90021-7

Gardner, W., Mulvey, E. P., & Shaw, E. C. (1995). Regression analyses of counts and rates: Poisson, overdispersed Poisson, and negative binomial models. *Psychological Bulletin, 118,* 392–404. http://dx.doi.org/10.1037/0033-2909.118.3.392

Harrison, D. A. (2002). Structure and timing in limited range dependent variables: Regression models for predicting if and when. In F. Drasgow & N. Schmitt (Eds.), *Measuring and analyzing behavior in organizations: Advances in measurement and data analysis* (pp. 446–497). San Francisco, CA: Jossey-Bass.

Hilbe, J. (1998). Robust variance estimators for MLE Poisson and negative binomial regression. *Stata Technical Bulletin, 45,* 26–28.

Hitt, M. A., Beamish, P. W., Jackson, S. E., & Mathieu, J. E. (2007). Building theoretical and empirical bridges across levels: Multilevel research in management. *Academy of Management Journal, 50,* 1385–1399. http://dx.doi.org/10.5465/AMJ.2007.28166219

Hofmann, D. (1997). An overview of the logic and rationale of hierarchical linear models. *Journal of Management, 23,* 723–744. http://dx.doi.org/10.1177/014920639702300602

Horton, N. J., & Lipsitz, S. R. (1999). Review of software to fit generalized estimating equation regression models. *The American Statistician, 18,* 160–169.

Huang, F. L. (2014). Further understanding factors associated with grade retention: Birthday effects and socioemotional skills. *Journal of Applied Developmental Psychology, 35,* 79–93. http://dx.doi.org/10.1016/j.appdev.2013.12.004

Lee, T. W., Mitchell, T. R., Sablynski, C. J., Burton, J. P., & Holtom, B. C. (2004). The effects of job embeddedness on organizational citizenship, job performance, volitional absences, and voluntary turnover. *Academy of Management Journal, 47,* 711–722. http://dx.doi.org/10.5465/20159613

Marcel, J. J., & Cowen, A. P. (2014). Cleaning house or jumping ship? Understanding board upheaval following financial fraud. *Strategic Management Journal, 35,* 926–937. http://dx.doi.org/10.1002/smj.2126

Mathieu, J. E., & Chen, G. (2011). The etiology of the multilevel paradigm in management research. *Journal of Management, 37,* 610–641. http://dx.doi.org/10.1177/0149206310364663

McCullagh, P., & Nelder, J. A. (1989). *Generalized linear models* (2nd ed.). London, England: Chapman and Hall.

Moore, C. B., Bell, R. G., Filatotchev, I., & Rasheed, A. A. (2012). Foreign IPO capital market choice: Understanding the institutional fit of corporate governance. *Strategic Management Journal, 33,* 914–937. http://dx.doi.org/10.1002/smj.1953

Ndofor, H. A., Vanevenhoven, J., & Barker, V. L., III. (2013). Software firm turnarounds in the 1990s: An analysis of reversing decline in a growing, dynamic industry. *Strategic Management Journal, 34,* 1123–1133. http://dx.doi.org/10.1002/smj.2050

Pindyck, R. S., & Rubinfeld, D. L. (1998). *Econometric models and economic forecasts* (4th ed.). Boston, MA: Irwin, McGraw-Hill.

Raudenbush, S. W., & Bryk, A. S. (2002). *Hierarchical linear models: Applications and data analysis methods* (2nd ed.). Thousand Oaks, CA: Sage.

Rodríguez, G., & Goldman, N. (1995). An assessment of estimation procedures for multilevel models with binary responses. *Journal of the Royal Statistical Society. Series A (General), 158,* 73–89. http://dx.doi.org/10.2307/2983404

Rose, E. L., & Ito, K. (2008). Competitive interactions: The international investment patterns of Japanese automobile manufacturers. *Journal of International Business Studies, 39,* 864–879. http://dx.doi.org/10.1057/palgrave.jibs.8400391

Sorensen, J. B., & Stuart, T. E. (2000). Aging, obsolescence, and organizational innovation. *Administrative Science Quarterly, 45,* 81–112. http://dx.doi.org/10.2307/2666980

Tosi, H. L. (1992). *The environment/organization/person contingency model: A meso approach to the study of organizations.* Greenwich, CT: JAI Press.

Tseloni, A., & Pease, K. (2003). Repeat personal victimization: "Boosts" or "flags"? *British Journal of Criminology, 43,* 196–212. http://dx.doi.org/10.1093/bjc/43.1.196

Wadhwa, A., & Kotha, S. (2006). Knowledge creation through external venturing: Evidence from the telecommunications equipment manufacturing industry. *Academy of Management Journal, 49,* 819–835. http://dx.doi.org/10.5465/AMJ.2006.22083132

Wang, M., Liao, H., Zhan, Y., & Shi, J. (2011). Daily customer mistreatment and employee sabotage against customers: Examining emotion and resource perspectives. *Academy of Management Journal, 54,* 312–334. http://dx.doi.org/10.5465/AMJ.2011.60263093

Watson, D., Clark, L. A., & Tellegen, A. (1988). Development and validation of brief measures of positive and negative affect: The PANAS scales. *Journal of Personality and Social Psychology, 54,* 1063–1070. http://dx.doi.org/10.1037/0022-3514.54.6.1063

Wedderburn, R. W. M. (1974). Quasi-likelihood functions, generalized linear models, and the Gauss-Newton method. *Biometrika, 61,* 439–447.

Xia, J., Dawley, D. D., Jiang, H., Ma, R., & Boal, K. B. (2016). Resolving a dilemma of signaling bankrupt-firm emergence: A dynamic integrative view. *Strategic Management Journal, 37,* 1754–1764. http://dx.doi.org/10.1002/smj.2406

Zeger, S. L., & Liang, K. Y. (1986). Longitudinal data analysis for discrete and continuous outcomes. *Biometrics, 42,* 121–130. http://dx.doi.org/10.2307/2531248

A TEMPORAL PERSPECTIVE ON EMERGENCE: USING THREE-LEVEL MIXED-EFFECTS MODELS TO TRACK CONSENSUS EMERGENCE IN GROUPS

Jonas W. B. Lang and Paul D. Bliese

Social psychologists, applied psychologists, and organizational researchers are interested in *multilevel processes*—interactional processes that occur across different hierarchical levels in organizations. Multilevel processes are central to understanding the social dynamics that underlie group and organizational functioning. The theoretical literature typically distinguishes between two types of multilevel processes. *Top-down processes* describe how characteristics of higher level units in an organization, such as teams, work groups, or divisions, influence and shape behavior and perceptions at lower levels. For instance, the work climate in work units may alter whether individuals' perceptions of work stressors have a strong or weak relationship to their individual-level work strains (e.g., Bliese & Jex, 2002).

Bottom-up processes, in contrast, describe how lower level units in organizations interact to jointly create characteristics of higher level units (Klein & Kozlowski, 2000; Kozlowski, 2012). Psychologists have long been interested in psychological constructs at group and higher organizational levels (Chen, Mathieu, & Bliese, 2005). Unlike individual constructs that may develop over long periods as an individual matures (e.g., personality traits, crystalized intelligence), psychological group constructs usually start to develop when a group is formed

or when some significant event occurs in a group. Thus, many psychological group constructs are based on perceptions or feelings of group members that develop over relatively short periods—a pattern that can be described as *consensus emergence*. For instance, group members may develop shared perceptions of how interactions in the group should take place and in so doing develop a group-specific work climate.

One important idea in the literature surrounding consensus emergence is that psychological group constructs are often characterized by shared perceptions or feelings. Although not all group-level constructs require the idea of shared perceptions, and the literature has differentiated between several different types of bottom-up processes, many group-level constructs used in social psychology and organizational research include the assumption that groups should develop some form of consensus about perceptions and affect (Bliese, 2000; Chan, 1998; Chen et al., 2005; Festinger, 1954; LeBreton & Senter, 2008; Morgeson & Hofmann, 1999). The literature (Klein & Kozlowski, 2000) especially uses the term *compilation constructs* to refer to these types of group-level constructs. The term *compilation* implies that individuals that interact in a group create something new that did not exist before.

http://dx.doi.org/10.1037/0000115-023
The Handbook of Multilevel Theory, Measurement, and Analysis, S. E. Humphrey and J. M. LeBreton (Editors-in-Chief)

In a typical scenario, repeated interactions among group members produce a common view of group-related issues that defines the social environment or climate of the group. Compilation constructs are commonly separated from composition constructs. *Composition constructs* are merely a combination of elements of the group (e.g., the maximum score on an IQ test in the group or the size of the group) and thus are simply the average or sum of their parts and do not require the idea that individuals develop a consensus. The notion that a shared climate should develop over time is apparent when researchers use terms such as *emergence* or *emergent states* to refer to group-level constructs (Humphrey & Aime, 2014; Kozlowski, 2015; Kozlowski & Chao, 2012; Ployhart & Moliterno, 2011). The term *bottom-up process* also implies that a temporal process occurs through the interaction of the group members that leads to the creation of something novel. In this chapter, we focus on the development of consensus over time and define *consensus emergence* as a pattern of increased similarity among group-member ratings (e.g., affect, perceptions) over time.

An important corollary to these ideas is that from both a theoretical perspective and a model-building and testing perspective, researchers have to be able to test both for the presence and absence of consensus emergence. That is, although a broad literature base has suggested that consensus emergence should occur, it is important for theory development to be able to test whether consensus emergence is stronger or weaker or even absent in different situations. At present, however, the multilevel methods typically used for studying consensus emergence are limited when it comes to modeling temporal processes. Most quantitative multilevel research on emergence assesses emergence retrospectively (Kozlowski, Chao, Grand, Braun, & Kuljanin, 2013). Existing methods are typically based on the intraclass correlation coefficient, type 1 (ICC(1); Bliese, 2000; LeBreton & Senter, 2008). The problem with the ICC(1) is that the index does not directly incorporate a temporal element and can thus only be used to assess whether consensus exists at a particular point.

When ICC(1) values are estimated separately for each time point, even an increase in ICC(1) values over time does not necessarily indicate

that consensus emergence has occurred (Cronin, Weingart, & Todorova, 2011; Humphrey & Aime, 2014; Kozlowski et al., 2013). Indeed, a recent review focusing on changes in ICC(1) values over time found limited support for the theoretical notion that changes in these values occur in typical organizational data (Allen & O'Neill, 2015). As an aside, the ICC(2) suffers from similar limitations as the ICC(1) because the ICC(2) is a direct function of the ICC(1) and the group size, so assuming group sizes remain constant, any pattern evident in the ICC(1) will also be evident in the ICC(2). From our perspective, the ICC(1) is typically more convenient with respect to substantive interpretation because it can be interpreted as the proportion of variance in a construct that can be explained by group characteristics.

In this chapter, we describe a multilevel approach that can address the limitations of the ICC(1) when studying consensus emergence. (Note again that we are equally interested in dissensus emergence and that the approach we suggest identifies both consensus and dissensus emergence, but to avoid repetition we simply refer to *consensus emergence*.) The chapter builds on work described more extensively by Lang, Bliese, and de Voogt (2018). The goals of the chapter are to (a) provide a basic introduction to the methods by demonstrating the core ideas in a step-by-step manner and (b) illustrate the core principles behind these methods. The chapter accomplishes these goals by applying the methods to simulated data and two real data sets. We start by explaining why the ICC(1) is limited when the goal is to model consensus emergence over time. We demonstrate these limitations using a simulated example in which two sets of groups have a similar pattern of increasing ICC(1) values, but only one set of groups reflects a pattern of consensus emergence. On the basis of these insights, we introduce the consensus emergence model as an approach that addresses the limitations of trying to interpret serial ICC(1) values and allows researchers to identify consensus emergence patterns. We provide example code in Appendix 22.2 using the open-source nlme package (Pinheiro & Bates, 2000) in R (R Foundation, n.d.).

We also provide two real data examples. Our first real data example uses a classic social psychology study in which we apply the emergence model to what was arguably one of the first studies of consensus emergence—Sherif's (1935) examination of the development of group norms in perception. Our second real data example applies the three-level emergence model to test for consensus emergence in team cohesion ratings of 32 student project teams (246 group members) who worked together for an extended time and were surveyed three times (708 observations).

STUDYING CONSENSUS EMERGENCE USING THE ICC(1)

As noted, existing methods for studying the consensus emergence in perceptions or affect typically rely on the ICC(1). The ICC(1) is a basic statistic from the multilevel literature that can be estimated on the basis of an intercept-only multilevel model. The intercept-only multilevel model can be written as follows:

$$\text{Level 1: } Y_{ij} = \beta_{0j} + e_{ij} \quad (22.1)$$

$$\text{Level 2: } \beta_{0j} = \gamma_{00} + u_{0j},$$

where

$$e_{ij} \overset{iid}{\sim} N(0, \sigma^2) \quad (22.2)$$

$$u_{0j} \overset{iid}{\sim} N(0, \tau_{00}) \quad (22.3)$$

and defines the response Y_{ij} for person i in group j as the product of an intercept γ_{00}, the group-specific value u_{0j}, and the residual error e_{ij}. The variance of the group-specific values τ_{00} is the group variance, and the variance of the residual error e_{ij} residual variance is the individual variance, σ^2. Using these variance components, the ICC(1) can be estimated using the formula

$$\text{ICC}(1) = \tau_{00}/(\tau_{00} + \sigma^2). \quad (22.4)$$

As indicated by the formula, the ICC(1) captures the percentage of variance that group membership explains in the overall variance (i.e., the proportion of variance in Y_{ij} that resides between groups).

When ICC(1) is high, members of the same group are similar to each other and different from other groups. In contrast, when ICC(1) is low, members of the same group may or may not be similar to one another, and there is little difference among groups.

As noted, ICC(1) values are useful when the goal is to quantify similarity or group effects at a particular point; however, when it comes to studying changes in consensus emergence over time, ICC(1) is problematic because change in ICC(1) values can result from group means becoming more or less similar over time (an increase or reduction in τ_{00}) or from individuals in groups becoming more or less similar over time (an increase or decreases in σ^2). When a researcher relies on ICC(1) values estimated at each time point to estimate consensus emergence, it not possible to tell whether an increased ICC(1) is the product of consensus emergence associated with a systematic reduction in σ^2 or the product of group mean divergence associated with a systematic increase in τ_{00} (Cronin et al., 2011; Humphrey & Aime, 2014; Kozlowski et al., 2013). It is not clear how often this confound occurs, but a recent review studying changes in ICC(1) values over time in the literature revealed limited evidence for temporal changes in ICC(1) values in groups (Allen & O'Neill, 2015).

Figures 22.1 and 22.2 illustrate the limitations of using changes in the ICC(1) as a measure of consensus emergence. Figure 22.1 shows data with groups that develop opinions that are increasingly similar. The pattern in Figure 22.1 represents consensus emergence reflected in the ICC(1) with values for each measurement occasion at .08, .07, .19, .27, and .33 for T1 to T5, respectively. Figure 22.2, illustrates the limitations of ICC(1) as a measure of consensus emergence. Notice in Figure 22.2 that the data within groups do not show a trend similar to that illustrated in Figure 22.1. Indeed, in Figure 22.2, there is no clear tendency for an increase in consensus in each of the groups; nonetheless, the data in Figure 22.2 show an ICC(1) trend similar to the pattern from Figure 22.1, with the ICC(1) in Figure 22.2 being .06, .09, .16, .23, and .46 at T1 to T5, respectively.

The reason Figure 22.2 shows an increase in ICC(1) values is that τ_{00} (between-group variance)

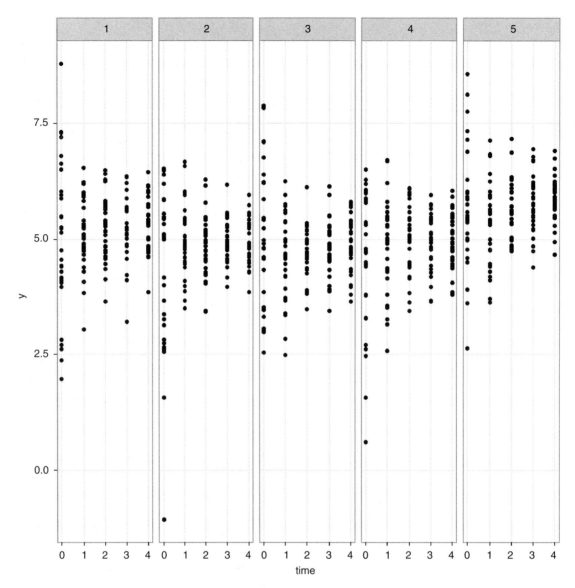

FIGURE 22.1.   Data Set 1: A data set including five groups with 20 members each measured at five time points.

increases over time. In contrast, the data in Figure 22.1 show an increase in the ICC(1) values because σ^2 (residual error) systematically decreases. In other words, in Figure 22.1, group members develop consensus. In Figure 22.2, the groups do not reach a consensus, but the differences between groups systematically increase. We believe these types of confounds are common. For instance, many European countries have systems with several political parties. The members of the same polit-ical parties often show a considerable degree of dissensus. At the same time, different political parties in a country often disagree. The ICC(1)

cannot differentiate between a situation in which the party members of each party discuss and develop a shared understanding, but the political parties remain apart from a situation in which the level of dissensus within the parties stays the same but the political parties drift further apart.

ADDRESSING THE LIMITATIONS OF THE ICC(1)

One limitation of the ICC(1) is that the measure takes both the within-group variance and the between-group variance into account. An intuitive way to

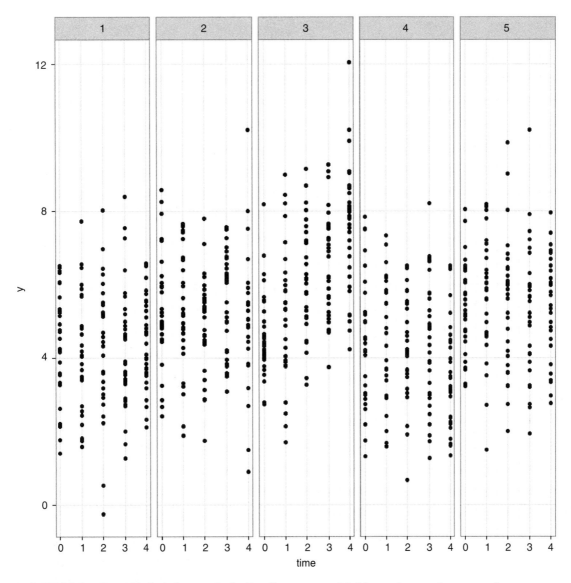

FIGURE 22.2. Data Set 2: A data set including five groups with 20 members each measured at five time points.

address this problem is to only focus on the within-group variance by using the within-group standard deviation as a measure of sharedness. This approach would not fully account for a potential scenario in which the between-group variance would also be decreasing so that group membership explains the

same amount of variance over time, but this approach can nevertheless provide important insights about the within-group variance in isolation.[1]

However, another limitation of the ICC(1) is that the measure only assesses the level of sharedness at snapshots in time without providing

[1]A measure of sharedness used in the organizational literature that is related to the within-group *SD* are agreement indices like the r_{wg} index (James, Demaree, & Wolf, 1993) and several similar indices (Bliese, 2000; LeBreton & Senter, 2008). Agreement indices are in large part based on the within-group variance and do not take the between-group variance into account and thus come close to relying on the within-group *SD*. Specifically, r_{wg} is designed for Likert-response formats and compares the variability of response categories with a theoretical null distribution ($r_{wg} = 1 -$ [observed group variance/expected random variance]). In an ideal scenario with big groups, equal group sizes and a large number of response categories, r_{wg} is a linear function of (or equivalent to) the within-group *SD*. In practice, r_{wg} can be different from the within-person *SD* because the observed within-group *SD*s can exceed the theoretically assumed *SD* of the default distribution. The agreement index is then set to 0 (see LeBreton, James, & Lindell, 2005; LeBreton & Senter, 2008). This scenario is known as *truncation* in the literature and can affect r_{wg} estimates.

researchers with a tool to model and test shared-ness over time and the degree to which team and individual characteristics contribute to sharedness. In theory, a researcher could estimate the within-group standard deviation, the between-group standard deviation, and the group mean and separately model trends in these three estimates using ordinary least squares regression analyses (for the between-group standard deviation) and growth models (for the mean and the within-group standard deviation).

We believe that a more elegant approach is to build an integrative multilevel model for consensus emergence that includes all three processes. An important advantage of such a model is that it takes all three processes into account simultaneously and thus directly and comprehensively captures the situation in Figure 22.1 and Figure 22.2 in the context of a multilevel model with random effects that can be optimized using a joint maximum like-lihood function. Furthermore, such an approach allows researchers to conduct overall tests of consensus emergence and to test novel hypotheses (e.g., predictors of consensus emergence at the individual and group level).

We refer to the approach as the *consensus emergence model* (CEM). The CEM is a multilevel growth model that uses variance functions to model changes in residual variances over time (Carroll & Ruppert, 1988; Pinheiro & Bates, 2000; Zuur, Ieno, Walker, Saveliev, & Smith, 2009). The growth model part of the model captures systematic changes in the between-group variance over time, and the variance functions capture changes in the within-group or residual variance over time. In so doing, the CEM approach explicitly models both variance components that constitute the ICC(1).

The use of variance functions in the CEM model (Lang et al., 2018) is new for organizational research in the sense that the changes in residual variance are of substantive interest for the analyses. Although the method is well established in statistical texts and biological research (Pinheiro & Bates, 2000), organizational research has typically discussed changes in residual variances as a way to address violations of the statistical assumptions behind mixed-effects models (Bliese & Ployhart, 2002). In contrast, researchers in

other fields such as aging research (Rast, MacDonald, & Hofer, 2012; Rast & Zimprich, 2011) and health research (Hedeker & Mermelstein, 2007; Hedeker, Mermelstein, & Demirtas, 2012; Hoffman, 2007) have used variance functions to understand variability around person means over time. Variance functions have also been used to study variability in cross-sectional data on groups (Raudenbush & Bryk, 1987) and to understand differential reactions to clinical treatments (Kim & Seltzer, 2011). Substantive interest in variations in residual variances and the use of variance functions to study these variations is accordingly not new. The novel aspect of the CEM, however, is to combine growth models and variance functions in a way that allows one to systematically delineate different sources of variance change over time to test consensus emergence.

The Two-Level Consensus Emergence Model

As noted, one intuitive way to test for the emergence of consensus in groups over time would be to estimate ICC(1)s at various measurement occasions. A pattern of increasing ICC(1) values suggests a pattern of emergence in which group members' perceptions become more consistent. Unfortunately, estimating ICC(1) values at each measurement occasion would lead to ambiguity as to whether (a) the individuals within the groups were becoming more similar over time or (b) the differences between the groups were increasing.

The most basic form of the CEM addresses this ambiguity using a two-level multilevel model estimated over a longitudinal data set that adds two elements: (a) a time variable that accounts for change in the group means over time and (b) a variance function to account for changes in the residual variance over time. The estimate of residual variance over time provides evidence of emergence (see Raudenbush & Bryk, 1987).

The two-level CEM can be written as follows:

$$\text{Level 1: } Y_{tij} = \beta_{00j} + \beta_{10j}\text{TIME}_t + e_{tij} \qquad (22.5)$$

$$\text{Level 2: } \beta_{00j} = \gamma_{000} + u_{00j}$$

$$\beta_{10j} = \gamma_{100} + u_{10j}$$

$$e_{tij} \overset{iid}{\sim} N\left(0, \sigma^2 \exp[2\delta_1 TIME_t]\right) \qquad (22.6)$$

$$\begin{pmatrix} u_{00j} \\ u_{10j} \end{pmatrix} \overset{iid}{\sim} N \left(\begin{bmatrix} 0 \\ 0 \end{bmatrix}, \begin{bmatrix} \tau_{00} & \tau_{01} \\ \tau_{10} & \tau_{11} \end{bmatrix} \right). \qquad (22.7)$$

The model thus specifies that the response of person i in group j at measurement occasion t is a function of a common intercept γ_{000}, one fixed-effects predictor γ_{100} ($TIME_i$), a group random effect u_{00j}, a group-specific random slope u_{10j}, ($TIME_t$), and the residual e_{tij} that changes as a function of $TIME_t$ with variance function weight δ_1. TIME is typically coded 0 at the origin with a 1-point increase for each occasion (0, 1, 2, 3, etc.), though other coding schemes are possible.[2]

The purpose of the $TIME_t$ variable in the CEM is to account for linear change in the latent group mean over time. The inclusion of this change term essentially makes the model a type of growth model (Bliese & Ployhart, 2002; Lang & Bliese, 2009; Singer & Willett, 2003). Where the CEM fundamentally differs from most treatments of growth models is that the CEM requires the $TIME_i$ slope covariate to vary randomly among groups rather than among individuals.

The variance function weight (δ_1) in the CEM reflects the systematic change in the residual variance over time. A positive estimate implies increased variability and thus dissensus over time, whereas a negative estimate implies reduced variability and thus consensus emergence. Because the CEM incorporates random variability in the group trend, systematic changes in the residual variance over time can be interpreted as person-level deviation from the group trend or, in other words, as evidence of group-level emergence. To model changes in the residual variance over time as a function of the variable $TIME_t$, the model uses a common and flexible exponential variance function (Pinheiro & Bates, 2000). One advantage of the exponential variance function is that it allows the time variables to start with 0, which facilitates the interpretation of model

parameters. The second advantage of the exponential variance function is that it ensures that variance estimates for the residual variance σ_e^2 cannot be negative because the exponential function can never be smaller than 0. When $TIME_t$ is coded 0 at the origin of time and increases by 1 with each measurement occasion (0, 1, 2, 3, etc.), the interpretation of δ_1 is relatively straightforward. Negative values of δ_1 can be interpreted as an approximately linear decrease in the amount of residual variance with each measurement occasion (and thus consensus emergence). In contrast, positive values for δ_1 indicate variance function weights associated with an approximate linear increase in residual variances (and thus dissensus emergence).

Table 22.1 provides estimates for the basic two-level CEM for the data sets shown in Figure 22.1 and Figure 22.2. Recall that both data sets showed a similar pattern of increasing ICC(1) values even though the patterns in Figure 22.1 and Figure 22.2 clearly describe two different situations. Table 22.1 shows how the CEM approach can address the ambiguity in approaches tracking changes in values like the ICC(1) over time. The values in Table 22.1 are the parameter estimates for the basic two-level CEM in the two data sets (Figure 22.1 and Figure 22.2).

In Data Set 1 (Figure 22.1), the results suggest a pattern of emergence with a negative δ_1 weight. The residual variance specifically decreased from $1.711 * \exp(2 * -0.247 * 0) = 1.711$ at T1 to $1.711 * \exp(2 * -0.247 * 4) = 0.237$ at T5. However, Data Set 1 shows no evidence for an increase in the variance between groups as the group slope variance is effectively 0 (see Table 22.1). Figure 22.3 shows the same data as Figure 22.1 but adds the within-group linear trend for time that is estimated by the CEM for each of the five groups. As indicated by Figure 22.3, the groups show a similar trend. The inclusion of the within-group linear time trend in Figure 22.3 also makes it apparent that the residual variation around the group trend decreases over time.

[2]The variable $TIME_t$ in the model specification omits a subscript for the person and the group because the model specification we present here assumes that the data is time-structured (i.e., there are fixed points in time at which the variables were measured). In situations in which the model is used with unstructured data and the time of measurement occasions varies across groups and individuals, it is necessary to add subscripts for the person and the group to the $TIME_t$ variable (i.e., $TIME_{tij}$).

TABLE 22.1

Two-Level Consensus Emergence Models Fitted to the Data Sets Shown in Figure 22.1 and Figure 22.2

Parameters	Data Set 1 (shown in Figure 22.1)		Data Set 2 (shown in Figure 22.2)	
	Model 1 (null model)	Model 2 (consensus emergence)	Model 1 (null model)	Model 2 (consensus emergence)
Intercept, γ_{000}	4.94**	4.94**	4.85**	4.85**
TIME, γ_{100}	0.06**	0.06**	0.09	0.09
Group intercept variance, τ_{00}	1.32	1.39	0.20	0.20
Group slope variance for TIME, τ_{11}	0.00	0.00	0.12	0.12
Covariance, τ_{01}	0.00	0.00	−0.03	−0.03
Residual variance, σ^2	0.85	1.71	2.47	2.41
TIME, δ_1		−0.25		0.006
logLik	−1,011.84	−907.39	−1,417.53	−1,417.48
df	6	7	6	7
χ^2 vs. previous model		208.89**		0.11

Note. Five groups with 30 persons measured at five measurement occasions in both data sets (750 observations). **$p < .01$.

The two-level CEM estimates for Data Set 2 (Figure 22.2) are also provided in Table 22.1. The δ_1 weight for Data Set 2 is 0.006 and thus indicates no substantive change in the residual variance. In contrast, the group slope variance for Data Set 2 was 0.116, indicating a substantive amount of variability between the five groups. Figure 22.4 shows the data from Figure 22.2 with the group trend from the CEM added to the graph, illustrating the different trends in the five groups. In conclusion, the CEM can identify a situation in which groups reach consensus over time and separate this situation from a situation in which merely groups vary in their trends.

A key feature of the CEM is that the significance of δ_1 can conveniently be tested using a log-likelihood ratio test (χ^2 difference test). This test compares the fit of a CEM with a model that does not include δ_1 and thus constrains the residual variance σ_e^2 to be homogenous, $e_{tij} \sim N(0, \sigma^2)$. This log-likelihood ratio test provides a formal overall test of consensus emergence. For our demonstration Data Set 1, this test was highly significant, χ^2 ($df = 1$) = 208.9, $p < .001$. The same test was not significant for Data Set 2, χ^2 ($df = 1$) = 0.1, $p = 0.74$.

The Three-Level Consensus Emergence Model

The two-level CEM model is the most basic and simple form of the CEM. One extension of this basic form of the model that may frequently be useful is to control for the possibility that persons within the same group differ systematically when the observation starts. Although controlling for person effects will likely not change the results in most cases, controlling for person-level effects often makes model estimation more robust and efficient (Bliese & Hanges, 2004; Bliese, Maltarich, & Hendricks, 2018). The three-level version of the CEM can be written as follows[3]:

$$\text{Level 1: } Y_{tij} = \pi_{0ij} + \pi_{1ij}\text{TIME}_t + e_{tij} \quad (22.8)$$

$$\text{Level 2: } \pi_{0ij} = \beta_{00j} + r_{0ij}$$

$$\pi_{1ij} = \beta_{10j}$$

$$\text{Level 3: } \beta_{00j} = \gamma_{000} + u_{00j}$$

$$\beta_{10j} = \gamma_{100} + u_{10j}$$

---

[3]Lang, Bliese, and de Voogt (2018) discussed an alternative model based on Goldstein (2011) that produces similar results without estimating a variance term.

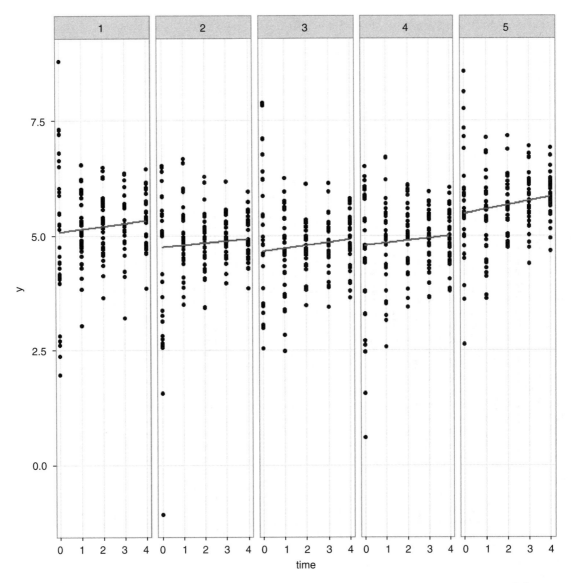

FIGURE 22.3.   Data Set 1 and group-specific trends from a two-level consensus emergence model.

$$e_{tij} \overset{iid}{\sim} N\left(0, \sigma^2 \exp\left[2\delta_1 \text{TIME}_t\right]\right) \quad (22.9)$$

$$r_{0ij} \overset{iid}{\sim} N\left(0, \tau_{00}\right) \quad (22.10)$$

$$\begin{pmatrix} u_{00j} \\ u_{10j} \end{pmatrix} \overset{iid}{\sim} N\left(\begin{bmatrix} 0 \\ 0 \end{bmatrix}, \begin{bmatrix} \upsilon_{00} & \upsilon_{10} \\ \upsilon_{01} & \upsilon_{11} \end{bmatrix} \right). \quad (22.11)$$

Notice that the only difference between the two-level version of the CEM and the three-level version is the addition of a person random intercept effect r_{0ij}. The three-level CEM accordingly functions like the two-level CEM. However, the inclusion of different person intercepts in the three-level CEM typically

increases power to detect consensus emergence. To demonstrate this phenomenon, we fit the three-level CEM to Data Set 1 and Data Set 2. Results are shown in Table 22.2. As indicated by Table 22.2, the consensus emergence trend in Data Set 1 was more pronounced after the inclusion of the person intercept variance ($\delta_1 = -0.59$ in the three-level CEM in Table 22.2 vs. $\delta_1 = -0.25$ for the two-level CEM in Table 22.1). Furthermore, the size of the log-likelihood ratio for the χ^2 difference test between the model with and without the consensus emergence trend more than doubled ($\chi^2 = 208.89$ for the two-level model in Table 22.1 vs. $\chi^2 = 564.49$ in Table 22.2).

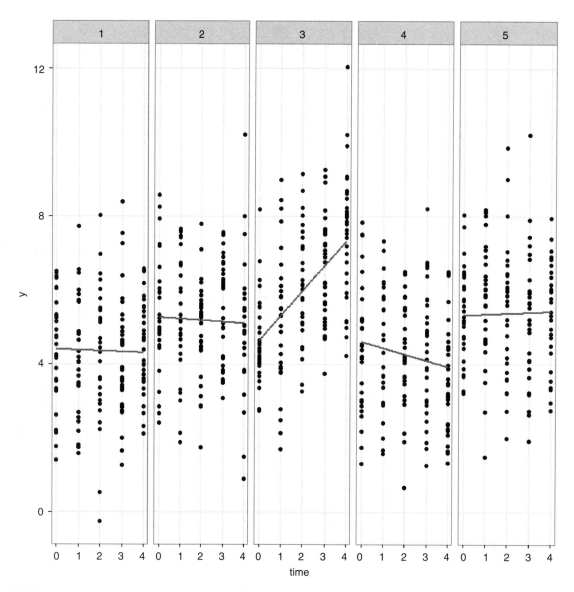

FIGURE 22.4.   Data Set 2 and group-specific trends from a two-level consensus emergence model.

To illustrate how the three-level CEM increases power to detect emergent effects, it is informative to examine Figure 22.5. The figure shows that although the residuals in the two-level CEM are defined relative to the group trend, the three-level CEM model takes an individual person intercept deviation into account and compares the residual deviations to a different level for each person. A-priori differences in potential response sets among persons are accordingly controlled and are not captured in the residual variance in the three-level CEM. The three-level CEM works analogously to add a control variable in a multiple regression analysis. The control variable reduces the error variance and thereby makes the detection of effects of the other predictors easier.

Figure 22.6 applies what is shown in Figure 22.5 to Data Set 2 (without a consensus emergence effect) and compares the residual variances in these data with a person-specific intercept. As indicated in Figure 22.6 and also shown in Table 22.2, the inclusion of a person intercept did not affect the conclusions regarding Data Set 2. The group slope variance in this data set remained the same ($v_{01} = 0.12$), and the χ^2 difference test for the consensus emergence trend was still not significant for these data (compare Table 22.1 with Table 22.2).

TABLE 22.2

Three-Level Consensus Emergence Models Fitted to the Data Sets Shown in Figure 22.1 and Figure 22.2

Parameters	Data Set 1 (shown in Figure 22.1)		Data Set 2 (shown in Figure 22.2)	
	Model 1 (null model)	Model 2 (consensus emergence)	Model 1 (null model)	Model 2 (consensus emergence)
Intercept, γ_{000}	4.94**	4.94**	4.85**	4.85**
TIME, γ_{100}	0.06**	0.06**	0.09	0.09
Group intercept variance, υ_{00}	0.12	0.11	0.19	0.19
Group slope variance for TIME, υ_{11}	0.00	0.001	0.12	0.12
Covariance, υ_{01}	0.00	0.00	–0.03	–0.03
Person intercept variance, τ_{00}	0.29	0.29	0.46	0.47
Residual variance, σ^2	0.56	1.84	2.02	1.85
TIME, δ_1		–0.59		0.02
logLik	–951.06	–668.810	–1,398.01	–1,397.49
df	7	8	7	8
χ^2 vs. previous model		564.51**		1.04

Note. Five groups with 30 persons measured at five measurement occasions in both data sets (750 observations).
**$p < .01$.

Relationships Between the Consensus Emergence Model and the ICC(1)

The CEM approach can be understood as a direct extension of the ICC(1). The three-level version of the CEM is particularly similar to the ICC(1). One way to view the three-level CEM model is to consider the CEM to be an ICC(1) that substitutes the residual error e_{tij} estimated in the typical model for the ICC(1) with two separate error components: one for the persons across measurement occasions r_{0ij} and one for each specific measurement occasion e_{tij} (this change is apparent when one compares Equation 22.4 for the basic model used to estimate the ICC(1) with Equation 22.10). As a result, the model is a three-level model with measurements at Level 1 nested in persons at Level 2, and persons at Level 2 nested in groups at Level 3.

The relations between the CEM and the ICC(1) can also formally be shown. In the basic CEM framework, it is possible to specify an ICC coefficient:

$$\text{ICCEM}_t = \left(\upsilon_{00} + 2\upsilon_{01}\text{TIME}_t + 2\upsilon_{11}\text{TIME}_t^2\right)/\sigma_{\text{TOTAL}_t^2}. \quad (22.12)$$

The ICCEM_t is the model-based ICC coefficient at time point t. In the numerator (before the / slash), the formula (Equation 22.12) includes the intercept

variance as in the commonly used ICC(1) coefficient (υ_{00}). In addition, the numerator includes variance that results from the slope and that changes over time ($\upsilon_{11}\text{TIME}_t^2$). Finally, the formula includes the covariance between the intercept and the slope ($2\upsilon_{01}\text{TIME}_t$). The covariance between the intercept and the slope can be positive or negative and, accordingly, the numerator of the ICCEM_t—the group variance—can either increase or decrease over time.

The denominator of the ICCEM_t formula in Equation 22.12 includes the total predicted variance from the CEM model. This variance consists of the group variance from the numerator ($\upsilon_{00} + 2\upsilon_{01}\text{TIME}_t + \upsilon_{11}\text{TIME}_t^2$) and the person variance (τ_{00}) and the error variance ($\sigma^2\exp[2\delta_1\text{TIME}_t]$):

$$\sigma_{\text{TOTAL}_t^2} = \upsilon_{00} + 2\upsilon_{01}\text{TIME}_t + \upsilon_{11}\text{TIME}_t^2$$

$$+ \tau_{00} + \sigma^2 exp(2\delta_1\text{TIME}_t). \quad (22.13)$$

The ICCEM_i coefficient is conceptually analogous to the ICC(1) estimated at specific times and provides an estimate of group variance relative to total variance. Total variance is sometimes labeled the *composite residual* (Singer & Willett, 2003) and captures the predicted variance from all model variance components at a particular time. Notice

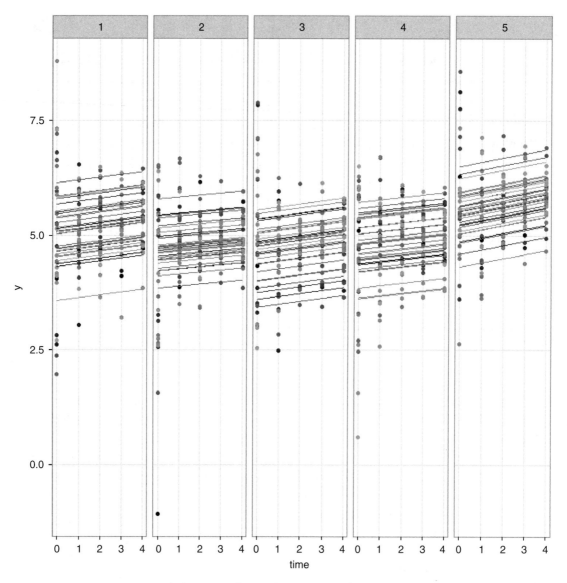

FIGURE 22.5. Data Set 1 and group-specific trends accounting for person intercept variance from a three-level consensus emergence model.

in Equation 22.12 and Equation 22.13 that three variance components in the formula for the $ICCEM_t$ change as a function of time—the residual variance σ^2, the random slope variance for the group slope υ_{11}, and the covariance of the random slope variance with the intercept variance for the group slope υ_{01}. Changes in the $ICCEM_t$ can accordingly result from any of these variance components.

An advantage of the $ICCEM_t$ over the ordinary ICC(1) is that the $ICCEM_t$ is model based and thus more robust to sample variation across measurement occasions. That is, the $ICCEM_t$ is estimated using the coefficients from a single CEM model,

whereas estimating ICC(1) for each time point requires estimating separate models and thus is more prone to sample variation. Despite the fact that $ICCEM_t$ is more robust to sample variation, it still shares the fundamental ambiguity associated with the ICC(1) in that it is not possible to discern whether changes result from group-level change or change in group-member variability. As noted previously, we therefore recommend directly focusing on the residual variance change term δ_1 because this change term directly captures systematic change in the residual variance while accounting for the other trends in the data, can be

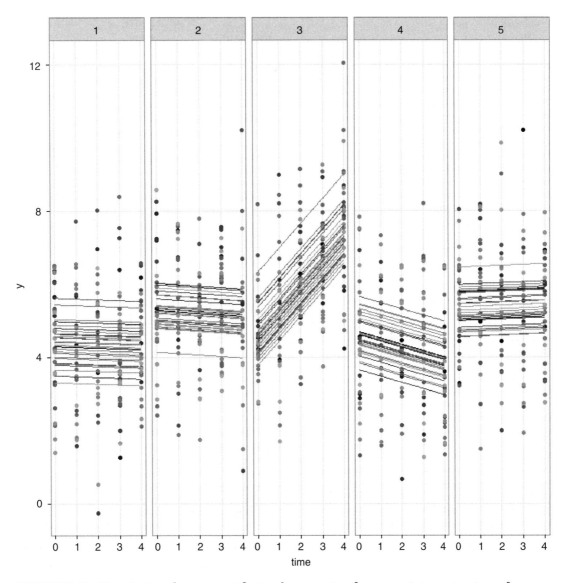

FIGURE 22.6. Data Set 2 and group-specific trends accounting for person intercept variance from a three-level consensus emergence model.

tested for significance, and thus provides direct evidence for consensus emergence.

Model Estimation

The CEM model can be estimated in a variety of software programs. In our examples, we used restricted maximum likelihood estimation, the nlme package (Pinheiro & Bates, 2000), and the L-BFGS-B optimization method in the R environment (R Foundation, n.d.). However, it is also possible to estimate the model in many other software programs. Examples of software programs that can estimate CEMs include M*plus* (Muthén, 1994)

and NLMIXED in SAS. In Appendices 22.1 and 22.2, we provide example code for nlme and three of the four data sets in this chapter. The fourth data set is available from the authors on request. M*plus* code is included in Lang et al. (2018) and also available from the authors.

EMPIRICAL EXAMPLES

Empirical research using CEM requires longitudinal data for groups. The likelihood that consensus emergence effects occur in organizational data may depend on a variety of factors, including the nature of the construct of interest, how long groups have been together, and the nature of the work. As a starting point, we analyze two data sets using the CEM to demonstrate the types of research questions the CEM can test.

Autokinetic Data

Possibly one of the first studies of the emergence of group consensus was Sherif's (1935) study of the autokinetic effect. The *autokinetic effect* occurs when individuals watch a small point of light in an otherwise dark environment. The point of light then appears to move in the dark environment even when no actual movement occurs. Sherif used this effect for his research on group consensus and asked groups of individuals to estimate the amount of movement. The data we analyze is taken from the figure shown on page 33 in Sherif's book chapter and includes eight three-person groups. This figure is shown in Figure 22.7 in this chapter. As indicated in Figure 22.7, four groups first worked on the task individually and then performed the task three times in group sessions. The participants in the other four groups directly started as a group and then completed one session alone. Our analyses only focus on the sessions that the participants completed in groups. Sherif originally only used descriptive analyses of his data. Figure 22.7 shows why Sherif was successful in convincing other researchers of the importance of his findings. Arguably, the effects in the data are strong.

Table 22.3 includes the CEM-based analyses of the data. We used the three-level CEM. The results in Table 22.3 indicate that the data show a strong trend in the residual variance of $\delta_1 = -1.02$. The δ_1 value of -1.02 indicates change with each measurement occasion relative to the baseline. At baseline, the weight for the variance function reduces to 1 because TIME is 0 at baseline and $\exp(2 \times 0 \times -1.02) = \exp(0) = 1$. The value of -1.02 indicates the degree to which the residual variance changes relative to the baseline residual variance. Across the three measurement occasions of the study, there was thus a decrease in residual variance from $1.70 \times \exp(2 \times -1.02 \times 0) = 1.70$ at TIME = 0 to $1.70 \times \exp(2 \times -1.02 \times 2) = 0.03$ at TIME = 2.

To formally test the significance of the residual variance trend, we compared a null model with homogenous residual variance to the model that included an exponential time trend in the residual variance. Results are shown in Table 22.3 and revealed that the model that included the consensus emergence trend had a significantly better fit to the data, $\chi^2 = 28.53$, $p < .001$.

To evaluate how these findings would compare with conclusions we would have reached relying on ICC values, we estimated the ICC(1) and the ICCEM at each time point. ICC(1) values were .75, .91, and .99 at TIME = 0, TIME = 1, and TIME = 2, respectively. ICCEM values were .39, .86, and .98 at TIME = 0, TIME = 1, and TIME = 2, respectively. These values indicate that the conclusion one would draw using ICC(1) would not differ for this classic data set. However, this finding is arguably a result of the extreme residual variance trend in the data that results from the controlled environment of the laboratory. Nevertheless, the example shows the fact that the CEM provides a useful overall model test and an overall summary of effect size (in the form of the δ_1 value).

Student-Team Data

Although the Sherif (1935) data set is an interesting example, the effects in this data set are arguably extreme and are likely not representative for typical consensus emergence in effects in organizational data. Our second example is a more typical example and includes 236 students who worked together on a research project in 32 teams for 6 weeks. The teams were surveyed three times. Our analyses focus on a three-item cohesion measure. The three items were adopted from Britt and Dawson (2005) who developed the measure on the basis of an earlier scale (Podsakoff & MacKenzie, 1994). An example item is "The members of my team are cooperative with each other" (Britt & Dawson, 2005, p. 212). The items were answered on a 7-point Likert scale. Alpha reliabilities were .88, .86, and .87 at TIME = 0, TIME = 1, and TIME = 2, respectively.

Figure 22.8 graphs the data for each group. Note that the graph depicts the observations slightly misplaced such that overlapping observations become visible. From Figure 22.8 alone, it is not clear whether a consensus emergence trend exists in this data. In addition, the figure also shows that some variation in the group trends exists in these

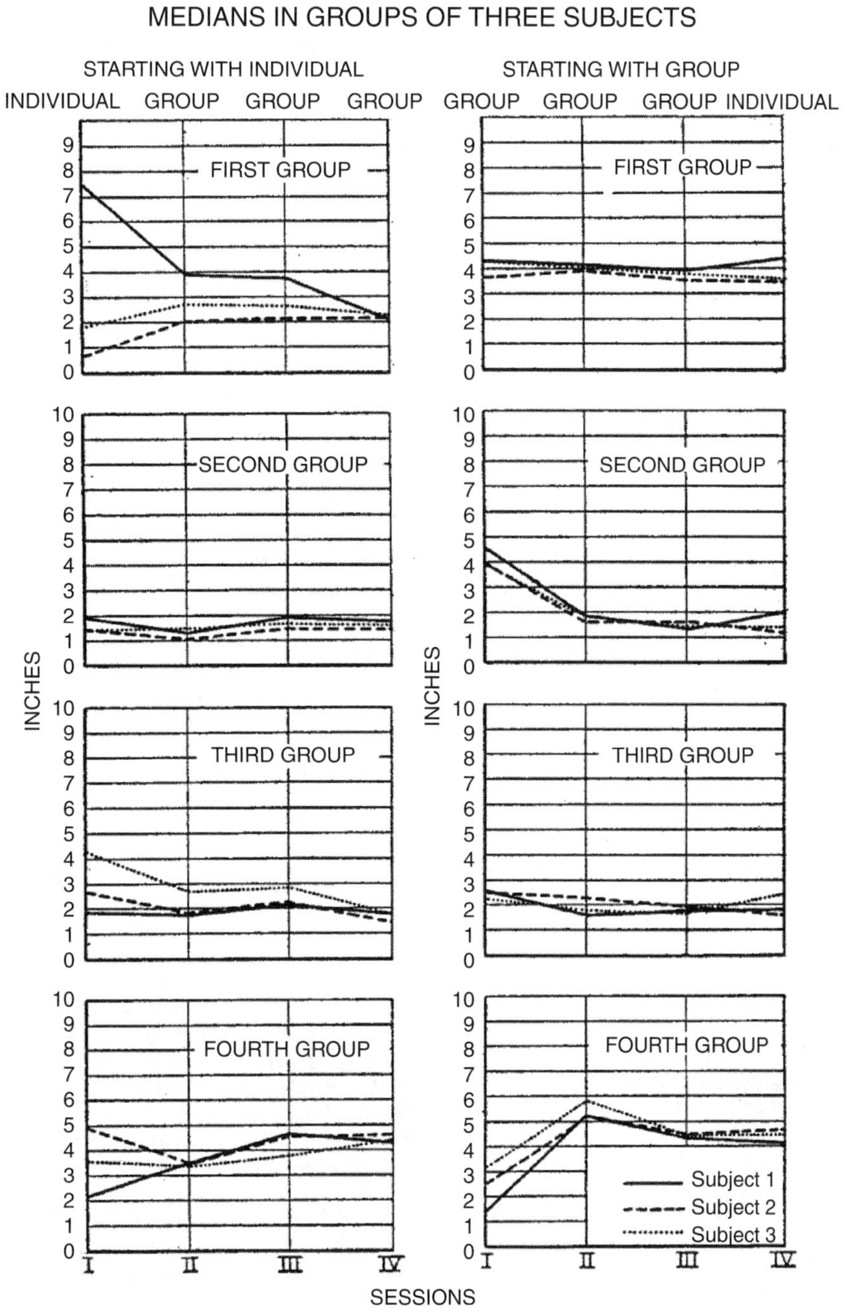
MEDIANS IN GROUPS OF THREE SUBJECTS
STARTING WITH INDIVIDUAL
STARTING WITH GROUP
INDIVIDUAL GROUP GROUP GROUP
GROUP GROUP GROUP INDIVIDUAL
FIRST GROUP
SECOND GROUP
THIRD GROUP
FOURTH GROUP
INCHES
Subject 1
Subject 2
Subject 3
I II III IV
SESSIONS

FIGURE 22.7. Graph. From "A Study of Some Social Factors in Perception," by M. Sherif, 1935, *Archives de Psychologie*, *27*, p. 33. In the public domain.

data. CEM results are shown in Table 22.4. Notice that a significant consensus emergence trend existed in the data with $\delta_1 = -.15$, $\chi^2 = 10.51$, $p < .01$. The residual variance decreased from $0.45 \times \exp(2 \times -0.15 \times 0) = 0.45$ at TIME = 0 to $0.45 \times \exp(2 \times -0.15 \times 2) = 0.25$ at TIME = 2. Despite the significant consensus emergence effect in the data, the ICC values did not clearly show an emergence trend. ICC(1) estimated at snapshots in time was .17, .21, and .19 at TIME = 0, TIME = 1, and TIME = 2, respectively. The ICCEM values were .17, .17, and .25 at TIME = 0, TIME = 1, and TIME = 2, respectively. The student-team data on cohesion clearly illustrate that the CEM can be a useful tool for detecting consensus emergence that has important advantages over ICC values.

TABLE 22.3

Autokinetic Effect Data From Sherif (1935): Three-Level Consensus Emergence Model

Parameters	Model 1 (null model)	Model 2 (consensus emergence)
Intercept, γ_{000}	2.95**	3.19**
TIME, γ_{100}	−0.08	−0.24*
Group intercept variance, υ_{00}	0.72	1.08
Group slope variance for TIME, υ_{11}	0.40	2.36
Covariance, υ_{01}	−0.05	0.13
Person intercept variance, τ_{00}	0.00	0.00
Residual variance, σ^2	3.47	1.70
TIME, δ_1		−1.02
logLik	−84.17	−69.90
df	7	8
χ^2 vs. previous model		28.53**

Note. Eight groups with 3 persons measured at 3 measurement occasions (72 observations).
*$p < .05$. **$p < .01$.

LINKING PREDICTORS TO THE CONSENSUS EMERGENCE MODEL

We believe that there is considerable value in being able to test for consensus emergence using a formal omnibus test (the χ^2 difference test) of an easily interpretable effect size measure (δ_1). Nonetheless, an additional important extension of the CEM is to add predictors of consensus emergence to the model. For instance, we may be interested in whether the groups that had an individual session before they worked together as a group showed quicker convergence than the groups that did not in the Sherif (1935) data. CEMs that add predictors, therefore, allow researchers to more fully integrate theory into test convergence in longitudinal research. The following is a model specification that adds a group-level predictor to the three-level CEM:

$$\text{Level 1}: Y_{tij} = \pi_{0ij} + \pi_{1ij}\text{TIME}_t + e_{tij} \quad (22.14)$$

$$\text{Level 2}: \pi_{0ij} = \beta_{00j} + r_{0ij}$$

$$\pi_{1ij} = \beta_{10j}$$

$$\text{Level 3}: \beta_{00j} = \gamma_{000} + \gamma_{010}(\text{PRED}_j) + u_{00j}$$

$$\beta_{10j} = \gamma_{100} + \gamma_{110}(\text{PRED}_j) + u_{10j}$$

$$e_{tij} \overset{iid}{\sim} N(0, \ \sigma^2\exp[2\delta_1\text{TIME}_t]$$

$$\exp[2\delta_2\text{PRED}_j]$$

$$\exp[2\delta_3\text{TIME}_t\text{PRED}_j]) \quad (22.15)$$

$$r_{0ij} \overset{iid}{\sim} N(0, \tau_{00}) \quad (22.16)$$

$$\begin{pmatrix} u_{00j} \\ u_{10j} \end{pmatrix} \overset{iid}{\sim} N\left(\begin{bmatrix} 0 \\ 0 \end{bmatrix}, \begin{bmatrix} \upsilon_{00} & \upsilon_{01} \\ \upsilon_{10} & \upsilon_{11} \end{bmatrix} \right). \quad (22.17)$$

Notice that the model specification adds the group-level predictor not only in the residual variance but also in the fixed-effects specification of the model. We recommend this type of model specification to ensure that group differences do not result from trend differences instead of residual variance differences. The core hypothesis of a systematic difference in consensus emergence is tested using the Predictor × Time interaction in the residual variance specification. The residual variance specification in this type of model includes not one but three exponential variance functions. When the δ effects are close to 0 or 0, each of the predictors has no effect on the residual variance because $\exp(0) = 1$. The specification of the residual variance thus functions conceptually like a regression equation.

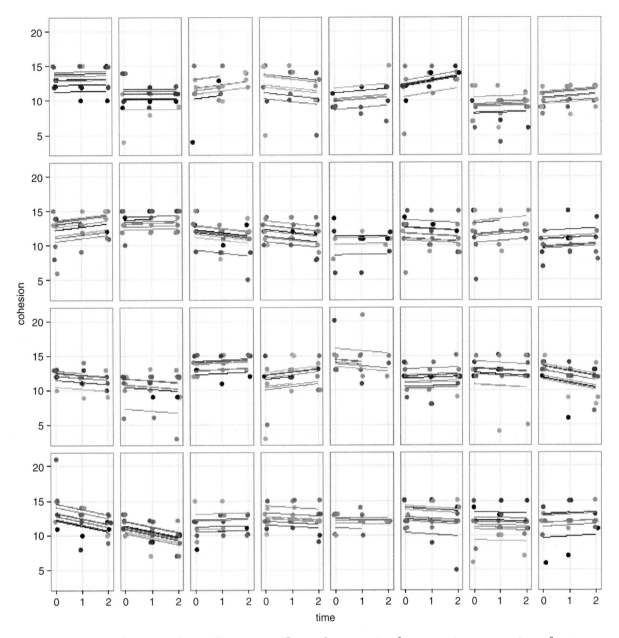

FIGURE 22.8. Student-team data and group-specific trends accounting for person intercept variance from a three-level consensus emergence model.

Table 22.5 applies the described model to the Sherif (1935) data. As the predictor, we used a dichotomous predictor that contrasted whether the members of the groups had started with an individual session before they worked together as a group (coded 0) or directly started with group sessions (coded 1). As indicated by the log-likelihood test in Table 22.5, the Predictor/Condition × Time interaction was significant in this data set, $\chi^2 = 3.94$, $p < .05$. Groups with participants who worked on

individual sessions before they worked in a group showed a decrease from 2.61 at TIME = 0 to 0.02 at TIME = 2 (calculations are as follows: [2.61 × exp(2 × −1.21 × 0) × exp(2 × −0.72 × 0) × exp(2 × 0.58 × 0 × 0) = 2.61 at TIME = 0], [2.61 × exp(2 × −1.21 × 2) × exp(2 × −0.72 × 0) × exp(2 × 0.58 × 2 × 0) = 0.02 at TIME = 2]). In contrast, groups with participants who did not work on individual sessions before they worked in a group showed a decrease from 0.62 at TIME = 0 to 0.05 at TIME = 2 (calculations are as

TABLE 22.4

Student-Team Data: Three-Level Consensus Emergence Model

Parameters	Model 1 (null model)	Model 2 (consensus emergence)
Intercept, γ_{000}	3.94**	3.95**
TIME, γ_{100}	−0.01	−0.02
Group intercept variance, υ_{00}	0.14	0.13
Group slope variance for TIME, υ_{11}	0.03	0.03
Covariance, υ_{01}	−0.03	−0.03
Person intercept variance, τ_{00}	0.17	0.18
Residual variance, σ^2	0.34	0.45
TIME, δ_1		−0.15
logLik	−771.60	−766.35
df	7	8
χ^2 vs. previous model		10.50**

Note. 705 observations at Level 1, 243 students at Level 2, and 32 teams at Level 3.
**$p < .01$.

TABLE 22.5

Autokinetic Effect Data From Sherif (1935): Three-Level Consensus Emergence Model With a Predictor for Consensus Emergence

Parameters	Model 3	Model 4
Intercept, γ_{000}	3.49**	3.53**
TIME, γ_{100}	−0.30	−0.32*
CONDITION, γ_{010}	−0.63	−0.78
TIME × CONDITION (start with individual session = 0, start with group session = 1), γ_{110}	0.14	0.22
Group intercept variance, υ_{00}	1.07	1.35
Group slope variance for TIME, υ_{11}	0.05	0.05
Covariance, υ_{01}	0.17	0.09
Person intercept variance, τ_{00}	0.00	0.00
Residual variance, σ^2	1.77	2.61
TIME, δ_1	−0.95	−1.21
CONDITION, δ_2	−0.19	−0.72
TIME × CONDITION δ_3		0.58
logLik	−68.83	−66.87
df	11	12
χ^2 vs. previous model		3.94*

Note. Eight groups with 3 persons measured at 3 measurement occasions (72 observations).
*$p < .05$. **$p < .01$.

follows [2.61 × exp(2 × −1.21 × 0) × exp(2 × −0.72 × 1) × exp(2 × 0.58 × 0 × 1) = 0.62 at TIME = 0], [2.61 × exp(2 −1.21 × 2) × exp(2 × −0.72 × 1) × exp(2 × 0.58 × 2 × 1) = 0.05 at TIME = 2]).

The log-likelihood test examining whether the experimental condition was related to changes in variance combined with the specific calculations of variance over time provided a formal, model-based test of Sherif's (1935) observations. Moreover, the models show that individuals who started out providing estimates individually had considerable variability (2.61) that quickly converged when they started working in groups (0.02). In contrast, individuals who started in groups had considerably less initial variability (0.62) that also converged over time (0.05). Although these results are completely in line with Sherif's conclusions, we believe that the ability to formally test these ideas has considerable applicability in other situations that may not be as visually evident as those observed by Sherif.

In addition to predicting consensus emergence, researchers may occasionally also be interested in using consensus emergence in a group or team as a predictor of something that happens in the future. One approach for addressing research questions of this type is to fit an extended version of the CEM that estimates group-specific consensus emergence coefficients by substituting weights=varComb(varExp(form = ~ time|group),varIdent(form=~1|group)) rather than weights=varExp(form = ~ time) in nlme. The coefficient from this model can then potentially be used in subsequent analyses. Appendix 22.2 includes example code for fitting this type of model.

DISCUSSION

In this chapter, we described how researchers can study consensus emergence using an extension of the standard multilevel methods. We explained and illustrated the limitations of ICC(1) values, and we described a basic two-level form and an extended three-level form of the CEM. The CEM uses variance functions and a growth model specification to delineate changes in between-group and within-group (residual) variability over time. The model

provides a formal statistical test of consensus emergence and an effect size measure that quantifies the amount of reduction in the residual variance with each measurement occasion, the δ_1 statistic. We also showed how predictors can be added to the CEM to test explanatory theories of consensus emergence.

An important advantage of the CEM approach is that it directly extends multilevel methodology to formally test a phenomenon (group emergence effects) that is at the core of a wide variety of theories but which has been difficult to test formally. Applying the CEM requires some advanced understanding of multilevel methods; however, multilevel methods are widely applied within the field, and we believe that the examples and R code will allow researchers to run these types of analyses on other data. In short, we anticipate that the CEM approach will provide a basis for future multilevel studies on consensus emergence in organizations and experimental research on groups and will also provide a foundation for developing a more thorough understanding of temporal social dynamics in organizations.

APPENDIX 22.1: R CODE FOR THE EXAMPLE DATA SETS

Note: The following code yields the reported findings in R version 3.3.1 on Windows, but results may slightly vary across different versions of R and different platforms.

In the following code, the model components correspond to the following elements of the model formulas in the text.

l3n = number of groups
l2n = number of individuals in each group
l1n = number of measurement time points in each individual
gamma000 = γ_{000}
vu00 = variance of u_{00j} or υ_{00}
vu01 = variance of u_{01j} or υ_{11}
vu0001 = covariance of u_{00j} and u_{01j} or υ_{11}
vr0 = variance of r_{0ij} or τ_{11}
delta = δ_1

```
gendat <- function(l3n,l2n,l1n,gamma000,pi01,
    vu00,vu01,vu0100,vr0,ve,delta){
dat=expand.grid(time = 0:(l1n-1),
    person = 1:l2n,group = 1:l3n)
u <- MASS::mvrnorm(l3n, c(0,0),
matrix(c(vu00,vu0100,vu0100,vu01), 2),
    empirical=T)
r<-rep(rnorm(l2n*l3n,0,sd=sqrt(vr0)),each=l1n)
e<-rnorm(l1n*l2n*l3n,0,sd=sqrt(ve*exp(2*delta*d
    at$time)))
dat$y<-gamma000+pi01*dat$time+u[,1]
    [dat[,3]]+u[,2][dat[,3]]*dat$time+r+e
return(dat)
}

set.seed(123456)
dataset1<-gendat(l3n=5,l2n=30,l1n=5,gamma000=5,
    pi01=0.05,vu00=0.1,vu01=0,vu0100=0,vr0=0.3,
    ve=2,delta=-0.60)

set.seed(765432)
dataset2<-gendat(l3n=5,l2n=30,l1n=5,gamma000=5
    ,pi01=0.05, vu00=0.1,vu01=0.1,
    vu0100=0,vr0=0.3,ve=2,delta=0)

sherifdat=expand.grid(person = 1:3,time = 0:2,
    group = 1:8)
sherifdat$y<-c(4.0,2.7,2.0,3.8,2.6,2.1,2.0,2.4,2.3,1.3,
    1.5,1.1,2.0,1.6,1.5,1.8,1.5,1.4,2.9,1.9,1.9,2.9,2.1,
    2.0,1.9,1.7,1.9,3.5,3.4,3.6,4.7,3.8,4.6,4.4,4.4,4.6,
    4.3,4.3,3.6,4.1,4.0,3.9,4.0,3.9,3.5,4.5,4.0,4.0,1.9,
    1.8,1.6,1.4,1.6,1.5,2.5,2.5,2.2,2.2,1.6,1.8,1.9,1.8,
    1.8,3.1,2.6,1.5,5.8,5.2,5.2,4.4,4.4,4.4)
sherifdat$condition<-rep(c(1,0),each=36)
```

APPENDIX 22.2: R CODE FOR RUNNING THE ANALYSES

```
library(nlme)

twolevel<-lme(y ~ time, random = list(group=
    pdLogChol(~time)),data=dataset1,
control=lmeControl(opt="optim",maxIter=
    3000,msMaxIter=3000))
twolevelCEM<-update(twolevel,weights=
    varExp(form = ~ time))
summary(twolevelCEM)
anova(twolevel,twolevelCEM)

threelevel<-lme(y ~ time, random = list(group=
    pdLogChol( time),person=pdIdent( 1)),
data=dataset1,control=lmeControl(opt=
    "optim",maxIter=3000, msMaxIter=3000))
threelevelCEM<-update(threelevel,weights=
    varExp(form = ~ time))
summary(threelevelCEM)
anova(threelevel,threelevelCEM)
threelevelCEMic<-update(threelevelCEM,
    weights=varComb(varExp(form =
    ~ time|group),varIdent(form=~1|group)))
summary(threelevelCEMic)

threelevelCEMwithPRED1<-lme(y
    ~ time*condition, random =
    list(group=pdLogChol(~time),

person=pdIdent(~1)),data=sherifdat,control=
    lmeControl(opt="optim",maxIter=3000,
    msMaxIter=3000),

weights=varComb(varExp(form = ~ time),
    varExp(form = ~ condition)))
threelevelCEMwithPRED2<-update
    (threelevelCEMwithPRED1,
weights=varComb(varExp(form = ~ time),
    varExp(form = ~ condition),
varExp(form = ~ time*condition)))
summary(threelevelCEMwithPRED2)
anova(threelevelCEMwithPRED1,
    threelevelCEMwithPRED2)
```

References

Allen, N. J., & O'Neill, T. A. (2015). The trajectory of emergence of shared group-level constructs. *Small Group Research, 46*, 352–390. http://dx.doi.org/10.1177/1046496415584973

Bliese, P. D. (2000). Within-group agreement, non-independence, and reliability: Implications for data aggregation and analysis. In K. J. Klein & S. W. J. Kozlowski (Eds.), *Multilevel theory, research, and methods in organizations: Foundations, extensions, and new directions* (pp. 349–381). San Francisco, CA: Jossey-Bass.

Bliese, P. D., & Hanges, P. J. (2004). Being both too liberal and too conservative: The perils of treating grouped data as though they were independent. *Organizational Research Methods, 7*, 400–417. http://dx.doi.org/10.1177/1094428104268542

Bliese, P. D., & Jex, S. M. (2002). Incorporating a multi-level perspective into occupational stress research: Theoretical, methodological, and practical implications. *Journal of Occupational Health Psychology, 7,* 265–276. http://dx.doi.org/10.1037/1076-8998.7.3.265

Bliese, P. D., Maltarich, M. A., & Hendricks, J. L. (2018). Back to basics with mixed-effects models: Nine take-away points. *Journal of Business and Psychology, 33,* 1–23. http://dx.doi.org/10.1007/s10869-017-9491-z

Bliese, P. D., & Ployhart, R. E. (2002). Growth modeling using random coefficient models: Model building, testing, and illustrations. *Organizational Research Methods, 5,* 362–387. http://dx.doi.org/10.1177/109442802237116

Britt, T. W., & Dawson, C. R. (2005). Predicting work—Family conflict from workload, job attitudes, group attributes, and health: A longitudinal study. *Military Psychology, 17,* 203–227. http://dx.doi.org/10.1207/s15327876mp1703_5

Carroll, R. J., & Ruppert, D. (1988). *Transformation and weighting in regression.* New York, NY: Chapman & Hall.

Chan, D. (1998). Functional relations among constructs in the same content domain at different levels of analysis: A typology of composition models. *Journal of Applied Psychology, 83,* 234–246. http://dx.doi.org/10.1037/0021-9010.83.2.234

Chen, G., Mathieu, J. E., & Bliese, P. D. (2005). A framework for conducting multilevel construct validation. In F. Dansereau & F. J. Yammarino (Eds.), *Research in multi-level issues: Volume 3. Multi-level issues in organizational behavior and processes* (pp. 273–303). Oxford, England: Elsevier.

Cronin, M. A., Weingart, L. R., & Todorova, G. (2011). Dynamics in groups: Are we there yet? *The Academy of Management Annals, 5,* 571–612. http://dx.doi.org/10.5465/19416520.2011.590297

Festinger, L. (1954). A theory of social comparison processes. *Human Relations, 7,* 117–140. http://dx.doi.org/10.1177/001872675400700202

Goldstein, H. (2011). *Multilevel statistical models* (4th ed.). Chichester, England: Wiley.

Hedeker, D., & Mermelstein, R. (2007). Mixed-effects regression models with heterogenous variance: Analyzing ecological momentary assessment (EMA) data of smoking. In T. D. Little, J. A. Bovaird, & N. A. Card (Eds.), *Modeling contextual effects in longitudinal studies* (pp. 183–206). Mahwah, NJ: Erlbaum.

Hedeker, D., Mermelstein, R. J., & Demirtas, H. (2012). Modeling between-subject and within-subject variances in ecological momentary assessment data using mixed-effects location scale models. *Statistics in Medicine, 31,* 3328–3336. http://dx.doi.org/10.1002/sim.5338

Hoffman, L. (2007). Multilevel models for examining individual differences in within-person variation and covariation over time. *Multivariate Behavioral Research, 42,* 609–629. http://dx.doi.org/10.1080/00273170701710072

Humphrey, S. E., & Aime, F. (2014). Team microdynamics: Toward an organizing approach to teamwork. *The Academy of Management Annals, 8,* 443–503. http://dx.doi.org/10.5465/19416520.2014.904140

James, L. R., Demaree, R. G., & Wolf, G. (1993). r_{wg}: An assessment of within-group interrater agreement. *Journal of Applied Psychology, 78,* 306–309. http://dx.doi.org/10.1037/0021-9010.78.2.306

Kim, J., & Seltzer, M. (2011). Examining heterogeneity in residual variance to detect differential response to treatments. *Psychological Methods, 16,* 192–208. http://dx.doi.org/10.1037/a0022656

Klein, K. J., & Kozlowski, S. W. J. (2000). From micro to meso: Critical steps in conceptualizing and conducting multilevel research. *Organizational Research Methods, 3,* 211–236. http://dx.doi.org/10.1177/109442810033001

Kozlowski, S. W. J. (2012). The nature of organizational psychology. In S. W. J. Kozlowski (Ed.), *The Oxford handbook of organizational psychology* (Vol. 1, pp. 3–21). New York, NY: Oxford University Press.

Kozlowski, S. W. J. (2015). Advancing research on team process dynamics: Theoretical, methodological, and measurement considerations. *Organizational Psychology Review, 5,* 270–299. http://dx.doi.org/10.1177/2041386614533586

Kozlowski, S. W. J., & Chao, G. T. (2012). The dynamics of emergence: Cognition and cohesion in work teams. *Managerial & Decision Economics, 33,* 335–354. http://dx.doi.org/10.1002/mde.2552

Kozlowski, S. W. J., Chao, G. T., Grand, J. A., Braun, M. T., & Kuljanin, G. (2013). Advancing multilevel research design: Capturing the dynamics of emergence. *Organizational Research Methods, 16,* 581–615. http://dx.doi.org/10.1177/1094428113493119

Lang, J. W. B., & Bliese, P. D. (2009). General mental ability and two types of adaptation to unforeseen change: Applying discontinuous growth models to the task-change paradigm. *Journal of Applied Psychology, 94,* 411–428. http://dx.doi.org/10.1037/a0013803

Lang, J. W. B., Bliese, P. D., & de Voogt, A. (2018). Modeling consensus emergence in groups using longitudinal multilevel methods. *Personnel Psychology, 71,* 255–281. http://dx.doi.org/10.1111/peps.12260

LeBreton, J. M., James, L. R., & Lindell, M. K. (2005). Recent issues regarding rWG, r*WG, rWG(J), and r*WG(J). *Organizational Research Methods, 8*, 128–138. http://dx.doi.org/10.1177/1094428104272181

LeBreton, J. M., & Senter, J. L. (2008). Answers to 20 questions about interrater reliability and interrater agreement. *Organizational Research Methods, 11*, 815–852. http://dx.doi.org/10.1177/1094428106296642

Morgeson, F., & Hofmann, D. (1999). The structure and function of collective constructs: Implications for multilevel research and theory development. *The Academy of Management Review, 24*, 249–265.

Muthén, B. O. (1994). Multilevel covariance structure analysis. *Sociological Methods & Research, 22*, 376–398. http://dx.doi.org/10.1177/0049124194022003006

Pinheiro, J. C., & Bates, D. M. (2000). *Mixed-effects models in S and S-PLUS*. New York, NY: Springer.

Ployhart, R. E., & Moliterno, T. P. (2011). Emergence of the human capital resource: A multilevel model. *The Academy of Management Review, 36*, 127–150. http://dx.doi.org/10.5465/amr.2009.0318

Podsakoff, P. M., & MacKenzie, S. B. (1994). An examination of the psychometric properties and nomological validity of some revised and reduced substitutes for leadership scales. *Journal of Applied Psychology, 79*, 702–713. http://dx.doi.org/10.1037/0021-9010.79.5.702

R Foundation. (n.d.). *R project for statistical computing*. Retrieved from http://www.r-project.org/

Rast, P., MacDonald, S. W. S., & Hofer, S. M. (2012). Intensive measurement designs for research on aging. *GeroPsych: The Journal of Gerontopsychology and Geriatric Psychiatry, 25*, 45–55. http://dx.doi.org/10.1024/1662-9647/a000054

Rast, P., & Zimprich, D. (2011). Modeling within-person variance in reaction time data of older adults. *GeroPsych: The Journal of Gerontopsychology and Geriatric Psychiatry, 24*, 169–176. http://dx.doi.org/10.1024/1662-9647/a000045

Raudenbush, S. W., & Bryk, A. S. (1987). Examining correlates of diversity. *Journal of Educational Statistics, 12*, 241–269. http://dx.doi.org/10.3102/10769986012003241

Sherif, M. (1935). A study of some social factors in perception. *Archives de Psychologie, 27*(187), 1–60.

Singer, J. D., & Willett, J. B. (2003). *Applied longitudinal data analysis: Modeling change and event occurrence*. New York, NY: Oxford University Press. http://dx.doi.org/10.1093/acprof:oso/9780195152968.001.0001

Zuur, A. F., Ieno, E. N., Walker, N., Saveliev, A. A., & Smith, G. M. (2009). *Mixed effects models and extensions in ecology with R*. New York, NY: Springer. http://dx.doi.org/10.1007/978-0-387-87458-6

SOCIAL NETWORK EFFECTS: COMPUTATIONAL MODELING OF NETWORK CONTAGION AND CLIMATE EMERGENCE

Daniel A. Newman and Wei Wang

Group-level psychological constructs (e.g., organizational climate, team motivation, classroom norms) reside at the group level-of-analysis, yet these constructs are measured via data collected at the individual level (e.g., employee perceptions of their work team or organization). Classically, these group-level constructs are believed to exist when there is high within-group agreement in the perceptions held by members of a collective (i.e., the consensus model of emergence). We present a formal theory of the emergence of group-level constructs that explicitly considers social networks. This dynamic computational model articulates the importance of network density, network contagion (spatial autocorrelation), cohesive network subgroups, brokering, and leadership/influence networks in the emergence of within-group agreement and organizational climate (as well as subgroup agreement and organizational microclimates). These factors offer a general etiology of group- and subgroup-level constructs. Model syntax is provided in the software R.

GROUP-LEVEL PSYCHOLOGICAL CONSTRUCTS AND WITHIN-GROUP AGREEMENT/THE CONSENSUS MODEL OF EMERGENCE

Contemporary multilevel theory and research (and to a growing extent, the entire field of organizational behavior itself; Porter & Schneider, 2014;

Rousseau, 2011) is built upon group-level psychological constructs (e.g., organizational climate, group satisfaction, team cohesion, leadership style). These concepts are proposed to exist at the group level-of-analysis (e.g., organization-level, department-level, and team-level concepts), but are typically measured using data collected at the individual level (see discussions by Bliese, 2000; James & Jones, 1974; Muthén, 1994; Ostroff, 1993). Most commonly, these group-level concepts are thought to emerge via consensus among group members (Chan, 1998; Kozlowski & Klein, 2000), where the very existence of the group-level concept inheres in the degree of perceptual within-group agreement among the individuals who belong to the group (James, 1982; James, Demaree, & Wolf, 1984; LeBreton, James, & Lindell, 2005; LeBreton & Senter, 2008). For example, if the members of a group agree in their perceptions about the degree to which the group has a safety climate (e.g., group mean = 3.7 on a 5-point Likert scale measuring safety climate), then this consensus degree of safety climate is considered a true property of the group itself. Conversely, without within-group agreement, there is no meaningful group-level climate.

But how does climate originate? That is, where does within-group agreement around the collective perception of a group-level property come from? And in particular, what is the role of social networks in the formation and maintenance of group climates and other group-level psychological constructs?

http://dx.doi.org/10.1037/0000115-024
The Handbook of Multilevel Theory, Measurement, and Analysis, S. E. Humphrey and J. M. LeBreton (Editors-in-Chief)

CLIMATE AS AN EXEMPLAR OF ALL GROUP-LEVEL PSYCHOLOGICAL PROPERTIES

Before we present our formal model of climate emergence, we should be clear that this chapter is not intended to narrowly, exclusively focus on the topic of organizational climate. Rather, organizational climate is an exemplar that represents all group-level psychological constructs. That is, we believe that many group-level constructs (e.g., group morale, classroom bullying norms, common expectations in a group therapy session) would emerge in the same fashion and via the same social network mechanisms that we describe in this chapter regarding organizational climate.

FORMAL THEORY AND COMPUTATIONAL MODELING OF THE FORMATION OF GROUP-LEVEL PROPERTIES

In this chapter, we offer a formal, mathematical theory of climate emergence, specifying how the structure and content of social networks among actors together determine the rate and final outcomes of the climate formation process. As such, this chapter takes its inspiration from the verbal theories of climate formation and consensus formation put forth by Schneider and Reichers (1983); James and Jones (1974); Festinger, Schacter, and Back (1950); Homans (1961); Berger and Luckmann (1966); Salancik and Pfeffer (1978); Weick (1979); Kenny (1991); and Newman, Hanges, Duan, and Ramesh (2008); our discussion is also related to Latané's (1996) work on dynamic social impact and Harrison and Carroll's (2002) work on the dynamics of cultural influence networks, but with greater emphasis in the current work on social network structure and network contagion.

In a nutshell, we articulate a theory in the form of a system of dynamic linear equations (DeShon, 2012; Fraley, 2002; van Geert, 1994, 1997), and we plot some prototypical outcomes from the theory over time using a simple computational model (Ilgen & Hulin, 2000). Formal theories

and computational models like the one advanced here were described by McGrath (1981; Runkel & McGrath, 1972) as *theoretical*—that is, this form of research is not empirical, in that there are no actors, no behaviors, and no contexts measured. Rather, this sort of theory marks an attempt "to model a particular concrete system (or set of concrete systems)" (McGrath, 1981, p. 188). Formal and computational models are a particularly useful form of theory (in comparison to potentially vague, verbal theories), because formal and computational models tend to be clear, precise, logically consistent, and easy to compare (Kreps, 1990, pp. 6–7) and can support the generation of hypotheses with these same characteristics (Carley, 1999; see discussion by Harrison, Lin, Carroll, & Carley, 2007; Hulin & Ilgen, 2000; Vancouver, Putka, & Scherbaum, 2005).

Network Contagion (ρ)

The current chapter takes its point of departure from a particular model of network contagion effects variously known as the *spatial regressive–autoregressive model, spatial lag model,* or *network effects model* (Anselin, 1988; Doreian, 1981; Doreian, Teuter, & Wang, 1984; Ord, 1975):

$$Y_i = \rho W_j Y_i + \beta_0 + \beta_1 X_i + \varepsilon_i, \qquad (23.1)$$

in which Y_i is an individual-level attribute vector (e.g., job satisfaction), β_1 is a regression slope that estimates the linear relationship between another individual attribute X_i (e.g., pay) and Y_i, β_0 is a regression intercept that gives the value of Y_i when all predictors (e.g., X_is) are equal to zero, and ε_i is a vector of residuals (individual-level errors of prediction). Importantly, the network effects or spatial autoregression model (Equation 23.1) differs from an ordinary regression model by the inclusion of the spatial autoregressive term $\rho W_j Y_i$, which is described below.

In Equation 23.1, W_j is an $N \times N$ square (Persons × Persons) adjacency matrix (e.g., W_j is a social network matrix). As such, W_j resides at the group level-of-analysis. In the example of a binary friendship matrix, the square W_j matrix would include an element "1" when an actor in a given row is sending a tie (i.e., a friendship nomination) to an actor in a given column.[1] All other elements in W_j (i.e., non-friendships) would be designated "0," as would the diagonal of the W_j matrix:

$$W_j = \begin{bmatrix} 0 & 1 & 1 \\ 1 & 0 & 0 \\ 0 & 0 & 0 \end{bmatrix} = \textit{friendship matrix.} \quad (23.2)$$

The elements of the W_j matrix in Equation 23.2 reveal that Person 1 has nominated Persons 2 and 3 as her friends, that Person 2 has indicated he is friends only with Person 1, and finally that Person 3 has nominated no friends.

Importantly, the matrix product W_jY_i, then, is a column vector in which each element contains the sum of all of one's friends' scores on Y_i. For example, suppose Y is a column vector of individual job satisfaction scores (rated on a 1-to-5 scale) with elements 3, 5, and 2:

$$Y = \begin{bmatrix} 3 \\ 5 \\ 2 \end{bmatrix}.$$

Then the matrix product, W_jY_i, would be

$$W_jY = \begin{bmatrix} 0 & 1 & 1 \\ 1 & 0 & 0 \\ 0 & 0 & 0 \end{bmatrix}\begin{bmatrix} 3 \\ 5 \\ 2 \end{bmatrix} = \begin{bmatrix} 0\cdot3+1\cdot5+1\cdot2 \\ 1\cdot3+0\cdot5+0\cdot2 \\ 0\cdot3+0\cdot5+0\cdot2 \end{bmatrix} = \begin{bmatrix} 7 \\ 3 \\ 0 \end{bmatrix}.$$

So, Person 1 has two friends (i.e., Persons 2 and 3), and the sum of these friends' satisfaction scores is 7. Person 2 has one friend (i.e., Person 1), and the sum of Person 2's friends' satisfaction scores

is 3. Person 3 has no friends, and the sum of his or her friends' satisfaction scores is thus 0. To repeat, W_jY_i is simply a column vector in which each element contains the sum of all of one's friends' scores on Y_i.

Finally, the coefficient ρ (see Equation 23.1) is the linear relationship between one's friends' scores on Y_i and one's own scores on Y_i (i.e., the spatial autoregression coefficient [i.e., controlling for other individual difference variables, X_i; see Equation 23.1]). The parameter ρ can thus be thought of as a network effect parameter or a "contagion" parameter (Leenders, 2002), because it indexes the relationship between (the sum of) one's peers' scores on Y_i (e.g., job satisfaction) and one's own score on Y_i (e.g., job satisfaction).[2] In the example above, the correlation between Y_i and W_jY_i turns out to be .25, suggesting contagion of job satisfaction. The larger the contagion parameter ρ, the greater the social influence from peers to the focal actor. For example, if Y_i is job satisfaction, then a large network contagion parameter (ρ) indicates that individuals' own job satisfaction can be predicted from their peers' job satisfaction.

Further, it is typical for researchers to *row-normalize* the adjacency matrix W (Anselin, 1988; LeSage, 1999) so that each nonempty row in the social network W_j sums to 1.0:

row-normalized W_j

$$= \begin{bmatrix} 0 & \frac{1}{2} & \frac{1}{2} \\ 1 & 0 & 0 \\ 0 & 0 & 0 \end{bmatrix}$$

$= \textit{row-normalized friendship matrix.} \quad (23.3)$

When W_j is row-normalized, then the matrix product W_jY_i becomes a column vector in which

---

[1] To clarify, note that although the actors in the rows of W_j are sending friendship nominations (or communication nominations) to the actors in the columns of W_j (e.g., the rows are the senders and the columns are the receivers of friendship nominations), the social influence itself might flow from the columns to the rows (i.e., I am influenced by those actors whom I nominate as friends).

[2] It is important to note that the network effects model in Equation 23.1 cannot be properly estimated via traditional ordinary least squares regression, and therefore requires special estimation routines (e.g., the *lnam* function in the R software package sna; Butts, 2008; see Anselin, 1988; Doreian, 1981; Kelejian & Prucha, 2002).

Newman and Wang

each element contains the mean of all of one's friends' scores on Y_i:

$$\text{row-normalized } W_j Y = \begin{bmatrix} 0 & \frac{1}{2} & \frac{1}{2} \\ 1 & 0 & 0 \\ 0 & 0 & 0 \end{bmatrix} \begin{bmatrix} 3 \\ 5 \\ 2 \end{bmatrix}$$

$$= \begin{bmatrix} 0 \cdot 3 + \frac{1}{2} \cdot 5 + \frac{1}{2} \cdot 2 \\ 1 \cdot 3 + 0 \cdot 5 + 0 \cdot 2 \\ 0 \cdot 3 + 0 \cdot 5 + 0 \cdot 2 \end{bmatrix}$$

$$= \begin{bmatrix} 3.5 \\ 3 \\ 0 \end{bmatrix}.$$

The act of row-normalizing W_j has the conceptual effect that the total amount of received influence is equal for all target actors (Leenders, 2002)—that is, everyone who has friends receives the same total amount of influence, regardless of their number of friends. In other words, the estimate of the contagion parameter (ρ) is influenced by peers' mean scores on Y_i rather than by peers' sum of scores on Y_i—which essentially decreases the effect of raw number of peers on the estimate of contagion.[3]

The network effects model has been occasionally implemented in past organizational research (Ibarra & Andrews, 1993; Mizruchi, Stearns, & Marquis, 2006; Newman, 2004; cf. Krackhardt, 1988), and scholars have called for increased future use of the model (Doh & Hahn, 2008). The model in Equation 23.1 has become increasingly easy to use in recent years, via the *lnam* function in the freely available R software package sna (Butts, 2008). Further, simulation work by Wang, Neuman, and Newman (2014) demonstrated the ease of successfully leveraging the network effects model because of its modest data requirements and its applicability to a diverse set of social networks. In particular, Wang et al. (2014) investigated the statistical power to detect network contagion effects (i.e., ρ) and showed that (a) social networks of modest size

($N = 40$) are typically adequate to detect network contagion and (b) network structure and network density have negligible unique effects on the power to detect network contagion, meaning that contagion can potentially be found for many types of networks.

Now that we have presented the network effects model (Equation 23.1) and the network contagion parameter ρ, we proceed by developing a formal theoretical model of the effects of network contagion (ρ) on the emergence of group-level psychological properties. This simplest form of our computational model specifies how climate emerges as a function of network contagion and network density.

Network Density (d)

Network density (d) is defined as the proportion of possible ties (between pairs of actors) that are actually present in a network. Density ranges from 0 to 1. A network with $d = 1$ has a tie or connection between every possible pair of actors, whereas a network with $d = .5$ has only half as many ties as the total number of pairs of actors. In a network with directed ties (i.e., an asymmetric network in which relationships are not necessarily reciprocated), the maximum number of ties is $N(N-1)$, whereas in a symmetric network (i.e., every relationship is reciprocal), the maximum number of unique ties is only $N(N-1)/2$.

Climate Strength

The theoretical model formulated in this chapter attempts to model a generic system by which group-level psychological properties emerge (in part) as a function of social networks. In other words, we model the role of social networks in the emergence of within-group agreement among individuals' perceptions of the group. The particular outcome variable we use in our simulation goes by many names, including *within-group agreement* (James & Jones, 1974; James et al., 1984), *shared assignment of psychological meaning* (James, 1982), *climate consensus* (Lindell & Brandt, 2000), and *climate strength* (Schneider, Salvaggio, & Subirats, 2002).

[3]Alternatively, Leenders (2002) suggested that it might sometimes be useful to column-normalize the W matrix in order to make the total amount of sent influence equal for all actors, but this is rarely done.

In other words, the social influence or contagion process that inheres in social networks should sometimes lead to eventual consensus among connected actors in the network. This consensus, when it involves within-group agreement among individuals' perceptions of a group attribute (e.g., organizational climate; James, 1982; James & Jones, 1974), is the hallmark of emergence of a group-level psychological property. As such, our theoretical model proposes that network contagion should produce increasing climate strength (smaller within-group standard deviations in climate perceptions) over time.

> *Proposition 1:* Network contagion (ρ) leads to within-group agreement (climate strength). Specifically, network contagion positively determines the rate of increase for climate strength.

Similarly, network density should enable the development of climate strength. Conceptually, this is because network density is the substrate upon which network contagion operates to yield consensus. As empirical evidence supporting this notion, we note that past researchers have found, at the group level-of-analysis, that (a) climate strength (for innovation climate) is positively related to a group's average ratings of social interaction and work interdependence (González-Romá, Peiró, & Tordera, 2002; Klein, Conn, Smith, & Sorra, 2001; i.e., climate strength is related to crude, nonsociometric measures of friendship network density, workflow or coordination network density, and work communication network density) and, more directly, that (b) climate strength (for safety climate) is correlated $r = .38$ with communication network density and $r = .32$ with friendship network density (Zohar & Tenne-Gazit, 2008). These positive observed relationships between network density and climate strength are consistent with our second proposition:

> *Proposition 2:* Network density (d) enables within-group agreement (climate strength) if there is network

contagion (ρ). Specifically, network density and network contagion positively interact to determine the rate of increase for climate strength.

FORMAL MODEL OF CLIMATE EMERGENCE

Our formal model of climate emergence is a linear dynamic system (i.e., a first-order difference equation, or vector autoregressive process), which we represent in state space form (DeShon, 2012; cf. Hannan & Deistler, 1988):

$$Y_{t+1} = AY_t + b, \qquad (23.4a)$$

where time (t) is represented in discrete time increments (e.g., minutes, days, years), Y_{t+1} is a column vector of N persons' scores on attribute Y at time $t + 1$, Y_t is a column vector of Y scores at the preceding time point (time t), A is a square $N \times N$ matrix called the *transition weight matrix*, and b is a column vector of time-invariant terms (aka "forcing terms"). As helpfully summarized by DeShon (2012), Equation 23.4a describes a deterministic system, in which individuals' trajectories of Y scores over time are completely determined by the column vector of initial conditions (Y_0), the weights in the transition matrix (A), and the vector of forcing term constants (b), with the weights in the transition matrix (A) being the primary focus of attention. The weights in the diagonal of the square transition matrix (A) describe the stability (or self-similarity) of each person's states over time, whereas the off-diagonal weights in the transition matrix (A) describe the interpersonal dynamics of the system.[4]

In order to be realistic, the weights in the transition matrix A should typically be between 1.0 and −1.0, and negative coefficients in the diagonal would represent an individual who oscillates, continually reversing her or his own perception (Y) over time (DeShon, 2012). It is desirable when a dynamic system has trajectories of Y that converge over time to a particular set of levels, known as a *steady state equilibrium*. Such system equilibria are

[4]Although we acknowledge that Equation 23.4a is fairly abstract at this point, we will provide a concrete example of how this equation works when we implement our computational model below.

considered stable if, after a shock or perturbing event, the trajectories return to their equilibrium states. Many organizational theories describe such perturbations or shocks (Landy, 1978; Lee & Mitchell, 1994; Weiss & Cropanzano, 1996) and thus could potentially be modeled using a linear dynamic system. DeShon (2012) pointed out that, mathematically speaking, a linear dynamic system will converge to a stable equilibrium whenever the absolute values of all the eigenvalues of the transition matrix (A) are less than 1.0, in which case the long-run steady states can be calculated as $[I - A]^{-1} b$ (where A and b are as defined above and I is the identity matrix—a square matrix containing all 0s but with 1s in the diagonal).

Putting the fancy math aside, the reader might notice at this point that there is a similarity between Equation 23.4a (the first-order difference equation describing a linear dynamic system) and Equation 23.1 (the network effects model). This potential equivalence can be seen more clearly if we rewrite Equation 23.4a as follows:

$$Y_{t+1} = \rho W Y_t + \beta Y_t + \varepsilon, \qquad (23.4b)$$

where the square $N \times N$ transition matrix, A, has now been decomposed into two parts: (a) the off-diagonal component of the transition matrix A now becomes $\rho W Y_t$, a term involving the social network W and the contagion parameter ρ, and (b) the diagonal component of the transition matrix A now becomes βY_t, a term involving the stability (or self-similarity) of each actor's Y score from one time period to the next. Note how Equation 23.4b is one form of the spatial lag or network effects model (i.e., Equation 23.1).[5]

To understand how Equation 23.4b works, we simulated data from $N = 30$ individuals who belong to the same group or organization and whose individual perceptions of that organization's climate (Y) are recorded for 20 consecutive time steps (e.g., 20 consecutive weeks). We drew our starting values (Y_0) from a random uniform distribution that ranged from 1 to 5 (simulating a 5-point Likert scale used to measure individual perceptions of organizational climate, starting at a point

in time before anyone has experienced the organizational climate—e.g., before the group has been formed). For the sake of the example, we then chose intuitively reasonable values for (a) network density ($d = .2$; i.e., each individual had roughly $dN = .2 \times 30 = 6$ peers, friends, or communication partners in the 30-person group), (b) the stability parameter in Equation 23.4b ($\beta = .9$ from one week to the next),[6] and (c) the network contagion parameter in Equation 23.4b ($\rho = .2$).

The simulated trajectories of organizational climate perceptions for the 30 individuals across the 20 time steps are shown in Figure 23.1. As seen in Figure 23.1, this model explodes. That is, using the chosen parameter values of contagion $\rho = .2$, density $d = .2$, and stability $\beta = .9$, the individual trajectories quickly go out of range (i.e., outside the simulated 1-to-5 scale that measures organizational climate), and they don't converge to an equilibrium state. Thus, the computational model with these parameter values is not realistic. For this reason, the model requires a tweak that will enable it to guarantee reasonable behavior, so that the perceptions of organizational climate will remain in the 1-to-5 range of the Likert scale we are simulating.

One handy solution to this problem is the following (inspired by a linear dynamic model from Fraley, 2002). First, note that the future state of Y (i.e., Y_{t+1}) is equal to the current state of Y (i.e., Y_t) plus the change in Y from the present to the future (i.e., ΔY_t):

$$Y_{t+1} = Y_t + \Delta Y_t. \qquad (23.5a)$$

Next—and this is the key step—we model the change in Y as proportional to the discrepancy between self (i.e., Y_t) and others (i.e., WY_t):

$$\Delta Y_t = \rho (W Y_t - Y_t) + \varepsilon. \qquad (23.5b)$$

This means that if my peers have a higher Y_t score than I do, I will adjust my Y_t score upward in the subsequent time step, by an amount proportional to the contagion parameter (ρ). The error term ε can

---

[5]For the sake of simplicity, we have dropped the intercept term (β_0) from Equation 23.1 when displaying Equation 23.4b.
[6]We note that the coefficients in this example are not standardized.

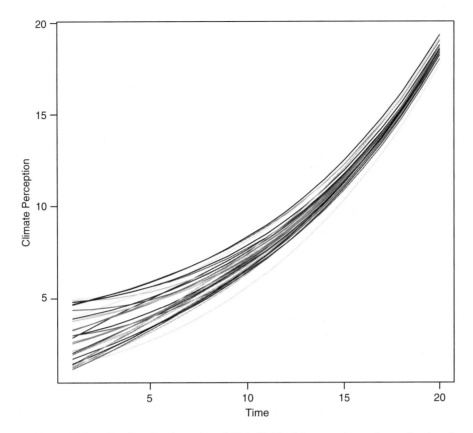

FIGURE 23.1.   Simulated trajectories of 30 individuals' perceptions of organizational climate (network contagion $\rho = .2$, network density $d = .2$, stability $\beta = .9$). This model explodes. Given the chosen parameter values, the individual trajectories quickly go out of range (outside the simulated 1-to-5 scale that measures organizational climate), and they don't converge to an equilibrium state. This model doesn't work.

be used to model the extent to which the process is nondeterministic—for example, when other outside events can influence an individual's score on Y_t from one time point to the next. Further, by substituting Equation 23.5b into Equation 23.5a, we get

$$Y_{t+1} = Y_t + \rho WY_t - \rho Y_t + \varepsilon, \qquad (23.5c)$$

which simplifies to

$$Y_{t+1} = \rho WY_t + (1 - \rho)Y_t + \varepsilon. \qquad (23.5d)$$

Note how Equation 23.5d is a special case of Equation 23.4b, where the stability parameter β has been constrained to equal $(1 - \rho)$. In other words, to prevent the model from exploding, we added a constraint to specify that when the dynamic contagion parameter (ρ) in the off-diagonal of the

transition matrix gets larger, the dynamic self-similarity or stability parameter in the diagonal of the transition matrix must get smaller by a proportional amount. That is, the model assumes that the more one's perceptions are driven by one's peers (contagion), the less they are driven by oneself (self-similarity).

A Computational Model of Climate Emergence

To investigate the behavior of our simple dynamic model of climate emergence, we next programmed the model to run in R (full syntax for the computational model is provided in Appendix 23.1). For the sake of labeling, we call this model CLiMATE, which is an acronym for Computational Linear Model of Aggregate True-score Emergence, and we note that the model can apply to the emergence of any group-level psychological construct derived under a consensus model (Chan, 1998).[7]

For the examples presented here, we simulated $N = 30$ group members across 20 time steps and drew the starting values of Y_0 from a random uniform distribution on the interval [1, 5]. To inspect the model, we will look at both the individual group members' trajectories of climate perceptions over time and the change in climate strength over time. Note that climate strength is indexed using the standard deviation (*SD*) of individual perceptions, so that climate strength (within-group agreement) is growing as the *SD* of climate perceptions falls toward zero.

No contagion ($\rho = 0$), medium density ($d = .2$). When we set the contagion parameter (ρ) to zero, the computational model produced no change in within-group agreement. This is seen in Figure 23.2a, left-hand side, where all 30 trajectories of individual climate perceptions simply carry forward the previous value over time (no change in climate perceptions). Likewise, the right-hand side of Figure 23.2a, shows that climate strength does not change over time, but holds steady at $SD = 1.2$ (i.e., the *SD* of a uniform distribution for a 5-point Likert scale, with no climate emergence).

Medium contagion ($\rho = .2$), medium density ($d = .2$). When the contagion parameter is set to a medium value of $\rho = .2$, the computational model reveals individual perceptions that converge to near-complete within-group agreement about the organizational climate within 20 time steps (see Figure 23.2b, left-hand side). In this theoretical model, network contagion produces within-group agreement and climate emergence. On the right-hand side of Figure 23.2b, the *SD* of individual perceptions drops to $SD = 0$, showing that climate strength eventually rises to its mathematical maximum value when there is network contagion.

High contagion ($\rho = .4$), medium density ($d = .2$). Under high contagion ($\rho = .4$), within-group agreement increases to near-maximum levels very quickly, in as few as 10 time steps (see Figure 23.2c).

Low contagion ($\rho = .1$), medium density ($d = .2$). When contagion is low ($\rho = .1$), within-group consensus is achieved very slowly, and climate strength gets only about halfway to its maximum by the end of 20 time steps (see Figure 23.2d).

Overall, it appears that the network contagion parameter (ρ) determines the speed or rate at which agreement is reached and climate emerges. As such, Figure 23.2 is consistent with Proposition 1.

Stochastic shocks. Before we turn our attention to the model's proposed effects of network density on climate emergence, we offer a brief digression about random error in the CLiMATE model. In particular, we note that the results presented in Figure 23.2 are deterministic, because the stochastic error term in Equation 23.5d was not modeled (i.e., we set $\varepsilon = 0$). When we do allow random variation into the model (i.e., when the residual term is drawn from a random normal distribution with the *SD* of ε set at $\sigma(\varepsilon) = .2$), we get the result shown in Figure 23.3b (left-hand side), where individual trajectories of climate perceptions are riddled with shocks at each time step. Although these individual perceptions do move toward convergence, they do not converge smoothly. Further, Figure 23.3b, right-hand side, shows that the addition of random error or events at each time step not only interrupts the smoothness of the climate emergence, but it also effectively prevents the model from achieving complete agreement (the *SD* for climate strength never goes to zero), because random variation is continually being reintroduced. We surmise that models containing such random error terms are much more realistic than the deterministic examples shown in Figure 23.2, but we nonetheless provide several deterministic (i.e., without random error) illustrations in the current chapter in order to make some particular emergence phenomena easier to see and understand. When looking at Figures 23.2 and 23.4, the reader should realize that things in the real world are likely much bumpier (i.e., Figure 23.3b, is more realistic).

Density effects. In Figure 23.4, we observe what happens to the model when network density is

[7]We point out that all group-level psychological constructs derived under a consensus model contain an aggregate, or group-level, true score (see LeBreton et al., 2005).

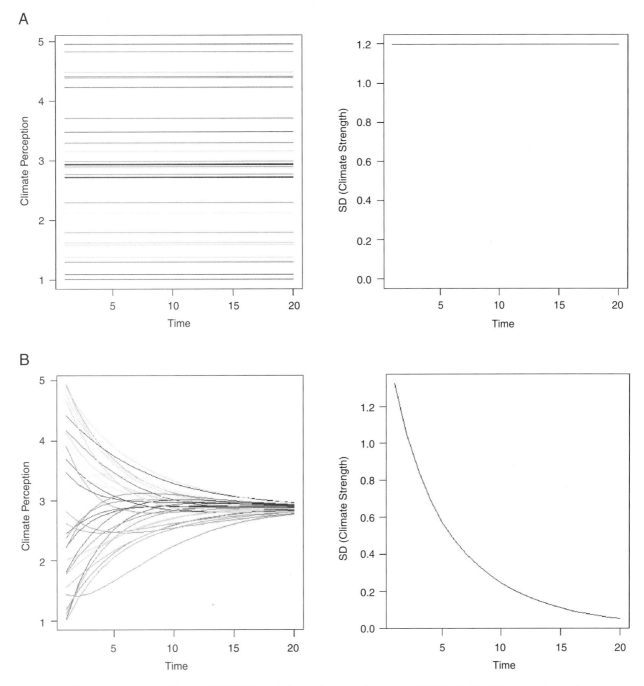

FIGURE 23.2. Contagion effects: CLiMATE model simulated trajectories of 30 individuals' perceptions of organizational climate. (a) No network contagion (ρ = .0), medium network density (d = .2). (b) Medium network contagion (ρ = .2), medium network density (d = .2). *SD* = standard deviation. (*continues*)

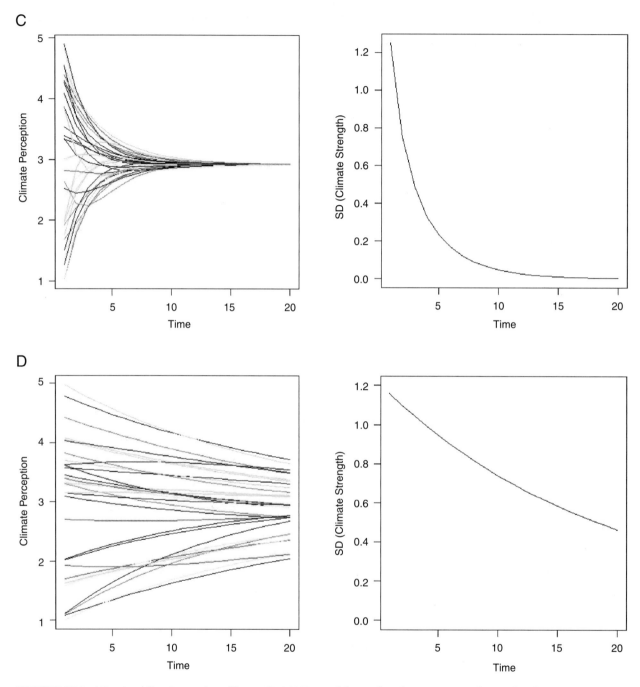

FIGURE 23.2. (*Continued*)   Contagion effects: CLiMATE model simulated trajectories of 30 individuals' perceptions of organizational climate. (c) High network contagion ($\rho = .4$), medium network density ($d = .2$). (d) Low network contagion ($\rho = .05$), medium network density ($d = .2$). *SD* = standard deviation.

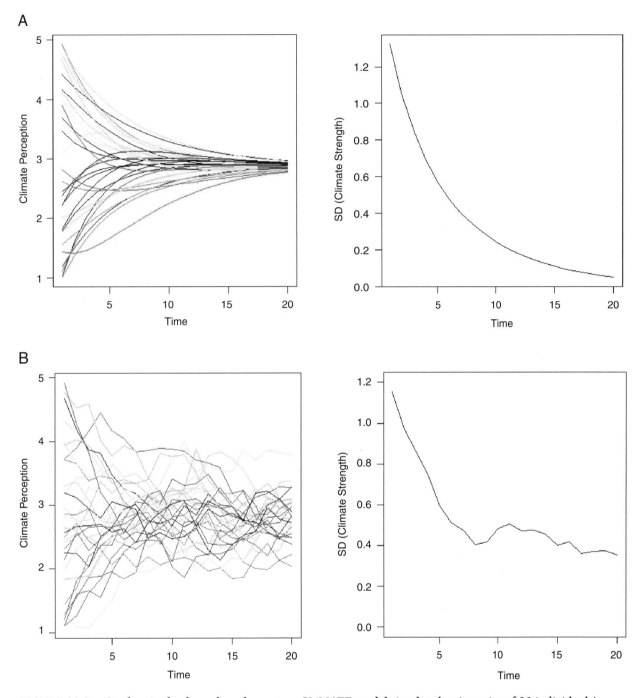

FIGURE 23.3.   Stochastic shocks and random error: CLiMATE model simulated trajectories of 30 individuals'
perceptions of organizational climate. (a) No error ($\varepsilon = 0$), medium contagion ($\rho = .2$), medium density ($d = .2$).
(b) Medium error ($\sigma(\varepsilon) = .2$), medium contagion ($\rho = .2$), medium density ($d = .2$). *SD* = standard deviation.

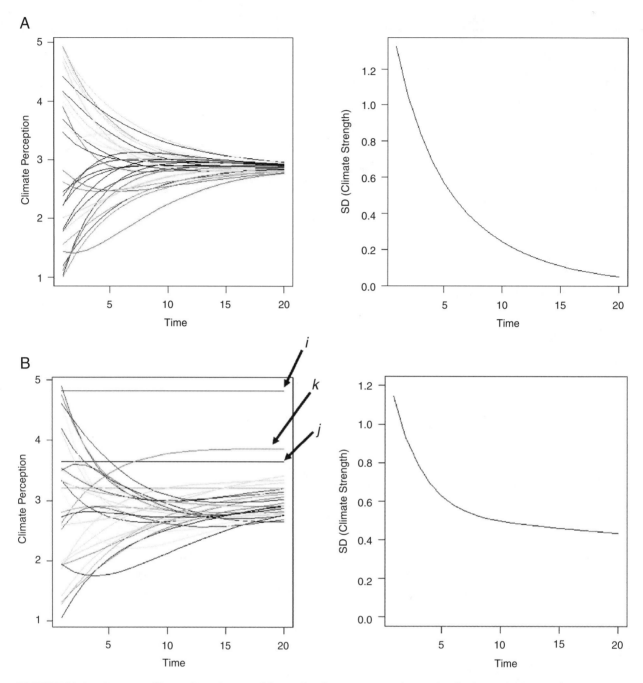

FIGURE 23.4. Density effects: CLiMATE model simulated trajectories of 30 individuals' perceptions of organizational climate. (a) Medium network contagion (ρ = .2), medium network density (d = .2). (b) Medium network contagion (ρ = .2), low network density (d = .1). Actors i, j, and k are explained in the text with the description of this figure. SD = standard deviation.

decreased. When the network becomes more sparse (less dense), we observe phenomena like those depicted in Figure 23.4b, left-hand side. In particular, in a low-density network (with fewer network ties overall), there is an increasing chance that several actors will not receive any social influence because they are not the recipients of any influence ties. These individuals need not be network isolates—indeed, in an asymmetric social network, it is possible to send influence ties but not be the recipient of any influence ties. In Figure 23.4b, Actors i and j are not receiving any social influence ties, and as such their climate perceptions simply carry forward across time, not converging to the group's overall mean. In a sparse network, the existence of these actors who are disconnected from social influence makes it impossible to achieve high rates of overall within-group agreement.

To exacerbate matters, it is also possible that these individual actors who are not following anyone's social influence may nonetheless be sending social influence to others in the network. Such is the case with Actor j, who receives no influence, but who himself or herself is sending influence to Actor k and thus brings Actor k's climate perception even further away from the group consensus. Altogether, low-density networks face two phenomena that impair the emergence of within-group agreement: (a) the increased frequency of aloof actors who are receiving no influence (Actors i and j) and (b) the fact that these aloof actors might be leading others astray (Actor j is influencing Actor k to move further from the group consensus). In Figure 23.4b, right-hand side, we see that the combined effects of these phenomena are to place a limit on the amount of consensus that can be reached. Overall, it appears that the network density parameter (*d*) determines the asymptote or limit of agreement that can be attained via contagion.

Contagion × density × time: A three-way interaction of climate emergence. In order to illustrate how our formal model of climate emergence gives rise to the interaction effect we specified in Proposition 2 above, we next generated 1,000 samples under each of four conditions (i.e., a 2 [high–low Contagion] × 2 [high–low Density]

design). We then plotted the mean time trajectories of climate strength across the 1,000 samples under each of the four conditions, with results shown in Figure 23.5. In Figure 23.5a, the illustration highlights the idea that network density governs the asymptote of climate strength, because low-density networks harbor more aloof actors who cannot be reached by social influence. Figure 23.5b, illustrates the model prediction that the network contagion parameter (ρ) governs the rate of climate strength because higher contagion leads group members to more quickly converge toward the group's asymptotic level of within-group perceptual consensus.

Network Structure (Random, Star, and Small World)

The example networks that we simulated up to this point in the chapter were all simple, random networks. Other network structures are possible and could give rise to distinct phenomena when simulating the emergence of group-level psychological constructs (e.g., organizational climate, group norms). We next review several alternative network structures (see Wang et al., 2014).

Random. The illustrations we provided in Figures 23.1 through 23.5 were all built from a model with random network structure, which is simulated from a binomial distribution with the probability of a tie set equal to the network density, and with diagonal elements of the network matrix *W* reset to zero. An example of this network structure is shown in Figure 23.6a. Random networks are useful for simple demonstrations, but they do not reflect typical human social networks found in the real world.

Star (modeling leadership). A star network, in its purest form, is a hub-and-spokes network in which one actor is connected to all other actors, but the other actors are not interconnected. Neuman and Mizruchi (2010) showed that the density of such a network is constrained to be 2/N but that denser star networks could be simulated by adding random ties among nonstars until the desired density is obtained. For example, Figure 23.6b depicts a star network with 50 nodes, to which 74 ties have been added in order to reach a density of .1.

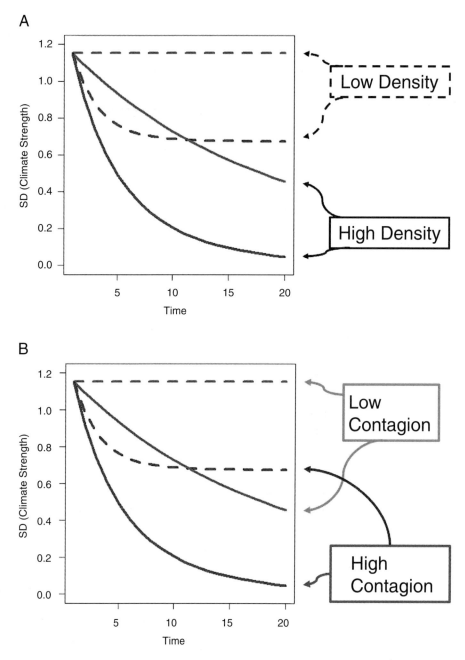

FIGURE 23.5.   Contagion × Density × Time interaction effect: Average of
1,000 replications from the CLiMATE model. (a) Comparison of high and low
network density (density determines asymptote). (b) Comparison of high
and low network contagion (contagion determines rate). *SD* = standard deviation.

When a star network structure is used for the adjacency matrix *W* in the CLiMATE computational model, it can represent a single actor with widespread social influence, such as a group leader. Indeed, DeShon (2012) proposed just such a model, in which the transition matrix from a linear dynamic model contained a single column of large off-diagonal elements to represent the influence that a single individual might have on all the other members of the group. This transition matrix (i.e., social network matrix) is not symmetric and is specified so that influence primarily (but not necessarily exclusively) flows in one direction from the leader to the followers. In such a network structure,

A

B

C

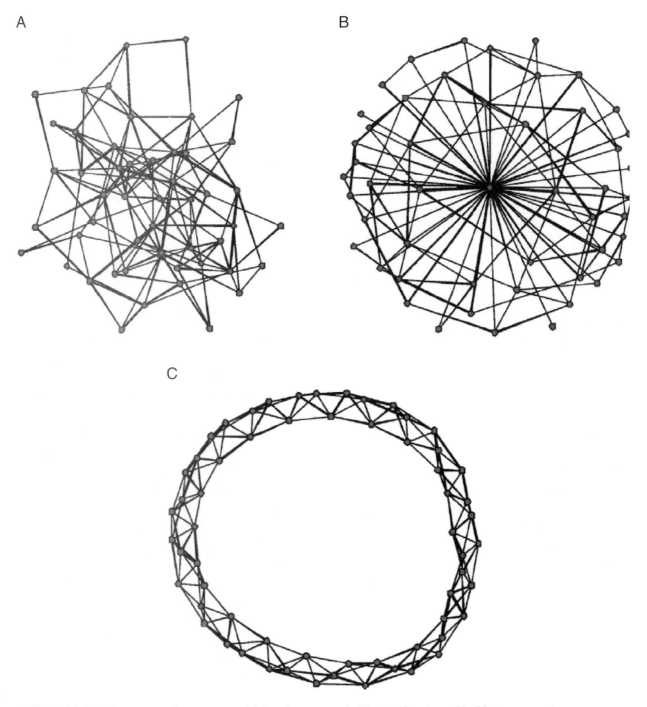

FIGURE 23.6.   Three network structures. (a) Random network (*N* = 50, density = .1). (b) Star network (*N* = 50, density = .1). (c) Small world network (*N* = 61, density = .1).

we would expect the leader's perceptions of the organizational climate to carry forward and not be influenced to any large degree by the followers (similar to Actors i and j in Figure 23.4b), but with an important caveat: Unlike actors i and j in Figure 23.4b, in the leadership scenario we would expect all of the group members to gravitate toward the position or climate perception espoused by the leader.

Small world (modeling subgroups and brokers).
The third network structure we address is called a *small world* network and is designed to approximate

real-world social networks—often characterized by (a) high clustering coefficients[8] but (b) small average path lengths[9] (Watts & Strogatz, 1998). The name "small world" comes from Milgram's (1967) small world experiment, which demonstrated short average path lengths in a large social system (i.e., six degrees of separation). In order to simulate small world networks, the researcher can begin with a ring lattice (Figure 23.6c) and then randomly rewire approximately 10% of the ties to achieve a short average path length (Watts & Strogatz, 1998; see Neuman & Mizruchi, 2010; Wang et al., 2014).

In small world networks, there are often cohesive subgroups that are loosely connected via brokers (cf. Burt, 1992). In such social networks, it is possible for distinct subgroup climates (LeBreton et al., 2005) or microclimates (Newman et al., 2008) to form. According to the formal model advanced in this chapter, in a small world network structure the likelihood of cohesive subgroup climates' consolidating into an overall organizational climate tends to be a function of the influence ties sent and received by brokers, who occupy the bridging positions between subgroups. For example, if a broker receives a lot of influence ties from Subgroup A and sends a lot of influence ties to Subgroup B, then the overall effect might be that Subgroup B changes toward perceptual consensus with the views previously held by Subgroup A (i.e., the broker becomes the agent for a subgroup-level influence process). Further, by selectively exercising their influence, brokers can be in a position to determine whether an overall climate gets formed or not.

CONCLUSION

The computational model we advance in this chapter shows how micro-level dyadic social influence phenomena give rise to macro-level properties of organizational climate emergence. We derived the following propositions: (a) Network contagion (ρ) determines the rate of consensus or climate strength

over time, (b) network density (d) determines the asymptote at which climate strength stops growing when contagion is in force, (c) the star network structure can create consensus around a single individual leader's climate perception, and (d) the small world network structure can produce local microclimates and subgroup-level contagion via brokers. R syntax was provided to enable easy use and extension of the linear dynamic model and formal theory by future researchers.

The model proposed in the current work has several limitations, which are areas for future research and extensions. Generally speaking, the limitations involve the fact that the model is exceedingly simple (this simplicity makes the model more artificial, but also easier to test empirically). The model essentially ignores personality and individual differences, the objective features of the organization that might be experienced in common by employees, and differential opportunity of employees to observe these organizational features (see Kenny, 1991), with the possible exception that these ignored factors might potentially be indirectly modeled by the initial states of individuals (Y_0), the network characteristics (W), and the stochastic shocks (ε). Another important limitation is that the social network (W) and the contagion parameter (ρ) are both treated as constants. Further, in the network effects model (Equation 23.1, Equation 23.5d), the social network (W) is exogenous, meaning that we are modeling social influence (i.e., changes in individual attribute Y, in response to the network W) but not modeling selection (i.e., in selection phenomena, the network ties are treated as a criterion variable—this would require a different model, such as stochastic actor-based models [see Schulte, Cohen, & Klein, 2012; Snijders, van de Bunt, & Steglich, 2010] or exponential random graph models [Contractor, Wasserman, & Faust, 2006; Lusher, Koskinen, & Robins, 2012]). A related limitation is that the current model does not permit us to treat the network as an open system with fluid membership (Humphrey & Aime, 2014). Finally, our model as

---

[8]A *clustering coefficient* is defined as the density of an ego network. For example, if an individual has k number of friends, then there are $k(k-1)$ possible directed ties among these friends. If only 50% of these possible ties actually exist, then that individual's clustering coefficient is .50.
[9]The *average path length* is the average distance between any pair of actors in a network, measured along the shortest path between the pair. It indexes the efficiency with which information (or diseases) can spread through the network.

1. We have presented a theory of the emergence of group-level psychological properties.
2. This theory is specified using a computational model, rather than vague verbal language (see Ilgen & Hulin, 2000).
3. The theory focuses on the following parameters: (a) social network contagion (ρ), (b) social network density (d), (c) social network structure (W), (d) random shocks and events (ε), and (e) time. The outcome variable is within-group agreement (e.g., climate strength).
4. The theory supports unique propositions:
   - Network contagion determines the rate (or velocity) of within-group agreement/climate emergence over time.
   - Network density determines the asymptote of within-group agreement/climate emergence over time.
   - Leadership and influence can be modeled via a star network structure, in which one individual possesses more influence than others. The model can accommodate the influence of individuals on groups.
   - Subgroup microclimates and influence brokerage can be modeled via a small world network structure, in which different subgroup climates can emerge in isolation, or one subgroup can influence another subgroup via a broker (or bridge). The model can also accommodate teams with either distinct or overlapping membership by directly specifying the dyadic communication networks, workflows, and so forth (using the W matrix).
5. This dynamic theoretical model can be adjusted by users (via the brief R syntax included in the appendix) as data accumulate on the various model parameters (e.g., contagion, time lags).
6. We recommend that multilevel researchers begin to measure social networks and estimate the network contagion parameter (ρ; Anselin, 1988; Butts, 2008; Wang, Neuman, & Newman, 2014) as a basis for understanding the origins of, and change in, group-level psychological constructs.

presently specified does not accommodate negative ties (Labianca & Brass, 2006). Despite these limitations, we hope that the current effort will stand as a user-friendly example of a formal model that can potentially offer some insight and clarity into dynamic theorizing about the emergence of group-level psychological properties as a function of social network structure, network density, and network contagion. A summary of our key messages is provided in Exhibit 23.1.

APPENDIX 23.1: R SYNTAX FOR FORMAL MODEL OF CLIMATE EMERGENCE

Paste the following text into R:

```
# Computational Linear Model of Aggregate True-
    score Emergence (CLiMATE)

# Parameters that can be configured are below

n = 30          # Number of people
iter = 20       # Number of time steps or iterations
rho = .2        # Contagion parameter
densityk = .2   # Probability of two people being
                    connected

stochast = 0    # 1 for Yes, 0 for No
```

```
#——————————————
# No need to configure parameters below
    this point
#——————————————

# This vector will hold the SD of Y across time
    sd.vec = rep(NA,iter)

# Create social network matrix
# with given size and density

    # W is raw connections (0, 1)

    W = matrix(rbinom(n*n,1,densityk),n,n,
        byrow=T)
    diag(W) <- 0

    # Row standardize W
    z<-apply(W,1,sum) + .000000000001
    W2 = W/z
    #diag(W2) = 0
    A = W2

# Starting values for y (T = 0)

    y = runif(n)*(5–1) + 1 # rnorm(n, 0, 1)

    # Create an empty matrix to hold Y scores for
        each person (rows) across time (columns)
```

```
Y = matrix(NA,n,iter, byrow=T)

   Y[,1] = y

# If someone has zero ties, put a 1 on diagonal

   for(j in 1:n){
   if(z[j] < .001){
   A[j,j] = 1
   }
   }

#————————————————
# Simulate dynamics across time
#————————————————

   for(i in 2:iter){
   Y[,i] = Y[,(i–1)] + rho*(A%*%Y[,(i–1)] –
       Y[,(i–1)]) + stochast*rnorm(n,0,.20)

   }

#————————————————
# Create graphs
#————————————————

   par(mfrow=c(1,2))   # 1 row, 2 columns
   plot(Y[1,],ylim=c(min(Y),max(Y)),type="n",
       xlab="Time",ylab="Climate Perception")
   # cycle through each person and plot his or her
       trajectory for Y
   for(i in 1:n){
   lines(Y[i,],col=i)
   }

# Compute SD of Y for each iteration

   for(i in 1:iter){
   sd.vec[i] = sd(Y[,i])
   }
   plot(sd.vec,type="l",xlab="Time", ylab="SD
   (Climate Strength)", ylim=c(0.0, 1.2))
```

References

Anselin, L. (1988). *Spatial econometrics: Methods and models*. Dordrecht, the Netherlands: Kluwer Academic. http://dx.doi.org/10.1007/978-94-015-7799-1

Berger, P. L., & Luckmann, T. (1966). *The social construction of reality: A treatise in the sociology of knowledge*. Garden City, NY: Anchor Books.

Bliese, P. D. (2000). Within-group agreement, non-independence, and reliability: Implications for data aggregation and analysis. In K. J. Klein & S. W. J. Kozlowski (Eds.), *Multilevel theory, research, and methods in organizations* (pp. 349–381). San Francisco, CA: Jossey-Bass.

Burt, R. (1992). *Structural holes: The social structure of competition*. Cambridge, MA: Harvard University Press.

Butts, C. T. (2008). Social network analysis with sna. *Journal of Statistical Software*, 24(6), 1–51. http://dx.doi.org/10.18637/jss.v024.i06

Carley, K. M. (1999). On generating hypotheses using computer simulations. *Systems Engineering*, 2, 69–77. http://dx.doi.org/10.1002/(SICI)1520-6858(1999)2:2<69::AID-SYS3>3.0.CO;2-0

Chan, D. (1998). Functional relations among constructs in the same content domain at different levels of analysis: A typology of composition models. *Journal of Applied Psychology*, 83, 234–246. http://dx.doi.org/10.1037/0021-9010.83.2.234

Contractor, N. S., Wasserman, S., & Faust, K. (2006). Testing multitheoretical, multilevel hypotheses about organizational networks: An analytic framework and empirical example. *The Academy of Management Review*, 31, 681–703. http://dx.doi.org/10.5465/AMR.2006.21318925

DeShon, R. P. (2012). Multivariate dynamics in organizational science. In S. W. J. Kozlowski (Ed.), *The Oxford handbook of organizational psychology* (pp. 117–142). New York, NY: Oxford University Press.

Doh, J. P., & Hahn, E. D. (2008). Using spatial methods in strategy research. *Organizational Research Methods*, 11, 659–681. http://dx.doi.org/10.1177/1094428107300340

Doreian, P. (1981). Estimating linear models with spatially distributed data. *Sociological Methodology*, 12, 359–388. http://dx.doi.org/10.2307/270747

Doreian, P., Teuter, K., & Wang, C.-S. (1984). Network autocorrelation models: Some Monte Carlo results. *Sociological Methods & Research*, 13, 155–200. http://dx.doi.org/10.1177/0049124184013002001

Festinger, L., Schacter, S., & Back, K. (1950). *Social pressures in informed groups: A study of a housing project*. New York, NY: Harper.

Fraley, R. C. (2002). Attachment stability from infancy to adulthood: Meta-analysis and dynamic modeling of developmental mechanisms. *Personality and Social Psychology Review*, 6, 123–151. http://dx.doi.org/10.1207/S15327957PSPR0602_03

González-Romá, V., Peiró, J. M., & Tordera, N. (2002). An examination of the antecedents and moderator influences of climate strength. *Journal of Applied Psychology*, 87, 465–473. http://dx.doi.org/10.1037/0021-9010.87.3.465

Hannan, E. J., & Deistler, M. (1988). *The statistical theory of linear systems*. New York, NY: Wiley.

Harrison, J. R., & Carroll, G. R. (2002). The dynamics of cultural influence networks. *Computational & Mathematical Organization Theory, 8*, 5–30. http://dx.doi.org/10.1023/A:1015142219808

Harrison, J. R., Lin, Z., Carroll, G. R., & Carley, K. M. (2007). Simulation modeling in organizational and management research. *The Academy of Management Review, 32*, 1229–1245. http://dx.doi.org/10.5465/AMR.2007.26586485

Homans, G. C. (1961). *Social behavior: Its elementary forms.* New York, NY: Harcourt Brace.

Hulin, C. L., & Ilgen, D. R. (2000). Introduction to computational modeling in organizations: The good that modeling does. In D. R. Ilgen & C. L. Hulin (Eds.), *Computational modeling of behavior in organizations: The third scientific discipline* (pp. 3–18). Washington, DC: American Psychological Association. http://dx.doi.org/10.1037/10375-001

Humphrey, S. E., & Aime, F. (2014). Team microdynamics: Toward an orienting approach to teamwork. *The Academy of Management Annals, 8*, 443–503. http://dx.doi.org/10.5465/19416520.2014.904140

Ibarra, H., & Andrews, S. B. (1993). Power, social influence, and sense making: Effects of network centrality and proximity on employee perceptions. *Administrative Science Quarterly, 38*, 277–303. http://dx.doi.org/10.2307/2393414

Ilgen, D. R., & Hulin, C. L. (Eds.). (2000). *Computational modeling of behavior in organizations: The third scientific discipline.* Washington, DC: American Psychological Association. http://dx.doi.org/10.1037/10375-000

James, L. R. (1982). Aggregation bias in estimates of perceptual agreement. *Journal of Applied Psychology, 67*, 219–229. http://dx.doi.org/10.1037/0021-9010.67.2.219

James, L. R., Demaree, R. G., & Wolf, G. (1984). Estimating within-group interrater reliability with and without response bias. *Journal of Applied Psychology, 69*, 85–98. http://dx.doi.org/10.1037/0021-9010.69.1.85

James, L. R., & Jones, A. P. (1974). Organizational climate: A review of theory and research. *Psychological Bulletin, 81*, 1096–1112. http://dx.doi.org/10.1037/h0037511

Kelejian, H. H., & Prucha, I. R. (2002). 2SLS and OLS in a spatial autoregressive model with equal spatial weights. *Regional Science and Urban Economics, 32*, 691–707. http://dx.doi.org/10.1016/S0166-0462(02)00003-0

Kenny, D. A. (1991). A general model of consensus and accuracy in interpersonal perception. *Psychological Review, 98*, 155–163. http://dx.doi.org/10.1037/0033-295X.98.2.155

Klein, K. J., Conn, A. B., Smith, D. B., & Sorra, J. S. (2001). Is everyone in agreement? An exploration of within-group agreement in employee perceptions of the work environment. *Journal of Applied Psychology, 86*, 3–16. http://dx.doi.org/10.1037/0021-9010.86.1.3

Kozlowski, S. W. J., & Klein, K. J. (2000). A multilevel approach to theory and research in organizations: Contextual, temporal, and emergent processes. In K. J. Klein & S. W. J. Kozlowski (Eds.), *Multilevel theory, research, and methods in organizations* (pp. 3–90). San Francisco, CA: Jossey-Bass.

Krackhardt, D. (1988). Predicting with networks: Non-parametric multiple regression analysis of dyadic data. *Social Networks, 10*, 359–381. http://dx.doi.org/10.1016/0378-8733(88)90004-4

Kreps, D. M. (1990). *A course in microeconomic theory.* Princeton, NJ: Princeton University Press.

Labianca, G., & Brass, D. J. (2006). Exploring the social ledger: Negative relationships and negative asymmetry in social networks in organizations. *The Academy of Management Review, 31*, 596–614. http://dx.doi.org/10.5465/AMR.2006.21318920

Landy, F. J. (1978). An opponent process theory of job satisfaction. *Journal of Applied Psychology, 63*, 533–547. http://dx.doi.org/10.1037/0021-9010.63.5.533

Latané, B. (1996). Dynamic social impact: The creation of culture by communication. *Journal of Communication, 46*(4), 13–25. http://dx.doi.org/10.1111/j.1460-2466.1996.tb01501.x

LeBreton, J. M., James, L. R., & Lindell, M. K. (2005). Recent issues regarding r_{WG}, r^*_{WG}, $r_{WG(J)}$, and $r^*_{WG(J)}$. *Organizational Research Methods, 8*, 128–138. http://dx.doi.org/10.1177/1094428104272181

LeBreton, J. M., & Senter, J. L. (2008). Answers to 20 questions about interrater reliability and interrater agreement. *Organizational Research Methods, 11*, 815–852. http://dx.doi.org/10.1177/1094428106296642

Lee, T. W., & Mitchell, T. R. (1994). An alternative approach: The unfolding model of voluntary employee turnover. *The Academy of Management Review, 19*, 51–89.

Leenders, R. A. J. (2002). Modeling social influence through network autocorrelation: Constructing the weight matrix. *Social Networks, 24*, 21–47. http://dx.doi.org/10.1016/S0378-8733(01)00049-1

LeSage, J. P. (1999). Spatial econometrics. In *Web book of regional science.* Morgantown, WV: Regional Research Institute, West Virginia University. Retrieved from http://www.rri.wvu.edu/WebBook/LeSage/spatial/wbook.pdf

Lindell, M. K., & Brandt, C. J. (2000). Climate quality and climate consensus as mediators of the relationship between organizational antecedents and outcomes. *Journal of Applied Psychology, 85*, 331–348. http://dx.doi.org/10.1037/0021-9010.85.3.331

Lusher, D., Koskinen, J., & Robins, G. (Eds.). (2012). *Exponential random graph models for social networks: Theory, methods, and applications.* New York, NY: Cambridge University Press. http://dx.doi.org/10.1017/CBO9780511894701

McGrath, J. E. (1981). Dilemmatics: The study of research choices and dilemmas. *American Behavioral Scientist, 25,* 179–210. http://dx.doi.org/10.1177/000276428102500205

Milgram, S. (1967). The small world problem. *Psychology Today, 1,* 61–67.

Mizruchi, M. S., Stearns, L. B., & Marquis, C. (2006). The conditional nature of embeddedness: A study of borrowing by large U.S. firms, 1973–1994. *American Sociological Review, 71,* 310–333. http://dx.doi.org/10.1177/000312240607100207

Muthén, B. (1994). Multilevel covariance structure analysis. *Sociological Methods & Research, 22,* 376–398. http://dx.doi.org/10.1177/0049124194022003006

Neuman, E. J., & Mizruchi, M. S. (2010). Structure and bias in the network autocorrelation model. *Social Networks, 32,* 290–300. http://dx.doi.org/10.1016/j.socnet.2010.04.003

Newman, D. A. (2004). *Is job (dis)satisfaction contagious? Simultaneous effects of social networks, task characteristics, and dispositions* (Unpublished doctoral dissertation). Pennsylvania State University, State College.

Newman, D. A., Hanges, P. J., Duan, L., & Ramesh, A. (2008). A network model of organizational climate: Friendship clusters, subgroup agreement, and climate schemas. In D. B. Smith (Ed.), *The people make the place: A festschrift for Benjamin Schneider* (pp. 101–126). New York, NY: Erlbaum.

Ord, K. (1975). Estimation methods for models of spatial interaction. *Journal of the American Statistical Association, 70,* 120–126. http://dx.doi.org/10.1080/01621459.1975.10480272

Ostroff, C. (1993). Comparing correlations based on individual-level and aggregated data. *Journal of Applied Psychology, 78,* 569–582. http://dx.doi.org/10.1037/0021-9010.78.4.569

Porter, L. W., & Schneider, B. (2014). What was, what is, and what may be in OP/OB. *Annual Review of Organizational Psychology and Organizational Behavior, 1,* 1–21. http://dx.doi.org/10.1146/annurev-orgpsych-031413-091302

Rousseau, D. M. (2011). Reinforcing the micro/macro bridge: Organizational thinking and pluralistic vehicles. *Journal of Management, 37,* 429–442. http://dx.doi.org/10.1177/0149206310372414

Runkel, P. J., & McGrath, J. E. (1972). *Research on human behavior: A systematic guide to method.* New York, NY: Holt.

Salancik, G. R., & Pfeffer, J. (1978). A social information processing approach to job attitudes and task design. *Administrative Science Quarterly, 23,* 224–253. http://dx.doi.org/10.2307/2392563

Schneider, B., & Reichers, A. A. (1983). On the etiology of climates. *Personnel Psychology, 36,* 19–39. http://dx.doi.org/10.1111/j.1744-6570.1983.tb00500.x

Schneider, B., Salvaggio, A. N., & Subirats, M. (2002). Climate strength: A new direction for climate research. *Journal of Applied Psychology, 87,* 220–229. http://dx.doi.org/10.1037/0021-9010.87.2.220

Schulte, M., Cohen, N. A., & Klein, K. J. (2012). The coevolution of network ties and perceptions of team psychological safety. *Organization Science, 23,* 564–581. http://dx.doi.org/10.1287/orsc.1100.0582

Snijders, T. A. B., van de Bunt, G. G., & Steglich, C. E. G. (2010). Introduction to stochastic actor-based models for network dynamics. *Social Networks, 32,* 44–60. http://dx.doi.org/10.1016/j.socnet.2009.02.004

Vancouver, J. B., Putka, D. J., & Scherbaum, C. A. (2005). Testing a computational model of the goal-level effect: An example of a neglected methodology. *Organizational Research Methods, 8,* 100–127. http://dx.doi.org/10.1177/1094428104271998

van Geert, P. (1994). *Dynamic systems of development.* New York, NY: Harvester Wheatsheaf.

van Geert, P. (1997). Time and theory in social psychology. *Psychological Inquiry, 8,* 143–151. http://dx.doi.org/10.1207/s15327965pli0802_11

Wang, W., Neuman, E. J., & Newman, D. A. (2014). Statistical power of the social network autocorrelation model. *Social Networks, 38,* 88–99. http://dx.doi.org/10.1016/j.socnet.2014.03.004

Watts, D. J., & Strogatz, S. H. (1998). Collective dynamics of "small-world" networks. *Nature, 393,* 440–442. http://dx.doi.org/10.1038/30918

Weick, K. E. (1979). *The social psychology of organizing.* Reading, MA: Addison-Wesley.

Weiss, H. M., & Cropanzano, R. (1996). Affective events theory: A theoretical discussion of the structure, causes and consequences of affective experiences at work. In B. M. Staw & L. L. Cummings (Eds.), *Research in organizational behavior* (pp. 1–74). Amsterdam, the Netherlands: Elsevier.

Zohar, D., & Tenne-Gazit, O. (2008). Transformational leadership and group interaction as climate antecedents: A social network analysis. *Journal of Applied Psychology, 93,* 744–757. http://dx.doi.org/10.1037/0021-9010.93.4.744

PART IV

REFLECTIONS ON MULTILEVEL RESEARCH

## CHAPTER 24

CROSS-LEVEL MODELS

Francis J. Yammarino and Janaki Gooty

Cross-level models are prevalent in social–behavioral–organizational sciences research. There are, however, at least two general views of these models, which have resulted in different conceptualizations and testing procedures. We refer to these different approaches and associated models here as *traditional* cross-level views, with a long history and derived mainly from established work in the physical or hard sciences, and *contemporary* cross-level views, with a shorter history and derived mainly from newer work in the social–behavioral or soft sciences.

Our purpose in this chapter is to explicate these different cross-level views and to attempt to combine the notions from these two general views of cross-level models to form an integrative cross-level view in which elements of both the traditional and contemporary views are included. We believe this is possible given that the two views are not necessarily contradictory but are more complementary, answering different questions and addressing different issues (detailed below). Our hope is that by explaining and better understanding these different perspectives on cross-level models, which have persisted into present times, we can begin to integrate them to enhance future theory building and theory testing in the social–behavioral–organizational sciences.

TRADITIONAL AND CONTEMPORARY CROSS-LEVEL VIEWS

The world of cross-level models—including theories, effects, and analyses—in the social–behavioral–organizational sciences shifted rather dramatically around the mid-1980s. Prior to that point in time, *cross level* had a particular meaning (conceptualization) and set of effects, based on testing procedures, that were adopted primarily from numerous physical or hard sciences, including physics, chemistry, biology, evolutionary studies, and computer and systems science (e.g., Gould, 2002; Miller, 1978; Wolfram, 2002; Yammarino & Dansereau, 2011). This older, established view is called *traditional* here, and it has had fairly widespread use in the social–behavioral–organizational sciences and continues today as one approach to cross-level theory building and theory testing (e.g., Behling, 1978; Chan, 1998; Dansereau, Alutto, & Yammarino, 1984; Dansereau, Cho, & Yammarino, 2006; Dansereau, Yammarino, & Kohles, 1999; Gould, 2002; Klein, Dansereau, & Hall, 1994; Miller, 1978; Mossholder & Bedeian, 1983; Roberts, Hulin, & Rousseau, 1978; Robinson, 1950; Thorndike, 1939; Wolfram, 2002; Yammarino, 1998, 2003; Yammarino & Dansereau, 2009, 2011).

We thank Fred Dansereau, James LeBreton, and Stephen Humphrey for helpful comments on earlier versions of this chapter and also thank Courtney Williams for formatting and checking help.
http://dx.doi.org/10.1037/0000115-025
The Handbook of Multilevel Theory, Measurement, and Analysis, S. E. Humphrey and J. M. LeBreton (Editors-in-Chief)

From about the mid-1980s on, however, another view of *cross level* became popular based primarily on more current work in the social–behavioral or soft sciences, including organizational sciences, education, sociology, political science, and to some extent economics; it used a different meaning (conceptualization) and consequently set about testing a different set of effects using a different set of testing procedures (e.g., Antonakis, Bendahan, Jacquart, & Lalive, 2010; Bollen & Brand, 2010; Bryk & Raudenbush, 1992; Gelman & Hill, 2007; Goldstein, 1987; Raudenbush & Bryk, 2002; Rousseau, 1985; Snijders & Bosker, 1999). This newer view is called *contemporary* here, and it has widespread use today in the social–behavioral–organizational sciences (e.g., Aguinis, Gottfredson, & Culpepper, 2013; Bliese, Chan, & Ployhart, 2007; Bryk & Raudenbush, 1992; Chen, Bliese, & Mathieu, 2005; Chen, Mathieu, & Bliese, 2004a, 2004b; Mathieu & Chen, 2011; Raudenbush & Bryk, 2002; Raudenbush, Bryk, Cheong, Congdon, & du Toit, 2004; Rousseau, 1985).

In a simple terminology sense, the traditional cross-level view treats associations among constructs that hold at more than one level as a cross-level effect. Traditional views of cross-level effects indicate that X and Y have the same relationship across different levels, such as individuals, groups, and organizations. For example, the work effort (X) put forth by an employee, teacher, or athlete can be positively related to performance (Y) at the individual level. This association is also plausible at multiple higher levels, such as at the dyad (e.g., both partners or an employee and supervisor exert higher effort, leading to better dyadic performance), group (e.g., team effort is associated with team performance), and organization (e.g., organizational effort or productivity is associated with organizational performance) levels.

In the contemporary cross-level view, unlike the traditional cross-level view, the term *cross level* is used to refer to the impact of a higher- (or lower-) level construct on a lower- (or higher-) level construct or relationship. Contemporary views of cross-level effects focus on directional effects (up or down) between X and Y (e.g., individual X impacts group Y; group X impacts individual Y). Continuing

the example above, cross-level effects of effort (X) on performance (Y) in the contemporary view could manifest as the cross-level effect of team effort on individual performance, or individual effort on team and organization performance. Also of note, in the contemporary view, the terms *multilevel* and *homologous* have been used at times to refer to an association between constructs within the same level that also holds between similar constructs at (or transfers across) multiple levels of analysis.

As such, traditional views of cross-level effects can be viewed as equivalent to contemporary views of multilevel or homologous effects. However, the specific conceptualization and testing of these traditional and contemporary cross-level views are more nuanced and complex than simple differences in terminology. As a consequence of these different cross-level views, confusion persists for researchers who may use one or the other view without fully understanding the nuances and differences between the two approaches (see, e.g., Chen et al., 2004a, 2004b, 2005, compared with Dansereau & Yammarino, 2000, 2004, and Yammarino & Dansereau, 2009, 2011).

Our primary ideas on the conceptualization and testing issues involved for these different traditional and contemporary views of cross-level models are summarized in Figure 24.1 and elaborated in Table 24.1. It is important to note that, given space limitations, we will not address issues of construct emergence per se from traditional or contemporary perspectives, which have been well covered elsewhere (see Dansereau et al., 1984, 1999; Fulmer & Ostroff, 2016; Klein & Kozlowski, 2000; Kozlowski, Chao, Grand, Braun, & Kuljanin, 2013; Morgeson & Hofmann, 1999; Yammarino & Dansereau, 2009, 2011). Likewise, although there are some subtle and nuanced differences across disciplines in the contemporary perspective with regard to random and fixed effects models (for extended discussions, see Antonakis et al., 2010; Gelman & Hill, 2007), there is a general use of the term *random coefficient models* (RCM) for testing in the contemporary perspective, which is used here. Hopefully, through the development of the conceptual and testing similarities and differences

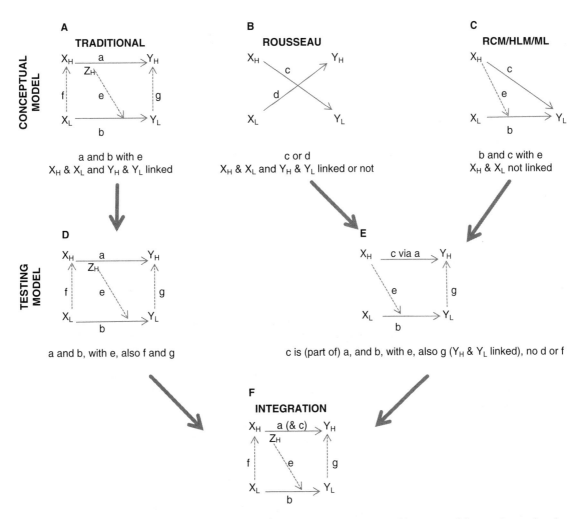

FIGURE 24.1. Cross-level models. H = higher level; HLM = hierarchical linear models; L = lower level; ML = multilevel models; RCM = random coefficient models.

between the traditional and contemporary cross-level approaches and their eventual combination here, we are able to clarify these issues in a way that improves future integrative cross-level theory building and theory testing.

Before detailing each cross-level view, a few points about Figure 24.1 may be helpful. The figure is divided into panels on the basis of conceptual models (i.e., types of models involving levels that are formulated based on theory) and testing models (i.e., variance and covariance decomposition and partitioning based on levels to empirically test the conceptual models) for the traditional and contemporary cross-level approaches. The conceptual (Figure 24.1a) and testing (Figure 24.1d) models for the traditional cross-level view are on the left side of the figure (also see "Traditional" column of

Table 24.1). For the contemporary cross-level view, there are two conceptual models, called "Rousseau" (Figure 24.1b) and "RCM/HLM/ML" (Figure 24.1c; where RCM is random coefficient models, HLM is hierarchical linear models, and ML is multilevel models), that essentially share a common testing model (Figure 24.1e), all shown on the right side of the figure (also see the "Contemporary" column of Table 24.1). The traditional and contemporary cross-level views are then merged to an integrative conceptual and testing cross-level view, called "Integration" (Figure 24.1f), at the bottom of the figure.

Also in Figure 24.1, two general levels of analysis are represented. The levels are simply referred to as higher (H) and lower (L) levels, as the actual levels involved could be any entities of interest such as

TABLE 24.1

Cross-Level Views

	Cross-level view	
Issue	Traditional (e.g., WABA)	Contemporary (e.g., RCM/HLM)
Aligned terms	Homology (theory) and ecological (data) views, isomorphism, composition models, cross-level effects	Multilevel models, random coefficient models, hierarchical linear and cross-classified models, cross-level models
Basic notions	$X_L \rightarrow Y_L$ and $X_H \rightarrow Y_H$	$X_L \rightarrow Y_H$ or $X_H \rightarrow Y_L$
	Relationships among variables hold at multiple (lower and higher) levels of analysis	Relationships of higher level variables with lower level variables
	Also:	Also:
	$X_L \rightarrow X_H$ and $Y_L \rightarrow Y_H$	$X_H \rightarrow [X_L \rightarrow Y_L]$
	$Z_H \rightarrow [X_L \rightarrow Y_L]$	
Key question	At what levels do variables and relationships operate?	Do higher- and individual-level variables affect individual-level outcomes?
Entities in models	Three choices: (a) homogeneity or wholes, (b) heterogeneity or parts, or (c) independent—test (after assertion) whether individual, within-unit, or between-unit level; also cross-level wholes, cross-level parts, or none	Two choices: (a) homogeneity or wholes or (b) independent—rely on theory (and justify with aggregation procedures) whether individual or unit level; also cross-level effects (wholes) or none
Unique and nonunique lower level entities	Unique and nonunique entities (e.g., independent and dependent dyads, respectively) can be analyzed	Unique entities (e.g., independent dyads) can be analyzed; CCM procedures for nonunique entities (e.g., dependent dyads)
Levels of analysis of variables	Tests (after assertion based on theory) whether individual, within-unit, or between-unit level	Rely on theory and justify with aggregation procedures whether individual or higher levels
Dependent variables	Any level	Individual level (Level 1)
Independent variables	Same level as dependent variable	Individual and higher levels (Level 1 and above)
Moderator and mediator variables	Same level as dependent variable and higher levels	Individual and higher levels
Longitudinal issues	Do levels of analysis change over time? Repeated measures study of any entities (tests for stability or change)	Do variables change over time for individuals? Repeated measures study of individuals (time as Level 1 for nonindependent data)
Basis of analysis	Tests of practical and statistical significance (ANOVA or correlation, regression approach)	Inferential statistical significance tests (e.g., maximum likelihood, algorithms)
Inferences for higher- and cross-level effects	More conservative than contemporary (RCM/HLM) view	More liberal than traditional (WABA) view

Note. ANOVA = analysis of variance; CCM = cross-classified models; H = higher level; HLM = hierarchical linear modeling; L = lower level; RCM = random coefficient modeling; WABA = within and between analysis.

individuals (persons), dyads (two-person groups), groups (teams), or collectives (e.g., functional areas, organizations, systems). To keep things simple, we focus on three variables, X (independent), Y (dependent), and Z (moderator), which again can be anything of interest and which are relevant at the higher and lower levels of analysis. For example, effort (X) and performance (Y) are standard variables that appear in multiple domains such as psychology, organizational sciences, education,

medicine, engineering, and sports. A moderator variable that can affect the direction and strength of effort–performance linkage could be, for instance, external resources (Z) such as support, opportunities, training, budgets, and extrinsic motivators. The lines that link the various variables and levels, Lines a to g, simply indicate linkages that can be bidirectional (covariance or correlation) or unidirectional (causal). (This notion also applies to the expressions below and in Table 24.1.) Solid

Lines a to d represent direct relationships, dashed Line e represents moderated relationships, and dashed Lines f and g represent linkages between the same variable at lower and higher levels. (The heavier lines between sections or panels in the figure simply indicate transitions from conceptual to testing to integration models.) These various relationships and linkages are detailed below for the traditional and contemporary cross-level views.

TRADITIONAL CROSS-LEVEL VIEW

Conceptual Model

The traditional cross-level conceptual model (Figure 24.1a and several rows of the "Traditional" column of Table 24.1) is usually expressed in terms of "homology" (for theory and conceptualization) or "ecological" (for data and testing), but also as "isomorphism" (more so in terms of theory and conceptualization) and "composition" models (more so in terms of data and testing). Behling (1978), Miller (1978), Mossholder and Bedeian (1983), and Dansereau et al. (1984), as well as early work by Robinson (1950), Thorndike (1939), and Roberts et al. (1978), either directly or indirectly discussed, implied, or used these terms and aligned them with the notion of *cross level*. This is the traditional use of the term in the physical sciences as well (see Gould, 2002; Miller, 1978; Wolfram, 2002; Yammarino & Dansereau, 2011); in this case, cross-level inference was often used as synonymous with ecological inference (see Behling, 1978; Dansereau et al., 1984, 2006; Mossholder & Bedeian, 1983; Roberts et al., 1978; Robinson, 1950; Thorndike, 1939). Many of these same scholars also conceptually discussed aggregation and disaggregation, homology and composition theories, and ecological inference and fallacies of the wrong level.

In particular, the meaning of *cross level* in these traditional approaches can be expressed as $X_L \rightarrow Y_L$ *and* $X_H \rightarrow Y_H$, which indicates that the X–Y relationship at the higher (indicated by the H subscript) and lower (indicated by the L subscript) levels (Lines a and b, respectively, in Figure 24.1a) hold and occur together (i.e., are both significant, though the values may not be identical). As such, the relationships among variables X and Y hold at multiple (higher and lower) levels simultaneously, and this constitutes

a cross-level effect in the traditional cross-level view. A classic example of this type of cross-level conceptualization is Einstein's equation $E = mc^2$ (where E is energy, m is mass, and c is speed of light), which holds at multiple levels of analysis (e.g., atomic for nuclear reactions, molecular for chemical reactions, and universe for planets and stars). Similarly, effort (X) can lead to (or be associated with) performance (Y) at the individual, dyad, group (team), and organization levels. Very simply, the form and association of effort and performance can be viewed as traversing levels, and their association remains positively related at each level.

Several of the previously cited scholars also dealt directly with isomorphism and composition (also see Chan's, 1998, work on additive, direct consensus, referent-shift consensus, and process composition models and Klein & Kozlowski's, 2000, framework on emergence). These can be expressed as $X_L \rightarrow X_H$ *and* $Y_L \rightarrow Y_H$, which indicates that there is a connection between X at lower and higher levels and between Y at lower and higher levels. In other words, Lines f and g, respectively (Figure 24.1a), are important elements of traditional cross-level views as the higher- and lower level connections for these variables then contribute to the higher and lower X–Y relationships (Lines a and b).

Traditional cross-level views also include cross-level moderator models and effects expressed as $Z_H \rightarrow [X_L \rightarrow Y_L]$, which indicates that Z at a higher level moderates the X–Y relationship at a lower level. In other words, Line e in Figure 24.1a constitutes the cross-level moderator effect in the traditional cross-level view. Ideally, Z is independent of both X and Y and occurs at a higher level (see Dansereau et al., 1984, 2006; Yammarino, 1998), but there are other possibilities (e.g., Z occurring at the same level as X and Y; see Schriesheim, 1995; Yammarino, 1998). For example, the external resources (Z) available to individuals might be independent of individuals' effort and moderate their effort–performance linkage, such that in contexts where individuals have easy access to resources, their effort–performance association is stronger. Academics, for instance, who have access to external resources such as funding, trained doctoral students, and software might be more apt to translate their effort into research productivity (i.e., performance). Similarly, in classroom settings, when teachers have access to school supplies, teaching assistants, and smaller class sizes, their effort might more readily impact their classroom performance.

Extending beyond two levels of analysis, Figure 24.2 shows traditional cross-level effects and cross-level moderator effects models for both three and four levels of analysis. For variables X and Y, in the three-level case, individual (e.g., students), group (e.g., classrooms), and collective (e.g., schools) levels are illustrated along with Z at the collective and group levels; in the four-level case, individual (e.g., students), dyad (e.g., student–teacher pairs), group (e.g., classrooms), and collective (e.g., schools) levels are illustrated along with Z at the collective, group, and dyad levels. Also shown in Figure 24.2 is one way to specify and test these traditional cross-level models and composition procedures via within and between analysis (WABA; e.g., Dansereau et al., 1984; Dansereau & Yammarino, 2000; Yammarino, 1998;

Yammarino & Markham, 1992) for the various levels (detailed below).

Testing Model: WABA Basics

The traditional cross-level testing model is shown in Figure 24.1d and several rows of the "Traditional" column of Table 24.1. There are a lot of ways to test such models, but in the social–behavioral–organizational sciences, one way is WABA. To test Line b, the total correlation (between lower level X and Y) is equal to the between component (of higher level X and Y) plus the within component (of higher level X and Y), as follows:

$$r_{xyl} = \eta_{bxh}\eta_{byh}r_{bxyh} + \eta_{wxh}\eta_{wyh}r_{wxyh}, \qquad (24.1)$$

where η_{bxh} and η_{byh} are the between etas (square root of eta squared from the analysis of variance [ANOVA]) for x and y for the higher level, η_{wxh} and η_{wyh} are the within etas (square root of one minus eta squared from the ANOVA) for x and y for the higher level, r_{bxyh} and r_{wxyh} are the between-cell correlation

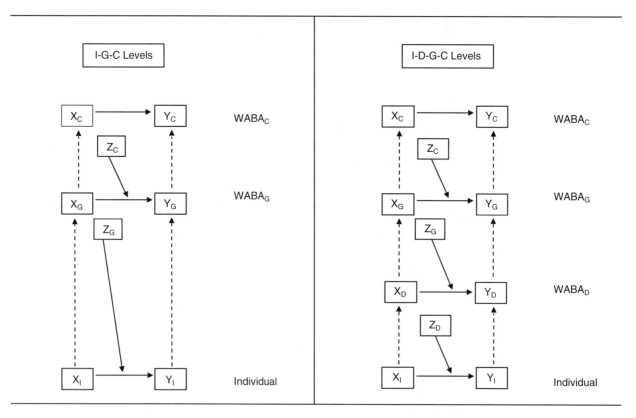

FIGURE 24.2. Within and between analysis (WABA) models: Type of traditional cross-level model for individual (I), dyad (D), group (G), and collective (C) levels.

(based on group means correlating the aggregated x and y scores or x_h and y_h) and within-cell correlation (or pooled within-groups correlation based on correlating the within-cell deviation scores for x and y from their cell mean scores or $x_i - x_h$ and $y_i - y_h$) between x and y for the higher level, and r_{xyl} is the raw score (total) correlation between x and y (the original raw scores) for the lower level. In Equation 24.1, r_{xy} technically and statistically occurs at the lower level and is partitioned into the other terms (within and between cells) that occur at the higher level (for a proof, see Dansereau et al., 1984). This partitioning process is then repeated for Line a, and if both effects represented by Lines a and b (Figure 24.1d) are evidenced (i.e., passed full testing procedures described below), then the inference is a cross-level effect.

In WABA, to draw inferences, a series of tests of practical and statistical significance are used. In addition to traditional F, Z, and t tests of the statistical significance of these various correlations and the relationships among the correlations, there are also unique tests of practical significance, or the magnitude of effects, called E, A, and R tests, based in coordinate-free geometry (not dependent on degrees of freedom). Moreover, just as one might set p value criteria such as $p < .05$ and $p < .01$ or report exact p values, in these later tests one can use 15° and 30° angle criteria or report exact angle values to draw inferences (for detailed explanation and justification, see Dansereau et al., 1984).

First, analogous to the F test of between and within etas, there is an E test of them:

$$E = \eta_{bxh}/\eta_{wxh} = cos\theta_{tbh}/cos\theta_{twh} = cot\theta_{tbh}$$
$$= sine\theta_{twh}/sine\theta_{tbh}, \quad (24.2)$$

where the etas are defined as above, and because correlations are equal to cosines of angles ($r_{xy} = cos\theta_{xy}$, where θ is the angle of the associated x and y vectors), the cosines ($cos\theta$), cotangents ($cot\theta$), and sines ($sine\theta$) of the various associated angles constitute the tests (for proofs and details, see Dansereau et al., 1984). The E test also equals Cohen's (1988) f effect size indicator (for a proof, see Dansereau & Yammarino, 2000).

Second, analogous to the Z test of independent between- and within-cell correlations, there is an A test of the difference between them:

$$A = \theta_{wxyh} - \theta_{bxyh} = cos^{-1}|r_{wxyh}| - cos^{-1}|r_{bxyh}|, \quad (24.3)$$

where the correlations and associated angles are as defined above. Here, the difference in inverse cosines is computed based on the absolute values of the pooled within-cells correlation and the between-cells correlation (for a detailed interpretation and inference drawing procedures, see Dansereau et al., 1984).

Third, analogous to the t tests of the within- and between-cell correlations separately, there are R tests of them:

$$R_{bxyh} = r_{bxyh}/\left(1 - r_{bxyh}^2\right)^{\frac{1}{2}} = cot\theta_{bxyh}$$
$$= cos\theta_{bxyh}/\left(1 - cos^2\theta_{bxyh}\right)^{\frac{1}{2}} \text{ and} \quad (24.4)$$

$$R_{wxyh} = r_{wxyh}/\left(1 - r_{wxyh}^2\right)^{\frac{1}{2}} = cot\theta_{wxyh}$$
$$= cos\theta_{wxyh}/\left(1 - cos^2\theta_{wxyh}\right)^{\frac{1}{2}}, \quad (24.5)$$

where the correlations, both between cells and within cells, as well as their associated angles, cotangents, and cosines, are as defined above (and with one-half power equal to the square root). Again, detailed descriptions, interpretations, and inference-drawing procedures were presented by Dansereau et al. (1984).

To test Line e (Figure 24.1d), the cross-level moderator effect, there are two options in WABA. If the moderator is a categorical variable, then WABA multiple relationship analysis (MRA) for categorical moderators (Dansereau et al., 1984; Yammarino, 1998; Yammarino et al., 2000) can be used. For example, in a simple scenario in which there are two conditions or categories composing the moderator Z, the following equations are used:

$$r_{xyl1} = \eta_{bxh1}\eta_{byh1}r_{bxyh1} + \eta_{wxh1}\eta_{wyh1}r_{wxyh1} \text{ and} \quad (24.6)$$

$$r_{xyl2} = \eta_{bxh2}\eta_{byh2}r_{bxyh2} + \eta_{wxh2}\eta_{wyh2}r_{wxyh2}. \quad (24.7)$$

The terms are as defined above for Equation 24.1, with the addition of the subscripts 1 and 2 denoting conditions Z_1 and Z_2, and the results are tested under each condition or category of Z and then tested against one another (i.e., conditions or categories Z_1 vs. Z_2) using various tests noted above (see Equations 24.2 to 24.5).

If the moderator variable is continuous, then a second option is used to test Line e (Figure 24.1d). In this case, WABA multivariate regression for a continuous moderator, labeled x_2 (with independent variable x_1 and dependent variable y; Schriesheim, 1995; Schriesheim, Castro, & Yammarino, 2000; Yammarino, 1998; Yammarino et al., 2000) is used:

$$r_{x1x2yl} = \eta_{bx1x2h}\eta_{byh}r_{bx1x2yh} + \eta_{wx1x2h}\eta_{wyh}r_{wx1x2yh}, \quad (24.8)$$

where the terms are the multivariate analogues to those in Equation 24.1; η_{bx1x2h} and η_{wx1x2h} are the multivariate between and within etas for the independent-moderator variable (cross-product linear combination) for the higher level; η_{byh} and η_{wyh} are the between and within etas for the dependent variable for the higher level; and $r_{bx1x2yh}$, $r_{wx1x2yh}$, and r_{x1x2yl} are the multivariate analogues for the between-cell, within-cell, and total (raw score) correlations, respectively. The exact computation of all these multivariate analogue terms is rather complex but was fully detailed and demonstrated by Schriesheim (1995). This second (multivariate) option, because it can be used to account for the categorical moderator case as well, is the one used in the sections below.

Likewise, Lines f and g (Figure 24.1d) can be examined using basic WABA aggregation procedures and tests or using the composition approaches presented by Chan (1998), who expanded upon additive, direct consensus, referent-shift consensus, and process composition models. Also relevant for these approaches to testing such effects is the work of LeBreton and Senter (2008).

CONTEMPORARY CROSS-LEVEL VIEW

Conceptual Model

The contemporary cross-level conceptual model (Figures 24.1b and 24.1c and several rows of the "Contemporary" column of Table 24.1) is expressed in terms of the work of Rousseau (1985) and RCM/HLM/ML views. Although nuanced differences exist in the RCM/HLM/ML world (see Antonakis et al., 2010; Gelman & Hill, 2007; Snijders & Bosker,

1999), these views have much in common with one another and with Rousseau's approach.

Beginning in the early to mid-1980s and then continuing to the present, Rousseau (1985), Bryk and Raudenbush (1992), and Goldstein (1987), among others (also see details in Gelman & Hill, 2007; Snijders & Bosker, 1999), altered the traditional meaning, testing, and use of the term *cross level*. In particular, *cross level* evolved to mean the expression $X_L \rightarrow Y_H$ or $X_H \rightarrow Y_L$, which indicates that lower level X and higher level Y are related or that higher level X and lower level Y are related. These two possibilities are generally not considered as occurring together or simultaneously; the focus is typically on one or the other. These are relationships of higher level variables with lower level variables and are shown for "Rousseau" in Figure 24.1b as Line d (X at lower level with Y at higher level) and Line c (X at higher level with Y at lower level). The latter (Line c) is still in vogue, but the former (Line d), although asserted as a conceptual possibility by Rousseau (1985), among others, has generally disappeared from the literature primarily because of testing issues associated with the RCM/HLM techniques (see below).

Line c (Figures 24.1b and 24.1c) constitutes the cross-level direct effect in the contemporary cross-level view. For the multilevel modeling view via RCM/HLM/ML, this is where Level 2 (e.g., group) entities impact Level 1 (e.g., individuals) entities and relationships. For example, Line c could illustrate that team effort (X_H) would facilitate individual performance (Y_L), a scenario often seen in sports teams. Note that the RCM/HLM/ML conceptualization in Figure 24.1c is limited to Line c because, in this view, the dependent variable (Y) must be at the lower level only. Clearly, other approaches in the contemporary view allow for Line d (Figure 24.1d) with the dependent variable (Y) at the higher level but do so with known testing limitations (noted below). For example, individual effort (X_L) facilitates team performance (Y_H) and is conceptually sound (Line d), yet this association has received far less attention because of testing complexities.

The contemporary cross-level view also includes cross-level moderator models (see Bryk & Raudenbush, 1992; Gelman & Hill, 2007; Goldstein,

1987; Raudenbush & Bryk, 2002), expressed as $X_H \to [X_L \to Y_L]$, which indicates that X at a higher level impacts (moderates) the X–Y relationship at a lower level. Line e (Figure 24.1c) constitutes the cross-level moderator effect in the contemporary cross-level view. Note that this contemporary cross-level moderator conceptualization involving X_H can be viewed as a special case of the traditional cross-level moderator conceptualization involving Z_H and shown as Line e in Figure 24.1a.

In the contemporary case, however, a variety of assumptions are made about higher level X (e.g., higher level effects are assumed to impact lower level relationships), which may be a grouping variable (i.e., not linked via isomorphism or composition) or, as an alternative, some assumed aggregate of lower level X (see Bryk & Raudenbush, 1992; Gelman & Hill, 2007; Goldstein, 1987; Raudenbush & Bryk, 2002; Snijders & Bosker, 1999). For example, team effort (X_H) could strengthen or weaken (depending on whether it is high or low) the positive association between individual effort (X_L) and performance (Y_L) in, for instance, classrooms, sports teams, and surgical units.

Unlike traditional cross-level models, no assumption of isomorphism exists in contemporary cross-level approaches. As such, the lower level variables could manifest via compositional or compilational processes at higher levels, and the association of X_L and Y_L could change. (Other moderator variables in the contemporary cross-level approach, different from X_H, would operate in a similar manner as the moderator Z_H in the traditional cross-level approach, as described above and thus not repeated here; for example, resource availability [or constraints] could strengthen [or dampen] the positive association between individual effort and performance.)

Extending beyond two levels of analysis, Figure 24.3 shows contemporary cross-level effects and cross-level moderator effects models for both three and four levels of analysis. For variables X and Y, in the three-level case,

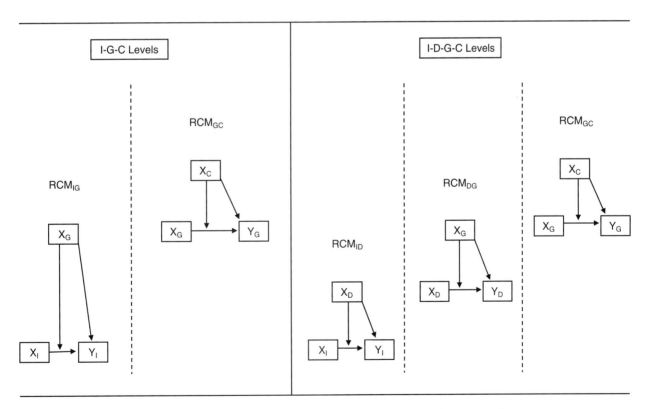

FIGURE 24.3. Random coefficient models (RCM) and hierarchical linear modeling: Type of contemporary cross-level model for individual (I), dyad (D), group (G), and collective (C) levels.

individual (e.g., students), group (e.g., classrooms), and collective (e.g., schools) levels are illustrated; in the four-level case, individual(e.g., students), dyad (e.g., student–teacher pairs), group (e.g., classrooms), and collective (e.g., schools) levels are illustrated. In these cases, X is shown as a grouping variable at higher levels. Also shown in Figure 24.3 is one way to specify and test these contemporary cross-level models via RCM (e.g., Bryk & Raudenbush, 1992; Gelman & Hill, 2007; Goldstein, 1987; Raudenbush & Bryk, 2002; Snijders & Bosker, 1999) for the various levels (detailed below).

Tentative Testing Model: RCM/HLM Basics

The contemporary cross-level testing model is shown in Figure 24.1e and several rows of the "Contemporary" column of Table 24.1. There are a number of ways to specify and test these models, but in social–behavioral–organizational sciences, one of the most commonly used techniques involves random coefficient (regression) modeling via hierarchical linear modeling, as well as R code (R Foundation for Statistical Computing, Vienna, Austria) and Stata (StataCorp, College Station, TX), among others. Before discussing the actual testing model below, in which Line c shifts to mimic Line a (as shown in Figure 24.1 with a Figure 24.1c to Figure 24.1e shift and also in Figure 24.1f), consider the tentative testing model that is routinely used in the literature. Focusing on Figures 24.1c and 24.1e, Lines b and c are being tested, along with Line e. Line d (Figure 24.1b), although conceptually viable and tested in early research, is typically no longer tested (as such, not shown in Figure 24.1e) because (a) it creates dependencies in the data (caused by distributing higher level scores [e.g., means] back to lower level entities) that lead to bias, problematic standard errors, erroneous indicators, statistical artifacts, and so forth and (b) the dependent variable must be only at the lower (e.g., individual) level (Level 1) in RCM/HLM models.

In this approach, for a general model (where Y = lower level dependent variable, X = lower level independent variable, and H = higher level

independent variable, which can be X_H or Z_H using the terms from above and as shown in Figures 24.1d and 24.1e), the within-unit effect, Line b (Figure 24.1e), is

$$\text{Level 1 } Y_{ij} = \beta_{0j} + \beta_{1j} X_{ij} + r_{ij}, \quad (24.9)$$

where β_{0j} is the unique (Level 1) intercept for Group j and β_{1j} is the unique (Level 1) slope for Group j. The cross-level main (direct) effect, or intercept-as-outcome, Line c, is

$$\text{Level 2 } \beta_{0j} = \gamma_{00} + \gamma_{01} H_j + U_{0j}, \quad (24.10)$$

where γ_{00} is the fixed or common (Level 2) intercept and γ_{01} is the fixed or common (Level 2) slope. The cross-level moderator effect, or slope-as-outcome, Line e, is

$$\text{Level 2 } \beta_{1j} = \gamma_{10} + \gamma_{11} H_j + U_{1j}, \quad (24.11)$$

where γ_{10} is the Level 2 intercept and γ_{11} is the Level 2 slope. Although this two-level model is frequently presented using separate equations for each level, it may also be represented using a mixed equation that substitutes Equations 24.10 and 24.11 into Equation 24.9:

$$Y_{ij} = \gamma_{00} + \gamma_{10} X_{ij} + \gamma_{01} H_j + \gamma_{11} X_{ij} H_j + U_{0j} + U_{1j} X_{ij} + r_{ij}, \quad (24.12)$$

where the terms are as defined above.

In addition, relevant for the contemporary cross-level model equations above, the within-unit variance, or Level 1 residual variance, is $\text{Var}(r_{ij})$ or σ^2. The between-unit variance, or Level 2 residual variance in intercepts, is $\text{Var}(U_{0j})$ or τ_{00}. The Level 2 residual variance in slopes is $\text{Var}(U_{1j})$. The variance of Y, intraclass correlation (ICC), and reliability that apply to the testing models are as follows (for details and interpretations, see Raudenbush & Bryk, 2002):

$$\text{Var}(Y) = \text{Var}(U_{0j} + r_{ij}) = \tau_{00} + \sigma^2, \quad (24.13)$$

$$\text{ICC} = \tau_{00} / (\tau_{00} + \sigma^2), \text{ and} \quad (24.14)$$

$$\text{Reliability} = \tau_{00} / (\tau_{00} + \sigma^2 / n_j), \quad (24.15)$$

where the terms are as defined above.

INTEGRATIVE CROSS-LEVEL VIEW

Differences and Similarities Between the Two Cross-Level Views

Given the two different views of cross-level models, traditional and contemporary, it is not surprising that confusion and sometimes controversy regarding cross-level models in terms of both conceptualization and testing resulted. For example, Chen et al. (2004a, 2004b, 2005) used the contemporary view of cross-level models, including a basic RCM/HLM approach, whereas Dansereau and Yammarino (2000, 2004) and Yammarino and Dansereau (2009, 2011) used the traditional cross-level view, including a WABA approach. These differing views resulted in a bit of a debate (also see Dansereau et al., 2006). Having clarified the key aspects and differences between these views, however, we can now begin to integrate them by highlighting some further similarities and differences between the traditional WABA–composition cross-level view and the contemporary RCM/HLM/ML cross-level view (see also Gooty & Yammarino, 2011; Yammarino & Gooty, 2017). This approach illustrates the potentially complementary nature of the two views, which address somewhat different issues and answer somewhat different questions, and offers the opportunity for integration.

The various similarities and differences among the characteristics of these traditional and contemporary cross-level views are shown in Table 24.1. In particular, as noted previously, the two cross-level views arise from different disciplinary and statistical traditions that are designed to test different types of cross-level questions. WABA, a type of traditional cross-level view, arises out of the hard or physical sciences and was implemented in the organization sciences, in which the focus is individual, dyad, group, and collective (e.g., organizational) behaviors. A key question in this case is whether variables and relationships operate at lower or higher levels of analysis or both. This approach relies on tests, after assertions based on theory, of whether various single-level and cross-level effects are relevant. For example, each variable, effort (X), performance (Y), and external resources (Z), could be tested empirically

for the level or levels at which they actually operate, despite theory asserting, for instance, that they reside at the individual level. In addition, the various associations among these variables— say, the effort–performance association—might manifest at some levels (e.g., individual and group) and not others (e.g., dyad) in a specific context or setting.

RCM, a type of contemporary cross-level view, arose out of and was implemented in the soft or behavioral sciences as well as educational research, a key basis of much multilevel work, where the focus is individual student achievement and performance. A key question in this case is whether higher- and individual-level variables affect individual-level outcomes. This approach relies on theory and empirical justification with aggregation procedures for individual or higher levels. Aggregation indices then might support or restrict the manifestation and use of constructs at higher levels, but note that this contemporary cross-level approach does not test whether, for example, the linkage between effort (X) and performance (Y) operates at each level, as does the traditional cross-level approach.

In the WABA cross-level view, there are three plausible views of entities: (a) homogeneity or wholes (e.g., whole groups in which members are the same or similar on elements or variables of interest and there are differences between groups), (b) heterogeneity or parts (e.g., group parts in which there is a relative positioning of, or dissimilarity among, members on elements or variables of interest within the groups), and (c) independent or none (e.g., groups are irrelevant, yet individuals may show differences on the elements or variables of interest). In this case, after identifying that entities (e.g., groups) are present, then one must decide or ask whether the entity partners (e.g., group members) are similar (wholes) versus dissimilar (parts) to one another. When considered at both higher and lower levels for relationships among variables (i.e., Lines a and b in Figures 24.1a, 24.1d, and 24.1f), this permits three plausible cross-level cases: The first case, cross-level wholes, refers to the situation in which Lines a and b are both based on whole entities (e.g., whole collectives and whole groups). The second case, cross-level parts, refers to the situation in which Line b is based on whole entities (e.g., whole groups) and Line a is based on entity parts (e.g., collective parts). Finally, the third case, none or no cross-level effects, exists when the relationships represented by Lines a and b are each based on independent entities (e.g., individuals and not groups or collectives). For additional details, interested readers are directed to Dansereau et al. (1984), Yammarino (1998), and Yammarino and Dansereau (2009).

In contrast, when considering the entities of focus in the RCM cross-level view, there are two plausible views: (a) homogeneity or wholes and (b) independent or none. Essentially, there are or are not focal entities (e.g., groups) present. In this case, when considered at both higher and lower levels for relationships among variables (i.e., Lines b and c in Figures 24.1c and 24.1e), this permits two plausible cross-level cases: The first is cross-level wholes in which Lines b and c (actually tested via Line a; see below) are based on whole entities; the second is none or no cross-level effects in which Lines b and c (actually tested via Line a; see below) are based on independent entities (e.g., individuals).

Both traditional and contemporary cross-level views are equipped to handle independent (unique) and dependent (nonunique) entities. Whereas traditional cross-level views such as WABA have always focused on both dependent and independent entities, contemporary cross-level views such as RCM/HLM were initially focused more on lower level entities uniquely nested within higher level entities, but they now also deal with nonunique higher level membership such as RCM by cross-classification (i.e., cross-classified models [CCM] via, for example, hierarchical cross-classified modeling [HCM]; see Gooty & Yammarino, 2011, 2016).

In terms of different types of variables, in traditional cross-level views such as WABA, dependent variables can operate at any level, independent variables operate at the same level as the dependent variable or higher levels, and mediator and moderator variables operate at the same level as the dependent variable or higher levels. In contrast, in contemporary cross-level views such as RCM/HLM, dependent variables operate at the individual level (i.e., Level 1), independent variables operate

at the individual or higher levels, and mediator and moderator variables operate at the individual or higher levels.

Another important cross-level issue is the theoretical specification and empirical test of potentially changing variables and shifting levels of analysis (entities such as individuals, groups, and collectives) over time (see Dansereau et al., 1999; Yammarino & Dansereau, 2011). Although much has been written about changing variables or constructs over time and strategies for analyzing these changes (e.g., Chan, 1998; Gelman & Hill, 2007; Raudenbush et al., 2004), relatively little has been written about changing entities (levels of analysis) over time (for exceptions, see Dansereau et al., 1984, 1999; Yammarino & Dansereau, 2009, 2011). A detailed discussion of these issues is beyond the scope here; suffice it to say that the traditional cross-level view has a more comprehensive and nuanced view of levels over time and the stability or change of these entities from a longitudinal perspective (e.g., Dansereau et al., 1999, dealt with a 16-cell matrix of possibilities; Gould, 2002, and Wolfram, 2002, dealt with numerous additional possibilities) than the contemporary cross-level view (e.g., Klein & Kozlowski, 2000, and Kozlowski et al., 2013, dealt with compilation and composition possibilities).

For data analysis, WABA, a type of traditional cross-level view, relies on tests of both statistical and practical significance, in which the latter tests, focused on effect sizes, are not dependent on degrees of freedom and are based in coordinate-free geometry, and WABA uses ANOVA and correlation or regression approaches. Likewise, for data analysis, RCM/HLM relies on inferential statistical significance tests using maximum likelihood and other algorithms and can include effect sizes. Using the various tests and criteria in these different cross-level views, traditional cross-level views (e.g., WABA) are typically more conservative (often involving more test criteria, both statistical and practical or magnitude based, and ruling out more alternative explanations such as three entity choices at more than one level of analysis; see Table 24.1) than contemporary cross-level views (e.g., RCM/HLM) when inferring higher level and cross-level effects. Our guess is that this less liberal approach is a result of the view in the hard or physical sciences that (traditional) cross-level effects are the most powerful in nature and the physical world, even more powerful than emergent effects (see Gould, 2002; Miller, 1978; Sayama, 2015; Wolfram, 2002; Yammarino & Dansereau, 2011). This is the case because (traditional) cross-level models and effects can explain many more things in much simpler ways (i.e., parsimonious explanations) and, as such, should be inferred only with very compelling evidence using a strong inference approach (see Dansereau et al., 1984; Sayama, 2015; Wolfram, 2002).

Actual Testing Model for Contemporary Cross-Level View

We can now further the integration of the two cross-level views by looking at the actual testing model for the contemporary cross-level view (see Figure 24.1e [note the shifting of Line c to mimic Line a] and the "Contemporary" column of Table 24.1). It is a bit different than the conceptual model, whether the Rousseau version (Figure 24.1b) or the RCM/HLM/M-L one (Figure 24.1c).

Specifically, how is Line c (Figures 24.1c and 24.1e), the contemporary cross-level main (direct) effect, actually tested? Simply, it is tested via Line a (Figures 24.1a and 24.1d), actually a portion of Line a, primarily the between-cell correlation, r_{bxyh}, but more generally the between-cell component, $\eta_{bxh} \eta_{byh} r_{bxyh}$, as defined above and expressed in Equation 24.1 for the traditional cross-level effect. Note that we are not claiming here that contemporary cross-level direct effects are not viable conceptually or even that they are actually not tested at all (for a somewhat alternative view, see LoPilato & Vandenberg, 2015). Empirically, however, the actual test of Line c mimics that of Line a given Equation 24.1. The conceptualization and logic of this view, admittedly nuanced, as well as the underlying statistical manipulations, are well beyond the scope here but have been detailed in various forms by others (see Dansereau et al., 1984, 2006; Gelman & Hill, 2007; Gooty & Yammarino, 2011; LoPilato & Vandenberg, 2015; Sayama, 2015; Snijders & Bosker, 1999; Wolfram, 2002).

In brief, the test or indicator from Equation 24.10 in RCM/HLM is essentially the same as the between-groups correlation from Equation 24.1 in WABA

(i.e., r_{bxy}). As such, this testing procedure in the contemporary cross-level view is a special case of the more comprehensive test in the traditional cross-level view. In terms of Figure 24.1, testing Line c (Figures 24.1c and 24.1e) is essentially the same thing as testing a portion of Line a (Figures 24.1a and 24.1d); moreover, as part of these testing procedures, it is important to justify any aggregation (as noted above) for the variables and relationships involved (i.e., Lines f and g in Figures 24.1d and 24.1e). Overall, this connection between the contemporary and traditional cross-level views means that all the diagonal lines in Figure 24.3, representing the cross-level main (direct) effect in contemporary cross-level models, are actually tested with (a portion of) all the higher level horizontal lines in Figure 24.2, which include the between-cell correlations from the traditional cross-level view.

INTEGRATIVE CROSS-LEVEL MODELS: CONCEPTUALIZATION AND TESTING

Given the above sections, a potential integration of these generally complementary traditional and contemporary cross-level views seems straightforward. As the two views of cross-level models ask and address different questions and issues, they are not incompatible and can be combined and used in a complementary and integrative way. Specifically, an integrative cross-level model combining the traditional and contemporary views for both conceptualization and testing purposes is shown in Figure 24.1f. Using the earlier example, with simply individual and group levels, effort (X) and performance (Y) are positively associated at the individual level, indicated by Line b; this association also manifests at the group level in the form of team-level association of team effort with team performance, indicated by Line a; the cross-level direct effect of team effort on individual performance is indicated by Line c as part of Line a. Line e then represents the cross-level moderating effect of external resources (Z) available at the team level that impacts the individual-level effort–performance relationship. This cross-level moderating effect could also be one of team effort moderating the individual effort–performance linkage. To summarize and generalize,

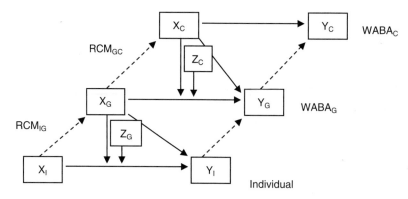

FIGURE 24.4. Integrative cross-level models: Within and between analysis (WABA) and random coefficient models (RCM) at the individual (I)–group (G)–collective (C) levels.

Lines a (with c as part of a), b, e, f, and g identify the integrative cross-level model components—that is, cross-level effect (Lines a and b together), cross-level moderator effect (Line e), and composition effects (Lines f and g). Essentially, the contemporary cross-level view then becomes a special case (based on some assumptions and a clarified testing procedure) of the more general traditional cross-level view.

Extending beyond two levels of analysis, Figures 24.4 and 24.5 show integrative cross-level

effects and cross-level moderator effects models, conceptually and in terms of testing, for both three and four levels of analysis. For variables *X* and *Y*, in the three-level case, individual, group, and collective levels are illustrated along with moderator *Z* at the collective and group levels; in the four-level case, individual, dyad, group, and collective levels are illustrated along with moderator *Z* at the collective, group, and dyad levels. In particular, Figures 24.4 and 24.5 include (a) traditional cross-

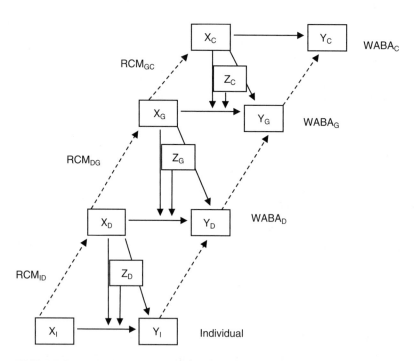

FIGURE 24.5. Integrative cross-level models: Within and between analysis (WABA) and random coefficient models (RCM) at the individual (I)–dyad (D)–group (G)–collective (C) levels.

level models (e.g., WABA approach including cross-level moderator), (b) composition models (e.g., Chan, 1998; LeBreton & Senter, 2008), and (c) contemporary cross-level models (e.g., RCM/ HLM approach including cross-level moderator). Below we provide some specification and testing details (all terms are defined as above) for these various level combinations for the integrative cross-level models. (For additional information and data sets, programming, and analyses involving some of these level combinations for both traditional [WABA] and contemporary [RCM/HLM] cross-level models, interested readers are directed to Gooty & Yammarino, 2011.)

Individual–Group–Collective

An integrative cross-level model for individual, group, and collective levels is shown in Figure 24.4. For individual and group levels (i = individuals, j = groups), the traditional cross-level model with cross-level moderator using the WABA approach is

$$r_{xyi} = \eta_{bxj}\eta_{byj}r_{bxyj} + \eta_{wxj}\eta_{wyj}r_{wxyj} \text{ and} \quad (24.16)$$

$$r_{x1x2yi} = \eta_{bx1x2j}\eta_{byj}r_{bx1x2yj} + \eta_{wx1x2j}\eta_{wyj}r_{wx1x2yj}. \quad (24.17)$$

For these same two levels, the contemporary cross-level model using the RCM/HLM approach is

$$\text{Level 1 } Y_{ij} = \beta_{0j} + \beta_{1j}X_{ij} + r_{ij}, \quad (24.18)$$

$$\text{Level 2 } \beta_{0j} = \gamma_{00} + \gamma_{01}H_j + U_{0j}, \text{ and} \quad (24.19)$$

$$\text{Level 2 } \beta_{1j} = \gamma_{10} + \gamma_{11}H_j + U_{1j}. \quad (24.20)$$

Note that the between-cell correlation from Equation 24.16, r_{bxyj}, can be viewed as testing the same effect as in Equation 24.19 (cross-level direct effect). Moreover, Equations 24.17 and 24.20 can be viewed as testing the same cross-level moderator effect when higher level X (from RCM) is comparable to Z (from WABA). (Also note that, in these cases and those presented below for the RCM approach, one should appropriately center the various indicators; for details and interpretations, see Gooty & Yammarino, 2011; Hofmann & Gavin, 1998; Raudenbush & Bryk, 2002.)

For group and collective levels (j = groups, k = collectives), the traditional cross-level model

with cross-level moderator using the WABA approach is

$$r_{xyj} = \eta_{bxk}\eta_{byk}r_{bxyk} + \eta_{wxk}\eta_{wyk}r_{wxyk} \text{ and} \quad (24.21)$$

$$r_{x1x2yj} = \eta_{bx1x2k}\eta_{byk}r_{bx1x2yk} + \eta_{wx1x2k}\eta_{wyk}r_{wx1x2yk}. \quad (24.22)$$

For these same two levels, the contemporary cross-level model using the RCM/HLM approach is

$$\text{Level 1 } Y_{jk} = \beta_{0k} + \beta_{1k}X_{jk} + r_{jk}, \quad (24.23)$$

$$\text{Level 2 } \beta_{0k} = \gamma_{00} + \gamma_{01}H_k + U_{0k}, \text{ and} \quad (24.24)$$

$$\text{Level 2 } \beta_{1k} = \gamma_{10} + \gamma_{11}H_k + U_{1k}. \quad (24.25)$$

Note that the between-cell correlation from Equation 24.21, r_{bxyk}, can be viewed as testing the same effect as in Equation 24.24 (cross-level direct effect). Moreover, Equations 24.22 and 24.25 can be viewed as testing the same cross-level moderator effect when higher level X (from RCM) is comparable to Z (from WABA).

For individual and collective levels (i = individual, k = collective, with groups not relevant or a focus), the traditional cross-level model with cross-level moderator using the WABA approach is

$$r_{xyi} = \eta_{bxk}\eta_{byk}r_{bxyk} + \eta_{wxk}\eta_{wyk}r_{wxyk} \text{ and} \quad (24.26)$$

$$r_{x1x2yi} = \eta_{bx1x2k}\eta_{byk}r_{bx1x2yk} + \eta_{wx1x2k}\eta_{wyk}r_{wx1x2yk}. \quad (24.27)$$

For these same two levels, the contemporary cross-level model using the RCM/HLM approach is

$$\text{Level 1 } Y_{ik} = \beta_{0k} + \beta_{1k}X_{ik} + r_{ik}, \quad (24.28)$$

$$\text{Level 2 } \beta_{0k} = \gamma_{00} + \gamma_{01}H_k + U_{0k}, \text{ and} \quad (24.29)$$

$$\text{Level 2 } \beta_{1k} = \gamma_{10} + \gamma_{11}H_k + U_{1k}. \quad (24.30)$$

Note that the between-cell correlation from Equation 24.26, r_{bxyk}, can be viewed as testing the same effect as in Equation 24.29 (cross-level direct effect). Moreover, Equations 24.27 and 24.30 can be viewed as testing the same cross-level moderator effect when higher level X (from RCM) is comparable to Z (from WABA).

Relatedly, WABA MRA (Dansereau et al., 1984; Yammarino, 1998; Yammarino et al., 2000) could also be added as options for Equations 24.17, 24.22, and 24.27 for testing cross-level moderator effects with categorical moderators. Also, a three-level RCM/HLM set of equations could be added (see the example in the section below and in Gooty & Yammarino, 2011). In addition, a three-level WABA set of equations could be added in which the between-group correlation from the second level is then used as the raw score correlation (i.e., input) and partitioned at the third level (for details, see Dansereau et al., 1984; Yammarino et al., 2000).

Individual–Dyad–Group–Collective

An integrative cross-level model for individual, dyad, group, and collective levels is shown in Figure 24.5. When the dyad level is involved, for the traditional WABA view, the equations hold for both dependent and independent dyads cases, and for the contemporary RCM/HLM view, the independent dyads case is illustrated first in this section, and the dependent dyads case is then illustrated below (also see Gooty & Yammarino, 2011; Krasikova & LeBreton, 2012; Yammarino & Gooty, 2017).

For individual and dyad levels (i = individuals [both sources; e.g., dating partners or subordinate and supervisor], d = dyads), the traditional cross-level model with cross-level moderator using the WABA approach is

$$r_{xyi} = \eta_{bxd}\eta_{byd}r_{bxyd} + \eta_{wxd}\eta_{wyd}r_{wxyd} \text{ and} \quad (24.31)$$

$$r_{x1x2yi} = \eta_{bx1x2d}\eta_{byd}r_{bx1x2yd} + \eta_{wx1x2d}\eta_{wyd}r_{wx1x2yd}. \quad (24.32)$$

For these same two levels, the contemporary cross-level model using the RCM/HLM approach is

$$\text{Level 1 } Y_{id} = \beta_{0d} + \beta_{1d}X_{id} + r_{id}, \quad (24.33)$$

$$\text{Level 2 } \beta_{0d} = \gamma_{00} + \gamma_{01}H_d + U_{0d}, \text{ and} \quad (24.34)$$

$$\text{Level 2 } \beta_{1d} = \gamma_{10} + \gamma_{11}H_d + U_{1d}. \quad (24.35)$$

Note that the between-cell correlation from Equation 24.31, r_{bxyd}, can be viewed as testing the same effect as in Equation 24.34 (cross-level direct effect). Moreover, Equations 24.32 and 24.35 can be viewed as testing the same cross-

level moderator effect when higher level X (from RCM) is comparable to Z (from WABA). Regarding Equations 24.34 and 24.35, although conceptually feasible and technically correct, these models are impossible to test with RCM/HLM because the lower (individuals) and higher (dyads) levels have the same degrees of freedom. We believe this is one of the reasons the dyad level is rarely studied as a level of analysis in such models. This, however, is not an issue for testing in WABA with Equations 24.31 and 24.32.

For dyad and group levels (d = dyads, j = groups), the traditional cross-level model with cross-level moderator using the WABA approach is

$$r_{xyd} = \eta_{bxj}\eta_{byj}r_{bxyj} + \eta_{wxj}\eta_{wyj}r_{wxyj} \text{ and} \quad (24.36)$$

$$r_{x1x2yd} = \eta_{bx1x2j}\eta_{byj}r_{bx1x2yj} + \eta_{wx1x2j}\eta_{wyj}r_{wx1x2yj}. \quad (24.37)$$

For these same two levels, the contemporary cross-level model using the RCM/HLM approach is

$$\text{Level 1 } Y_{dj} = \beta_{0j} + \beta_{1j}X_{dj} + r_{dj}, \quad (24.38)$$

$$\text{Level 2 } \beta_{0j} = \gamma_{00} + \gamma_{01}H_j + U_{0j}, \text{ and} \quad (24.39)$$

$$\text{Level 2 } \beta_{1j} = \gamma_{10} + \gamma_{11}H_j + U_{1j}. \quad (24.40)$$

Note that the between-cell correlation from Equation 24.36, r_{bxyj}, can be viewed as testing the same effect as in Equation 24.39 (cross-level direct effect). Moreover, Equations 24.37 and 24.40 can be viewed as testing the same cross-level moderator effect when higher level X (from RCM) is comparable to Z (from WABA).

For group and collective levels (j = groups, k = collectives), the traditional cross-level model with cross-level moderator using the WABA approach is

$$r_{xyj} = \eta_{bxk}\eta_{byk}r_{bxyk} + \eta_{wxk}\eta_{wyk}r_{wxyk} \text{ and} \quad (24.41)$$

$$r_{x1x2yj} = \eta_{bx1x2k}\eta_{byk}r_{bx1x2yk} + \eta_{wx1x2k}\eta_{wyk}r_{wx1x2yk}. \quad (24.42)$$

For these same two levels, the contemporary cross-level model using the RCM/HLM approach is

$$\text{Level 1 } Y_{jk} = \beta_{0k} + \beta_{1k}X_{jk} + r_{jk}, \quad (24.43)$$

Level 2 $\beta_{0k} = \gamma_{00} + \gamma_{01}H_k + U_{0k}$, and   (24.44)

Level 2 $\beta_{1k} = \gamma_{10} + \gamma_{11}H_k + U_{1k}$.   (24.45)

Note that the between-cell correlation from Equation 24.41, r_{bxyk}, can be viewed as testing the same effect as in Equation 24.44 (cross-level direct effect). Moreover, Equations 24.42 and 24.45 can be viewed as testing the same cross-level moderator effect when higher level X (from RCM) is comparable to Z (from WABA).

Relatedly, WABA MRA (Dansereau et al., 1984; Yammarino, 1998; Yammarino et al., 2000) could also be added as options for Equations 24.32, 24.37, and 24.42 for testing cross-level moderator effects with categorical moderators. Also, individual and group levels together and individual and collective levels together, for both cross-level views, are plausible (see Equations 24.16–24.20 and 24.26–24.30, respectively). Extensions are also possible for three-level and four-level WABA, including independent (unique) and dependent (nonunique) dyads (see Dansereau et al., 1984; Gooty & Yammarino, 2011; Yammarino et al., 2000). Likewise, extensions are possible for three-level and four-level RCM/HLM (see Bryk & Raudenbush, 1992; Gooty & Yammarino, 2011; Raudenbush & Bryk, 2002; Raudenbush et al., 2004; Snijders & Bosker, 1999), including the dependent dyads case, which requires cross-classified models equations for cross-classification in RCM (e.g., via HCM; see Gooty & Yammarino, 2011).

Although the implementation of all these analyses, including the various partitioning, distribution, and alignment of scores for the analyses, can be complex, extensive details and interpretations are provided in the citations noted above. Nevertheless, to illustrate the latter instances in the contemporary cross-level view using RCM (see Gooty & Yammarino, 2011), for the case of unique nesting (e.g., independent dyads) in a three-level model, the slope and intercept from the Level 1 regressions are modeled as Level 2 outcomes. A typical three-level unconditional model with, for example, individuals (i) nested in dyads (d) nested in groups (j) in RCM/HLM is as follows:

Level 1 : $Y_{idj} = \pi_{0dj} + e_{idj}$,   (24.46)

Level 2 : $\pi_{0dj} = \beta_{00j} + r_{0dj}$, and   (24.47)

Level 3 : $\beta_{00j} = \gamma_{000} + u_{00j}$.   (24.48)

For the nonunique nesting case in which cross-classification is required (e.g., dependent dyads), in a three-level model, individuals (i) are at Level 1, and the dyad (d) and group (j) entities now both occur at Level 2. A typical Level 1 and Level 2 unconditional model with individuals in dyads cross-classified by groups in RCM/CCM via HCM is as follows:

Level 1 : $Y_{idj} = \pi_{0dj} + e_{idj}$ and   (24.49)

Level 2 : $\pi_{0dj} = \theta_o + b_{00d} + c_{00j}$.   (24.50)

In this case, the column or group factor term (c_{00j}) is modeled simultaneously with the row or dyad factor term (b_{00d}), accounting for the dependency between dyads and the group simultaneously.

IMPLICATIONS FOR THEORY BUILDING AND THEORY TESTING

Although there are differences in conceptualization and testing approaches in the traditional and contemporary cross-level model views, there are also enough similarities and commonalities (e.g., some elements in the contemporary cross-level view can be viewed as special cases of more general elements in the traditional cross-level view) that they can be complementary and combined into an integrative cross-level models view. Why is this important? Simply, multiple levels of analysis and cross-level issues are critical in social–behavioral–organizational sciences research because theory and theory building considerations without levels are incomplete; likewise, data and theory testing considerations without levels of analysis are incomprehensible.

Research Questions

To address issues and concerns in this realm, including potential misunderstandings and controversies, we specified the conceptualization and testing procedures that underlie both traditional and contemporary cross-level models. The types of research questions that can be addressed with traditional cross-level approaches are summarized in the "Traditional" column in Table 24.1 and illustrated in Figures 24.1a and 24.1d and in Figure 24.2. These include questions (with some illustrations from the example used throughout) such as the following:

- At what higher and lower levels of analysis do variables operate? (For example, what are the levels of analysis of effort, performance, and external resources?)
- At what higher and lower levels of analysis do relationships among variables operate? (For example, does the association between effort and performance manifest at multiple higher levels, such as the dyad, group, and collective levels?)
- Are particular entities (levels of analysis) operating, and if so, are they operating as whole units or unit parts? (For example, is effort similar within a group and yet there are differences across groups in effort, or do members of each group display dissimilar effort?)
- Are cross-level effects operating, and if so, are they operating as cross-level wholes or cross-level parts? (For example, are the associations between effort and performance operating based on both individual differences and differences between groups, or based on individual differences and group parts in which individuals are dissimilar?)
- Are cross-level (higher and lower level), level-specific (lower but not higher level), or emergent (higher but not lower level) effects operating, and if so, are they operating in terms of whole units or unit parts?
- How can cross-level effects be tested when the dependent variable (e.g., performance) operates at a higher level of analysis?
- Do unique and nonunique nesting of lower level entities (e.g., individuals) affect variables (e.g., effort and performance) and relationships (e.g., effort–performance association) at various levels of analysis (e.g., dyads and groups)?
- Do levels of analysis (and variables) change over time? (For example, when individuals become more uniform in effort or performance over time because of training and homogenous

distribution of resources, do each of these variables then display only whole group-level effects later in time?)

The types of research questions that can be addressed with contemporary cross-level approaches are summarized in the "Contemporary" column in Table 24.1 and illustrated in Figures 24.1b, 24.1c, and 24.1e and in Figure 24.3. These include questions (with some illustrations from the example used throughout) such as the following:

- Do higher level variables, and in what proportion or contribution, affect the dependent variable that operates at a lower or lowest level of analysis? (For example, do team effort and team resources affect individual performance?)
- Are particular entities (levels of analysis) operating or not? (For example, do individual effort and performance manifest at the group or organization levels?)
- Are cross-level main (direct) effects (e.g., team effort to individual performance) operating?
- Are cross-level moderator effects (e.g., team effort moderates the individual effort–performance association) operating?
- Are cross-level (higher level independent variable to lower level dependent variable; e.g., team effort to individual performance) or level-specific (same-level independent to dependent variable; e.g., individual effort to performance) effects operating?
- How can cross-level effects be tested when the dependent variable (e.g., performance) operates at a lower or lowest (e.g., individual) level of analysis?
- Do unique and nonunique nesting of lower level entities (e.g., individuals) affect the dependent variable (e.g., performance) that operates at a lower or lowest level (e.g., individual) of analysis? (For example, is individual performance affected by multiple group memberships creating nonunique nesting?)
- Do variables (e.g., effort and performance) at a lower or lowest (e.g., individual) level of analysis change over time?

We then combined these complementary approaches into an integrative cross-level models view with conceptualization and testing elements. The research questions that can be addressed with the integrative cross-level approach are illustrated in Figure 24.1f and in Figures 24.4 and 24.5. These include questions (with some illustrations from the example used throughout) such as the following:

- All research questions noted above for both the traditional and contemporary cross-level approaches (see all of the previous examples).
- All research questions that involve unique and nonunique nesting of entities (levels of analysis). For example, individuals are routinely part of multiple higher level entities (e.g., different groups or teams). Such designs create challenges theoretically and empirically. Individual effort is positively associated with individual performance, and much of the organizational sciences assumes that individuals are neatly nested within unique higher level teams. The reality, however, of most teams today is that individuals might belong to multiple project teams at a single point in time or switch team memberships across time. How, then, for instance, does the individual effort–performance association change as a function of such multiple team memberships? These types of questions and designs are relatively less studied and are empirically plausible via the integrated conceptualizations and analytical techniques noted here for cross-classification models.
- All research questions that involve comparison or sequential testing between the traditional and contemporary cross-level approaches. For example, researchers could use both WABA and RCM-related aggregation statistics as complementary ways of assessing whether constructs manifest at theoretically specified levels of analyses. Extending this idea, triangulation of findings via both WABA and RCM approaches could provide more robust estimates of how associations among variables operate at multiple levels and manifest (traditional and contemporary) cross-level effects.

Because many, perhaps most, phenomena actually involve multiple levels of analysis and often manifest cross-level effects, whether viewed from traditional or contemporary or integrative perspectives, we offer some thoughts and recommendations to summarize the importance of these issues. In particular, levels of analysis and cross-level models and effects are not simply an analytical or testing issue. Levels of analysis and cross-level considerations begin with theory and conceptualization (i.e., theory building), and then continue with research design and measurement as well as data analysis and inference drawing (i.e., theory testing).

Theory

For theory and conceptualization in cross-level research, we have four recommendations for theory building.

First, define the level of analysis of the unit or units of interest, or, in the language of the traditional approach (and WABA), define the entity or entities to which theoretical generalizations apply. The key point here is that constructs and the associations among them may be limited to a single level, may emerge at higher levels (see Dansereau et al., 1984, 1999; Fulmer & Ostroff, 2016; Klein & Kozlowski, 2000; Kozlowski et al., 2013; Morgeson & Hofmann, 1999; Yammarino & Dansereau, 2009, 2011), or may manifest themselves in terms of cross-level effects whether from traditional (e.g., Gould, 2002; Miller, 1978; Wolfram, 2002; Yammarino & Dansereau, 2011) or contemporary (e.g., Bryk & Raudenbush, 1992; Gelman & Hill, 2007; Goldstein, 1987; Raudenbush & Bryk, 2002; Rousseau, 1985) perspectives. And when these cross-level models and effects are relevant, they may look and be tested very differently from one another. So, be very specific about what types of cross-level models are being conceptualized and eventually tested. The integrative cross-level model view presented here may be helpful in that regard.

Second, define the level of analysis of the associated concepts, constructs, variables, and relationships, keeping in mind that the level at which associations between constructs occur might be different from the level at which a single construct is defined or operates. For example, the leadership notion of leader–member exchange (LMX) originates at the dyadic level as a construct (defined as the quality of the exchange relationship in the dyad), is measured at the individual level (for followers and leaders), manifests at the dyad level (via compositional or compilational process from individual member ratings), and could impact individual-level associations (e.g., follower justice perceptions–performance relationships; see Gooty & Yammarino, 2016).

Third, keeping in mind that not all constructs and relationships among them are cross level, regardless of the particular cross-level view one holds, articulate such models and effects and provide a theoretical justification for how and why constructs and their associations cross levels. Again, an integrative cross-level view may be helpful.

Fourth, specify the boundary conditions, including and based upon levels of analysis for everything articulated in the preceding three recommendations. A key point often ignored in this regard is that the emergence of constructs and associations at higher levels and across time is conditional and not a given (Morgeson & Hofmann, 1999). For example, LMX might not always emerge at the dyad level when conceptualized as a consensus construct because leaders and followers rarely agree regarding their LMX (see Gooty & Yammarino, 2016).

Design and Measurement

The theoretical foundations outlined above lead to three recommendations regarding research design and measurement in cross-level research.

First, create research designs as well as measures at the same level of analysis depicted in the theory, models, and hypotheses. In some instances, this might be made possible because the construct exists only at the higher level (e.g., group size), and in other cases it might be derived from lower level ratings, as noted below.

Second, when the measurement of constructs at their appropriate level is not directly possible or feasible, then lower level ratings are combined in compositional or compilational processes to construct higher level measures (see Chan, 1998). Compositional models (except additive models) assume consensus in lower level ratings and require appropriate justification (e.g., consensus, agreement, aggregation) indices such as r_{wg}, ICC1, ICC2, and so

forth (for a detailed review, see LeBreton & Senter, 2008). Compilational models rely on variability and do not require such consensus justification but require reliable between-unit differences to be displayed.

Third, validate a measure, even an established measure, if it has been modified or adapted to account for various or different levels of analysis than originally intended (e.g., for a change in referent or entities).

Analyses

For data analysis in cross-level research, our recommendations for this aspect of theory testing are as follows: First, permit theory (variables, relationships, and levels of analysis) to determine the cross-level technique to be used. Second, use appropriate cross-level techniques, traditional or contemporary or integrative, for cross-level models if the entities of interest are at a level of analysis above the individual level.

Inferences

Our recommendations for drawing inferences in cross-level research are as follows: First, include levels of analysis both in theory and conceptualization (i.e., as the entities of focus) and in data and testing (i.e., as the samples and subjects of study). Second, state which relationships hold across different levels of analysis and in which ways in terms of cross-level models if appropriate (see Figures 24.1–24.5 for various options) or in terms of emergent and level-specific (single-level) models if relevant.

CONCLUSION

We have explicated the fundamental underlying notions as well as the conceptualization and testing formulations for both traditional and contemporary cross-level models, and then integrated them. The integrated cross-level models presented here, which view elements of contemporary cross-level models as a special case of more general elements of traditional cross-level models, merge traditional work from the physical or hard sciences with contemporary work from the social–behavioral or soft sciences in terms of both conceptualization and testing. As a consequence, we sought to help resolve some of the confusion and controversy that have inhibited the work of cross-level researchers in the social and behavioral sciences. We hope this integrated cross-level perspective will provide a scientific approach to enhance future cross-level models for theory building and theory testing in the social–behavioral–organizational sciences.

References

Aguinis, H., Gottfredson, R. K., & Culpepper, S. A. (2013). Best-practice recommendations for estimating cross-level interaction effects using multilevel modeling. *Journal of Management, 39,* 1490–1528. http://dx.doi.org/10.1177/0149206313478188

Antonakis, J., Bendahan, S., Jacquart, P., & Lalive, R. (2010). On making causal claims: A review and recommendations. *The Leadership Quarterly, 21,* 1086–1120. http://dx.doi.org/10.1016/j.leaqua.2010.10.010

Behling, O. (1978). Some problems in the philosophy of science of organizations. *The Academy of Management Review, 3,* 193–201. http://dx.doi.org/10.2307/257660

Bliese, P. D., Chan, D., & Ployhart, R. E. (2007). Multilevel methods: Future directions in measurement, longitudinal analyses, and nonnormal outcomes. *Organizational Research Methods, 10,* 551–563. http://dx.doi.org/10.1177/1094428107301102

Bollen, K. A., & Brand, J. E. (2010). A general panel model with random and fixed effects: A structural equations approach. *Social Forces, 89,* 1–34. http://dx.doi.org/10.1353/sof.2010.0072

Bryk, A. S., & Raudenbush, S. W. (1992). *Hierarchical linear models.* Newbury Park, CA: Sage.

Chan, D. (1998). Functional relations among constructs in the same content domain at different levels of analysis: A typology of composition models. *Journal of Applied Psychology, 83,* 234–246. http://dx.doi.org/10.1037/0021-9010.83.2.234

Chen, G., Bliese, P. D., & Mathieu, J. E. (2005). Conceptual framework and statistical procedures for delineating and testing multilevel theories of homology. *Organizational Research Methods, 8,* 375–409. http://dx.doi.org/10.1177/1094428105280056

Chen, G., Mathieu, J. E., & Bliese, P. D. (2004a). A framework for conducting multi-level construct validation. In F. J. Yammarino & F. Dansereau (Eds.), *Multi-level issues in organizational behavior and processes* (Research in Multi-level Issues, Vol. 3, pp. 273–303). Oxford, England: Emerald. http://dx.doi.org/10.1016/S1475-9144(04)03013-9

Chen, G., Mathieu, J. E., & Bliese, P. D. (2004b). Validating frogs and ponds in multi-level contexts: Some afterthoughts. In F. J. Yammarino & F. Dansereau (Eds.), *Multi-level issues in organizational behavior and processes* (Research in Multi-level Issues, Vol. 3, pp. 335–343). Oxford, England: Emerald. http://dx.doi.org/10.1016/s1475-9144(04)03016-4

Cohen, J. (1988). *Statistical power analysis for the behavioral sciences* (2nd ed.). Mahwah, NJ: Lawrence Erlbaum.

Dansereau, F., Alutto, J. A., & Yammarino, F. J. (1984). *Theory testing in organizational behavior: The varient approach.* Englewood Cliffs, NJ: Prentice-Hall.

Dansereau, F., Cho, J., & Yammarino, F. J. (2006). Avoiding the "fallacy of the wrong level": A within and between analysis (WABA) approach. *Group & Organization Management, 31,* 536–577. http://dx.doi.org/10.1177/1059601106291131

Dansereau, F., & Yammarino, F. J. (2000). Within and between analysis: The varient paradigm as an underlying approach to theory building and testing. In K. J. Klein & S. W. J. Kozlowski (Eds.), *Multilevel theory, research, and methods in organizations: Foundations, extensions, and new directions* (SIOP Frontiers Series, pp. 425–466). San Francisco, CA: Jossey-Bass.

Dansereau, F., & Yammarino, F. J. (2004). Overview: Multilevel issues in organizational behavior and processes. In F. J. Yammarino & F. Dansereau (Eds.), *Multilevel issues in organizational behavior and processes* (Research in Multi-level Issues, Vol. 3, pp. xiii–xxxiii). Oxford, England: Emerald. http://dx.doi.org/10.1016/s1475-9144(04)03024-3

Dansereau, F., Yammarino, F. J., & Kohles, J. (1999). Multiple levels of analysis from a longitudinal perspective: Some implications for theory building. *The Academy of Management Review, 24,* 346–357. http://dx.doi.org/10.2307/259086

Fulmer, C. A., & Ostroff, C. (2016). Convergence and emergence in organizations: An integrative framework and review. *Journal of Organizational Behavior, 37*(Suppl. 1), S122–S145. http://dx.doi.org/10.1002/job.1987

Gelman, A., & Hill, J. (2007). *Data analysis using regression and multilevel/hierarchical models.* New York, NY: Cambridge University Press.

Goldstein, H. (1987). *Multilevel models in educational and social research.* London, England: Griffin.

Gooty, J., & Yammarino, F. J. (2011). Dyads in organizational research: Conceptual issues and multilevel analyses. *Organizational Research Methods, 14,* 456–483. http://dx.doi.org/10.1177/1094428109358271

Gooty, J., & Yammarino, F. J. (2016). The leader–member exchange relationship: A multisource, cross-level investigation. *Journal of Management, 42*, 915–945. http://dx.doi.org/10.1177/0149206313503009

Gould, S. J. (2002). *The structure of evolutionary theory.* Cambridge, MA: Belknap Press of Harvard University Press.

Hofmann, D. A., & Gavin, M. B. (1998). Centering decisions in hierarchical linear models: Implications for research in organizations. *Journal of Management, 24*, 623–641. http://dx.doi.org/10.1177/014920639802400504

Klein, K. J., Dansereau, F., & Hall, R. J. (1994). Levels issues in theory development, data collection, and analysis. *The Academy of Management Review, 19*, 195–229. http://dx.doi.org/10.2307/258703

Klein, K. J., & Kozlowski, S. W. J. (2000). From micro to meso: Critical steps for conceptualizing and conducting multilevel research. *Organizational Research Methods, 3*, 211–236. http://dx.doi.org/10.1177/109442810033001

Kozlowski, S. W. J., Chao, G. T., Grand, J. A., Braun, M. T., & Kuljanin, G. (2013). Advancing multilevel research design: Capturing the dynamics of emergence. *Organizational Research Methods, 16*, 581–615. http://dx.doi.org/10.1177/1094428113493119

Krasikova, D. V., & LeBreton, J. M. (2012). Just the two of us: Misalignment of theory and methods in examining dyadic phenomena. *Journal of Applied Psychology, 97*, 739–757. http://dx.doi.org/10.1037/a0027962

LeBreton, J. M., & Senter, J. L. (2008). Answers to 20 questions about interrater reliability and interrater agreement. *Organizational Research Methods, 11*, 815–852. http://dx.doi.org/10.1177/1094428106296642

LoPilato, A. C., & Vandenberg, R. J. (2015). The not-so-direct cross-level direct effect. In C. E. Lance & R. J. Vandenberg (Eds.), *More statistical and methodological myths and urban legends* (pp. 292–310). New York, NY: Routledge.

Mathieu, J. E., & Chen, G. (2011). The etiology of the multilevel paradigm in management research. *Journal of Management, 37*, 610–641. http://dx.doi.org/10.1177/0149206310364663

Miller, J. G. (1978). *Living systems.* New York, NY: McGraw Hill.

Morgeson, F. P., & Hofmann, D. A. (1999). The structure and function of collective constructs: Implications for multilevel research and theory development. *The Academy of Management Review, 24*, 249–265. http://dx.doi.org/10.2307/259081

Mossholder, K. W., & Bedeian, A. G. (1983). Cross-level inference and organizational research: Perspectives on interpretation and application. *The Academy of Management Review, 8*, 547–558. http://dx.doi.org/10.2307/258256

Raudenbush, S. W., & Bryk, A. S. (2002). *Hierarchical linear models: Applications and data analysis methods* (2nd ed.). Thousand Oaks, CA: Sage.

Raudenbush, S. W., Bryk, A. S., Cheong, Y. F., Congdon, R., & du Toit, M. (2004). *HLM 6: Hierarchical linear and nonlinear modeling.* Lincolnwood, IL: Scientific Software International.

Roberts, K. H., Hulin, C. L., & Rousseau, D. M. (1978). *Developing an interdisciplinary science of organizations.* San Francisco, CA: Jossey Bass.

Robinson, W. S. (1950). Ecological correlations and the behavior of individuals. *American Sociological Review, 15*, 351–357. http://dx.doi.org/10.2307/2087176

Rousseau, D. M. (1985). Issues of level in organizational research: Multi-level and cross-level perspectives. *Research in Organizational Behavior, 7*, 1–37.

Sayama, H. (2015). *Introduction to modeling and analysis of complex systems.* Albany, NY: OpenSUNY. Retrieved from https://textbooks.opensuny.org/introduction-to-the-modeling-and-analysis-of-complex-systems/

Schriesheim, C. A. (1995). Multivariate and moderated within- and between-entity analysis (WABA) using hierarchical linear multiple regression. *The Leadership Quarterly, 6*, 1–18. http://dx.doi.org/10.1016/1048-9843(95)90002-0

Schriesheim, C. A., Castro, S. L., & Yammarino, F. J. (2000). Investigating contingencies: An examination of the impact of span of supervision and upward controllingness on leader–member exchange using traditional and multivariate within- and between-entities analysis. *Journal of Applied Psychology, 85*, 659–677. http://dx.doi.org/10.1037/0021-9010.85.5.659

Snijders, T. A. B., & Bosker, R. J. (1999). *Multilevel analysis: An introduction to basic and advanced multilevel modeling.* Thousand Oaks, CA: Sage.

Thorndike, E. L. (1939). On the fallacy of imputing the correlations found for a group to the individual or smaller groups composing them. *The American Journal of Psychology, 52*, 122–124. http://dx.doi.org/10.2307/1416673

Wolfram, S. (2002). *A new kind of science.* Champaign, IL: Wolfram Media.

Yammarino, F. J. (1998). Multivariate aspects of the varient/WABA approach: A discussion and leadership illustration. *The Leadership Quarterly, 9*, 203–227. http://dx.doi.org/10.1016/S1048-9843(98)90005-4

Yammarino, F. J. (2003). Modern data analytic techniques for multisource feedback. *Organizational Research*

Methods, 6, 6–14. http://dx.doi.org/10.1177/1094428102239423

Yammarino, F. J., & Dansereau, F. (2009). A new kind of OB (organizational behavior). In F. J. Yammarino & F. Dansereau (Eds.), *Multi-level issues in organizational behavior and leadership* (Research in Multi-Level Issues, Vol. 8, pp. 13–60). Oxford, England: Emerald. http://dx.doi.org/10.1108/S1475-9144(2009)0000008001

Yammarino, F. J., & Dansereau, F. (2011). Multi-level issues in evolutionary theory, organization science, and leadership. *The Leadership Quarterly, 22*, 1042–1057. http://dx.doi.org/10.1016/j.leaqua.2011.09.002

Yammarino, F. J., Dansereau, F., Schriesheim, C. A., Castro, S., Cogliser, C., DeChurch, L., & Zhou, X. T.

(2000). *Manual: DIG for WABA: DETECT interpretation guide for within and between analysis.* Williamsville, NY: The Institute for Theory Testing.

Yammarino, F. J., & Gooty, J. (2017). Multi-level issues and dyads in leadership research. In B. Schyns, R. Hall, & P. Neves (Eds.), *Handbook of methods in leadership research* (pp. 229–255). Cheltenham, England: Edward Elgar. http://dx.doi.org/10.4337/9781785367281.00018

Yammarino, F. J., & Markham, S. E. (1992). On the application of within and between analysis: Are absence and affect really group-based phenomena? *Journal of Applied Psychology, 77*, 168–176 (correction, 77, 426). http://dx.doi.org/10.1037/0021-9010.77.2.168

## CHAPTER 25

PANEL INTERVIEW: REFLECTIONS ON MULTILEVEL THEORY, MEASUREMENT, AND ANALYSIS

Organizer: *Michael E. Hoffman*
Panelists: *David Chan, Gilad Chen, Fred Dansereau,*
Denise Rousseau, and Benjamin Schneider

For the past 40 years, scholars across a wide array of disciplines within the social sciences have made critical contributions to multilevel research. These contributions were driven by the multilevel nature of many of the research questions studied in the social sciences. Consequently, a strong foundation in multilevel theory, measurement, and analysis is of critical importance. Despite this rising prominence within the social sciences, multilevel research is still not without its growing pains. Many of these growing pains will impact the future of research in the organizational sciences and, subsequently, influence the future research and careers of today's students and junior scholars.

It is with this audience and these thoughts in mind that the idea for the current chapter was conceived. This chapter was designed as both a look back and a look forward from the perspective of five of the most esteemed multilevel researchers working in the organizational and social sciences. As organizer, it was my good fortune to come up with questions and interview these distinguished panelists: David Chan from Singapore Management University, Gilad Chen from the University of Maryland, Fred Dansereau from the State University of New York at Buffalo, Denise Rousseau from Carnegie Mellon University, and Benjamin Schneider from the University of Maryland (emeritus). The interview questions were intended to elicit a conversation about how multilevel research

originally came to be (especially within the organizational sciences), how the field has grown since those early days, and where we might be going with multilevel research in the future. It is the goal of this chapter to provide junior scholars with context for the current state of multilevel research as well as advice for pursuing research and publications in this arena and for avoiding pitfalls best sidestepped along the way.

LOOKING BACK

Which specific scholars and articles have substantively influenced your conceptualization of multilevel research or the direction of the literature in a way that you think is fundamental for developing a research program involving multilevel phenomena and issues?

Benjamin Schneider: I want to clarify that when I began thinking about and doing work that now is referred to as *multilevel*, the big deal was to go up one level, and not to do more than one level at a time. So, in my early days in industrial psychology and what has come to be called I/O (industrial and organizational psychology) and OB (organizational behavior), which emerged later (see Porter & Schneider, 2014), we studied phenomena at only the individual level of analysis. We had little precedent in the field for thinking about, much less

http://dx.doi.org/10.1037/0000115-026
The Handbook of Multilevel Theory, Measurement, and Analysis, S. E. Humphrey and J. M. LeBreton (Editors-in-Chief)

conducting, quantitative research on psychologically relevant constructs at unit and organizational levels of analysis. Readers have to put themselves in this ancient mind-set to appreciate what follows.

The most important reading for me early on was Schein's (1965) book *Organizational Psychology*, which took me conceptually from a focus on individual differences as the essence of industrial psychology research to a focus on the larger social psychological environment in which people worked. His notion that organizations have philosophies (e.g., "social man," "self-actualizing man") that guide them in the way they operate vis-à-vis people had a profound impact on both my career in academics and private industry. He jumped the conceptual level of analysis from individual differences—the focus of industrial psychology in the 1960s, when I was a graduate student—while still retaining an emphasis on the psychology of people; he detailed the psychology of the environment and how organizations, not individuals, differed. Of course, he later was (and continues to be) a central figure in the development of the organizational culture construct (see the latest edition of his book; Schein, 2010), which in my opinion represents a further elaboration of his earlier writings.

In fact, the first measure of climate I tried to develop was one that detailed the behaviors to be expected in organizations for the different organizational philosophies Schein described. It did not work out well, and I never published anything based on it, but I could just picture what a "social man climate" was compared to a "self-actualizing man climate." Maybe I will try that again!

The second most important paper for me was by James and Jones (1974), with their important distinction between psychological climate and organizational climate. So, while researchers implicitly or explicitly followed Schein's (1965) conceptual lead, research continued to be done (primarily) at the individual level of analysis, including research on "organizational" climate. In James and Jones's article, it became painfully clear that such work was conceptually poor, and the methodological suggestions they made in the paper (frequently overlooked) clarified the importance

of being able to document the fact that a unit or organizational phenomenon actually existed—which James, Demaree, and Wolf (1984) made perfectly doable with their r_{wg} formulation.

Roberts, Hulin, and Rousseau's (1978) brief book was also very important to me and my work because it legitimized some of what I was also working on. That is to say, they revealed that traditional topics in industrial psychology (such as employee turnover) were valuable to study at the unit and organizational level of analysis, too. Here was Chuck Hulin (already then of guru status) and his students literally arguing that a focus only on individual differences and individual-level behavior actually sold the field short. Of course, Rousseau's (1985) chapter on multilevel and cross-level perspectives in the influential *Research in Organizational Behavior* series set the stage for much of the later movement to do unit- and organizational-level research in which organizations were conceptualized through appropriate psychological lenses.

Readers of the present book will likely not be familiar with Roberts et al.'s (1978) earlier book on which Rousseau's (1985) later thinking was based, but it is an informative historical read. I would also note here that my 1985 *Annual Review of Psychology* article on organizational behavior (Schneider, 1985) was organized around a multilevel model, but it certainly did not have the conceptual and methodological power of what Rousseau had done.

In summary, one has to appreciate the era in which I began thinking "one level up," much less multilevel, with regard to psychological theories and methods. We had no intraclass correlations (ICCs), no r_{wg}, no climate and culture; we only had a strange idea that there was more to understanding behavior in organizations than the individual differences of the people working in them.

Fred Dansereau: Some understanding of how a focus on multiple levels of analysis developed in the past may be helpful in deciding how to approach multiple levels of analysis in the present. Going back more than 70 years, there has been at least a tacit recognition of multiple levels in psychology in the traditional person–environment view of human behavior (for example, in Lewin's 1943 work). In this early work, the emphasis was largely on individual differences (or personality) as a lower level of analysis and on the environment as a higher level of analysis. At this stage, variations within a person over time were viewed as error (perhaps because of the view of personality as stable as well as the traditional experimental designs), yet environmental factors were recognized. The focus, then, was on the whole person (or personality). In many ways, this perspective remains the dominant view in psychology today. Schneider's (1975, p. 467) work about levels of analysis, unlike previous work, suggested the possibility that groups could be a level of analysis that goes beyond the individual or person level.

Nevertheless, it was Miller (1978) who, in more than 1,000 pages of seminal work, introduced a much more comprehensive and integrated framework for addressing levels of analysis. Miller, a biologist who is credited with originating the term *behavioral science*, reviewed work from multiple scientific disciplines; this diversity of resources, in turn, prompted him to offer a substantial enrichment over the simple person and environment approach applied in the past.

Regardless of one's view of the specifics of his approach, Miller (1978) offered three major conceptual and theoretical advances to the study of multiple levels of analysis. First, Miller examined the nature of multiple levels of analysis ranging from the cell to the person, the group, the organization, society, and the supranational system. This work raised the specter of a very large number of levels of analysis and expanded the very definition of multiple levels of analysis in specific terms beyond the person and the environment. In doing so, Miller moved the focus beyond two levels of analysis.

Second, Miller (1978) suggested that each of the levels can be viewed in terms of the parts that compose them. The parts were viewed as similar across levels with this approach. This concept expanded the definition of levels to include components or parts. Thus, each level could be viewed in terms of its components or parts, and, unlike with previous approaches, the variations within individuals (or persons, or groups, and so on) were not always viewed as error. At the same time, the traditional notion that, for example, it is conceptually and empirically plausible to focus

on whole persons rather than within-person differences remained valid, as did the idea of individual differences. Thus, Miller suggested that the units at one level can be viewed (a) in terms of the parts of the unit or (b) as whole units.

Third, Miller (1978) showed that levels need not be viewed conceptually and empirically from a reductionist view. He suggested that effects could be theorized and found to emerge or disappear from one level to the next. In some cases, effects at one level may be attributable to effects at higher levels or lower levels. In other words, what is observed could be viewed as attributable to neither the wholes nor the parts at the level being observed, but rather as an effect at higher or lower levels of analysis. Miller also articulated what might be termed, in the traditional sense, *cross-level effects*—that is, similar effects that manifest themselves at more than one level of analysis. Thus, effects may be (a) level specific (that is, be specific to one level), (b) emergent at one level (that is, hold at a given level but not at a lower level), or (c) cross level (that is, hold across multiple levels).

In summary, Miller's (1978) seminal work provided a conceptualization of multiple levels of analysis that includes multiple levels, multiple views at one level, and cross-level, level-specific, and emergent views of multiple levels of analysis. Popular approaches to this complex range of possibilities involve assuming away some of the complexity and then creating theories that involve a limited number of levels or considering only a wholes perspective on these levels. The purpose of the assumptions is to allow simplified modeling and data analysis that are based on untested assumptions. Approaches of this type abound; indeed, they can be found throughout the multilevel analysis literature. An alternative approach attempts to simultaneously account for Miller's three general views of levels effects in theory development and empirical testing. To move in this second direction, which will be the focus of my remaining responses here, requires allowing for multiple hypotheses and testing them simultaneously. A strong inference approach (Platt, 1964) represents one way to try to move in that direction. Nevertheless, Miller's seminal work remains a conceptual basis for multilevel research regardless of one's orientation toward the topic.

Denise Rousseau: In graduate school at the University of California, Berkeley, I rode the bus to school and back and to my job at Pacific Gas and Electric while reading *Sociotechnical Systems: Factors in Analysis, Design, and Management* by Kenyon B. De Greene (1973). I'd found it in a technical bookstore on Market Street in San Francisco, and *Sociotechnical Systems* helped me make sense of things. Its key idea is that failure to comprehend things as a whole was a root of many problems, economic, social, and personal. Some key ideas really resonated for me. There was a way to make complexity friendlier, by building multilevel models of organizations or society that comprised independent variables, dependent variables, and the relationships between them. These relationships could be based on established causal relations, but even if our best evidence were correlational, we still knew something useful.

As the title indicates, sociotechnical systems are joint products of social and technological activities, which need to be understood in relation to each other. I had a sociotechnical systems course in Berkeley's industrial engineering program taught by two fascinating Tavistock-influenced scholars, Steve Laner and Alfred Crossman. De Greene (1973) reinforced what they had taught regarding the nature of activities that define an organization (e.g., its purpose, direction, and evolution), but he provided models of organizations I continue to find useful.

De Greene (1973) described a management problem we have today: "We still lack the techniques to synthesize a major system. Judgments are made by managers, usually on a very intuitive basis, with minimum influence by systems scientists" (p. 152). The book walks through a series of analytic processes for making sense of organizational processes in order to identify problems, make changes, and learn what works. To this day, I think De Greene was correct in noting the need to monitor the effects of change, because any change is just one step in an ongoing process. But I think he missed the human emotional and political issues.

Gilad Chen: In 2011, John Mathieu and I coauthored an article in *Journal of Management*

that traced the etiology of the multilevel paradigm in management research. In it, we highlighted numerous key contributors to multilevel theory and thinking, measurement, and analyses, many of whom also contributed to this book. I do not have much to add beyond what is in that article, given that it answers this question broadly and with many examples. However, personally, my own multilevel research and thinking have been particularly influenced by (listed alphabetically) Paul Bliese, David Chan, David Hofmann, Katherine Klein, Steve Kozlowski, John Mathieu, and Robert Ployhart. These individuals influenced me not only through their published work (which is, of course, very influential and highly cited), but also through numerous conversations, mutual work, and feedback they have personally provided me on my work over the years.

David Chan: My conceptualization of multilevel issues has been most influenced by four pioneering works that laid the conceptual foundations for subsequent organizational research in the multilevel literature. Roberts and colleagues (1978) provided one of the earliest discussions of conceptual issues in multilevel research by explicating the fallacious inferences that may arise when aggregating or disaggregating data without adequate consideration of the appropriate level of analysis. Rousseau (1985) presented one of the earliest conceptual frameworks by explicating a typology consisting of composition models that specify the nature of a construct at multiple levels of analysis, cross-level models that specify causal relationships linking constructs that belong to different levels of analysis, and multilevel models that generalize interconstruct relationships from one level of analysis to another level of analysis. Klein, Dansereau, and Hall (1994) discussed the conceptual assumptions underlying specification of levels and linkages connecting theory, measurement, and data analysis. House, Rousseau, and Thomas-Hunt (1995) argued that understanding multilevel organizational phenomena requires examining "mesolevel" variables that intervene between microlevel variables and macrolevel variables, especially intervening variables related to social interactions. I believe it is fundamental for researchers to be familiar with these four pioneering works if they want to develop a research program involving multilevel phenomena or issues.

What do you think is the most influential article, chapter, or book relevant to multilevel research that may be relatively unknown or underutilized or that might come as a surprise to others? How has it affected your thinking, and why should others read it?

David Chan: Robinson (1950) is of fundamental relevance to multilevel research, but I suspect it is not read by many researchers who conduct multilevel studies. Published more than half a century ago in *American Sociological Review*, this article is one of the first empirical demonstrations of the *ecological fallacy*, which refers to mistakenly making substantive conclusions at the lower level from aggregated data analyzed at the higher level. Using data on ethnicity and literacy from different geographic regions, Robinson clearly showed the severity of erroneous conclusions when there is a mismatch or disconnect between the level of data analysis and the level of substantive conclusion. More generally, the article provides an excellent example and point of departure for discussing how the single-level approach to multilevel data has conceptual problems that often lead to inadequate or misleading inferences. The clarity and severity of the ecological fallacy, as well as its converse, the atomistic fallacy, has positively influenced my impression of multilevel research because it demonstrated to me the practical importance of attending to multilevel issues (for details on these two fallacies, see Chan, 2005).

Fred Dansereau: If one assumes that it is plausible that there are (a) multiple levels, (b) multiple views at one level (parts and wholes), and (c) various combinations of cross-level, level-specific, and emergent effects at multiple levels of analysis as described by Miller (1978), how can these perspectives simultaneously be accommodated and tested? One rarely cited approach that had the potential to support Miller's three plausible contributions is strong inference, a framework developed by a physicist (Platt, 1964). Given that multiple levels in living systems differ in important ways from the levels in physics (e.g., electrons), only certain parts of the strong inference approach are likely to be helpful in studying Miller's concepts. Nevertheless, an understanding of the strong inference approach has definite benefits in elucidating Miller's multilevel perspectives.

As Miller (1978) suggested that multiple levels, along with views of those levels separately and in combination, are possible, multiple hypotheses seem necessary. When applying the strong inference approach (Platt, 1964, p. 347), then, the first step is to create alternative hypotheses. Next, the following objective is established: to perform analyses in a study that, for each outcome from the study, will as nearly as possible exclude one or more of the original hypotheses. A study is then conducted to obtain the clearest results possible. At this point, the process seeks to rule out more alternative hypotheses. Overall, this approach involves generating alternative hypotheses and testing them against each other.

The material that follows attempts to draw out the implications and relevance of the strong inference approach for understanding multiple levels of analysis. When doing so, it is important to keep in mind that the strong inference approach focuses on trying to disprove a preferred theory. If the preferred theory fails to be disproved through this process, it is viewed as a stronger theory. A preferred theory includes three elements: (a) the selection of a single level or multiple levels of analysis, (b) a view of the units at each level as whole units or parts, and (c) the means by which effects of interest emerge or disappear at different levels. The application of the strong inference approach implies that a preferred theory should be tested to confirm that other plausible configurations of those levels do not apply. Thus, when applying a strong inference approach, it is not useful to assume away plausible alterative hypothesized levels; instead, it is necessary to test whether the alternative hypothesized levels are more likely than the preferred view.

This point illustrates a key difference between popular approaches and the strong inference approach. In popular approaches, one can simply assume away (without testing) alternative views on the basis of a preferred theory. In the strong inference approach, however, it is essential to show explicitly that the alternative hypothesized levels do not hold. This approach is helpful if one recognizes that—as Miller's (1978) work implies—multiple levels of analysis are plausible even if one ignores them or assumes them away. The specific application of this concept of strong inference to the multiple-levels approach of Miller became a major intellectual quest for me during my academic career.

Benjamin Schneider: In my humble opinion, the most important overlooked publication that revealed the possibilities and merits of the quantitative study of psychological concepts at higher levels of analysis is the country-level work by McClelland (1961). McClelland is unfortunately best known in the world of I/O and OB for the criticisms made of his need for achievement (nAch) work via the use of the Thematic Apperception Test as a predictor of it. But in his book *The Achieving Society* (McClelland, 1961), he documented achievement imagery coded in astonishingly creative ways as a correlate of country-level financial performance. For example, his theory predicted that the achievement imagery in folk myths would be correlated with country indicators of economic performance. Not having the myths available, he coded the stories in primers used to teach reading to children across countries and showed that the levels of achievement imagery in a country's primers were significantly correlated with later indicators of country economic performance. Later work on coding ancient pottery was not as effective, but the audacity in doing so remains for me a high point in what is possible given an appropriate theory and methodological creativity, and, of course, the book also reveals how subconscious phenomena can exist not only within individuals but within larger units of analysis of people in the aggregate—as Schein (2010) has been arguing for years.

In a similar vein, McGregor's (1960) and Argyris's (1957) books, though they were not books containing quantitative research, greatly influenced the way I began to think about people attributes as higher level organizational phenomena. I suppose I/O psychologists and OB scholars no longer read these books, but they should, because as with Schein (1965), they constitute the foundation for much of what has followed in our field. Both were students of Lewin (cf. Lewin, 1935, 1951), and his idea of life space is critical to an understanding of the idea that the world around us is central to who we are and how we behave. McGregor proposed that managers carry their subconscious impressions of what motivates people (the famous Theory X and Theory Y) around with them and operationalize those in the psychological work conditions they create for employees. Argyris made a similar argument, proposing that most organizations infantilize workers such that the full expression of who they are is not possible to be displayed. In both instances, we again see the focus on the importance of organizations for the aggregate psychology of the people in them—the same way we see in McClelland (1961) how the common experiences of people in a society can yield important consequences for those societies.

The effect on me of these readings is probably obvious: I became convinced that psychological phenomena exist at more than the individual level of analysis. McClelland's (1961) work probably impressed me for its audacity—think big and work at it. McGregor (1960) and Argyris (1957) revealed for me in relatively concrete terms that there were aggregate human effects of what management in organizations does on the people in them. Implicitly this told me that there would also be variability across organizations in these effects, resulting in both my work on organizational climate and the attraction–selection–attrition (ASA) model, topics I turn to later.

What do you believe is the most important contribution you have made to multilevel research? Where did the idea for this contribution originate? Did you have to overcome any major obstacles? We would love to hear the backstory behind how that contribution came to be, including any struggles or challenges that were present as you sought to get your ideas published.
Gilad Chen: Methodologically, I believe my two largest contributions include delineation of frameworks for developing and validating multilevel constructs (Chen,

Mathieu, & Bliese, 2004) and for testing multilevel homology (Chen, Bliese, & Mathieu, 2005). These contributions came about after my colleagues and I encountered roadblocks for conducting substantive multilevel research and from our not being sufficiently satisfied with solutions that were available at the time in the literature.

Substantively, I believe my multilevel research on motivation in teams (e.g., Chen & Kanfer, 2006; Chen, Kanfer, DeShon, Mathieu, & Kozlowski, 2009; Chen, Kirkman, Kanfer, Allen, & Rosen, 2007) has allowed for (a) greater integration between individual-level and team-level theories and models of motivation and (b) better understanding of how teams and individuals influence each other, as reflected by motivation and performance across levels. My interest in this research stemmed from my competitive swimming career, during which I witnessed firsthand the complex interplay (involving motivation and performance) between individuals and their teams. For instance, I noticed how my team's success and motivational climate greatly influenced my own motivation and performance in practice and competitions. As I started to study work and organizations in graduate school, it became clear to me that the same issues are often found in the context of work teams.

In trying to publish this work, a key challenge was to convince reviewers (and editors) that there was something new and worthwhile in this research. For example, we had to tell motivation scholars (who sometimes held a more psychological, and decontextualized, view of behavior) that the work team context can actually help explain additional and important individual variation in motivation and behavior. At the same time, team scholars focused on team-level outcomes and processes, and therefore we had to convince them that understanding individual variation in motivation and performance can translate (through emergence) into important team-level outcomes.

Benjamin Schneider: I think I have made both conceptual and substantive contributions in two areas, organizational climate and the ASA model (Schneider, 1987). I began my interest in climate as a graduate student and operationalized that interest in my dissertation proposal (Schneider &

Bartlett, 1968). The proposal won the Cattell Award (now, I think, called the Owens Award) because it proposed that the prediction of life insurance agent performance on the basis of individual differences predictors would be moderated by the climate of the life insurance agencies to which they were assigned. In the early work on the assessment of work climate in life insurance agencies, I assessed the degree to which participants working in different agencies agreed with their coworkers concerning the perceptions they had of work climates (Schneider & Bartlett, 1970), definitely one of the early attempts at looking at such within-unit issues.

As I pursued the dissertation research (the project was not completed until 5 years later, so I had to do another dissertation proposal in January of the year I received the PhD!), I saw that the conceptualization of climate was, to say the least, muddy. So, in 1975 I published an essay on climate in which (a) I carefully documented where the climate construct fit within the traditional schools of psychology (structuralism, functionalism, and gestalt), (b) I clearly stated that, on the basis of bandwidth theory, climate survey data had to be about a climate "for something" (e.g., safety, service) in order for it to have a chance of being related to that "something" (e.g., accidents, customer satisfaction), and (c) based on evidence from then-existing literature, I showed that aggregates of individual perceptions produced reliable unit or organizational scores (Schneider, 1975). The paper clearly lodged climate as a unit and organizationally relevant psychological construct (à la James & Jones, 1974), and this was especially true because I showed that structural variables (size, technology, levels in the hierarchy) had weak relationships with climate perceptions. I followed up these ideas about a climate "for something" as a unit or organizational level variable with empirical research showing the validity the climate for service construct had in the prediction of customer satisfaction at the bank branch level of analysis (Schneider, Parkington, & Buxton, 1980). I note with some pride that in this paper I documented the between-branch differences using analysis of variance. I believe this is one of the earliest demonstrations (along with Zohar, 1980) of the empirical usefulness of a climate "for something" construct above the individual level of analysis, a now-ubiquitous occurrence (Schneider, González-Romá, Ostroff, & West, 2017).

The second contribution I have made is the work I published on the ASA model (Schneider, 1987). I published several papers (Schneider, 1983a, 1983b) prior to the 1987 paper (which was my presidential address to Division 14 in 1985), but the 1987 version was the most straightforward presentation of the set of propositions concerning the model. This model made the argument that the way organizations look and feel is a function of the relatively homogenous personalities of the people in them and that this happens as the result of what was termed the *attraction–selection–attrition cycle*.

From my earliest days in graduate school, I was intrigued with the Person (*P*) × Situation (*S*) interaction model of human behavior (thus the dissertation proposal referred to earlier). The industrial psychology program I was in had lots of research about the *P* part of the framework but nothing on the *S* piece, so I began to think about the situation through the climate lens. What was true then (and is mostly still true to this day) was that the *P* and the *S* were conceptualized as separate phenomena. The conceptual breakthrough I had in melding the *P* and the *S* occurred slowly. It was influenced by Holland's (1966) early work on career environments, in which he logically deduced that people with similar career interests would naturally be in similar environments and that, because of the people in them, the environments would be different from other career environments. It was also influenced by me reading heavily in what was then called "interactional psychology" (e.g., Magnusson & Endler, 1977) and finding Bowers's (1973) magnificent paper. Bowers's paper was magnificent in two ways. First, it showed that the then-situationist movement in psychology (e.g., Mischel, 1968) was based on laboratory experiments that were deliberately created to produce strong situations, making it appear as if individual differences do not exist. Second, and more important for me, he argued that laboratory experiments require random assignment of people to treatments, but in the real world people choose themselves into and out of situations and are not randomly assigned to them. Aha! This insight, combined with Holland's notion

of career environments, is the foundation on which I built the ASA model. I tested the homogeneity hypothesis suggested by the ASA model and found support for it (Schneider, Smith, Taylor, & Fleenor, 1998), as have others (for a review, see Bradley-Geist & Landis, 2012). Blending the *P* and the *S* via the ASA model to propose that, as I titled the paper, "The People Make the Place," has been richly rewarding.

The papers I did on climate (Schneider, 1975) and the ASA model (Schneider, 1987) were, by 1998, two of the 10 most-cited papers published in the history of *Personnel Psychology* (see *Personnel Psychology*, 1998). I am pleased by this because both papers jumped the level of analysis within the classic traditional outlet for publications oriented toward individual differences, the tradition in which I was trained.

David Chan: I believe my main contribution is the typology of composition models proposed in Chan (1998b) for specifying the functional relations among constructs in the same content domain at different levels of analysis. The typology described five different basic forms that composition models can take and provided a framework for organizing, evaluating, and developing constructs and theories in multilevel research.

On the basis of citation count, substantive discussion in publications, and widespread use in empirical studies, I think the typology of composition models has provided researchers an organizing framework for existing focal constructs, facilitating scientific communication in multilevel research. Researchers can be more confident that they are referring to the same construct when it is explicated according to the same form of composition. Meaningful replications and extensions of current findings then are possible. Apparent contradictory findings may be reconciled, and debates may be clarified. Organizing existing constructs also aids accumulation of research findings by providing a framework for performing meaningful meta-analytic studies in multilevel research. The typology also provides a conceptual framework for developing and validating new focal constructs and multilevel theories. It could help compose new explanatory constructs from established ones. In addition, being cognizant of different models allows the researcher to consider alternative designs, measurements, and data analyses for testing competing hypotheses, modifying existing theories or developing new ones, or performing a more rigorous test of the original hypothesis. In short, I see the contribution of Chan (1998b) as helping to clarify conceptualizations and measurement of similar constructs at different levels of analysis.

On the origin of ideas and the backstory behind how this contribution came to be, my intellectual curiosity in multilevel issues actually goes back to the early 1980s when I was an undergraduate studying psychology, sociology, and philosophy. I was intrigued by the different levels of explanation that dominate different disciplines, and even different fields within psychology. I also wondered how so many professors in each discipline were so confident that their single level of explanation was the best, if not the only, reasonable account of reality. I was also particularly interested in discussions on paradigm clash, reductionism in levels of explanation, and fallacies of personification and reification when human characteristics are attributed to the higher level collective unit (e.g., organization) that the individual members jointly constitute. It was the early 1980s, and understandably, no one had mentioned to me the term *multilevel research*. My interest in multilevel issues then was conceptual rather than empirical in nature.

As a graduate student in the 1990s, I learned about the pioneering works that laid important foundations in multilevel research in the organizational sciences, particularly the four articles that I mentioned earlier (i.e., House et al., 1995; Klein et al., 1994; Roberts et al., 1978; Rousseau, 1985). These pioneering articles and other early works in multilevel research (e.g., James, 1982; Jones & James, 1979; Kozlowski & Hults, 1987; Ostroff, 1993; Schneider, 1990) led me to systematically think about multilevel phenomena in terms of explicitly linking conceptual and methodological issues. These thoughts on the linkages resulted in my conceptualization of the multilevel issues in the typology of composition models in Chan (1998b). My professional tendency to focus on construct validity issues, which has been developed over the years working with Neal Schmitt, also played an important role in how I adopted a construct

orientation approach to developing the different forms of composition models in the typology.

I should note that the contribution of the typology is just one of several conceptual developments in the multilevel literature. Several other frameworks published after Chan (1998b) provided important conceptual advances. For example, Morgeson and Hofmann (1999) provided a framework to conceptualize multilevel issues by distinguishing between the structure and functions of collective constructs. Kozlowski and Klein (2000) explicated the relationships between various concepts discussed in the multilevel literature and highlighted the complementary contributions by multiple frameworks including those of Chan (1998b) and Morgeson and Hofmann (1999). They provided a typology of emergence that identifies distinct aspects of the process of emergence and distinct forms of emergence involving multilevel constructs. Chen et al. (2005) offered a framework and described statistical procedures for testing homologous multilevel theories, which are theories of parallel relationships between parallel constructs at different levels of analysis.

Denise Rousseau: This is hard to answer because I think my work on multilevel issues in organizations is more synthetic, pulling together existing ideas in a way that helped organize what was already in the literature. This would be true for both of my *Research in Organizational Behavior* (*ROB*) chapters (House et al., 1995; Rousseau, 1985). You should note that I have very few peer-reviewed papers on levels, though a few, like my work with Bob Sutton, use cross-level methods in order to identify effects that are missed if we stay at just one level. I think of both *ROB* chapters as sort of tool kits for researchers; they're my mental tools for thinking about organizational issues. You know, one of the things I think would be helpful for graduate students to know is the sort of heuristics and routines other researchers use to organize their thinking about research problems. I think I have done my most interesting work by playing with flow diagrams of processes, like psychological contract formation or $N \times N$ tables of how a set of concepts relate, like I-deals and job crafting. I think the *ROB* chapters are about ways theories could be developed to tackle organizational research questions.

Fred Dansereau: My contribution focused on the application of the concept of strong inference (Platt, 1964) to the multiple-levels approach advocated by Miller (1978). The theoretical and conceptual underpinnings of this work appeared in the book by Dansereau, Alutto, and Yammarino (1984). The data analysis approach was described by Dansereau et al. (1986). A computer package to analyze data compatible with this application can be downloaded at no charge at https://www.binghamton.edu/som/cls/. Various elaborations and simplifications appear in the publications of Dansereau, Cho, and Yammarino (2006) and Dansereau and Yammarino (2000, 2006). Schriesheim (1995) also extended this approach to multivariate analysis, which further validated the methods portion of this inferential system.

With this approach, a significant hypothesized set of levels of analysis involving variables, entities, and their relationships can be expected at any level. To infer an effect at one level, other ways to view that level and other levels need to be conceptualized and tested as alternative hypotheses. Because this is a complex approach, an (admittedly oversimplified) illustration of the application may be helpful at this point. The previously cited publications and computer package provide much more detail about this approach.

As an example, first consider that units at any single level of analysis can be represented and theorized to be (a) whole units or (b) their parts within units. For instance, groups could be hypothesized to be the applicable entity for two variables as well as to be whole units—that is, a traditional homogeneous group. As an alternative, at the same group level, the hypothesis might state that the units can be viewed in terms of parts, in which the individuals in groups are interdependent but not homogeneous—the traditional "frog pond" view (Firebaugh, 1978). Second, because there are potentially other levels of analysis above or below the group level of interest, it is possible to decide whether an effect of interest is specific to that group level and does not apply above or below that level. Thus, there are three alternatives at each level: parts, wholes, and reject level (there are two different ways to define *reject level* in the approach that are defined in more detail in elaborations cited previously).

For a three-level case, then, at each level one can select an alternative at a level of interest. The selection of one alternative at both the higher and lower levels results in a multilevel theory that allows for parts or wholes that may or may not also include higher or lower levels. For example, in the case of a hypothesized group-level effect that involves individuals becoming homogenized into groups, the following selections at each level could be made:

- Lower level alternatives (e.g., person level):
  - Wholes (*selected for this example*)
  - Parts
  - Level does not apply
- Middle level alternatives (e.g., group level):
  - Wholes (*selected for this example*)
  - Parts
  - Level does not apply
- Higher level alternatives (e.g., department level):
  - Wholes
  - Parts
  - Level does not apply (*selected for this example*).

In this example, the proposed theory is about homogenized groups (middle level) formed by persons (lower level), but the groups are not based on departmental differences (higher level).

Using this approach, multiple hypotheses involving other theories that are implicit in the alternatives at each level or multiple levels are empirically tested against the illustrative proposed group theory. In other words, in the example, the test would assess whether the alternatives at each level are or are not more likely than the one selected. To support the theory in the example, the alternatives not selected would have to fail empirically. The books and articles referenced earlier describe how this selection is done on the basis of theory and data as well as the logic underlying this approach of applying strong inference to these multiple levels of analysis. Further description of this approach is also found in Chapter 24 of this volume.

Two recent illustrations of research that use this more exhaustive wholes-and-parts approach to testing alternative levels of analysis include the work by Markham and colleagues. Markham, Markham, and Smith (2015) examined dyadic configurations of subordinate feedback reports, whereas Markham, Smith, Markham, and Braekkan (2014) similarly looked at rater group effects to determine whether they could be characterized as whole feedback groups. The approach is actually considerably more complicated than presented here, but the present discussion is intended to provide a window into what I consider to be a major contribution of applying the strong inference approach to multiple levels of analysis.

In contrast to the strong inference approach, other popular approaches to levels tend to focus on the development of theories that cut across multiple levels in assumed—but not in directly tested—ways. The numerous empirical methods currently used in the field that were developed and associated with these theories tend to be based on modeling that assumes away another level or set of levels. In other words, a set of levels (and parts or wholes at that level) are assumed away, with only the salient levels (or level) assumed to hold. A significant result obtained involving variables and their relationships is then seen as supportive of the salient level or set of levels despite the lack of comprehensive testing.

Given the dominance of the popular assumptive approaches in the field, the alternative strong inference–based approach has raised a variety of questions and spurred vigorous debates, some of which have been described by Dansereau and Yammarino (1998a, 1998b, 2003, 2005, 2007; Yammarino & Dansereau, 2002, 2004, 2006, 2008a, 2008b, 2009). Emotions that were and remain extremely heated about these issues arose in the course of the debate over these approaches. Undoubtedly, such emotions will persist for the foreseeable future regarding the two contrasting general views about levels of analysis. These emotions are understandable and perhaps so vociferous, in part, because these approaches raise fundamental scientific questions about the strength of the previous studies and the results based on these two approaches.

If you knew then (in the early days of multilevel research) what you know now, how would your path have changed?

Fred Dansereau: Miller's (1978) work on levels of analysis and Platt's (1964) work on strong inferences were both largely based on a physical sciences–based approach to knowledge creation. That scientific view is rejected by some social scientists. At the beginning of their works, Miller and Platt discussed the difference between their perspectives and those promoted by some social scientists. Unfortunately, advocating this type of view in the social sciences can lead to some unique problems. To illustrate one such possibility, at one point in a presentation I said (to a social scientist), "If your view is correct, and if you jumped out the window and your constructed view of reality rejected gravity, would you not still fall?" A conference participant rebutted my assertion by insisting that the ability to test (and support) theories by trying to disprove them can apply only to the physical sciences, not to the social sciences.

This somewhat typical reaction to the strong inference approach voiced by some researchers became incredibly hostile at certain points during my career. Some members of the field preferred the view that as long as scientists agree about something, such as levels of analysis, consensus is all that is necessary to continue to carry out their research. For them, the issue of whether the levels exist in space and time was a moot point. Groups need not exist at all—they are abstract constructs; they are not necessarily collections of individuals. When I approached a chaired professor at a major institution who also took a physical sciences view and I asked about this perspective, he offered the following advice: "Never try to teach colleagues to accept a strong inference approach; doing so wastes your time and annoys the person you are trying to teach." His intention was not to demean those who disagree with the strong inference approach, but rather to point out that it is not helpful to make others uncomfortable with their own positions about science.

If I had fully realized early on how strongly some researchers would react to this approach, I might have devoted more attention to presenting the strong inference approach in social sciences in a way that would have been seen as helpful. If I had fully recognized the fundamental and polarizing differences between these two views, I would have been careful to seek publication of my work in outlets that also valued a physical sciences approach, as reflected by their editorial boards. Alternatively, in some journals it would have been possible to present the strong inference approach by addressing it from a constructed reality perspective as well as from a strong inference approach. As a result, it might have been possible to publish articles sooner than was the case. Needless to say, persistence in trying to publish on this topic is a requirement if the author hopes that his or her ideas will ever see the light of day.

Benjamin Schneider: I am going to respond to a similar question: How have things changed vis-à-vis multilevel research? When I began this kind of work back in the mid-1960s, it was already clear that the phenomena of interest to us simultaneously existed at different levels of analysis and that those levels impacted each other as well. But we did not have the computer power to study these issues. The first time I looked at interrater agreement (Schneider & Bartlett, 1970) on climate in life insurance agencies, I had to randomly choose two agents from each of the agencies and then submit their data (on punch cards) to obtain the correlation across agencies for two people per agency. I then had to do that 10 more times just to get some indication of the stability of the relationship. Today you can choose 500 random samples and push a button and get the distribution of the relationships in about .03 seconds. The point is that computing power has made all of this possible. I am not surprised by what is being studied and at the different levels of analysis, but I am surprised by (a) the dedication to the individual as the fundamental level of analysis, (b) the relative failure to do multivariable work at multiple levels, and (c) the relative failure to be looking at reciprocity between the variables we study and the outcomes we study, an issue I address in some detail later.

LOOKING FORWARD

What do you see as the most important multilevel issues or topics that will need to be addressed in the near future?

David Chan: I agree with the claim or premise that organizational phenomena are inherently multilevel in nature. However, I would add that organizational phenomena are also inherently multidimensional and temporal in nature. I have always considered a multilevel conceptualization as one of three equally important approaches that we need to explicitly

and simultaneously adopt, or at least pay attention to, when examining a substantive organizational phenomenon. The other two approaches are (a) a construct orientation that focuses on the dimensionality of the constructs and (b) a dynamic orientation that examines the different facets of changes over time that the constructs may undergo. In my view, the most important issue or topic that multilevel research should address in the near future is to explicitly incorporate construct dimensionality and changes over time into the study.

In many situations, this is not just about adding layers of complexity to enrich the theory of the phenomenon under study. Instead, it is about making accurate inferences and preventing misleading ones by taking into account fundamental issues of construct validity and the realistic nature of the construct as the process of change unfolds over time (Chan, 1998a, 2014b). For example, if basic issues related to measurement invariance (i.e., the psychometric equivalence of assessments taken across multiple groups or multiple waves of data collection) are not addressed when the number or nature of the construct dimensions changes across levels or over time, the measurement and analyses will likely result in misleading substantive conclusions.

The tendency to approach a phenomenon from a single lens is not unique to multilevel research. The neglect to consider multiple approaches is particularly noteworthy in the area of modeling changes in job performance dimensionality over time, given the amount of attention that researchers have focused on performance dimensionality and, separately, on performance dynamics (Chan, 2013). However, if the researcher is able to address construct dimensionality and changes over time when studying a multilevel phenomenon, it is likely to open up many fruitful venues for future research (Chan, 2011). For example, changes over time may exist in complex ways in cross-level situations. Chan (2014a) provided two such examples. One example is when changes over time at one level (e.g., subcultures) affect the changes over time or eventual outcome at another level (e.g., organizational culture). Another example concerns changes over time in an inherently cross-level construct such as person–organization fit in culture dimensions. Person–organization fit constructs are composite constructs consisting of the lower level person component and the higher level organization component. The cross-level nature of the construct raises issues of how different rates of change or different types of change occurring at different levels (or components) impact the cross-level (composite) construct.

Gilad Chen: How to conceptualize, empirically study, and analyze more complex multilevel influences in work organizations (e.g., in the many circumstances in which individuals work in multiple teams at the same time, examining contextual or top-down influences on individuals, as well as bottom-up influences on individuals across teams). Mathieu and Chen (2011) provided additional thoughts relevant to this question.

Fred Dansereau: Three types of work would be helpful for future work. First, it would be interesting to examine the numerous popular approaches that assume away some or multiple levels of analysis to see whether or how results differ on the basis of the specific approaches used. Such an assessment would require attention to what is being assumed away. To address this issue, researchers would apply more than one existing modeling approach to levels of analysis in one study on one set of data, thereby gaining a better idea of how the various modeling approaches are both similar and different. Such an approach could result in the specification of assumptions about multiple levels built into some of the popular, more assumptive types of analyses.

A second potentially fruitful line of investigation in the future might focus on testing at least some theories at multiple levels of analysis and across levels using a strong inference approach to multiple levels (e.g., Chapter 24, this volume).

Third, nothing prevents future studies from using the strong inference–based approach to test theories in tandem with use of approaches that are more assumptive to test some of the tacit assumptions.

Benjamin Schneider: I am no statistician so can only think conceptually, but the three most important issues requiring attention in multilevel work (especially in the fields of I/O psychology and OB) are (a) multivariable work, not just multilevel work; (b) a focus on important organizationally

relevant outcomes; and (c) exploration of the impact of outcomes on the variables we typically study as "causes" (i.e., potential reciprocal influences).

By *multivariable work* I mean that we need to stop studying only one variable at a time at different levels of analysis but rather do multivariable work at different levels of analysis. For example, in research on organizational climate, following Schneider's (1975) idea of assessing a climate "for something," scholars have studied only one such climate at a time (Kuenzi & Schminke, 2009). So, we have studies of service climate and safety climate and fairness climate, but rarely do we have studies simultaneously of fairness and service climate (Schneider et al., 2017) and their potentially supportive effects on employee turnover at different levels of analysis and customer satisfaction at different levels of analysis.

Further, there is an unfortunate inclination in the academic literature to become enamored of the concepts we study and a relative ignoring of important organizational consequences. For example, hierarchical linear modeling was invented to study the simultaneous impact of individual and situational variables on individual-level performance—again revealing the bias to studying individuals—and only recently have studies begun to emerge in which individual and situational variables are used in combination at different levels of analysis to predict unit or organizational outcomes (Liao & Chuang, 2007). The problem is that unit and organizational samples are difficult to obtain, so we persist in studying individual outcomes, and at that, they tend to be important only to the researchers. That is, managers in companies want to know how the company is doing compared with the marketplace in which they function, and we have not been good at clarifying how the microfoundations of organizational behavior we study get reflected in such competitive advantage (Ployhart & Hale, 2014).

Finally, I fear we have lived in a left-to-right world in which our boxes and arrows end in outcomes; we study the microfoundations of important consequences or outcomes and do so at different levels of analysis, but we almost never study the impact of consequences and outcomes on the microfoundations. When employees serve satisfied customers, is there no effect on employee satisfaction? Yes, there is, and the so-called outside-in effect is larger than the inside-out effect (Zablah, Carlson, Donavan, Maxham, & Brown, 2016). When organizations are competitively successful in their marketplaces, does that not influence the aggregate job satisfaction for those there? Yes, it does, with the financial success of companies having a consistently larger effect on employee satisfaction than the reverse (Schneider, Hanges, Smith, & Salvaggio, 2003). In the world of I/O and OB, we have paid scarce attention at all to the fact that individuals and units or organizations and their consequences and outcomes reciprocate and evolve and change over time, and thus we know little about how those changes emerge and occur and the influence of different levels of analysis on those changes. We would do well to pay more attention to how organizations and their members evolve and change over time and the ways reciprocity may operate prior to concluding from our sophisticated multilevel structural equation models that the arrows always go from left to right (Aldrich, 1999).

Give us a bold prediction: Twenty years from now, multilevel research will . . .

Denise Rousseau: Twenty years from now, multilevel research will have a time machine. I am hopeful that simulations will be included in organizational research publications on a more regular basis. It is one thing to theorize with words and another to specify and test how relationships evolve over time. I am working now with Carnegie Mellon colleagues who use simulations to supplement fieldwork on the effects positive and negative workplace incentives have on employee behavior. It is like having a time machine!

David Chan: I believe that 20 years from now, multilevel research in the organizational sciences will be much more common in the micro areas, such as those in the field of organizational behavior, but remain relatively rare in the macro areas, such as those in the field of strategy.

Benjamin Schneider: . . . be ubiquitous. In a recent review of the literature in *Journal of Applied Psychology* (on climate; Schneider et al., 2017), we discovered that much of the research on climate in the last 15 years has become multilevel, and I see no reason why that will not be true in research on other topics. I also hope (but do not predict it will be true) that the research is not only multilevel but multivariable with multilevel outcomes and foci.

Gilad Chen: . . . be able to explain more complex multilevel phenomena, which transcend multiple organizational and work and nonwork units and systems.

Fred Dansereau: In the future, it seems likely that the popular assumptive approaches of the past will continue to be applied in future studies. More and more modeling approaches are likely to be developed that are predisposed to favor whatever theories are proposed. In turn, effects will be assumed at one or several levels, and whether the real effects might be observed at another level will not be tested. This kind of narrowly defined approach has potentially very negative consequences. As one example, consider the situation in which efforts are targeted at the group level, yet the real effects are found at the individual level. Certainly, the amount of time wasted in group meetings addressing problems that might better be handled at the individual level are familiar to almost all individuals who have ever worked.

This future seems likely, given the track record of the past. The current situation—at least in the leadership literature—does not suggest that testing alternative hypotheses will become a major approach. Specifically, Dionne et al. (2014) showed that only 17% of leadership studies over a 25-year period tested for multiple levels simultaneously. In contrast, Dionne et al. reported a change in that a larger number of studies at least explicitly considered levels of analysis in some way over time than in the past. It would not be a problem if this prediction failed to become reality.

The application of the strong inference approach outside the domain of organizational behavior and leadership does have appeal, however—for example, in business and engineering. To the extent that this approach can analyze and test hypotheses about entities as well as variables, it would seem destined to be very attractive to business researchers who model dynamic systems using both visualization and simulation tools (Markham, 1998, 2002). This new audience includes operations researchers, change management specialists, industrial system engineers, database designers, and organizational architects, to name just a few.

What paradigm shifts do you see in the future for multilevel research? What might facilitate (or force) this shift, and how might junior researchers prepare for this shift now?

David Chan: The increasing use of big data in science and practice will motivate or force researchers to learn novel data collection methods and analytical procedures such as visual analytics, agent-based modeling, and other computational modeling methodologies. I believe the real paradigm shift for multilevel research arising from the ubiquitous use of big data is conceptual rather than driven by novel technologies or techniques. To me, the basic paradigm-shift question is this: What are the different ways in which the characteristics of big data (e.g., volume, velocity, variety) could lead to a qualitative change in the way multilevel research is conducted in terms of generating and testing research hypotheses? Many possibilities can come to mind if we apply multilevel conceptualizations (e.g., composition models, structure and function of collective constructs, emergence) to big-data studies to investigate phenomena such as crowd behaviors, collective movements, and contagion.

To prepare for this paradigm shift, I have two suggestions for multilevel researchers. First, we need to adopt a multidisciplinary orientation and to do so earlier rather than later. We need to go beyond our colleagues in the organizational, social, and behavioral sciences to learn from and work with academics and practitioners in the computational sciences. Second, given the dynamic nature of big data, we need to adopt a dynamic approach to the way we think about multilevel theories, design, measurement, and analysis. This adds to the urgency in what I explained earlier about the need for multilevel research to incorporate issues

of changes over time in their research. Both the multidisciplinary and dynamic approaches should be given more emphasis in graduate school training in multilevel research methods.

With respect to your multilevel research, has there been anything you have wanted to say, but could not get past the reviewers and editors for one reason or another? This is your chance to tell the field.

Benjamin Schneider: There is something I want to tell journal editors and journal reviewers: Get over your obsession with the individual level of analysis. From my very earliest studies to the present, I have received reviews that I cannot believe. For example, in my early linkage of service climate to customer satisfaction (Schneider et al., 1980) across 27 branches of a bank, I was told the sample size was too small. In a recent submission of a paper on employee engagement at the company level of analysis, I was told that it was inappropriate to study engagement as a company-level phenomenon! And most recently, I submitted a paper on personality homogeneity (the ASA model; Schneider, 1987) linking aggregate personality in companies to financial returns for those same companies. This time I was told I did not present evidence that the personality measure I used predicted individual-level performance! Really, are these editors and reviewers not paying any attention to the need for us to study the behavioral consequences of aggregates of people in organizations? Are editors and reviewers so enamored of the world of academe that they fail to understand that our work has the potential to have utility for companies but that this will be true only if we show it to be true (Ployhart & Schneider, 2012)?

Fred Dansereau: My hopes for the future represent my reaction to being asked by individuals for advice about whether they should act at the individual, group, department, division, corporate, or societal level, or at some combination of these levels. When I have tried to answer such questions, I have found very few data that address these issues directly. If researchers devote themselves to theorizing about and testing among alternative multiple levels of analysis, however, answers to such questions might be based on analysis of data rather than representing purely theoretical assumptions and preferences. Most of the studies from the recent past seem to suggest that the value of this approach is being ignored. Time will tell whether researchers broaden their views to embrace the opportunities offered by this innovative strategy. Nevertheless, if it were embraced, it would become possible to have greater assurance that, when interventions are undertaken at one level for some variables or allocations, those actions are truly warranted.

David Chan: I have not tried saying it in a manuscript, so I do not know if it could get past the reviewers and editors. I would want to say that although it is true that probably all phenomena of interest in organizational research are inherently multilevel, it is not true that all research questions about the phenomena, and therefore the data analytic techniques, need to be multilevel in nature.

ADVICE FOR THOSE PURSUING MULTILEVEL RESEARCH

For those who are new to conducting multilevel research, what might be some barriers that you experienced, and how could those be avoided?

Benjamin Schneider: If you focus the research effort at the individual level of analysis for the outcome, you are alright usually with regard to sample size. If you study teams or units, and especially the organizational level, the reviewers will kill you on sample size. If you aggregate individual-level perceptions to obtain a unit score, you must point out in your paper that reliable (ICC1 and ICC2; r_{wg}) aggregate data are more reliable than the sample size because of the fact that power is a function not only of sample size, but of data reliability as well.

Denise Rousseau: Don't let people tell you that it is too hard to collect multilevel data. I have found it relatively straightforward to do fieldwork looking into cross-level effects (bottom-up or top-down) using interviews, surveys, or archival data attached to individual, unit, or dyadic levels. Take a look at what some clever folks like Bob Liden and Sandy Wayne and their students are doing to look at nested effects of teams, managers, and employees for inspiration.

Fred Dansereau: Attempting to publish multiple-levels research is difficult because researchers often have a particular level that they prefer—the individual, the group, or something else. Entire analytic procedures are then based on assumptions that favor a particular preferred level of analysis and ignore other levels. With this perspective, researchers need to justify what they are doing based only on their theory and the assumptions of that theory. In such a case, introducing and testing for levels that are part of the situation but are not typically part of the theory may raise in the reviewer's mind (mistaken) questions about whether the theory is clear and fully driving the analyses. To introduce and assess alternative views of levels, then, carries considerable risk when the goal is publishing results within a reasonable period of time. A reviewer may very well have been the person who originally tested a theory in a particular way and will defend that work as a legitimate construction accepted in the field, rejecting your results and approach as part of that defense and not necessarily on a scientific basis.

As a result, attempts to publish papers that focus on testing among alternative hypothesized levels are likely to irritate many reviewers. In contrast, if researchers follow currently used methods based on their theory, their efforts will typically be deemed acceptable and their publication efforts may find a warmer reception.

One way around this problem is to test among alternative hypothesized levels but also use the more assumptive approaches. The problem with this strategy is that the results from the applications of the two approaches may differ. Because discrepant results will raise questions among reviewers, from a career perspective it might be best to wait until receiving tenure before trying to publish studies that fully test alternative hypotheses. In any case, I think that it is best to always work closely with very bright and supportive colleagues with a similar scientific point of view, which I was truly fortunate to be able to do throughout my career.

Are there suggestions or life lessons that you would like to pass along to junior researchers?

Gilad Chen: Multilevel phenomena are complex and can sometimes be flat-out nasty and difficult to fully grasp and study. However, they reflect real-life realities in work organizations, with all their messiness. That is what makes multilevel research both challenging and fascinating. Studying multilevel phenomena provides scholars with unique opportunities to contribute to our literature, and hence can be exciting and instrumental to junior scholars in the field. Along these lines, I have also found that when conducting complex multilevel research on important phenomena, reviewers sometimes cut you more slack and allow you to publish work that may not be perfect from statistical or methodological standpoints, yet can nonetheless add to our knowledge in important ways. In other words, embrace the messiness multilevel research entails, and go on studying important and complex multilevel phenomena. There are many, many more opportunities for discoveries and contributions ahead of us in this field.

Denise Rousseau: I would look to biology for insights into multilevel effects. The populations studied have large numbers, and often short life cycles, and lots of environmental effects on behavior and responses can be studied.

David Chan: In the literature on multilevel methods, there is much focus on different aggregation methods, such as the use of various within-group agreement indices and different data analytic techniques such as hierarchical linear modeling techniques and multilevel structural equation modeling. However, the technical understanding of multilevel measurement and analytical strategies is necessary but not sufficient for advancing specific fields of substantive research. Conceptual issues and methodological issues in multilevel research are inextricably linked. To adequately examine multilevel phenomena, the methodological issues and choices concerning measurement and analysis should be grounded in the conceptual bases for the focal constructs.

CONCLUSION

Although it is clear from the responses that the panelists all brought unique perspectives, experiences, and insights to the conversation, a few common themes emerged across their

various responses. First, despite the progress that researchers have made in addressing theoretical, measurement, and analytic issues since the early days of multilevel research and the increasingly frequent use of multilevel methods, it can still be difficult to publish multilevel studies. As discussed, reviewers and editors often become fixated with a specific level of analysis—most often, the individual level. It can also be particularly difficult if the great majority of prior research in the respective research area consists of theoretical work that does not account for the multilevel nature of the phenomena and is applicable only at a single level. Additionally, it is not uncommon to see reviewers bemoan the lack of sample size at the highest level of analysis or dispute the level at which a construct is appropriate solely because of past conceptualizations of the construct. Although these are certainly important considerations that require their due diligence, there appears to be, at times, a general reluctance to shift one's way of thinking to a multilevel perspective.

Second, the panelists wrote of the value of the diversity of backgrounds and scientific viewpoints. In fact, as evidence of this, panelists offered details of their own differing backgrounds in terms of graduate school research, courses, and literature they read. The specific paths they each traveled led them to unique perspectives, and they often drew connections to how those differences heavily influenced their work and their understanding of the multilevel nature of psychological constructs. Further, the panelists also highlighted the value to be gained from looking not only outside of one's primary research interests, but also outside of one's field. In short, diversity of perspective can be conducive to great progress.

The final theme that recurred across many responses was that theory, measurement, and analysis are inseparably interconnected. The panelists stated this either directly or indirectly in the majority of their responses. When investigating multilevel phenomena, the researcher must have a firm conceptual understanding of the focal constructs, their multilevel nature, and how to best coordinate measurement and analysis of these constructs. As the panelists discussed, advances in multilevel theory over the past few decades—

thanks in large part to the efforts of the panelists—have helped lay the groundwork for how multilevel constructs should be measured and analyzed.

In summary, researchers interested in multilevel methods have more to consider than just learning a new analytical approach. A thorough understanding of multilevel theory, measurement, and analysis is becoming increasingly vital in the organizational sciences. Even though the publication process for multilevel research can be difficult at times, it is becoming increasingly clear that much of what is studied in the social sciences is inherently multilevel. Further, bringing a diverse background to multilevel research and seeking insights outside of one's immediate research area or discipline can be highly beneficial to the researcher's understanding. Hopefully, the advice and wisdom offered here from the esteemed panelists can help aid researchers in more efficiently navigating the multilevel waters.

References

Aldrich, H. (1999). *Organizations evolving.* Thousand Oaks, CA: Sage.

Argyris, C. (1957). *Personality and organization.* New York: Harper & Bros.

Bowers, K. S. (1973). Situationism in psychology: An analysis and a critique. *Psychological Review, 80,* 307–336. http://dx.doi.org/10.1037/h0035592

Bradley-Geist, J. C., & Landis, R. S. (2012). Homogeneity of personality in occupations and organizations: A comparison of alternative statistical tests. *Journal of Business and Psychology, 27,* 149–159. http://dx.doi.org/10.1007/s10869-011-9233-6

Chan, D. (1998a). The conceptualization and analysis of change over time: An integrative approach incorporating longitudinal means and covariance structures analysis (LMACS) and multiple indicator latent growth modeling (MLGM). *Organizational Research Methods, 1,* 421–483. http://dx.doi.org/10.1177/109442819814004

Chan, D. (1998b). Functional relations among constructs in the same content domain at different levels of analysis: A typology of composition models. *Journal of Applied Psychology, 83,* 234–246. http://dx.doi.org/10.1037/0021-9010.83.2.234

Chan, D. (2005). Multilevel research. In F. T. L. Leong & J. T. Austin (Eds.), *The psychology research handbook* (2nd ed., pp. 401–418). Thousand Oaks, CA: Sage.

Chan, D. (2011). Longitudinal assessment of changes in job performance and work attitudes: Conceptual and methodological issues. *International Review of Industrial and Organizational Psychology, 26,* 93–117.

Chan, D. (2013). Advances in modeling dimensionality and dynamics of job performance. In K. J. Ford, J. Hollenbeck, & A. M. Ryan (Eds.), *The psychology of work* (pp. 211–228). Washington, DC: American Psychological Association.

Chan, D. (2014a). Multilevel and aggregation issues in climate and culture research. In B. Schneider & K. M. Babera (Eds.), *The Oxford handbook of organizational climate and culture research* (pp. 484–495). New York, NY: Oxford University Press.

Chan, D. (2014b). Time and methodological choices. In A. J. Shipp & Y. Fried (Eds.), *Time and work (Vol. 2): How time impacts groups, organizations, and methodological choices* (pp. 146–176). New York, NY: Psychology Press.

Chen, G., Bliese, P. D., & Mathieu, J. E. (2005). Conceptual framework and statistical procedures for delineating and testing multilevel theories of homology. *Organizational Research Methods, 8,* 375–409. http://dx.doi.org/10.1177/1094428105280056

Chen, G., & Kanfer, R. (2006). Toward a systems theory of motivated behavior in work teams. *Research in Organizational Behavior, 27,* 223–267. http://dx.doi.org/10.1016/S0191-3085(06)27006-0

Chen, G., Kanfer, R., DeShon, R. P., Mathieu, J. E., & Kozlowski, S. W. J. (2009). The motivating potential of teams: Test and extension of Chen & Kanfer's (2006) cross-level model of motivation in teams. *Organizational Behavior and Human Decision Processes, 110,* 45–55. http://dx.doi.org/10.1016/j.obhdp.2009.06.006

Chen, G., Kirkman, B. L., Kanfer, R., Allen, D., & Rosen, B. (2007). A multilevel study of leadership, empowerment, and performance in teams. *Journal of Applied Psychology, 92,* 331–346. http://dx.doi.org/10.1037/0021-9010.92.2.331

Chen, G., Mathieu, J. E., & Bliese, P. D. (2004). A framework for conducting multi-level construct validation. In F. J. Yammarino & F. Dansereau (Eds.), *Research in multilevel issues: Multilevel issues in organizational behavior and processes* (Vol. 3, pp. 273–303). Oxford, England: Elsevier. http://dx.doi.org/10.1016/S1475-9144(04)03013-9

Dansereau, F., Alutto, J., & Yammarino, F. (1984). *Theory testing in organizational behavior: The varient approach.* Englewood Cliffs, NJ: Prentice-Hall.

Dansereau, F., Chandrasekaran, G., Dumas, M., Coleman, D., Ehrlich, S., & Bagchi, D. (1986). *DETECT = Data enquiry that tests entity and correlational/causal theories: Program and application and user's guide.* Buffalo, NY: Institute for Theory Testing. Available at https://www.binghamton.edu/som/cls/

Dansereau, F., Cho, J., & Yammarino, F. (2006). Avoiding the fallacy of the wrong level: A within and between analysis (WABA) approach. *Group & Organization Management, 31,* 536–577. http://dx.doi.org/10.1177/1059601106291131

Dansereau, F., & Yammarino, F. (Eds.). (1998a). *Leadership: The multiple-level approaches: Classical and new wave* (Vol. A). Stamford, CT: JAI Press.

Dansereau, F., & Yammarino, F. (Eds.). (1998b). *Leadership: The multiple-level approaches: Contemporary and alternative* (Vol. B). Stamford, CT: JAI Press.

Dansereau, F., & Yammarino, F. (2000). Within and between analysis: The varient paradigm as an underlying approach to theory building and testing. In K. Klein & S. Kozlowski (Eds.), *Multilevel theory, research, and methods in organizations: Foundations, extensions, and new directions* (pp. 425–466). San Francisco, CA: Jossey-Bass.

Dansereau, F., & Yammarino, F. (2003). *Multi-level issues in organizational behavior and strategy* (Research in Multi-Level Issues, Vol. 2). Oxford, England: Emerald.

Dansereau, F., & Yammarino, F. (2005). *Multi-level issues in strategy and methods* (Research in Multi-Level Issues, Vol. 4). Oxford, England: Emerald.

Dansereau, F., & Yammarino, F. (2006). Is more discussion about levels of analysis really necessary? When is such discussion sufficient? *The Leadership Quarterly, 17,* 537–552. http://dx.doi.org/10.1016/j.leaqua.2006.07.002

Dansereau, F., & Yammarino, F. (2007). *Multi-level issues in organizations and time* (Research in Multi-Level Issues, Vol. 6). Oxford, England: Emerald.

De Greene, K. B. (1973). *Sociotechnical systems: Factors in analysis, design, and management.* New York, NY: Prentice Hall.

Dionne, S., Gupta, A., Sotak, K., Shirreffs, A., Serban, A., Hao, C., . . . Yammarino, F. (2014). A 25-year perspective on levels of analysis in leadership research. *The Leadership Quarterly, 25,* 6–35. http://dx.doi.org/10.1016/j.leaqua.2013.11.002

Firebaugh, G. (1978). A rule for inferring individual-level relationships from aggregate data. *American Sociological Review, 43,* 557–572. http://dx.doi.org/10.2307/2094779

Holland, J. L. (1966). *The psychology of vocational choice.* Waltham, MA: Blaisdell.

Hollenbeck, J. R. (1998). *Personnel Psychology*'s citation leading articles: The first five decades. *Personnel Psychology, 51,* 818–819. http://dx.doi.org/10.1111/j.1744-6570.1998.tb00736.x

House, R., Rousseau, D. M., & Thomas-Hunt, M. (1995). The meso paradigm: A framework for the integration of micro and macro organizational behavior. In L. L. Cummings & E. M. Staw (Eds.), *Research in organizational behavior* (Vol. 17, pp. 71–114). Greenwich, CT: JAI Press.

James, L. R. (1982). Aggregation bias in estimates of perceptual agreement. *Journal of Applied Psychology, 67,* 219–229. http://dx.doi.org/10.1037/0021-9010.67.2.219

James, L. R., Demaree, R. G., & Wolf, G. (1984). Estimating within-group interrater reliability with and without response bias. *Journal of Applied Psychology, 69,* 85–98. http://dx.doi.org/10.1037/0021-9010.69.1.85

James, L. R., & Jones, A. P. (1974). Organizational climate: A review of theory and research. *Psychological Bulletin, 81,* 1096–1112. http://dx.doi.org/10.1037/h0037511

Jones, A. P., & James, L. R. (1979). Psychological climate: Dimensions and relationships of individual and aggregated work environment perceptions. *Organizational Behavior and Human Performance, 23,* 201–250. http://dx.doi.org/10.1016/0030-5073(79)90056-4

Klein, K. J., Dansereau, F., & Hall, R. J. (1994). Levels issues in theory development, data collection, and analysis. *Academy of Management Review, 19,* 195–229.

Kozlowski, S. W. J., & Hults, B. M. (1987). An exploration of climates for technical updating and performance. *Personnel Psychology, 40,* 539–563. http://dx.doi.org/10.1111/j.1744-6570.1987.tb00614.x

Kozlowski, S. W. J., & Klein, K. J. (2000). A multilevel approach to theory and research in organizations: Contextual, temporal, and emergent processes. In K. J. Klein & S. W. J. Kozlowski (Eds.), *Multilevel theory, research, and methods in organizations* (pp. 3–90). San Francisco, CA: Jossey-Bass.

Kuenzi, M., & Schminke, M. (2009). Assembling fragments into a lens: A review, critique, and proposed research agenda for the organizational work climate literature. *Journal of Management, 35,* 634–717. http://dx.doi.org/10.1177/0149206308330559

Lewin, K. (1935). *Dynamic theory of personality.* New York, NY: McGraw-Hill.

Lewin, K. (1943). Defining the field at a given time. *Psychological Review, 50,* 292–310. http://dx.doi.org/10.1037/h0062738

Lewin, K. (1951). *Field theory in social science.* New York, NY: Harper & Row.

Liao, H., & Chuang, A. (2007). Transforming service employees and climate: A multilevel, multisource examination of transformational leadership in building long-term service relationships. *Journal of Applied Psychology, 92,* 1006–1019. http://dx.doi.org/10.1037/0021-9010.92.4.1006

Magnusson, D., & Endler, N. S. (Eds.). (1977). *Personality at the crossroads: Current issues in interactional psychology*. Hillsdale, NJ: Lawrence Erlbaum.

Markham, S. E. (1998). The scientific visualization of organizations: A rationale for a new approach to organizational modeling. *Decision Sciences, 29*, 1–23. http://dx.doi.org/10.1111/j.1540-5915.1998.tb01342.x

Markham, S. E. (2002). Multi-level simulation analysis issues: Four themes. In F. Dansereau & F. J. Yammarino (Eds.), *The many faces of multi-level issues* (*Research in Multi-Level Issues*, Vol. 1, pp. 387–396). Oxford, England: Emerald. http://dx.doi.org/10.1016/S1475-9144(02)01044-5

Markham, S. E., Markham, I. S., & Smith, J. W. (2015). At the crux of dyadic leadership: Self–other agreement of leaders and direct reports—Analyzing 360-degree feedback. *The Leadership Quarterly, 26*, 958–977. http://dx.doi.org/10.1016/j.leaqua.2015.10.001

Markham, S. E., Smith, J. W., Markham, I. S., & Braekkan, K. F. (2014). A new approach to analyzing the Achilles' heel of multisource feedback programs: Can we really trust ratings of leaders at the group level of analysis? *The Leadership Quarterly, 25*, 1120–1142. http://dx.doi.org/10.1016/j.leaqua.2014.10.003

Mathieu, J. E., & Chen, G. (2011). The etiology of the multilevel paradigm in management research. *Journal of Management, 37*, 610–641. http://dx.doi.org/10.1177/0149206310364663

McClelland, D. C. (1961). *The achieving society*. Princeton, NJ: Van Nostrand. http://dx.doi.org/10.1037/14359-000

McGregor, D. M. (1960). *The human side of enterprise*. New York, NY: McGraw-Hill.

Miller, M. (1978). *Living systems*. New York, NY: McGraw-Hill.

Mischel, W. (1968). *Personality and assessment*. New York, NY: Wiley.

Morgeson, F. P., & Hofmann, D. A. (1999). The structure and function of collective constructs: Implications for multilevel research and theory development. *The Academy of Management Review, 24*, 249–265. http://dx.doi.org/10.2307/259081

Ostroff, C. (1993). Comparing correlations based on individual-level and aggregated data. *Journal of Applied Psychology, 78*, 569–582. http://dx.doi.org/10.1037/0021-9010.78.4.569

Platt, J. R. (1964). Strong inference: Certain systematic methods of scientific thinking may produce much more rapid progress than others. *Science, 146*, 347–353. http://dx.doi.org/10.1126/science.146.3642.347

Ployhart, R. E., & Hale, D., Jr. (2014). The fascinating psychological microfoundations of strategy and competitive advantage. *Annual Review of Organizational Psychology and Organizational Behavior, 1*, 145–172. http://dx.doi.org/10.1146/annurev-orgpsych-031413-091312

Ployhart, R. E., & Schneider, B. (2012). The social and organizational context of personnel selection. In N. Schmitt (Ed.), *The Oxford handbook of personnel assessment and selection* (pp. 48–67). New York, NY: Oxford University Press. http://dx.doi.org/10.1093/oxfordhb/9780199732579.013.0004

Porter, L. W., & Schneider, B. (2014). What was, what is, and what may be in OP/OB. *Annual Review of Organizational Psychology and Organizational Behavior, 1*, 1–21. http://dx.doi.org/10.1146/annurev-orgpsych-031413-091302

Roberts, K. H., Hulin, C. L., & Rousseau, D. M. (1978). *Developing an interdisciplinary science of organizations*. San Francisco, CA: Jossey-Bass.

Robinson, W. S. (1950). Ecological correlations and the behavior of individuals. *American Sociological Review, 15*, 351–357. http://dx.doi.org/10.2307/2087176

Rousseau, D. M. (1985). Issues of level in organizational research: Multi-level and cross-level perspectives. In L. L. Cummings & B. Staw (Eds.), *Research in organizational behavior* (Vol. 7, pp. 1–37). Greenwich, CT: JAI Press.

Schein, E. H. (1965). *Organizational psychology*. Englewood Cliffs, NJ: Prentice-Hall.

Schein, E. H. (2010). *Organizational culture and leadership* (4th ed.). San Francisco, CA: Jossey-Bass.

Schneider, B. (1975). Organizational climates: An essay. *Personnel Psychology, 28*, 447–479. http://dx.doi.org/10.1111/j.1744-6570.1975.tb01386.x

Schneider, B. (1983a). Interactional psychology and organizational behavior. In L. L. Cummings & B. Staw (Eds.), *Research in organizational behavior* (Vol. 5, pp. 1–32). Greenwich, CT: JAI Press.

Schneider, B. (1983b). An interactionist perspective on organizational effectiveness. In K. Cameron & D. S. Whetten (Eds.), *Organizational effectiveness* (pp. 27–54). New York, NY: Academic Press. http://dx.doi.org/10.1016/B978-0-12-157180-1.50007-0

Schneider, B. (1985). Organizational behavior. *Annual Review of Psychology, 36*, 573–611. http://dx.doi.org/10.1146/annurev.ps.36.020185.003041

Schneider, B. (1987). The people make the place. *Personnel Psychology, 40*, 437–453. http://dx.doi.org/10.1111/j.1744-6570.1987.tb00609.x

Schneider, B. (1990). The climate for service: An application of the climate construct. In B. Schneider (Ed.), *Organizational climate and culture* (pp. 383–412). San Francisco, CA: Jossey-Bass.

Schneider, B., & Bartlett, C. J. (1968). Individual differences and organizational climate: I. The research plan and questionnaire development. *Personnel Psychology, 21*, 323–333. http://dx.doi.org/10.1111/j.1744-6570.1968.tb02033.x

Schneider, B., & Bartlett, C. J. (1970). Individual differences and organizational climate II: Measurement of organizational climate by the multi-trait, multi-rater matrix. *Personnel Psychology, 23*, 493–512. http://dx.doi.org/10.1111/j.1744-6570.1970.tb01368.x

Schneider, B., González-Romá, V., Ostroff, C., & West, M. A. (2017). Organizational climate and culture: Reflections on the history of the constructs in the *Journal of Applied Psychology. Journal of Applied Psychology, 102*, 468–482. http://dx.doi.org/10.1037/apl0000090

Schneider, B., Hanges, P. J., Smith, D. B., & Salvaggio, A. N. (2003). Which comes first: Employee attitudes or organizational financial and market performance? *Journal of Applied Psychology, 88*, 836–851. http://dx.doi.org/10.1037/0021-9010.88.5.836

Schneider, B., Parkington, J. P., & Buxton, V. M. (1980). Employee and customer perceptions of service in banks. *Administrative Science Quarterly, 25*, 252–267. http://dx.doi.org/10.2307/2392454

Schneider, B., Smith, D. B., Taylor, S., & Fleenor, J. (1998). Personality and organizations: A test of the homogeneity of personality hypothesis. *Journal of Applied Psychology, 83*, 462–470. http://dx.doi.org/10.1037/0021-9010.83.3.462

Schriesheim, C. (1995). Multivariate and moderated within- and between-entity analysis (WABA) using hierarchical linear multiple regression. *The Leadership Quarterly, 6*, 1–18. http://dx.doi.org/10.1016/1048-9843(95)90002-0

Yammarino, F., & Dansereau, F. (Eds.). (2002). *The many faces of multi-level issues* (Research in Multi-Level Issues, Vol. 1). Oxford, England: Emerald.

Yammarino, F., & Dansereau, F. (Eds.). (2004). *Multi-level issues in organizational behavior and processes* (*Research in Multi-Level Issues*, Vol. 3). Oxford, England: Emerald.

Yammarino, F., & Dansereau, F. (Eds.). (2006). *Multi-level issues in social systems* (Research in Multi-Level Issues, Vol. 5). Oxford, England: Emerald.

Yammarino, F., & Dansereau, F. (2008a). Introduction to multi-level issues in creativity and innovation. In M. Mumford, S. Hunter, & E. Bedell-Avers (Eds.), *Multi-level issues in creativity and innovation* (*Research in Multi-Level Issues*, Vol. 7, pp. xiii–xx). Oxford, England: Emerald.

Yammarino, F., & Dansereau, F. (2008b). Multi-level nature of and multi-level approaches to leadership. *The Leadership Quarterly, 19*, 135–141. http://dx.doi.org/10.1016/j.leaqua.2008.01.001

Yammarino, F., & Dansereau, F. (Eds.). (2009). *Multi-level issues in organizational behavior and leadership* (*Research in Multi-Level Issues*, Vol. 8). Oxford, England: Emerald. http://dx.doi.org/10.1108/S1475-9144(2009)8

Zablah, A. R., Carlson, B. D., Donavan, D. T., Maxham, J. G., III, & Brown, T. J. (2016). A cross-lagged test of the association between customer satisfaction and employee job satisfaction in a relational context. *Journal of Applied Psychology, 101*, 743–755. http://dx.doi.org/10.1037/apl0000079

Zohar, D. (1980). Safety climate in industrial organizations: Theoretical and applied implications. *Journal of Applied Psychology, 65*, 96–102. http://dx.doi.org/10.1037/0021-9010.65.1.96

Index

Brown, N. A., 79
Browne, W. J., 332
Bryk, A. S., 365, 397, 456, 457, 460, 462, 464, 570
Building-block approach to SEM, 466
Burba, M., 182
Burke, M. J., 291
Burt, R. S., 195
Busing, F., 332
Butterfly effect, 122
Butts, M. M., 308, 315
Buxton, V. M., 593
Bystander effects, 51

Cannon-Bowers, J. A., 166
Canonical link function, 503
Canonical parameter (θ), 501
Canonical situation perspective on context, 68
    and CAPTION model, 74
    and Chinese idiom approach, 76
    and perceived qualities of situations approach, 78
    and SAAP framework, 80
    and Situational Eight DIAMONDS approach, 77
    and situational strength, 81
    in ten Berge and De Raad's approach, 83
CAPTION model, 73–74, 83
CAPTION scale, 74
CAPTIONs short form, 74
Career environments, 594
Careless responses, 235
Carter, D. R., 178
Carter, N. M., 126
Carter, N. T., 178
Case-by-variable data matrices, 190
CATA (computer-aided text analysis), 178, 179
Catastrophe theory, 132
Categorical variables, in social relations model, 435–438
Causal direction, context and, 69
Cause and effect relationships
    in complexity science, 127
    covariance in, 21–22
    explanations of, 17–21
    path diagram for modeling, 91
    temporal precedence in, 22–26
CEM. *See* Consensus emergence model
Centering
    cluster-mean, 321
    grand-mean, 362, 401

group-mean, 362, 401
of predictors, 335
within-group, 482
Centrality
    betweenness, 193, 194
    cross-level effects of, 197
    in cross-level moderator model, 213
    degree, 196, 204
    eigenvector, 194
    isomorphism for, 196
    social network analysis of, 128
Centralization, 192–193
Central tendency bias, 263
CFA. *See* Confirmatory factor analysis
CFA full measurement model, 464–466
CFA test of conceptual model, 466–468
Chan, D., 258–260, 319–320, 570, 590–591, 594–595, 598–603
Chandler, M. M., 308
Change
    catastrophic, 96
    in complexity science, 116
    discontinuous, 25, 121, 123
    endogenous, 93, 100–101, 104–105, 108–109
    planned, 92–93
    temporal, in groups, 521
Chao, G. T., 152, 172–173
Characteristics, in metatheories of context, 70, 80, 85
Chen, G., 166, 256–259, 268–270, 272, 573, 590, 592–593, 595, 599, 600, 602–603
Chiles, T. H., 121
Cho, J., 596
Christian, L. M., 234
Christiansen, J., 129
CIs. *See* Confidence intervals
Clark, M. R., 134
Clark, P. C., 353
Class 1 constructs, 254
Class I networks, 207, 208, 213
Class 2 constructs, 255–256
Class II networks, 207, 208, 214–215
Class 3 constructs, 256
Class III networks, 207–210
Class 4 constructs. *See* Multilevel constructs
Class IV networks, 207, 209, 210
Class V networks, 207, 209, 211, 212
Class VI networks, 207, 209, 211
Classes, in metatheories of context, 70, 76, 85
Climate consensus, social network in, 544–545

Climate emergence. *See also* Organizational climate
    formal model of, 545–556
    R syntax for formal model of, 557–558
CLiMATE model, 547–553
    limitations of, 556
    network contagion effects in, 548–550, 553
    network density effects in, 548, 552, 553
    network structure and, 553–556
    random error in, 548, 551
    R syntax for, 557–558
    stochastic shocks in, 548, 551
Climate strength, 544–545
Closed systems, 18
Clustered data, 458, 481, 513
Clustered variance, 53
Clustering coefficients, 556n8
Cluster-mean centering, 321
Clusters, of organizational units, 226–227
Cluster sampling design, adaptive, 233
Coalescing phase, 175
Codeterminism, 115, 119–120
Coefficient examination, in homology testing, 271–272
Coff, R. W., 151
Cognitive and affective trust study, 429–439
    analytical approach in, 429–430
    and complexity of dyadic data analysis, 438–439
    data preparation for, 430–432
    null models in, 432–435
    prediction models in, 435–438
    R code for, 441–444
Cognitive attributional approach to context, 74, 76
Cognitive demands of situation, 86
Cohen, M., 341
Cohesion
    CEM-based data analysis on, 533–536
    as Class 3 construct, 256
    in job satisfaction and leadership style example, 365
    in trait aggression and counterproductive work behaviors example, 393–394
Cole, M. S., 460
Coleman, J. S., 156, 188, 202, 215–216
Coleman's boat model, 215–216
Collective attitudes and responses, in internal context, 49–50, 54
Collective behavior, 56
Collective constructs, forms of, 182

Ghandour, L., 313
Ghoshal, S., 192, 194, 197
Gibson, C. B., 179
Gilmore, R., 133
gllam software, 374
GLMMs. *See* Generalized linear mixed
    models
Global constructs, 205
Global dynamics, 174
Global unit properties, 241, 284
Global variables, 368
Glomb, T. M., 320
gls function, 400, 405, 407
Goldstein, H., 570
Goldstein, K., 41
Gomes, D., 126
Goodwin, G. F., 166
Goossen, M. C., 216
Grand, J. A., 152
Grand-mean centering, 362, 401
Granovetter, M., 192, 195, 196
Gray, B., 195
Greer, L. L., 259
Griffin, M. A., 255
Grigoriou, K., 145, 146
Grosser, T. J., 195
Group emergence effects, 537
Group interaction, individual interactions
    as, 193–194
Group level of analysis
    in contemporary conceptual
        cross-level model, 571, 572
    and group-level psychological
        constructs, 541
    in integrative cross-level model,
        576–579
    of interpersonal perception and
        behavior, 425
    in multilevel structural modeling
        example, 455
    research questions suited to, 14
    with social relations model, 436–437
    in traditional conceptual cross-level
        model, 568
    within-person research methods for,
        319–320
Group-level properties, computational
    modeling of, 542–545
Group-level psychological constructs,
    519, 541
Group-mean centering, 362, 401
Group mean differences, nonindepen-
    dence and, 283–284
Group performance
    as Class 2 construct, 255

four-stage mediation model of trust
    propensity and, 105–110
Group size, as Class 2 construct, 255, 256
Growth modeling, temporally nested con-
    structs in, 254
Groysberg, B., 148
Gulati, A., 125

Haas, M. R., 178
Hackman, J. R., 16–17
Hakoyama, S., 353
Hale, D., Jr., 148
Hall, G. S., 141
Hall, R. J., 225, 590
Halverson, R. R., 297, 355
Hamaker, E., 320
Hambleton, R. K., 243
Hanges, P. J., 33, 135
Hansen, M. T., 192
Harrison, D. A., 166
Hartman, M. J., 353
Harzing, 2006, 244
Heck, R. H., 449, 456, 457, 462, 471
Hedberg, E. C., 334
Hedges, L. V., 334
Heffner, T. S., 166
Heimeriks, K. H., 145
Heisenberg, W., 129
Helfat, C. E., 147
Hench, T. J., 121
Hesterly, W. S., 151–153
Heterogeneity
    in organizational sciences, 141
    as topic in management research, 143
    in WABA cross-level view, 573
Heterogeneous parts model, 214
Heteroskedastic (nonconstant) variance,
    497
Hidden variables, in artificial neural
    networks, 134
Hierachical linear modeling and models
    (HLM), 151, 599. *See also* Multilevel
    regression (MLR) modeling
    in cognitive trust study, 429
    and generalized linear modeling, 498
    multilevel analysis with M*plus* vs.,
        450–451
    and nonnormal data, 495
    RCM/HLM/ML conceptual model,
        565, 570
    RCM/HLM testing model, 572
Hierarchical nesting, of data, 389
Hierarchical structures, levels in, 11–12
Hierarchical systems, tightly coupled
    levels in, 16

Higher level (HL) analysis
    in contemporary cross-level
        conceptual model, 570
    of cross-level model, 565, 566
    in traditional cross-level conceptual
        model, 567
Higher level node constructs, 205–206
Higher levels, defined, 12
High involvement work processes
    (HIWP), 452–471
Hinzsz, V. B., 173, 177
HIWP (high involvement work
    processes), 452–471
HL analysis. *See* Higher level analysis
HLM. *See* Hierachical linear modeling and
    models
Hoffart, G. C., 102
Hofmann, D., 506, 590
Hofmann, D. A., 172, 595
Holland, J. L., 594
Hollenbeck, J. R., 105, 467
Homeostatic breakdowns, 25–26
Homogeneity, 165, 573, 574, 596
Homologous constructs, 564
Homologous models of multilevel
    systems, 151
Homology
    and construct validation, 260
    in traditional cross-level view, 567
    in within-person research, 305
Homology models in nomological
    networks, 268–272
Homology testing, 270–272, 593
Homophily, 49–50
Houchin, K., 117
House, R., 163, 590, 595
House, R. J., 19, 242
Howe, M., 467
Hox, J. J., 332, 333, 335
Huang, L., 176
Hulin, C. L., 21, 588
Humphrey, S. E., 105
Hunter, J. E., 264
Huy, Q. N., 92
Hybrid models of homology, 269, 272
Hypothesis testing
    in multilevel regression modeling,
        411–413
    with multilevel structural equation
        modeling, 456, 463–471
    multiparameter tests in multiple
        imputation, 381
    with multiply imputed data, 373
    with nonnormal data, 495
    with social relations models, 435–438